# THE OXFORD

## Portuguese
## Dictionary

*Also available*

THE OXFORD DESK DICTIONARY AND THESAURUS

THE OXFORD ESSENTIAL DICTIONARY

THE OXFORD ESSENTIAL QUOTATIONS DICTIONARY

THE OXFORD ESSENTIAL SPELLING DICTIONARY

THE OXFORD ESSENTIAL THESAURUS

THE OXFORD FRENCH DICTIONARY

THE OXFORD GERMAN DICTIONARY

THE OXFORD ITALIAN DICTIONARY

THE OXFORD RUSSIAN DICTIONARY

THE OXFORD SPANISH DICTIONARY

# THE OXFORD

# Portuguese Dictionary

PORTUGUESE–ENGLISH
*Compiled by John Whitlam*

ENGLISH–PORTUGUESE
*Compiled by Lia Correia Raitt*

**B**
BERKLEY BOOKS, NEW YORK

## THE OXFORD PORTUGUESE DICTIONARY

A Berkley Book / published in mass market paperback
by arrangement with Oxford University Press, Inc.

PRINTING HISTORY
Berkley edition / August 1998

Copyright © 1996, 1998 by Oxford University Press.
First published in 1996 as *The Oxford Paperback Portuguese Dictionary*.
Oxford is a registered trademark of Oxford University Press, Inc.
All rights reserved. No part of this publication may be reproduced,
stored in a retrieval system, or transmitted, in any form or by any
means, electronic, mechanical, photocopying, recording, or otherwise
without the prior written permission of Oxford University Press, Inc
For information address: Oxford University Press, Inc.,
198 Madison Avenue, New York, New York 10016.

The Penguin Putnam Inc. World Wide Web site address is
http://www.penguinputnam.com

ISBN: 0-425-16389-X

BERKLEY®
Berkley Books are published by The Berkley Publishing Group,
a member of Penguin Putnam Inc.,
200 Madison Avenue, New York, New York 10016.
BERKLEY and the "B" design
are trademarks belonging to Berkley Publishing Corporation.

PRINTED IN THE UNITED STATES OF AMERICA

10  9  8  7  6  5  4  3  2  1

# Contents • Índice

# Preface

*The Oxford Paperback Portuguese Dictionary* has been written for speakers of both Portuguese and English and contains the most useful words and expressions in use today.

The dictionary provides a handy and comprehensive reference work for tourists, students, and business people who require quick and reliable answers to their translation needs.

Thanks are due to: Dr John Sykes, Prof. A. W. Raitt, Commander Virgílio Correia, Marcelo Affonso, Eng. Pedro Carvalho, Eng. Vasco Carvalho, Dr Iva Correia, Dr Ida Reis de Carvalho, Eng. J. Reis de Carvalho, Prof. A. Falcão, Bishop Manuel Falcão, Dr M. Luísa Falcão, Prof. J. Ferraz, Prof. M. de Lourdes Ferraz, Drs Ana and Jorge Fonseca, Mr Robert Howes, Irene Lakhani, Eng. Hugo Pires, Prof. M. Kaura Pires, Dr M. Alexandre Pires, Ambassador L. Pazos Alonso, Dr Teresa Pinto Pereira, Dr Isabel Tully, Carlos Wallenstein, Ligia Xavier, and Dr H. Martins and the members of his Mesa Lusófona at St Antony's College, Oxford.

# Prefácio

O *Oxford Paperback Portuguese Dictionary* foi escrito por pessoas de língua portuguesa e inglesa, e contém as palavras e expressões mais úteis em uso atualmente.

O dicionário constitui uma obra de referência prática e abrangente para turistas, estudantes e pessoas de negócios que necessitam de respostas rápidas e confiáveis para as suas traduções.

Agradecimentos a: Dr John Sykes, Prof. A. W. Raitt, Comandante Virgílio Correia, Marcelo Affonso, Eng. Pedro Carvalho, Eng. Vasco Carvalho, Dr Iva Correia, Dr Ida Reis de Carvalho, Eng. J. Reis de Carvalho, Prof. A. Falcão, Bispo Manuel Falcão, Dr M. Luísa Falcão, Prof. J. Ferraz, Prof. M. de Lourdes Ferraz, Drs Ana e Jorge Fonseca, Mr Robert Howes, Eng. Hugo Pires, Prof. M. Laura Pires, Dr M. Alexandre Pires, Embaixador L. Pazos Alonso, Dr Teresa Pinto Pereira, Dr Isabel Tully, Carlos Wallenstein, e Dr H. Martins e os membros de sua Mesa Lusófona do St Antony's College, em Oxford.

# Introduction

The swung dash (~) is used to replace a headword, or that part of a headword preceding the vertical bar ( | ).

In both English and Portuguese, only irregular plural forms are given. Plural forms of Portuguese nouns and adjectives ending in a single vowel are formed by adding an *s* (e.g. *livro, livros*). Those ending in *n, r, s* where the stress falls on the final syllable, and *z*, add *es* (e.g. *mulher, mulheres, falaz, falazes*). Nouns and adjectives ending in *m* change the final *m* to *ns* (e.g. *homem, homens, bom, bons*). Most of those ending in *ão* change their ending to *ões* (e.g. *estação, estações*).

Portuguese nouns and adjectives ending in an unstressed *o* form the feminine by changing the *o* to *a* (e.g. *belo, bela*). Those ending in *or* become *ora* (e.g. *trabalhador, trabalhadora*). All other masculine-feminine changes are shown at the main headword.

English and Portuguese pronunciation is given by means of the International Phonetic Alphabet. It is shown for all headwords, and for those derived words whose pronunciation is not easily deduced from that of a headword.

Portuguese verb tables will be found in the appendix.

# Introdução

O sinal (~) é usado para substituir o verbete, ou parte deste precedendo a barra vertical (|).

Tanto em inglês como em português, somente as formas irregulares do plural são dadas. As formas regulares do plural dos substantivos ingleses recebem um *s* (ex. *teacher*, *teachers*), ou *es* quando terminarem em *ch*, *sh*, *s*, *ss*, *us*, *x* ou *z* (ex. *sash*, *sashes*). Os substantivos terminados em *y* e precedidos por uma consoante, mudam no plural para *ies* (ex. *baby*, *babies*).

O passado e o particípio passado dos verbos regulares ingleses são formados pelo acréscimo de *ed* á forma infinitiva (ex. *last*, *lasted*). Os verbos terminados em *e* recebem *d* (ex. *move*, *moved*). Aqueles terminados em *y* têm o *y* substituído por *ied* (*carry*, *carried*). As formas irregulares dos verbos aparecem no dicionário em ordem alfabética, remetidas à forma infinitiva, e também, na lista de verbos no apêndice.

As pronúncias inglesa e portuguesa são dadas em acordo com o Alfabeto Fonético Internacional. A pronúncia é dada para todos os verbetes, assim como para aquelas palavras derivadas cuja pronúncia não seja facilmente deduzida a partir do verbete.

# Proprietary terms

This dictionary includes some words which are, or are asserted to be, proprietary names or trade marks. Their inclusion does not imply that they have acquired for legal purposes a non-proprietary or general significance, nor is any other judgement implied concerning their legal status. In cases where the editor has some evidence that a word is used as a proprietary name or trade mark this is indicated by the label *propr*, but no judgement concerning the legal status of such words is made or implied thereby.

# Nomes comerciais

Este dicionário inclui algumas palavras que são, ou acredita-se ser, nomes comerciais ou marcas registradas. A sua inclusão no dicionário não implica que elas tenham adquirido para fins legais um significado geral ou não-comercial, assim como não afeta em nenhum dos conceitos implícitos o seu status legal.

Nos casos em que o editor tenha prova suficiente de que uma palavra seja usada como um nome comercial ou marca registrada, este emprego é indicado pela etiqueta *propr*, mas nenhuma apreciação relativa ao status legal de tais palavras é feita ou sugerida por esta indicação.

# Portuguese Pronunciation

## Vowels and Diphthongs

| | | | |
|---|---|---|---|
| a, à, á, â | /ã/ | chamam, ambos, antes | 1) before *m* at the end of a word, or before *m* or *n* and another consonant, is nasalized |
| | /a/ | aba, à, acolá, desânimo | 2) in other positions is like *a* in English r*a*ther |
| ã | /ã/ | irmã | is nasalized |
| e | /ẽ/ | sem, venda | 1) before *m* at the end of a word, or before *m* or *n* and another consonant, is nasalized |
| | /i/ | arte | 2) at the end of a word is like *y* in English happ*y* |
| | /e/ | menas | 3) in other positions is like *e* in English th*ey* |
| é | /ɛ/ | artéria | is like *e* in English g*e*t |
| ê | /e/ | fêmur | is like *e* in English th*ey* |
| i | /ĩ/ | sim, vindo | 1) before *m* at the end of a word, or before *m* or *n* and another consonant, is nasalized |
| | /i/ | fila | 2) in other positions is like *ee* in English s*ee* |
| o | /õ/ | com, sombra, onda | 1) before *m* at the end of a word, or before *m* or *n* and another consonant, is nasalized |
| | /u/ | muito | 2) at the end of a word, unstressed, is like *u* in English r*u*le |

xii

| | | | |
|---|---|---|---|
| | /o/ | como**v**er | 3) in other positions, unstressed, is like *o* in English p**o**le |
| | /o/ | b**o**b**o** | 4) stressed, is like *o* in English p**o**le or *o* in sh**o**p |
| | /ɔ/ | l**o**ja | |
| ó | /ɔ/ | **ó**pera | is like *o* in English p**o**le |
| ô | /o/ | t**ô**nica | is like *o* in English p**o**le |
| u, ú | | g**u**erra, g**u**isado, q**u**e, q**u**ilo | 1) is silent in *gue*, and *gui, que, qui* |
| | /u/ | m**u**la, p**ú**rpura | 2) in other positions is like *u* in English r**u**le |
| ü gü | /gw/ | ung**ü**ento | in the combinations *güe* and *güi* is like *g* in English g**o**t, followed by English *w* |
| | /kw/ | tranq**üi**lo | in the combinations *qüe* and *qüi* is like *qu* in English q**u**een |
| ãe | /ãj/ | m**ãe**, p**ãe**s, alem**ãe**s | is like *y* in English b**y**, but nasalized |
| ai | /aj/ | v**ai**, p**ai**, s**ai**, c**ai**ta | is like *y* in English b**y** |
| ao, au | /aw/ | **ao**s, **au**todefesa | is like *ow* in English h**ow** |
| ão | /ãw/ | n**ão** | is like *ow* in English h**ow**, but nasalized |
| ei | /ej/ | l**ei** | is like *ey* in English th**ey** |
| eu | /ew/ | d**eu**s, fl**eu**gma | both vowels pronounced separately |
| oẽ | /õj/ | eleiç**õe**s | is like *oi* in English c**oi**n, but nasalized |
| oi | /oj/ | n**oi**te | is like *oi* in English c**oi**n |
| ou | /o/ | p**ou**co | is like *o* in English p**o**le |

**Consonants**

| b | /b/ | **b**anho | is like *b* in English **b**all |

| | | | |
|---|---|---|---|
| c | /s/ | *c*inza, *c*em | 1) before *e* or *i* is like *s* in English *s*it |
| | /k/ | *c*asa | 2) in other positions is like *c* in English *c*at |
| ç | /s/ | esta*ç*ão | is like *s* in English *s*it |
| ch | /ʃ/ | *ch*á | is like *sh* in English *sh*out |
| d | /dʒ/ | *d*izer, don*d*e | 1) before *i* or final unstressed *e* is like *j* in English *j*oin |
| | /d/ | *d*ar | 2) in other positions is like *d* in English *d*og |
| f | /f/ | *f*alar | is like *f* in English *f*all |
| g | /ʒ/ | a*g*ente, *g*iro | 1) before *e* or *i* is like *s* in English vi*s*ion |
| | /g/ | *g*ato | 2) in other positions is like *g* in English *g*et |
| h | | *h*aver | is silent in Portuguese, but see *ch*, *lh*, *nh* |
| j | /ʒ/ | *j*unta | is like *s* in English vi*s*ion |
| k | /k/ | *k*it | is like English *k* in *k*ey |
| l | /w/ | fa*l*ta | 1) between a vowel and a consonant, or following a vowel at the end of a word, is like *w* in English *w*ater |
| | /l/ | *l*ata | 2) in other positions is like *l* in English *l*ike |
| l | /ʎ/ | ca*l*har | is like *ll*i in English mi*lli*on |
| m | | a*m*bas/ãbuʃ/ co*m* /kõ/ | 1) between a vowel and a consonant, or after a vowel at the end of a word, *m* nasalizes the preceding vowel |
| | /m/ | *m*ato, *m*ão | 2) in other positions is like *m* in English *m*other |
| n | | ci*n*za /'sīza/ | 1) between a vowel and a consonant, *n* nasalizes the preceding vowel |

| | /n/ | be*nig*no | 2) in other positions is like *n* in English *n*ear |
| nh | /ɲ/ | ba*nh*o | is like *ni* in English opi*ni*on |
| p | /p/ | *p*az | is like *p* in English *p*oor |
| q | /k/ | *q*ue, in*q*uieto | 1) *qu* before *e* or *i* is like English *k* |
| | /kw/ | *q*uase, *q*uórum | 2) *qu* before *a* or *o*, or *qü* before *e* or *i*, is like *qu* in English *qu*een |
| r | /r/ | apa*r*ato, go*r*do | 1) between two vowels, or between a vowel and a consonant, is trilled |
| | /x/ | *r*ato, ga*rr*a, mel*r*o, gen*r*o, Is*r*ael | 2) at the beginning of a word, or in *rr*, or after *l*, *n*, or *s*, is like *ch* in Scottish lo*ch* |
| s | /ʃ/ | depoi*s* | at the end of a word is like *sh* in English *sh*oot |
| | /z/ | a*s*a, de*s*de, abi*s*mo, I*s*rael | 2) between two vowels, or before *b, d, g, l, m, n, r, v*, is like *z* in English *z*ebra |
| | /s/ | *s*uave | 3) in other positions is like *s* in English *s*it |
| t | /tʃ/ | *t*io, an*t*es | 1) before *i* or final unstressed *e* is like *ch* in English *ch*eese |
| | /tʃi/ | ki*t* | 2) at the end of a word is like *chy* in English it*chy* |
| | /t/ | a*t*ar | 3) in other positions is like *t* in English *t*ap |
| v | /v/ | lu*v*a | is like *v* in English *v*ain |
| w | /u/ | *w*att | is shorter than English *w* |
| x | /z/ | e*x*ato, e*x*emplo | 1) in the prefix *ex* before a vowel, is pronounced like *z* in *z*ero |

| | | | |
|---|---|---|---|
| | /ʃ/ | xícara, baixo, peixe, frouxo | 2) at the beginning of a word or after *ai*, *ei* or *ou*, is pronounced like *sh* in *sh*ow |
| | /s/ | explodir, auxiliar | 3) is like *s* in English *s*it |
| | /ks/ | axila, fixo | 4) is like *x* in English e*x*it |
| | | | 5) in the combination *xce*, *xci*, *x* is not pronounced in Portuguese e.g. e*x*celente, e*x*citar |
| z | /s/ | falaz | 1) at the end of a word, is like *s* in English *s*it |
| | /z/ | dizer | 2) in other positions, is like English *z* |

# Pronuncia Inglesa

## Vogals e Ditongos

| | | |
|---|---|---|
| /iː/ | see, tea | como *i* em g*i*ro |
| /ɪ/ | sit, happy | é um som mais breve do que *i* em l*i* |
| /e/ | set | como *e* em t*é*pido |
| /æ/ | hat | é um som mais breve do que *a* em *a*mor |
| /aː/ | arm, calm | como *a* em c*a*rtaz |
| /ɒ/ | got | como *o* em ex*ó*tico |
| /ɔː/ | saw, more | como *o* em c*o*rte |
| /ʊ/ | put, look | como *u* em m*u*rro |
| /uː/ | too, due | como *u* em d*u*ro |
| /ʌ/ | cup, some | como *a* em p*a*no |
| /ɜː/ | firm, fur | como *e* em enx*e*rto |
| /ə/ | ago, weather | como *e* no português europeu part*e* |
| /eɪ/ | page, pain, pay | como *ei* em l*ei*te |
| /əʊ/ | home, roam | é um som mais longo do que *o* em c*o*ma |
| /aɪ/ | fine, by, guy | como *ai* em s*ai* |
| /aɪə/ | fire, tyre | como *ai* em s*ai* seguido por /ə/ |
| /aʊ/ | now, shout | como *au* em *au*la |
| /aʊə/ | hour, flower | como *au* em *au*la seguido por /ə/ |
| /ɔɪ/ | join, boy | como *oi* em d*ói* |
| /ɪə/ | dear, here, beer | como *ia* em d*ia* |
| /eə/ | hair, care, bear, there | como *e* em et*é*reo |
| /ʊə/ | poor, during | como *ua* em s*ua* |

## Consoantes

| | | |
|---|---|---|
| /p/ | sna*p* | como *p* em *p*ato |
| /b/ | *b*ath | como *b* em *b*ala |
| /t/ | *t*ap | como *t* em *t*ela |
| /d/ | *d*ip | como *d* em *d*ar |
| /k/ | *c*at, *k*ite, stoma*ch*, pi*que* | como *c* em *c*asa |
| /ks/ | e*x*ercise | como *x* em a*x*ila |
| /g/ | *g*ot | como *g* em *g*ato |
| /tʃ/ | *ch*in | como *t* em *t*io |
| /dʒ/ | *J*une, general, *j*u*dg*e | como *d* em *d*izer |
| /f/ | *f*all | como *f* em *f*aca |
| /v/ | *v*ine, o*f* | como *v* em *v*aca |
| /θ/ | *th*in, mo*th* | não tem equivalente, soa como um *s* entre os dentes |
| /ð/ | *th*is | não tem equivalente, soa como um *z* entre os dentes |
| /s/ | *s*o, voi*c*e | como *s* em *s*uave |
| /z/ | *z*oo, ro*s*e | como *z* em fa*z*er |
| /ʃ/ | *sh*e, lun*ch* | como *ch* em *ch*egar |
| /ʒ/ | mea*s*ure, vi*s*ion | como *j* em *j*amais |
| /h/ | *h*ow | *h* aspirado |
| /m/ | *m*an | como *m* em *m*ala |
| /n/ | *n*o*n*e | como *n* em *n*ada |
| /ŋ/ | si*n*g | como *n* em ci*n*to |
| /l/ | *l*eg | como *l* em *l*uva |
| /r/ | *r*ed, *w*rite | como *r* em ca*r*a |
| /j/ | *y*es, *y*oke | como *i* em *i*oga |
| /w/ | *w*eather, s*w*itch | como *u* ég*u*a |

# European Portuguese

Brazilian Portuguese, which is used in this dictionary, differs in a number of respects from that used in Portugal and the rest of the Portuguese-speaking world. These differences affect both spelling and pronunciation. Spelling variations appear on the Portuguese–English side. In so far as they affect pronunciation, the main variants are:

Brazilian Portuguese often omits the letters *b*, *c*, *m*, and *p*, which are retained by European Portuguese:

|   | **Brazilian** | **European** |
|---|---|---|
| b | sutil | su*b*til |
| c | a*ç*ão | ac*c*ão |
|   | ato | ac*t*o |
|   | elétrico | elé*c*trico |
| m | indenizar | inde*m*nizar |
| p | batismo | ba*p*tismo |
|   | exceção | exce*p*ção |

Letters *c* and *p* in such variant forms are usually silent, hence acto /'atu/, ba'ptismo /batiʒmu/. However, *c* is pronounced in the combination *ect*, hence eléctrico /i'lektriku/.

The combinations *güi* and *qüi* become *gu* and *qu*:

| **Brazilian** | **European** |
|---|---|
| un*gü*ento | un*gu*ento |
| tran*qü*ilo | tran*qu*ilo |

However, they are still pronounced /gw/ and /kw/ respectively.

The other main differences in pronunciation are:

| d | /d/ | *d*ar, *d*izer, bal*d*e, *d*onde | 1) at the beginning of a word, or after *l*, or *n*, is like *d* in English *d*og |
|---|---|---|---|

| | /ð/ | ci*dade*, me*d*roso | 2) in other positions is a sound between *d* in English *d*og and *th* in English *th*is |
|---|---|---|---|
| e | /ə/ | a*r*te | at the end of a word, is like *e* in English quarre*l* |
| r | /rr/ | *r*ato, ga*rr*a, mel*r*o, gen*r*o, Is*r*ael, guel*r*a, ten*r*o, is*r*aelense | at the beginning of a word, or in *rr*, or after *l*, *n*, or *s*, is strongly trilled |
| s | /ʃ/ | depoi*s*, a*s*co, ra*s*par, co*s*tura | 1) at the end of a word, or before *c*, *f*, *p*, *qu*, or *t*, is like English *sh* |
| | /ʒ/ | de*s*de, I*s*lã abi*s*mo, I*s*rael | 2) before *b*, *d*, *g*, *l*, *m*, *n*, *r*, or *v* is like *s* in English vi*s*ion |
| t | /t/ | a*t*ar, an*t*es, *t*io | is like *t* in English *t*ap |
| z | /ʃ/ | fala*z* | at the end of a word, is like *sh* in English *sh*ake |

# Abbreviations •
# Abreviaturas

| adjective | a | adjetivo |
|---|---|---|
| abbreviation | abbr/abr | abreviatura |
| something | aco | alguma coisa |
| adverb | adv | advérbio |
| somebody, someone | alg | algúem |
| article | art | artigo |
| American (English) | Amer | (inglês) americano |
| anatomy | anat | anatomia |
| architecture | arquit | arquitetura |
| astrology | astr/astrol | astrologia |
| motoring | auto | automobilismo |
| aviation | aviat | aviação |
| Brazilian Portuguese | B | português do Brasil |
| biology | biol | biologia |
| botany | bot | botânica |
| Brazilian Portuguese | Bras | português do Brasil |
| cinema | cine | cinema |
| colloquial | colloq | coloquial |
| commerce | comm/com | comércio |
| computing | comput | computação |
| conjunction | conj | conjunção |
| cookery | culin | cozinha |
| electricity | electr/eletr | eletricidade |
| feminine | f | feminina |
| familiar | fam | familiar |
| figurative | fig | figurativo |
| geography | geog | geografia |
| grammar | gramm/gram | gramática |

| infinitive | inf | infinitivo |
|---|---|---|
| interjection | int | interjeição |
| interrogative | interr | interrogativo |
| invariable | invar | invariável |
| legal, law | jur/jurid | jurídico |
| language | lang | linguagem |
| literal | lit | literal |
| masculine | m | masculino |
| mathematics | mat | matemática |
| mechanics | mech | mecânica |
| medicine | med | medicina |
| military | mil | militar |
| music | mus | música |
| noun | n | substantivo |
| nautical | naut | náutico |
| negative | neg | negativo |
| oneself | o.s. | se, si mesmo |
| European Portuguese | P | português de Portugal |
| pejorative | pej | pejorativo |
| philosophy | phil | filosofia |
| plural | pl | plural |
| politics | pol | política |
| European Portuguese | Port | português de Portugal |
| past participle | pp | particípio passado |
| prefix | pref | prefixo |
| preposition | prep | preposição |
| present | pres | presente |
| present participle | pres p | particípio presente |
| pronoun | pron | pronome |
| psychology | psych/psic | psicologia |

| | | |
|---|---|---|
| past tense | pt | pretérito |
| relative | rel | relativo |
| religion | relig | religião |
| somebody | sb | alguém |
| singular | sing | singular |
| slang | sl | gíria |
| someone | s.o. | alguém |
| something | sth | alguma coisa |
| subjunctive | subj | subjuntivo |
| technology | techn/tecn | tecnologia |
| theatre | theat/teat | teatro |
| television | TV | televisão |
| university | univ | universidade |
| auxiliary verb | v aux | verbo auxiliar |
| intransitive verb | vi | verbo intransitivo |
| pronominal verb | vpr | verbo pronominal |
| transitive verb | vt | verbo transitivo |
| transitive & intransitive verb | vt/i | verbo transitivo e intransitivo |

# A

**a**[1] /a/ *artigo* the □ *pron* (*mulher*) her; (*coisa*) it; (*você*) you

**a**[2] /a/ *prep* (*para*) to; (*em*) at; **às 3 horas** at 3 o'clock; **à noite** at night; **a lápis** in pencil; **a mão** by hand

**à** /a/ = **a**[2] + **a**[1]

**aba** /'aba/ *f* (*de chapéu*) brim; (*de camisa*) tail; (*de mesa*) flap

**abacate** /aba'katʃi/ *m* avocado (pear)

**abacaxi** /abaka'ʃi/ *m* pineapple; (*fam: problema*) pain, headache

**aba|de** /a'badʒi/ *m* abbot; **~dia** *f* abbey

**aba|fado** /aba'fadu/ *a* (*tempo*) humid, close; (*quarto*) stuffy; **~far** *vt* (*asfixiar*) stifle; muffle <*som*>; smother <*fogo*>; suppress <*informação*>; cover up <*escândalo, assunto*>

**abagunçar** /abagũ'sar/ *vt* mess up

**abaixar** /aba'ʃar/ *vt* lower; turn down <*som, rádio*>□*vi* **~-se** *vpr* bend down

**abaixo** /a'baʃu/ *adv* down; **~ de** below; **mais ~** further down; **~-assinado** *m* petition

**abajur** /aba'ʒur/ *m* (*quebra-luz*) lampshade; (*lâmpada*) (table) lamp

**aba|lar** /aba'lar/ *vt* shake; (*fig*) shock; **~lar-se** *vpr* be shocked, be shaken; **~lo** *m* shock

**abanar** /aba'nar/ *vt* shake, wave; wag <*rabo*>; (*com leque*) fan

**abando|nar** /abãdo'nar/ *vt* abandon; (*deixar*) leave; **~no** /o/ *m* abandonment; (*estado*) neglect

**abarcar** /abar'kar/ *vt* comprise, cover

**abarro|tado** /abaxo'tadu/ *a* crammed full; (*lotado*) crowded, packed; **~tar** *vt* cram full, stuff

**abastado** /abas'tadu/ *a* wealthy

**abaste|cer** /abaste'ser/ *vt* supply; fuel <*motor*>; fill up (with petrol) <*carro*>; refuel <*avião*>; **~cimento** *m* supply; (*de carro, avião*) refuelling

**aba|ter** /aba'ter/ *vt* knock down; cut down, fell <*árvore*>; shoot down <*avião, ave*>; slaughter <*gado*>; knock down, cut <*preço*>; (*fig*) get s.o. down, wear s.o. out; <*má notícia*> sadden s.o.; <*doença*> lay s.o. low, knock the stuffing out of s.o.; **~tido** *a* dispirited, dejected; <*cara*> haggard, worn;

**~timento** *m* dejection; (*de preço*) reduction

**abaulado** /abaw'ladu/ *a* convex; <*estrada*> cambered

**abcesso** /ab'sɛsu/ *m* (*Port*) veja **abscesso**

**abdi|cação** /abidʒika'sãw/ *f* abdication; **~car** *vt/i* abdicate

**abdômen** /abi'domẽ/ *m* abdomen

**abecedário** /abese'dariu/ *m* alphabet, ABC

**abeirar-se** /abe'rarsi/ *vr* draw near

**abe|lha** /a'beʎa/ *f* bee; **~lhudo** *a* inquisitive, nosy

**abençoar** /abẽso'ar/ *vt* bless

**aber|to** /a'bɛrtu/ *pp de* **abrir** □ *a* open; <*céu*> clear; <*gás, torneira*> on; <*sinal*> green; **~tura** *f* opening; (*foto*) aperture; (*pol*) liberalization

**abeto** /a'betu/ *m* fir (tree)

**abis|mado** /abiz'madu/ *a* astonished; **~mo** *m* abyss

**abjeto** /abi'ʒɛtu/ *a* abject

**abóbada** /a'bɔbada/ *f* vault

**abobalhado** /aboba'ʎadu/ *a* silly

**abóbora** /a'bɔbora/ *f* pumpkin

**abobrinha** /abo'briɲa/ *f* courgette, (*Amer*) zucchini

**abo|lição** /aboli'sãw/ *f* abolition; **~lir** *vt* abolish

**abomi|nação** /abomina'sãw/ *f* abomination; **~nável** (*pl* **~náveis**) *a* abominable

**abo|nar** /abo'nar/ *vt* guarantee <*dívida*>; give a bonus to <*empregado*>; **~no** /o/ *m* guarantee; (*no salário*) bonus; (*subsídio*) allowance, benefit; (*reforço*) endorsement

**abordar** /abor'dar/ *vt* approach <*pessoa*>; broach, tackle <*assunto*>; (*naut*) board

**aborre|cer** /aboxe'ser/ *vt* (*irritar*) annoy; (*entediar*) bore; **~cer-se** *vpr* get annoyed; get bored; **~cido** *a* annoyed; bored; **~cimento** *m* annoyance; boredom

**abor|tar** /abor'tar/ *vi* miscarry, have a miscarriage □ *vt* abort; **~to** /o/ *m* abortion; (*natural*) miscarriage

**aboto|adura** /abotoa'dura/ *f* cufflink; **~ar** *vt* button (up) □ *vi* bud

**abra|çar** /abra'sar/ *vt* hug, embrace;

embrace <*causa*>; **~ço** *m* hug, embrace

**abrandar** /abrã'dar/ *vt* ease <*dor*>; temper <*calor, frio*>; mollify, appease, placate <*povo*>; tone down, smooth over <*escândalo*> □ *vi* <*dor*> ease; <*calor, frio*> become less extreme; <*tempestade*> die down

**abranger** /abrã'ʒer/ *vt* cover; (*entender*) take in, grasp; **~ a** extend to

**abrasileirar** /abrazile'rar/ *vt* Brazilianize

**abre-|garrafas** /abriga'xafas/ *m invar* (Port) bottle-opener; **~latas** *m invar* (Port) can-opener

**abreugrafia** /abrewgra'fia/ *f* X-ray

**abrevi|ar** /abrevi'ar/ *vt* abbreviate <*palavra*>; abridge <*livro*>; **~atura** *f* abbreviation

**abridor** /abri'dor/ *m* **~ (de lata)** can-opener; **~ de garrafa** bottle-opener

**abri|gar** /abri'gar/ *vt* shelter; house <*sem-teto*>; **~gar-se** *vpr* (take) shelter; **~go** *m* shelter

**abril** /a'briw/ *m* April

**abrir** /a'brir/ *vt* open; (*a chave*) unlock; turn on <*gás, torneira*>; make <*buraco, exceção*> □ *vi* open; <*céu, tempo*> clear (up); <*sinal*> turn green; **~-se** *vpr* open; (*desabafar*) open up

**abrupto** /a'bruptu/ *a* abrupt

**abrutalhado** /abruta'ʎadu/ *a* <*sapato*> heavy; (*pessoa*) coarse

**abscesso** /abi'sesu/ *m* abscess

**absolu|tamente** /abisoluta'mẽtʃi/ *adv* absolutely; (*não*) not at all; **~to** *a* absolute; **em ~to** not at all, absolutely not

**absol|ver** /abisow'ver/ *vt* absolve; (*jurid*) acquit; **~vição** *f* absolution; (*jurid*) acquittal

**absor|ção** /abisor'sãw/ *f* absorption; **~to** *a* absorbed; **~vente** *a* <*tecido*> absorbent; <*livro*> absorbing; **~ver** *vt* absorb; **~ver-se** *vpr* get absorbed

**abs|têmio** /abis'temiu/ *a* abstemious; (*de álcool*) teetotal □ *m* teetotaller; **~tenção** *f* abstention; **~tencionista** *a* abstaining □ *m/f* abstainer; **~ter-se** *vpr* abstain; **~ter-se de** refrain from; **~tinência** *f* abstinence

**abstra|ção** /abistra'sãw/ *f* abstraction; (*mental*) distraction; **~ir** *vt* separate; **~to** *a* abstract

**absurdo** /abi'surdu/ *a* absurd □ *m* nonsense

**abun|dância** /abũ'dãsia/ *f* abundance; **~dante** *a* abundant; **~dar** *vi* abound

**abu|sar** /abu'zar/ *vi* go too far; **~sar de** abuse; (*aproveitar-se*) take advantage of; **~so** *m* abuse

**abutre** /a'butri/ *m* vulture

**aca|bado** /aka'badu/ *a* finished;

(*exausto*) exhausted; (*velho*) decrepit; **~bamento** *m* finish; **~bar** *vt* finish □ *vi* finish, end; (*esgotar-se*) run out; **~bar-se** *vpr* end, be over; (*esgotar-se*) run out; **~bar com** put an end to, end; (*abolir, matar*) do away with; split up with <*namorado*>; wipe out <*adversário*>; **~bou de chegar** he has just arrived; **~bar fazendo** *or* **por fazer** end up doing

**acabrunhado** /akabru'ɲadu/ *a* dejected

**aca|demia** /akade'mia/ *f* academy; (*de ginástica etc*) gym; **~dêmico** *a* & *m* academic

**açafrão** /asa'frãw/ *m* saffron

**acalentar** /akalẽ'tar/ *vt* lull to sleep <*bebê*>; cherish <*esperanças*>; have in mind <*planos*>

**acalmar** /akaw'mar/ *vt* calm (down) □ *vi* <*vento*> drop; <*mar*> grow calm; **~-se** *vpr* calm down

**acam|pamento** /akãpa'mẽtu/ *m* camp; (*ato*) camping; **~par** *vi* camp

**aca|nhado** /aka'ɲadu/ *a* shy; **~nhamento** *m* shyness; **~nhar-se** *vpr* be shy

**ação** /a'sãw/ *f* action; (*jurid*) lawsuit; (*com*) share

**acariciar** /akarisi'ar/ *vt* (*com a mão*) caress, stroke; (*adular*) make a fuss of; cherish <*esperanças*>

**acarretar** /akaxe'tar/ *vt* bring, cause

**acasalar** /akaza'lar/ *vt* mate; **~-se** *vpr* mate

**acaso** /a'kazu/ *m* chance; **ao ~** at random; **por ~** by chance

**aca|tamento** /akata'mẽtu/ *m* respect, deference; **~tar** *vt* respect, defer to <*pessoa, opinião*>; obey, abide by <*leis, ordens*>; take in <*criança*>

**acc-, acç-** (*Port*) *veja* **ac-, aç-**

**acautelar-se** /akawte'larsi/ *vpr* be cautious

**acei|tação** /asejta'sãw/ *f* acceptance; **~tar** *vt* accept; **~tável** (*pl* **~táveis**) *a* acceptable

**acele|ração** /aselera'sãw/ *f* acceleration; **~rador** *m* accelerator; **~rar** *vi* accelerate □ *vt* speed up

**acenar** /ase'nar/ *vi* signal; (*saudando*) wave; **~ com** promise, offer

**acender** /asẽ'der/ *vt* light <*cigarro, fogo, vela*>; switch on <*luz*>; heat up <*debate*>

**aceno** /a'senu/ *m* signal; (*de saudação*) wave

**acen|to** /a'sẽtu/ *m* accent; **~tuar** *vt* accentuate; accent <*letra*>

**acepção** /asep'sãw/ *f* sense

**acepipes** /ase'pipʃ/ *m pl* (Port) cocktail snacks

**acerca** /a'serka/ **~ de** *prep* about, concerning

**acercar-se** /aser'karsi/ *vpr* ~ **de** approach

**acertar** /aser'tar/ *vt* find <*(com o) caminho*, *(a) casa*>; put right, set <*relógio*>; get right <*pergunta*>; guess (correctly) <*solução*>; hit <*alvo*>; make <*acordo, negócio*>; fix, arrange <*encontro*> □ *vi* (*ter razão*) be right; (*atingir o alvo*) hit the mark; ~ **com** find, happen upon; ~ **em** hit

**acervo** /a'servu/ *m* collection; (*jurid*) estate

**aceso** /a'sezu/ *pp de* **acender** □ *a* <*luz*> on; <*fogo*> alight

**aces|sar** /ase'sar/ *vt* access; ~**sível** (*pl* ~**síveis**) *a* accessible; affordable <*preço*>; ~**so** /ɛ/ *m* access; (*de raiva, tosse*) fit; (*de febre*) attack; ~**sório** *a & m* accessory

**acetona** /ase'tona/ *f* (*para unhas*) nail varnish remover

**achado** /a'ʃadu/ *m* find

**achaque** /a'ʃaki/ *m* ailment

**achar** /a'ʃar/ *vt* find; (*pensar*) think; ~**-se** *vpr* (*estar*) be; (*considerar-se*) think that one is; **acho que sim/não** I think so/I don't think so

**achatar** /aʃa'tar/ *vt* flatten; cut <*salário*>

**aciden|tado** /asidẽ'tadu/ *a* rough <*terreno*>; bumpy <*estrada*>; eventful <*viagem, vida*>; injured <*pessoa*>; ~**tal** (*pl* ~**tais**) *a* accidental; ~**te** *m* accident

**acidez** /asi'des/ *f* acidity

**ácido** /'asidu/ *a & m* acid

**acima** /a'sima/ *adv* above; ~ **de** above; **mais** ~ higher up

**acio|nar** /asio'nar/ *vt* operate; (*jurid*) sue; ~**nista** *m/f* shareholder

**acirrado** /asi'xadu/ *a* stiff, tough

**acla|mação** /aklama'sãw/ *f* acclaim; (*de rei*) acclamation; ~**mar** *vt* acclaim

**aclarar** /akla'rar/ *vt* clarify, clear up □ *vi* clear up; ~**-se** *vpr* become clear

**aclimatar** /aklima'tar/ *vt* acclimatize, (*Amer*) acclimate; ~**-se** *vpr* get acclimatized, (*Amer*) get acclimated

**aço** /'asu/ *m* steel; ~ **inoxidável** stainless steel

**acocorar-se** /akoko'rarsi/ *vpr* squat (down)

**acolá** /ako'la/ *adv* over there

**acolcho|ado** /akowʃo'adu/ *m* quilt; ~**ar** *vt* quilt; upholster <*móveis*>

**aco|lhedor** /akoʎe'dor/ *a* welcoming; ~**lher** *vt* welcome <*hóspede*>; take in <*criança, refugiado*>; accept <*decisão, convite*>; respond to <*pedido*>; ~**lhida** *f*, ~**lhimento** *m* welcome; (*abrigo*) refuge

**acomodar** /akomo'dar/ *vt* accommodate; (*ordenar*) arrange; (*tornar cô-*

*modo*) make comfortable; ~**-se** *vpr* make o.s. comfortable

**acompa|nhamento** /akõpaɲa'mẽtu/ *m* (*mus*) accompaniment; (*prato*) side dish; (*comitiva*) escort; ~**nhante** *m/f* companion; (*mus*) accompanist; ~**nhar** *vt* accompany, go with; watch <*jogo, progresso*>; keep up with <*eventos, caso*>; keep up with, follow <*aula, conversa*>; share <*política, opinião*>; (*mus*) accompany; **a estrada ~nha o rio** the road runs alongside the river

**aconche|gante** /akõʃe'gãtʃi/ *a* cosy, (*Amer*) cozy; ~**gar** *vt* (*chegar a si*) cuddle; (*agasalhar*) wrap up; (*na cama*) tuck up; (*tornar cômodo*) make comfortable; ~**gar-se** *vpr* ensconce o.s.; ~**gar-se com** snuggle up to; ~**go** /e/ *m* cosiness, (*Amer*) coziness; (*abraço*) cuddle

**acondicionar** /akõdʒisio'nar/ *vt* condition; pack, package <*mercadoria*>

**aconse|lhar** /akõse'ʎar/ *vt* advise; ~**lhar-se** *vpr* consult; ~**lhar alg a** advise s.o. to; ~**lhar aco a alg** recommend sth to s.o.; ~**lhável** (*pl* ~**lháveis**) *a* advisable

**aconte|cer** /akõte'ser/ *vi* happen; ~**cimento** *m* event

**acordar** /akor'dar/ *vt/i* wake up

**acorde** /a'kordʒi/ *m* chord

**acordeão** /akordʒi'ãw/ *m* accordion

**acordo** /a'kordu/ *m* agreement; **de ~ com** in agreement with <*pessoa*>; in accordance with <*lei etc*>; **estar de ~** agree

**Açores** /a'soris/ *m pl* Azores

**açoriano** /asori'ano/ *a & m* Azorean

**acorrentar** /akoxẽ'tar/ *vt* chain (up)

**acossar** /ako'sar/ *vt* hound, badger

**acos|tamento** /akosta'mẽtu/ *m* hard shoulder, (*Amer*) berm; ~**tar-se** *vpr* lean back

**acostu|mado** /akostu'madu/ *a* usual, customary; **estar ~mado a** be used to; ~**mar** *vt* accustom; ~**mar-se a** get used to

**acotovelar** /akotove'lar/ *vt* (*empurrar*) jostle; (*para avisar*) nudge

**açou|gue** /a'sogi/ *m* butcher's (shop); ~**gueiro** *m* butcher

**acovardar** /akovar'dar/ *vt* cow, intimidate

**acre** /'akri/ *a* <*gosto*> bitter; <*aroma*> acrid, pungent; <*tom*> harsh

**acredi|tar** /akredʒi'tar/ *vt* believe; accredit <*representante*>; ~**tar em** believe <*pessoa, história*>; believe in <*Deus, fantasmas*>; (*ter confiança*) have faith in; ~**tável** (*pl* ~**táveis**) *a* believable

**acre-doce** /akri'dosi/ *a* sweet and sour

**acrescentar** /akrese'tar/ vt add

**acres|cer** /akre'ser/ vt (juntar) add; (aumentar) increase □ vi increase; **~cido de** with the addition of; **~ce que** add to that the fact that

**acréscimo** /a'krɛsimu/ m addition; (aumento) increase

**acriançado** /akriã'sadu/ a childish

**acrílico** /a'kriliku/ a acrylic

**acroba|cia** /akroba'sia/ f acrobatics; **~ta** m/f acrobat

**act-** (Port) veja **at-**

**acuar** /aku'ar/ vt corner

**açúcar** /a'sukar/ m sugar

**açuca|rar** /asuka'rar/ vt sweeten; sugar <café, chá>; **~reiro** m sugar bowl

**açude** /a'sudʒi/ m dam

**acudir** /aku'dʒir/ vt/i **~ (a)** come to the rescue (of)

**acumular** /akumu'lar/ vt accumulate; combine <cargos>

**acupuntura** /akupũ'tura/ f acupuncture

**acu|sação** /akuza'sãw/ f accusation; **~sar** vt accuse; (jurid) charge; (revelar) reveal, show up; acknowledge <recebimento>

**acústi|ca** /a'kustʃika/ f acoustics; **~co** a acoustic

**adap|tação** /adapta'sãw/ f adaptation; **~tado** a (criança) well-adjusted; **~tar** vt adapt; (para encaixar) tailor; **~tar-se** vpr adapt; **~tável** (pl **~táveis**) a adaptable

**adega** /a'dɛga/ f wine cellar

**adentro** /a'dẽtru/ adv inside; **selva ~** into the jungle

**adepto** /a'dɛptu/ m follower; (Port: de equipa) supporter

**ade|quado** /ade'kwadu/ a appropriate, suitable; **~quar** vt adapt, tailor

**adereços** /ade'resus/ m pl props

**ade|rente** /ade'rẽtʃi/ m/f follower; **~rir** vi (colar) stick; join <a partido, causa>; follow <a moda>; **~são** f adhesion; (apoio) support; **~sivo** a sticky, adhesive □ m sticker

**ades|trado** /ades'tradu/ a skilled; **~trador** m trainer; **~trar** vt train; break in <cavalo>

**adeus** /a'dews/ int goodbye □ m goodbye, farewell

**adian|tado** /adʒiã'tadu/ a advanced; <relógio> fast; **chegar ~tado** be early; **~tamento** m progress; (pagamento) advance; **~tar** vt advance <dinheiro>; put forward <relógio>; bring forward <data, reunião>; get ahead with <trabalho> □ vi <relógio> gain; (ter efeito) be of use; **~tar-se** vpr progress, get ahead; **não ~ta (fazer)** it's no use (doing); **~te** adv ahead

**adia|r** /adʒi'ar/ vt postpone; adjourn <sessão>; **~mento** m postponement, adjournment

**adi|ção** /adʒi'sãw/ f addition; **~cionar** vt add; **~do** m attaché

**adivi|nhação** /adʒiviɲa'sãw/ f guesswork; (por adivinho) fortune-telling; **~nhar** vt guess; tell <futuro, sorte>; read <pensamento>; **~nho** m fortune-teller

**adjetivo** /adʒe'tʃivu/ m adjective

**adminis|tração** /adʒiministra'sãw/ f administration; (de empresas) management; **~trador** m administrator; manager; **~trar** vt administer; manage <empresa>

**admi|ração** /adʒimira'sãw/ f admiration; (assombro) wonder(ment); **~rado** a admired; (surpreso) amazed, surprised; **~rador** m admirer □ a admiring; **~rar** vt admire; (assombrar) amaze; **~rar-se** vpr be amazed; **~rável** (pl **~ráveis**) a admirable; (assombroso) amazing

**admis|são** /adʒimi'sãw/ f admission; (de escola) intake; **~sível** (pl **~síveis**) a admissible

**admitir** /adʒimi'tʃir/ vt admit; (permitir) permit, allow; (contratar) take on

**adoção** /ado'sãw/ f adoption

**ado|çar** /ado'sar/ vt sweeten; **~cicado** a slightly sweet

**adoecer** /adoe'ser/ vi fall ill □ vt make ill

**adoles|cência** /adole'sẽsia/ f adolescence; **~cente** a & m adolescent

**adopt-** (Port) veja **adot-**

**adorar** /ado'rar/ vt (amar) adore; worship <deus>; (fam: gostar de) love

**adorme|cer** /adorme'ser/ vi fall asleep; <perna> go to sleep, go numb; **~cido** a sleeping; <perna> numb

**ador|nar** /ador'nar/ vt adorn; **~no** /o/ m adornment

**ado|tar** /ado'tar/ vt adopt; **~tivo** a adopted

**adquirir** /adʒiki'rir/ vt acquire

**adu|bar** /adu'bar/ vt fertilize; **~bo** m fertilizer

**adu|lação** /adula'sãw/ f flattery; (do público) adulation; **~lar** vt make a fuss of; (com palavras) flatter

**adulterar** /aduwte'rar/ vt adulterate; cook, doctor <contas> □ vi commit adultery

**adúltero** /a'duwteru/ m adulterer (f -ess) □ a adulterous

**adul|tério** /aduw'tɛriu/ m adultery; **~to** a & m adult

**advento** /adʒi'vẽtu/ m advent

**advérbio** /adʒi'vɛrbiu/ m adverb

adver|sário /adʒiver'sariu/ m opponent; (*inimigo*) adversary; ~sidade *f* adversity; ~so *a* adverse; (*adversário*) opposed

adver|tência /adʒiver'tẽsia/ *f* warning; ~tir *vt* warn

advo|cacia /adʒivoka'sia/ *f* legal practice; ~gado *m* lawyer; ~gar *vt* advocate; (*jurid*) plead □ *vi* practise law

aéreo /a'ɛriu/ *a* air

aero|dinâmica /aerodʒi'namika/ *f* aerodynamics; ~dinâmico *a* aerodynamic; ~dromo *m* airfield; ~moça /o/ *f* air hostess; ~nauta *m* airman (*f* -woman); ~náutica *f* ( *força*) air force; (*ciência*) aeronautics; ~nave *f* aircraft; ~porto /o/ *m* airport

aeros|sol /aero'sɔw/ (*pl* ~sóis) *m* aerosol

afabilidade /afabili'dadʒi/ *f* friendliness, kindness

afagar /afa'gar/ *vt* stroke

afamado /afa'madu/ *a* renowned, famed

afas|tado /afas'tadu/ *a* remote; <*parente*> distant; ~tado de (far) away from; ~tamento *m* removal; (*distância*) distance; (*de candidato*) rejection; ~tar *vt* move away; (*tirar*) remove; ward off <*perigo, ameaça*>; put out of one's mind <*idéia*>; ~tar-se *vpr* move away; (*distanciar-se*) distance o.s.; (*de cargo*) step down

afá|vel /a'favew/ (*pl* ~veis) *a* friendly, genial

afazeres /afa'zeris/ *m pl* business; ~ domésticos (household) chores

afect- (*Port*) *veja* afet-

Afeganistão /afeganis'tãw/ *m* Afghanistan

afe|gão /afe'gãw/ *a & m* (*f* ~gã) Afghan

afeição /afej'sãw/ *f* affection, fondness

afeiçoado /afejsu'adu/ *a* (*devoto*) devoted; (*amoroso*) fond

afeminado /afemi'nadu/ *a* effeminate

aferir /afe'rir/ *vt* check, inspect <*pesos, medidas*>; (*avaliar*) assess; (*cotejar*) compare

aferrar /afe'xar/ *vt* grasp; ~-se a cling to

afe|tação /afeta'sãw/ *f* affectation; ~tado *a* affected; ~tar *vt* affect; ~tivo *a* (*carinhoso*) affectionate; (*sentimental*) emotional; ~to /ɛ/ *m* affection; ~tuoso /o/ *a* affectionate

afi|ado /afi'adu/ *a* sharp; skilled <*pessoa*>; ~ar *vt* sharpen

aficionado /afisio'nadu/ *m* enthusiast

afilhado /afi'ʎadu/ *m* godson (*f* -daughter)

afili|ação /afilia'sãw/ *f* affiliation; ~ada *f* affiliate; ~ar *vt* affiliate

afim /a'fĩ/ *a* related, similar

afinado /afi'nadu/ *a* in tune

afinal /afi'naw/ *adv* ~ (de contas) ( *por fim*) in the end; (*pensando bem*) after all

afinar /afi'nar/ *vt* tune □ *vi* taper

afinco /a'fĩku/ *m* perseverance, determination

afinidade /afini'dadʒi/ *f* affinity

afir|mação /afirma'sãw/ *f* assertion; ~mar *vt* claim, assert; ~mativo *a* affirmative

afivelar /afive'lar/ *vt* buckle

afixar /afik'sar/ *vt* stick, post

afli|ção /afli'sãw/ *f* (*física*) affliction; (*cuidado*) anxiety; ~gir *vt* <*doença*> afflict; (*inquietar*) trouble; ~gir-se *vpr* worry; ~to *a* troubled, worried

afluente /aflu'ẽtʃi/ *m* tributary

afo|bação /afoba'sãw/ *f* fluster, flap; ~bado *a* in a flap, flustered; ~bar *vt* fluster; ~bar-se *vpr* get flustered, get in a flap

afo|gado /afo'gadu/ *a* drowned; morrer ~gado drown; ~gador *m* choke; ~gar *vt/i* drown; (*auto*) flood; ~gar-se *vpr* (*matar-se*) drown o.s.

afoito /a'fojtu/ *a* bold, daring

afora /a'fɔra/ *adv* pelo mundo ~ throughout the world

afortunado /afortu'nadu/ *a* fortunate

afresco /a'fresku/ *m* fresco

África /'afrika/ *f* Africa; ~ do Sul South Africa

africano /afri'kanu/ *a & m* African

afrodisíaco /afrodʒi'ziaku/ *a & m* aphrodisiac

afron|ta /a'frõta/ *f* affront, insult; ~tar *vt* affront, insult

afrouxar /afro'ʃar/ *vt/i* loosen; (*de rapidez*) slow down; (*de disciplina*) relax

afta /'afta/ *f* (mouth) ulcer

afugentar /afuʒẽ'tar/ *vt* drive away; rout <*inimigo*>

afundar /afũ'dar/ *vt* sink; ~-se *vpr* sink

agachar /aga'ʃar/ *vi* ~-se *vpr* bend down

agarrar /aga'xar/ *vt* grab, snatch; ~-se *vpr* ~-se a cling to, hold on to

agasa|lhar /agaza'ʎar/ *vt* ~lhar-se *vpr* wrap up (warmly); ~lho *m* (*casaco*) coat; (*suéter*) sweater

agência /a'ʒẽsia/ *f* agency; ~ de correio post office; ~ de viagens travel agency

agenda /a'ʒẽda/ *f* diary

agente /a'ʒẽtʃi/ *m/f* agent

ágil /'aʒiw/ (*pl* ágeis) *a* <*pessoa*> agile; <*serviço*> quick, efficient

agili|dade /aʒili'dadʒi/ *f* agility; (*rapidez*) speed; ~zar *vt* speed up, streamline

ágio /'aʒiu/ *m* premium

**agiota** /aʒiˈɔta/ m/f loan shark

**agir** /aˈʒir/ vi act

**agi|tado** /aʒiˈtadu/ a agitated; <*mar*> rough; **~tar** vt wave <*braços*>; wag <*rabo*>; shake <*garrafa*>; (*perturbar*) agitate; **~tar-se** vpr get agitated; <*mar*> get rough

**aglome|ração** /aglomeraˈsãw/ f collection; (*de pessoas*) crowd; **~rar** collect; **~rar-se** vpr gather

**agonia** /agoˈnia/ f anguish; (*da morte*) death throes

**agora** /aˈgɔra/ adv now; (*há pouco*) just now; **~ mesmo** right now; **de ~ em diante** from now on; **até ~** so far, up till now

**agosto** /aˈgostu/ m August

**agouro** /aˈgoru/ m omen

**agraciar** /agrasiˈar/ vt decorate

**agra|dar** /agraˈdar/ vt please; (*fazer agrados*) be nice to, fuss over □ vi be pleasing, please; (*cair no gosto*) go down well; **~dável** (pl **~dáveis**) a pleasant

**agrade|cer** /agradeˈser/ vt **~cer aco a alg, ~cer a alg por aco** thank s.o. for sth □ vi say thank you; **~cido** a grateful; **~cimento** m gratitude; pl thanks

**agrado** /aˈgradu/ m **fazer ~s** a be nice to, make a fuss of

**agrafa|r** /agraˈfar/ vt (*Port*) staple; **~dor** m stapler

**agrário** /aˈgrariu/ a land, agrarian

**agra|vante** /agraˈvãtʃi/ a aggravating □ f aggravating circumstance; **~var** vt aggravate, make worse; **~var-se** vpr get worse

**agredir** /agreˈdʒir/ vt attack

**agregado** /agreˈgadu/ m (*em casa*) lodger

**agres|são** /agreˈsãw/ f aggression; (*ataque*) assault; **~sivo** a aggressive; **~sor** m aggressor

**agreste** /aˈgrɛstʃi/ a rural

**agrião** /agriˈãw/ m watercress

**agrícola** /aˈgrikola/ a agricultural

**agricul|tor** /agrikuwˈtor/ m farmer; **~tura** f agriculture, farming

**agridoce** /agriˈdosi/ a bittersweet

**agropecuá|ria** /agropekuˈaria/ f farming; **~rio** a agricultural

**agru|pamento** /agrupaˈmẽtu/ m grouping; **~par** vt group; **~par-se** vpr group (together)

**água** /ˈagwa/ f water; **dar ~ na boca** be mouthwatering; **ir por ~ abaixo** go down the drain; **~ benta** holy water; **~ doce** fresh water; **~ mineral** mineral water; **~ salgada** salt water; **~ sanitária** household bleach

**aguaceiro** /agwaˈseru/ m downpour

**água-de-|-coco** /agwadʒiˈkoku/ f coconut water; **~-colônia** f eau de cologne

**aguado** /aˈgwadu/ a watery

**aguardar** /agwarˈdar/ vt wait for, await □ vi wait

**aguardente** /agwarˈdẽtʃi/ f spirit

**aguarrás** /agwaˈxas/ m turpentine

**água-viva** /agwaˈviva/ f jellyfish

**agu|çado** /aguˈsadu/ a pointed; <*sentidos*> acute; **~çar** vt sharpen; **~deza** f sharpness; (*mental*) perceptiveness; **~do** a sharp; <*som*> shrill; (*fig*) acute

**agüentar** /agwẽˈtar/ vt stand, put up with; hold <*peso*> □ vi <*pessoa*> hold out; <*suporte*> hold

**águia** /ˈagia/ f eagle

**agulha** /aˈguʎa/ f needle

**ai** /aj/ m sigh; (*de dor*) groan □ int ah!; (*de dor*) ouch!

**aí** /aˈi/ adv there; (*então*) then

**aidético** /ajˈdɛtʃiku/ a suffering from Aids □ m Aids sufferer

**AIDS** /ˈajdʒis/ f Aids

**ainda** /aˈida/ adv still; **melhor ~** even better; **não ... ~** not ... yet; **~ assim** even so; **~ bem** just as well; **~ por cima** moreover, in addition; **~ que** even if

**aipim** /ajˈpĩ/ m cassava

**aipo** /ˈajpu/ m celery

**ajeitar** /aʒejˈtar/ vt (*arrumar*) sort out; (*arranjar*) arrange; (*ajustar*) adjust; **~-se** vpr adapt; (*dar certo*) turn out right, sort s.os. out

**ajoe|lhado** /aʒoeˈʎadu/ a kneeling (down); **~lhar** vi, **~lhar-se** vpr kneel (down)

**aju|da** /aˈʒuda/ f help; **~dante** m/f helper; **~dar** vt help

**ajuizado** /aʒuiˈzadu/ a sensible

**ajus|tar** /aʒusˈtar/ vt adjust; settle <*disputa*>; take in <*roupa*>; **~tar-se** vpr conform; **~tável** (pl **~táveis**) a adjustable; **~te** m adjustment; (*acordo*) settlement

**ala** /ˈala/ f wing

**ala|gação** /alagaˈsãw/ f flooding; **~gadiço** a marshy □ m marsh; **~gar** vt flood

**alameda** /alaˈmeda/ f avenue

**álamo** /ˈalamu/ m poplar (tree)

**alarde** /aˈlardʒi/ m **fazer ~ de** flaunt; make a big thing of <*notícia*>; **~ar** vt/i flaunt

**alargar** /alarˈgar/ vt widen; (*fig*) broaden; let out <*roupa*>

**alarido** /alaˈridu/ m outcry

**alar|ma** /aˈlarma/ m alarm; **~mante** a alarming; **~mar** vt alarm; **~me** m alarm; **~mista** a & m alarmist

**alastrar** /alasˈtrar/ vt scatter; (*disseminar*) spread □ vi spread

**alavanca** /ala'vãka/ f lever; ~ **de mudanças** gear lever

**alban|ês** /awba'nes/ a & m (f ~**esa**) Albanian

**Albânia** /aw'bania/ f Albania

**albergue** /aw'bɛrgi/ m hostel

**álbum** /'awbũ/ m album

**alça** /'awsa/ f handle; (de roupa) strap; (de fusil) sight

**alcachofra** /awka'ʃofra/ f artichoke

**alçada** /aw'sada/ f competence, power

**álcali** /'awkali/ m alkali

**alcan|çar** /awkã'sar/ vt reach; (conseguir) attain; (compreender) understand □ vi reach; ~**cável** (pl ~**cáveis**) a reachable; attainable; ~**ce** m reach; (de tiro) range; (importância) consequence; (compreensão) understanding

**alcaparra** /awka'paxa/ f caper

**alcatra** /aw'katra/ f rump steak

**alcatrão** /awka'trãw/ m tar

**álcool** /'awkow/ m alcohol

**alcoó|latra** /awko'ɔlatra/ m/f alcoholic; ~**lico** a & m alcoholic

**alcunha** /aw'kuɲa/ f nickname

**aldeia** /aw'deja/ f village

**aleatório** /alia'tɔriu/ a random, arbitrary

**alecrim** /ale'krĩ/ m rosemary

**ale|gação** /alega'sãw/ f allegation; ~**gar** vt allege

**ale|goria** /alego'ria/ f allegory; ~**górico** a allegorical

**ale|grar** /ale'grar/ vt cheer up; brighten up <casa>; ~**grar-se** vpr cheer up; ~**gre** /ɛ/ a cheerful; <cores> bright; ~**gria** f joy

**alei|jado** /ale'ʒadu/ a crippled □ m cripple; ~**jar** vt cripple

**alei|tamento** /alejta'mẽtu/ m breast-feeding; ~**tar** vt breast-feed

**além** /a'lẽj/ adv beyond; ~ **de** (ao lado de lá de) beyond; (mais de) over; (ademais de) apart from

**Alemanha** /ale'maɲa/ f Germany

**alemão** /ale'mãw/ (pl ~**mães**) a & m (f ~**mã**) German

**alen|tador** /alẽta'dor/ a encouraging; ~**tar** vt encourage; ~**tar-se** vpr cheer up; ~**to** m courage; (fôlego) breath

**alergia** /aler'ʒia/ f allergy

**alérgico** /a'lɛrʒiku/ a allergic (a to)

**aler|ta** /a'lɛrta/ a & m alert □ adv on the alert; ~**tar** vt alert

**alfa|bético** /awfa'bɛtʃiku/ a alphabetical; ~**betização** f literacy; ~**betizar** vt teach to read and write; ~**beto** m alphabet

**alface** /aw'fasi/ f lettuce

**alfaiate** /awfaj'atʃi/ m tailor

**al|fândega** /aw'fãdʒiga/ f customs;

~**fandegário** a customs □ m customs officer

**alfine|tada** /awfine'tada/ f prick; (dor) stabbing pain; (fig) dig; ~**te** /e/ m pin; ~**te de segurança** safety pin

**alforreca** /alfo'xeka/ f (Port) jellyfish

**alga** /'awga/ f seaweed

**algarismo** /awga'rizmu/ m numeral

**algazarra** /awga'zaxa/ f uproar, racket

**alge|mar** /awʒe'mar/ vt handcuff; ~**mas** /e/ f pl handcuffs

**algibeira** /alʒi'bejra/ f (Port) pocket

**algo** /'awgu/ pron something; (numa pergunta) anything □ adv somewhat

**algodão** /awgo'dãw/ m cotton; ~(-**doce**) candy floss, (Amer) cotton candy; ~ (**hidrófilo**) cotton wool, (Amer) absorbent cotton

**alguém** /aw'gẽj/ pron somebody, someone; (numa pergunta) anybody, anyone

**al|gum** /aw'gũ/ (f ~**guma**) a some; (numa pergunta) any; (nenhum) no, not one □ pron pl some; ~**guma coisa** something

**algures** /aw'guris/ adv somewhere

**alheio** /a'ʎeju/ a (de outra pessoa) someone else's; (de outras pessoas) other people's; ~ **a** a foreign to; (impróprio) irrelevant to; (desatento) unaware of; ~ **de** removed from

**alho** /'aʎu/ m garlic; ~-**poró** m leek

**ali** /a'li/ adv (over) there

**ali|ado** /ali'adu/ a allied □ m ally; ~**ança** f alliance; (anel) wedding ring; ~**ar** vt, ~**ar-se** vpr ally

**aliás** /a'ljaʃ/ adv (além disso) what's more, furthermore; (no entanto) however; (diga-se de passagem) by the way, incidentally; (senão) otherwise

**álibi** /'alibi/ m alibi

**alicate** /ali'katʃi/ m pliers; ~ **de unhas** nail clippers

**alicerce** /ali'sɛrsi/ m foundation; (fig) basis

**alie|nado** /alie'nadu/ a alienated; (demente) insane; ~**nar** vt alienate; transfer <bens>; ~**nígena** a & m/f alien

**alimen|tação** /alimẽta'sãw/ f (ato) feeding; (comida) food; (tecn) supply; ~**tar** a food; <hábitos> eating □ vt feed; (fig) nurture; ~**tar-se de** live on; ~**tício** a gêneros ~**tícios** foodstuffs; ~**to** m food

**ali|nhado** /ali'ɲadu/ a aligned; <pessoa> smart, (Amer) sharp; ~**nhar** vt align

**alíquota** /a'likwota/ f (de imposto) bracket

**alisar** /ali'zar/ vt smooth (out); straighten <cabelo>

**alistar** /alisˈtar/ *vt* recruit; **~-se** *vpr* enlist

**aliviar** /aliviˈar/ *vt* relieve

**alívio** /aˈliviu/ *m* relief

**alma** /ˈawma/ *f* soul

**almanaque** /awmaˈnaki/ *m* yearbook

**almejar** /awmeˈʒar/ *vt* long for

**almirante** /awmiˈrãtʃi/ *m* admiral

**almo|çar** /awmoˈsar/ *vi* have lunch □ *vt* have for lunch; **~ço** /o/ *m* lunch

**almofada** /awmoˈfada/ *f* cushion; (*Port: de cama*) pillow

**almôndega** /awˈmõdʒiga/ *f* meatball

**almoxarifado** /awmoʃariˈfadu/ *m* storeroom

**alô** /aˈlo/ *int* hallo

**alocar** /aloˈkar/ *vt* allocate

**alo|jamento** /aloʒaˈmẽtu/ *m* accommodation, (*Amer*) accommodations, (*habitação*) housing; **~jar** *vt* accommodate; house <*sem-teto*>; **~jar-se** *vpr* stay

**alongar** /alõˈgar/ *vt* lengthen; extend, stretch out <*braço*>

**alpendre** /awˈpẽdri/ *m* shed; (*pórtico*) porch

**Alpes** /ˈawpis/ *m pl* Alps

**alpinis|mo** /awpiˈnizmu/ *m* mountaineering; **~ta** *m/f* mountaineer

**alqueire** /awˈkeri/ *m = 4.84 hectares*, (*in São Paulo = 2.42 hectares*)

**alquimi|a** /awkiˈmia/ *f* alchemy; **~sta** *mf* alchemist

**alta** /ˈawta/ *f* rise; **dar ~ a** discharge; **ter ~** be discharged

**altar** /awˈtar/ *m* altar

**alterar** /awteˈrar/ *vt* alter; (*falsificar*) falsify; **~-se** *vpr* change; (*zangar-se*) get angry

**alter|nado** /awterˈnadu/ *a* alternate; **~nar** *vt/i*, **~nar-se** *vpr* alternate; **~nativa** *f* alternative; **~nativo** *a* alternative; <*corrente*> alternating

**al|teza** /awˈteza/ *f* highness; **~titude** *f* altitude

**alti|vez** /awtʃiˈves/ *f* arrogance; **~vo** *a* arrogant; (*elevado*) majestic

**alto** /ˈawtu/ *a* high; <*pessoa*> tall; <*barulho*> loud □ *adv* high; <*falar*> loud(ly); <*ler*> aloud □ *m* top; **os ~s e baixos** the ups and downs □ *int* halt!; **~-falante** *m* loudspeaker

**altura** /awˈtura/ *f* height; (*momento*) moment; **ser à ~ de** be up to

**aluci|nação** /alusinaˈsãw/ *f* hallucination; **~nante** *a* mind-boggling, crazy

**aludir** /aluˈdʒir/ *vi* allude (**a** to)

**alu|gar** /aluˈgar/ *vt* rent <*casa*>; hire, rent <*carro*>; <*locador*> let, rent out, hire out; **~guel** (*Port*), **~guer** /ɛ/ *m* rent; (*ato*) renting

**alumiar** /alumiˈar/ *vt* light (up)

**alumínio** /aluˈminiu/ *m* aluminium, (*Amer*) aluminum

**aluno** /aˈlunu/ *m* pupil

**alusão** /aluˈzãw/ *f* allusion (**a** to)

**alvará** /awvaˈra/ *m* permit, licence

**alve|jante** /awveˈʒãtʃi/ *m* bleach; **~jar** *vt* bleach; (*visar*) aim at

**alvenaria** /awvenaˈria/ *f* masonry

**alvo** /ˈawvu/ *m* target

**alvorada** /awvoˈrada/ *f* dawn

**alvoro|çar** /awvoroˈsar/ *vt* stir up, agitate; (*entusiasmar*) excite; **~ço** /o/ *m* (*tumulto*) uproar; (*entusiasmo*) excitement

**amabilidade** /amabiliˈdadʒi/ *f* kindness

**amaci|ante** /amasiˈãtʃi/ *m* (*de roupa*) (fabric) conditioner; **~ar** *vt* soften; run in <*carro*>

**amador** /amaˈdor/ *a & m* amateur; **~ismo** *m* amateurism; **~ístico** *a* amateurish

**amadurecer** /amadureˈser/ *vt/i* <*fruta*> ripen; (*fig*) mature

**âmago** /ˈamagu/ *m* heart, core; (*da questão*) crux

**amaldiçoar** /amawdʒisoˈar/ *vt* curse

**amamentar** /amamẽˈtar/ *vt* breastfeed

**amanhã** /amaˈɲã/ *m & adv* tomorrow; **depois de ~** the day after tomorrow

**amanhecer** /amaɲeˈser/ *vi & m* dawn

**amansar** /amãˈsar/ *vt* tame; (*fig*) placate <*pessoa*>

**a|mante** /aˈmãtʃi/ *m/f* lover; **~mar** *vt/i* love

**amarelo** /amaˈrɛlu/ *a & m* yellow

**amar|go** /aˈmargu/ *a* bitter; **~gura** *f* bitterness; **~gurar** *vt* embitter; (*sofrer*) endure

**amarrar** /amaˈxar/ *vt* tie (up); (*naut*) moor; **~ a cara** frown, scowl

**amarrotar** /amaxoˈtar/ *vt* crease

**amassar** /amaˈsar/ *vt* crush, squash; screw up <*papel*>; crease <*roupa*>; dent <*carro*>; knead <*pão*>; mash <*batatas*>

**amá|vel** /aˈmavew/ (*pl* **~veis**) *a* kind

**Ama|zonas** /amaˈzonas/ *m* Amazon; **~zônia** *f* Amazonia

**âmbar** /ˈabar/ *m* amber

**ambi|ção** /ãbiˈsãw/ *f* ambition; **~cionar** *vt* aspire to; **~cioso** /o/ *a* ambitious

**ambien|tal** /ãbiẽˈtaw/ (*pl* **~tais**) *a* environmental; **~tar** *vt* set <*filme, livro*>; set up <*casa*>; **~tar-se** *vpr* settle in; **~te** *m* environment; (*atmosfera*) atmosphere

**am|bigüidade** /ãbigwiˈdadʒi/ *f* ambiguity; **~bíguo** *a* ambiguous

**âmbito** /ˈabitu/ *m* scope, range

**ambos** /ˈabus/ *a & pron* both

**ambu|lância** /ābu'lãsia/ *f* ambulance; **~lante** *a* (*que anda*) walking; <*músico*> wandering; <*venda*> mobile; **~latório** *m* out-patient clinic

**amea|ça** /ami'asa/ *f* threat; **~çador** *a* threatening; **~çar** *vt* threaten

**ameba** /a'mɛba/ *f* amoeba

**amedrontar** /amedrõ'tar/ *vt* scare; **~-se** *vpr* get scared

**ameixa** /a'mɛʃa/ *f* plum; (*passa*) prune

**amém** /a'mẽj/ *int* amen □ *m* agreement; **dizer ~ a** go along with

**amêndoa** /a'mẽdoa/ *f* almond

**amendoim** /amẽdo'ĩ/ *m* peanut

**ame|nidade** /ameni'dadʒi/ *f* pleasantness; *pl* pleasantries, small talk; **~nizar** *vt* ease; calm <*ânimos*>; settle <*disputa*>; tone down <*repreensão*>; **~no** /e/ *a* pleasant; mild <*clima*>

**América** /a'mɛrika/ *f* America; **~ do Norte/Sul** North/South America

**america|nizar** /amerikani'zar/ *vt* Americanize; **~no** *a* & *m* American

**amestrar** /ames'trar/ *vt* train

**ametista** /ame'tʃista/ *f* amethyst

**amianto** /ami'ãtu/ *m* asbestos

**ami|gar-se** /ami'garsi/ *vpr* make friends; **~gável** (*pl* **~gáveis**) *a* amicable

**amígdala** /a'migdala/ *f* tonsil

**amigdalite** /amigda'litʃi/ *f* tonsillitis

**amigo** /a'migu/ *a* friendly □ *m* friend; **~ da onça** false friend

**amistoso** /amis'tozu/ *a* & *m* friendly

**amiúde** /ami'udʒi/ *adv* often

**amizade** /ami'zadʒi/ *f* friendship

**amnésia** /ami'nɛzia/ *f* amnesia

**amnistia** /amnis'tia/ *f* (*Port*) *veja* **anistia**

**amo|lação** /amola'sãw/ *f* annoyance; **~lante** *a* annoying; **~lar** *vt* annoy, bother; sharpen <*faca*>; **~lar-se** *vpr* get annoyed

**amolecer** /amole'ser/ *vt/i* soften

**amol|gadura** /amowga'dura/ *f* dent; **~gar** *vt* dent

**amoníaco** /amo'niaku/ *m* ammonia

**amontoar** /amõto'ar/ *vt* pile up; amass <*riquezas*>; **~-se** *vpr* pile up

**amor** /a'mor/ *m* love; **~ próprio** self-esteem

**amora** /a'mɔra/ *f* **~ preta**, (*Port*) **~ silvestre** blackberry

**amordaçar** /amorda'sar/ *vt* gag

**amoroso** /amo'rozu/ *adj* loving

**amor-perfeito** /amorper'fejtu/ *m* pansy

**amorte|cedor** /amortese'dor/ *m* shock absorber; **~cer** *vt* deaden; absorb <*impacto*>; break <*queda*> □ *vi* fade

**amostra** /a'mɔstra/ *f* sample

**ampa|rar** /ãpa'rar/ *vt* support; (*fig*) protect; **~rar-se** *vpr* lean; **~ro** *m* (*apoio*) support; (*proteção*) protection; (*ajuda*) aid

**ampère** /ã'pɛri/ *m* amp(ere)

**ampli|ação** /ãplia'sãw/ *f* (*de foto*) enlargement; (*de casa*) extension; **~ar** *vt* enlarge <*foto*>; extend <*casa*>; broaden <*conhecimentos*>

**amplifi|cador** /ãplifika'dor/ *m* amplifier; **~car** *vt* amplify

**amplo** /'ãplu/ *a* <*sala*> spacious; <*roupa*> full; <*sentido, conhecimento*> broad

**ampola** /ã'pola/ *f* ampoule

**amputar** /ãpu'tar/ *vt* amputate

**Amsterdã** /amister'dã/, (*Port*) **Amsterdão** /amiʃter'dãw/ *f* Amsterdam

**amu|ado** /amu'adu/ *a* in a sulk, sulky; **~ar** *vi* sulk

**amuleto** /amu'leto/ *m* charm

**amuo** /a'muu/ *m* sulk

**ana|crônico** /ana'kroniku/ *a* anachronistic; **~cronismo** *m* anachronism

**anais** /a'najs/ *m pl* annals

**analfabeto** /anawfa'bɛtu/ *a* & *m* illiterate

**analisar** /anali'zar/ *vt* analyse

**análise** /a'nalizi/ *f* analysis

**ana|lista** /ana'lista/ *m/f* analyst; **~lítico** *a* analytical

**analogia** /analo'ʒia/ *f* analogy

**análogo** /a'nalogu/ *a* analogous

**ananás** /ana'naʃ/ *m invar* (*Port*) pineapple

**anão** /a'nãw/ *a* & *m* (*f* **anã**) dwarf

**anarquia** /anar'kia/ *f* anarchy; (*fig*) chaos

**anárquico** /a'narkiku/ *a* anarchic

**anarquista** /anar'kista/ *m/f* anarchist

**ana|tomia** /anato'mia/ *f* anatomy; **~tômico** *a* anatomical

**anca** /'ãka/ *f* (*de pessoa*) hip; (*de animal*) rump

**anchova** /ã'ʃova/ *f* anchovy

**ancinho** /ã'siɲu/ *m* rake

**âncora** /'ãkora/ *f* anchor

**anco|radouro** /ãkora'doru/ *m* anchorage; **~rar** *vt/i* anchor

**andaime** /ã'dajmi/ *m* scaffolding

**an|damento** /ãda'mẽtu/ *m* (*progresso*) progress; (*rumo*) course; **dar ~damento a** set in motion; **~dar** *m* (*jeito de andar*) gait, walk; (*de prédio*) floor; (*Port: apartamento*) flat, (*Amer*) apartment □ *vi* (*ir a pé*) walk; (*de trem, ônibus*) travel; (*a cavalo, de bicicleta*) ride; (*funcionar, progredir*) go; **ele anda deprimido** he's been depressed lately

**Andes** /'ãdʒis/ *m pl* Andes

**andorinha** /ãdo'riɲa/ *f* swallow

**anedota** /ane'dæta/ *f* anecdote

**anel** /a'nɛw/ (*pl* **anéis**) *m* ring; (*no cabelo*) curl; ~ **viário** ringroad

**anelado** /ane'ladu/ *a* curly

**anemia** /ane'mia/ *f* anaemia

**anêmico** /a'nemiku/ *a* anaemic

**anes|tesia** /aneste'zia/ *f* anaesthesia; (*droga*) anaesthetic; ~**tesiar** *vt* anaesthetize; ~**tésico** *a* & *m* anaesthetic; ~**tesista** *m/f* anaesthetist

**ane|xar** /anek'sar/ *vt* annex <*terras*>; (*em carta*) enclose; (*juntar*) attach; ~**xo** /ɛ/ *a* attached; (*em carta*) enclosed □ *m* annexe; (*em carta*) enclosure

**anfíbio** /ã'fibiu/ *a* amphibious □ *m* amphibian

**anfiteatro** /ãfitʃi'atru/ *m* amphitheatre; (*no teatro*) dress circle

**anfi|trião** /ãfitri'ãw/ *m* (*f* ~**triã**) host (*f* -ess)

**angariar** /ãgari'ar/ *vt* raise <*fundos*>; canvass for <*votos*>; win <*adeptos, simpatia*>

**angli|cano** /ãgli'kanu/ *a* & *m* Anglican; ~**cismo** *m* Anglicism

**anglo-saxônico** /ãglusak'soniku/ *a* Anglo-Saxon

**Angola** /ã'gola/ *f* Angola

**angolano** /ãgo'lanu/ *a* & *m* Angolan

**angra** /'ãgra/ *f* inlet, cove

**angular** /ãgu'lar/ *a* angular

**ângulo** /'ãgulu/ *m* angle

**angústia** /ã'gustʃia/ *f* anguish, anxiety

**angustiante** /ãgustʃi'ãtʃi/ *a* distressing; <*momento*> anxious

**ani|mado** /ani'madu/ *a* (*vivo*) lively; (*alegre*) cheerful; (*entusiasmado*) enthusiastic; ~**mador** *a* encouraging □ *m* presenter; ~**mal** (*pl* ~**mais**) *a* & *m* animal; ~**mar** *vt* encourage; liven up <*festa*>; ~**mar-se** *vpr* cheer up; <*festa*> liven up

**ânimo** /'animu/ *m* courage, spirit; *pl* tempers

**animosidade** /animozi'dadʒi/ *f* animosity

**aniquilar** /aniki'lar/ *vt* destroy; (*prostrar*) shatter

**anis** /a'nis/ *m* aniseed

**anistia** /anis'tʃia/ *f* amnesty

**aniver|sariante** /aniversari'ãtʃi/ *m/f* birthday boy (*f* girl); ~**sário** *m* birthday; (*de casamento etc*) anniversary

**anjo** /'ãʒu/ *m* angel

**ano** /'anu/ *m* year; **fazer** ~**s** have a birthday; ~ **bissexto** leap year; ~ **letivo** academic year; ~**-bom** New Year

**anoite|cer** /anojte'ser/ *m* nightfall □ *vi* ~**ceu** night fell

**anomalia** /anoma'lia/ *f* anomaly

**anonimato** /anoni'matu/ *m* anonymity

**anônimo** /a'nonimu/ *a* anonymous

**anor|mal** /anor'maw/ (*pl* ~**mais**) *a* abnormal

**ano|tação** /anota'sãw/ *f* note; ~**tar** *vt* note down, write down

**ânsia** /'ãsia/ *f* anxiety; (*desejo*) longing; ~**s de vômito** nausea

**ansi|ar** /ãsi'ar/ *vi* ~ **por** long for; ~**edade** *f* anxiety; (*desejo*) eagerness; ~**oso** /o/ *a* anxious

**antártico** /ã'tartʃiku/ *a* & *m* Antarctic

**antebraço** /ãtʃi'brasu/ *m* forearm

**antece|dência** /ãtese'dẽsia/ *f* com ~**dência** in advance; ~**dente** *a* preceding; ~**dentes** *m pl* record, past

**antecessor** /ãtese'sor/ *m* (*f* ~**a**) predecessor

**anteci|pação** /ãtʃisipa'sãw/ *f* anticipation; **com** ~**pação** in advance; ~**padamente** *adv* in advance; ~**pado** *a* advance; ~**par** *vt* anticipate, forestall; (*adiantar*) bring forward; ~**par-se** *vpr* be previous

**antena** /ã'tena/ *f* aerial, (*Amer*) antenna; (*de inseto*) feeler

**anteontem** /ãtʃi'õtẽ/ *adv* the day before yesterday

**antepassado** /ãtʃipa'sadu/ *m* ancestor

**anterior** /ãteri'or/ *a* previous; (*dianteiro*) front

**antes** /'ãtʃis/ *adv* before; (*ao contrário*) rather; ~ **de/que** before

**ante-sala** /ãtʃi'sala/ *f* ante-room

**anti|biótico** /ãtʃibi'otʃiku/ *a* & *m* antibiotic; ~**caspa** *a* anti-dandruff; ~**concepcional** (*pl* ~**concepcionais**) *a* & *m* contraceptive; ~**congelante** *m* antifreeze; ~**corpo** *m* antibody

**antídoto** /ã'tʃidotu/ *m* antidote

**antiético** /ãtʃi'ɛtʃiku/ *a* unethical

**antigamente** /ãtʃiga'mẽtʃi/ *adv* formerly

**anti|go** /ã'tʃigu/ *a* old; (*da antiguidade*) ancient; <*móveis etc*> antique; (*anterior*) former; ~**guidade** *f* antiquity; (*numa firma*) seniority; *pl* (*monumentos*) antiquities; (*móveis etc*) antiques

**anti-|higiênico** /ãtʃiʒi'eniku/ *a* unhygienic; ~**histamínico** *a* & *m* antihistamine; ~**horário** *a* anticlockwise

**antilhano** /ãtʃi'ʎanu/ *a* & *m* West Indian

**Antilhas** /ã'tʃiʎas/ *f pl* West Indies

**anti|patia** /ãtʃipa'tʃia/ *f* dislike; ~**pático** *a* unpleasant, unfriendly

**antiquado** /ātʃi'kwadu/ *a* antiquated, out-dated

**anti-|semitismo** /ātʃisemi'tʃizmu/ *m* anti-Semitism; **~séptico** *a* & *m* antiseptic; **~social** (*pl* **~sociais**) *a* antisocial

**antítese** /ā'tʃitezi/ *f* antithesis

**antologia** /ātolo'ʒia/ *f* anthology

**antônimo** /ā'tonimu/ *m* antonym

**antro** /'ātru/ *m* cavern; (*de animal*) lair; (*de ladrões*) den

**antro|pófago** /ātro'pɔfagu/ *a* man-eating; **~pologia** *f* anthropology; **~pólogo** *m* anthropologist

**anu|al** /anu'aw/ (*pl* **~ais**) *a* annual, yearly

**anu|lação** /anula'sāw/ *f* cancellation; **~lar** *vt* cancel; annul <*casamento*>; (*compensar*) cancel out □ *m* ring finger

**anunciar** /anūsi'ar/ *vt* announce; advertise <*produto*>

**anúncio** /a'nūsiu/ *m* announcement; (*propaganda, classificado*) advert(isement); (*cartaz*) notice

**ânus** /'anus/ *m invar* anus

**an|zol** /ā'zow/ (*pl* **~zóis**) *m* fish-hook

**aonde** /a'ōdʒi/ *adv* where

**apadrinhar** /apadri'ɲar/ *vt* be godfather to <*afilhado*>; be best man for <*noivo*>; (*proteger*) protect; (*patrocinar*) support

**apa|gado** /apa'gadu/ *a* <*fogo*> out; <*luz, TV*> off; (*indistinto*) faint; <*pessoa*> dull; **~gar** *vt* put out <*cigarro, fogo*>; blow out <*vela*>; switch off <*luz, TV*>; rub out <*erro*>; clean <*quadro-negro*>; **~gar-se** *vpr* <*fogo, luz*> go out; <*lembrança*> fade; (*desmaiar*) pass out; (*fam: dormir*) nod off

**apaixo|nado** /apaʃo'nadu/ *a* in love (**por** with); **~nante** *a* captivating; **~nar-se** *vpr* fall in love (**por** with)

**apalpar** /apaw'par/ *vt* touch, feel; <*médico*> examine

**apanhar** /apa'ɲar/ *vt* catch; (*do chão*) pick up; pick <*flores, frutas*>; (*ir buscar*) pick up; (*alcançar*) catch up □ *vi* be beaten

**aparafusar** /aparafu'zar/ *vt* screw

**apa|ra-lápis** /apara'lapiʃ/ *m invar* (*Port*) pencil sharpener; **~rar** *vt* catch <*bola*>; parry <*golpe*>; trim <*cabelo*>; sharpen <*lápis*>

**aparato** /apa'ratu/ *m* pomp, ceremony

**apare|cer** /apare'ser/ *vi* appear; **~ça!** do drop in!; **~cimento** *m* appearance

**apare|lhagem** /apare'ʎaʒẽ/ *f* equipment; **~lhar** *vt* equip; **~lho** /e/ *m* apparatus; (*máquina*) machine; (*de chá*) set, service; (*fone*) phone

**aparência** /apa'rēsia/ *f* appearance; **na ~** apparently

**aparen|tado** /aparē'tadu/ *a* related; **~tar** *vt* show; (*fingir*) feign; **~te** *a* apparent

**apar|tamento** /aparta'mētu/ *m* flat, (*Amer*) apartment; **~tar** *vt*, **~tar-se** *vpr* separate; **~te** *m* aside

**apatia** /apa'tʃia/ *f* apathy

**apático** /a'patʃiku/ *a* apathetic

**apavo|rante** /apavo'rātʃi/ *a* terrifying; **~rar** *vt* terrify; **~rar-se** *vpr* be terrified

**apaziguar** /apazi'gwar/ *vt* appease

**apear-se** /api'arsi/ *vpr* (*de cavalo*) dismount; (*de ônibus*) alight

**ape|gar-se** /ape'garsi/ *vpr* become attached (**a** to); **~go** /e/ *m* attachment

**ape|lação** /apela'sāw/ *f* appeal; (*fig*) exhibitionism; **~lar** *vi* appeal (**de** against); **~lar para** appeal to; (*fig*) resort to

**apeli|dar** /apeli'dar/ *vt* nickname; **~do** *m* nickname

**apelo** /a'pelu/ *m* appeal

**apenas** /a'penas/ *adv* only

**apêndice** /a'pēdʒisi/ *m* appendix

**apendicite** /apēdʒi'sitʃi/ *f* appendicitis

**aperceber-se** /aperse'bersi/ *vpr* **~(de)** notice, realize

**aperfeiçoar** /aperfejso'ar/ *vt* perfect

**aperitivo** /aperi'tʃivu/ *m* aperitif

**aper|tado** /aper'tadu/ *a* tight; (*sem dinheiro*) hard-up; **~tar** *vt* (*segurar*) hold tight; tighten <*cinto*>; press <*botão*>; squeeze <*esponja*>; take in <*vestido*>; fasten <*cinto de segurança*>; step up <*vigilância*>; cut down on <*despesas*>; break <*coração*>; (*fig*) pressurize <*pessoa*> □ *vi* <*sapato*> pinch; <*chuva, frio*> get worse; <*estrada*> narrow; **~tar-se** *vpr* (*gastar menos*) tighten one's belt; (*não ter dinheiro*) feel the pinch; **~tar a mão de alg** shake hands with s.o.; **~to** /e/ *m* pressure; (*de botão*) press; (*dificuldade*) tight spot, jam; **~to de mãos** handshake

**apesar** /ape'zar/ **~ de** *prep* in spite of

**apeti|te** /ape'tʃitʃi/ *m* appetite; **~toso** /o/ *a* appetizing

**apetrechos** /ape'treʃus/ *m pl* gear; (*de pesca*) tackle

**apimentado** /apimē'tadu/ *a* spicy, hot

**apinhar** /api'ɲar/ *vt* crowd, pack; **~se** *vpr* crowd

**api|tar** /api'tar/ *vi* whistle □ *vt* referee <*jogo*>; **~to** *m* whistle

**aplanar** /apla'nar/ *vt* level <*terreno*>; (*fig*) smooth <*caminho*>; smooth over <*problema*>

**aplau|dir** /aplaw'dʒir/ *vt* applaud; **~so(s)** *m* (*pl*) applause

**apli|cação** /aplika'sāw/ *f* application; (*de dinheiro*) investment; (*de lei*) enforcement; ~**car** vt apply; invest <*dinheiro*>; enforce <*lei*>; ~**car-se** vpr apply (**a** to); (*ao estudo etc*) apply o.s. (**a** to); ~**que m** hairpiece

**apoderar-se** /apode'rarsi/ vpr ~ **de** take possession of; <*raiva*> take hold of

**apodrecer** /apodre'ser/ vt/i rot

**apoi|ar** /apoj'ar/ vt lean; ( fig) support; (*basear*) base; ~**ar-se** vpr ~**ar-se em** lean on; ( fig) be based on, rest on; ~**o m** support

**apólice** /a'polisi/ f policy; (*ação*) bond

**apon|tador** /apõta'dor/ m pencil sharpener; ~**tar** vt (*com o dedo*) point at, point to; point out <*erro, caso interessante*>; aim <*arma*>; name <*nomes*>; put forward <*razão*> □ vi <*sol, planta*> come up; (*com o dedo*) point (**para** to)

**apoquentar** /apokē'tar/ vt annoy

**aporrinhar** /apoxi'ɲar/ vt annoy

**após** /a'pɔs/ adv after; **loção ~-barba** after-shave (lotion)

**aposen|tado** /apozē'tadu/ a retired □ m pensioner; ~**tadoria** f retirement; (*pensão*) pension; ~**tar** vt, ~**tar-se** vpr retire; ~**to** m room

**após-guerra** /apɔz'gɛxa/ m post-war period

**apos|ta** /a'pɔsta/ f bet; ~**tar** vt bet (**em** on); ( fig) have faith (**em** in)

**apostila** /apos'tʃila/ f revision aid, book of key facts

**apóstolo** /a'pɔstolu/ m apostle

**apóstrofo** /a'pɔstrofu/ m apostrophe

**apre|ciação** /apresia'sãw/ f appreciation; ~**ciar** vt appreciate; think highly of <*pessoa*>; ~**ciativo** a appreciative; ~**ciável** (*pl* ~**ciáveis**) a appreciable; ~**ço** /e/ m regard

**apreen|der** /apriē'der/ vt seize <*contrabando*>; apprehend <*criminoso*>; grasp <*sentido*>; ~**são** f apprehension; (*de contrabando*) seizure; ~**sivo** a apprehensive

**apregoar** /aprego'ar/ vt proclaim; cry <*mercadoria*>

**apren|der** /aprē'der/ vt/i learn; ~**diz** m/f (*de ofício*) apprentice; (*de direção*) learner; ~**dizado** m, ~**dizagem** f (*de ofício*) apprenticeship; (*de profissão*) training; (*escolar*) learning

**apresen|tação** /aprezēta'sãw/ f presentation; (*teatral etc*) performance; (*de pessoas*) introduction; ~**tador** m presenter; ~**tar** vt present; introduce <*pessoa*>; ~**tar-se** vpr (*identificar-se*) introduce o.s.; <*ocasião, problema*> present o.s., arise; ~**tar-se a** report to <*polícia etc*>; go in for <*exame*>; stand for <*eleição*>; ~**tável** (*pl* ~**táveis**) a presentable

**apres|sado** /apre'sadu/ a hurried; ~**sar** vt hurry; ~**sar-se** vpr hurry (up)

**aprimorar** /aprimo'rar/ vt perfect, refine

**aprofundar** /aprofũ'dar/ vt deepen; study carefully <*questão*>; ~**-se** vpr get deeper; ~**-se em** go deeper into

**aprontar** /aprõ'tar/ vt get ready; pick <*briga*> □ vi act up; ~**-se** vpr get ready

**apropriado** /apropri'adu/ a appropriate, suitable

**apro|vação** /aprova'sãw/ f approval; (*num exame*) pass; ~**var** vt approve of; approve <*lei*> □ vi make the grade; **ser ~vado** (*num exame*) pass

**aprovei|tador** /aprovejta'dor/ m opportunist; ~**tamento** m utilization; ~**tar** vt take advantage of; take <*ocasião*>; (*utilizar*) use □ vi make the most of it; ( *Port: adiantar*) be of use; ~**tar-se** vpr take advantage (**de** of); ~**te!** (*divirta-se*) have a good time!

**aproxi|mação** /aprosima'sãw/ f (*chegada*) approach; (*estimativa*) approximation; ~**mado** a <*valor*> approximate; ~**mar** vt move nearer; (*aliar*) bring together; ~**mar-se** vpr approach, get nearer (**de** to)

**ap|tidão** /aptʃi'dãw/ f aptitude, suitability; ~**to** a suitable

**apunhalar** /apuɲa'lar/ vt stab

**apu|rado** /apu'radu/ a refined; ~**rar** vt (*aprimorar*) refine; (*descobrir*) ascertain; investigate <*caso*>; collect <*dinheiro*>; count <*votos*>; ~**rar-se** vpr (*com a roupa*) dress smartly; ~**ro** m refinement; (*no vestir*) elegance; (*dificuldade*) difficulty; *pl* trouble

**aquarela** /akwa'rɛla/ f watercolour

**aquariano** /akwari'anu/ a & m Aquarian

**aquário** /a'kwariu/ m aquarium; **Aquário** Aquarius

**aquartelar** /akwarte'lar/ vt billet

**aquático** /a'kwatʃiku/ a aquatic, water

**aque|cedor** /akese'dor/ m heater; ~**cer** vt heat □ vi, ~**cer-se** vpr heat up; ~**cimento** m heating

**aqueduto** /ake'dutu/ m aqueduct

**aquele** /a'keli/ a that; *pl* those □ pron that one; *pl* those; ~ **que** the one that

**àquele** = **a²** + **aquele**

**aqui** /a'ki/ adv here

**aquilo** /a'kilu/ pron that

**àquilo** = **a²** + **aquilo**

**aquisi|ção** /akizi'sãw/ f acquisition; ~**tivo** a **poder ~tivo** purchasing power

**ar** /ar/ m air; (*aspecto*) look, air; (*Port: no carro*) choke; **ao ~ livre** in the open air; **no** ~ (*fig*) up in the air; (*TV*) on air; ~ **condicionado** air conditioning

**árabe** /'arabi/ *a & m* Arab; (*ling*) Arabic

**Arábia** /a'rabia/ *f* Arabia; ~ **Saudita** Saudi Arabia

**arado** /a'radu/ *m* plough, (*Amer*) plow

**aragem** /a'raʒẽ/ *f* breeze

**arame** /a'rami/ *m* wire; ~ **farpado** barbed wire

**aranha** /a'raɲa/ *f* spider

**arar** /a'rar/ *vt* plough, (*Amer*) plow

**arara** /a'rara/ *f* parrot

**arbi|trar** /arbi'trar/ *vt/i* referee <*jogo*>; arbitrate <*disputa*>; ~**trá-rio** *a* arbitrary

**arbítrio** /ar'bitriu/ *m* judgement; **livre** ~ free will

**árbitro** /'arbitru/ *m* arbiter <*da moda etc*>; (*jurid*) arbitrator; (*de futebol*) referee; (*de tênis*) umpire

**arborizado** /arbori'zadu/ *a* wooded, green; <*rua*> tree-lined

**arbusto** /ar'bustu/ *m* shrub

**ar|ca** /'arka/ *f* ~**ca de Noé** Noah's Ark; ~**cada** *f* (*galeria*) arcade; (*arco*) arch

**arcaico** /ar'kajku/ *a* archaic

**arcar** /ar'kar/ *vt* ~ **com** deal with

**arcebispo** /arse'bispu/ *m* archbishop

**arco** /'arku/ *m* (*arquit*) arch; (*arma, mus*) bow; (*eletr, mat*) arc; ~**da-velha** *m* **coisa do** ~**-da-velha** amazing thing; ~**-íris** *m invar* rainbow

**ar|dente** /ar'dẽtʃi/ *a* burning; (*fig*) ardent; ~**der** *vi* burn; <*olhos, ferida*> sting

**ar|dil** /ar'dʒiw/ (*pl* ~**dis**) *m* trick, ruse

**ardor** /ar'dor/ *m* heat; (*fig*) ardour; **com** ~ ardently

**árduo** /'arduu/ *a* strenuous, arduous

**área** /'aria/ *f* area; (**grande**) ~ penalty area; ~ (**de serviço**) yard

**arear** /ari'ar/ *vt* scour <*panela*>

**areia** /a'reja/ *f* sand

**arejar** /are'ʒar/ *vt air* □ *vi*, ~**-se** *vpr* get some air; (*descansar*) have a breather

**are|na** /a'rena/ *f* arena; ~**noso** /o/ *a* sandy

**arenque** /a'rēki/ *m* herring

**argamassa** /arga'masa/ *f* mortar

**Argélia** /ar'ʒɛlia/ *f* Algeria

**argelino** /arʒe'linu/ *a & m* Algerian

**Argentina** /arʒē'tʃina/ *f* Argentina

**argentino** /arʒē'tʃinu/ *a & m* Argentinian

**argila** /ar'ʒila/ *f* clay

**argola** /ar'gɔla/ *f* ring

**argumen|tar** /argumē'tar/ *vt/i* argue; ~**to** *m* argument; (*de filme etc*) subject-matter

**ariano** /ari'anu/ *a & m* (*do signo Aries*) Arian

**árido** /'aridu/ *a* arid; barren <*deserto*>; (*fig*) dull, dry

**Aries** /'aris/ *f* Aries

**arisco** /a'risku/ *a* timid

**aristo|cracia** /aristokra'sia/ *f* aristocracy; ~**crata** *m/f* aristocrat; ~**crático** *a* aristocratic

**aritmética** /aritʃ'mɛtʃika/ *f* arithmetic

**arma** /'arma/ *f* weapon; *pl* arms; ~ **de fogo** firearm

**ar|mação** /arma'sãw/ *f* frame; (*de óculos*) frames; (*naut*) rigging; ~**madilha** *f* trap; ~**madura** *f* suit of armour; (*armação*) framework; ~**mar** *vt* (*dar armas a*) arm; (*montar*) put up, assemble; set up <*máquina*>; set, lay <*armadilha*>; fit out <*navio*>; hatch <*plano, complô*>; cause <*briga*>; ~**mar-se** *vpr* arm o.s.

**armarinho** /arma'riɲu/ *m* haberdashery, (*Amer*) notions

**armário** /ar'mariu/ *m* cupboard; (*de roupa*) wardrobe

**arma|zém** /arma'zẽj/ *m* warehouse; (*loja*) general store; (*depósito*) storeroom; ~**zenagem** *f*, ~**zenamento** *m* storage; ~**zenar** *vt* store

**Armênia** /ar'menia/ *f* Armenia

**armênio** /ar'meniu/ *a & m* Armenian

**aro** /'aru/ *m* (*de roda, óculos*) rim; (*de porta*) frame

**aro|ma** /a'roma/ *f* aroma; (*perfume*) fragrance; ~**mático** *a* aromatic; fragrant

**ar|pão** /ar'pãw/ *m* harpoon; ~**poar** *vt* harpoon

**arquear** /arki'ar/ *vt* arch; ~**-se** *vpr* bend, bow

**arque|ologia** /arkiolo'ʒia/ *f* archaeology; ~**ológico** *a* archaeological; ~**ólogo** *m* archaeologist

**arquétipo** /ar'kɛtʃipu/ *m* archetype

**arquibancada** /arkibã'kada/ *f* terraces, (*Amer*) bleachers

**arquipélago** /arki'pɛlagu/ *m* archipelago

**arquite|tar** /arkite'tar/ *vt* think up; ~**to** /ɛ/ *m* architect; ~**tônico** *a* architectural; ~**tura** *f* architecture

**arqui|var** /arki'var/ *vt* file <*plano, processo*>; shelve <*plano, processo*>; ~**vista** *m/f* archivist; ~**vo** *m* file; (*conjunto*) files; (*móvel*) filing cabinet; *pl* (*do Estado etc*) archives

**arran|cada** /axã'kada/ *f* lurch; (*de atleta, fig*) spurt; ~**car** *vt* pull out <*cabelo etc*>; pull off <*botão etc*>; pull up <*erva daninha etc*>; take out <*dente*>; (*das mãos de alg*) wrench, snatch; extract <*confissão, dinheiro*> □ *vi* <*carro*> roar off; <*pessoa*> take off; (*dar solavanco*) lurch forward; ~**car-se** *vpr* take off; ~**co** *m* pull, tug; *veja* ~**cada**

**arranha-céu** /axaɲa'sɛw/ *m* skyscraper

**arra|nhadura** /axaɲa'dura/ *f* scratch; ~**nhão** *m* scratch; ~**nhar** *vt* scratch; have a smattering of <*língua*>

**arran|jar** /axã'ʒar/ *vt* arrange; (*achar*) get, find; (*resolver*) settle, sort out; ~**jar-se** *vpr* manage; ~**jo** *m* arrangement

**arrasar** /axa'zar/ *vt* devastate; raze, flatten <*casa, cidade*>; ~**se** *vpr* be devastated

**arrastar** /axas'tar/ *vt* drag; <*corrente, avalancha*> sweep away; (*atrair*) draw □ *vi* trail; ~**-se** *vpr* crawl; <*tempo*> drag; <*processo*> drag out

**arreba|tador** /axebata'dor/ *a* entrancing; shocking <*notícia*>; ~**tar** *vt* (*enlevar*) entrance, send; (*chocar*) shock

**arreben|tação** /axebẽta'sãw/ *f* surf; ~**tar** *vi* <*bomba*> explode; <*corda*> snap, break; <*balão, pessoa*> burst; <*onda*> break; <*guerra, incêndio*> break out □ *vt* snap, break <*corda*>; burst <*balão*>; break down <*porta*>

**arrebitar** /axebi'tar/ *vt* turn up <*nariz*>; prick up <*orelhas*>

**arreca|dação** /axekada'sãw/ *f* (*dinheiro*) tax revenue; ~**dar** *vt* collect

**arredar** /axe'dar/ *vt* **não ~ pé** stand one's ground

**arredio** /axe'dʒiu/ *a* withdrawn

**arredondar** /axedõ'dar/ *vt* round up <*quantia*>; round off <*ângulo*>

**arredores** /axe'dɔris/ *m pl* surroundings; (*de cidade*) outskirts

**arrefecer** /axefe'ser/ *vt/i* cool

**arregaçar** /axega'sar/ *vt* roll up

**arrega|lado** /axega'ladu/ *a* <*olhos*> wide; ~**lar** *vt* ~**lar os olhos se** wide-eyed with amazement

**arreganhar** /axega'ɲar/ *vt* bare <*dentes*>; ~**-se** *vpr* grin

**arrema|tar** /axema'tar/ *vt* finish off; (*no tricô*) cast off; ~**te** *m* conclusion; (*na costura*) finishing off; (*no futebol*) finishing

**arremes|sar** /axeme'sar/ *vt* hurl; ~**so** /e/ *m* throw

**arrepen|der-se** /axepẽ'dersi/ *vpr* be sorry; <*pecador*> repent; ~**der-se de regret**; ~**dido** *a* sorry; <*pecador*> repentant; ~**dimento** *m* regret; (*de pecado, crime*) repentance

**arrepi|ado** /axepi'adu/ *a* <*cabelo*> standing on end; <*pele, pessoa*> covered in goose pimples; ~**ar** *vt* (*dar calafrios*) make shudder; make stand on end <*cabelo*>; **me** ~**a (a pele)** it

gives me goose pimples; ~**ar-se** *vpr* (*estremecer*) shudder; <*cabelo*> stand on end; (*na pele*) get goose pimples; ~**o** *m* shudder; **me dá** ~**os** it makes me shudder

**arris|cado** /axis'kadu/ *a* risky; ~**car** *vt* risk; ~**car-se** *vpr* take a risk, risk it; ~**car-se a fazer** risk doing

**arro|char** /axo'ʃar/ *vt* tighten up □ *vi* be tough; ~**cho** /o/ *m* squeeze

**arro|gância** /axo'gãsia/ *f* arrogance; ~**gante** *a* arrogant

**arro|jado** /axo'ʒadu/ *a* bold; ~**jar** *vt* throw

**arrombar** /axõ'bar/ *vt* break down <*porta*>; break into <*casa*>; crack <*cofre*>

**arro|tar** /axo'tar/ *vi* burp, belch; ~**to** /o/ *m* burp

**arroz** /a'xoz/ *m* rice; ~ **doce** rice pudding; ~**al** (*pl* ~**ais**) *m* rice field

**arrua|ça** /axu'asa/ *f* riot; ~**ceiro** *m* rioter

**arruela** /axu'ɛla/ *f* washer

**arruinar** /axui'nar/ *vt* ruin; ~**-se** *vpr* be ruined

**arru|madeira** /axuma'dera/ *f* (*de hotel*) chambermaid; ~**mar** *vt* tidy (up) <*casa*>; sort out <*papéis, vida*>; pack <*mala*>; (*achar*) find, get; make up <*desculpa*>; (*vestir*) dress up; ~**mar-se** *vpr* (*aprontar-se*) get ready; (*na vida*) sort o.s. out

**arse|nal** /arse'naw/ (*pl* ~**nais**) *m* arsenal

**arsênio** /ar'seniu/ *m* arsenic

**arte** /'artʃi/ *f* art; **fazer** ~ <*criança*> get up to mischief; ~**fato** *m* product, article

**arteiro** /ar'teru/ *a* mischievous

**artéria** /ar'tɛria/ *f* artery

**artesa|nal** /arteza'naw/ (*pl* ~**nais**) *a* craft; ~**nato** *m* craftwork

**arte|são** /arte'zãw/ (*pl* ~**s**) *m* (*f* ~**sã**) artisan, craftsman (*f* -woman)

**ártico** /'artʃiku/ *a & m* arctic

**articu|lação** /artʃikula'sãw/ *f* articulation; (*anat, tecn*) joint; ~**lar** *vt* articulate

**arti|ficial** /artʃifisi'aw/ (*pl* ~**ficiais**) *a* artificial; ~**fício** *m* trick

**artigo** /ar'tʃigu/ *m* article; (*com*) item

**arti|lharia** /artʃiʎa'ria/ *f* artillery; ~**lheiro** *m* (*mil*) gunner; (*no futebol*) striker

**artimanha** /artʃi'maɲa/ *f* trick; (*método*) clever way

**ar|tista** /ar'tʃista/ *m/f* artist; ~**tístico** *a* artistic

**artrite** /ar'tritʃi/ *f* arthritis

**árvore** /'arvori/ *f* tree

**arvoredo** /arvo'redu/ *m* grove

**as** /as/ *artigo & pron veja* **a**[1]

**ás** /as/ *m* ace

às = a² + as
**asa** /'aza/ f wing; (de xícara) handle; ~**-delta** f hang-glider
**ascen|dência** /asẽ'dẽsia/ f ancestry; (superioridade) ascendancy; ~**dente** a rising; ~**der** vi rise; ascend <ao trono>; ~**são** f rise; (relig) Ascension; **em** ~**são** rising; (fig) up and coming; ~**sor** m lift, (Amer) elevator; ~**sorista** m/f lift operator
**asco** /'asku/ m revulsion, disgust; **dar** ~ be revolting
**asfalto** /as'fawtu/ m asphalt
**asfixiar** /asfiksi'ar/ vt/i asphyxiate
**Asia** /'azia/ f Asia
**asiático** /azi'atʃiku/ a & m Asian
**asilo** /a'zilu/ m (refúgio) asylum; (de velhos, crianças) home
**as|ma** /'azma/ f asthma; ~**mático** a & m asthmatic
**asneira** /az'nera/ f stupidity; (uma) stupid thing
**aspas** /'aspas/ f pl inverted commas
**aspargo** /as'pargu/ m asparagus
**aspecto** /as'pɛktu/ m appearance, look; (de um problema) aspect
**aspereza** /aspe'reza/ f roughness; (do clima, de um som) harshness; (fig) rudeness
**áspero** /'asperu/ a rough; <clima, som> harsh; (fig) rude
**aspi|ração** /aspira'sãw/ f aspiration; (med) inhalation; ~**rador** m vacuum cleaner; ~**rar** vt inhale, breathe in <ar, fumaça>; suck up <líquido>; ~**rar a** aspire to
**aspirina** /aspi'rina/ f aspirin
**asqueroso** /aske'rozu/ a revolting, disgusting
**assa|do** /a'sadu/ a & m roast; ~**dura** f (na pele) sore patch
**assalariado** /asalari'adu/ a salaried □ m salaried worker
**assal|tante** /asaw'tãtʃi/ m robber; (na rua) mugger; (de casa) burglar; ~**tar** vt rob; burgle, (Amer) burglarize <casa>; ~**to** m (roubo) robbery; (a uma casa) burglary; (ataque) assault; (no boxe) round
**assanhado** /asa'ɲadu/ a worked up; <criança> excitable; (erótico) amorous
**assar** /a'sar/ vt roast
**assassi|nar** /asasi'nar/ vt murder; (pol) assassinate; ~**nato** m murder; (pol) assassination; ~**no** m murderer; (pol) assassin
**asseado** /asi'adu/ a well-groomed
**as|sediar** /asedʒi'ar/ vt besiege <cidade>; (fig) pester; ~**sédio** m siege; (fig) pestering
**assegurar** /asegu'rar/ vt (tornar seguro) secure; (afirmar) guarantee; ~ **a alg aco/que** assure s.o. of sth/

that; ~**-se de/que** make sure of/that
**assembléia** /asẽ'blɛja/ f (pol) assembly; (com) meeting
**assemelhar** /aseme'ʎar/ vt liken; ~**se** vpr be alike; ~**se a** resemble, be like
**assen|tar** /asẽ'tar/ vt (estabelecer) establish, define; settle <povo>; lay <tijolo> □ vi <pó> settle; ~**tar-se** vpr settle down; ~**tar com** go with; ~**tar a** <roupa> suit; ~**to** m seat; (fig) basis; **tomar** ~**to** take a seat; <pó> settle
**assen|tir** /asẽ'tʃir/ vi agree; ~**timento** m agreement
**assessor** /ase'sor/ m adviser; ~**ar** vt advise
**assexuado** /aseksu'adu/ a asexual
**assiduidade** /asidui'dadʒi/ f (à escola) regular attendance; (diligência) diligence
**assíduo** /a'siduu/ a (que freqüenta) regular; (diligente) assiduous
**assim** /a'sĩ/ adv like this, like that; (portanto) therefore; **e** ~ **por diante** and so on; ~ **como** as well as; ~ **que** as soon as
**assimétrico** /asi'mɛtriku/ a asymmetrical
**assimilar** /asimi'lar/ vt assimilate; ~**se** vpr be assimilated
**assinalar** /asina'lar/ vt (marcar) mark; (distinguir) distinguish; (apontar) point out
**assi|nante** /asi'nãtʃi/ m/f subscriber; ~**nar** vt/i sign; ~**natura** f (nome) signature; (de revista) subscription
**assis|tência** /asis'tẽsia/ f assistance; (presença) attendance; (público) audience; ~**tente** a assistant □ m/f assistant; ~**tente social** social worker; ~**tir (a)** vt/i (ver) watch; (presenciar) attend; assist <doente>
**assoalho** /aso'aʎu/ m floor
**assoar** /aso'ar/ vt ~ **o nariz**, (Port) ~**se** blow one's nose
**assobi|ar** /asobi'ar/ vt/i whistle; ~**o** m whistle
**associ|ação** /asosia'sãw/ f association; ~**ado** a & m associate; ~**ar** vt associate (a with); ~**ar-se** vpr associate; (com) go into partnership (a with)
**assolar** /aso'lar/ vt devastate
**assom|bração** /asõbra'sãw/ f ghost; ~**brar** vt astonish, amaze; ~**brar-se** vpr be amazed; ~**bro** m amazement, astonishment; (coisa) marvel; ~**broso** /o/ a astonishing, amazing
**assoprar** /aso'prar/ vi blow □ vt blow; blow out <vela>
**assovi-** veja assobi-
**assu|mido** /asu'midu/ a (confesso) confirmed, self-confessed; ~**mir** vt

assume, take on; accept, admit
*<defeito>* □ *vi* take office

**assunto** /a'sũtu/ *m* subject; (*negócio*)
matter

**assus|tador** /asusta'dor/ *a* frighten-
ing; **~tar** *vt* frighten, scare; **~tar-se**
*vpr* get frightened, get scared

**asterisco** /aste'risku/ *m* asterisk

**as|tral** /as'traw/ ( *pl* **~trais**) *m* ( *fam*)
state of mind; **~tro** *m* star; **~tro-
logia** *f* astrology; **~trólogo** *m* astro-
loger; **~tronauta** *m/f* astronaut;
**~tronave** *f* spaceship; **~tronomia** *f*
astronomy; **~tronômico** *a* astro-
nomical; **~trônomo** *m* astronomer

**as|túcia** /as'tusia/ *f* cunning; **~tuto** *a*
cunning; (*comerciante*) astute

**ata** /'ata/ *f* minutes

**ata|ca|dista** /ataka'dʒista/ *m/f* whole-
saler; **~do** *m* **por** **~do** wholesale

**ata|cante** /ata'kãtʃi/ *a* attacking □ *m/
f* attacker; **~car** *vt* attack; tackle
*<problema>*

**atadura** /ata'dura/ *f* bandage

**ata|lhar** /ata'ʎar/ *vi* take a shortcut;
**~lho** *m* shortcut

**ataque** /a'taki/ *m* attack; (*de raiva,
riso*) fit

**atar** /a'tar/ *vt* tie

**atarantado** /atarã'tadu/ *a* flustered,
in a flap

**atarefado** /atare'fadu/ *a* busy

**atarracado** /ataxa'kadu/ *a* stocky

**atarraxar** /ataxa'ʃar/ *vt* screw

**até** /a'tɛ/ *prep* (up) to, as far as;
(*tempo*) until □ *adv* even; **~ logo**
goodbye; **~ que** until

**atéia** /a'tɛja/ *a & f veja* **ateu**

**ateliê** /ateli'e/ *m* studio

**atemorizar** /atemori'zar/ *vt* frighten

**Atenas** /a'tenas/ *f* Athens

**aten|ção** /atẽ'sãw/ *f* attention; *pl* (*bon-
dade*) thoughtfulness; **com ~ção**
attentively; **~cioso** *a* thoughtful, considerate

**aten|der** /atẽ'der/ **~der** (**a**) *vt/i* an-
swer *<telefone, porta>*; answer to
*<nome>*; serve *<freguês>*; see
*<paciente, visitante>*; grant, meet
*<pedido>*; heed *<conselho>*; **~di-
mento** *m* service; (*de médico etc*) con-
sultation

**aten|tado** /atẽ'tadu/ *m* murder at-
tempt; (*pol*) assassination attempt;
(*ataque*) attack (**contra** on); **~tar** *vi*
**~tar contra** make an attempt on

**atento** /a'tẽtu/ *a* attentive; **~ a** mind-
ful of

**aterrador** /atexa'dor/ *a* terrifying

**ater|ragem** /ate'xaʒẽ/ *f* (*Port*)
landing; **~rar** *vi* (*Port*) land

**aterris|sagem** /atexi'saʒẽ/ *f* landing;
**~sar** *vi* land

**ater-se** /a'tersi/ *vpr* **~ a** keep to, go by

**ates|tado** /ates'tadu/ *m* certificate;
**~tar** *vt* attest (to)

**ateu** /a'tew/ *a & m* ( *f* **atéia**) atheist

**atiçar** /atʃi'sar/ *vt* poke *<fogo>*; stir up
*<ódio, discórdia>*; arouse *<pessoa>*

**atinar** /atʃi'nar/ *vt* work out, guess;
**~ com** find; **~ em** notice

**atingir** /atʃĩ'ʒir/ *vt* reach; hit *<alvo>*;
(*conseguir*) attain; (*afetar*) affect

**atirar** /atʃi'rar/ *vt* throw □ *vi* shoot;
**~ em** fire at

**atitude** /atʃi'tudʒi/ *f* attitude; **tomar
uma ~** take action

**ati|va** /a'tʃiva/ *f* active service; **~var**
*vt* activate; **~vidade** *f* activity; **~vo** *a*
active □ *m* (*com*) assets

**Atlântico** /at'lãtʃiku/ *m* Atlantic

**atlas** /'atlas/ *m* atlas

**at|leta** /at'leta/ *m/f* athlete; **~lético** *a*
a...letic; **~letismo** *m* athletics

**atmosfera** /atʃimos'fɛra/ *f* atmo-
sphere

**ato** /'atu/ *m* act; (*ação*) action; **no ~**
on the spot

**ato|lar** /ato'lar/ *vt* bog down; **~lar-se**
*vpr* get bogged down; **~leiro** *m* bog;
( *fig*) fix, spot of trouble

**atômico** /a'tomiku/ *a* atomic

**atomizador** /atomiza'dor/ *m* atom-
izer spray

**átomo** /'atomu/ *m* atom

**atônito** /a'tonitu/ *a* astonished,
stunned

**ator** /a'tor/ *m* actor

**atordoar** /atordo'ar/ *vt* *<golpe, noti-
cia>* stun; *<som>* deafen; (*alucinar*)
bewilder

**atormentar** /atormẽ'tar/ *vt* plague,
torment

**atração** /atra'sãw/ *f* attraction

**atracar** /atra'kar/ *vt/i* (*naut*) moor; **~-
se** *vpr* grapple; ( *fam*) neck

**atractivo** (*Port*) *veja* **atrativo**

**atraente** /atra'ẽtʃi/ *a* attractive

**atraiçoar** /atrajso'ar/ *vt* betray

**atrair** /atra'ir/ *vt* attract

**atrapalhar** /atrapa'ʎar/ *vt/i* (*confundir*) confuse; (*estorvar*) hinder; (*perturbar*) disturb; **~-se** *vpr* get mixed
up

**atrás** /a'traʃ/ *adv* behind; (*no fundo*)
at the back; **~ de** behind; (*depois de,
no encalço de*) after; **um mês ~ a**
month ago; **ficar ~** be left behind

**atra|sado** /atra'zadu/ *a* late; (*relógio,
criança*) backward; *<relógio>* slow;
*<pagamento>* overdue; *<idéias>* old-
fashioned; **~sar** *vt* delay; put back
*<relógio>* □ *vi* be late; *<relógio>*
lose; **~sar-se** *vpr* be late; (*num trabalho*) get behind; (*no pagar*) get into
arrears; **~so** *m* delay; (*de país etc*)
backwardness; *pl* (*com*) arrears; **com
~so** late

atrativo /atra'tʃivu/ *m* attraction

através /atra'vɛs/ ~ de *prep* through; (*de um lado ao outro*) across

atravessado /atrave'sadu/ *a* <*espinha*> stuck; estar com alg ~ na garganta be fed up with s.o.

atravessar /atrave'sar/ *vt* go through; cross <*rua, rio*>

atre|ver-se /atre'versi/ *vpr* dare; ~ver-se a dare to; ~vido *a* daring; (*insolente*) impudent; ~vimento *m* daring, boldness; (*insolência*) impudence

atribu|ir /atribu'ir/ *vt* attribute (a to); confer <*prêmio, poderes*> (a on); attach <*importância*> (a to); ~to *m* attribute

atrito /a'tritu/ *m* friction; (*desavença*) disagreement

atriz /a'tris/ *f* actress

atrocidade /atrosi'dadʒi/ *f* atrocity

atrope|lar /atrope'lar/ *vt* run over, knock down <*pedestre*>; (*empurrar*) jostle; mix up <*palavras*>; ~lamento *m* (*de pedestre*) running over; ~lo /e/ *m* scramble

atroz /a'trɔs/ *a* awful, terrible; heinous <*crime*>; cruel <*pessoa*>

atuação /atua'sãw/ *f* (*ação*) action; (*desempenho*) performance

atu|al /atu'aw/ (*pl* ~ais) *a* current, present; <*assunto, interesse*> topical; <*pessoa, carro*> up-to-date; ~alidade *f* (*presente*) present (time); (*de um livro*) topicality; *pl* current affairs; ~alizado *a* up-to-date; ~alizar *vt* update; ~alizar-se *vpr* bring o.s. up to date; ~almente *adv* at present, currently

atum /a'tũ/ *m* tuna

aturdir /atur'dʒir/ *vt veja* atordoar

audácia /aw'dasia/ *f* boldness; (*insolência*) audacity

audi|ção /awdʒi'sãw/ *f* hearing; (*concerto*) recital; ~ência *f* audience; (*jurid*) hearing

audiovisu|al /awdʒiovizu'aw/ (*pl* ~ais) *a* audiovisual

auditório /awdʒi'tɔriu/ *m* auditorium; programa de ~ variety show

auge /'awʒi/ *m* peak, height

aula /'awla/ *f* class, lesson; dar ~ teach

aumen|tar /awmẽ'tar/ *vt* increase; raise <*preço, salário*>; extend <*casa*>; (*com lente*) magnify; (*acrescentar*) add □ *vi* increase; <*preço, salário*> go up; ~to *m* increase; (*de salário*) rise, (*Amer*) raise

au|sência /aw'zẽsia/ *f* absence; ~sente *a* absent □ *m/f* absentee

aus|pícios /aws'pisius/ *m pl* auspices; ~picioso /o/ *a* auspicious

auste|ridade /awsteri'dadʒi/ *f* austerity; ~ro /ɛ/ *a* austere

Austrália /aw'stralia/ *f* Australia

australiano /awstrali'anu/ *a & m* Australian

Austria /'awstria/ *f* Austria

austríaco /aws'triaku/ *a & m* Austrian

autarquia /awtar'kia/ *f* public authority

autêntico /aw'tẽtʃiku/ *a* authentic; genuine <*pessoa*>; true <*fato*>

autobio|grafia /awtobiogra'fia/ *f* autobiography; ~gráfico *a* autobiographical

autocarro /awto'kaxu/ *m* (*Port*) bus

autocrata /awto'krata/ *a* autocratic

autodefesa /awtode'feza/ *f* self-defence

autodidata /awtodʒi'data/ *a & m/f* self-taught (person)

autódromo /aw'tɔdromu/ *m* race track

auto-escola /awtois'kɔla/ *f* driving school

auto-estrada /awtois'trada/ *f* motorway, (*Amer*) expressway

autógrafo /aw'tɔgrafu/ *m* autograph

auto|mação /awtoma'sãw/ *f* automation; ~mático *a* automatic; ~matizar *vt* automate

auto|mobilismo /awtomobi'lizmu/ *m* motoring; (*esporte*) motor racing; ~móvel (*pl* ~móveis) *m* motor car, (*Amer*) automobile

au|tonomia /awtono'mia/ *f* autonomy; ~tônomo *a* autonomous; <*trabalhador*> selfemployed

autopeça /awto'pɛsa/ *f* car spare

autópsia /aw'tɔpsia/ *f* autopsy

autor /aw'tor/ *m* (*f* ~a) author; (*de crime*) perpetrator; (*jurid*) plaintiff

auto-retrato /awtoxe'tratu/ *m* self-portrait

autoria /awto'ria/ *f* authorship; (*de crime*) responsibility (de for)

autori|dade /awtori'dadʒi/ *f* authority; ~zação *f* authorization; ~zar *vt* authorize

autuar /awtu'ar/ *vt* sue

au|xiliar /awsili'ar/ *a* auxiliary □ *m/f* assistant □ *vt* assist; ~xílio *m* assistance, aid

aval /a'vaw/ (*pl* avais) *m* endorsement; (*com*) guarantee

avali|ação /avalia'sãw/ *f* (*de preço*) valuation; (*fig*) evaluation; ~ar *vt* value <*quadro etc*> (em at); assess <*danos, riscos*>; (*fig*) evaluate

avan|çar /avã'sar/ *vt* move forward □ *vi* move forward; (*mil, fig*) advance; ~çar a (*montar*) amount to; ~ço *m* advance

avar|eza /ava'reza/ *f* meanness; ~ento *a* mean

**ava|ria** /ava'ria/ *f* damage; (*de máquina*) breakdown; **~riado** *a* damaged; *<máquina>* out of order; *<carro>* broken down; **~riar** *vt* damage □ *vi* be damaged; *<máquina>* break down

**ave** /'avi/ *f* bird; **~ de rapina** bird of prey

**aveia** /a'veja/ *f* oats

**avelã** /ave'lã/ *f* hazelnut

**avenida** /ave'nida/ *f* avenue

**aven|tal** /avẽ'taw/ (*pl* **~tais**) *m* apron

**aventu|ra** /avẽ'tura/ *f* adventure; (*amorosa*) fling; **~rar** *vt* venture; **~rar-se** *vpr* venture (**a** to); **~reiro** *a* adventurous □ *m* adventurer

**averiguar** /averi'gwar/ *vt* check (out)

**avermelhado** /averme'ʎadu/ *a* reddish

**aver|são** /aver'sãw/ *f* aversion; **~so a** averse (**a** to)

**aves|sas** /a'vɛsas/ **às ~sas** the wrong way round; (*de cabeça para baixo*) upside down; **~so** /e/ *m* **ao ~so** inside out

**avestruz** /aves'trus/ *m* ostrich

**avi|ação** /avia'sãw/ *f* aviation; **~ão m** (aero)plane, (*Amer*) (air)plane; **~ão a jato** jet

**avi|dez** /avi'des/ *f* (*cobiça*) greediness; **~do** *a* greedy

**avi|sar** /avi'zar/ *vt* (*informar*) tell, let know; (*advertir*) warn; **~so** *m* notice; (*advertência*) warning

**avistar** /avis'tar/ *vt* catch sight of

**avo** /'avu/ *m* **um doze ~s** one twelfth

**avó** /a'vɔ/ *f* grandmother; **~s** *m pl* grandparents

**avô** /a'vo/ *m* grandfather

**avoado** /avo'adu/ *a* dizzy, scatterbrained

**avulso** /a'vuwsu/ *a* loose, odd

**avultado** /avuw'tadu/ *a* bulky

**axila** /ak'sila/ *f* armpit

**azaléia** /aza'lɛja/ *f* azalea

**azar** /a'zar/ *m* bad luck; **ter ~** be unlucky; **~ado, ~ento** *a* unlucky

**aze|dar** /aze'dar/ *vt* sour □ *vi* go sour; **~do** /e/ *a* sour

**azei|te** /a'zejtʃi/ *m* oil; **~tona** /o/ *f* olive

**azevinho** /aze'viɲu/ *m* holly

**azia** /a'zia/ *f* heartburn

**azucrinar** /azukri'nar/ *vt* annoy

**azul** /a'zuw/ (*pl* **azuis**) *a* blue

**azulejo** /azu'leʒu/ *m* (ceramic) tile

**azul-marinho** /azuwma'riɲu/ *a* *invar* navy blue

# B

**babá** /ba'ba/ *f* nanny; **~ eletrônica** baby alarm

**ba|bado** /ba'badu/ *m* frill; **~bador** *m* bib; **~bar** *vt/i*, **~bar-se** *vpr* drool (**por** over); *<bebê>* dribble; **~beiro** (*Port*) *m* bib

**baby-sitter** /bejbi'siter/ (*pl* **~s**) *m/f* babysitter

**bacalhau** /baka'ʎaw/ *m* cod

**bacana** /ba'kana/ (*fam*) *a* great

**bacha|rel** /baʃa'rɛw/ (*pl* **~réis**) bachelor; **~relado** *m* bachelor's degree; **~relar-se** *vpr* graduate

**bacia** /ba'sia/ *f* basin; (*da privada*) bowl; (*anat*) pelvis

**baço** /'basu/ *m* spleen

**bacon** /'bejkõ/ *m* bacon

**bactéria** /bak'tɛria/ *f* bacterium; *pl* bacteria

**bada|lado** /bada'ladu/ *a* (*fam*) talked about; **~lar** *vt* ring *<sino>* □ *vi* ring; (*fam*) go out and about; **~lativo** (*fam*) *a* fun-loving, gadabout

**badejo** /ba'deʒu/ *m* sea bass

**baderna** /ba'dɛrna/ *f* (*tumulto*) commotion; (*desordem*) mess

**badulaque** /badu'laki/ *m* trinket

**bafafá** /bafa'fa/ (*fam*) *m* to-do, kerfuffle

**ba|fo** /'bafu/ *m* bad breath; **~fômetro** *m* Breathalyser; **~forada** *f* puff

**bagaço** /ba'gasu/ *m* pulp; (*Port: aguardente*) brandy

**baga|geiro** /baga'ʒeru/ *m* (*de carro*) roofrack; (*Port: homem*) porter; **~gem** *f* luggage; (*cultural etc*) baggage

**bagatela** /baga'tɛla/ *f* trifle

**Bagdá** /bagi'da/ *f* Baghdad

**bago** /'bagu/ *m* berry; (*de chumbo*) pellet

**bagulho** /ba'guʎu/ *m* piece of junk; *pl* junk; **ele é um ~** he's as ugly as sin

**bagun|ça** /ba'gũsa/ *f* mess; **~çar** *vt* mess up; **~ceiro** *a* messy □ *m* messer

**baía** /ba'ia/ *f* bay

**baiano** /ba'janu/ *a & m* Bahian

**baila** /'bajla/ *f* **trazer/vir à ~** bring/come up

**bai|lar** /baj'lar/ *vt/i* dance; **~larino** *m* ballet dancer; **~le** *m* dance; (*de gala*) ball

**bainha** /ba'iɲa/ *f* (*de vestido*) hem; (*de arma*) sheath

**baioneta** /bajo'neta/ *f* bayonet

**bairro** /'bajxu/ *m* neighbourhood, area

**baixa** /'baʃa/ *f* drop, fall; (*de guerra*) casualty; (*dispensa*) discharge; **~-mar** *f* low tide

**baixar** /ba'ʃar/ *vt* lower; issue *<ordem>*; pass *<lei>* □ *vi* drop, fall; (*fam: pintar*) turn up

**baixaria** /baʃa'ria/ *f* sordidness; (*uma*) sordid thing

**baixela** /ba'ʃɛla/ *f* set of cutlery

**baixeza** /ba'ʃeza/ *f* baseness

**baixo** /'baʃu/ a low; <pessoa> short; <som, voz> quiet, soft; <cabeça, olhos> lowered; (vil) sordid □ adv low; <falar> softly, quietly □ m bass; **em ~** underneath; (em casa) downstairs; **em ~ de** under; **para ~** down; (em casa) downstairs; **por ~ de** under(neath)

**baju|lador** /baʒula'dor/ a obsequious □ m sycophant; **~lar** vt fawn on

**bala** /'bala/ f (de revólver) bullet; (doce) sweet

**balada** /ba'lada/ f ballad

**balaio** /ba'laju/ m linen basket

**balan|ça** /ba'lãsa/ f scales; **Balança** (signo) Libra; **~ça de pagamentos** balance of payments; **~çar** vt/i (no ar) swing; (numa cadeira etc) rock; <carro, avião> shake; <navio> roll; **~çar-se** vpr swing; **~cete** /e/ m trial balance; **~ço** m (com) balance sheet; (brinquedo) swing; (movimento no ar) swinging; (de carro, avião) shaking; (de navio) rolling; (de cadeira) rocking; **fazer um ~ço de** (fig) take stock of

**balangandã** /balãgã'dã/ m bauble

**balão** /ba'lãw/ m balloon; **soltar um ~-de-ensaio** (fig) put out feelers

**balar** /ba'lar/ vi bleat

**balbu|ciar** /bawbusi'ar/ vt/i babble; **~cio** m babble, babbling

**balbúrdia** /baw'burdʒia/ f hubbub

**bal|cão** /baw'kãw/ m (em loja) counter; (de informações, bilhetes) desk; (de cozinha) worktop, (Amer) counter; (no teatro) circle; **~conista** m/f shop assistant

**balde** /'bawdʒi/ m bucket

**baldeação** /bawdʒia'sãw/ f **fazer ~** change (trains)

**baldio** /baw'dʒiu/ a fallow; **terreno ~** (piece of) waste ground

**balé** /ba'lɛ/ m ballet

**balear** /bali'ar/ vt shoot

**baleia** /ba'leja/ f whale

**balido** /ba'lidu/ m bleat, bleating

**balísti|ca** /ba'listʃika/ f ballistics; **~co** a ballistic

**bali|za** /ba'liza/ f marker; (luminosa) beacon; **~zar** vt mark out

**balneário** /bawni'ariu/ m seaside resort

**balofo** /ba'lofu/ a fat, tubby

**baloiço, balouço** /ba'lojsu, ba'losu/ (Port) m (de criança) swing

**balsa** /'bawsa/ f (de madeira etc) raft; (que vai e vem) ferry

**bálsamo** /'bawsamu/ m balm

**báltico** /'bawtʃiku/ a & m Baltic

**baluarte** /balu'artʃi/ m bulwark

**bambo** /'bãbu/ a loose, slack; <pernas> limp; <mesa> wobbly

**bambo|lê** /bãbo'le/ m hula hoop;

**~lear** vi <pessoa> sway, totter; <coisa> wobble

**bambu** /bã'bu/ m bamboo

**ba|nal** /ba'naw/ (pl **~nais**) a banal; **~nalidade** f banality

**bana|na** /ba'nana/ f banana □ (fam) m/f wimp; **~nada** f banana fudge; **~neira** f banana tree; **plantar ~neira** do a handstand

**banca** /'bãka/ f (de trabalho) bench; (de jornais) newsstand; **~ examinadora** examining board; **~da** f (pol) bench

**bancar** /bã'kar/ vt (custear) finance; (fazer papel de) play; (fingir) pretend

**bancário** /bã'kariu/ a bank □ m bank employee

**bancarrota** /bãka'xota/ f bankruptcy; **ir à ~** go bankrupt

**banco** /'bãku/ m (com) bank; (no parque) bench; (na cozinha, num bar) stool; (de bicicleta) saddle; (de carro) seat; **~ de areia** sandbank; **~ de dados** database

**banda** /'bãda/ f band; (lado) side; **~ sideways on; nestas ~s** in these parts; **~ desenhada** (Port) cartoon

**bandei|ra** /bã'dera/ f flag; (divisa) banner; **dar ~ra** (fam) give o.s. away; **~rante** m/f pioneer □ f girl guide; **~rinha** m linesman

**bandeja** /bã'deʒa/ f tray

**bandido** /bã'dʒidu/ m bandit

**bando** /'bãdu/ m (de pessoas) band; (de pássaros) flock

**bandolim** /bãdo'lĩ/ m mandolin

**bangalô** /bãga'lo/ m bungalow

**Bangcoc** /bã'koki/ f Bangkok

**bangue-bangue** /bãgi'bãgi/ (fam) m western

**banguela** /bã'gela/ a toothless

**banha** /'bana/ f lard; pl (no corpo) flab

**banhar** /ba'nar/ vt (molhar) bathe; (lavar) bath; **~-se** vpr bathe

**banhei|ra** /ba'nera/ f bath, (Amer) bathtub; **~ro** m bathroom; (Port) lifeguard

**banhista** /ba'nista/ m/f bather

**banho** /'banu/ m bath; (no mar) bathe, dip; **tomar ~** have a bath; (no chuveiro) have a shower; **tomar um ~ de loja/cultura** go on a shopping/cultural spree; **~ de espuma** bubble bath; **~ de sol** sunbathing; **~-maria** (pl **~s-maria**) m bain marie

**ba|nimento** /bani'mẽtu/ m banishment; **~nir** vt banish

**banjo** /'bãʒu/ m banjo

**banqueiro** /bã'keru/ m banker

**banqueta** /bã'keta/ f foot-stool

**banque|te** /bã'ketʃi/ m banquet; **~teiro** m caterer

**banzé** /bã'zɛ/ (fam) m commotion, uproar

**bapt-** (*Port*) *veja* **bat-**

**baque** /'baki/ *m* thud, crash; (*revés*) blow; **~ar** *vi* topple over □ *vt* hit hard, knock for six

**bar** /bar/ *m* bar

**barafunda** /bara'fũda/ *f* jumble; (*barulho*) racket

**bara|lhada** /bara'ʎada/ *f* jumble; **~lho** *m* pack of cards, (*Amer*) deck of cards

**barão** /ba'rãw/ *m* baron

**barata** /ba'rata/ *f* cockroach

**bara|tear** /barat∫i'ar/ *vt* cheapen; **~teiro** *a* cheap

**baratinar** /barat∫i'nar/ *vt* fluster; (*transtornar*) rattle, shake up

**barato** /ba'ratu/ *a* cheap □ *adv* cheaply □ (*fam*) *m* **um ~** great; **que ~!** that's brilliant!

**barba** /'barba/ *f* beard; *pl* (*de g to etc*) whiskers; **fazer a ~** shave; **~da** *f* walkover; (*cavalo*) favourite; **~do** *a* bearded

**barbante** /bar'bãt∫i/ *m* string

**bar|baridade** /barbari'dadʒi/ *f* barbarity; (*fam: muito dinheiro*) fortune; **~bárie** *f*, **~barismo** *m* barbarism

**bárbaro** /'barbaru/ *m* barbarian □ *a* barbaric; (*fam: forte, bom*) terrific

**barbatana** /barba'tana/ *f* fin

**bar|beador** /barbia'dor/ *m* shaver; **~bear** *vt* shave; **~bear-se** *vpr* shave; **~bearia** *f* barber's shop; **~beiragem** (*fam*) *f* bit of bad driving; **~beiro** *m* barber; (*fam: motorista*) bad driver

**bar|ca** /'barka/ *f* barge; (*balsa*) ferry; **~caça** *f* barge; **~co** *m* boat; **~co a motor** motorboat; **~co a remo/vela** rowing/sailing boat, (*Amer*) rowboat/sailboat

**barga|nha** /bar'gaɲa/ *f* bargain; **~nhar** *vt/i* bargain

**barítono** /ba'ritonu/ *m* baritone

**barômetro** /ba'rometru/ *m* barometer

**baronesa** /baro'neza/ *f* baroness

**barra** /'baxa/ *f* bar; (*sinal gráfico*) slash, stroke; (*fam: situação*) situation; **segurar a ~** hold out; **forçar a ~** force the issue

**barra|ca** /ba'xaka/ *f* (*de acampar*) tent; (*na feira*) stall; (*casinha*) hut; (*guarda-sol*) sunshade; **~cão** *m* shed; **~co** *m* shack, shanty

**barragem** /ba'xaʒẽ/ *f* (*represa*) dam

**barra-pesada** /baxape'zada/ (*fam*) *a invar* <*bairro*> rough; <*pessoa*> shady; (*difícil*) tough

**bar|rar** /ba'xar/ *vt* bar; **~reira** *f* barrier; (*em corrida*) hurdle; (*em futebol*) wall

**barrento** /ba'xẽtu/ *a* muddy

**barricada** /baxi'kada/ *f* barricade

**barri|ga** /ba'xiga/ *f* stomach, (*Amer*) belly; **~ga da perna** calf; **~gudo** *a* pot-bellied

**bar|ril** /ba'xiw/ (*pl* **~ris**) *m* barrel

**barro** /'baxu/ *m* (*argila*) clay; (*lama*) mud

**barroco** /ba'xoku/ *a & m* baroque

**barrote** /ba'xɔt∫i/ *m* beam, joist

**baru|lheira** /baru'ʎera/ *f* racket, din; **~lhento** *a* noisy; **~lho** *m* noise

**base** /'bazi/ *f* base; (*fig: fundamento*) basis; **com ~ em** on the basis of; **na ~ de** based on; **~ado** *a* based; (*firme*) well-founded □ (*fam*) *m* joint; **~ar** *vt* base; **~ar-se em** be based on

**básico** /'baziku/ *a* basic

**basquete** /bas'kɛt∫i/ *m*, **basquetebol** /basketʃi'bɔw/ *m* basketball

**bas|ta** /'basta/ *m* **dar um ~ta em** call a halt to; **~tante** *a* (*muito*) quite a lot of; (*suficiente*) enough □ *adv* (*com adjetivo, advérbio*) quite; (*com verbo*) quite a lot; (*suficientemente*) enough

**bastão** /bas'tãw/ *m* stick; (*num revezamento, de comando*) baton

**bastar** /bas'tar/ *vi* be enough

**bastidores** /bast∫i'doris/ *m pl* (*no teatro*) wings; **nos ~** (*fig*) behind the scenes

**bata** /'bata/ *f* (*de mulher*) smock; (*de médico etc*) overall

**bata|lha** /ba'taʎa/ *f* battle; **~lhador** *a* plucky, feisty □ *m* fighter; **~lhão** *m* battalion; **~lhar** *vi* battle; (*esforçar-se*) fight hard □ *vt* fight hard to get

**batata** /ba'tata/ *f* potato; **~ doce** sweet potato; **~ frita** chips, (*Amer*) French fries; (*salgadinhos*) crisps, (*Amer*) potato chips

**bate-boca** /bat∫i'boka/ *m* row, argument

**bate|deira** /bate'dera/ *f* whisk; (*de manteiga*) churn; **~dor** *m* (*policial etc*) outrider; (*no criquete*) batsman; (*no beisebol*) batter; (*de caça*) beater; **~dor de carteiras** pickpocket

**batelada** /bate'lada/ *f* batch; **~s de** heaps of

**batente** /ba'tẽt∫i/ *m* (*de porta*) doorway; **para o/no ~** (*fam: ao trabalho*) to/at work

**bate-papo** /bat∫i'papu/ *m* chat.

**bater** /ba'ter/ *vt* beat; stamp <*pé*>; slam <*porta*>; strike <*horas*>; take <*foto*>; flap <*asas*>; (*datilografar*) type; (*lavar*) wash; (*usar muito*) wear a lot <*roupa*>; (*fam*) pinch <*carteira*> □ *vi* <*coração*> beat; <*porta*> slam; <*janela*> bang; <*horas*> strike; <*sino*> ring; (*à porta*) knock; (*com o carro*) crash; **~-se** *vpr* (*lutar*) fight; **~ à máquina** type; **~ à**

*ou* **na porta** knock at the door; ~ **em** hit; harp on *<assunto>*; *<luz, sol>* shine on; ~ **com o carro** crash one's car, have a crash; ~ **com a cabeça** bang one's head; **ele batia os dentes de frio** his teeth were chattering with cold; **ele não bate bem** ( *fam*) he's not all there

**bate|ria** /bate'ria/ *f* (*eletr*) battery; (*mus*) drums; ~**ria de cozinha** kitchen utensils; ~**rista** *m/f* drummer

**bati|da** /ba'tʃida/ *f* beat; (*à porta*) knock; (*no carro*) crash; (*policial*) raid; (*bebida*) cocktail of rum, sugar and fruit juice; ~**do** *a* beaten; *<roupa>* well worn; *<assunto>* hackneyed □ *m* ~**do de leite** (*Port*) milkshake

**batina** /ba'tʃina/ *f* cassock

**ba|tismo** /ba'tʃizmu/ *m* baptism; ~**tizado** *m* christening; ~**tizar** *vt* baptize; (*pôr nome*) christen

**batom** /ba'tõ/ *m* lipstick

**batu|cada** /batu'kada/ *f* samba percussion group; ~**car** *vt/i* drum in a samba rhythm; ~**que** *m* samba rhythm

**batuta** /ba'tuta/ *f* baton; **sob a ~ de** under the direction of

**baú** /ba'u/ *m* trunk

**baunilha** /baw'niʎa/ *f* vanilla

**bazar** /ba'zar/ *m* bazaar; (*loja*) stationery and haberdashery shop

**bê-a-bá** /bea'ba/ *m* ABC

**bea|titude** /beatʃi'tudʒi/ *f* ( *felicidade*) bliss; (*devoção*) piety, devoutness; ~**to** *a* (*devoto*) pious, devout; ( *feliz*) blissful

**bêbado** /'bebadu/ *a & m* drunk

**bebê** /be'be/ *m* baby; ~ **de proveta** test-tube baby

**bebe|deira** /bebe'dera/ *f* (*estado*) drunkenness; (*ato*) drinking bout; ~**dor** *m* drinker; ~**douro** *m* drinking fountain

**beber** /be'ber/ *vt/i* drink

**bebericar** /beberi'kar/ *vt/i* sip

**bebida** /be'bida/ *f* drink

**beca** /'bɛka/ *f* gown

**beça** /'bɛsa/ *f* **à ~** ( *fam*) (*com substantivo*) loads of; (*com adjetivo*) really; (*com verbo*) a lot

**beco** /'beku/ *m* alley; ~ **sem saída** dead end

**bedelho** /be'deʎu/ *m* **meter o ~ (em)** stick one's oar in(to)

**bege** /'bɛʒi/ *a invar* beige

**bei|cinho** /bej'siɲu/ *m* **fazer ~cinho** pout; ~**ço** *m* lip; ~**çudo** *a* thicklipped

**beija-flor** /bejʒa'flor/ *m* hummingbird

**bei|jar** /be'ʒar/ *vt* kiss; ~**jo** *m* kiss; ~**joca** /ɔ/ *f* peck

**bei|ra** /'bera/ *f* edge; ( *fig: do desastre etc*) verge, brink; **à ~ra de** at the edge of; ( *fig*) on the verge of; ~**rada** *f* edge; ~**ra-mar** *f* seaside; ~**rar** *vt* ( *ficar*) border (on); (*andar*) skirt; ( *fig*) border on, verge on; **ele está ~rando os 30 anos** he's nearing thirty

**beisebol** /beijsi'bɔw/ *m* baseball

**belas-artes** /bɛlaʃ'artʃiʃ/ *f pl* fine arts

**beldade** /bew'dadʒi/ *f*, **beleza** /be-'leza/ *f* beauty

**belga** /'bɛwga/ *a & m* Belgian

**Bélgica** /'bɛwʒika/ *f* Belgium

**beliche** /be'liʃi/ *m* bunk

**bélico** /'bɛliku/ *a* war

**belicoso** /beli'kozu/ *a* warlike

**belis|cão** /belis'kãw/ *m* pinch; ~**car** *vt* pinch; nibble *<comida>*

**Belize** /be'lizi/ *m* Belize

**belo** /'bɛlu/ *a* beautiful

**beltrano** /bew'tranu/ *m* such-and-such

**bem** /bẽj/ *adv* well; (*bastante*) quite; (*muito*) very □ *m* good; *pl* goods, property; **está ~** (it's) fine, OK; **fazer ~ a** be good for; **tudo ~?** ( *fam*) how's things?; **se ~ que** even though; ~ **feito (por você)** ( *fam*) it serves you right; **muito ~!** well done!; **de ~ com alg** on good terms with s.o.; ~ **como** as well as

**bem|-apessoado** /bẽjapeso'adu/ *a* nice-looking; ~**-comportado** *a* well-behaved; ~**-disposto** *a* keen, willing; ~**-estar** *m* well-being; ~**-humorado** *a* good-humoured; ~**-intencionado** *a* well-intentioned; ~**-passado** *a* *<carne>* well-done; ~**-sucedido** *a* successful; ~**-vindo** *a* welcome; ~**-visto** *a* well thought of

**bênção** /'bẽsãw/ ( *pl* ~**s**) *f* blessing

**bendito** /bẽ'dʒitu/ *a* blessed

**benefi|cência** /benefi'sẽsia/ *f* (*bondade*) goodness, kindness; (*caridade*) charity; ~**cente** *a* *<associação>* charitable; *<concerto, feira>* charity; ~**ciado** *m* beneficiary; ~**ciar** *vt* benefit; ~**ciar-se** *vpr* benefit (**de** from)

**benefício** /bene'fisiu/ *m* benefit; **em ~ de** in aid of

**benéfico** /be'nɛfiku/ *a* beneficial (**a** to)

**benevolência** /benevo'lẽsia/ *f* benevolence

**benévolo** /be'nɛvolu/ *a* benevolent

**benfeitor** /bẽfej'tor/ *m* benefactor

**bengala** /bẽ'gala/ *f* walking stick; (*pão*) French stick

**benigno** /be'niginu/ *a* benign

**ben|to** /'bẽtu/ *a* blessed; *<água>* holy; ~**zer** *vt* bless; ~**zer-se** *vpr* cross o.s.

**berço** /'bersu/ *m* (*de embalar*) cradle; (*caminha*) cot; ( *fig*) birthplace; **ter ~** be from a good family

**berimbau** /berĩ'baw/ *m Brazilian percussion instrument shaped like a bow*

**berinjela** /berĩ'ʒɛla/ *f* aubergine, (*Amer*) eggplant

**Berlim** /ber'lĩ/ *f* Berlin

**berma** /'bɛrma/ (*Port*) *f* hard shoulder, (*Amer*) berm

**bermuda** /ber'muda/ *f* Bermuda shorts

**Berna** /'bɛrna/ *f* Berne

**ber|rante** /be'xãtʃi/ *a* loud, flashy; ~**rar** *vi* <*pessoa*> shout; <*criança*> bawl; <*boi*> bellow; ~**reiro** *m* (*gritaria*) yelling, shouting; (*choro*) crying, bawling; ~**ro** /ε/ *m* yell, shout; (*de boi*) bellow; **aos** ~**ros** shouting

**besouro** /be'zoru/ *m* beetle

**bes|ta** /'besta/ *a* (*idiota*) stupid; (*cheio de si*) full of o.s.; (*pedante*) pretentious □ *f* (*pessoa*) dimwit, numbskull; **ficar** ~**ta** (*fam*) be taken aback; ~**teira** *f* stupidity; (*uma*) stupid thing; **falar** ~**teira** talk rubbish; ~**tial** (*pl* ~**tiais**) *a* bestial; ~**tificar** *vt* astound, dumbfound

**besuntar** /bezũ'tar/ *vt* coat; (*sujar*) smear

**betão** /be'tãw/ (*Port*) *m* concrete

**beterraba** /bete'xaba/ *f* beetroot

**betoneira** /beto'nera/ *f* cement mixer

**bexiga** /be'ʃiga/ *f* bladder

**bezerro** /be'zeru/ *m* calf

**bibelô** /bibe'lo/ *m* ornament

**Bíblia** /'biblia/ *f* Bible

**bíblico** /'bibliku/ *a* biblical

**biblio|grafia** /bibliogra'fia/ *f* bibliography; ~**teca** /ε/ *f* library; ~**tecário** *m* librarian □ *a* library

**bica** /'bika/ *f* tap; (*Port: cafezinho*) espresso; **suar em** ~**s** drip with sweat

**bicama** /bi'kama/ *f* truckle bed

**bicar** /bi'kar/ *vt* peck

**bíceps** /'bisɛps/ *m invar* biceps

**bicha** /'biʃa/ *f* (*Port: fila*) queue; (*Bras: fam*) queer, fairy

**bicheiro** /bi'ʃeru/ *m* organizer of illegal numbers game, racketeer

**bicho** /'biʃu/ *m* animal; (*inseto*) insect, (*Amer*) bug; **que** ~ **te mordeu?** what's got into you?; ~**-da-seda** (*pl* ~**s-da-seda**) *m* silkworm; ~**-de-sete-cabeças** (*fam*) *m* big deal, big thing; ~**-do-mato** (*pl* ~**s-do-mato**) *m* very shy person

**bicicleta** /bisi'klɛta/ *f* bicycle, bike

**bico** /'biku/ *m* (*de ave*) beak; (*de faca*) point; (*de sapato*) toe; (*de bule*) spout; (*de caneta*) nib; (*do seio*) nipple; (*de gás*) jet; (*fam*) (*emprego*) odd job, sideline; (*boca*) mouth

**bidê** /bi'de/ *m* bidet

**bidimensio|nal** /bidʒimẽsio'naw/ (*pl* ~**nais**) *a* two-dimensional

**biela** /bi'ɛla/ *f* connecting rod

**Bielo-Rússia** /bielo'xusia/ *f* Byelorussia

**bielo-russo** /bielo'xusu/ *a* & *m* Byelorussian

**bie|nal** /bie'naw/ (*pl* ~**nais**) *a* biennial □ *f* biennial art exhibition

**bife** /'bifi/ *m* steak

**bifo|cal** /bifo'kaw/ (*pl* ~**cais**) *a* bifocal

**bifur|cação** /bifurka'sãw/ *f* fork; ~**car-se** *vpr* fork

**bigamia** /biga'mia/ *f* bigamy

**bígamo** /'bigamu/ *a* bigamous □ *m* bigamist

**bigo|de** /bi'gɔdʒi/ *m* moustache; ~**dudo** *a* with a big moustache

**bigorna** /bi'gɔrna/ *f* anvil

**bijuteria** /biʒute'ria/ *f* costume jewellery

**bila|teral** /bilate'raw/ (*pl* ~**rais**) *a* bilateral

**bilhão** /bi'ʎãw/ *m* thousand million, (*Amer*) billion

**bilhar** /bi'ʎar/ *m* pool, billiards

**bilhe|te** /bi'ʎetʃi/ *m* ticket; (*recado*) note; ~**te de ida e volta** return ticket, (*Amer*) round-trip ticket; **o** ~**te azul** (*fam*) the sack; ~**teria** *f*, (*Port*) ~**teira** *f* (*no cinema, teatro*) box office; (*na estação*) ticket office

**bilíngüe** /bi'lĩgwi/ *a* bilingual

**bilionário** /bilio'nariu/ *a* & *m* billionaire

**bílis** /'bilis/ *f* bile

**binário** /bi'nariu/ *a* binary

**bingo** /'bĩgu/ *m* bingo

**binóculo** /bi'nɔkulu/ *m* binoculars

**biodegradá|vel** /biodegra'davew/ (*pl* ~**veis**) *a* biodegradable

**bio|grafia** /biogra'fia/ *f* biography; ~**gráfico** *a* biographical

**biógrafo** /bi'ɔgrafu/ *m* biographer

**bio|logia** /biolo'ʒia/ *f* biology; ~**lógico** *a* biological

**biólogo** /bi'ɔlogu/ *m* biologist

**biombo** /bi'õbu/ *m* screen

**biônico** /bi'oniku/ *a* bionic; (*pol*) unelected

**biópsia** /bi'ɔpsia/ *f* biopsy

**bioquími|ca** /bio'kimika/ *f* biochemistry; ~**co** *a* biochemical □ *m* biochemist

**biquíni** /bi'kini/ *m* bikini

**birma|nês** /birma'nes/ *a* & *m* (*f* ~**nesa**) Burmese

**Birmânia** /bir'mania/ *f* Burma

**birô** /bi'ro/ *m* bureau

**bir|ra** /'bixa/ *f* wilfulness; **fazer** ~**ra** have a tantrum; ~**rento** *a* wilful

**biruta** /bi'ruta/ (*fam*) *a* crazy □ *f* windsock

**bis** /bis/ *int* encore!, more! □ *m invar* encore

**bisa|vó** /biza'vɔ/ *f* great-grandmother; **~vós** *m pl* great-grandparents; **~vô** *m* great-grandfather

**bisbilho|tar** /bizbiʎo'tar/ *vt* pry into □ *vi* pry; **~teiro** *a* prying □ *m* busybody; **~tice** *f* prying

**bisca|te** /bis'katʃi/ *m* odd job; **~teiro** *m* odd-job man

**biscoito** /bis'kojtu/ *m* biscuit, (*Amer*) cookie

**bisnaga** /biz'naga/ *f* (*pão*) bridge roll; (*tubo*) tube

**bisne|ta** /biz'nɛta/ *f* great-granddaughter; **~to** /ɛ/ *m* great-grandson; *pl* great-grandchildren

**bis|pado** /bis'padu/ *m* bishopric; **~po** *m* bishop

**bissexto** /bi'sestu/ *a* occasional; **ano ~** leap year

**bissexu|al** /biseksu'aw/ (*pl* **~ais**) *a* & *m/f* bisexual

**bisturi** /bistu'ri/ *m* scalpel

**bito|la** /bi'tɔla/ *f* gauge; **~lado** *a* narrow-minded

**bizarro** /bi'zaxu/ *a* bizarre

**blablablá** /blabla'bla/ (*fam*) *m* chit-chat

**black** /'blɛki/ *m* black market; **~tie** *m* evening dress

**blas|femar** /blasfe'mar/ ˈ*vi* blaspheme; **~fêmia** *f* blasphemy; **~femo** /e/ *a* blasphemous □ *m* blasphemer

**blecaute** /ble'kawtʃi/ *m* power cut

**ble|far** /ble'far/ *vi* bluff; **~fe** /ɛ/ *m* bluff

**blin|dado** /bli'dadu/ *a* armoured; **~dagem** *f* armour-plating

**blitz** /blits/ *f invar* police spot-check (on vehicles)

**blo|co** /'blɔku/ *m* block; (*pol*) bloc; (*de papel*) pad; (*no carnaval*) section; **~quear** *vt* block; (*mil*) blockade; **~queio** *m* blockage; (*psic*) mental block; (*mil*) blockade

**blusa** /'bluza/ *f* shirt; (*de mulher*) blouse; (*de lã*) sweater

**boa** /'boa/ *f de* bom; **numa ~** (*fam*) well; (*sem problemas*) easily; **estar numa ~** (*fam*) be doing fine; **~gente** (*fam*) *a invar* nice; **~-pinta** (*pl* **~s-pintas**) (*fam*) *a* nice-looking; **~-praça** (*pl* **~s-praças**) (*fam*) *a* friendly, sociable

**boate** /bo'atʃi/ *f* nightclub

**boato** /bo'atu/ *m* rumour

**boa|-nova** /boa'nɔva/ (*pl* **~s-novas**) *f* good news; **~-vida** (*pl* **~s-vidas**) *m/f* good-for-nothing, waster; **~zinha** *f* sweet, kind

**bo|bagem** /bo'baʒẽ/ *f* silliness; (*uma*) silly thing; **~beada** *f* slip-up; **~bear** *vi* slip up; **~beira** *f veja* bobagem

**bobe** /'bɔbi/ *m* curler, roller

**bobina** /bo'bina/ *f* reel; (*eletr*) coil

**bobo** /'bobu/ *a* silly □ *m* fool; (*da corte*) jester; **~ca** /ɔ/ (*fam*) *a* stupid □ *m/f* twit

**bo|ca** /'boka/ *f* mouth; (*no fogão*) ring; **~ca da noite** nightfall; **~cado** *m* (*na boca*) mouthful; (*pedaço*) piece, bit; **~cal** (*pl* **~cais**) *m* mouthpiece

**boce|jar** /bose'ʒar/ *vi* yawn; **~jo** /e/ *m* yawn

**boche|cha** /bo'ʃeʃa/ *f* cheek; **~char** *vi* rinse one's mouth; **~cho** /e/ *m* mouthwash; **~chudo** *a* with puffy cheeks

**bodas** /'bodas/ *f pl* wedding anniversary; **~ de prata/ouro** silver/golden wedding

**bode** /'bɔdʒi/ *m* (billy) goat; **~ expiatório** scapegoat

**bodega** /bo'dɛga/ *f* (*de bebidas*) off-licence, (*Amer*) liquor store; (*de secos e molhados*) grocer's shop, corner shop

**boêmio** /bo'emiu/ *a* & *m* Bohemian

**bofe|tada** /bofe'tada/ *f*, **bofe|tão** /bofe'tãw/ *m* slap; **~tear** *vt* slap

**boi** /boj/ *m* bullock, (*Amer*) steer

**bói** /bɔj/ *m* office boy

**bóia** /'bɔja/ *f* (*de balizamento*) buoy; (*de cortiça, isopor etc*) float; (*câmara de borracha*) rubber ring; (*de braço*) armband, water wing; (*na caixa-d'água*) ballcock; (*fam: comida*) grub; **~ salva-vidas** lifebelt; **~-fria** (*pl* **~s-frias**) *m/f* itinerant farm labourer

**boiar** /bo'jar/ *vt/i* float; (*fam*) be lost

**boico|tar** /bojko'tar/ *vt* boycott; **~te** /ɔ/ *m* boycott

**boiler** /'bojler/ (*pl* **~s**) *m* boiler

**boina** /'bojna/ *f* beret

**bo|jo** /'boʒu/ *m* bulge; **~judo** *a* (*cheio*) bulging; (*arredondado*) bulbous

**bola** /'bɔla/ *f* ball; **dar ~ para** (*fam*) give attention to *<pessoa>*; care about *<coisa>*; **~ de gude** marble; **~ de neve** snowball

**bolacha** /bo'laʃa/ *f* (*biscoito*) biscuit, (*Amer*) cookie; (*descanso*) beermat; (*fam: tapa*) slap

**bo|lada** /bo'lada/ *f* large sum of money; **~lar** *vt* think up, devise

**boléia** /bo'lɛja/ *f* cab; (*Port: carona*) lift

**boletim** /bole'tʃĩ/ *m* bulletin; (*escolar*) report

**bolha** /'boʎa/ *f* bubble; (*na pele*) blister □ (*fam*) *m/f* pain

**boliche** /bo'liʃi/ *m* skittles

**Bolívia** /bo'livia/ *f* Bolivia

**boliviano** /bolivi'anu/ *a* & *m* Bolivian

**bolo** /'bolu/ *m* cake

**bo|lor** /bo'lor/ *m* mould, mildew; **~lorento** *a* mouldy

**bolota** /bo'lɔta/ f (*glande*) acorn; (*bolinha*) little ball

**bol|sa** /'bowsa/ f bag; ~**sa (de estudo)** scholarship; ~**sa (de valores)** stock exchange; ~**sista** m/f, (*Port*) ~**seiro** m scholarship student; ~**so** /o/ m pocket

**bom** /bõ/ a (f **boa**) good; (*de saúde*) well; <*comida*> nice; **está** ~ that's fine

**bomba¹** /'bõba/ f (*explosiva*) bomb; (*doce*) eclair; (*fig*) bombshell; **levar** ~ (*fam*) fail

**bomba²** /'bõba/ f (*de bombear*) pump

**Bombaim** /bõba'ĩ/ f Bombay

**bombar|dear** /bõbardʒi'ar/ vt bombard; (*do ar*) bomb; ~**deio** m bombardment; (*do ar*) bombing

**bomba|-relógio** /bõbaxe'lɔʒiu/ (*pl* ~**s-relógio**) f time bomb

**bom|bear** /bõbi'ar/ vt pump; ~**beiro** m fireman; (*encanador*) plumber

**bombom** /bõ'bõ/ m chocolate

**bombordo** /bõ'bordu/ m port

**bondade** /bõ'dadʒi/ f goodness

**bonde** /'bõdʒi/ m tram; (*teleférico*) cable car

**bondoso** /bõ'dozu/ a good(-hearted)

**boné** /bo'nɛ/ m cap

**bone|ca** /bo'nɛka/ f doll; ~**co** /ɛ/ m dummy

**bonificação** /bonifika'sãw/ f bonus

**bonito** /bo'nitu/ a <*mulher*> pretty; <*homem*> handsome; <*tempo, casa etc*> lovely

**bônus** /'bonus/ m invar bonus

**boqui|aberto** /bokia'bɛrtu/ a openmouthed, flabbergasted; ~**nha** f snack

**borboleta** /borbo'leta/ f butterfly; (*roleta*) turnstile

**borbotão** /borbo'tãw/ m spurt

**borbu|lha** /bor'buʎa/ f bubble; ~**lhar** vi bubble

**borda** /'bɔrda/ f edge; ~**do** a edged; (*à linha*) embroidered □ m embroidery

**bordão** /bor'dãw/ m (*frase*) catchphrase

**bordar** /bor'dar/ vt (*à linha*) embroider

**bor|del** /bor'dɛw/ (*pl* ~**déis**) m brothel

**bordo** /'bɔrdu/ m a ~ aboard

**borra** /'bɔxa/ f dregs; (*de café*) grounds

**borra|cha** /bo'xaʃa/ f rubber; ~**cheiro** m tyre fitter

**bor|rão** /bo'xãw/ m (*de tinta*) blot; (*rascunho*) rough draft; ~**rar** vt (*sujar*) blot; (*riscar*) cross out; (*pintar*) daub

**borrasca** /bo'xaska/ f squall

**borri|far** /boxi'far/ vt sprinkle; ~**fo** m sprinkling

**bosque** /'bɔski/ m wood

**bosta** /'bɔsta/ f (*de animal*) dung; (*chulo*) crap

**bota** /'bɔta/ f boot

**botâni|ca** /bo'tanika/ f botany; ~**co** a botanical □ m botanist

**bo|tão** /bo'tãw/ m button; (*de flor*) bud; **falar com os seus** ~**tões** say to o.s.

**botar** /bo'tar/ vt put; put on <*roupa*>; set <*mesa, despertador*>; lay <*ovo*>; find <*defeito*>

**bote¹** /'bɔtʃi/ m (*barco*) dinghy; ~ **salva-vidas** lifeboat; (*de borracha*) liferaft

**bote²** /'bɔtʃi/ m (*de animal etc*) lunge

**botequim** /butʃi'kĩ/ m bar

**botoeira** /boto'era/ f buttonhole

**boxe** /'bɔksi/ m boxing; ~**ador** m boxer

**brabo** /'brabu/ a <*animal*> ferocious; <*calor, sol*> fierce; <*doença*> bad; <*prova, experiência*> tough; (*zangado*) angry

**bra|çada** /bra'sada/ f armful; (*em natação*) stroke; ~**cadeira** (*faixa*) armband; (*ferragem*) bracket; (*de atleta*) sweatband; ~**cal** (*pl* ~**çais**) a manual; ~**celete** /e/ m bracelet; ~**ço** m arm; ~**ço direito** (*fig: pessoa*) right-hand man

**bra|dar** /bra'dar/ vt/i shout; ~**do** m shout

**braguilha** /bra'giʎa/ f fly, flies

**braile** /'brajli/ m Braille

**bra|mido** /bra'midu/ m roar; ~**mir** vi roar

**branco** /'brãku/ a white □ m (*homem*) white man; (*espaço*) blank; **em** ~ <*cheque etc*> blank; **noite em** ~ sleepless night

**bran|do** /'brãdu/ a gentle; <*doença*> mild; (*indulgente*) lenient, soft; ~**dura** f gentleness; (*indulgência*) softness, leniency

**brasa** /'braza/ f **em** ~ red-hot; **mandar** ~ (*fam*) go to town

**brasão** /bra'zãw/ m coat of arms

**braseiro** /bra'zeru/ m brasier

**Brasil** /bra'ziw/ m Brazil

**brasi|leiro** /brazi'leru/ a & m Brazilian; ~**liense** a & m/f (person) from Brasília

**bra|vata** /bra'vata/ f bravado; ~**vio** a wild; <*mar*> rough; ~**vo** a (*corajoso*) brave; (*zangado*) angry; <*mar*> rough; ~**vura** f bravery

**breca** /'brɛka/ f **levado da** ~ very naughty

**brecar** /bre'kar/ vt stop <*carro*>; (*fig*) curb □ vi brake

**brecha** /'brɛʃa/ f gap; (*na lei*) loophole

**bre|ga** /'brɛga/ (*fam*) a tacky, naff; ~**guice** (*fam*) f tack, tackiness

**brejo** /'brɛʒu/ *m* marsh; **ir para o ~** (*fig*) go down the drain

**brenha** /'brɛɲa/ *f* thicket

**breque** /'brɛki/ *m* brake

**breu** /brew/ *m* tar, pitch

**bre|ve** /'brɛvi/ *a* short, brief; **em ~ve** soon, shortly; **~vidade** *f* shortness, brevity

**briga** /'briga/ *f* fight; (*bate-boca*) argument

**briga|da** /bri'gada/ *f* brigade; **~deiro** *m* brigadier; (*doce*) chocolate truffle

**bri|gão** /bri'gãw/ *a* (*f* **~gona**) belligerent; (*na fala*) argumentative □ *m* (*f* **~gona**) troublemaker; **~gar** *vi* fight; (*com palavras*) argue; *<cores>* clash

**bri|lhante** /bri'ʎãtʃi/ *a* (*reluzente*) shiny; (*fig*) brilliant; **~lhar** *vi* shine; **~lho** *m* (*de sapatos etc*) shine; (*dos olhos, de metais*) gleam; (*das estrelas*) brightness; (*de uma cor*) brilliance; (*fig: esplendor*) splendour

**brin|cadeira** /brĩka'dera/ *f* (*piada*) joke; (*brinquedo, jogo*) game; **de ~ cadeira** for fun; **~calhão** (*f* **~calhona**) *a* playful □ *m* joker; **~car** *vi* (*divertir-se*) play; (*gracejar*) joke

**brinco** /'brĩku/ *m* earring

**brin|dar** /brĩ'dar/ *vt* (*saudar*) toast, drink to; (*presentear*) give a gift to; **~dar alg com aco** afford s.o. sth; (*de presente*) give s.o. sth as a gift; **~de** *m* (*saudação*) toast; (*presente*) free gift

**brinquedo** /brĩ'kedu/ *m* toy

**brio** /'briu/ *m* self-esteem, character; **~so** /o/ *a* self-confident

**brisa** /'briza/ *f* breeze

**britadeira** /brita'dera/ *f* pneumatic drill

**britânico** /bri'taniku/ *a* British □ *m* Briton; **os ~s** the British

**broca** /'brɔka/ *f* drill

**broche** /'brɔʃi/ *m* brooch

**brochura** /bro'ʃura/ *f* **livro de ~** paperback

**brócolis** /'brɔkulis/ *m pl*, (*Port*) **brócolos** /'brɔkuluʃ/ *m pl* broccoli

**bron|ca** /'brõka/ (*fam*) *f* telling-off; **dar uma ~ca em alg** tell s.o. off; **~co** *a* coarse, rough

**bronquite** /brõ'kitʃi/ *f* bronchitis

**bronze** /'brõzi/ *m* bronze; **~ado** *a* tanned, brown □ *m* (*sun*)tan; **~ador** *a* tanning □ *m* suntan lotion; **~amento** *m* tanning; **~ar** *vt* tan; **~ar-se** *vpr* go brown, tan

**bro|tar** /bro'tar/ *vt* sprout *<folhas, flores>*; spout *<lágrimas, palavras>* □ *vi* *<planta>* sprout; *<água>* spout; *<idéias>* pop up; **~tinho** (*fam*) *m* youngster; **~to** /o/ *m* shoot; (*fam*) youngster

**broxa** /'brɔʃa/ *f* (large) paint brush □ (*fam*) *a* impotent

**bruços** /'brusus/ **de ~** face down

**bru|ma** /'bruma/ *f* mist; **~moso** /o/ *a* misty

**brusco** /'brusku/ *a* brusque, abrupt

**bru|tal** /bru'taw/ (*pl* **~tais**) *a* brutal; **~talidade** *f* brutality; **~to** *a* *<feições>* coarse; *<homem>* brutish; *<tom, comentário>* aggressive; *<petróleo>* crude; *<peso, lucro, salário>* gross □ *m* brute

**bruxa** /'bruʃa/ *f* witch; (*feia*) hag; **~ria** *f* witchcraft

**Bruxelas** /bru'ʃɛlas/ *f* Brussels

**bruxo** /'bruʃu/ *m* wizard

**bruxulear** /bruʃuli'ar/ *vi* flicker

**bucha** /'buʃa/ *f* (*tampão*) bung; (*para paredes*) rawlplug (R); **acertar na ~** (*fam*) hit the nail on the head

**bucho** /'buʃu/ *m* gut; **~ de boi** tripe

**budis|mo** /bu'dʒizmu/ *m* Buddhism; **~ta** *a* & *m/f* Buddhist

**bueiro** /bu'eru/ *m* storm drain

**búfalo** /'bufalu/ *m* buffalo

**bu|fante** /bu'fãtʃi/ *a* full, puffed; **~far** *vi* snort; (*reclamar*) grumble, moan

**bufê** /bu'fe/ *m* (*refeição*) buffet; (*serviço*) catering service; (*móvel*) sideboard

**bugiganga** /buʒi'gãga/ *f* knickknack

**bujão** /bu'ʒãw/ *m* **~ de gás** gas cylinder

**bula** /'bula/ *f* (*de remédio*) directions; (*do Papa*) bull

**bulbo** /'buwbu/ *m* bulb

**bule** /'buli/ *m* (*de chá*) teapot; (*de café etc*) pot

**Bulgária** /buw'garia/ *f* Bulgaria

**búlgaro** /'buwgaru/ *a* & *m* Bulgarian

**bulhufas** /bu'ʎufas/ (*fam*) *pron* nothing

**bulício** /bu'lisiu/ *m* bustle

**bumbum** /bũ'bũ/ (*fam*) *m* bottom, bum

**bunda** /'bũda/ *f* bottom

**buquê** /bu'ke/ *m* bouquet

**buraco** /bu'raku/ *m* hole; (*de agulha*) eye; (*jogo de cartas*) rummy; **~ da fechadura** keyhole

**burburinho** /burbu'riɲu/ *m* (*de vozes*) hubbub

**bur|guês** /bur'ges/ *a* & *m* (*f* **~guesa**) bourgeois; **~guesia** *f* bourgeoisie

**burlar** /bur'lar/ *vt* get round *<lei>*; get past *<defesas, vigilância>*

**buro|cracia** /burokra'sia/ *f* bureaucracy; **~crata** *m/f* bureaucrat; **~crático** *a* bureaucratic; **~cratizar** *vt* make bureaucratic

**bur|rice** /bu'xisi/ *f* stupidity; (*uma*) stupid thing; **~ro** *a* stupid; (*ignorante*) dim □ *m* (*animal*) donkey; (*pessoa*) halfwit, dunce; **~ro de carga** (*fig*) workhorse

**bus|ca** /'buska/ *f* search; **dar ~ca em**
search; **~ca-pé** *m* banger; **~car** *vt*
fetch; (*de carro*) pick up; **mandar**
**~car** send for

**bússola** /'busola/ *f* compass; (*fig*)
guide

**busto** /'bustu/ *m* bust

**butique** /bu'tʃiki/ *f* boutique

**buzi|na** /bu'zina/ *f* horn; **~nada** *f*
toot (of the horn); **~nar** *vi* sound
the horn, toot the horn

# C

**cá** /ka/ *adv* here; **o lado de ~** this
side; **para ~** here; **de ~ para lá** back
and forth; **de lá para ~** since then; **~**
**entre nós** between you and me

**ca|bal** /ka'baw/ (*pl* **~bais**) *a* com-
plete, full; <*prova*> conclusive

**cabana** /ka'bana/ *f* hut; (*casinha no*
*campo*) cottage

**cabeça** /ka'besa/ *f* head; (*de lista*) top;
(*pessoa inteligente*) mind □ *m/f* (*chefe*)
ringleader; (*integrante mais inteli-*
*gente*) brains; **de ~** <*saber*> off the
top of one's head; <*calcular*> in one's
head; **de ~ para baixo** upside down;
**deu-lhe na ~ de** he took it into his
head to; **esquentar a ~** (*fam*) get
worked up; **fazer a ~ de alg** convince s.o.; **quebrar a ~** rack one's
brains; **subir à ~** go to s.o.'s head;
**ter a ~ no lugar** have one's head
screwed on; **~da** *f* (*no futebol*)
header; (*pancada*) head butt; **dar**
**uma ~da no teto** bang one's head on
the ceiling; **~-de-porco** (*pl* **~s-de-**
**porco**) *f* tenement; **~-de-vento** (*pl*
**~s-de-vento**) *m/f* scatterbrain,
airhead; **~lho** *m* heading

**cabe|cear** /kabesi'ar/ *vt* head <*bola*>;
**~ceira** *f* head; **~çudo** *a* pigheaded

**cabe|dal** /kabe'daw/ (*pl* **~dais**) *m*
wealth

**cabelei|ra** /kabe'lera/ *f* head of hair;
(*peruca*) wig; **~reiro** *m* hairdresser

**cabe|lo** /ka'belu/. *m* hair; **cortar o**
**~lo** have one's hair cut; **~ludo** *a*
hairy; (*difícil*) complicated; <*palavra,*
*piada*> dirty

**caber** /ka'ber/ *vi* fit; (*ter cabimento*) be
fitting; **~ a** <*mérito, parte*> be due to;
<*tarefa*> fall to; **cabe a você ir** it is
up to you to go; **~ em alg** <*roupa*> fit
s.o.

**cabide** /ka'bidʒi/ *m* (*peça de madeira,*
*arame etc*) hanger; (*móvel*) hat stand;
(*na parede*) coat rack

**cabimento** /kabi'mẽtu/ *m* **ter ~** be
fitting, be appropriate; **não ter ~** be
out of the question

**cabine** /ka'bini/ *f* cabin; (*de avião*)
cockpit; (*de loja*) changing room; **~**
**telefônica** phone box, (*Amer*) phone
booth

**cabisbaixo** /kabiz'baʃu/ *a* crestfallen

**cabí|vel** /ka'bivew/ (*pl* **~veis**) *a* ap-
propriate, fitting

**cabo**[1] /'kabu/ *m* (*militar*) corporal; **ao**
**~ de** after; **levar a ~** carry out; **~**
**eleitoral** campaign worker

**cabo**[2] /'kabu/ *m* (*fio*) cable; (*de panela*
*etc*) handle; **TV por ~** cable TV; **~ de**
**extensão** extension lead; **~ de força**
tug of war

**caboclo** /ka'boklu/ *a & m* mestizo

**ca|bra** /'kabra/ *f* goat; **~brito** *m* kid

**ca|ça** /'kasa/ *f* (*atividade*) hunting; (*ca-*
*çada*) hunt; (*animais*) game □ *m*
(*avião*) fighter; **à ~ça de** in pursuit
of; **~ça das bruxas** (*fig*) witch hunt;
**~çador** *m* hunter; **~ça-minas** *m* in-
*var* minesweeper; **~ça-níqueis** *m* in-
*var* slot machine; **~çar** *vt* hunt
<*animais, criminoso etc*>; (*procurar*)
hunt for □ *vi* hunt

**cacareco** /kaka'rɛku/ *m* piece of junk;
*pl* junk

**cacare|jar** /kakare'ʒar/ *vi* cluck; **~jo**
/e/ *m* clucking

**caçarola** /kasa'rɔla/ *f* saucepan

**cacau** /ka'kaw/ *m* cocoa

**cace|tada** /kase'tada/ *f* blow with a
club; (*fig*) annoyance; **~te** /e/ *m* club
□ (*fam*) *int* damn

**cachaça** /ka'ʃasa/ *f* white rum

**cachê** /ka'ʃe/ *m* fee

**cache|col** /kaʃe'kɔw/ (*pl* **~cóis**) *m*
scarf

**cachimbo** /ka'ʃĩbu/ *m* pipe

**cacho** /'kaʃu/ *m* (*de banana, uva*)
bunch; (*de cabelo*) lock; (*fam: caso*)
affair

**cachoeira** /kaʃo'era/ *f* waterfall

**cachor|rinho** /kaʃo'xiɲu/ *m* (*nado*)
doggy paddle; **~ro** /o/ *m* dog; (*Port*)
puppy; (*pessoa*) scoundrel; **~ro-**
**quente** (*pl* **~ros-quentes**) *m* hot dog

**cacife** /ka'sifi/ *m* (*fig*) pull

**caci|que** /ka'siki/ *m* (*índio*) chief; (*po-*
*lítico*) boss; **~quia** *f* leadership

**caco** /'kaku/ *m* shard; (*pessoa*) old
crock

**cacto** /'kaktu/ *m* cactus

**caçula** /ka'sula/ *m/f* youngest child □
*a* youngest

**cada** /'kada/ *a* each; **~ duas horas**
every two hours; **custam £5 ~ (um)**
they cost £5 each; **~ vez mais** more
and more; **~ vez mais fácil** easier
and easier; **ele fala ~ coisa** (*fam*)
he says the most amazing things

**cadafalso** /kada'fawsu/ *m* gallows

**cadarço** /ka'darsu/ *m* shoelace

**cadas|trar** /kadas'trar/ *vt* register;
**~tro** *m* register; (*ato*) registration;

(*policial, bancário*) records, files; (*imobiliário*) land register

ca|dáver /ka'daver/ *m* (dead) body, corpse; ~**daverico** *a* cadaverous, corpse-like; <*exame*> post-mortem

cadê /ka'de/ ( *fam*) *adv* where is/ are...?

cadeado /kadʒi'adu/ *m* padlock

cadeia /ka'deja/ *f* (*de eventos, lojas etc*) chain; ( *prisão*) prison; (*rádio, TV*) network

cadeira /ka'dera/ *f* (*móvel*) chair; (*no teatro*) stall; (*de político*) seat; ( *função de professor*) chair; (*matéria*) subject; *pl* (*anat*) hips; ~ **de balanço** rocking chair; ~ **de rodas** wheelchair; ~ **elétrica** electric chair

ca|dência /ka'dẽsia/ *f* (*mus, da voz*) cadence; (*compasso*) rhythm; ~**denciado** *a* rhythmic; <*passos*> measured

cader|neta /kader'neta/ *f* notebook; (*de professor*) register; (*de banco*) passbook; ~**neta de poupança** savings account; ~**no** /ɛ/ *m* exercise book; (*pequeno*) notebook; (*no jornal*) section

cadete /ka'detʃi/ *m* cadet

cadu|car /kadu'kar/ *vi* <*pessoa*> become senile; <*contrato*> lapse; ~**co** *a* <*pessoa*> senile; <*contrato*> lapsed; ~**quice** *f* senility

cafajeste /kafa'ʒestʃi/ *m* swine

ca|fé /ka'fɛ/ *m* coffee; (*botequim*) café; ~**fé da manhã** breakfast; **tomar** ~**fé** have breakfast; ~**fé-com-leite** *a invar* coffee-coloured, light brown □ *m* white coffee; ~**feeiro** *a* coffee □ *m* coffee plant; ~**feicultura** *f* coffee-growing; ~**feína** *f* caffein(e)

cafetã /kafe'tã/ *m* caftan

cafetão /kafe'tãw/ *m* pimp

cafe|teira /kafe'tera/ *f* coffee pot; ~**zal** (*pl* ~**zais**) *m* coffee plantation; ~**zinho** *m* small black coffee

cafo|na /ka'fona/ ( *fam*) *a* naff, tacky; ~**nice** *f* tackiness; (*coisa*) tacky thing

cágado /'kagadu/ *m* turtle

caiar /kaj'ar/ *vt* whitewash

cãibra /'kãjbra/ *f* cramp

caí|da /ka'ida/ *f* fall; *veja* **queda**; ~**do** *a* <*árvore etc*> fallen; <*beiços etc*> drooping; (*deprimido*) dejected; (*apaixonado*) smitten

caimento /kaj'mẽtu/ *m* fall

caipi|ra /kaj'pira/ *a* <*pessoa*> countrified; <*festa, música*> country; <*sotaque*> rural □ *m/f* country person; (*depreciativo*) country bumpkin; ~**rinha** *f* cachaça with limes, sugar and ice

cair /ka'ir/ *vi* fall; <*dente, cabelo*> fall out; <*botão etc*> fall off; <*comércio, trânsito etc*> fall off; <*tecido, cortina*>

hang; ~ **bem/mal** <*roupa*> go well/ badly; <*ato, dito*> go down well, badly; **estou caindo de sono** I'm really sleepy

cais /kajs/ *m* quay; (*Port: na estação*) platform

caixa /'kaʃa/ *f* box; (*de loja etc*) cash-desk □ *m/f* cashier; ~ **de correio** letter box; ~ **de mudanças**, (*Port*) ~ **de velocidades** gear box; ~ **postal** post office box, PO Box; ~**-d'água** (*pl* ~**s-d'água**) *f* water tank; ~**-forte** (*pl* ~**s-fortes**) *f* vault

cai|xão /ka'ʃãw/ *m* coffin; ~**xeiro** *m* (*em loja*) assistant; salesman; ~**xilho** *m* frame; ~**xote** /ɔ/ *m* crate

caju /ka'ʒu/ *m* cashew fruit; ~**eiro** *m* cashew tree

cal /kaw/ *f* lime

calado /ka'ladu/ *a* quiet

calafrio /kala'friu/ *m* shudder, shiver

calami|dade /kalami'dadʒi/ *f* calamity; ~**toso** /o/ *a* calamitous

calar /ka'lar/ *vi* be quiet □ *vt* keep quiet about <*segredo, sentimento*>; silence <*pessoa*>; ~**-se** *vpr* go quiet

calça /'kawsa/ *f* trousers, (*Amer*) pants

calça|da /kaw'sada/ *f* pavement, (*Amer*) sidewalk; (*Port: rua*) roadway; ~**dão** *m* pedestrian precinct; ~**deira** *f* shoe-horn; ~**do** *a* paved □ *m* shoe; *pl* footwear

calcanhar /kawka'ɲar/ *m* heel

calção /kaw'sãw/ *m* shorts; ~ **de banho** swimming trunks

calcar /kaw'kar/ *vt* (*pisar*) trample; (*comprimir*) press; ~ **aco em** ( *fig*) base sth on, model sth on

calçar /kaw'sar/ *vt* put on <*sapatos, luvas*>; take <*número*>; pave <*rua*>; (*com calço*) wedge □ *vi* <*sapato*> fit; ~**-se** *vpr* put one's shoes on

calcário /kaw'kariu/ *m* limestone □ *a* <*água*> hard

calças /'kawsas/ *f pl veja* **calça**

calcinha /kaw'siɲa/ *f* knickers, (*Amer*) panties

cálcio /'kawsiu/ *m* calcium

calço /'kawsu/ *m* wedge

calcu|ladora /kawkula'dora/ *f* calculator; ~**lar** *vt/i* calculate; ~**lista** *a* calculating □ *m/f* opportunist

cálculo /'kawkulu/ *m* calculation; (*diferencial*) calculus; (*med*) stone

cal|da /'kawda/ *f* syrup; *pl* hot springs; ~**deira** *f* boiler; ~**deirão** *m* cauldron; ~**do** *m* (*sopa*) broth; (*suco*) juice; ~**do de carne/galinha** beef/ chicken stock

calefação /kalefa'sãw/ *f* heating

caleidoscópio /kalejdos'kɔpiu/ *m* kaleidoscope

**calejado** /kale'ʒadu/ a <mãos> calloused; <pessoa> experienced

**calendário** /kalẽ'dariu/ m calendar

**calha** /'kaʎa/ f (no telhado) gutter; (sulco) gulley

**calhamaço** /kaʎa'masu/ m tome

**calhambeque** /kaʎã'bɛki/ (fam) m banger

**calhar** /ka'ʎar/ vi **calhou que** it so happened that; **calhou pegar em o mesmo trem** they happened to get the same train; ~ **de** happen to; **vir a ~** come at the right time

**cali|brado** /kali'bradu/ a (bêbado) tipsy; ~**brar** vt calibrate; check (the pressure of) <pneu>; ~**bre** m calibre; **coisas desse** ~**bre** things of this order

**cálice** /'kalisi/ m (copo) liqueur glass; (na missa) chalice

**caligrafia** /kaligra'fia/ f (letra) handwriting; (arte) calligraphy

**calista** /ka'lista/ m/f chiropodist, (Amer) podiatrist

**cal|ma** /'kawma/ f calm; **com** ~**ma** calmly ☐ int calm down; ~**mante** m tranquilizer; ~**mo** a calm

**calo** /'kalu/ m (na mão) callus; (no pé) corn

**calombo** /ka'lõbu/ m bump

**calor** /ka'lor/ m heat; (agradável, fig) warmth; **estar com** ~ be hot

**calo|rento** /kalo'rẽtu/ a <pessoa> sensitive to heat; <lugar> hot; ~**ria** f calorie; ~**roso** /o/ a warm; <protesto> lively

**calota** /ka'lɔta/ f hubcap

**calo|te** /ka'lɔtʃi/ m bad debt; ~**teiro** m bad risk

**calouro** /ka'loru/ m (na faculdade) freshman; (em outros ramos) novice

**ca|lúnia** /ka'lunia/ f slander; ~**luniar** vt slander; ~**lunioso** /o/ a slanderous

**cal|vície** /kaw'visi/ f baldness; ~**vo** a bald

**cama** /'kama/ f bed; ~ **de casal/solteiro** double/single bed; ~-**beliche** (pl ~**s-beliches**) f bunk bed

**camada** /ka'mada/ f layer; (de tinta) coat

**câmara** /'kamara/ f chamber; (fotográfica) camera; **em** ~ **lenta** in slow motion; ~ **municipal** town council; (Port) town hall

**camarada** /kama'rada/ a friendly ☐ m/f comrade; ~**gem** f comradeship; (convivência agradável) camaraderie

**câmara-de-ar** /kamaradʒi'ar/ (pl **câmaras-de-ar**) f inner tube

**camarão** /kama'rãw/ m shrimp; (maior) prawn

**cama|reira** /kama'rera/ f chambermaid; ~**rim** m dressing room;

~**rote** /ɔ/ m (no teatro) box; (num navio) cabin

**cambada** /kã'bada/ f gang, horde

**cambalacho** /kãba'laʃu/ m scam

**camba|lear** /kãbali'ar/ vi stagger; ~**lhota** f somersault

**cambi|al** /kãbi'aw/ (pl ~**ais**) a exchange; ~**ante** m shade; ~**ar** vt change

**câmbio** /'kãbiu/ m exchange; (taxa) rate of exchange; ~ **oficial/paralelo** official/black market exchange rate

**cambista** /kã'bista/ m/f (de entradas) ticket-tout, (Amer) scalper; (de dinheiro) money changer

**Camboja** /kã'bɔʒa/ m Cambodia

**cambojano** /kãbo'ʒanu/ a & m Cambodian

**camburão** /kãbu'rãw/ m police van

**camélia** /ka'mɛlia/ f camelia

**camelo** /ka'melu/ m camel

**camelô** /kame'lo/ m street vendor

**camião** /kami'ãw/ (Port) m veja **caminhão**

**caminhada** /kami'nada/ f walk

**caminhão** /kami'nãw/ m lorry, (Amer) truck

**cami|nhar** /kami'nar/ vi walk; (fig) advance, progress; ~**nho** m way; (estrada) road; (trilho) path; **a** ~**nho** on the way; **a meio** ~**nho** halfway; ~**nho de ferro** (Port) railway, (Amer) railroad

**caminho|neiro** /kaminɔ'neru/ m lorry driver, (Amer) truck driver; ~**nete** /ɛ/ f van

**camio|neta** /kamio'neta/ f van; ~**nista** (Port) m/f veja **caminhoneiro**

**cami|sa** /ka'miza/ f shirt; ~**sa-de-força** (pl ~**sas-de-força**) f straitjacket; ~**sa-de-vênus** (pl ~**sas-de-vênus**) f condom; ~**seta** /e/ f T-shirt; (de baixo) vest; ~**sinha** (fam) f condom; ~**sola** /ɔ/ f nightdress; (Port) sweater

**camomila** /kamo'mila/ f camomile

**campainha** /kãpa'ina/ f bell; (da porta) doorbell

**campanário** /kãpa'nariu/ m belfry

**campanha** /kã'pana/ f campaign

**campe|ão** /kãpi'ãw/ m (f ~ã) champion; ~**onato** m championship

**campestre** /kã'pɛstri/ a rural; ~**pina** f grassland

**cam|ping** /'kãpī/ m camping; (lugar) campsite; ~**pismo** (Port) m camping

**campo** /'kãpu/ m field; (interior) country; (de futebol) pitch; (de golfe) course; ~ **de concentração** concentration camp; ~**nês** m (f ~**nesa**) peasant

**camu|flagem** /kamu'flaʒē/ f camouflage; ~**flar** vt camouflage

**camundongo** /kamū'dõgu/ m mouse

**cana** /'kana/ f cane; ~ **de açúcar** sugar cane

**Canadá** /kana'da/ m Canada

**canadense** /kana'dẽsi/ a & m Canadian

**ca|nal** /ka'naw/ (pl ~**nais**) m channel; (hidrovia) canal

**canalha** /ka'naʎa/ m/f scoundrel

**cana|lização** /kanaliza'sãw/ f piping; ~**zador** (Port) m plumber; ~**zar** vt channel < líquido, esforço, recursos>; canalize <rio>; pipe for water and drainage <cidade>

**canário** /ka'nariu/ m canary

**canastrão** /kanas'trãw/ m (f ~**trona**) ham actor (f actress)

**canavi|al** /kanavi'aw/ (pl ~**ais**) m cane field; ~**eiro** a sugar cane

**canção** /kã'sãw/ f song

**cance|lamento** /kãsela'mẽtu/ m cancellation; ~**lar** vt cancel; (riscar) cross out

**câncer** /'kãser/ m cancer; **Câncer** (signo) Cancer

**cance|riano** /kãseri'anu/ a & m Cancerian; ~**rígeno** a carcinogenic; ~**roso** /o/ a cancerous □ m person with cancer

**cancro** /'kãkru/ m (Port: câncer) cancer; (fig) canker

**candango** /kã'dãgu/ m person from Brasília

**cande|eiro** /kãdʒi'eru/ m (oil-)lamp; ~**labro** m candelabra

**candida|tar-se** /kãdʒida'tarsi/ vpr (a vaga) apply (a for); (à presidência etc) stand, (Amer) run (a for); ~**to** m candidate (a for); (a vaga) applicant (a for); ~**tura** f candidature; (a vaga) application (a for)

**cândido** /'kãdʒidu/ a innocent

**candomblé** /kãdo'blɛ/ m Afro-Brazilian cult; (reunião) candomble meeting

**candura** /kã'dura/ f innocence

**cane|ca** /ka'nɛka/ f mug; ~**co** /ɛ/ m tankard

**canela¹** /ka'nɛla/ f (condimento) cinnamon

**canela²** /ka'nɛla/ f (da perna) shin; ~**da** f **dar uma ~da em alg** kick s.o. in the shins; **dar uma ~da em aco** hit one's shins on sth

**cane|ta** /ka'neta/ f pen; ~ **esferográfica** ball-point pen; ~**ta-tinteiro** (pl ~**tas-tinteiro**) f fountain pen

**cangote** /kã'gotʃi/ m nape of the neck

**canguru** /kãgu'ru/ m kangaroo

**canhão** /ka'ɲãw/ m (arma) cannon; (vale) canyon

**canhoto** /ka'ɲotu/ a left-handed □ m (talão) stub

**cani|bal** /kani'baw/ (pl ~**bais**) m/f cannibal; ~**balismo** m cannibalism

**caniço** /ka'nisu/ m reed; (pessoa) skinny person

**canícula** /ka'nikula/ f heat wave

**ca|nil** /ka'niw/ (pl ~**nis**) m kennel

**canivete** /kani'vetʃi/ m penknife

**canja** /'kãʒa/ f chicken soup; (fam) piece of cake

**canjica** /kã'ʒika/ f corn porridge

**cano** /'kanu/ m pipe; (de bota) top; (de arma de fogo) barrel

**cano|a** /ka'noa/ f canoe; ~**agem** f canoeing; ~**ista** m/f canoeist

**canonizar** /kanoni'zar/ vt canonize

**can|saço** /kã'sasu/ m tiredness; ~**sado** a tired; ~**sar** vt tire; (aborrecer) bore □ vi, ~**sar-se** vpr get tired; ~**sativo** a tiring; (aborrecido) boring; ~**seira** f tiredness; (lida) toil

**can|tada** /kã'tada/ f (fam) chat-up; ~**tar** vt/i sing; (fam) chat up

**cântaro** /'kãtaru/ m **chover a ~s** pour down, bucket down

**cantarolar** /kãtaro'lar/ vt/i hum

**cantei|ra** /kã'tera/ f quarry; ~**ro** m (de flores) flowerbed; (artífice) stonemason; ~**ro de obras** site office

**cantiga** /kã'tʃiga/ f ballad

**can|til** /kã'tʃiw/ (pl ~**tis**) m canteen; ~**tina** f canteen

**canto¹** /'kãtu/ m (ângulo) corner

**can|to²** /'kãtu/ m (cantar) singing; ~**tor** m singer; ~**toria** f singing

**canudo** /ka'nudu/ m (de beber) straw; (tubo) tube; (fam: diploma) diploma

**cão** /kãw/ (pl **cães**) m dog

**caolho** /ka'oʎu/ a one-eyed

**ca|os** /kaws/ m chaos; ~**ótico** a chaotic

**capa** /'kapa/ f (de livro, revista) cover; (roupa sem mangas) cape; ~ **de chuva** raincoat

**capacete** /kapa'setʃi/ m helmet

**capacho** /ka'paʃu/ m doormat

**capaci|dade** /kapasi'dadʒi/ f capacity; (aptidão) ability; ~**tar** vt enable; (convencer) convince

**capataz** /kapa'tas/ m foreman

**capaz** /ka'pas/ a capable (**de** of); **ser ~ de** (poder) be able to; (ser provável) be likely to

**cape|la** /ka'pɛla/ f chapel; ~**lão** (pl ~**lães**) m chaplain

**capen|ga** /ka'pẽga/ a doddery; ~**gar** vi dodder

**capeta** /ka'peta/ m (diabo) devil; (criança) little devil

**capilar** /kapi'lar/ a hair

**ca|pim** /ka'pĩ/ m grass; ~**pinar** vt/i weed

**capi|tal** /kapi'taw/ (pl ~**tais**) a & m/f capital; ~**talismo** m capitalism; ~**talista** a & m/f capitalist; ~**talizar** vt (com) capitalize; (aproveitar) capitalize on

**capi|tanear** /kapitani'ar/ *vt* captain
*<navio>*; (*fig*) lead; **~tania** *f*
captaincy; **~tania do porto** port
authority; **~tão** (*pl* **~tães**) *m* captain

**capitulação** /kapitula'sãw/ *f* capitulation, surrender

**capítulo** /ka'pitulu/ *m* chapter; (*de telenovela*) episode

**capô** /ka'po/ *m* bonnet, (*Amer*) hood

**capoeira** /kapo'era/ *f* Brazilian kickboxing

**capo|ta** /ka'pɔta/ *f* roof; **~tar** *vi* overturn

**capote** /ka'pɔtʃi/ *m* overcoat

**capri|char** /kapri'ʃar/ *vi* excel o.s.;
**~cho m** (*em esmero*) care; (*desejo*) whim;
(*teimosia*) contrariness; **~choso** /o/ *a*
(*cheio de caprichos*) capricious; (*com
esmero*) painstaking, meticulous

**Capricórnio** /kapri'kɔrniu/ *m* Capricorn

**capricorniano** /kaprikorni'anu/ *a &
m* Capricorn

**cápsula** /'kapsula/ *f* capsule

**cap|tar** /kap'tar/ *vt* pick up *<emissão,
sinais>*; tap *<água>*; catch, grasp
*<sentido>*; win *<simpatia, admiração>*; **~tura** *f* capture; **~turar** *vt*
capture

**capuz** /ka'pus/ *m* hood

**caquético** /ka'kɛtʃiku/ *a* brokendown, on one's last legs

**caqui** /ka'ki/ *m* persimmon

**cáqui** /'kaki/ *a invar & m* khaki

**cara** /'kara/ *f* face; (*aparência*) look;
(*ousadia*) cheek □ (*fam*) *m* guy; **~ a
~** face to face; **de ~** straightaway;
**dar de ~ com** run into; **está na ~**
it's obvious; **fechar a ~** frown; **~ de
pau** cheek; **~ de tacho** (*fam*) sheepish look

**cara|col** /kara'kɔw/ (*pl* **~cóis**) *m* snail

**caracte|re** /karak'tɛri/ *m* character;
**~rística** *f* characteristic, feature;
**~rístico** *a* characteristic; **~rizar** *vt*
characterize; **~rizar-se** *vpr* be characterized

**cara-de-pau** /karadʒi'paw/ (*pl* **caras-de-pau**) *a* cheeky, brazen

**caramba** /ka'rãba/ *int* (*de espanto*)
wow; (*de desagrado*) damn

**caramelo** /kara'mɛlu/ *m* caramel;
(*bala*) toffee

**caramujo** /kara'muʒu/ *m* water snail

**caranguejo** /karã'geʒu/ *m* crab

**caratê** /kara'te/ *m* karate

**caráter** /ka'rater/ *m* character

**caravana** /kara'vana/ *f* caravan

**car|boidrato** /karboi'dratu/ *m*
carbohydrate; **~bono** /o/ *m* carbon

**carbu|rador** /karbura'dor/ *m* carburettor, (*Amer*) carburator; **~rante** *m*
fuel

**carcaça** /kar'kasa/ *f* carcass; (*de navio etc*) frame

**cárcere** /'karseri/ *m* jail

**carcereiro** /karse'reru/ *m* jailer,
warder

**carcomido** /karko'midu/ *a* wormeaten; *<rosto>* pock-marked

**cardápio** /kar'dapiu/ *m* menu

**carde|al** /kardʒi'aw/ (*pl* **~ais**) *a* cardinal

**cardíaco** /kar'dʒiaku/ *a* cardiac; **ataque ~** heart attack

**cardio|lógico** /kardʒio'lɔʒiku/ *a*
heart; **~logista** *m/f* heart specialist,
cardiologist

**cardume** /kar'dumi/ *m* shoal

**careca** /ka'rɛka/ *a* bald □ *f* bald
patch

**ca|recer** /kare'ser/ **~recer de** *vt* lack;
**~rência** *f* lack; (*social*) deprivation;
(*afetiva*) lack of affection; **~rente** *a*
lacking; (*socialmente*) deprived; (*afetivamente*) in need of affection

**carestia** /kares'tʃia/ *f* high cost; (*geral*) high cost of living; (*escassez*)
shortage

**careta** /ka'reta/ *f* grimace □ *a* (*fam*)
straight, square

**car|ga** /'karga/ *f* load; (*mercadorias*)
cargo; (*elétrica*) charge; (*de cavalaria*)
charge; (*de caneta*) refill; (*fig*)
burden; **~ga horária** workload;
**~go m** (*função*) post, job; **a ~go de**
in the charge of; **~gueiro** *m* (*navio*)
cargo ship, freighter

**cariar** /kari'ar/ *vi* decay

**Caribe** /ka'ribi/ *m* Caribbean

**caricatu|ra** /karika'tura/ *f* caricature; **~rar** *vt* caricature; **~rista**
*m/f* caricaturist

**carícia** /ka'risia/ *f* (*com a mão*)
stroke, caress; (*carinho*) affection

**cari|dade** /kari'dadʒi/ *f* charity; **obra
de ~dade** charity; **~doso** /o/ *a*
charitable

**cárie** /'kari/ *f* tooth decay

**carim|bar** /karĩ'bar/ *vt* stamp; postmark *<carta>*; **~bo m** stamp; (*do correio*) postmark

**cari|nho** /ka'riɲu/ *m* affection; (*um
caress*) **~nhoso** /o/ *a* affectionate

**carioca** /kari'ɔka/ *a* from Rio de Janeiro □ *m/f* person from Rio de Janeiro □ (*Port*) *m* weak coffee

**caris|ma** /ka'rizma/ *m* charisma;
**~mático** *a* charismatic

**carna|val** /karna'vaw/ (*pl* **~vais**) *m*
carnival; **~valesco** /e/ *a* carnival;
*<roupa>* over the top, overdone □ *m*
carnival organizer

**car|ne** /'karni/ *f* (*humana etc*) flesh;
(*comida*) meat; **~neiro** *m* sheep; (*macho*) ram; (*como comida*) mutton;
**~niça** *f* carrion; **~nificina** *f*

slaughter; ~**nívoro** a carnivorous □
m carnivore; ~**nudo** a fleshy
**caro** /'karu/ a expensive; (*querido*)
dear □ adv <*custar, cobrar*> a lot;
<*comprar, vender*> at a high price;
**pagar** ~ pay a high price (for)
**caroço** /ka'rosu/ m (*de pêssego etc*)
stone; (*de maçã*) core; (*em sopa, molho
etc*) lump
**carona** /ka'rona/ f lift
**carpete** /kar'petʃi/ m fitted carpet
**carpin|taria** /karpita'ria/ f car-
pentry; ~**teiro** m carpenter
**carran|ca** /ka'xãka/ f scowl; ~**cudo** a
<*cara*> scowling; <*pessoa*> sullen
**carrapato** /kaxa'patu/ m (*animal*)
tick; (*fig*) hanger-on
**carrasco** /ka'xasku/ m executioner;
(*fig*) butcher
**carre|gado** /kaxe'gadu/ a <*céu*>
dark, black; <*cor*> dark; <*ambiente*>
tense; ~**gador** m porter; ~**gamento**
m loading; (*carga*) load; ~**gar** vt load
<*navio, arma, máquina fotográfica*>;
(*levar*) carry; charge <*bateria,
pilha*>; ~**gar em** overdo; pronounce
strongly <*letra*>; (*Port*) press
**carreira** /ka'xera/ f career
**carre|tel** /kaxe'tɛw/ (*pl* ~**téis**) m reel
**car|ril** /ka'xiw/ (*pl* ~**ris**) (*Port*) m rail
**carrinho** /ka'xiɲu/ m (*para baga-
gem, compras*) trolley; (*de criança*)
pram; ~ **de mão** wheel-barrow
**carro** /'kaxu/ m car; (*de bois*) cart; ~
**alegórico** float; ~ **esporte** sports
car; ~ **fúnebre** hearse; ~**ça** /ɔ/ f
cart; ~**ceria** f bodywork; ~**chefe**
(*pl* ~**s-chefes**) m (*no carnaval*) main
float; (*fig*) centrepiece; ~**-forte** (*pl*
~**s-fortes**) m security van
**carros|sel** /kaxo'sɛw/ (*pl* ~**séis**) m
merry-go-round
**carruagem** /kaxu'aʒẽ/ f carriage,
coach
**carta** /'karta/ f letter; (*mapa*) chart;
(*do baralho*) card; ~ **branca** (*fig*)
carte blanche; ~ **de condução** (*Port*)
driving licence, (*Amer*) driver's
license; ~**-bomba** (*pl* ~**s-bomba**) f
letter bomb; ~**da** f (*fig*) move
**cartão** /kar'tãw/ m card; (*Port: papelão*) cardboard; ~ **de crédito** credit
card; ~ **de visita** visiting card; ~**-
postal** (*pl* **cartões-postais**) m postcard
**car|taz** /kar'tas/ m poster, (*Amer*) bill;
**em** ~ showing, (*Amer*) playing;
~**teira** f (*para dinheiro*) wallet; (*cartão*) card; (*mesa*) desk; ~**teira de
identidade** identity card; ~**teira de
motorista** driving licence, (*Amer*)
driver's license; ~**teiro** m postman
**car|tel** /kar'tɛw/ (*pl* ~**téis**) m cartel
**cárter** /'karter/ m sump

**carto|la** /kar'tɔla/ f top hat □ m
director; ~**lina** f card; ~**mante** m/f
tarot reader, fortune-teller
**cartório** /kar'tɔriu/ m registry office
**cartucho** /kar'tuʃu/ m cartridge; (*de
dinamite*) stick; (*de amendoim etc*) bag
**car|tum** /kar'tũ/ m cartoon;
~**tunista** m/f cartoonist
**caruncho** /ka'rũʃu/ m woodcorm
**carvalho** /kar'vaʎu/ m oak
**car|vão** /kar'vãw/ m coal; (*de desenho*)
charcoal; ~**voeiro** a coal
**casa** /'kaza/ f house; (*comercial*) firm;
(*de tabuleiro*) square; (*de botão*) hole;
**em** ~ at home; **para** ~ home; **na** ~
**dos 30 anos** in one's thirties; ~ **da
moeda** mint; ~ **de banho** (*Port*)
bathroom; ~ **de campo** country
house; ~ **de saúde** private hospital;
~ **decimal** decimal place; ~ **popular** council house
**casaco** /ka'zaku/ m (*sobretudo*) coat;
(*paletó*) jacket; (*de lã*) pullover
**ca|sal** /ka'zaw/ (*pl* ~**sais**) m couple;
~**samento** m marriage; (*cerimônia*)
wedding; ~**sar** vt marry; (*fig*) combine □ vi get married; (*fig*) go
together; ~**sar-se** upr get married;
(*fig*) combine; ~**sar-se com** marry
**casarão** /kaza'rãw/ m mansion
**casca** /'kaska/ f (*de árvore*) bark; (*de
laranja, limão*) peel; (*de banana*)
skin; (*de noz, ovo*) shell; (*de milho*)
husk; (*de pão*) crust; (*de ferida*) scab
**cascalho** /kas'kaʎu/ m gravel
**cascata** /kas'kata/ f waterfall; (*fam*)
fib
**casca|vel** /kaska'vɛw/ (*pl* ~**véis**) m
(*cobra*) rattlesnake □ f (*mulher*) shrew
**casco** /'kasku/ m (*de cavalo etc*) hoof;
(*de navio*) hull; (*garrafa vazia*) empty
**ca|sebre** /ka'zɛbri/ m hovel, shack;
~**seiro** a <*comida*> home-made;
<*pessoa*> home-loving; <*vida*> home
□ m housekeeper
**caserna** /ka'zɛrna/ f barracks
**casmurro** /kaz'muxu/ a sullen
**caso** /'kazu/ m case; (*amoroso*) affair;
(*conto*) story □ conj in case; **em todo
ou qualquer** ~ in any case; **fazer** ~
**de** take notice of; **vir ao** ~ be
relevant; ~ **contrário** otherwise
**casório** /ka'zɔriu/ (*fam*) m wedding
**caspa** /'kaspa/ f dandruff
**casquinha** /kas'kiɲa/ f (*de sorvete*)
cone, cornet
**cassar** /ka'sar/ vt revoke, withdraw
<*direitos, autorização*>; ban <*polí-
tico*>
**cassete** /ka'sɛtʃi/ m cassette
**cassetete** /kase'tɛtʃi/ m truncheon,
(*Amer*) nightstick
**cassino** /ka'sinu/ m casino; ~ **de ofi-
ciais** officers' mess

castanha 32 celeuma

**casta|nha** /kaſˈtaɲa/ f chestnut; **~nha de caju** cashew nut; **~nha-do-pará** (pl **~nhas-do-pará**) f Brazil nut; **~nheiro** m chestnut tree; **~nho** a chestnut(-coloured); **~nholas** /ɔ/ f pl castanets

**castelhano** /kasteˈʎanu/ a & m Castilian

**castelo** /kasˈtɛlu/ m castle

**casti|çal** /kastʃiˈsaw/ (pl **~çais**) m candlestick

**cas|tidade** /kastʃiˈdadʒi/ f chastity; **~tigar** vt punish; **~tigo** m punishment; **~to** a chaste

**castor** /kasˈtor/ m beaver

**castrar** /kasˈtrar/ vt castrate

**casu|al** /kazuˈaw/ (pl **~ais**) a chance; (fortuito) fortuitous; **~alidade** f chance

**casulo** /kaˈzulu/ m (de larva) cocoon

**cata** /ˈkata/ f à ~ **de** in search of

**cata|lão** /kataˈlãw/ (pl **~lães**) a & m (f **~lã**) Catalan

**catalisador** /katalizaˈdor/ m catalyst; (de carro) catalytic convertor

**catalogar** /kataloˈgar/ vt catalogue

**catálogo** /kaˈtalogu/ m catalogue; (de telefones) phone book

**Catalunha** /kataˈluɲa/ f Catalonia

**catapora** /kataˈpora/ f chicken pox

**catar** /kaˈtar/ vt (procurar) search for; (recolher) gather; (do chão) pick up; sort ‹arroz, café›

**catarata** /kataˈrata/ f waterfall; (no olho) cataract

**catarro** /kaˈtaxu/ m catarrh

**catástrofe** /kaˈtastrofi/ f catastrophe

**catastrófico** /katasˈtrɔfiku/ a catastrophic

**catecismo** /kateˈsizmu/ m catechism

**cátedra** /ˈkatedra/ f chair

**cate|dral** /kateˈdraw/ (pl **~drais**) f cathedral; **~drático** m professor

**cate|goria** /kategoˈria/ f category; (social) class; (qualidade) quality; **~górico** a categorical; **~gorizar** vt categorize

**catinga** /kaˈtʃĩga/ f body odour, stink

**cati|vante** /katʃiˈvãtʃi/ a captivating; **~var** vt captivate; **~veiro** m captivity; **~vo** a & m captive

**catolicismo** /katoliˈsizmu/ m Catholicism

**católico** /kaˈtɔliku/ a & m Catholic

**catorze** /kaˈtorzi/ a & m fourteen

**cau|da** /ˈkawda/ f tail; **~dal** (pl **~dais**) m torrent

**caule** /ˈkawli/ m stem

**cau|sa** /ˈkawza/ f cause; (jurid) case; **por ~sa de** because of; **~sar** vt cause

**caute|la** /kawˈtɛla/ f caution; (documento) ticket; **~loso** /o/ a cautious, careful

**cava** /ˈkava/ f armhole

**cava|do** /kaˈvadu/ a ‹vestido› low-cut; ‹olhos› deep-set; **~dor** a hard-working □ m hard worker

**cava|laria** /kavalaˈria/ f cavalry; **~lariça** f stable; **~leiro** m horseman; (na Idade Média) knight

**cavalete** /kavaˈletʃi/ m easel

**caval|gadura** /kavawgaˈdura/ f mount; **~gar** vt/i ride; sit astride ‹muro, banco›; (saltar) jump

**cavalhei|resco** /kavaʎeˈresku/ a gallant, gentlemanly; **~ro** m gentleman □ a gallant, gentlemanly

**cavalo** /kaˈvalu/ m horse; **a ~** on horseback; **~-vapor** (pl **~s-vapor**) horsepower

**cavanhaque** /kavaˈɲaki/ m goatee

**cavaquinho** /kavaˈkiɲu/ m ukulele

**cavar** /kaˈvar/ vt dig; (fig) go all out for □ vi dig; (fig) go all out; **~ em** (vasculhar) delve into; **~ a vida** make a living

**caveira** /kaˈvera/ f skull

**caverna** /kaˈvɛrna/ f cavern

**caviar** /kaviˈar/ m caviar

**cavidade** /kaviˈdadʒi/ f cavity

**cavilha** /kaˈviʎa/ f peg

**cavo** /ˈkavu/ a hollow

**cavoucar** /kavoˈkar/ vt excavate

**caxemira** /kaʃeˈmira/ f cashmere

**caxumba** /kaˈʃũba/ f mumps

**cear** /siˈar/ vt have for supper □ vi have supper

**cebo|la** /seˈbola/ f onion; **~linha** f spring onion

**ceder** /seˈder/ vt give up; (dar) give; (emprestar) lend □ vi (não resistir) give way; **~ a** yield to

**cedilha** /seˈdʒiʎa/ f cedilla

**cedo** /ˈsedu/ adv early; **mais ~ ou mais tarde** sooner or later

**cedro** /ˈsɛdru/ m cedar

**cédula** /ˈsɛdula/ f (de banco) note, (Amer) bill; (eleitoral) ballot paper

**ce|gar** /seˈgar/ vt blind; blunt ‹faca›; **~go** /ɛ/ a blind; ‹faca› blunt □ m blind man; **às ~gas** blindly

**cegonha** /seˈgoɲa/ f stork

**cegueira** /seˈgera/ f blindness

**ceia** /ˈseja/ f supper

**cei|fa** /ˈsejfa/ f harvest; (massacre) slaughter; **~far** vt reap; claim ‹vidas›; (matar) mow down

**cela** /ˈsɛla/ f cell

**cele|bração** /selebraˈsãw/ f celebration; **~brar** vt celebrate

**célebre** /ˈsɛlebri/ a celebrated

**celebridade** /selebriˈdadʒi/ f celebrity

**celeiro** /seˈleru/ m granary

**célere** /ˈsɛleri/ a swift, fast

**celeste** /seˈlɛstʃi/ a celestial

**celeuma** /seˈlewma/ f pandemonium

**celibato** /seli'batu/ *m* celibacy

**celofane** /selo'fani/ *m* cellophane

**celta** /'sɛwta/ *a* Celtic □ *m/f* Celt □ *m* (*língua*) Celtic

**célula** /'sɛlula/ *f* cell

**celu|lar** /selu'lar/ *a* cellular; ~**lite** *f* cellulite; ~**lose** /ɔ/ *f* cellulose

**cem** /sẽj/ *a* & *m* hundred

**cemitério** /semi'tɛriu/ *m* cemetery; (*fig*) graveyard

**cena** /'sena/ *f* scene; (*palco*) stage; **em** ~ on stage

**cenário** /se'nariu/ *m* scenery; (*de crime etc*) scene

**cênico** /'seniku/ *a* stage

**cenoura** /se'nora/ *f* carrot

**cen|so** /'sẽsu/ *m* census; ~**sor** *m* censor; ~**sura** *f* (*de jornais etc*) censorship; (*órgão*) censor(s); (*condenação*) censure; ~**surar** *vt* censor <*jornal, filme etc*>; (*condenar*) censure

**centavo** /sẽ'tavu/ *m* cent

**centeio** /sẽ'teju/ *m* rye

**centelha** /sẽ'teʎa/ *f* spark; (*fig: de gênio etc*) flash

**cente|na** /sẽ'tena/ *f* hundred; **uma ~na de** about a hundred; **às ~nas** in their hundreds; ~**nário** *m* centenary

**centésimo** /sẽ'tɛzimu/ *a* hundredth

**centí|grado** /sẽ'tʃigradu/ *m* centigrade; ~**litro** *m* centilitre; ~**metro** *m* centimetre

**cento** /'sẽtu/ *a* & *m* hundred; **por** ~ per cent

**cen|tral** /sẽ'traw/ (*pl* ~**trais**) *a* central; ~**tralizar** *vt* centralize; ~**trar** *vt* centre; ~**tro** *m* centre

**cepti-** (*Port*) *veja* **ceti-**

**cera** /'sera/ *f* wax; **fazer** ~ waste time, faff about

**cerâmi|ca** /se'ramika/ *f* ceramics, pottery; ~**co** *a* ceramic

**cer|ca** /'serka/ *f* fence; ~**ca viva** hedge □ *adv* ~**ca de** around, about; ~**cado** *m* enclosure; (*para criança*) playpen; ~**car** *vt* surround; (*com muro, cerca*) enclose; (*assediar*) besiege

**cercear** /sersi'ar/ *vt* (*fig*) curtail, restrict

**cerco** /'serku/ *m* (*mil*) siege; (*policial*) dragnet

**cere|al** /seri'aw/ (*pl* ~**ais**) *m* cereal

**cere|bral** /sere'braw/ (*pl* ~**brais**) *a* cerebral

**cérebro** /'sɛrebru/ *m* brain; (*inteligência*) intellect

**cere|ja** /se'reʒa/ *f* cherry; ~**jeira** *f* cherry tree

**cerimônia** /seri'monia/ *f* ceremony; **sem** ~ unceremoniously; **fazer** ~ stand on ceremony

**cerimoni|al** /serimoni'aw/ (*pl* ~**ais**) *a* & *m* ceremonial; ~**oso** /o/ *a* ceremonious

**cer|rado** /se'xadu/ *a* <*barba, mata*> thick; <*punho, dentes*> clenched □ *m* scrubland; ~**rar** *vt* close; ~**rar-se** *vpr* close; <*noites, trevas*> close in

**certeiro** /ser'teru/ *a* well-aimed, accurate

**certeza** /ser'teza/ *f* certainty; **com** ~ certainly; **ter** ~ be sure (**de** of; **de que** that)

**certidão** /sertʃi'dãw/ *f* certificate; ~ **de nascimento** birth certificate

**certifi|cado** /sertʃifi'kadu/ *m* certificate; ~**car** *vt* certify; ~**car-se de** make sure of

**certo** /'sɛrtu/ *a* (*correto*) right; (*seguro*) certain; (*algum*) a certain □ *adv* right; **dar** ~ work

**cerveja** /ser'veʒa/ *f* beer; ~**ria** *f* brewery; (*bar*) pub

**cervo** /'sɛrvu/ *m* deer

**cer|zidura** /serzi'dura/ *f* darning; ~**zir** *vt* darn

**cesariana** /sezari'ana/ *f* Caesarian

**césio** /'sɛziu/ *m* caesium

**cessar** /se'sar/ *vt/i* cease

**ces|ta** /'sesta/ *f* basket; (*de comida*) hamper; ~**to** /e/ *m* basket; ~**to de lixo** wastepaper basket

**ceticismo** /setʃi'sizmu/ *m* scepticism

**cético** /'sɛtʃiku/ *a* sceptical □ *m* sceptic

**cetim** /se'tʃĩ/ *m* satin

**céu** /sɛw/ *m* sky; (*na religião*) heaven; ~ **da boca** roof of the mouth

**cevada** /se'vada/ *f* barley

**chá** /ʃa/ *m* tea

**chacal** /ʃa'kaw/ (*pl* ~**cais**) *m* jackal

**chácara** /'ʃakara/ *f* smallholding; (*casa*) country cottage

**chaci|na** /ʃa'sina/ *f* slaughter; ~**nar** *vt* slaughter

**chá-de-bar** /ʃadʒi'bar/ (*pl* ~**s-de-bar**) *m* bachelor party; ~**-de-panela** (*pl* ~**s-de-panela**) *m* hen night, (*Amer*) wedding shower

**chafariz** /ʃafa'ris/ *m* fountain

**chaga** /'ʃaga/ *f* sore

**chaleira** /ʃa'lera/ *f* kettle

**chama** /'ʃama/ *f* flame

**cha|mada** /ʃa'mada/ *f* call; (*dos presentes*) roll call; (*dos alunos*) register; ~**mado** *m* call □ *a* (*depois do substantivo*) called; (*antes do substantivo*) so-called; ~**mar** *vt* call; (*para sair etc*) ask, invite; attract <*atenção*> □ *vi* call; <*telefone*> ring; ~**mar-se** *vpr* be called; ~**mariz** *m* decoy; ~**mativo** *a* showy, flashy

**chamejar** /ʃame'ʒar/ *vi* flare

**chaminé** /ʃami'nɛ/ *f* (*de casa, fábrica*) chimney; (*de navio, trem*) funnel

**champanhe** /ʃãˈpaɲi/ *m* champagne

**champu** /ʃãˈpu/ (*Port*) *m* shampoo

**chamuscar** /ʃamusˈkar/ *vt* singe, scorch

**chance** /ˈʃãsi/ *f* chance

**chanceler** /ʃãseˈler/ *m* chancellor

**chanchada** /ʃãˈʃada/ *f* (*peça*) second-rate play; (*filme*) B movie

**chanta|gear** /ʃãtaʒiˈar/ *vt* blackmail; ~**gem** *f* blackmail; ~**gista** *m/f* blackmailer

**chão** /ʃãw/ (*pl* ~**s**) *m* ground; (*dentro de casa etc*) floor

**chapa** /ˈʃapa/ *f* sheet; (*foto*) plate; ~ **eleitoral** electoral list; (*de matrícula* (*Port*) number plate, (*Amer*) license plate □ ( *fam*) *m* mate

**chapéu** /ʃaˈpɛw/ *m* hat

**charada** /ʃaˈrada/ *f* riddle

**char|ge** /ˈʃarʒi/ *f* (political) cartoon; ~**gista** *m/f* cartoonist

**charla|tanismo** /ʃarlataˈnizmu/ *m* charlatanism; ~**tão** (*pl* ~**tães**) *m* ( *f* ~**tona**) charlatan

**char|me** /ˈʃarmi/ *m* charm; **fazer** ~**me** turn on the charm; ~**moso** /o/ *a* charming

**charneca** /ʃarˈnɛka/ *f* moor

**charuto** /ʃaˈrutu/ *m* cigar

**chassi** /ʃaˈsi/ *m* chassis

**chata** /ˈʃata/ *f* (*barca*) barge

**chate|ação** /ʃatʃiaˈsãw/ *f* annoyance; ~**ar** *vt* annoy; ~**ar-se** *vpr* get annoyed

**cha|tice** /ʃaˈtʃisi/ *f* nuisance; ~**to** *a* (*tedioso*) boring; (*irritante*) annoying; (*mal-educado*) rude; (*plano*) flat

**chauvinis|mo** /ʃoviˈnizmu/ *m* chauvinism; ~**ta** *m/f* chauvinist □ *a* chauvinistic

**cha|vão** /ʃaˈvãw/ *m* cliché; ~**ve** *f* key; ( *ferramenta*) spanner; ~**ve de fenda** screwdriver; ~**ve inglesa** wrench; ~**veiro** *m* (*aro*) keyring; (*pessoa*) locksmith

**chávena** /ˈʃavena/ *f* soup bowl; (*Port: xícara*) cup

**checar** /ʃeˈkar/ *vt* check

**che|fe** /ˈʃɛfi/ *m/f* (*patrão*) boss; (*gerente*) manager; (*dirigente*) leader; ~**fia** *f* leadership; (*de empresa*) management; (*sede*) headquarters; ~**fiar** *vt* lead; **be in charge of** <*trabalho*>

**che|gada** /ʃeˈgada/ *f* arrival; ~**gado** *a* <*amigo, relação*> close; ~**gar** *vi* arrive; (*deslocar-se*) move up; (*ser suficiente*) be enough □ *vt* bring up <*prato, cadeira*>; ~**gar a fazer** go as far as doing; **aonde você quer** ~**gar?** what are you driving at?; ~**gar lá** ( *fig*) make it

**cheia** /ˈʃeja/ *f* flood

**cheio** /ˈʃeju/ *a* full; ( *fam: farto*) fed up

**chei|rar** /ʃeˈrar/ *vt/i* smell (**a** of); ~**roso** /o/ *a* scented

**cheque** /ˈʃɛki/ *m* cheque, (*Amer*) check; ~ **de viagem** traveller's cheque; ~ **em branco** blank cheque

**chi|ado** /ʃiˈadu/ *m* (*de pneus, freios*) screech; (*de porta*) squeak; (*de vapor, numa fita*) hiss; ~**ar** *vi* <*porta*> squeak; <*pneus, freios*> screech; <*vapor, fita*> hiss; <*fritura*> sizzle; ( *fam: reclamar*) grumble, moan

**chiclete** /ʃiˈklɛtʃi/ *m* chewing gum; ~ **de bola** bubble gum

**chico|tada** /ʃikoˈtada/ *f* lash; ~**te** /ɔ/ *m* whip; ~**tear** *vt* whip

**chi|frar** /ʃiˈfrar/ ( *fam*) *vt* cheat on <*marido, esposa*>; two-time <*namorado, namorada*>; ~**fre** *m* horn; ~**frudo** *a* horned; ( *fam*) cuckolded □ *m* cuckold

**Chile** /ˈʃili/ *m* Chile

**chileno** /ʃiˈlenu/ *a* & *m* Chilean

**chilique** /ʃiˈliki/ ( *fam*) *m* funny turn

**chil|rear** /ʃiwxiˈar/ *vi* chirp, twitter; ~**reio** *m* chirping, twittering

**chimarrão** /ʃimaˈxãw/ *m* unsweetened maté tea

**chimpanzé** /ʃĩpãˈzɛ/ *m* chimpanzee

**China** /ˈʃina/ *f* China

**chinelo** /ʃiˈnɛlu/ *m* slipper

**chi|nês** /ʃiˈnes/ *a* & *m* ( *f* ~**nesa**) Chinese

**chinfrim** /ʃĩˈfrĩ/ *a* tatty, shoddy

**chio** /ˈʃiu/ *m* squeak; (*de pneus*) screech; (*de vapor*) hiss

**chique** /ˈʃiki/ *a* <*pessoa, aparência, roupa*> smart, (*Amer*) sharp; <*hotel, bairro, loja etc*> smart, up-market, posh

**chiqueiro** /ʃiˈkeru/ *m* pigsty

**chis|pa** /ˈʃispa/ *f* flash; ~**pada** *f* dash; ~**par** *vi* (*soltar chispas*) flash; (*correr*) dash

**choca|lhar** /ʃokaˈʎar/ *vt/i* rattle; ~**lho** *m* rattle

**cho|cante** /ʃoˈkãtʃi/ *a* shocking; ( *fam*) incredible; ~**car** *vt/i* hatch <*ovos*>; (*ultrajar*) shock; ~**car-se** *vpr* <*carros etc*> crash; <*teorias etc*> clash

**chocho** /ˈʃoʃu/ *a* dull, insipid

**chocolate** /ʃokoˈlatʃi/ *m* chocolate

**chofer** /ʃoˈfer/ *m* chauffeur

**chope** /ˈʃopi/ *m* draught lager

**choque** /ˈʃɔki/ *m* shock; (*colisão*) collision; (*conflito*) clash

**cho|radeira** /ʃoraˈdera/ *f* fit of crying; ~**ramingar** *vi* whine; ~**ramingas** *m/f invar* whiner; ~**rão** *m* (*salgueiro*) weeping willow □ *a* (~**rona**) tearful; ~**rar** *vi* cry; ~**ro** /o/ *m* crying; ~**roso** /o/ *a* tearful

**chouriço** /ʃoˈrisu/ *m* black pudding; (*Port*) sausage

**chover** /ʃo'ver/ *vi* rain
**chuchu** /ʃu'ʃu/ *m* chayote
**chucrute** /ʃu'krutʃi/ *m* sauerkraut
**chumaço** /ʃu'masu/ *m* wad
**chum|bado** /ʃũ'badu/ (*fam*) *a* knocked out; **~bar** (*Port*) *vt* fill <*dente*>; fail <*aluno*> □ *vi* <*aluno*> fail; **~bo** *m* lead; (*Port*: *obturação*) filling
**chu|par** /ʃu'par/ *vt* suck; <*esponja*> suck up; **~peta** /e/ *f* dummy, (*Amer*) pacifier
**churras|caria** /ʃuxaska'ria/ *f* barbecue restaurant; **~co** *m* barbecue; **~queira** *f* barbecue; **~quinho** *m* kebab
**chu|tar** /ʃu'tar/ *vt/i* kick; (*fam: adivinhar*) guess; **~te** *m* kick; **~teira** *f* football boot
**chu|va** /'ʃuva/ *f* rain; **~va de pedra** hail; **~varada** *f* torrential rainstorm; **~veiro** *m* shower; **~viscar** *vi* drizzle; **~visco** *m* drizzle; **~voso** /o/ *a* rainy
**cica|triz** /sika'tris/ *f* scar; **~trizar** *vt* scar □ *vi* <*ferida*> heal
**cic|lismo** /si'klizmu/ *m* cycling; **~lista** *m/f* cyclist; **~lo** *m* cycle; **~lone** /o/ *m* cyclone; **~lovia** *f* cycle lane
**cida|dania** /sidada'nia/ *f* citizenship; **~dão** (*pl* **~dãos**) *m* (*f* **~dã**) citizen; **~de** *f* town; (*grande*) city; **~dela** /ɛ/ *f* citadel
**ciência** /si'ẽsia/ *f* science
**cien|te** /si'ẽtʃi/ *a* aware; **~tífico** *a* scientific; **~tista** *m/f* scientist
**ci|fra** /'sifra/ *f* figure; (*código*) cipher; **~frão** *m* dollar sign; **~frar** *vt* encode
**cigano** /si'ganu/ *a & m* gypsy
**cigarra** /si'gaxa/ *f* cicada; (*dispositivo*) buzzer
**cigar|reira** /siga'xera/ *f* cigarette case; **~ro** *m* cigarette
**cilada** /si'lada/ *f* trap; (*estratagema*) trick
**cilindrada** /sili'drada/ *f* (engine) capacity
**cilíndrico** /si'lĩdriku/ *a* cylindrical
**cilindro** /si'lĩdru/ *m* cylinder; (*rolo*) roller
**cílio** /'siliu/ *m* eyelash
**cima** /'sima/ *f* **em ~** on top; (*na casa*) upstairs; **em ~ de** on, on top of; **para ~** up; (*na casa*) upstairs; **por ~** over the top; **por ~ de** over; **de ~** from above; **ainda por ~** moreover
**címbalo** /'sĩbalu/ *m* cymbal
**cimeira** /si'mera/ *f* crest; (*Port: cúpula*) summit
**cimen|tar** /simẽ'tar/ *vt* cement; **~to** *m* cement
**cinco** /'sĩku/ *a & m* five

**cine|asta** /sini'asta/ *m/f* film-maker; **~ma** /e/ *m* cinema
**Cingapura** /sĩga'pura/ *f* Singapore
**cínico** /'siniku/ *a* cynical □ *m* cynic
**cinismo** /si'nizmu/ *m* cynicism
**cinqüen|ta** /sĩ'kwẽta/ *a & m* fifty; **~tão** *a & m* (*f* **~tona**) fifty-year-old
**cinti|lante** /sĩtʃi'lãtʃi/ *a* glittering; **~lar** *vi* glitter
**cin|to** /'sĩtu/ *m* belt; **~to de segurança** seatbelt; **~tura** *f* waist; **~turão** *m* belt
**cin|za** /'sĩza/ *f* ash □ *a invar* grey; **~zeiro** *m* ashtray
**cin|zel** /sĩ'zɛw/ (*pl* **~zéis**) *m* chisel; **~zelar** *vt* carve
**cinzento** /sĩ'zẽtu/ *a* grey
**cipó** /si'pɔ/ *m* vine, liana; **~poal** (*pl* **~poais**) *m* jungle
**cipreste** /si'prɛstʃi/ *m* cypress
**cipriota** /sipri'ota/ *a & m* Cypriot
**ciranda** /si'rãda/ *f* (*fig*) merry-go-round
**cir|cense** /sir'sẽsi/ *a* circus; **~co** *m* circus
**circu|ito** /sir'kuitu/ *m* circuit; **~lação** *f* circulation; **~lar** *a & f* circular □ *vt* circulate □ *vi* <*dinheiro, sangue*> circulate; <*carro*> drive; <*ônibus*> run; <*trânsito*> move; <*pessoa*> go round
**círculo** /'sirkulu/ *m* circle
**circunci|dar** /sirkũsi'dar/ *vt* circumcise; **~ção** *f* circumcision
**circun|dar** /sirkũ'dar/ *vt* surround; **~ferência** *f* circumference; **~flexo** /eks/ *a & m* circumflex; **~scrição** *f* district; **~scrição eleitoral** constituency; **~specto** /ɛ/ *a* circumspect; **~stância** *f* circumstance; **~stanciado** *a* detailed; **~stancial** (*pl* **~stanciais**) *a* circumstantial; **~stante** *m/f* bystander
**cirrose** /si'xɔzi/ *f* cirrhosis
**cirur|gia** /sirur'ʒia/ *f* surgery; **~gião** *m* (*f* **~giã**) surgeon
**cirúrgico** /si'rurʒiku/ *a* surgical
**cisão** /si'zãw/ *f* split, division
**cisco** /'sisku/ *m* speck
**cisma**[1] /'sizma/ *m* schism
**cis|ma**[2] /'sizma/ *f* (*mania*) fixation; (*devaneio*) imagining, daydream; (*prevenção*) irrational dislike; (*de criança*) whim; **~mar** *vt/i* be lost in thought; <*criança*> be insistent; **~mar em** brood over; **~mar de ou em fazer** insist on doing; **~mar que** insist on thinking that; **~mar com alg** take a dislike to s.o.
**cisne** /'sizni/ *m* swan
**cistite** /sis'tʃitʃi/ *f* cystitis
**ci|tação** /sita'sãw/ *f* quotation; (*jurid*) summons; **~tar** *vt* quote; (*jurid*) summon

**ciúme** /si'umi/ *m* jealousy; **ter ~s de** be jealous of

**ciu|meira** /siu'mera/ *f* fit of jealousy; **~mento** *a* jealous

**cívico** /'siviku/ *a* civic

**ci|vil** /si'viw/ (*pl ~vis*) *a* civil □ *m* civilian; **~vilidade** *f* civility

**civili|zação** /siviliza'sãw/ *f* civilization; **~zado** *a* civilized; **~zar** *vt* civilize

**civismo** /si'vizmu/ *m* public spirit

**cla|mar** /kla'mar/ *vt/i* cry out, clamour (**por** for); **~mor** *m* outcry; **~moroso** /o/ *a* <*protesto*> loud, noisy; <*erro, injustiça*> blatant

**clandestino** /klãdes'tʃinu/ *a* clandestine

**cla|ra** /'klara/ *f* egg white; **~rabóia** *f* skylight; **~rão** *m* flash; **~rear** *vt* brighten; clarify <*questão*> □ *vi* brighten up; (*fazer-se dia*) become light; **~reira** *f* clearing; **~reza** /e/ *f* clarity; **~ridade** *f* brightness; (*do dia*) daylight

**cla|rim** /kla'rĩ/ *m* bugle; **~rinete** /e/ *m* clarinet

**clarividente** /klarivi'dẽtʃi/ *m/f* clairvoyant

**claro** /'klaru/ *a* clear; <*luz*> bright; <*cor*> light □ *adv* clearly □ *int* of course; **~ que sim/não** of course/of course not; **às claras** openly; **noite em ~** sleepless night; **já é dia ~** it's already daylight

**classe** /'klasi/ *f* class; **~ média** middle class

**clássico** /'klasiku/ *a* classical; (*famoso, exemplar*) classic □ *m* classic

**classifi|cação** /klasifika'sãw/ *f* classification; (*numa competição esportiva*) placing, place; **~cado** *a* classified; <*candidato*> successful; <*esportista, time*> qualified; **~car** *vt* classify; (*considerar*) describe (**de** as); **~car-se** *vpr* <*candidato, esportista*> qualify; (*chamar-se*) describe o.s. (**de** as); **~catório** *a* qualifying

**classudo** /kla'sudu/ (*fam*) *a* classy

**claustro|fobia** /klawstrofo'bia/ *f* claustrophobia; **~fóbico** *a* claustrophobic

**cláusula** /'klawzula/ *f* clause

**cla|ve** /'klavi/ *f* clef; **~vícula** *f* collar bone

**cle|mência** /kle'mẽsia/ *f* clemency; **~mente** *a* <*pessoa*> lenient; <*tempo*> clement

**cleptomaníaco** /kleptoma'niaku/ *m* kleptomaniac

**clérigo** /'klɛrigu/ *m* cleric, clergyman

**clero** /'klɛru/ *m* clergy

**clien|te** /kli'ẽtʃi/ *m/f* (*de loja*) customer; (*de advogado, empresa*) client;

**~tela** /ɛ/ *f* (*de loja*) customers; (*de restaurante, empresa*) clientele

**cli|ma** /'klima/ *m* climate; **~mático** *a* climatic

**clímax** /'klimaks/ *m invar* climax

**clíni|ca** /'klinika/ *f* clinic; **~ca geral** general practice; **~co** *a* clinical □ *m* **~co geral** general practitioner, GP

**clipe** /'klipi/ *m* clip; (*para papéis*) paper clip

**clone** /'kloni/ *m* clone

**cloro** /'klɔru/ *m* chlorine

**close** /'klɔzi/ *m* close-up

**clube** /'klubi/ *m* club

**coação** /koa'sãw/ *f* coercion

**coadjuvante** /koadʒu'vãtʃi/ *a* <*ator*> supporting □ *m/f* (*em peça, filme*) co-star; (*em crime*) accomplice

**coador** /koa'dor/ *m* strainer; (*de legumes*) colander; (*de café*) filter bag

**coadunar** /koadu'nar/ *vt* combine

**coagir** /koa'ʒir/ *vt* compel

**coagular** /koagu'lar/ *vt/i* clot; **~-se** *vpr* clot

**coágulo** /ko'agulu/ *m* clot

**coalhar** /koa'ʎar/ *vt/i* curdle; **~-se** *vpr* curdle

**coalizão** /koali'zãw/ *f* coalition

**coar** /ko'ar/ *vt* strain

**coaxar** /koa'ʃar/ *vi* croak □ *m* croaking

**cobaia** /ko'baja/ *f* guinea pig

**cober|ta** /ko'bɛrta/ *f* (*de cama*) bed-cover; (*de navio*) deck; **~to** /ɛ/ *a* covered □ *pp de* cobrir; **~tor** *m* blanket; **~tura** *f* (*revestimento*) covering; (*reportagem*) coverage; (*seguro*) cover; (*apartamento*) penthouse

**cobi|ça** /ko'bisa/ *f* greed, covetousness; **~çar** *vt* covet; **~çoso** /o/ *a* covetous

**cobra** /'kɔbra/ *f* snake

**co|brador** /kobra'dor/ *m* (*no ônibus*) conductor; **~brança** *f* (*de dívida*) collection; (*de preço*) charging; (*de atitudes*) asking for something in return (**de** for); **~brança de pênalti/falta** penalty (kick)/free kick; **~brar** *vt* collect <*dívida*>; ask for <*coisa prometida*>; take <*pênalti*>; **~brar aco a alg** (*em dinheiro*) charge s.o. for sth; (*fig*) make s.o. pay for sth; **~brar uma falta** (*no futebol*) take a free kick

**cobre** /'kɔbri/ *m* copper

**cobrir** /ko'brir/ *vt* cover; **~-se** *vpr* <*pessoa*> cover o.s. up; <*coisa*> be covered

**cocaína** /koka'ina/ *f* cocaine

**coçar** /ko'sar/ *vt* scratch □ *vi* (*esfregar-se*) scratch; (*comichar*) itch; **~-se** *vpr* scratch o.s.

**cócegas** /'kɔsegas/ *f pl* **fazer ~ em** tickle; **sentir ~** be ticklish

**coceira** /ko'sera/ *f* itch
**cochi|char** /koʃi'ʃar/ *vt/i* whisper; ∼**cho** *m* whisper
**cochi|lada** /koʃi'lada/ *f* doze; ∼**lar** *vi* doze; ∼**lo** *m* snooze
**coco** /'koku/ *m* coconut
**cócoras** /'kokoras/ *f pl* **de** ∼ squatting; **ficar de** ∼ squat
**côdea** /'kodʒia/ *f* crust
**codificar** /kodʒifi'kar/ *vt* encode <*mensagem*>; codify <*leis*>
**código** /'kodʒigu/ *m* code; ∼ **de barras** bar code
**codinome** /kodʒi'nomi/ *m* codename
**coeficiente** /koefisi'ẽtʃi/ *m* coefficient; ( *fig: fator*) factor
**coelho** /ko'eʎu/ *m* rabbit
**coentro** /ko'ẽtru/ *m* coriander
**coerção** /koer'sãw/ *f* coercion
**coe|rência** /koe'rẽsia/ *f* ( *lógica*) coherence; ( *conseqüência*) consistency; ∼**rente** *a* ( *lógico*) coherent; ( *conseqüente*) consistent
**coexis|tência** /koezis'tẽsia/ *f* coexistence; ∼**tir** *vi* coexist
**cofre** /'kofri/ *m* safe; ( *de dinheiro público*) coffer
**cogi|tação** /koʒita'sãw/ *f* contemplation; **fora de** ∼ **tação** out of the question; ∼**tar** *vt/i* contemplate
**cogumelo** /kogu'mɛlu/ *m* mushroom
**coibir** /koi'bir/ *vt* restrict; ∼**-se de** keep o.s. from
**coice** /'kojsi/ *m* kick
**coinci|dência** /koĩsi'dẽsia/ *f* coincidence; ∼**dir** *vi* coincide
**coisa** /'kojza/ *f* thing
**coitado** /koj'tadu/ *m* poor thing; ∼ **do pai** poor father
**cola** /'kɔla/ *f* glue; ( *cópia*) crib
**colabo|ração** /kolabora'sãw/ *f* collaboration; ( *de escritor etc*) contribution; ∼**rador** *m* collaborator; ( *em jornal, livro*) contributor; ∼**rar** *vi* collaborate; ( *em jornal, livro*) contribute (**em** to)
**colagem** /ko'laʒẽ/ *f* collage
**colágeno** /ko'laʒenu/ *m* collagen
**colapso** /ko'lapsu/ *m* collapse
**colar¹** /ko'lar/ *m* necklace
**colar²** /ko'lar/ *vt* ( *grudar*) stick; ( *copiar*) crib □ *vi* stick; ( *copiar*) crib; <*desculpa etc*> stand up, stick
**colarinho** /kola'riɲu/ *m* collar; ( *de cerveja*) head
**colate|ral** /kolate'raw/ ( *pl* ∼**rais**) *a* **efeito** ∼**ral** side effect
**col|cha** /'kowʃa/ *f* bedspread; ∼**chão** *m* mattress
**colchete** /kow'ʃetʃi/ *m* fastener; ( *sinal de pontuação*) square bracket; ∼ **de pressão** press stud, popper
**colchonete** /kowʃo'nɛtʃi/ *m* (foldaway) mattress

**coldre** /'kowdri/ *m* holster
**cole|ção** /kole'sãw/ *f* collection; ∼**cionador** *m* collector; ∼**cionar** *vt* collect
**colega** /ko'lɛga/ *m/f* ( *amigo*) friend; ( *de trabalho*) colleague
**colegi|al** /koleʒi'aw/ ( *pl* ∼**ais**) *a* school □ *m/f* schoolboy ( *f* -girl)
**colégio** /ko'lɛʒiu/ *m* secondary school, ( *Amer*) high school
**coleira** /ko'lera/ *f* collar
**cólera** /'kɔlera/ *f* ( *doença*) cholera; ( *raiva*) fury
**colérico** /ko'lɛriku/ *a* ( *furioso*) furious □ *m* ( *doente*) cholera victim
**colesterol** /koleste'rɔw/ *m* cholesterol
**cole|ta** /ko'lɛta/ *f* collection; ∼**tânea** *f* collection; ∼**tar** *vt* collect
**colete** /ko'letʃi/ *m* waistcoat, ( *Amer*) vest; ∼ **salva-vidas** life-jacket, ( *Amer*) life-preserver
**coletivo** /kole'tʃivu/ *a* collective; <*transporte*> public □ *m* bus
**colheita** /ko'ʎejta/ *f* harvest; ( *produtos colhidos*) crop
**colher¹** /ko'ʎɛr/ *f* spoon
**colher²** /ko'ʎɛr/ *vt* pick <*flores, frutos*>; gather <*informações*>
**colherada** /koʎe'rada/ *f* spoonful
**colibri** /koli'bri/ *m* hummingbird
**cólica** /'kɔlika/ *f* colic
**colidir** /koli'dʒir/ *vi* collide
**coli|gação** /koliga'sãw/ *f* ( *pol*) coalition; ∼**gado** *m* ( *pol*) coalition partner; ∼**gar** *vt* bring together; ∼**gar-se** *vpr* join forces; ( *pol*) form a coalition
**colina** /ko'lina/ *f* hill
**colírio** /ko'liriu/ *m* eyewash
**colisão** /koli'zãw/ *f* collision
**collant** /ko'lã/ ( *pl* ∼**s**) *m* body; ( *de ginástica*) leotard
**colmeia** /kow'meja/ *f* beehive
**colo** /'kɔlu/ *f* ( *regaço*) lap; ( *pescoço*) neck
**colo|cação** /koloka'sãw/ *f* placing; ( *emprego*) position; ( *exposição de fatos*) statement; ( *de aparelho, pneus, carpete etc*) fitting; ∼**cado** *a* placed; **o primeiro** ∼**cado** ( *em ranking*) person in first place; ∼**cador** *m* fitter; ∼**car** put; fit <*aparelho, pneus, carpete etc*>; put forward, state <*opinião, idéias*>; ( *empregar*) get a job for
**Colômbia** /ko'lõbia/ *f* Colombia
**colombiano** /kolõbi'anu/ *a & m* Colombian
**cólon** /'kɔlõ/ *m* colon
**colônia¹** /ko'lonia/ *f* ( *colonos*) colony
**colônia²** /ko'lonia/ *f* ( *perfume*) cologne
**coloni|al** /koloni'aw/ ( *pl* ∼**ais**) *a* colonial; ∼**alismo** *m* colonialism;

~**alista** *a & m/f* colonialist; ~**zar** *vt* colonize

**colono** /ko'lonu/ *m* settler, colonist; (*lavrador*) tenant farmer

**coloqui|al** /koloki'aw/ (*pl* ~**ais**) *a* colloquial

**colóquio** /ko'lɔkiu/ *m* (*conversa*) conversation; (*congresso*) conference

**colo|rido** /kolo'ridu/ *a* colourful □ *m* colouring; ~**rir** *vt* colour

**colu|na** /ko'luna/ *f* column; (*vertebral*) spine; ~**nável** (*pl* ~**náveis**) *a* famous □ *m/f* celebrity; ~**nista** *m/f* columnist

**com** /kõ/ *prep* with; **o comentário foi comigo** the comment was meant for me; **você está ~ a chave?** have you got the key?; ~ **seis anos de idade** at six years of age

**coma** /'koma/ *f* coma

**comadre** /ko'madri/ *f* (*madrinha*) godmother of one's child; (*mãe do afilhado*) mother of one's godchild; (*urinol*) bedpan

**coman|dante** /komã'dãtʃi/ *m* commander; ~**dar** *vt* lead; (*ordenar*) command; (*elevar-se acima de*) dominate; ~**do** *m* command; (*grupo*) commando group

**comba|te** /kõ'batʃi/ *m* combat; (*a drogas, doença etc*) fight (**a** against); ~**ter** *vt/i* fight; ~**ter-se** *vpr* fight

**combi|nação** /kõbina'sãw/ *f* combination; (*acordo*) arrangement; (*plano*) scheme; (*roupa*) petticoat; ~**nar** *vt* (*juntar*) combine; (*ajustar*) arrange □ *vi* go together, match; ~**nar com** go with, match; ~**nar de sair** arrange to go out; ~**nar-se** *vpr* (*juntar-se*) combine; (*harmonizar-se*) go together, match

**comboio** /kõ'boju/ *m* convoy; (*Port: trem*) train

**combustí|vel** /kõbus'tʃivew/ (*pl* ~**veis**) *m* fuel

**come|çar** /kome'sar/ *vt/i* start, begin; ~**ço** /e/ *m* beginning, start

**comédia** /ko'mɛdʒia/ *f* comedy

**comediante** /komedʒi'ãtʃi/ *m/f* comedian (*f* comedienne)

**comemo|ração** /komemora'sãw/ *f* (*celebração*) celebration; (*lembrança*) commemoration; ~**rar** *vt* (*festejar*) celebrate; (*lembrar*) commemorate; ~**rativo** *a* commemorative

**comen|tar** /komẽ'tar/ *vt* comment on; (*falar mal de*) make comments about; ~**tário** *m* comment; (*de texto, na TV etc*) commentary; **sem ~tários** no comment; ~**tarista** *m/f* commentator

**comer** /ko'mer/ *vt* eat; <*ferrugem etc*> eat away; take <*peça de xadrez*> □ *vi* eat; ~**-se** *vpr* (*de raiva etc*) be

consumed (**de** with); **dar de ~ a** feed

**comerci|al** /komersi'aw/ (*pl* ~**ais**) *a & m* commercial; ~**alizar** *vt* market; ~**ante** *m/f* trader; ~**ar** *vi* do business, trade; ~**ário** *m* shopworker

**comércio** /ko'mersiu/ *m* (*atividade*) trade; (*loja etc*) business; (*lojas*) shops

**comes** /'komis/ *m pl* ~ **e bebes** (*fam*) food and drink; ~**tíveis** *m pl* foods, food; ~**tível** (*pl* ~**tíveis**) *a* edible

**cometa** /ko'meta/ *m* comet

**cometer** /kome'ter/ *vt* commit <*crime*>; make <*erro*>

**comichão** /komi'ʃãw/ *f* itch

**comício** /ko'misiu/ *m* rally

**cômico** /'komiku/ *a* (*de comédia*) comic; (*engraçado*) comical

**comida** /ko'mida/ *f* food; (*uma*) meal

**comigo = com + mim**

**comi|lão** /komi'lãw/ *a* (*f* ~**lona**) greedy □ *m* (*f* ~**lona**) glutton

**cominho** /ko'miɲu/ *m* cummin

**comiserar-se** /komize'rarsi/ *vpr* commiserate (**de** with)

**comis|são** /komi'sãw/ *f* commission; ~**sário** *m* commissioner; ~**sário de bordo** (*aéreo*) steward; (*de navio*) purser; ~**sionar** *vt* commission

**comi|tê** /komi'te/ *m* committee; ~**tiva** *f* group; (*de uma pessoa*) retinue

**como** /'komu/ *adv* (*na condição de*) as; (*da mesma forma que*) like; (*de que maneira*) how □ *conj* as; ~? (*pedindo repetição*) pardon?; ~ **se** as if; **assim ~** as well as

**cômoda** /'komoda/ *f* chest of drawers, (*Amer*) bureau

**como|didade** /komodʒi'dadʒi/ *f* comfort; (*conveniência*) convenience; ~**dismo** *m* complacency; ~**dista** *a* complacent

**cômodo** /'komodu/ *a* comfortable; (*conveniente*) convenient □ *m* (*aposento*) room

**como|vente** /komo'vẽtʃi/ *a* moving; ~**ver** *vt* move □ *vi* be moving; ~**ver-se** *vpr* be moved

**compacto** /kõ'paktu/ *a* compact □ *m* single

**compadecer-se** /kõpade'sersi/ *vpr* feel pity (**de** for)

**compadre** /kõ'padri/ *m* (*padrinho*) godfather of one's child; (*pai do afilhado*) father of one's godchild

**compaixão** /kõpaj'ʃãw/ *f* compassion

**companhei|rismo** /kõpaɲe'rizmu/ *m* companionship; ~**ro** *m* (*de viagem etc*) companion; (*amigo*) friend, mate

**companhia** /kõpa'ɲia/ *f* company; **fazer ~ a alg** keep s.o. company

**compa|ração** /kõpara'sãw/ *f* comparison; ~**rar** *vt* compare; ~**rativo**

*a* comparative; **~rável** (*pl* **~ráveis**) *a* comparable

**compare|cer** /kõpare'ser/ *vi* appear; **~cer a** attend; **~cimento** *m* attendance

**comparsa** /kõ'parsa/ *m/f* (*ator*) bit player; (*cúmplice*) sidekick

**comparti|lhar** /kõpartʃi'ʎar/ *vt/i* share (**de** in); **~mento** *m* compartment

**compassado** /kõpa'sadu/ *a* (*medido*) measured; (*ritmado*) regular

**compassivo** /kõpa'sivu/ *a* compassionate

**compasso** /kõ'pasu/ *m* (*mus*) beat, time; (*instrumento*) compass, pair of compasses

**compatí|vel** /kõpa'tʃivew/ (*pl* **~veis**) *a* compatible

**compatriota** /kõpatri'ɔta/ *m/f* compatriot, fellow countryman (*f* -woman)

**compelir** /kõpe'lir/ *vt* compel

**compene|tração** /kõpenetra'sãw/ *f* conviction; **~trar** *vt* convince; **~trar-se** *vpr* convince o.s.

**compen|sação** /kõpẽsa'sãw/ *f* compensation; (*de cheques*) clearing; **~sar** *vt* make up for <*defeitos, danos*>; offset <*peso, gastos*>; clear <*cheques*> □ *vi* <*crime*> pay

**compe|tência** /kõpe'tẽsia/ *f* competence; **~tente** *a* competent

**compe|tição** /kõpetʃi'sãw/ *f* competition; **~tidor** *m* competitor; **~tir** *vi* compete; **~tir a** be up to; **~tividade** *f* competitiveness; **~titivo** *a* competitive

**compla|cência** /kõpla'sẽsia/ *f* complaisance; **~cente** *a* obliging

**complemen|tar** /kõplemẽ'tar/ *vt* complement □ *a* complementary; **~to** *m* complement

**comple|tar** /kõple'tar/ *vt* complete; top up <*copo, tanque etc*>; **~tar 20 anos** turn 20; **~to** /ɛ/ *a* complete; (*cheio*) full up; **por ~to** completely; **escrever por ~to** write out in full

**comple|xado** /kõplek'sadu/ *a* with a complex; **~xidade** *f* complexity; **~xo** /ɛ/ *a* & *m* complex

**compli|cação** /kõplika'sãw/ *f* complication; **~cado** *a* complicated; **~car** *vt* complicate; **~car-se** *vpr* get complicated

**complô** /kõ'plo/ *m* conspiracy, plot

**com|ponente** /kõpo'nẽtʃi/ *a* & *m* component; **~por** *vt/i* compose; **~por-se** *vpr* (*controlar-se*) compose o.s.; **~por-se de** be composed of

**compor|tamento** /kõporta'mẽtu/ *m* behaviour; **~tar** *vt* hold; bear <*dor, prejuízo*>; **~tar-se** *vpr* behave

**composi|ção** /kõpozi'sãw/ *f* composi-

tion; (*acordo*) conciliation; **~tor** *m* (*de música*) composer; (*gráfico*) compositor

**compos|to** /kõ'postu/ *pp de* **compor** □ *a* compound; <*pessoa*> level-headed □ *m* compound; **~to de** made up of; **~tura** *f* composure

**compota** /kõ'pɔta/ *f* fruit in syrup

**com|pra** /'kõpra/ *f* purchase; *pl* shopping; **fazer ~pras** go shopping; **~prador** *m* buyer; **~prar** *vt* buy; bribe <*oficial, juiz*>; pick <*briga*>

**compreen|der** /kõprič'der/ *vt* (*conter em si*) contain; (*estender-se a*) cover, take in; (*entender*) understand; **~são** *f* understanding; **~sível** (*pl* **~síveis**) *a* understandable; **~sivo** *a* understanding

**compres|sa** /kõ'prɛsa/ *f* compress; **~são** *f* compression; **~sor** *m* compressor; **rolo ~sor** steamroller

**compri|do** /kõ'pridu/ *a* long; **~mento** *m* length

**compri|mido** /kõpri'midu/ *m* pill, tablet □ *a* <*ar*> compressed; **~mir** *vt* (*apertar*) press; (*reduzir o volume de*) compress

**comprome|tedor** /kõpromete'dor/ *a* compromising; **~ter** *vt* (*envolver*) involve; (*prejudicar*) compromise; **~ter alg a fazer** commit s.o. to doing; **~ter-se** *vpr* (*obrigar-se*) commit o.s.; (*prejudicar-se*) compromise o.s.; **~tido** *a* (*ocupado*) busy; (*noivo*) spoken for

**compromisso** /kõpro'misu/ *m* commitment; (*encontro marcado*) appointment; **sem ~** without obligation

**compro|vação** /kõprova'sãw/ *f* proof; **~vante** *m* receipt; **~var** *vt* prove

**compul|são** /kõpuw'sãw/ *f* compulsion; **~sivo** *a* compulsive; **~sório** *a* compulsory

**compu|tação** /kõputa'sãw/ *f* computation; (*matéria, ramo*) computing; **~tador** *m* computer; **~tadorizar** *vt* computerize; **~tar** *vt* compute

**comum** /ko'mũ/ *a* common; (*não especial*) ordinary; **fora do ~** out of the ordinary; **em ~** <*trabalho*> joint; <*atuar*> jointly; **ter muito em ~** have a lot in common

**comungar** /komũ'gar/ *vi* take communion

**comunhão** /komu'ɲãw/ *f* communion; (*relig*) (Holy) Communion

**comuni|cação** /komunika'sãw/ *f* communication; **~cação social/visual** media studies/ graphic design; **~cado** *m* notice; (*pol*) communiqué; **~car** *vt* communicate; (*unir*) connect □ *vi*, **~car-se** *vpr* communicate; **~cativo** *a* communicative comu|nidade /komuni'dadʒi/ f community; ~nismo m communism; ~nista a & m/f communist; ~ nitário a (da comunidade) community; (para todos juntos) communal

côncavo /'kõkavu/ a concave

conce|ber /kõse'ber/ vt conceive; (imaginar) conceive of □ vi conceive; ~bível (pl ~bíveis) a conceivable

conceder /kõse'der/ vt grant; ~ em accede to

concei|to /kõ'sejtu/ m concept; (opinião) opinion; (fama) reputation; ~tuado a highly thought of; ~tuar vt (imaginar) conceptualize; (avaliar) assess

concen|tração /kõsẽtra'sãw/ f concentration; (de jogadores) training camp; ~trar vt concentrate; ~trar-se vpr concentrate

concepção /kõsep'sãw/ f conception; (opinião) view

concernir /kõser'nir/ vt ~ a concern

concerto /kõ'sertu/ m concert

conces|são /kõse'sãw/ f concession; ~sionária f dealership; ~sionário m dealer

concha /'kõʃa/ f (de molusco) shell; (colher) ladle

concili|ação /kõsilia'sãw/ f conciliation; ~ador a conciliatory; ~ar vt reconcile

concílio /kõ'siliu/ m council

conci|são /kõsi'zãw/ f conciseness; ~so a concise

conclamar /kõkla'mar/ vt call <eleição, greve>; call upon <pessoa>

conclu|dente /kõklu'dẽtʃi/ a conclusive; ~ir vt/i conclude; ~são f conclusion; ~sivo a concluding

concor|dância /kõkor'dãsia/ f agreement; ~dante a consistent; ~dar vi agree (em to) □ vt bring into line; ~data f abrir ~data go into liquidation

concórdia /kõ'kɔrdʒia/ f concord

concor|rência /kõko'xẽsia/ f competition (a for); ~rente a competing; ~rer vi compete (a for); ~rer para contribute to; ~rido a popular

concre|tizar /kõkretʃi'zar/ vt realize; ~tizar-se vpr be realized; ~to /ɛ/ a & m concrete

concurso /kõ'kursu/ m contest; (prova) competition

con|dado /kõ'dadu/ m county; ~de m count

condeco|ração /kõdekora'sãw/ f decoration; ~rar vt decorate

conde|nação /kõdena'sãw/ f condemnation; (jurid) conviction; ~nar vt condemn; (jurid) convict

conden|sação /kõdẽsa'sãw/ f condensation; ~sar vt condense; ~sar-se vpr condense

condescen|dência /kõdesẽ'dẽsia/ f acquiescence; ~dente a acquiescent; ~der vi acquiesce; ~der a comply with <pedido, desejo>; ~der a ir condescend to go

condessa /kõ'desa/ f countess

condi|ção /kõdʒi'sãw/ f condition; (qualidade) capacity; ter ~ção ou ~ções para be able to; em boas ~ções in good condition; ~cionado a conditioned; ~cional (pl ~cionais) a conditional; ~cionamento m conditioning

condimen|tar /kõdʒimẽ'tar/ vt season; ~to m seasoning

condoer-se /kõdo'ersi/ vpr ~ de feel sorry for

condolência /kõdo'lẽsia/ f sympathy; pl condolences

condomínio /kõdo'miniu/ m (taxa) service charge

condu|ção /kõdu'sãw/ f (de carro etc) driving; (transporte) transport; ~cente a conducive (a to); ~ta f conduct; ~to m conduit; ~tor m (de carro) driver; (eletr) conductor; ~zir vt lead; drive <carro>; (eletr) conduct □ vi (de carro) drive; (levar) lead (a to)

cone /'koni/ m cone

conectar /konek'tar/ vt connect

cone|xão /konek'sãw/ f connection; ~xo /ɛ/ a connected

confec|ção /kõfek'sãw/ f (roupa) off-the-peg outfit; (loja) clothes shop, boutique; (fábrica) clothes manufacturer; ~cionar vt make

confederação /kõfedera'sãw/ f confederation

confei|tar /kõfej'tar/ vt ice; ~taria f cake shop; ~teiro m confectioner

confe|rência /kõfe'rẽsia/ f conference; (palestra) lecture; ~rencista m/f speaker

conferir /kõfe'rir/ vt check (com against); (conceder) confer (a on) □ vi (controlar) check; (estar exato) tally

confes|sar /kõfe'sar/ vt/i confess; ~sar-se vpr confess; ~sionário m confessional; ~sor m confessor

confete /kõ'fɛtʃi/ m confetti

confi|ança /kõfi'ãsa/ f (convicção) confidence; (fé) trust; ~ante a confident (em of); ~ar (dar) entrust; ~ar em trust; ~ável (pl ~áveis) a reliable; ~dência f confidence; ~dencial (pl ~denciais) a confidential; ~denciar vt tell in confidence; ~dente m/f confidant (f confidante)

configu|ração /kõfigura'sãw/ f configuration; ~rar vt (representar) represent; (formar) shape; (comput) configure

**con|finar** /kõfi'nar/ *vi* ~**finar com** border on; ~**fins** *m pl* borders
**confir|mação** /kõfirma'sãw/ *f* confirmation; ~**mar** *vt* confirm; ~**mar-se** *vpr* be confirmed
**confis|car** /kõfis'kar/ *vt* confiscate; ~**co** *m* confiscation
**confissão** /kõfi'sãw/ *f* confession
**confla|gração** /kõflagra'sãw/ *f* conflagration; ~**grar** *vt* set alight; (*fig*) throw into turmoil
**confli|tante** /kõfli'tãtʃi/ *a* conflicting; ~**to** *m* conflict
**confor|mação** /kõforma'sãw/ *f* resignation; ~**mado** *a* resigned (**com** to); ~**mar** *vt* adapt (**a** to); ~**mar-se com** conform to < *regra, política*>; resign o.s. to, come to terms with < *destino, evento*>; ~**me** /ɔ/ *prep* according to □ *conj* depending on; ~**me** it depends; ~**midade** *f* conformity; ~**mismo** *m* conformism; ~**mista** *a* & *m/f* conformist
**confor|tar** /kõfor'tar/ *vt* comfort; ~**tável** (*pl* ~**táveis**) *a* comfortable; ~**to** /o/ *m* comfort
**confraternizar** /kõfraterni'zar/ *vi* fraternize
**confron|tação** /kõfrõta'sãw/ *f* confrontation; ~**tar** *vt* confront; (*comparar*) compare; ~**to** *m* confrontation; (*comparação*) comparison
**con|fundir** /kõfũ'dʒir/ *vt* confuse; ~**fundir-se** *vpr* get confused; ~**fusão** *f* confusion; (*desordem*) mess; (*tumulto*) commotion; ~**fuso** *a* (*confundido*) confused; (*que confunde*) confusing
**conge|lador** /kõʒela'dor/ *m* freezer; ~**lamento** *m* (*de preços etc*) freeze; ~**lar** *vt* freeze; ~**lar-se** *vpr* freeze
**congênito** /kõ'ʒenitu/ *a* congenital
**congestão** /kõʒes'tãw/ *f* congestion
**congestio|nado** /kõʒestʃio'nadu/ *a* < *rua, cidade*> congested; < *pessoa, rosto*> flushed; < *olhos*> bloodshot; ~**namento** *m* (*de trânsito*) traffic jam; ~**nar** *vt* congest; ~**nar-se** *vpr* < *rua*> get congested; < *rosto*> flush
**conglomerado** /kõglome'radu/ *m* conglomerate
**congratular** /kõgratu'lar/ *vt* congratulate (**por** on)
**congre|gação** /kõgrega'sãw/ *f* (*na igreja*) congregation; (*reunião*) gathering; ~**gar** *vt* bring together; ~**gar-se** *vpr* congregate
**congresso** /kõ'grɛsu/ *m* congress
**conhaque** /ko'ɲaki/ *m* brandy
**conhe|cedor** /koɲese'dor/ *a* knowing □ *m* connoisseur; ~**cer** *vt* know; (*ser apresentado a*) get to know; (*visitar*) go to, visit; ~**cido** *a* known; (*famoso*) well-known □ *m* acquaintance;

~**cimento** *m* knowledge; **tomar** ~**cimento de** learn of; **travar** ~**cimento com alg** make s.o.'s acquaintance, become acquainted with s.o.
**cônico** /'koniku/ *a* conical
**coni|vência** /koni'vẽsia/ *f* connivance; ~**vente** *a* conniving (**em** at)
**conjetu|ra** /kõʒe'tura/ *f* conjecture; ~**rar** *vt/i* conjecture
**conju|gação** /kõʒuga'sãw/ *f* (*ling*) conjugation; ~**gar** *vt* conjugate < *verbo*>
**cônjuge** /'kõʒuʒi/ *m/f* spouse
**conjun|ção** /kõʒũ'sãw/ *f* conjunction; ~**tivo** *a* & *m* subjunctive; ~**to** *a* joint □ *m* set; (*roupa*) outfit; (*musical*) group; **o** ~**to de** the body of; **em** ~**to** jointly; ~**tura** *f* state of affairs; (*econômica*) state of the economy
**conosco** = **com** + **nós**
**cono|tação** /konota'sãw/ *f* connotation; ~**tar** *vt* connote
**conquanto** /kõ'kwãtu/ *conj* although, even though
**conquis|ta** /kõ'kista/ *f* conquest; (*proeza*) achievement; ~**tador** *m* conqueror □ *a* conquering; ~**tar** *vt* conquer < *terra, país*>; win < *riqueza, independência*>; win over < *pessoa*>
**consa|gração** /kõsagra'sãw/ *f* (*de uma igreja*) consecration; (*dedicação*) dedication; ~**grado** *a* < *artista, expressão*> established; ~**grar** *vt* consecrate < *igreja*>; establish < *artista, estilo*>; (*dedicar*) dedicate (**a** to); ~**grar-se a** dedicate o.s. to
**consci|ência** /kõsi'ẽsia/ *f* (*moralidade*) conscience; (*sentidos*) consciousness; (*no trabalho*) conscientiousness; (*de um fato etc*) awareness; ~**encioso** /o/ *a* conscientious; ~**ente** *a* conscious; ~**entizar** *vt* make aware (**de** of); ~**entizar-se** *vpr* become aware (**de** of)
**consecutivo** /kõseku'tʃivu/ *a* consecutive
**conse|guinte** /kõse'gĩtʃi/ *a* **por** ~**guinte** consequently; ~**guir** *vt* get; ~**guir fazer** manage to do □ *vi* succeed
**conse|lheiro** /kõse'ʎeru/ *m* counsellor, adviser; ~**lho** /e/ *m* piece of advice; *pl* advice; (*órgão*) council
**consen|so** /kõ'sẽsu/ *m* consensus; ~**timento** *m* consent; ~**tir** *vt* allow □ *vi* consent (**em** to)
**conse|qüência** /kõse'kwẽsia/ *f* consequence; **por** ~**qüência** consequently; ~**qüente** *a* consequent; (*coerente*) consistent
**conser|tar** /kõser'tar/ *vt* repair; ~**to** /e/ *m* repair

conser|va /kõˈsɛrva/ f (em vidro) preserve; (em lata) tinned food; ~vação f preservation; ~vador a & m conservative; ~vadorismo m conservatism; ~vante a & m preservative; ~var vt preserve; (manter, guardar) keep; ~var-se vpr keep; ~vatório m conservatory

conside|ração /kõsideraˈsãw/ f consideration; (estima) esteem; levar em ~ração take into consideration; ~rar vt consider; (estimar) think highly of □ vi consider; ~rar-se vpr consider o.s.; ~rável (pl ~ráveis) a considerable

consig|nação /kõsignaˈsãw/ f consignment; ~nar vt consign

consigo = com + si

consis|tência /kõsisˈtẽsia/ f consistency; ~tente a firm; ~tir vi consist (em in)

consoante /kõsoˈãtʃi/ f consonant

conso|lação /kõsolaˈsãw/ f consolation; ~lador a consoling; ~lar vt console; ~lar-se vpr console o.s.

consolidar /kõsoliˈdar/ vt consolidate; mend <fratura>

consolo /kõˈsolu/ m consolation

consórcio /kõˈsɔrsiu/ m consortium

consorte /kõˈsɔrtʃi/ m/f consort

conspícuo /kõsˈpikuu/ a conspicuous

conspi|ração /kõspiraˈsãw/ f conspiracy; ~rador m conspirator; ~rar vi conspire

cons|tância /kõsˈtãsia/ f constancy; ~tante a & f constant; ~tar vi (em lista etc) appear; não me ~ta I am not aware; ~ta que it is said that; ~tar de consist of

consta|tação /kõstataˈsãw/ f observation; ~tar vt note, notice; certify <óbito>

conste|lação /kõstelaˈsãw/ f constellation; ~lado a star-studded

conster|nação /kõsternaˈsãw/ f consternation; ~nar vt dismay

consti|pação /kõstʃipaˈsãw/ f (Port: resfriado) cold; ~pado a (resfriado) with a cold; (no intestino) constipated; ~par-se vpr (Port: resfriarse) get a cold

constitu|cional /kõstʃitusioˈnaw/ (pl ~cionais) a constitutional; ~ição f constitution; ~inte a constituent □ f Constituinte Constituent Assembly; ~ir vt form <governo, sociedade>; (representar) constitute; (nomear) appoint

constran|gedor /kõstrãʒeˈdor/ a embarrassing; ~ger vt embarrass; (coagir) constrain; ~ger-se vpr get embarrassed; ~gimento m (embaraço) embarrassment; (coação) constraint

constru|ção /kõstruˈsãw/ f construction; (terreno) building site; ~ir vt build <casa, prédio>; (fig) construct; ~tivo a constructive; ~tor m builder; ~tora f building firm

cônsul /ˈkõsuw/ (pl ~es) m consul

consulado /kõsuˈladu/ m consulate

consul|ta /kõˈsuwta/ f consultation; ~tar vt consult; ~tor m consultant; ~toria f consultancy; ~tório m (médico) surgery, (Amer) office

consu|mação /kõsumaˈsãw/ f (taxa) minimum charge; ~mado a fato ~mado fait accompli; ~mar vt accomplish <projeto>; carry out <crime, sacrifício>; consummate <casamento>

consu|midor /kõsumiˈdor/ a & m consumer; ~mir vt consume; take up <tempo>; ~mismo m consumerism; ~mista a & m/f consumerist; ~mo m consumption

conta /ˈkõta/ f (a pagar) bill; (bancária) account; (contagem) count; (de vidro etc) bead; pl (com) accounts; em ~ economical; por ~ de on account of; por ~ própria on one's own account; ajustar ~s settle up; dar ~ de (fig) be up to; dar ~ do recado (fam) deliver the goods; dar-se ~ de realize; fazer de ~ pretend; ficar por ~ de be left to; levar ou ter em ~ take into account; prestar ~s de account for; tomar ~ de take care of; ~ bancária bank account; ~ corrente current account

contabili|dade /kõtabiliˈdadʒi/ f accountancy; (contas) accounts; (seção) accounts department; ~lista (Port) m/f accountant; ~lizar vt write up <quantia>; (fig) notch up

contact- (Port) veja contat-

conta|dor /kõtaˈdor/ m (pessoa) accountant; (de luz etc) meter; ~gem f counting; (de pontos num jogo) scoring; ~gem regressiva countdown

contagi|ante /kõtaʒiˈãtʃi/ a infectious; ~ar vt infect; ~ar-se vpr become infected

contágio /kõˈtaʒiu/ m infection

contagioso /kõtaʒiˈozu/ a contagious

contami|nação /kõtaminaˈsãw/ f contamination; ~nar vt contaminate

contanto /kõˈtãtu/ adv ~ que provided that

contar /kõˈtar/ vt/i count; (narrar) tell; ~ com count on

conta|tar /kõtaˈtar/ vt contact; ~to m contact; entrar em ~to com get in touch with; tomar ~to com come into contact with

contem|plação /kõtẽplaˈsãw/ f contemplation; ~plar vt (considerar) contemplate; (*dizer respeito a*) concern; ~**plar alg com** treat s.o. to □ *vi* ponder; ~**plativo** *a* contemplative

**contemporâneo** /kõtẽpo'raniu/ *a* & *m* contemporary

**contenção** /kõtẽ'sãw/ *f* containment

**conten|cioso** /kõtẽsi'ozu/ *a* contentious; ~**da** *f* dispute

**conten|tamento** /kõtẽta'mẽtu/ *m* contentment; ~**tar** *vt* satisfy; ~**tar-se** *upr* be content; ~**te** *a* (*feliz*) happy; (*satisfeito*) content; ~**to** *m a* ~**to** satisfactorily

**conter** /kõ'ter/ *vt* contain; ~**-se** *upr* contain o.s.

**conterrâneo** /kõte'xaniu/ *m* fellow countryman (*f* -woman)

**contestar** /kõtes'tar/ *vt* question; (*jurid*) contest

**conteúdo** /kõte'udu/ *m* (*de recipiente*) contents; (*fig: de carta etc*) content

**contexto** /kõ'testu/ *m* context

**contigo** = **com** + **ti**

**continência** /kõtʃi'nẽsia/ *f* (*mil*) salute

**continen|tal** /kõtʃinẽ'taw/ (*pl* ~**tais**) *a* continental; ~**te** *m* continent

**contin|gência** /kõtʃĩ'ʒẽsia/ *f* contingency; ~**gente** *a* (*eventual*) possible; (*incerto*) contingent □ *m* contingent

**continu|ação** /kõtʃinua'sãw/ *f* continuation; ~**ar** *vt/i* continue; **eles** ~**am ricos** they are still rich; ~**idade** *f* continuity

**contínuo** /kõ'tʃinuu/ *a* continuous □ *m* office junior

**con|tista** /kõ'tʃista/ *m/f* (short) story writer; ~**to** *m* (short) story; ~**to de fadas** fairy tale; ~**to-do-vigário** (*pl* ~**tos-do-vigário**) *m* confidence trick, swindle

**contorcer** /kõtor'ser/ *vt* twist; ~**-se** *upr* (*de dor*) writhe

**contor|nar** /kõtor'nar/ *vt* go round; (*fig*) get round <*obstáculo, problema*>; (*cercar*) surround; (*delinear*) outline; ~**no** /o/ *m* outline; (*da paisagem*) contour

**contra** /'kõtra/ *prep* against

**contra-|atacar** /kõtrata'kar/ *vt* counterattack; ~**-ataque** *m* counterattack

**contrabaixo** /kõtra'baʃu/ *m* double bass

**contrabalançar** /kõtrabalã'sar/ *vt* counterbalance

**contraban|dear** /kõtrabãdʒi'ar/ *vt* smuggle; ~**dista** *m/f* smuggler; ~**do** *m* (*ato*) smuggling; (*artigos*) contraband

**contração** /kõtra'sãw/ *f* contraction

**contracenar** /kõtrase'nar/ *vi* ~ **com** play up to

**contraceptivo** /kõtrasep'tʃivu/ *a* & *m* contraceptive

**contracheque** /kõtra'ʃɛki/ *m* pay slip

**contradi|ção** /kõtradʒi'sãw/ *f* contradiction; ~**tório** *a* contradictory; ~**zer** *vt* contradict; ~**zer-se** *upr* <*pessoa*> contradict o.s.; <*idéias etc*> be contradictory

**contragosto** /kõtra'gostu/ *m a* ~ reluctantly

**contrair** /kõtra'ir/ *vt* contract; pick up <*hábito, vício*>; ~**-se** *upr* contract

**contramão** /kõtra'mãw/ *f* opposite direction □ *a invar* one way

**contramestre** /kõtra'mɛstri/ *m* supervisor; (*em navio*) bosun

**contra-ofensiva** /kõtraofẽ'siva/ *f* counter-offensive

**contrapartida** /kõtrapar'tʃida/ *f* (*fig*) compensation; **em** ~ on the other hand

**contraproducente** /kõtraprodu'sẽtʃi/ *a* counter-productive

**contrari|ar** /kõtrari'ar/ *vt* go against, run counter to; (*aborrecer*) annoy; ~**edade** *f* adversity; (*aborrecimento*) annoyance

**contrário** /kõ'trariu/ *a* opposite; (*desfavorável*) adverse; ~ **a** contrary to; <*pessoa*> opposed to □ *m* opposite; **pelo** *ou* **ao** ~ **on the contrary; ao** ~ **de** contrary to; **em** ~ to the contrary

**contras|tante** /kõtras'tãtʃi/ *a* contrasting; ~**tar** *vt/i* contrast; ~**te** *m* contrast

**contra|tante** /kõtra'tãtʃi/ *m/f* contractor; ~**tar** *vt* employ, take on <*operários*>

**contra|tempo** /kõtra'tẽpu/ *m* hitch

**contra|to** /kõ'tratu/ *m* contract; ~**tual** (*pl* ~**tuais**) *a* contractual

**contraven|ção** /kõtravẽ'sãw/ *f* contravention; ~**tor** *m* offender

**contribu|ição** /kõtribui'sãw/ *f* contribution; ~**inte** *m/f* contributor; (*pagador de impostos*) taxpayer; ~**ir** *vt* contribute □ *vi* contribute; (*pagar impostos*) pay tax

**contrição** /kõtri'sãw/ *f* contrition

**contro|lar** /kõtro'lar/ *vt* control; (*fiscalizar*) check; ~**le** /o/, (*Port*) ~**lo** /o/ *m* control; (*fiscalização*) check

**contro|vérsia** /kõtro'vɛrsia/ *f* controversy; ~**verso** /ɛ/ *a* controversial

**contudo** /kõ'tudu/ *conj* nevertheless

**contundir** /kõtũ'dʒir/ *vt* (*dar hematoma em*) bruise; injure <*jogador*>; ~**se** *upr* bruise o.s.; <*jogador*> get injured

**conturbado** /kõtur'badu/ *a* troubled

**contu|são** /kõtu'zãw/ *f* bruise; (*de jogador*) injury; ~**so** *a* bruised; <*jogador*> injured

**convales|cença** /kõvale'sẽsa/ f convalescence; **~cer** vi convalesce

**convenção** /kõvẽ'sãw/ f convention

**conven|cer** /kõvẽ'ser/ vt convince; **~cido** a (convicto) convinced; (metido) conceited; **~cimento** m (convicção) conviction; (imodéstia) conceitedness

**convencio|nal** /kõvẽsio'naw/ (pl **~nais**) a conventional

**conveni|ência** /kõveni'ẽsia/ f convenience; **~ente** a convenient; (cabível) appropriate

**convênio** /kõ'veniu/ m agreement

**convento** /kõ'vẽtu/ m convent

**convergir** /kõver'ʒir/ vi converge

**conver|sa** /kõ'vɛrsa/ f conversation; **a ~sa dele** the things he says; **~sa fiada** idle talk; **~sação** f conversation; **~sado** a <pessoa> talkative; <assunto> talked about; **~sador** a talkative

**conversão** /kõver'sãw/ f conversion

**conversar** /kõver'sar/ vi talk

**conver|sível** /kõver'sivew/ (pl **~síveis**) a & m convertible; **~ter** vt convert; **~ter-se** vpr be converted; **~tido** m convert

**con|vés** /kõ'vɛs/ (pl **~veses**) m deck

**convexo** /kõ'vɛksu/ a convex

**convic|ção** /kõvik'sãw/ f conviction; **~to** a convinced; (ferrenho) confirmed; <criminoso> convicted

**convi|dado** /kõvi'dadu/ m guest; **~dar** vt invite; **~dativo** a inviting

**convincente** /kõvĩ'sẽtʃi/ a convincing

**convir** /kõ'vir/ vi (ficar bem) be appropriate; (concordar) agree (**em** on); **~ a** suit, be convenient for; **convém notar que** one should note that

**convite** /kõ'vitʃi/ m invitation

**convi|vência** /kõvi'vẽsia/ f coexistence; (relação) close contact; **~ver** vi coexist; (ter relações) associate (**com** with)

**convívio** /kõ'viviu/ m association (**com** with)

**convocar** /kõvo'kar/ vt call <eleições, greve>; call upon <pessoa> (**a** to); (ao serviço militar) call up

**convosco** = **com + vós**

**convul|são** /kõvuw'sãw/ f (do corpo) convulsion; (da sociedade etc) upheaval; **~sionar** vt convulse <corpo>; (fig) churn up; **~sivo** a convulsive

**cooper** /'kuper/ m jogging; **fazer ~** go jogging

**coope|ração** /koopera'sãw/ f cooperation; **~rar** vi cooperate; **~rativa** f cooperative; **~rativo** a cooperative

**coorde|nação** /koordena'sãw/ f coordination; **~nada** f coordinate; **~nar** vt coordinate

**copa** /'kɔpa/ f (de árvore) top; (aposento) breakfast room; (torneio) cup; pl (naipe) hearts; **a Copa (do Mundo)** the World Cup; **~-cozinha** (pl **~s-cozinhas**) f kitchen-diner

**cópia** /'kɔpia/ f copy

**copiar** /kopi'ar/ vt copy

**co-piloto** /kopi'lotu/ m co-pilot

**copioso** /kopi'ozu/ a ample; <refeição> substantial

**copo** /'kɔpu/ m glass

**coque** /'kɔki/ m (penteado) bun

**coqueiro** /ko'keru/ m coconut palm

**coqueluche** /koke'luʃi/ f (doença) whooping cough; (mania) fad

**coque|tel** /koke'tɛw/ (pl **~téis**) m cocktail; (reunião) cocktail party

**cor**[1] /kɔr/ m **de ~** by heart

**cor**[2] /kor/ f colour; **TV a ~es** colour TV; **pessoa de ~** coloured person

**coração** /kora'sãw/ m heart

**cora|gem** /ko'raʒẽ/ f courage; **~joso** /o/ a courageous

**co|ral**[1] /ko'raw/ (pl **~rais**) m (animal) coral

**co|ral**[2] /ko'raw/ (pl **~rais**) m (de cantores) choir □ a choral

**co|rante** /ko'rãtʃi/ a & m colouring; **~rar** vt colour □ vi blush

**cor|da** /'kɔrda/ f rope; (mus) string; (para roupa lavada) clothes line; **dar ~da em** wind <relógio>; **~da bamba** tightrope; **~das vocais** vocal chords; **~dão** m cord; (de sapatos) lace; (policial) cordon

**cordeiro** /kor'deru/ m lamb

**cor|del** /kor'dɛw/ (pl **~déis**) (Port) m string; **literatura de ~del** trash

**cor-de-rosa** /kordʒi'rɔza/ a invar pink

**cordi|al** /kordʒi'aw/ (pl **~ais**) a & m cordial; **~alidade** f cordiality

**cordilheira** /kordʒi'ʎera/ f chain of mountains

**coreano** /kori'anu/ a & m Korean

**Coréia** /ko'rɛja/ f Korea

**core|ografia** /koriogra'fia/ f choreography; **~ógrafo** m choreographer

**coreto** /ko'retu/ m bandstand

**coriza** /ko'riza/ f runny nose

**corja** /'kɔrʒa/ f pack; (de pessoas) rabble

**córner** /'kɔrner/ m corner

**coro** /'koru/ m chorus

**coro|a** /ko'roa/ f crown; (de flores etc) wreath □ (fam) m/f old man (f woman); **~ação** f coronation; **~ar** vt crown

**coro|nel** /koro'nɛw/ (pl **~néis**) m colonel

**coronha** /ko'roɲa/ f butt

**corpete** /kor'petʃi/ m bodice

**corpo** /'korpu/ m body; (físico de mulher) figure; (físico de homem) physique; ~ **de bombeiros** fire brigade; ~ **diplomático** diplomatic corps; ~ **docente** teaching staff, (*Amer*) faculty; ~**a-** ~ *m invar* pitched battle; ~**ral** (*pl* ~**rais**) a physical; (*pena*) corporal

**corpu|lência** /korpu'lēsia/ *f* stoutness; ~**lento** *a* stout

**correção** /koxe'sāw/ *f* correction

**corre-corre** /kɔxi'kɔxi/ *m* (*debandada*) stampede; (*correria*) rush

**correct-** (*Port*) *veja* corret-

**corre|diço** /koxe'dʒisu/ *a* <*porta*> sliding; ~**dor** *m* (*atleta*) runner; (*passagem*) corridor

**correia** /ko'xeja/ *f* strap; (*peça de máquina*) belt; (*para cachorro*) lead, (*Amer*) leash

**correio** /ko'xeju/ *m* post, mail; (*repartição*) post office; **pôr no** ~ post, (*Amer*) mail; ~ **aéreo** air mail

**correlação** /koxela'sāw/ *f* correlation

**correligionário** /koxeliʒio'nariu/ *m* party colleague

**corrente** /ko'xētʃi/ *a* <*água*> running; <*mês, conta*> current; <*estilo*> fluid; (*usual*) common □ *f* (*de água, eletricidade*) current; (*cadeia*) chain; ~ **de ar** draught; ~**za** /e/ *f* current; (*de ar*) draught

**cor|rer** /ko'xer/ *vi* (*à pé*) run; (*de carro*) drive fast, speed; (*fazer rápido*) rush; <*água, sangue*> flow; <*tempo*> elapse; <*boato*> go round □ *vt* draw <*cortina*>; run <*risco*>; ~**reria** *f* rush

**correspon|dência** /koxespō'dēsia/ *f* correspondence; ~**dente** *a* corresponding □ *m/f* correspondent; (*equivalente*) equivalent; ~**der** *vi* ~**der** **a** correspond to; (*retribuir*) return; ~**der-se** *vpr* correspond (**com** with)

**corre|tivo** /koxe'tʃivu/ *a* corrective □ *m* punishment; ~**to** /ɛ/ *a* correct

**corretor** /koxe'tor/ *m* broker; ~ **de imóveis** estate agent, (*Amer*) realtor

**corrida** /ko'xida/ *f* (*prova*) race; (*ação de correr*) run; (*de taxi*) ride

**corrigir** /koxi'ʒir/ *vt* correct

**corrimão** /koxi'mãw/ (*pl* ~**s**) *m* handrail; (*de escada*) banister

**corriqueiro** /koxi'keru/ *a* ordinary, run-of-the-mill

**corroborar** /koxobo'rar/ *vt* corroborate

**corroer** /koxo'er/ *vt* corrode <*metal*>; (*fig*) erode; ~-**se** *vpr* corrode; (*fig*) erode

**corromper** /koxō'per/ *vt* corrupt; ~-**se** *vpr* be corrupted

**corro|são** /koxo'zāw/ *f* (*de metal*) corrosion; (*fig*) erosion; ~**sivo** *a* corrosive

**corrup|ção** /koxup'sāw/ *f* corruption; ~**to** *a* corrupt

**cor|tada** /kor'tada/ *f* (*em tênis*) smash; (*em pessoa*) put-down; ~**tante** *a* cutting; ~**tar** *vt* cut; cut off <*luz, telefone, perna etc*>; cut down <*árvore*>; cut out <*efeito, vício*>; take away <*prazer*>; (*com o carro*) cut up; (*desprezar*) cut dead □ *vi* cut; ~**tar o cabelo** (*no cabeleireiro*) get one's hair cut; (*gume*) cut; (*gume*) blade; (*desenho*) cross-section; **sem** ~**te** <*faca*> blunt; ~**te de cabelo** haircut

**cor|te²** /'kortʃi/ *f* court; ~**tejar** *vt* court; ~**tejo** /e/ *m* (*séquito*) retinue; (*fúnebre*) cortège; ~**tês** *a* (*f* ~**tesa**) courteous, polite; ~**tesão** (*pl* ~**tesãos**) *m* courtier; ~**tesia** *f* courtesy

**corti|ça** /kor'tʃisa/ *f* cork; ~**ço** *m* (*casa popular*) slum tenement

**cortina** /kor'tʃina/ *f* curtain

**cortisona** /kortʃi'zona/ *f* cortisone

**coruja** /ko'ruʒa/ *f* owl □ *a* <*pai, mãe*> proud, doting

**coruscar** /korus'kar/ *vi* flash

**corvo** /'korvu/ *m* crow

**cós** /kɔs/ *m invar* waistband

**coser** /ko'zer/ *vt/i* sew

**cosmético** /koz'metʃiku/ *a & m* cosmetic

**cósmico** /'kɔzmiku/ *a* cosmic

**cosmo** /'kɔzmu/ *m* cosmos; ~**nauta** *m/f* cosmonaut; ~**polita** *a* cosmopolitan □ *m/f* globetrotter

**costa** /'kɔsta/ *f* coast; *pl* (*dorso*) back; **Costa do Marfim** Ivory Coast; **Costa Rica** Costa Rica

**costarriquenho** /kostaxi'keɲu/ *a & m* Costa Rican

**cos|teiro** /kos'teru/ *a* coastal; ~**tela** /ɛ/ *f* rib; ~**teleta** /e/ *f* chop; *pl* (*suíças*) sideburns; ~**telinha** *f* (*de porco*) spare rib

**costu|mar** /kostu'mar/ *vt* ~**ma fazer** he usually does; ~**mava fazer** he used to do; ~**me** *m* (*uso*) custom; (*traje*) costume; **de** ~**me** usually; **como de** ~**me** as usual; **ter o** ~**me de** have a habit of; ~**meiro** *a* customary

**costu|ra** /kos'tura/ *f* sewing; ~**rar** *vt/i* sew; ~**reira** *f* (*mulher*) dressmaker; (*caixa*) needlework box

**co|ta** /'kɔta/ *f* quota; ~**tação** *f* (*preço*) rate; (*apreço*) rating; ~**tado** *a* <*ação*> quoted; (*conceituado*) highly rated; ~**tar** *vt* rate; quote <*ações*>

**cote|jar** /kote'ʒar/ *vt* compare; ~**jo** /e/ *m* comparison

**cotidiano** /kotʃidʒi'anu/ *a* everyday □ *m* everyday life

**cotonete** /koto'nɛtʃi/ *m* cotton bud

**cotove|lada** /kotove'lada/ *f* (*para abrir caminho*) shove; (*para chamar atenção*) nudge; **~lo** /e/ *m* elbow

**coura|ça** /ko'rasa/ *f* (*armadura*) breastplate; (*de navio, animal*) armour; **~çado** (*Port*) *m* battleship

**couro** /'koru/ *m* leather; **~ cabeludo** scalp

**couve** /'kovi/ *f* spring greens; **~-de-bruxelas** (*pl* **~s-de-bruxelas**) *f* Brussels sprout; **~-flor** (*pl* **~s-flores**) *f* cauliflower

**couvert** /ku'vɛr/ (*pl* **~s**) *m* cover charge

**cova** /'kɔva/ *f* (*buraco*) pit; (*sepultura*) grave

**covar|de** /ko'vardʒi/ *m/f* coward □ *a* cowardly; **~dia** *f* cowardice

**coveiro** /ko'veru/ *m* gravedigger

**covil** /ko'viw/ (*pl* **~vis**) *m* den, lair

**covinha** /ko'viɲa/ *f* dimple

**co|xa** /'koʃa/ *f* thigh; **~xear** *vi* hobble

**coxia** /ko'ʃia/ *f* aisle

**coxo** /'koʃu/ *a* hobbling; **ser ~** hobble

**co|zer** /ko'zer/ *vt/i* cook; **~zido** *m* stew, casserole

**cozi|nha** /ko'ziɲa/ *f* (*aposento*) kitchen; (*comida, ação*) cooking; (*arte*) cookery; **~nhar** *vt/i* cook; **~nheiro** *m* cook

**crachá** /kra'ʃa/ *m* badge, (*Amer*) button

**crânio** /'kraniu/ *m* skull; (*pessoa*) genius

**crápula** /'krapula/ *m/f* scoundrel

**craque** /'kraki/ *m* (*de futebol*) soccer star; (*fam*) expert

**crase** /'krazi/ *f* contraction; **a com ~** a grave (à)

**crasso** /'krasu/ *a* crass

**cratera** /kra'tɛra/ *f* crater

**cravar** /kra'var/ *vt* drive in *<prego>*; dig *<unha>*; stick *<estaca>*; **~ com os olhos** stare at; **~-se** *vpr* stick

**cravejar** /krave'ʒar/ *vt* nail; (*com balas*) spray, riddle

**cravo**[1] /'kravu/ *m* (*flor*) carnation; (*condimento*) clove

**cravo**[2] /'kravu/ *m* (*na pele*) blackhead; (*prego*) nail

**cravo**[3] /'kravu/ *m* (*instrumento*) harpsichord

**creche** /'krɛʃi/ *f* crèche

**credenci|ais** /kredẽsi'ajs/ *f pl* credentials; **~ar** *vt* qualify

**credi|ário** /kredʒi'ariu/ *m* hire purchase agreement, credit plan; **~bilidade** *f* credibility; **~tar** *vt* credit

**crédito** /'krɛdʒitu/ *m* credit; **a ~** on credit

**cre|do** /'krɛdu/ *m* creed □ *int* heavens; **~dor** *m* creditor □ *a* *<saldo>* credit

**crédulo** /'krɛdulu/ *a* gullible

**cre|mação** /krema'sãw/ *f* cremation; **~mar** *vt* cremate; **~matório** *m* crematorium

**cre|me** /'kremi/ *a invar* & *m* cream; **~me Chantilly** whipped cream; **~me de leite** (sterilized) cream; **~moso** /o/ *a* creamy

**cren|ça** /'krẽsa/ *f* belief; **~dice** *f* superstition; **~te** *m* believer; (*protestante*) Protestant □ *a* religious; (*protestante*) Protestant; **estar ~te que** believe that

**crepe** /'krɛpi/ *m* crepe

**crepitar** /krepi'tar/ *vi* crackle

**crepom** /kre'põ/ *m* crepe; **papel ~** tissue paper

**crepúsculo** /kre'puskulu/ *m* twilight

**crer** /krer/ *vt/i* believe (**em** in); **creio que** I think (that); **~-se** *vpr* believe o.s. to be

**cres|cendo** /kre'sẽdu/ *m* crescendo; **~cente** *a* growing □ *m* crescent; **~cer** *vi* grow; *<bolo>* rise; **~cido** *a* grown; **~cimento** *m* growth

**crespo** /'krespu/ *a* *<cabelo>* frizzy; *<mar>* choppy

**cretino** /kre'tʃinu/ *m* cretin

**cria** /'kria/ *f* baby; *pl* young

**criação** /kria'sãw/ *f* creation; (*educação*) upbringing; (*de animais*) raising; (*gado*) livestock

**criado** /kri'adu/ *m* servant; **~-mudo** (*pl* **~s-mudos**) *m* bedside table

**criador** /kria'dor/ *m* creator; (*de animais*) farmer, breeder

**crian|ça** /kri'ãsa/ *f* child □ *a* childish; **~çada** *f* kids; **~cice** *f* childishness; (*uma*) childish thing

**criar** /kri'ar/ *vt* (*fazer*) create; bring up *<filhos>*; rear *<animais>*; grow *<planta>*; pluck up *<coragem>*; **~-se** *vpr* be brought up, grow up

**criati|vidade** /kriatʃivi'dadʒi/ *f* creativity; **~vo** *a* creative

**criatura** /kria'tura/ *f* creature

**crime** /'krimi/ *m* crime

**crimi|nal** /krimi'naw/ (*pl* **~nais**) *a* criminal; **~nalidade** *f* crime; **~noso** *m* criminal

**crina** /'krina/ *f* mane

**crioulo** /kri'olu/ *a* & *m* creole; (*negro*) black

**cripta** /'kripta/ *f* crypt

**crisálida** /kri'zalida/ *f* chrysalis

**crisântemo** /kri'zãtemu/ *m* chrysanthemum

**crise** /'krizi/ *f* crisis

**cris|ma** /'krizma/ *f* confirmation; **~mar** *vt* confirm; **~mar-se** *vpr* get confirmed

**crista** /'krista/ *f* crest

**cris|tal** /kris'taw/ (*pl* **~tais**) *m* crystal; (*vidro*) glass; **~talino** *a* crystal-clear; **~talizar** *vt/i* crystallize cris|tandade /kristă'dadʒi/ f Christendom; ~tão (pl ~tãos) a & m (f ~tã) Christian; ~tianismo m Christianity

Cristo /'kristu/ m Christ

cri|tério /kri'tɛriu/ m discretion; (norma) criterion; ~terioso a perceptive, discerning

crítica /'kritʃika/ f criticism; (análise) critique; (de filme, livro) review; (críticos) critics

criticar /kritʃi'kar/ vt criticize; review <filme, livro>

crítico /'kritʃiku/ a critical □ m critic

crivar /kri'var/ vt (furar) riddle

crí|vel /'krivew/ (pl ~veis) a credible

crivo /'krivu/ m sieve; (fig) scrutiny

crocante /kro'kãtʃi/ a crunchy

crochê /kro'ʃe/ m crochet

crocodilo /kroko'dʒilu/ m crocodile

cromo /'kromu/ m chrome

cromossomo /kromo'somu/ m chromosome

crôni|ca /'kronika/ f (histórica) chronicle; (no jornal) feature; (conto) short story; ~co a chronic

cronista /kro'nista/ m/f (de jornal) feature writer; (contista) short story writer; (historiador) chronicler

crono|grama /krono'grama/ m schedule; ~logia f chronology; ~lógico a chronological; ~metrar vt time

cronômetro /kro'nometru/ m stopwatch

croquete /kro'kɛtʃi/ m savoury meatball in breadcrumbs

croqui /kro'ki/ m sketch

crosta /'krosta/ f crust; (em ferida) scab

cru /kru/ a (f ~a) raw; <luz, tom, palavra> harsh; crude; <verdade> unvarnished, plain

cruci|al /krusi'aw/ (pl ~ais) a crucial

crucifi|cação /krusifika'sãw/ f crucifixion; ~car vt crucify; ~xo /ks/ m crucifix

cru|el /kru'ɛw/ (pl ~éis) a cruel; ~eldade f cruelty; ~ento a bloody

crupe /'krupi/ m croup

crustáceos /krus'tasius/ m pl shellfish

cruz /krus/ f cross

cruza|da /kru'zada/ f crusade; ~do¹ m (soldado) crusader

cru|zado² /kru'zadu/ m (moeda) cruzado; ~zador m cruiser; ~zamento m (de ruas) crossroads, junction, (Amer) intersection; (de raças) cross; ~zar vt cross □ vi <navio> cruise; ~zar com pass; ~zar-se vpr cross; <pessoas> pass each other;

~zeiro m (moeda) cruzeiro; (viagem) cruise; (cruz) cross

cu /ku/ m (chulo) arse, (Amer) ass

Cuba /'kuba/ f Cuba

cubano /ku'banu/ a & m Cuban

cúbico /'kubiku/ a cubic

cubículo /ku'bikulu/ m cubicle

cubis|mo /ku'bizmu/ m cubism; ~ta a & m/f cubist

cubo /'kubu/ m cube; (de roda) hub

cuca /'kuka/ (fam) f head

cuco /'kuku/ m cuckoo; (relógio) cuckoo clock

cu|-de-ferro /kudʒi'fɛxu/ (pl ~s-de-ferro) (fam) m swot

cueca /ku'ɛka/ f underpants; pl (Port: de mulher) knickers

cueiro /ku'eru/ m baby wrap

cuia /'kuia/ f gourd

cuidado /kui'dadu/ m care; com ~ carefully; ter ou tomar ~ be careful; ~so /o/ a careful

cuidar /kui'dar/ vi ~ de take care of; ~-se vpr look after o.s.

cujo /'kuʒu/ pron whose

culatra /ku'latra/ f breech; sair pela ~ (fig) backfire

culiná|ria /kuli'naria/ f cookery; ~rio a culinary

culmi|nância /kuwmi'nãsia/ f culmination; ~nante a culminating; ~nar vi culminate (em in)

cul|pa /'kuwpa/ f guilt; foi ~pa minha it was my fault; ter ~pa de be to blame for; ~pabilidade f guilt; ~pado a guilty □ m culprit; ~par vt blame (de for); (na justiça) find guilty (de of); ~par-se vpr take the blame (de for); ~pável (pl ~páveis) a culpable, guilty

culti|var /kuwtʃi'var/ vt cultivate; grow <plantas>; ~vo m cultivation; (de plantas) growing

cul|to /'kuwtu/ a cultured □ m cult; ~tura f culture; (de terra) cultivation; ~tural (pl ~turais) a cultural

cumbuca /kũ'buka/ f bowl

cume /'kumi/ m peak

cúmplice /'kũplisi/ m/f accomplice

cumplicidade /kũplisi'dadʒi/ f complicity

cumprimen|tar /kũprimẽ'tar/ vt/i (saudar) greet; (parabenizar) compliment; ~to m (saudação) greeting; (elogio) compliment; (de lei, ordem) compliance (de with); (de promessa, palavra) fulfilment

cumprir /kũ'prir/ vt keep <promessa, palavra>; comply with <lei, ordem>; do <dever>; carry out <obrigações>; serve <pena>; ~ com keep to □ vi cumpre-nos ir we should go; ~-se vpr be fulfilled

**cúmulo** /'kumulu/ *m* height; **é o ~!** that's the limit!

**cunha** /'kuɲa/ *f* wedge

**cunha|da** /ku'ɲada/ *f* sister-in-law; **~do** *m* brother-in-law

**cunhar** /ku'ɲar/ *vt* coin <*palavra, expressão*>; mint <*moedas*>

**cunho** /'kuɲu/ *m* hallmark

**cupim** /ku'pĩ/ *m* termite

**cupom** /ku'põ/ *m* coupon

**cúpula** /'kupula/ *f* (*de abóbada*) dome; (*de abajur*) shade; (*chefia*) leadership; **(reunião de) ~** summit (meeting)

**cura** /'kura/ *f* cure □ *m* curate, priest

**curandeiro** /kurã'deru/ *m* (*religioso*) faith-healer; (*índio*) medicine man; (*charlatão*) quack

**curar** /ku'rar/ *vt* cure; dress <*ferida*>; **~-se** *vpr* be cured

**curativo** /kura'tʃivu/ *m* dressing

**curá|vel** /ku'ravew/ (*pl* ~**veis**) *a* curable

**curin|ga** /ku'rĩga/ *m* wild card; **~gão** *m* joker

**curio|sidade** /kuriozi'dadʒi/ *f* curiosity; **~so** /o/ *a* curious □ *m* (*espectador*) onlooker

**cur|ral** /ku'xaw/ (*pl* ~**rais**) *m* pen

**currículo** /ku'xikulu/ *m* curriculum; (*resumo*) curriculum vitae, CV

**cur|sar** /kur'sar/ *vt* attend <*escola, aula*>; study <*matéria*>; **~so** *m* course; **~sor** *m* cursor

**curta|-metragem** /kurtame'traʒẽ/ (*pl* ~**s-metragens**) *m* short (film)

**cur|tição** /kurtʃi'sãw/ (*fam*) *f* enjoyment; **~tir** *vt* (*fam*) enjoy; tan <*couro*>

**curto** /'kurtu/ *a* short; <*conhecimento, inteligência*> limited; **~-circuito** (*pl* ~**s-circuitos**) *m* short circuit

**cur|va** /'kurva/ *f* curve; (*de estrada, rio*) bend; **~va fechada** hairpin bend; **~var** *vt* bend; **~var-se** *vpr* bend; (*fig*) bow (**a** to); **~vo** *a* curved; <*estrada*> winding

**cus|parada** /kuspa'rada/ *f* spit; **~pe** *m* spit, spittle; **~pir** *vt/i* spit

**cus|ta** /'kusta/ *f* **à ~ta de** at the expense of; **~tar** *vt* cost □ *vi* (*ser difícil*) be hard; **~tar a fazer** (*ter dificuldade*) find it hard to do; (*demorar*) take a long time to do; **~tear** *vt* finance, fund; **~teio** *m* funding; (*relação de despesas*) costing; **~to** *m* cost; **a ~to** with difficulty

**custódia** /kus'tɔdʒia/ *f* custody

**cutelo** /ku'tɛlu/ *m* cleaver

**cutícula** /ku'tʃikula/ *f* cuticle

**cútis** /'kutʃis/ *f invar* complexion

**cutucar** /kutu'kar/ *vt* (*com o cotovelo,*

*joelho*) nudge; (*com o dedo*) poke; (*com instrumento*) prod

**czar** /zar/ *m* tsar

# D

**da** = **de** + **a**

**dádiva** /'dadʒiva/ *f* gift; (*donativo*) donation

**dado** /'dadu/ *m* (*de jogar*) die, dice; (*informação*) fact, piece of information; *pl* data

**daí** /da'i/ *adv* (*no espaço*) from there; (*no tempo*) then; **~ por diante** from then on; **e ~?** (*fam*) so what?

**dali** /da'li/ *adv* from over there

**dália** /'dalia/ *f* dahlia

**dal|tônico** /daw'toniku/ *a* colourblind; **~tonismo** *m* colour-blindness

**dama** /'dama/ *f* lady; (*em jogos*) queen; *pl* (*jogo*) draughts, (*Amer*) checkers; **~ de honra** bridesmaid

**da|nado** /da'nadu/ *a* damned; (*zangado*) angry; (*travesso*) naughty; **~nar-se** *vpr* get angry; **~ne-se!** (*fam*) who cares?

**dan|ça** /'dãsa/ *f* dance; **~çar** *vt* dance □ *vi* dance; (*fam*) miss out; <*coisa*> go by the board; <*crimonoso*> get caught; **~çarino** *m* dancer; **~ceteria** *f* discotheque

**da|nificar** /danifi'kar/ *vt* damage; **~ninho** *a* undesirable; **~no** *m* (*pl*) damage; **~noso** /o/ *a* damaging

**dantes** /'dãtʃis/ *adv* formerly

**daquela(s), daquele(s)** = **de** + **aquela(s), aquele(s)**

**daqui** /da'ki/ *adv* from here; **~ a 2 dias** in 2 days(' time); **~ a pouco** in a minute; **~ em diante** from now on

**daquilo** = **de** + **aquilo**

**dar** /dar/ *vt* give; have <*dormida, lida etc*>; do <*pulo, cambalhota etc*>; cause <*problemas*>; produce <*frutas, leite*>; deal <*cartas*>; (*lecionar*) teach □ *vi* (*ser possível*) be possible; (*ser suficiente*) be enough; **~ com** come across; **~ em** lead to; **ele dá para ator** he'd make a good actor; **~ por** (*considerar como*) consider to be; (*reparar em*) notice; **~-se** *vpr* <*coisa*> happen; <*pessoa*> get on

**dardo** /'dardu/ *m* dart; (*no atletismo*) javelin

**das** = **de** + **as**

**da|ta** /'data/ *f* date; **de longa ~** long since; **~tar** *vt/i* date

**dati|lografar** /datʃilogra'far/ *vt/i* type; **~lografia** *f* typing; **~lógrafo** *m* typist

**de** /dʒi/ *prep* of; (*procedência*) from; **~ carro** by car; **trabalho ~ repórter** I work as a reporter

**debaixo** /dʒi'baʃu/ *adv* below; **~ de** under

**debalde** /dʒi'bawdʒi/ *adv* in vain

**debandada** /debã'dada/ *f* stampede

**deba|te** /de'batʃi/ *m* debate; **~ter** *vt* debate; **~ter-se** *vpr* grapple

**debelar** /debe'lar/ *vt* overcome

**dé|bil** /'dɛbiw/ (*pl* **~beis**) *a* feeble; **~bil mental** retarded (person)

**debili|dade** /debili'dadʒi/ *f* debility; **~tar** *vt* debilitate; **~tar-se** *vpr* become debilitated

**debitar** /debi'tar/ *vt* debit

**débito** /'dɛbitu/ *m* debit

**debo|chado** /debo'ʃadu/ *a* sardonic; **~char** *vt* mock; **~che** /ɔ/ *m* jibe

**debruar** /debru'ar/ *vt/i* edge

**debruçar-se** /debru'sarsi/ *vpr* bend over; **~ sobre** study

**debrum** /de'brũ/ *m* edging

**debulhar** /debu'ʎar/ *vt* thresh

**debu|tante** /debu'tãtʃi/ *f* debutante; **~tar** *vi* debut, make one's debut

**década** /'dɛkada/ *f* decade; **a ~ dos 60** the sixties

**deca|dência** /deka'dẽsia/ *f* decadence; **~dente** *a* decadent

**decair** /deka'ir/ *vi* decline; (*degringolar*) go downhill; <*planta*> wilt

**decal|car** /dekaw'kar/ *vt* trace; **~que** *m* tracing

**decapitar** /dekapi'tar/ *vt* decapitate

**decatlo** /de'katlu/ *m* decathlon

**de|cência** /de'sẽsia/ *f* decency; **~cente** *a* decent

**decepar** /dese'par/ *vt* cut off

**decep|ção** /desep'sãw/ *f* disappointment; **~cionar** *vt* disappoint; **~cionar-se** *vpr* be disappointed

**decerto** /dʒi'sɛrtu/ *adv* certainly

**deci|dido** /desi'dʒidu/ *a* <*pessoa*> determined; **~dir** *vt/i* decide; **~dir-se** *vpr* make up one's mind; **~dir-se por** decide on

**decíduo** /de'siduu/ *a* deciduous

**decifrar** /desi'frar/ *vt* decipher

**deci|mal** /desi'maw/ (*pl* **~mais**) *a* & *m* decimal

**décimo** /'dɛsimu/ *a* & *m* tenth; **~ primeiro** eleventh; **~ segundo** twelfth; **~ terceiro** thirteenth; **~ quarto** fourteenth; **~ quinto** fifteenth; **~ sexto** sixteenth; **~ sétimo** seventeenth; **~ oitavo** eighteenth; **~ nono** nineteenth

**deci|são** /desi'zãw/ *f* decision; **~sivo** *a* decisive

**decla|ração** /deklara'sãw/ *f* declaration; **~rado** *a* <*inimigo*> sworn; <*crente*> avowed; <*ladrão*> self-confessed; **~rar** *vt* declare

**decli|nação** /deklina'sãw/ *f* declension; **~nar** *vt* **~nar (de)** de-

cline □ *vi* decline; <*sol*> go down; <*chão*> slope down

**declínio** /de'kliniu/ *m* decline

**declive** /de'klivi/ *m* (downward) slope, incline

**decodificar** /dekodʒifi'kar/ *vt* decode

**deco|lagem** /deko'laʒẽ/ *f* take-off; **~lar** *vi* take off; (*fig*) get off the ground

**decom|por** /dekõ'por/ *vt* break down; contort <*feições*>; **~por-se** *vpr* break down; <*cadáver*> decompose; **~ posição** *f* (*de cadáver*) decomposition

**deco|ração** /dekora'sãw/ *f* decoration; (*aprendizagem*) learning by heart; **~rar** *vt* (*adornar*) decorate; (*aprender*) learn by heart, memorize; **~rativo** *a* decorative; **~reba** /ɛ/ (*fam*) *f* rote-learning; **~ro** /o/ *m* decorum; **~roso** /o/ *a* decorous

**decor|rência** /deko'xẽsia/ *f* consequence; **~rente** *a* resulting (de from); **~rer** *vi* <*tempo*> elapse; <*acontecimento*> pass off; (*resultar*) result (de from) □ *m* **no ~rer de** in the course of; **com o ~rer do tempo** in time, with the passing of time

**deco|tado** /deko'tadu/ *a* low-cut; **~te** /ɔ/ *m* neckline

**decrépito** /de'krɛpitu/ *a* decrepit

**decres|cente** /dekre'sẽtʃi/ *a* decreasing; **~cer** *vi* decrease

**decre|tar** /dekre'tar/ *vt* decree; declare <*estado de sítio*>; **~to** /ɛ/ *m* decree; **~to-lei** (*pl* **~tos-leis**) *m* act

**decurso** /de'kursu/ *m* course

**de|dal** /de'daw/ (*pl* **~dais**) *m* thimble; **~dão** *m* (*da mão*) thumb; (*do pé*) big toe

**dedetizar** /dedetʃi'zar/ *vt* spray with insecticide

**dedi|cação** /dedʒika'sãw/ *f* dedication; **~car** *vt* dedicate; devote <*tempo*>; **~car-se** *vpr* dedicate o.s. (a to); **~catória** *f* dedication

**dedilhar** /dedʒi'ʎar/ *vt* pluck

**dedo** /'dedu/ *m* finger; (*do pé*) toe; **cheio de ~s** all fingers and thumbs; (*sem graça*) awkward; **~-duro** (*pl* **~s-duros**) *m* sneak; (*político, criminoso*) informer

**dedução** /dedu'sãw/ *f* deduction

**dedurar** /dedu'rar/ *vt* sneak on; (*à polícia*) inform on

**dedu|tivo** /dedu'tʃivu/ *a* deductive; **~zir** *vt* (*descontar*) deduct; (*concluir*) deduce

**defa|sado** /defa'zadu/ *a* out of step; **~sagem** *f* gap, lag

**defecar** /defe'kar/ *vi* defecate

**defei|to** /de'fejtu/ *m* defect; **botar ~to em** find fault with; **~tuoso** /o/ *a* defective

**defen|der** /defẽ'der/ *vt* defend; **~der-se** *vpr* (*virar-se*) fend for o.s.; (*contra-atacar*) defend o.s. (**de** against); **~siva** *f* **na ~siva** on the defensive; **~sor** *m* defender; (*advogado*) defence counsel

**defe|rência** /defe'rẽsia/ *f* deference; **~rente** *a* deferential

**defesa** /de'feza/ *f* defence □ *m* defender

**defici|ência** /defisi'ẽsia/ *f* deficiency; **~ente** *a* deficient; (*física ou mentalmente*) handicapped □ *m/f* handicapped person

**déficit** /'dɛfisitʃi/ (*pl* **~s**) *m* deficit

**deficitário** /defisitʃi'ariu/ *a* in deficit; <*empresa*> loss-making

**definhar** /defi'ɲar/ *vi* waste away; <*planta*> wither

**defi|nição** /defini'sãw/ *f* definition; **~nir** *vt* define; **~nir-se** *vpr* (*descrever-se*) define o.s.; (*decidir-se*) come to a decision; (*explicar-se*) make one's position clear; **~nitivo** *a* definitive; **~nível** (*pl* **~níveis**) *a* definable

**defla|ção** /defla'sãw/ *f* deflation; **~cionário** *a* deflationary

**deflagrar** /defla'grar/ *vt* set off □ *vi* break out

**defor|mar** /defor'mar/ *vt* misshape; deform <*corpo*>; distort <*imagem*>; **~midade** *f* deformity

**defraudar** /defraw'dar/ *vt* defraud (**de** of)

**defron|tar** /defrõ'tar/ *vt* **~tar com** face; **~te** *adv* opposite; **~te de** opposite

**defumar** /defu'mar/ *vt* smoke

**defunto** /de'fũtu/ *a & m* deceased

**dege|lar** /deʒe'lar/ *vt/i* thaw; **~lo** /e/ *m* thaw

**degeneração** /deʒenera'sãw/ *f* degeneration

**degenerar** /deʒene'rar/ *vi* degenerate (**em** into)

**degolar** /dego'lar/ *vt* cut the throat of

**degra|dação** /degrada'sãw/ *f* degradation; **~dante** *a* degrading; **~dar** *vt* degrade

**degrau** /de'graw/ *m* step

**degringolar** /degrĩgo'lar/ *vi* deteriorate, go downhill

**degustar** /degus'tar/ *vt* taste

**dei|tada** /dej'tada/ *f* lie-down; **~tado** *a* lying down; (*dormindo*) in bed; (*fam: preguiçoso*) idle; **~tar** *vt* lay down; (*na cama*) put to bed; (*pôr*) put; (*Port: jogar*) throw □ *vi*, **~tar-se** *vpr* lie down; (*ir para cama*) go to bed

**dei|xa** /'deʃa/ *f* cue; **~xar** *vt* leave; (*permitir*) let; **~xar de** (*parar*) stop; (*omitir*) fail; **não pôde ~xar de rir** he couldn't help laughing; **~xar alg**

**nervoso** make s.o. annoyed; **~xar cair** drop; **~xar a desejar** leave a lot to be desired; **~xa (para lá)** (*fam*) never mind, forget it

**dela(s) = de + ela(s)**

**delatar** /dela'tar/ *vt* report

**délavé** /dela've/ *a invar* faded

**dele(s) = de + ele(s)**

**dele|gação** /delega'sãw/ *f* delegation; **~gacia** *f* police station; **~gado** *m* delegate; **~gado de polícia** police chief; **~gar** *vt* delegate

**delei|tar** /delej'tar/ *vt* delight; **~tar-se** *vpr* delight (**com** in); **~te** *m* delight; **~toso** /o/ *a* delightful

**delgado** /dew'gadu/ *a* slender

**delibe|ração** /delibera'sãw/ *f* deliberation; **~rar** *vt/i* deliberate

**delica|deza** /delika'deza/ *f* delicacy; (*cortesia*) politeness; **~do** *a* delicate; (*cortês*) polite

**delícia** /de'lisia/ *f* delight; **ser uma ~** <*comida*> be delicious; <*sol etc*> be lovely

**delici|ar** /delisi'ar/ *vt* delight; **~ar-se** delight (**com** in); **~oso** /o/ *a* delightful, lovely; <*comida*> delicious

**deline|ador** /delinia'dor/ *m* eye-liner; **~ar** *vt* outline

**delin|qüência** /delĩ'kwẽsia/ *f* delinquency; **~qüente** *a & m* delinquent

**deli|rante** /deli'rãtʃi/ *a* rapturous; (*med*) delirious; **~rar** *vi* go into raptures; <*doente*> be delirious

**delírio** /de'liriu/ *m* (*febre*) delirium; (*excitação*) raptures

**delito** /de'litu/ *m* crime

**delonga** /de'lõga/ *f* delay

**delta** /'dɛwta/ *f* delta

**dema|gogia** /demago'ʒia/ *f* demagogy; **~gógico** *a* demagogic; **~gogo** /o/ *m* demagogue

**demais** /dʒi'majs/ *a & adv* (*muito*) very much; (*em demasia*) too much; **os ~** the rest, the others; **é ~!** (*fam*) it's great!

**deman|da** /de'mãda/ *f* demand; (*jurid*) action; **~dar** *vt* sue

**demão** /de'mãw/ *f* coat

**demar|car** /demar'kar/ *vt* demarcate; **~catório** *a* demarcation

**demasia** /dema'zia/ *f* excess; **em ~** too much, (much, many)

**de|mência** /de'mẽsia/ *f* insanity; (*med*) dementia; **~mente** *a* insane; (*med*) demented

**demissão** /demi'sãw/ *f* sacking, dismissal; **pedir ~** resign

**demitir** /demi'tʃir/ *vt* sack, dismiss; **~-se** *vpr* resign

**demo|cracia** /demokra'sia/ *f* democracy; **~crata** *m/f* democrat; **~crático** *a* democratic; **~cratizar**

*vt* democratize; **~grafia** *f* demography; **~gráfico** *a* demographic
**demo|lição** /demoli'sãw/ *f* demolition; **~lir** *vt* demolish
**demônio** /de'moniu/ *m* demon
**demons|tração** /demõstra'sãw/ *f* demonstration; **~trar** *vt* demonstrate; **~trativo** *a* demonstrative
**demo|ra** /de'mɔra/ *f* delay; **~rado** *a* lengthy; **~rar** *vi* (*levar*) take; (*tardar a voltar, terminar etc*) be long; (*levar muito tempo*) take a long time □ *vt* delay
**dendê** /dẽ'de/ *m* (*óleo*) palm oil
**denegrir** /dene'grir/ *vt* denigrate
**dengoso** /dẽ'gozu/ *a* coy
**dengue** /'dẽgi/ *m* dengue
**denomi|nação** /denomina'sãw/ *f* denomination; **~nar** *vt* name
**denotar** /deno'tar/ *vt* denote
**den|sidade** /dẽsi'dadʒi/ *f* density; **~so** *a* dense
**den|tado** /dẽ'tadu/ *a* serrated; **~tadura** *f* (set of) teeth; (*postiça*) dentures, false teeth; **~tal** (*pl* **~tais**) *a* dental; **~tário** *a* dental; **~te** *m* tooth; (*de alho*) clove; **~te do siso** wisdom tooth; **~tição** *f* teething; (*dentadura*) teeth; **~tífrico** *m* toothpaste; **~tista** *m/f* dentist
**dentre** = **de** + **entre**
**dentro** /'dẽtru/ *adv* inside; **lá ~** in there; **por ~** on the inside; **~ de** inside; (*tempo*) within
**dentu|ça** /dẽ'tusa/ *f* buck teeth; **~ço** *a* with buck teeth
**denúncia** /de'nũsia/ *f* (*à polícia etc*) report; (*na imprensa etc*) disclosure
**denunciar** /denũsi'ar/ *vt* (*à polícia etc*) report; (*na imprensa etc*) denounce
**deparar** /depa'rar/ *vi* **~ com** come across
**departamento** /departa'mẽtu/ *m* department
**depauperar** /depawpe'rar/ *vt* impoverish
**depenar** /depe'nar/ *vt* pluck <*aves*>; (*roubar*) fleece
**depen|dência** /depẽ'dẽsia/ *f* dependence; *pl* premises; **~dente** *a* dependent (**de** on) □ *m/f* dependant; **~der** *vi* depend (**de** on)
**depi|lação** /depila'sãw/ *f* depilation; **~lar** *vt* depilate; **~latório** *m* depilatory cream
**deplo|rar** /deplo'rar/ *vt* deplore; **~rável** (*pl* **~ráveis**) *a* deplorable
**de|poente** /depo'ẽtʃi/ *m/f* witness; **~poimento** *m* (*à polícia*) statement; (*na justiça, fig*) testimony
**depois** /de'pojs/ *adv* after(wards); **~ de** after; **~ que** after
**depor** /de'por/ *vi* (*na polícia*) make a statement; (*na justiça*) give evidence, testify □ *vt* lay down <*armas*>; depose <*rei, presidente*>
**depor|tação** /deporta'sãw/ *f* deportation; **~tar** *vt* deport
**deposi|tante** /depozi'tãtʃi/ *m/f* depositor; **~tar** *vt* deposit; cast <*voto*>; place <*confiança*>
**depósito** /de'pɔzitu/ *m* deposit; (*armazém*) warehouse
**depra|vação** /deprava'sãw/ *f* depravity; **~vado** *a* depraved; **~var** *vt* deprave
**depre|ciação** /depresia'sãw/ *f* (*perda de valor*) depreciation; (*menosprezo*) deprecation; **~ciar** *vt* (*desvalorizar*) devalue; (*menosprezar*) deprecate; **~ciar-se** *vpr* <*bens*> depreciate; <*pessoa*> deprecate o.s.; **~ciativo** *a* deprecatory
**depre|dação** /depreda'sãw/ *f* depredation; **~dar** *vt* wreck
**depressa** /dʒi'presa/ *adv* fast, quickly
**depres|são** /depre'sãw/ *f* depression; **~sivo** *a* depressive
**depri|mente** /depri'mẽtʃi/ *a* depressing; **~mido** *a* depressed; **~mir** *vt* depress; **~mir-se** *vpr* get depressed
**depurar** /depu'rar/ *vt* purify
**depu|tação** /deputa'sãw/ *f* deputation; **~tado** *m* deputy, MP, (*Amer*) congressman (*f* -woman); **~tar** *vt* delegate
**deque** /'dɛki/ *m* (sun)deck
**deri|va** /de'riva/ *f* **à ~va** adrift; **andar à ~va** drift; **~vação** *f* derivation; **~var** *vt* derive; (*desviar*) divert □ *vi*, **~var-se** *vpr* derive, be derived (**de** from); <*navio*> drift
**dermatolo|gia** /dermatolo'ʒia/ *f* dermatology; **~gista** *m/f* dermatologist
**derradeiro** /dexa'deru/ *a* last, final
**derra|mamento** /dexama'mẽtu/ *m* spill, spillage; **~mamento de sangue** bloodshed; **~mar** *vt* spill; shed <*lágrimas*>; **~mar-se** *vpr* spill; **~me** *m* spill, spillage; **~me cerebral** stroke
**derra|pagem** /dexa'paʒẽ/ *f* skidding; (*uma*) skid; **~par** *vi* skid
**derreter** /dexe'ter/ *vt* melt; **~-se** *vpr* melt
**derro|ta** /de'xɔta/ *f* defeat; **~tar** *vt* defeat; **~tismo** *m* defeatism; **~tista** *a* & *m/f* defeatist
**derrubar** /dexu'bar/ *vt* knock down; bring down <*governo*>
**desaba|far** /dʒizaba'far/ *vi* speak one's mind; **~fo** *m* outburst
**desa|bamento** /dʒizaba'mẽtu/ *m* collapse; **~bar** *vi* collapse; <*chuva*> pour down

**desabotoar** /dʒiaboto'ar/ vt unbutton

**desabri|gado** /dʒizabri'gadu/ a homeless; ~**gar** vt make homeless

**desabrochar** /dʒizabro'ʃar/ vi blossom, bloom

**desaca|tar** /dʒizaka'tar/ vt defy; ~**to** m (de pessoa) disrespect; (da lei etc) disregard

**desacerto** /dʒiza'sertu/ m mistake

**desacompanhado** /dʒizakõpa-'ɲadu/ a unaccompanied

**desaconse|lhar** /dʒizakõse'ʎar/ vt advise against; ~**lhável** (pl ~**lháveis**) a inadvisable

**desacor|dado** /dʒizakor'dadu/ a unconscious; ~**do** /o/ m disagreement

**desacostu|mado** /dʒizakostu'madu/ a unaccustomed; ~**mar** vt ~**mar alg de** break s.o. of the habit of; ~**mar-se de** get out of the habit of

**desacreditar** /dʒizakredʒi'tar/ vt discredit

**desafeto** /dʒiza'fɛtu/ m disaffection

**desafi|ador** /dʒizafia'dor/ a <tarefa> challenging; <pessoa> defiant; ~**ar** vt challenge; (fazer face a) defy <perigo, morte>

**desafi|nado** /dʒizafi'nadu/ a out of tune; ~**nar** vi (cantando) sing out of tune; (tocando) play out of tune □ vt put out of tune

**desafio** /dʒiza'fiu/ m challenge

**desafivelar** /dʒizafive'lar/ vt unbuckle

**desafo|gar** /dʒizafo'gar/ vt vent; (desapertar) relieve; ~**gar-se** vpr give vent to one's feelings; ~**go** /o/ m (alívio) relief

**desafo|rado** /dʒizafo'radu/ a cheeky; ~**ro** /o/ m cheek; (um) liberty

**desafortunado** /dʒizafortu'nadu/ a unfortunate

**desagra|dar** /dʒizagra'dar/ vt displease; ~**dável** (pl ~**dáveis**) a unpleasant; ~**do** m displeasure

**desagravo** m redress, amends

**desagregar** /dʒizagre'gar/ vt split up; ~**-se** vpr split up

**desaguar** /dʒiza'gwar/ vt drain □ vi <rio> flow (em into)

**desajeitado** /dʒizaʒej'tadu/ a clumsy

**desajuizado** /dʒizaʒui'zadu/ a foolish

**desajus|tado** /dʒizaʒus'tadu/ a (psic) maladjusted; ~**te** m (psic) maladjustment

**desalen|tar** /dʒizalẽ'tar/ vt dishearten; ~**tar-se** vpr get disheartened; ~**to** m discouragement

**desali|nhado** /dʒizali'ɲadu/ a untidy; ~**nho** m untidiness

**desalojar** /dʒizalo'ʒar/ vt turn out <inquilino>; flush out <inimigo, ladrões>

**desamarrar** /dʒizama'xar/ vt untie □ vi cast off

**desamarrotar** /dʒizamaxo'tar/ vt smooth out

**desamassar** /dʒizama'sar/ vt smooth out

**desambientado** /dʒizãbiẽ'tadu/ a unsettled

**desampa|rar** /dʒizãpa'rar/ vt abandon; ~**ro** m abandonment

**desandar** /dʒizã'dar/ vi <molho> separ əte; ~ **a** start to

**de|sanimar** /dʒizani'mar/ vt discourage □ vi <pessoa> lose heart; <fato> be disc.·raging; ~**sânimo** m discouragement

**desapaixonado** /dʒizapaʃo'nadu/ a dispassionate

**desaparafusar** /dʒizaparafu'zar/ vt unscrew

**desapare|cer** /dʒizapare'ser/ vi disappear; ~**cimento** m disappearance

**desapego** /dʒiza'pegu/ m detachment; (indiferença) indifference

**desapercebido** /dʒizaperse'bidu/ a unnoticed

**desapertar** /dʒizaper'tar/ vt loosen

**desapon|tamento** /dʒizapõta'mẽtu/ m disapointment; ~**tar** vt disappoint

**desapropriar** /dʒizapropri'ar/ vt expropriate

**desapro|vação** /dʒizaprova'sãw/ f disapproval; ~**var** vt disapprove of

**desaproveitado** /dʒizaprovej'tadu/ a wasted

**desar|mamento** /dʒizarma'mẽtu/ m disarmament; ~**mar** vt disarm; take down <barraca>

**desarran|jar** /dʒizaxã'ʒar/ vt mess up; upset <estômago>; ~**jo** m mess; (do estômago) upset

**desarregaçar** /dʒizaxega'sar/ vt roll down

**desarru|mado** /dʒizaxu'madu/ a untidy; ~**mar** vt untidy; unpack <mala>

**desarticular** /dʒizartʃiku'lar/ vt dislocate

**desarvorado** /dʒizarvo'radu/ a disoriented, at a loss

**desassociar** /dʒizasosi'ar/ vt disassociate; ~**-se** vpr disassociate o.s.

**desas|trado** /dʒizas'tradu/ a accident-prone; ~**tre** m disaster; ~**troso** /o/ a disastrous

**desatar** /dʒiza'tar/ vt untie; ~ **a chorar** dissolve in tears

**desatarraxar** /dʒizataxa'ʃar/ vt unscrew

**desaten|cioso** /dʒizatẽsi'ozu/ a inattentive; ~**to** a oblivious (a to)

**desati|nar** /dʒizatʃi'nar/ vt bewilder □ vi not think straight; ~**no** m mental aberration, bewilderment; (um) folly

**desativar** /dʒizatʃi'var/ *vt* deactivate; shut down <*fábrica*>

**desatrelar** /dʒizatre'lar/ *vt* unhitch

**desatualizado** /dʒizatuali'zadu/ *a* out-of-date

**desavença** /dʒiza'vẽsa/ *f* disagreement

**desavergonhado** /dʒizavergo'ɲadu/ *a* shameless

**desbancar** /dʒizbã'kar/ *vt* outdo

**desbaratar** /dʒizbara'tar/ *vt* (*desperdiçar*) waste

**desbocado** /dʒizbo'kadu/ *a* outspoken

**desbotar** /dʒizbo'tar/ *vt/i* fade

**desbra|vador** /dʒizbrava'dor/ *m* explorer; ~**var** *vt* explore

**desbun|dante** /dʒizbũ'dãtʃi/ (*fam*) *a* mind-blowing; ~**dar** (*fam*) *vt* blow the mind of □ *vi* flip, freak out; ~**de** (*fam*) *m* knockout

**descabido** /dʒiska'bidu/ *a* inappropriate

**descalabro** /dʒiska'labru/ *m* débâcle

**descalço** /dʒis'kawsu/ *a* barefoot

**descambar** /dʒiskã'bar/ *vi* deteriorate, degenerate

**descan|sar** /dʒiskã'sar/ *vt/i* rest; ~**so** *m* rest; (*de prato, copo*) mat

**desca|rado** /dʒiska'radu/ *a* blatant; ~**ramento** *m* cheek

**descarga** /dʒis'karga/ *f* (*eletr*) discharge; (*da privada*) flush; **dar** ~ flush (the toilet)

**descarregar** /dʒiskaxe'gar/ *vt* unload <*mercadorias*>; discharge <*poluentes*>; vent <*raiva*> □ *vi* <*bateria*> go flat; ~ **em cima de alg** take it out on s.o.

**descarrilhar** /dʒiskaxi'ʎar/ *vt/i* derail

**descar|tar** /dʒiskar'tar/ *vt* discard; ~**tável** (*pl* ~**táveis**) *a* disposable

**descascar** /dʒiskas'kar/ *vt* peel <*frutas, batatas*>; shell <*nozes*> □ *vi* <*pessoa, pele*> peel

**descaso** /dʒis'kazu/ *m* indifference

**descen|dência** /dʒisẽ'dẽsia/ *f* descent; ~**dente** *a* descended □ *m/f* descendant; ~**der** *vi* descend (**de** from)

**descentralizar** /dʒisẽtrali'zar/ *vt* decentralize

**des|cer** /de'ser/ *vi* go down; <*avião*> descend; (*do ônibus, trem*) get off; (*do carro*) get out □ *vt* go down <*escada, ladeira*>; ~**cida** *f* descent

**desclassificar** /dʒisklasifi'kar/ *vt* disqualify

**desco|berta** /dʒisko'bɛrta/ *f* discovery; ~**berto** /ɛ/ *a* uncovered; <*conta*> overdrawn; **a** ~**berto** overdrawn; ~**bridor** *m* discoverer; ~**brimento** *m* discovery; ~**brir** *vt* discover; (*expor*) uncover

**descolar** /dʒisko'lar/ *vt* unstick; (*fam*) (*dar*) give; (*arranjar*) get hold of, rustle up; (*Port*) <*avião*> take off

**descom|por** /dʒiskõ'por/ *vt* (*censurar*) scold; ~**-se** *vpr* <*pessoa*> lose one's composure; ~**postura** *f* (*estado*) loss of composure; (*censura*) talking-to

**descomprometido** /dʒiskõprome'tʃidu/ *a* free

**descomu|nal** /dʒiskomu'naw/ (*pl* ~**nais**) *a* extraordinary; (*grande*) huge

**desconcentrar** /dʒiskõsẽ'trar/ *vt* distract

**desconcer|tante** /dʒiskõser'tãtʃi/ *a* disconcerting; ~**tar** *vt* disconcert

**desconexo** /dʒisko'nɛksu/ *a* incoherent

**desconfi|ado** /dʒiskõfi'adu/ *a* suspicious; ~**ança** *f* mistrust; ~**ar** *vi* suspect

**desconfor|tável** /dʒiskõfor'tavew/ (*pl* ~**táveis**) *a* uncomfortable; ~**to** /o/ *m* discomfort

**descongelar** /dʒiskõʒe'lar/ *vt* defrost <*geladeira*>; thaw <*comida*>

**descongestio|nante** /dʒiskõʒestʃio'nãtʃi/ *a* & *m* decongestant; ~**nar** *vt* decongest

**desconhe|cer** /dʒiskoɲe'ser/ *vt* not know; ~**cido** *a* unknown □ *m* stranger

**desconsiderar** /dʒiskõside'rar/ *vt* ignore

**desconsolado** /dʒiskõso'ladu/ *a* disconsolate

**descontar** /dʒiskõ'tar/ *vt* deduct; (*não levar em conta*) discount

**desconten|tamento** /dʒiskõtẽta'mẽtu/ *m* discontent; ~**te** *a* discontent

**desconto** /dʒis'kõtu/ *m* discount; **dar um** ~ (*fig*) make allowances

**descontra|ção** /dʒiskõtra'sãw/ *f* informality; ~**ído** *a* informal, casual; ~**ir** *vt* relax; ~**ir-se** *vpr* relax

**descontro|lar-se** /dʒiskõtro'larsi/ *vpr* <*pessoa*> lose control; <*coisa*> go out of control; ~**le** /o/ *m* lack of control

**desconversar** /dʒiskõver'sar/ *vi* change the subject

**descortesia** /dʒiskorte'zia/ *f* rudeness

**descostu|rar** /dʒiskostu'rar/ *vt* unrip, ~**rar-se** *vpr* come undone

**descrédito** /dʒis'krɛdʒitu/ *m* discredit

**descren|ça** /dʒis'krẽsa/ *f* disbelief; ~**te** *a* sceptical, disbelieving

**des|crever** /dʒiskre'ver/ *vt* describe; ~**crição** *f* description; ~**critivo** *a* descriptive

**descui|dado** /dʒiskui'dadu/ *a* careless; ~**dar** *vt* neglect; ~**do** *m* carelessness; (*um*) oversight

**descul|pa** /dʒis'kuwpa/ f excuse; pe-
  dir ~pas apologize; ~par vt excuse;
  ~pe! sorry!; ~par-se vpr apologize;
  ~pável (pl ~páveis) a excusable
**desde** /'dezdʒi/ prep since; ~ que
  since
**des|dém** /dez'dẽj/ m disdain;
  ~denhar vt disdain; ~nhoso /o/ a
  disdainful
**desdentado** /dʒizdẽ'tadu/ a toothless
**desdita** /dʒiz'dʒita/ f unhappiness
**desdizer** /dʒizdʒi'zer/ vt take back,
  withdraw □ vi take back what one
  said
**desdo|bramento** /dʒizdobra'mẽtu/ m
  implication; ~brar vt (abrir) unfold;
  break down <dados, contas>; ~brar-
  se vpr unfold; (empenhar-se) go to a
  lot of trouble, bend over backwards
**dese|jar** /deze'ʒar/ vt want; (apaixo-
  nadamente) desire; ~jar aco a alg
  wish s.o. sth; ~jável (pl ~jáveis) a
  desirable; ~jo /e/ m wish; (forte)
  desire; ~joso /o/ a desirous
**deselegante** /dʒizele'gãtʃi/ a inel-
  egant
**desemaranhar** /dʒizemara'nar/ vt
  untangle
**desembara|çado** /dʒizɪbara'sadu/ a
  <pessoa> confident, nonchalant;
  ~çar-se vpr rid o.s. (de of); ~ço m
  confidence, ease
**desembar|car** /dʒizɪbar'kar/ vt/i
  disembark; ~que m disembarkation;
  (seção do aeroporto) arrivals
**desembocar** /dʒizɪbo'kar/ vi flow
**desembol|sar** /dʒizɪbow'sar/ vt
  spend, pay out; ~so /o/ m expenditure
**desembrulhar** /dʒizɪbru'ʎar/ vt unwrap
**desembuchar** /dʒizɪbu'ʃar/ (fam) vi
  (desabafar) get things off one's chest;
  (falar logo) spit it out
**desempacotar** /dʒizɪpako'tar/ vt unpack
**desempatar** /dʒizɪpa'tar/ vt decide
  <jogo>
**desempe|nhar** /dʒizɪpe'nar/ vt per-
  form; play <papel>; ~nho m performance
**desempre|gado** /dʒizɪpre'gadu/ a un-
  employed; ~go /e/ m unemployment
**desencadear** /dʒizɪkadʒi'ar/ vt set
  off, trigger
**desencaminhar** /dʒizɪkami'nar/ vt
  lead astray; embezzle <dinheiro>
**desencantar** /dʒizɪkã'tar/ vt disenchant
**desencon|trar-se** /dʒizɪkõ'trarsi/ vpr
  miss each other, fail to meet; ~tro m
  failure to meet
**desencorajar** /dʒizɪkora'ʒar/ vt discourage

**desenferrujar** /dʒizɪfexu'ʒar/ vt de-
  rust <metal>; stretch <pernas>; brush
  up <língua>
**desenfreado** /dʒizɪfri'adu/ a unbridled
**desenganar** /dʒizɪga'nar/ vt dis-
  abuse; declare incurable <doente>
**desengonçado** /dʒizɪgõ'sadu/ a
  <pessoa> ungainly
**desengre|nado** /dʒizɪgre'nadu/ a
  <carro> in neutral; ~nar vt put in
  neutral <carro>; (tec) disengage
**dese|nhar** /deze'nar/ vt draw;
  ~nhista m/f drawer; (industrial)
  designer; ~nho /e/ m drawing
**desenlace** /dʒizɪ'lasi/ m dénouement,
  outcome
**desenredar** /dʒizɪxe'dar/ vt unravel
**desenrolar** /dʒizɪxo'lar/ vt unroll
  <rolo>
**desenten|der** /dʒizɪtẽ'der/ vt mis-
  understand; ~der-se vpr (não se dar
  bem) not get on; ~dimento m misunderstanding
**desenterrar** /dʒizɪte'xar/ vt dig up
  <cadáver>; unearth <informação>
**desentortar** /dʒizɪtor'tar/ vt
  straighten out
**desentupir** /dʒizɪtu'pir/ vt unblock
**desenvol|to** /dʒizɪ'vowtu/ a casual,
  nonchalant; ~tura f casualness, non-
  chalance; com ~tura nonchal-
  antly; ~ver vt develop; ~ver-se
  vpr develop; ~vimento m develop-
  ment
**desequi|librado** a unbalanced;
  ~librar vt unbalance; ~librar-se
  vpr become unbalanced; ~líbrio m
  imbalance
**deser|ção** /dezer'sãw/ f desertion;
  ~tar vt/i desert; ~to /ɛ/ a deserted;
  ilha ~ta desert island □ m desert;
  ~tor m deserter
**desespe|rado** /dʒizispe'radu/ a
  desperate; ~rador a hopeless; ~rar
  vt (desesperança) make despair □ vi,
  ~rar-se vpr despair; ~ro /e/ m despair
**desestabilizar** /dʒizistabili'zar/ vt
  destabilize
**desestimular** /dʒizistʃimu'lar/ vt discourage
**desfal|car** /dʒisfaw'kar/ vt embezzle;
  ~que m embezzlement
**desfal|ecer** /dʒisfale'ser/ vt (des-
  maiar) faint; ~ecimento m faint
**desfavor** /dʒisfa'vor/ m disfavour
**desfavo|rável** /dʒisfavo'ravew/ (pl
  ~ráveis) a unfavourable; ~recer vt
  be unfavourable to; treat less favour-
  ably <minorias etc>
**desfazer** /dʒisfa'zer/ vt undo; unpack
  <mala>; strip <cama>; break
  <contrato>; clear up <mistério>; ~se

*vpr* come undone; <*casamento*> break up; <*sonhos*> crumble; **∼-se em lágrimas** dissolve into tears

**desfe|char** /dʒisfe'ʃar/ *vt* throw <*murro, olhar*>; **∼cho** /e/ *m* outcome, dénouement

**desfeita** /dʒis'fejta/ *f* slight, insult

**desferir** /dʒisfe'rir/ *vt* give <*pontapé*>; launch <*ataque*>; fire <*flecha*>

**desfiar** /dʒisfi'ar/ *vt* pick the meat off <*frango*>; **∼-se** *vpr* <*tecido*> fray

**desfigurar** /dʒisfigu'rar/ *vt* disfigure; (*fig*) distort

**desfi|ladeiro** /dʒisfila'deru/ *m* pass; **∼lar** *vi* parade; **∼le** *m* parade; **∼le de modas** fashion show

**desflorestamento** /dʒisfloresta'mẽtu/ *m* deforestation

**desforra** /dʒis'fɔxa/ *f* revenge

**desfraldar** /dʒisfraw'dar/ *vt* unfurl

**desfrutar** /dʒisfru'tar/ *vt* enjoy

**desgas|tante** /dʒizgas'tãtʃi/ *a* wearing, stressful; **∼tar** *vt* wear out; **∼te** *m* (*de máquina etc*) wear and tear; (*de pessoa*) stress and strain

**desgosto** /dʒiz'gostu/ *m* sorrow

**desgovernar-se** /dʒizgover'narsi/ *vpr* go out of control

**desgraça** /dʒiz'grasa/ *f* misfortune; **∼do** *a* wretched □ *m* wretch

**desgravar** /dʒizgra'var/ *vt* erase

**desgrenhado** /dʒizgre'ɲadu/ *a* unkempt

**desgrudar** /dʒizgru'dar/ *vt* unstick; **∼-se** *vpr* <*pessoa*> tear o.s. away

**desidra|tação** /dʒizidrata'sãw/ *f* dehydration; **∼tar** *vt* dehydrate

**desig|nação** /dezigna'sãw/ *f* designation; **∼nar** *vt* designate

**desi|gual** /dʒizi'gwaw/ (*pl* **∼guais**) *a* unequal; <*terreno*> uneven; **∼gualdade** *f* inequality; (*de terreno*) unevenness

**desilu|dir** /dʒizilu'dʒir/ *vt* disillusion; **∼são** *f* disillusionment

**desinfe|tante** /dʒizĩfe'tãtʃi/ *a & m* disinfectant; **∼tar** *vt* disinfect

**desinibido** /dʒizini'bidu/ *a* uninhibited

**desintegrar-se** /dʒizĩte'grarsi/ *vpr* disintegrate

**desinteres|sado** /dʒizĩtere'sadu/ *a* uninterested; **∼sante** *a* uninteresting; **∼sar-se** *vpr* lose interest (**de** in); **∼se** /e/ *m* disinterest

**desis|tência** /dezis'tẽsia/ *f* giving up; **∼tir** *vt/i* **∼tir** (**de**) give up

**desle|al** /dʒizli'aw/ (*pl* **∼ais**) *a* disloyal; **∼aldade** *f* disloyalty

**deslei|xado** /dʒizle'ʃadu/ *a* sloppy; (*no vestir*) scruffy; **∼xo** *m* carelessness; (*no vestir*) scruffiness

**desli|gado** /dʒizli'gadu/ *a* <*luz, TV*> off; <*pessoa*> absent-minded; **∼gar** *vt*

turn off <*luz, TV, motor*>; hang up, put down <*telefone*> □ *vi* (*ao telefonar*) hang up, put the phone down

**deslindar** /dʒizlĩ'dar/ *vt* clear up, solve

**desli|zante** /dʒizli'zãtʃi/ *a* slippery; <*inflação*> creeping; **∼zar** *vi* slip; **∼zar-se** *vpr* creep; **∼ze** *m* slip; (*fig: erro*) slip-up

**deslo|cado** *a* <*membro*> dislocated; (*fig*) out of place; **∼car** *vt* move; (*med*) dislocate; **∼car-se** *vpr* move

**deslum|brado** /dʒizlũ'bradu/ *a* (*fig*) starry-eyed; **∼bramento** *m* (*fig*) wonderment; **∼brante** *a* dazzling; **∼brar** *vt* dazzle; **∼brar-se** *vpr* (*fig*) be dazzled

**desmai|ado** /dʒizmaj'adu/ *a* unconscious; **∼ar** *vi* faint; **∼o** *m* faint

**desman|cha-prazeres** /dʒizmãʃapra'zeris/ *m/f invar* spoilsport; **∼char** *vt* break up; break off <*noivado*>; shatter <*sonhos*>; **∼char-se** *vpr* break up; (*no ar, na água, em lágrimas*) dissolve

**desmantelar** /dʒizmãte'lar/ *vt* dismantle

**desmarcar** /dʒizmar'kar/ *vt* cancel <*encontro*>

**desmascarar** /dʒizmaske'rar/ *vt* unmask

**desma|tamento** /dʒizmata'mẽtu/ *m* deforestation; **∼tar** *vt* clear (of forest)

**desmedido** /dʒizme'didu/ *a* excessive

**desmemoriado** /dʒizmemori'adu/ *a* forgetful

**desmen|tido** /dʒizmẽ'tʃidu/ *m* denial; **∼tir** *vt* deny

**desmiolado** /dʒizmio'ladu/ *a* brainless

**desmontar** /dʒizmõ'tar/ *vt* dismantle

**desmorali|zante** /dʒizmorali'zãtʃi/ *a* demoralizing; **∼zar** *vt* demoralize

**desmoro|namento** /dʒizmorona'mẽtu/ *m* collapse; **∼nar** *vt* destroy; **∼nar-se** *vpr* collapse

**desnatar** /dʒizna'tar/ *vi* skim <*leite*>

**desnecessário** /dʒiznese'sariu/ *a* unnecessary

**desní|vel** /dʒiz'nivew/ (*pl* **∼veis**) *m* difference in height

**desnortear** /dʒiznortʃi'ar/ *vt* disorientate, (*Amer*) disorient

**desnutrição** /dʒiznutri'sãw/ *f* malnutrition

**desobe|decer** /dʒizobede'ser/ *vt/i* **∼decer (a)** disobey; **∼diência** *f* disobedience; **∼diente** *a* disobedient

**desobrigar** /dʒizobri'gar/ *vt* release (**de** from)

**desobstruir** /dʒizobistru'ir/ *vt* unblock; empty <*casa*>

**desocupado** /dʒizoku'padu/ a unoccupied

**desodorante** /dʒizodo'rātʃi/ m, (Port) **desodorizante** /dʒizoduri'zātʃi/ m deodorant

**deso|lação** /dezola'sãw/ f desolation; **~lado** a <lugar> desolate; <pessoa> desolated; **~lar** vt desolate

**desones|tidade** /dʒizonestʃi'dadʒi/ f dishonesty; **~to** /ɛ/ a dishonest

**deson|ra** /dʒi'zõxa/ f dishonour; **~rar** vt dishonour; **~roso** /o/ a dishonourable

**desor|deiro** /dʒizor'deru/ a troublemaking □ m troublemaker; **~dem** f disorder; **~denado** a disorganized; <vida> disordered; **~denar** vt disorganize

**desorgani|zação** /dʒizorganiza'sãw/ f disorganization; **~zar** vt disorganize; **~zar-se** vpr get disorganized

**desorientar** /dʒizoriẽ'tar/ vt disorientate, (Amer) disorient

**desossar** /dʒizo'sar/ vt bone

**deso|va** /dʒi'zɔva/ f roe; **~var** vi spawn

**despa|chado** /dʒispa'ʃadu/ a efficient; **~chante** m/f (de mercadorias) shipping agent; (de documentos) documentation agent; **~char** vt deal with; dispatch, forward <mercadorias>; **~cho** m dispatch

**desparafusar** /dʒisparafu'zar/ vt unscrew

**despedaçar** /dʒispeda'sar/ vt (rasgar) tear to pieces; (quebrar) smash; **~-se** vpr <vidro, vaso> smash; <papel, tecido> tear

**despe|dida** /dʒispe'dʒida/ f farewell; **~dida de solteiro** stag night, (Amer) bachelor party; **~dir** vt dismiss; sack <empregado>; **~dir-se** vpr say goodbye (de to)

**despei|tado** /dʒispej'tadu/ a spiteful; **~to** m spite; **a ~to de** despite, in spite of

**despe|jar** /dʒispe'ʒar/ vt pour out <líquido>; empty <recipiente>; evict <inquilino>; **~jo** /e/ m (de inquilino) eviction

**despencar** /dʒispẽ'kar/ vi plummet

**despender** /dʒispẽ'der/ vt spend <dinheiro>

**despensa** /dʒis'pẽsa/ f pantry, larder

**despentear** /dʒispẽtʃi'ar/ vt mess up <cabelo>; mess up the hair of <pessoa>

**despercebido** /dʒisperse'bidu/ a unnoticed

**desper|diçar** /dʒisperdʒi'sar/ vt waste; **~dício** m waste

**desper|tador** /dʒisperta'dor/ m alarm clock; **~tar** vt rouse <pessoa>;

(fig) arouse <interesse, suspeitas etc> □ vi awake

**despesa** /dʒis'peza/ f expense

**des|pido** /des'pidu/ a bare, stripped (**de** of); **~pir** vt strip (**de** of); strip off <roupa>; **~pir-se** vpr strip (off), get undressed

**despo|jar** /dʒispo'ʒar/ vt strip (**de** of); **~jar-se** vpr divest o.s. (**de** of); **~jo** /o/ m spoils, booty; **~jos mortais** mortal remains

**despontar** /dʒispõ'tar/ vi emerge

**despor|tista** /dʒispur'tiʃta/ (Port) m/f sportsman (f -woman); **~tivo** (Port) a sporting; **~to** /o/ (Port) m sport; **carro de ~to** sports car

**déspota** /'dɛspota/ m/f despot

**despótico** /des'pɔtʃiku/ a despotic

**despovoar** /dʒispovo'ar/ vt depopulate

**desprender** /dʒisprẽ'der/ vt detach; (da parede) take down; **~-se** vpr come off; (fig) detach o.s.

**despreocupado** /dʒisprioku'padu/ a unconcerned

**despreparado** /dʒisprepa'radu/ a unprepared

**despretensioso** /dʒispretẽsi'ozu/ a unpretentious

**desprestigiar** /dʒisprestʃiʒi'ar/ vt discredit

**desprevenido** /dʒispreve'nidu/ a off one's guard, unprepared; **apanhar ~** catch unawares

**despre|zar** /dʒispre'zar/ vt despise; (ignorar) ignore; **~zível** (pl **~zíveis**) a despicable; **~zo** /e/ m contempt

**desproporção** /dʒispropor'sãw/ f disproportion

**desproporcio|nado** /dʒisproporsio'nadu/ a disproportionate; **~nal** (pl **~nais**) a disproportional

**despropositado** /dʒispropozi'tadu/ a (absurdo) preposterous

**desprovido** /dʒispro'vidu/ a **~ de** without

**desqualificar** /dʒiskwalifi'kar/ vt disqualify

**desqui|tar-se** /dʒiski'tarsi/ vpr (legally) separate; **~te** m (legal) separation

**desrespei|tar** /dʒizxespej'tar/ vt not respect; (ignorar) disregard; **~to** m disrespect; **~toso** /o/ a disrespectful

**dessa(s), desse(s)** = **de** + **essa(s), esse(s)**

**desta** = **de** + **esta**

**desta|camento** /dʒistaka'mẽtu/ m detachment; **~car** vt detach; (ressaltar) bring out, make stand out; **~car-se** vpr (desprender-se) come off; <corredor> break away; (sobressair) stand out (**sobre** against); **~cável** (pl

~cáveis/ a detachable; <caderno> pull-out

destam|pado /dʒistã'padu/ a (panela) uncovered; ~par vt remove the lid of

destapar /dʒista'par/ vt uncover

destaque /dʒis'taki/ m prominence; (coisa, pessoa) highlight; (do notícia-rio) headline

destas, deste = de + estas, este

destemido /dʒiste'midu/ a intrepid, courageous

desterrar /dʒiste'xar/ vt (exilar) exile

destes = de + estes

destilar /desti'lar/ vt distil; ~ia f distillery

desti|nado /destʃi'nadu/ a (fadado) destined; ~nar vt intend, mean (para for); ~natário m addressee; ~no m (de viagem) destination; (sorte) fate

destituir /destʃitu'ir/ vt remove

desto|ante /dʒisto'ãtʃi/ a <sons> discordant; <cores> clashing; ~ar vi ~ar de clash with

destrancar /dʒistrã'kar/ vt unlock

destreza /des'treza/ f skill

destrinchar /dʒistrĩ'ʃar/ vt (expor) dissect; (resolver) sort out

destro /'destru/ a skilful

destro|çar /dʒistro'sar/ vt wreck; ~ços m pl wreckage

destronar /dʒistro'nar/ vt depose

destroncar /dʒistrõ'kar/ vt rick

destru|ição /dʒistrui'sãw/ f destruction; ~idor a destructive □ m destroyer; ~ir vt destroy

desumano /dʒizu'manu/ a inhuman; (cruel) inhumane

desunião /dʒizuni'ãw/ f disunity

desu|sado /dʒizu'zadu/ a disused; ~so m disuse

desvairado /dʒizvaj'radu/ a delirious, raving

desvalori|zação /dʒizvaloriza'sãw/ f devaluation; ~zar vt devalue

desvanta|gem /dʒizvã'taʒẽ/ f disadvantage; ~joso /o/ a disadvantageous

desve|lar /dʒizve'lar/ vt unveil; uncover <segredo>; ~lar-se vpr go to a lot of trouble; ~lo /e/ m great care

desvencilhar /dʒizvẽsi'ʎar/ vt extricate, free

desvendar /dʒizvẽ'dar/ vt reveal <segredo>; solve <mistério>

desventura /dʒizvẽ'tura/ f misfortune; (infelicidade) unhappiness

desviar /dʒizvi'ar/ vt divert <trânsito, rio, atenção, dinheiro>; avert <golpe, suspeitas, olhos>; ~se vpr deviate; <do tema> digress

desvincular /dʒizvĩku'lar/ vt free

desvio /dʒiz'viu/ m diversion; (do trânsito) diversion, (Amer) detour; (linha ferroviária) siding

desvirtuar /dʒizvirtu'ar/ vt misrepresent <verdade>

deta|lhado /deta'ʎadu/ a detailed; ~lhar vt detail; ~lhe m detail

detec|tar /detek'tar/ vt detect; ~tive (Port) m veja detetive; ~tor m detector

de|tenção /detẽ'sãw/ f (prisão) detention; ~tentor m holder; ~ter vt (ter) hold; (prender) detain

detergente /deter'ʒẽtʃi/ m detergent

deterio|ração /deteriora'sãw/ f deterioration; ~rar vt damage; ~rar-se vpr deteriorate

determi|nação /determina'sãw/ f determination; ~nado a (certo) certain; (resoluto) determined; ~nar vt determine

detestar /detes'tar/ vt hate

detetive /dete'tʃivi/ m detective

detido /de'tʃidu/ pp de deter □ a thorough □ m detainee

detonar /deto'nar/ vt detonate; (fam: criticar) pull to pieces □ vi detonate

detrás /de'traʃ/ adv behind □ prep ~ de behind

detrito /de'tritu/ m detritus

deturpar /detur'par/ vt misrepresent, distort

deus /dews/ m (f deusa) god (f goddess); ~dará m ao ~dará at the mercy of chance

devagar /dʒiva'gar/ adv slowly

deva|near /devani'ar/ vi daydream; ~neio m daydream

devas|sar /deva'sar/ vt expose; ~sidão f debauchery; ~so a debauched

devastar /devas'tar/ vt devastate

de|vedor /deve'dor/ a debit □ m debtor; ~ver vt owe □ vaux ~ve fazer (obrigação) he has to do; ~ve chegar (probabilidade) he should arrive; ~ve ser (suposição) he must be; ~ve ter ido he must have gone; ~v(er)ia fazer he ought to do; ~v(er)ia ter feito he ought to have done; ~vidamente adv duly; ~vido a due (a to)

devoção /devo'sãw/ f devotion

de|volução /devolu'sãw/ f return; ~volver vt return

devorar /devo'rar/ vt devour

devo|tar /devo'tar/ vt devote; ~tar-se vpr devote o.s. (a to); ~to /ɔ/ a devout

dez /dɛs/ a & m ten

dezanove /dza'nɔv/ (Port) a & m nineteen

dezas|seis /dza'sejʃ/ (Port) a & m sixteen; ~sete /ɛ/ (Port) a & m seventeen

dezembro /de'zẽbru/ m December

**deze|na** /de'zena/ *f* ten; **uma ~ (de)** about ten; **~nove** /ɔ/ *a & m* nineteen

**dezes|seis** /dʒize'sejs/ *a & m* sixteen; **~sete** /ɛ/ *a & m* seventeen

**dezoito** /dʒi'zojtu/ *a & m* eighteen

**dia** /'dʒia/ *m* day; **de ~** by day; **(no) ~ 20 de julho** (on) July 20th; **~ de folga** day off; **~ útil** working day; **~-a-~** *m* everyday life

**dia|bete** /dʒia'bɛtʃi/ *f* diabetes; **~bético** *a & m* diabetic

**dia|bo** /dʒi'abu/ *m* devil; **~bólico** *a* diabolical, devilish; **~brete** /e/ *m* little devil; **~brura** *f (de criança)* bit of mischief; *pl* mischief

**diadema** /dʒia'dema/ *m* tiara

**diafragma** /dʒia'fragima/ *m* diaphragm

**dia|gnosticar** /dʒiagnostʃi'kar/ *vt* diagnose; **~gnóstico** *m* diagnosis □ *a* diagnostic

**diago|nal** /dʒiago'naw/ ( *pl* **~nais**) *a & f* diagonal

**diagra|ma** /dʒia'grama/ *m* diagram; **~mação** *f* design; **~mador** *m* designer; **~mar** *vt* design *<livro, revista>*

**dialect-** (*Port*) *veja* **dialet-**

**dia|lética** /dʒia'lɛtʃika/ *f* dialectics; **~leto** /ɛ/ *m* dialect

**dialogar** /dʒialo'gar/ *vi* talk; (*pol*) hold talks

**diálogo** /dʒi'alogu/ *m* dialogue

**diamante** /dʒia'mãtʃi/ *m* diamond

**diâmetro** /dʒi'ametru/ *m* diameter

**dian|te** /dʒi'ãtʃi/ *adv* **de ... em ~te** from ... on(wards); **~te de** (*enfrentando*) faced with; ( *perante*) before; **~teira** *f* lead; **~teiro** *a* front

**diapasão** /dʒiapa'zãw/ *m* tuningfork

**diapositivo** /dʒiapozi'tʃivu/ *m* transparency

**diá|ria** /dʒi'aria/ *f* daily rate; **~rio** *a* daily

**diarista** /dʒia'rista/ *m/f* day labourer; ( *faxineira*) daily (help)

**diarréia** /dʒia'xɛja/ *f* diarrhoea

**dica** /'dʒika/ *f* tip, hint

**dicção** /dʒik'sãw/ *f* diction

**dicionário** /dʒisio'nariu/ *m* dictionary

**didáti|ca** /dʒi'datʃika/ *f* teaching methodology; **~co** *a* teaching; *<livro>* educational; *<estilo>* didactic

**die|ta** /dʒi'sta/ *f* diet; **de ~ta** on a diet; **~tista** *m/f* dietician

**difa|mação** /dʒifama'sãw/ *f* defamation; **~mar** *vt* defame; **~matório** *a* defamatory

**diferen|ça** /dʒife'rẽsa/ *f* difference; **~cial** ( *pl* **~ciais**) *a & f* differential; **~ciar** *vt* differentiate; **~ciar-se** *vpr* differ; **~te** *a* different

**dife|rimento** /dʒiferi'mẽtu/ *m* deferment; **~rir** *vt* defer □ *vi* differ

**difí|cil** /dʒi'fisiw/ ( *pl* **~ceis**) *a* difficult; (*improvável*) unlikely

**dificilmente** /dʒifisiw'mẽtʃi/ *adv* **~ poderá fazê-lo** he's unlikely to be able to do it

**dificul|dade** /dʒifikuw'dadʒi/ *f* difficulty; **~tar** *vt* make difficult

**difteria** /dʒifte'ria/ *f* diphtheria

**difun|dir** /dʒifũ'dʒir/ *vt* spread; ( *pela rádio*) broadcast; diffuse *<luz, calor>*; **~dir-se** *vpr* spread

**difu|são** /dʒifu'zãw/ *f* diffusion; **~so** *a* diffuse

**dige|rir** /dʒiʒe'rir/ *vt* digest; **~rível** ( *pl* **~ríveis**) *a* digestible

**diges|tão** /dʒiʒes'tãw/ *f* digestion; **~tivo** *a* digestive

**digi|tal** /dʒiʒi'taw/ ( *pl* **~tais**) *a* digital; **impressão ~tal** fingerprint; **~tar** *vt* key

**dígito** /'dʒiʒitu/ *m* digit

**digladiar** /dʒigladʒi'ar/ *vi* do battle

**dig|nar-se** /dʒig'narsi/ *vpr* deign (de to); **~nidade** *f* dignity; **~nificar** *vt* dignify; **~no** *a* worthy (de of); (*decoroso*) dignified

**dilace|rante** /dʒilase'rãtʃi/ *a <dor>* excruciating; **~rar** *vt* tear to pieces

**dilapidar** /dʒilapi'dar/ *vt* squander

**dilatar** /dʒila'tar/ *vt* expand; (*med*) dilate; **~se** *vpr* expand; (*med*) dilate

**dilema** /dʒi'lema/ *m* dilemma

**diletante** /dʒile'tãtʃi/ *a & m/f* dilettante

**dili|gência** /dʒili'ʒẽsia/ *f* diligence; (*carruagem*) stagecoach; **~gente** *a* diligent, hard-working

**diluir** /dʒilu'ir/ *vt* dilute

**dilúvio** /dʒi'luviu/ *m* deluge

**dimen|são** /dʒimẽ'sãw/ *f* dimension; **~sionar** *vt* size up

**diminu|ição** /dʒiminui'sãw/ *f* reduction; **~ir** *vt* reduce □ *vi* lessen; *<carro, motorista>* slow down; **~tivo** *a & m* diminutive; **~to** *a* minute

**Dinamarca** /dʒina'marka/ *f* Denmark

**dinamar|quês** /dʒinamar'kes/ ( *f* **~quesa**) *a* Danish □ *m* Dane

**dinâmi|ca** /dʒi'namika/ *f* dynamics; **~co** *a* dynamic

**dina|mismo** /dʒina'mizmu/ *m* dynamism; **~mite** *f* dynamite

**dínamo** /'dʒinamu/ *m* dynamo

**dinastia** /dʒinas'tʃia/ *f* dynasty

**dinda** /'dʒĩda/ ( *fam*) *f* godmother

**dinheiro** /dʒi'ɲeru/ *m* money

**dinossauro** /dʒino'sawru/ *m* dinosaur

**diocese** /dʒio'sɛzi/ *f* diocese

**dióxido** /dʒi'ɔksidu/ *m* dioxide; **~ de carbono** carbon dioxide

**diplo|ma** /dʒi'ploma/ *m* diploma; **~macia** *f* diplomacy; **~mar-se** *vpr* take one's diploma; **~mata** *m/f* diplomat □ *a* diplomatic; **~mático** *a* diplomatic

**direção** /dʒire'sãw/ *f* (*sentido*) direction; (*de empresa*) management; (*condução de carro*) driving; (*manuseio do volante*) steering

**direct-** (*Port*) *veja* **diret-**

**direi|ta** /dʒi'rejta/ *f* right; **~tinho** *adv* exactly right; **~tista** *a* rightwing □ *m/f* rightwinger, rightist; **~to** *a* right; (*ereto*) straight □ *adv* properly □ *m* right

**dire|tas** /dʒi'rɛtas/ *f pl* direct (presidential) elections; **~to** *a* direct □ *adv* directly; **~tor** *m* director; (*de escola*) headteacher; (*de jornal*) editor; **~tor-gerente** managing director; **~toria** *f* (*diretores*) board of directors; (*sala*) boardroom; **~tório** *m* directory; **~triz** *f* directive

**diri|gente** /dʒiri'ʒẽtʃi/ *a* leading □ *m/f* leader; **~gir** *vt* direct; manage <*empresa*>; drive <*carro*>; **~gir-se** *vpr* (*ir*) make one's way; **~gir-se a** (*falar com*) address

**dis|cagem** /dʒis'kaʒẽ/ *f* dialling; **~car** *vt/i* dial

**discente** /dʒi'sẽtʃi/ *a* **corpo ~** student body

**discer|nimento** /dʒiserni'mẽtu/ *m* discernment; **~nir** *vt* discern

**discipli|na** /dʒisi'plina/ *f* discipline; **~nador** *a* disciplinary; **~nar** *vt* discipline

**discípulo** /dʒi'sipulu/ *m* disciple

**disc-jóquei** /dʒisk'ʒɔkej/ *m* disc-jockey

**disco** /'dʒisku/ *m* disc; (*de música*) record; (*no atletismo*) discus □ (*fam*) *f* disco; **~ flexível/rígido** floppy/hard disk; **~ laser** CD, compact disc; **~ voador** flying saucer

**discor|dante** /dʒiskor'dãtʃi/ *a* conflicting; **~dar** *vi* disagree (**de** with)

**discote|ca** /dʒisko'tɛka/ *f* discotheque; **~cário** *m* DJ

**discre|pância** /dʒiskre'pãsia/ *f* discrepancy; **~pante** *a* inconsistent; **~par** *vi* diverge (**de** from)

**dis|creto** /dʒis'krɛtu/ *a* discreet; **~crição** *f* discretion

**discrimi|nação** /dʒiskrimina'sãw/ *f* discrimination; (*descrição*) description; **~nar** *vt* discriminate; **~natório** *a* discriminatory

**discur|sar** /dʒiskur'sar/ *vi* speak; **~so** *m* speech

**discussão** /dʒisku'sãw/ *f* discussion; (*briga*) argument

**discu|tir** /dʒisku'tʃir/ *vt/i* discuss; (*brigar*) argue; **~tível** (*pl* **~tíveis**) *a* debatable

**disenteria** /dʒizẽte'ria/ *f* dysentery

**disfar|çar** /dʒisfar'sar/ *vt* disguise; **~çar-se** *vpr* disguise o.s.; **~ce** *m* disguise

**dis|léxico** /dʒiz'lɛtʃiku/ *a* & *m* dyslexic; **~lexia** *f* dyslexia; **~léxico** *a* & *m* dyslexic

**dispa|rada** /dʒispa'rada/ *f* bolt; **~rado** *adv* **o melhor ~rado** the best by a long way; **~rar** *vt* fire <*arma*> □ *vi* (*com arma*) fire; <*preços, inflação*> shoot up; <*corredor*> surge ahead

**disparate** /dʒispa'ratʃi/ *m* piece of nonsense; *pl* nonsense

**dis|pêndio** /dʒis'pẽdʒiu/ *m* expenditure; **~pendioso** /o/ *a* costly

**dispen|sa** /dʒis'pẽsa/ *f* exemption; **~sar** *vt* (*distribuir*) dispense; (*isentar*) exempt (**de** from); (*prescindir de*) dispense with; **~sável** (*pl* **~sáveis**) *a* dispensable

**dispersar** /dʒisper'sar/ *vt* disperse; waste <*energias*> □ *vi*, **~-se** *vpr* disperse

**disperso** /dʒis'pɛrsu/ *adj* scattered

**dispo|nibilidade** /dʒisponibili'dadʒi/ *f* availability; **~nível** (*pl* **~níveis**) *a* available

**dis|por** /dʒis'por/ *vt* arrange □ *vi* **~por de** have at one's disposal; **~por-se** *vpr* form up □ *m* **ao seu ~por** at your disposal; **~posição** *f* (*vontade*) willingness; (*arranjo*) arrangement; (*de espírito*) frame of mind; (*de testamento etc*) provision; **à ~posição de alg** at s.o.'s disposal; **~positivo** *m* device; **~posto** *a* prepared, willing (**a** to)

**dispu|ta** /dʒis'puta/ *f* dispute; **~tar** *vt* dispute; (*tentar ganhar*) compete for

**disquete** /dʒis'ketʃi/ *m* diskette, floppy (disk)

**dissabores** /dʒisa'boris/ *m pl* troubles

**disseminar** /dʒisemi'nar/ *vt* disseminate

**dissertação** /dʒiserta'sãw/ *f* dissertation, lecture

**dissi|dência** /dʒisi'dẽsia/ *f* dissidence; **~dente** *a* & *m* dissident

**dissídio** /dʒi'sidʒiu/ *m* dispute

**dissimular** /dʒisimu'lar/ *vt* hide □ *vi* dissimulate

**disso** = **de** + **isso**

**dissipar** /dʒisi'par/ *vt* clear <*nevoeiro*>; dispel <*dúvidas, suspeitas, ilusões*>; dissipate <*fortuna*>; **~-se** *vpr* <*nevoeiro*> clear; <*dúvidas etc*> be dispelled

**dissolu|ção** /dʒisolu'sãw/ *f* dissolution; **~to** *a* dissolute

**dissolver** /dʒisow'ver/ *vt* dissolve; **~-se** *vpr* dissolve

**dissuadir** /dʒisua'dʒir/ *vt* dissuade (**de** from)

**distância** /dʒis'tãsia/ f distance

**distan|ciar** /dʒistãsi'ar/ vt distance; **~ciar-se** vpr distance o.s.; **~te** a distant

**disten|der** /dʒistẽ'der/ vt stretch <*pernas*>; relax <*músculo*>; **~der-se** vpr relax; **~são** f (*med*) pull; **~são muscular** pulled muscle

**distin|ção** /dʒistʃ'ĩsãw/ f distinction; **~guir** vt distinguish (**de** from); **~guir-se** vpr distinguish o.s.; **~tivo** a distinctive □ m badge; **~to** a distinct; <*senhor*> distinguished

**disto** = **de** + **isto**

**distor|ção** /dʒistor'sãw/ f distortion; **~cer** vt distort

**distra|ção** /dʒistra'sãw/ f distraction; **~ído** a absent-minded; **~ir** vt distract; (*divertir*) amuse; **~ir-se** vpr be distracted; (*divertir-se*) amuse o.s.

**distribu|ição** /dʒistribui'sãw/ f distribution; **~idor** m distributor; **~idora** f distributor, distribution company; **~ir** vt distribute

**distrito** /dʒis'tritu/ m district

**distúrbio** /dʒis'turbiu/ m trouble

**di|tado** /dʒi'tadu/ m dictation; (*provérbio*) saying; **~tador** m dictator; **~tadura** f dictatorship; **~tame** m dictate; **~tar** vt dictate; **~tatorial** (*pl* **~tatoriais**) a dictatorial

**dito** /'dʒitu/ a **~ e feito** no sooner said than done □ m remark

**ditongo** /dʒi'tõgu/ m diphthong

**DIU** /'dʒiu/ m IUD, coil

**diurno** /dʒi'urnu/ a day

**divã** /dʒi'vã/ m couch

**divagar** /dʒiva'gar/ vi digress

**diver|gência** /dʒiver'ʒẽsia/ a divergence; **~gente** a divergent; **~gir** vi diverge (**de** from); **~são** f diversion; (*divertimento*) amusement; **~sidade** f diversity, **~sificar** vt/i diversify; **~so** /ɛ/ a (*diferente*) diverse; *pl* (*vários*) several; **~tido** a (*engraçado*) funny; (*que se curte*) enjoyable; **~timento** m enjoyment, fun; (*um*) amusement; **~tir** vt amuse; **~tir-se** vpr enjoy o.s., have fun

**dívida** /'dʒivida/ f debt; **~ externa** foreign debt

**divi|dendo** /dʒivi'dẽdu/ m dividend; **~dido** a <*pessoa*> torn; **~dir** vt divide; (*compartilhar*) share; **~dir-se** vpr be divided

**divindade** /dʒivĩ'dadʒi/ f divinity

**divino** /dʒi'vinu/ a divine

**divi|sa** /dʒi'viza/ f (*lema*) motto; (*galão*) stripes; (*fronteira*) border; *pl* foreign currency; **~são** f division; **~sória** f partition; **~sório** a dividing

**divorci|ado** /dʒivorsi'adu/ a divorced □ m divorcé (f divorcée); **~ar** vt

divorce; **~ar-se** vpr get divorced; **~ar-se de** divorce

**divórcio** /dʒi'vɔrsiu/ m divorce

**divul|gado** /dʒivuw'gadu/ a widespread; **~gar** vt spread; publish <*notícia*>; divulge <*segredo*>; **~gar-se** vpr be spread

**dizer** /dʒi'zer/ vt say; **~ a alg que** tell sb that; **~ para alg fazer** tell s.o. to do □ vi **~ com** go with; **~-se** vpr claim to be □ m saying

**dizimar** /dʒizi'mar/ vt decimate

**do** = **de** +o

**dó** /dɔ/ m pity; **dar ~** be pitiful; **ter ~ de** feel sorry for

**do|ação** /doa'sãw/ f donation; **~ador** m donor; **~ar** vt donate

**do|bra** /'dɔbra/ f fold; (*de calça*) turn-up, (*Amer*) cuff; **~bradiça** f hinge; **~bradiço** a pliable; **~brado** a (*duplo*) double; **~brar** vt (*duplicar*) double; (*fazer dobra em*) fold; (*curvar*) bend; go round <*esquina*>; ring <*sinos*>; (*Port*) dub <*filme*> □ vi double; <*sinos*> ring; **~brar-se** vpr bend; **~bro** m double

**doca** /'dɔka/ f dock

**doce** /'dɔsi/ a sweet; <*água*> fresh □ m sweet; **~ de leite** fudge

**docente** /do'sẽtʃi/ a teaching; **corpo ~** teaching staff, (*Amer*) faculty

**dó|cil** /'dɔsiw/ (*pl* **~ceis**) a docile

**documen|tação** /dokumẽta'sãw/ f documentation; **~tar** vt document; **~tário** a & m documentary; **~to** m document

**doçura** /do'sura/ f sweetness

**dodói** /do'dɔj/ (*fam*) m **ter ~** have a pain □ a poorly, ill

**doen|ça** /do'ẽsa/ f illness; (*infecciosa, fig*) disease; **~te** a ill; **~tio** a <*criança, aspecto*> sickly; <*interesse, curiosidade*> morbid

**doer** /do'er/ vi hurt; <*cabeça, músculo*> ache

**dog|ma** /'dɔgima/ m dogma; **~mático** a dogmatic

**doido** /'dojdu/ a crazy

**dois** /dojs/ a & m (f **duas**) two

**dólar** /'dɔlar/ m dollar

**dolo|rido** /dolo'ridu/ a sore; **~roso** /o/ a painful

**dom** /dõ/ m gift

**do|mador** /doma'dor/ m tamer; **~mar** vt tame

**doméstica** /do'mɛstʃika/ f housemaid

**domesticar** /domestʃi'kar/ vt domesticate

**doméstico** /do'mɛstʃiku/ a domestic

**domi|ciliar** /domisili'ar/ a home; **~cílio** m home

**domi|nação** /domina'sãw/ f domination; **~nador** a domineering; **~nante** a dominant; **~nar** vt dom-

inate; have a command of <*língua*>;
**~nar-se** *vpr* control o.s.
**domin|go** /do'mĩgu/ *m* Sunday;
**~gueiro** *a* Sunday
**domini|cal** /domini'kaw/ (*pl* **~cais**)
*a* Sunday; **~cano** *a* & *m* Dominican
**domínio** /do'miniu/ *m* command
**dona** /'dona/ *f* owner; **Dona** (*com
nome*) Miss; **~ de casa** *f* housewife
**donativo** /dona'tʃivu/ *m* donation
**donde** /'dõdʒi/ *adv* from where; (*motivo*) from whence
**dono** /'donu/ *m* owner
**donzela** /dõ'zɛla/ *f* maiden
**dopar** /do'par/ *vt* drug
**dor** /dor/ *f* pain; (*menos aguda*) ache;
**~ de cabeça** headache
**dor|mente** /dor'mẽtʃi/ *a* numb □ *m*
sleeper; **~mida** *f* sleep; **~minhoco**
/o/ *m* sleepyhead; **~mir** *vi* sleep;
**~mitar** *vi* doze; **~mitório** *m* bedroom; (*comunitário*) dormitory
**dorso** /'dorsu/ *m* back; (*de livro*) spine
**dos = de + os**
**do|sagem** /do'zaʒẽ/ *f* dosage; **~sar** *vt*
moderate; **~se** /ɔ/ *f* dose; (*de uísque
etc*) shot, measure
**dossiê** /dosi'e/ *m* file
**do|tação** /dota'sãw/ *f* endowment;
**~tado** *a* gifted; **~tado de** endowed
with; **~tar** *vt* endow (**de** with); **~te**
/ɔ/ *m* (*de noiva*) dowry; (*dom*) endowment
**dou|rado** /do'radu/ *a* (*de cor*) golden;
(*revestido de ouro*) gilded, gilt □ *m* gilt;
**~rar** *vt* gild
**dou|to** /'dotu/ *a* learned; **~tor** *m*
doctor; **~torado** *m* doctorate, PhD;
**~trina** *f* doctrine; **~trinar** *vt* indoctrinate
**doze** /'dozi/ *a* & *m* twelve
**dragão** /dra'gãw/ *m* dragon
**dragar** /dra'gar/ *vt* dredge
**drágea** /'draʒia/ *f* lozenge
**dra|ma** /'drama/ *m* drama; **~malhão**
*m* melodrama; **~mático** *a* dramatic;
**~matizar** *vt* dramatize; **~maturgo**
*m* dramatist, playwright
**drapeado** /drapi'adu/ *a* draped
**drástico** /'drastʃiku/ *a* drastic
**dre|nagem** /dre'naʒẽ/ *f* drainage;
**~nar** *vt* drain; **~no** /ɛ/ *m* drain
**driblar** /dri'blar/ *vt* (*em futebol*)
dribble round, beat; (*fig*) get round
**drinque** /'drĩki/ *m* drink
**drive** /'drajvi/ *m* disk drive
**dro|ga** /'drɔga/ *f* drug; (*fam*) (*coisa
sem valor*) dead loss; (*coisa chata*)
drag □ *int* damn; **~gado** *a* on drugs
□ *m* drug addict; **~gar** *vt* drug;
**~gar-se** *vpr* take drugs; **~garia** *f*
dispensing chemist's, pharmacy
**duas** /'duas/ *veja* **dois**
**dúbio** /'dubiu/ *a* dubious

**dub|lagem** /du'blaʒẽ/ *f* dubbing;
**~lar** *vt* dub <*filme*>; mime
<*música*>; **~lê** *m* double
**ducentésimo** /dusẽ'tɛzimu/ *a* two-
hundredth
**ducha** /'duʃa/ *f* shower
**ducto** /'duktu/ *m* duct
**duelo** /du'ɛlu/ *m* duel
**duende** /du'ẽdʒi/ *m* elf
**dueto** /du'etu/ *m* duet
**duna** /'duna/ *f* dune
**duodécimo** /duo'dɛsimu/ *a* twelfth
**duodeno** /duo'dɛnu/ *m* duodenum
**dupla** /'dupla/ *f* pair, duo; <*no tênis*>
doubles
**duplex** /du'plɛks/ *a invar* two-floor □
*m invar* two-floor apartment, (*Amer*)
duplex
**dupli|car** /dupli'kar/ *vt/i* double;
**~cidade** *f* duplicity; **~cata** *f* duplicate
**duplo** /'duplu/ *a* double
**duque** /'duki/ *m* duke; **~sa** /e/ *f* duchess
**du|ração** /dura'sãw/ *f* duration;
**~radouro** *a* lasting; **~rante** *prep*
during; **~rar** *vi* last; **~rável** (*pl
~ráveis*) *a* durable
**durex** /du'rɛks/ *m invar* sellotape
**du|reza** /du'reza/ *f* hardness; **~ro** *a*
hard; (*fam: sem dinheiro*) hard up,
broke
**dúvida** /'duvida/ *f* doubt; (*pergunta*)
query
**duvi|dar** /duvi'dar/ *vt/i* doubt;
**~doso** /o/ *a* doubtful
**duzentos** /du'zẽtus/ *a* & *m* two hundred
**dúzia** /'duzia/ *f* dozen

# E

**e** /i/ *conj* and
**ébano** /'ɛbanu/ *m* ebony
**ébrio** /'ɛbriu/ *a* drunk □ *m* drunkard
**ebulição** /ebuli'sãw/ *f* boiling
**eclesiástico** /eklezi'astʃiku/ *a* ecclesiastical
**eclético** /e'klɛtʃiku/ *a* eclectic
**eclip|sar** /eklip'sar/ *vt* eclipse; **~se** *m*
eclipse
**eclodir** /eklo'dʒir/ *vi* emerge; (*estourar*) break out; open
**eco** /'ɛku/ *m* echo; **ter ~** have
repercussions; **~ar** *vt/i* echo
**eco|logia** /ekolo'ʒia/ *f* ecology;
**~lógico** *a* ecological; **~logista** *m/f*
ecologist
**eco|nomia** /ekono'mia/ *f* economy;
(*ciência*) economics; *pl* (*dinheiro poupado*) savings; **~nômico** *a* economic;
(*rentável, barato*) economical; **~nomista** *m/f* economist; **~nomizar** *vt*
save □ *vi* economize

**écran** /ɛ'krã/ (*Port*) *m* screen
**eczema** /ek'zema/ *m* eczema
**edição** /edʒi'sãw/ *f* edition; (*de filmes*) editing
**edificante** /edʒifi'kãtʃi/ *a* edifying
**edifício** /edʒi'fisiu/ *m* building
**Edimburgo** /edʒĩ'burgu/ *f* Edinburgh
**edi|tal** /edʒi'taw/ (*pl* ~tais) *m* announcement; ~tar *vt* publish; (*comput*) edit; ~to *m* edict; ~tor *m* publisher; ~tora *f* publishing company; ~torial (*pl* ~toriais) *a* publishing □ *m* editorial
**edredom** /edre'dõ/ *m*, (*Port*) **edredão** /edre'dãw/ *m* quilt
**educa|ção** /eduka'sãw/ *f* (*ensino*) education; (*polidez*) good manners; **é falta de** ~ção it's rude; ~cional (*pl* ~cionais) *a* education
**edu|cado** /edu'kadu/ *a* polite; ~car *vt* educate; ~cativo *a* educational
**efeito** /e'fejtu/ *m* effect; **fazer** ~ have an effect; **para todos os** ~s to all intents and purposes; ~ **colateral** side effect; ~ **estufa** greenhouse effect
**efêmero** /e'fêmeru/ *a* ephemeral
**efeminado** /efemi'nadu/ *a* effeminate
**efervescente** /eferve'stʃi/ *a* effervescent
**efe|tivar** /efetʃi'var/ *vt* bring into effect; (*contratar*) make a permanent member of staff; ~tivo *a* real, effective; <*cargo, empregado*> permanent; ~tuar *vt* carry out, effect
**efi|cácia** /efi'kasia/ *f* effectiveness; ~caz *a* effective
**efici|ência** /efisi'ẽsia/ *f* efficiency; ~ente *a* efficient
**efígie** /e'fiɡi/ *f* effigy
**efusivo** /efu'zivu/ *a* effusive
**Egeu** /e'ʒew/ *a & m* Aegean
**égide** /'ɛʒidʒi/ *f* aegis
**egípcio** /e'ʒipsiu/ *a & m* Egyptian
**Egito** /e'ʒitu/ *m* Egypt
**ego** /'ɛɡu/ *m* ego; ~cêntrico *a* self-centred, egocentric; ~ísmo *m* selfishness; ~ísta *a* selfish □ *m/f* egoist □ *m* (*de rádio etc*) earplug
**égua** /'ɛɡwa/ *f* mare
**eis** /ejs/ *adv* (*aqui está*) here is/are; (*isso é*) that is
**eixo** /'ejʃu/ *m* axle; (*mat, entre cidades*) axis; **pôr nos** ~s set straight
**ela** /'ɛla/ *pron* she; (*coisa*) it; (*com preposição*) her; (*coisa*) it
**elaborar** /elabo'rar/ *vt* (*fazer*) make, produce; (*desenvolver*) work out
**elasticidade** /elastʃisi'dadʒi/ *f* (*de coisa*) elasticity; (*de pessoa*) suppleness
**elástico** /e'lastʃiku/ *a* elastic □ *m* (*de borracha*) elastic band; (*de calcinha etc*) elastic
**ele** /'eli/ *pron* he; (*coisa*) it; (*com preposição*) him; (*coisa*) it

**electr-** (*Port*) *veja* **eletr-**
**eléctrico** /i'lɛktriku/ (*Port*) *m* tram, (*Amer*) streetcar □ *a veja* **elétrico**
**elefante** /ele'fãtʃi/ *m* elephant
**ele|gância** /ele'gãsia/ *f* elegance; ~gante *a* elegant
**eleger** /ele'ʒer/ *vt* elect; ~-se *vpr* get elected
**elegia** /ele'ʒia/ *f* elegy
**elei|ção** /elej'sãw/ *f* election; ~to *a* elected, elect; <*povo*> chosen; ~tor *m* voter; ~torado *m* electorate; ~toral (*pl* ~torais) *a* electoral
**elemen|tar** /elemẽ'tar/ *a* elementary; ~to *m* element
**elenco** /e'lẽku/ *m* (*de filme, peça*) cast
**eletri|cidade** /eletrisi'dadʒi/ *f* electricity; ~cista *m/f* electrician
**elétrico** /e'lɛtriku/ *a* electric
**eletri|ficar** /eletrifi'kar/ *vt* electrify; ~zar *vt* electrify
**eletro** /e'lɛtru/ *m* ECG; ~cutar *vt* electrocute; ~do /o/ *m* electrode; ~domésticos *m pl* electrical appliances
**eletrôni|ca** /ele'tronika/ *f* electronics; ~co *a* electronic
**ele|vação** /eleva'sãw/ *f* elevation; (*aumento*) rise; ~vado *a* high; <*sentimento, estilo*> elevated; ~vador *m* lift, (*Amer*) elevator; ~var *vt* raise; (*promover*) elevate; ~var-se *vpr* rise
**elimi|nar** /elimi'nar/ *vt* eliminate; ~natória *f* heat; ~natório *a* eliminatory
**elipse** /e'lipsi/ *f* ellipse
**elíptico** /e'liptʃiku/ *a* elliptical
**eli|te** /e'litʃi/ *f* elite; ~tismo *m* elitism; ~tista *a & m/f* elitist
**elmo** /'ɛwmu/ *m* helmet
**elo** /'ɛlu/ *m* link
**elo|giar** /eloʒi'ar/ *vt* praise; ~giar **alg por** compliment s.o. on; ~gio *m* (*louvor*) praise; (*um*) compliment; ~gioso /o/ *a* complimentary
**elo|quência** /elo'kwẽsia/ *f* eloquence; ~quente *a* eloquent
**eluci|dar** /elusi'dar/ *vt* elucidate; ~dativo *a* elucidating
**em** /j/ *prep* in; (*sobre*) on; **ela está no Eduardo** she's at Eduardo's (house); **de casa** ~ **casa** from house to house; **aumentar** ~ **10%** increase by 10%
**emagre|cer** /emagre'ser/ *vi* lose weight, get thinner □ *vt* make thinner; ~cimento *m* slimming
**emanar** /ema'nar/ *vi* emanate (**de** from)
**emanci|pação** /emãsipa'sãw/ *f* emancipation; ~par *vt* emancipate; ~par-se *vpr* become emancipated
**emara|nhado** /emara'nadu/ *a* tangled □ *m* tangle; ~nhar *vt* tangle; (*envolver*) entangle; ~nhar-se *vpr* get

tangled up; (*envolver-se*) become entangled (*em in*)

**embaçar** /ība'sar/, (*Port*) **embaciar** /ībasi'ar/ *vt* steam up <*vidro*> □ *vi* <*vidro*> steam up; <*olhos*> grow misty

**embainhar** /ībaȝ'ɲar/ *vt* hem <*vestido, calça*>

**embaixa|da** /ība'ʃada/ *f* embassy; ~**dor** *m* ambassador; ~**triz** *f* ambassador; (*esposa*) ambassador's wife

**embaixo** /ī'baʃu/ *adv* underneath; (*em casa*) downstairs; ~ **de** under

**emba|lagem** /ība'laȝē/ *f* packaging; ~**lar**[1] *vt* pack

**emba|lar**[2] /ība'lar/ *vt* rock <*criança*>; ~**lo** *m* (*fig*) excitement, thrill

**embalsamar** /ībawsa'mar/ *vt* embalm

**embara|çar** /ībara'sar/ *vt* embarrass; ~**çar-se** *vpr* get embarrassed (*com by*); ~**ço** *m* embarrassment; ~**çoso** /o/ *a* embarrassing

**embaralhar** /ībara'ʎar/ *vt* muddle up; shuffle <*cartas*>; ~**-se** *vpr* get muddled up

**embar|cação** /ībarka'sãw/ *f* vessel; ~**cadouro** *m* wharf; ~**car** *vt/i* board, embark

**embar|gado** /ībar'gadu/ *a* <*voz*> faltering; ~**go** *m* embargo

**embarque** /ī'barki/ *m* boarding; (*seção do aeroporto*) departures

**embasba|cado** /ībazba'kadu/ *a* openmouthed; ~**car-se** *vpr* be left openmouthed

**embate** /ī'batʃi/ *m* (*de carros etc*) crash; (*fig*) clash

**embebedar** /ībebe'dar/ *vt* make drunk; ~**-se** *vpr* get drunk

**embeber** /ībe'ber/ *vt* soak; ~**-se de** soak up; ~**-se em** get absorbed in

**embele|zador** /ībeleza'dor/ *a* <*cirurgia*> cosmetic; ~**zar** *vt* embellish; spruce up <*casa*>; ~**zar-se** *vpr* make o.s. beautiful

**embevecer** /ībeve'ser/ *vt* captivate, engross; ~**-se** *vpr* get engrossed, be captivated

**emblema** /ē'blema/ *m* emblem

**embocadura** /ī boka'dura/ *f* (*de instrumento*) mouthpiece; (*de freio*) bit; (*de rio*) mouth; (*de rua*) entrance

**êmbolo** /'ēbulu/ *m* piston

**embolsar** /ībow'sar/ *vt* pocket; (*reembolsar*) reimburse

**embora** /ī'bɔra/ *adv* away □ *conj* although

**emborcar** /ībor'kar/ *vi* overturn; <*barco*> capsize

**emboscada** /ībos'kada/ *f* ambush

**embrai|agem** /ībraj'aȝē/ (*Port*) *f veja* **embreagem**; ~**ar** (*Port*) *vi veja* **embrear**

**embre|agem** /ēbri'aȝe/ *f* clutch; ~**ar** *vi* let in the clutch

**embria|gar** /ēbria'gar/ *vt* intoxicate; ~**gar-se** *vpr* get drunk, become intoxicated; ~**guez** /e/ *f* drunkenness; ~**guez no volante** drunken driving

**embri|ão** /ēbri'āw/ *m* embryo; ~**onário** *a* embryonic

**embro|mação** /ībroma'sãw/ *f* flannel; ~**mar** *vt* flannel, string along; (*enganar*) con □ *vi* stall, drag one's feet

**embru|lhada** /ībru'ʎada/ *f* muddle; ~**lhar** *vt* wrap up <*pacote*>; upset <*estômago*>; (*confundir*) muddle up; ~**lhar-se** *vpr* <*pessoa*> get muddled up; ~**lho** *m* parcel; (*fig*) mix-up

**embur|rado** /ību'xadu/ *a* sulky; ~**rar** *vi* sulk

**embuste** /ī'bustʃi/ *m* hoax, put-up job

**embu|tido** /ību'tʃidu/ *a* built-in, fitted; ~**tir** *vt* build in, fit

**emen|da** /e'mēda/ *f* correction, improvement; (*de lei*) amendment; ~**dar** *vt* correct; amend <*lei*>; ~**dar-se** *vpr* mend one's ways

**ementa** /i'mēta/ (*Port*) *f* menu

**emer|gência** /emer'ȝēsia/ *f* emergency; ~**gente** *a* emergent; ~**gir** *vi* surface

**emi|gração** /emigra'sãw/ *f* emigration; (*de aves etc*) migration; ~**grado** *a* & *m* émigré; ~**grante** *a* & *m/f* emigrant; ~**grar** *vi* emigrate; <*aves, animais*> migrate

**emi|nência** /emi'nēsia/ *f* eminence; ~**nente** *a* eminent

**emis|são** /emi'sãw/ *f* (*de ações etc*) issue; (*na rádio, TV*) transmission, broadcast; (*de som, gases*) emission; ~**sário** *m* emissary; ~**sor** *m* transmitter; ~**sora** *f* (*de rádio*) radio station; (*de TV*) TV station

**emitir** /emi'tʃir/ *vt* issue <*ações, selos etc*>; emit <*sons*>; (*pela rádio, TV*) transmit, broadcast

**emoção** /emo'sãw/ *f* emotion; (*excitação*) excitement

**emocio|nal** /emosio'naw/ (*pl* ~**nais**) *a* emotional; ~**nante** *a* (*excitante*) exciting; (*comovente*) touching, emotional; ~**nar** *vt* (*excitar*) excite; (*comover*) move, touch; ~**nar-se** *vpr* get emotional

**emoldurar** /emowdu'rar/ *vt* frame

**emotivo** /emo'tʃivu/ *a* emotional

**empacar** /īpa'kar/ *vi* <*cavalo*> baulk; <*negociações etc*> grind to a halt; <*orador*> dry up

**empacotar** /īpako'tar/ *vt* pack up; (*pôr em pacotes*) packet

**empa|da** /ē'pada/ *f* pie; ~**dão** *m* (large) pie

**empalhar** /īpa'ʎar/ *vt* stuff

**empalidecer** /īpalide'ser/ *vi* turn pale

empanar¹ /ẽpa'nar/ vt tarnish, dull

empanar² /ẽpa'nar/ vt cook in batter <carne etc>

empanturrar /ĩpãtu'xar/ vt stuff; ~-se vpr stuff o.s. (de with)

empapar /ĩpa'par/ vt soak

empa|tar /ẽpa'tar/ vt draw <jogo> □ vi <times> draw; <corredores> tie; ~te m (em jogo) draw; (em corrida, votação) tie; (em xadrez, fig) stalemate

empatia /ẽpa'tʃia/ f empathy

empecilho /ẽpe'siʎu/ m hindrance

empenar /ẽpe'nar/ vt/i warp

empe|nhar /ĩpe'ɲar/ vt (penhorar) pawn; (prometer) pledge; ~nhar-se vpr do one's utmost (em to); ~nho /e/ (compromisso) pledge; (diligência) effort, commitment

emperrar /ĩpe'xar/ vt make stick □ vi stick

emperti|gado /ĩpertʃi'gadu/ a upright; ~gar-se vpr stand up straight

empilhar /ĩpi'ʎar/ vt pile up

empi|nado /ĩpi'nadu/ a erect; (íngreme) sheer, steep; <nariz> turned-up; (fig) stuck-up; ~nar vt stand up-right; fly <pipa>; tip up <copo>

empírico /ẽ'piriku/ a empirical

emplacar /ĩpla'kar/ vt notch up <pontos, sucessos, anos>; license <carro>

emplastro /ĩ'plastru/ m surgical plaster; ~ de nicotina nicotine patch

empobre|cer /ĩpobre'ser/ vt impoverish; ~cimento m impoverishment

empoleirar /ĩpole'rar/ vt perch; ~-se vpr perch

empol|gação /ĩpowga'sãw/ f fascination; ~gante a fascinating; ~gar vt fascinate

empossar /ĩpo'sar/ vt swear in

empreen|dedor /ẽpriẽde'dor/ a enterprising □ m entrepreneur; ~der vt undertake; ~dimento m undertaking

empre|gada /ĩpre'gada/ f (doméstica) maid; ~gado m employee; ~gador m employer; ~gar vt employ; ~gar-se vpr get a job; ~gatício a vínculo ~gatício contract of employment; ~go /e/ m (trabalho) job; (uso) use; ~guismo m patronage

emprei|tada /ĩprej'tada/ f commission, contract; (empreendimento) venture; ~teira f contractor, firm of contractors; ~teiro m contractor

empre|sa /ĩ'preza/ f company; ~sariado m business community; ~sarial (pl ~sariais) a business; ~sário m businessman; (de cantor etc) manager

empres|tado /ĩpres'tadu/ a on loan; pedir ~tado (ask to) borrow; tomar ~tado borrow; ~tar vt lend

empréstimo /ĩ'prestʃimu/ m loan

empur|rão /ĩpu'xãw/ m push; ~rar vt push

emular /emu'lar/ vt emulate

enamorado /enamo'radu/ a (apaixonado) in love

encabeçar /ĩkabe'sar/ vt head

encabu|lado /ĩkabu'ladu/ a shy; ~lar vt embarrass; ~lar-se vpr be shy

encadear /ĩkade'ar/ vt chain ou link together

encader|nação /ĩkaderna'sãw/ f binding; ~nado a bound; (com capa dura) hardback; ~nar vt bind

encai|xar /ĩka'ʃar/ vt/i fit; ~xe m (cavidade) socket; (juntura) joint

encalço /ĩ'kawsu/ m pursuit; no ~ de in pursuit of

encalhar /ĩka'ʎar/ vi <barco> run aground; (fig) get bogged down; <mercadoria> not sell; (fam: ficar solteiro) be left on the shelf

encaminhar /ĩkami'ɲar/ vt (dirigir) steer, direct; (remeter) pass on; set in motion <processo>; ~-se vpr set out

encana|dor /ĩkana'dor/ m plumber; ~mento m plumbing

encan|tador /ĩkãta'dor/ a enchanting; ~tamento m enchantment; ~tar vt enchant; ~to m charm

encaraco|lado /ĩkarako'ladu/ a curly; ~lar vt curl; ~lar-se vpr curl up

encarar /ĩka'rar/ vt confront, face

encarcerar /ĩkarse'rar/ vt imprison

encardido /ĩkar'dʒidu/ a grimy

encarecidamente /ĩkaresida'mẽtʃi/ adv insistently

encargo /ĩ'kargu/ m task, responsibility

encar|nação /ĩkarna'sãw/ f (do espírito) incarnation; (de um personagem) embodiment; ~nar vt embody; play <papel>

encarre|gado /ĩkaxe'gadu/ a in charge (de of) □ m person in charge; (de operários) foreman; ~gado de negócios chargé d'affaires; ~gar vt ~gar alg de put s.o. in charge of; ~gar-se de undertake to

encarte /ĩ'kartʃi/ m insert

ence|nação /ĩsena'sãw/ f (de peça) production; (fingimento) playacting; ~nar vt put on ou it on

ence|radeira /ĩsera'dera/ f floor polisher; ~rar vt wax

encer|rado /ĩse'xadu/ a <assunto> closed; ~ramento m close; ~rar vt close; ~rar-se vpr close

encharcar /ĩʃar'kar/ vt soak

en|chente /ẽ'ʃẽtʃi/ f flood; ~cher vt fill; (fam) annoy □ (fam) vi be annoying; ~cher-se vpr fill up; (fam: fartar-se) get fed up (de with)

**enciclopédia** /ẽsiklo'pɛdʒia/ f encyclopaedia

**enco|berto** /ĩko'bɛrtu/ a <céu, tempo> overcast; **~brir** vt cover up □ vi <tempo> become overcast

**encolher** /ĩko'ʎer/ vt shrug <ombros>; pull up <pernas>; shrink <roupa> □ vi <roupa> shrink; **~se** vpr (de medo) shrink; (de frio) huddle; (espremer-se) squeeze up

**encomen|da** /ĩko'mẽda/ f order; **de** ou **sob ~da** to order; **~dar** vt order (a from)

**encon|trão** /ĩkõ'trãw/ m bump; (empurrão) shove; **~trar** vt (achar) find; (ver) meet; **~trar com** meet; **~trar-se** vpr (ver-se) meet; (estar) be; **~tro** m meeting; (mil) encounter; **ir ao ~tro de** go to meet; (fig) meet; **ir de ~tro a** run into; (fig) go up against

**encorajar** /ĩkora'ʒar/ vt encourage

**encor|pado** /ĩkor'padu/ a stocky; <vinho> full-bodied; **~par** vt/i fill out

**encos|ta** /ĩ'kɔsta/ f slope; **~tar** vt (apoiar) lean; park <carro>; leave on the latch <porta>; (pôr de lado) put aside □ vi <carro> pull in; **~tar-se** vpr lean; **~to** /o/ m back

**encra|vado** /ĩkra'vadu/ a <unha, pêlo> ingrowing; **~var** vt stick

**encren|ca** /ĩ'krẽka/ f fix, jam; pl trouble; **~car** vt get into trouble <pessoa>; complicate <situação> □ vi <situação> get complicated; <carro> break down; **~car-se** vpr <pessoa> get into trouble; **~queiro** m troublemaker

**encres|pado** /ĩkres'padu/ a <mar> choppy; **~par** vt frizz <cabelo>; **~par-se** vpr <cabelo> go frizzy; <mar> get choppy

**encruzilhada** /ĩkruzi'ʎada/ f crossroads

**encurralar** /ĩkuxa'lar/ vt hem in, pen in

**encurtar** /ĩkur'tar/ vt shorten

**endere|çar** /ĩdere'sar/ vt address; **~ço** /e/ m address

**endinheirado** /ĩdʒiɲe'radu/ a well-off

**endireitar** /ĩdʒirej'tar/ vt straighten; **~se** vpr straighten up

**endivi|dado** /ĩdʒivi'dadu/ a in debt; **~dar** vt put into debt; **~dar-se** vpr get into debt

**endoidecer** /ĩdojde'ser/ vi get mad

**endos|sar** /ĩdo'sar/ vt endorse; **~so** /o/ m endorsement

**endurecer** /ĩdure'ser/ vt/i harden

**ener|gético** /ener'ʒɛtʃiku/ a energy; **~gia** f energy

**enérgico** /e'nɛrʒiku/ a vigorous; <remédio, discurso> powerful

**enevoado** /enevu'adu/ a (com névoa) misty; (com nuvens) cloudy

**enfarte** /ĩ'fartʃi/ m heart attack

**ênfase** /'ẽfazi/ f emphasis; **dar ~ a** emphasize

**enfático** /ẽ'fatʃiku/ a emphatic

**enfatizar** /ẽfatʃi'zar/ vt emphasize

**enfei|tar** /ĩfej'tar/ vt decorate; **~tar-se** vpr dress up; **~te** m decoration

**enfeitiçar** /ĩfejtʃi'sar/ vt bewitch

**enfer|magem** /ĩfer'maʒẽ/ f nursing; **~maria** f ward; **~meira** f nurse; **~meiro** m male nurse; **~midade** f illness; **~mo** a sick □ m patient

**enferru|jado** /ĩfexu'ʒadu/ a rusty; **~jar** vt/i rust

**enfezado** /ĩfe'zadu/ a bad-tempered

**enfiar** /ẽfi'ar/ vt put; slip on <roupa>; thread <agulha>; string <pérolas>

**enfileirar** /ĩfilej'rar/ vt line up; **~se** vpr line up

**enfim** /ẽ'fĩ/ adv (finalmente) finally; (resumindo) anyway

**enfo|car** /ĩfo'kar/ vt tackle; **~que** m approach

**enfor|camento** /ĩforka'mẽtu/ m hanging; **~car** vt hang; **~car-se** vpr hang o.s.

**enfraquecer** /ĩfrake'ser/ vt/i weaken

**enfrentar** /ĩfrẽ'tar/ vt face

**enfumaçado** /ĩfuma'sadu/ a smoky

**enfurecer** /ĩfure'ser/ vt infuriate; **~se** vpr get furious

**enga|jamento** /ĩgaʒa'mẽtu/ m commitment; **~jado** a committed; **~jar-se** vpr get involved (em in)

**engalfinhar-se** /ĩgawfi'ɲarsi/ vpr grapple

**enga|nado** /ĩga'nadu/ a (errado) mistaken; **~nar** vt deceive; cheat on <marido, esposa>; stave off <fome>; **~nar-se** vpr be mistaken; **~no** m (erro) mistake; (desonestidade) deception

**engarra|famento** /ĩgaxafa'mẽtu/ m traffic jam; **~far** vt bottle <vinho etc>; block <trânsito>

**engas|gar** /ĩgaz'gar/ vt choke □ vi choke; <motor> backfire; **~go** m choking

**engastar** /ĩgaʃ'tar/ vt set <jóias>

**engatar** /ĩga'tar/ vt hitch <reboque etc> (a to); engage <marcha>

**engatinhar** /ĩgatʃi'ɲar/ vi crawl; (fig) start out

**engave|tamento** /ĩgaveta'mẽtu/ m pile-up; **~tar** vt shelve

**engelhar** /ĩʒe'ʎar/ vi (pele) wrinkle

**enge|nharia** /ĩʒeɲa'ria/ f engineering; **~nheiro** m engineer; **~nho** /e/ m (de pessoa) ingenuity; (de açúcar) sugar mill; (máquina) device; **~nhoca** /ɔ/ f gadget; **~nhoso** a ingenious

**engessar** /ĩʒe'sar/ *vt* put in plaster

**engodo** /ĩ'godu/ *m* lure

**engolir** /ĩgo'lir/ *vt/i* swallow; ~ **em seco** gulp

**engomar** /ĩgo'mar/ *vt* press; (*com goma*) starch

**engordar** /ĩgor'dar/ *vt* make fat; fatten <*animais*> □ *vi* <*pessoa*> put on weight; <*comida*> be fattening

**engraçado** /ĩgra'sadu/ *a* funny

**engradado** /ĩgra'dadu/ *m* crate

**engravidar** /ĩgravi'dar/ *vt* make pregnant □ *vi* get pregnant

**engraxar** /ĩgra'ʃar/ *vt* polish

**engre|nado** /ĩgre'nadu/ *a* <*carro*> in gear; ~**nagem** *f* gear; (*fig*) mechanism; ~**nar** *vt* put into gear <*carro*>; strike up <*conversa*>; ~**nar-se** *vpr* mesh; (*fig*) <*pessoas*> get on

**engrossar** /ĩgro'sar/ *vt* thicken; raise <*voz*> □ *vi* thicken; <*pessoa*> turn nasty

**enguia** /ẽ'gia/ *f* eel

**engui|çar** /ẽgi'sar/ *vi* break down; ~**ço** *m* breakdown

**enig|ma** /e'nigima/ *m* enigma; ~**mático** *a* enigmatic

**enjaular** /ĩʒaw'lar/ *vt* cage

**enjo|ar** /ĩʒo'ar/ *vt* sicken □ *vi*, ~**ar-se** *vpr* get sick (**de** *of*); ~**ativo** *a* <*comida*> sickly; <*livro etc*> boring

**enjôo** /ĩ'ʒou/ *m* sickness

**enlameado** /ĩlami'adu/ *a* muddy

**enlatado** /ĩla'tadu/ *a* tinned, canned; ~**s** *m pl* tinned foods

**enle|var** /ẽle'var/ *vt* enthral; ~**vo** /e/ *m* rapture

**enlouquecer** /ĩloke'ser/ *vt* drive mad □ *vi* go mad

**enluarado** /ĩlua'radu/ *a* moonlit

**enor|me** /e'normi/ *a* enormous; ~**midade** *f* enormity

**enquadrar** /ĩkwa'drar/ *vt* fit □ *vi*, ~**se** *vpr* fit in

**enquanto** /ĩ'kwãtu/ *conj* while; ~ **isso** meanwhile; **por** ~ for the time being

**enquête** /ã'kɛtʃi/ *f* survey

**enraivecer** /ĩxajve'ser/ *vt* enrage

**enredo** /ẽ'redu/ *m* plot

**enrijecer** /ĩxiʒe'ser/ *vt* stiffen; ~**se** *vpr* stiffen

**enrique|cer** /ĩxike'ser/ *vt* (*dar dinheiro a*) make rich; (*fig*) enrich □ *vi* get rich; ~**cimento** *m* enrichment

**enro|lado** /ĩxo'ladu/ *a* complicated; ~**lar** *vt* (*envolver*) roll up; (*complicar*) complicate; (*enganar*) cheat; ~**lar-se** *vpr* (*envolver-se*) roll up; (*confundir-se*) get mixed up

**enroscar** /ĩxos'kar/ *vt* twist

**enrouquecer** /ĩxoke'ser/ *vi* go hoarse

**enrugar** /ĩxu'gar/ *vt* wrinkle <*pele, tecido*>; furrow <*testa*>

**enrustido** /ĩxus'tʃidu/ *a* repressed

**ensaboar** /ĩsabo'ar/ *vt* soap

**ensai|ar** /ĩsaj'ar/ *vt* (*provar*) try out; (*repetir*) rehearse; ~**o** *m* (*prova*) test; (*repetição*) rehearsal; (*escrito*) essay

**ensangüentado** /ĩsãgwẽ'tadu/ *a* bloody, bloodstained

**enseada** /ĩsi'ada/ *f* inlet

**ensebado** /ĩse'badu/ *a* greasy

**ensimesmado** /ĩsimez'madu/ *a* lost in thought

**ensi|nar** /ĩsi'nar/ *vt/i* teach (**aco a alg** *s.o. sth*); ~**nar alg a nadar** teach s.o. to swim; ~**no** *m* teaching; (*em geral*) education

**ensolarado** /ĩsola'radu/ *a* sunny

**enso|pado** /ĩso'padu/ *a* soaked □ *m* stew; ~**par** *vt* soak

**ensurde|cedor** /ĩsurdese'dor/ *a* deafening; ~**cer** *vt* deafen □ *vi* go deaf

**entabular** /ĩtabu'lar/ *vt* open, start

**entalar** /ĩta'lar/ *vt* wedge, jam; (*em apertos*) get; ~**se** *vpr* get wedged, get jammed; (*em apertos*) get caught up

**entalhar** /ĩta'ʎar/ *vt* carve

**entanto** /ĩ'tãtu/ *m* **no** ~ however

**então** /ĩ'tãw/ *adv* then; (*nesse caso*) so

**entardecer** /ĩtarde'ser/ *m* sunset

**ente** /'ẽtʃi/ *m* being

**entea|da** /ẽtʃi'ada/ *f* stepdaughter; ~**do** *m* stepson

**entedi|ante** /ĩtedʒi'ãtʃi/ *a* boring; ~**ar** *vt* bore; ~**ar-se** *vpr* get bored

**enten|der** /ĩtẽ'der/ *vt* understand; ~**der-se** *vpr* (*dar-se bem*) get on (**com** *with*); **dar a** ~ **der** give to understand; ~**der de futebol** know about football; ~**dimento** *m* understanding

**enternecedor** /ĩternese'dor/ *a* touching

**enter|rar** /ĩte'xar/ *vt* bury; ~**ro** /e/ *m* burial; (*cerimônia*) funeral

**entidade** /ĩtʃi'dadʒi/ *f* entity; (*órgão*) body

**entornar** /ĩtor'nar/ *vt* tip over, spill

**entorpe|cente** /ĩtorpe'sẽtʃi/ *m* drug, narcotic; ~**cer** *vt* numb

**entortar** /ĩtor'tar/ *vt* make crooked

**entrada** /ẽ'trada/ *f* entry; (*onde se entra*) entrance; (*bilhete*) ticket; (*prato*) starter; (*pagamento*) deposit; *pl* (*no cabelo*) receding hairline; **dar** ~ **a** enter; ~ **proibida** no entry

**entranhas** /ĩ'traɲas/ *f pl* entrails

**entrar** /ẽ'trar/ *vi* go/come in; ~ **com** enter <*dados*>; put in <*dinheiro*>; ~ **em detalhes** go into details; ~ **em vigor** come into force

**entravar** /ẽtra'var/ *vt* hamper

**entre** /'ẽtri/ *prep* between; (*em meio a*) among

**entreaberto** /ẽtria'bɛrtu/ *a* half-open

**entrecortar** /ẽtrikor'tar/ *vt* intersperse; (*cruzar*) intersect

**entre|ga** /ĩ'trɛga/ *f* delivery; (*rendição*) surrender; **~ga a domicílio** home delivery; **~gar** *vt* hand over; deliver <*mercadorias, cartas*>; hand in <*caderno, trabalho escolar*>; **~gar-se** *vpr* give o.s. up (**a** to); **~gue** *pp de* **entregar**

**entrelaçar** /ẽtrela'sar/ *vt* intertwine; clasp <*mãos*>

**entrelinhas** /ẽtri'liɲas/ *f pl* **ler nas ~** read between the lines

**entremear** /ẽtrimi'ar/ *vt* intersperse

**entreolhar-se** /ẽtrio'ʎarsi/ *vpr* look at one another

**entretanto** /ẽtre'tãtu/ *conj* however

**entre|tenimento** /ẽtreteni'mẽtu/ *m* entertainment; **~ter** *vt* entertain

**entrever** /ẽtre'ver/ *vt* glimpse

**entrevis|ta** /ẽtre'vista/ *f* interview; **~tador** *m* interviewer; **~tar** *vt* interview

**entristecer** /ĩtriste'ser/ *vt* sadden □ *vi* be saddened (**com** by)

**entroncamento** /ĩtrõka'mẽtu/ *m* junction

**entrosar** /ĩtro'zar/ *vt/i* integrate

**entu|lhar** /ĩtu'ʎar/ *vt* cram (**de** with); **~lho** *m* rubble

**entupir** /ĩtu'pir/ *vt* block; **~pir-se** *vpr* get blocked; (*de comida*) stuff o.s. (**de** with)

**enturmar-se** /ĩtur'marsi/ *vpr* mix in, fit in

**entusias|mar** /ĩtuziaz'mar/ *vt* fill with enthusiasm; **~mar-se** *vpr* get enthusiastic (**com** about); **~mo** *m* enthusiasm; **~ta** *m/f* enthusiast □ *a* enthusiastic

**entusiástico** /ĩtuzi'astʃiku/ *a* enthusiastic

**enumerar** /enume'rar/ *vt* enumerate

**envelope** /ẽve'lɔpi/ *m* envelope

**envelhecer** /ĩveʎe'ser/ *vt/i* age

**envenenar** /ĩvene'nar/ *vt* poison; (*fam*) soup up <*carro*>

**envergadura** /ĩverga'dura/ *f* wingspan; (*fig*) scale

**envergo|nhado** /ĩvergo'ɲadu/ *a* ashamed; (*constrangido*) embarrassed; **~nhar** *vt* disgrace; (*constranger*) embarrass; **~nhar-se** *vpr* be ashamed; (*acanhar-se*) get embarrassed

**envernizar** /ĩverni'zar/ *vt* varnish

**en|viado** /ẽvi'adu/ *m* envoy; **~viar** *vt* send; **~vio** *m* (*ato*) sending; (*remessa*) consignment

**envidraçar** /ĩvidra'sar/ *vt* glaze

**enviesado** /ĩvie'zadu/ *a* (*não vertical*) slanting; (*torto*) crooked

**envol|vente** /ĩvow'vẽtʃi/ *a* compelling, gripping; **~ver** *vt* (*embrulhar*) wrap; (*enredar*) involve; **~ver-se** *vpr* (*enrolar-se*) wrap o.s.; (*enredar-se*) get involved; **~vimento** *m* involvement

**enxada** /ẽ'ʃada/ *f* hoe

**enxaguar** /ẽʃa'gwar/ *vt* rinse

**enxame** /ẽ'ʃami/ *m* swarm

**enxaqueca** /ẽʃa'keka/ *f* migraine

**enxergar** /ĩʃer'gar/ *vt/i* see

**enxer|tar** /ĩʃer'tar/ *vt* graft; **~to** /e/ *m* graft

**enxotar** /ĩʃo'tar/ *vt* drive away

**enxofre** /ẽ'ʃofri/ *m* sulphur

**enxo|val** /ẽʃo'vaw/ ( *pl* **~vais**) *m* (*de noiva*) trousseau; (*de bebê*) layette

**enxugar** /ĩʃu'gar/ *vt* dry; **~-se** *vpr* dry o.s.

**enxurrada** /ĩʃu'xada/ *f* torrent; (*fig*) flood

**enxuto** /ĩ'ʃutu/ *a* dry; <*corpo*> shapely

**enzima** /ẽ'zima/ *f* enzyme

**epicentro** /epi'sẽtru/ *m* epicentre

**épico** /'ɛpiku/ *a* epic

**epidemia** /epide'mia/ *f* epidemic

**epi|lepsia** /epilep'sia/ *f* epilepsy; **~léptico** *a & m* epileptic

**epílogo** /e'pilogu/ *m* epilogue

**episódio** /epi'zɔdʒiu/ *m* episode

**epitáfio** /epi'tafiu/ *m* epitaph

**época** /'ɛpoca/ *f* time; (*da história*) age, period; **fazer ~** make history; **móveis da ~** period furniture

**epopéia** /epo'pɛja/ *f* epic

**equação** /ekwa'sãw/ *f* equation

**equador** /ekwa'dor/ *m* equator; **o Equador** Ecuador

**equatori|al** /ekwatori'aw/ (*pl* **~ais**) *a* equatorial; **~ano** *a & m* Ecuadorian

**equilibrar** /ekili'brar/ *vt* balance; **~-se** *vpr* balance

**equilíbrio** /eki'libriu/ *m* balance

**equipa** /e'kipa/ (*Port*) *f* team

**equi|pamento** /ekipa'mẽtu/ *m* equipment; **~par** *vt* equip

**equiparar** /ekipa'rar/ *vt* equate (**com** with); **~-se** *vpr* compare (**a** with)

**equipe** /e'kipi/ *f* team

**equitação** /ekita'sãw/ *f* riding

**equiva|lência** /ekiva'lẽsia/ *f* equivalence; **~lente** *a* equivalent; **~ler** *vi* be equivalent (**a** to)

**equivo|cado** /ekivo'kadu/ *a* mistaken; **~car-se** *vpr* make a mistake

**equívoco** /e'kivoku/ *a* equivocal □ *m* mistake

**era** /'ɛra/ *f* era

**erário** /e'rariu/ *m* exchequer

**ereção** /ere'sãw/ *f* erection

**eremita** /ere'mita/ *m/f* hermit

**ereto** /e'rɛtu/ *a* erect

**erguer** /er'ger/ *vt* raise; erect <*monumento etc*>; **~-se** *vpr* rise

**eri|çado** /eri'sadu/ *a* bristling; **~çar-se** *vpr* bristle

**ermo** /'ermu/ *a* deserted □ *m* wilderness

**erosão** /ero'zãw/ *f* erosion

**erótico** /e'rɔtʃiku/ *a* erotic

**erotismo** /ero'tʃizmu/ *m* eroticism

**er|rado** /e'xadu/ *a* wrong; **~rante** *a* wandering; **~rar** *vt* (*não fazer certo*) get wrong; miss <*alvo*> □ *vi* (*enganar-se*) be wrong; (*vaguear*) wander; **~ro** /e/ *m* mistake; **fazer um ~ro** make a mistake; **~rôneo** *a* erroneous

**erudi|ção** /erudʒi'sãw/ *f* learning; **~to** *a* learned; <*música*> classical □ *m* scholar

**erupção** /erup'sãw/ *f* (*vulcânica*) eruption; (*cutânea*) rash

**erva** /'ɛrva/ *f* herb; **~ daninha** weed; **~-doce** *f* aniseed

**ervilha** /er'viʎa/ *f* pea

**esban|jador** /izbãʒa'dor/ *a* extravagant □ *m* spendthrift; **~jar** *vt* squander; burst with <*saúde, imaginação, energia etc*>

**esbar|rão** /izba'xãw/ *m* bump; **~rar** *vi* **~rar com** *ou* **em** bump into <*pessoa*>; come up against <*problema*>

**esbelto** /iz'bɛwtu/ *a* svelte

**esbo|çar** /izbo'sar/ *vt* sketch <*desenho etc*>; outline <*plano etc*>; **~çar um sorriso** give a hint of a smile; **~ço** /o/ *m* (*desenho*) sketch; (*plano*) outline; (*de um sorriso*) hint

**esbofetear** /izbofetʃi'ar/ *vt* slap

**esborrachar** /izboxa'ʃar/ *vt* squash; **~-se** *vpr* crash

**esbravejar** /izbrave'ʒar/ *vi* rant, rail

**esbura|cado** /izbura'kadu/ *a* full of holes; **~car** *vt* make holes in

**esbuga|lhado** /izbuga'ʎadu/ *a* <*olhos*> bulging; **~lhar-se** *vpr* <*olhos*> pop out

**escabroso** /iska'brozu/ *a* (*fig*) difficult, tough

**escada** /is'kada/ *f* (*dentro de casa*) stairs; (*na rua*) steps; (*de mão*) ladder; **de incêndio** fire escape; **~ rolante** escalator; **~ria** *f* staircase

**escafan|drista** /iskafã'drista/ *m/f* diver; **~dro** *m* diving suit

**escala** /is'kala/ *f* scale; (*de navio*) port of call; (*de avião*) stopover; **fazer ~** stop over; **sem ~** <*vôo*> non-stop

**esca|lada** /iska'lada/ *f* (*fig*) escalation; **~lão** *m* echelon, level; **~lar** *vt* (*subir a*) scale; (*designar*) select

**escaldar** /iskaw'dar/ *vt* scald; blanch <*vegetais*>

**escalfar** /iskaw'far/ *vt* poach

**escalonar** /iskalo'nar/ *vt* schedule <*pagamento*>

**escama** /is'kama/ *f* scale

**escanca|rado** /iskãka'radu/ *a* wide open; **~rar** *vt* open wide

**escandalizar** /iskãdali'zar/ *vt* scandalize; **~-se** *vpr* be scandalized

**escândalo** /is'kãdalu/ *m* (*vexame*) scandal; (*tumulto*) fuss, uproar; **fazer um ~** make a scene

**escandaloso** /iskãda'lozu/ *a* (*chocante*) scandalous; (*espalhafatoso*) outrageous, loud

**Escandinávia** /iskãdʒi'navia/ *f* Scandinavia

**escandinavo** /iskãdʒi'navu/ *a* & *m* Scandinavian

**escanga|lhado** /iskãga'ʎadu/ *a* broken; **~lhar** *vt* break up; **~lhar-se** *vpr* fall to pieces; **~lhar-se de rir** split one's sides laughing

**escaninho** /iska'niɲu/ *m* pigeonhole

**escanteio** /iskã'teju/ *m* corner

**esca|pada** /iska'pada/ *f* (*fuga*) escape; (*aventura*) escapade; **~pamento** *m* exhaust; **~par** *vi* **~par a** *ou* **de** (*livrar-se*) escape from; (*evitar*) escape; **~pou-lhe a palavra** the word slipped out; **o copo ~pou-me das mãos** the glass slipped out of my hands; **o nome me ~pa** the name escapes me; **~par de boa** have a narrow escape; **~patória** *f* way out; (*desculpa*) pretext; **~pe** *m* escape; (*de carro etc*) exhaust; **~pulir** *vi* escape (*de* from)

**escaramuça** /iskara'musa/ *f* skirmish

**escaravelho** /iskara'veʎu/ *m* beetle

**escarcéu** /iskar'sɛw/ *m* uproar, fuss

**escarlate** /iskar'latʃi/ *a* scarlet

**escarnecer** /iskarne'ser/ *vt* mock

**escárnio** /is'karniu/ *m* derision

**escarpado** /iskar'padu/ *a* steep

**escarrado** /iska'xadu/ *m* **ele é o pai ~** he's the spitting image of his father

**escarro** /is'kaxu/ *m* phlegm

**escas|sear** /iskasi'ar/ *vi* run short; **~sez** *f* shortage; **~so** *a* (*raro*) scarce; (*ralo*) scant

**esca|vadeira** /iskava'dera/ *f* digger; **~var** *vt* excavate

**esclare|cer** /isklare'ser/ *vt* explain <*fatos*>; enlighten <*pessoa*>; **~cer-se** *vpr* <*fato*> be explained; <*pessoa*> find out; **~cimento** *m* (*de pessoas*) enlightenment; (*de fatos*) explanation

**esclerosado** /isklero'zadu/ *a* senile

**escoar** /isko'ar/ *vt/i* drain

**esco|cês** /isko'ses/ *a* (*f* **~cesa**) Scottish □ *m* (*f* **~cesa**) Scot

**Escócia** /is'kɔsia/ *f* Scotland

**esco|la** /is'kɔla/ *f* school; **~la de samba** samba school; **~lar** *a* school □ *m/f* schoolchild; **~laridade** *f* schooling

**esco|lha** /is'koʎa/ *f* choice; **~lher** *vt* choose

**escol|ta** /is'kɔwta/ *f* escort; **~tar** *vt* escort

**escombros** /is'kõbrus/ *m pl* debris

**escon|de-esconde** /iskõdʒis'kõdʒi/ *m* hide-and-seek; **~der** *vt* hide; **~der-se** *vpr* hide; **~derijo** *m* hiding place; (*de bandidos*) hideout; **~didas** *f pl* **às ~didas** secretly

**esco|ra** /is'kɔra/ *f* prop; **~rar** *vt* prop up; **~rar-se** *vpr* <*argumento etc*> be based (**em** on)

**escore** /is'kɔri/ *m* score

**escória** /is'kɔria/ *f* scum, dross

**escori|ação** /iskoria'sãw/ *f* graze, abrasion; **~ar** *vt* graze

**escorpião** /iskorpi'ãw/ *m* scorpion; **Escorpião** Scorpio

**escorredor** /iskoxe'dor/ *m* drainer

**escorrega** /isko'xega/ *m* slide

**escorre|gador** /iskoxega'dor/ *m* slide; **~gão** *m* slip; **~gar** *vi* slip

**escor|rer** /isko'xer/ *vt* drain □ *vi* trickle; **~rido** *a* <*cabelo*> straight

**escoteiro** /isko'teru/ *m* boy scout

**escotilha** /isko'tʃiʎa/ *f* hatch

**esco|va** /is'kova/ *f* brush; **fazer ~va no cabelo** blow-dry one's hair; **~va de dentes** toothbrush; **~var** *vt* brush; **~vinha** *f* **cabelo à ~vinha** crew-cut

**escra|chado** /iskra'ʃadu/ (*fam*) *a* outspoken; **~char** (*fam*) *vt* tell off

**escra|vatura** /iskrava'tura/ *f* slavery; **~vidão** *f* slavery; **~vizar** *vt* enslave; **~vo** *m* slave

**escre|vente** /iskre'vẽtʃi/ *m/f* clerk; **~ver** *vt/i* write

**escri|ta** /is'krita/ *f* writing; **~to** *pp de* **escrever** □ *a* written; **por ~to** in writing; **~tor** *m* writer; **~tório** *m* office; (*numa casa*) study

**escritu|ra** /iskri'tura/ *f* (*a Bíblia*) scripture; (*contrato*) deed; **~ração** *f* bookkeeping; **~rar** *vt* keep, write up <*contas*>; draw up <*documento*>

**escri|vaninha** /iskriva'niɲa/ *f* bureau, writing desk; **~vão** *m* (*f ~vã*) registrar

**escrúpulo** /is'krupulu/ *m* scruple

**escrupuloso** /iskrupu'lozu/ *a* scrupulous

**escrutínio** /iskru'tʃiniu/ *m* ballot

**escu|dar** /isku'dar/ *vt* shield; **~deria** *f* team; **~do** *m* shield; (*moeda*) escudo

**escula|chado** /iskula'ʃadu/ (*fam*) *a* sloppy; **~char** (*fam*) *vt* mess up <*coisa*>; tell off <*pessoa*>; **~cho** (*fam*) *m* (*bagunça*) mess; (*bronca*) telling-off

**escul|pir** /iskuw'pir/ *vt* sculpt; **~tor** *m* sculptor; **~tura** *f* sculpture; **~tural** (*pl* **~turais**) *a* statuesque

**escuma** /is'kuma/ *f* scum; **~deira** *f* skimmer

**escuna** /is'kuna/ *f* schooner

**escu|ras** /is'kuras/ *f pl* **às ~ras** in the dark; **~recer** *vt* darken □ *vi* get dark; **~ridão** *f* darkness; **~ro** *a & m* dark

**escuso** /is'kuzu/ *a* shady

**escu|ta** /is'kuta/ *f* listening; **estar à ~ta** be listening; **~ta telefônica** phone tapping; **~tar** *vt* (*perceber*) hear; (*prestar atenção a*) listen to □ *vi* (*poder ouvir*) hear; (*prestar atenção*) listen

**esdrúxulo** /iz'druʃulu/ *a* weird

**esfacelar** /isfase'lar/ *vt* wreck

**esfalfar** /isfaw'far/ *vt* wear out; **~-se** *vpr* get worn out

**esfaquear** /isfaki'ar/ *vt* stab

**esfarelar** /isfare'lar/ *vt* crumble; **~-se** *vpr* crumble

**esfarrapado** /isfaxa'padu/ *a* ragged; <*desculpa*> lame

**es|fera** /is'fɛra/ *f* sphere; **~férico** *a* spherical

**esferográfi|co** /isfero'grafiku/ *a* **caneta ~ca** ball-point pen

**esfiapar** /isfia'par/ *vt* fray; **~-se** *vpr* fray

**esfinge** /is'fĩʒi/ *f* sphinx

**esfolar** /isfo'lar/ *vt* skin; (*fig*) overcharge

**esfomeado** /isfomi'adu/ *a* starving, famished

**esfor|çar-se** /isfor'sarsi/ *vpr* make an effort; **~ço** /o/ *m* effort; **fazer ~ço** make an effort

**esfre|gaço** /isfre'gasu/ *m* smear; **~gar** *vt* rub; (*para limpar*) scrub

**esfriar** /isfri'ar/ *vt* cool □ *vi* cool (down); (*sentir frio*) get cold

**esfumaçado** /isfuma'sadu/ *a* smoky

**esfuziante** /isfuzi'ãtʃi/ *a* irrepressible, exuberant

**esganar** /izga'nar/ *vt* throttle

**esganiçado** /izgani'sadu/ *a* shrill

**esgarçar** /izgar'sar/ *vt/i* fray

**esgo|tado** /izgo'tadu/ *a* exhausted; <*estoque, lotação*> sold out; **~tamento** *m* exhaustion; **~tamento nervoso** nervous breakdown; **~tar** *vt* exhaust; (*gastar*) use up; **~tar-se** *vpr* <*pessoa*> become exhausted; <*estoque, lotação*> sell out; <*recursos, provisões*> run out; **~to** /o/ *m* drain; (*de detritos*) sewer

**esgri|ma** /iz'grima/ *f* fencing; **~mir** *vt* brandish □ *vi* fence; **~mista** *m/f* fencer

**esgrouvinhado** /izgrovi'ɲadu/ *a* tousled, dishevelled

**esgueirar-se** /izge'rarsi/ *vpr* slip, sneak

**esguelha** /iz'geʎa/ *f* **de ~** askew; <*olhar*> askance

**esgui|char** /izgi'ʃar/ *vt/i* spurt, squirt; **~cho** *m* jet, spurt

esguio /iz'giʊ/ a slender
eslavo /iz'lavu/ a Slavic □ m Slav
esmaecer /izmaj'ser/ vi fade
esma|gador /izmaga'dor/ a <vitória, maioria> overwhelming; <provas> incontrovertible; ~gar vt crush
esmalte /iz'mawtʃi/ m enamel; ~ de unhas nail varnish
esmeralda /izme'rawda/ f emerald
esme|rar-se /izme'rarsi/ vpr take great care (em over); ~ro /e/ m great care
esmigalhar /izmiga'ʎar/ vt crumble <pão etc>; shatter <vidro, copo>; ~-se vpr <pão etc> crumble; <vidro, copo> shatter
esmiuçar /izmiu'sar/ vt examine in detail
esmo /'ezmu/ m a ~ <escolher> at random; <andar> aimlessly; <falar> nonsense
esmola /iz'mɔla/ f donation; pl charity
esmorecer /izmore'ser/ vi flag
esmurrar /izmu'xar/ vt punch
esno|bar /izno'bar/ vt snub □ vi be snobbish; ~be /iz'nɔbi/ a snobbish □ m/f snob; ~bismo m snobbishness
esotérico /ezo'tɛriku/ a esoteric
espa|çar /ispa'sar/ vt space out; make less frequent <visitas, consultas etc>; ~cial (pl ~ciais) a space; ~ço m space; (cultural etc) venue; ~çoso /o/ a spacious
espada /is'pada/ f sword; pl (naipe) spades; ~chim m swordsman
espádua /is'padua/ f shoulder blade
espaguete /ispa'getʃi/ m spaghetti
espaire|cer /ispajre'ser/ vt amuse □ vi relax; (dar uma volta) go for a walk; ~cimento m recreation
espaldar /ispaw'dar/ m back
espalhafato /ispaʎa'fatu/ m (barulho) fuss, uproar; (de roupa etc) extravagance; ~so /o/ a (barulhento) noisy, rowdy; (ostentoso) extravagant
espalhar /ispa'ʎar/ vt scatter; spread <notícia, terror etc>; shed <luz>; ~-se vpr spread; <pessoas> spread out
espa|nador /ispana'dor/ m feather duster; ~nar vt dust
espan|camento /ispãka'mẽtu/ m beating; ~car vt beat up
Espanha /is'paɲa/ f Spain
espa|nhol /ispa'ɲɔw/ (pl ~nhóis) a (f ~nhola) Spanish □ m (f ~nhola) Spaniard; (língua) Spanish; os ~nhóis the Spanish
espan|talho /ispã'taʎu/ m scarecrow; ~tar vt (admirar) amaze; (assustar) scare; (afugentar) drive away; ~tar-se vpr (admirar-se) be amazed; (assustar-se) get scared; ~to m (susto) fright; (admiração) amazement; ~toso /o/ a amazing

esparadrapo /ispara'drapu/ m sticking plaster
espargo /is'pargu/ (Port) m asparagus
esparramar /ispaxa'mar/ vt scatter; ~-se vpr be scattered, spread
espartano /ispar'tanu/ a spartan
espartilho /ispar'tʃiʎu/ m corset
espas|mo /is'pazmu/ m spasm; ~módico a spasmodic
espatifar /ispatʃi'far/ vt smash; ~-se vpr smash; <carro, avião> crash
especi|al /ispesi'aw/ (pl ~ais) a special; ~alidade f speciality; ~alista m/f specialist
especiali|zado /ispesiali'zadu/ a specialized; (mão-de-obra) skilled; ~zar-se vpr specialize (em in)
especiaria /ispesia'ria/ f spice
espécie /is'pɛsi/ f sort, kind; (de animais) species
especifi|cação /ispesifika'sãw/ f specification; ~car vt specify
específico /ispe'sifiku/ a specific
espécime /is'pesimi/ m specimen
espectador /ispekta'dor/ m (de TV) viewer; (de jogo, espetáculo) spectator; (de acidente etc) onlooker
espectro /is'pɛktru/ m (fantasma) spectre; (de cores) spectrum
especu|lação /ispekula'sãw/ f speculation; ~lador m speculator; ~lar vi speculate (sobre on); ~lativo a speculative
espe|lhar /ispe'ʎar/ vt mirror; ~lhar-se vpr be mirrored; ~lho /e/ m mirror; ~lho retrovisor rearview mirror
espelunca /ispe'lũka/ (fam) f dive
espera /is'pɛra/ f wait; à ~ de waiting for
esperan|ça /ispe'rãsa/ f hope; ~çoso /o/ a hopeful
esperar /ispe'rar/ vt (aguardar) wait for; (desejar) hope for; (contar com) expect □ vi wait (por for); fazer alg ~ keep s.o. waiting; espero que ele venha I hope (that) he comes; espero que sim/não I hope so/not
esperma /is'pɛrma/ m sperm
espernear /isperni'ar/ vi kick; (fig: reclamar) kick up
esper|talhão /isperta'ʎãw/ m (f ~talhona) wise guy; ~teza /e/ f cleverness; (uma) clever move; ~to /e/ a clever
espes|so /is'pesu/ a thick; ~sura f thickness
espe|tacular /ispetaku'lar/ a spectacular; ~táculo m (no teatro etc) show; (cena impressionante) spectacle; ~taculoso /o/ a spectacular
espe|tar /ispe'tar/ vt (cravar) stick; (furar) skewer; ~tar-se vpr (cravar-se) stick; (ferir-se) prick o.s.; ~tinho

*m* skewer; (*de carne etc*) kebab; **~to** /e/ *m* spit

**espevitado** /ispevi'tadu/ *a* cheeky

**espezinhar** /ispezi'ɲar/ *vt* walk all over

**espi|a** /is'pia/ *m/f* spy; **~ão** *m* (*f ~ã*) spy; **~ada** *f* peep; **~ar** *vt* (*observar*) spy on; (*aguardar*) watch for □ *vi* peer, peep

**espicaçar** /ispika'sar/ *vt* goad <*pessoa*>; excite <*imaginação, curiosidade*>

**espichar** /ispi'ʃar/ *vt* stretch □ *vi* shoot up; **~-se** *vpr* stretch out

**espiga** /is'piga/ *f* (*de trigo etc*) ear; (*de milho*) cob

**espina|fração** /ispinafra'sãw/ (*fam*) *f* telling-off; **~frar** (*fam*) *vt* tell off; **~fre** *m* spinach

**espingarda** /ispĩ'garda/ *f* rifle, shotgun

**espinha** /is'piɲa/ *f* (*de peixe*) bone; (*na pele*) spot; **~ dorsal** spine

**espinho** /is'piɲu/ *m* thorn; **~so** /o/ *a* thorny; (*fig*) difficult, tough

**espio|nagem** /ispio'naʒẽ/ *f* espionage, spying; **~nar** *vt* spy on □ *vi* spy

**espi|ral** /ispi'raw/ (*pl* **~rais**) *a & f* spiral

**espírita** /is'pirita/ *a & m/f* spiritualist

**espiritismo** /ispiri'tʃizmu/ *m* spiritualism

**espírito** /is'piritu/ *m* spirit; (*graça*) wit

**espiritu|al** /ispiritu'aw/ (*pl* **~ais**) *a* spiritual; **~oso** /o/ *a* witty

**espir|rar** /ispi'xar/ *vt* spurt □ *vi* <*pessoa*> sneeze; <*lama, tinta etc*> spatter; <*fogo, lenha, fritura etc*> spit; **~ro** *m* sneeze

**esplêndido** /is'plẽdʒidu/ *a* splendid

**esplendor** /isplẽ'dor/ *m* splendour

**espoleta** /ispo'leta/ *f* fuse

**espoliar** /ispoli'ar/ *vt* plunder, pillage

**espólio** /is'pɔliu/ *m* (*herdado*) estate; (*roubado*) spoils

**espon|ja** /is'põʒa/ *f* sponge; **~joso** /o/ *a* spongy

**espon|taneidade** /ispõtanej'dadʒi/ *f* spontaneity; **~tâneo** *a* spontaneous

**espora** /is'pora/ *f* spur

**esporádico** /ispo'radʒiku/ *a* sporadic

**esporear** /ispori'ar/ *vt* spur on

**espor|te** /is'portʃi/ *m* sport □ *a invar* <*roupa*> casual; **carro ~te** sports car; **~tista** *m/f* sportsman (*f* -woman); **~tiva** *f* sense of humour; **~tivo** *a* sporting

**espo|sa** /is'poza/ *f* wife; **~so** *m* husband

**espregui|çadeira** /ispregisa'dera/ *f* (*tipo cadeira*) deckchair; (*tipo cama*) sun lounger; **~çar-se** *vpr* stretch

**esprei|ta** /is'prejta/ *f* **ficar à ~ta** lie in wait; **~tar** *vt* stalk <*caça, vítima*>; spy on <*vizinhos, inimigos etc*>; look out for <*ocasião*> □ *vi* peep, spy

**espre|medor** /ispreme'dor/ *m* squeezer; **~mer** *vt* squeeze; wring out <*roupa*>; squash <*pessoa*>; **~mer-se** *vpr* squeeze up

**espu|ma** /is'puma/ *f* foam; **~ma de borracha** foam rubber; **~mante** *a* <*vinho*> sparkling; **~mar** *vi* foam, froth

**espúrio** /is'puriu/ *a* spurious

**esqua|dra** /is'kwadra/ *f* squad; **~dra de polícia** (*Port*) police station; **~drão** *m* squadron; **~dria** *f* doors and windows; **~drinhar** *vt* explore; **~dro** *m* set square

**esqualidez** /iskwali'des/ *f* squalor

**esquálido** /is'kwalidu/ *a* squalid

**esquartejar** /iskwarte'ʒar/ *vt* chop up

**esque|cer** /iske'ser/ *vt/i* forget; **~cer-se de** forget; **~cido** *a* forgotten; (*com memória fraca*) forgetful; **~cimento** *m* oblivion; (*memória fraca*) forgetfulness

**esque|lético** /iske'lɛtʃiku/ *a* skinny, skeleton-like; **~leto** /e/ *m* skeleton

**esque|ma** /is'kema/ *m* outline, draft; (*operação*) scheme; **~ma de segurança** security operation; **~mático** *a* schematic

**esquentar** /iskẽ'tar/ *vt* warm up □ *vi* warm up; <*roupa*> be warm; **~-se** *vpr* get annoyed; **~ a cabeça** (*fam*) get worked up

**esquer|da** /is'kerda/ *f* left; **à ~da** (*posição*) on the left; (*direção*) to the left; **~dista** *a* left-wing □ *m/f* left-winger; **~do** /e/ *a* left

**esqui** /is'ki/ *m* ski; (*esporte*) skiing; **~ aquático** water skiing; **~ador** *m* skier; **~ar** *vi* ski

**esquilo** /is'kilu/ *m* squirrel

**esquina** /is'kina/ *f* corner

**esquisi|tice** /iskizi'tʃisi/ *f* strangeness; (*uma*) strange thing; **~to** *a* strange

**esqui|var-se** /iski'varsi/ *vpr* dodge out of the way; **~var-se de** dodge; **~vo** *a* elusive; <*pessoa*> aloof, antisocial

**esquizo|frenia** /iskizofre'nia/ *f* schizophrenia; **~frênico** *a & m* schizophrenic

**es|sa** /'ɛsa/ *pron* that (one); **~sa é boa** that's a good one; **~sa não** come off it; **por ~sas e outras** for these and other reasons; **~se** /e/ *a* that; *pl* those; (*fam: este*) this; *pl* these □ *pron* that one; *pl* those; (*fam: este*) this one; *pl* these

**essência** /e'sẽsia/ *f* essence

**essenci|al** /esẽsi'aw/ (*pl* ~**ais**) *a* essential; **o** ~**al** what is essential

**estabele|cer** /istabele'ser/ *vt* establish; ~**cer-se** *vpr* establish o.s.; ~**cimento** *m* establishment

**estabili|dade** /istabili'dadʒi/ *f* stability; ~**zar** *vt* stabilize; ~**zar-se** *vpr* stabilize

**estábulo** /is'tabulu/ *m* cowshed

**estaca** /is'taka/ *f* stake; (*de barraca*) peg; **voltar à** ~ **zero** go back to square one

**estação** /ista'sãw/ *f* (*do ano*) season; (*ferroviária etc*) station; ~ **balneária** seaside resort

**estacar** /ista'kar/ *vi* stop short

**estacio|namento** /istasiona'mẽtu/ *m* (*ação*) parking; (*lugar*) car park, (*Amer*) parking lot; ~**nar** *vt/i* park

**estada** /is'tada/ *f*, **estadia** /ista'dʒia/ *f* stay

**estádio** /is'tadʒiu/ *m* stadium

**esta|dista** /ista'dʒista/ *m/f* statesman (*f* -woman); ~**do** *m* state; ~**do civil** marital status; ~**do de espírito** state of mind; **Estados Unidos da América** United States of America; **Estado-Maior** *m* Staff; ~**dual** (*pl* ~**duais**) *a* state

**esta|fa** /is'tafa/ *f* exhaustion; ~**fante** *a* exhausting; ~**far** *vt* tire out; ~**far-se** *vpr* get tired out

**estagi|ar** /istaʒi'ar/ *vi* do a traineeship; ~**ário** *m* trainee

**estágio** /is'taʒiu/ *m* traineeship

**estag|nado** /istagi'nadu/ *a* stagnant; ~**nar** *vi* stagnate

**estalagem** /ista'laʒẽ/ *f* inn

**estalar** /ista'lar/ *vt* (*quebrar*) crack; (*fazer barulho com*) click □ *vi* crack

**estaleiro** /ista'leru/ *m* shipyard

**estalo** /is'talu/ *m* crack; (*de dedos, língua*) click; **me deu um** ~ it clicked (in my mind)

**estam|pa** /is'tãpa/ *f* print; ~**pado** *a* <*tecido*> patterned □ *m* (*desenho*) pattern; (*tecido*) print; ~**par** *vt* print

**estampido** /istã'pidu/ *m* bang

**estancar** /istã'kar/ *vt* staunch; ~**se** *vpr* dry up

**estância** /is'tãsia/ *f* ~ **hidromineral** spa

**estandarte** /istã'dartʃi/ *m* banner

**estanho** /is'taɲu/ *m* tin

**estanque** /is'tãki/ *a* watertight

**estante** /is'tãtʃi/ *f* bookcase

**estapafúrdio** /istapa'furdʒiu/ *a* weird, odd

**estar** /is'tar/ *vi* be; (~ **em casa**) be in; **está chovendo**, (*Port*) **está a chover** it's raining; ~ **com** have; ~ **com calor/sono** be hot/sleepy; ~ **para terminar** be about to finish; **ele não está para ninguém** he's not avail-

able to see anyone; **o trabalho está por terminar** the work is yet to be finished

**estardalhaço** /istarda'ʎasu/ *m* (*barulho*) fuss; (*ostentação*) extravagance

**estarre|cedor** /istaxese'dor/ *a* horrifying; ~**cer** *vt* horrify; ~**cer-se** *vpr* be horrified

**esta|tal** /ista'taw/ (*pl* ~**tais**) *a* state-owned □ *f* state company

**estate|lado** /istate'ladu/ *a* sprawling; ~**lar** *vt* knock down; ~**lar-se** *vpr* sprawling

**estático** /is'tatʃiku/ *a* static

**estatísti|ca** /ista'tʃistʃika/ *f* statistics; ~**co** *a* statistical

**estati|zação** /istatʃiza'sãw/ *f* nationalization; ~**zar** *vt* nationalize

**estátua** /is'tatua/ *f* statue

**estatueta** /istatu'eta/ *f* statuette

**estatura** /ista'tura/ *f* stature

**estatuto** /ista'tutu/ *m* statute

**está|vel** /is'tavew/ (*pl* ~**veis**) *a* stable

**este**[1] /'estʃi/ *m a invar* & *m* east

**este**[2] /'estʃi/ *a* this; *pl* these □ *pron* this one; *pl* these; (*mencionado por último*) the latter

**esteio** /is'teju/ *m* prop; (*fig*) mainstay

**esteira** /is'tera/ *f* (*tapete*) mat; (*rastro*) wake

**estelionato** /istelio'natu/ *m* fraud

**estender** /istẽ'der/ *vt* (*desdobrar*) spread out; (*alongar*) stretch; (*ampliar*) extend; hold out <*mão*>; hang out <*roupa*>; roll out <*massa*>; draw out <*conversa*>; ~**se** *vpr* (*deitar-se*) stretch out; (*ir longe*) stretch, extend; ~**se sobre** dwell on

**esteno|datilógrafo** /istenodatʃi'lɔgrafu/ *m* shorthand typist; ~**grafia** *f* shorthand

**estepe** /is'tɛpi/ *m* spare wheel

**esterco** /is'terku/ *m* dung

**estéreo** /is'tɛriu/ *a invar* stereo

**estere|otipado** /isteriotʃi'padu/ *a* stereotypical; ~**ótipo** *m* stereotype

**esté|ril** /is'tɛriw/ (*pl* ~**reis**) *a* sterile

**esterili|dade** /isterili'dadʒi/ *f* sterility; ~**zar** *vt* sterilize

**esterli|no** /ister'lino/ *a* **libra** ~**na** pound sterling

**esteróide** /iste'rɔjdʒi/ *m* steroid

**estética** /is'tɛtʃika/ *f* aesthetics

**esteticista** /istetʃi'sista/ *m/f* beautician

**estético** /is'tɛtʃiku/ *a* aesthetic

**estetoscópio** /istetos'kɔpiu/ *m* stethoscope

**estiagem** /istʃi'aʒẽ/ *f* dry spell

**estibordo** /istʃi'bɔrdu/ *m* starboard

**esti|cada** /istʃi'kada/ *f* **dar uma** ~**cada** go on; ~**car** *vt* stretch □ (*fam*) *vi* go on; ~**car-se** *vpr* stretch out

estigma /is'tʃigima/ m stigma;
~tizar vt brand (de as)
estilha|çar /istʃiʎa'sar/ vt shatter;
~çar-se vpr shatter; ~ço m shard,
fragment
estilingue /istʃi'lĩgi/ m catapult
estilis|mo /istʃi'lizmu/ m fashion
design; ~ta m/f fashion designer
esti|lístico /istʃi'listʃiku/ a stylistic;
~lizar vt stylize; ~lo m style; ~lo
de vida lifestyle
esti|ma /es'tʃima/ f esteem; ~mação
f estimation; cachorro de ~mação
pet dog; ~mado a esteemed; Estima-
do Senhor Dear Sir; ~mar vt value
<bens, jóias etc> (em at); estimate
<valor, preço etc> (em at); think
highly of <pessoa>; ~mativa f estimate
estimu|lante /istʃimu'lãtʃi/ a stimu-
lating □ m stimulant; ~lar vt stimulate; (incentivar) encourage
estímulo /is'tʃimulu/ m stimulus; (incentivo) incentive
estio /is'tʃiu/ m summer
estipu|lação /istʃipula'sãw/ f stipu-
lation; ~lar vt stipulate
estirar /istʃi'rar/ vt stretch; ~-se vpr
stretch
estirpe /is'tʃirpi/ f stock, line
estivador /istʃiva'dor/ m docker
estocada /isto'kada/ f thrust
estocar /isto'kar/ vt stock □ vi stock
up
Estocolmo /isto'kɔwmu/ f Stockholm
esto|far /isto'far/ vt upholster
<móveis>; ~fo /o/ m upholstery
estóico /is'tɔjku/ a & m stoic
estojo /is'toʒu/ m case
estômago /is'tomagu/ m stomach
Estônia /is'tonia/ f Estonia
estonte|ante /istõtʃi'ãtʃi/ a stunning,
mind-boggling; ~ar vt stun
estopim /isto'pĩ/ m fuse; (fig) flash-
point
estoque /is'tɔki/ m stock
estore /is'tɔri/ m blind
estória /is'tɔria/ f story
estor|var /istor'var/ vt hinder; ob-
struct <entrada, trânsito>; ~vo /o/
m hindrance
estou|rado /isto'radu/ a <pessoa>
explosive; ~rar vi <bomba, escândalo, pessoa> blow up; <pneu> burst;
<guerra> break out; <moda, cantor
etc> make it big; ~ro m (de bomba,
moda etc) explosion; (de pessoa) outburst; (de pneu) blowout; (de guerra)
outbreak
estrábico /is'trabiku/ a <olhos>
squinty; <pessoa> squint-eyed
estrabismo /istra'bizmu/ m squint
estraçalhar /istrasa'ʎar/ vt tear to
pieces

estrada /is'trada/ f road; ~ de ferro
railway, (Amer) railroad; ~ de
rodagem highway; ~ de terra dirt
road
estrado /is'tradu/ m podium; (de
cama) base
estraga-prazeres /istragapra'zeris/
m/f invar spoilsport
estragão /istra'gãw/ m tarragon
estra|gar /istra'gar/ vt (tornar desa-
gradável) spoil; (acabar com) ruin □
vi (quebrar) break; (apodrecer) go off;
~go m damage; pl damage; (da guerra, do tempo) ravages
estrangeiro /istrã'ʒeru/ a foreign □
m foreigner; do ~ from abroad; para
o/no ~ abroad
estrangular /istrãgu'lar/ vt strangle
estra|nhar /istra'ɲar/ vt (achar es-
tranho) find strange; (não se adaptar
a) find it hard to get used to; (não se
sentir à vontade com) be shy with;
~nhar que find it strange that; estou te ~nhando that's not like you;
não é de se ~nhar it's not
surprising; ~nheza /e/ f (esquisitice)
strangeness; (surpresa) surprise;
~nho a strange □ m stranger
estratagema /istrata'ʒema/ m stratagem
estraté|gia /istra'tɛʒia/ f strategy;
~gico a strategic
estrato /is'tratu/ m (camada)
stratum; (nuvem) stratus; ~sfera f
stratosphere
estre|ante /istri'ãtʃi/ a new □ m/f
newcomer; ~ar vt première <peça,
filme>; embark on <carreira>; wear
for the first time <roupa> □ vi <pes-
soa> make one's début; <filme, peça>
open
estrebaria /istreba'ria/ f stable
estréia /is'trɛja/ f (de pessoa) début;
(de filme, peça) première
estrei|tar /istrej'tar/ vt narrow; take
in <vestido>; make closer <relações,
laços> □ vi narrow; ~tar-se vpr <re-
lações> become closer; ~to a narrow;
<relações, laços> close; <saia>
straight □ m strait
estre|la /is'trela/ f star; ~lado a
<céu> starry; <ovo> fried; ~lado
por <filme etc> starring; ~la-do-
mar (pl ~las-do-mar) f starfish;
~lar vt fry <ovo>; star in <filme,
peça>; ~lato m stardom; ~lismo m
star quality
estreme|cer /istreme'ser/ vt shake;
strain <relações, amizade> □ vi shudder; <relações, amizade> become
strained; ~cimento m shudder; (de
relações, amizade) strain
estrepar-se /istre'parsi/ (fam) vpr
come a cropper

estrépito /iʃˈtrɛpitu/ m noise; com ~ noisily

estrepitoso /iʃtrepiˈtozu/ a noisy; <sucesso etc> resounding

estres|sante /iʃtreˈsãtʃi/ a stressful; ~sar vt stress; ~se /ɛ/ m stress

estria /iʃˈtria/ f streak; (no corpo) stretch mark

estribeira /iʃtriˈbera/ f stirrup; perder as ~s lose control

estribilho /iʃtriˈbiʎu/ m chorus

estribo /iʃˈtribu/ m stirrup

estridente /iʃtriˈdẽtʃi/ a strident

estripulia /iʃtripuˈlia/ f antic

estrito /iʃˈtritu/ a strict

estrofe /iʃˈtrɔfi/ f stanza, verse

estrogonofe /iʃtrogoˈnɔfi/ m stroganoff

estrógeno /iʃˈtrɔʒenu/ m oestrogen

estron|do /iʃˈtrõdu/ m crash; ~doso /o/ a loud; <aplausos> thunderous; <sucesso, fracasso> resounding

estropiar /iʃtropiˈar/ vt cripple <pessoa>; mangle <palavras>

estrume /iʃˈtrumi/ m manure

estrutu|ra /iʃtruˈtura/ f structure; ~ral (pl ~rais) a structural; ~rar vt structure

estuário /iʃtuˈariu/ m estuary

estudan|te /iʃtuˈdãtʃi/ m/f student; ~til (pl ~tis) a student

estudar /iʃtuˈdar/ vt/i study

estúdio /iʃˈtudʒiu/ m studio

estu|dioso /iʃtudʒiˈozu/ a studious □ m scholar; ~do m study

estufa /iʃˈtufa/ f (para plantas) greenhouse; (de aquecimento) stove; ~do m stew

estupefato /iʃtupeˈfatu/ a dumbfounded

estupendo /iʃteˈpẽdu/ a stupendous

estupidez /iʃtupiˈdes/ f (grosseria) rudeness; (uma) rude thing; (burrice) stupidity; (uma) stupid thing

estúpido /iʃˈtupidu/ a (grosso) rude, coarse; (burro) stupid □ m lout

estupor /iʃtuˈpor/ m stupor

estu|prador /iʃtupraˈdor/ m rapist; ~prar vt rape; ~pro m rape

esturricar /iʃtuxiˈkar/ vt parch

esvair-se /iʒvaˈirsi/ vpr fade; ~ em sangue bleed to death

esvaziar /iʒvaziˈar/ vt empty; ~se vpr empty

esverdeado /iʒverdʒiˈadu/ a greenish

esvoa|çante /iʒvoaˈsãtʃi/ a <cabelo> fly-away; ~çar vi flutter

eta /ˈeta/ int what a

etapa /eˈtapa/ f stage; (de corrida, turnê etc) leg

etário /eˈtariu/ a age

éter /ˈɛter/ m ether

etéreo /eˈtɛriu/ a ethereal

eter|nidade /eterniˈdadʒi/ f eternity; ~no /ɛ/ a eternal

éti|ca /ˈɛtʃika/ f ethics; ~co a ethical

etimo|logia /etʃimoloˈʒia/ f etymology; ~lógico a etymological

etíope /eˈtʃiopi/ a & m/f Ethiopian

Etiópia /eˈtʃiɔpia/ f Ethiopia

etique|ta /etʃiˈketa/ f (rótulo) label; (bons modos) etiquette; ~tar vt label

étnico /ˈɛtʃiniku/ a ethnic

eu /ew/ pron I □ m self; mais alto do que ~ taller than me; sou ~ it's me

EUA m pl USA

eucalipto /ewkaˈliptu/ m eucalyptus

eufemismo /ewfeˈmizmu/ m euphemism

euforia /ewfoˈria/ f euphoria

Europa /ewˈrɔpa/ f Europe

euro|peu /ewroˈpew/ a & m (f ~péia) European

eutanásia /ewtaˈnazia/ f euthanasia

evacu|ação /evakuaˈsãw/ f evacuation; ~ar vt evacuate

evadir /evaˈdʒir/ vt evade; ~se vpr escape (de from)

evan|gelho /evãˈʒeʎu/ m gospel; ~gélico a evangelical

evaporar /evapoˈrar/ vt evaporate; ~se vpr evaporate

eva|são /evaˈzãw/ f escape; (fiscal etc) evasion; ~são escolar truancy; ~siva f excuse; ~sivo a evasive

even|to /eˈvẽtu/ m event; ~tual (pl ~tuais) a possible; ~tualidade f eventuality

evidência /eviˈdẽsia/ f evidence

eviden|ciar /evidẽsiˈar/ vt show up; ~ciar-se vpr show up; ~te a obvious, evident

evi|tar /eviˈtar/ vt avoid; ~tar de beber avoid drinking; ~tável (pl ~táveis) a avoidable

evocar /evoˈkar/ vt call to mind, evoke <passado etc>; call up <espíritos etc>

evolu|ção /evoluˈsãw/ f evolution; ~ir vi evolve

exacerbar /ezaserˈbar/ vt exacerbate

exage|rado /ezaʒeˈradu/ a over the top; ~rar vt (atribuir proporções irreais a) exaggerate; (fazer em excesso) overdo □ vi (ao falar) exaggerate; (exceder-se) overdo it; ~ro /e/ m exaggeration

exa|lação /ezalaˈsãw/ f fume; (agradável) scent; ~lar vt give off <perfume etc>

exal|tação /ezawtaˈsãw/ f (excitação) agitation; (engrandecimento) exaltation; ~tar vt (excitar) agitate; (enfurecer) infuriate; (louvar) exalt; ~tar-se vpr (excitar-se) get agitated; (enfurecer-se) get furious

exa|me /eˈzami/ m examination; (na escola) exam(ination); ~me de

**sangue** blood test; **∼minar** *vt* examine

**exaspe|ração** /ezaspera'sãw/ *f* exasperation; **∼rar** *vt* exasperate; **∼rar-se** *vpr* get exasperated

**exa|tidão** /ezatʃi'dãw/ *f* exactness; **∼to** *a* exact

**exaurir** /ezaw'rir/ *vt* exhaust; **∼-se** *vpr* become exhausted

**exaus|tivo** /ezaws'tʃivu/ *a* <*estudo*> exhaustive; <*trabalho*> exhausting; **∼to** *a* exhausted

**exceção** /ese'sãw/ *f* exception; **abrir ∼** make an exception; **com ∼ de** with the exception of

**exce|dente** /ese'dẽtʃi/ *a & m* excess, surplus; **∼der** *vt* exceed; **∼der-se** *vpr* overdo it

**exce|lência** /ese'lẽsia/ *f* excellence; (*tratamento*) excellency; **∼lente** *a* excellent

**excentricidade** /esẽtrisi'dadʒi/ *f* eccentricity

**excêntrico** /e'sẽtriku/ *a & m* eccentric

**excep|ção** /iʃsɛ'sãw/ (*Port*) *f veja* **exceção**; **∼cional** (*pl* **∼cionais**) *a* exceptional; (*deficiente*) handicapped

**exces|sivo** /ese'sivu/ *a* excessive; **∼so** /ɛ/ *m* excess; **∼so de bagagem** excess baggage; **∼so de velocidade** speeding

**exce|to** /e'sɛtu/ *prep* except; **∼tuar** *vt* except

**exci|tação** /esita'sãw/ *f* excitement; **∼tante** *a* exciting; **∼tar** *vt* excite; **∼tar-se** *vpr* get excited

**excla|mação** /isklama'sãw/ *f* exclamation; **∼mar** *vt/i* exclaim

**exclu|ir** /isklu'ir/ *vt* exclude; **∼são** *f* exclusion; **com ∼são de** with the exclusion of; **∼sividade** *f* exclusive rights; **com ∼sividade** exclusively; **∼sivo** *a* exclusive; **∼so** *a* excluded

**excomungar** /iskomũ'gar/ *vt* excommunicate

**excremento** /iskre'mẽtu/ *m* excrement

**excur|são** /iskur'sãw/ *f* excursion; (*a pé*) hike, walk; **∼sionista** *m/f* day-tripper; (*a pé*) hiker, walker

**execu|ção** /ezeku'sãw/ *f* execution; **∼tante** *m/f* performer; **∼tar** *vt* carry out <*ordem, plano etc*>; perform <*papel, música*>; execute <*preso, criminoso etc*>; **∼tivo** *a & m* executive

**exem|plar** /ezẽ'plar/ *a* exemplary □ *m* (*de espécie*) example; (*de livro, jornal etc*) copy; **∼plificar** *vt* exemplify

**exemplo** /e'zẽplu/ *m* example; **a ∼ de** following the example of; **por ∼** for example; **dar o ∼** set an example

**exeqüi|vel** /eze'kwivew/ (*pl* **∼veis**) *a* feasible

**exer|cer** /ezer'ser/ *vt* exercise; exert <*pressão, influência*>; carry on <*profissão*>; **∼cício** *m* exercise; (*mil*) drill; (*de profissão*) practice; (*financeiro*) financial year; **∼citar** *vt* exercise; practise <*ofício*>; **∼citar-se** *vpr* train

**exército** /e'zɛrsitu/ *m* army

**exibição** /ezibi'sãw/ *f* (*de filme, passaporte etc*) showing; (*de talento, força, ostentação*) show

**exibicionis|mo** /ezibisio'nizmu/ *m* exhibitionism; **∼ta** *a & m/f* exhibitionist

**exi|bido** /ezi'bidu/ *a* <*pessoa*> pretentious □ *m* show-off; **∼bir** *vt* show; (*ostentar*) show off; **∼bir-se** *vpr* (*ostentar-se*) show off

**exi|gência** /ezi'ʒẽsia/ *f* demand; **∼gente** *a* demanding; **∼gir** *vt* demand

**exíguo** /e'zigwu/ *a* (*muito pequeno*) tiny; (*escasso*) minimal

**exi|lado** /ezi'ladu/ *a* exiled □ *m* exile; **∼lar** *vt* exile; **∼lar-se** *vpr* go into exile

**exílio** /e'ziliu/ *m* exile

**exímio** /e'zimiu/ *a* distinguished

**eximir** /ezi'mir/ *vt* exempt (**de** from); **∼-se de** get out of

**exis|tência** /ezis'tẽsia/ *f* existence; **∼tencial** (*pl* **∼tenciais**) *a* existential; **∼tente** *a* existing; **∼tir** *vi* exist

**êxito** /'ezitu/ *m* success; (*música, filme etc*) hit; **ter ∼** succeed

**êxodo** /'ezodu/ *m* exodus

**exonerar** /ezone'rar/ *vt* (*de cargo*) dismiss, sack; **∼-se** *vpr* resign

**exorbitante** /ezorbi'tãtʃi/ *a* exorbitant

**exor|cismo** /ezor'sizmu/ *m* exorcism; **∼cista** *m/f* exorcist; **∼cizar** *vt* exorcize

**exótico** /e'zɔtʃiku/ *a* exotic

**expan|dir** /ispã'dʒir/ *vt* spread; **∼dir-se** *vpr* spread; <*pessoa*> open up; **∼dir-se sobre** expand upon; **∼são** *f* expansion; **∼sivo** *a* expansive, open

**expatri|ado** /ispatri'adu/ *a & m* expatriate; **∼ar-se** *vpr* leave one's country

**expectativa** /ispekta'tʃiva/ *f* expectation; **na ∼ de** expecting; **estar na ∼** wait to see what happens; **∼ de vida** life expectancy

**expedição** /ispedʒi'sãw/ *f* (*de encomendas, cartas*) dispatch; (*de passaporte, diploma etc*) issue; (*viagem*) expedition

**expediente** /ispedʒi'ẽtʃi/ *a* <*pessoa*> resourceful □ *m* (*horário*) working hours; (*meios*) expedient; **meio ∼** part-time

**expe|dir** /ispe'dʒir/ *vt* dispatch < *encomendas, cartas*>; issue < *passaporte, diploma*>; **~dito** *a* prompt, quick

**expelir** /ispe'lir/ *vt* expel

**experi|ência** /isperi'ẽsia/ *f* experience; (*teste, tentativa*) experiment; **~ente** *a* experienced

**experimen|tação** /isperimẽta'sãw/ *f* experimentation; **~tado** *a* experienced; **~tar** *vt* (*provar*) try out; try on < *roupa*>; try < *comida*>; (*sentir, viver*) experience; **~to** *m* experiment

**expi|ar** /espi'ar/ *vt* atone for; **~atório** *a* **bode ~atório** scapegoat

**expi|ração** /espira'sãw/ *f* (*vencimento*) expiry; (*de ar*) exhalation; **~rar** *vt* exhale □ *vi* (*morrer, vencer*) expire; (*expelir ar*) breath out, exhale

**expli|cação** /isplika'sãw/ *f* explanation; **~car** *vt* explain; **~car-se** *vpr* explain o.s.; **~cável** (*pl* **~cáveis**) *a* explainable

**explicitar** /isplisi'tar/ *vt* set out

**explícito** /is'plisitu/ *a* explicit

**explo|dir** /isplo'dʒir/ *vt* explode □ *vi* explode; < *ator etc*> make it big

**explo|ração** /isplora'sãw/ *f* (*uso, abuso*) exploitation; (*pesquisa*) exploration; **~rar** *vt* (*tirar proveito de*) exploit; (*esquadrinhar*) explore

**explo|são** /isplo'zãw/ *f* explosion; **~sivo** *a & m* explosive

**expor** /es'por/ *vt* (*sujeitar, arriscar*) expose (**a** to); display < *mercadorias*>; exhibit < *obras de arte*>; (*explicar*) expound; **~ a vida** risk one's life; **~-se** *vpr* expose o.s. (**a** to)

**expor|tação** /isporta'sãw/ *f* export; **~tador** *a* exporting □ *m* exporter; **~tadora** *f* export company; **~tar** *vt* export

**exposi|ção** /ispozi'sãw/ *f* (*de arte etc*) exhibition; (*de mercadorias*) display; (*de filme fotográfico*) exposure; (*explicação*) exposition; **~tor** *m* exhibitor

**exposto** /is'postu/ *a* exposed (**a** to); < *mercadoria, obra de arte*> on display

**expres|são** /ispre'sãw/ *f* expression; **~sar** *vt* express; **~sar-se** *vpr* express o.s.; **~sivo** *a* expressive; < *número, quantia*> significant; **~so** /ε/ *a & m* express

**exprimir** /ispri'mir/ *vt* express; **~-se** *vpr* express o.s.

**expropriar** /ispropri'ar/ *vt* expropriate

**expul|são** /ispuw'sãw/ *f* expulsion; (*de jogador*) sending off; **~sar** *vt* (*de escola, partido, país etc*) expel; (*de clube, bar, festa etc*) throw out; (*de jogo*) send off; **~so** *pp* de **expulsar**

**expur|gar** /ispur'gar/ *vt* purge; expurgate < *livro*>; **~go** *m* purge

**êxtase** /'estazi/ *f* ecstasy

**extasiado** /istazi'adu/ *a* ecstatic

**exten|são** /istẽ'sãw/ *f* extension; (*tamanho, alcance, duração*) extent; (*de terreno*) expanse; **~sivo** *a* extensive; **~so** *a* extensive; **por ~so** in full

**extenu|ante** /istenu'ãtʃi/ *a* wearing, tiring; **~ar** *vt* tire out; **~ar-se** *vpr* tire o.s. out

**exterior** /isteri'or/ *a* outside, exterior; < *aparência*> outward; < *relações, comércio etc*> foreign □ *m* outside, exterior; (*de pessoa*) exterior; **o ~** (*outros países*) abroad; **para o/no ~** abroad

**exter|minar** /istermi'nar/ *vt* exterminate; **~mínio** *m* extermination

**exter|nar** /ister'nar/ *vt* show; **~na** /ε/ *f* location shot; **~no** /ε/ *a* external; < *dívida etc*> foreign □ *m* day-pupil

**extin|ção** /istʃi'sãw/ *f* extinction; **~guir** *vt* extinguish < *fogo*>; wipe out < *dívida, animal, povo*>; **~guir-se** *vpr* < *fogo, luz*> go out; < *animal, planta*> become extinct; **~to** *a* extinct; < *organização, pessoa*> defunct; **~tor** *m* fire extinguisher

**extirpar** /istʃir'par/ *vt* remove < *tumor etc*>; uproot < *ervas daninhas*>; eradicate < *abusos*>

**extor|quir** /istor'kir/ *vt* extort; **~são** *f* extortion

**extra** /'εstra/ *a & m/f* extra; **horas ~s** overtime

**extração** /istra'sãw/ *f* extraction; (*da loteria*) draw

**extraconju|gal** /istrakõʒu'gaw/ (*pl* **~gais**) *a* extramarital

**extracurricular** /istrakuxiku'lar/ *a* extracurricular

**extradi|ção** /istradʒi'sãw/ *f* extradition; **~tar** *vt* extradite

**extrair** /istra'ir/ *vt* extract; draw < *números da loteria*>

**extrajudici|al** /istraʒudʒisi'aw/ (*pl* **~ais**) *a* out-of-court; **~almente** *adv* out of court

**extraordinário** /istraordʒi'nariu/ *a* extraordinary

**extrapolar** /istrapo'lar/ *vt* (*exceder*) overstep; (*calcular*) extrapolate □ *vi* overstep the mark, go too far

**extra-sensori|al** /istrasẽsori'aw/ (*pl* **~ais**) *a* extra-sensory

**extraterrestre** /estrate'xestri/ *a & m* extraterrestrial

**extrato** /is'tratu/ *m* extract; (*de conta*) statement

**extrava|gância** /istrava'gãsia/ *f* extravagance; **~gante** *a* extravagant

**extravasar** /istrava'zar/ *vt* release, let out < *emoções, sentimentos*> □ *vi* overflow

**extra|viado** /istravi'adu/ *a* lost; **~viar** *vt* lose, mislay < *papéis, car-*

*ta*>; lead astray <*pessoa*>; embezzle <*dinheiro*>; ~**viar-se** *vpr* go astray; <*carta*> get lost; ~**vio** *m* (*perda*) misplacement; (*de dinheiro*) embezzlement

**extre|midade** /estremi'dadʒi/ *f* end; (*do corpo*) extremity; ~**mismo** *m* extremism; ~**mista** *a* & *m/f* extremist; ~**mo** /e/ *a* & *m* extreme; **o Extremo Oriente** the Far East; ~**moso** /o/ *a* doting

**extrovertido** /istrover'tʃido/ *a* & *m* extrovert

**exube|rância** /ezube'rãsia/ *f* exuberance; ~**rante** *a* exuberant

**exultar** /ezuw'tar/ *vi* exult

**exumar** /ezu'mar/ *vt* exhume <*cadáver*>; dig up <*documentos etc*>

# F

**fã** /fã/ *m/f* fan

**fábrica** /'fabrika/ *f* factory

**fabri|cação** /fabrika'sãw/ *f* manufacture; ~**cante** *m/f* manufacturer; ~**car** *vt* manufacture; (*inventar*) fabricate

**fábula** /'fabula/ *f* fable; (*fam: dinheirão*) fortune

**fabuloso** /fabu'lozu/ *a* fabulous

**faca** /'faka/ *f* knife; ~**da** *f* knife blow; **dar uma ~da em** (*fig*) get some money off

**façanha** /fa'saɲa/ *f* feat

**facção** /fak'sãw/ *f* faction

**face** /'fasi/ *f* face; (*do rosto*) cheek; ~**ta** /e/ *f* facet

**fachada** /fa'ʃada/ *f* façade

**facho** /'faʃu/ *m* beam

**faci|al** /fasi'aw/ (*pl* ~**ais**) *a* facial

**fá|cil** /'fasiw/ (*pl* ~**ceis**) *a* easy; <*pessoa*> easy-going

**facili|dade** /fasili'dadʒi/ *f* ease; (*talento*) facility; ~**tar** *vt* facilitate

**fã-clube** /fã'klubi/ *m* fan club

**fac-símile** /fak'simili/ *m* facsimile; (*fax*) fax

**fact-** (*Port*) *veja* **fat-**

**facul|dade** /fakuw'dadʒi/ *f* (*mental etc*) faculty; (*escola*) university, (*Amer*) college; **fazer ~dade** go to university; ~**tativo** *a* optional

**fada** /'fada/ *f* fairy; ~**do** *a* destined, doomed; ~**madrinha** (*pl* ~**s-madrinhas**) *f* fairy godmother

**fadiga** /fa'dʒiga/ *f* fatigue

**fa|dista** /fa'dʒista/ *m/f* fado singer; ~**do** *m* fado

**fagote** /fa'ɡɔtʃi/ *m* bassoon

**fagulha** /fa'ɡuʎa/ *f* spark

**faia** /'faja/ *f* beech

**faisão** /faj'zãw/ *m* pheasant

**faísca** /fa'iska/ *f* spark

**fais|cante** /fajs'kãtʃi/ *a* sparkling; ~**car** *vi* spark; (*cintilar*) sparkle

**faixa** /'faʃa/ *f* strip; (*cinto*) sash; (*em karatê, judô*) belt; (*da estrada*) lane; (*para pedestres*) zebra crossing, (*Amer*) crosswalk; (*atadura*) bandage; (*de disco*) track; ~ **etária** age group

**fajuto** /fa'ʒutu/ (*fam*) *a* fake

**fala** /'fala/ *f* speech

**falácia** /fa'lasia/ *f* fallacy

**fa|lado** /fa'ladu/ *a* <*língua*> spoken; <*caso, pessoa*> talked about; ~**lante** *a* talkative; ~**lar** *vt/i* speak; (*dizer*) say; ~**lar com** talk to; ~**lar de** *ou* **em** talk about; **por ~lar em** speaking of; **sem ~lar em** not to mention; ~**lou!** (*fam*) OK!; ~**latório** *m* (*boatos*) talk; (*som de vozes*) talking

**falaz** /fa'las/ *a* fallacious

**falcão** /faw'kãw/ *m* falcon

**falcatrua** /fawka'trua/ *f* swindle

**fale|cer** /fale'ser/ *vi* die, pass away; ~**cido** *a* & *m* deceased; ~**cimento** *m* death

**falência** /fa'lẽsia/ *f* bankruptcy; **ir à ~** go bankrupt

**falésia** /fa'lɛzia/ *f* cliff

**fa|lha** /'faʎa/ *f* fault; (*omissão*) failure; ~**lhar** *vi* fail; ~**lho** *a* faulty

**fálico** /'faliku/ *a* phallic

**fa|lido** /fa'lidu/ *a* & *m* bankrupt; ~**lir** *vi* go bankrupt; ~**lível** (*pl* ~**líveis**) *a* fallible

**falo** /'falu/ *m* phallus

**fal|sário** /faw'sariu/ *m* forger; ~**sear** *vt* falsify; ~**sete** *m* falsetto; ~**sidade** *f* falseness; (*mentira*) falsehood

**falsifi|cação** /fawsifika'sãw/ *f* forgery; ~**cador** *m* forger; ~**car** *vt* falsify; forge <*documentos, notas*>

**falso** /'fawsu/ *a* false

**fal|ta** /'fawta/ *f* lack; (*em futebol*) foul; **em ~ta** at fault; **por ~ta de** for lack of; **sem ~ta** without fail; **fazer ~ta** be needed; **sentir a ~ta de** miss; ~**tar** *vi* be missing; <*aluno*> be absent; ~**tam dois dias para** it's two days until; **me ~ta ...** I don't have ...; ~**tar a** miss <*aula etc*>; break <*palavra, promessa*>; ~**to** *a* short (**de** of)

**fa|ma** /'fama/ *f* reputation; (*celebridade*) fame; ~**migerado** *a* notorious

**família** /fa'milia/ *f* family

**famili|ar** /famili'ar/ *a* familiar; (*de família*) family; ~**aridade** *f* familiarity; ~**arizar** *vt* familiarize; ~**arizar-se** *vpr* familiarize o.s.

**faminto** /fa'mĩtu/ *a* starving

**famoso** /fa'mozu/ *a* famous

**fanático** /fa'natʃiku/ *a* fanatical □ *m* fanatic

**fanatismo** /fana'tʃizmu/ *m* fanaticism

**fanfarrão** /fãfaˈxãw/ *m* braggart

**fanhoso** /faˈɲozu/ *a* nasal; **ser ~** talk through one's nose

**fanta|sia** /fãtaˈzia/ *f* ( *faculdade*) imagination; (*devaneio*) fantasy; (*roupa*) fancy dress; **~siar** *vt* dream up □ *vi* fantasize; **~siar-se** *vpr* dress up (**de** as); **~sioso** /o/ *a* fanciful; <*pessoa*> imaginative; **~sista** *a* imaginative

**fantasma** /fãˈtazma/ *m* ghost; **~górico** *a* ghostly

**fantástico** /fãˈtastʃiku/ *a* fantastic

**fantoche** /fãˈtɔʃi/ *m* puppet

**faqueiro** /faˈkeru/ *m* canteen of cutlery

**fara|ó** /faraˈɔ/ *m* pharaoh; **~ônico** *a* ( *fig*) of epic proportions

**farda** /ˈfarda/ *f* uniform; **~do** *a* uniformed

**fardo** /ˈfardu/ *m* ( *fig*) burden

**fare|jador** /fareʒaˈdor/ *a* **cão ~jador** sniffer dog; **~jar** *vt* sniff out □ *vi* sniff

**farelo** /faˈrɛlu/ *m* bran; (*de pão*) crumb; (*de madeira*) sawdust

**farfalhar** /farfaˈʎar/ *vi* rustle

**farináceo** /fariˈnasiu/ *a* starchy; **~s** *m pl* starchy foods

**farin|ge** /faˈrĩʒi/ *f* pharynx; **~gite** *f* pharyngitis

**farinha** /faˈriɲa/ *f* flour; **~ de rosca** breadcrumbs

**far|macêutico** /farmaˈsewtʃiku/ *a* pharmaceutical □ *m* ( *pessoa*) pharmacist; **~mácia** *f* ( *loja*) chemist's, (*Amer*) pharmacy; (*ciência*) pharmacy

**faro** /ˈfaru/ *m* sense of smell; ( *fig*) nose

**faroeste** /faroˈɛstʃi/ *m* ( *filme*) western; (*região*) wild west

**faro|fa** /faˈrɔfa/ *f* fried manioc flour; **~feiro** ( *fam*) *m* day-tripper

**fa|rol** /faˈrɔw/ ( *pl* **~róis**) *m* (*de carro*) headlight; (*de trânsito*) traffic light; (*à beira-mar*) lighthouse; **~rol alto** full beam; **~rol baixo** dipped beam; **~roleiro** *a* boastful □ *m* bighead; **~rolete** /e/ *m*, (*Port*) **~rolim** *m* side-light; (*traseiro*) tail-light

**farpa** /ˈfarpa/ *f* splinter; (*de metal, fig*) barb; **~do** *a* **arame ~do** barbed wire

**farra** /ˈfaxa/ ( *fam*) *f* partying; **cair na ~** go out and party

**farrapo** /faˈxapu/ *m* rag

**far|rear** /faxiˈar/ ( *fam*) *vi* party; **~rista** ( *fam*) *m/f* raver

**far|sa** /ˈfarsa/ *f* ( *peça*) farce; ( *fingimento*) pretence; **~sante** *m/f* (*brincalhão*) joker; ( *pessoa sem seriedade*) unreliable character

**far|tar** /farˈtar/ *vt* satiate; **~tar-se** *vpr* (*saciar-se*) gorge o.s. (**de** with); (*cansar*) tire (**de** of); **~to** *a* (*abundante*) plentiful; (*cansado*) fed up (**de** with); **~tura** *f* abundance

**fascículo** /faˈsikulu/ *m* instalment

**fasci|nação** /fasinaˈsãw/ *f* fascination; **~nante** *a* fascinating; **~nar** *vt* fascinate

**fascínio** /faˈsiniu/ *m* fascination

**fas|cismo** /faˈsizmu/ *m* fascism; **~cista** *a* & *m/f* fascist

**fase** /ˈfazi/ *f* phase

**fa|tal** /faˈtaw/ ( *pl* **~tais**) *a* fatal; **~talismo** *m* fatalism; **~talista** *a* fatalistic □ *m/f* fatalist; **~talmente** *adv* inevitably

**fatia** /faˈtʃia/ *f* slice

**fatídico** /faˈtʃidʒiku/ *a* fateful

**fati|gante** /fatʃiˈgãtʃi/ *a* tiring; **~gar** *vt* tire, fatigue

**fato**[1] /ˈfatu/ *m* fact; **de ~** as a matter of fact, in fact; **~ consumado** fait accompli

**fato**[2] /ˈfatu/ (*Port*) *m* suit

**fator** /faˈtor/ *m* factor

**fátuo** /ˈfatuu/ *a* fatuous

**fatu|ra** /faˈtura/ *f* invoice; **~ramento** *m* turnover; **~rar** *vt* invoice for <*encomenda*>; make <*dinheiro*>; ( *fig: emplacar*) notch up □ *vi* ( *fam*) rake it in

**fauna** /ˈfawna/ *f* fauna

**fava** /ˈfava/ *f* broad bean; **mandar alg às ~s** tell s.o. where to get off

**favela** /faˈvɛla/ *f* shanty town; **~do** *m* shanty-dweller

**favo** /ˈfavu/ *m* honeycomb

**favor** /faˈvor/ *m* favour; **a ~ de** in favour of; **por ~** please; **faça ~** please

**favo|rável** /favoˈravew/ ( *pl* **~ráveis**) *a* favourable; **~recer** *vt* favour; **~ritismo** *m* favouritism; **~rito** *a* & *m* favourite

**faxi|na** /faˈʃina/ *f* clean-up; **~neiro** *m* cleaner

**fazen|da** /faˈzẽda/ *f* (*de café, gado etc*) farm; (*tecido*) fabric, material; ( *pública*) treasury; **~deiro** *m* farmer

**fazer** /faˈzer/ *vt* do; ( *produzir*) make; ask <*pergunta*>; **~-se** *vpr* (*tornar-se*) become; **~-se de** make o.s. out to be; **~ anos** have a birthday; **~ 20 anos** be twenty; **faz dois dias que ele está aqui** he's been here for two days; **faz dez anos que ele morreu** it's ten years since he died; **tanto faz** it doesn't matter

**faz-tudo** /fasˈtudu/ *m/f invar* jack of all trades

**fé** /fɛ/ *f* faith

**fe|bre** /ˈfɛbri/ *f* fever; **~bre amarela** yellow fever; **~bre do feno** hay fever; **~bril** ( *pl* **~bris**) *a* feverish

**fe|chado** /feˈʃadu/ *a* closed; <*curva*> sharp; <*sinal*> red; <*torneira*> off; <*tempo*> overcast; <*cara*> stern; <*pessoa*> reserved; **~chadura** *f* lock; ~**chamento** *m* closure; ~**char** *vt* close, shut; turn off <*torneira*>; do up <*calça, casaco*>; close <*negócio*> □ *vi* close, shut; <*sinal*> go red; <*tempo*> cloud over; ~**char à chave** lock; ~**char a cara** frown; ~**cho** /e/ *m* fastener; ~**cho ecler** zip

**fécula** /'fɛkula/ *f* starch

**fecun|dar** /fekũ'dar/ *vt* fertilize; ~**do** *a* fertile

**feder** /fe'der/ *vi* stink

**fede|ração** /federa'sãw/ *f* federation; ~**ral** (*pl* ~**rais**) *a* federal; (*fam*) huge; ~**rativo** *a* federal

**fedor** /fe'dor/ *m* stink, stench; ~**ento** *a* stinking

**feérico** /fe'ɛriku/ *a* magical

**feições** /fej'sõjs/ *f pl* features

**fei|jão** /fe'ʒãw/ *m* bean; (*coletivo*) beans; ~**joada** *f* bean stew; ~**joeiro** *m* bean plant

**feio** /'feju/ *a* ugly; <*palavra, situação, tempo*> nasty; <*olhar*> dirty; ~**so** /o/ *a* plain

**fei|ra** /'fera/ *f* market; (*industrial*) trade fair; ~**rante** *m/f* market trader

**feiti|çaria** /fejtʃi'sera/ *f* magic; ~**ceira** *f* witch; ~**ceiro** *m* wizard □ *a* bewitching; ~**ço** *m* spell

**fei|tio** /fej'tʃiu/ *m* (*de pessoa*) make-up; ~**to** *pp de* **fazer** □ *m* (*ato*) deed; (*proeza*) feat □ *conj* like; **bem** ~**to por ele** (it) serves him right; ~**tura** *f* making

**feiúra** /fej'ura/ *f* ugliness

**feixe** /'fejʃi/ *m* bundle

**fel** /fɛw/ *f* gall; (*fig*) bitterness

**felicidade** /felisi'dadʒi/ *f* happiness

**felici|tações** /felisita'sõjs/ *f pl* congratulations; ~**tar** *vt* congratulate (**por** on)

**felino** /fe'linu/ *a* feline

**feliz** /fe'lis/ *a* happy; ~**ardo** *a* lucky; ~**mente** *adv* fortunately

**fel|pa** /'fewpa/ *f* (*de pano*) nap; (*penugem*) down, fluff; ~**pudo** *a* fluffy

**feltro** /'fewtru/ *m* felt

**fêmea** /'femia/ *a & f* female

**femi|nil** /femi'niw/ (*pl* ~**nis**) *a* feminine; ~**nilidade** *f* femininity; ~**nino** *a* female; <*palavra*> feminine; ~**nismo** *m* feminism; ~**nista** *a & m/f* feminist

**fêmur** /'femur/ *m* femur

**fen|da** /'fẽda/ *f* crack; ~**der** *vt/i* split, crack

**feno** /'fenu/ *m* hay

**fenome|nal** /fenome'naw/ (*pl* ~**nais**) *a* phenomenal

**fenômeno** /fe'nomenu/ *m* phenomenon

**fera** /'fɛra/ *f* wild beast; **ficar uma** ~ get really angry; **ser** ~ **em** (*fam*) be brilliant at

**féretro** /'fɛretru/ *m* coffin

**feriado** /feri'adu/ *m* public holiday

**férias** /'fɛrias/ *f pl* holiday(s), (*Amer*) vacation; **de** ~ on holiday; **tirar** ~ take a holiday

**feri|da** /fe'rida/ *f* injury; (*com arma*) wound; ~**do** *a* injured; (*mil*) wounded □ *m* injured person; **os** ~**dos** the injured; (*mil*) the wounded; ~**r** *vt* injure; (*com arma*) wound; (*magoar*) hurt

**fermen|tar** /fermẽ'tar/ *vt/i* ferment; ~**to** *m* yeast; (*fig*) ferment; ~**to em pó** baking powder

**fe|rocidade** /ferosi'dadʒi/ *f* ferocity; ~**roz** *a* ferocious

**fer|rado** /fe'xadu/ *a* **estou** ~**rado** (*fam*) I've had it; ~**rado no sono** fast asleep; ~**radura** *f* horseshoe; ~**ragem** *f* ironwork; *pl* hardware; ~**ramenta** *f* tool; (*coletivo*) tools; ~**rão** *m* (*de abelha*) sting; ~**rar** *vt* brand <*gado*>; shoe <*cavalo*>; ~**rar-se** (*fam*) *vpr* come a cropper; ~**reiro** *m* blacksmith; ~**renho** *a* <*partidário etc*> staunch; <*vontade*> iron

**férreo** /'fɛxiu/ *a* iron

**ferro** /'fɛxu/ *m* iron; ~**lho** /o/ *m* bolt; ~-**velho** (*pl* ~**s-velhos**) *m* (*pessoa*) scrap-metal dealer; (*lugar*) scrap-metal yard; ~**via** *f* railway, (*Amer*) railroad; ~**viário** *a* railway □ *m* railway worker

**ferrugem** /fe'xuʒẽ/ *f* rust

**fér|til** /'fɛrtʃiw/ (*pl* ~**teis**) *a* fertile

**fertili|dade** /fertʃili'dadʒi/ *f* fertility; ~**zante** *m* fertilizer; ~**zar** *vt* fertilize

**fer|vente** /fer'vẽtʃi/ *a* boiling; ~**ver** *vi* boil; (*de raiva*) seethe; ~**vilhar** *vi* bubble; ~**vilhar de** swarm with; ~**vor** *m* fervour; ~**vura** *f* boiling

**fes|ta** /'fɛsta/ *f* party; (*religiosa*) festival; ~**tejar** *vt/i* celebrate; (*acolher*) fete; ~**tejo** /e/ *m* celebration; ~**tim** *m* feast; ~**tival** (*pl* ~**tivais**) *m* festival; ~**tividade** *f* festivity; ~**tivo** *a* festive

**feti|che** /fe'tʃiʃi/ *m* fetish; ~**chismo** *m* fetishism; ~**chista** *m/f* fetishist □ *a* fetishistic

**fétido** /'fɛtʃidu/ *a* fetid

**feto**¹ /'fɛtu/ *m* (*no útero*) foetus

**feto**² /'fɛtu/ (*Port*) *m* (*planta*) fern

**feu|dal** /few'daw/ (*pl* ~**dais**) *a* feudal; ~**dalismo** *m* feudalism

**fevereiro** /feve'reru/ *m* February

**fezes** /'fɛzis/ *f pl* faeces

**fiação** /fia'sãw/ *f* (*eletr*) wiring; (*fábrica*) mill

**fia|do** /fi'adu/ *a* <*conversa*> idle □ *adv* <*comprar*> on credit; ~**dor** *m* guarantor

**fiambre** /fi'ãbri/ *m* cooked ham

**fiança** /fi'ãsa/ f surety; (*jurid*) bail
**fiapo** /fi'apu/ m thread
**fiar** /fi'ar/ vt spin <*lã etc*>
**fiasco** /fi'asku/ m fiasco
**fibra** /'fibra/ f fibre
**ficar** /fi'kar/ vi (*tornar-se*) become; (*estar, ser*) be; (*manter-se*) stay; ~ **fazendo** keep (on) doing; ~ **com** keep; get <*impressão, vontade*>; ~ **com medo** get scared; ~ **de fazer** arrange to do; ~ **para** be left for; ~ **bom** turn out well; (*recuperar-se*) get better; ~ **bem** look good
**fic|ção** /fik'sãw/ f fiction; ~**ção científica** science fiction; ~**cionista** m/f fiction writer
**fi|cha** /'fiʃa/ f (*de telefone*) token; (*de jogo*) chip; (*da caixa*) ticket; (*de fichário*) file card; (*na polícia*) record; (*Port: tomada*) plug; ~**chário** m, (*Port*) ~**cheiro** m file; (*móvel*) filing cabinet
**fictício** /fik'tʃisiu/ a fictitious
**fidalgo** /fi'dalgu/ m nobleman
**fide|digno** /fide'dʒignu/ a trustworthy; ~**lidade** f fidelity
**fiduciário** /fidusi'ariu/ a fiduciary □ m trustee
**fi|el** /fi'ɛw/ (*pl* ~**éis**) a faithful □ m os ~**éis** (*na igreja*) the congregation
**figa** /'figa/ f talisman
**fígado** /'figadu/ f liver
**fi|go** /'figu/ m fig; ~**gueira** f fig tree
**figu|ra** /fi'gura/ f figure; (*carta de jogo*) face card; (*fam: pessoa*) character; **fazer (má)** ~**ra** make a (bad) impression; ~**rado** a figurative; ~**rante** m/f extra; ~**rão** m big shot; ~**rar** vi appear, figure; ~**rativo** a figurative; ~**rinha** f sticker; ~**rino** m fashion plate; (*de filme, peça*) costume design; (*fig*) model; **como manda o** ~**rino** as it should be
**fila** /'fila/ f line; (*de espera*) queue, (*Amer*) line; (*fileira*) row; **fazer** ~ queue up, (*Amer*) stand in line; ~ **indiana** single file
**filamento** /fila'mẽtu/ m filament
**filante** /fi'lãtʃi/ (*fam*) m/f sponger
**filan|tropia** /filãtro'pia/ f philanthropy; ~**trópico** a philanthropic; ~**tropo** /o/ m philanthropist
**filão** /fi'lãw/ m (*de ouro*) seam; (*fig*) money-spinner
**filar** /fi'lar/ (*fam*) vt sponge, cadge
**filar|mônica** /filar'monika/ f philharmonic (orchestra); ~**mônico** a philharmonic
**filate|lia** /filate'lia/ f philately; ~**lista** m/f philatelist
**filé** /fi'lɛ/ m fillet
**fileira** /fi'lera/ f row
**filete** /fi'letʃi/ m fillet
**fi|lha** /'fiʎa/ f daughter; ~**lho** m son; pl (*crianças*) children; ~**lho da puta**

(*chulo*) bastard, (*Amer*) son of a bitch; ~**lho de criação** foster child; ~**lho único** only child; ~**lhote** m (*de cão*) pup; (*de lobo etc*) cub; pl young
**fili|ação** /filia'sãw/ f affiliation; ~**al** (*pl* ~**ais**) a filial □ f branch
**Filipinas** /fili'pinas/ f pl Philippines
**filipino** /fili'pinu/ a & m Filipino
**fil|madora** /fiwma'dora/ f camcorder; ~**magem** f filming; ~**mar** vt/i film; ~**me** m film
**fi|lologia** /filolo'ʒia/ f philology; ~**lólogo** m philologist
**filo|sofar** /filozo'far/ vi philosophize; ~**sofia** f philosophy; ~**sófico** a philosophical
**filósofo** /fi'lozofu/ m philosopher
**fil|trar** /fiw'trar/ vt filter; ~**tro** m fil-ʼer
**fi**\_ /fĩ/ m end; **a** ~ **de** (*para*) in order to; **estar a** ~ **de** fancy; **por** ~ finally; **sem** ~ endless; **ter** ~ come to an end; ~ **de semana** weekend
**fi|nado** /fi'nadu/ a & m deceased, departed; ~**nal** (*pl* ~**nais**) a final □ m end □ f final; ~**nalista** m/f finalist; ~**nalizar** vt/i finish
**finan|ças** /fi'nãsas/ f pl finances; ~**ceiro** a financial □ m financier; ~**ciamento** m financing; (*um*) loan; ~**ciar** vt finance; ~**cista** m/f financier
**fincar** /fĩ'kar/ vt plant; ~ **o pé** (*fig*) dig one's heels in
**findar** /fĩ'dar/ vt/i end
**fineza** /fi'neza/ f finesse; (*favor*) kindness
**fin|gido** /fĩ'ʒidu/ a feigned; <*pessoa*> insincere; ~**gimento** m pretence; ~**gir** vt pretend; feign <*doença etc*> □ vi pretend; ~**gir-se de** pretend to be
**finito** /fi'nitu/ a finite
**finlan|dês** /filã'des/ a (*f* ~**desa**) Finnish □ m (*f* ~**desa**) Finn; (*língua*) Finnish
**Finlândia** /fi'lãdʒia/ f Finland
**fi|ninho** /fi'niɲu/ adv **sair de** ~**ninho** slip away; ~**no** a (*não grosso*) thin; <*areia, pó etc*> fine; (*refinado*) refined; ~**nório** a crafty; ~**nura** f thinness; fineness
**fio** /'fiu/ m thread; (*elétrico*) wire; (*de sangue, água*) trickle; (*de luz, esperança*) glimmer; (*de navalha etc*) edge; **horas a** ~ hours on end
**fir|ma** /'firma/ f firm; (*assinatura*) signature; ~**mamento** m firmament; ~**mar** vt fix; (*basear*) base □ vi settle; ~**mar-se** vpr be based (em on); ~**me a** firm; <*tempo*> settled □ adv firmly; ~**meza** f firmness
**fis|cal** /fis'kaw/ (*pl* ~**cais**) m inspector; ~**calização** f inspection;

**~calizar** *vt* inspect; **~co** *m* inland revenue, (*Amer*) internal revenue service

**fis|gada** /fiz'gada/ *f* stabbing pain; **~gar** *vt* hook

**físi|ca** /'fizika/ *f* physics; **~co** *a* physical □ *m* (*pessoa*) physicist; (*corpo*) physique

**fisio|nomia** /fizio'nomia/ *f* face; **~nomista** *m/f* ser **~nomista** have a good memory for faces; **~terapeuta** *m/f* physiotherapist; **~terapia** *f* physiotherapy

**fissura** /fi'sura/ *f* fissure; ( *fam*) craving; **~do** *a* **~do em** ( *fam*) mad about

**fita** /'fita/ *f* tape; ( *fam: encenação*) playacting; **fazer ~** ( *fam*) put on an act; **~ adesiva** (*Port*) adhesive tape; **~ métrica** tape measure

**fitar** /fi'tar/ *vt* stare at

**fivela** /fi'vɛla/ *f* buckle

**fi|xador** /fiksa'dor/ *m* (*de cabelo*) setting lotion; (*de fotos*) fixative; **~xar** *vt* fix; stick up <*cartaz*>; **~xo** *a* fixed

**flácido** /'flasidu/ *a* flabby

**flagelo** /fla'ʒɛlu/ *m* scourge

**fla|grante** /fla'grãtʃi/ *a* flagrant; **apanhar em ~grante (delito)** catch in the act; **~grar** *vt* catch

**flame|jante** /flame'ʒãtʃi/ *a* blazing; **~jar** *vi* blaze

**flamengo** /fla'mẽgu/ *a* Flemish □ *m* Fleming; (*língua*) Flemish

**flamingo** /fla'mĩgu/ *m* flamingo

**flâmula** /'flamula/ *f* pennant

**flanco** /'flãku/ *m* flank

**flanela** /fla'nɛla/ *f* flannel

**flanquear** /flãki'ar/ *vt* flank

**flash** /flɛʃ/ *m invar* flash

**flau|ta** /'flawta/ *f* flute; **~tista** *m/f* flautist

**flecha** /'flɛʃa/ *f* arrow

**fler|tar** /fler'tar/ *vi* flirt; **~te** *m* flirtation

**fleuma** /'flewma/ *f* phlegm

**fle|xão** /flek'sãw/ *f* press-up, (*Amer*) push-up; (*ling*) inflection; **~xibilidade** *f* flexibility; **~xionar** *vt/i* flex <*perna, braço*>; (*ling*) inflect; **~xível** (*pl* **~xíveis**) *a* flexible

**fliperama** /flipe'rama/ *m* pinball machine

**floco** /'flɔku/ *m* flake

**flor** /flor/ *f* flower; **a fina ~** the cream; **à ~ da pele** ( *fig*) on edge

**flo|ra** /'flɔra/ *f* flora; **~reado** *a* full of flowers; ( *fig*) florid; **~reio** *m* clever turn of phrase; **~rescer** *vi* flower; **~resta** /ɛ/ *f* forest; **~restal** (*pl* **~restais**) *a* forest; **~rido** *a* in flower; ( *fig*) florid; **~rir** *vi* flower

**flotilha** /flo'tʃiʎa/ *f* flotilla

**fluência** /flu'ẽsia/ *f* fluency; **~ente** *a* fluent

**flui|dez** /flui'des/ *f* fluidity; **~do** *a* & *m* fluid

**fluir** /flu'ir/ *vi* flow

**fluminense** /flumi'nẽsi/ *a* & *m* (person) from Rio de Janeiro state

**fluorescente** /fluore'sẽtʃi/ *a* fluorescent

**flutu|ação** /flutua'sãw/ *f* fluctuation; **~ante** *a* floating; **~ar** *vi* float; <*bandeira*> flutter; (*hesitar*) waver

**fluvi|al** /fluvi'aw/ (*pl* **~ais**) *a* river

**fluxo** /'fluksu/ *m* flow; **~grama** *m* flowchart

**fobia** /fo'bia/ *f* phobia

**foca** /'fɔka/ *f* seal

**focalizar** /fokali'zar/ *vt* focus on

**focinho** /fo'siɲu/ *m* snout

**foco** /'fɔku/ *m* focus; ( *fig*) centre

**fofo** /'fofu/ *a* soft; <*pessoa*> cuddly

**fofo|ca** /fo'fɔka/ *f* piece of gossip; *pl* gossip; **~car** *vi* gossip; **~queiro** *m* gossip □ *a* gossipy

**fo|gão** /fo'gãw/ *m* stove; (*de cozinhar*) cooker; **~go** /o/ *m* fire; **tem ~go?** have you got a light?; **ser ~go** ( *fam*) (*ser chato*) be a pain in the neck; (*ser incrível*) be amazing; **~gos de artifício** fireworks; **~goso** /o/ *a* fiery; **~gueira** *f* bonfire; **~guete** /e/ *m* rocket

**foice** /'fojsi/ *f* scythe

**fol|clore** /fow'klɔri/ *m* folklore; **~clórico** *a* folk

**fole** /'fɔli/ *m* bellows

**fôlego** /'folegu/ *m* breath; ( *fig*) stamina

**fol|ga** /'fɔwga/ *f* rest, break; ( *fam: cara-de-pau*) cheek; **~gado** *a* <*roupa*> full, loose; <*vida*> leisurely; ( *fam: atrevido*) cheeky; **~gar** *vt* loosen □ *vi* have time off

**fo|lha** /'foʎa/ *f* leaf; (*de papel*) sheet; **novo em ~lha** brand new; **~lha de pagamento** payroll; **~lhagem** *f* foliage; **~lhear** *vt* leaf through; **~lheto** /e/ *m* pamphlet; **~lhinha** *f* tear-off calendar; **~lhudo** *a* leafy

**foli|a** /fo'lia/ *f* revelry; **~ão** *m* ( *f* **~ona**) reveller

**folículo** /fo'likulu/ *m* follicle

**fome** /'fomi/ *f* hunger; **estar com ~** be hungry

**fomentar** /fomẽ'tar/ *vt* foment

**fone** /'foni/ *m* (*do telefone*) receiver; (*de rádio etc*) headphones

**fonema** /fo'nema/ *m* phoneme

**fonéti|ca** /fo'nɛtʃika/ *f* phonetics; **~co** *a* phonetic

**fonologia** /fonolo'ʒia/ *f* phonology

**fonte** /'fõtʃi/ *f* (*de água*) spring; ( *fig*) source

**fora** /'fɔra/ *adv* outside; (*não em casa*) out; (*viajando*) away □ *prep* except; **dar um ~** drop a clanger; **dar um**

~ **em alg** cut s.o. dead; chuck
<*namorado*>; **por** ~ on the outside;
~-**de-lei** m/f invar outlaw
**foragido** /fora'ʒidu/ a at large, on the
run □ m fugitive
**forasteiro** /foras'teru/ m outsider
**forca** /'forka/ f gallows
**for|ça** /'forsa/ f (*vigor*) strength; (*vio-
lência*) force; (*elétrica*) power; **dar
uma** ~**ça a alg** help s.o. out; **fazer**
~**ça** make an effort; ~**ças armadas**
armed forces; ~**çar** vt force; ~**ça-
tarefa** (pl ~**ças-tarefa**) f task force
**fórceps** /'forseps/ m invar forceps
**forçoso** /for'sozu/ a forced
**for|ja** /'forʒa/ f forge; ~**jar** vt forge
**forma** /'forma/ f form; (*contorno*)
shape; (*maneira*) way; **de qualquer**
~ anyway; **manter a** ~ keep fit
**fôrma** /'forma/ f mould; (*de cozinha*)
baking tin
**for|mação** /forma'sãw/ f formation;
(*educação*) education; (*profissionalizante*) training; ~**mado** m graduate;
~**mal** (pl ~**mais**) a formal;
~**malidade** f formality; ~**malizar**
vt formalize; ~**mar** vt form; (*educar*)
educate; ~**mar-se** vpr be formed;
<*estudante*> graduate; ~**mato** m
format; ~**matura** f graduation
**formidá|vel** /formi'davew/ (pl
~**veis**) a formidable; (*muito bom*) tremendous
**formi|ga** /for'miga/ f ant; ~-
**gamento** m pins and needles; ~**gar**
vi swarm (**de** with); <*perna, mão etc*>
tingle; ~**gueiro** m ants' nest
**formosura** /formo'zura/ f beauty
**fórmula** /'formula/ f formula
**formu|lação** /formula'sãw/ f for-
mulation; ~**lar** vt formulate;
~**lário** m form
**fornalha** /for'naʎa/ f furnace
**forne|cedor** /fornese'dor/ m supplier;
~**cer** vt supply; ~**cer aco a alg** supply s.o. with sth; ~**cimento** m supply
**forno** /'fornu/ m oven; (*para louça
etc*) kiln
**foro** /'foru/ m forum
**forra** /'fɔxa/ f **ir à** ~ get one's own
back
**for|ragem** /fo'xaʒẽ/ f fodder; ~**rar** vt
line <*roupa, caixa etc*>; cover <*sofá
etc*>; carpet <*assoalho, sala etc*>; ~**ro**
/o/ m (*de roupa, caixa etc*) lining;
(*de sofá etc*) cover; (*carpete*) (fitted)
carpet
**forró** /fo'xɔ/ m type of Brazilian dance
**fortale|cer** /fortale'ser/ vt strengthen;
~**cimento** m strengthening; ~**za** /e/
f fort-ress
**for|te** /'fortʃi/ a strong; <*golpe*> hard;
<*chuva*> heavy; <*físico*> muscular □
adv strongly; <*bater, chover*> hard □

m (*militar*) fort; (*habilidade*) strong
point, forte; ~**tificação** f fortifica-
tion; ~**tificar** vt fortify
**fortu|ito** /for'tuitu/ a chance; ~**na** f
fortune
**fosco** /'fosku/ a dull; <*vidro*> frosted
**fosfato** /fos'fatu/ m phosphate
**fósforo** /'fɔsforu/ m match; (*elemento
químico*) phosphor
**fossa** /'fosa/ f pit; **na** ~ (*fig*) miserable, depressed
**fós|sil** /'fɔsiw/ (pl ~**seis**) m fossil
**fosso** /'fosu/ m ditch; (*de castelo*) moat
**foto** /'fɔtu/ f photo; ~**cópia** f photocopy; ~**copiadora** f photocopier;
~**copiar** vt photocopy; ~**gênico** a
photogenic; ~**grafar** vt photograph;
~**grafia** f photography; ~**gráfico** a
photographic
**fotógrafo** /fo'tɔgrafu/ m photo-
grapher
**foz** /fos/ f mouth
**fração** /fra'sãw/ f fraction
**fracas|sado** /fraka'sadu/ a failed □ m
failure; ~**sar** vi fail; ~**so** m failure
**fracionar** /frasio'nar/ vt break up
**fraco** /'fraku/ a weak; <*luz, som*>
faint; <*mediocre*> poor □ m weakness,
weak spot
**fract-** (*Port*) veja **frat-**
**frade** /'fradʒi/ m friar
**fragata** /fra'gata/ f frigate
**frá|gil** /'fraʒiw/ (pl ~**geis**) a fragile;
<*pessoa*> frail
**fragilidade** /fraʒili'dadʒi/ f fragility;
(*de pessoa*) frailty
**fragmen|tar** /fragmẽ'tar/ vt frag-
ment; ~**tar-se** vpr fragment; ~**to** m
fragment
**fra|grância** /fra'grãsia/ f fragrance;
~**grante** a fragrant
**fralda** /'frawda/ f nappy, (*Amer*) diaper
**framboesa** /frãbo'eza/ f raspberry
**França** /'frãsa/ f France
**fran|cês** /frã'ses/ a (f ~**cesa**) French
□ m (f ~**cesa**) Frenchman (f
-woman); (*língua*) French; **os** ~**ceses**
the French
**franco** /'frãku/ a (*honesto*) frank; (*óbvio*) clear; (*gratuito*) free □ m franc;
~-**atirador** (pl ~-**atiradores**) m
sniper; (*fig*) maverick
**frangalho** /frã'gaʎu/ m tatter
**frango** /'frãgu/ m chicken
**franja** /'frãʒa/ f fringe; (*do cabelo*)
fringe, (*Amer*) bangs
**fran|quear** /frãki'ar/ vt frank
<*carta*>; ~**queza** /e/ f frankness;
~**quia** f (*de cartas*) franking; (*jur*)
franchise
**fran|zino** /frã'zinu/ a skinny; ~**zir** vt
gather <*tecido*>; wrinkle <*testa*>
**fraque** /'fraki/ m morning suit

fraqueza /fra'keza/ f weakness; (de luz, som) faintness

frasco /'frasku/ m bottle

frase /'frazi/ f (oração) sentence; (locução) phrase; ~ado m phrasing

frasqueira /fras'kera/ f vanity case

frater|nal /frater'naw/ a (pl ~nais) a fraternal; ~nidade f fraternity; ~nizar vi fraternize; ~no a fraternal

fratu|ra /fra'tura/ f fracture; ~rar vt fracture; ~rar-se vpr fracture

frau|dar /fraw'dar/ vt defraud; ~de f fraud; ~dulento a fraudulent

frear /fri'ar/ vt/i brake

freezer /'frizer/ m freezer

fre|guês /fre'ges/ m (f ~guesa) customer; ~guesia f (de loja etc) clientele; (paróquia) parish

frei /frej/ m brother

freio /'freju/ m brake; (de cavalo) bit

freira /'frera/ f nun

freixo /'freʃu/ m ash

fremir /fre'mir/ vi shake

frêmito /'fremitu/ m wave

frenesi /frene'zi/ m frenzy

frenético /fre'nɛtʃiku/ a frantic

frente /'frẽtʃi/ f front; em ~ a ou de in front of; para a ~ forward; pela ~ ahead; fazer ~ a face

freqüência /fre'kwẽsia/ f frequency; (assiduidade) attendance; com muita ~ often

freqüen|tador /frekwẽta'dor/ m regular visitor (de to); ~tar vt frequent; (cursar) attend; ~te a frequent

fres|cão /fres'kãw/ m air-conditioned coach; ~co /e/ a <comida etc> fresh; <vento, água, quarto> cool; (fam) (afetado) affected; (exigente) fussy; ~cobol m kind of racquetball; ~cor m freshness; ~cura f (fam) (afetação) affectation; (ser exigente) fussiness; (coisa sem importância) trifle

fresta /'frɛsta/ f slit

fre|tar /fre'tar/ vt charter <avião>; hire <caminhão>; ~te /ɛ/ m freight; (aluguel de avião) charter; (de caminhão) hire

frevo /'frevu/ m type of Brazilian dance

fria /'fria/ (fam) f difficult situation, spot; ~gem f chill

fric|ção /frik'sãw/ f friction; ~cionar vt rub

fri|eira /fri'era/ f chilblain; ~eza /e/ f coldness

frigideira /friʒi'dera/ f frying pan

frígido /'friʒidu/ a frigid

frigorífico /frigo'rifiku/ m cold store, refrigerator, fridge

frincha /'frĩʃa/ f chink

frio /'friu/ a & m cold; estar com ~ be cold; ~rento a sensitive to the cold

frisar /fri'zar/ vt (enfatizar) stress; crimp <cabelo>

friso /'frizu/ m frieze

fri|tada /fri'tada/ f fry-up; ~tar vt fry; ~tas f pl chips, (Amer) French fries; ~to a fried; está ~to (fam) he's had it; ~tura f fried food

frivolidade /frivoli'dadʒi/ f frivolity; frívolo a frivolous

fronha /'froɲa/ f pillowcase

fronte /'frõtʃi/ f forehead, brow

frontei|ra /frõ'tera/ f border; ~riço a border

frota /'frɔta/ f fleet

frou|xidão /froʃi'dãw/ f looseness; (moral) laxity; ~xo a loose; <regulamento> lax; <pessoa> lackadaisical

fru|gal /fru'gaw/ (pl ~gais) a frugal; ~galidade f frugality

frus|tração /frustra'sãw/ f frustration; ~trante a frustrating; ~trar vt frustrate

fru|ta /'fruta/ f fruit; ~ta-do-conde (pl ~tas-do-conde) f sweetsop; ~ta-pão (pl ~tas-pão) f breadfruit; ~teira f fruitbowl; ~tífero a (fig) fruitful; ~to m fruit

fubá /fu'ba/ m maize flour

fu|car /fu'sar/ vi nose around; ~ças (fam) f pl face, chops

fu|ga /'fuga/ f escape; ~gaz a fleeting; ~gida f escape; ~gir vi run away; (soltar-se) escape; ~gir a avoid; ~gitivo a & m fugitive

fulano /fu'lanu/ m whatever his name is

fuleiro /fu'leru/ a down-market, cheap and cheerful

fulgor /fuw'gor/ m brightness; (fig) splendour

fuligem /fu'liʒẽ/ f soot

fulmi|nante /fuwmi'nãtʃi/ a devastating; ~nar vt strike down; (fig) devastate; ~nado por um raio struck by lightning □ vi (criticar) rail

fu|maça /fu'masa/ f smoke; ~maceira f cloud of smoke; ~mante, (Port) ~mador m smoker; ~mar vt/i smoke; ~mê a invar smoked; ~megar vi smoke; ~mo m (tabaco) tobacco; (Port: fumaça) smoke; (fumar) smoking

função /fũ'sãw/ f function; em ~ de as a result of; fazer as funções de function as

funcho /'fũʃu/ m fennel

funcio|nal /fũsio'naw/ (pl ~nais) a functional; ~nalismo m civil service; ~namento m working; ~nar vi work; ~nário m employee; ~nário público civil servant

fun|dação /fũda'sãw/ f foundation; ~dador m founder □ a founding

**fundamen|tal** /fũdamẽ'taw/ (*pl* ~**tais**) *a* fundamental; ~**tar** *vt* (*basear*) base; (*justificar*) substantiate; ~**to** *m* foundation

**fun|dar** /fũ'dar/ *vt* (*criar*) found; (*basear*) base; ~**dar-se** *vpr* be based (**em** on); ~**dear** *vi* drop anchor, anchor; ~**dilho** *m* seat

**fundir** /fũ'dʒir/ *vt* melt <*ouro, ferro*>; cast <*sino, estátua*>; (*juntar*) merge; ~**-se** *vpr* <*ouro, ferro*> melt; (*juntarse*) merge

**fundo** /'fũdu/ *a* deep □ *m* (*parte de baixo*) bottom; (*parte de trás*) back; (*de quadro, foto*) background; (*de dinheiro*) fund; **no** ~ basically; ~**s** *m pl* (*da casa etc*) back; (*recursos*) funds

**fúnebre** /'funebri/ *a* funereal

**funerário** /fune'rariu/ *a* funeraí

**funesto** /fu'nɛstu/ *a* fatal

**fungar** /fũ'gar/ *vt/i* sniff

**fungo** /'fũgu/ *m* fungus

**fu|nil** /fu'niw/ (*pl* ~**nis**) *m* funnel; ~**nilaria** *f* panel-beating; (*oficina*) bodyshop

**furacão** /fura'kãw/ *m* hurricane

**furado** /fu'radu/ *a* **papo** ~ (*fam*) hot air

**furão** /fu'rãw/ *m* (*animal*) ferret

**furar** /fu'rar/ *vt* pierce <*orelha etc*>; puncture <*pneu*>; make a hole in <*roupa etc*>; jump <*fila*>; break <*greve*> □ *vi* <*roupa etc*> go into a hole; <*pneu*> puncture; (*fam*) <*programa*> fall through

**fur|gão** /fur'gãw/ *m* van; ~**goneta** /e/ (*Port*) *f* van

**fúria** /'furia/ *f* fury

**furioso** /furi'ozu/ *a* furious

**furo** /'furu/ *m* hole; (*de pneu*) puncture; (*jornalístico*) scoop; (*fam: gafe*) blunder, faux pas; **dar um** ~ put one's foot in it

**furor** /fu'ror/ *m* furore

**fur|ta-cor** /furta'kor/ *a invar* iridescent; ~**tar** *vt* steal; ~**tivo** *a* furtive; ~**to** *m* theft

**furúnculo** /fu'rũkulu/ *m* boil

**fusão** /fu'zãw/ *f* fusion; (*de empresas*) merger

**fusca** /'fuska/ *f* VW beetle

**fuselagem** /fuze'laʒẽ/ *f* fuselage

**fusí|vel** /fu'zivew/ (*pl* ~**veis**) *m* fuse

**fuso** /'fuzu/ *m* spindle; ~ **horário** time zone

**fustigar** /fustʃi'gar/ *vt* lash; (*fig: com palavras*) lash out at

**futebol** /futʃi'bɔw/ *m* football; ~**ístico** *a* football

**fú|til** /'futʃiw/ (*pl* ~**teis**) *a* frivolous, inane

**futilidade** /futʃili'dadʒi/ *f* frivolity, inanity; (*uma*) frivolous thing

**futu|rismo** /futu'rizmu/ *m* futurism;

~**rista** *a* & *m* futurist; ~**rístico** *a* futuristic; ~**ro** *a* & *m* future

**fu|zil** /fu'ziw/ (*pl* ~**zis**) *m* rifle; ~**zilamento** *m* shooting; ~**zilar** *vt* shoot □ *vi* flash; ~**zileiro** *m* rifleman; ~**zileiro naval** marine

**fuzuê** /fuzu'e/ *m* commotion

# G

**gabar-se** /ga'barsi/ *vpr* boast (**de** of)

**gabarito** /gaba'ritu/ *m* calibre

**gabinete** /gabi'netʃi/ *m* (*em casa*) study; (*ɛ critório*) office; (*ministros*) cabinet

**gado** /'gadu/ *m* livestock; (*bovino*) cattle

**gaélico** /ga'ɛliku/ *a* & *m* Gaelic

**gafanhoto** /gafa'ɲotu/ *m* (*pequeno*) grasshopper; (*grande*) locust

**gafe** /'gafi/ *f* faux pas, gaffe

**gafieira** /gafi'era/ *f* dance; (*salão*) dance hall

**gagá** /ga'ga/ *a* (*fam*) senile

**ga|go** /'gagu/ *a* stuttering □ *m* stutterer; ~**gueira** *f* stutter; ~**guejar** *vi* stutter

**gaiato** /gaj'atu/ *a* funny

**gaiola** /gaj'ɔla/ *f* cage

**gaita** /'gajta/ *f* ~ **de foles** bagpipes

**gaivota** /gaj'vɔta/ *f* seagull

**gajo** /'gaʒu/ *m* (*Port*) guy, bloke

**gala** /'gala/ *f* **festa de** ~ gala; **roupa de** ~ formal dress

**galã** /ga'lã/ *m* leading man

**galan|tear** /galãtʃi'ar/ *vt* woo; ~**teio** *m* wooing; (*um*) courtesy

**galão** /ga'lãw/ *m* (*enfeite*) braid; (*mil*) stripe; (*medida*) gallon; (*Port: café*) white coffee

**galáxia** /ga'laksia/ *f* galaxy

**galé** /ga'lɛ/ *f* galley

**galego** /ga'legu/ *a* & *m* Galician

**galera** /ga'lɛra/ *f* (*fam*) crowd

**galeria** /gale'ria/ *f* gallery

**Gales** /'galis/ *m* **País de** ~ Wales

**ga|lês** /ga'les/ *a* (*f* ~**lesa**) Welsh □ *m* (*f* ~**lesa**) Welshman (*f* -woman); (*língua*) Welsh

**galeto** /ga'letu/ *m* spring chicken

**galgar** /gaw'gar/ *vt* (*transpor*) jump over; climb <*escada*>

**galgo** /'gawgu/ *m* greyhound

**galheteiro** /gaʎe'teru/ *m* cruet stand

**galho** /'gaʎu/ *m* branch; **quebrar um** ~ (*fam*) help out

**galináceos** /gali'nasius/ *m pl* poultry

**gali|nha** /ga'liɲa/ *f* chicken; ~**nheiro** *m* chicken coop

**galo** /'galu/ *m* cock; (*inchação*) bump

**galocha** /ga'lɔʃa/ *f* Wellington boot

**galo|pante** /galo'pãtʃi/ *a* galloping; ~**par** *vi* gallop; ~**pe** /ɔ/ *m* gallop

**galpão** /gaw'pãw/ *m* shed
**galvanizar** /gawvani'zar/ *vt* galvanize
**gama** /'gama/ *f* (*musical*) scale; (*fig*) range
**gamado** /ga'madu/ *a* besotted (**por** with)
**gamão** /ga'mãw/ *m* backgammon
**gamar** /ga'mar/ *vi* fall in love (**por** with)
**gana** /'gana/ *f* desire
**ganância** /ga'nãsia/ *f* greed
**ganancioso** /ganãsi'ozu/ *a* greedy
**gancho** /'gãʃu/ *m* hook
**gangorra** /gã'goxa/ *f* seesaw
**gangrena** /gã'grena/ *f* gangrene
**gangue** /'gãgi/ *m* gang
**ga|nhador** /gaɲa'dor/ *m* winner □ *a* winning; **~nhar** *vt* win <*corrida, prêmio*>; earn <*salário*>; get <*presente*>; gain <*vantagem, tempo, amigo*> □ *vi* win; **~nhar a vida** earn a living; **~nha-pão** *m* livelihood; **~nho** *m* gain; *pl* (*no jogo*) winnings □ *pp de* **ganhar**
**ga|nido** *m* squeal; (*de cachorro*) yelp; **~nir** *vi* squeal; <*cachorro*> yelp
**ganso** /'gãsu/ *m* goose
**gara|gem** /ga'raʒẽ/ *f* garage; **~gista** *m/f* garage attendant
**garanhão** /gara'ɲãw/ *m* stallion
**garan|tia** /garã'tʃia/ *f* guarantee; **~tir** *vt* guarantee
**garatujar** /garatu'ʒar/ *vt* scribble
**gar|bo** /'garbu/ *m* grace; **~boso** *a* graceful
**garça** /'garsa/ *f* heron
**gar|com** /gar'sõ/ *m* waiter; **~conete** /ɛ/ *f* waitress
**gar|fada** /gar'fada/ *f* forkful; **~fo** *m* fork
**gargalhada** /garga'ʎada/ *f* gale of laughter; **rir às ~s** roar with laughter
**gargalo** /gar'galu/ *m* bottleneck; **tomar no ~** drink out of the bottle
**garganta** /gar'gãta/ *f* throat
**gargare|jar** /gargare'ʒar/ *vi* gargle; **~jo** /e/ *m* gargle
**gari** /ga'ri/ *m/f* (*lixeiro*) dustman, (*Amer*) garbage collector; (*varredor de rua*) roadsweeper, (*Amer*) streetsweeper
**garim|par** /garĩ'par/ *vi* prospect; **~peiro** *m* prospector; **~po** *m* mine
**garo|a** /ga'roa/ *f* drizzle; **~ar** *vi* drizzle
**garo|ta** /ga'rota/ *f* girl; **~to** /o/ *m* boy; (*Port: café*) coffee with milk
**garoupa** /ga'ropa/ *f* grouper
**garra** /'gaxa/ *f* claw; (*fig*) drive, determination; *pl* (*poder*) clutches
**garra|fa** /ga'xafa/ *f* bottle; **~fada** *f* blow with a bottle; **~fão** *m* flagon

**garrancho** /ga'xãʃu/ *m* scrawl
**garrido** /ga'xidu/ *a* (*alegre*) lively
**garupa** /ga'rupa/ *f* (*de animal*) rump; (*de moto*) pillion seat
**gás** /gas/ *m* gas; *pl* (*intestinais*) wind, (*Amer*) gas; **~ lacrimogêneo** tear gas
**gasóleo** /ga'zɔliu/ *m* diesel oil
**gasolina** /gazo'lina/ *f* petrol
**gaso|sa** /ga'zɔza/ *f* fizzy lemonade, (*Amer*) soda; **~so** *a* gaseous; <*bebida*> fizzy
**gáspea** /'gaspia/ *f* upper
**gas|tador** /gasta'dor/ *a* & *m* spendthrift; **~tar** *vt* spend <*dinheiro, tempo*>; use up <*energia*>; wear out <*roupa, sapatos*>; **~to** *m* expense; *pl* spending, expenditure; **dar para o ~to** do
**gastrenterite** /gastrẽte'ritʃi/ *f* gastroenteritis
**gástrico** /'gastriku/ *a* gastric
**gastrite** /gas'tritʃi/ *f* gastritis
**gastronomia** /gastrono'mia/ *f* gastronomy
**ga|ta** /'gata/ *f* cat; (*fam*) sexy woman; **~tão** *m* (*fam*) hunk
**gatilho** /ga'tʃiʎu/ *m* trigger
**ga|tinha** /ga'tʃina/ *f* (*fam*) sexy woman; **~to** *m* cat; (*fam*) hunk; **fazer alg de ~to-sapato** treat s.o. like a doormat
**gatuno** /ga'tunu/ *m* crook □ *a* crooked
**gaúcho** /ga'uʃu/ *a* & *m* (person) from Rio Grande do Sul
**gaveta** /ga'veta/ *f* drawer
**gavião** /gavi'ãw/ *m* hawk
**gaze** /'gazi/ *f* gauze
**gazela** /ga'zɛla/ *f* gazelle
**gazeta** /ga'zeta/ *f* gazette
**geada** /ʒi'ada/ *f* frost
**ge|ladeira** /ʒela'dera/ *f* fridge; **~lado** *a* frozen; (*muito frio*) freezing □ *m* (*Port*) ice cream; **~lar** *vt/i* freeze
**gelati|na** /ʒela'tʃina/ *f* (*sobremesa*) jelly; (*pó*) gelatine; **~noso** /o/ *a* gooey
**geléia** /ʒe'lɛja/ *f* jam
**ge|leira** /ʒe'lera/ *f* glacier; **~lo** /e/ *m* ice
**gema** /'ʒema/ *f* (*de ovo*) yolk; (*pedra*) gem; **carioca da ~** carioca born and bred; **~da** *f* egg yolk whisked with sugar
**gêmeo** /'ʒemiu/ *a* & *m* twin; **Gêmeos** (*signo*) Gemini
**ge|mer** /ʒe'mer/ *vi* moan, groan; **~mido** *m* moan, groan
**gene** /'ʒɛni/ *m* gene; **~alogia** *f* genealogy; **~alógico** *a* genealogical; **árvore ~alógica** family tree
**Genebra** /ʒe'nebra/ *f* Geneva
**gene|ral** /ʒene'raw/ (*pl* **~rais**) *m* general; **~ralidade** *f* generality; **~ralização** *f* generalization;

**~ralizar** *vt/i* generalize; **~ralizar-se** *upr* become generalized

**genérico** /ʒeˈnɛriku/ *a* generic

**gênero** /ˈʒeneru/ *m* type, kind; (*gramatical*) gender; (*literário*) genre; *pl* goods; **~s alimentícios** foodstuffs; **ela não faz o meu ~** she's not my type

**gene|rosidade** /ʒenerozi'dadʒi/ *f* generosity; **~roso** /o/ *a* generous

**genéti|ca** /ʒeˈnɛtʃika/ *f* genetics; **~co** *a* genetic

**gengibre** /ʒẽ'ʒibri/ *m* ginger

**gengiva** /ʒẽ'ʒiva/ *f* gum

**geni|al** /ʒeni'aw/ (*pl* **~ais**) *a* brilliant

**gênio** /ˈʒeniu/ *m* genius; (*temperamento*) temperament

**genioso** /ʒeni'ozu/ *a* temperamental

**geni|tal** /ʒeni'taw/ (*pl* **~tais**) *a* genital

**genitivo** /ʒeni'tʃivu/ *a & m* genitive

**genocídio** /ʒenoˈsidʒiu/ *m* genocide

**genro** /ˈʒẽxu/ *m* son-in-law

**gente** /ˈʒẽtʃi/ *f* people; (*fam*) folks; **a ~** (*sujeito*) we; (*objeto*) us □ *interj* (*fam*) gosh

**gen|til** /ʒẽ'tʃiw/ (*pl* **~tis**) *a* kind; **~tileza** /e/ *f* kindness

**genuíno** /ʒenu'inu/ *a* genuine

**geo|grafia** /ʒeogra'fia/ *f* geography; **~gráfico** *a* geographical

**geógrafo** /ʒe'ɔgrafu/ *m* geographer

**geo|logia** /ʒeolo'ʒia/ *f* geology; **~lógico** *a* geological

**geólogo** /ʒe'ɔlogu/ *m* geologist

**geo|metria** /ʒeome'tria/ *f* geometry; **~métrico** *a* geometrical; **~político** *a* geopolitical

**Geórgia** /ʒi'ɔrʒia/ *f* Georgia

**georgiano** /ʒiorʒi'anu/ *a & m* Georgian

**gera|ção** /ʒera'sãw/ *f* generation; **~dor** *m* generator

**ge|ral** /ʒe'raw/ (*pl* **~rais**) *a* general □ *f* (*limpeza*) spring-clean; **em ~ral** in general

**gerânio** /ʒe'raniu/ *m* geranium

**gerar** /ʒe'rar/ *vt* create; generate <*eletricidade*>

**gerência** /ʒe'rẽsia/ *f* management

**gerenci|ador** /ʒerẽsia'dor/ *m* manager; **~al** (*pl* **~ais**) *a* management; **~ar** *vt* manage

**gerente** /ʒe'rẽtʃi/ *m* manager □ *a* managing

**gergelim** /ʒerʒe'lĩ/ *m* sesame

**geri|atria** /ʒeria'tria/ *f* geriatrics; **~átrico** *a* geriatric

**geringonça** /ʒerĩ'gõsa/ *f* contraption

**gerir** /ʒe'rir/ *vt* manage

**germânico** /ʒer'maniku/ *a* Germanic

**ger|me** /ˈʒɛrmi/ *m* germ; **~me de trigo** wheatgerm; **~minar** *vi* germinate

**gerúndio** /ʒe'rũdʒiu/ *m* gerund

**gesso** /ˈʒesu/ *m* plaster

**ges|tação** /ʒesta'sãw/ *f* gestation; **~tante** *f* pregnant woman

**gestão** /ʒes'tãw/ *f* management

**ges|ticular** *vi* gesticulate; **~to** /ˈʒɛstu/ *m* gesture

**gibi** /ʒi'bi/ *m* (*fam*) comic

**Gibraltar** /ʒibraw'tar/ *f* Gibraltar

**gigan|te** /ʒi'gãtʃi/ *a & m* giant; **~tesco** /e/ *a* gigantic

**gilete** /ʒi'lɛtʃi/ *f* razor blade □ *a & m/f* (*fam*) bisexual

**gim** /ʒĩ/ *m* gin

**ginásio** /ʒi'naziu/ *m* (*escola*) secondary school; (*de ginástica*) gymnasium

**ginasta** /ʒi'nasta/ *m/f* gymnast

**ginásti|ca** /ʒi'nastʃika/ *f* gymnastics; (*aeróbica*) aerobics; **~co** *a* gymnastic

**ginecolo|gia** /ʒinekolo'ʒia/ *f* gynaecology; **~gista** *m/f* gynaecologist

**gingar** /ʒĩ'gar/ *vi* sway

**gira-discos** /ʒira'diʃkuʃ/ *m invar* (*Port*) record player

**girafa** /ʒi'rafa/ *f* giraffe

**gi|rar** /ʒi'rar/ *vt/i* spin, revolve; **~rassol** (*pl* **~rassóis**) *m* sunflower; **~ratório** *a* revolving

**gíria** /ˈʒiria/ *f* slang; (*uma ~*) slang expression

**giro** /ˈʒiru/ *m* spin, turn □ *a* (*Port fam*) great

**giz** /ʒis/ *m* chalk

**gla|cê** /gla'se/ *m* icing; **~cial** (*pl* **~ciais**) *a* icy

**glamour** /gla'mur/ *m* glamour; **~oso** /o/ *a* glamorous

**glândula** /ˈglãdula/ *f* gland

**glandular** /glãdu'lar/ *a* glandular

**glicerina** /glise'rina/ *f* glycerine

**glicose** /gli'kɔzi/ *f* glucose

**glo|bal** /glo'baw/ (*pl* **~bais**) *a* (*mundial*) global; <*preço etc*> overall; **~bo** /o/ *m* globe; **~bo ocular** eyeball

**glóbulo** /ˈglɔbulu/ *m* globule; (*do sangue*) corpuscle

**glória** /ˈglɔria/ *f* glory

**glori|ficar** /glorifi'kar/ *vt* glorify; **~oso** /o/ *a* glorious

**glossário** /glo'sariu/ *m* glossary

**glu|tão** /glu'tãw/ *m* (*f* **~tona**) glutton □ *a* (*f* **~tona**) greedy

**gnomo** /gi'nomu/ *m* gnome

**godê** /go'de/ *a* flared

**goela** /go'ɛla/ *f* gullet

**gogó** /go'gɔ/ *m* (*fam*) Adam's apple

**goia|ba** /goj'aba/ *f* guava; **~bada** *f* guava jelly; **~beira** *f* guava tree

**gol** /'gow/ (*pl* **~s**) *m* goal

**gola** /ˈgɔla/ *f* collar

**gole** /ˈgɔli/ *m* mouthful

**go|lear** /goli'ar/ *vt* thrash; **~leiro** *m* goalkeeper

**golfe** /ˈgowfi/ *m* golf

**golfinho** /gow'fiɲu/ *m* dolphin

**golfista** /gow'fista/ *m/f* golfer
**golo** /'golu/ *m* (*Port*) goal
**golpe** /'gɔwpi/ *m* blow; (*manobra*) trick; ~ **(de estado)** coup (d'état); ~ **de mestre** masterstroke; ~ **de vento** gust of wind; ~**ar** *vt* hit
**goma** /'goma/ *f* gum; (*para roupa*) starch
**gomo** /'gomu/ *m* segment
**gôndola** /'gõdola/ *f* rack
**gongo** /'gõgu/ *m* gong
**gonorréia** /gono'xɛja/ *f* gonorrhea
**gonzo** /'gõzu/ *m* hinge
**gorar** /go'rar/ *vi* go wrong, fail
**gor|do** /'gordu/ *a* fat; ~**ducho** *a* plump
**gordu|ra** /gor'dura/ *f* fat; ~**rento** *a* greasy; ~**roso** /u/ *a* fatty; <*pele*> greasy, oily
**gorgolejar** /gorgole'ʒar/ *vi* gurgle
**gorila** /go'rila/ *m* gorilla
**gor|jear** /gorʒi'ar/ *vi* twitter; ~**jeio** *m* twittering
**gorjeta** /gor'ʒeta/ *f* tip
**gorro** /'goxu/ *m* hat
**gos|ma** /'gɔzma/ *f* slime; ~**mento** *a* slimy
**gos|tar** /gos'tar/ *vi* ~**tar de** like; ~**to** /o/ *m* taste; (*prazer*) pleasure; **para o meu** ~**to** for my taste; **ter** ~**to de** taste of; ~**toso** *a* nice; <*comida*> nice, tasty; (*fam*) <*pessoa*> gorgeous
**go|ta** /'gota/ *f* drop; (*que cai*) drip; (*doença*) gout; **foi a** ~**ta d'água** (*fig*) it was the last straw; ~**teira** *f* (*buraco*) leak; (*cano*) gutter; ~**tejar** *vi* drip; <*telhado*> leak □ *vt* drip
**gótico** /'gɔtʃiku/ *a* Gothic
**gotícula** /go'tʃikula/ *f* droplet
**gover|nador** /governa'dor/ *m* governor; ~**namental** (*pl* ~**namentais**) *a* government; ~**nanta** *f* housekeeper; ~**nante** *a* ruling □ *m/f* ruler; ~**nar** *vt* govern; ~**nista** *a* government □ *m/f* government supporter; ~**no** /e/ *m* government
**go|zação** /goza'sãw/ *f* joking; (*uma*) send-up; ~**zado** *a* funny; ~**zar** *vt* ~**zar (de)** enjoy; (*fam: zombar de*) make fun of □ *vi* (*ter orgasmo*) come; ~**zo** *m* (*prazer*) enjoyment; (*posse*) possession; (*orgasmo*) orgasm; **ser um** ~**zo** be funny
**Grã-Bretanha** /grãbre'taɲa/ *f* Great Britain
**graça** /'grasa/ *f* grace; (*piada*) joke; (*humor*) humour, funny side; (*jur*) pardon; **de** ~ for nothing; **sem** ~ (*enfadonho*) dull; (*não engraçado*) unfunny; (*envergonhado*) embarrassed; **ser uma** ~ be lovely; **ter** ~ be funny; **não tem** ~ **sair sozinho** it's no fun to go out alone; ~**s a** thanks to

**grace|jar** /grase'ʒar/ *vi* joke; ~**jo** /e/ *m* joke
**graci|nha** /gra'siɲa/ *f* ser uma ~**nha** be sweet; ~**oso** /o/ *a* gracious
**grada|ção** /grada'sãw/ *f* gradation; ~**tivo** *a* gradual
**grade** /'gradʒi/ *f* grille, grating; (*cerca*) railings; **atrás das** ~**s** behind bars; ~**ado** *a* <*janela*> barred
**grado** /'gradu/ *m* **de bom/mau** ~ willingly/unwillingly
**gradu|ação** /gradua'sãw/ *f* graduation; (*mil*) rank; (*variação*) gradation; ~**ado** *a* <*escala*> graduated; <*estudante*> graduate; <*militar*> high-ranking; (*eminente*) respected; ~**al** (*pl* ~**ais**) *a* gradual; ~**ar** *vt* graduate <*escala*>; (*ordenar*) grade; (*regular*) regulate; ~**ar-se** *vpr* <*estudante*> graduate
**grafia** /gra'fia/ *f* spelling
**gráfi|ca** /'grafika/ *f* (*arte*) graphics; (*oficina*) print shop; ~**co** *a* graphic □ *m* (*pessoa*) printer; (*diagrama*) graph; *pl* (*de computador*) graphics
**grã-fino** /grã'finu/ (*fam*) *a* posh, upper-class □ *m* posh person
**grafite** /gra'fitʃi/ *f* (*mineral*) graphite; (*de lápis*) lead; (*pichação*) piece of graffiti
**gra|fologia** /grafolo'ʒia/ *f* graphology; ~**fólogo** *m* graphologist
**grama**[1] /'grama/ *m* gramme
**grama**[2] /'grama/ *f* grass; ~**do** *m* lawn; (*campo de futebol*) field
**gramática** /gra'matʃika/ *f* grammar
**gramati|cal** /gramatʃi'kaw/ (*pl* ~**cais**) *a* grammatical
**gram|peador** /grãpia'dor/ *m* stapler; ~**pear** *vt* staple <*papéis etc*>; tap <*telefone*>; ~**po** *m* (*de cabelo*) hairclip; (*para papéis etc*) staple; (*ferramenta*) clamp
**grana** /'grana/ *f* (*fam*) cash
**granada** /gra'nada/ *f* (*projétil*) grenade; (*pedra*) garnet
**gran|dalhão** /grãda'sãw/ *a* (*f* ~**dalhona**) enormous; ~**dão** *a* (*f* ~**dona**) huge; ~**de** *a* big; (*fig*) <*escritor, amor etc*> great; ~**deza** /e/ *f* greatness; (*tamanho*) magnitude; ~**dioso** /o/ *a* grand
**granel** /gra'nɛw/ *m* **a** ~ in bulk
**granito** /gra'nitu/ *m* granite
**granizo** /gra'nizu/ *m* hail
**gran|ja** /'grãʒa/ *f* farm; ~**jear** *vt* win, gain
**granulado** /granu'ladu/ *a* granulated
**grânulo** /'granulu/ *m* granule
**grão** /grãw/ (*pl* ~**s**) *m* grain; (*de café*) bean; ~**-de-bico** (*pl* ~**s-de-bico**) *m* chickpea
**grasnar** /graz'nar/ *vi* <*pato*> quack; <*rã*> croak; <*corvo*> caw

**grati|dão** /gratʃiˈdãw/ f gratitude; **~ficação** f (dinheiro a mais) gratuity; (recompensa) gratification; **~ficante** a gratifying; **~ficar** vt (dar dinheiro a) give a gratuity to; (recompensar) gratify

**gratinado** /gratʃiˈnadu/ a & m gratin

**grátis** /ˈgratʃis/ adv free

**grato** /ˈgratu/ a grateful

**gratuito** /graˈtuito/ a (de graça) free; (sem motivo) gratuitous

**grau** /graw/ m degree; **escola de 1°/2° ~** primary/secondary school

**graúdo** /graˈudu/ a big; (importante) important

**gra|vação** /graˈvasãw/ f (de som) recording; (de desenhos etc) engraving; **~vador** m (pessoa) engraver; (máquina) tape recorder; **~vadora** f record company; **~var** vt record <música, disco>; (fixar na memória) memorize; (estampar) engrave

**gravata** /graˈvata/ f tie; (golpe) stranglehold; **~ borboleta** bowtie

**grave** /ˈgravi/ a serious; <voz, som> deep; <acento> grave

**grávida** /ˈgravida/ f pregnant

**gravidade** /graviˈdadʒi/ f gravity

**gravidez** /graviˈdes/ f pregnancy

**gravura** /graˈvura/ f engraving; (em livro) illustration

**graxa** /ˈgraʃa/ f (de sapatos) polish; (de lubrificar) grease

**Grécia** /ˈgrɛsia/ f Greece

**grego** /ˈgregu/ a & m Greek

**grei** /grej/ f flock

**gre|lha** /ˈgrɛʎa/ f grill; **~lhado** a grilled □ m grill; **~lhar** vt grill

**grêmio** /ˈgremiu/ m guild, association

**grená** /greˈna/ a & m dark red

**gre|ta** /ˈgreta/ f crack; **~tar** vt/i crack

**gre|ve** /ˈgrɛvi/ f strike; **entrar em ~ve** go on strike; **~ve de fome** hunger strike; **~vista** m/f striker

**gri|fado** /griˈfadu/ a in italics; **~far** vt italicize

**griffe** /ˈgrifi/ f label, line

**gri|lado** /griˈladu/ a (fam) hung-up; **~lar** (fam) vt bug; **~lar-se** vpr get hung-up (com about)

**grilhão** /griˈʎãw/ m fetter

**grilo** /ˈgrilu/ m (bicho) cricket; (fam) (preocupação) hang-up; (problema) hassle; (barulho) squeak

**grinalda** /griˈnawda/ f garland

**gringo** /ˈgrĩgu/ (fam) a foreign □ m foreigner

**gri|pado** /griˈpadu/ a **estar/ficar ~pado** have/get the flu; **~par-se** vpr get the flu; **~pe** f flu, influenza

**grisalho** /griˈzaʎu/ a grey

**gri|tante** /griˈtãtʃi/ a <erro> glaring, gross; <cor> loud, garish; **~tar** vt/i shout; (de medo) scream; **~taria** f

shouting; **~to** m shout; (de medo) scream; **aos ~tos** in a loud voice; **no ~to** (fam) by force

**grogue** /ˈgrɔgi/ a groggy

**grosa** /ˈgrɔza/ f gross

**groselha** /groˈzɛʎa/ f (vermelha) redcurrant; (espinhosa) gooseberry; **~ negra** blackcurrant

**gros|seiro** /groˈseru/ a rude; (tosco, malfeito) rough; **~seria** f rudeness; (uma) rude thing; **~so** /o/ a thick; <voz> deep; (fam) <pessoa, atitude> rude; **~sura** f thickness; (fam: grosseria) rudeness

**grotesco** /groˈtesku/ a grotesque

**grua** /ˈgrua/ f crane

**gru|dado** /gruˈdadu/ a stuck; (fig) very attached (em to); **~dar** vt/i stick; **~de** m glue; **~dento** a sticky

**gru|nhido** /gruˈɲidu/ m grunt; **~nhir** vi grunt

**grupo** /ˈgrupu/ m group

**gruta** /ˈgruta/ f cave

**guaraná** /gwaraˈna/ m guarana

**guarani** /gwaraˈni/ a & m/f Guarani

**guarda** /ˈgwarda/ f guard □ m/f guard; (policial) policeman (f -woman); **~ costeira** coastguard; **~chuva** m umbrella; **~costas** m invar bodyguard; **~dor** m parking attendant; **~florestal** (pl **~s-florestais**) m/f forest ranger; **~louça** m china cupboard; **~napo** m napkin, serviette; **~noturno** (pl **~s-noturnos**) m night watchman

**guardar** /gwarˈdar/ vt (pôr no lugar) put away; (conservar) keep; (vigiar) guard; (não esquecer) remember; **~-se de** guard against

**guarda|-redes** /ˈgwarda-ˈxedʃ/ m invar (Port) goalkeeper; **~roupa** m wardrobe; **~sol** (pl **~sóis**) m sunshade

**guardi|ão** /gwardʒiˈãw/ (pl **~ães** ou **~ões**) m (f **~ã**) guardian

**guarita** /gwaˈrita/ f sentry box

**guar|necer** /gwarneˈser/ vt (fortificar) garrison; (munir) equip; (enfeitar) garnish; **~nição** f (mil) garrison; (enfeite) garnish

**Guatemala** /gwateˈmala/ f Guatemala

**guatemalteco** /gwatemalˈtɛku/ a & m Guatemalan

**gude** /ˈgudʒi/ m **bola de ~** marble

**guelra** /ˈgɛwxa/ f gill

**guer|ra** /ˈgɛxa/ f war; **~reiro** m warrior □ a warlike; **~rilha** f guerrilla war; **~rilheiro** a & m guerrilla

**gueto** /ˈgetu/ m ghetto

**guia** /ˈgia/ m/f guide □ m guide(book) □ f delivery note

**Guiana** /giˈana/ f Guyana

**guianense** /giaˈnẽsi/ a & m/f Guyanan

**guiar** /gi'ar/ *vt* guide; drive <*veículo*> □ *vi* drive; **~-se** *vpr* be guided
**guichê** /gi'ʃe/ *m* window
**guidom** /gi'dõ/, (*Port*) **guidão** /gi'dãw/ *m* handlebars
**guilhotina** /giʎo'tʃina/ *f* guillotine
**guimba** /'gĩba/ *f* butt
**guinada** /gi'nada/ *f* change of direction; **dar uma ~** change direction
**guinchar[1]** /gĩ'ʃar/ *vi* squeal; <*freios*> screech
**guinchar[2]** /gĩ'ʃar/ *vt* tow <*carro*>; (*içar*) winch
**guincho[1]** /'gĩʃu/ *m* squeal; (*de freios*) screech
**guincho[2]** /'gĩʃu/ *m* (*máquina*) winch; (*veículo*) tow truck
**guin|dar** /gĩ'dar/ *vt* hoist; **~daste** *m* crane
**Guiné** /gi'nɛ/ *f* Guinea
**gui|sado** /gi'zadu/ *m* stew; **~sar** *vt* stew
**guitar|ra** /gi'taxa/ *f* (electric) guitar; **~rista** *m/f* guitarist
**guizo** /'gizu/ *m* bell
**gu|la** /'gula/ *f* greed; **~lodice** *f* greed; **~loseima** *f* delicacy; **~loso** /o/ *a* greedy
**gume** /'gumi/ *m* cutting edge
**guri** /gu'ri/ *m* boy; **~a** *f* girl
**guru** /gu'ru/ *m* guru
**gutu|ral** /gutu'raw/ (*pl* **~rais**) *a* guttural

# H

**há|bil** /'abiw/ (*pl* **~beis**) *a* clever, skilful
**habili|dade** /abili'dadʒi/ *f* skill; **ter ~dade com** be good with; **~doso** /o/ *a* skilful; **~tação** *f* qualification; **~tar** *vt* qualify
**habi|tação** /abita'sãw/ *f* housing; (*casa*) dwelling; **~tacional** (*pl* **~tacionais**) *a* housing; **~tante** *m/f* inhabitant; **~tar** *vt* inhabit □ *vi* live; **~tável** (*pl* **~táveis**) *a* habitable
**hábito** /'abitu/ *m* habit
**habitu|al** /abitu'aw/ (*pl* **~ais**) *a* habitual; **~ar** *vt* accustom (**a** to); **~ar-se** *vpr* get accustomed (**a** to)
**hadoque** /a'dɔki/ *m* haddock
**Haia** /'aja/ *f* the Hague
**Haiti** /aj'tʃi/ *m* Haiti
**haitiano** /ajtʃi'anu/ *a & m* Haitian
**hálito** /'alitu/ *m* breath
**halitose** /ali'tɔzi/ *f* halitosis
**hall** /xɔw/ (*pl* **~s**) *m* hall; (*de hotel*) foyer
**halte|re** /aw'tɛri/ *m* dumbbell; **~rofilismo** *m* weight lifting; **~rofilista** *m/f* weight lifter
**hambúrguer** /ã'burger/ *m* hamburger

**hangar** /ã'gar/ *m* hangar
**haras** /'aras/ *m invar* stud farm
**hardware** /'xarduer/ *m* hardware
**harmo|nia** /armo'nia/ *f* harmony; **~nioso** /o/ *a* harmonious; **~nizar** *vt* harmonize; (*conciliar*) reconcile; **~nizar-se** *vpr* (*combinar*) tone in; (*concordar*) coincide
**har|pa** /'arpa/ *f* harp; **~pista** *m/f* harpist
**haste** /'astʃi/ *m* pole; (*de planta*) stem, stalk; **~ar** *vt* hoist, raise
**Havaí** /ava'i/ *m* Hawaii
**havaiano** /avaj'anu/ *a & m* Hawaiian
**haver** /a'ver/ *m* credit; *pl* possessions □ *vt* (*auxiliar*) **havia sido** it had been; (*impessoal*) **há** there is/are; **ele trabalha aqui há anos** he's been working here for years; **ela morreu há vinte anos (atrás)** she died twenty years ago
**haxixe** /a'ʃiʃi/ *m* hashish
**he|braico** /e'brajku/ *a & m* Hebrew; **~breu** *a & m* (*f* **~bréia**) Hebrew
**hectare** /ek'tari/ *m* hectare
**hediondo** /edʒi'õdu/ *a* hideous
**hein** /ẽj/ *int* eh
**hélice** /'ɛlisi/ *f* propeller
**helicóptero** /eli'kɔpteru/ *m* helicopter
**hélio** /'ɛliu/ *m* helium
**heliporto** /eli'portu/ *m* heliport
**hem** /ẽj/ *int* eh
**hematoma** /ema'toma/ *m* bruise
**hemisfério** /emis'fɛriu/ *m* hemisphere; **Hemisfério Norte/Sul** Northern/Southern Hemisphere
**hemo|filia** /emofi'lia/ *f* haemophilia; **~fílico** *a & m* haemophiliac; **~globina** *f* haemoglobin; **~grama** *m* blood count
**hemor|ragia** /emoxa'ʒia/ *f* haemorrhage; **~róidas** *f pl* haemorrhoids
**hené** /e'ne/ *m* henna
**hepatite** /epa'tʃitʃi/ *f* hepatitis
**hera** /'ɛra/ *f* ivy
**heráldi|ca** /e'rawdʒika/ *f* heraldry; **~co** *a* heraldic
**herança** /e'rãsa/ *f* inheritance; (*de um povo etc*) heritage
**her|bicida** /erbi'sida/ *m* weedkiller; **~bívoro** *a* herbivorous □ *m* herbivore
**her|dar** /er'dar/ *vt* inherit; **~deiro** *m* heir
**hereditário** /eredʒi'tariu/ *a* hereditary
**here|ge** /e'rɛʒi/ *m/f* heretic; **~sia** *f* heresy
**herético** /e'rɛtʃiku/ *a* heretical
**hermético** /er'mɛtʃiku/ *a* airtight; (*fig*) obscure
**hérnia** /'ɛrnia/ *f* hernia
**herói** /e'rɔj/ *m* hero; **~co** *a* heroic

**hero|ína** /ero'ina/ f (*mulher*) heroine; (*droga*) heroin; **~ismo** m heroism

**herpes** /'ɛrpis/ m *invar* herpes; **~-zoster** m shingles

**hesi|tação** /ezita'sãw/ f hesitation; **~tante** a hesitant; **~tar** vi hesitate

**hetero|doxo** /etero'dɔksu/ a unorthodox; **~gêneo** a heterogeneous

**heterossexu|al** /eteroseksu'aw/ (*pl* **~ais**) a & m heterosexual

**hexago|nal** /eksago'naw/ (*pl* **~nais**) a hexagonal

**hexágono** /e'ksagonu/ m hexagon

**hiato** /i'atu/ m hiatus

**hiber|nação** /iberna'sãw/ f hibernation; **~nar** vi hibernate

**híbrido** /'ibridu/ a & m hybrid

**hidrante** /i'drãtʃi/ m fire hydrant

**hidra|tante** /idra'tãtʃi/ a moisturising □ m moisturizer; **~tar** vt moisturize <*pele*>; **~to** m **~to de carbono** carbohydrate

**hidráuli|ca** /i'drawlika/ f hydraulics; **~co** a hydraulic

**hidrelétri|ca** /idre'lɛtrika/ f hydroelectric power station; **~co** a hydroelectric

**hidro|avião** /idroavi'ãw/ m seaplane; **~carboneto** /e/ m hydrocarbon

**hidrófilo** /i'drɔfilu/ a absorbent; **algodão ~** cotton wool, (*Amer*) absorbent cotton

**hidrofobia** /idrofo'bia/ f rabies

**hidro|gênio** /idro'ʒeniu/ m hydrogen; **~massagem** f banheira de **~massagem** jacuzzi; **~via** f waterway

**hiena** /i'ena/ f hyena

**hierarquia** /ierar'kia/ f hierarchy

**hieróglifo** /ie'rɔglifu/ m hieroglyphic

**hifen** /'ifẽ/ m hyphen

**higi|ene** /iʒi'eni/ f hygiene; **~ênico** a hygienic

**hilari|ante** /ilari'ãtʃi/ a hilarious; **~dade** f hilarity

**Himalaia** /ima'laja/ m Himalayas

**hin|di** /ĩ'dʒi/ m Hindi; **~du** a a m/f Hindu; **~duísmo** m Hinduism; **~duísta** a a m/f Hindu

**hino** /'inu/ m hymn; **~ nacional** national anthem

**hipermercado** /ipermer'kadu/ m hypermarket

**hipersensí|vel** /ipersẽ'sivew/ (*pl* **~veis**) a hypersensitive

**hipertensão** /ipertẽ'sãw/ f hypertension

**hípico** /'ipiku/ a horseriding

**hipismo** /i'piʒmu/ m horseriding; (*corridas*) horseracing

**hip|nose** /ipi'nɔzi/ f hypnosis; **~nótico** a hypnotic; **~notismo** m hypnotism; **~notizador** m hypnotist; **~notizar** vt hypnotize

**hipocondríaco** /ipokõ'driaku/ a & m hypochondriac

**hipocrisia** /ipokri'zia/ f hypocrisy

**hipócrita** /i'pɔkrita/ m/f hypocrite □ a hypocritical

**hipódromo** /i'pɔdromu/ m race course, (*Amer*) race track

**hipopótamo** /ipo'pɔtamu/ m hippopotamus

**hipote|ca** /ipo'tɛka/ f mortgage; **~car** vt mortgage; **~cário** a mortgage

**hipotermia** /ipoter'mia/ f hypothermia

**hipótese** /i'pɔtezi/ f hypothesis; **na ~ de** in the event of; **na pior das ~s** at worst

**hipotético** /ipo'tɛtʃiku/ a hypothetical

**hirto** /'irtu/ adj rigid, stiff

**hispânico** /is'paniku/ a Hispanic

**histamina** /ista'mina/ f histamine

**his|terectomia** /isterekto'mia/ f hysterectomy; **~teria** f hysteria; **~térico** a hysterical; **~terismo** m hysteria

**his|tória** /is'tɔria/ f (*do passado*) history; (*conto*) story; pl (*amolação*) trouble; **~toriador** m historian; **~tórico** a historical; (*marcante*) historic □ m history

**hoje** /'oʒi/ adv today; **~ em dia** nowadays; **~ de manhã** this morning; **~ à noite** tonight

**Holanda** /o'lãda/ f Holland

**holan|dês** /olã'des/ a (f **~desa**) Dutch □ m (f **~desa**) Dutchman (f -woman); (*língua*) Dutch; **os ~deses** the Dutch

**holding** /'xɔwdʒĩ/ (*pl* **~s**) f holding company

**holerite** /ole'ritʃi/ m pay slip

**holo|causto** /olo'kawstu/ m holocaust; **~fote** /ɔ/ m spotlight; **~grama** m hologram

**homem** /'omẽ/ m man; **~ de negócios** businessman; **~-rã** (*pl* **homens-rã**) m frogman

**homena|gear** /omenaʒi'ar/ vt pay tribute to; **~gem** f tribute; **em ~gem a** in honour of

**homeo|pata** /omio'pata/ m/f homoeopath; **~patia** f homoeopathy; **~pático** a homoeopathic

**homérico** /o'mɛriku/ a (*estrondoso*) booming; (*extraordinário*) phenomenal

**homi|cida** /omi'sida/ a homicidal □ m/f murderer; **~cídio** m homicide; **~cídio involuntário** manslaughter

**homo|geneizado** /omoʒenej'zadu/ a <*leite*> homogenized; **~gêneo** a homogeneous

**homologar** /omolo'gar/ vt ratify

**homólogo** /o'mɔlogu/ *m* opposite number □ *a* equivalent

**homônimo** /o'monimu/ *m* (*xará*) namesake; (*vocábulo*) homonym

**homossexu|al** /omoseksu'aw/ (*pl* ~ais) *a* & *m* homosexual; ~alismo *m* homosexuality

**Honduras** /õ'duras/ *f* Honduras

**hondurenho** /õdu'reɲu/ *a* & *m* Honduran

**hones|tidade** /onestʃi'dadʒi/ *f* honesty; ~to /ɛ/ *a* honest

**hono|rário** /ono'rariu/ *a* honorary; ~rários *m pl* fees; ~rífico *a* honorific

**hon|ra** /'õxa/ *f* honour; ~radez *f* honesty, integrity; ~rado *a* honourable; ~rar *vt* honour; ~roso /o/ *a* honourable

**hóquei** /'ɔkej/ *m* (field) hockey; ~ sobre gelo ice hockey; ~ sobre patins roller hockey

**hora** /'ɔra/ *f* (*unidade de tempo*) hour; (*ocasião*) time; **que ~s são?** what's the time?; **a que ~s?** at what time?; **às três ~s** at three o'clock; **dizer as ~s** tell the time; **tem ~s?** do you have the time?; **de ~ em ~** every hour; **em cima da ~** at the last minute; **na ~** (*naquele momento*) at the time; (*no ato*) on the spot; (*a tempo*) on time; **está na ~ de ir** it's time to go; **na ~ H** (*no momento certo*) at just the right moment; (*no momento crítico*) at the crucial moment; **meia ~** half an hour; **toda ~** all the time; **fazer ~** kill time; **marcar ~** make an appointment; **perder a ~** lose track of time; **não tenho ~** my time is my own; **não vejo a ~ de ir** I can't wait to go; ~s extras overtime; ~s vagas spare time

**horário** /o'rariu/ *a* hourly; **km ~s** km per hour □ *m* (*hora*) time; (*tabela*) timetable; (*de trabalho etc*) hours; ~ nobre prime time

**horda** /'ɔrda/ *f* horde

**horista** /o'rista/ *a* paid by the hour □ *m/f* worker paid by the hour

**horizon|tal** /orizõ'taw/ (*pl* ~tais) *a* & *f* horizontal; ~te *m* horizon

**hor|monal** /ormo'naw/ (*pl* ~monais) *a* hormonal; ~mônio *m* hormone

**horóscopo** /o'rɔskopu/ *m* horoscope

**horrendo** /o'xẽdu/ *a* horrid

**horripi|lante** /oxipi'lãtʃi/ *a* horrifying; ~lar *vt* horrify

**horrí|vel** /o'xivew/ (*pl* ~veis) *a* horrible, awful

**horror** /o'xor/ *m* horror (**a** of); (*coisa horrorosa*) horrible thing; **ser um ~** be awful; **que ~!** how awful!

**horro|rizar** /oxori'zar/ *vt/i* horrify;
~rizar-se *vpr* be horrified; ~roso /o/ *a* horrible

**horta** /'ɔrta/ *f* vegetable plot; ~ comercial market garden, (*Amer*) truck farm; ~liça *f* vegetable

**hortelã** /orte'lã/ *f* mint; ~-pimenta peppermint

**horti|cultor** /ortʃikuw'tor/ *m* horticulturalist; ~cultura *f* horticulture; ~frutigranjeiros *m pl* fruit and vegetables; ~granjeiros *m pl* vegetables

**horto** /'ɔrtu/ *m* market garden; (*viveiro*) nursery

**hospe|dagem** /ospe'daʒẽ/ *f* accommodation; ~dar *vt* put up; ~dar-se *vpr* stay

**hóspede** /'ɔspidʒi/ *m/f* guest

**hospe|deira** /ospe'dera/ *f* landlady; ~ra de bordo (*Port*) stewardess; ~ro *m* landlord

**hospício** /os'pisiu/ *m* (*de loucos*) asylum

**hospi|tal** /ospi'taw/ (*pl* ~tais) *m* hospital; ~talar *a* hospital; ~taleiro *a* hospitable; ~talidade *f* hospitality; ~talizar *vt* hospitalize

**hóstia** /'ɔstʃia/ *f* Host, Communion wafer

**hos|til** /os'tʃiw/ (*pl* ~tis) *a* hostile; ~tilidade *f* hostility; ~tilizar *vt* antagonize

**ho|tel** /o'tɛw/ (*pl* ~téis) *m* hotel; ~teleiro *a* hotel □ *m* hotelier

**huma|nidade** /umani'dadʒi/ *f* humanity; ~nismo *m* humanism; ~nista *a* & *m/f* humanist; ~nitário *a* & *m* humanitarian; ~nizar *vt* humanize; ~no *a* human; (*compassivo*) humane; ~nos *m pl* humans

**húmido** /'umidu/ *adj* (*Port*) humid

**humil|dade** /umiw'dadʒi/ *f* humility; ~de *a* humble

**humi|lhação** /umiʎa'sãw/ *f* humiliation; ~lhante *a* humiliating; ~lhar *vt* humiliate

**humor** /u'mor/ *m* humour; (*disposição do espírito*) mood; **de bom/mau ~** in a good/bad mood

**humo|rismo** /umo'rizmu/ *m* humour; ~rista *m/f* (*no palco*) comedian; (*escritor*) humorist; ~rístico *a* humorous

**húngaro** /'ũgaru/ *a* & *m* Hungarian

**Hungria** /ũ'gria/ *f* Hungary

**hurra** /'uxa/ *int* hurrah □ *m* cheer

# I

**ia|te** /i'atʃi/ *m* yacht; ~tismo *m* yachting; ~tista *m/f* yachtsman (*f* -woman)

**ibérico** /i'bɛriku/ *a & m* Iberian
**ibope** /i'bɔpi/ *m* **dar ~** (*fam*) be popular
**içar** /i'sar/ *vt* hoist
**iceberg** /ajs'bɛrgi/ (*pl* **~s**) *m* iceberg
**ícone** /'ikoni/ *m* icon
**iconoclasta** /ikono'klasta/ *m/f* iconoclast □ *a* iconoclastic
**icterícia** /ikte'risia/ *f* jaundice
**ida** /'ida/ *f* going; **na ~** on the way there; **~ e volta** return, (*Amer*) round trip
**idade** /i'dadʒi/ *f* age; **meia ~** middle age; **homem de meia ~** middle-aged man; **senhor de ~** elderly man; **Idade Média** Middle Ages
**ide|al** /ide'aw/ (*pl* **~ais**) *a & m* ideal; **~alismo** *m* idealism; **~alista** *m/f* idealist □ *a* idealistic; **~alizar** *vt* (*criar*) devise; (*sublimar*) idealize; **~ar** *vt* devise; **~ário** *m* ideas
**idéia** /i'dɛja/ *f* idea; **mudar de ~** change one's mind
**idem** /'idẽ/ *adv* ditto
**idêntico** /i'dẽtʃiku/ *a* identical
**identi|dade** /idẽtʃi'dadʒi/ *f* identity; **~ficar** *vt* identify; **~ficar-se** *vpr* identify (**com** with)
**ideo|logia** /ideolo'ʒia/ *f* ideology; **~lógico** *a* ideological
**idílico** /i'dʒiliku/ *a* idyllic
**idílio** /i'dʒiliu/ *m* idyll
**idio|ma** /idʒi'oma/ *m* language; **~mático** *a* idiomatic
**idio|ta** /idʒi'ota/ *m/f* idiot □ *a* idiotic; **~tice** *f* stupidity; (*uma*) stupid thing
**idola|trar** /idola'trar/ *vt* idolize; **~tria** *f* idolatry
**ídolo** /'idulu/ *m* idol
**idôneo** /i'doniu/ *a* suitable
**idoso** /i'dozu/ *a* elderly
**Iêmen** /i'emẽ/ *m* Yemen
**iemenita** /ieme'nita/ *a & m/f* Yemeni
**iene** /i'ɛni/ *m* yen
**iglu** /i'glu/ *m* igloo
**ignição** /igni'sãw/ *f* ignition
**ignomínia** /igno'minia/ *f* ignominy
**igno|rância** /igno'rãsia/ *f* ignorance; **~rante** *a* ignorant; **~rar** (*desconsiderar*) ignore; (*desconhecer*) not know
**igreja** /i'greʒa/ *f* church
**igu|al** /i'gwaw/ (*pl* **~ais**) *a* equal; (*em aparência*) identical; (*liso*) even □ *m/f* equal; **por ~** al equally; **~alar** *vt* equal; level <*terreno*>; **~alar(-se) a** be equal to; **~aldade** *f* equality; **~alitário** *a* egalitarian; **~almente** *adv* equally; (*como resposta*) the same to you; **~alzinho** *a* exactly the same (a as)
**iguaria** /igwa'ria/ *f* delicacy
**iídiche** /i'idiʃi/ *m* Yiddish
**ile|gal** /ile'gaw/ (*pl* **~gais**) *a* illegal; **~galidade** *f* illegality

**ilegítimo** /ile'ʒitʃimu/ *a* illegitimate
**ilegí|vel** /ile'ʒivew/ (*pl* **~veis**) *a* illegible
**ileso** /i'lɛzu/ *a* unhurt
**iletrado** /ile'tradu/ *adj & m* illiterate
**ilha** /'iʎa/ *f* island
**ilharga** /i'ʎarga/ *f* side
**ilhéu** /i'ʎɛw/ *m* (*f* **ilhoa**) islander
**ilhós** /i'ʎɔs/ *m invar* eyelet
**ilhota** /i'ʎɔta/ *f* small island
**ilícito** /i'lisitu/ *a* illicit
**ilimitado** /ilimi'tadu/ *a* unlimited
**ilógico** /i'lɔʒiku/ *a* illogical
**iludir** /ilu'dʒir/ *vt* delude; **~-se** *vpr* delude o.s.
**ilumi|nação** /ilumina'sãw/ *f* lighting; (*inspiração*) enlightenment; **~nar** *vt* light up, illuminate; (*inspirar*) enlighten
**ilu|são** /ilu'zãw/ *f* illusion; (*sonho*) delusion; **~sionista** *m/f* illusionist; **~sório** *a* illusory
**ilus|tração** /ilustra'sãw/ *f* illustration; (*erudição*) learning; **~trador** *m* illustrator; **~trar** *vt* illustrate; **~trativo** *a* illustrative; **~tre** *a* illustrious; **~tríssimo senhor** Dear Sir
**ímã** /'imã/ *m* magnet
**imaculado** /imaku'ladu/ *a* immaculate
**imagem** /i'maʒẽ/ *f* image; (*da TV*) picture
**imagi|nação** /imaʒina'sãw/ *f* imagination; **~nar** *vt* imagine; **~nário** *a* imaginary; **~nativo** *a* imaginative; **~nável** (*pl* **~náveis**) *a* imaginable; **~noso** /o/ *a* imaginative
**imatu|ridade** /imaturi'dadʒi/ *f* immaturity; **~ro** *a* immature
**imbatí|vel** /ĩba'tʃivew/ (*pl* **~veis**) *a* unbeatable
**imbe|cil** /ĩbe'siw/ (*pl* **~cis**) *a* stupid □ *m/f* imbecile
**imberbe** /ĩ'bɛrbi/ *adj* (*sem barba*) beardless
**imbricar** /ĩbri'kar/ *vt* overlap; **~-se** *vpr* overlap
**imedia|ções** /imedʒia'sõjs/ *f pl* vicinity; **~tamente** *adv* immediately; **~to** *a* immediate
**imemori|al** /imemori'aw/ (*pl* **~ais**) *a* immemorial
**imen|sidão** /imẽsi'dãw/ *f* vastness; **~so** *a* immense
**imergir** /imer'ʒir/ *vt* immerse
**imi|gração** /imigra'sãw/ *f* immigration; **~grante** *a & m/f* immigrant; **~grar** *vi* immigrate
**imi|nência** /imi'nẽsia/ *f* imminence; **~nente** *a* imminent
**imiscuir-se** /imisku'irsi/ *vpr* interfere
**imi|tação** /imita'sãw/ *f* imitation; **~tador** *m* imitator; **~tar** *vt* imitate

**imobili|ária** /imobili'aria/ f estate agent's, (*Amer*) realtor; **~ário** *a* property; **~dade** f immobility; **~zar** *vt* immobilize

**imo|ral** /imo'raw/ (*pl* **~rais**) *a* immoral; **~ralidade** f immorality

**imor|tal** /imor'taw/ (*pl* **~tais**) *a* immortal □ *m/f* member of the Brazilian Academy of Letters; **~talidade** f immortality; **~talizar** *vt* immortalize

**imó|vel** /i'mɔvew/ (*pl* **~veis**) *a* motionless, immobile □ *m* building, property; *pl* property, real estate

**impaci|ência** /impasi'ēsia/ f impatience; **~entar-se** *vpr* get impatient; **~ente** *a* impatient

**impacto** /ī'paktu/, (*Port*) **impacte** /ī'paktʃi/ *m* impact

**impagá|vel** /ī̃pa'gavew/ (*pl* **~veis**) *a* priceless

**ímpar** /'ī̃par/ *a* unique; <*número*> odd

**imparci|al** /ī̃parsi'aw/ (*pl* **~ais**) *a* impartial; **~alidade** f impartiality

**impasse** /ī̃'pasi/ *m* impasse

**impassí|vel** /ī̃pa'sivew/ (*pl* **~veis**) *a* impassive

**impecá|vel** /ī̃pe'kavew/ (*pl* **~veis**) *a* impeccable

**impe|dido** /ī̃pe'dʒidu/ *a* <*rua*> blocked; (*Port*: *ocupado*) engaged, (*Amer*) busy; (*no futebol*) offside; **~dimento** *m* prevention; (*estorvo*) obstruction; (*no futebol*) offside position; **~dir** *vt* stop; (*estorvar*) hinder; block <*rua*>; **~dir alg de ir** *ou* **que alg vá** stop s.o. going

**impelir** /ī̃pe'lir/ *vt* drive

**impenetrá|vel** /ī̃pene'travew/ (*pl* **~veis**) *a* impenetrable

**impensá|vel** /ī̃pē'savew/ (*pl* **~veis**) *a* unthinkable

**impe|rador** /ī̃pera'dor/ *m* emperor; **~rar** *vi* reign, rule; **~rativo** *a* & *m* imperative; **~ratriz** f empress

**imperceptí|vel** /ī̃persep'tʃivew/ (*pl* **~veis**) *a* imperceptible

**imperdí|vel** /ī̃per'dʒivew/ (*pl* **~veis**) *a* unmissable

**imperdoá|vel** /ī̃perdo'avew/ (*pl* **~veis**) *a* unforgivable

**imperfei|ção** /ī̃perfej'sāw/ f imperfection; **~to** *a* & *m* imperfect

**imperi|al** /ī̃peri'aw/ (*pl* **~ais**) *a* imperial; **~alismo** *m* imperialism; **~alista** *a* & *m/f* imperialist

**império** /ī̃'pɛriu/ *m* empire

**imperioso** /ī̃peri'ozu/ *a* imperious; <*necessidade*> pressing

**imperme|abilizar** /ī̃permiabili'zar/ *vt* waterproof; **~ável** (*pl* **~áveis**) *a* waterproof; (*fig*) impervious (**a** to) □ *m* raincoat

**imperti|nência** /ī̃pertʃi'nēsia/ f impertinence; **~nente** *a* impertinent

**impesso|al** /ī̃peso'aw/ (*pl* **~ais**) *a* impersonal

**ímpeto** /'ī̃petu/ *m* (*vontade*) urge, impulse; (*de emoção*) surge; (*movimento*) start; (*na física*) impetus

**impetuo|sidade** /ī̃petuozi'dadʒi/ f impetuosity; **~so** *a/o* impetuous

**impiedoso** /ī̃pie'dozu/ *a* merciless

**impingir** /ī̃pī'ʒir/ *vt* foist (**a** on)

**implacá|vel** /ī̃pla'kavew/ (*pl* **~veis**) *a* implacable

**implan|tar** /ī̃plā'tar/ *vt* introduce; (*no corpo*) implant; **~te** *m* implant

**implemen|tar** /ī̃plemē'tar/ *vt* implement; **~to** *m* implement

**impli|cação** /ī̃plika'sāw/ f implication; **~cância** f (*ato*) harassment; (*antipatia*) grudge; **estar de ~cância com** have it in for; **~cante** *a* troublesome □ *m/f* troublemaker; **~car** *vt* (*comprometer*) implicate; **~car (em)** (*dar a entender*) imply; (*acarretar, exigir*) involve; **~car com** (*provocar*) pick on; (*antipatizar*) not get on with

**implícito** /ī̃'plisitu/ *a* implicit

**implorar** /ī̃plo'rar/ *vt* plead for (**a** from)

**imponente** /ī̃po'nētʃi/ *a* imposing

**impopular** /ī̃popu'lar/ *a* unpopular

**impor** /ī̃'por/ *vt* impose (**a** on); command <*respeito*>; **~-se** *vpr* assert o.s.

**impor|tação** /ī̃porta'sāw/ f import; **~tador** *m* importer; **~tadora** f import company; **~tados** *m pl* imported goods; **~tância** f importance; (*quantia*) amount; **ter ~tância** be important; **~tante** *a* important; **~tar** *vt* import <*mercadorias*> □ *vi* matter; **~tar em** (*montar a*) amount to; (*resultar em*) lead to; **~tar-se (com)** mind

**importu|nar** /ī̃portu'nar/ *vt* bother; **~no** *a* annoying

**imposição** /ī̃pozi'sāw/ f imposition

**impossibili|dade** /ī̃posibili'dadʒi/ f impossibility; **~tar** *vt* make impossible; **~tar alg de ir, ~tar a alg ir** prevent s.o. from going, make it impossible for s.o. to go

**impossí|vel** /ī̃po'sivew/ (*pl* **~veis**) *a* impossible

**impos|to** /ī̃'postu/ *m* tax; **~to de renda** income tax; **~to sobre o valor acrescentado** (*Port*) VAT; **~tor** *m* impostor; **~tura** f deception

**impo|tência** /ī̃po'tēsia/ f impotence; **~tente** *a* impotent

**impreci|são** /ī̃presi'zāw/ f imprecision; **~so** *a* imprecise

**impregnar** /ī̃preg'nar/ *vt* impregnate

**imprensa** /ī̃'prēsa/ f press; **~ marrom** gutter press

**imprescindí|vel** /ĩpresĩ'dʒivew/ (*pl* ~**veis**) *a* essential
**impres|são** /ĩpre'sãw/ *f* impression; (*no prelo*) printing; ~**são digital** fingerprint; ~**sionante** *a* (*imponente*) impressive; (*comovente*) striking; ~**sionar** *vt* (*causar admiração*) impress; (*comover*) make an impression on; ~**sionar-se** *vpr* be impressed (**com** by); ~**sionável** (*pl* ~**sionáveis**) *a* impressionable; ~**sionismo** *m* impressionism; ~**sionista** *a* & *m/f* impressionist; ~**so** *a* printed □ *m* printed sheet; *pl* printed matter; ~**sor** *m* printer; ~**sora** *f* printer
**impresta|vel** /ĩpres'tavew/ (*pl* ~**veis**) *a* useless
**impre|visível** /ĩprevi'zivew/ (*pl* ~**visíveis**) *a* unpredictable; ~**visto** *a* unforeseen □ *m* unforeseen circumstance
**imprimir** /ĩpri'mir/ *vt* print
**impropério** /ĩpro'pɛriu/ *m* term of abuse; *pl* abuse
**impróprio** /ĩ'prɔpriu/ *a* improper; (*inadequado*) unsuitable (**para** for)
**imprová|vel** /ĩpro'vavew/ (*pl* ~**veis**) *a* unlikely
**improvi|sação** /ĩproviza'sãw/ *f* improvisation; ~**sar** *vt/i* improvise; ~**so** *m* **de** ~**so** on the spur of the moment
**impru|dência** /ĩpru'dẽsia/ *f* recklessness; ~**dente** *a* reckless
**impul|sionar** /ĩpuwsio'nar/ *vt* drive; ~**sivo** *a* impulsive; ~**so** *m* impulse
**impu|ne** /ĩ'puni/ *a* unpunished; ~**nidade** *f* impunity
**impu|reza** /ĩpu'reza/ *f* impurity; ~**ro** *a* impure
**imun|dície** /imũ'dʒisi/ *f* filth; ~**do** *a* filthy
**imu|ne** /i'muni/ *a* immune (**a** to); ~**nidade** *f* immunity; ~**nizar** *vt* immunize
**inabalá|vel** /inaba'lavew/ (*pl* ~**veis**) *a* unshakeable
**iná|bil** /i'nabiw/ (*pl* ~**bis**) *a* (*desafeitado*) clumsy
**inabitado** /inabi'tadu/ *a* uninhabited
**inacabado** /inaka'badu/ *a* unfinished
**inaceitá|vel** /inasej'tavew/ (*pl* ~**veis**) *a* unacceptable
**inacessí|vel** /inase'sivew/ (*pl* ~**veis**) *a* inaccessible
**inacreditá|vel** /inakredʒi'tavew/ (*pl* ~**veis**) *a* unbelievable
**inadequado** /inade'kwadu/ *a* unsuitable
**inadmissí|vel** /inadʒimi'sivew/ (*pl* ~**veis**) *a* inadmissible
**inadvertência** /inadʒiver'tẽsia/ *f* oversight
**inalar** /ina'lar/ *vt* inhale

**inalcançá|vel** /inawkã'savew/ (*pl* ~**veis**) *a* unattainable
**inalterá|vel** /inawte'ravew/ (*pl* ~**veis**) *a* unchangeable
**inanição** /inani'sãw/ *f* starvation
**inanimado** /inani'madu/ *a* inanimate
**inapto** /i'naptu/ *a* (*incapaz*) unfit
**inati|vidade** /inatʃivi'dadʒi/ *f* inactivity; ~**vo** *a* inactive
**inato** /i'natu/ *a* innate
**inaudito** /inaw'dʒitu/ *a* unheard of
**inaugu|ração** /inawgura'sãw/ *f* inauguration; ~**ral** (*pl* ~**rais**) *a* inaugural; ~**rar** *vt* inaugurate
**incabí|vel** /ĩka'bivew/ (*pl* ~**veis**) *a* inappropriate
**incalculá|vel** /ĩkawku'lavew/ (*pl* ~**veis**) *a* incalculable
**incandescente** /ĩkãde'sẽtʃi/ *a* red-hot
**incansá|vel** /ĩkã'savew/ (*pl* ~**veis**) *a* tireless
**incapaci|tado** /ĩkapasi'tadu/ *a* <*pessoa*> disabled; ~**tar** *vt* incapacitate
**incauto** /ĩ'kawtu/ *a* reckless
**incendi|ar** /ĩsẽdʒi'ar/ *vt* set alight; ~**ar-se** *vpr* catch fire; ~**ário** *a* incendiary; (*fig*) <*discurso*> inflammatory □ *m* arsonist; (*fig*) agitator
**incêndio** /ĩ'sẽdʒiu/ *m* fire
**incenso** /ĩ'sẽsu/ *m* incense
**incenti|var** /ĩsẽtʃi'var/ *vt* encourage; ~**vo** *m* incentive
**incer|teza** /ĩser'teza/ *f* uncertainty; ~**to** /ɛ/ *a* uncertain
**inces|to** /ĩ'sɛstu/ *m* incest; ~**tuoso** /o/ *a* incestuous
**in|chação** /ĩʃa'sãw/ *f* swelling; ~**char** *vt/i* swell
**inci|dência** /ĩsi'dẽsia/ *f* incidence; ~**dente** *m* incident; ~**dir** *vi* ~**dir em** <*luz*> shine on; <*imposto*> be payable on
**incinerar** /ĩsine'rar/ *vt* incinerate
**inci|são** /ĩsi'zãw/ *f* incision; ~**sivo** *a* incisive
**incitar** /ĩsi'tar/ *vt* incite
**incli|nação** /ĩklina'sãw/ *f* (*do chão*) incline; (*da cabeça*) nod; (*propensão*) inclination; ~**nado** *a* <*chão*> sloping; <*edifício*> leaning; (*propenso*) inclined (**a** to); ~**nar** *vt* tilt; nod <*cabeça*> □ *vi* <*chão*> slope; <*edifício*> lean; (*tender*) incline (**para** towards); ~**nar-se** *vpr* lean
**inclu|ir** /ĩklu'ir/ *vt* include; ~**são** *f* inclusion; ~**sive** *prep* including □ *adv* inclusive; (*até*) even; ~**so** *a* included
**incoe|rência** /ĩkoe'rẽsia/ *f* (*falta de nexo*) incoherence; (*inconseqüência*) inconsistency; ~**rente** *a* (*sem nexo*) incoherent; (*inconseqüente*) inconsistent

**incógni|ta** /ĩ'kɔgnita/ *f* unknown; ~**to** *adv* incognito

**incolor** /ĩko'lor/ *a* colourless

**incólume** /ĩ'kɔlumi/ *a* unscathed

**incomodar** /ĩkomo'dar/ *vt* bother □ *vi* be a nuisance; ~**-se** *vpr* (*dar-se ao trabalho*) bother (em to); ~**-se** (com) be bothered (by), mind

**incômodo** /ĩ'komodu/ *a* (*desagradável*) tiresome; (*sem conforto*) uncomfortable □ *m* nuisance

**incompa|rável** /ĩkõpa'ravew/ (*pl* ~**ráveis**) *a* incomparable; ~**tível** (*pl* ~**tíveis**) *a* incompatible

**incompe|tência** /ĩkõpe'tẽsia/ *f* incompetence; ~**tente** *a* incompetent

**incompleto** /ĩkõ'plɛtu/ *a* incomplete

**incompreensí|vel** /ĩkõprĩẽ'sivew/ (*pl* ~**veis**) *a* incomprehensible

**inconcebí|vel** /ĩkõse'bivew/ (*pl* ~**veis**) *a* inconceivable

**incondicio|nal** /ĩkõdʒisio'naw/ (*pl* ~**nais**) *a* unconditional; <*fã, partidário*> firm

**inconformado** /ĩkõfor'madu/ *a* unreconciled (com to)

**inconfundí|vel** /ĩkõfũ'dʒivew/ (*pl* ~**veis**) *a* unmistakeable

**inconsciente** /ĩkõsi'ẽtʃi/ *a & m* unconscious

**inconseqüente** /ĩkõse'kwẽtʃi/ *a* inconsistent

**incons|tância** /ĩkõs'tãsia/ *f* changeability; ~**tante** *a* changeable

**inconstitucio|nal** /ĩkõstʃitusio'naw/ (*pl* ~**nais**) *a* unconstitutional

**incontestá|vel** /ĩkõtes'tavew/ (*pl* ~**veis**) *a* indisputable

**inconveniente** /ĩkõveni'ẽtʃi/ *a* (*difícil*) inconvenient; (*desagradável*) annoying, tiresome; (*indecente*) unseemly □ *m* drawback

**incorporar** /ĩkorpo'rar/ *vt* incorporate

**incorrer** /ĩko'xer/ *vi* ~ em <*multa etc*> incur

**incorrigí|vel** /ĩkoxi'ʒivew/(*pl* ~**veis**) *a* incorrigible

**incrédulo** /ĩ'krɛdulu/ *a* incredulous

**incremen|tado** /ĩkremẽ'tadu/ *a* (*fam*) stylish; ~**tar** *vt* build up; (*fam*) jazz up; ~**to** *m* development, growth

**incriminar** /ĩkrimi'nar/ *vt* incriminate

**incrí|vel** /ĩ'krivew/ (*pl* ~**veis**) *a* incredible

**incu|bação** /ĩkuba'sãw/ *f* incubation; ~**badora** *f* incubator; ~**bar** *vt/i* incubate

**inculto** /ĩ'kuwtu/ *a* <*pessoa*> uneducated; <*terreno*> uncultivated

**incum|bência** /ĩkũ'bẽsia/ *f* task; ~**bir** *vt* ~**bir alg de** aco/**de ir** as-

sign s.o. sth/to go □ *vi* ~**bir a** be up to; ~**bir-se de** take on

**incurá|vel** /ĩku'ravew/ (*pl* ~**veis**) *a* incurable

**incursão** /ĩkur'sãw/ *f* incursion

**incutir** /ĩku'tʃir/ *vt* instil (em in)

**indagar** /ĩda'gar/ *vt* inquire (into)

**inde|cência** /ĩde'sẽsia/ *f* indecency; ~**cente** *a* indecent

**indecifrá|vel** /ĩdesi'fravew/ (*pl* ~**veis**) *a* indecipherable

**indeciso** /ĩde'sizu/ *a* undecided

**indecoroso** /ĩdeko'rozu/ *a* indecorous

**indefi|nido** /ĩdefi'nidu/ *a* indefinite; ~**nível** (*pl* ~**níveis**) *a* indefinable

**indelé|vel** /ĩde'lɛvew/ (*pl* ~**veis**) *a* indelible

**indelica|deza** /ĩdelika'deza/ *f* impoliteness; (*uma*) impolite thing; ~**do** *a* impolite

**indeni|zação** /ĩdeniza'sãw/ *f* compensation; ~**zar** *vt* compensate

**indepen|dência** /ĩdepẽ'dẽsia/ *f* independence; ~**dente** *a* independent

**indescriti|vel** /ĩdʒiskri'tʃivew/ (*pl* ~**veis**) *a* indescribable

**indesculpá|vel** /ĩdʒiskuw'pavew/ (*pl* ~**veis**) *a* inexcusable

**indesejá|vel** /ĩdeze'ʒavew/ (*pl* ~**veis**) *a* undesirable

**indestruti|vel** /ĩdʒistru'tʃivew/ (*pl* ~**veis**) *a* indestructible

**indeterminado** /ĩdetermi'nadu/ *a* indeterminate

**indevido** /ĩde'vidu/ *a* undue

**indexar** /ĩdek'sar/ *vt* index; index-link <*salário, preços*>

**Índia** /'ĩdʒia/ *f* India

**indiano** /ĩdʒi'anu/ *a & m* Indian

**indi|cação** /ĩdʒika'sãw/ *f* indication; (*do caminho*) directions; (*nomeação*) nomination; (*recomendação*) recommendation; ~**cador** *m* indicator; (*dedo*) index finger □ *a* indicative (de of); ~**car** *vt* indicate; (*para cargo, prêmio*) nominate (**para** for); (*recomendar*) recommend; ~**cativo** *a & m* indicative

**índice** /'ĩdʒisi/ *m* (*taxa*) rate; (*em livro etc*) index; ~ **de audiência** ratings

**indiciar** /ĩdʒisi'ar/ *vt* charge

**indício** /ĩ'dʒisiu/ *m* sign, indication; (*de crime*) clue

**indife|rença** /ĩdʒife'rẽsa/ *f* indifference; ~**rente** *a* indifferent

**indígena** /ĩ'dʒiʒena/ *a* indigenous, native □ *m/f* native

**indiges|tão** /ĩdʒiʒes'tãw/ *f* indigestion; ~**to** *a* indigestible; (*fig*) heavy-going

**indig|nação** /ĩdʒigna'sãw/ *f* indignation; ~**nado** *a* indignant; ~**nar** *vt* make indignant; ~**nar-se** *vpr* get indignant (**com** about)

**indig|nidade** /ĩdʒigni'dadʒi/ *f* indignity; ~**no** *a* <*pessoa*> unworthy; <*ato*> despicable

**índio** /'ĩdʒiu/ *a* & *m* Indian

**indire|ta** /ĩdʒi'rɛta/ *f* hint; ~**to** /ɛ/ *a* indirect

**indis|creto** /ĩdʒis'krɛtu/ *a* indiscreet; ~**crição** *f* indiscretion

**indiscriminado** /ĩdʒiskrimi'nadu/ *a* indiscriminate

**indiscuti|vel** /ĩdʒisku'tʃivew/ (*pl* ~**veis**) *a* unquestionable

**indispensá|vel** /ĩdʒispẽ'savew/ (*pl* ~**veis**) *a* indispensable

**indisponí|vel** /ĩdʒispo'nivew/ (*pl* ~**veis**) *a* unavailable

**indis|por** /ĩdʒis'por/ *vt* upset; ~**por alg contra** turn s.o. against; ~**por-se** *vpr* fall out (**com** with); ~**posição** *f* indisposition; ~**posto** *a* (*doente*) indisposed

**indistinto** /ĩdʒis'tʃĩtu/ *a* indistinct

**individu|al** /ĩdʒividu'aw/ (*pl* ~**ais**) *a* individual; ~**alidade** *f* individuality; ~**alismo** *m* individualism; ~**alista** *a* & *m/f* individualist

**indivíduo** /ĩdʒi'viduu/ *m* individual

**indizí|vel** /ĩdʒi'zivew/ (*pl* ~**veis**) *a* unspeakable

**índole** /'ĩdoli/ *f* nature

**indo|lência** /ĩdo'lẽsia/ *f* indolence; ~**lente** *a* indolent

**indolor** /ĩdo'lor/ *a* painless

**Indonésia** /ĩdo'nɛzia/ *f* Indonesia

**indonésio** /ĩdo'nɛziu/ *a* & *m* Indonesian

**indubitá|vel** /ĩdubi'tavew/ (*pl* ~**veis**) *a* undoubted

**indul|gência** /ĩduw'ʒẽsia/ *f* indulgence; ~**gente** *a* indulgent

**indulto** /ĩ'duwtu/ *m* pardon

**indumentária** /ĩdumẽ'taria/ *f* outfit

**indústria** /ĩ'dustria/ *f* industry

**industri|al** /ĩdustri'aw/ (*pl* ~**ais**) *a* industrial □ *m/f* industrialist; ~**alizado** *a* <*país*> industrialized; <*mercadoria*> manufactured; <*comida*> processed; ~**alizar** *vt* industrialize <*país, agricultura etc*>; process <*comida, lixo etc*>; ~**oso** /o/ *a* industrious

**induzir** /ĩdu'zir/ *vt* (*persuadir*) induce; (*inferir*) infer (**de** from); ~ **em erro** lead astray, mislead s.o.

**inebriante** /inebri'ãtʃi/ *a* intoxicating

**inédito** /i'nɛdʒitu/ *a* unheard-of, unprecedented; (*não publicado*) unpublished

**ineficaz** /inefi'kas/ *a* ineffective

**inefici|ência** /inefisi'ẽsia/ *f* inefficiency; ~**ente** *a* inefficient

**inegá|vel** /ine'gavew/ (*pl* ~**veis**) *a* undeniable

**inépcia** /i'nɛpsia/ *f* ineptitude

**inepto** /i'nɛptu/ *a* inept

**inequívoco** /ine'kivoku/ *a* unmistakeable

**inércia** /i'nɛrsia/ *f* inertia

**inerente** /ine'rẽtʃi/ *a* inherent (**a** in)

**inerte** /i'nɛrtʃi/ *a* inert

**inesgotá|vel** /inezgo'tavew/ (*pl* ~**veis**) *a* inexhaustible

**inesperado** /inespe'radu/ *a* unexpected

**inesquecí|vel** /ineske'sivew/ (*pl* ~**veis**) *a* unforgettable

**inevitá|vel** /inevi'tavew/ (*pl* ~**veis**) *a* inevitable

**inexato** /ine'zatu/ *a* inaccurate

**inexis|tência** /inezis'tẽsia/ *f* lack; ~**tente** *a* non-existent

**inexperi|ência** /inisperi'ẽsia/ *f* inexperience; ~**ente** *a* inexperienced

**inexpressivo** /inespre'sivu/ *a* expressionless

**infalí|vel** /ĩfa'livew/ (*pl* ~**veis**) *a* infallible

**infame** /ĩ'fami/ *a* despicable; (*péssimo*) dreadful

**infâmia** /ĩ'famia/ *f* disgrace

**infância** /ĩ'fãsia/ *f* childhood

**infantaria** /ĩfãta'ria/ *f* infantry

**infan|til** /ĩfa'tʃiw/ *a* <*roupa, livro*> children's; (*bobo*) childish; ~**tilidade** *f* childishness; (*uma*) childish thing

**infarto** /ĩ'fartu/ *m* heart attack

**infec|ção** /ĩfek'sãw/ *f* infection; ~**cionar** *vt* infect; ~**cioso** *a* infectious

**infeliz** /ĩfe'lis/ *a* (*não contente*) unhappy; (*inconveniente*) unfortunate; (*desgraçado*) wretched □ *m* (*desgraçado*) wretch; ~**mente** *adv* unfortunately

**inferi|or** /ĩferi'or/ *a* lower; (*em qualidade*) inferior (**a** to); ~**oridade** *f* inferiority

**inferir** /ĩfe'rir/ *vt* infer

**infer|nal** /ĩfer'naw/ (*pl* ~**nais**) *a* infernal; ~**nizar** *vt* ~**nizar a vida dele** make his life hell; ~**no** /ɛ/ *m* hell

**infér|til** /ĩ'fɛrtʃiw/ (*pl* ~**teis**) *a* infertile

**infertilidade** /ĩfertʃili'dadʒi/ *f* infertility

**infestar** /ĩfes'tar/ *vt* infest

**infetar** /ĩfe'tar/ *vt* infect

**infidelidade** /ĩfideli'dadʒi/ *f* infidelity

**infi|el** /ĩfi'ɛw/ (*pl* ~**éis**) *a* unfaithful

**infiltrar** /ĩfiw'trar/ *vt* infiltrate; ~**-se em** infiltrate

**ínfimo** /'ĩfimu/ *a* lowest; (*muito pequeno*) tiny

**infindá|vel** /ĩfĩ'davew/ (*pl* ~**veis**) *a* unending

infinidade /ĩfini'dadʒi/ f infinity; **uma ~ de** an infinite number of

infini|tesimal /ĩfinitezi'maw/ (pl ~tesimais) a infinitesimal; ~tivo a & m infinitive; ~to a infinite □ m infinity

infla|ção /ĩfla'sãw/ f inflation; ~cionar vt inflate; ~cionário a inflationary; ~cionista a & m/f inflationist

infla|mação /ĩflama'sãw/ f inflammation; ~mar vt inflame; ~mar-se vpr become inflamed; ~matório a inflammatory; ~mável (pl ~máveis) a inflammable

in|flar vt inflate; ~flar-se vpr inflate; ~flável (pl ~fláveis) a inflatable

infle|xibilidade /ĩfleksibili'dadʒi/ f inflexibility; ~xível (pl ~xíveis) a inflexible

infligir /ĩfli'ʒir/ vt inflict (**a** on)

influência /ĩflu'êsia/ f influence

influen|ciar /ĩfluêsi'ar/ vt ~ciar (em) influence; ~ciar-se vpr be influenced; ~ciável (pl ~ciáveis) a open to influence; ~te a influential

influir /ĩflu'ir/ vi ~ em ou sobre influence

informação /ĩforma'sãw/ f information; (uma) a piece of information; (mil) intelligence; pl information

infor|mal /ĩfor'maw/ (pl ~mais) a informal; ~malidade f informality

infor|mar /ĩfor'mar/ vt inform; ~mar-se vpr find out (**de** about); ~mática f information technology; ~mativo a informative; ~matizar vt computerize; ~me m (mil) piece of intelligence

infortúnio /ĩfor'tuniu/ m misfortune

infração /ĩfra'sãw/ f infringement

infra-estrutura /ĩfraistru'tura/ f infrastructure

infrator /ĩfra'tor/ m offender

infravermelho /ĩfraver'meʎu/ a infrared

infringir /ĩfrĩ'ʒir/ vt infringe

infrutífero /ĩfru'tʃiferu/ a fruitless

infundado /ĩfũ'dadu/ a unfounded

infundir /ĩfũ'dʒir/ vt (insuflar) infuse; (incutir) instil

infusão /ĩfu'zãw/ f infusion

ingenuidade /ĩʒenui'dadʒi/ f naivety

ingênuo /ĩ'ʒenuu/ a naive

Inglaterra /ĩgla'texa/ f England

ingerir /ĩʒe'rir/ vt ingest; (engolir) swallow

in|glês /ĩ'gles/ a (f ~glesa) English □ m (f ~glesa) Englishman (f -woman); (língua) English; **os ~gleses** the English

ingra|tidão /ĩgratʃi'dãw/ f ingratitude; ~to a ungrateful

ingrediente /ĩgredʒi'ẽtʃi/ m ingredient

íngreme /'ĩgrimi/ a steep

ingres|sar /ĩgre'sar/ vi ~sar em join; ~so m entry; (bilhete) ticket

inhame /i'ɲami/ m yam

ini|bição /inibi'sãw/ f inhibition; ~bir vt inhibit

inici|ado /inisi'adu/ m initiate; ~al (pl ~ais) a & f initial; ~ar vt (começar) begin; (em ciência, seita etc) initiate (**em** into) □ vi begin; ~ativa f initiative

início /i'nisiu/ m beginning

inigualá|vel /inigwa'lavew/ (pl ~veis) a unparalleled

inimaginá|vel /inimaʒi'navew/ (pl ~veis) a unimaginable

inimi|go /ini'migu/ a & m enemy; ~zade f enmity

ininterrupto /inĩte'xuptu/ a continuous

inje|ção /ĩʒe'sãw/ f injection; ~tado a <olhos> bloodshot; ~tar vt inject; ~tável (pl ~táveis) a <droga> intravenous

injúria /ĩ'ʒuria/ f insult

injuriar /ĩʒuri'ar/ vt insult

injus|tiça /ĩʒus'tʃisa/ f injustice; ~tiçado a wronged; ~to a unfair, unjust

ino|cência /ino'sêsia/ f innocence; ~centar vt clear (**de** of); ~cente a innocent

inocular /inoku'lar/ vt inoculate

inócuo /i'nɔkuu/ a harmless

inodoro /ino'dɔru/ a odourless

inofensivo /inofẽ'sivu/ a harmless

inoportuno /inopor'tunu/ a inopportune

inorgânico /inor'ganiku/ a inorganic

inóspito /i'nɔspitu/ a inhospitable

ino|vação /inova'sãw/ f innovation; ~var vt/i innovate

inoxidá|vel /inoksi'davew/ (pl ~veis) a <aço> stainless

inquérito /ĩ'keritu/ m inquiry

inquie|tação /ĩkieta'sãw/ f concern; ~tador, ~tante a worrying; ~tar vt worry; ~tar-se vpr worry; ~to /ɛ/ a uneasy

inquili|nato /ĩkili'natu/ m tenancy; ~no m tenant

inquirir /ĩki'rir/ vt cross-examine <testemunha>

Inquisição /ĩkizi'sãw/ f a ~ the Inquisition

insaciá|vel /ĩsasi'avew/ (pl ~veis) a insatiable

insalubre /ĩsa'lubri/ a unhealthy

insatis|fação /ĩsatʃisfa'sãw/ f dissatisfaction; ~fatório a unsatisfactory; ~feito a dissatisfied ins|crever /ĩskre'ver/ vt (registrar) register; (gravar) inscribe; ~crever-se vpr register; (em escola etc) enrol; ~crição f (registro) registration; (em clube, escola) enrolment; (em monumento etc) inscription

insegu|rança /ĩsegu'rãsa/ f insecurity; ~ro a insecure

insemi|nação /ĩsemina'sãw/ f insemination; ~nar vt inseminate

insen|satez /ĩsẽsa'tes/ f folly; ~sato a foolish; ~sibilidade f insensitivity; ~sível (pl ~síveis) a insensitive

insepará|vel /ĩsepa'ravew/ (pl ~veis) a inseparable

inserção /ĩser'sãw/ f insertion

inserir /ĩse'rir/ vt insert; enter <dados>

inse|ticida /ĩsetʃi'sida/ m insecticide; ~to /ε/ m insect

insígnia /ĩ'signia/ f insignia

insignifi|cância /ĩsignifi'kãsia/ f insignificance; ~cante a insignificant

insincero /ĩsĩ'sεru/ a insincere

insinu|ante /ĩsinu'ãtʃi/ a suggestive; ~ar vt/i insinuate

insípido /ĩ'sipidu/ a insipid

insis|tência /ĩsis'tẽsia/ f insistence; ~tente a insistent; ~tir vt/i insist (em on)

insolação /ĩsola'sãw/ f sunstroke

inso|lência /ĩso'lẽsia/ f insolence; ~lente a insolent

insólito /ĩ'sɔlitu/ a unusual

insolú|vel /ĩso'luvew/ (pl ~veis) a insoluble

insone /ĩ'sɔni/ a <noite> sleepless; <pessoa> insomniac □ m/f insomniac

insônia /ĩ'sonia/ f insomnia

insosso /ĩ'sosu/ a bland; (sem sabor) tasteless; (sem sal) unsalted

inspe|ção /ĩspe'sãw/ f inspection; ~cionar vt inspect; ~tor m inspector

inspi|ração /ĩspira'sãw/ f inspiration; ~rar vt inspire; ~rar-se vpr take inspiration (em from)

instabilidade /ĩstabili'dadʒi/ f instability

insta|lação /ĩstala'sãw/ f installation; ~lar vt install; ~lar-se vpr install o.s.

instan|tâneo /ĩstã'taniu/ a instant; ~te m instant

instaurar /ĩstaw'rar/ vt set up

instá|vel /ĩ'stavew/ (pl ~veis) a unstable; <tempo> unsettled

insti|gação /ĩstʃiga'sãw/ f instigation; ~gante a stimulating; ~gar vt incite

instin|tivo /ĩstʃĩ'tʃivu/ a instinctive; ~to m instinct

institu|cional /ĩstʃitusio'naw/ (pl ~cionais) a institutional; ~ição f

institution; ~ir vt set up; set <prazo>; ~to m institute

instru|ção /ĩstru'sãw/ f instruction; ~ir vt instruct; train <recrutas>; (informar) advise (sobre of)

instrumen|tal /ĩstrumẽ'taw/ (pl ~tais) a instrumental; ~tista m/f instrumentalist; ~to m instrument

instru|tivo /ĩstru'tʃivu/ a instructive; ~tor m instructor

insubstitu|ível /ĩsubistʃitu'ivew/ (pl ~veis) a irreplaceable

insucesso /ĩsu'sesu/ m failure

insufici|ência /ĩsufisi'ẽsia/ f insufficiency; (dos órgãos) failure; ~ente a insufficient

insulina /ĩsu'lina/ f insulin

insul|tar /ĩsuw'tar/ vt insult; ~to m insult

insuperá|vel /ĩsupe'ravew/ (pl ~veis) a <problema> insurmountable; <qualidade> unsurpassed

insuportá|vel /ĩsupor'tavew/ (pl ~veis) a unbearable

insur|gente /ĩsur'ʒẽtʃi/ a & m/f insurgent; ~gir-se vpr rise up, revolt; ~reição f insurrection

intato /ĩ'tatu/ a intact

íntegra /'ĩtegra/ f full text; na ~ in full

inte|gração /ĩtegra'sãw/ f integration; ~gral (pl ~grais) a whole; arroz/pão ~gral brown rice/bread; ~grante a integral □ m/f member; ~grar vt make up, form; ~grar-se em become a part of; ~gridade f integrity

íntegro /'ĩtegru/ a honest

intei|ramente /ĩtera'mẽtʃi/ adv completely; ~rar vt (informar) fill in, inform (de about); ~rar-se vpr find out (de about); ~riço a in one piece; ~ro a whole

intelec|to /ĩte'lεktu/ m intellect; ~tual (pl ~tuais) a & m/f intellectual

inteli|gência /ĩteli'ʒẽsia/ f intelligence; ~gente a clever, intelligent; ~gível (pl ~gíveis) a intelligible

intem|périe /ĩtẽ'peri/ f bad weather; ~pestivo a ill-timed

inten|ção /ĩtẽ'sãw/ f intention; segundas ~ções ulterior motives

intencio|nado /ĩtẽsio'nadu/ a bem ~nado well-meaning; ~nal (pl ~nais) a intentional; ~nar vt intend

inten|sidade /ĩtẽsi'dadʒi/ f intensity; ~sificar vt intensify; ~sificar-se vpr intensify; ~sivo a intensive; ~so a intense

intento /ĩ'tẽtu/ m intention

intera|ção /ĩtera'sãw/ f interaction; ~gir vi interact; ~tivo a interactive

**inter|calar** /ĩterka'lar/ vt insert; **~câmbio** m exchange; **~ceptar** vt intercept

**intercontinen|tal** /ĩterkõtʃinẽ'taw/ (pl **~tais**) a intercontinental

**interdepen|dência** /ĩterdepẽ'dẽsia/ f interdependence; **~dente** a interdependent

**interdi|ção** /ĩterdʒi'sãw/ f closure; (jurid) injunction; **~tar** vt close <rua etc>; (proibir) ban

**interes|sante** /ĩtere'sãtʃi/ a interesting; **~sar** vt interest □ vi be relevant; **~sar-se** vpr be interested (em ou por in); **~se** /e/ m interest; (próprio) self-interest; **~seiro** a self-seeking

**interestadu|al** /ĩteristadu'aw/ (pl **~ais**) a interstate

**interface** /ĩter'fasi/ f interface

**interfe|rência** /ĩterfe'rẽsia/ f interference; **~rir** vi interfere

**interfone** /ĩter'fɔni/ m intercom

**ínterim** /'ĩterĩ/ m interim; **nesse ~** in the interim

**interino** /ĩte'rinu/ a temporary

**interior** /ĩteri'or/ a inner; (dentro do país) internal, domestic □ m inside; (do país) country, interior

**inter|jeição** /ĩterʒej'sãw/ f interjection; **~ligar** vt interconnect; **~locutor** m interlocutor; **~mediário** a & m intermediary

**intermédio** /ĩter'mɛdʒiu/ m **por ~ de** through

**intermina|vel** /ĩtermi'navew/ (pl **~veis**) a interminable

**intermitente** /ĩtermi'tẽtʃi/ a intermittent

**internacio|nal** /ĩternasio'naw/ (pl **~nais**) a international

**inter|nar** /ĩter'nar/ vt intern <preso>; admit to hospital <doente>; **~nato** m boarding school; **~no** a internal

**interpelar** /ĩterpe'lar/ vt question

**interpor** /ĩter'por/ vt interpose; **~-se** vpr intervene

**interpre|tação** /ĩterpreta'sãw/ f interpretation; **~tar** vt interpret; perform <papel, música>; **intérprete** m/f (de línguas) interpreter; (de teatro etc) performer

**interro|gação** /ĩterroga'sãw/ f interrogation; **~gar** vt interrogate, question; **~gativo** a interrogative; **~gatório** m interrogation

**inter|romper** /ĩterõ'per/ vt interrupt; **~rupção** f interruption; **~ruptor** m switch

**interurbano** /ĩterur'banu/ a long-distance □ m trunk call

**intervalo** /ĩter'valu/ m interval

**inter|venção** /ĩtervẽ'sãw/ f intervention; **~vir** vi intervene

**intesti|nal** /ĩtestʃi'naw/ (pl **~nais**) a intestinal; **~no** m intestine

**inti|mação** /ĩtʃima'sãw/ f (da justiça) summons; **~mar** vt order; (à justiça) summon

**intimidade** /ĩtʃimi'dadʒi/ f intimacy; (entre amigos) closeness; (vida íntima) private life; **ter ~ com** be close to

**intimidar** /ĩtʃimi'dar/ vt intimidate; **~-se** vpr be intimidated

**íntimo** /'ĩtʃimu/ a intimate; <amigo> close; <vida> private □ m close friend

**intitular** /ĩtʃitu'lar/ vt entitle

**intocá|vel** /ĩto'kavew/ (pl **~veis**) a untouchable

**intole|rância** /ĩtole'rãsia/ f intolerance; **~rante** a intolerant; **~rável** (pl **~ráveis**) a intolerable

**intoxi|cação** /ĩtoksika'sãw/ f poisoning; **~cação alimentar** food poisoning; **~car** vt poison

**intragá|vel** /ĩtra'gavew/ (pl **~veis**) a <comida> inedible; <pessoa> unbearable

**intransigente** /ĩtrãzi'ʒẽtʃi/ a uncompromising

**intransi|tável** /ĩtrãzi'tavew/ (pl **~táveis**) a impassable; **~tivo** a intransitive

**intratá|vel** /ĩtra'tavew/ (pl **~veis**) a <pessoa> difficult

**intra-uterino** /ĩtraute'rinu/ a **dispositivo ~** intra-uterine device, IUD

**intrépido** /ĩ'trɛpidu/ a intrepid

**intri|ga** /ĩ'triga/ f intrigue; (enredo) plot; **~gante** a intriguing; **~gar** vt intrigue

**intrincado** /ĩtrĩ'kadu/ a intricate

**intrínseco** /ĩ'trĩsiku/ a intrinsic

**introdu|ção** /ĩtrodu'sãw/ f introduction; **~tório** a introductory; **~zir** vt introduce

**introme|ter-se** /ĩtrome'tersi/ vpr interfere; **~tido** a interfering □ m busybody

**introspec|ção** /ĩtrospek'sãw/ f introspection; **~tivo** a introspective

**introvertido** /ĩtrover'tʃidu/ a introverted □ m introvert

**intruso** /ĩ'truzu/ a intrusive □ m intruder

**intu|ição** /ĩtui'sãw/ f intuition; **~ir** vt intuit; **~itivo** a intuitive; **~to** m purpose

**inumano** /inu'manu/ a inhuman

**inumerá|vel** /inume'ravew/ (pl **~veis**) a innumerable

**inúmero** /i'numeru/ a countless

**inun|dação** /inũda'sãw/ f flood; **~dar** vt/i flood

**inusitado** /inuzi'tadu/ a unusual

**inú|til** /i'nutʃiw/ (pl **~teis**) a useless

**inutilmente** /inutʃiw'mētʃi/ *adv* in vain

**inutilizar** /inutʃili'zar/ *vt* render useless; damage *<aparelho>*; thwart *<esforços>*

**invadir** /iva'dʒir/ *vt* invade

**invali|dar** /ivali'dar/ *vt* invalidate; disable *<pessoa>*; ~**dez** /e/ *f* disability

**inválido** /ĩ'validu/ *a & m* invalid

**invariá|vel** /ivari'avew/ (*pl* ~**veis**) *a* invariable

**inva|são** /iva'zãw/ *f* invasion; ~**sor** *m* invader □ *a* invading

**inve|ja** /ĩ'veʒa/ *f* envy; ~**jar** *vt* envy; ~**jável** (*pl* ~**jáveis**) *a* enviable; ~**joso** /o/ *a* envious

**inven|ção** /ivē'sãw/ *f* invention; ~**tar** *vt* invent; ~**tário** *m* inventory; ~**tivo** *a* inventive; ~**tor** *m* inventor

**inver|nar** /ĩver'nar/ *vi* winter, spend the winter; ~**no** /ɛ/ *m* winter

**inverossí|mil** /ivero'simiw/ (*pl* ~**meis**) *a* improbable

**inver|são** /ĩver'sãw/ *f* inversion; ~**so** *a* inverse; *<ordem>* reverse □ *m* reverse; ~**ter** *vt* reverse; (*colocar de cabeça para baixo*) invert

**invertebrado** /ĩverte'bradu/ *a & m* invertebrate

**invés** /ĩ'vɛs/ *m* **ao ~ de** instead of

**investida** /ĩvestʃida/ *f* attack

**investidura** /ĩvestʃi'dura/ *f* investiture

**investi|gação** /ĩvestʃiga'sãw/ *f* investigation; ~**gar** *vt* investigate

**inves|timento** /ĩvestʃi'mētu/ *m* investment; ~**tir** *vt/i* invest; ~**tir contra** attack

**inveterado** /ĩvete'radu/ *a* inveterate

**inviá|vel** /ĩvi'avew/ (*pl* ~**veis**) *a* impracticable

**invicto** /ĩ'viktu/ *a* unbeaten

**invisí|vel** /ĩvi'zivew/ (*pl* ~**veis**) *a* invisible

**invocar** /ĩvo'kar/ *vt* invoke; (*fam*) pester

**invólucro** /ĩ'vɔlukru/ *m* covering

**involuntário** /ĩvolũ'tariu/ *a* involuntary

**invulnerá|vel** /ĩvuwne'ravew/ (*pl* ~**veis**) *a* invulnerable

**iodo** /i'odu/ *m* iodine

**ioga** /i'ɔga/ *f* yoga

**iogurte** /io'gurtʃi/ *m* yoghurt

**ir** /ir/ *vi* go; ~**-se** *vpr* go away; **vou voltar** I will come back; **vou melhorando** I am (gradually) getting better

**ira** /'ira/ *f* wrath

**Irã** /i'rã/ *m* Iran

**iraniano** /irani'anu/ *a & m* Iranian

**Irão** /i'rãw/ *m* (*Port*) Iran

**Iraque** /i'raki/ *m* Iraq

**iraquiano** /iraki'anu/ *a & m* Iraqui

**Irlanda** /ir'lãda/ *f* Ireland

**irlan|dês** /irlã'des/ *a* (*f* ~**desa**) Irish □ *m* (*f* ~**desa**) Irishman (*f* -woman); (*língua*) Irish; **os** ~**deses** the Irish

**irmã** /ir'mã/ *f* sister

**irmandade** /irmã'dadʒi/ *f* (*associação*) brotherhood

**irmão** /ir'mãw/ (*pl* ~**s**) *m* brother

**ironia** /iro'nia/ *f* irony

**irônico** /i'roniku/ *a* ironic

**irracio|nal** /ixasio'naw/ (*pl* ~**nais**) *a* irrational

**irradiar** /ixadʒi'ar/ *vt* radiate; (*pelo rádio*) broadcast □ *vi* shine; ~**-se** *vpr* spread, radiate

**irre|al** /ixe'aw/ (*pl* ~**ais**) *a* unreal

**irreconhecí|vel** /ixekoɲe'sivew/ (*pl* ~**veis**) *a* unrecognizable

**irrecuperá|vel** /ixekupe'ravew/ (*pl* ~**veis**) *a* irretrievable

**irrefletido** /ixefle'tʃidu/ *a* rash

**irregu|lar** /ixegu'lar/ *a* irregular; (*inconstante*) erratic; ~**laridade** *f* irregularity

**irrelevante** /ixele'vãtʃi/ *a* irrelevant

**irrepará|vel** /ixepa'ravew/ (*pl* ~**veis**) *a* irreparable

**irrepreensí|vel** /ixepriē'sivew/ (*pl* ~**veis**) *a* irreproachable

**irrequieto** /ixeki'ɛtu/ *a* restless

**irresistí|vel** /ixezis'tʃivew/ (*pl* ~**veis**) *a* irresistible

**irresoluto** /ixezo'lutu/ *a* *<questão>* unresolved; *<pessoa>* indecisive

**irresponsá|vel** /ixespõ'savew/ (*pl* ~**veis**) *a* irresponsible

**irreverente** /ixeve'rētʃi/ *a* irreverent

**irri|gação** /ixiga'sãw/ *f* irrigation; ~**gar** *vt* irrigate

**irrisório** /ixi'zɔriu/ *a* derisory

**irri|tação** /ixita'sãw/ *f* irritation; ~**tadiço** *a* irritable; ~**tante** *a* irritating; ~**tar** *vt* irritate; ~**tar-se** *vpr* get irritated

**irromper** /ixõ'per/ *vi* ~ **em** burst into

**isca** /'iska/ *f* bait

**isen|ção** /izē'sãw/ *f* exemption; ~**tar** *vt* exempt; ~**to** *a* exempt

**Islã** /iz'lã/ *m* Islam

**islâmico** /iz'lamiku/ *a* Islamic

**isla|mismo** /izla'mizmu/ *m* Islam; ~**mita** *a & m/f* Muslim

**islan|dês** /izlã'des/ *a* (*f* ~**desa**) Icelandic □ *m* (*f* ~**desa**) Icelander; (*língua*) Icelandic

**Islândia** /iz'lãdʒia/ *f* Iceland

**iso|lamento** /izola'mētu/ *m* isolation; (*eletr*) insulation; ~**lante** *a* insulating; ~**lar** *vt* isolate; (*eletr*) insulate □ *vi* (*contra azar*) touch wood, (*Amer*) knock on wood

**isopor** /izo'por/ *m* polystyrene

**isqueiro** /is'keru/ *m* lighter

Israel /izraˈɛw/ m Israel
israe|lense /izrajˈlẽsi/ a & m/f Israeli; ~lita a & m/f Israelite
isso /ˈisu/ pron that; por ~ therefore
isto /ˈistu/ pron this; ~ é that is
Itália /iˈtalia/ f Italy
italiano /italiˈanu/ a & m Italian
itálico /iˈtaliku/ a & m italic
item /ˈitẽ/ m item
itine|rante /itʃineˈrãtʃi/ a itinerant; ~rário m itinerary
Iugoslávia /iugozˈlavia/ f Yugoslavia
iugoslavo /iugozˈlavu/ a & m Yugoslavian

# J

já /ʒa/ adv already; (agora) right away □ conj on the other hand; desde ~ from now on; ~ não no longer; ~ que since; ~, ~ in no time
jabuticaba /ʒabutʃiˈkaba/ f jabuticaba
jaca /ˈʒaka/ f jack fruit
jacaré /ʒakaˈrɛ/ m alligator
jacinto /ʒaˈsĩtu/ m hyacinth
jactância /ʒakˈtãsia/ f boasting
jade /ˈʒadʒi/ m jade
jaguar /ʒaguˈar/ m jaguar
jagunço /ʒaˈgũsu/ m hired gunman
jamais /ʒaˈmajs/ adv never
Jamaica /ʒaˈmajka/ f Jamaica
jamaicano /ʒamajˈkanu/ a & m Jamaican
jamanta /ʒaˈmãta/ f juggernaut
janeiro /ʒaˈneru/ m January
janela /ʒaˈnɛla/ f window
jangada /ʒãˈgada/ f (fishing) raft
janta /ˈʒãta/ f ( fam) dinner
jantar /ʒãˈtar/ m dinner □ vi have dinner □ vt have for dinner
Japão /ʒaˈpãw/ m Japan
japo|na /ʒaˈpɔna/ f pea jacket □ m/f ( fam) Japanese; ~nês a & m ( f ~nesa) Japanese
jaqueira /ʒaˈkera/ f jack-fruit tree
jaqueta /ʒaˈketa/ f jacket
jarda /ˈʒarda/ f yard
jar|dim /ʒarˈdʒĩ/ m garden; ~dim-de-infância (pl ~dins-de-infância) f kindergarten
jardi|nagem /ʒardʒiˈnaʒẽ/ f gardening; ~nar vi garden; ~neira f (calça) dungarees; (vestido) pinafore dress, (Amer) jumper; (ônibus) open-sided bus; ( para flores) flower stand; ~neiro m gardener
jargão /ʒarˈgãw/ m jargon
jar|ra /ˈʒaxa/ f pot; ~ro m jug
jasmim /ʒazˈmĩ/ m jasmine
jato /ˈʒatu/ m jet
jaula /ˈʒawla/ f cage

ja|zer /ʒaˈzer/ vi lie; ~zida f deposit; ~zigo m grave
jazz /dʒaz/ m jazz; ~ista m/f jazz artist; ~ístico a jazzy
jeca /ˈʒɛka/ m/f country bumpkin □ a countrified; (cafona) tacky; ~-tatu m/f country bumpkin
jei|tão /ʒejˈtãw/ m ( fam) individual style; ~tinho m knack; ~to m way; (de pessoa) manner; (habilidade) skill; de qualquer ~to anyway; de ~to nenhum no way; pelo ~to by the looks of things; sem ~to awkward; dar um ~to find a way; dar um ~to em (arrumar) tidy up; (consertar) fix; (torcer) twist <pé etc>; ter ~to de look like; ter ou levar ~to para be good at; tomar ~to pull one's socks up; ~toso /o/ a skilful; (de aparência) elegant
je|juar /ʒeʒuˈar/ vi fast; ~jum m fast
Jeová /ʒioˈva/ m testemunha de ~ Jehovah's witness
jérsei /ˈʒersej/ m jersey
jesuíta /ʒezuˈita/ a & m/f Jesuit
Jesus /ʒeˈzus/ m Jesus
jibóia /ʒiˈbɔja/ f boa constrictor
jiboiar /ʒibojˈar/ vi have a rest to let one's dinner go down
jiló /ʒiˈlɔ/ m okra
jipe /ˈʒipi/ m jeep
jiu-jitsu /ʒiuˈʒitsu/ m jiu-jitsu
joa|lheiro /ʒoaˈʎeru/ m jeweller; ~lheria f jeweller's (shop)
joaninha /ʒoaˈnina/ f ladybird, (Amer) ladybug; (alfinete) safety pin
joão-ninguém /ʒoãwnĩˈgẽj/ (pl joões-ninguém) m nobody
jocoso /ʒoˈkozu/ a jocular
joe|lhada /ʒoeˈʎada/ f blow with the knee; ~lheira f kneepad; ~lho /e/ m knee; de ~lhos kneeling
jo|gada /ʒoˈgada/ f move; ~gado a <pessoa> flat out; (papéis, roupa etc> lying around; ~gador m player; (no cassino etc) gambler; ~gar vt play; (atirar) throw; (arriscar no jogo) gamble □ vi play; (no cassino etc) gamble; (balançar) toss; ~gar fora throw away; ~gatina f gambling
jogging /ˈʒɔgĩ/ m (cooper) jogging; (roupa) track suit
jogo /ˈʒogu/ m (partida) game; (ação de jogar) play; (jogatina) gambling; (conjunto) set; em ~ at stake; ~ de cintura ( fig) flexibility, room to manoeuvre; ~ de luz lighting effects; ~ do bicho illegal numbers game; Jogos Olímpicos Olympic Games; ~da-velha m noughts and crosses
joguete /ʒoˈgetʃi/ m plaything
jóia /ˈʒɔja/ f jewel; ( propina) entry fee □ a ( fam) great

**joio** /ˈʒoju/ *m* chaff; **separar o ~ do trigo** separate the wheat from the chaff

**jóquei** /ˈʒɔkej/ *m* (*pessoa*) jockey; (*lugar*) race course

**Jordânia** /ʒorˈdania/ *f* Jordan

**jordaniano** /ʒordaniˈanu/ *a & m* Jordanian

**jor|nada** /ʒorˈnada/ *f* (*viagem*) journey; **~nada de trabalho** working day; (*pl* **~nais**) *m* newspaper; (*na TV*) news

**jorna|leco** /ʒornaˈlɛku/ *m* rag, scandal sheet; **~leiro** *m* (*vendedor*) newsagent, (*Amer*) newsdealer; (*entregador*) paperboy; **~lismo** *m* journalism; **~lista** *m/f* journalist; **~lístico** *a* journalistic

**jor|rar** /ʒoˈxar/ *vi* gush, spurt; **~ro** /ˈʒoxu/ *m* spurt

**jota** /ˈʒɔta/ *m* letter J

**jovem** /ˈʒovẽ/ *a* young; (*criado por jovens*) youth □ *m/f* young man (*f* -woman); *pl* young people

**jovi|al** /ʒoviˈaw/ (*pl* **~ais**) *a* jovial

**juba** /ˈʒuba/ *f* mane

**jubileu** /ʒubiˈlew/ *m* jubilee

**júbilo** /ˈʒubilu/ *m* joy

**ju|daico** /ʒuˈdajku/ *a* Jewish; **~daísmo** *m* Judaism; **~deu** *a* (*f* **~dia**) Jewish □ *m* (*f* **~dia**) Jew; **~diação** *f* ill-treatment; (*uma*) terrible thing; **~diar** *vi* **~diar de** ill-treat

**judici|al** /ʒudʒisiˈaw/ (*pl* **~ais**) *a* judicial; **~ário** *a* judicial □ *m* judiciary; **~oso** /o/ *a* judicious

**judô** /ʒuˈdo/ *m* judo

**judoca** /ʒuˈdɔka/ *m/f* judo player

**jugo** /ˈʒugu/ *m* yoke

**juiz** /ʒuˈis/ *m* (*f* **juíza**) judge; (*em jogos*) referee

**juizado** /ʒuiˈzadu/ *m* court

**juízo** /ʒuˈizu/ *m* judgement; (*tino*) sense; (*tribunal*) court; **perder o ~** lose one's head; **ter ~** be sensible; **tomar** *ou* **criar ~** come to one's senses

**jujuba** /ʒuˈʒuba/ *f* (*bala*) fruit jelly

**jul|gamento** /ʒuwgaˈmẽtu/ *m* judgement; **~gar** *vt* judge; pass judgement on <*réu*>; (*imaginar*) think; **~gar-se** *vpr* consider o.s.

**julho** /ˈʒuʎu/ *m* July

**jumento** /ʒuˈmẽtu/ *m* donkey

**junção** /ʒũˈsãw/ *f* join; (*ação*) joining

**junco** /ˈʒũku/ *m* reed

**junho** /ˈʒuɲu/ *m* June

**juni|no** /ʒuˈninu/ *a* **festa ~na** St John's Day festival

**júnior** /ˈʒunior/ *a & m* junior

**jun|ta** /ˈʒũta/ *f* board; (*pol*) junta; **~tar** *vt* (*acrescentar*) add; (*uma coisa a outra*) join; (*uma coisa com outra*)

combine; save up <*dinheiro*>; gather up <*papéis, lixo etc*> □ *vi* gather; **~tar-se** *vpr* join together; <*multidão*> gather; <*casal*> live together; **~tar-se a** join; **~to** *a* together □ *adv* together; **~to a** next to; **~to com** together with

**ju|ra** /ˈʒura/ *f* vow; **~rado** *m* juror; **~ramentado** *a* accredited; **~ramento** *m* oath; **~rar** *vt/i* swear; **~ra?** (*fam*) really?

**júri** /ˈʒuri/ *m* jury

**jurídico** /ʒuˈridʒiku/ *a* legal

**juris|consulto** /ʒuriskõˈsuwtu/ *m* legal advisor; **~dição** *f* jurisdiction; **~prudência** *f* jurisprudence; **~ta** *m/f* jurist

**juros** /ˈʒurus/ *m pl* interest

**jus** /ʒus/ *m* **fazer ~ a** live up to

**jusante** /ʒuˈzãtʃi/ *f* **a ~** downstream

**justamente** /ʒustaˈmẽtʃi/ *adv* exactly; (*com justiça*) fairly

**justapor** /ʒustaˈpor/ *vt* juxtapose

**justi|ça** /ʒusˈtʃisa/ *f* (*perante a lei*) justice; (*para com outros*) fairness; (*tribunal*) court; **~ceiro** *a* fairminded □ *m* vigilante

**justifi|cação** /ʒustʃifikaˈsãw/ *f* justification; **~car** *vt* justify; **~cativa** *f* justification; **~cável** (*pl* **~cáveis**) *a* justifiable

**justo** /ˈʒustu/ *a* fair; (*apertado*) tight □ *adv* just

**juve|nil** /ʒuveˈniw/ (*pl* **~nis**) *a* youthful; (*para jovens*) for young people; <*time, torneio*> junior □ *m* junior championship

**juventude** /ʒuvẽˈtudʒi/ *f* youth

# K

**karaokê** /karaoˈke/ *m* karaoke

**kart** /ˈkartʃi/ (*pl* **~s**) *m* go-kart

**ketchup** /keˈtʃupi/ *m* ketchup

**kit** /ˈkitʃi/ (*pl* **~s**) *m* kit

**kitchenette** /kitʃeˈnɛtʃi/ *f* bedsitter

**Kuwait** /kuˈwajtʃi/ *m* Kuwait

**kuwaitiano** /kuwajtʃiˈanu/ *a & m* Kuwaiti

# L

**lá** /la/ *adv* there; **até ~** <*ir*> there; <*esperar etc*> until then; **por ~** (*naquela direção*) that way; (*naquele lugar*) around there; **~ fora** outside; **sei ~** how should I know?

**lã** /lã/ *f* wool

**labareda** /labaˈreda/ *f* flame

**lábia** /ˈlabia/ *f* flannel; **ter ~** have the gift of the gab

**lábio** /ˈlabio/ *m* lip

abirinto /labi'rītu/ *m* labyrinth

aboratório /labora'tɔriu/ *m* laboratory

aborioso /labori'ozu/ *a* hard-working

abu|ta /la'buta/ *f* drudgery; ~tar *vi* slog

aca /'laka/ *f* lacquer

açada /la'sada/ *f* slipknot

acaio /la'kaju/ *m* lackey

a|çar /la'sar/ *vt* lasso <*boi*>; ~ço *m* bow; (*de vaqueiro*) lasso; (*vínculo*) tie

acônico /la'koniku/ *a* laconic

acraia /la'kraja/ *f* centipede

a|crar /la'krar/ *vt* seal; ~cre *m* (*substância*) sealing wax; ( *fechamento*) seal

acri|mejar /lakrime'ʒar/ *vi* water; ~mogêneo *a* <*gás*> tear; <*filme*> tearjerking; ~moso /o/ *a* tearful

ácteo /'laktʃiu/ *a* milk; Via Láctea Milky Way

acticínio /laktʃi'siniu/ *m veja* laticínio

acuna /la'kuna/ *f* gap

adainha /la'iɲa/ *f* litany

a|dear /ladʒi'ar/ *vt* flank; sidestep <*dificuldade*>; ~deira *f* slope

ado /'ladu/ *m* side; o ~ de cá/lá this/that side; ao ~ de beside; ~ a ~ side by side; para este ~ this way; por outro ~ on the other hand

a|drão /la'drãw/ *m* ( *f* ~dra) thief; (*tubo*) overflow pipe □ *a* thieving

adrar /la'drar/ *vi* bark

adri|lhar /ladri'ʎar/ *vt* tile; ~lho *m* tile

adroagem /ladro'aʒẽ/ *f* stealing

agar|ta /la'garta/ *f* caterpillar; (*numa roda*) caterpillar track; ~tear *vi* bask in the sun; ~tixa *f* gecko; ~to *m* lizard

ago /'lagu/ *m* lake

agoa /la'goa/ *f* lagoon

agos|ta /la'gosta/ *f* lobster; ~tim *m* crayfish, (*Amer*) crawfish

ágrima /'lagrima/ *f* tear

aia /'laja/ *f* kind

aico /'lajku/ *adj* <*pessoa*> lay; <*ensino*> secular

aivos /'lajvus/ *m pl* traces

aje /'laʒi/ *m* flagstone; ~ar *vt* pave

ajota /la'ʒɔta/ *f* small paving stone

ama /'lama/ *f* mud; ~çal (*pl* ~çais) *m* bog; ~cento *a* muddy

amba|da /lã'bada/ *f* lambada; ~teria *f* lambada club

am|ber /lã'bɛr/ *vt* lick; ~bida *f* lick

ambreta /lã'breta/ *f* moped

ambris /lã'bris/ *m pl* panelling

ambuzar /lãbu'zar/ *vt* smear; ~-se *vpr* get sticky

amen|tar /lamẽ'tar/ *vt* (*lastimar*) lament; (*sentir*) be sorry; ~tar-se de lament; ~tável (*pl* ~táveis) *a* lamentable; ~to *m* lament

lâmina /'lamina/ *f* blade; (*de persiana*) slat

laminar /lami'nar/ *vt* laminate

lâmpada /'lãpada/ *f* light bulb; (*abajur*) lamp

lampe|jar /lãpe'ʒar/ *vi* flash; ~jo /e/ *m* flash

lampião /lãpi'ãw/ *m* lantern

lamúria /la'muria/ *f* moaning

lamuriar-se /lamuri'arsi/ *vpr* moan (de about)

lan|ça /'lãsa/ *f* spear; ~çamento *m* (*de navio, foguete, produto*) launch; (*de filme, disco*) release; (*novo produto*) new line; (*novo filme, disco*) release; (*novo livro*) new title; (*em livro comercial*) entry; ~çar *vt* (*atirar*) throw; launch <*navio, foguete, novo produto, livro*>; release <*filme, disco*>; (*em livro comercial*) enter; (*em leilão*) bid; ~çar mão de make use of; ~ce *m* (*num filme, jogo*) bit, moment; (*episódio*) episode; (*questão*) matter; (*jogada*) move; (*em leilão*) bid; (*de escada*) flight; (*de casas*) row

lancha /'lãʃa/ *f* launch

lan|char /lã'ʃar/ *vi* have a snack □ *vt* have a snack of; ~che *m* snack; ~chonete /ɛ/ *f* snack bar

lancinante /lãsi'nãtʃi/ *a* <*dor*> shooting; <*grito*> piercing

lânguido /'lãgidu/ *a* languid

lantejoula /lãte'ʒola/ *f* sequin

lanter|na /lã'tɛrna/ *f* lantern; (*de bolso*) torch, (*Amer*) flashlight; ~nagem *f* panel-beating; (*oficina*) body-shop; ~ninha *m/f* usher ( *f* usherette)

lanugem /la'nuʒẽ/ *f* down

lapela /la'pɛla/ *f* lapel

lapi|dar /lapi'dar/ *vt* cut <*pedra preciosa*>; ( *fig*) polish

lápide /'lapidʒi/ *f* tombstone

lápis /'lapis/ *m invar* pencil

lapiseira /lapi'zera/ *f* propelling pencil; (*caixa*) pencil box

Lapônia /la'ponia/ *f* Lappland

lapso /'lapsu/ *m* lapse

la|quê /la'ke/ *m* lacquer; ~quear *vt* lacquer

lar /lar/ *m* home

laran|ja /la'rãʒa/ *f* orange □ *a invar* orange; ~jada *f* orangeade; ~jeira *f* orange tree

lareira /la'rera/ *f* hearth, fireplace

lar|gada /lar'gada/ *f* start; dar a ~gada start off; ~gar *vt* (*soltar*) let go of; give up <*estudos, emprego etc*>; ~gar de fumar give up smoking; ~go *a* wide; <*roupa*> loose □ *m* (*praça*) square; ao ~go (*no alto-mar*) out at sea; ~gura *f* width

larin|ge /la'rĩʒi/ *f* larynx; ~gite *f* laryngitis

larva /'larva/ *f* larva

**lasanha** /la'zaɲa/ f lasagna
**las|ca** /'laska/ f chip; **~car** vt/i chip; **de ~car** (fam) awful
**lástima** /'lastʃima/ f shame
**lastro** /'lastru/ m ballast
**la|ta** /'lata/ f (material) tin; (recipiente) tin, (Amer) can; **~ta de lixo** dustbin, (Amer) trash can; **~tão** m brass
**late|jante** /late'ʒatʃi/ a throbbing; **~jar** vi throb
**latente** /la'tẽtʃi/ a latent
**late|ral** /late'raw/ (pl **~rais**) a side, lateral
**laticínio** /latʃi'siniu/ m dairy product
**latido** /la'tʃidu/ m bark
**lati|fundiário** /latʃifũdʒi'ariu/ a landowning □ m landowner; **~fúndio** m estate
**latim** /la'tʃĩ/ m Latin
**latino** /la'tʃinu/ a & m Latin; **~americano** a & m Latin American
**latir** /la'tʃir/ vi bark
**latitude** /latʃi'tudʒi/ f latitude
**lauda** /'lawda/ f side
**laudo** /'lawdu/ m report, findings
**lava** /'lava/ f lava
**lava|bo** /la'vabu/ m toilet; **~dora** f washing machine; **~gem** f washing; **~gem a seco** dry cleaning; **~gem cerebral** brainwashing
**lavanda** /la'vãda/ f lavender
**lavanderia** /lavãde'ria/ f laundry
**lavar** /la'var/ vt wash; **~ a seco** dry-clean; **~-se** vpr wash
**lavatório** /lava'tɔriu/ m (Port) wash-basin
**lavoura** /la'vora/ f (agricultura) farming; (terreno) field
**lav|rador** /lavra'dor/ m farmhand; **~rar** vt work; draw up <documento>
**laxante** /la'ʃãtʃi/ a & m laxative
**lazer** /la'zer/ m leisure
**le|al** /le'aw/ (pl **~ais**) a loyal; **~aldade** f loyalty
**leão** /le'ãw/ m lion; **Leão** (signo) Leo; **~-de-chácara** (pl leões-de-chácara) m bouncer
**lebre** /'lɛbri/ f hare
**lecionar** /lesio'nar/ vt/i teach
**le|gação** /lega'sãw/ f legation; **~gado** m (pessoa) legate; (herança) legacy
**le|gal** /le'gaw/ (pl **~gais**) a legal; (fam) good; <pessoa> nice; **tá ~gal** OK; **~galidade** f legality; **~galizar** vt legalize
**legar** /le'gar/ vt bequeath
**legenda** /le'ʒẽda/ f (de quadro) caption; (de filme) subtitle; (inscrição) inscription
**legi|ão** /leʒi'ãw/ f legion; **~onário** m (romano) legionary; (da legião estrangeira) legionnaire
**legis|lação** /leʒizla'sãw/ f legislation; **~lador** m legislator; **~lar** vi

legislate; **~lativo** a legislative □ m legislature; **~latura** f legislature; **~ta** m/f legal expert
**legiti|mar** /leʒitʃi'mar/ vt legitimize; **~midade** f legitimacy
**legítimo** /le'ʒitʃimu/ a legitimate
**legí|vel** /le'ʒivew/ (pl **~veis**) a legible
**légua** /'lɛgwa/ f league
**legume** /le'gumi/ m vegetable
**lei** /lej/ f law
**leigo** /'lejgu/ a lay □ m layman
**lei|lão** /lej'lãw/ m auction; **~loar** vt auction; **~loeiro** m auctioneer
**leitão** /lej'tãw/ m sucking pig
**lei|te** /'lejtʃi/ m milk; **~te condensa-do/desnatado** condensed/skimmed milk; **~teira** f (jarro) milk jug; (panela) milk saucepan; **~teiro** m milkman □ a <vaca> dairy
**leito** /'lejtu/ m bed
**leitor** /lej'tor/ m reader
**leitoso** /lej'tozu/ a milky
**leitura** /lej'tura/ f (ação) reading; (material) reading matter
**lema** /'lema/ m motto
**lem|brança** /lẽ'brãsa/ f memory; (presente) souvenir; **~brar** vt/i remember; **~brar-se de** remember; **~brar aco a alg** remind s.o. of sth; **~brete** /e/ m reminder
**leme** /'lemi/ m rudder
**len|ço** /'lẽsu/ m (para o nariz) handkerchief; (para vestir) scarf; **~çol** /ɔ/ (pl **~çóis**) m sheet
**len|da** /'lẽda/ f legend; **~dário** a legendary
**lenha** /'leɲa/ f firewood; (uma) log; **~dor** m woodcutter
**lente** /'lẽtʃi/ f lens; **~ de contato** contact lens
**lentidão** /lẽtʃi'dãw/ f slowness
**lentilha** /lẽ'tʃiʎa/ f lentil
**lento** /'lẽtu/ a slow
**leoa** /le'oa/ f lioness
**leopardo** /lio'pardu/ m leopard
**le|pra** /'lɛpra/ f leprosy; **~proso** /o/ a leprous □ m leper
**leque** /'lɛki/ m fan; (fig) array
**ler** /ler/ vt/i read
**ler|deza** /ler'deza/ f sluggishness; **~do** /ɛ/ a sluggish
**le|são** /le'zãw/ f lesion, injury; **~sar** vt damage
**lésbi|ca** /'lɛzbika/ f lesbian; **~co** a lesbian
**lesionar** /lezio'nar/ vt injure
**lesma** /'lezma/ f slug
**leste** /'lɛstʃi/ m east
**le|tal** /le'taw/ (pl **~tais**) a lethal
**le|tão** /le'tãw/ a & m (f **~tã**) Latvian
**letargia** /letar'ʒia/ f lethargy
**letivo** /le'tʃivu/ a **ano ~** academic year

**Letônia** /le'tonia/ *f* Latvia
**letra** /'letra/ *f* letter; (*de música*) lyrics, words; (*caligrafia*) writing; **Letras** Modern Languages; **ao pé da ~** literally; **com todas as ~s** in no uncertain terms; **tirar de ~** take in one's stride; **~ de fôrma** block letter
**letreiro** /le'treru/ *m* sign
**leucemia** /lewse'mia/ *f* leukaemia
**leva** /ɛ/ *f* batch
**levado** /le'vadu/ *a* naughty
**levan|tamento** /levãta'mẽtu/ *m* (*enquete*) survey; (*rebelião*) uprising; **~tamento de pesos** weightlifting; **~tar** *vt* raise; lift <*peso*> □ *vi* get up; **~tar-se** *vpr* get up; (*revoltar-se*) rise up
**levante** /le'vãtʃi/ *m* east
**levar** /le'var/ *vt* take; lead <*vida*>; get <*tapa, susto etc*> □ *vi* lead (**a** to)
**leve** /'lɛvi/ *a* light; (*não grave*) slight; **de ~** lightly
**levedura** /leve'dura/ *f* yeast
**leveza** /le'veza/ *f* lightness
**levi|andade** /leviã'dadʒi/ *f* frivolity; **~ano** *a* frivolous
**levitar** /levi'tar/ *vi* levitate
**lexi|cal** /leksi'kaw/ (*pl* **~cais**) *a* lexical
**lêxico** /'leksiku/ *m* lexicon
**lexicografia** /leksikogra'fia/ *f* lexicography
**lhe** /ʎi/ *pron* (*a ele*) to him; (*a ela*) to her; (*a você*) to you; **~s** *pron* to them; (*a vocês*) to you
**liba|nês** /liba'nes/ *a & m* (*f* **~nesa**) Lebanese
**Líbano** /'libanu/ *m* Lebanon
**libélula** /li'bɛlula/ *f* dragonfly
**libe|ração** /libera'sãw/ *f* release; **~ral** (*pl* **~rais**) *a & m* liberal; **~ralismo** *m* liberalism; **~ralizar** *vt* liberalize; **~rar** *vt* release
**liberdade** /liber'dadʒi/ *f* freedom; **pôr em ~** set free; **~ condicional** probation
**líbero** /'liberu/ *m* sweeper
**liber|tação** /liberta'sãw/ *f* liberation; **~tar** *vt* free
**Líbia** /'libia/ *f* Libya
**líbio** /'libiu/ *a & m* Libyan
**libi|dinoso** /libidʒi'nozu/ *a* lecherous; **~do** *f* libido
**li|bra** /'libra/ *f* pound; **Libra** (*signo*) Libra; **~briano** *a & m* Libran
**lição** /li'sãw/ *f* lesson
**licen|ça** /li'sẽsa/ *f* leave; (*documento*) licence; **com ~ça** excuse me; **de ~ça** on leave; **sob ~ça** under licence; **~ciar** *vt* (*autorizar*) license; (*dar férias a*) give leave to; **~ciar-se** *vpr* (*tirar férias*) take leave; (*formar-se*) graduate; **~ciatura** *f* degree; **~cioso** /o/ *a* licentious

**liceu** /li'sew/ *m* (*Port*) secondary school, (*Amer*) high school
**licor** /li'kor/ *m* liqueur
**lida** /'lida/ *f* slog, grind; (*leitura*) read
**lidar** /li'dar/ *vt/i* **~ com** deal with
**lide** /'lidʒi/ *f* (*trabalho*) work
**líder** /'lider/ *m/f* leader
**lide|rança** /lide'rãsa/ *f* (*de partido etc*) leadership; (*em corrida, jogo etc*) lead; **~rar** *vt* lead
**lido** /'lidu/ *a* well-read
**liga** /'liga/ *f* (*aliança*) league; (*tira*) garter; (*presilha*) suspender; (*de metais*) alloy
**li|gação** /liga'sãw/ *f* connection; (*telefônica*) call; (*amorosa*) liaison; **~gada** *f* call, ring; **~gado** *a* <*luz, TV*> on; **~gado em** attached to <*pessoa*>; hooked on <*droga*>; **~gamento** *m* ligament; **~gar** *vt* join, connect; switch on <*luz, TV etc*>; start up <*carro*>; bind <*amigos*> □ *vi* ring up, call; **~gar para** (*telefonar*) ring, call; (*dar importância*) care about; (*dar atenção*) pay attention to; **~gar-se** *vpr* join
**ligeiro** /li'ʒeru/ *a* light; <*ferida, melhora*> slight; (*ágil*) nimble
**lilás** /li'las/ *m* lilac □ *a invar* mauve
**lima¹** /'lima/ *f* (*ferramenta*) file
**lima²** /'lima/ *f* (*fruta*) sweet orange
**limão** /li'mãw/ *m* lime; (*amarelo*) lemon
**limar** /li'mar/ *vt* file
**limeira** /li'mera/ *f* sweet orange tree
**limiar** /limi'ar/ *m* threshold
**limi|tação** /limita'sãw/ *f* limitation; **~tar** *vt* limit; **~tar-se** *vpr* limit o.s.; **~tar(-se) com** border on; **~te** *m* limit; (*de terreno*) boundary; **passar dos ~tes** go too far; **~te de velocidade** speed limit
**limo|eiro** /limo'eru/ *m* lime tree; **~nada** *f* lemonade
**lim|pador** /lĩpa'dor/ *m* **~pador de pára-brisas** windscreen wiper; **~par** *vt* clean; wipe <*lágrimas, suor*>; (*fig*) clean up <*cidade, organização*>; **~peza** /e/ *f* (*ato*) cleaning; (*qualidade*) cleanness; (*fig*) clean-up; **~peza pública** sanitation; **~po** *a* clean; <*céu, consciência*> clear; <*lucro*> net, clear; (*fig*) pure; **passar a ~po** write up <*trabalho*>; (*fig*) sort out <*vida*>; **tirar a ~po** get to the bottom of <*caso*>
**limusine** /limu'zini/ *f* limousine
**lince** /'lĩsi/ *m* lynx
**lindo** /'lĩdu/ *a* beautiful
**linear** /lini'ar/ *a* linear
**lingote** /lĩ'gotʃi/ *m* ingot
**língua** /'lĩgwa/ *f* (*na boca*) tongue; (*idioma*) language; **~ materna** mother tongue

**linguado** /lĩˈgwadu/ *m* sole
**lingua|gem** /lĩˈgwaʒẽ/ *f* language;
~**jar** *m* speech, dialect
**lingüeta** /lĩˈgweta/ *f* bolt
**lingüiça** /lĩˈgwisa/ *f* pork sausage
**lin|güista** /lĩˈgwiʃta/ *m/f* linguist;
~**güística** *f* linguistics; ~**güístico** *a*
linguistic
**linha** /ˈliɲa/ *f* line; ( *fio* ) thread; **per-**
**der a** ~ lose one's cool; ~ **aérea**
airline; ~ **de fogo** firing line; ~ **de**
**montagem** assembly line; ~**gem** *f*
lineage
**linho** /ˈliɲu/ *m* linen; ( *planta* ) flax
**linóleo** /liˈnɔliu/ *m* lino(leum)
**lipoaspiração** /lipoaspiraˈsãw/ *f* lipo-
suction
**liqui|dação** /likidaˈsãw/ *f* liquida-
tion; ( *de loja* ) clearance sale; ( *de con-*
*ta* ) settlement; ~**dar** *vt* liquidate;
settle <*conta*>; pay off <*dívida*>; sell
off, clear <*mercadorias*>
**liqüidificador** /likwidʒifikaˈdor/ *m*
liquidizer
**líquido** /ˈlikidu/ *a* liquid; <*lucro, sa-*
*lário*> net □ *m* liquid
**líri|ca** /ˈlirika/ *f* ( *mus* ) lyrics; ( *poesia* )
lyric poetry; ~**co** *a* lyrical; <*poesia*>
lyric
**lírio** /ˈliriu/ *m* lily
**Lisboa** /liʒˈboa/ *f* Lisbon
**lisboeta** /liʒboˈeta/ *a* & *m/f* (person)
from Lisbon
**liso** /ˈlizu/ *a* smooth; ( *sem desenho* )
plain; <*cabelo*> straight; ( *fam: duro* )
broke
**lison|ja** /liˈzõʒa/ *f* flattery; ~**jear** *vt*
flatter
**lista** /ˈlista/ *f* list; ( *listra* ) stripe; ~
**telefônica** telephone directory
**listra** /ˈlistra/ *f* stripe; ~**do** *a* striped,
stripey
**lite|ral** /liteˈraw/ ( *pl* ~**rais** ) *a* literal;
~**rário** *a* literary; ~**ratura** *f* literature
**litígio** /liˈtʃiʒiu/ *m* dispute; ( *jurid* )
lawsuit
**lito|ral** /litoˈraw/ ( *pl* ~**rais** ) *m*
coastline; ~**râneo** *a* coastal
**litro** /ˈlitru/ *m* litre
**Lituânia** /lituˈania/ *f* Lithuania
**lituano** /lituˈanu/ *a* & *m* Lithuanian
**living** /ˈlivĩ/ ( *pl* ~**s** ) *m* living room
**livrar** /liˈvrar/ *vt* free; ( *salvar* ) save;
~**-se** *vpr* escape; ~**-se de** get rid of
**livraria** /livraˈria/ *f* bookshop
**livre** /ˈlivri/ *a* free; ~ **de impostos**
tax-free; ~**-arbítrio** *m* free will
**liv|reiro** /liˈvreru/ *m* bookseller; ~**ro**
*m* book; ~**ro de consulta** reference
book; ~**ro de cozinha** cookery book;
~**ro de texto** text book
**li|xa** /ˈliʃa/ *f* ( *de unhas* ) emery board;
( *para madeira etc* ) sandpaper; ~**xar**

*vt* sand <*madeira*>; file <*unhas*>; **es-**
**tou me** ~**xando** ( *fam* ) I couldn't
care less
**li|xeira** /liˈʃera/ *f* dustbin, ( *Amer* )
garbage can; ~**xeiro** *m* dustman,
( *Amer* ) garbage collector; ~**xo** rubbish, ( *Amer* ) garbage; ( *atômico* ) waste
**lobisomem** /lobiˈzomẽ/ *m* werewolf
**lobo** /ˈlobu/ *m* wolf; ~**-marinho** ( *pl*
~**s-marinhos** ) *m* sea lion
**lóbulo** /ˈlɔbulu/ *m* lobe
**lo|cação** /lokaˈsãw/ *f* ( *de imóvel* )
lease; ( *de carro* ) rental; ~**cador** *m*
( *de casa* ) landlord; ~**cadora** *f* rental
company; ( *de vídeos* ) video shop
**lo|cal** /loˈkaw/ ( *pl* ~**cais** ) *a* local □ *m*
site; ( *de um acidente etc* ) scene;
~**calidade** *f* locality; ~**calização** *f*
location; ~**calizar** *vt* locate; ~**cali-**
**zar-se** *vpr* ( *orientar-se* ) get one's bear-
ings
**loção** /loˈsãw/ *f* lotion; ~ **apósbarba**
aftershave lotion
**locatário** /lokaˈtariu/ *m* ( *de imóvel* )
tenant; ( *de carro etc* ) hirer
**locomo|tiva** /lokomoˈtʃiva/ *f* loco-
motive; ~**ver-se** *vpr* get around
**locu|ção** /lokuˈsãw/ *f* phrase; ~**tor** *m*
announcer
**lodo** /ˈlodu/ *m* mud; ~**so** /o/ *a* muddy
**logaritmo** /logaˈritʃimu/ *m* logar-
ithm
**lógi|ca** /ˈlɔʒika/ *f* logic; ~**co** *a* logical
**logo** /ˈlɔgu/ *adv* ( *em seguida* ) straightaway; ( *em breve* ) soon; ( *justamente* )
just; ~ **mais** later; ~ **antes/depois**
just before/straight after; ~ **que** as
soon as; **até** ~ goodbye
**logotipo** /logoˈtʃipu/ *m* logo
**logradouro** /lograˈdoru/ *m* public
place
**loiro** /ˈlojru/ *a veja* **louro**
**lo|ja** /ˈlɔʒa/ *f* shop, ( *Amer* ) store; ~**ja**
**de departamentos** department store;
~**ja maçônica** masonic lodge;
~**jista** *m/f* shopkeeper
**lom|bada** /lõˈbada/ *f* ( *de livro* ) spine;
( *na rua* ) speed bump; ~**binho** *m*
tenderloin; ~**bo** *m* back; ( *carne* ) loin
**lona** /ˈlona/ *f* canvas
**Londres** /ˈlõdris/ *f* London
**londrino** /lõˈdrinu/ *a* London □ *m*
Londoner
**longa-metragem** /lõgameˈtraʒẽ/ ( *pl*
**longas-metragens** ) *m* feature film
**longe** /ˈlõʒi/ *adv* far, a long way; **de** ~
from a distance; ( *por muito* ) by far; ~
**disso** far from it
**longevidade** /lõʒeviˈdadʒi/ *f* longevity
**longínquo** /lõˈʒĩkwu/ *a* distant
**longitude** /lõʒiˈtudʒi/ *f* longitude
**longo** /ˈlõgu/ *a* long □ *m* long dress; **ao**
~ **de** along; ( *durante* ) through, over

**lontra** /'lõtra/ *f* otter
**lorde** /'lɔrdʒi/ *m* lord
**lorota** /lo'rɔta/ (*fam*) *f* fib
**losango** /lo'zãgu/ *m* diamond
**lo|tação** /lota'sãw/ *f* capacity; (*ônibus*) bus; **~tação esgotada** full house; **~tado** *a* crowded; < *teatro, ônibus*> full; **~tar** *vt* fill □ *vi* fill up
**lote** /'lɔtʃi/ *m* (*quinhão*) portion; (*de terreno*) plot, (*Amer*) lot; (*em leilão*) lot; (*porção de coisas*) batch
**loteria** /lote'ria/ *f* lottery
**louça** /'losa/ *f* china; (*pratos etc*) crockery; **lavar a ~** wash up, (*Amer*) do the dishes
**lou|co** /'loku/ *a* mad, crazy □ *m* madman; **estou ~co para ir** (*fam*) I'm dying to go; **~cura** *f* madness; (*uma*) crazy thing
**louro** /'loru/ *a* blond □ *m* laurel; (*condimento*) bayleaf
**lou|var** /lo'var/ *vt* praise; **~vável** (*pl* **~váveis**) *a* praiseworthy; **~vor** /o/ *m* praise
**lua** /'lua/ *f* moon; **~-de-mel** *f* honeymoon
**lu|ar** /lu'ar/ *m* moonlight; **~arento** *a* moonlit
**lubrifi|cação** /lubrifika'sãw/ *f* lubrication; **~cante** *a* lubricating □ *m* lubricant; **~car** *vt* lubricate
**lucidez** /lusi'des/ *f* lucidity
**lúcido** /'lusidu/ *a* lucid
**lu|crar** /lu'krar/ *vi* profit (com by); **~cratividade** *f* profitability; **~crativo** *a* profitable, lucrative; **~cro** *m* profit
**ludibriar** /ludʒibri'ar/ *vt* cheat
**lúdico** /'ludʒiku/ *a* playful
**lugar** /lu'gar/ *m* place; (*espaço*) room; **em ~ de** in place of; **em primeiro ~** in the first place; **em algum ~** somewhere; **em todo ~** everywhere; **dar ~ a** give rise to; **ter ~** take place
**lugarejo** /luga'reʒu/ *m* village
**lúgubre** /'lugubri/ *a* gloomy, dismal
**lula** /'lula/ *f* squid
**lume** /'lumi/ *m* fire
**luminária** /lumi'naria/ *f* light, lamp; *pl* illuminations
**luminoso** /lumi'nozu/ *a* luminous; < *idéia*> brilliant
**lunar** /lu'nar/ *a* lunar □ *m* mole
**lupa** /'lupa/ *f* magnifying glass
**lusco-fusco** /lusku'fusku/ *m* twilight
**lusitano** /luzi'tanu/, **luso** /'luzu/ *a* & *m* Portuguese
**lus|trar** /lus'trar/ *vt* shine, polish; **~tre** *m* shine; (*fig*) lustre; (*luminária*) light, lamp; **~troso** /o/ *a* shiny
**lu|ta** /'luta/ *f* fight, struggle; **~ta livre** wrestling; **~tador** *m* fighter; (*de luta livre*) wrestler; **~tar** *vi* fight □ *vt* do < *judô etc*>

**luto** /'lutu/ *m* mourning
**luva** /'luva/ *f* glove
**luxação** /luʃa'sãw/ *f* dislocation
**Luxemburgo** /luʃẽ'burgu/ *m* Luxembourg
**luxembur|guês** /luʃẽbur'ges/ *a* ( *f* **~guesa**) Luxemburg □ *m* ( *f* **~guesa**) Luxemburger; (*língua*) Luxemburgish
**luxo** /'luʃu/ *m* luxury; **hotel de ~** luxury hotel; **cheio de ~** (*fam*) fussy
**luxuoso** /luʃu'ozu/ *a* luxurious
**luxúria** /lu'ʃuria/ *f* lust
**luxuriante** /luʃuri'ãtʃi/ *a* lush
**luz** /lus/ *f* light; **à ~ de** by the light of < *velas etc*>; in the light of < *fatos etc*>; **dar à ~** give birth to
**luzidio** /luzi'dʒio/ *a* shiny
**luzir** /lu'zir/ *vi* shine

# M

**maca** /'maka/ *f* stretcher
**maçã** /ma'sã/ *f* apple
**macabro** /ma'kabru/ *a* macabre
**maca|cão** /maka'kãw/ *m* (*de trabalho*) overalls, (*Amer*) coveralls; (*tipo de calça*) dungarees; (*roupa inteiriça*) jumpsuit; (*para bebê*) romper suit; **~co** *m* monkey; (*aparelho*) jack
**maçada** /ma'sada/ *f* bore
**maçaneta** /masa'neta/ *f* doorknob
**maçante** /ma'sãtʃi/ *a* boring
**macar|rão** /maka'xãw/ *m* pasta; (*espaguete*) spaghetti; **~ronada** *f* pasta with tomato sauce and cheese
**macarrônico** /maka'xoniku/ *a* broken
**macete** /ma'setʃi/ *m* trick
**machado** /ma'ʃadu/ *m* axe
**ma|chão** /ma'ʃãw/ *a* tough □ *m* tough guy; **~chismo** *m* machismo; **~chista** *a* chauvinistic □ *m* male chauvinist; **~cho** *a* male; < *homem*> macho □ *m* male
**machu|cado** /maʃu'kadu/ *m* injury; (*na pele*) sore patch; **~car** *vt/i* hurt; **~car-se** *vpr* hurt o.s.
**maci|ço** /ma'sisu/ *a* solid; < *dose etc*> massive □ *m* massif
**macieira** /masi'era/ *f* apple tree
**maciez** /masi'es/ *f* softness
**macilento** /masi'lẽtu/ *a* haggard
**macio** /ma'siu/ *a* soft; < *carne*> tender
**maço** /'masu/ *m* (*de cigarros*) packet; (*de notas*) bundle
**ma|çom** /ma'sõ/ *m* freemason; **~çonaria** *f* freemasonry
**maconha** /ma'koɲa/ *f* marijuana
**maçônico** /ma'soniku/ *a* masonic
**má-criação** /makria'sãw/ *f* rudeness
**macrobiótico** /makrobi'ɔtʃiku/ *a* macrobiotic

**macum|ba** /ma'kũba/ *f* Afro-Brazilian cult; (*uma*) spell; **~beiro** *m* follower of macumba □ *a* macumba

**madame** /ma'dami/ *f* lady

**Madeira** /ma'dera/ *f* Madeira

**madeira** /ma'dera/ *f* wood □ *m* (*vinho*) Madeira; **~ de lei** hardwood

**madeirense** /made'rẽsi/ *a & m* Madeiran

**madeixa** /ma'deʃa/ *f* lock

**madrasta** /ma'drasta/ *f* stepmother

**madrepérola** /madre'pɛrola/ *f* mother of pearl

**madressilva** /madre'siwva/ *f* honeysuckle

**Madri** /ma'dri/ *f* Madrid

**madrinha** /ma'driɲa/ *f* (*de batismo*) godmother; (*de casamento*) bridesmaid

**madru|gada** /madru'gada/ *f* early morning; **~gador** *m* early riser; **~gar** *vi* get up early

**maduro** /ma'duru/ *a* <*fruta*> ripe; <*pessoa*> mature

**mãe** /mãj/ *f* mother; **~-de-santo** (*pl* **~s-de-santo**) *f* macumba priestess

**maes|tria** /majs'tria/ *f* expertise; **~tro** *m* conductor

**máfia** /'mafia/ *f* mafia

**magazine** /maga'zini/ *m* department store

**magia** /ma'ʒia/ *f* magic

**mági|ca** /'maʒika/ *f* magic; (*uma*) magic trick; **~co** *a* magic □ *m* magician

**magis|tério** /maʒis'tɛriu/ *m* teaching; (*professores*) teachers; **~trado** *m* magistrate

**magnânimo** /mag'nanimu/ *a* magnanimous

**magnata** /mag'nata/ *m* magnate

**magnésio** /mag'nɛziu/ *m* magnesium

**mag|nético** /mag'nɛtʃiku/ *a* magnetic; **~netismo** *m* magnetism; **~netizar** *vt* magnetize; (*fig*) mesmerize

**mag|nificência** /magnifi'sẽsia/ *f* magnificence; **~nífico** *a* magnificent

**magnitude** /magni'tudʒi/ *f* magnitude

**mago** /'magu/ *m* magician; **os reis ~s** the Three Wise Men

**mágoa** /'magoa/ *f* sorrow

**magoar** /mago'ar/ *vt/i* hurt; **~-se** *vpr* be hurt

**ma|gricela** /magri'sɛla/ *a* skinny; **~gro** *a* thin; <*leite*> skimmed; <*carne*> lean; (*fig*) meagre

**maio** /'maju/ *m* May

**maiô** /ma'jo/ *m* swimsuit

**maionese** /majo'nɛzi/ *f* mayonnaise

**maior** /ma'jɔr/ *a* bigger; <*escritor, amor etc*> greater; **o ~ carro** the biggest car; **o ~ escritor** the greatest writer; **~ de idade** of age

**Maiorca** /ma'jɔrka/ *f* Majorca

**maio|ria** /majo'ria/ *f* majority; **a ~ria dos brasileiros** most Brazilians; **~ridade** *f* majority, adulthood

**mais** /majs/ *adv & pron* more; **~ dois** two more; **dois dias a ~** two more days; **não trabalho ~** I don't work any more; **~ ou menos** more or less

**maisena** /maj'zena/ *f* cornflour, (*Amer*) cornstarch

**maître** /mɛtr/ *m* head waiter

**maiúscula** /ma'juskula/ *f* capital letter

**majes|tade** /maʒes'tadʒi/ *f* majesty; **~toso** *a* majestic

**major** /ma'jɔr/ *m* major

**majoritário** /maʒori'tariu/ *a* majority

**mal** /maw/ *adv* badly; (*quase não*) hardly □ *conj* hardly □ *m* evil; (*doença*) sickness; **não faz a ~** never mind; **levar a ~** take offence at; **passar ~** be sick

**mala** /'mala/ *f* suitcase; (*do carro*) boot, (*Amer*) trunk; **~ aérea** air courier

**malabaris|mo** /malaba'rizmu/ *m* juggling act; **~ta** *m/f* juggler

**malagradecido** /malagrade'sidu/ *a* ungrateful

**malagueta** /mala'geta/ *f* chilli pepper

**malaio** /ma'laju/ *a & m* Malay

**Malaísia** /mala'izia/ *f* Malaysia

**malaísio** /mala'iziu/ *a & m* Malaysian

**malan|dragem** /malã'draʒẽ/ *f* hustling; (*uma*) clever trick; **~dro** *a* cunning □ *m* hustler

**malária** /ma'laria/ *f* malaria

**mal-assombrado** /malaso'bradu/ *a* haunted

**Malavi** /mala'vi/ *m* Malawi

**malcriado** /mawkri'adu/ *a* rude

**mal|dade** /maw'dadʒi/ *f* wickedness; (*uma*) wicked thing; **por ~dade** out of spite; **~dição** *f* curse; **~dito** *a* cursed, damned; **~doso** /o/ *a* wicked

**maleá|vel** /mali'avew/ (*pl* **~veis**) *a* malleable

**maledicência** /maledi'sẽsia/ *f* malicious gossip

**maléfico** /ma'lɛfiku/ *a* evil; (*prejudicial*) harmful

**mal-encarado** /malĩka'radu/ *a* shady, dubious □ *m* shady character

**mal-entendido** /malĩtẽ'dʒidu/ *m* misunderstanding

**mal-estar** /malis'tar/ *m* (*doença*) ailment; (*constrangimento*) discomfort

**maleta** /ma'leta/ *f* overnight bag

**malévolo** /ma'lɛvolu/ *a* malevolent

**malfei|to** /maw'fejtu/ *a* badly done; <*roupa etc*> badly made; (*fig*) wrongful; **~tor** *m* wrongdoer; **~toria** *f* wrongdoing

**ma|lha** /'maʎa/ f (ponto) stitch; (tricô) knitting; (tecido) jersey; (casaco) jumper, (Amer) sweater; (para ginástica) leotard; (de rede) mesh; **fazer ~lha** knit; **~lhado** a <animal> dappled; <roque> heavy; **~lhar** vt beat; thresh <trigo etc> □ vi (fam) work out

**mal-humorado** /malumo'radu/ a in a bad mood, grumpy

**malícia** /ma'lisia/ f (má índole) malice; (astúcia) guile; (humor) innuendo

**malicioso** /malisi'ozu/ a (mau) malicious; (astuto) crafty; (que põe malícia) dirty-minded

**maligno** /ma'liginu/ a malignant

**malmequer** /mawme'ker/ m marigold

**maloca** /ma'lɔka/ f Indian village

**malo|grar-se** /malo'grarsi/ vpr go wrong, fail; **~gro** /o/ m failure

**mal-passado** /mawpa'sadu/ a <carne> rare

**Malta** /'mawta/ f Malta

**malte** /'mawtʃi/ m malt

**maltrapilho** /mawtra'piʎu/ a scruffy

**maltratar** /mawtra'tar/ vt ill-treat, mistreat

**malu|co** /ma'luku/ a mad, crazy □ m madman; **~quice** f madness; (uma) crazy thing

**malvado** /maw'vadu/ a wicked

**malver|sação** /mawversa'sãw/ f mismanagement; (de fundos) misappropriation; **~sar** vt mismanage; misappropriate <dinheiro>

**Malvinas** /maw'vinas/ f pl Falklands

**mamadeira** /mama'dera/ f (baby's) bottle

**mamãe** /ma'mãj/ f mum

**mamão** /ma'mãw/ m papaya

**ma|mar** /ma'mar/ vi suckle; **~mata** f (fam) fiddle

**mamífero** /ma'miferu/ m mammal

**mamilo** /ma'milu/ m nipple

**mamoeiro** /mamo'eru/ m papaya tree

**manada** /ma'nada/ f herd

**mananci|al** /manãsi'aw/ (pl **~ais**) m spring; (fig) rich source

**man|cada** /mã'kada/ f blunder; **~car** vi limp; **~car-se** vpr (fam) take the hint, get the message

**Mancha** /'mãʃa/ f **o canal da ~** the English Channel

**man|cha** /'mãʃa/ f stain; (na pele) mark; **~char** vt stain

**manchete** /mã'ʃetʃi/ f headline

**manco** /'mãku/ a lame □ m cripple

**mandachuva** /mãda'ʃuva/ m (fam) bigwig; (chefe) boss

**man|dado** /mã'dadu/ m order; **~dado de busca** search warrant; **~dado de prisão** arrest warrant; **~damento** m commandment; **~dante** m/f person

in charge; **~dão** a (f **~dona**) bossy; **~dar** vt (pedir) order; (enviar) send □ vi be in charge; **~dar-se** vpr (fam) take off; **~dar buscar** fetch; **~dar dizer** send word; **~dar alg ir** tell s.o. to go; **~dar ver** (fam) go to town; **~dar em alg** order s.o. about; **~dato** m mandate

**mandíbula** /mã'dʒibula/ f (lower) jaw

**mandioca** /mãdʒi'ɔka/ f manioc

**maneira** /ma'nera/ f way; pl (boas) manners; **desta ~** in this way; **de qualquer ~** anyway

**mane|jar** /mane'ʒar/ vt handle; operate <máquina>; **~jável** (pl **~jáveis**) a manageable; **~jo** /e/ m handling

**manequim** /mane'kĩ/ m (boneco) dummy; (medida) size □ m/f mannequin, model

**maneta** /ma'neta/ a one-armed □ m/f person with one arm

**manga¹** /'mãga/ f (de roupa) sleeve

**manga²** /'mãga/ f (fruta) mango

**manganês** /mãga'nes/ m manganese

**mangue** /'mãgi/ m mangrove swamp

**mangueira¹** /mã'gera/ f (tubo) hose

**mangueira²** /mã'gera/ f (árvore) mango tree

**manha** /'maɲa/ f tantrum

**manhã** /ma'ɲã/ f morning; **de ~** in the morning

**manhoso** /ma'ɲozu/ a wilful

**mania** /ma'nia/ f (moda) craze; (doença) mania

**maníaco** /ma'niaku/ a manic □ m maniac; **~-depressivo** a & m manic depressive

**manicômio** /mani'komiu/ m lunatic asylum

**manicura** /mani'kura/ f manicure; (pessoa) manicurist

**manifes|tação** /manifesta'sãw/ f manifestation; (passeata) demonstration; **~tante** m/f demonstrator; **~tar** vt manifest, demonstrate; **~tar-se** vpr (revelar-se) manifest o.s.; (exprimir-se) express an opinion; **~to** /ɛ/ a manifest, clear □ m manifesto

**manipular** /manipu'lar/ vt manipulate

**manjedoura** /mãʒe'dora/ f manger

**manjericão** /mãʒeri'kãw/ m basil

**mano|bra** /ma'nɔbra/ f manoeuvre; **~brar** vt manoeuvre; **~brista** m/f parking valet

**mansão** /mã'sãw/ f mansion

**man|sidão** /mãsi'dãw/ f gentleness; (do mar) calm; **~sinho** adv **de ~sinho** (devagar) slowly; (de leve) gently; (de fininho) stealthily; **~so** a gentle; <mar> calm; <animal> tame

**manta** /'mãta/ f blanket; (casaco) cloak

mantei|ga /mã'tejga/ f butter; ~gueira f butter dish

manter /mã'ter/ vt keep; ~-se vpr keep; (sustentar-se) keep o.s.

mantimentos /mãtʃi'mẽtus/ m pl provisions

manto /'mãtu/ m mantle

manu|al /manu'aw/ (pl ~ais) a & m manual; ~fatura f manufacture; (fábrica) factory; ~faturar vt manufacture

manuscrito /manus'kritu/ a hand-written □ m manuscript

manu|sear /manuzi'ar/ vt handle; ~seio m handling

manutenção /manutẽ'sãw/ f maintenance; (de prédio) upkeep

mão /mãw/ (pl ~s) f hand; (do trânsito) direction; (de tinta) coat; abrir ~ de give up; agüentar a ~ hang on; dar a ~ a alg hold s.o.'s hand; (cumprimentando) shake s.o.'s hand; deixar alg na ~ let s.o. down; enfiar ou meter a ~ em hit, slap; lançar ~ de make use of; escrito à ~ written by hand; ter à ~ have to hand; de ~s dadas hand in hand; em segunda ~ second-hand; fora de ~ out of the way; ~ única one way; ~-de-obra f labour

mapa /'mapa/ m map

maquete /ma'kɛtʃi/ f model

maqui|agem /maki'aʒẽ/ f make-up; ~ar vt make up; ~ar-se vpr put on make-up

maquiavélico /makia'vɛliku/ a Machiavellian

maqui|lagem, ~lar, (Port) ~lhagem, ~lhar veja maqui|agem, ~ar

máquina /'makina/ f machine; (ferroviária) engine; escrever à ~ type; ~ de costura sewing machine; ~ de escrever typewriter; ~ de lavar (roupa) washing machine; ~ de lavar pratos dishwasher; ~ fotográfica camera

maqui|nação /makina'sãw/ f machination; ~nal (pl ~nais) a mechanical; ~nar vt/i plot; ~naria f machinery; ~nista m/f (ferroviário) engine driver; (de navio) engineer

mar /mar/ m sea

maracu|já /maraku'ʒa/ m passion fruit; ~jazeiro m passion-fruit plant

marasmo /ma'razmu/ f stagnation

marato|na /mara'tona/ f marathon; ~nista m/f marathon runner

maravi|lha /mara'viʎa/ f marvel; às mil ~lhas wonderfully; ~lhar vt amaze; ~lhar-se vpr marvel (de at); ~lhoso /o/ a marvellous

mar|ca /'marka/ f (sinal) mark; (de carro, máquina) make; (de cigarro, sabão etc) brand; ~ca registrada registered trademark; ~cação f marking; (Port: discagem) dialling; ~cador m marker; (em livro) bookmark; (placar) scoreboard; (jogador) scorer; ~cante a outstanding; ~capasso m pacemaker; ~car vt mark; arrange <hora, encontro, jantar etc>; score <gol, ponto>; (Port: discar) dial; <relógio, termômetro> show; brand <gado>; (observar) keep a close eye on; (impressionar) leave one's mark on □ vi make one's mark; ~car época make history; ~car hora make an appointment; ~car o compasso beat time; ~car os pontos keep the score

marce|naria /marsena'ria/ f cabinet-making; (oficina) cabinet maker's workshop; ~neiro m cabinet maker

mar|cha /'marʃa/ f march; (de carro) gear; pôr-se em ~cha get going; ~cha à ré, (Port) ~cha atrás reverse; ~char vi march

marci|al /marsi'aw/ (pl ~ais) a martial; ~ano a & m Martian

marco¹ /'marku/ m (sinal) landmark

marco² /'marku/ m (moeda) mark

março /'marsu/ m March

maré /ma'rɛ/ f tide

mare|chal /mare'ʃaw/ (pl ~chais) m marshal

maresia /mare'zia/ f smell of the sea

marfim /mar'fĩ/ m ivory

margarida /marga'rida/ f daisy; (para impressora) daisywheel

margarina /marga'rina/ f margarine

mar|gem /'marʒẽ/ f (de rio) bank; (de lago) shore; (parte em branco, fig) margin; ~ginal (pl ~ginais) a marginal; (delinqüente) delinquent □ m/f delinquent □ f (rua) riverside road; ~ginalidade f delinquency; ~ginalizar vt marginalize

marido /ma'ridu/ m husband

marimbondo /marĩ'bõdu/ m hornet

marina /ma'rina/ f marina

mari|nha /ma'riɲa/ f navy; ~nha mercante merchant navy; ~nheiro m sailor; ~nho a marine

marionete /mario'nɛtʃi/ f puppet

mariposa /mari'poza/ f moth

mariscos /ma'riskus/ m seafood

mari|tal /mari'taw/ (pl ~tais) a marital

marítimo /ma'ritʃimu/ a sea; <cidade> seaside

marmanjo /mar'mãʒu/ m grown-up

marme|lada /marme'lada/ f (fam) fix; ~lo /ɛ/ m quince

marmita /mar'mita/ f (de soldado) mess tin; (de trabalhador) lunchbox

mármore /'marmori/ m marble

marmóreo /mar'mɔriu/ a marble

marquise /mar'kizi/ f awning

marreco /ma'xɛku/ m wild duck

**Marrocos** /ma'xɔkus/ *m* Morocco

**marrom** /ma'xõ/ *a* & *m* brown

**marroquino** /maxo'kinu/ *a* & *m* Moroccan

**Marte** /'martʃi/ *m* Mars

**marte|lada** /marte'lada/ *f* hammer blow; **~lar** *vt/i* hammer; **~lar em** ( *fig*) go on and on about; **~lo** /ɛ/ *m* hammer

**mártir** /'martʃir/ *m/f* martyr

**mar|tírio** /mar'tʃiriu/ *m* martyrdom; ( *fig*) torture; **~tirizar** *vt* martyr; ( *fig*) torture

**marujo** /ma'ruʒu/ *m* sailor

**mar|xismo** /mark'sizmu/ *m* Marxism; **~xista** *a* & *m/f* Marxist

**mas** /mas/ *conj* but

**mascar** /mas'kar/ *vt* chew

**máscara** /'maskara/ *f* mask; (*tratamento facial*) face-pack

**mascarar** /maska'rar/ *vt* mask

**mascate** /mas'katʃi/ *m* street vendor

**mascavo** /mas'kavu/ *a* **açúcar ~** brown sugar

**mascote** /mas'kɔtʃi/ *f* mascot

**masculino** /masku'linu/ *a* male; ( *para homens*) men's; *<palavra>* masculine □ *m* masculine

**másculo** /'maskulu/ *a* masculine

**masmorra** /maz'moxa/ *f* dungeon

**masoquis|mo** /mazo'kizmu/ *m* masochism; **~ta** *m/f* masochist □ *a* masochistic

**massa** /'masa/ *f* mass; (*de pão*) dough; (*de torta, empada*) pastry; (*macarrão etc*) pasta; **cultura de ~** mass culture; **em ~** en masse; **as ~s** the masses

**massa|crante** /masa'krãtʃi/ *a* gruelling; **~crar** *vt* massacre; ( *fig: maçar*) wear out; **~cre** *m* massacre

**massa|gear** /masaʒi'ar/ *vt* massage; **~gem** *f* massage; **~gista** *m/f* masseur ( *f* masseuse)

**mastigar** /mastʃi'gar/ *vt* chew; (*ponderar*) chew over

**mastro** /'mastru/ *m* mast; (*de bandeira*) flagpole

**mastur|bação** /masturba'sãw/ *f* masturbation; **~bar-se** *vpr* masturbate

**mata** /'mata/ *f* forest

**mata-borrão** /matabo'xãw/ *m* blotting paper

**matadouro** /mata'doru/ *m* slaughterhouse

**mata|gal** /mata'gaw/ ( *pl* **~gais**) *m* thicket

**mata-moscas** /mata'moskas/ *m invar* fly spray

**ma|tança** /ma'tãsa/ *f* slaughter; **~tar** *vt* kill; satisfy *<fome>*; quench *<sede>*; guess *<charada>*; ( *fazer nas coxas*) dash off; ( *fam*) skive off *<aula, serviço>* □ *vi* kill

**mata-ratos** /mata'xatus/ *m invar* rat poison

**mate¹** /'matʃi/ *m* (*chá*) maté

**mate²** /'matʃi/ *a invar* matt

**matemáti|ca** /mate'matʃika/ *f* mathematics; **~co** *a* mathematical □ *m* mathematician

**matéria** /ma'tɛria/ *f* (*assunto, disciplina*) subject; (*no jornal*) article; (*substância*) matter; (*usada para fazer algo*) material; **em ~ de** in the way of

**materi|al** /materi'aw/ ( *pl* **~ais**) *m* materials □ *a* material; **~alismo** *m* materialism; **~alista** *a* materialistic □ *m/f* materialist; **~alizar-se** *vpr* materialize

**matéria-prima** /matɛria'prima/ ( *pl* **matérias-primas**) *f* raw material

**mater|nal** /mater'naw/ ( *pl* **~nais**) *a* maternal; **~nidade** *f* maternity; (*clínica*) maternity hospital; **~no** /ɛ/ *a* maternal; **língua ~na** mother tongue

**mati|nal** /matʃi'naw/ ( *pl* **~nais**) *a* morning; **~nê** *f* matinée

**matiz** /ma'tʃis/ *m* shade; (*político*) colouring; (*pontinha: de ironia etc*) tinge

**matizar** /matʃi'zar/ *vt* tinge (**de** with)

**mato** /'matu/ *m* scrubland, bush

**matraca** /ma'traka/ *f* rattle; (*tagarela*) chatterbox

**matreiro** /ma'treru/ *a* cunning

**matriar|ca** /matri'arka/ *f* matriarch; **~cal** ( *pl* **~cais**) *a* matriarchal

**matrícula** /ma'trikula/ *f* enrolment; (*taxa*) enrolment fee; (*Port: de carro*) number plate, ( *Amer*) license plate

**matricular** /matriku'lar/ *vt* enrol; **~se** *vpr* enrol

**matri|monial** /matrimoni'aw/ ( *pl* **~moniais**) *a* marriage; **~mônio** *m* marriage

**matriz** /ma'tris/ *f* matrix; (*útero*) womb; (*sede*) head office

**maturidade** /maturi'dadʒi/ *f* maturity

**matutino** /matu'tʃinu/ *a* morning □ *m* morning paper

**matuto** /ma'tutu/ *a* countrified □ *m* country bumpkin

**mau** /maw/ *a* ( *f* **má**) bad; **~-caráter** *m invar* bad lot □ *a invar* no-good; **~-olhado** *m* evil eye

**mausoléu** /mawzo'lɛw/ *m* mausoleum

**maus-tratos** /maws'tratus/ *m pl* ill-treatment

**maxilar** /maksi'lar/ *m* jaw

**máxima** /'masima/ *f* maxim

**maximizar** /masimi'zar/ *vt* maximize; (*exagerar*) play up

**máximo** /'masimu/ *a* (*antes do substantivo*) utmost, greatest; (*depois do substantivo*) maximum □ *m*

**maximum; o ~** (*fam: o melhor*) really something; **ao ~** to the maximum; **no ~** at most

**maxixe** /maˈʃiʃi/ *m* gherkin

**me** /mi/ *pron* me; (*indireto*) (to) me; (*reflexivo*) myself

**meada** /miˈada/ *f* skein; **perder o fio da ~** lose one's thread

**meados** /miˈadus/ *m pl* ~ **de maio** mid-May

**meandro** /miˈãdru/ *f* meander; *pl* (*fig*) twists and turns

**mecâni|ca** /meˈkanika/ *f* mechanics; **~co** *a* mechanical □ *m* mechanic

**meca|nismo** /mekaˈnizmu/ *m* mechanism; **~nizar** *vt* mechanize

**mecenas** /meˈsɛnas/ *m invar* patron

**mecha** /ˈmɛʃa/ *f* (*de vela*) wick; (*de bomba*) fuse; (*porção de cabelos*) lock; (*cabelo tingido*) highlight; **~do** *a* highlighted

**meda|lha** /meˈdaʎa/ *f* medal; **~lhão** *m* medallion; (*jóia*) locket

**média** /ˈmɛdʒia/ *f* average; (*café*) white coffee; **em ~** on average

**medi|ação** /medʒiaˈsãw/ *f* mediation; **~ador** *m* mediator; **~ante** *prep* through, by; **~ar** *vi* mediate

**medica|ção** /medʒikaˈsãw/ *f* medication; **~mento** *m* medicine

**medição** /medʒiˈsãw/ *f* measurement

**medicar** /medʒiˈkar/ *vt* treat □ *vi* practise medicine; **~se** *vpr* dose o.s. up

**medici|na** /medʒiˈsina/ *f* medicine; **~na legal** forensic medicine; **~nal** (*pl* **~nais**) *a* medicinal

**médico** /ˈmɛdʒiku/ *m* doctor □ *a* medical; **~-legal** (*pl* **~-legais**) *a* forensic; **~-legista** (*pl* **~s-legistas**) *m/f* forensic scientist

**medi|da** /meˈdʒida/ *f* measure; (*dimensão*) measurement; **à ~da que** as; **sob ~da** made to measure; **tirar as ~das de alg** take s.o.'s measurements; **~dor** *m* meter

**medie|val** /medʒieˈvaw/ (*pl* **~vais**) *a* medieval

**médio** /ˈmɛdʒiu/ *a* (*típico*) average; <*tamanho, prazo*> medium; <*classe, dedo*> middle

**medíocre** /meˈdʒiɔkri/ *a* mediocre

**mediocridade** /medʒiokriˈdadʒi/ *f* mediocrity

**medir** /meˈdʒir/ *vt* measure; weigh <*palavras*> □ *vi* measure; **~se** *vpr* measure o.s.; **quanto você mede?** how tall are you?

**medi|tação** /medʒitaˈsãw/ *f* meditation; **~tar** *vi* meditate

**mediterrâneo** /medʒiteˈxaniu/ *a* Mediterranean □ *m* **o Mediterrâneo** the Mediterranean

**médium** /ˈmɛdʒiũ/ *m/f* medium

**medo** /ˈmedu/ *m* fear; **ter ~ de** be

afraid of; **com ~** afraid; **~nho** /o/ *a* frightful

**medroso** /meˈdrozu/ *a* fearful, timid

**medula** /meˈdula/ *f* marrow

**megalomania** /megalomaˈnia/ *f* megalomania

**meia** /ˈmeja/ *f* (*comprida*) stocking; (*curta*) sock; (*seis*) six; **~-calça** (*pl* **~s-calças**) *f* tights, (*Amer*) pantihose; **~-idade** *f* middle age; **~-noite** *f* midnight; **~-volta** (*pl* **~s-voltas**) *f* about-turn

**mei|go** /ˈmejgu/ *a* sweet; **~guice** *f* sweetness

**meio** /ˈmeju/ *a* half □ *adv* rather □ *m* (*centro*) middle; (*ambiente*) environment; (*recurso*) means; **~ litro** half a litre; **dois meses e ~** two and a half months; **em ~ a** amid; **por ~ de** through; **o ~ ambiente** the environment; **os ~s de comunicação** the media; **~-dia** *m* midday; **~-fio** *m* kerb; **~-termo** *m* (*acordo*) compromise

**mel** /mɛw/ *m* honey

**mela|ço** /meˈlasu/ *m* molasses; **~do** *a* sticky □ *m* treacle

**melancia** /melãˈsia/ *f* watermelon

**melan|colia** /melãkoˈlia/ *f* melancholy; **~cólico** *a* melancholy

**melão** /meˈlãw/ *m* melon

**melar** /meˈlar/ *vt* make sticky

**melhor** /meˈʎɔr/ *a & adv* better; **o ~** the best

**melho|ra** /meˈʎɔra/ *f* improvement; **~ras!** get well soon!; **~ramento** *m* improvement; **~rar** *vt* improve □ *vi* improve; <*doente*> get better

**melin|drar** /melĩˈdrar/ *vt* hurt; **~drar-se** *vpr* be hurt; **~droso** /o/ *a* delicate; <*pessoa*> sensitive

**melodi|a** /meloˈdʒia/ *f* melody; **~oso** /o/ *a* melodious

**melodra|ma** /meloˈdrama/ *m* melodrama; **~mático** *a* melodramatic

**meloso** /meˈlozu/ *a* sickly sweet

**melro** /ˈmɛwxu/ *m* blackbird

**membrana** /mẽˈbrana/ *f* membrane

**membro** /ˈmẽbru/ *m* member; (*braço, perna*) limb

**memo|rando** /memoˈrãdu/ *m* memo; **~rável** (*pl* **~ráveis**) *a* memorable

**memória** /meˈmɔria/ *f* memory; *pl* (*autobiografia*) memoirs

**men|ção** /mẽˈsãw/ *f* mention; **fazer ~ção de** mention; **~cionar** *vt* mention

**mendi|cância** /mẽdʒiˈkãsia/ *f* begging; **~gar** *vi* beg; **~go** *m* beggar

**menina** /meˈnina/ *f* girl; **a ~ dos olhos de alg** the apple of s.o.'s eye

**meningite** /menĩˈʒitʃi/ *f* meningitis

**meni|nice** /meniˈnisi/ *f* (*idade*) childhood; **~no** *m* boy

**menopausa** /meno'pawza/ *f* menopause

**menor** /me'nɔr/ *a* smaller □ *m/f* minor; **o/a ~** the smallest; (*mínimo*) the slightest, the least

**menos** /'menos/ *adv & pron* less □ *prep* except; **dois dias a ~** two days less; **a ~ que** unless; **ao** *ou* **pelo ~** at least; **o ~ bonito** the least pretty; **~prezar** *vt* look down upon; **~prezo** /e/ *m* disdain

**mensa|geiro** /mẽsa'ʒeru/ *m* messenger; **~gem** *f* message

**men|sal** /mẽ'saw/ (*pl* **~sais**) *a* monthly; **~salidade** *f* monthly payment; **~salmente** *adv* monthly

**menstru|ação** /mẽstrua'sãw/ *f* menstruation; **~ada a estar ~ada** be having one's period; **~al** (*pl* **~ais**) *a* menstrual; **~ar** *vi* menstruate

**menta** /'mẽta/ *f* mint

**men|tal** /mẽ'taw/ (*pl* **~tais**) *a* mental; **~talidade** *f* mentality; **~te** *f* mind

**men|tir** /mẽ'tʃir/ *vi* lie; **~tira** *f* lie; **~tiroso** /o/ *a* lying □ *m* liar

**mentor** /mẽ'tor/ *m* mentor

**mercado** /mer'kadu/ *m* market; **~ria** *f* commodity; *pl* goods

**mercan|te** /mer'kãtʃi/ *a* merchant; **~til** (*pl* **~tis**) *a* mercantile; **~tilismo** *m* commercialism

**mercê** /mer'se/ *f* **à ~ de** at the mercy of

**merce|aria** /mersia'ria/ *f* grocer's; **~eiro** *m* grocer

**mercenário** /merse'nariu/ *a & m* mercenary

**mercúrio** /mer'kuriu/ *m* mercury; **Mercúrio** Mercury

**merda** /'merda/ *f* (*chulo*) shit

**mere|cedor** /merese'dor/ *a* deserving; **~cer** *vt* deserve □ *vi* be deserving; **~cimento** *m* merit

**merenda** /me'rẽda/ *f* packed lunch; **~ escolar** school dinner

**mere|trício** /mere'trisiu/ *m* prostitution; **~triz** *f* prostitute

**mergu|lhador** /merguʎa'dor/ *m* diver; **~lhar** *vt* dip (**em** into) □ *vi* (*na água*) dive; (*no trabalho*) bury o.s.; **~lho** *m* dive; (*esporte*) diving; (*banho de mar*) dip

**meridi|ano** /meridʒi'anu/ *m* meridian; **~onal** (*pl* **~onais**) *a* southern

**mérito** /'mɛritu/ *m* merit

**merluza** /mer'luza/ *f* hake

**mero** /'mɛru/ *a* mere

**mês** /mes/ (*pl* **meses**) *m* month

**mesa** /'meza/ *f* table; (*de trabalho*) desk; **~ de centro** coffee table; **~ de jantar** dining table; **~ telefônica** switchboard

**mesada** /me'zada/ *f* monthly allowance

**mescla** /'mɛskla/ *f* mixture, blend

**mesmice** /mez'misi/ *f* sameness

**mesmo** /'mezmu/ *a* same □ *adv* (*até*) even; (*justamente*) right; (*de verdade*) really; **você ~** you yourself; **hoje ~** this very day; **~ assim** even so; **~ que** even if; **dá no ~** it comes to the same thing; **fiquei na mesma** I'm none the wiser

**mesqui|nharia** /meskiɲa'ria/ *f* meanness; (*uma*) mean thing; **~nho** *a* mean

**mesquita** /mes'kita/ *f* mosque

**Messias** /me'sias/ *m* Messiah

**mesti|çagem** /mestʃi'saʒẽ/ *f* interbreeding; **~ço** *a* <*pessoa*> of mixed race; <*animal*> crossbred □ *m* (*pessoa*) person of mixed race; (*animal*) mongrel

**mes|trado** /mes'tradu/ *m* master's degree; **~tre** /ε/ *m* (*f* **~tra**) master (*f* mistress); (*de escola*) teacher □ *a* main; <*chave*> master; **~tre-de-obras** (*pl* **~tres-de-obras**) *m* foreman; **~tre-sala** (*pl* **~tres-salas**) *m* master of ceremonies (*in carnival procession*); **~tria** *f* expertise

**meta** /'mɛta/ *f* (*de corrida*) finishing post; (*gol, fig*) goal

**meta|bólico** /meta'bɔliku/ *a* metabolic; **~bolismo** *m* metabolism

**metade** /me'tadʒi/ *f* half; **pela ~** halfway

**metafísi|ca** /meta'fizika/ *f* metaphysics; **~co** *a* metaphysical

**metáfora** /me'tafora/ *f* metaphor

**metafórico** /meta'fɔriku/ *a* metaphorical

**me|tal** /me'taw/ (*pl* **~tais**) *m* metal; *pl* (*numa orquestra*) brass; **~tálico** *a* metallic

**meta|lurgia** /metalur'ʒia/ *f* metallurgy; **~lúrgica** *f* metal works; **~lúrgico** *a* metallurgical □ *m* metalworker

**metamorfose** /metamor'fɔzi/ *f* metamorphosis

**metano** /me'tanu/ *m* methane

**meteórico** /mete'ɔriku/ *a* meteoric

**meteoro** /mete'ɔru/ *m* meteor; **~logia** *f* meteorology; **~lógico** *a* meteorological; **~logista** *m/f* (*cientista*) meteorologist; (*na TV*) weather forecaster

**meter** /me'ter/ *vt* put; **~-se** *vpr* (*envolver-se*) get (**em** into); (*intrometer-se*) meddle (**em** in); **~ medo** be frightening

**meticuloso** /metʃiku'lozu/ *a* meticulous

**metido** /me'tʃidu/ *a* snobbish; **ele é ~ a perito** he thinks he's an expert

**metódico** /me'tɔdʒiku/ *a* methodical

**metodista** /meto'dʒista/ *a & m/f* Methodist

**método** /ˈmɛtodu/ *m* method

**metra|lhadora** /metraʎaˈdora/ *f* machine gun; **~lhar** *vt* machine-gun

**métri|co** /ˈmɛtriku/ *a* metric; **fita ~ca** tape measure

**metro**[1] /ˈmɛtru/ *m* metre

**metro**[2] /ˈmɛtru/ *m* (*Port: metropolitano*) underground, (*Amer*) subway

**metrô** /meˈtro/ *m* underground, (*Amer*) subway

**metrópole** /meˈtrɔpoli/ *f* metropolis

**metropolitano** /metropoliˈtanu/ *a* metropolitan □ *m* (*Port*) underground, (*Amer*) subway

**meu** /mew/ *a* (*f* **minha**) my □ *pron* (*f* **minha**) mine; **um amigo ~** a friend of mine; **fico na minha** (*fam*) I keep myself to myself

**mexer** /meˈʃer/ *vt* move; (*com colher etc*) stir □ *vi* move; **~-se** *vpr* move; (*apressar-se*) get a move on; **~ com** (*comover*) affect, get to; (*brincar com*) tease; (*trabalhar com*) work with; **~ em** touch

**mexeri|ca** /meʃeˈrika/ *f* tangerine; **~car** *vi* gossip; **~co** *m* piece of gossip; *pl* gossip; **~queiro** *a* gossiping □ *m* gossip

**mexicano** /meʃiˈkanu/ *a & m* Mexican

**México** /ˈmɛʃiku/ *m* Mexico

**mexido** /meˈʃidu/ *a* **ovos ~s** scrambled eggs

**mexilhão** /meʃiˈʎɐ̃w/ *m* mussel

**mi|ado** /miˈadu/ *m* miaow; **~ar** *vi* miaow

**micróbio** /miˈkrɔbiu/ *m* microbe

**micro|cosmo** /mikroˈkɔzmu/ *m* microcosm; **~empresa** /e/ *f* small business; **~empresário** *m* small businessman; **~filme** *m* microfilm; **~fone** *m* microphone; **~onda** *f* microwave; **(forno de) ~s** *m* microwave (oven); **~ônibus** *m* *invar* minibus; **~processador** *m* microprocessor

**microrganismo** /mikrorgaˈnizmu/ *m* microorganism

**microscó|pico** /mikrosˈkɔpiku/ *a* microscopic; **~pio** *m* microscope

**mídia** /ˈmidʒia/ *f* media

**migalha** /miˈgaʎa/ *f* crumb

**mi|gração** /migraˈsɐ̃w/ *f* migration; **~grar** *vi* migrate; **~gratório** *a* migratory

**mi|jar** /miˈʒar/ *vi* (*fam*) pee; **~jar-se** *vpr* wet o.s.; **~jo** *m* (*fam*) pee

**mil** /miw/ *a & m* *invar* thousand; **estar a ~** be on top form

**mila|gre** /miˈlagri/ *m* miracle; **~groso** /o/ *a* miraculous

**milênio** /miˈleniu/ *m* millennium

**milésimo** /miˈlɛzimu/ *a* thousandth

**milha** /ˈmiʎa/ *f* mile

**milhão** /miˈʎɐ̃w/ *m* million; **um ~ de dólares** a million dollars

**milhar** /miˈʎar/ *m* thousand; **~es de vezes** thousands of times; **aos ~es** in their thousands

**milho** /ˈmiʎo/ *m* maize, (*Amer*) corn

**milico** /miˈliku/ *m* (*fam*) military man; **os ~s** the military

**mili|grama** /miliˈgrama/ *m* milligram; **~litro** *m* millilitre; **~metro** /e/ *m* millimetre

**milionário** /milioˈnariu/ *a & m* millionaire

**mili|tante** /miliˈtɐ̃tʃi/ *a & m* militant; **~tar** *a* military □ *m* soldier

**mim** /mĩ/ *pron* me

**mimar** /miˈmar/ *vt* spoil

**mímica** /ˈmimika/ *f* mime; (*brincadeira*) charades

**mi|na** /ˈmina/ *f* mine; **~nar** *vt* mine; (*fig: prejudicar*) undermine

**mindinho** /mĩˈdʒiɲu/ *m* little finger, (*Amer*) pinkie

**mineiro** /miˈneru/ *a* mining; (*de MG*) from Minas Gerais □ *m* miner; (*de MG*) person from Minas Gerais

**mine|ração** /mineraˈsɐ̃w/ *f* mining; **~ral** (*pl* **~rais**) *a & m* mineral; **~rar** *vt/i* mine

**minério** /miˈnɛriu/ *m* ore

**mingau** /mĩˈgaw/ *m* porridge

**mingua** /ˈmĩgwa/ *f* lack

**minguante** /mĩˈgwɐ̃tʃi/ *a* **quarto ~** last quarter

**minguar** /mĩˈgwar/ *vi* dwindle

**minha** /ˈmiɲa/ *a & pron veja* **meu**

**minhoca** /miˈɲɔka/ *f* worm

**miniatura** /miniaˈtura/ *f* miniature

**mini|malista** /minimaˈlista/ *a & m/f* minimalist; **~mizar** *vt* minimize; (*subestimar*) play down

**mínimo** /ˈminimu/ *a* (*muito pequeno*) tiny; (*mais baixo*) minimum □ *m* minimum; **a mínima idéia** the slightest idea; **no ~** at least

**minissaia** /miniˈsaja/ *f* miniskirt

**minis|terial** /ministeriˈaw/ (*pl* **~teriais**) *a* ministerial; **~tério** *m* ministry; **Ministério do Interior** Home Office, (*Amer*) Department of the Interior

**minis|trar** /minisˈtrar/ *vt* administer; **~tro** *m* minister; **primeiro ~tro** prime minister

**Minorca** /miˈnɔrka/ *f* Menorca

**mino|ritário** /minoriˈtariu/ *a* minority; **~ria** *f* minority

**minúcia** /miˈnusia/ *f* detail

**minucioso** /minusiˈozu/ *a* thorough

**minúscu|la** /miˈnuskula/ *f* small letter; **~lo** *a* <*letra*> small; (*muito pequeno*) minuscule

**minuta** /miˈnuta/ *f* (*rascunho*) rough draft

**minuto** /mi'nutu/ *m* minute
**miolo** /mi'olu/ *f* (*de fruta*) flesh; (*de pão*) crumb; *pl* brains
**míope** /'miopi/ *a* short-sighted
**miopia** /mio'pia/ *f* myopia
**mira** /'mira/ *f* sight; **ter em ~** have one's sights on
**mirabolante** /mirabo'lãtʃi/ *a* amazing; <*idéias, plano*> grandiose
**mi|ragem** /mi'raʒẽ/ *f* mirage; **~rante** *m* lookout; **~rar** *vt* look at; **~rar-se** *vpr* look at o.s.
**mirim** /mi'rĩ/ *a* little
**miscelânea** /mise'lania/ *f* miscellany
**miscigenação** /misiʒena'sãw/ *f* inter-breeding
**mise-en-plis** /mizã'pli/ *m* shampoo and set
**miserá|vel** /mize'ravew/ (*pl* ~**veis**) *a* miserable
**miséria** /mi'zɛria/ *f* misery; (*pobreza*) poverty; **uma ~** (*pouco dinheiro*) a pittance; **chorar ~** claim poverty
**miseri|córdia** /mizeri'kɔrdʒia/ *f* mercy; **~cordioso** *a* merciful
**misógino** /mi'zɔʒinu/ *m* misogynist □ *a* misogynistic
**miss** /'misi/ *f* beauty queen
**missa** /'misa/ *f* mass
**missão** /mi'sãw/ *f* mission
**mís|sil** /'misiw/ (*pl* ~**seis**) *m* missile; **~sil de longo alcance** long-range missile
**missionário** /misio'nariu/ *m* missionary
**missiva** /mi'siva/ *f* missive
**mis|tério** /mis'tɛriu/ *m* mystery; **~terioso** /o/ *a* mysterious; **~ticismo** *m* mysticism
**místico** /'mistʃiku/ *m* mystic □ *a* mystical
**misto** /'mistu/ *a* mixed □ *m* mix; **~ quente** toasted ham and cheese sandwich
**mistu|ra** /mis'tura/ *f* mixture; **~rar** *vt* mix; (*confundir*) mix up; **~rar-se** *vpr* mix (**com** with)
**mítico** /'mitʃiku/ *a* mythical
**mito** /'mitu/ *m* myth; **~logia** *f* mythology; **~lógico** *a* mythological
**miudezas** /miu'dezas/ *f pl* odds and ends
**miúdo** /mi'udu/ *a* tiny, minute; <*chuva*> fine; <*despesas*> minor □ *m* (*criança*) child, little one; *pl* (*de galinha*) giblets; **trocar em ~s** go into detail
**mixaria** /miʃa'ria/ *f* (*fam*) (*soma irrisória*) pittance
**mixórdia** /mi'ʃɔrdʒia/ *f* muddle
**mnemônico** /ne'moniku/ *a* mnemonic
**mobilar** /mobi'lar/ *vt* (*Port*) furnish

**mobília** /mo'bilia/ *f* furniture
**mobili|ar** /mobili'ar/ *vt* furnish; **~ário** *m* furniture
**mobili|dade** /mobili'dadʒi/ *f* mobility; **~zar** *vt* mobilize
**moça** /'mosa/ *f* girl
**moçambicano** /mosãbi'kanu/ *a* & *m* Mozambican
**Moçambique** /mosã'biki/ *m* Mozambique
**moção** /mo'sãw/ *f* motion
**mochila** /mo'ʃila/ *f* rucksack
**moço** /'mosu/ *a* young □ *m* boy, lad
**moda** /'mɔda/ *f* fashion; **na ~** fashionable
**modalidade** /modali'dadʒi/ *f* (*esporte*) event
**mode|lagem** /mode'laʒẽ/ *f* modelling; **~lar** *vt* model (**a** on); **~lar-se** *vpr* model o.s. (**a** on) □ *a* model; **~lo** /e/ *m* model
**mode|ração** /modera'sãw/ *f* moderation; **~rado** *a* moderate; **~rar** *vt* moderate; reduce <*velocidade, despesas*>; **~rar-se** *vpr* restrain oneself
**moder|nidade** /moderni'dadʒi/ *f* modernity; **~nismo** *m* modernism; **~nista** *a* & *m/f* modernist; **~nizar** *vt* modernize; **~no** /ɛ/ *a* modern
**modess** /'mɔdʒis/ *m invar* sanitary towel
**modéstia** /mo'dɛstʃia/ *f* modesty
**modesto** /mo'dɛstu/ *a* modest
**módico** /'mɔdʒiku/ *a* modest
**modifi|cação** /modʒifika'sãw/ *f* modification; **~car** *vt* modify
**mo|dismo** /mo'dʒizmu/ *m* idiom; **~dista** *f* dressmaker
**modo** /'mɔdu/ *m* way; (*ling*) mood; *pl* (*maneiras*) manners
**modular** /modu'lar/ *vt* modulate □ *a* modular
**módulo** /'mɔdulu/ *m* module
**moeda** /mo'eda/ *f* (*peça de metal*) coin; (*dinheiro*) currency
**mo|edor** /moe'dor/ *m* **~edor de café** coffee-grinder; **~edor de carne** mincer; **~er** *vt* grind <*café, trigo*>; squeeze <*cana*>; mince <*carne*>; (*bater*) beat
**mo|fado** /mo'fadu/ *a* mouldy; **~far** *vi* moulder; **~fo** /o/ *m* mould
**mogno** /'mɔgnu/ *m* mahogany
**moinho** /mo'iɲu/ *m* mill; **~ de vento** windmill
**moisés** /moj'zɛs/ *m invar* carry-cot
**moita** /'mojta/ *f* bush
**mola** /'mɔla/ *f* spring
**mol|dar** /mow'dar/ *vt* mould; cast <*metal*>; **~de** /ɔ/ *m* mould; (*para costura etc*) pattern
**moldu|ra** /mow'dura/ *f* frame; **~rar** *vt* frame

**mole** /'mɔli/ *a* soft; <*pessoa*> listless; (*fam*) (*fácil*) easy □ *adv* easily; **é ~?** (*fam*) can you believe it?

**molécula** /mo'lɛkula/ *f* molecule

**moleque** /mo'lɛki/ *m* (*menino*) lad; (*de rua*) urchin; (*homem*) scoundrel

**molestar** /moles'tar/ *vt* bother

**moléstia** /mo'lɛstʃia/ *f* disease

**moletom** /mole'tõ/ *m* (*tecido*) knitted cotton; (*blusa*) sweatshirt

**moleza** /mo'leza/ *f* softness; (*de pessoa*) laziness; **viver na ~** lead a cushy life; **ser ~** be easy

**mo|lhado** /mo'ʎadu/ *a* wet; **~lhar** *vt* wet; **~lhar-se** *vpr* get wet

**molho¹** /'mɔʎu/ *m* (*de chaves*) bunch; (*de palha*) sheaf

**molho²** /'mɔʎu/ *m* sauce; (*para salada*) dressing; **deixar de ~** leave in soak <*roupa*>; **~ inglês** Woʼcester sauce

**molusco** /mo'lusku/ *m* mollusc

**momen|tâneo** /mome'taniu/ *a* momentary; **~to** *m* moment; (*força*) momentum

**Mônaco** /'monaku/ *m* Monaco

**monar|ca** /mo'narka/ *m/f* monarch; **~quia** *f* monarchy; **~quista** *a* & *m/f* monarchist

**monástico** /mo'nastʃiku/ *a* monastic

**monção** /mõ'sãw/ *f* monsoon

**mone|tário** /mone'tariu/ *a* monetary; **~tarismo** *m* monetarism; **~tarista** *a* & *m/f* monetarist

**monge** /'mõʒi/ *m* monk

**monitor** /moni'tor/ *m* monitor; **~ de vídeo** VDU

**monitorar** /monito'rar/ *vt* monitor

**mono|cromo** /mono'krɔmu/ *a* monochrome; **~gamia** *f* monogamy

**monógamo** /mo'nɔgamu/ *a* monogamous

**monograma** /mono'grama/ *m* monogram

**monólogo** /mo'nɔlogu/ *m* monologue

**mononucleose** /mononukli'ɔzi/ *f* glandular fever

**mono|pólio** /mono'pɔliu/ *m* monopoly; **~polizar** *vt* monopolize

**monossílabo** /mono'silabu/ *a* monosyllabic □ *m* monosyllable

**monotonia** /monoto'nia/ *f* monotony

**monótono** /mo'nɔtonu/ *a* monotonous

**monóxido** /mo'nɔksidu/ *m* **~ de carbono** carbon monoxide

**mons|tro** /'mõstru/ *m* monster; **~truosidade** *f* monstrosity; **~truoso** /o/ *a* monstrous

**monta|dor** /mõta'dor/ *m* (*de cinema*) editor; **~dora** *f* assembly company; **~gem** *f* assembly; (*de filme*) editing; (*de peça teatral*) production

**monta|nha** /mõ'taɲa/ *f* mountain;

**~nha-russa** (*pl* **~nhas-russas**) *f* roller coaster; **~nhismo** *m* mountaineering; **~nhoso** /o/ *a* mountainous

**mon|tante** /mõ'tãtʃi/ *m* amount □ *a* rising; **a ~tante** upstream; **~tão** *m* heap; **~tar** *vt* ride <*cavalo, bicicleta*>; assemble <*peças, máquina*>; put up <*barraca*>; set up <*empresa, escritório*>; mount <*guarda, diamante*>; put on <*espetáculo, peça*>; edit <*filme*> □ *vi* ride; **~tar a** <*dívidas etc*> amount to; **~tar em** (*subir em*) mount; **~taria** *f* mount; **~te** *m* heap; **um ~te de coisas** (*fam*) loads of things; **o Monte Branco** Mont Blanc

**Montevidéu** /mõtʃivi'dɛw/ *f* Montevideo

**montra** /'mõtra/ *f* (*Port*) shop window

**monumen|tal** /monumẽ'taw/ (*pl* **~tais**) *a* monumental; **~to** *m* monument

**mora|da** /mo'rada/ *f* dwelling; (*Port*) address; **~dia** *f* dwelling; **~dor** *m* resident

**mo|ral** /mo'raw/ (*pl* **~rais**) *a* moral □ *f* (*ética*) morals; (*de uma história*) moral □ *m* (*ânimo*) morale; (*de pessoa*) moral sense; **~ralidade** *f* morality; **~ralista** *a* moralistic □ *m/f* moralist; **~ralizar** *vi* moralize

**morango** /mo'rãgu/ *m* strawberry

**morar** /mo'rar/ *vi* live

**moratória** /mora'tɔria/ *f* moratorium

**mórbido** /'mɔrbidu/ *a* morbid

**morcego** /mor'segu/ *m* bat

**mor|daça** /mor'dasa/ *f* gag; (*para cão*) muzzle; **~daz** *a* scathing; **~der** *vt/i* bite; **~dida** *f* bite

**mordo|mia** /mordo'mia/ *f* (*no emprego*) perk; (*de casa etc*) comfort; **~mo** /o/ *m* butler

**more|na** /mo'rena/ *f* brunette; **~no** *a* dark; (*bronzeado*) brown □ *m* dark person

**morfina** /mor'fina/ *f* morphine

**moribundo** /mori'bũdu/ *a* dying

**moringa** /mo'rĩga/ *f* water jug

**morma|cento** /morma'sẽtu/ *a* sultry; **~ço** *m* sultry weather

**morno** /'mornu/ *a* lukewarm

**moro|sidade** /morozi'dadʒi/ *f* slowness; **~so** /o/ *a* slow

**morrer** /mo'xer/ *vi* die; <*luz, dia, ardor, esperança etc*> fade; <*carro*> stall

**morro** /'moxu/ *m* hill; (*fig: favela*) slum

**mortadela** /morta'dɛla/ *f* mortadella, salami

**mor|tal** /mor'taw/ (*pl* **~tais**) *a* & *m* mortal; **~talha** *f* shroud; **~talidade** *f* mortality; **~tandade** *f* slaughter; **~te** /ɔ/ *f* death; **~tífero** *a* deadly; **~tificar** *vt* mortify; **~to** /o/ *a* dead

**mosaico** /mo'zajku/ *m* mosaic

**mosca** /'moska/ *f* fly

**Moscou** /mos'ku/, (*Port*) **Moscovo** /moʃ'kovu/ *f* Moscow

**mosquito** /mos'kitu/ *m* mosquito

**mostarda** /mos'tarda/ *f* mustard

**mosteiro** /mos'teru/ *m* monastery

**mos|tra** /'mɔstra/ *f* display; **dar** ~**tras de** show signs of; **pôr à** ~**tra** show up; ~**trador** *m* face, dial; ~**trar** *vt* show; ~**trar-se** *vpr* (*revelar-se*) show o.s. to be; (*exibir-se*) show off; ~**truário** *m* display case

**mo|tel** /mo'tɛw/ (*pl* ~**téis**) *m* motel

**motim** /mo'tʃĩ/ *m* riot; (*na marinha*) mutiny

**moti|vação** /motʃiva'sãw/ *f* motivation; ~**var** *vt* (*incentivar*) motivate; (*provocar*) cause; ~**vo** *m* (*razão*) reason; (*estímulo*) motive; (*na arte, música*) motif; **dar** ~**vo de** give cause for

**moto** /'mɔtu/ *f* motorbike; ~**ca** /mo'tɔka/ *f* ( *fam*) motorbike

**motoci|cleta** /motosi'kleta/ *f* motorcycle; ~**clismo** *m* motorcycling; ~**clista** *m/f* motorcyclist

**motoqueiro** /moto'keru/ *m* ( *fam*) biker

**motor** /mo'tor/ *m* (*de carro, avião etc*) engine; (*elétrico*) motor □ *a* ( *f* **motriz**) <*força*> driving; (*anat*) motor; ~ **de arranque** starter motor; ~ **de popa** outboard motor

**moto|rista** /moto'rista/ *m/f* driver; ~**rizado** *a* motorized; ~**rizar** *vt* motorize

**movedi|ço** /move'dʒisu/ *a* unstable, moving; **areia** ~**ça** quicksand

**mó|vel** /'mɔvew/ (*pl* ~**veis**) *a* <*peça, parte*> moving; <*tropas*> mobile; <*festa*> movable □ *m* piece of furniture; *pl* furniture

**mo|ver** /mo'ver/ *vt* move; (*impulsionar, fig*) drive; ~**ver-se** *vpr* move; ~**vido** *a* driven; ~**vido a álcool** alcohol-powered

**movimen|tação** /movimẽta'sãw/ *f* bustle; ~**tado** *a* <*rua, loja*> busy; <*música*> up-beat, lively; <*pessoa, sessão*> lively; ~**tar** *vt* liven up; ~**tar-se** *vpr* move; ~**to** *m* movement; (*tecn*) motion; (*na rua etc*) activity

**muam|ba** /mu'ãba/ *f* contraband; ~**beiro** *m* smuggler

**muco** /'muku/ *m* mucus

**muçulmano** /musuw'manu/ *a & m* Muslim

**mu|da** /'muda/ *f* (*planta*) seedling; ~**da de roupa** change of clothes; ~**dança** *f* change; (*de casa*) move; (*de carro*) transmission; ~**dar** *vt/i* change; ~**dar de assunto** change the subject; ~**dar** (*de casa*) move (house); ~**dar de cor** change colour;

~**dar de idéia** change one's mind; ~**dar de lugar** change places; ~**dar de roupa** change (clothes); ~**dar-se** *vpr* move

**mu|dez** /mu'des/ *f* silence; ~**do** *a* silent; (*deficiente*) dumb; <*telefone*> dead □ *m* mute

**mu|gido** /mu'ʒidu/ *m* moo; ~**gir** *vi* moo

**muito** /'mũitu/ *a* a lot of; *pl* many □ *pron* a lot □ *adv* (*com adjetivo, advérbio*) very; (*com verbo*) a lot; ~ **maior** much bigger; ~ **tempo** a long time

**mula** /'mula/ *f* mule

**mulato** /mu'latu/ *a & m* mulatto

**muleta** /mu'leta/ *f* crutch

**mulher** /mu'ʎer/ *f* woman; (*esposa*) wife

**mulherengo** /muʎe'rẽgu/ *a* womanizing □ *m* womanizer, ladies' man

**mul|ta** /'muwta/ *f* fine; ~**tar** *vt* fine

**multicolor** /muwtʃiko'lor/ *a* multicoloured

**multidão** /muwtʃi'dãw/ *f* crowd

**multinacio|nal** /muwtʃinasio-'naw/ (*pl* ~**nais**) *a & f* multinational

**multipli|cação** /muwtʃiplika-'sãw/ *f* multiplication; ~**car** *vt* multiply; ~**car-se** *vpr* multiply; ~**cidade** *f* multiplicity

**múltiplo** /'muwtʃiplu/ *a & m* multiple

**multirraci|al** /muwtʃixasi'aw/ (*pl* ~**ais**) *a* multiracial

**múmia** /'mumia/ *f* mummy

**mun|dano** /mũ'danu/ *a* <*prazeres etc*> worldly; <*vida, mulher*> society; ~**dial** (*pl* ~**diais**) *a* world □ *m* world championship; ~**do** *m* world; **todo** (**o**) ~**do** everybody

**munição** /muni'sãw/ *f* ammunition

**muni|cipal** /munisi'paw/ (*pl* ~**cipais**) *a* municipal; ~**cípio** *m* (*lugar*) borough, community; (*prédio*) town hall; (*autoridade*) local authority

**munir** /mu'nir/ *vt* provide (**de** with); ~**-se** *vpr* equip o.s. (**de** with)

**mu|ral** /mu'raw/ (*pl* ~**rais**) *a & m* mural; ~**ralha** *f* wall

**mur|char** /mur'ʃar/ *vi* <*planta*> wither, wilt; <*salada*> go limp; <*beleza*> fade □ *vt* wither, wilt <*planta*>; ~**cho** *a* <*planta*> wilting; <*pessoa*> broken

**mur|murar** /murmu'rar/ *vi* murmur; (*queixar-se*) mutter □ *vt* murmur; ~**múrio** *m* murmur

**muro** /'muru/ *m* wall

**murro** /'muxu/ *m* punch

**musa** /'muza/ *f* muse

**muscu|lação** /muskula'sãw/ *f* weight-training; ~**lar** *a* muscular; ~**latura** *f* musculature

**músculo** /'muskulu/ *m* muscle

**musculoso** /musku'lozu/ *a* muscular
**museu** /mu'zew/ *m* museum
**musgo** /'muzgu/ *m* moss
**música** /'muzika/ *f* music; (*uma*) song; ~ **de câmara** chamber music; ~ **de fundo** background music; ~ **clássica** *ou* **erudita** classical music
**musi|cal** /muzi'kaw/ (*pl* ~**cais**) *a* & *m* musical; ~**car** *vt* set to music
**músico** /'muziku/ *m* musician □ *a* musical
**musse** /'musi/ *f* mousse
**mutilar** /mutʃi'lar/ *vt* mutilate; maim <*pessoa*>
**mutirão** /mutʃi'rãw/ *m* joint effort
**mútuo** /'mutuu/ *a* mutual
**muxoxo** /mu'ʃoʃu/ *m* **fazer** ~ tut

# N

**na** = em + a
**nabo** /'nabu/ *m* turnip
**nação** /na'sãw/ *f* nation
**nacio|nal** /nasio'naw/ (*pl* ~**nais**) *a* national; (*brasileiro*) home-produced; ~**nalidade** *f* nationality; ~**nalismo** *m* nationalism; ~**nalista** *a* & *m/f* nationalist; ~**nalizar** *vt* nationalize
**naco** /'naku/ *m* chunk
**nada** /'nada/ *pron* nothing □ *adv* not at all; **de** ~ (*não há de quê*) don't mention it; **que** ~!, ~ **disso!** no way!
**na|dadeira** /nada'dera/ *f* (*de peixe*) fin; (*de mergulhador*) flipper; ~**dador** *m* swimmer; ~**dar** *vi* swim
**nádegas** /'nadegas/ *f pl* buttocks
**nado** /'nadu/ *m* ~ **borboleta** butterfly stroke; ~ **de costas** backstroke; ~ **de peito** breaststroke; **atravessar a** ~ swim across
**náilon** /'najlõ/ *m* nylon
**naipe** /'najpi/ *m* (*em jogo de cartas*) suit
**namo|rada** /namo'rada/ *f* girlfriend; ~**rado** *m* boyfriend; ~**rador** *a* amorous □ *m* ladies' man; ~**rar** *vt* (*ter relação com*) go out with; (*cobiçar*) eye up □ *vi* <*casal*> (*ter relação*) go out together; (*beijar-se etc*) kiss and cuddle; <*homem*> have a girlfriend; <*mulher*> have a boyfriend; ~**ro** /o/ *m* relationship
**nanar** /na'nar/ *vi* (*col*) sleep
**nanico** /na'niku/ *a* tiny
**não** /nãw/ *adv* not; (*resposta*) no □ *m* no; ~**-alinhado** *a* non-aligned; ~**-conformista** *a* & *m/f* non-conformist
**naquela, naquele, naquilo** = em + aquela, aquele, aquilo
**narci|sismo** /narsi'zizmu/ *m* narcissism; ~**sista** *m/f* narcissist □ *a* narcissistic; ~**so** *m* narcissus
**narcótico** /nar'kɔtʃiku/ *a* & *m* narcotic

**nari|gudo** /nari'gudu/ *a* with a big nose; **ser** ~**gudo** have a big nose; ~**na** *f* nostril
**nariz** /na'ris/ *m* nose
**nar|ração** /naxa'sãw/ *f* narration; ~**rador** *m* narrator; ~**rar** *vt* narrate; ~**rativa** *f* narrative; ~**rativo** *a* narrative
**nas** = em + as
**na|sal** /na'zaw/ (*pl* ~**sais**) *a* nasal; ~**salizar** *vt* nasalize
**nas|cença** /na'sẽsa/ *f* birth; ~**cente** *a* nascent □ *f* source; ~**cer** *vi* be born; <*dente, espinha*> grow; <*planta*> sprout; <*sol, lua*> rise; <*dia*> dawn; (*fig*) <*empresa, projeto etc*> come into being □ *m* o ~**cer do sol** sunrise; ~**cimento** *m* birth
**nata** /'nata/ *f* cream
**natação** /nata'sãw/ *f* swimming
**Natal** /na'taw/ *m* Christmas
**na|tal** /na'taw/ (*pl* ~**tais**) *a* <*país, terra*> native
**nata|lício** /nata'lisiu/ *a* & *m* birthday; ~**lidade** *f* **índice de** ~**lidade** birth rate; ~**lino** *a* Christmas
**nati|vidade** /natʃivi'dadʒi/ *f* nativity; ~**vo** *a* & *m* native
**nato** /'natu/ *a* born
**natu|ral** /natu'raw/ (*pl* ~**rais**) *a* natural; (*oriundo*) originating (**de** from) □ *m* native (**de** of)
**natura|lidade** /naturali'dadʒi/ *f* naturalness; **com** ~**lidade** matter-of-factly; **de** ~**lidade carioca** born in Rio de Janeiro; ~**lismo** *m* naturalism; ~**lista** *a* & *m/f* naturalist; ~**lizar** *vt* naturalize; ~**lizar-se** *vpr* become naturalized
**natureza** /natu'reza/ *f* nature; ~ **morta** still life
**naturis|mo** /natu'rizmu/ *m* naturism; ~**ta** *m/f* naturist
**nau|fragar** /nawfra'gar/ *vi* <*navio*> be wrecked; <*tripulação*> be ship-wrecked; (*fig*) <*plano, casamento etc*> founder; ~**frágio** *m* shipwreck; (*fig*) failure
**náufrago** /'nawfragu/ *m* castaway
**náusea** /'nawzia/ *f* nausea
**nauseabundo** /nawzia'bũdu/ *a* nauseating
**náuti|ca** /'nawtʃika/ *f* navigation; ~**co** *a* nautical
**na|val** /na'vaw/ (*pl* ~**vais**) *a* naval; **construção** ~**val** shipbuilding
**navalha** /na'vaʎa/ *f* razor; ~**da** *f* cut with a razor
**nave** /'navi/ *f* nave; ~ **espacial** space-ship
**nave|gação** /navega'sãw/ *f* navigation; (*tráfego*) shipping; ~**gador** *m* navigator; ~**gante** *m/f* seafarer; ~**gar** *vt* navigate; sail <*mar*> □ *vi*

sail; (*traçar o rumo*) navigate; ~**gável**
(*pl* ~**gáveis**) *a* navigable
**navio** /na'viu/ *m* ship; ~ **cargueiro**
cargo ship; ~ **de guerra** warship; ~
**petroleiro** oil tanker
**nazista** /na'zista/, (*Port*) **nazi** /na'zi/ *a*
& *m/f* Nazi
**neblina** /ne'blina/ *f* mist
**nebulo|sa** /nebu'lɔza/ *f* nebula;
~**sidade** *f* cloud; ~**so** /o/ *a* cloudy;
(*fig*) obscure
**neces|saire** /nese'sɛr/ *m* toilet bag;
~**sário** *a* necessary; ~**sidade** *f* necessity; (*que se impõe*) need; (*pobreza*)
need; ~**sitado** *a* needy □ *m* person in
need; ~**sitar** *vt* require; (*tornar ne-*
*cessário*) necessitate; ~**sitar de** need
**necro|lógio** /nekro'lɔʒiu/ *m* obituary
column; ~**tério** *m* mortuary, (*Amer*)
morgue
**néctar** /'nɛktar/ *m* nectar
**nectarina** /nekta'rina/ *f* nectarine
**nefasto** /ne'fastu/ *a* fatal
**ne|gação** /nega'sãw/ *f* denial; (*ling*)
negation; **ser uma** ~**gação em** be
hopeless at; ~**gar** *vt* deny; ~**gar-se**
**a** refuse to; ~**gativa** *f* refusal; (*ling*)
negative; ~**gativo** *a* & *m* negative
**negli|gência** /negli'ʒẽsia/ *f* negli-
gence; ~**genciar** *vt* neglect; ~**gente**
*a* negligent
**negoci|ação** /negosia'sãw/ *f* negotia-
tion; ~**ador** *m* negotiator; ~**ante** *m/f*
dealer (de in); ~**ar** *vt/i* negotiate;
~**ar em** deal in; ~**ata** *f* shady deal;
~**ável** (*pl* ~**áveis**) *a* negotiable
**negócio** /ne'gɔsiu/ *m* deal; (*fam: coi-*
*sa*) thing; *pl* business; **a** *ou* **de** ~**s**
<*viajar*> on business
**negocista** /nego'sista/ *m* wheeler-
dealer □ *a* wheeler-dealing
**ne|grito** /ne'gritu/ *m* bold; ~**gro** /e/ *a*
& *m* black; (*de raça*) Negro
**nela, nele** = **em + ela, ele**
**nem** /nẽj/ *adv* not even □ *conj* ~ ... ~
... neither ... nor ...; ~ **sempre** not
always; ~ **todos** not all; ~ **que** not
even if; **que** ~ like; ~ **eu** nor do I
**nenê** /ne'ne/, **neném** /ne'nẽj/ *m* baby
**nenhum** /ne'ɲũ/ *a* (*f* **nenhuma**) no □
*pron* (*f* **nenhuma**) not one; ~ **dos**
**dois** neither of them; ~ **erro** no mistakes; **erro** ~ no mistakes at all, not
a single mistake; ~ **lugar** nowhere
**nenúfar** /ne'nufar/ *m* waterlily
**neologismo** /neolo'ʒizmu/ *m* neolo-
gism
**néon** /'nɛõ/ *m* neon
**neozelan|dês** /neozelã'des/ *a* (*f*
~**desa**) New Zealand □ *m* (*f* ~**desa**)
New Zealander
**Nepal** /ne'paw/ *m* Nepal
**nervo** /'nervu/ *m* nerve; ~**sismo** *m*
(*chateação*) annoyance; (*medo*) nerv-

ousness; ~**so** /o/ *a* <*sistema, doença*>
nervous; (*chateado*) annoyed; (*medro-*
*so*) nervous; **deixar alg** ~**so** get on
s.o.'s nerves
**nessa(s), nesse(s)** = **em + essa(s),**
**esse(s)**
**nesta(s), neste(s)** = **em + esta(s),**
**este(s)**
**ne|ta** /'nɛta/ *f* granddaughter; ~**to** /ɛ/
*m* grandson; *pl* grandchildren
**neuro|logia** /newrolo'ʒia/ *f* neuro-
logy; ~**lógico** *a* neurological;
~**logista** *m/f* neurologist
**neu|rose** /new'rɔzi/ *f* neurosis;
~**rótico** *a* neurotic
**neutrali|dade** /newtrali'dadʒi/ *f*
neutrality; ~**zar** *vt* neutralize
**neutrão** /new'trãw/ *m* (*Port*) *veja*
**nêutron**
**neutro** /'newtru/ *a* neutral
**nêutron** /'newtrõ/ *m* neutron
**ne|vada** /ne'vada/ *f* snowfall; ~**vado**
*a* snow-covered; ~**var** *vi* snow;
~**vasca** *f* snowstorm; ~**ve** /ɛ/ *f* snow
**névoa** /'nɛvoa/ *f* haze
**nevoeiro** /nevo'eru/ *m* fog
**nexo** /'nɛksu/ *m* connection; **sem** ~
incoherent
**Nicarágua** /nika'ragwa/ *f* Nicaragua
**nicaragüense** /nikara'gwẽsi/ *a* & *m/*
*f* Nicaraguan
**nicho** /'niʃu/ *m* niche
**nicotina** /niko'tʃina/ *f* nicotine
**Níger** /'niʒer/ *m* Niger
**Nigéria** /ni'ʒɛria/ *f* Nigeria
**nigeriano** /niʒeri'anu/ *a* & *m* Niger-
ian
**Nilo** /'nilu/ *m* Nile
**ninar** /ni'nar/ *vt* lull to sleep
**ninfa** /'nĩfa/ *f* nymph
**ninguém** /nĩ'gẽj/ *pron* no-one, nobody
**ninhada** /nĩ'ɲada/ *f* brood
**ninharia** /niɲa'ria/ *f* trifle
**ninho** /'niɲu/ *m* nest
**níquel** /'nikew/ *m* nickel
**nisei** /ni'sej/ *a* & *m/f* Japanese Brazilian
**nisso** = **em + isso**
**nisto** = **em + isto**
**nitidez** /nitʃi'des/ *f* (*de imagem etc*)
sharpness
**nítido** /'nitʃidu/ *a* <*imagem, foto*>
sharp; <*diferença, melhora*> distinct,
clear
**nitrogênio** /nitro'ʒeniu/ *m* nitrogen
**ní|vel** /'nivew/ (*pl* ~**veis**) *m* level; **a**
~**vel de** in terms of
**nivelamento** /nivela'mẽtu/ *m* level-
ling
**nivelar** /nive'lar/ *vt* level
**no** = **em + o**
**nó** /nɔ/ *m* knot; **dar um** ~ tie a knot;
~ **dos dedos** knuckle; **um** ~ **na gar-**
**ganta** a lump in one's throat

**nobre** /'nɔbri/ *a* noble; *<bairro>* exclusive □ *m/f* noble; **~za** /e/ *f* nobility

**noção** /no'sãw/ *f* notion; *pl* (*rudimentos*) elements

**nocaute** /no'kawtʃi/ *m* knockout; **pôr alg ~** knock s.o. out; **~ar** *vt* knock out

**nocivo** /no'sivu/ *a* harmful

**nódoa** /'nodoa/ *f* (*Port*) stain

**nogueira** /no'gera/ *f* (*árvore*) walnut tree

**noi|tada** /noj'tada/ *f* night; **~te** *f* night; (*antes de dormir*) evening; **à ou de ~te** at night; (*antes de dormir*) in the evening; **hoje à ~te** tonight; **ontem à ~te** last night; **boa ~te** (*ao chegar*) good evening; (*ao despedir-se*) good night; **~te em branco** *ou* **claro** sleepless night

**noi|vado** /noj'vadu/ *m* engagement; **~va** *f* fiancée; (*no casamento*) bride; **~vo** *m* fiancé; (*no casamento*) bridegroom; **os ~vos** the engaged couple; (*no casamento*) the bride and groom; **ficar ~vo** get engaged

**no|jento** /no'ʒẽtu/ *a* disgusting; **~jo** /o/ *m* disgust

**nômade** /'nomadʒi/ *m/f* nomad □ *a* nomadic

**nome** /'nomi/ *m* name; **de ~** by name; **em ~ de** in the name of; **~ comercial** trade name; **~ de batismo** Christian name; **~ de guerra** professional name

**nome|ação** /nomia'sãw/ *f* appointment; **~ar** *vt* (*para cargo*) appoint; (*chamar pelo nome*) name

**nomi|nal** /nomi'naw/ (*pl* **~nais**) *a* nominal

**nonagésimo** /nona'ʒɛzimu/ *a* ninetieth

**nono** /'nonu/ *a & m* ninth

**nora** /'nɔra/ *f* daughter-in-law

**nordes|te** /nor'dɛstʃi/ *m* northeast; **~tino** *a* Northeastern □ *m* person from the Northeast (*of Brazil*)

**nórdico** /'nɔrdʒiku/ *a* Nordic

**nor|ma** /'nɔrma/ *f* norm; **~mal** (*pl* **~mais**) *a* normal

**normali|dade** /normali'dadʒi/ *f* normality; **~zar** *vt* bring back to normal; normalize *<relações diplomáticas>*; **~zar-se** *vpr* return to normal

**noroeste** /noro'ɛstʃi/ *a & m* northwest

**norte** /'nɔrtʃi/ *a & m* north; **~africano** *a & m* North African; **~americano** *a & m* North American; **~-coreano** *a & m* North Korean

**nortista** /nor'tʃista/ *a* Northern □ *m/f* Northerner

**Noruega** /noru'ɛga/ *f* Norway

**norue|guês** /norue'ges/ *a & m* (*f* **~guesa**) Norwegian

**nos**[1] **= em + os**

**nos**[2] /nus/ *pron* us; (*indireto*) (to) us; (*reflexivo*) ourselves

**nós** /nɔs/ *pron* we; (*depois de preposição*) us

**nos|sa** /'nɔsa/ *int* gosh; **~so** /ɔ/ *a* our □ *pron* ours

**nos|talgia** /nostaw'ʒia/ *f* nostalgia; **~tálgico** *a* nostalgic

**nota** /'nɔta/ *f* note; (*na escola etc*) mark; (*conta*) bill; **custar uma ~ (preta)** (*fam*) cost a bomb; **tomar ~** take note (**de** of); **~ fiscal** receipt

**no|tação** /nota'sãw/ *f* notation; **~tar** *vt* notice, note; **fazer ~tar** point out; **~tável** (*pl* **~táveis**) *a & m/f* notable

**notícia** /no'tʃisia/ *f* piece of news; *pl* news

**notici|ar** /notʃi'sjar/ *vt* report; **~ário** *m* (*na TV*) news; (*em jornal*) news section; **~arista** *m/f* (*na TV*) newsreader; (*em jornal*) news reporter; **~oso** /o/ *a* **agência ~osa** news agency

**notifi|cação** /notʃifika'sãw/ *f* notification; **~car** *vt* notify

**notívago** /no'tʃivagu/ *a* nocturnal □ *m* night person

**notório** /no'tɔriu/ *a* well-known

**noturno** /no'turnu/ *a* night; *<animal>* nocturnal

**nova** /'nɔva/ *f* piece of news; **~mente** *adv* again

**novato** /no'vatu/ *m* novice

**nove** /'nɔvi/ *a & m* nine; **~centos** *a & m* nine hundred

**novela** /no'vɛla/ *f* (*na TV*) soap opera; (*livro*) novella

**novembro** /no'vẽbru/ *m* November

**noventa** /no'vẽta/ *a & m* ninety

**noviço** /no'visu/ *m* novice

**novidade** /novi'dadʒi/ *f* novelty; (*notícia*) piece of news; *pl* (*notícias*) news

**novilho** /no'viʎu/ *m* calf

**novo** /'novu/ *a* new; (*jovem*) young; **de ~** again; **~ em folha** brand new

**noz** /nɔs/ *f* walnut; **~ moscada** nutmeg

**nu** /nu/ *a* (*f* **~a**) *<corpo, pessoa>* naked; *<braço, parede, quarto>* bare □ *m* nude; **~ em pêlo** stark naked; **a verdade ~a e crua** the plain truth

**nuança** /nu'ãsa/ *f* nuance

**nu|blado** /nu'bladu/ *a* cloudy; **~blar** *vt* cloud; **~blar-se** *vpr* cloud over

**nuca** /'nuka/ *f* nape of the neck

**nuclear** /nukli'ar/ *a* nuclear

**núcleo** /'nukliu/ *m* nucleus

**nu|dez** /nu'des/ *f* nakedness; (*na TV etc*) nudity; (*da parede etc*) bareness; **~dismo** *m* nudism; **~dista** *m/f* nudist

**nulo** /'nulu/ *a* void

**num, numa(s) = em + um, uma(s)**

**nume|ral** /nume'raw/ (*pl* ~**rais**) *a* & *m* numeral; ~**rar** *vt* number

**numérico** /nu'mɛriku/ *a* numerical

**número** /'numeru/ *m* number; (*de jornal, revista*) issue; (*de sapatos*) size; (*espetáculo*) act; **fazer** ~ make up the numbers

**numeroso** /nume'rozu/ *a* numerous

**nunca** /'nũka/ *adv* never; ~ **mais** never again

**nuns** = **em** + **uns**

**nupci|al** /nupsi'aw/ (*pl* ~**ais**) *a* bridal

**núpcias** /'nupsias/ *f pl* marriage

**nu|trição** /nutri'sãw/ *f* nutrition; ~**trir** *vt* nourish; (*fig*) harbour <*ódio, esperança*>; ~**tritivo** *a* nourishing; <*valor*> nutritional

**nuvem** /'nuvẽ/ *f* cloud

# O

**o** /u/ *artigo* the □ *pron* (*homem*) him; (*coisa*) it; (*você*) you; ~ **que** (*a coisa que*) what; (*aquele que*) the one that; ~ **quê?** what?; **meu livro e** ~ **do João** my book and John's (one)

**ó** /ɔ/ *int* (*fam*) look

**ô** /o/ *int* oh

**oásis** /o'azis/ *m invar* oasis

**oba** /'oba/ *int* great

**obcecar** /obise'kar/ *vt* obsess

**obe|decer** /obede'ser/ *vt* ~**decer a** obey; ~**diência** *f* obedience; ~**diente** *a* obedient

**obe|sidade** /obezi'dadʒi/ *f* obesity; ~**so** /e/ *a* obese

**óbito** /'ɔbitu/ *m* death

**obituário** /obitu'ariu/ *m* obituary

**obje|ção** /obiʒe'sãw/ *f* objection; ~**tar** *vt/i* object (**a** to)

**objeti|va** /obiʒe'tʃiva/ *f* lens; ~**vidade** *f* objectivity; ~**vo** *a* & *m* objective

**objeto** /obi'ʒɛtu/ *m* object

**oblíquo** /o'blikwu/ *a* oblique; <*olhar*> sidelong

**obliterar** /oblite'rar/ *vt* obliterate

**oblongo** /o'blõgu/ *a* oblong

**obo|é** /obo'ɛ/ *m* oboe; ~**ísta** *m/f* oboist

**obra** /'ɔbra/ *f* work; **em** ~**s** being renovated; ~ **de arte** work of art; ~ **de caridade** charity; ~**prima** (*pl* ~**s-primas**) *f* masterpiece

**obri|gação** /obriga'sãw/ *f* obligation; (*título*) bond; ~**gado** *int* thank you; (*não querendo*) no thank you; ~**gar** *vt* force, oblige (**a** to); ~**gar-se** *vpr* undertake (**a** to); ~**gatório** *a* obligatory, compulsory

**obsce|nidade** /obiseni'dadʒi/ *f* obscenity; ~**no** /e/ *a* obscene

**obscu|ridade** /obiskuri'dadʒi/ *f* obscurity; ~**ro** *a* obscure

**obséquio** /obi'sɛkiu/ *m* favour

**obsequioso** /obiseki'ozu/ *a* obsequious

**obser|vação** /obiserva'sãw/ *f* observation; ~**vador** *a* observant □ *m* observer; ~**vância** *f* observance; ~**var** *vt* observe; ~**vatório** *m* observatory

**obses|são** /obise'sãw/ *f* obsession; ~**sivo** *a* obsessive

**obsoleto** /obiso'letu/ *a* obsolete

**obstáculo** /obis'takulu/ *m* obstacle

**obstar** /obis'tar/ *vt* stand in the way (**a** of)

**obs|tetra** /obis'tɛtra/ *m/f* obstetrician; ~**tetrícia** *f* obstetrics; ~**tétrico** *a* obstetric

**obsti|nação** /obistina'sãw/ *f* obstinacy; ~**nado** *a* obstinate; ~**nar-se** *vpr* insist (**em** on)

**obstru|ção** /obistru'sãw/ *f* obstruction; ~**ir** *vt* obstruct

**ob|tenção** /obitẽ'sãw/ *f* obtaining; ~**ter** *vt* obtain

**obtu|ração** /obitura'sãw/ *f* filling; ~**rador** *m* shutter; ~**rar** *vt* fill <*dente*>

**obtuso** /obi'tuzu/ *a* obtuse

**óbvio** /'ɔbviu/ *a* obvious

**ocasi|ão** /okazi'ãw/ *f* occasion; (*oportunidade*) opportunity; (*compra*) bargain; ~**onal** (*pl* ~**onais**) *a* chance; ~**onar** *vt* cause

**Oceania** /osia'nia/ *f* Oceania

**oce|ânico** /osi'aniku/ *a* ocean; ~**ano** *m* ocean

**ociden|tal** /osidẽ'taw/ (*pl* ~**tais**) *a* western □ *m/f* Westerner; ~**te** *m* West

**ócio** /'ɔsiu/ *m* (*lazer*) leisure; (*falta de trabalho*) idleness

**ocioso** /osi'ozu/ *a* idle □ *m* idler

**oco** /'oku/ *a* hollow; <*cabeça*> empty

**ocor|rência** /oko'xẽsia/ *f* occurrence; ~**rer** *vi* occur (**a** to)

**ocu|lar** /oku'lar/ *a* **testemunha** ~**lar** eye witness; ~**lista** *m/f* optician

**óculos** /'ɔkulus/ *m pl* glasses; ~ **de sol** sunglasses

**ocul|tar** /okuw'tar/ *vt* conceal; ~**to** *a* hidden; (*sobrenatural*) occult

**ocu|pação** /okupa'sãw/ *f* occupation; ~**pado** *a* <*pessoa*> busy; <*cadeira*> taken; <*telefone*> engaged, (*Amer*) busy; ~**par** *vt* occupy; take up <*tempo, espaço*>; hold <*cargo*>; ~**par-se** *vpr* keep busy; ~**par-se com** *ou* **de** be involved with <*política, literatura etc*>; take care of <*cliente, doente, problema*>; occupy one's time with <*leitura, palavras cruzadas etc*>

**ode** /'ɔdʒi/ *f* ode

**odiar** /o'dʒi'ar/ vt hate

**ódio** /'ɔdʒiu/ m hatred, hate; (raiva) anger

**odioso** /odʒi'ozu/ a hateful

**odontologia** /odõtolo'ʒia/ f dentistry

**odor** /o'dor/ m odour

**oeste** /o'ɛstʃi/ a & m west

**ofe|gante** /ofe'gãtʃi/ a panting; ~gar vi pant

**ofen|der** /ofẽ'der/ vt offend; ~der-se vpr take offence; ~sa f insult; ~siva f offensive; ~sivo a offensive

**ofere|cer** /ofere'ser/ vt offer; ~cer-se vpr <pessoa> offer o.s. (como as); <ocasião> arise; ~cer-se para ajudar offer to help; ~cimento m offer

**oferenda** /ofe'rẽda/ f offering

**oferta** /o'fɛrta/ f offer; em ~ on offer; a ~ e a demanda supply and demand

**ofici|al** /ofisi'aw/ (pl ~ais) a official □ m officer; ~alizar vt make official; ~ar vi officiate

**oficina** /ofi'sina/ f workshop; (para carros) garage, (Amer) shop

**ofício** /o'fisiu/ m (profissão) trade; (na igreja) service

**oficioso** /ofisi'ozu/ a unofficial

**ofus|cante** /ofus'kãtʃi/ a dazzling; ~car vt dazzle <pessoa>; obscure <sol etc>; (fig: eclipsar) outshine

**oi** /oj/ int (cumprimento) hi; (resposta) yes?

**oi|tavo** /oi'tavu/ a & m eighth; ~tenta a & m eighty; ~to a & m eight; ~tocentos a & m eight hundred

**olá** /o'la/ int hello

**olaria** /ola'ria/ f pottery

**óleo** /'ɔliu/ m oil

**oleo|duto** /oliu'dutu/ m oil pipeline; ~so /o/ a oily

**olfato** /ow'fatu/ m sense of smell

**olhada** /o'ʎada/ f look; dar uma ~ have a look

**olhar** /o'ʎar/ vt look at; (assistir) watch □ vi look □ m look; ~ para look at; ~ por look after; e olhe lá (fam) and that's pushing it

**olheiras** /o'ʎeras/ f pl dark rings under one's eyes

**olho** /'oʎu/ m eye; a ~ nu with the naked eye; custar os ~s da cara cost a fortune; ficar de ~ keep an eye out; ficar de ~ em keep an eye on; pôr alg no ~ da rua throw s.o. out; não pregar o ~ not sleep a wink; ~ gordo ou grande envy; ~ mágico peephole; ~ roxo black eye

**Olimpíada** /oli'piada/ f Olympic Games

**olímpico** /o'lĩpiku/ a <jogos, vila> Olympic; (fig) blithe

**oliveira** /oli'vera/ f olive tree

**olmo** /'owmu/ m elm

**om|breira** /õ'brera/ f (para roupa) shoulder pad; ~bro m shoulder; dar de ~bros shrug one's shoulders

**omelete** /ome'lɛtʃi/, (Port) omeleta /ome'leta/ f omelette

**omis|são** /omi'sãw/ f omission; ~so a negligent, remiss

**omitir** /omi'tʃir/ vt omit

**omni-** (Port) veja oni-

**omoplata** /omo'plata/ f shoulder blade

**onça¹** /'õsa/ f (peso) ounce

**onça²** /'õsa/ f (animal) jaguar

**onda** /'õda/ f wave; pegar ~ (fam) surf

**onde** /'õdʒi/ adv where; por ~? which way?; ~ quer que wherever

**ondu|lação** /õdula'sãw/ f undulation; (do cabelo) wave; ~lado a wavy; ~lante a undulating; ~lar vt wave <cabelo> □ vi undulate

**onerar** /one'rar/ vt burden

**ônibus** /'onibus/ m invar bus; ~ espacial space shuttle

**onipotente** /onipo'tẽtʃi/ a omnipotent

**onírico** /o'niriku/ a dreamlike

**onisciente** /onisi'ẽtʃi/ a omniscient

**onomatopéia** /onomato'pɛja/ f onomatopoeia

**ontem** /'õtẽ/ adv yesterday

**onze** /'õzi/ a & m eleven

**opaco** /o'paku/ a opaque

**opala** /o'pala/ f opal

**opção** /opi'sãw/ f option

**ópera** /'ɔpera/ f opera

**ope|ração** /opera'sãw/ f operation; (bancária etc) transaction; ~rador m operator; ~rar vt operate; operate on <doente>; work <milagre> □ vi operate; ~rar-se vpr (acontecer) come about; (fazer operação) have an operation; ~rário a working □ m worker

**opereta** /ope'reta/ f operetta

**opinar** /opi'nar/ vt think □ vi express one's opinion

**opinião** /opini'ãw/ f opinion; na minha ~ in my opinion; ~ pública public opinion

**ópio** /'ɔpiu/ m opium

**opor** /o'por/ vt put up <resistência, argumento>; (pôr em contraste) contrast (a with); ~-se a (não aprovar) oppose; (ser diferente) contrast with

**oportu|nidade** /oportuni'dadʒi/ f opportunity; ~nista a & m/f opportunist; ~no a opportune

**oposi|ção** /opozi'sãw/ f opposition (a to); ~cionista a opposition □ m/f opposition politician

**oposto** /o'postu/ a & m opposite

**opres|são** /opreˈsãw/ f oppression; (*no peito*) tightness; **~sivo** a oppressive; **~sor** m oppressor

**oprimir** /opriˈmir/ vt oppress; (*com trabalho*) weigh down □ vi be oppressive

**optar** /opiˈtar/ vi opt (**por** for); **~ por ir** opt to go

**óptica, óptico** *veja* ótica, ótico

**opu|lência** /opuˈlẽsia/ f opulence; **~lento** a opulent

**ora** /ˈɔra/ adv & conj now □ int come; **~ essa!** come now!; **~ ..., ~ ...** first ..., then

**oração** /oraˈsãw/ f (*prece*) prayer; (*discurso*) oration; (*frase*) clause

**oráculo** /oˈrakulu/ m oracle

**orador** /oraˈdor/ m orator

**oral** /oˈraw/ (*pl* **orais**) a & f oral

**orar** /oˈrar/ vi pray

**órbita** /ˈɔrbita/ f orbit; (*do olho*) socket

**orçamen|tário** /orsamẽˈtariu/ a budgetary; **~to** m (*plano financeiro*) budget; (*previsão dos custos*) estimate

**orçar** /orˈsar/ vt estimate (**em** at)

**ordeiro** /orˈderu/ a orderly

**ordem** /ˈɔrdẽ/ f order; **por ~ alfabética** in alphabetical order; **~ de pagamento** banker's draft; **~ do dia** agenda

**orde|nação** /ordenaˈsãw/ f ordering; (*de padre*) ordination; **~nado** a ordered □ m wages; **~nar** vt order; put in order <*papéis, livros etc*>; ordain <*padre*>

**ordenhar** /ordeˈɲar/ vt milk

**ordinário** /ordʒiˈnariu/ a (*normal*) ordinary; (*grosseiro*) vulgar; (*de má qualidade*) inferior; (*sem caráter*) rough

**orégano** /oˈrɛganu/ m oregano

**ore|lha** /oˈreʎa/ f ear; **~lhão** m phone booth; **~lhudo** a with big ears; **ser ~lhudo** have big ears

**orfanato** /orfaˈnatu/ m orphanage

**ór|fão** /ˈɔrfãw/ (*pl* **~fãos**) a & m (*f* **~fã**) orphan

**orgânico** /orˈgɐniku/ a organic

**orga|nismo** /orgaˈnizmu/ m organism; (*do Estado etc*) institution; **~nista** m/f organist

**organi|zação** /organizaˈsãw/ f organization; **~zador** a organizing □ m organizer; **~zar** vt organize

**órgão** /ˈɔrgãw/ (*pl* **~s**) m organ; (*do Estado etc*) body

**orgasmo** /orˈgazmu/ m orgasm

**orgia** /orˈʒia/ f orgy

**orgu|lhar** /orguˈʎar/ vt make proud; **~lhar-se** vpr be proud (**de** of); **~lho** m pride; **~lhoso** /o/ a proud

**orien|tação** /oriẽtaˈsãw/ f orientation; (*direção*) direction; (*vocacional etc*) guidance; **~tador** m advisor; **~tal** (*pl* **~tais**) a eastern; (*da Ásia*) oriental; **~tar** vt direct; (*aconselhar*) advise; (*situar*) position; **~tar-se** get one's bearings; **~tar-se por** be guided by; **~te** m east; **Oriente Médio** Middle East; **Extremo Oriente** Far East

**orifício** /oriˈfisiu/ m opening; (*no corpo*) orifice

**origem** /oˈriʒẽ/ f origin; **dar ~ a** give rise to; **ter ~** originate

**origi|nal** /oriʒiˈnaw/ (*pl* **~nais**) a & m original; **~nalidade** f originality; **~nar** vt give rise to; **~nar-se** vpr originate; **~nário** a <*planta, animal*> native (**de** to); <*pessoa*> originating (**de** from)

**oriundo** /oˈrjũdu/ a originating (**de** from)

**orla** /ˈɔrla/ f border; **~ marítima** seafront

**ornamen|tação** /ornamẽtaˈsãw/ f ornamentation; **~tal** (*pl* **~tais**) a ornamental; **~tar** vt decorate; **~to** m ornament

**orques|tra** /orˈkɛstra/ f orchestra; **~tra sinfônica** symphony orchestra; **~tral** (*pl* **~trais**) a orchestral; **~trar** vt orchestrate

**orquídea** /orˈkidʒia/ f orchid

**ortodoxo** /ortoˈdɔksu/ a orthodox

**orto|grafia** /ortograˈfia/ f spelling, orthography; **~gráfico** a orthographic

**orto|pedia** /ortopeˈdʒia/ f orthopaedics; **~pédico** a orthopaedic; **~pedista** m/f orthopaedic surgeon

**orvalho** /orˈvaʎu/ m dew

**os** /us/ *artigo* & *pron veja* o

**oscilar** /osiˈlar/ vi oscillate

**ósseo** /ˈɔsiu/ a bone

**os|so** /ˈosu/ m bone; **~sudo** a bony

**ostensivo** /ostẽˈsivu/ a ostensible

**osten|tação** /ostẽtaˈsãw/ f ostentation; **~tar** vt show off; **~toso** a showy, ostentatious

**osteopata** /ostʃioˈpata/ m/f osteopath

**ostra** /ˈostra/ f oyster

**ostracismo** /ostraˈsizmu/ m ostracism

**otário** /oˈtariu/ m (*fam*) fool

**óti|ca** /ˈɔtʃika/ f (*ciência*) optics; (*loja*) optician's; (*ponto de vista*) viewpoint; **~co** a optical

**otimis|mo** /otʃiˈmizmu/ m optimism; **~ta** m/f optimist □ a optimistic

**ótimo** /ˈɔtʃimu/ a excellent

**otorrino** /otoˈxinu/ m ear, nose and throat specialist

**ou** /o/ conj or; **~ ... ~ ...** either... or...; **~ seja** in other words

**ouriço** /oˈrisu/ m hedgehog; **~do-mar** (*pl* **~s-do-mar**) m sea urchin

**ouri|ves** /o'rivis/ *m/f invar* jeweller; ~**vesaria** *f* (*loja*) jeweller's

**ouro** /'oru/ *m* gold; *pl* (*naipe*) diamonds; **de ~** golden

**ou|sadia** /oza'dʒia/ *f* daring; (*uma*) daring step; ~**sado** *a* daring; ~**sar** *vt/i* dare

**outdoor** /'awtdor/ (*pl* ~s) *m* billboard

**outo|nal** /oto'naw/ (*pl* ~**nais**) *a* autumnal; ~**no** /o/ *m* autumn, (*Amer*) fall

**outorgar** /otor'gar/ *vt* grant

**ou|trem** /o'trẽj/ *pron* (*outro*) someone else; (*outros*) others; ~**tro** *a* other □ *pron* (*um*) another (one); *pl* others; ~**tro copo** another glass; ~**tra coisa** something else; ~**tro dia** the other day; **no ~tro dia** the next day; ~**tra vez** again; ~**trora** *adv* once upon a time; ~**trossim** *adv* equally

**outubro** /o'tubru/ *m* October

**ou|vido** /o'vidu/ *m* ear; **de ~vido** by ear; **dar ~vidos a** listen to; ~**vinte** *m/f* listener; ~**vir** *vt* hear; (*atentamente*) listen to □ *vi* hear; ~**vir dizer que** hear that; ~**vir falar de** hear of

**ovação** /ova'sãw/ *f* ovation

**oval** /o'vaw/ (*pl* **ovais**) *a & f* oval

**ovário** /o'variu/ *m* ovary

**ovelha** /o'veʎa/ *f* sheep

**óvni** /'ɔvni/ *m* UFO

**ovo** /'ovu/ *m* egg; ~ **cozido/frito/ mexido/pochê** boiled/fried/ scrambled/poached egg

**oxi|genar** /oksiʒe'nar/ *vt* bleach <*cabelo*>; ~**gênio** *m* oxygen

**ozônio** /o'zoniu/ *m* ozone

# P

**pá** /pa/ *f* spade; (*de hélice*) blade; (*de moinho*) sail □ *m* (Port: *fam*) mate

**pacato** /pa'katu/ *a* quiet

**paci|ência** /pasi'ẽsia/ *f* patience; ~**ente** *a & m/f* patient

**pacificar** /pasifi'kar/ *vt* pacify

**pacífico** /pa'sifiku/ *a* peaceful; **Oceano Pacífico** Pacific Ocean; **ponto ~** undisturbed point

**pacifis|mo** /pasi'fizmu/ *m* pacifism; ~**ta** *a & m/f* pacifist

**paço** /'pasu/ *m* palace

**pacote** /pa'kɔtʃi/ *m* (*de biscoitos etc*) packet; (*mandado pelo correio*) parcel; (*econômico, turístico, software*) package

**pacto** /'paktu/ *m* pact

**padaria** /pada'ria/ *f* baker's (shop), bakery

**padecer** /pade'ser/ *vt/i* suffer

**padeiro** /pa'deru/ *m* baker

**padiola** /padʒi'ɔla/ *f* stretcher

**padrão** /pa'drãw/ *m* standard; (*desenho*) pattern

**padrasto** /pa'drastu/ *m* stepfather

**padre** /'padri/ *m* priest

**padrinho** /pa'drinu/ *m* (*de batismo*) godfather; (*de casamento*) best man

**padroeiro** /padro'eru/ *m* patron saint

**padronizar** /padroni'zar/ *vt* standardize

**paetê** /paj'te/ *m* sequin

**paga** /'paga/ *f* pay; ~**mento** *m* payment

**pa|gão** /pa'gãw/ (*pl* ~**gãos**) *a & m* (*f* ~**gã**) pagan

**pagar** /pa'gar/ *vt* pay for <*compra, erro etc*>; pay <*dívida, conta, empregado etc*>; pay back <*empréstimo*>; repay <*gentileza etc*> □ *vi* pay; **eu pago para ver** I'll believe it when I see it

**página** /'paʒina/ *f* page

**pago** /'pagu/ *a* paid □ *pp de* **pagar**

**pagode** /pa'gɔdʒi/ *m* (*torre*) pagoda; (*fam*) singalong

**pai** /paj/ *m* father; *pl* (*pai e mãe*) parents; ~**-de-santo** (*pl* ~**s-de-santo**) *m* macumba priest

**pai|nel** /paj'nɛw/ (*pl* ~**néis**) *m* panel; (*de carro*) dashboard

**paio** /'paju/ *m* pork sausage

**pairar** /paj'rar/ *vi* hover

**país** /pa'is/ *m* country; **País de Gales** Wales; **Países Baixos** Netherlands

**paisa|gem** /paj'zaʒẽ/ *f* landscape; ~**gista** *m/f* landscape gardener

**paisana** /paj'zana/ *f* à ~ <*policial*> in plain clothes; <*soldado*> in civilian clothes

**paixão** /pa'ʃãw/ *f* passion

**pala** /'pala/ *f* (*de boné*) peak; (*de automóvel*) sun visor

**palácio** /pa'lasiu/ *m* palace

**paladar** /pala'dar/ *m* palate, taste

**palanque** /pa'lãki/ *m* stand

**palavra** /pa'lavra/ *f* word; **pedir a ~** ask to speak; **ter ~** be reliable; **tomar a ~** start to speak; **sem ~** <*pessoa*> unreliable; ~ **de ordem** watchword; ~**s cruzadas** crossword

**palavrão** /pala'vrãw/ *m* swearword

**palco** /'pawku/ *m* stage

**palestino** /pales'tʃinu/ *a & m* Palestinian

**palestra** /pa'lɛstra/ *f* lecture

**paleta** /pa'leta/ *f* palette

**paletó** /pale'tɔ/ *m* jacket

**palha** /'paʎa/ *f* straw

**palha|çada** /paʎa'sada/ *f* joke; ~**ço** *m* clown

**paliativo** /palia'tʃivu/ *a & m* palliative

**palidez** /pali'des/ *f* paleness

**pálido** /'palidu/ *a* pale

**pali|tar** /pali'tar/ *vt* pick □ *vi* pick one's teeth; **~teiro** *m* toothpick holder; **~to** *m* (*para dentes*) toothpick; (*de fósforo*) matchstick; (*pessoa magra*) beanpole

**pal|ma** /'pawma/ *f* palm; *pl* (*aplauso*) clapping; **bater ~mas** clap; **~meira** *f* palm tree; **~mito** *m* palm heart; **~mo** *m* span; **~mo a ~mo** inch by inch

**palpá|vel** /paw'pavew/ (*pl* **~veis**) *a* palpable

**pálpebra** /'pawpebra/ *f* eyelid

**palpi|tação** /pawpita'sãw/ *f* palpitation; **~tante** *a* (*fig*) thrilling; **~tar** *vi* (*coração*) flutter; (*pessoa*) tremble; (*dar palpite*) stick one's oar in; **~te** *m* (*pressentimento*) hunch; (*no jogo etc*) tip; **dar ~te** stick one's oar in

**panacéia** /pana'sɛja/ *f* panacea

**Panamá** /pana'ma/ *m* Panama

**panamenho** /pana'meɲu/ *a & m* Panamanian

**pan-americano** /panameri'kanu/ *a* Pan-American

**pança** /'pãsa/ *f* paunch

**pancada** /pã'kada/ *f* blow; **~ d'água** downpour; **~ria** *f* fight, punch-up

**pâncreas** /'pãkrias/ *m invar* pancreas

**pançudo** /pã'sudu/ *a* paunchy

**panda** /'pãda/ *f* panda

**pandarecos** /pãda'rɛkus/ *m pl* **aos** *ou* **em ~** battered

**pandeiro** /pã'deru/ *m* tambourine

**pandemônio** /pãde'moniu/ *m* pandemonium

**pane** /'pani/ *f* breakdown

**panela** /pa'nɛla/ *f* saucepan; **~ de pressão** pressure cooker

**panfleto** /pã'fletu/ *m* pamphlet

**pânico** /'paniku/ *m* panic; **em ~** in a panic; **entrar em ~** panic

**panifica|ção** /panifika'sãw/ *f* bakery; **~dora** *f* bakery

**pano** /'panu/ *m* cloth; **~ de fundo** backdrop; **~ de pó** duster; **~ de pratos** tea towel

**pano|rama** /pano'rama/ *m* panorama; **~râmico** *a* panoramic

**panqueca** /pã'kɛka/ *f* pancake

**panta|nal** /pãta'naw/ (*pl* **~nais**) *m* marshland

**pântano** /'pãtanu/ *m* marsh

**pantanoso** /pãta'nozu/ *a* marshy

**pantera** /pã'tɛra/ *f* panther

**pão** /pãw/ (*pl* **pães**) *m* bread; **~ de fôrma** sliced loaf; **~ integral** brown bread; **~-de-ló** *m* sponge cake; **~duro** (*pl* **pães-duros**) (*fam*) *a* stingy, tight-fisted □ *m/f* skinflint; **~zinho** *m* bread roll

**Papa** /'papa/ *m* Pope

**papa** /'papa/ *f* (*de nenem*) food; (*arroz etc*) mush

**papagaio** /papa'gaju/ *m* parrot

**papai** /pa'paj/ *m* dad, daddy; **Papai Noël** Father Christmas

**papar** /pa'par/ *vt/i* (*fam*) eat

**papari|car** /papari'kar/ *vt* pamper; **~cos** *m pl* pampering

**pa|pel** /pa'pɛw/ (*pl* **~péis**) *m* (*de escrever etc*) paper; (*um*) piece of paper; (*numa peça, filme*) part; (*fig: função*) role; **de ~ pel passado** officially; **~pel de alumínio** aluminium foil; **~pel higiênico** toilet paper; **~pelada** *f* paperwork; **~pelão** *m* cardboard; **~pelaria** *f* stationer's (shop); **~pelzinho** *m* scrap of paper

**papo** /'papu/ *f* (*fam: conversa*) talk; (*do rosto*) double chin; **bater um ~** (*fam*) have a chat; **~ furado** idle talk

**papoula** /pa'pola/ *f* poppy

**páprica** /'paprika/ *f* paprika

**paque|ra** /pa'kɛra/ *f* (*fam*) pick-up; **~rador** *a* flirtatious □ *m* flirt; **~rar** *vt* flirt with <*pessoa*>; eye up <*vestido, carro etc*> □ *vi* flirt

**paquista|nês** /pakista'nes/ *a & m* (*f* **~nesa**) Pakistani

**Paquistão** /pakis'tãw/ *m* Pakistan

**par** /par/ *a* even □ *m* pair; (*parceiro*) partner; **a ~ de** up to date with <*notícias etc*>; **sem ~** unequalled

**para** /'para/ *prep* for; (*a*) to; **~ que** that; **~ quê?** what for?; **~ casa** home; **estar ~ sair** be about to leave; **era ~ eu ir** I was supposed to go

**para|benizar** /parabeni'zar/ *vt* congratulate (**por** on); **~béns** *m pl* congratulations

**parábola** /pa'rabola/ *f* (*conto*) parable; (*curva*) parabola

**parabóli|co** /para'bɔliku/ *a* **antena ~ca** satellite dish

**pára|-brisa** /para'briza/ *m* windscreen, (*Amer*) windshield; **~choque** *m* bumper

**para|da** /pa'rada/ *f* stop; (*interrupção*) stoppage; (*militar*) parade; (*fam: coisa difícil*) ordeal, challenge; **~da cardíaca** cardiac arrest; **~deiro** *m* whereabouts

**paradisíaco** /paradʒi'ziaku/ *a* idyllic

**parado** /pa'radu/ *a* <*trânsito, carro*> at a standstill, stopped; (*fig*) <*pessoa*> dull; **ficar ~** <*pessoa*> stand still; <*trânsito*> come to a standstill; (*fig: deixar de trabalhar*) stop work

**parado|xal** /paradok'saw/ (*pl* **~xais**) *a* paradoxical; **~xo** /ɔ/ *m* paradox

**parafina** /para'fina/ *f* paraffin

**paráfrase** /pa'rafrazi/ *f* paraphrase

**parafrasear** /parafrazi'ar/ *vt* paraphrase

**parafuso** /para'fuzu/ *f* screw; **entrar em ~** get into a state

**para|gem** /pa'raʒẽ/ *f* (*Port: parada*) stop; **nestas ~gens** in these parts

**parágrafo** /pa'ragrafu/ *m* paragraph

**Paraguai** /para'gwaj/ *m* Paraguay

**paraguaio** /para'gwaju/ *a & m* Paraguayan

**paraíso** /para'izu/ *m* paradise

**pára-lama** /para'lama/ *m* (*de carro*) wing, (*Amer*) fender; (*de bicicleta*) mudguard

**parale|la** /para'lɛla/ *f* parallel; *pl* (*aparelho*) parallel bars; **~lepípedo** *m* paving stone; **~lo** /ɛ/ *a & m* parallel

**para|lisar** /parali'zar/ *vt* paralyse; bring to a halt *<fábrica, produção>*; **~lisar-se** *vpr* become paralysed; *<fábrica, produção>* grind to a halt; **~lisia** *f* paralysis; **~lítico** *a & m* paralytic

**paranói|a** /para'nɔja/ *f* paranoia; **~co** *a* paranoid

**parapeito** /para'pejtu/ *m* (*muro*) parapet; (*da janela*) window-sill

**pára-que|das** /para'kɛdas/ *m invar* parachute; **~dista** *m/f* parachutist; (*militar*) paratrooper

**parar** /pa'rar/ *vt/i* stop; **~ de fumar** stop smoking; **ir ~** end up

**pára-raios** /para'xajus/ *m invar* lightning conductor

**parasita** /para'zita/ *a & m/f* parasite

**parceiro** /par'seru/ *m* partner

**parce|la** /par'sɛla/ *f* (*de terreno*) plot; (*prestação*) instalment; **~lar** *vt* spread *<pagamento>*

**parceria** /parse'ria/ *f* partnership

**parci|al** /parsi'aw/ (*pl* **~ais**) *a* partial; (*partidário*) biased; **~alidade** *f* bias

**parco** /'parku/ *a* frugal; *<recursos>* scant

**par|dal** /par'daw/ (*pl* **~dais**) *m* sparrow; **~do** *a* *<papel>* brown; *<pessoa>* mulatto

**pare|cer** /pare'ser/ *vi* (*ter aparência de*) seem; (*ter semelhança com*) be like; **~cer-se com** look like, resemble □ *m* opinion; **~cido** *a* similar (**com** to)

**parede** /pa'redʒi/ *f* wall

**paren|te** /pa'rẽtʃi/ *m/f* relative, relation; **~tesco** /e/ *m* relationship

**parêntese** /pa'rẽtʃizi/ *f* parenthesis; *pl* (*sinais*) brackets, parentheses

**paridade** /pari'dadʒi/ *f* parity

**parir** /pa'rir/ *vt* give birth to □ *vi* give birth

**parlamen|tar** /parlamẽ'tar/ *a* parliamentary □ *m/f* member of parliament; **~tarismo** *m* parliamentary system; **~to** *m* parliament

**parmesão** /parme'zãw/ *a & m* (**queijo**) **~** Parmesan (cheese)

**paródia** /pa'rɔdʒia/ *f* parody

**parodiar** /parodʒi'ar/ *vt* parody

**paróquia** /pa'rɔkia/ *f* parish

**parque** /'parki/ *m* park

**parte** /'partʃi/ *f* part; (*quinhão*) share; (*num litígio, contrato*) party; **a maior ~** de most of; **à ~** (*de lado*) aside; (*separadamente*) separately; **um erro da sua ~** a mistake on your part; **em ~** in part; **em alguma ~** somewhere; **por toda ~** everywhere; **por ~ do pai** on one's father's side; **fazer ~ de** be part of; **tomar ~ em** take part in

**parteira** /par'tera/ *f* midwife

**partici|pação** /partʃisipa'sãw/ *f* participation; (*numa empresa, nos lucros*) share; **~pante** *a* participating □ *m/f* participant; **~par** *vi* take part (**de** *ou* **em** in)

**particípio** /partʃi'sipiu/ *m* participle

**partícula** /par'tʃikula/ *f* particle

**particu|lar** /partʃiku'lar/ *a* private; (*especial*) unusual □ *m* (*pessoa*) private individual; *pl* (*detalhes*) particulars; **em ~lar** (*especialmente*) in particular; (*a sós*) in private; **~laridade** *f* peculiarity

**partida** /par'tʃida/ *f* (*saída*) departure; (*de corrida*) start; (*de futebol, xadrez etc*) match; **dar ~ em** start up

**par|tidário** /partʃi'dariu/ *a* partisan □ *m* supporter; **~tido** *a* broken □ *m* (*político*) party; (*casamento, par*) match; **tirar ~tido de** benefit from; **tomar o ~tido de** side with; **~tilha** *f* division; **~tir** *vi* (*sair*) depart; *<corredor>* start □ *vt* break; **~tir-se** *vpr* break; **a ~tir de ...** from ... onwards; **~tir para** (*fam*) resort to; **~tir para outra** do something different, change direction; **~titura** *f* score

**parto** /'partu/ *m* birth

**parvo** /'parvu/ *a* (*Port*) stupid

**Páscoa** /'paskoa/ *f* Easter

**pas|mar** /paz'mar/ *vt* amaze; **~marse** *vpr* be amazed (**com** at); **~mo** *a* amazed □ *m* amazement

**passa** /'pasa/ *f* raisin

**pas|sada** /pa'sada/ *f* **dar uma ~sada em** call in at; **~sadeira** *f* (*mulher*) woman who irons; (*Port: faixa*) zebra crossing, (*Amer*) crosswalk; **~sado** *a* *<ano, mês, semana>* last; *<tempo, particípio etc>* past; *<fruta, comida>* off □ *m* past; **são duas horas ~sadas** it's gone two o'clock; **bem/mal ~sado** *<bife>* well done/rare

**passa|geiro** /pasa'ʒeru/ *m* passenger □ *a* passing; **~gem** *f* passage; (*bilhete*) ticket; **de ~gem** *<dizer etc>* in passing; **estar de ~gem** be passing

through; ~**gem de ida e volta** return ticket, (*Amer*) round trip ticket
**passaporte** /pasa'pɔrtʃi/ *m* passport
**passar** /pa'sar/ *vt* pass; spend <*tempo*>; cross <*ponte, rio*>; (*a ferro*) iron <*roupa etc*>; (*aplicar*) put on <*creme, batom etc*> □ *vi* pass; <*dor, medo, chuva etc*> go; (*ser aceitável*) be passable □ *m* passing; ~**se** *vpr* happen; **passou a beber muito** he started to drink a lot; **passei dos 30 anos** I'm over thirty; **não passa de um boato** it's nothing more than a rumour; ~ **por** go through; go along <*rua*>; (*ser considerado*) be taken for; **fazer-se** ~ **por** pass o.s. off as; ~ **por cima de** (*fig*) overlook; ~ **sem** do without
**passarela** /pasa'rɛla/ *f* (*sobre rua*) footbridge; (*para desfile de moda*) catwalk
**pássaro** /'pasaru/ *m* bird
**passatempo** /pasa'tẽpu/ *m* pastime
**passe** /'pasi/ *m* pass
**pas|sear** /pasi'ar/ *vi* go out and about; (*viajar*) travel around □ *vt* take for a walk; ~**seata** *f* protest march; ~**seio** *m* outing; (*volta a pé*) walk; (*volta de carro*) drive; **dar um** ~**seio** (*a pé*) go for a walk; (*de carro*) go for a drive
**passio|nal** /pasio'naw/ (*pl* ~**nais**) *a* **crime** ~**nal** crime of passion
**passista** /pa'sista/ *m/f* dancer
**passí|vel** /pa'sivew/ (*pl* ~**veis**) *a* ~**vel de** subject to
**passi|vidade** /pasivi'dadʒi/ *f* passivity; ~**vo** *a* passive □ *m* (*com*) liabilities; (*ling*) passive
**passo** /'pasu/ *m* step; (*velocidade*) pace; (*barulho*) footstep; ~ **a** ~ step by step; **a dois** ~**s de** a stone's throw from; **dar um** ~ take a step
**pasta** /'pasta/ *f* (*matéria*) paste; (*bolsa*) briefcase; (*fichário*) folder; **ministro sem** ~ minister without portfolio; ~ **de dentes** toothpaste
**pas|tagem** /pas'taʒẽ/ *f* pasture; ~**tar** *vi* graze
**pas|tel** /pas'tɛw/ (*pl* ~**téis**) *m* (*para comer*) samosa; (*Port: doce*) pastry; (*para desenhar*) pastel; ~**telão** *m* (*comédia*) slapstick; ~**telaria** *f* (*loja*) samosa vendor, (*Port*) pastry shop; (*Port: pastéis*) pastries
**pasteurizado** /pastewri'zadu/ *a* pasteurized
**pastilha** /pas'tʃiʎa/ *f* pastille
**pas|to** /'pastu/ *m* (*erva*) fodder, feed; (*lugar*) pasture; ~**tor** *m* (*de gado*) shepherd; (*clérigo*) vicar; ~**tor alemão** (*cachorro*) Alsatian; ~**toral** (*pl* ~**torais**) *a* pastoral
**pata** /'pata/ *f* paw; ~**da** *f* kick
**patamar** /pata'mar/ *m* landing; (*fig*) level

**patê** /pa'te/ *m* pâté
**patente** /pa'tẽtʃi/ *a* obvious □ *f* (*mil*) rank; (*de invenção*) patent; ~**ar** *vt* patent <*produto, invenção*>
**pater|nal** /pater'naw/ (*pl* ~**nais**) *a* paternal; ~**nidade** *f* paternity; ~**no** /ɛ/ *a* paternal
**pate|ta** /pa'tɛta/ *a* daft, silly □ *m/f* fool; ~**tice** *f* stupidity; (*uma*) silly thing
**patético** /pa'tɛtʃiku/ *a* pathetic
**patíbulo** /pa'tʃibulu/ *m* gallows
**pati|faria** /patʃifa'ria/ *f* roguishness; (*uma*) dirty trick; ~**fe** *m* scoundrel
**patim** /pa'tʃĩ/ *m* skate; ~ **de rodas** roller skate
**pati|nação** /patʃina'sãw/ *f* skating; (*rinque*) skating rink; ~**nador** *m* skater; ~**nar** *vi* skate; <*carro*> skid; ~**nete** /ɛ/ *m* skateboard
**pátio** /'patʃiu/ *m* courtyard; (*de escola*) playground
**pato** /'patu/ *m* duck
**pato|logia** /patolo'ʒia/ *f* pathology; ~**lógico** *a* pathological; ~**logista** *m/f* pathologist
**patrão** /pa'trãw/ *m* boss
**pátria** /'patria/ *f* homeland
**patriar|ca** /patri'arka/ *m* patriarch; ~**cal** (*pl* ~**cais**) *a* patriarchal
**patrimônio** /patri'moniu/ *m* (*bens*) estate, property; (*fig: herança*) heritage
**patri|ota** /patri'ɔta/ *m/f* patriot; ~**ótico** *a* patriotic; ~**otismo** *m* patriotism
**patroa** /pa'troa/ *f* boss; (*fam: esposa*) missus, wife
**patro|cinador** /patrosina'dor/ *m* sponsor; ~**cinar** *vt* sponsor; ~**cínio** *m* sponsorship
**patru|lha** /pa'truʎa/ *f* patrol; ~**lhar** *vt/i* patrol
**pau** /paw/ *m* stick; (*fam: cruzeiro*) cruzeiro; (*chulo: pênis*) prick; *pl* (*naipe*) clubs; **a meio** ~ at half mast; **rachar** ~ (*fam: brigar*) row, fight like cat and dog; ~**lada** *f* blow with a stick
**paulista** /paw'lista/ *a & m/f* (*person*) from (the state of) São Paulo; ~**no a** *& m* (*person*) from (the city of) São Paulo
**pausa** /'pawza/ *f* pause; ~**do** *a* slow
**pauta** /'pawta/ *f* (*em papel*) lines; (*de música*) stave; (*fig: de discussão etc*) agenda; ~**do** *a* <*papel*> lined
**pavão** /pa'vãw/ *m* peacock
**pavilhão** /paviʎãw/ *m* pavilion; (*no jardim*) summerhouse
**pavimen|tar** /pavimẽ'tar/ *vt* pave; ~**to** *m* floor; (*de rua etc*) surface
**pavio** /pa'viu/ *m* wick
**pavor** /pa'vor/ *m* terror; **ter** ~ **de** be terrified of; ~**oso** /o/ *a* dreadful

**paz** /pas/ f peace; **fazer as ~es** make up

**pé** /pɛ/ m foot; (planta) plant; (de móvel) leg; **a ~** on foot; **ao ~ da letra** literally; **estar de ~** <festa etc> be on; **ficar de ~** stand up; **em ~** standing (up); **em ~ de igualdade** on an equal footing

**peão** /pi'ãw/ m (Port: pedestre) pedestrian; (no xadrez) pawn

**peça** /'pɛsa/ f piece; (de máquina, carro etc) part; (teatral) play; **pregar uma ~ em** play a trick on; **~ de reposição** spare part; **~ de vestuário** item of clothing

**pe|cado** /pe'kadu/ m sin; **~cador** m sinner; **~caminoso** /o/ a sinful; **~car** vi (contra a religião) sin; (fig) fall down

**pechin|cha** /pe'ʃiʃa/ f bargain; **~char** vi bargain, haggle

**peçonhento** /peso'ɲetu/ a animais **~s** vermin

**pecu|ária** /peku'aria/ f livestock-farming; **~ário** a livestock; **~arista** m/f livestock farmer

**peculi|ar** /pekuli'ar/ a peculiar; **~aridade** f peculiarity

**pecúlio** /pe'kuliu/ m savings

**pedaço** /pe'dasu/ m piece; **aos ~s** in pieces; **cair aos ~s** fall to pieces

**pedágio** /pe'daʒiu/ m toll; (cabine) tollbooth

**peda|gogia** /pedago'ʒia/ f education; **~gógico** a educational; **~gogo** /o/ m educationalist

**pe|dal** /pe'daw/ (pl ~dais) m pedal; **~dalar** vt/i pedal

**pedante** /pe'dãtʃi/ a pretentious □ m/f pseud

**pé|-de-atleta** /pɛdʒiat'lɛta/ m athlete's foot; **~-de-meia** (pl ~s-de-meia) m nest egg; **~-de-pato** (pl ~s-de-pato) m flipper

**pederneira** /peder'nera/ f flint

**pedes|tal** /pedes'taw/ (pl ~tais) m pedestal

**pedestre** /pe'dɛstri/ a & m/f pedestrian

**pé|-de-vento** /pɛdʒi'vẽtu/ (pl ~s-de-vento) m gust of wind

**pedia|tra** /pedʒi'atra/ m/f paediatrician; **~tria** f paediatrics

**pedicuro** /pedʒi'kuru/ m chiropodist, (Amer) podiatrist

**pe|dido** /pe'dʒidu/ m request; (encomenda) order; **a ~dido de** at the request of; **~dido de demissão** resignation; **~dido de desculpa** apology; **~dir** vt ask for; (num restaurante etc) order □ vi ask; (num restaurante etc) order; **~dir aco a alg** ask s.o. for sth; **~dir para alg ir** ask s.o. to go; **~dir desculpa** apologize; **~dir em casamento** propose to

**pedinte** /pe'dʒĩtʃi/ m/f beggar

**pedra** /'pɛdra/ f stone; **~ de gelo** ice cube; **chuva de ~** hail; **~ pomes** pumice stone

**pedregoso** /pedre'gozu/ a stony

**pedreiro** /pe'dreru/ m builder

**pegada** /pe'gada/ f footprint; (de goleiro) save

**pegajoso** /pega'ʒozu/ a sticky

**pegar** /pe'gar/ vt get; catch <bola, doença, ladrão, ônibus>; (segurar) get hold of; pick up <emissora, hábito, mania> □ vi (aderir) stick; <doença> be catching; <moda> catch on; <carro, motor> start; <mentira, desculpa> stick; **~-se** vpr come to blows; **~ bem/mal** go down well/badly; **~ fogo** catch fire; **pega essa rua** take that street; **~ em** grab; **~ no sono** get to sleep

**pego** /'pɛgu/ pp de **pegar**

**pei|dar** /pej'dar/ vi (chulo) fart; **~do** m (chulo) fart

**pei|to** /'pejtu/ m chest; (seio) breast; (fig: coragem) guts; **~toril** (pl ~toris) m window-sill; **~tudo** a <mulher> busty; (fig: corajoso) gutsy

**pei|xaria** /pe'ʃaria/ f fishmonger's; **~xe** m fish; **Peixes** (signo) Pisces; **~xeiro** m fishmonger

**pela** = **por** + **a**

**pelado** /pe'ladu/ a (nu) naked, in the nude

**pelan|ca** /pe'lãka/ f roll of fat; pl flab; **~cudo** a flabby

**pelar** /pe'lar/ vt peel <fruta, batata>; skin <animal>; (fam: tomar dinheiro de) fleece

**pelas** = **por** + **as**

**pele** /'pɛli/ f skin; (como roupa) fur; **~teiro** m furrier; **~teria** f furrier's

**pelica** /pe'lika/ f **luvas de ~** kid gloves

**pelicano** /peli'kanu/ m pelican

**película** /pe'likula/ f skin

**pelo** = **por** + **o**

**pêlo** /'pelu/ m hair; (de animal) coat; **nu em ~** stark naked; **montar em ~** ride bareback

**pelos** = **por** + **os**

**pelotão** /pelo'tãw/ m platoon

**pelúcia** /pe'lusia/ f **bicho de ~** soft toy, fluffy animal

**peludo** /pe'ludu/ a hairy

**pena¹** /'pena/ f (de ave) feather; (de caneta) nib

**pena²** /'pena/ f (castigo) penalty; (de amor etc) pang; **é uma ~ que** it's a pity that; **que ~!** what a pity!; **dar ~** be upsetting; **estar com ou ter ~ de** feel sorry for; **(não) vale a ~** it's (not) worth it; **vale a ~ tentar** it's worth trying; **~ de morte** death penalty

**penada** /pe'nada/ *f* stroke of the pen

**pe|nal** /pe'naw/ (*pl* **~nais**) *a* penal; **~nalidade** *f* penalty; **~nalizar** *vt* penalize

**pênalti** /'penawtʃi/ *m* penalty

**penar** /pe'nar/ *vi* suffer

**pen|dente** /pẽ'dẽtʃi/ *a* hanging; (*fig: causa*) pending; **~der** *vi* hang; (*inclinar-se*) slope; (*tender*) be inclined (**a** to); **~dor** *m* inclination

**pêndulo** /'pẽdulu/ *m* pendulum

**pendu|rado** /pẽdu'radu/ *a* hanging; (*fam: por fazer, pagar*) outstanding; **~rar** *vt* hang (up); (*fam*) put on the slate <*compra*> □ *vi* (*fam*) pay later; **~ricalho** *m* pendant

**penedo** /pe'nedu/ *m* rock

**penei|ra** /pe'nera/ *f* sieve; **~rar** *vt* sieve, sift □ *vi* drizzle

**pene|tra** /pe'nɛtra/ *m/f* (*fam*) gatecrasher; **~tração** *f* penetration; (*fig*) perspicacity; **~trante** *a* <*som, olhar*> piercing; <*dor*> sharp; <*ferida*> deep; <*frio*> biting; <*análise, espírito*> incisive, perceptive; **~trar** *vt* penetrate □ *vi* **~trar em** enter <*casa*>; (*fig*) penetrate

**penhasco** /pe'ɲasku/ *m* cliff

**penhoar** /peɲo'ar/ *m* dressing gown

**penhor** /pe'ɲor/ *m* pledge; **casa de ~es** pawnshop

**penicilina** /penisi'lina/ *f* penicillin

**penico** /pe'niku/ *m* potty

**península** /pe'nĩsula/ *f* peninsula

**pênis** /'penis/ *m invar* penis

**penitência** /peni'tẽsia/ *f* (*arrependimento*) penitence; (*expiação*) penance

**penitenciá|ria** /penitẽsi'aria/ *f* prison; **~rio** *a* prison □ *m* prisoner

**penoso** /pe'nozu/ *a* <*experiência, tarefa, assunto*> painful; <*trabalho, viagem*> hard, difficult

**pensa|dor** /pẽsa'dor/ *m* thinker; **~mento** *m* thought

**pensão** /pẽ'sãw/ *f* (*renda*) pension; (*hotel*) guesthouse; **~ (alimentícia)** (*paga por ex-marido*) alimony; **~ completa** full board

**pen|sar** /pẽ'sar/ *vt/i* think (**em** *of ou* about); **~sativo** *a* thoughtful, pensive

**pên|sil** /'pẽsiw/ (*pl* **~seis**) *a* **ponte ~sil** suspension bridge

**penso** /'pẽsu/ *m* (*curativo*) dressing

**pentágono** /pẽ'tagonu/ *m* pentagon

**pentatlo** /pẽ'tatlu/ *m* pentathlon

**pente** /'pẽtʃi/ *m* comb; **~adeira** *f* dressing table; **~ado** *m* hairstyle, hairdo; **~ar** *vt* comb; **~ar-se** *vpr* do one's hair; (*com pente*) comb one's hair

**Pentecostes** /pẽte'kɔstʃis/ *m* Whitsun

**pente-fino** /pẽtʃi'finu/ *m* **passar a ~** go over with a fine-tooth comb

**pente|lhar** /pẽte'ʎar/ *vt* (*fam*) bother; **~lho** /e/ *m* pubic hair; (*fam: pessoa inconveniente*) pain (in the neck)

**penugem** /pe'nuʒẽ/ *f* down

**penúltimo** /pe'nuwtʃimu/ *a* last but one, penultimate

**penumbra** /pe'nũbra/ *f* half-light

**penúria** /pe'nuria/ *f* penury, extreme poverty

**pepino** /pe'pinu/ *m* cucumber

**pepita** /pe'pita/ *f* nugget

**peque|nez** /peke'nes/ *f* smallness; (*fig*) pettiness; **~nininho** *a* tiny; **~no** /e/ *a* small; (*mesquinho*) petty

**Pequim** /pe'kĩ/ *f* Peking, Beijing

**pequinês** /peki'nes/ *m* Pekinese

**pêra** /'pera/ *f* pear

**perambular** /perãbu'lar/ *vi* wander

**perante** /pe'rãtʃi/ *prep* before

**percalço** /per'kawsu/ *m* pitfall

**perceber** /perse'ber/ *vt* realize; (*Port: entender*) understand; (*psiqu*) perceive

**percen|tagem** /persẽ'taʒẽ/ *f* percentage; **~tual** (*pl* **~tuais**) *a & m* percentage

**percep|ção** /persep'sãw/ *f* perception; **~tível** (*pl* **~tíveis**) *a* perceptible

**percevejo** /perse'veʒu/ *m* (*bicho*) bedbug; (*tachinha*) drawing pin, (*Amer*) thumbtack

**per|correr** /perko'xer/ *vt* cross; cover <*distância*>; (*viajar por*) travel through; **~curso** *m* journey

**percus|são** /perku'sãw/ *f* percussion; **~sionista** *m/f* percussionist

**percutir** /perku'tʃir/ *vt* strike

**perda** /'perda/ *f* loss; **~ de tempo** waste of time

**perdão** /per'dãw/ *f* pardon

**perder** /per'der/ *vt* lose; (*não chegar a ver, pegar*) miss <*ônibus, programa na TV etc*>; waste <*tempo*> □ *vi* lose; **~-se** *vpr* get lost; **~-se de alg** lose s.o.; **~ aco de vista** lose sight of sth

**perdiz** /per'dʒis/ *f* partridge

**perdoar** /perdo'ar/ *vt* forgive (**aco a alg** s.o. for sth)

**perdulário** /perdu'lariu/ *a & m* spendthrift

**perdurar** /perdu'rar/ *vi* endure; <*coisa ruim*> persist

**pere|cer** /pere'ser/ *vi* perish; **~cível** (*pl* **~cíveis**) *a* perishable

**peregri|nação** /peregrina'sãw/ *f* peregrination; (*romaria*) pilgrimage; **~nar** *vi* roam; (*por motivos religiosos*) go on a pilgrimage; **~no** *m* pilgrim

**pereira** /pe'rera/ *f* pear tree

**peremptório** /perẽp'tɔriu/ *a* peremptory

**perene** /pe'reni/ *a* perennial

**perereca** /pere'rɛka/ *f* tree frog

**perfazer** /perfa'zer/ vt make up

**perfeccionis|mo** /perfeksio'nizmu/ m perfectionism; **~ta** a & m/f perfectionist

**perfei|ção** /perfej'sãw/ f perfection; **~to** a & m perfect

**per|fil** /per'fiw/ (pl **~fis**) m profile; **~filar** vt line up; **~filar-se** vpr line up

**perfu|mado** /perfu'madu/ a <flor, ar> fragrant; <sabonete etc> scented; <pessoa> with perfume on; **~mar** vt perfume; **~mar-se** vpr put perfume on; **~maria** f perfumery; ( fam) trimmings, frills; **~me** m perfume

**perfu|rador** /perfura'dor/ m punch; **~rar** vt punch <papel, bilhete>; drill through <chão>; perforate <úlcera, pulmão etc>; **~ratriz** f drill

**pergaminho** /perga'miɲu/ m parchment

**pergun|ta** /per'gũta/ f question; **fazer uma ~ta** ask a question; **~tar** vt/i ask; **~tar aco a alg** ask s.o. sth; **~tar por** ask after

**perícia** /pe'risia/ f (mestria) expertise; (inspeção) investigation; ( peritos) experts

**perici|al** /perisi'aw/ (pl **~ais**) a expert

**pericli|tante** /perikli'tãtʃi/ a precarious; **~tar** vi be at risk

**peri|feria** /perife'ria/ f periphery; (da cidade) outskirts; **~férico** a & m peripheral

**perigo** /pe'rigu/ m danger; **~so** /o/ a dangerous

**perímetro** /pe'rimetru/ m perimeter

**periódico** /peri'ɔdʒiku/ a periodic □ m periodical

**período** /pe'riodu/ m period; **trabalhar meio ~** work part-time

**peripécias** /peri'pɛsias/ f pl ups and downs, vicissitudes

**periquito** /peri'kitu/ m parakeet; (de estimação) budgerigar

**periscópio** /peris'kɔpiu/ m periscope

**perito** /pe'ritu/ a & m expert (**em at**)

**per|jurar** /perʒu'rar/ vi commit perjury; **~júrio** m perjury; **~juro** m perjurer

**perma|necer** /permane'ser/ vi remain; **~nência** f permanence; (estadia) stay; **~nente** a permanent □ f perm

**permeá|vel** /permi'avew/ (pl **~veis**) a permeable

**permis|são** /permi'sãw/ f permission; **~sível** (pl **~síveis**) a permissible; **~sivo** a permissive

**permitir** /permi'tʃir/ vt allow, permit; **~ a alg ir** allow s.o. to go

**permutar** /permu'tar/ vt exchange

**perna** /'pɛrna/ f leg

**pernicioso** /pernisi'ozu/ a pernicious

**per|nil** /per'niw/ (pl **~nis**) m leg

**pernilongo** /perni'lõgu/ m (large) mosquito

**pernoi|tar** /pernoj'tar/ vi spend the night; **~te** m overnight stay

**pérola** /'pɛrola/ f pearl

**perpendicular** /perpẽdʒiku'lar/ a perpendicular

**perpetrar** /perpe'trar/ vt perpetrate

**perpetu|ar** /perpetu'ar/ vt perpetuate; **~idade** f perpetuity

**perpétu|o** /per'pɛtuu/ a perpetual; **prisão ~a** life imprisonment

**perple|xidade** /perpleksi'dadʒi/ f puzzlement; **~xo** /ɛ/ a puzzled

**persa** /'pɛrsa/ a & m/f Persian

**perse|guição** /persegi'sãw/ f pursuit; (de minorias etc) persecution; **~guidor** m pursuer; (de minorias etc) persecutor; **~guir** vt pursue; persecute <minoria, seita etc>

**perseve|rança** /perseve'rãsa/ f perseverance; **~rante** a persevering; **~rar** vi persevere

**persiana** /persi'ana/ f blind

**pérsico** /'pɛrsiku/ a **Golfo Pérsico** Persian Gulf

**persignar-se** /persig'narsi/ vt cross o.s.

**persis|tência** /persis'tẽsia/ f persistence; **~tente** a persistent; **~tir** vi persist

**perso|nagem** /perso'naʒẽ/ m/f (pessoa famosa) personality; (em livro, filme etc) character; **~nalidade** f personality; **~nalizar** vt personalize; **~nificar** vt personify

**perspectiva** /perspek'tʃiva/ f (na arte, ponto de vista) perspective; (possibilidade) prospect

**perspi|cácia** /perspi'kasia/ f insight, perceptiveness; **~caz** a perceptive

**persua|dir** /persua'dʒir/ vt persuade (**alg a** s.o. to); **~são** f persuasion; **~sivo** a persuasive

**perten|cente** /pertẽ'sẽtʃi/ a belonging (**a** to); (que tem a ver com) pertaining (**a** to); **~cer** vi belong (**a** to); (referir-se) pertain (**a** to); **~ces** m pl belongings

**perto** /'pɛrtu/ adv near (**de** to); **aqui ~** near here, nearby; **de ~** closely; <ver> close up

**pertur|bação** /perturba'sãw/ f disturbance; (do espírito) anxiety; **~bado** a <pessoa> unsettled, troubled; **~bar** vt disturb; **~bar-se** vpr get upset, be perturbed

**Peru** /pe'ru/ m Peru

**peru** /pe'ru/ m turkey

**perua** /pe'rua/ f (carro grande) estate car, (Amer) station wagon; (caminho-

*nete*) van; ( *para escolares etc*) minibus; ( *fam: mulher*) brassy woman
**peruano** /peru'ano/ *a & m* Peruvian
**peruca** /pe'ruka/ *f* wig
**perver|são** /perver'sãw/ *f* perversion; **~so** *a* perverse; **~ter** *vt* pervert
**pesadelo** /peza'delu/ *m* nightmare
**pesado** /pe'zadu/ *a* heavy; <*estilo, livro*> heavy-going □ *adv* heavily
**pêsames** /'pezamis/ *m pl* condolences
**pesar**¹ /pe'zar/ *vt* weigh; ( *fig: avaliar*) weigh up □ *vi* weigh; (*influir*) carry weight; **~ sobre** <*ameaça etc*> hang over; **~-se** *vpr* weigh o.s.
**pesar**² /pe'zar/ *m* sorrow; **~oso** /o/ *a* sorry, sorrowful
**pes|ca** /'pɛska/ *f* fishing; **ir à ~ca** go fishing; **~cador** *m* fisherman; **~car** *vt* catch; (*retirar da água*) fish out □ *vi* fish; ( *fam*) (*entender*) understand; (*cochilar*) nod off; **~car de** ( *fam*) know all about
**pescoço** /pes'kosu/ *m* neck
**peseta** /pe'zeta/ *f* peseta
**peso** /'pezu/ *m* weight; **de ~** ( *fig*) <*pessoa*> influential; <*livro, argumento*> authoritative
**pesqueiro** /pes'keru/ *a* fishing
**pesqui|sa** /pes'kiza/ *f* research; (*uma*) study; *pl* research; **~sa de mercado** market research; **~sador** *m* researcher; **~sar** *vt/i* research
**pêssego** /'pesigu/ *m* peach
**pessegueiro** /pesi'geru/ *m* peach tree
**pessimis|mo** /pesi'mizmu/ *m* pessimism; **~ta** *a* pessimistic □ *m/f* pessimist
**péssimo** /'pɛsimu/ *a* terrible, awful
**pesso|a** /pe'soa/ *f* person; *pl* people; **em ~a** in person; **~al** (*pl* **~ais**) *a* personal □ *m* staff; ( *fam*) folks
**pesta|na** /pes'tana/ *f* eyelash; **tirar uma ~na** ( *fam*) have a nap; **~nejar** *vi* blink; **sem ~nejar** ( *fig*) without batting an eyelid
**pes|te** /'pɛstʃi/ *f* (*doença*) plague; (*criança etc*) pest; **~ticida** *m* pesticide
**pétala** /'pɛtala/ *f* petal
**peteca** /pe'tɛka/ *f* kind of shuttlecock; (*jogo*) kind of badminton played with the hand
**peteleco** /pete'lɛku/ *m* flick
**petição** /petʃi'sãw/ *f* petition
**petisco** /pe'tʃisku/ *m* savoury, titbit
**petrificar** /petrifi'kar/ *vt* petrify; (*de surpresa*) stun; **~-se** *vpr* be petrified; (*de surpresa*) be stunned
**petroleiro** /petro'leru/ *a* oil □ *m* oil tanker
**petróleo** /pe'trɔliu/ *m* oil, petroleum; **~ bruto** crude oil
**petrolífero** /petro'liferu/ *a* oil-producing

**petroquími|ca** /petro'kimika/ *f* petrochemicals; **~co** *a* petrochemical
**petu|lância** /petu'lãsia/ *f* cheek; **~lante** *a* cheeky
**peúga** /pi'uga/ *f* (*Port*) sock
**pevide** /pe'vidʒi/ *f* (*Port*) pip
**pia** /'pia/ *f* (*do banheiro*) washbasin; (*da cozinha*) sink; **~ batismal** font
**piada** /pi'ada/ *f* joke
**pia|nista** /pia'nista/ *m/f* pianist; **~no** *m* piano; **~no de cauda** grand piano
**piar** /pi'ar/ *vi* <*pinto*> cheep; <*coruja*> hoot
**picada** /pi'kada/ *f* (*de agulha, alfinete etc*) prick; (*de abelha, vespa*) sting; (*de mosquito, cobra*) bite; (*de heroína*) shot; (*de avião*) nosedive; **o fim da ~** ( *fig*) the limit
**picadeiro** /pika'deru/ *m* ring
**picante** /pi'kãtʃi/ *a* <*comida*> hot, spicy; <*piada*> risqué; <*filme, livro*> raunchy
**pica-pau** /pika'paw/ *m* woodpecker
**picar** /pi'kar/ *vt* (*com agulha, alfinete etc*) prick; <*abelha, vespa, urtiga*> sting; <*mosquito, cobra*> bite; <*pássaro*> peck; chop <*carne, alho etc*>; shred <*papel*> □ *vi* <*peixe*> bite; <*lã, cobertor*> prickle
**picareta** /pika'reta/ *f* pickaxe
**pi|chação** /piʃa'sãw/ *f* piece of graffiti; *pl* graffiti; **~char** *vt* spray with graffiti <*muro, prédio*>; spray <*grafite, desenho*>; **~che** *m* pitch
**picles** /'piklis/ *m pl* pickles
**pico** /'piku/ *m* peak; **20 anos e ~** (*Port*) just over 20
**picolé** /piko'lɛ/ *m* ice lolly
**pico|tar** /piko'tar/ *vt* perforate; **~te** /ɔ/ *m* perforations
**pie|dade** /pie'dadʒi/ *f* (*religiosidade*) piety; (*compaixão*) pity; **~doso** /o/ *a* merciful, compassionate
**pie|gas** /pi'ɛgas/ *a invar* <*filme, livro*> sentimental, schmaltzy; <*pessoa*> soppy; **~guice** *f* sentimentality
**pifar** /pi'far/ *vi* ( *fam*) break down, go wrong
**pigar|rear** /pigaxi'ar/ *vi* clear one's throat; **~ro** *m* frog in the throat
**pigmento** /pig'mẽtu/ *m* pigment
**pig|meu** /pig'mew/ *a & m* ( *f* **~méia**) pygmy
**pijama** /pi'ʒama/ *m* pyjamas
**pilantra** /pi'lãtra/ *m/f* ( *fam*) crook
**pilão** /pi'lãw/ *m* (*na cozinha*) pestle; (*na construção*) ram
**pilar** /pi'lar/ *m* pillar
**pilastra** /pi'lastra/ *f* pillar
**pileque** /pi'lɛki/ *m* drinking session; **tomar um ~** get drunk
**pilha** /'piʎa/ *f* (*monte*) pile; (*elétrica*) battery
**pilhar** /pi'ʎar/ *vt* pillage

**pilhéria** /pi'ʎɛria/ *f* joke
**pilotar** /pilo'tar/ *vt* fly, pilot <*avião*>; drive <*carro*>
**pilotis** /pilo'tʃis/ *m pl* pillars
**piloto** /pi'lotu/ *m* pilot; (*de carro*) driver; (*de gás*) pilot light □ *a invar* pilot
**pílula** /'pilula/ *f* pill
**pimen|ta** /pi'mẽta/ *f* pepper; **~ta de Caiena** cayenne pepper; **~ta-do-reino** *f* black pepper; **~ta-malagueta** (*pl* **~tas-malagueta**) *f* chilli pepper; **~tão** *m* (bell) pepper; **~teira** *f* pepper pot
**pinacoteca** /pinako'tɛka/ *f* art gallery
**pin|ça** /'pĩsa/ (*para tirar pêlos*) tweezers; (*para segurar*) tongs; (*de siri etc*) pincer; **~çar** *vt* pluck <*sobrancelhas*>
**pin|cel** /pĩ'sɛw/ (*pl* **~céis**) *m* brush; **~celada** *f* brush stroke; **~celar** *vt* paint
**pin|ga** /'pĩga/ *f* Brazilian rum; **~gado** *a* <*café*> with a dash of milk; **~gar** *vi* drip; (*começar a chover*) spit (with rain) □ *vt* drip; **~gente** *m* pendant; **~go** *m* drop; (*no i*) dot
**pingue-pongue** /pĩgi'põgi/ *m* table tennis
**pingüim** /pĩ'gwĩ/ *m* penguin
**pi|nha** /'piɲa/ *f* pine cone; **~nheiro** *f* pine tree; **~nho** *m* pine
**pino** /'pinu/ *m* pin; (*para trancar carro*) lock; **a ~** upright; **bater ~** <*carro*> knock
**pin|ta** /'pĩta/ *f* (*sinal*) mole; (*fam: aparência*) look; **~tar** *vt* paint; dye <*cabelo*>; put make-up on <*rosto, olhos*> □ *vi* paint; (*fam*) <*pessoa*> show up; <*problema, oportunidade*> crop up; **~tar-se** *vpr* put on make-up
**pintarroxo** /pĩta'xoʃu/ *m* robin
**pinto** /'pĩtu/ *m* chick
**pin|tor** /pĩ'tor/ *m* painter; **~tura** *f* painting
**pio¹** /'piu/ *m* (*de pinto*) cheep; (*de coruja*) hoot
**pio²** /'piu/ *a* pious
**piolho** /pi'oʎu/ *m* louse
**pioneiro** /pio'neru/ *m* pioneer □ *a* pioneering
**pior** /pi'ɔr/ *a & adv* worse; **o ~** the worst
**pio|ra** /pi'ɔra/ *f* worsening; **~rar** *vt* make worse, worsen □ *vi* get worse, worsen
**pipa** /'pipa/ *f* (*que voa*) kite; (*de vinho*) cask
**pipilar** /pipi'lar/ *vi* chirp
**pipo|ca** /pi'pɔka/ *f* popcorn; **~car** *vi* spring up; **~queiro** *m* popcorn seller
**pique** /'piki/ *m* (*disposição*) energy; **a ~** vertically; **ir a ~** <*navio*> sink

**piquenique** /piki'niki/ *m* picnic
**pique|te** /pi'ketʃi/ *m* picket; **~teiro** *m* picket
**pirado** /pi'radu/ *a* (*fam*) crazy
**pirâmide** /pi'ramidʒi/ *f* pyramid
**piranha** /pi'raɲa/ *f* piranha; (*fam: mulher*) maneater
**pirar** /pi'rar/ (*fam*) *vi* flip out, go mad
**pirata** /pi'rata/ *a & m/f* pirate; **~ria** *f* piracy
**pires** /'piris/ *m invar* saucer
**pirilampo** /piri'lãpu/ *m* glow-worm
**Pirineus** /piri'news/ *m pl* Pyrenees
**pirra|ça** /pi'xasa/ *f* spiteful act; **fazer ~ça** be spiteful; **~cento** *a* spiteful
**pirueta** /piru'eta/ *f* pirouette
**pirulito** /piru'litu/ *m* lollipop
**pi|sada** /pi'zada/ *f* step; (*rastro*) footprint; **~sar** *vt* tread on; tread <*uvas, palco*>; (*esmagar*) trample on □ *vi* step; **~sar em** step on; (*entrar*) set foot in
**pis|cadela** /piska'dɛla/ *f* wink; **~capisca** *m* indicator; **~car** *vi* (*com o olho*) wink; (*pestanejar*) blink; <*estrela, luz*> twinkle; <*motorista*> indicate □ *m* num **~car de olhos** in a flash
**piscicultura** /pisikuw'tura/ *f* fish farming; (*lugar*) fish farm
**piscina** /pi'sina/ *f* swimming pool
**piso** /'pizu/ *m* floor
**pisotear** /pizotʃi'ar/ *vt* trample
**pista** /'pista/ *f* track; (*da estrada*) carriageway; (*para aviões*) runway; (*de circo*) ring; (*dica*) clue; **~ de dança** dancefloor
**pistache** /pis'taʃi/ *m*, **pistacho** /pis'taʃu/ *m* pistachio (nut)
**pisto|la** /pis'tɔla/ *f* pistol; (*para pintar*) spray gun; **~lão** *m* influential contact; **~leiro** *m* gunman
**pitada** /pi'tada/ *f* pinch
**piteira** /pi'tera/ *f* cigarette-holder
**pitoresco** /pito'resku/ *a* picturesque
**pitu** /pi'tu/ *m* crayfish
**pivete** /pi'vetʃi/ *m/f* child thief
**pivô** /pi'vo/ *m* pivot
**pixaim** /piʃa'ĩ/ *a* frizzy
**pizza** /'pitsa/ *f* pizza; **~ria** *f* pizzeria
**placa** /'plaka/ *f* plate; (*de carro*) number plate, (*Amer*) license plate; (*comemorativa*) plaque; (*em computador*) board; **~ de sinalização** roadsign
**placar** /pla'kar/ *m* scoreboard; (*escore*) scoreline
**plácido** /'plasidu/ *a* placid
**plagi|ário** /plaʒi'ariu/ *m* plagiarist; **~ar** *vt* plagiarize
**plágio** /'plaʒiu/ *m* plagiarism
**plaina** /'plajna/ *f* plane
**planador** /plana'dor/ *m* glider
**planalto** /pla'nawtu/ *m* plateau
**planar** /pla'nar/ *vi* glide

**planeamento, planear** (*Port*) *veja* **planejamento, planejar**

**plane|jamento** /planeʒa'mẽtu/ *m* planning; **~jamento familiar** family planning; **~jar** *vt* plan

**planeta** /pla'neta/ *m* planet

**planície** /pla'nisi/ *f* plain

**planificar** /planifi'kar/ *vt* (*programar*) plan (out)

**planilha** /pla'niʎa/ *f* spreadsheet

**plano** /'planu/ *a* flat □ *m* plan; (*superfície, nível*) plane; **primeiro ~** foreground

**planta** /'plãta/ *f* plant; (*do pé*) sole; (*de edifício*) ground plan; **~ção** *f* (*ato*) planting; (*terreno*) plantation; **~do a deixar alg ~do** (*fam*) keep s.o. waiting around

**plantão** /plã'tãw/ *m* duty; (*noturno*) night duty; **estar de ~** be on duty

**plantar** /plã'tar/ *vt* plant

**plas|ma** /'plazma/ *m* plasma; **~mar** *vt* mould, shape

**plásti|ca** /'plastʃika/ *f* face-lift; **~co** *a & m* plastic

**plataforma** /plata'fɔrma/ *f* platform

**plátano** /'platanu/ *m* plane tree

**platéia** /pla'tɛja/ *f* audience; (*parte do teatro*) stalls, (*Amer*) orchestra

**platina** /pla'tʃina/ *f* platinum; **~dos** *m pl* points

**platônico** /pla'toniku/ *a* platonic

**plausí|vel** /plaw'zivew/ (*pl* **~veis**) *a* plausible

**ple|be** /'plɛbi/ *f* common people; **~beu** *a* (*f* **~béia**) plebeian □ *m* (*f* **~béia**) commoner; **~biscito** *m* plebiscite

**plei|tear** /plejtʃi'ar/ *vt* contest; **~to m** (*litígio*) case; (*eleitoral*) contest

**ple|namente** /plena'mẽtʃi/ *adv* fully; **~nário** *a* plenary □ *m* plenary assembly; **~no** /e/ *a* full; **em ~no verão** in the middle of summer

**plissado** /pli'sadu/ *a* pleated

**pluma** /'pluma/ *f* feather; **~gem** *f* plumage

**plu|ral** /plu'raw/ (*pl* **~rais**) *a & m* plural

**plutônio** /plu'toniu/ *m* plutonium

**pluvi|al** /pluvi'aw/ (*pl* **~ais**) *a* rain

**pneu** /pi'new/ *m* tyre; **~mático** *a* pneumatic □ *m* tyre

**pneumonia** /pineumo'nia/ *f* pneumonia

**pó** /pɔ/ *f* powder; (*poeira*) dust; **leite em ~** powdered milk

**pobre** /'pɔbri/ *a* poor □ *m/f* poor man (*f* woman); **os ~s** the poor; **~za** /e/ *f* poverty

**poça** /'posa/ *f* pool; (*deixada pela chuva*) puddle

**poção** /po'sãw/ *f* potion

**pocilga** /po'siwga/ *f* pigsty

**poço** /'posu/ *f* (*de água, petróleo*) well; (*de mina, elevador*) shaft

**podar** /po'dar/ *vt* prune

**pó-de-arroz** /pɔdʒia'xoz/ *m* (face) powder

**poder** /po'der/ *m* power □ *v aux* can, be able; (*eventualidade*) may; **ele pode/podia/poderá vir** he can/could/might come; **ele pôde vir** he was able to come; **pode ser que** it may be that; **~ com** stand up to; **em ~ de alg** in sb's possession; **estar no ~** be in power

**pode|rio** /pode'riu/ *m* might; **~roso** /o/ *a* powerful

**pódio** /'pɔdʒiu/ *m* podium

**podre** /'podri/ *a* rotten; (*fam*) (*cansado*) exhausted; (*doente*) grotty; **~ de rico** filthy rich; **~s** *m pl* faults

**poei|ra** /po'era/ *f* dust; **~rento** *a* dusty

**poe|ma** /po'ema/ *m* poem; **~sia** *f* (*arte*) poetry; (*poema*) poem; **~ta** *m* poet

**poético** /po'ɛtʃiku/ *a* poetic

**poetisa** /poe'tʃiza/ *f* poetess

**pois** /pojs/ *conj* as, since; **~ é** that's right; **~ não** of course; **~ não?** can I help you?; **~ sim** certainly not

**polaco** /pu'laku/ (*Port*) *a* Polish □ *m* Pole; (*língua*) Polish

**polar** /po'lar/ *a* polar

**polarizar** /polari'zar/ *vt* polarize; **~-se** *vpr* polarize

**pole|gada** /pole'gada/ *f* inch; **~gar** *m* thumb

**poleiro** /po'leru/ *m* perch

**polêmi|ca** /po'lemika/ *f* controversy, debate; **~co** *a* controversial

**pólen** /'pɔlẽ/ *m* pollen

**polícia** /po'lisia/ *f* police □ *m/f* policeman (*f* -woman)

**polici|al** /polisi'aw/ (*pl* **~ais**) *a* <*carro, inquérito etc*> police; <*romance, filme*> detective □ *m/f* policeman (*f* -woman); **~amento** *m* policing; **~ar** *vt* police

**poli|dez** /poli'des/ *f* politeness; **~do** *a* polite

**poli|gamia** /poliga'mia/ *f* polygamy; **~glota** *a & m/f* polyglot

**Polinésia** /poli'nɛzia/ *f* Polynesia

**polinésio** /poli'nɛziu/ *a & m* Polynesian

**pólio** /'pɔliu/ *f* polio

**polir** /po'lir/ *vt* polish

**polissílabo** /poli'silabu/ *m* polysyllable

**políti|ca** /po'litʃika/ *f* politics; (*uma*) policy; **~co** *a* political □ *m* politician

**pólo**[1] /'polu/ *m* pole

**pólo**[2] /'polu/ *m* (*jogo*) polo; **~ aquático** water polo

**polo|nês** /polo'nes/ *a* ( *f* **~nesa**) Polish □ *m* ( *f* **~nesa**) Pole; (*língua*) Polish

**Polônia** /po'lonia/ *f* Poland

**polpa** /'powpa/ *f* pulp

**poltrona** /pow'trona/ *f* armchair

**polu|ente** /polu'ētʃi/ *a & m* pollutant; **~ição** *f* pollution; **~ir** *vt* pollute

**polvilhar** /powvi'ʎar/ *vt* sprinkle

**polvo** /'powvu/ *m* octopus

**pólvora** /'pɔwvora/ *f* gunpowder

**polvorosa** /powvo'rɔza/ *f* uproar; **em ~** in uproar; <*pessoa*> in a flap

**pomada** /po'mada/ *f* ointment

**pomar** /po'mar/ *m* orchard

**pom|ba** /'põba/ *f* dove; **~bo** *m* pigeon

**pomo-de-Adão** /pomudʃia'dãw/ *m* Adam's apple

**pom|pa** /'põpa/ *f* pomp; **~poso** /o/ *a* pompous

**ponche** /'põʃi/ *m* punch

**ponderar** /põde'rar/ *vt/i* ponder

**pônei** /'ponej/ *m* pony

**ponta** /'põta/ *f* end; (*de faca, prego*) point; (*de nariz, dedo, língua*) tip; (*de sapato*) toe; (*Cin, Teat: papel curto*) walk-on part; (*no campo de futebol*) wing; (*jogador*) winger; **na ~ dos pés** on tip-toe; **uma ~ de** a touch of <*ironia etc*>; **agüentar as ~s** ( *fam*) hold on; **~cabeça** /e/ *f* **de ~-cabeça** upside down

**pontada** /põ'tada/ *f* (*dor*) twinge

**pontapé** /põta'pɛ/ *m* kick; **~ inicial** kick-off

**pontaria** /põta'ria/ *f* aim; **fazer ~** take aim

**ponte** /'põtʃi/ *f* bridge; **~ aérea** shuttle; (*em tempo de guerra*) airlift; **~ de safena** heart bypass; **~ pênsil** suspension bridge

**ponteiro** /põ'teru/ *m* pointer; (*de relógio*) hand

**pontiagudo** /põtʃia'gudu/ *a* sharp

**pontilhado** /põtʃi'ʎadu/ *a* dotted

**ponto** /'põtu/ *m* point; (*de costura, tricô*) stitch; (*no final de uma frase*) full stop, (*Amer*) period; (*sinalzinho, no i*) dot; (*de ônibus*) stop; (*no teatro*) prompter; **a ~ de** on the point of; **ao ~** <*carne*> medium; **até certo ~** to a certain extent; **às duas em ~** at exactly two o'clock; **dormir no ~** ( *fam*) miss the boat; **entregar os ~s** ( *fam*) give up; **fazer ~** ( *fam*) hang out; **dois ~s** colon; **~ de exclamação/interrogação** exclamation/question mark; **~ de táxi** taxi rank, (*Amer*) taxi stand; **~ de vista** point of view; **~ morto** neutral; **~-e-vírgula** *m* semicolon

**pontu|ação** /põtua'sãw/ *f* punctuation; **~al** (*pl* **~ais**) *a* punctual; **~alidade** *f* punctuality; **~ar** *vt* punctuate

**pontudo** /põ'tudu/ *a* pointed

**popa** /'popa/ *f* stern

**popu|lação** /popula'sãw/ *f* population; **~lacional** (*pl* **~lacionais**) *a* population; **~lar** *a* popular; **~laridade** *f* popularity; **~larizar** *vt* popularize; **~larizar-se** *vpr* become popular

**pôquer** /'poker/ *m* poker

**por** /por/ *prep* for; (*através de*) through; (*indicando meio, agente*) by; (*motivo*) out of; **~ ano/mês/** *etc* per year/month/*etc*; **~ cento** per cent; **~ aqui** (*nesta área*) around here; (*nesta direção*) this way; **~ dentro/fora** on the inside/outside; **~ isso** for this reason; **~ sorte** luckily; **~ que** why; **~ mais caro que seja** however expensive it may be; **está ~ acontecer/fazer** it is yet to happen/to be done

**pôr** /por/ *vt* put; put on <*roupa, chapéu, óculos*>; lay <*mesa, ovos*> □ **~ o ~ do sol** sunset; **~-se** *vpr* <*sol*> set; **~-se a** a start to; **~-se a caminho** set off

**porão** /po'rãw/ *m* (*de prédio*) basement; (*de casa*) cellar; (*de navio*) hold

**porca** /'pɔrka/ *f* (*de parafuso*) nut; (*animal*) sow

**porção** /por'sãw/ *f* portion; **uma ~ de** (*muitos*) a lot of

**porcaria** /porka'ria/ *f* (*sujeira*) filth; (*coisa malfeita*) piece of trash; *pl* trash

**porcelana** /porse'lana/ *f* china

**porcentagem** /porsē'taʒē/ *f* percentage

**porco** /'porku/ *a* filthy □ *m* (*animal, fig*) pig; (*carne*) pork; **~-espinho** (*pl* **~s-espinhos**) *m* porcupine

**porém** /po'rēj/ *conj* however

**pormenor** /porme'nɔr/ *m* detail

**por|nô** /por'no/ *a* porn □ *m* porn film; **~nografia** *f* pornography; **~nográfico** *a* pornographic

**poro** /'pɔru/ *m* pore; **~so** /o/ *a* porous

**por|quanto** /por'kwãtu/ *conj* since; **~que** /por'ki/ *conj* because; (*Port: por quê?*) why; **~quê** /por'ke/ *adv* (*Port*) why □ *m* reason why

**porquinho|-da-índia** /porkinuda-'idʒia/ (*pl* **~s-da-índia**) *m* guinea pig

**porrada** /po'xada/ *f* ( *fam*) beating

**porre** /'pɔxi/ *m* ( *fam*) drinking session, booze-up; **de ~** drunk; **tomar um ~** get drunk

**porta** /'pɔrta/ *f* door

**porta-aviões** /pɔrtavi'õjs/ *m invar* aircraft carrier

**portador** /porta'dor/ *m* bearer

**portagem** /por'taʒē/ *f* (*Port*) toll

**porta|chaves** /pɔrta'ʃavis/ *m invar* key-holder *ou* key-ring; **~-jóias** *m in-**

*var* jewellery box; **~-lápis** *m invar* pencil holder; **~-luvas** *m invar* glove compartment; **~-malas** *m invar* boot, (*Amer*) trunk; **~-níqueis** *m invar* purse
**portanto** /porˈtãtu/ *conj* therefore
**portão** /porˈtãw/ *m* gate
**portar** /porˈtar/ *vt* carry; **~-se** *vpr* behave
**porta|-retrato** /pɔrtaxeˈtratu/ *m* photo frame; **~-revistas** *m invar* magazine rack
**portaria** /portaˈria/ *f* (*entrada*) entrance; (*decreto*) decree
**portá|til** (*pl* **~teis**) *a* portable
**porta|-toalhas** /portatoˈaʎas/ *m invar* towel rail; **~-voz** *m/f* spokesman (*f* -woman)
**porte** /ˈpɔrtʃi/ *m* (*frete*) carriage; (*de cartas etc*) postage; (*de pessoa*) bearing; (*dimensão*) scale; **de grande/pequeno ~** large-/small-scale
**porteiro** /porˈteru/ *m* doorman; **~ eletrônico** entryphone
**porto** /ˈpɔrtu/ *m* port; **o Porto** Oporto; **~ de escala** port of call; **Porto Rico** *m* Puerto Rico; **~-riquenho** /e/ *a & m* Puertorican
**portuense** /portuˈẽsi/ *a & m/f* (person) from Oporto
**Portugal** /portuˈgaw/ *m* Portugal
**portu|guês** /portuˈges/ *a & m* (*f* **~guesa**) Portuguese
**portuário** /portuˈariu/ *a* port □ *m* dock worker, docker
**po|sar** /poˈzar/ *vi* pose; **~se** /o/ *f* pose; (*de filme*) exposure
**pós-datar** /pɔzdaˈtar/ *vt* postdate
**pós-escrito** /pɔzisˈkritu/ *m* postscript
**pós-gradua|ção** /pɔzgraduaˈsãw/ *f* postgraduation; **~do** *a & m* postgraduate
**pós-guerra** /pɔzˈgɛxa/ *m* post-war period; **a Europa do ~** post-war Europe
**posi|ção** /poziˈsãw/ *f* position; **~cionar** *vt* position; **~tivo** *a & m* positive
**posologia** /pozoloˈʒia/ *f* dosage
**pos|sante** /poˈsãtʃi/ *a* powerful; **~se** /ɔ/ *f* (*de casa etc*) possession, ownership; (*do presidente etc*) swearing in; *pl* (*pertences*) possessions; **tomar ~se** take office; **tomar ~se de** take possession of
**posses|são** /poseˈsãw/ *f* possession; **~sivo** *a* possessive; **~so** /ɛ/ *a* possessed; (*com raiva*) furious
**possibili|dade** /posibiliˈdadʒi/ *f* possibility; **~tar** *vt* make possible
**possí|vel** /poˈsivew/ (*pl* **~veis**) *a* possible; **fazer todo o ~vel** do one's best
**possuir** /posuˈir/ *vt* possess; (*ser dono de*) own

**posta** /ˈpɔsta/ *f* (*de peixe*) steak
**pos|tal** /posˈtaw/ (*pl* **~tais**) *a* postal □ *m* postcard
**postar** /posˈtar/ *vt* place; **~-se** *vpr* position o.s.
**poste** /ˈpɔstʃi/ *m* post
**pôster** /ˈpostɛr/ *m* poster
**posteri|dade** /posteriˈdadʒi/ *f* posterity; **~or** *a* (*no tempo*) subsequent, later; (*no espaço*) rear; **~ormente** *adv* subsequently
**postiço** /posˈtʃisu/ *a* false
**posto** /ˈpostu/ *m* post; **~ de gasolina** petrol station, (*Amer*) gas station; **~ de saúde** health centre □ *pp de* **pôr**; **~ que** although
**póstumo** /ˈpɔstumu/ *a* posthumous
**postura** /posˈtura/ *f* posture
**potá|vel** /poˈtavew/ (*pl* **~veis**) *a* **água ~vel** drinking water
**pote** /ˈpɔtʃi/ *m* pot; (*de vidro*) jar
**potência** /poˈtẽsia/ *f* power
**poten|cial** /potẽsiˈaw/ (*pl* **~ciais**) *a & m* potential; **~te** *a* potent
**potro** /ˈpotru/ *m* foal
**pouco** /ˈpoku/ *a & pron* little; *pl* few □ *adv* not much □ *m* **um ~** a little; **~ a ~** little by little; **aos ~s** gradually; **daqui a ~** shortly; **por ~** almost; **~ tempo** a short time
**pou|pança** /poˈpãsa/ *f* saving; (*conta*) savings account; **~par** *vt* save; spare <*vida*>
**pouquinho** /poˈkiɲu/ *m* **um ~ (de)** a little
**pou|sada** /poˈzada/ *f* inn; **~sar** *vi* land; **~so** *m* landing
**po|vão** /poˈvãw/ *m* common people; **~vo** /o/ *m* people
**povo|ação** /povoaˈsãw/ *f* settlement; **~ar** *vt* populate
**poxa** /ˈpɔʃa/ *int* gosh
**pra** /pra/ *prep* (*fam*) *veja* **para**
**praça** /ˈprasa/ *f* (*largo*) square; (*mercado*) market □ *m* (*soldado*) private
**prado** /ˈpradu/ *m* meadow
**pra-frente** /praˈfrẽtʃi/ *a invar* (*fam*) with it, modern
**praga** /ˈpraga/ *f* curse; (*inseto, doença, pessoa*) pest
**prag|mático** /pragˈmatʃiku/ *a* pragmatic; **~matismo** *m* pragmatism
**praguejar** /prageˈʒar/ *vt/i* curse
**praia** /ˈpraja/ *f* beach
**pran|cha** /ˈprãʃa/ *f* plank; (*de surfe*) board; **~cheta** /e/ *f* drawing board
**pranto** /ˈprãtu/ *m* weeping
**pra|ta** /ˈprata/ *f* silver; **~taria** *f* (*coisas de prata*) silverware; **~teado** *a* silver-plated; (*cor*) silver
**prateleira** /prateˈlera/ *f* shelf
**prática** /ˈpratʃika/ *f* practice; **na ~** in practice

**prati|cante** /pratʃi'kãtʃi/ *a* practising □ *m/f* apprentice; (*de esporte etc*) player; **∼car** *vt* practise; (*cometer, executar*) carry out □ *vi* practise; **∼cável** (*pl* **∼cáveis**) *a* practicable

**prático** /'pratʃiku/ *a* practical

**prato** /'pratu/ *m* (*objeto*) plate; (*comida*) dish; (*parte de uma refeição*) course; (*do toca-discos*) turntable; *pl* (*instrumento*) cymbals; **∼ fundo** dish; **∼ principal** main course

**praxe** /'praʃi/ *f* normal practice; **de ∼** usually

**prazer** /pra'zer/ *m* pleasure; **muito ∼ (em conhecê-lo)** pleased to meet you; **∼oso** /o/ *a* pleasurable

**prazo** /'prazu/ *m* term, time; **a ∼** <*compra etc*> on credit; **a curto/ longo ∼** in the short/long term; **último ∼** deadline

**preâmbulo** /pri'ãbulu/ *m* preamble

**precário** /pre'kariu/ *a* precarious

**precaução** /prekaw'sãw/ *f* precaution

**preca|ver-se** /preka'versi/ *vpr* take precautions (**de** against); **∼vido** *a* cautious

**prece** /'prɛsi/ *f* prayer

**prece|dência** /prese'dẽsia/ *f* precedence; **∼dente** *a* preceding □ *m* precedent; **∼der** *vt/i* precede

**preceito** /pre'sejtu/ *m* precept

**precioso** /presi'ozu/ *a* precious

**precipício** /presi'pisiu/ *m* precipice

**precipi|tação** /presipita'sãw/ *f* haste; (*chuva etc*) precipitation; **∼tado** *a* <*fuga*> headlong; <*decisão, ato*> hasty, rash; **∼tar** *vt* (*lançar*) throw; (*antecipar*) hasten; **∼tar-se** *vpr* (*lançar-se*) throw o.s.; (*apressar-se*) rush; (*agir sem pensar*) act rashly

**precisão** /presi'zãw/ *f* precision, accuracy

**precisamente** /presiza'mẽtʃi/ *adv* precisely

**preci|sar** /presi'zar/ *vt* (*necessitar*) need; (*indicar com exatidão*) specify □ *vi* be necessary; **∼sar de** need; **∼so ir** I have to go; **∼sa-se** wanted; **∼so** *a* (*exato*) precise; (*necessário*) necessary

**preço** /'presu/ *m* price; **∼ de custo** cost price; **∼ fixo** set price

**precoce** /pre'kɔsi/ *a* <*fruto*> early; <*velhice, calvície etc*> premature; <*criança*> precocious

**precon|cebido** /prekõse'bidu/ *a* preconceived; **∼ceito** *m* prejudice; **∼ceituoso** *a* prejudiced

**preconizar** /prekoni'zar/ *vt* advocate

**precursor** /prekur'sor/ *m* forerunner

**preda|dor** /preda'dor/ *m* predator; **∼tório** *a* predatory

**predecessor** /predese'sor/ *m* predecessor

**predestinar** /predestʃi'nar/ *vt* predestine

**predeterminar** /predetermi'nar/ *vt* predetermine

**predição** /predʒi'sãw/ *f* prediction

**predile|ção** /predʒile'sãw/ *f* preference; **∼to** /ɛ/ *a* favourite

**prédio** /'prɛdʒiu/ *m* building

**predis|por** /predʒis'por/ *vt* prepare (**para** for); (*tornar parcial*) prejudice (**contra** against); **∼por-se** *vpr* prepare o.s.; **∼posto** *a* predisposed; (*contra*) prejudiced

**predizer** /predʒi'zer/ *vt* predict, foretell

**predomi|nância** /predomi'nãsia/ *f* predominance; **∼nante** *a* predominant; **∼nar** *vi* predominate

**predomínio** /predo'miniu/ *m* predominance

**preencher** /priẽ'ʃer/ *vt* fill; fill in, (*Amer*) fill out <*formulário*>; meet <*requisitos*>

**pré|-escola** /prɛis'kɔla/ *f* infant school, (*Amer*) pre-school; **∼escolar** *a* pre-school; **∼estréia** *f* preview; **∼fabricado** *a* prefabricated

**prefácio** /pre'fasiu/ *m* preface

**prefei|to** /pre'fejtu/ *m* mayor; **∼tura** *f* prefecture; (*prédio*) town hall

**prefe|rência** /prefe'rẽsia/ *f* preference; (*direito no trânsito*) right of way; **de ∼rência** preferably; **∼rencial** (*pl* **∼renciais**) *a* preferential; <*rua*> main; **∼rido** *a* favourite; **∼rir** *vt* prefer (**a** to); **∼rível** (*pl* **∼ríveis**) *a* preferable

**prefixo** /pre'fiksu/ *m* prefix

**prega** /'prɛga/ *f* pleat

**pregador**[1] /prega'dor/ *m* (*de roupa*) peg

**pre|gador**[2] /prega'dor/ *m* (*quem prega*) preacher; **∼gão** *m* (*de vendedor*) cry; **o ∼gão** (*na bolsa de valores*) trading; (*em leilão*) bidding

**pregar**[1] /pre'gar/ *vt* fix; (*com prego*) nail; sew on <*botão*>; **não ∼ olho** not sleep a wink; **∼ uma peça em** play a trick on; **∼ um susto em alg** give s.o. a fright

**pregar**[2] /pre'gar/ *vt/i* preach

**prego** /'prɛgu/ *m* nail

**pregui|ça** /pre'gisa/ *f* laziness; (*bicho*) sloth; **estou com ∼ça de ir** I can't be bothered to go; **∼çoso** *a* lazy

**pré-histórico** /prɛjs'tɔriku/ *a* prehistoric

**preia-mar** /preja'mar/ *f* high tide

**prejudi|car** /preʒudʒi'kar/ *vt* harm; damage <*saúde*>; **∼car-se** *vpr* harm o.s.; **∼cial** (*pl* **∼ciais**) *a* harmful, damaging (**a** to)

**prejuízo** /pre3u'izu/ *m* damage; (*financeiro*) loss; **em ~ de** to the detriment of

**prejulgar** /preʒuw'gar/ *vt* prejudge

**preliminar** /prelimi'nar/ *a* & *m/f* preliminary

**prelo** /'prɛlu/ *m* printing press; **no ~** being printed

**prelúdio** /pre'ludʒiu/ *m* prelude

**prematuro** /prema'turu/ *a* premature

**premeditar** /premedʒi'tar/ *vt* premeditate

**premente** /pre'mẽtʃi/ *a* pressing

**premi|ado** /premi'adu/ *a* <*romance, atleta etc*> prize-winning; <*bilhete, número etc*> winning □ *m* prize-winner; **~ar** *vt* award a prize to <*romance, atleta etc*>; reward <*honestidade, mérito*>

**prêmio** /'premiu/ *m* prize; (*de seguro*) premium; **Grande Prêmio** (*de F1*) Grand Prix

**premissa** /pre'misa/ *f* premiss

**premonição** /premoni'sãw/ *f* premonition

**pré-na|tal** /prɛna'taw/ (*pl* ~**tais**) *a* antenatal, (*Amer*) prenatal

**prenda** /'prẽda/ *f* (*Port*) present; **~s domésticas** household chores; **~do** *a* domesticated

**pren|dedor** /prẽde'dor/ *m* clip; **~dedor de roupa** clothes peg; **~der** *vt* (*pregar*) fix; (*capturar*) arrest; (*atar*) tie up <*cachorro*>; tie back <*cabelo*>; (*restringir*) restrict; (*ligar afetivamente*) bind; **~der** (**a atenção de**) **alg** grab s.o.('s attention)

**prenhe** /'prɛɲi/ *a* pregnant

**prenome** /pre'nomi/ *m* first name

**pren|sa** /'prẽsa/ *f* press; **~sar** *vt* press

**preocu|pação** /preokupa'sãw/ *f* concern; **~pante** *a* worrying; **~par** *vt* worry; **~par-se** *vpr* worry (**com** about)

**prepa|ração** /prepara'sãw/ *f* preparation; **~rado** *m* preparation; **~rar** *vt* prepare; **~rar-se** *vpr* prepare, get ready; **~rativos** *m pl* preparations; (*competência*) knowledge; **~ro físico** physical fitness

**preponderar** /prepõde'rar/ *vi* prevail (**sobre** over)

**preposição** /prepozi'sãw/ *f* preposition

**prerrogativa** /prexoga'tʃiva/ *f* prerogative

**presa** /'preza/ *f* (*de caça*) prey; (*de cobra*) fang; (*de elefante*) tusk; **~ de guerra** spoils of war

**prescin|dir** /presĩ'dʒir/ *vi* **~dir de** dispense with; **~dível** (*pl* ~**díveis**) *a* dispensable

**pres|crever** /preskre'ver/ *vt* prescribe; **~crição** *f* prescription; (*norma*) rule

**presen|ça** /pre'zẽsa/ *f* presence; **~ça de espírito** presence of mind; **~ciar** *vt* (*estar presente a*) be present at; (*testemunhar*) witness; **~te** *a* & *m* present; **~tear** *vt* **~tear alg** (**com aco**) give s.o. (sth as) a present

**presépio** /pre'zɛpiu/ *m* crib

**preser|vação** /prezerva'sãw/ *f* preservation; **~var** *vt* preserve, protect; **~vativo** *m* (*em comida*) preservative; (*camisinha*) condom

**presi|dência** /prezi'dẽsia/ *f* presidency; (*de uma reunião*) chair; **~dencial** (*pl* ~**denciais**) *a* presidential; **~dencialismo** *m* presidential system; **~dente** *m* (*f* ~**denta**) president; (*de uma reunião*) chairperson

**presidiário** /prezidʒi'ariu/ *m* convict

**presídio** /pre'zidʒiu/ *m* prison

**presidir** /prezi'dʒir/ *vi* preside (**a** over)

**presilha** /pre'ziʎa/ *f* fastener; (*de cabelo*) slide

**preso** /'prezu/ *pp* **de prender** □ *m* prisoner; **ficar ~** get stuck; <*saia, corda etc*> get caught

**pressa** /'prɛsa/ *f* hurry; **às ~s** in a hurry, hurriedly; **estar com** *ou* **ter ~** be in a hurry

**presságio** /pre'saʒiu/ *m* omen

**pressão** /pre'sãw/ *f* pressure; **fazer ~ sobre** put pressure on; **~ arterial** blood pressure

**pressen|timento** /presẽtʃi'mẽtu/ *m* premonition, feeling; **~tir** *vt* sense

**pressionar** /presio'nar/ *vt* press <*botão*>; pressure <*pessoa*>

**pressupor** /presu'por/ *vt* <*pessoa*> presume; <*coisa*> presuppose

**pressurizado** /presuri'zadu/ *a* pressurized

**pres|tação** /presta'sãw/ *f* repayment, instalment; **~tar** *vt* render <*contas, serviço*> □ *vi* be of use; **não ~ta** he/it is no good; **~tar atenção** pay attention; **~tar juramento** take an oath; **~tativo** *a* helpful; **~tável** (*pl* ~**táveis**) *a* serviceable

**prestes** /'prɛstʃis/ *a invar* **~ a** about to

**prestidigita|ção** /prestʃidʒiʒita'sãw/ *f* conjuring; **~dor** *m* conjurer

**pres|tigiar** /prestʃiʒi'ar/ *vt* give prestige to; **~tígio** *m* prestige; **~tigioso** /o/ *a* prestigious

**préstimo** /'prɛstʃimu/ *m* merit

**presumir** /prezu'mir/ *vt* presume

**presun|ção** /prezũ'sãw/ *f* presumption; **~çoso** /o/ *a* presumptuous

**presunto** /pre'zũtu/ *m* ham

**pretendente** /pretĕ'dētʃi/ *m/f* (*candidato*) candidate, applicant

**preten|der** /pretĕ'der/ *vt* intend; **~são** *f* pretension; **~sioso** /o/ *a* pretentious

**preterir** /prete'rir/ *vt* disregard

**pretérito** /pre'tεritu/ *m* preterite

**pretexto** /pre'testu/ *m* pretext

**preto** /'pretu/ *a & m* black; **~-e-branco** *a invar* black and white

**prevalecer** /prevale'ser/ *vi* prevail

**prevenção** /prevĕ'sãw/ *f* (*impedimento*) prevention; (*parcialidade*) bias

**prevenir** /preve'nir/ *vt* (*evitar*) prevent; (*avisar*) warn; **~-se** *vpr* take precautions

**preventivo** /prevĕ'tʃivu/ *a* preventive

**prever** /pre'ver/ *vt* foresee, predict

**previdência** /previ'dēsia/ *f* foresight; **~ social** social security

**prévio** /'previu/ *a* prior

**previ|são** /previ'zãw/ *f* prediction, forecast; **~são do tempo** weather forecast; **~sível** (*pl* **~síveis**) *a* predictable

**pre|zado** /pre'zadu/ *a* esteemed; **Prezado Senhor** Dear Sir; **~zar** *vt* think highly of; **~zar-se** *vpr* have self-respect

**prima** /'prima/ *f* cousin

**primário** /pri'mariu/ *a* primary; (*fundamental*) basic

**primata** /pri'mata/ *m* primate

**primave|ra** /prima'vera/ *f* spring; (*flor*) primrose; **~ril** (*pl* **~ris**) *a* spring

**primazia** /prima'zia/ *f* primacy

**primei|ra** /pri'mera/ *f* (*marcha*) first (gear); **de ~ra** first-rate; **<carne>** prime; **~ra-dama** (*pl* **~ras-damas**) *f* first lady; **~ranista** *m/f* first-year (student); **~ro** *a & adv* first; **no dia ~ro de maio** on the first of May; **em ~ro lugar** (*para começar*) in the first place; (*numa corrida, competição*) in first place; **~ro de tudo** first of all; **~ros socorros** first aid; **~ro-ministro** (*pl* **~ros-ministros**) *m* (*f* **~ra-ministra**) prime-minister

**primitivo** /primi'tʃivu/ *a* primitive

**primo** /'primu/ *m* cousin □ *a* **número ~** prime number; **~gênito** *a & m* first-born

**primor** /pri'mor/ *m* perfection

**primordi|al** /primordʒi'aw/ (*pl* **~ais**) *a* (*primitivo*) primordial; (*fundamental*) fundamental

**primoroso** /primo'rozu/ *a* exquisite

**princesa** /prĩ'seza/ *f* princess

**princi|pado** /prĩsipi'adu/ *m* principality; **~pal** (*pl* **~pais**) *a* main □ *m* principal

**príncipe** /'prĩsipi/ *m* prince

**principiante** /prĩsipi'ãtʃi/ *m/f* beginner

**princípio** /prĩ'sipiu/ *m* (*início*) beginning; (*regra*) principle; **em ~** in principle; **por ~** on principle

**priori|dade** /priori'dadʒi/ *f* priority; **~tário** *a* priority

**prisão** /pri'zãw/ *f* (*ato de prender*) arrest; (*cadeia*) prison; (*encarceramento*) imprisonment; **~ perpétua** life imprisonment; **~ de ventre** constipation

**prisioneiro** /prizio'neru/ *m* prisoner

**prisma** /'prizma/ *m* prism

**privação** /priva'sãw/ *f* deprivation

**privacidade** /privasi'dadʒi/ *f* privacy

**pri|vada** /pri'vada/ *f* toilet; **~vado** *a* private; **~vado de** deprived of; **~var** *vt* deprive (**de** of); **~var-se** *vpr* deprive o.s. (**de** of)

**privati|vo** /priva'tʃivu/ *a* private; **~zar** *vt* privatize

**privi|legiado** /privileʒi'adu/ *a* privileged; **<tratamento>** preferential; **~legiar** *vt* favour; **~légio** *m* privilege

**pro** (*fam*) = **para + o**

**pró** /prɔ/ *adv* for □ *m* **os ~s e os contras** the pros and cons

**proa** /'proa/ *f* bow, prow

**probabilidade** /probabili'dadʒi/ *f* probability

**proble|ma** /pro'blema/ *m* problem; **~mático** *a* problematic

**proce|dência** /prose'dēsia/ *f* origin; **~dente a** logical; **~dente de** coming from; **~der** *vi* proceed; (*comportar-se*) behave; (*na justiça*) take legal action; **~der de** come from; **~dimento** *m* procedure; (*comportamento*) behaviour; (*na justiça*) proceedings

**proces|sador** /prosesa'dor/ *m* processor; **~sador de texto** word processor; **~samento** *m* processing; (*na justiça*) prosecution; **~samento de dados** data processing; **~sar** *vt* process; (*por crime*) prosecute; (*por causa civil*) sue; **~so** /ε/ *m* process; (*criminal*) trial; (*civil*) lawsuit

**procla|mação** /proklama'sãw/ *f* proclamation; **~mar** *vt* proclaim

**procri|ação** /prokria'sãw/ *f* procreation; **~ar** *vt/i* procreate

**procu|ra** /pro'kura/ *f* search; (*de produto*) demand; **à ~ra de** in search of; **~ração** *f* power of attorney; **~rado** *a* sought after, in demand; **~rado pela polícia** wanted by the police; **~rador** *m* (*mandatário*) proxy; (*advogado*) public prosecutor; **~rar** *vt* look for; (*contatar*) get in touch with; (*ir visitar*) lookup; **~rar saber** try to find out

**prodígio** /pro'dʒiʒiu/ *m* wonder; (*pessoa*) prodigy

**prodigioso** /prɔdʒiʒi'ozu/ *a* prodigious

**pródigo** /'prɔdigu/ *a* lavish, extravagant

**produ|ção** /produ'sãw/ *f* production; **~tividade** *f* productivity; **~tivo** *a* productive; **~to** *m* product; *(renda)* proceeds; **~to nacional bruto** gross national product; **~tos agrícolas** agricultural produce; **~tor** *m* producer □ *a* **país ~tor de trigo** wheat-producing country; **~zido** *a* ( *fam: arrumado*) done up; **~zir** *vt* produce

**proeminente** /proemi'nẽtʃi/ *a* prominent

**proeza** /pro'eza/ *f* achievement

**profa|nar** /profa'nar/ *vt* desecrate; **~no** *a* profane

**profecia** /profe'sia/ *f* prophecy

**proferir** /profe'rir/ *vt* utter; give *<discurso, palestra>*; pass *<sentença>*

**profes|sar** /profe'sar/ *vt* profess; **~so** /ε/ *a* professed; *<político etc>* seasoned; **~sor** *m* teacher; **~sor catedrático** professor

**pro|feta** /pro'fεta/ *m* prophet; **~fético** *a* prophetic; **~fetizar** *vt* prophesy

**profissão** /profi'sãw/ *f* profession

**profissio|nal** /profisio'naw/ ( *pl* **~nais**) *a* & *m/f* professional; **~nalismo** *m* professionalism; **~nalizante** *a* vocational; **~nalizar-se** *vpr* *<esportista etc>* turn professional

**profun|didade** /profũdʒi'dadʒi/ *f* depth; **~do** *a* deep; *<sentimento etc>* profound

**profusão** /profu'zãw/ *f* profusion

**prog|nosticar** /prognostʃi'kar/ *vt* forecast; **~nóstico** *m* forecast; *(med )* prognosis

**progra|ma** /pro'grama/ *m* programme; *(de computador)* program; *(diversão)* thing to do; **~mação** *f* programming; **~mador** *m* programmer; **~mar** *vt* plan; program *<computador etc>*; **~mável** ( *pl* **~máveis**) *a* programmable

**progredir** /progre'dʒir/ *vi* progress

**progres|são** /progre'sãw/ *f* progression; **~sista** *a* & *m/f* progressive; **~sivo** *a* progressive; **~so** /ε/ *m* progress

**proi|bição** /proibi'sãw/ *f* ban *(de on)*; **~bido** *a* forbidden; **~bir** *vt* forbid (**alg de** s.o. to); ban *<livro, importações etc>*; **~bitivo** *a* prohibitive

**proje|ção** /proʒe'sãw/ *f* projection; **~tar** *vt* plan *<viagem, estrada etc>*; design *<casa, carro etc>*; project *<filme, luz>*

**projé|til** /pro'ʒεtʃiw/ ( *pl* **~teis**) *m* projectile

**proje|tista** /proʒe'tʃista/ *m/f* designer; **~to** /ε/ *m* project; *(de casa, carro)* design; **~to de lei** bill; **~tor** *m* projector

**prol** /prɔw/ *m* **em ~ de** on behalf of

**prole** /'prɔli/ *f* offspring; **~tariado** *m* proletariat; **~tário** *a* & *m* proletarian

**prolife|ração** /prolifera'sãw/ *f* proliferation; **~rar** *vi* proliferate

**prolífico** /pro'lifiku/ *a* prolific

**prolixo** /pro'liksu/ *a* verbose, long-winded

**prólogo** /'prɔlogu/ *m* prologue

**prolon|gado** /prolõ'gadu/ *a* prolonged; **~gar** *vt* prolong; **~gar-se** *vpr* go on

**promessa** /pro'mεsa/ *f* promise

**prome|tedor** /promete'dor/ *a* promising; **~ter** *vt* promise □ *vi* *(dar esperança)* show promise; **~ter voltar** promise to return

**promíscuo** /pro'miskuu/ *a* promiscuous

**promis|sor** /promi'sor/ *a* promising; **~sória** *f* promissory note

**promoção** /promo'sãw/ *f* promotion

**promontório** /promõ'tɔriu/ *m* promontory

**promo|tor** /promo'tor/ *m* promoter; *(advogado)* prosecutor; **~ver** *vt* promote

**promulgar** /promuw'gar/ *vt* promulgate

**prono|me** /pro'nomi/ *m* pronoun; **~minal** ( *pl* **~minais**) *a* pronominal

**pron|tidão** /prõtʃi'dãw/ *f* readiness; **com ~tidão** promptly; **estar de ~tidão** be at the ready; **~tificar** *vt* get ready; **~tificar-se** *vpr* volunteer (**a** to; **para** for); **~to** *a* ready; *(rápido)* prompt □ *int* that's that; **~to-socorro** ( *pl* **~tos-socorros**) *m* casualty department; *(Port: reboque)* towtruck; **~tuário** *m* *(manual)* manual, handbook; *(médico)* notes; *(policial)* record, file

**pronúncia** /pro'nũsia/ *f* pronunciation

**pronunci|ado** /pronũsi'adu/ *a* pronounced; **~amento** *m* pronouncement; **~ar** *vt* pronounce

**propagar** /propa'gar/ *vt* propagate *<espécie>*; spread *<notícia, idéia, fé>*; **~-se** *vpr* spread; *<espécie>* propagate

**propen|são** /propẽ'sãw/ *f* propensity; **~so** *a* inclined (**a** to)

**pro|piciar** /propisi'ar/ *vt* provide; **~pício** *a* propitious

**propina** /pro'pina/ *f* bribe; *(Port: escolar)* fee

**propor** /pro'por/ *vt* propose; **~-se** set o.s. *<objetivo>*; **~-se a estudar** set out to study

**proporção** /propor'sãw/ f proportion

**proporcio|nado** /proporsio'nadu/ a proportionate (**a** to); **bem ~nado** well proportioned; **~nal** (pl **~nais**) a proportional; **~nar** vt provide

**proposi|ção** /propozi'sãw/ f proposition; **~tado** a, **~tal** (pl **~tais**) a intentional

**propósito** /pro'pɔzitu/ m intention; **a ~** by the way; **a ~ de** on the subject of; **chegar a ~** arrive at the right time; **de ~** on purpose

**proposta** /pro'pɔsta/ f proposal

**propriamente** /propria'mẽtʃi/ adv strictly; **a casa ~ dita** the house proper

**proprie|dade** /proprie'dadʒi/ f property; (direito sobre bens) ownership; **~tário** m owner; (de casa alugada) landlord

**próprio** /'prɔpriu/ a (de si) own; <sentido> literal; <nome> proper; **meu ~ carro** my own car; **um carro ~** a car of my own; **o ~ rei** the king himself; **~ a** peculiar to; **~ para** suited to

**prorro|gação** /proxoga'sãw/ f extension; (de dívida) deferment; (em futebol etc) extra time; **~gar** vt extend <prazo>; defer <pagamento>

**pro|sa** /'prɔza/ f prose; **~sador** m prose writer; **~saico** a prosaic

**proscrever** /proskre'ver/ vt proscribe

**prospecto** /pros'pɛktu/ m (livro) brochure; (folheto) leaflet

**prospe|rar** /prospe'rar/ vi prosper; **~ridade** f prosperity

**próspero** /'prɔsperu/ a prosperous

**prosse|guimento** /prosegi'mẽtu/ m continuation; **~guir** vt continue □ vi proceed, go on

**prostitu|ição** /prostʃitui'sãw/ f prostitution; **~ta** f prostitute

**pros|tração** /prostra'sãw/ f debility; **~trado** a prostrate; **~trar** vt prostrate; (enfraquecer) debilitate; **~trar-se** vpr prostrate o.s.

**protago|nista** /protago'nista/ m/f protagonist; **~nizar** vt be at the centre of <acontecimento>; feature in <peça, filme>

**prote|ção** /prote'sãw/ f protection; **~cionismo** m protectionism; **~cionista** a & m/f protectionist; **~ger** vt protect; **~gido** m protégé

**proteína** /prote'ina/ f protein

**protelar** /prote'lar/ vt put off

**protes|tante** /protes'tãtʃi/ a & m/f Protestant; **~tar** vt/i protest; **~to** /ɛ/ m protest

**protetor** /prote'tor/ m protector □ a protective

**protocolo** /proto'kɔlu/ m protocol; (registro) register

**protótipo** /pro'tɔtʃipu/ m prototype

**protuberância** /protube'rãsia/ f bulge

**pro|va** /'prɔva/ f (que comprova) proof; (teste) trial; (exame) exam; (esportiva) competition; (de livro etc) proof; pl (na justiça) evidence; **à ~va de bala** bulletproof; **pôr à ~va** put to the test; **~vado** a proven; **~var** vt try <comida>; try on <roupa>; try out <carro, novo sistema etc>; (comprovar) prove

**prová|vel** /pro'vavew/ (pl **~veis**) a probable

**proveito** /pro'vejtu/ m profit, advantage; **tirar ~ de** (beneficiar-se) profit from; (explorar) take advantage of; **~so** /o/ a useful

**proveni|ência** /proveni'ẽsia/ f origin; **~ente** a originating (**de** from)

**proventos** /pro'vẽtus/ m pl proceeds

**prover** /pro'ver/ vt provide (**de** with)

**provérbio** /pro'vɛrbiu/ m proverb

**proveta** /pro'veta/ f test tube; **bebê de ~** test-tube baby

**provi|dência** /provi'dẽsia/ f (medida) measure, step; (divina) providence; **tomar ~dências** take steps, take action; **~denciar** vt (prover) get hold of, provide; (resolver) see to, take care of □ vi take action

**província** /pro'vĩsia/ f province; (longe da cidade) provinces

**provinci|al** /provĩsi'aw/ (pl **~ais**) a provincial; **~ano** a & m provincial

**provir** /pro'vir/ vi come (**de** from); (resultar) be due (**de** to)

**provi|são** /provi'zãw/ f provision; **~sório** a provisional

**provo|cação** /provoka'sãw/ f provocation; **~cador, ~cante** a provocative; **~car** vt provoke; (ocasionar) cause

**proximidade** /prosimi'dadʒi/ f closeness; pl (imediações) vicinity

**próximo** /'prɔsimo/ a (no tempo) next; (perto) near, close (**de** to); <parente> close; <futuro> near □ m neighbour, fellow man

**pru|dência** /pru'dẽsia/ f prudence; **~dente** a prudent

**prumo** /'prumu/ m plumb line; **a ~** vertically

**prurido** /pru'ridu/ m itch

**pseudônimo** /pisew'donimu/ m pseudonym

**psica|nálise** /pisika'nalizi/ f psychoanalysis; **~nalista** m/f psychoanalyst

**psi|cologia** /pisikolo'ʒia/ f psychology; **~cológico** a psychological; **~cólogo** m psychologist

**psico|pata** /pisiko'pata/ m/f psychopath; **~se** /ɔ/ f psychosis; **~terapeuta** m/f psychotherapist; **~terapia** f psycho-therapy

**psicótico** /pisiˈkɔtʃiku/ *a* & *m* psychotic

**psique** /piˈsiki/ *f* psyche

**psiqui|atra** /pisikiˈatra/ *m/f* psychiatrist; **~atria** *f* psychiatry; **~átrico** *a* psychiatric

**psíquico** /piˈsikiku/ *a* psychological

**pua** /ˈpua/ *f* bit

**puberdade** /puberˈdadʒi/ *f* puberty

**publi|cação** /publikaˈsãw/ *f* publication; **~car** *vt* publish

**publici|dade** /publisiˈdadʒi/ *f* publicity; (*reclame*) advertising; **~tário** *a* publicity; (*de reclame*) advertising □ *m* advertising executive

**público** /ˈpubliku/ *a* public □ *m* public; (*platéia*) audience; **em ~** in public; **o grande ~** the general public

**pudera** /puˈdɛra/ *int* no wonder!

**pudico** /puˈdʒiku/ *a* prudish

**pudim** /puˈdʒĩ/ *m* pudding

**pudor** /puˈdor/ *m* modesty, shame

**pue|ril** /pueˈriw/ (*pl* **~ris**) *a* puerile

**pugilis|mo** /puʒiˈlizmu/ *m* boxing; **~ta** *m* boxer

**pu|ído** /puˈidu/ *a* worn through; **~ir** *vt* wear through

**pujan|ça** /puˈʒãsa/ *f* power; **~te** *a* powerful; (*de saúde*) robust

**pular** /puˈlar/ *vt* jump (over); (*omitir*) skip □ *vi* jump; **~ de contente** jump for joy; **~ carnaval** celebrate Carnival; **~ corda** skip

**pulga** /ˈpuwga/ *f* flea

**pulmão** /puwˈmãw/ *m* lung

**pulo** /ˈpulu/ *m* jump; **dar um ~ em** drop by; **dar ~s** jump up and down

**pulôver** /puˈlover/ *m* pullover

**púlpito** /ˈpuwpitu/ *m* pulpit

**pul|sar** /puwˈsar/ *vi* pulsate; **~seira** *f* bracelet; **~so** *m* (*do braço*) wrist; (*batimento arterial*) pulse

**pulular** /puluˈlar/ *vi* swarm (**de** with)

**pulveri|zador** /puwveriza'dor/ *m* spray; **~zar** *vt* spray <*líquido*>; (*reduzir a pó, fig*) pulverize

**pun|gente** /pũˈʒẽtʃi/ *a* consuming; **~gir** *vt* afflict

**pu|nhado** /puˈɲadu/ *m* handful; **~nhal** (*pl* **~nhais**) *m* dagger; **~nhalada** *f* stab wound; **~nho** *m* fist; (*de camisa etc*) cuff; (*de espada*) hilt

**pu|nição** /puniˈsãw/ *f* punishment; **~nir** *vt* punish; **~nitivo** *a* punitive

**pupila** /puˈpila/ *f* pupil

**purê** /puˈre/ *m* purée; **~ de batata** mashed potato

**pureza** /puˈreza/ *f* purity

**pur|gante** /purˈgãtʃi/ *a* & *m* purgative; **~gar** *vt* purge; **~gatório** *m* purgatory

**purificar** /purifiˈkar/ *vt* purify

**puritano** /puriˈtanu/ *a* & *m* puritan

**puro** /ˈpuru/ *a* pure; <*aguardente*> neat; **~ e simples** pure and simple; **~-sangue** (*pl* **~s-sangues**) *a* & *m* thoroughbred

**púrpura** /ˈpurpura/ *a* purple

**purpurina** /purpuˈrina/ *f* glitter

**purulento** /puruˈlẽtu/ *a* festering

**pus** /pus/ *m* pus

**pusilânime** /puziˈlanimi/ *a* faint-hearted

**pústula** /ˈpustula/ *f* pimple

**puta** /ˈputa/ *f* whore □ *a invar* (*fam*) **um ~ carro** one hell of a car; **filho da ~** (*chulo*) bastard; **~ que (o) pariu!** (*chulo*) fucking hell!

**puto** /ˈputu/ *a* (*fam*) furious

**putrefazer** /putrefaˈzer/ *vi* putrefy

**puxa** /ˈpuʃa/ *int* gosh

**pu|xado** /puˈʃadu/ *a* (*fam*) <*exame*> tough; <*trabalho*> hard; <*aluguel, preço*> steep; **~xador** *m* handle; **~xão** *m* pull, tug; **~xa-puxa** *m* toffee; **~xar** *vt* pull; strike up <*conversa*>; bring up <*assunto*>; **~xar de uma perna** limp; **~xar para** (*parecer com*) take after; **~xar por** (*exigir muito de*) push (hard); **~xa-saco** *m* (*fam*) creep

# Q

**QI** /ke i/ *m* IQ

**quadra** /ˈkwadra/ *f* (*de tênis etc*) court; (*quarteirão*) block; **~do** *a* & *m* square

**quadragésimo** /kwadraˈʒɛzimu/ *a* fortieth

**qua|dril** /kwaˈdriw/ (*pl* **~dris**) *m* hip

**quadrilha** /kwaˈdriʎa/ *f* (*bando*) gang; (*dança*) square dance

**quadrinho** /kwaˈdriɲu/ *m* frame; **história em ~s** comic strip

**quadro** /ˈkwadru/ *m* picture; (*pintado*) painting; (*tabela*) table; (*pessoal*) staff; (*equipe*) team; (*de uma peça*) scene; **~-negro** (*pl* **~s-negros**) *m* blackboard

**quadruplicar** /kwadrupliˈkar/ *vt/i* quadruple

**quádruplo** /ˈkwadruplu/ *a* quadruple; **~s** *m pl* (*crianças*) quads

**qual** /kwaw/ (*pl* **quais**) *pron* which (one); **o/a ~** (*coisa*) that, which; (*pessoa*) that, who; **~ é o seu nome?** what's your name?; **seja ~ for a decisão** whatever the decision may be

**qualidade** /kwaliˈdadʒi/ *f* quality; **na ~ de** in one's capacity as, as

**qualifi|cação** /kwalifikaˈsãw/ *f* qualification; **~car** *vt* qualify; (*descrever*) describe (**de** as); **~car-se** *vpr* qualify

**qualitativo** /kwalita'tʃivu/ *a* qualitative

**qualquer** /kwaw'kɛr/ (*pl* **quaisquer**) *a* any; **um livro ∼** any old book; **∼ um** any one

**quando** /'kwãdu/ *adv & conj* when; **∼ quer que** whenever; **∼ de** at the time of; **∼ muito** at most

**quantia** /kwã'tʃia/ *f* amount

**quanti|dade** /kwãtʃi'dadʒi/ *f* quantity; **uma ∼dade de** a lot of; **em ∼dade** in large amounts; **∼ficar** *vt* quantify; **∼tativo** *a* quantitative

**quanto** /'kwãtu/ *adv & pron* how much; *pl* how many; **∼ tempo** how long?; **∼ mais barato melhor** the cheaper the better; **tão alto ∼ eu** as tall as me; **∼ ri!** how I laughed!; **∼ a** as for; **∼ antes** as soon as possible

**quaren|ta** /kwa'rēta/ *a & m* forty; **∼tão** *a & m* (*f* **∼tona**) forty-year-old; **∼tena** /e/ *f* quarantine

**quaresma** /kwa'rezma/ *f* Lent

**quarta** /'kwarta/ *f* (*dia*) Wednesday; (*marcha*) fourth (gear); **∼-de-final** (*pl* **∼s-de-final**) *f* quarter final; **∼-feira** (*pl* **∼s-feiras**) *f* Wednesday

**quartanista** /kwarta'nista/ *m/f* fourth-year (student)

**quarteirão** /kwarte'rãw/ *m* block

**quar|tel** /kwar'tɛw/ (*pl* **∼téis**) *m* barracks; **∼tel-general** (*pl* **∼téis-generais**) *m* headquarters

**quarteto** /kwar'tetu/ *m* quartet; **∼ de cordas** string quartet

**quarto** /'kwartu/ *a* fourth □ *m* (*parte*) quarter; (*aposento*) bedroom; (*guarda*) watch; **são três e/menos um ∼** (*Port*) it's quarter past/to three; **∼ de banho** (*Port*) bathroom; **∼ de hora** quarter of an hour; **∼ de hóspedes** guest room

**quartzo** /'kwartzu/ *m* quartz

**quase** /'kwazi/ *adv* almost, nearly; **∼ nada/nunca** hardly anything/ever

**quatro** /'kwatru/ *a & m* four; **de ∼** (*no chão*) on all fours; **∼centos** *a & m* four hundred

**que** /ki/ *a* which, what; **∼ dia é hoje?** what's the date today?; **∼ homem!** what a man!; **∼ triste!** how sad! □ *pron* what; **∼ é ∼ é?** what is it? □ *pron rel* (*coisa*) which, that; (*pessoa*) who, that; (*interrogativo*) what; **o dia em ∼ ...** the day when/that ... □ *conj* that; (*porque*) because; **espero ∼ sim/não** I hope so/not

**quê** /ke/ *pron* what □ *m* **um ∼** something; **não tem de ∼** don't mention it

**quebra** /'kɛbra/ *f* break; (*de empresa, banco*) crash; (*de força*) cut; **de ∼** in addition; **∼-cabeça** *m* jigsaw (puzzle); (*fig*) puzzle; **∼diço** *a* breakable; **∼do** *a* broken; <*carro*> broken down;

**∼dos** *m pl* small change; **∼-galho** (*fam*) *m* stopgap; **∼-mar** *m* breakwater; **∼-molas** *m invar* speed bump; **∼-nozes** *m invar* nutcrackers; **∼-pau** (*fam*) *m* row; **∼-quebra** *m* riot

**quebrar** /ke'brar/ *vt* break □ *vi* break; <*carro etc*> break down; <*banco, empresa etc*> crash, go bust; **∼-se** *vpr* break

**queda** /'kɛda/ *f* fall; **ter uma ∼ por** have a soft spot for; **∼-de-braço** *f* arm wrestling

**quei|jeira** /ke'ʒera/ *f* cheese dish; **∼jo** *m* cheese; **∼jo prato** cheddar; **∼jo-de-minas** *m* Cheshire cheese

**queima** /'kejma/ *f* burning; **∼da** *f* forest fire; **∼do** *a* burnt; (*bronzeado*) tanned, brown; **cheiro de ∼do** smell of burning

**queimar** /kej'mar/ *vt* burn; (*bronzear*) tan □ *vi* burn; <*lâmpada*> go; <*fusível*> blow; **∼-se** *vpr* burn o.s.; (*bronzear-se*) go brown

**queima-roupa** /kejma'xopa/ *f* à **∼** point-blank

**quei|xa** /'keʃa/ *f* complaint; **∼xar-se** *vpr* complain (**de** about)

**queixo** /'keʃu/ *m* chin; **bater o ∼** shiver

**queixoso** /ke'ʃozu/ *a* plaintive □ *m* plaintiff

**quem** /kēj/ *pron* who; (*a pessoa que*) anyone who, he who; **de ∼ é este livro?** whose is this book?; **∼ quer que** whoever; **seja ∼ for** whoever it is; **∼ falou isso fui eu** it was me who said that; **∼ me dera (que) ...** I wish ..., if only

**Quênia** /'kenia/ *m* Kenya

**queniano** /keni'anu/ *a & m* Kenyan

**quen|tão** /kē'tãw/ *m* mulled wine; **∼te** *a* hot; (*com calor agradável*) warm; **∼tura** *f* heat

**quepe** /'kɛpi/ *m* cap

**quer** /kɛr/ *conj* **∼ ... ∼ ...** whether ... or ...

**querer** /ke'rer/ *vt/i* want; **quero ir** I want to go; **quero que você vá** I want you to go; **eu queria falar com o Sr X** I'd like to speak to Mr X; **vai ∼ vir amanhã?** do you want to come tomorrow?; **vou ∼ um cafezinho** I'd like a coffee; **se você quiser** if you want; **queira sentar** do sit down; **∼ dizer** mean; **quer dizer** (*isto é*) that is to say, I mean

**querido** /ke'ridu/ *a* dear □ *m* darling

**quermesse** /ker'mɛsi/ *f* fête, fair

**querosene** /kero'zeni/ *m* kerosene

**questão** /kes'tãw/ *f* question; (*assunto*) matter; **em ∼** in question; **fazer ∼ de** really want to; **não faço ∼ de ir** I don't mind not going

**questio|nar** /kestʃio'nar/ *vt/i* question; **~nário** *m* questionnaire; **~ná·vel** (*pl* **~náveis**) *a* questionable

**quiabo** /ki'abu/ *m* okra

**quibe** /'kibi/ *m* savoury meatball

**quicar** /ki'kar/ *vt/i* bounce

**quiche** /'kiʃi/ *f* quiche

**quie|to** /ki'etu/ *a* (*calado*) quiet; (*imóvel*) still; **~tude** *f* quiet

**quilate** /ki'latʃi/ *m* carat; (*fig*) calibre

**quilha** /'kiʎa/ *f* keel

**quilo** /'kilo/ *m* kilo; **~grama** *m* kilogram; **~metragem** *f* mileage; **~métrico** *a* mile-long

**quilômetro** /ki'lometru/ *m* kilometre

**quimbanda** /kĩ'bãda/ *m* Afro-Brazilian cult

**qui|mera** /ki'mɛra/ *f* fantasy; **~mérico** *a* fanciful

**quími|ca** /'kimika/ *f* chemistry; **~co** *a* chemical □ *m* chemist

**quimioterapia** /kimiotera'pia/ *f* chemotherapy

**quimono** /ki'mɔnu/ *m* kimono

**quina** /'kina/ *f* **de ~** edgeways

**quindim** /kĩ'dʒĩ/ *m* sweet made of coconut, sugar and egg yolks

**quinhão** /ki'ɲãw/ *m* share

**quinhentos** /ki'ɲẽtus/ *a & m* five hundred

**quinina** /ki'nina/ *f* quinine

**qüinquagésimo** /kwĩkwa'ʒezimu/ *a* fiftieth

**quinquilharias** /kĩkiʎa'rias/ *f pl* knick-knacks

**quinta**[1] /'kĩta/ *f* (*fazenda*) farm

**quinta**[2] /'kĩta/ *f* (*dia*) Thursday; **~-feira** (*pl* **~s-feiras**) *f* Thursday

**quin|tal** /kĩ'taw/ (*pl* **~tais**) *m* backyard

**quinteiro** /kĩ'tajru/ *m* (*Port*) farmer

**quinteto** /kĩ'tetu/ *m* quintet

**quin|to** /'kĩtu/ *a & m* fifth; **~tuplo** *a* fivefold; **~tuplos** *m pl* (*crianças*) quins

**quinze** /'kĩzi/ *a & m* fifteen; **às dez e ~** at quarter past ten; **são ~ para as dez** it's quarter to ten; **~na** /e/ *f* fortnight; **~nal** (*pl* **~nais**) *a* fortnightly; **~nalmente** *adv* fortnightly

**quiosque** /ki'ɔski/ *m* (*banca*) kiosk; (*no jardim*) gazebo

**quiro|mância** /kiro'mãsia/ *f* palmistry; **~mante** *m/f* palmist

**quisto** /'kistu/ *m* cyst

**quitan|da** /ki'tãda/ *f* grocer's (shop); **~deiro** *m* grocer

**qui|tar** /ki'tar/ *vt* pay off <*dívida*>; **~te** *a* **estar ~te** be quits

**quociente** /kwosi'ẽtʃi/ *m* quotient

**quórum** /'kwɔrũ/ *m* quorum

# R

**rã** /xã/ *f* frog

**rabanete** /xaba'netʃi/ *m* radish

**rabear** /xabi'ar/ *vi* <*caminhão*> jack-knife

**rabino** /xa'binu/ *m* rabbi

**rabis|car** /xabis'kar/ *vt* scribble □ *vi* (*escrever mal*) scribble; (*fazer desenhos*) doodle; **~co** *m* doodle

**rabo** /'xabu/ *m* (*de animal*) tail; **com o ~ do olho** out of the corner of one's eye; **~-de-cavalo** (*pl* **~s-de-cavalo**) *m* pony tail

**rabugento** /xabu'ʒẽtu/ *a* grumpy

**raça** /'xasa/ *f* (*de homens*) race; (*de animais*) breed

**ração** /xa'sãw/ *f* (*de comida*) ration; (*para animal*) food

**racha** /'xaʃa/ *f* crack; **~dura** *f* crack

**rachar** /xa'ʃar/ *vt* (*dividir*) split; (*abrir fendas em*) crack; chop <*lenha*>; split <*despesas*> □ *vi* (*dividir-se*) split; (*apresentar fendas*) crack; (*ao pagar*) split the cost

**raci|al** /xasi'aw/ (*pl* **~ais**) *a* racial

**racio|cinar** /xasiosi'nar/ *vi* reason; **~cínio** *m* reasoning; **~nal** (*pl* **~nais**) *a* rational; **~nalizar** *vt* rationalize

**racio|namento** /xasiona'mẽtu/ *m* rationing; **~nar** *vt* ration

**racis|mo** /xa'sizmu/ *m* racism; **~ta** *a & m/f* racist

**radar** /xa'dar/ *m* radar

**radia|ção** /xadʒia'sãw/ *f* radiation; **~dor** *m* radiator

**radialista** /xadʒia'lista/ *m/f* radio announcer

**radiante** /xadʒi'ãtʃi/ *a* (*de alegria*) overjoyed

**radi|cal** /xadʒi'kaw/ (*pl* **~cais**) *a & m* radical; **~car-se** *vpr* settle

**rádio**[1] /'xadʒiu/ *m* radio □ *f* radio station

**rádio**[2] /'xadʒiu/ *m* (*elemento*) radium

**radioati|vidade** /xadioatʃivi'dadʒi/ *f* radioactivity; **~vo** *a* radioactive

**radiodifusão** /xadʒiodʒifu'zãw/ *f* broadcasting

**radiogra|far** /radʒiogra'far/ *vt* X-ray <*pulmões, osso etc*>; radio <*mensagem*>; **~fia** *f* X-ray

**radiolo|gia** /radʒiolo'ʒia/ *f* radiology; **~gista** *m/f* radiologist

**radio|novela** /xadʒiono'vɛla/ *f* radio serial; **~patrulha** *f* patrol car; **~táxi** *m* radio taxi; **~terapia** *f* radiotherapy, ray treatment

**raia** /'xaja/ *f* (*em corrida*) lane; (*peixe*) ray

**rainha** /xaˈiɲa/ f queen; **~-mãe** f queen mother

**raio** /ˈxaju/ m (de luz etc) ray; (de círculo) radius; (de roda) spoke; (relâmpago) bolt of lightning; **~ de ação** range

**rai|va** /ˈxajva/ f rage; (doença) rabies; **estar com ~va** be furious (de with); **ter ~va de alg** have it in for s.o.; **~voso** a furious; <cachorro> rabid

**raiz** /xaˈiz/ f root; **~ quadrada/cúbica** square/cube root

**rajada** /xaˈʒada/ f (de vento) gust; (de tiros) burst

**ra|lador** /xalaˈdor/ m grater; **~lar** vt grate

**ralé** /xaˈlɛ/ f rabble

**ralhar** /xaˈʎar/ vi scold

**ralo¹** /ˈxalu/ m (ralador) grater; (de escoamento) drain

**ralo²** /ˈxalu/ a <cabelo> thinning; <sopa, tecido> thin; <vegetação> sparse; <café> weak

**ra|mal** /xaˈmaw/ (pl ~mais) m (telefone) extension; (de ferrovia) branch line

**ramalhete** /xamaˈʎetʃi/ m posy, bouquet

**ramifi|cação** /xamifikaˈsãw/ f branch; **~car-se** vi branch off

**ramo** /ˈxamu/ m branch; (profissional etc) field; (buquê) bunch; **Domingo de Ramos** Palm Sunday

**rampa** /ˈxãpa/ f ramp

**rancor** /xãˈkor/ m resentment; **~oso** /o/ a resentful

**rançoso** /xãˈsozu/ a rancid

**ran|ger** /xãˈʒer/ vt grind <dentes> □ vi creak; **~gido** m creak

**ranhura** /xaˈɲura/ f groove; (para moedas) slot

**ranzinza** /xãˈzĩza/ a cantankerous

**rapariga** /xapaˈriga/ f (Port) girl

**rapaz** /xaˈpas/ m boy

**rapé** /xaˈpɛ/ m snuff

**rapidez** /xapiˈdes/ f speed

**rápido** /ˈxapidu/ a fast □ adv <fazer> quickly; <andar> fast

**rapina** /xaˈpina/ f ave de **~** bird of prey

**rapo|sa** /xaˈpoza/ f vixen; **~so** m fox

**rapsódia** /xapˈsɔdʒia/ f rhapsody

**rap|tar** /xapˈtar/ vt abduct, kidnap <criança>; **~to** m abduction, kidnapping (de criança)

**raquete** /xaˈkɛtʃi/ f, (Port) **raqueta** /xaˈketa/ f racquet

**raquítico** /xaˈkitʃiku/ a puny

**ra|ramente** /xaraˈmetʃi/ adv rarely; **~ridade** f rarity; **~ro** a rare □ adv rarely

**rascunho** /xasˈkuɲu/ m rough version, draft

**ras|gado** /xazˈgadu/ a torn; (fig)

<elogios etc> effusive; **~gão** m tear; **~gar** vt tear; (em pedaços) tear up □ vi, **~gar-se** vpr tear; **~go** m tear; (fig) burst

**raso** /ˈxazu/ a <água> shallow; <sapato> flat; <colher etc> level

**ras|pão** /xasˈpãw/ m graze; **atingir de ~pão** graze; **~par** vt shave <cabeça, pêlos>; plane <madeira>; (para limpar) scrape; (tocar de leve) graze; **~par em** scrape

**ras|teiro** /xasˈteru/ a <planta> creeping; <animal> crawling; **~tejante** a crawling; <voz> slurred; **~tejar** vi crawl

**rasto** /ˈxastu/ m veja **rastro**

**ras|trear** /xastriˈar/ vt track <satélite etc>; scan <céu, corpo etc>; **~tro** m trail

**ratear¹** /xatʃiˈar/ vi <motor> miss

**ra|tear²** /xatʃiˈar/ vt share; **~teio** m sharing

**ratifi|cação** /xatʃifikaˈsãw/ f ratification; **~car** vt ratify

**rato** /ˈxatu/ m rat; (camundongo) mouse; **~eira** f mousetrap

**ravina** /xaˈvina/ f ravine

**razão** /xaˈzãw/ f reason; (proporção) ratio □ m ledger; **à ~ de** at the rate of; **em ~ de** on account of; **ter ~** be right; **não ter ~** be wrong

**razoá|vel** /xazoˈavew/ (pl ~veis) a reasonable

**ré¹** /xɛ/ f (na justiça) defendant

**ré²** /xɛ/ f (marcha) reverse; **dar ~** reverse

**reabastecer** /xeabasteˈser/ vt/i refuel

**reabilitar** /xeabiliˈtar/ vt rehabilitate

**rea|ção** /xeaˈsãw/ f reaction; **~ção em cadeia** chain reaction; **~cionário** a & m reactionary

**readmitir** /xeadʒimiˈtʃir/ vt reinstate <funcionário>

**reagir** /xeaˈʒir/ vi react; <doente> respond

**reajus|tar** /xeaʒusˈtar/ vt readjust; **~te** m adjustment

**re|al** /xeˈaw/ (pl ~ais) a (verdadeiro) real; (da realeza) royal

**real|çar** /xeawˈsar/ vt highlight; **~ce** m prominence

**realejo** /xeaˈleʒu/ m barrel organ

**realeza** /xeaˈleza/ f royalty

**realidade** /xealiˈdadʒi/ f reality

**realimentação** /xealimẽtaˈsãw/ f feedback

**realis|mo** /xeaˈlizmu/ m realism; **~ta** a realistic □ m/f realist

**reali|zado** /xealiˈzadu/ a <pessoa> fulfilled; **~zar** vt (fazer) carry out, (tornar real) realize <sonho, capital>; **~zar-se** vpr <sonho> come true; <pessoa> fulfil o.s.; <casamento, reunião etc> take place

**realmente** /xeaw'mẽtʃi/ *adv* really

**reaparecer** /xeapare'ser/ *vi* reappear

**reativar** /xeatʃi'var/ *vt* reactivate

**reaver** /xea'ver/ *vt* get back

**reavivar** /xeavi'var/ *vt* revive

**rebaixar** /xeba'ʃar/ *vt* lower <*preço*>; (*fig*) demean □ *vi* <*preços*> drop; **~se** *vpr* demean o.s.

**rebanho** /xe'baɲu/ *m* herd; (*fiéis*) flock

**reba|te** /xe'batʃi/ *m* alarm; **~ter** *vt* return <*bola*>; refute <*acusação*>; (*à máquina*) retype

**rebelar-se** /xebe'larsi/ *vpr* rebel

**rebel|de** /xe'bɛwdʒi/ *a* rebellious □ *m/f* rebel; **~dia** *f* rebelliousness

**rebelião** /xebeli'ãw/ *f* rebellion

**reben|tar** /xebẽ'tar/ *vt/i veja* **arrebentar**; **~to** *m* (*de planta*) shoot; (*descendente*) offspring

**rebite** /xe'bitʃi/ *m* rivet

**rebobinar** /xebobi'nar/ *vt* rewind

**rebo|cador** /xeboka'dor/ *m* tug; **~car** *vt* (*tirar*) tow; (*cobrir com reboco*) plaster; **~co** /o/ *m* plaster

**rebolar** /xebo'lar/ *vi* swing one's hips

**reboque** /xe'bɔki/ *m* towing; (*veículo a ~*) trailer; (*com guindaste*) tow-truck; **a ~** on tow

**rebuçado** /xebu'sadu/ *m* (*Port*) sweet, (*Amer*) candy

**rebuliço** /xebu'lisu/ *m* commotion

**rebuscado** /xebus'kadu/ *a* récherché

**recado** /xe'kadu/ *m* message

**reca|ída** /xeka'ida/ *f* relapse; **~ir** *vi* relapse; <*acento, culpa*> fall

**recal|cado** /xekaw'kadu/ *a* repressed; **~car** *vt* repress

**recanto** /xe'kãtu/ *m* nook, recess

**recapitular** /xekapitu'lar/ *vt* review □ *vi* recap

**reca|tado** /xeka'tadu/ *a* reserved, withdrawn; **~to** *m* reserve

**recear** /xesi'ar/ *vt/i* fear (*por* for)

**rece|ber** /xese'ber/ *vt* receive; entertain <*convidados*> □ *vi* (*~ber salário*) get paid; (*~ber convidados*) entertain; **~bimento** *m* receipt

**receio** /xe'seju/ *m* fear

**recei|ta** /xe'sejta/ *f* (*de cozinha*) recipe; (*médica*) prescription; (*dinheiro*) revenue; **~tar** *vt* prescribe

**recém|-casados** /xesẽjka'zadus/ *m pl* newly-weds; **~-chegado** *m* new-comer; **~-nascido** *a* newborn □ *m* newborn child, baby

**recente** /xe'sẽtʃi/ *a* recent; **~mente** *adv* recently

**receoso** /xese'ozu/ *a* (*apreensivo*) afraid

**recep|ção** /xesep'sãw/ *f* reception; (*Port: de carta*) receipt; **~cionar** *vt* receive; **~cionista** *m/f* receptionist; **~táculo** *m* receptacle; **~tivo** *a* receptive; **~tor** *m* receiver

**reces|são** /xese'sãw/ *f* recession; **~so** /ɛ/ *m* recess

**re|chear** /xeʃi'ar/ *vt* stuff <*frango, assado*>; fill <*empada*>; **~cheio** *m* (*para frango etc*) stuffing; (*de empada etc*) filling

**rechonchudo** /xeʃõ'ʃudu/ *a* plump

**recibo** /xe'sibu/ *m* receipt

**reciclar** /xesik'lar/ *vt* recycle

**recife** /xe'sifi/ *m* reef

**recinto** /xe'sĩtu/ *m* enclosure

**recipiente** /xesipi'ẽtʃi/ *m* container

**reciprocar** /xesipro'kar/ *vt* reciprocate

**recíproco** /xe'siproku/ *a* reciprocal; <*sentimento*> mutual

**reci|tal** /xesi'taw/ (*pl* **~tais**) *m* recital; **~tar** *vt* recite

**recla|mação** /xeklama'sãw/ *f* complaint; (*no seguro*) claim; **~mar** *vt* claim □ *vi* complain (**de** about); (*no seguro*) claim; **~me** *m*, (*Port*) **~mo** *m* advertising

**reclinar-se** /xekli'narsi/ *vpr* recline

**recluso** /xe'kluzu/ *a* reclusive □ *m* recluse

**recobrar** /xeko'brar/ *vt* recover; **~se** *vpr* recover

**recolher** /xeko'ʎer/ *vt* collect; (*retirar*) withdraw; **~-se** *vpr* retire

**recomeçar** /xekome'sar/ *vt/i* start again

**recomen|dação** /xekomẽda'sãw/ *f* recommendation; **~dar** *vt* recommend; **~dável** (*pl* **~dáveis**) *a* advisable

**recompen|sa** /xekõ'pẽsa/ *f* reward; **~sar** *vt* reward

**reconcili|ação** /xekõsilia'sãw/ *f* reconciliation; **~ar** *vt* reconcile; **~ar-se** *vpr* be reconciled

**reconhe|cer** /xekoɲe'ser/ *vt* recognize; (*admitir*) acknowledge; (*mil*) reconnoitre; identify <*corpo*>; **~cimento** *m* recognition; (*gratidão*) gratitude; (*mil*) reconnaissance; (*de corpo*) identification; **~cível** (*pl* **~cíveis**) *a* recognizable

**reconsiderar** /xekõside'rar/ *vt/i* reconsider

**reconstituinte** /xekõstʃitu'ĩtʃi/ *m* tonic

**reconstituir** /xekõstʃitu'ir/ *vt* reform; reconstruct <*crime, cena*>

**reconstruir** /xekõstru'ir/ *vt* rebuild

**recor|dação** /xekorda'sãw/ *f* recollection; (*objeto*) memento; **~dar** *vt* recollect; **~dar-se (de)** recall

**recor|de** /xe'kɔrdʒi/ *a invar* & *m* record; **~dista** *a* record-breaking □ *m/f* record-holder

**recorrer** /xeko'xer/ *vi* **~ a** turn to <*médico, amigo*>; resort to <*violência, tática*>; **~ de** appeal against

**recor|tar** /xekor'tar/ *vt* cut out; **~te** /ɔ/ *m* cutting, (*Amer*) clipping

**recostar** /xekos'tar/ *vt* lean back; **~se** *vpr* lean back

**recreio** /xe'kreju/ *m* recreation; (*na escola*) break

**recriar** /xekri'ar/ *vt* recreate

**recriminação** /xekrimina'sãw/ *f* recrimination

**recrudescer** /xekrude'ser/ *vi* intensify

**recru|ta** /xe'kruta/ *m/f* recruit; **~tamento** *m* recruitment; **~tar** *vt* recruit

**recu|ar** /xeku'ar/ *vi* move back; <*tropas*> retreat; (*no tempo*) go back; (*ceder*) back down; (*não cumprir*) back out (**de** of) □ *vt* move back; **~o** *m* retreat; (*fig: de intento*) climbdown

**recupe|ração** /xekupera'sãw/ *f* recovery; **~rar** *vt* recover; make up <*atraso, tempo perdido*>; **~rar-se** *vpr* recover (**de** from)

**recurso** /xe'kursu/ *m* resort; (*coisa útil*) resource; (*na justiça*) appeal; *pl* resources

**recu|sa** /xe'kuza/ *f* refusal; **~sar** *vt* refuse; turn down <*convite, oferta*>; **~sar-se** *vpr* refuse (**a** to)

**reda|ção** /xeda'sãw/ *f* (*de livro, contrato*) draft; (*pessoal*) editorial staff; (*seção*) editorial department; (*na escola*) composition; **~tor** *m* editor

**rede** /'xedʒi/ *f* net; (*para deitar*) hammock; (*fig: sistema*) network

**rédea** /'xedʒia/ *f* rein

**redemoinho** /xedemo'iɲu/ *m veja* **rodamoinho**

**reden|ção** /xedẽ'sãw/ *f* redemption; **~tor** *a* redeeming □ *m* redeemer

**redigir** /xedʒi'ʒir/ *vt* draw up <*contrato*>; write <*artigo*>; edit <*dicionário*>

**redimir** /xedʒi'mir/ *vt* redeem

**redobrar** /xedo'brar/ *vt* redouble

**redon|deza** /xedõ'deza/ *f* roundness; *pl* vicinity; **~do** *a* round

**redor** /xe'dor/ *m* **ao** *ou* **em ~ de** around

**redução** /xedu'sãw/ *f* reduction

**redun|dante** /xedũ'dãtʃi/ *a* redundant; **~dar** *vi* **~dar em** develop into

**redu|zido** /xedu'zidu/ *a* limited; (*pequeno*) small; **~zir** *vt* reduce; **~zir-se** *vpr* (*ficar reduzido*) be reduced (**a** to); (*resumir-se*) come down (**a** to)

**reeleger** /xeele'ʒer/ *vt* re-elect; **~se** *vpr* be re-elected

**reeleição** /xeelej'sãw/ *f* re-election

**reembol|sar** /xeẽbow'sar/ *vt* reimburse <*pessoa*>; refund <*dinheiro*>; **~so** /o/ *m* refund; **~so postal** cash on delivery

**reencarnação** /xeẽkarna'sãw/ *f* reincarnation

**reentrância** /xeẽ'trãsia/ *f* recess

**reescalonar** /xeeskalo'nar/ *vt* reschedule

**reescrever** /xeeskre'ver/ *vt* rewrite

**refastelar-se** /xefaste'larsi/ *vpr* stretch out

**refazer** /xefa'zer/ *vt* redo; rebuild <*vida*>; **~se** *vpr* recover (**de** from)

**refei|ção** /xefej'sãw/ *f* meal; **~tório** *m* dining hall

**refém** /xe'fẽj/ *m* hostage

**referência** /xefe'rẽsia/ *f* reference; **com ~ a** with reference to

**referendum** /xefe'rẽdũ/ *m* referendum

**refe|rente** /xefe'rẽtʃi/ *a* **~rente a** regarding; **~rir** *vt* report; **~rir-se** *vpr* refer (**a** to)

**refestelar-se** /xefeste'larsi/ *vpr* (*Port*) *veja* **refastelar-se**

**re|fil** /xe'fiw/ (*pl* **~fis**) *m* refill

**refi|nado** /xefi'nadu/ *a* refined; **~namento** *m* refinement; **~nar** *vt* refine; **~naria** *f* refinery

**refle|tido** /xefle'tʃidu/ *a* <*decisão*> well-thought-out; <*pessoa*> thoughtful; **~tir** *vt/i* reflect; **~tir-se** *vpr* be reflected; **~xão** /ks/ *f* reflection; **~xivo** /ks/ *a* reflexive; **~xo** /eks/ *a* <*luz*> reflected; <*ação*> reflex □ *m* (*de luz etc*) reflection; (*físico*) reflex; (*no cabelo*) streak

**refluxo** /xe'fluksu/ *m* ebb

**refo|gado** /xefo'gadu/ *m* lightly fried mixture of onions and garlic; **~gar** *vt* fry lightly

**refor|çar** /xefor'sar/ *vt* reinforce; **~ço** /o/ *m* reinforcement

**refor|ma** /xe'fɔrma/ *f* (*da lei etc*) reform; (*na casa etc*) renovation; (*de militar*) discharge; (*pensão*) pension; **~ma ministerial** cabinet reshuffle; **~mado** *a* reformed; (*Port: aposentado*) retired □ *m* (*Port*) pensioner; **~mar** *vt* reform <*lei, sistema etc*>; renovate <*casa, prédio*>; (*Port: aposentar*) retire; **~mar-se** *vpr* (*Port: aposentar-se*) retire; <*criminoso*> reform; **~matório** *m* reform school; **~mista** *a* & *m/f* reformist

**refratário** /xefra'tariu/ *a* <*tigela etc*> ovenproof, heatproof

**refrear** /xefri'ar/ *vt* rein in <*cavalo*>; (*fig*) curb, keep in check <*paixões etc*>; **~se** *vpr* restrain o.s.

**refrega** /xe'frega/ *f* clash, fight

**refres|cante** /xefres'kãtʃi/ *a* refreshing; **~car** *vt* freshen, cool <*ar*>; refresh <*pessoa, memória etc*> □ *vi* get cooler; **~car-se** *vpr* refresh o.s.; **~co** /e/ *m* (*bebida*) soft drink; *pl* refreshments

**refrige|rado** /xefriʒe'radu/ *a* cooled; <*casa etc*> air-conditioned; (*na geladeira*) refrigerated; **~rador** *m* refrigerator; **~rante** *m* soft drink; **~rar** *vt* keep cool; (*na geladeira*) refrigerate

**refugi|ado** /xefuʒi'adu/ *m* refugee; **~ar-se** *vpr* take refuge

**refúgio** /xe'fuʒiu/ *m* refuge

**refugo** /xe'fugu/ *m* waste, refuse

**refutar** /xefu'tar/ *vt* refute

**regaço** /xe'gasu/ *m* lap

**regador** /xega'dor/ *m* watering can

**regalia** /xega'lia/ *f* privilege

**regar** /xe'gar/ *vt* water

**regata** /xe'gata/ *f* regatta

**regatear** /xegatʃi'ar/ *vi* bargain, haggle

**re|gência** /xe'ʒesia/ *f* (*de verbo etc*) government; **~gente** *m/f* (*de orquestra*) conductor; **~ger** *vt* govern □ *vi* rule

**região** /xeʒi'ãw/ *f* region; (*de cidade etc*) area

**regi|me** /xe'ʒimi/ *m* regime; (*dieta*) diet; **fazer ~me** diet; **~mento** *m* (*militar*) regiment; (*regulamento*) regulations

**régio** /'xɛʒiu/ *a* regal

**regio|nal** /xeʒio'naw/ (*pl* **~nais**) *a* regional

**regis|trador** /xeʒistra'dor/ *a* **caixa ~tradora** cash register; **~trar** *vt* register; (*anotar*) record; **~tro** *m* (*lista*) register; (*de um fato, em banco de dados*) record; (*ato de ~trar*) registration

**rego** /'xegu/ *m* (*de arado*) furrow; (*de roda*) rut; (*para escoamento*) ditch

**regozi|jar** /xegozi'ʒar/ *vt* delight; **~jar-se** *vpr* be delighted; **~jo** *m* delight

**regra** /'xɛgra/ *f* rule; *pl* (*menstruações*) periods; **em ~** as a rule

**regres|sar** /xegre'sar/ *vi* return; **~sivo** *a* regressive; **contagem ~siva** countdown; **~so** /ɛ/ *m* return

**régua** /'xɛgwa/ *f* ruler

**regu|lagem** /xegu'laʒẽ/ *f* (*de carro*) tuning; **~lamento** *m* regulations; **~lar** *a* regular; <*estatura, qualidade etc*> average □ *vt* regulate; tune <*carro, motor*>; set <*relógio*> □ *vi* work; **~lar-se por** go by, be guided by; **~laridade** *f* regularity; **~larizar** *vt* regularize

**regurgitar** /xegurʒi'tar/ *vt* bring up

**rei** /xej/ *m* king; **~nado** *m* reign

**reincidir** /xeĩsi'dʒir/ *vi* <*criminoso*> reoffend

**reino** /'xejnu/ *m* kingdom; (*fig: da fantasia etc*) realm; **Reino Unido** United Kingdom

**reiterar** /xejte'rar/ *vt* reiterate

**reitor** /xej'tor/ *m* chancellor, (*Amer*) president

**reivindi|cação** /xejvĩdʒika'sãw/ *f* demand; **~car** *vt* claim, demand

**rejei|ção** /xeʒej'sãw/ *f* rejection; **~tar** *vt* reject

**rejuvenescer** /xeʒuvene'ser/ *vt* rejuvenate □ *vi* be rejuvenated

**relação** /xela'sãw/ *f* relationship; (*relatório*) account; (*lista*) list; *pl* relations; **com** *ou* **em ~ a** in relation to, regarding

**relacio|namento** /xelasiona'mẽtu/ *m* relationship; **~nar** *vt* relate (**com** to); (*listar*) list; **~nar-se** *vpr* relate (**com** to)

**relações-públicas** /xelasõjs-'publikas/ *m/f invar* public-relations person

**relâmpago** /xe'lãpagu/ *m* flash of lightning; *pl* lightning □ *a* lightning; **num ~** in a flash

**relampejar** /xelãpe'ʒar/ *vi* flash; **relampejou** there was a flash of lightning

**relance** /xe'lãsi/ *m* glance; **olhar de ~** glance (at)

**rela|tar** /xela'tar/ *vt* relate; **~tivo** *a* relative; **~to** *m* account; **~tório** *m* report

**rela|xado** /xela'ʃadu/ *a* relaxed; <*disciplina*> lax; <*pessoa*> lazy, complacent; **~xamento** *m* (*físico*) relaxation; (*de pessoa*) complacency; **~xante** *a* relaxing □ *m* tranquillizer; **~xar** *vt* relax □ *vi* (*descansar*) relax; (*tornar-se omisso*) get complacent; **~xar-se** *vpr* relax; **~xe** *m* relaxation

**reles** /'xɛlis/ *a invar* <*gente*> common; <*ação*> despicable

**rele|vância** /xele'vãsia/ *f* relevance; **~vante** *a* relevant; **~var** *vt* emphasize; **~vo** /e/ *m* relief; (*importância*) prominence

**religi|ão** /xeliʒi'ãw/ *f* religion; **~oso** /o/ *a* religious

**relin|char** /xelĩ'ʃar/ *vi* neigh; **~cho** *m* neighing

**relíquia** /xe'likia/ *f* relic

**relógio** /xe'lɔʒiu/ *m* clock; (*de pulso*) watch

**relu|tância** /xelu'tãsia/ *f* reluctance; **~tante** *a* reluctant; **~tar** *vi* be reluctant (**em** to)

**reluzente** /xelu'zẽtʃi/ *a* shining, gleaming

**relva** /'xɛwva/ *f* grass; **~do** *m* lawn

**remador** /xema'dor/ *m* rower

**remanescente** /xemane'sẽtʃi/ *a* remaining □ *m* remainder

**remar** /xe'mar/ *vt/i* row

**rema|tar** /xema'tar/ *vt* finish off; **~te** *m* finish; (*adorno*) finishing touch; (*de piada*) punch line

**remediar** /xemedʒi'ar/ vt remedy

**remédio** /xe'mɛdʒiu/ m (contra doen-ça) medicine, drug; (a probiema etc) remedy

**remelento** /xeme'lẽtu/ a bleary

**remen|dar** /xemẽ'dar/ vt mend; (com pedaço de pano) patch; **~do** m mend; (pedaço de pano) patch

**remessa** /xe'mɛsa/ f (de mercadorias) shipment; (de dinheiro) remittance

**reme|tente** /xeme'tẽtʃi/ m/f sender; **~ter** vt send <mercadorias, dinheiro etc>; refer <leitor> (a to)

**remexer** /xeme'ʃer/ vt shuffle <papéis>; stir up <poeira, lama>; wave <braços> □ vi rummage; **~-se** vpr move around

**reminiscência** /xemini'sẽsia/ f reminiscence

**remir** /xe'mir/ vt redeem; **~·e** vpr redeem o.s.

**remissão** /xemi'sãw/ f (de pecados) redemption; (de doença, pena) remission; (num livro) cross-reference

**remo** /'xemu/ m oar; (esporte) rowing

**remoção** /xemo'sãw/ f removal

**remoinho** /xemo'iɲu/ m (Port) veja **rodamoinho**

**remontar** /xemõ'tar/ vi **~ a** <coisa> date back to; <pessoa> think back to

**remorso** /xe'mɔrsu/ m remorse

**remo|to** /xe'mɔtu/ a remote; **~ver** vt remove

**remune|ração** /xemunera'sãw/ f payment; **~rador** a profitable; **~rar** vt pay

**rena** /'xena/ f reindeer

**re|nal** /xe'naw/ (pl **~nais**) a renal, kidney

**Renascença** /xena'sẽsa/ f Renaissance

**renas|cer** /xena'ser/ vi be reborn; **~cimento** m rebirth

**renda**[1] /'xẽda/ f (tecido) lace

**ren|da**[2] /'xẽda/ f income; (Port: aluguel) rent; **~der** bring in, yield <lucro>; earn <juros>; fetch <preço>; bring <resultado> □ vi <investimento, trabalho, negócio> pay off; <comida> go a long way; <produto comprado> give value for money; **~der-se** vpr surrender; **~dição** f surrender; **~dimento** m (renda) income; (de investimento, terreno) yield; (de motor etc) output; (de produto comprado) value for money; **~doso** /o/ a profitable

**rene|gado** /xene'gadu/ a & m renegade; **~gar** vt renounce

**renhido** /xe'ɲidu/ a hard-fought

**Reno** /'xenu/ m Rhine

**reno|mado** /xeno'madu/ a renowned; **~me** /o/ m renown

**reno|vação** /xenova'sãw/ f renewal; **~var** vt renew

**renque** /'xẽki/ m row

**ren|tabilidade** /xẽtabili'dadʒi/ f profitability; **~tável** (pl **~táveis**) a profitable

**rente** /'xẽtʃi/ adv **~ a** close to □ a <cabelo> cropped

**renúncia** /xe'nũsia/ f renunciation (a of); (a cargo) resignation (a from)

**renunciar** /xenũsi'ar/ vi <presidente etc> resign; **~ a** give up; waive <direito>

**reorganizar** /xeorgani'zar/ vt reorganize

**repa|ração** /xepara'sãw/ f reparation; (conserto) repair; **~rar** vt (consertar) repair; make up for <ofensa, injustiça, erro>; make good <danos, prejuízo> □ vi **~rar (em)** notice; **~ro** m (conserto) repair

**repar|tição** /xepartʃi'sãw/ f division; (seção do governo) department; **~tir** vt divide up

**repassar** /xepa'sar/ vt revise <matéria, lição>

**repatriar** /xepatri'ar/ vt repatriate

**repe|lente** /xepe'lẽtʃi/ a & m repellent; **~lir** vt repel; reject <idéia, proposta etc>

**repensar** /xepẽ'sar/ vt/i rethink

**repen|te** /xe'pẽtʃi/ m **de ~te** suddenly; (fam: talvez) maybe; **~tino** a sudden

**reper|cussão** /xeperku'sãw/ f repercussion; **~cutir** vi <som> reverberate; (fig: ter efeito) have repercussions

**repertório** /xeper'tɔriu/ m (músico etc) repertoire; (lista) list

**repe|tição** /xepetʃi'sãw/ f repetition; **~tido** a repeated; **~tidas vezes** repeatedly; **~tir** vt repeat □ vi (ao comer) have seconds; **~tir-se** vpr <pessoa> repeat o.s.; <fato, acontecimento> recur; **~titivo** a repetitive

**repi|car** /xepi'kar/ vt/i ring; **~que** m ring

**replay** /xe'plej/ (pl **~s**) m action replay

**repleto** /xe'plɛtu/ a full up

**réplica** /'xɛplika/ f reply; (cópia) replica

**replicar** /xepli'kar/ vt answer □ vi reply

**repolho** /xe'poʎu/ m cabbage

**repor** /xe'por/ vt (num lugar) put back; (substituir) replace

**reportagem** /xepor'taʒẽ/ f (uma) report; (ato) reporting

**repórter** /xe'pɔrter/ m/f reporter

**reposição** /xepozi'sãw/ f replacement

**repou|sar** /xepo'sar/ vt/i rest; **~so** m rest

**repreen|der** /xepriẽ'der/ vt rebuke, reprimand; **~são** f rebuke, reprimand; ~**sível** (*pl* ~**síveis**) *a* reprehensible

**represa** /xe'preza/ *f* dam

**represália** /xepre'zalia/ *f* reprisal

**represen|tação** /xeprezẽta'sãw/ *f* representation; (*espetáculo*) performance; (*ofício de ator*) acting; ~**tante** *m/f* representative; ~**tar** *vt* represent; (*no teatro*) perform <*peça*>; play <*papel, personagem*> □ *vi* <*ator*> act; ~**tativo** *a* representative

**repres|são** /xepre'sãw/ *f* repression; ~**sivo** *a* repressive

**repri|mido** /xepri'midu/ *a* repressed; ~**mir** *vt* repress

**reprise** /xe'prizi/ *f* (*na TV*) repeat; (*de filme*) rerun

**reprodu|ção** /xeprodu'sãw/ *f* reproduction; ~**zir** *vt* reproduce; ~**zir-se** *vpr* (*multiplicar-se*) reproduce; (*repetir-se*) recur

**repro|vação** /xeprova'sãw/ *f* disapproval; (*em exame*) failure; ~**var** *vt* (*rejeitar*) disapprove of; (*em exame*) fail; **ser** ~**vado** <*aluno*> fail

**rép|til** /'xɛptʃiw/ (*pl* ~**teis**) *m* reptile

**república** /xe'publika/ *f* republic; (*de estudantes*) hall of residence

**republicano** /xepubli'kanu/ *a* & *m* republican

**repudiar** /xepudʒi'ar/ *vt* disown; repudiate <*esposa*>

**repug|nância** /xepug'nãsia/ *f* repugnance; ~**nante** *a* repugnant

**repul|sa** /xe'puwsa/ *f* repulsion; (*recusa*) rejection; ~**sivo** *a* repulsive

**reputação** /xeputa'sãw/ *f* reputation

**requebrar** /xeke'brar/ *vt* swing; ~**-se** *vpr* sway

**requeijão** /xeke'ʒãw/ *m* cheese spread, cottage cheese

**reque|rer** /xeke'rer/ *vt* (*pedir*) apply for; (*exigir*) require; ~**rimento** *m* application

**requin|tado** /xekĩ'tadu/ *a* refined; ~**tar** *vt* refine; ~**te** *m* refinement

**requisi|ção** /xekizi'sãw/ *f* requisition; ~**tar** *vt* requisition; ~**to** *m* requirement

**rês** /xes/ (*pl* **reses**) *m* head of cattle; *pl* cattle

**rescindir** /xesĩ'dʒir/ *vt* rescind

**rés-do-chão** /xɛzdu'ʃãw/ *m* *invar* (*Port*) ground floor, (*Amer*) first floor

**rese|nha** /xe'zeɲa/ *f* review; ~**nhar** *vt* review

**reser|va** /xe'zɛrva/ *f* reserve; (*em hotel, avião etc, ressalva*) reservation; ~**var** *vt* reserve; ~**vatório** *m* reservoir; ~**vista** *m/f* reservist

**resfri|ado** /xesfri'adu/ *a* **estar** ~**ado** have a cold □ *m* cold; ~**ar** *vt* cool □ *vi* get cold; (*tornar-se morno*) cool down; ~**ar-se** *vpr* catch a cold

**resga|tar** /xezga'tar/ *vt* (*salvar*) rescue; (*remir*) redeem; ~**te** *m* (*salvamento*) rescue; (*pago por refém*) ransom; (*remissão*) redemption

**resguardar** /xezgwar'dar/ *vt* protect; ~**-se** *vpr* protect o.s. (**de** from)

**residência** /xezi'dẽsia/ *f* residence

**residen|cial** /xezidẽsi'aw/ (*pl* ~**ciais**) *a* <*bairro*> residential; <*telefone etc*> home; ~**te** *a* & *m/f* resident

**residir** /xezi'dʒir/ *vi* reside

**resíduo** /xe'ziduu/ *m* residue

**resig|nação** /xezigna'sãw/ *f* resignation; ~**nado** *a* resigned; ~**nar-se** *vpr* resign o.s. (**com** to)

**resina** /xe'zina/ *f* resin

**resis|tência** /xezis'tẽsia/ *f* resistance; (*de atleta, mental*) endurance; (*de material, objeto*) toughness; ~**tente** *a* strong, tough; <*tecido, roupa*> hardwearing; <*planta*> hardy; ~**tente a** resistant to; ~**tir** *vi* (*opor* ~**tência**) resist; (*aguentar*) withstand; <*objeto*> hold; ~**tir a** (*combater*) resist; (*aguentar*) withstand; ~**tir ao tempo** stand the test of time

**resmun|gar** /xezmũ'gar/ *vi* grumble; ~**go** *m* grumbling

**resolu|ção** /xezolu'sãw/ *f* resolution; (*firmeza*) resolve; (*de problema*) solution; ~**to** *a* resolute; ~**to a** resolved to

**resolver** /xezow'ver/ *vt* (*esclarecer*) sort out; solve <*problema, enigma*>; (*decidir*) decide; ~**-se** *vpr* make up one's mind (**a** to)

**respaldo** /xes'pawdu/ *m* (*de cadeira*) back; (*fig: apoio*) backing

**respectivo** /xespek'tʃivu/ *a* respective

**respei|tabilidade** /xespejtabili'dadʒi/ *f* respectability; ~**tador** *a* respectful; ~**tar** *vt* respect; ~**tável** (*pl* ~**táveis**) *a* respectable; ~**to** *m* respect (**por** for); **a** ~**to de** about; a **este** ~**to** in this respect; **com** ~**to a** with regard to; **dizer** ~**to a** concern; ~**toso** /o/ *a* respectful

**respin|gar** /xespĩ'gar/ *vt/i* splash; ~**go** *m* splash

**respi|ração** /xespira'sãw/ *f* breathing; ~**rador** *m* respirator; ~**rar** *vt/i* breathe; ~**ratório** *a* respiratory; ~**ro** *m* breath; (*descanso*) break, breather

**resplande|cente** /xesplãde'sẽtʃi/ *a* resplendent; ~**cer** *vi* shine

**resplendor** /xesplẽ'dor/ *m* brilliance; (*fig*) glory

**respon|dão** /xespõ'dãw/ *a* (*f* ~**dona**) cheeky; ~**der** *vt/i* answer; (*com insolência*) answer back; ~**der a** answer; ~**der por** answer for, take responsibility for

**responsabili|dade** /xespôsabili-'dadʒi/ *f* responsibility; **~zar** *vt* hold responsible (**por** for); **~zar-se** *vpr* take responsibility (**por** for)

**responsá|vel** /xespô'savew/ (*pl* **~veis**) *a* responsible (**por** for)

**resposta** /xes'pɔsta/ *f* answer

**resquício** /xes'kisiu/ *m* vestige, remnant

**ressabiado** /xesabi'adu/ *a* wary, suspicious

**ressaca** /xe'saka/ *f* (*depois de beber*) hangover; (*do mar*) undertow

**ressaltar** /xesaw'tar/ *vt* emphasize □ *vi* stand out

**ressalva** /xe'sawva/ *f* reservation, proviso; (*proteção*) safeguard

**ressarcir** /xesar'sir/ *vt* refund

**resse|cado** /xese'kadu/ *a* <*terra*> parched; <*pele*> dry; **~car** *vt/i* dry up

**ressen|tido** /xesẽ'tʃidu/ *a* resentful; **~timento** *m* resentment; **~tir-se de** (*ofender-se*) resent; (*ser influenciado*) show the effects of

**ressequido** /xese'kidu/ *a veja* **ressecado**

**resso|ar** /xeso'ar/ *vi* resound; **~nância** *f* resonance; **~nante** *a* resonant; **~nar** *vi* (*Port*) snore

**ressurgimento** /xesurʒi'mẽtu/ *m* resurgence

**ressurreição** /xesuxej'sãw/ *f* resurrection

**ressuscitar** /xesusi'tar/ *vt* revive

**restabele|cer** /xestabele'ser/ *vt* restore; restore to health <*doente*>; **~cer-se** *vpr* recover; **~cimento** *m* restoration; (*de doente*) recovery

**res|tante** /xes'tãtʃi/ *a* remaining □ *m* remainder; **~tar** *vi* remain; **~ta-me dizer que** ... it remains for me to say that

**restau|ração** /xestawra'sãw/ *f* restoration; **~rante** *m* restaurant; **~rar** *vt* restore

**restitu|ição** /xestʃitui'sãw/ *f* return, restitution; **~ir** *vt* (*devolver*) return; restore <*forma, força etc*>; reinstate <*funcionário*>

**resto** /'xestu/ *m* rest; *pl* (*de comida*) left-overs; (*de cadáver*) remains; **de ~** besides

**restrição** /xestri'sãw/ *f* restriction

**restringir** /xestrĩ'ʒir/ *vt* restrict

**restrito** /xes'tritu/ *a* restricted

**resul|tado** /xezuw'tadu/ *m* result; **~tante** *a* resulting (**de** from); **~tar** *vi* result (**de** from; **em** in)

**resu|mir** /xezu'mir/ *vt* (*abreviar*) summarize; (*conter em poucas palavras*) sum up; **~mir-se em** (*ser expresso em poucas palavras*) be summed up; **~mir-se em** (*ser*

*apenas*) come down to; **~mo** *m* summary; **em ~mo** briefly

**resvalar** /xezva'lar/ *vi* (*sem querer*) slip; (*deslizar*) slide

**reta** /'xɛta/ *f* (*linha*) straight line; (*de pista etc*) straight; **~ final** home straight

**retaguarda** /xeta'gwarda/ *f* rearguard

**retalho** /xe'taʎu/ *m* scrap; **a ~** (*Port*) retail

**retaliação** /xetalia'sãw/ *f* retaliation

**retangular** /xetãgu'lar/ *a* rectangular

**retângulo** /xe'tãgulu/ *m* rectangle

**retar|dado** /xetar'dadu/ *a* retarded □ *m* retard; **~dar** *vt* delay; **~datário** *m* latecomer

**retenção** /xetẽ'sãw/ *f* retention

**reter** /xe'ter/ *vt* keep <*pessoa*>; hold back <*águas, riso, lágrimas*>; (*na memória*) retain; **~se** *vpr* restrain o.s.

**rete|sado** /xete'zadu/ *a* taut; **~sar** *vt* pull taut

**reticência** /xetʃi'sẽsia/ *f* reticence

**reti|dão** /xetʃi'dãw/ *f* rectitude; **~ficar** *vt* rectify

**reti|rada** /xetʃi'rada/ *f* (*de tropas*) retreat; (*de dinheiro*) withdrawal; **~rado** *a* secluded; **~rar** *vt* withdraw; (*afastar*) move away; **~rar-se** *vpr* <*tropas*> retreat; (*afastar-se*) withdraw; (*de uma atividade*) retire; **~ro** *m* retreat

**reto** /'xɛtu/ *a* <*linha etc*> straight; <*pessoa*> honest

**retocar** /xeto'kar/ *vt* touch up <*desenho, maquiagem etc*>; alter <*texto*>

**reto|mada** /xeto'mada/ *f* (*continuação*) resumption; (*reconquista*) retaking; **~mar** *vt* (*continuar com*) resume; (*conquistar de novo*) retake

**retoque** /xe'tɔki/ *m* finishing touch

**retorcer** /xetor'ser/ *vt* twist; **~se** *vpr* writhe

**retóri|ca** /xe'tɔrika/ *f* rhetoric; **~co** *a* rhetorical

**retor|nar** /xetor'nar/ *vi* return; **~no** *m* return; (*na estrada*) turning place; **dar ~no** do a U-turn

**retrair** /xetra'ir/ *vt* retract, withdraw; **~se** *vpr* (*recuar*) withdraw; (*encolher-se*) retract

**retrasa|do** /xetra'zadu/ *a* **a semana ~da** the week before last

**retratar[1]** /xetra'tar/ *vt* (*desdizer*) retract

**retra|tar[2]** /xetra'tar/ *vt* (*em quadro, livro*) portray, depict; **~to** *m* portrait; (*foto*) photo; (*representação*) portrayal; **~to falado** identikit picture

**retribuir** /xetribu'ir/ *vt* return <*favor, visita*>; repay <*gentileza*>

**retroativo** /xetroa't∫ivu/ *a* retroactive; <*pagamento*> backdated

**retro|ceder** /xetrose'der/ *vi* retreat; (*desistir*) back down; ~**cesso** /ε/ *m* retreat; (*ao passado*) regression

**retrógrado** /xe'trɔgradu/ *a* retrograde

**retrospec|tiva** /xetrospek't∫iva/ *f* retrospective; ~**tivo** *a* retrospective; ~**to** /ε/ *m* look back; **em** ~**to** in retrospect

**retrovisor** /xetrovi'zor/ *a* & *m* (**espelho**) ~ rear-view mirror

**retrucar** /xetru'kar/ *vt/i* retort

**retum|bante** /xetũ'bãt∫i/ *a* resounding; ~**bar** *vi* resound

**réu** /'xεw/ *m* ( *f* ré) defendant

**reumatismo** /xewma't∫izmu/ *m* rheumatism

**reu|nião** /xeuni'ãw/ *f* meeting; (*descontraída*) get-together; (*de família*) reunion; ~**nião de cúpula** summit meeting; ~**nir** *vt* bring together <*pessoas*>; combine <*qualidades*>; ~**nir-se** *vpr* meet; <*amigos, familiares*> get together; ~**nir-se** a join

**revanche** /xe'vã∫i/ *f* revenge; (*jogo*) return match

**reveillon** /xeve'jõ/ (*pl* ~**s**) *m* New Year's Eve

**reve|lação** /xevela'sãw/ *f* revelation; (*de fotos*) developing; (*novo talento*) promising newcomer; ~**lar** *vt* reveal; develop <*filme, fotos*>; ~**lar-se** *vpr* (*vir a ser*) turn out to be

**revelia** /xeve'lia/ *f* à ~ by default; à ~ de without the knowledge of

**reven|dedor** /xevẽde'dor/ *m* dealer; ~**der** *vt* resell

**rever** /xe'ver/ *vt* (*ver de novo*) see again; (*revisar*) revise; (*examinar*) check

**reve|rência** /xeve'resia/ *f* reverence; (*movimento do busto*) bow; (*dobrando os joelhos*) curtsey; ~**rente** *a* reverent

**reverso** /xe'vεrsu/ *m* reverse; **o** ~ **da medalha** the other side of the coin

**revés** /xe'vεs/ (*pl* **reveses**) *m* setback

**reves|timento** /xevest∫i'mẽtu/ *m* covering; ~**tir** *vt* cover

**reve|zamento** /xeveza'mẽtu/ *m* alternation; ~**zar** *vt/i* alternate; ~**zar-se** *vpr* alternate

**revi|dar** /xevi'dar/ *vt* return <*golpe, insulto*>; refute <*crítica*>; (*retrucar*) retort □ *vi* hit back; ~**de** *m* response

**revigorar** /xevigo'rar/ *vt* strengthen □ *vi*, ~**-se** *vpr* regain one's strength

**revi|rar** /xevi'rar/ *vt* turn out <*bolsos, gavetas*>; turn over <*terra*>; turn inside out <*roupa*>; roll <*olhos*>; ~**rar-se** *vpr* toss and turn; ~**ravolta** /ɔ/ *f* (*na política etc*) about-face, about-turn; (*da situação*) turnabout, dramatic change

**revi|são** /xevi'zãw/ *f* (*de lições etc*) revision; (*de máquina, motor*) overhaul; (*de carro*) service; ~**são de provas** proofreading; ~**sar** *vt* revise <*provas, lições*>; service <*carro*>; ~**sor** *m* (*de bilhetes*) ticket inspector; ~**sor de provas** proofreader

**revis|ta** /xe'vista/ *f* (*para ler*) magazine; (*teatral*) revue; (*de tropas etc*) review; **passar** ~**ta** a review; ~**tar** *vt* search

**reviver** /xevi'ver/ *vt* relive □ *vi* revive

**revogar** /xevo'gar/ *vt* revoke <*lei*>; cancel <*ordem*>

**revol|ta** /xe'vɔwta/ *f* (*rebelião*) revolt; (*indignação*) disgust; ~**tante** *a* disgusting; ~**tar** *vt* disgust; ~**tar-se** *vpr* (*rebelar-se*) revolt; (*indignar-se*) be disgusted; ~**to** /o/ *a* <*casa, gaveta*> upside down; <*cabelo*> dishevelled; <*mar*> rough; <*mundo, região*> troubled; <*anos*> turbulent

**revolu|ção** /xevolu'sãw/ *f* revolution; ~**cionar** *vt* revolutionize; ~**cionário** *a* & *m* revolutionary

**revolver** /xevow'ver/ *vt* turn over <*terra*>; roll <*olhos*>; go through <*gavetas, arquivos*>

**revólver** /xe'vɔwver/ *m* revolver

**re|za** /'xεza/ *f* prayer; ~**zar** *vi* pray □ *vt* say <*missa, oração*>; (*dizer*) state

**riacho** /xi'a∫u/ *m* stream

**ribalta** /xi'bawta/ *f* footlights

**ribanceira** /xibã'sera/ *f* embankment

**ribombar** /xibõ'bar/ *vi* rumble

**rico** /'xiku/ *a* rich □ *m* rich man; **os** ~**s** the rich

**ricochete** /xiko'∫et∫i/ *m* ricochet; ~**ar** *vi* ricochet

**ricota** /xi'kɔta/ *f* curd cheese, ricotta

**ridicularizar** /xidʒikulari'zar/ *vt* ridicule

**ridículo** /xi'dʒikulu/ *a* ridiculous

**ri|fa** /'xifa/ *f* raffle; ~**far** *vt* raffle

**rifão** /xi'fãw/ *m* saying

**rifle** /'xifli/ *m* rifle

**rigidez** /xiʒi'des/ *f* rigidity

**rígido** /'xiʒidu/ *a* rigid

**rigor** /xi'gor/ *m* severity; (*meticulosidade*) rigour; **vestido a** ~ evening dress; **de** ~ essential

**rigoroso** /xigo'rozu/ *a* strict; <*inverno, pena*> severe, harsh; <*lógica, estudo*> rigorous

**rijo** /'xiʒu/ *a* stiff; <*músculos*> firm

**rim** /xĩ/ *m* kidney; *pl* (*parte das costas*) small of the back

**ri|ma** /'xima/ *f* rhyme; ~**mar** *vt/i* rhyme

**rí|mel** /'ximew/ (*pl* ~**meis**) *m* mascara

**ringue** /'xĩgi/ *m* ring

**rinoceronte** /xinose'rõtʃi/ *m* rhinoceros

**rinque** /'xĩki/ *m* rink

**rio** /'xio/ *m* river

**riqueza** /xi'keza/ *f* wealth; *(qualidade)* richness; *pl* riches

**rir** /xir/ *vi* laugh (**de** at)

**risada** /xi'zada/ *f* laugh, laughter; **dar
~** laugh

**ris|ca** /'xiska/ *f* stroke; *(listra)* stripe;
*(do cabelo)* parting; **à ~ca** to the
letter; **~car** *vt* (*apagar*) cross out
<*erro*>; strike <*fósforo*>; scratch
<*mesa, carro etc*>; write off <*amigo
etc*>; **~co¹** *m* (*na parede etc*) scratch;
*(no papel)* line; *(esboço)* sketch

**risco²** /'xisku/ *m* risk

**riso** /'xizu/ *m* laugh; **~nho** /o/ *a* smil-
ing

**ríspido** /'xispidu/ *a* harsh

**rítmico** /'xitʃmiku/ *a* rhythmic

**ritmo** /'xitʃimu/ *m* rhythm

**rito** /'xitu/ *m* rite

**ritu|al** /xitu'aw/ (*pl* **~ais**) *a* & *m*
ritual

**ri|val** /xi'vaw/ (*pl* **~vais**) *a* & *m/f*
rival; **~validade** *f* rivalry; **~-
valizar** *vt* rival □ *vi* vie (**com** with)

**rixa** /'xiʃa/ *f* fight

**robô** /xo'bo/ *m* robot

**robusto** /xo'bustu/ *a* robust

**roça** /'xɔsa/ *f* (*campo*) country

**rocambole** /xokã'bɔli/ *m* roll

**roçar** /xo'sar/ *vt* graze; **~ em** brush
against

**ro|cha** /'xɔʃa/ *f* rock; **~chedo** /e/ *m*
cliff

**roda** /'xɔda/ *f* (*de carro etc*) wheel; *(de
amigos etc*) circle; **~ dentada** cog;
**~da** *f* round; **~do** *a* **saia ~da** full
skirt; **~-gigante** (*pl* **~s-gigantes**) *f*
big wheel, *(Amer)* ferris wheel;
**~moinho** *m* (*de vento*) whirlwind;
*(na água)* whirlpool; *( fig)* whirl,
swirl; **~pé** *m* skirting board, *(Amer)*
baseboard

**rodar** /xo'dar/ *vt* (*fazer girar*) spin;
*(viajar por)* go round; do <*quilometragem*>; shoot <*filme*>; run
<*programa*> □ *vi* (*girar*) spin; *(de car-
ro)* drive round

**rodear** /xodʒi'ar/ *vt* (*circundar*) surround; *(andar ao redor de)* go round

**rodeio** /xo'deju/ *m* (*ao falar*) circum-
locution; *(de gado)* round-up; **falar
sem ~s** talk straight

**rodela** /xo'dɛla/ *f* (*de limão etc*) slice;
*( peça de metal)* washer

**rodízio** /xo'dʒiziu/ *m* rota

**rodo** /'xodu/ *m* rake

**rodopiar** /xodopi'ar/ *vi* spin round

**rodovi|a** /xodo'via/ *f* highway; **~ária**
*f* bus station; **~ário** *a* road; **polícia
~ária** traffic police

**ro|edor** /xoe'dor/ *m* rodent; **~er** *vt*
gnaw; bite <*unhas*>; *( fig)* eat away

**rogar** /xo'gar/ *vi* request

**rojão** /xo'ʒãw/ *m* rocket

**rol** /xɔw/ (*pl* **róis**) *m* roll

**rolar** /xo'lar/ *vt* roll □ *vi* roll; *( fam)*
*(acontecer)* happen

**roldana** /xow'dana/ *f* pulley

**roleta** /xo'leta/ *f* ( *jogo*) roulette; *(borboleta)* turnstile

**rolha** /'xoʎa/ *f* cork

**roliço** /xo'lisu/ *a* <*objeto*> cylindrical; <*pessoa*> plump

**rolo** /'xolu/ *m* (*de filme, tecido etc*) roll;
*(máquina, bobe)* roller; **~ compres-
sor** steamroller; **~ de massa** rolling
pin

**Roma** /'xoma/ *f* Rome

**romã** /xo'mã/ *f* pomegranate

**roman|ce** /xo'mãsi/ *m* (*livro*) novel;
*(caso)* romance; **~cista** *m/f* novelist

**romano** /xo'manu/ *a* & *m* Roman

**romântico** /xo'mãtʃiku/ *a* romantic

**romantismo** /xomã'tʃizmu/ *m*
*(amor)* romance; *(idealismo)* romanti-
cism

**romaria** /xoma'ria/ *f* pilgrimage

**rombo** /'xõbu/ *m* hole

**Romênia** /xo'menia/ *f* Romania

**romeno** /xo'menu/ *a* & *m* Romanian

**rom|per** /xõ'per/ *vt* break; break off
<*relações*> □ *vi* <*dia*> break; <*sol*>
rise; **~per com** break up with;
**~pimento** *m* break; *(de relações)*
breaking off

**ron|car** /xõ'kar/ *vi* (*ao dormir*) snore;
<*estômago*> rumble; **~co** *m* snoring;
*(um)* snore; *(de motor)* roar

**ron|da** /'xõda/ *f* round, patrol; **~dar**
*vt* (*patrulhar*) patrol; *(espreitar)*
prowl around □ *vi* <*vigia etc*> patrol;
<*animal, ladrão*> prowl around

**ronronar** /xõxo'nar/ *vi* purr

**roque¹** /'xɔki/ *m* (*em xadrez*) rook

**ro|que²** /'xɔki/ *m* (*música*) rock;
**~queiro** *m* rock musician

**rosa** /'xɔza/ *f* rose □ *a invar* pink; **~do**
*a* rosy; <*vinho*> rosé

**rosário** /xo'zariu/ *m* rosary

**rosbife** /xoz'bifi/ *m* roast beef

**rosca** /'xoska/ *f* (*de parafuso*) thread;
*(biscoito)* rusk; **farinha de ~** breadcrumbs

**roseira** /xo'zera/ *f* rosebush

**roseta** /xo'zeta/ *f* rosette

**rosnar** /xoz'nar/ *vi* <*cachorro*>
growl; <*pessoa*> snarl

**rosto** /'xostu/ *m* face

**rota** /'xɔta/ *f* route

**rota|ção** /xota'sãw/ *f* rotation;
**~tividade** *f* turnround; **~tivo** *a* ro-
tating

**rotei|rista** /xote'rista/ *m/f* script-
writer; **~ro** *m* (*de viagem*) itinerary;

(*de filme, peça*) script; (*de discussão etc*) outline
**roti|na** /xo'tʃina/ *f* routine; **~neiro** *a* routine
**rótula** /'xɔtula/ *f* kneecap
**rotular** /xotu'lar/ *vt* label (**de as**)
**rótulo** /'xɔtulu/ *m* label
**rou|bar** /xo'bar/ *vt* steal <*dinheiro, carro etc*>; rob <*pessoa, loja etc*> □ *vi* steal; (*em jogo*) cheat; **~bo** *m* theft, robbery
**rouco** /'xoku/ *a* hoarse; <*voz*> gravelly
**rou|pa** /'xopa/ *f* clothes; (*uma*) outfit; **~pa de baixo** underwear; **~pa de cama** bedclothes; **~pão** *m* dressing gown
**rouquidão** /xoki'dãw/ *f* hoarseness
**rouxi|nol** /xoʃi'nɔw/ (*pl* **~nóis**) *m* nightingale
**roxo** /'xoʃu/ *a* purple
**rua** /'xua/ *f* street
**rubéola** /xu'bɛola/ *f* German measles
**rubi** /xu'bi/ *m* ruby
**rude** /'xudʒi/ *a* rude
**rudimentos** /xudʒi'mẽtus/ *m pl* rudiments, basics
**ruela** /xu'ɛla/ *f* backstreet
**rufar** /xu'far/ *vi* <*tambor*> roll □ *m* roll
**ruga** /'xuga/ *f* (*na pele*) wrinkle; (*na roupa*) crease
**ru|gido** /xu'ʒidu/ *m* roar; **~gir** *vi* roar
**ruibarbo** /xui'barbu/ *m* rhubarb
**ruído** /xu'idu/ *m* noise
**ruidoso** /xui'dozu/ *a* noisy
**ruim** /xu'ĩ/ *a* bad
**ruína** /xu'ina/ *f* ruin
**ruivo** /'xuivu/ *a* <*cabelo*> red; <*pessoa*> red-haired □ *m* redhead
**rulê** /xu'le/ *a* **a gola ~** roll-neck
**rum** /xũ/ *m* rum
**ru|mar** /xu'mar/ *vi* head (**para** for); **~mo** *m* course; **~mo a** heading for; **sem ~mo** <*vida*> aimless; <*andar*> aimlessly
**rumor** /xu'mor/ *m* (*da rua, de vozes*) hum; (*do trânsito*) rumble; (*boato*) rumour
**ru|ral** /xu'raw/ (*pl* **~rais**) *a* rural
**rusga** /'xuzga/ *f* quarrel, disagreement
**rush** /xaʃ/ *m* rush hour
**Rússia** /'xusia/ *f* Russia
**russo** /'xusu/ *a* & *m* Russian
**rústico** /'xustʃiku/ *a* rustic

# S

**Saará** /saa'ra/ *m* Sahara
**sábado** /'sabadu/ *m* Saturday
**sabão** /sa'bãw/ *m* soap; **~ em pó** soap powder

**sabatina** /saba'tʃina/ *f* test
**sabedoria** /sabedo'ria/ *f* wisdom
**saber** /sa'ber/ *vt/i* know (**de** about); (*descobrir*) find out (**de** about) □ *m* knowledge; **eu sei cantar** I know how to sing, I can sing; **sei lá** I've no idea; **que eu saiba** as far as I know
**sabiá** /sabi'a/ *m* thrush
**sabi|chão** /sabi'ʃãw/ *a* & *m* (*f* **~chona**) know-it-all
**sábio** /'sabiu/ *a* wise □ *m* wise man
**sabone|te** /sabo'netʃi/ *m* bar of soap; **~teira** *f* soapdish
**sabor** /sa'bor/ *m* flavour; **ao ~ de** at the mercy of
**sabo|rear** /sabori'ar/ *vt* savour; **~roso** *a* tasty
**sabo|tador** /sabota'dor/ *m* saboteur; **~tagem** *f* sabotage; **~tar** *vt* sabotage
**saca** /'saka/ *f* sack
**sacada** /sa'kada/ *f* balcony
**sa|cal** /sa'kaw/ (*pl* **~cais**) *a* (*fam*) boring
**saca|na** /sa'kana/ (*fam*) *a* (*desonesto*) devious; (*lascivo*) dirty-minded, naughty □ *m/f* rogue; **~nagem** (*fam*) *f* (*esperteza*) trickery; (*sexo*) sex; (*uma*) dirty trick; **~near** (*fam*) *vt* (*enganar*) do the dirty on; (*amolar*) take the mickey out of
**sacar** /sa'kar/ *vt/i* withdraw <*dinheiro*>; draw <*arma*>; (*em tênis, vôlei etc*) serve; (*fam*) (*entender*) understand
**saçaricar** /sasari'kar/ *vi* play around
**sacarina** /saka'rina/ *f* saccharine
**saca-rolhas** /saka'xoʎas/ *m invar* corkscrew
**sacer|dócio** /saser'dɔsiu/ *m* priesthood; **~dote** /ɔ/ *m* priest; **~dotisa** *f* priestess
**sachê** /sa'ʃe/ *m* sachet
**saciar** /sasi'ar/ *vt* satisfy
**saco** /'saku/ *m* bag; **que ~!** (*fam*) what a pain!; **estar de ~ cheio (de)** (*fam*) be fed up (with), be sick (of); **encher o ~ de alg** (*fam*) get on s.o.'s nerves; **puxar o ~ de alg** (*fam*) suck up to s.o.; **~ de dormir** sleeping bag; **~la** /ɔ/ *f* bag; **~lão** *m* wholesale fruit and vegetable market; **~lejar** *vt* shake
**sacramento** /sakra'mẽtu/ *m* sacrament
**sacri|ficar** /sakrifi'kar/ *vt* sacrifice; have put down <*cachorro etc*>; **~fício** *m* sacrifice; **~légio** *m* sacrilege
**sacrílego** /sa'krilegu/ *a* sacrilegious
**sacro** /'sakru/ *a* <*música*> religious
**sacrossanto** /sakro'sãtu/ *a* sacrosanct
**sacu|dida** /saku'dʒida/ *f* shake; **~dir** *vt* shake

**sádico** /'sadʒiku/ *a* sadistic □ *m* sadist
**sadio** /sa'dʒiu/ *a* healthy
**sadismo** /sa'dʒizmu/ *m* sadism
**safa|deza** /safa'deza/ *f (desonestidade)* deviousness; *(libertinagem)* indecency; *(uma)* dirty trick; **~do** *a (desonesto)* devious; *(lascivo)* dirty-minded; *(esperto)* quick; <*criança*> naughty
**safena** /sa'fɛna/ *f* **ponte de ~** heart bypass; **~do** *m* bypass patient
**safira** /sa'fira/ *f* sapphire
**safra** /'safra/ *f* crop
**sagitariano** /saʒitari'anu/ *a & m* Sagittarian
**Sagitário** /saʒi'tariu/ *m* Sagittarius
**sagrado** /sa'gradu/ *a* sacred
**saguão** /sa'gwãw/ *m (de teatro, hotel)* foyer, *(Amer)* lobby; *(de estação, aeroporto)* concourse
**saia** /'saja/ *f* skirt; **~-calça** (*pl* **~s-calças**) *f* culottes
**saída** /sa'ida/ *f (partida)* departure; *(porta, fig)* way out; **de ~** at the outset; **estar de ~** be on one's way out
**sair** /sa'ir/ *vi (de dentro)* go/come out; *(partir)* leave; *(desprender-se)* come off; <*mancha*> come out; *(resultar)* turn out; **~-se** *vpr* fare; **~-se com** *(dizer)* come out with; **~ mais barato** work out cheaper
**sal** /saw/ (*pl* **sais**) *m* salt; **~ de frutas** Epsom salts
**sala** /'sala/ *f (numa casa)* lounge; *(num lugar público)* hall; *(classe)* class; **fazer ~ a** entertain; **~ (de aula)** classroom; **~ de embarque** departure lounge; **~ de espera** waiting room; **~ de jantar** dining room; **~ de operação** operating theatre
**sala|da** /sa'lada/ *f* salad; *(fig)* jumble, mishmash; **~da de frutas** fruit salad; **~deira** *f* salad bowl
**sala-e-quarto** /sali'kwartu/ *m* two-room flat
**sala|me** /sa'lami/ *m* salami; **~minho** *m* pepperoni
**salão** /sa'lãw/ *m* hall; *(de cabeleireiro)* salon; *(de carros)* show; **~ de beleza** beauty salon
**salari|al** /salari'aw/ (*pl* **~ais**) *a* wage
**salário** /sa'lariu/ *m* salary
**sal|dar** /saw'dar/ *vt* settle; **~do** *m* balance
**saleiro** /sa'leru/ *m* salt cellar
**sal|gadinhos** /sawga'dʒinus/ *m pl* snacks; **~gado** *a* salty; <*preço*> exorbitant; **~gar** *vt* salt
**salgueiro** /saw'geru/ *m* willow; **~ chorão** weeping willow
**saliência** /sali'ẽsia/ *f* projection
**salien|tar** /saliẽ'tar/ *vt (deixar claro)* point out; *(acentuar)* highlight; **~tar-**

**se** *vpr* distinguish o.s.; **~te** *a* prominent
**saliva** /sa'liva/ *f* saliva
**salmão** /saw'mãw/ *m* salmon
**salmo** /'sawmu/ *m* psalm
**salmonela** /sawmo'nɛla/ *f* salmonella
**salmoura** /saw'mora/ *f* brine
**salpicar** /sawpi'kar/ *vt* sprinkle; *(sem querer)* spatter
**salsa** /'sawsa/ *f* parsley
**salsicha** /saw'siʃa/ *f* sausage
**saltar** /saw'tar/ *vt (pular)* jump; *(omitir)* skip □ *vi* jump; **~ à vista** be obvious; **~ do ônibus** get off the bus
**saltear** /sawtʃi'ar/ *vt* sauté <*batatas etc*>
**saltitar** /sawtʃi'tar/ *vi* hop
**salto** /'sawtu/ *m (pulo)* jump; *(de sapato)* heel; **~ com vara** pole vault; **~ em altura** high jump; **~ em distância** long jump; **~-mortal** (*pl* **~s-mortais**) *m* somersault
**salu|bre** /sa'lubri/ *a* healthy; **~tar** *a* salutary
**salva¹** /'sawva/ *f (de canhões)* salvo; *(bandeja)* salver; **~ de palmas** round of applause
**salva²** /'sawva/ *f (erva)* sage
**salva|ção** /sawva'sãw/ *f* salvation; **~dor** *m* saviour
**salvaguar|da** /sawva'gwarda/ *f* safeguard; **~dar** *vt* safeguard
**sal|vamento** /sawva'mẽtu/ *m* rescue; *(de navio)* salvage; **~var** *vt* save; **~var-se** *vpr* escape; **~va-vidas** *m invar (bóia)* lifebelt □ *m/f (pessoa)* lifeguard □ *a* **barco ~va-vidas** lifeboat; **~vo** *a* safe □ *prep* save; **a ~vo** safe
**samambaia** /samã'baja/ *f* fern
**sam|ba** /'sãba/ *m* samba; **~ba-canção** (*pl* **~bas-canção**) *m* slow samba □ *a invar* **cueca ~ba-canção** boxer shorts; **~ba-enredo** (*pl* **~bas-enredo**) *m* samba story; **~bar** *vi* samba; **~bista** *m/f (dançarino)* samba dancer; *(compositor)* composer of sambas; **~bódromo** *m* Carnival parade ground
**samovar** /samo'var/ *m* tea urn
**sanar** /sa'nar/ *vt* cure
**san|ção** /sã'sãw/ *f* sanction; **~cionar** *vt* sanction
**sandália** /sã'dalia/ *f* sandal
**sandes** /'sãdiʃ/ *f invar (Port)* sandwich
**sanduíche** /sãdu'iʃi/ *m* sandwich
**sane|amento** /sania'mẽtu/ *m (esgotos)* sanitation; *(de finanças)* rehabilitation; **~ar** *vt* set straight <*finanças*>
**sanfona** /sã'fona/ *f (instrumento)* accordion; *(tricô)* ribbing; **~do** *a* <*porta*> folding; <*pulôver*> ribbed
**san|grar** /sã'grar/ *vt/i* bleed; **~grento** *a* bloody; <*carne*> rare;

~gria /f bloodshed; (de dinheiro) extortion
sangue /'sãgi/ m blood; ~ pisado bruise; ~frio m cool, coolness
sanguessuga /sãgi'suga/ f leech
sanguinário /sãgi'nariu/ a bloodthirsty
sanguíneo /sã'giniu/ a blood
sanidade /sani'dadʒi/ f sanity
sanitário /sani'tariu/ a sanitary; ~s mpl toilets
san|tidade /sãtʃi'dadʒi/ f sanctity; ~tificar vt sanctify; ~to a holy □ m saint; todo ~to dia every single day; ~tuário m sanctuary
São /sãw/ a Saint
são /sãw/ (pl ~s) a (f sã) healthy; (mentalmente) sane; <conselho> sound
sapata /sa'pata/ f shoe; ~ria f shoe shop
sapate|ado /sapatʃi'adu/ m tap dancing; ~ador m tap dancer; ~ar vi tap one's feet; (dançar) tap-dance
sapa|teiro /sapa'teru/ m shoemaker; ~tilha f pump; ~tilha de balé ballet shoe; ~to m shoe
sapeca /sa'pɛka/ a saucy
sa|pinho /sa'piɲu/ m thrush; ~po m toad
saque¹ /'saki/ m (do banco) withdrawal; (em tênis, vôlei etc) serve
saque² /'saki/ m (de loja etc) looting; ~ar vt loot
saraiva /sa'rajva/ f hail; ~da f hailstorm; uma ~da de a hail of
sarampo /sa'rãpu/ m measles
sarar /sa'rar/ vt cure □ vi get better; <ferida> heal
sar|casmo /sar'kazmu/ m sarcasm; ~cástico a sarcastic
sarda /'sarda/ f freckle
Sardenha /sar'deɲa/ f Sardinia
sardento /sar'dẽtu/ a freckled
sardinha /sar'dʒiɲa/ f sardine
sardônico /sar'doniku/ a sardonic
sargento /sar'ʒẽtu/ m sergeant
sarjeta /sar'ʒeta/ f gutter
Satanás /sata'nas/ m Satan
satânico /sa'taniku/ a satanic
satélite /sa'tɛlitʃi/ a & m satellite
sátira /'satʃira/ f satire
satírico /sa'tʃiriku/ a satirical
satirizar /satʃiri'zar/ vt satirize
satisfa|ção /satʃisfa'sãw/ f satisfaction; dar ~ções a answer to; ~tório a satisfactory; ~zer vt ~zer (a) satisfy □ vi be satisfactory; ~zer-se vpr be satisfied
satisfeito /satʃis'fejtu/ a satisfied; (contente) content; (de comida) full
saturar /satu'rar/ vt saturate
Saturno /sa'turnu/ m Saturn
saudação /sawda'sãw/ f greeting

saudade /saw'dadʒi/ f longing; (lembrança) nostalgia; estar com ~s de miss; matar ~s catch up
saudar /saw'dar/ vt greet
saudá|vel /saw'davew/ (pl ~veis) a healthy
saúde /sa'udʒi/ f health □ int (ao beber) cheers; (ao espirrar) bless you
saudo|sismo /sawdo'zizmu/ m nostalgia; ~so /o/ a longing; estar ~so de miss; o nosso ~so amigo our much-missed friend
sauna /'sawna/ f sauna
saxofo|ne /sakso'foni/ m saxophone; ~nista m/f saxophonist
sazo|nado /sazo'nadu/ a seasoned; ~nal (pl ~nais) a seasonal
se¹ /si/ conj if; não sei ~ ... I don't know if/whether
se² /si/ pron (ele mesmo) himself; (ela mesma) herself; (você mesmo) yourself; (eles/elas) themselves; (vocês) yourselves; (um ao outro) each other; dorme-~ tarde no Brasil people go to bed late in Brazil; aqui ~ fala inglês English is spoken here
sebo /'sebu/ m (sujeira) grease; (livraria) secondhand bookshop; ~so /o/ a greasy; <pessoa> slimy
seca /'seka/ f drought; ~dor m ~dor de cabelo hairdryer; ~dora f tumble dryer
secar /se'kar/ vt/i dry
sec|ção /sek'sãw/ f veja seção; ~cionar vt split up
seco /'seku/ a dry; <resposta, tom> curt; <pessoa, caráter> cold; <barulho, pancada> dull; estar ~ por I'm dying for
secretaria /sekreta'ria/ f (de empresa) general office; (ministério) department
secretá|ria /sekre'taria/ f secretary; ~ria eletrônica ansaphone; ~rio m secretary
secreto /se'krɛtu/ a secret
secular /seku'lar/ a (não religioso) secular; (antigo) age-old
século /'sɛkulu/ m century; pl (muito tempo) ages
secundário /sekũ'dariu/ a secondary
secura /se'kura/ f dryness; estar com uma ~ de be longing for/to
seda /'seda/ f silk
sedativo /seda'tʃivu/ a & m sedative
sede¹ /'sɛdʒi/ f headquarters; (local do governo) seat
sede² /'sedʒi/ f thirst (de for); estar com ~ be thirsty
sedentário /sedẽ'tariu/ a sedentary
sedento /se'dẽtu/ a thirsty (de for)
sediar /sedʒi'ar/ vt host

**sedimen|tar** /sedʒimẽ'tar/ vt consolidate; **~to** m sediment
**sedoso** /se'dozu/ a silky
**sedu|ção** /sedu'sãw/ f seduction; **~tor** a seductive; **~zir** vt seduce
**segmento** /seg'mẽtu/ m segment
**segredo** /se'gredu/ m secret; (de cofre etc) combination
**segregar** /segre'gar/ vt segregate
**segui|da** /se'gida/ f em **~da** (imediatamente) straight away; (depois) next; **~do** a followed (de by); **cinco horas ~das** five hours running; **~dor** m follower; **~mento** m continuation; **dar ~mento a** go on with
**se|guinte** /se'gĩtʃi/ a following; <dia, semana etc> next; **~guir** vt/i follow; (continuar) continue; **~guir-se** vpr follow; **~guir em frente** (ir embora) go; (indicação na rua) go straight ahead
**segun|da** /se'gũda/ f (dia) Monday; (marcha) second; **de ~da** second-rate; **~da-feira** (pl **~das-feiras**) f Monday; **~do** a & m second □ adv secondly □ prep according to □ conj according to what; **~das intenções** ulterior motives; **de ~da mão** second-hand
**segu|rança** /segu'rãsa/ f security; (estado de seguro) safety; (certeza) assurance □ m/f security guard; **~rar** vt hold; **~rar-se** vpr (controlar-se) control o.s.; **~rar-se em** hold on to; **~ro** a secure; ( fora de perigo) safe; (com certeza) sure □ m insurance; **estar no ~ro** <bens> be insured; **fazer ~ro de** insure; **~ro-desemprego** m un-employment benefit
**seio** /'seju/ m breast, bosom; **no ~ de** within
**seis** /sejs/ a & m six; **~centos** a & m six hundred
**seita** /'sejta/ f sect
**seixo** /'sejʃu/ m pebble
**sela** /'sɛla/ f saddle
**selar**¹ /se'lar/ vt saddle <cavalo>
**selar**² /se'lar/ vt seal; ( franquear) stamp
**sele|ção** /sele'sãw/ f selection; (time) team; **~cionar** vt select; **~to** /ɛ/ a select
**selim** /se'lĩ/ m saddle
**selo** /'selu/ m seal; ( postal) stamp; (de discos) label
**selva** /'sɛwva/ f jungle; **~gem** a wild; **~geria** f savagery
**sem** /sẽj/ prep without; **~ eu saber** without me knowing; **ficar ~ dinheiro** run out of money
**semáforo** /se'maforu/ m (na rua) traffic lights; (de ferrovia) signal
**sema|na** /se'mana/ f week; **~nal** (pl **~nais**) a weekly; **~nalmente** adv weekly; **~nário** m weekly
**semear** /semi'ar/ vt sow
**semelhan|ça** /seme'ʎãsa/ f similarity; **~te** a similar; (tal) such
**sêmen** /'semẽ/ m semen
**semente** /se'mẽtʃi/ f seed; (em fruta) pip
**semestre** /se'mɛstri/ m six months; (da faculdade etc) term, (Amer) semester
**semi|círculo** /semi'sirkulu/ m semicircle; **~final** (pl **~finais**) f semi-final
**seminário** /semi'nariu/ m (aula) seminar; (colégio religioso) seminary
**sem-número** /sẽ'numeru/ m **um ~ de** innumerable
**sempre** /'sẽpri/ adv always; **como ~** as usual; **para ~** for ever; **~ que** whenever
**sem|-terra** /sẽ'tɛxa/ m/f invar landless labourer; **~-teto** a homeless □ m/f homeless person; **~-vergonha** a invar brazen □ m/f invar scoundrel
**sena|do** /se'nadu/ m senate; **~dor** m senator
**senão** /si'nãw/ conj otherwise; (mas antes) but rather □ m snag
**senda** /'sẽda/ f path
**senha** /'seɲa/ f ( palavra) password; (número) code; (sinal ) signal
**senhor** /se'ɲor/ m gentleman; (homem idoso) older man; (tratamento) sir □ a ( f **~a**) mighty; **Senhor** (com nome) Mr; (Deus) Lord; **o ~** (você) you
**senho|ra** /se'ɲora/ f lady; (mulher idosa) older woman; (tratamento) madam; **Senhora** (com nome) Mrs; a **~ra** (você) you; **nossa ~ra!** ( fam) gosh; **~ria** f Vossa Senhoria you; **~rita** f young lady; (tratamento) miss; **Senhorita** (com nome) Miss
**se|nil** (pl **~nis**) a senile; **~nilidade** f senility
**sensação** /sẽsa'sãw/ f sensation
**sensacio|nal** /sẽsasio'naw/ ( pl **~nais**) a sensational; **~nalismo** m sensationalism; **~nalista** a sensationalist
**sen|sato** /sẽ'satu/ a sensible; **~sibilidade** f sensitivity; **~sível** ( pl **~síveis**) a sensitive; (que se pode sentir) noticeable; **~so** m sense; **~sual** (pl **~suais**) a sensual
**sen|tado** /sẽ'tadu/ a sitting; **~tar** vt/i sit; **~tar-se** vpr sit down
**sentença** /sẽ'tẽsa/ f sentence
**sentido** /sẽ'tʃidu/ m sense; (direção) direction □ a hurt; **fazer** ou **ter ~** make sense
**sentimen|tal** /sẽtʃimẽ'taw/ ( pl **~tais**) a sentimental; **vida ~tal** love life; **~to** m feeling

**sentinela** /sẽtʃi'nɛla/ f sentry
**sentir** /sẽ'tʃir/ vt feel; (notar) sense; smell <cheiro>; taste <gosto>; tell <diferença>; (ficar magoado por) be hurt by □ vi feel; **~-se** vpr feel; **sinto muito** I'm very sorry
**sepa|ração** /separa'sãw/ f separation; **~rado** a separate; <casal> separated; **~rar** vt separate; **~rar-se** vpr separate
**séptico** /'sɛptʃiku/ a septic
**sepul|tar** /sepuw'tar/ vt bury; **~tura** f grave
**seqüência** /se'kwẽsia/ f sequence
**sequer** /se'kɛr/ adv nem **~** not even
**seqües|trador** /sekwestra'dor/ m kidnapper; (de avião) hijacker; **~trar** vt kidnap <pessoa>; hijack <avião>; sequestrate <bens>; **~tro** /ɛ/ m (de pessoa) kidnapping; (de avião) hijack; (de bens) sequestration
**ser** /ser/ vi be □ m being; (como resposta) yes; **você gosta, não é?** you like it, don't you?; **ele foi morto** he was killed; **será que ele volta?** I wonder if he's coming back; **ou seja** in other words; **a não ~** except; **a não ~ que** unless; **não sou de fofocar** I'm not one to gossip
**sereia** /se'reja/ f mermaid
**serenata** /sere'nata/ f serenade
**sereno** /se'renu/ a serene; <tempo> fine
**série** /'sɛri/ f series; (na escola) grade; **fora de ~** (fam) incredible
**seriedade** /serie'dadʒi/ f seriousness
**serin|ga** /se'rĩga/ f syringe; **~gueiro** m rubber tapper
**sério** /'sɛriu/ a serious; (responsável) responsible; **~?** really?; **falar ~** be serious; **levar a ~** take seriously
**sermão** /ser'mãw/ m sermon
**serpen|te** /ser'pẽtʃi/ f serpent; **~tear** vi wind; **~tina** f streamer
**serra¹** /'sɛxa/ f (montanhas) mountain range
**serra²** /'sɛxa/ f (de serrar) saw; **~gem** f sawdust; **~lheiro** m locksmith
**serrano** /se'xanu/ a mountain
**serrar** /se'xar/ vt saw
**ser|tanejo** /serta'neʒu/ a from the backwoods □ m backwoodsman; **~tão** m backwoods
**servente** /ser'vẽtʃi/ m/f labourer
**Sérvia** /'sɛrvia/ f Serbia
**servi|çal** /servi'saw/ (pl **~çais**) a helpful □ m/f servant; **~ço** m service; (trabalho) work; (tarefa) job; **estar de ~ço** be on duty; **~dor** m servant
**ser|vil** /ser'viw/ (pl **~vis**) a servile
**sérvio** /'sɛrviu/ a & m Serbian
**servir** /ser'vir/ vt serve □ vi serve; (ser adequado) do; (ser útil) be of use; <roupa, sapato etc> fit; **~-se**

vpr (ao comer etc) help o.s. (**de** to); **~-se de** make use of; **~ como** ou **de** serve as; **para que serve isso?** what is this (used) for?
**sessão** /se'sãw/ f session; (no cinema) showing, performance
**sessenta** /se'sẽta/ a & m sixty
**seta** /'sɛta/ f arrow; (de carro) indicator
**sete** /'sɛtʃi/ a & m seven; **~centos** a & m seven hundred
**setembro** /se'tẽbru/ m September
**setenta** /se'tẽta/ a & m seventy
**sétimo** /'sɛtʃimu/ a seventh
**setuagésimo** /setua'ʒɛzimu/ a seventieth
**setor** /se'tor/ m sector
**seu** /sew/ a (f **sua**) (dele) his; (dela) her; (de coisa) its; (deles) their; (de você, de vocês) your □ pron (dele) his; (dela) hers; (deles) theirs; (de você, de vocês) yours; **~ idiota!** you idiot!; **seu João** Mr John
**seve|ridade** /severi'dadʒi/ f severity; **~ro** /ɛ/ a severe
**sexagésimo** /seksa'ʒɛzimu/ a sixtieth
**sexo** /'sɛksu/ m sex; **fazer ~** have sex
**sex|ta** /'sesta/ f Friday; **~ta-feira** (pl **~tas-feiras**) f Friday; **Sexta-feira Santa** Good Friday; **~to** /e/ a & m sixth
**sexu|al** /seksu'aw/ (pl **~ais**) a sexual; **vida ~al** sex life
**sexy** /'sɛksi/ a invar sexy
**shopping** /'ʃɔpĩ/ (pl **~s**) m shopping centre, (Amer) mall
**short** /'ʃɔrtʃi/ m (pl **~s**) shorts; **um ~** a pair of shorts
**show** /'ʃou/ (pl **~s**) m show; (de música) concert
**si** /si/ pron (ele) himself; (ela) herself; (coisa) itself; (você) yourself; (eles) themselves; (vocês) yourselves; (qualquer pessoa) oneself; **em ~** in itself; **fora de ~** beside o.s.; **cheio de ~** full of o.s.; **voltar a ~** come round
**sibilar** /sibi'lar/ vi hiss
**SIDA** /'sida/ f (Port) AIDS
**side|ral** /side'raw/ (pl **~rais**) a espaço **~ral** outer space.
**siderurgia** /siderur'ʒia/ f iron and steel industry
**siderúrgi|ca** /side'rurʒika/ f steelworks; **~co** a iron and steel □ m steelworker
**sifão** /si'fãw/ m syphon
**sífilis** /'sifilis/ f syphilis
**sigilo** /si'ʒilu/ m secrecy; **~so** /o/ a secret
**sigla** /'sigla/ f acronym
**signatário** /signa'tariu/ m signatory
**signifi|cação** /signifika'sãw/ f significance; **~cado** m meaning; **~car** vt mean; **~cativo** a significant

**signo** /'signu/ *m* sign
**sílaba** /'silaba/ *f* syllable
**silenciar** /silẽsi'ar/ *vt* silence
**silêncio** /si'lẽsiu/ *m* silence
**silencioso** /silẽsi'ozu/ *a* silent □ *m*
silencer, (*Amer*) muffler
**silhueta** /siʎu'eta/ *f* silhouette
**silício** /si'lisiu/ *m* silicon
**silicone** /sili'kɔni/ *m* silicone
**silo** /'silu/ *m* silo
**silvar** /siw'var/ *vi* hiss
**sil|vestre** /siw'vɛstri/ *a* wild; **~vi-
cultura** *f* forestry
**sim** /sĩ/ *adv* yes; **acho que ~** I think
so
**simbólico** /sĩ'bɔliku/ *a* symbolic
**simbo|lismo** /sĩbo'lizmu/ *m* sym-
bolism; **~lizar** *vt* symbolize
**símbolo** /'sĩbolu/ *m* symbol
**si|metria** /sime'tria/ *f* symmetry;
**~métrico** *a* symmetrical
**similar** /simi'lar/ *a* similar
**sim|patia** /sĩpa'tʃia/ *f* (*qualidade*)
pleasantness; (*afeto*) fondness (*por*
for); (*compreensão, apoio*) sympathy;
*pl* sympathies; **ter ~patia por** a
fond of; **~pático** *a* nice
**simpati|zante** /sĩpatʃi'zãtʃi/ *a* sym-
pathetic □ *m/f* sympathizer; **~zar** *vi*
**~zar com** take a liking to <*pessoa*>;
sympathize with <*idéias, partido etc*>
**simples** /'sĩplis/ *a invar* simple; (*único*) single □ *f* (*no tênis etc*) singles;
**~mente** *adv* simply
**simpli|cidade** /sĩplisi'dadʒi/ *f* sim-
plicity; **~ficar** *vt* simplify
**simplório** /sĩ'plɔriu/ *a* simple
**simpósio** /sĩ'pɔziu/ *m* symposium
**simu|lação** /simula'sãw/ *f* simula-
tion; **~lar** *vt* simulate
**simultâneo** /simuw'taniu/ *a* simultaneous
**sina** /'sina/ *f* fate
**sinagoga** /sina'gɔga/ *f* synagogue
**si|nal** /si'naw/ (*pl* **~nais**) *m* sign;
(*aviso, de rádio etc*) signal; (*de trânsito*) traffic light; (*no telefone*) tone;
(*dinheiro*) deposit; (*na pele*) mole;
**por ~nal** as a matter of fact; **~nal
de pontuação** punctuation mark;
**~naleira** *f* traffic lights;
**~nalização** *f* (*na rua*) road signs;
**~nalizar** *vt* signal; signpost <*rua,
cidade*>
**since|ridade** /sĩseri'dadʒi/ *f* sin-
cerity; **~ro** /ɛ/ *a* sincere
**sincro|nia** /sĩkro'nia/ *f* synchron-
ization; **~nizar** *vt* synchronize
**sindi|cal** /sĩdʒi'kaw/ (*pl* **~cais**) *a*
trade union; **~calismo** *m* trade un-
ionism; **~calista** *m/f* trade unionist;
**~calizar** *vt* unionize; **~cato** *m* trade
union
**síndico** /'sĩdʒiku/ *m* house manager

**síndrome** /'sĩdromi/ *f* syndrome
**sineta** /si'neta/ *f* bell
**sin|fonia** /sĩfo'nia/ *f* symphony;
**~fônica** *f* symphony orchestra
**singe|leza** /sĩʒe'leza/ *f* simplicity;
**~lo** /ɛ/ *a* simple
**singu|lar** /sĩgu'lar/ *a* singular; (*estra-
nho*) peculiar; **~larizar** *vt* single out
**sinis|trado** /sinis'tradu/ *a* damaged;
**~tro** *a* sinister □ *m* accident
**sino** /'sinu/ *m* bell
**sinônimo** /si'nonimu/ *a* synonymous
□ *m* synonym
**sintaxe** /sĩ'taksi/ *f* syntax
**síntese** /'sĩtezi/ *f* synthesis
**sin|tético** /sĩ'tɛtʃiku/ *a* (*artificial*)
synthetic; (*resumido*) concise; **~
tetizar** *vt* summarize
**sinto|ma** /sĩ'toma/ *m* symptom;
**~mático** *a* symptomatic
**sintoni|zador** /sĩtoniza'dor/ *m* tuner;
**~zar** *vt* tune <*rádio, TV*>; tune in to
<*emissora*> □ *vi* be in tune (**com**
with)
**sinuca** /si'nuka/ *f* snooker
**sinuoso** /sinu'ozu/ *a* winding
**sinusite** /sinu'zitʃi/ *f* sinusitis
**sirene** /si'rɛni/ *f* siren
**siri** /si'ri/ *m* crab
**Síria** /'siria/ *f* Syria
**sírio** /'siriu/ *a & m* Syrian
**siso** /'sizu/ *m* good sense
**siste|ma** /sis'tema/ *m* system;
**~mático** *a* systematic
**sisudo** /si'zudu/ *a* serious
**sítio** /'sitʃiu/ *m* (*chácara*) farm; (*Port:
local*) place; **estado de ~** state of
siege
**situ|ação** /situa'sãw/ *f* situation; (*no
governo*) party in power; **~ar** *vt*
situate; **~ar-se** *vpr* be situated;
<*pessoa*> position o.s.
**smoking** /iz'mɔkĩ/ (*pl* **~s**) *m* dinner
jacket, (*Amer*) tuxedo
**só** /sɔ/ *a* alone; (*sentindo solidão*)
lonely □ *adv* only; **um ~ voto** one
single vote; **~ um carro** only one
car; **a ~s** alone; **imagina ~** just
imagine; **~ que** except (that)
**soalho** /so'aʎu/ *m* floor
**soar** /so'ar/ *vt/i* sound
**sob** /'sobi/ *prep* under
**sobera|nia** /sobera'nia/ *f* sover-
eignty; **~no** *a & m* sovereign
**soberbo** /so'berbu/ *a* <*pessoa*>
haughty; (*magnífico*) splendid
**sobra** /'sɔbra/ *f* surplus; *pl* leftovers;
**tempo de ~** (*muito*) plenty of time;
**ficar de ~** be left over; **ter aco de ~**
(*sobrando*) have sth left over
**sobraçar** /sobra'sar/ *vt* carry under
one's arm
**sobrado** /so'bradu/ *m* (*casa*) house;
(*andar*) upper floor

**sobrancelha** /sobrã'seʎa/ f eyebrow

**so|brar** /so'brar/ vi be left; **~bram-me dois** I have two left

**sobre** /'sobri/ prep (em cima de) on; (por cima de, acima de) over; (acerca de) about

**sobreaviso** /sobria'vizu/ m **estar de ~** be on one's guard

**sobrecapa** /sobri'kapa/ f dust jacket

**sobrecarregar** /sobrikaxe'gar/ vt overload

**sobreloja** /sobri'lɔʒa/ f mezzanine

**sobremesa** /sobri'meza/ f dessert

**sobrenatu|ral** /sobrinatu'raw/ (pl **~rais**) a supernatural

**sobrenome** /sobri'nomi/ m surname

**sobrepor** /sobri'por/ vt superimpose

**sobrepujar** /sobripu'ʒar/ vt (em altura) tower over; (em valor, número etc) surpass; overwhelm <adversário>; overcome <problemas>

**sobrescritar** /sobriskri'tar/ vt address

**sobressair** /sobrisa'ir/ vi stand out; **~-se** vpr stand out

**sobressalente** /sobrisa'lẽtʃi/ a spare

**sobressal|tar** /sobrisaw'tar/ vt startle; **~tar-se** vpr be startled; **~to** m (movimento) start; (susto) fright

**sobretaxa** /sobri'taʃa/ f surcharge

**sobretudo** /sobri'tudu/ adv above all □ m overcoat

**sobrevir** /sobri'vir/ vi happen suddenly; (seguir) ensue; **~ a** follow

**sobrevi|vência** /sobrivi'vẽsia/ f survival; **~vente** a surviving □ m/f survivor; **~ver** vt/i **~ver (a)** survive

**sobrevoar** /sobrivo'ar/ vt fly over

**sobri|nha** /so'briɲa/ f niece; **~nho** m nephew

**sóbrio** /'sɔbriu/ a sober

**socar** /so'kar/ vt (esmurrar) punch; (amassar) crush

**soci|al** /sosi'aw/ (pl **~ais**) a social; **camisa ~al** dress shirt; **~alismo** m socialism; **~alista** a & m/f socialist; **~alite** /-a'lajtʃi/ m/f socialite; **~ável** (pl **~áveis**) a sociable

**sociedade** /sosie'dadʒi/ f society; (parceria) partnership; **~ anônima** limited company

**sócio** /'sɔsiu/ m (de empresa) partner; (de clube) member

**socio-econômico** /sosioeko'nomiku/ a socio-economic

**soci|ologia** /sosiolo'ʒia/ f sociology; **~ológico** a sociological; **~ólogo** m sociologist

**soco** /'soku/ m punch; **dar um ~ em** punch

**socor|rer** /soko'xer/ vt help; **~ro** m aid □ int help; **primeiros ~ros** first aid

**soda** /'sɔda/ f (água) soda water; **~ cáustica** caustic soda

**sódio** /'sɔdʒiu/ m sodium

**sofá** /so'fa/ m sofa; **~-cama** (pl **~s-camas**) m sofa-bed

**sofisticado** /sofistʃi'kadu/ a sophisticated

**so|fredor** /sofre'dor/ a martyred; **~frer** vt suffer <dor, derrota, danos etc>; have <acidente>; undergo <operação, mudança etc> □ vi suffer; **~frer de** suffer from <doença>; have trouble with <coração etc>; **~frido** a long-suffering; **~frimento** m suffering; **~frível** (pl **~fríveis**) a passable

**soft** /'sɔftʃi/ (pl **~s**) m software package; **~ware** m software; (um) software package

**so|gra** /'sɔgra/ f mother-in-law; **~gro** /o/ m father-in-law; **~gros** /ɔ/ m pl in-laws

**soja** /'sɔʒa/ f soya, (Amer) soy

**sol** /sɔw/ (pl **sóis**) m sun; **faz ~** it's sunny

**sola** /'sɔla/ f sole; **~do** a <bolo> flat

**solapar** /sola'par/ vt undermine

**solar¹** /so'lar/ a solar

**solar²** /so'lar/ vt sole <sapato> □ vi <bolo> go flat

**solavanco** /sola'vãku/ m jolt; **dar ~s** jolt

**soldado** /sow'dadu/ m soldier

**sol|dadura** /sowda'dura/ f weld; **~dar** vt weld

**soldo** /'sowdu/ m pay

**soleira** /so'lera/ f doorstep

**sole|ne** /so'leni/ a solemn; **~nidade** f (cerimônia) ceremony; (qualidade) solemnity

**soletrar** /sole'trar/ vt spell

**solici|tação** /solisita'sãw/ f request (de for); (por escrito) application (de for); **~tante** m/f applicant; **~tar** vt request; (por escrito) apply for

**solícito** /so'lisitu/ a helpful

**solidão** /soli'dãw/ f loneliness

**soli|dariedade** /solidarie'dadʒi/ f solidarity; **~dário** a supportive (com of)

**soli|dez** /soli'des/ f solidity; **~dificar** vt solidify; **~dificar-se** vpr solidify

**sólido** /'sɔlidu/ a & m solid

**solista** /so'lista/ m/f soloist

**solitá|ria** /soli'taria/ f (verme) tapeworm; (cela) solitary confinement; **~rio** a solitary

**solo¹** /'sɔlu/ m (terra) soil; (chão) ground

**solo²** /'sɔlu/ m solo

**soltar** /sow'tar/ vt let go <prisioneiros, animal etc>; let loose <cães>; (deixar de segurar) let go of; loosen <gravata, corda etc>; let down

*<cabelo>*; let out *<grito, suspiro etc>*; let off *<foguetes>*; tell *<piada>*; take off *<freio>*; **~-se** *vpr <peça, parafuso>* come loose; *<pessoa>* let o.s. go

**soltei|ra** /sow'tera/ *f* single woman; **~rão** *m* bachelor; **~ro** *a* single □ *m* single man; **~rona** *f* spinster

**solto** /'sowtu/ *a (livre)* free; *<cães>* loose; *<cabelo>* down; *<arroz>* fluffy; *(frouxo)* loose; *(à vontade)* relaxed; *(abandonado)* abandoned; **correr ~** run wild

**solução** /solu'sãw/ *f* solution

**soluçar** /solu'sar/ *vi (ao chorar)* sob; *(engasgar)* hiccup

**solucionar** /solusio'nar/ *vt* solve

**soluço** /so'lusu/ *m (ao chorar)* sob; *(engasgo)* hiccup; **estar com ~s** have the hiccups

**solú|vel** /so'luvew/ *(pl ~veis) a* soluble

**solvente** /sow'vẽtʃi/ *a & m* solvent

**som** /sõ/ *m* sound; *(aparelho)* stereo; **um ~** *(fam) (música)* a bit of music

**so|ma** /'soma/ *f* sum; **~mar** *vt* add up *<números etc>*; *(ter como soma)* add up to

**sombra** /'sõbra/ *f* shadow; *(área abrigada do sol)* shade; **à ~ de** in the shade of; **sem ~ de dúvida** without a shadow of a doubt

**sombre|ado** /sõbri'adu/ *a* shady □ *m* shading; **~ar** *vt* shade

**sombrinha** /sõ'briɲa/ *f* parasol

**sombrio** /sõ'briu/ *a* gloomy

**somente** /so'mẽtʃi/ *adv* only

**sonâmbulo** /so'nãbulu/ *m* sleepwalker

**sonante** /so'nãtʃi/ *a* **moeda ~** hard cash

**sonata** /so'nata/ *f* sonata

**son|da** /'sõda/ *f* probe; **~dagem** *f (no mar)* sounding; *(de terreno)* survey; **~dagem de opinião** opinion poll; **~dar** *vt* probe; sound *<profundeza>*; *(fig)* sound out *<pessoas, opiniões etc>*

**soneca** /so'nɛka/ *f* nap; **tirar uma ~** have a nap

**sone|gação** /sonega'sãw/ *f (de impostos)* tax evasion; **~gador** *m* tax dodger; **~gar** *vt* withhold

**soneto** /so'netu/ *m* sonnet

**so|nhador** /soɲa'dor/ *a* dreamy □ *m* dreamer; **~nhar** *vt/i* dream (com about); **~nho** /'soɲu/ *m* dream; *(doce)* doughnut

**sono** /'sonu/ *m* sleep; **estar com ~** be sleepy; **pegar no ~** get to sleep; **~lento** *a* sleepy

**sono|plastia** /sonoplas'tʃia/ *f* sound effects; **~ridade** *f* sound quality; **~ro** /ɔ/ *a* sound; *<voz>* sonorous; *<consoante>* voiced

**sonso** /'sõsu/ *a* devious

**sopa** /'sopa/ *f* soup

**sopapo** /so'papu/ *m* slap; **dar um ~ em** slap

**sopé** /so'pɛ/ *m* foot

**sopeira** /so'pera/ *f* soup tureen

**soprano** /so'pranu/ *m/f* soprano

**so|prar** /so'prar/ *vt* blow *<folhas etc>*; blow up *<balão>*; blow out *<vela>* □ *vi* blow; **~pro** *m* blow; *(de vento)* puff; **instrumento de ~pro** wind instrument

**soquete¹** /so'kɛtʃi/ *f* ankle sock

**soquete²** /so'kɛtʃi/ *m* socket

**sordidez** /sordʒi'des/ *f* sordidness; *(imundície)* squalor

**sórdido** /'sordʒidu/ *a (reles)* sordid; *(imundo)* squalid

**soro** /'soru/ *m (remédio)* serum; *(de leite)* whey

**sorrateiro** /soxa'teru/ *a* crafty

**sor|ridente** /soxi'dẽtʃi/ *a* smiling; **~rir** *vi* smile; **~riso** *m* smile

**sorte** /'sortʃi/ *f* luck; *(destino)* fate; **pessoa de ~** lucky person; **por ~** luckily; **ter** *ou* **dar ~** be lucky; **tive a ~ de conhecê-lo** I was lucky enough to meet him; **tirar a ~** draw lots; **trazer** *ou* **dar ~** bring good luck

**sor|tear** /sortʃi'ar/ *vt* draw for *<prêmio>*; select in a draw *<pessoa>*; **~teio** *m* draw

**sorti|do** /sor'tʃidu/ *a* assorted; **~mento** *m* assortment

**sorumbático** /sorũ'batʃiku/ *a* sombre, gloomy

**sorver** /sor'ver/ *vt* sip *<bebida>*

**sósia** /'sɔzia/ *m/f* double

**soslaio** /soz'laju/ *m* **de ~** sideways; *<olhar>* askance

**sosse|gado** /sose'gadu/ *a <vida>* quiet; **ficar ~gado** *<pessoa>* rest assured; **~gar** *vt* reassure □ *vi* rest; **~go** /e/ *m* peace

**sótão** /'sotãw/ *(pl ~s) m* attic, loft

**sotaque** /so'taki/ *m* accent

**soterrar** /sote'xar/ *vt* bury

**soutien** /suti'ã/ *(pl ~s) m (Port)* bra

**sova|co** /so'vaku/ *m* armpit; **~queira** *f* BO, body odour

**soviético** /sovi'ɛtʃiku/ *a & m* Soviet

**sovi|na** /so'vina/ *a* stingy, mean, *(Amer)* cheap □ *m/f* cheapskate; **~nice** *f* stinginess, meanness, *(Amer)* cheapness

**sozinho** /so'ziɲu/ *a (sem ninguém)* alone, on one's own; *(por si próprio)* by o.s.; **falar ~** talk to o.s.

**spray** /is'prej/ *(pl ~s) m* spray

**squash** /is'kwɛʃ/ *m* squash

**stand** /is'tãdʒi/ *(pl ~s) m* stand

**status** /is'tatus/ *m* status

**stripper** /is'triper/ *(pl ~s) m/f* stripper

**strip-tease** /istripi't∫izi/ *m* striptease

**sua** /'sua/ *a & pron veja* **seu**

**su|ado** /su'adu/ *a* <*pessoa, roupa*> sweaty; (*fig*) hard-earned; **~ar** *vt/i* sweat; **~ar por/para** (*fig*) work hard for/to; **~ar frio** come out in a cold sweat

**sua|ve** /su'avi/ *a* <*toque, subida*> gentle; <*gosto, cheiro, dor, inverno*> mild; <*música, voz*> soft; <*vinho*> smooth; <*trabalho*> light; <*prestações*> easy; **~vidade** *f* gentleness; mildness; softness; smoothness; *veja* **suave**; **~vizar** *vt* soften; soothe <*dor, pessoa*>

**subalterno** /subaw'tɛrnu/ *a & m* subordinate

**subconsciente** /subikõsi'ẽt∫i/ *a & m* subconscious

**subdesenvolvido** /subidʒizĩvow- 'vidu/ *a* underdeveloped

**súbdito** /'subditu/ *m* (*Port*) *veja* **súdito**

**subdividir** /subidʒivi'dʒir/ *vt* subdivide

**subemprego** /subĩ'pregu/ *m* menial job

**subemprei|tar** /subĩprej'tar/ *vt* subcontract; **~teiro** *m* subcontractor

**subenten|der** /subĩtẽ'der/ *vt* infer; **~dido** *a* implied □ *m* insinuation

**subestimar** /subest∫i'mar/ *vt* underestimate

**su|bida** /su'bida/ *f* (*ação*) ascent; (*ladeira*) incline; (*de preços etc, fig*) rise; **~bir** *vi* go up; <*rio, águas*> rise □ *vt* go up, climb; **~bir em** climb <*árvore*>; get up onto <*mesa*>; get on <*ônibus*>

**súbito** /'subitu/ *a* sudden; **(de)** **~** suddenly

**subjacente** /subiʒa'sẽt∫i/ *a* underlying

**subjeti|vidade** /subiʒet∫ivi'dadʒi/ *f* subjectivity; **~vo** *a* subjective

**subjugar** /subiʒu'gar/ *vt* subjugate

**subjuntivo** /subiʒũ't∫ivu/ *a & m* subjunctive

**sublevar-se** /suble'varsi/ *vpr* rise up

**sublime** /su'blimi/ *a* sublime

**subli|nhado** /subli'ɲadu/ *m* underlining; **~nhar** *vt* underline

**sublocar** /sublo'kar/ *vt/i* sublet

**submarino** /subima'rinu/ *a* underwater □ *m* submarine

**submer|gir** /subimer'ʒir/ *vt* submerge; **~gir-se** *vpr* submerge; **~so** *a* submerged

**submeter** /subime'ter/ *vt* subject (**a** to); put down, subdue <*povo, rebeldes etc*>; submit <*projeto*>; **~se** *vpr* (*render-se*) submit; **~se a** (*sofrer*) undergo

**submis|são** /subimi'sãw/ *f* submission; **~so** *a* submissive

**submundo** /subi'mũdu/ *m* underworld

**subnutrição** /subinutri'sãw/ *f* malnutrition

**subordi|nado** /subordʒi'nadu/ *a & m* subordinate; **~nar** *vt* subordinate (**a** to)

**subor|nar** /subor'nar/ *vt* bribe; **~no** /o/ *m* bribe

**subproduto** /subipro'dutu/ *m* byproduct

**subs|crever** /subiskre'ver/ *vt* sign <*carta etc*>; subscribe to <*opinião*>; subscribe <*dinheiro*> (**para** to); **~crever-se** *vpr* sign one's name; **~crição** *f* subscription; **~crito** *pp de* **~crever**

**subseqüente** /subise'kwẽt∫i/ *a* subsequent

**subserviente** /subiservi'ẽt∫i/ *a* subservient

**subsidiar** /subisidʒi'ar/ *vt* subsidize

**subsidiá|ria** /subisidʒi'aria/ *f* subsidiary; **~rio** *a* subsidiary

**subsídio** /subi'sidʒiu/ *m* subsidy

**subsistência** /subisis'tẽsia/ *f* subsistence

**subsolo** /subi'sɔlu/ *m* (*porão*) basement

**substância** /subis'tãsia/ *f* substance

**substan|cial** /subistãsi'aw/ (*pl* **~ciais**) *a* substantial; **~tivo** *m* noun

**substitu|ição** /subist∫itui'sãw/ *f* replacement; substitution; **~ir** *vt* (*pôr B no lugar de A*) replace (**A por B** A with B); (*usar B em vez de A*) substitute (**A por B** B for A); **~to a & m** substitute

**subterfúgio** /subiter'fuʒiu/ *m* subterfuge

**subterrâneo** /subite'xaniu/ *a* underground

**sub|til** /sub'til/ (*pl* **~tis**) *a* (*Port*) *veja* **sutil**

**subtra|ção** /subitra'sãw/ *f* subtraction; **~ir** *vt* subtract <*números*>; (*roubar*) steal

**suburbano** /subur'banu/ *a* suburban

**subúrbio** /su'burbiu/ *m* suburbs

**subven|ção** /subivẽ'sãw/ *f* grant, subsidy; **~cionar** *vt* subsidize

**subver|são** /subiver'sãw/ *f* subversion; **~sivo** *a & m* subversive

**suca|ta** /su'kata/ *f* scrap metal; **~tear** *vt* scrap

**sucção** /suk'sãw/ *f* suction

**suce|der** /suse'der/ *vi* (*acontecer*) happen □ *vt* **~der a** succeed <*rei etc*>; (*vir depois*) follow; **~der-se** *vpr* follow on from one another; **~dido** *a* **bem ~dido** successful

**suces|são** /suse'sãw/ *f* succession; **~sivo** *a* successive; **~so** /ɛ/ *m* success; (*música*) hit; **fazer** *ou* **ter ~so** be successful; **~sor** *m* successor

**sucinto** /su'sĩtu/ *a* succinct

**suco** /'suku/ *m* juice

**suculento** /suku'lẽtu/ *a* juicy

**sucumbir** /sukũ'bir/ *vi* succumb (**a** to)

**sucur|sal** /sukur'saw/ (*pl* **~sais**) *f* branch

**Sudão** /su'dãw/ *m* Sudan

**sudário** /su'dariu/ *m* shroud

**sudeste** /su'dɛstʃi/ *a & m* southeast; **o Sudeste Asiático** Southeast Asia

**súdito** /'sudʒitu/ *m* subject

**sudoeste** /sudo'ɛstʃi/ *a & m* southwest

**Suécia** /su'ɛsia/ *f* Sweden

**sueco** /su'ɛku/ *a & m* Swedish

**suéter** /su'ɛter/ *m/f* sweater

**sufici|ência** /sufisi'ẽsia/ *f* sufficiency; **~ente** *a* enough, sufficient; **o ~ente** enough

**sufixo** /su'fiksu/ *m* suffix

**suflê** /su'fle/ *m* soufflé

**sufo|cante** /sufo'kãtʃi/ *a* stifling; **~car** *vt* (*asfixiar*) suffocate; (*fig*) stifle □ *vi* suffocate; **~co** /o/ *m* hassle; **estar num ~co** be having a tough time

**sufrágio** /su'fraʒiu/ *m* suffrage

**sugar** /su'gar/ *vt* suck

**sugerir** /suʒe'rir/ *vt* suggest

**suges|tão** /suʒes'tãw/ *f* suggestion; **dar uma ~tão** make a suggestion; **~tivo** *a* suggestive

**Suíça** /su'isa/ *f* Switzerland

**suíças** /su'isas/ *f pl* sideburns

**sui|cida** /sui'sida/ *a* suicidal □ *m/f* suicide (victim); **~cidar-se** *vpr* commit suicide; **~cídio** *m* suicide

**suíço** /su'isu/ *a & m* Swiss

**suíno** /su'inu/ *a & m* pig

**suíte** /su'itʃi/ *f* suite

**su|jar** /su'ʒar/ *vt* dirty; (*fig*) sully <*reputação etc*> □ *vi*, **~jar-se** *vpr* get dirty; **~jar-se com alg** queer one's pitch with s.o.; **~jeira** *f* dirt; (*uma*) dirty trick

**sujei|tar** /suʒej'tar/ *vt* subject (**a** to); **~tar-se** *vpr* subject o.s. (**a** to); **~to** *a* subject (**a** to) □ *m* (*de oração*) subject; (*pessoa*) person

**su|jidade** /suʒi'dadʒi/ *f* (*Port*) dirt; **~jo** *a* dirty

**sul** /suw/ *a invar & m* south; **~-africano** *a & m* South African; **~-americano** *a & m* South American; **~-coreano** *a & m* South Korean

**sul|car** /suw'kar/ *vt* furrow <*testa*>; **~co** *m* furrow

**sulfúrico** /suw'furiku/ *a* sulphuric

**sulista** /su'lista/ *a* southern □ *m/f* southerner

**sultão** /suw'tãw/ *m* sultan

**sumário** /su'mariu/ *a* <*justiça*> summary; <*roupa*> skimpy, brief

**su|miço** /su'misu/ *m* disappearance; **dar ~miço em** spirit away; **tomar chá de ~miço** disappear; **~mido** *a* <*cor, voz*> faint; **ele anda ~mido** he's disappeared; **~mir** *vi* disappear

**sumo** /'sumu/ *m* (*Port*) juice

**sumptuoso** /sũtu'ozu/ *a* (*Port*) *veja* **suntuoso**

**sunga** /'sũga/ *f* swimming trunks

**suntuoso** /sũtu'ozu/ *a* sumptuous

**suor** /su'or/ *m* sweat

**superar** /supe'rar/ *vt* overcome <*dificuldade etc*>; surpass <*expectativa, pessoa*>

**superá|vel** /supe'ravew/ (*pl* **~veis**) *a* surmountable; **~vit** (*pl* **~vits**) *m* surplus

**superestimar** /superestʃi'mar/ *vt* overestimate

**superestrutura** /superistru'tura/ *f* superstructure

**superfici|al** /superfisi'aw/ (*pl* **~ais**) *a* superficial

**superfície** /super'fisi/ *f* surface; (*medida*) area

**supérfluo** /su'pɛrfluu/ *a* superfluous

**superintendência** /superĩtẽ'dẽsia/ *f* bureau

**superi|or** /superi'or/ *a* (*de cima*) upper; <*ensino*> higher; <*número, temperatura etc*> greater (**a** than); (*melhor*) superior (**a** to) □ *m* superior; **~oridade** *f* superiority

**superlativo** /superla'tʃivu/ *a & m* superlative

**superlota|ção** /superlota'sãw/ *f* overcrowding; **~do** *a* overcrowded

**supermercado** /supermer'kadu/ *m* supermarket

**superpotência** /superpo'tẽsia/ *f* superpower

**superpovoado** /superpovo'adu/ *a* overpopulated

**supersecreto** /superse'krɛtu/ *a* top secret

**supersensí|vel** /supersẽ'sivew/ (*pl* **~veis**) *a* oversensitive

**supersônico** /super'soniku/ *a* supersonic

**supersti|ção** /superstʃi'sãw/ *f* superstition; **~cioso** /o/ *a* superstitious

**supervi|são** /supervi'zãw/ *f* supervision; **~sionar** *vt* supervise; **~sor** *m* supervisor

**supetão** /supe'tãw/ *m* **de ~** all of a sudden

**suplantar** /suplã'tar/ *vt* supplant

**suplemen|tar** /suplemẽ'tar/ *a* supplementary □ *vt* supplement; **~to** *m* supplement

**suplente** /su'plẽtʃi/ *a* & *m/f* substitute

**supletivo** /suple'tʃivu/ *a* supplementary; **ensino** ∼ adult education

**súplica** /'suplika/ *f* plea; **tom de** ∼ pleading tone

**suplicar** /supli'kar/ *vt* plead for; (*em juízo*) petition for

**suplício** /su'plisiu/ *m* torture; (*fig: aflição*) torment

**supor** /su'por/ *vt* suppose

**supor|tar** /supor'tar/ *vt* (*sustentar*) support; (*tolerar*) stand, bear; ∼**tável** (*pl* ∼**táveis**) *a* bearable; ∼**te** /ɔ/ *m* support

**suposição** /supozi'sãw/ *f* supposition

**supositório** /supozi'tɔriu/ *m* suppository

**supos|tamente** /suposta'mẽtʃi/ *adv* supposedly; ∼**to** /o/ *a* supposed; ∼**to que** supposing that

**supre|macia** /suprema'sia/ *f* supremacy; ∼**mo** /e/ *a* supreme

**supressão** /supre'sãw/ *f* (*de lei, cargo, privilégio*) abolition; (*de jornal, informação, nomes*) suppression; (*de palavras, cláusula*) deletion

**suprimento** /supri'mẽtu/ *m* supply

**suprimir** /supri'mir/ *vt* abolish <*lei, cargo, privilégio*>; suppress <*jornal, informação, nomes*>; delete <*palavras, cláusula*>

**suprir** /su'prir/ *vt* provide for <*família, necessidades*>; make up for <*falta*>; make up <*quantia*>; supply <*o que falta*>; (*substituir*) take the place of; ∼ **alg de** provide s.o. with; ∼ **A por B** substitute B for A

**supurar** /supu'rar/ *vi* turn septic

**sur|dez** /sur'des/ *f* deafness; ∼**do** *a* deaf; <*consoante*> voiceless □ *m* deaf person; **os** ∼**dos** the deaf; ∼**do-mudo** (*pl* ∼**dos-mudos**) *a* deaf and dumb □ *m* deaf-mute

**sur|fe** /'surfi/ *m* surfing; ∼**fista** *m/f* surfer

**sur|gimento** /surʒi'mẽtu/ *m* appearance; ∼**gir** *vi* arise; ∼**gir à mente** spring to mind

**Suriname** /suri'nami/ *m* Surinam

**surpreen|dente** /surpriẽ'dẽtʃi/ *a* surprising; ∼**der** *vt* surprise □ *vi* be surprising; ∼**der-se** *vpr* be surprised (**de** at)

**surpre|sa** /sur'preza/ *f* surprise; **de** ∼**sa** by surprise; ∼**so** /e/ *a* surprised

**sur|ra** /'suxa/ *f* thrashing; ∼**rado** *a* <*roupa*> worn-out; ∼**rar** *vt* thrash <*pessoa*>; wear out <*roupa*>

**surrealis|mo** /suxea'lizmu/ *m* surrealism; ∼**ta** *a* & *m/f* surrealist

**surtir** /sur'tʃir/ *vt* produce; ∼ **efeito** be effective

**surto** /'surtu/ *m* outbreak

**suscept-** (*Port*) *veja* **suscet-**

**susce|tibilidade** /susetʃibili'dadʒi/ *f* (*de pessoa*) sensitivity; ∼**tível** (*pl* ∼**tíveis**) *a* <*pessoa*> touchy, sensitive; ∼**tível de** open to

**suscitar** /susi'tar/ *vt* cause; raise <*dúvida, suspeita*>

**suspei|ta** /sus'pejta/ *f* suspicion; ∼**tar** *vt/i* ∼**tar** (**de**) suspect; ∼**to** *a* suspicious; (*duvidoso*) suspect □ *m* suspect; ∼**toso** /o/ *a* suspicious

**suspen|der** /suspẽ'der/ *vt* suspend; ∼**são** *f* suspension; ∼**se** *m* suspense; ∼**so** *a* suspended; ∼**sórios** *m pl* braces, (*Amer*) suspenders

**suspi|rar** /suspi'rar/ *vi* sigh; ∼**rar por** long for; ∼**ro** *m* sigh; (*doce*) meringue

**sussur|rar** /susu'xar/ *vt/i* whisper; ∼**ro** *m* whisper

**sustar** /sus'tar/ *vt/i* stop

**susten|táculo** /sustẽ'takulu/ *m* mainstay; ∼**tar** *vt* support; (*afirmar*) maintain; ∼**to** *m* support; (*ganhapão*) livelihood

**susto** /'sustu/ *m* fright

**sutiã** /sutʃi'ã/ *m* bra

**su|til** /su'tʃiw/ (*pl* ∼**tis**) *a* subtle; ∼**tileza** /e/ *f* subtlety

**sutu|ra** /su'tura/ *f* suture; ∼**rar** *vt* suture

# T

**tá** /ta/ *int* (*fam*) OK; *veja* **estar**

**taba|caria** /tabaka'ria/ *f* tobacconist's; ∼**co** *m* tobacco

**tabefe** /ta'bɛfi/ *m* slap

**tabe|la** /ta'bɛla/ *f* table; ∼**lar** *vt* tabulate

**tablado** /ta'bladu/ *m* platform

**tabu** /ta'bu/ *a* & *m* taboo

**tábua** /'tabua/ *f* board; ∼ **de passar roupa** ironing board

**tabuleiro** /tabu'leru/ *m* (*de xadrez etc*) board

**tabuleta** /tabu'lɛta/ *f* (*letreiro*) sign

**taça** /'tasa/ *f* (*prêmio*) cup; (*de champanhe etc*) glass

**ta|cada** /ta'kada/ *f* shot; **de uma** ∼**cada** in one go; ∼**car** *vt* hit <*bola*>; (*fam*) throw

**tacha** /'taʃa/ *f* tack

**tachar** /ta'ʃar/ *vt* brand (**de** as)

**tachinha** /ta'ʃina/ *f* drawing pin, (*Amer*) thumbtack

**tácito** /'tasitu/ *a* tacit

**taciturno** /tasi'turnu/ *a* taciturn

**taco** /'taku/ *m* (*de golfe*) club; (*de bilhar*) cue; (*de hóquei*) stick

**tact-** (*Port*) *veja* **tat-**

**tagare|la** /taga'rɛla/ *a* chatty, talkative □ *m/f* chatterbox; ∼**lar** *vi* chatter

**tailan|dês** /tajlã'des/ *a* & *m* ( *f* ~**desa**) Thai

**Tailândia** /taj'lãdʒia/ *f* Thailand

**tailleur** /ta'jɛr/ ( *pl* ~ **s**) *m* suit

**Taiti** /taj'tʃi/ *m* Tahiti

**tal** /taw/ ( *pl* **tais**) *a* such; **que** ~? what do you think?, (*Port*) how are you?; **que** ~ **uma cerveja?** how about a beer?; ~ **como** such as; ~ **qual** just like; **um** ~ **de João** someone called John; **e** ~ **e** and so on

**tala** /'tala/ *f* splint

**talão** /ta'lãw/ *m* stub; ~ **de cheques** chequebook

**talco** /'tawku/ *m* talc

**talen|to** /ta'lẽtu/ *m* talent; ~**toso** /o/ *a* talented

**talhar** /ta'ʎar/ *vt* slice <*dedo, carne*>; carve <*pedra, imagem*>

**talharim** /taʎa'rĩ/ *m* tagliatelle

**talher** /ta'ʎɛr/ *m* set of cutlery; *pl* cutlery

**talho** /'taʎu/ *m* (*Port*) butcher's

**talismã** /taliz'mã/ *m* charm, talisman

**talo** /'talu/ *m* stalk

**talvez** /taw'ves/ *adv* perhaps; ~ **ele venha amanhã** he may come tomorrow

**tamanco** /ta'mãku/ *m* clog

**tamanho** /ta'maɲu/ *m* size □ *adj* such

**tâmara** /'tamara/ *f* date

**tamarindo** /tama'rĩdu/ *m* tamarind

**também** /tã'bẽj/ *adv* also; ~ **não** not ... either, neither

**tam|bor** /tã'bor/ *m* drum; ~**borilar** *vi* <*dedos*> drum; <*chuva*> patter; ~**borim** *m* tambourine

**Tâmisa** /'tamiza/ *m* Thames

**tam|pa** /'tãpa/ *f* lid; ~**pão** *m* (*vaginal*) tampon; ~**par** *vt* put the lid on <*recipiente*>; (*tapar*) cover; ~**pinha** *f* top□ *m/f* ( *fam*) shorthouse

**tampouco** /tã'poku/ *adv* nor, neither

**tanga** /'tãga/ *f* G-string; (*avental*) loincloth

**tangente** /tã'ʒẽtʃi/ *f* tangent; **pela** ~ ( *fig*) narrowly

**tangerina** /tãʒe'rina/ *f* tangerine

**tango** /'tãgu/ *m* tango

**tanque** /'tãki/ *m* tank; ( *para lavar roupa*) sink

**tanto** /'tãtu/ *a* & *pron* so much; *pl* so many □ *adv* so much; ~ ... **como** ... both ... and ...; ~ **(...) quanto** as much (...) as; ~ **melhor** so much the better; ~ **tempo** so long; **vinte e** ~**s anos** twenty odd years; **nem** ~ not as much; **um** ~ **difícil** somewhat difficult; ~ **que** to the extent that

**Tanzânia** /tã'zania/ *f* Tanzania

**tão** /tãw/ *adv* so; ~ **grande quanto** as big as; ~**somente** *adv* solely

**tapa** /'tapa/ *m ou f* slap; **dar um** ~ **em** slap

**tapar** /ta'par/ *vt* (*cobrir*) cover; block <*luz, vista*>; cork <*garrafa*>

**tapeçaria** /tapesa'ria/ *f* (*pano*) tapestry; (*loja*) carpet shop

**tape|tar** /tape'tar/ *vt* carpet; ~**te** /e/ *m* carpet

**tapioca** /tapi'ɔka/ *f* tapioca

**tapume** /ta'pumi/ *m* fence

**taquicardia** /takikar'dʒia/ *f* palpitations

**taquigra|far** /takigra'far/ *vt/i* write in shorthand; ~**fia** *f* shorthand

**tara** /'tara/ *f* fetish; ~**do** *a* sex-crazed □ *m* sex maniac; **ser** ~**do por** be crazy about

**tar|dar** /tar'dar/ *vi* (*atrasar*) be late; (*demorar muito*) be long □ *vt* delay; ~**dar a responder** take a long time to answer, be a long time answering; **o mais** ~**dar** at the latest; **sem mais** ~**dar** without further delay; ~**de** *adv* late □ *f* afternoon; **hoje à** ~**de** this afternoon; ~**de da noite** late at night; ~**dinha** *f* late afternoon; ~**dio** *a* late

**tarefa** /ta'rɛfa/ *f* task, job

**tarifa** /ta'rifa/ *f* tariff; ~ **de embarque** airport tax

**tarimbado** /tarĩ'badu/ *a* experienced

**tarja** /'tarʒa/ *f* strip

**ta|rô** /ta'ro/ *m* tarot; ~**rólogo** *m* tarot reader

**tartamu|dear** /tartamudʒi'ar/ *vi* stammer; ~**do** *a* stammering □ *m* stammerer

**tártaro** /'tartaru/ *m* tartar

**tartaruga** /tarta'ruga/ *f* (*bicho*) turtle; (*material*) tortoiseshell

**tatear** /tatʃi'ar/ *vt* feel □ *vi* feel one's way

**táti|ca** /'tatʃika/ *f* tactics; ~**co** *a* tactical

**tá|til** /'tatʃiw/ ( *pl* ~**teis**) *a* tactile

**tato** /'tatu/ *m* (*sentido*) touch; (*diplomacia*) tact

**tatu** /ta'tu/ *m* armadillo

**tatu|ador** /tatua'dor/ *m* tattooist; ~**agem** *f* tattoo; ~**ar** *vt* tattoo

**tauromaquia** /tawroma'kia/ *f* bullfighting

**taxa** /'taʃa/ *f* (*a pagar*) charge; (*índice*) rate; ~ **de câmbio** exchange rate; ~ **de juros** interest rate; ~ **rodoviária** road tax

**taxar** /ta'ʃar/ *vt* tax

**taxativo** /taʃa'tʃivu/ *a* firm, categorical

**táxi** /'taksi/ *m* taxi

**taxiar** /taksi'ar/ *vi* taxi

**taxímetro** /tak'simetru/ *m* taxi meter

**taxista** /tak'sista/ *m/f* taxi driver

**tchã** /tʃã/ *m* ( *fam*) special something

**tchau** /tʃaw/ *int* goodbye, bye

**tcheco** /'tʃɛku/ *a* & *m* Czech

**Tchecoslováquia** /tʃekoslo'vakia/ f Czechoslovakia

**te** /tʃi/ *pron* you; (*a ti*) to you

**tear** /tʃi'ar/ *m* loom

**tea|tral** /tʃia'traw/ (*pl* ~**trais**) *a* theatrical; <*grupo*> theatre; ~**tro** *m* theatre; ~**trólogo** *m* playwright

**tece|lagem** /tese'laʒẽ/ *f* (*trabalho*) weaving; (*fábrica*) textile factory; ~**lão** *m* (*f* ~**lã**) weaver

**te|cer** /te'ser/ *vt/i* weave; ~**cido** *m* cloth; (*no corpo*) tissue

**te|cla** /'tɛkla/ *f* key; ~**cladista** *m/f* (*músico*) keyboard player; (*de computador*) keyboard operator; ~**clado** *m* keyboard; ~**clar** *vt* key (in)

**técni|ca** /'tɛknika/ *f* technique; ~**co** *a* technical □ *m* specialist; (*de time*) manager; (*que mexe com máquinas*) technician

**tecno|crata** /tekno'krata/ *m/f* technocrat; ~**logia** *f* technology; ~**lógico** *a* technological

**teco-teco** /tɛku'tɛku/ *m* light aircraft

**tecto** /'tɛtu/ *m* (*Port*) *veja* **teto**

**tédio** /'tɛdʒiu/ *m* boredom

**tedioso** /tedʒi'ozu/ *a* boring, tedious

**Teerã** /tee'rã/ *f* Teheran

**teia** /'teja/ *f* web

**tei|ma** /'tejma/ *f* persistence; ~**mar** *vi* insist; ~**mar em** ir insist on going; ~**mosia** *f* stubbornness; ~**moso** /o/ *a* stubborn; <*ruído*> insistent

**teixo** /'tejʃu/ *m* yew

**Tejo** /'teʒu/ *m* Tagus

**tela** /'tɛla/ *f* (*de cinema, TV etc*) screen; (*tecido, pintura*) canvas

**telecoman|dado** /telekomã'dadu/ *a* remote-controlled; ~**do** *m* remote control

**telecomunicação** /telekomunika-'sãw/ *f* telecommunication

**teleférico** /tele'fɛriku/ *m* cable car

**telefo|nar** /telefo'nar/ *vi* telephone; ~**nar para alg** phone s.o.; ~**ne** /o/ *m* telephone; (*número*) phone number; ~**ne celular** cell phone; ~**ne sem fio** cordless phone; ~**nema** /e/ *m* phone call; ~**nia** *f* telephone technology

**telefôni|co** /tele'foniku/ *a* telephone; **cabine** ~**ca** phone box, (*Amer*) phone booth; **mesa** ~**ca** switchboard

**telefonista** /telefo'nista/ *m/f* (*da companhia telefônica*) operator; (*dentro de empresa etc*) telephonist

**tele|grafar** /telegra'far/ *vt/i* telegraph; ~**gráfico** *a* telegraphic

**telégrafo** /te'lɛgrafu/ *m* telegraph

**tele|grama** /tele'grama/ *m* telegram; ~**guiado** *a* remote- controlled

**telejor|nal** /teleʒor'naw/ (*pl* ~**nais**) *m* television news

**tele|novela** /teleno'vɛla/ *f* TV soap opera; ~**objetiva** *f* telephoto lens

**tele|patia** /telepa'tʃia/ *f* telepathy; ~**pático** *a* telepathic

**telescó|pico** /teles'kɔpiku/ *a* telescopic; ~**pio** *m* telescope

**telespectador** /telespekta'dor/ *m* television viewer □ *a* viewing

**televi|são** /televi'zãw/ *f* television; ~**são a cabo** cable television; ~**sionar** *vt* televise; ~**sivo** *a* television; ~**sor** *m* television set

**telex** /te'lɛks/ *m invar* telex

**telha** /'teʎa/ *f* tile; ~**do** *m* roof

**te|ma** /'tema/ *m* theme; ~**mático** *a* thematic

**temer** /te'mer/ *vt* fear □ *vi* be afraid; ~**por** fear for

**teme|rário** /teme'rariu/ *a* reckless; ~**ridade** *f* recklessness; ~**roso** /o/ *a* fearful

**te|mido** /te'midu/ *a* feared; ~**mível** (*pl* ~**míveis**) *a* fearsome; ~**mor** *m* fear

**tempão** /tẽ'pãw/ *m* **um** ~ a long time

**temperado** /tẽpe'radu/ *a* <*clima*> temperate □ *pp de* **temperar**

**temperamen|tal** /tẽperamẽ'taw/ (*pl* ~**tais**) *a* temperamental; ~**to** *m* temperament

**temperar** /tẽpe'rar/ *vt* season <*comida*>; temper <*aço*>

**temperatura** /tẽpera'tura/ *f* temperature

**tempero** /tẽ'peru/ *m* seasoning

**templo** /'tẽplu/ *m* temple

**tempo** /'tẽpu/ *m* (*período*) time; (*atmosférico* ) weather; (*do verbo*) tense; (*de jogo*) half; **ao mesmo** ~ at the same time; **nesse meio** ~ in the meantime; **o** ~ **todo** all the time; **de todos os** ~**s** of all time; **quanto** ~ how long; **muito/pouco** ~ a long/ short time; ~ **integral** full time

**têmpora** /'tẽpora/ *f* temple

**tempo|rada** /tẽpo'rada/ *f* (*sazão*) season; (*tempo*) while; ~**ral** (*pl* ~**rais**) *a* temporal □ *m* storm; ~**rário** *a* temporary

**te|nacidade** /tenasi'dadʒi/ *f* tenacity; ~**naz** *a* tenacious □ *f* tongs

**tenção** /tẽ'sãw/ *f* intention

**tencionar** /tẽsio'nar/ *vt* intend

**tenda** /'tẽda/ *f* tent

**tendão** /tẽ'dãw/ *m* tendon; ~ **de Aquiles** Achilles tendon

**tendência** /tẽ'dẽsia/ *f* (*moda*) trend; (*propensão*) tendency

**tendencioso** /tẽdẽsi'ozu/ *a* tendentious

**ten|der** /tě'der/ *vi* tend (**para to-wards**); **~de a engordar** he tends to get fat; **o tempo ~de a ficar bom** the weather is improving

**tenebroso** /tene'brozu/ *a* dark; (*fig: terrível*) dreadful

**tenente** /te'nětʃi/ *m/f* lieutenant

**tênis** /'tenis/ *m invar* (*jogo*) tennis; (*sapato*) trainer; **um ~** (*par*) a pair of trainers; **~ de mesa** table tennis

**tenista** /te'nista/ *m/f* tennis player

**tenor** /te'nor/ *m* tenor

**tenro** /'tẽxu/ *a* tender

**ten|são** /tẽ'sãw/ *f* tension; **~são** (**arterial**) blood pressure; **~so** *a* tense

**tentação** /tẽta'sãw/ *f* temptation

**tentáculo** /tẽ'tacalu/ *m* tentacle

**ten|tador** /tẽta'dor/ *a* tempting; **~tar** *vt* try; (*seduzir*) tempt □ *vi* try; **~tativa** *f* attempt; **~tativo** *a* tentative

**tênue** /'tenui/ *a* faint

**teo|logia** /teolo'ʒia/ *f* theology; **~lógico** *a* theological

**teólogo** /te'ɔlogu/ *m* theologian

**teor** /te'or/ *m* (*de gordura etc*) content; (*de carta, discurso*) drift

**teo|rema** /teo'rema/ *m* theorem; **~ria** *f* theory

**teórico** /te'oriku/ *a* theoretical

**teorizar** /teori'zar/ *vt* theorize

**tépido** /'tɛpidu/ *a* tepid

**ter** /ter/ *vt* have; **tenho vinte anos** I am twenty (years old); **~ medo/sede** be afraid/thirsty; **tenho que** *ou* **de ir** I have to go; **tem** (*há*) there is/are; **não tem de quê** don't mention it; **~ a ver com** have to do with

**tera|peuta** /tera'peuta/ *m/f* therapist; **~pêutico** *a* therapeutic; **~pia** *f* therapy

**terça** /'tersa/ *f* Tuesday; **~-feira** (*pl ~s-feiras*) *f* Tuesday; **Terça-Feira Gorda** Shrove Tues- day

**tercei|ra** /ter'sera/ *f* (*marcha*) third; **~ranista** *m/f* third-year; **~ro** *a* third □ *m* third party

**terço** /'tersu/ *m* third

**ter|çol** (*pl ~çóis*) *m* stye

**tergal** /ter'gaw/ *m* Terylene

**térmico** /'tɛrmiku/ *a* thermal; **garrafa ~ca** Thermos flask

**termi|nal** /termi'naw/ (*pl ~nais*) *a & m* terminal; **~nal de vídeo** VDU; **~nante** *a* definite; **~nar** *vt* finish □ *vi* <*pessoa, coisa*> finish; <*coisa*> end; **~nar com alg** (*cortar relação*) break up with s.o.

**ter|minologia** /terminolo'ʒia/ *f* terminology; **~mo**[1] /'termu/ *m* term; **pôr ~mo a** put an end to; **meio ~mo** compromise

**termo**[2] /'termu/ *m* (*Port*) Thermos flask

**ter|mômetro** /ter'mometru/ *m* thermometer; **~mostato** *m* thermostat

**terno**[1] /'ternu/ *m* suit

**ter|no**[2] /'tɛrnu/ *a* tender; **~nura** *f* tenderness

**terra** /'texa/ *f* land; (*solo, elétrico*) earth; (*chão*) ground; **a Terra** Earth; **por ~** on the ground; **~ natal** homeland

**terraço** /te'xasu/ *m* terrace

**terra|cota** /texa'kɔta/ *f* terracotta; **~moto** /texa'mɔtu/ *m* (*Port*) earthquake; **~plenagem** *f* earth moving

**terreiro** /te'xeru/ *m* meeting place for Afro-Brazilian cults

**terremoto** /texe'mɔtu/ *m* earthquake

**terreno** /te'xenu/ *a* earthly □ *m* ground; (*geog*) terrain; (*um*) piece of land; **~ baldio** piece of waste ground

**térreo** /'tɛxiu/ *a* ground-floor; (**andar**) **~** ground floor, (*Amer*) first floor

**terrestre** /te'xɛstri/ *a* <*animal, batalha, forças*> land; (*da Terra*) of the Earth, the Earth's; <*alegrias etc*> earthly

**terrificante** /texifi'kãtʃi/ *a* terrifying

**terrina** /te'xina/ *f* tureen

**territori|al** /texitori'aw/ (*pl ~ais*) *a* territorial

**território** /texi'toriu/ *m* territory

**terri|vel** /te'xivew/ (*pl ~veis*) *a* terrible

**terror** /te'xor/ *m* terror; **filme de ~** horror film

**terroris|mo** /texo'rizmu/ *m* terrorism; **~ta** *a & m/f* terrorist

**tese** /'tɛzi/ *f* theory; (*escrita*) thesis

**teso** /'tezu/ *a* (*apertado*) taut; (*rígido*) stiff

**tesoura** /te'zora/ *f* scissors; **uma ~** a pair of scissors

**tesou|reiro** /tezo'reru/ *m* treasurer; **~ro** *m* treasure; (*do Estado*) treasury

**testa** /'tɛsta/ *f* forehead; **~-de-ferro** (*pl ~s-de-ferro*) *m* frontman

**testamento** /tɛsta'mẽtu/ *m* will; (*na Bíblia*) testament

**tes|tar** /tɛs'tar/ *vt* test; **~te** /ɛ/ *m* test

**testemu|nha** /tɛste'muɲa/ *f* witness; **~nha ocular** eye witness; **~nhar** *vt* bear witness to □ *vi* testify; **~nho** *m* evidence, testimony

**testículo** /tɛs'tʃikulu/ *m* testicle

**teta** /'teta/ *f* teat

**tétano** /'tɛtanu/ *m* tetanus

**teto** /'tɛtu/ *m* ceiling; **~ solar** sun roof

**tétrico** /'tɛtriku/ *a* (*triste*) dismal; (*medonho*) horrible

**teu** /tew/ (*f tua*) *a* your □ *pron* yours

**têx|til** /'testʃiw/ (*pl ~teis*) *m* textile

**tex|to** /'testu/ *m* text; **~tura** *f* texture

**texugo** /te'ʃugu/ *m* badger

**tez** /tes/ *f* complexion

**ti** /tʃi/ *pron* you

**tia** /'tʃia/ *f* aunt; **~-avó** (*pl* **~s-avós**) *f* great aunt

**tiara** /tʃi'ara/ *f* tiara

**tíbia** /'tʃibia/ *f* shinbone

**ticar** /tʃi'kar/ *vt* tick

**tico** /'tʃiku/ *m* **um ~ de** a little bit of

**tiete** /tʃi'etʃi/ *m/f* fan

**tifo** /'tʃifu/ *m* typhoid

**tigela** /tʃi'ʒɛla/ *f* bowl; **de meia ~** smalltime

**tigre** /'tʃigri/ *m* tiger; **~sa** /e/ *f* tigress

**tijolo** /tʃi'ʒolu/ *m* brick

**til** /tʃiw/ (*pl* **tis**) *m* tilde

**tilintar** /tʃili'tar/ *vi* jingle □ *m* jingling

**timão** /tʃi'mãw/ *m* tiller

**timbre** /'tʃibri/ *m* (*insígnia*) crest; (*em papel*) heading; (*de som*) tone; (*de vogal*) quality

**time** /'tʃimi/ *m* team

**timidez** /tʃimi'des/ *f* shyness

**tímido** /'tʃimidu/ *a* shy

**tímpano** /'tʃĩpanu/ *m* (*tambor*) kettledrum; (*no ouvido*) eardrum

**tina** /'tʃina/ *f* vat

**tingir** /tʃi'ʒir/ *vt* dye <*tecido, cabelo*>; (*fig*) tinge

**ti|nido** /tʃi'nidu/ *m* tinkling; **~nir** *vi* tinkle; <*ouvidos*> ring; (*tremer*) tremble; **estar ~nindo** (*fig*) be in peak condition

**tino** /'tʃinu/ *m* sense, judgement; **ter ~ para** have a flair for

**tin|ta** /'tʃita/ *f* (*para pintar*) paint; (*para escrever*) ink; (*para tingir*) dye; **~teiro** *m* inkwell

**tintim** /tʃi'tʃi/ *m* **contar ~ por ~** give a blow-by-blow account of

**tin|to** /'tʃitu/ *a* dyed; <*vinho*> red; **~tura** *f* dye; (*fig*) tinge; **~turaria** *f* dry cleaner's

**tio** /'tʃiu/ *m* uncle; *pl* (**~ e tia**) uncle and aunt; **~-avô** (*pl* **~s-avôs**) *m* great uncle

**típico** /'tʃipiku/ *a* typical

**tipo** /'tʃipu/ *m* type

**tipóia** /tʃi'pɔja/ *f* sling

**tique** /'tʃiki/ *m* (*sinal*) tick; (*do rosto etc*) twitch

**tíquete** /'tʃiketʃi/ *m* ticket

**tiquinho** /tʃi'kiɲu/ *m* **um ~ de** a tiny bit of

**tira** /'tʃira/ *f* strip □ *m/f* (*fam*) copper, (*Amer*) cop

**tiracolo** /tʃira'kɔlu/ *m* **a ~** <*bolsa*> over one's shoulder; <*pessoa*> in tow

**tiragem** /tʃi'raʒẽ/ *f* (*de jornal*) circulation

**tira|-gosto** /tʃira'gostu/ *m* snack; **~-manchas** *m invar* stain remover

**ti|rania** /tʃira'nia/ *f* tyranny; **~rânico** *a* tyrannical; **~rano** *m* tyrant

**tirar** /tʃi'rar/ *vt* (*afastar*) take away; (*de dentro*) take out; take off <*roupa, sapato, tampa*>; take <*foto, cópia, férias*>; clear <*mesa*>; get <*nota, diploma, salário*>; get out <*mancha*>

**tiritar** /tʃiri'tar/ *vi* shiver

**tiro** /'tʃiru/ *m* shot; **~ ao alvo** shooting; **é ~ e queda** (*fam*) it can't fail; **~teio** *m* shoot-out

**titânio** /tʃi'taniu/ *m* titanium

**títere** /'tʃiteri/ *m* puppet

**ti|tia** /tʃi'tʃia/ *f* auntie; **~tio** *m* uncle

**tititi** /tʃitʃi'tʃi/ *m* (*fam*) talk

**titubear** /tʃitubi'ar/ *vi* stagger, totter; (*fig: hesitar*) waver

**titular** /tʃitu'lar/ *m/f* title holder; (*de time*) captain □ *vt* title

**título** /'tʃitulu/ *m* title; (*obrigação*) bond; **a ~ de** on the basis of; **a ~ pessoal** on a personal basis

**toa** /'toa/ *f* **à ~** (*sem rumo*) aimlessly; (*ao acaso*) at random; (*sem motivo*) without reason; (*em vão*) for nothing; (*desocupado*) at a loose end; (*de repente*) out of the blue

**toada** /to'ada/ *f* melody

**toalete** /toa'letʃi/ *m* toilet

**toalha** /to'aʎa/ *f* towel; **~ de mesa** tablecloth

**tobogã** /tobo'gã/ *m* (*rampa*) slide; (*trenó*) toboggan

**toca** /'tɔka/ *f* burrow

**toca|-discos** /toka'dʒiskus/ *m invar* record player; **~-fitas** *m invar* tape player

**tocaia** /to'kaja/ *f* ambush

**tocante** /to'kãtʃi/ *a* (*enternecedor*) moving

**tocar** /to'kar/ *vt* touch; play <*piano, música, disco etc*>; ring <*campainha*> □ *vi* touch; <*pianista, música, disco etc*> play; <*campainha, telefone, sino*> ring; **~-se** *vpr* take the hint; (*mancar-se*) take the hint; **~ a** (*dizer respeito*) concern; **~ em** touch; touch on <*assunto*>

**tocha** /'tɔʃa/ *f* torch

**toco** /'tɔku/ *m* (*de árvore*) stump; (*de cigarro*) butt

**toda** /'toda/ *f* **a ~** at full speed

**todavia** /toda'via/ *conj* however

**todo** /'todu/ *a* all; (*cada*) every; *pl* all; **~ o dinheiro** all the money; **~ dia**, **~s os dias** every day; **~s os alunos** all the pupils; **o dia ~** all day; **em ~ lugar** everywhere; **~ mundo**, **~s everyone**; **~s nós** all of us; **ao ~** in all; **~-poderoso** *a* almighty

**tofe** /'tɔfi/ *m* toffee

**toga** /'tɔga/ *f* gown; (*de romano*) toga

**toicinho** /toj'siɲu/ *m* bacon

**toldo** /'towdu/ *m* awning

**tole|rância** /tole'rãsia/ f tolerance; **~rante** a tolerant; **~rar** vt tolerate; **~rável** (pl **~ráveis**) a tolerable

**to|lice** /to'lisi/ f foolishness; (uma) foolish thing; **~lo** /o/ a foolish □ m fool

**tom** /tõ/ m tone

**to|mada** /to'mada/ f (conquista) capture; (elétrica) plughole; (de filme) shot; **~mar** vt take; (beber) drink; **~mar café** have breakfast

**tomara** /to'mara/ int I hope so; **~ que** let's hope that; **~-que-caia** a invar <vestido> strapless

**tomate** /to'matʃi/ m tomato

**tom|bar** /tõ'bar/ vt (derrubar) knock down; list <edifício> □ vi fall over; **~bo** m fall; **levar um ~bo** have a fall

**tomilho** /to'miʎu/ m thyme

**tomo** /'tomu/ m volume

**tona** /'tona/ f **trazer à ~** bring up; **vir à ~** emerge

**tonalidade** /tonali'dadʒi/ f (de música) key; (de cor) shade

**to|nel** /to'nɛw/ (pl **~néis**) m cask; **~nelada** f tonne

**tôni|ca** /'tonika/ f tonic; (fig: assunto) keynote; **~co** a & m tonic

**tonificar** /tonifi'kar/ vt tone up

**ton|tear** /tõtʃi'ar/ vt **~tear alg** make s.o.'s head spin; **~teira** f dizziness; **~to** a (zonzo) dizzy; (bobo) stupid; (atrapalhado) flustered; **~tura** f dizziness

**to|pada** /to'pada/ f trip; **dar uma ~pada em** stub one's toe on; **~par** vt agree to, accept; **~par com** bump into <pessoa>; come across <coisa>

**topázio** /to'paziu/ m topaz

**topete** /to'petʃi/ m quiff

**tópico** /'tɔpiku/ a topical □ m topic

**topless** /topi'lɛs/ a invar & adv topless

**topo** /'topu/ m top

**topografia** /topogra'fia/ f topography

**topônimo** /to'ponimu/ m place name

**toque** /'tɔki/ m touch; (da campainha, do telefone) ring; (de instrumento) playing; **dar um ~ em** (fam) have a word with

**Tóquio** /'tɔkiu/ f Tokyo

**tora** /'tɔra/ f log

**toranja** /to'rãʒa/ f grapefruit

**tórax** /'tɔraks/ m invar thorax

**tor|ção** /tor'sãw/ f (do braço etc) sprain; **~cedor** m supporter; **~cer** vt twist; (machucar) sprain; (espremer) wring <roupa>; (centrifugar) spin <roupa> □ vi (gritar) cheer (**por** for); (desejar sucesso) keep one's fingers crossed (**por** for; **para que** that); **~cer-se** vpr twist about;

**~cicolo** /ɔ/ m stiff neck; **~cida** f (torção) twist; (torcedores) supporters; (gritaria) cheering

**tormen|ta** /tor'mẽta/ f storm; **~to** m torment; **~toso** /o/ a stormy

**tornado** /tor'nadu/ m tornado

**tornar** /tor'nar/ vt make; **~-se** vpr become

**torne|ado** /torni'adu/ a **bem ~ado** shapely; **~ar** vt turn

**torneio** /tor'neju/ m tournament

**torneira** /tor'nera/ f tap, (Amer) faucet

**torniquete** /torni'ketʃi/ m (para ferido) tourniquet; (Port: de entrada) turnstile

**torno** /'tornu/ m lathe; (de ceramista) wheel; **em ~ de** around

**tornozelo** /torno'zelu/ m ankle

**toró** /to'rɔ/ m downpour

**torpe** /'torpi/ a dirty

**torpe|dear** /torpedʒi'ar/ vt torpedo; **~do** /e/ m torpedo

**torpor** /tor'por/ m torpor

**torra|da** /to'xada/ f piece of toast; pl toast; **~deira** f toaster

**torrão** /to'xãw/ m (de terra) turf; (de açúcar) lump

**torrar** /to'xar/ vt toast <pão>; roast <café>; blow <dinheiro>; sell off <mercadorias>

**torre** /'toxi/ f tower; (em xadrez) rook; **~ de controle** control tower; **~ão** m turret

**torrefação** /toxefa'sãw/ f (ação) roasting; (fábrica) coffee-roasting plant

**torren|cial** /toxẽsi'aw/ (pl **~ciais**) a torrential; **~te** f torrent

**torresmo** /to'xezmu/ m crackling

**tórrido** /'tɔxidu/ a torrid

**torrone** /to'xoni/ m nougat

**torso** /'torsu/ m torso

**torta** /'tɔrta/ f pie, tart

**tor|to** /'tɔrtu/ a crooked; **a ~ e a direito** left, right and centre; **~tuoso** a winding

**tortu|ra** /tor'tura/ f torture; **~rador** m torturer; **~rar** vt torture

**to|sa** /'tɔza/ f (de cachorro) clipping; (de ovelhas) shearing; **~são** m fleece; **~sar** vt clip <cachorro>; shear <ovelhas>; crop <cabelo>

**tosco** /'tosku/ a rough, coarse

**tosquiar** /toski'ar/ vt shear <ovelha>

**tos|se** /'tɔsi/ f cough; **~se de cachorro** whooping cough; **~sir** vi cough

**tostão** /tos'tãw/ m penny

**tostar** /tos'tar/ vt brown <carne>; tan <pele, pessoa>; **~-se** vpr (ao sol) go brown

**to|tal** /to'taw/ (pl **~tais**) a & m total

**totali|dade** /totali'dadʒi/ f entirety; **~tário** a totalitarian; **~zar** vt total

**touca** /'toka/ f bonnet; (de freira) wimple; ~ de banho bathing cap; ~dor m dressing table

**toupeira** /to'pera/ f mole

**tou|rada** /to'rada/ f bullfight; ~reiro m bullfighter; ~ro m bull; **Touro** (signo) Taurus

**tóxico** /'tɔksiku/ a toxic □ m toxic substance

**toxicômano** /toksi'komanu/ m drug addict

**toxina** /tok'sina/ f toxin

**traba|lhador** /trabaʎa'dor/ a <pessoa> hard-working; <classe> working □ m worker; ~lhar vt work □ vi work; (numa peça, filme) act; ~lheira f big job; ~lhista a labour; ~lho m work; (um) (na escola) assignment; **dar-se o ~lho de** go to the trouble of; ~lho de parto labour; ~lhos forçados hard labour; ~lhoso a laborious

**traça** /'trasa/ f moth

**tração** /tra'sãw/ f traction

**tra|çar** /tra'sar/ vt draw; draw up <plano>; set out <ordens>; ~ço m stroke; (entre frases) dash; (vestígio) trace; (característica) trait; pl (do rosto) features

**tractor** /tra'tor/ m (Port) veja **trator**

**tradi|ção** /tradʒi'sãw/ f tradition; ~cional (pl ~cionais) a traditional

**tradu|ção** /tradu'sãw/ f translation; ~tor m translator; ~zir vt/i translate (de from; para into)

**trafe|gar** /trafe'gar/ vi run; ~gável (pl ~gáveis) a open to traffic

**tráfego** /'trafegu/ m traffic

**trafi|cância** /trafi'kãsia/ f trafficking; ~cante m/f trafficker; ~car vt/i traffic (com in)

**tráfico** /'trafiku/ m traffic

**tra|gada** /tra'gada/ f (de bebida) swallow; (de cigarro) drag; ~gar vt swallow; inhale <fumaça>

**tragédia** /tra'ʒedʒia/ f tragedy

**trágico** /'traʒiku/ a tragic

**trago** /'tragu/ m (de bebida) swallow; (de cigarro) drag; **de um** ~ in one go

**trai|ção** /traj'sãw/ f (ato) betrayal; (deslealdade) treachery; (da pátria) treason; ~çoeiro a treacherous; ~dor a treacherous □ m traitor

**trailer** /'trejler/ (pl ~s) m (de filme etc) trailer; (casa móvel) caravan, (Amer) trailer

**traineira** /traj'nera/ f trawler

**training** /'trejnĩ/ (pl ~s) m track suit

**trair** /tra'ir/ vt betray; be unfaithful to <marido, mulher>; ~se vpr give o.s. away

**tra|jar** /tra'ʒar/ vt wear; ~jar-se vpr dress (de in); ~je m outfit; ~je a

rigor evening dress; ~je espacial space suit

**traje|to** /tra'ʒɛtu/ m (percurso) journey; (caminho) route; ~tória f trajectory; (fig) course

**tralha** /'traʎa/ f (trastes) junk

**tra|ma** /'trama/ f plot; ~mar vt/i plot

**trambi|que** /trã'biki/ (fam) m con; ~queiro (fam) m con artist

**tramitar** /trami'tar/ vi be processed

**trâmites** /'tramitʃis/ m pl channels

**tramóia** /tra'mɔja/ f scheme

**trampolim** /trãpo'lĩ/ m (de ginástica) trampoline; (de piscina, fig) springboard

**tranca** /'trãka/ f bolt; (em carro) lock

**trança** /'trãsa/ f (de cabelo) plait

**tran|cafiar** /trãkafi'ar/ vt lock up; ~car vt lock; cancel <matrícula>

**trançar** /trã'sar/ vt plait <cabelo>; weave <palha etc>

**tranco** /'trãku/ m jolt; **aos ~s e barrancos** in fits and starts

**tranqueira** /trã'kera/ f junk

**tranqüi|lidade** /trãkwili'dadʒi/ f tranquillity; ~lizador a reassuring; ~lizante m tranquillizer □ a reassuring; ~lizar vt reassure; ~lizar-se vpr be reassured; ~lo a <bairro, sono> peaceful; <pessoa, voz, mar> calm; <consciência> clear; <sucesso, lucro> sure-fire □ adv with no trouble

**transa** /'trãza/ f (fam) (negócio) deal; (caso) affair; ~ção f transaction; ~do a (fam) <roupa, pessoa, casa> stylish; <relação> healthy

**Transamazônica** /trãzama'zonika/ f trans-Amazonian highway

**transar** /trã'zar/ (fam) vt set up; do <drogas> □ vi (negociar) deal; (fazer sexo) have sex

**transatlântico** /trãzat'lãtʃiku/ a transatlantic □ m liner

**transbordar** /trãzbor'dar/ vi overflow

**transcen|dental** /trãsẽdẽ'taw/ (pl ~dentais) a transcendental; ~der vt/i ~der (a) transcend

**trans|crever** /trãskre'ver/ vt transcribe; ~crição f transcription; ~crito a transcribed □ m transcript

**transe** /'trãzi/ m trance

**transeunte** /trãzi'ũtʃi/ m/f passer-by

**transfe|rência** /trãsfe'rẽsia/ f transfer; ~ridor m protractor; ~rir vt transfer; ~rir-se vpr transfer

**transfor|mação** /trãsforma'sãw/ f transformation; ~mador m transformer; ~mar vt transform; ~mar-se vpr be transformed

**trânsfuga** /'trãsfuga/ m/f deserter; (de um país) defector

**transfusão** /trãsfu'zãw/ *f* transfusion

**trans|gredir** /trãzgre'dʒir/ *vt* infringe; **~gressão** *f* infringement

**transi|ção** /trãzi'sãw/ *f* transition; **~cional** (*pl* **~cionais**) *a* transitional

**transi|gente** /trãzi'ʒẽtʃi/ *a* open to compromise; **~gir** *vi* compromise

**transis|tor** /trãzis'tor/ *m* transistor; **~torizado** *a* transistorized

**transi|tar** /trãzi'tar/ *vi* pass; **~tável** (*pl* **~táveis**) *a* passable; **~tivo** *a* transitive

**trânsito** /'trãzitu/ *m* traffic; **em ~** in transit

**transitório** /trãzi'toriu/ *a* transitory

**translúcido** /trãz'lusidu/ *a* translucent

**transmis|são** /trãzmi'sãw/ *f* transmission; **~sor** *m* transmitter

**transmitir** /trãzmi'tʃir/ *vt* transmit <*programa, calor, doença*>; convey <*notícia, ordens*>; transfer <*herança, direito*>; **~-se** *vpr* <*doença*> be transmitted

**transpa|recer** /trãspare'ser/ *vi* be visible; (*fig*) <*emoção, verdade*> come out; **~rência** *f* transparency; **~rente** *a* transparent

**transpi|ração** /trãspira'sãw/ *f* perspiration; **~rar** *vt* exude □ *vi* (*suar*) perspire; <*notícia*> trickle through; <*verdade*> come out

**transplan|tar** /trãsplã'tar/ *vt* transplant; **~te** *m* transplant

**transpor** /trãs'por/ *vt* cross <*rio, fronteira*>; get over <*obstáculo, dificuldade*>; transpose <*letras, música*>

**transpor|tadora** /trãsporta'dora/ *f* transport company; **~tar** *vt* transport; (*em contas*) carry forward; **~te** *m* transport; **~te coletivo** public transport

**transposto** /trãs'postu/ *pp de* transpor

**transtor|nar** /trãstor'nar/ *vt* mess up <*papéis, casa*>; disrupt <*rotina, ambiente*>; disturb, upset <*pessoa*>; **~nar-se** *vpr* <*pessoa*> be rattled; **~no** /o/ *m* (*de casa, rotina*) disruption; (*de pessoa*) disturbance; (*contratempo*) upset

**transver|sal** /trãzver'saw/ (*pl* **~sais**) *a* (**rua**) **~sal** cross street; **~so** /ɛ/ *a* transverse

**transvi|ado** /trãzvi'adu/ *a* wayward; **~ar** *vt* lead astray

**trapa|ça** /tra'pasa/ *f* swindle; **~cear** *vi* cheat; **~ceiro** *a* crooked □ *m* cheat

**trapa|lhada** /trapa'ʎada/ *f* bungle; **~lhão** *a* (*f* **~lhona**) bungling □ *m* (*f* **~lhona**) bungler

**trapézio** /tra'peziu/ *m* trapeze

**trapezista** /trape'zista/ *m/f* trapeze artist

**trapo** /'trapu/ *m* rag

**traquéia** /tra'kɛja/ *f* windpipe, trachea

**traquejo** /tra'keʒu/ *m* knack

**traquinas** /tra'kinas/ *a invar* mischievous

**trás** /tras/ *adv* **de ~** from behind; **a roda de ~** the back wheel; **de ~ para frente** back to front; **para ~** backwards; **deixar para ~** leave behind; **por ~ de** behind

**traseiro** /tra'zeru/ *a* rear, back □ *m* bottom

**trasladar** /trazla'dar/ *vt* transport

**traspas|sado** /traspa'sadu/ *a* <*paletó*> double-breasted; **~sar** *vt* pierce

**traste** /'trastʃi/ *m* (*pessoa*) pain; (*coisa*) piece of junk

**tra|tado** /tra'tadu/ *m* (*pacto*) treaty; (*estudo*) treatise; **~tamento** *m* treatment; (*título*) title; **~tar** *vt* treat; negotiate <*preço, venda*> □ *vi* (*manter relações*) have dealings (**com** with); (*combinar*) negotiate (**com** with); **~tar de** deal with; **~tar alg de** *ou* **por** address s.o. as; **~tar de voltar** (*tentar*) seek to return; (*resolver*) decide to return; **~tar-se de** be a matter of; **~tável** (*pl* **~táveis**) *a* <*doença*> treatable; <*pessoa*> accommodating; **~tos** *m pl* **maus ~tos** illtreatment

**trator** /tra'tor/ *m* tractor

**trauma** /'trawma/ *m* trauma; **~tizante** *a* traumatic; **~tizar** *vt* traumatize

**tra|vão** /tra'vãw/ *m* (*Port*) brake; **~var** *vt* lock <*rodas, músculos*>; stop <*carro*>; block <*passagem*>; strike up <*amizade, conversa*>; wage <*luta, combate*> □ *vi* (*Port*) brake

**trave** /'travi/ *f* beam, joist; (*do gol*) crossbar

**traves|sa** /tra'vesa/ *f* (*trave*) crossbar; (*rua*) side street; (*prato*) dish; (*pente*) slide; **~são** *m* dash; **~seiro** *m* pillow; **~sia** *f* crossing; **~so** /e/ *a* <*criança*> naughty; **~sura** *f* prank; *pl* mischief

**travesti** /traves'tʃi/ *m* transvestite; (*artista*) drag artist; **~do** *a* in drag

**trazer** /tra'zer/ *vt* bring; bear <*nome, ferida*>; wear <*barba, chapéu, cabelo curto*>

**trecho** /'treʃu/ *m* (*de livro etc*) passage; (*de rua etc*) stretch

**treco** /'trɛku/ (*fam*) *m* (*coisa*) thing; (*ataque*) turn

**trégua** /'trɛgwa/ *f* truce; (*fig*) respite

**trei|nador** /trejna'dor/ *m* trainer; **~namento** *m* training; **~nar** *vt* train <*atleta, animal*>; practise <*língua etc*> □ *vi* <*atleta*> train;

**trejeito** /tre'ʒejtu/ *m* grimace
**trela** /'trɛla/ *f* lead, (*Amer*) leash
**treliça** /tre'lisa/ *f* trellis
**trem** /trẽj/ *m* train; ~ **de aterrissagem** undercarriage; ~ **de carga** goods train, (*Amer*) freight train
**trema** /'trema/ *m* dieresis
**treme|deira** /treme'dera/ *f* shiver; ~**licar** *vi* tremble; ~**luzir** *vi* glimmer, flicker
**tremendo** /tre'mẽdu/ *a* tremendous
**tre|mer** /tre'mer/ *vi* tremble; <*terra*> shake; ~**mor** *m* tremor; (*tremedeira*) shiver; ~**mular** *vi* <*bandeira*> flutter; <*luz, estrela*> glimmer, flicker
**trêmulo** /'tremulu/ *a* trembling; <*luz*> flickering
**trena** /'trena/ *f* tape measure
**trenó** /tre'nɔ/ *m* sledge, (*Amer*) sled; (*puxado a cavalos etc*) sleigh
**tre|padeira** /trepa'dera/ *f* climbing plant; ~**par** *vt* climb □ *vi* climb; (*chulo*) fuck
**três** /tres/ *a & m* three
**tresloucado** /trezlo'kadu/ *a* deranged
**trevas** /'trɛvas/ *f pl* darkness
**trevo** /'trevu/ *m* (*planta*) clover; (*rodoviário*) interchange
**treze** /'trezi/ *a & m* thirteen
**trezentos** /tre'zẽtus/ *a & m* three hundred
**triagem** /tri'aʒẽ/ *f* (*escolha*) selection; (*separação*) sorting; **fazer uma ~ de** sort
**tri|angular** /triãgu'lar/ *a* triangular; ~**ângulo** *m* triangle
**tri|bal** /tri'baw/ (*pl* ~**bais**) *a* tribal; ~**bo** *f* tribe
**tribu|na** /tri'buna/ *f* rostrum; ~**nal** (*pl* ~**nais**) *m* court
**tribu|tação** /tributa'sãw/ *f* taxation; ~**tar** *vt* tax; ~**tário** *a* tax □ *m* tributary; ~**to** *m* tribute
**tri|cô** /tri'ko/ *m* knitting; **artigos de** ~**cô** knitwear; ~**cotar** *vt/i* knit
**tridimensio|nal** /tridʒimẽsio'naw/ (*pl* ~**nais**) *a* three- dimensional
**trigêmeo** /tri'ʒemiu/ *m* triplet
**trigésimo** /tri'ʒezimu/ *a* thirtieth
**tri|go** /'trigu/ *m* wheat; ~**gueiro** *a* dark
**trilha** /'triʎa/ *f* path; (*pista, de disco*) track; ~ **sonora** soundtrack
**trilhão** /tri'ʎãw/ *m* billion, (*Amer*) trillion
**trilho** /'triʎu/ *m* track
**trilogia** /trilo'ʒia/ *f* trilogy
**trimes|tral** /trimes'traw/ (*pl* ~**trais**) *a* quarterly; ~**tre** /ɛ/ *m* quarter; (*do ano letivo*) term
**trincar** /trĩ'kar/ *vt/i* crack

**trincheira** /trĩ'ʃera/ *f* trench
**trinco** /'trĩku/ *m* latch
**trindade** /trĩ'dadʒi/ *f* trinity
**trinta** /'trĩta/ *a & m* thirty
**trio** /'triu/ *m* trio; ~ **elétrico** music float
**tripa** /'tripa/ *f* gut
**tripé** /tri'pɛ/ *m* tripod
**tripli|car** /tripli'kar/ *vt/i*, ~**car-se** *vpr* treble; ~**cata** *f* triplicate
**triplo** /'triplu/ *a & m* triple
**tripu|lação** /tripula'sãw/ *f* crew; ~**lante** *m/f* crew member; ~**lar** *vt* man
**triste** /'tristʃi/ *a* sad; ~**za** /e/ *f* sadness; **é uma ~za** (*fam*) it's pathetic
**tritu|rador** /tritura'dor/ *m* (*de papel*) shredder; ~**rador de lixo** waste disposal unit; ~**rar** *vt* shred <*legumes, papel*>; grind up <*lixo*>
**triun|fal** /triũ'faw/ (*pl* ~**fais**) *a* triumphal; ~**fante** *a* triumphant; ~**far** *vi* triumph; ~**fo** *m* triumph
**trivi|al** /trivi'aw/ (*pl* ~**ais**) *a* trivial; ~**alidade** *f* triviality; *pl* trivia
**triz** /tris/ *m* **por um** ~ narrowly, by a hair's breadth; **não foi atropelado por um** ~ he narrowly missed being knocked down
**tro|ca** /'trɔka/ *f* exchange; **em** ~**ca de** in exchange for; ~**cadilho** *m* pun; ~**cado** *m* change; ~**cador** *m* conductor; ~**car** *vt* (*dar e receber*) exchange (**por** for); change <*dinheiro, lençóis, lâmpada, lugares etc*>; (*transpor*) change round; (*confundir*) mix up; ~**car-se** *vpr* change; ~**car de roupa/trem/lugar** change clothes/trains/places; ~**ca-troca** *m* swap; ~**co** /o/ *m* change; **a** ~**co de quê?** what for?; **dar o** ~**co em alg** pay s.o. back
**troço** /'trɔsu/ (*fam*) *m* (*coisa*) thing; (*ataque*) turn; **me deu um** ~ I had a funny turn
**troféu** /tro'fɛw/ *m* trophy
**trólebus** /'trɔlebus/ *m invar* trolley bus
**trom|ba** /'trõba/ *f* (*de elefante*) trunk; (*cara amarrada*) long face; ~**bada** *f* crash; ~**ba-d'água** (*pl* ~**bas-d'água**) *f* downpour; ~**badinha** *m* bag snatcher; ~**bar** *vi* ~**bar com** crash into <*poste, carro*>; bump into <*pessoa*>
**trombo|ne** /trõ'bɔni/ *m* trombone; ~**nista** *m/f* trombonist
**trompa** /'trõpa/ *f* French horn; ~ **de Falópio** fallopian tube
**trompe|te** /trõ'petʃi/ *m* trumpet; ~**tista** *m/f* trumpeter
**tron|co** /'trõku/ *m* trunk; ~**cudo** *a* stocky
**trono** /'tronu/ *m* throne

**tropa** /'trɔpa/ *f* troop; (*exército*) army; *pl* troops; ∼ **de choque** riot police
**trope|ção** /trope'sãw/ *m* trip; (*erro*) slip-up; ∼**çar** *vi* trip; (*errar*) slip up; ∼**ço** /e/ *m* stumbling block
**trôpego** /'tropegu/ *a* unsteady
**tropi|cal** /tropi'kaw/ (*pl* ∼**cais**) *a* tropical
**trópico** /'trɔpiku/ *m* tropic
**tro|tar** /tro'tar/ *vi* trot; ∼**te** /ɔ/ *m* (*de cavalo*) trot; (*de estudantes*) practical joke; (*mentira*) hoax
**trouxa** /'troʃa/ *f* (*de roupa etc*) bundle □ *m/f* (*fam*) sucker □ *a* (*fam*) gullible
**tro|vão** /tro'vãw/ *m* clap of thunder; *pl* thunder; ∼**vejar** *vi* thunder; ∼**voada** *f* thunderstorm; ∼**voar** *vi* thunder
**trucidar** /trusi'dar/ *vt* slaughter
**trucu|lência** /truku'lẽsia/ *f* barbarity; ∼**lento** *a* (*cruel*) barbaric; (*brigão*) belligerent
**trufa** /'trufa/ *f* truffle
**trunfo** /'trũfu/ *m* trump; (*fig*) trump card
**truque** /'truki/ *m* trick
**truta** /'truta/ *f* trout
**tu** /tu/ *pron* you
**tua** /'tua/ *veja* **teu**
**tuba** /'tuba/ *f* tuba
**tubarão** /tuba'rãw/ *m* shark
**tubá|rio** /tu'bariu/ *a* **gravidez** ∼**ria** ectopic pregnancy
**tuberculose** /tubercu'lɔzi/ *f* tuberculosis
**tubo** /'tubu/ *m* tube; (*no corpo*) duct
**tubulação** /tubula'sãw/ *f* ducting
**tucano** /tu'kanu/ *m* toucan
**tudo** /'tudu/ *pron* everything; ∼ **bem?** (*cumprimento*) how are things?; ∼ **de bom** all the best; **em** ∼ **quanto é lugar** all over the place
**tufão** /tu'fãw/ *m* typhoon
**tulipa** /tu'lipa/ *f* tulip
**tumba** /'tũba/ *f* tomb
**tumor** /tu'mor/ *m* tumour; ∼ **cerebral** brain tumour
**túmulo** /'tumulu/ *m* grave
**tumul|to** /tu'muwtu/ *m* commotion; (*motim*) riot; ∼**tuado** *a* disorderly, rowdy; ∼**tuar** *vt* disrupt □ *vi* cause a commotion; ∼**tuoso** *a* tumultuous
**tú|nel** /'tunew/ (*pl* ∼**neis**) *m* tunnel
**túnica** /'tunika/ *f* tunic
**Tunísia** /tu'nizia/ *f* Tunisia
**tupiniquim** /tupini'ki/ *a* Brazilian
**turbante** /tur'bãtʃi/ *m* turban
**turbilhão** /turbi'ʎãw/ *m* whirlwind
**turbina** /tur'bina/ *f* turbine
**turbu|lência** /turbu'lẽsia/ *f* turbulence; ∼**lento** *a* turbulent
**turco** /'turku/ *a* & *m* Turkish
**turfa** /'turfa/ *f* peat
**turfe** /'turfe/ *m* horse-racing
**turis|mo** /tu'rizmu/ *m* tourism; **fazer**

∼**mo** go sightseeing; ∼**ta** *m/f* tourist
**turístico** /tu'ristʃiku/ *a* <*ponto, indústria*> tourist; <*viagem*> sightseeing
**turma** /'turma/ *f* group; (*na escola*) class
**turnê** /tur'ne/ *f* tour
**turno** /'turnu/ *m* (*de trabalho*) shift; (*de competição, eleição*) round
**turquesa** /tur'keza/ *m/f* & *a* invar turquoise
**Turquia** /tur'kia/ *f* Turkey
**turra** /'tuxa/ *f* **às** ∼**s com** at loggerheads with
**tur|var** /tur'var/ *vt* cloud; ∼**vo** *a* cloudy
**tutano** /tu'tanu/ *m* marrow
**tutela** /tu'tɛla/ *f* guardianship
**tutor** /tu'tor/ *m* guardian
**tutu** /tu'tu/ *m* (*vestido*) tutu; (*prato*) beans with bacon and manioc flour
**TV** /te've/ *f* TV

# U

**ubíquo** /u'bikwu/ *a* ubiquitous
**Ucrânia** /u'krania/ *f* Ukraine
**ucraniano** /ukrani'anu/ *a* & *m* Ukrainian
**ué** /u'ɛ/ *int* hang on
**ufa** /'ufa/ *int* phew
**ufanis|mo** /ufa'nizmu/ *m* chauvinism; ∼**ta** *a* & *m/f* chauvinist
**Uganda** /u'gãda/ *m* Uganda
**ui** /ui/ *int* (*de dor*) ouch; (*de nojo*) ugh; (*de espanto*) oh
**uísque** /u'iski/ *m* whisky
**ui|var** /ui'var/ *vi* howl; ∼**vo** *m* howl
**úlcera** /'uwsera/ *f* ulcer
**ulterior** /uwteri'or/ *a* further
**ulti|mamente** /uwtʃima'mẽtʃi/ *adv* recently; ∼**mar** *vt* finalize; ∼**mato** *m* ultimatum
**último** /'uwtʃimu/ *a* last; <*moda, notícia etc*> latest; **em** ∼ **caso** as a last resort; **nos** ∼**s anos** in recent years; **por** ∼ last
**ultra|jante** /uwtra'ʒãtʃi/ *a* offensive; ∼**jar** *vt* offend; ∼**je** *m* outrage
**ultraleve** /uwtra'lɛvi/ *m* microlite
**ultra|mar** /uwtra'mar/ *m* overseas; ∼**marino** *a* overseas
**ultrapas|sado** /uwtrapa'sadu/ *a* outdated; ∼**sagem** *f* overtaking, (*Amer*) passing; ∼**sar** *vt* (*de carro*) overtake, (*Amer*) pass; (*ser superior a*) surpass; (*exceder*) exceed; (*extrapolar*) go beyond □ *vi* overtake, (*Amer*) pass
**ultra-sonografia** /uwtrasonogra-'fia/ *f* ultrasound scan
**ultravioleta** /uwtravio'leta/ *a* ultraviolet

**ulu|lante** /ulu'lãtʃi/ a (fig) blatant; **~lar** vi wail

**um** /ũ/ (f **uma**; m pl **uns**, f pl **umas**) art a, an; pl some □ a & pron one; **~ ao outro** one another; **vieram umas 20 pessoas** about 20 people came

**umbanda** /ũ'bãda/ m Afro-Brazilian cult

**umbigo** /ũ'bigu/ m navel

**umbili|cal** /ũbili'kaw/ (pl **~cais**) a umbilical

**umedecer** /umede'ser/ vt moisten; **~-se** vpr moisten

**umidade** /umi'dadʒi/ f moisture; (desagradável) damp; (do ar) humidity

**úmido** /'umidu/ a moist; <parede, roupa etc> damp; <ar, clima> humid

**unânime** /u'nanimi/ a unanimous

**unanimidade** /unanimi'dadʒi/ f unanimity

**undécimo** /ũ'dɛsimu/ a eleventh

**ungüento** /ũ'gwẽtu/ m ointment

**unha** /'uɲa/ f nail; (de animal, utensílio) claw

**unhar** /u'ɲar/ vt claw

**união** /uni'ãw/ f union; (concórdia) unity; (ato de unir) joining

**unicamente** /unika'mẽtʃi/ adv only

**único** /'uniku/ a only; (ímpar) unique

**uni|dade** /uni'dadʒi/ f unit; **~do** a united; <família> close

**unifi|cação** /unifika'sãw/ f unification; **~car** vt unify

**unifor|me** /uni'fɔrmi/ a uniform; <superfície> even □ m uniform; **~midade** f uniformity; **~mizado** a <policial etc> uniformed; (padronizado) standardized; **~zar** vt (padronizar) standardize

**unilate|ral** /unilate'raw/ (pl **~rais**) a unilateral

**unir** /u'nir/ vt unite <povo, nações, família etc>; (ligar, casar) join; (combinar) combine (a ou com with); **~-se** vpr (aliar-se) unite (a with); (juntar-se) join together; (combinar-se) combine (a ou com with)

**unissex** /uni'sɛks/ a invar unisex

**uníssono** /u'nisonu/ m **em ~** in unison

**univer|sal** /univer'saw/ (pl **~sais**) a universal

**universi|dade** /universi'dadʒi/ f university; **~tário** a university □ m university student

**universo** /uni'vɛrsu/ m universe

**untar** /ũ'tar/ vt grease <fôrma>; spread <pão>; smear <corpo, rosto etc>

**upa** /'upa/ int (incentivando) upsa-daisy; (ao cair algo etc) whoops

**urânio** /u'raniu/ m uranium

**Urano** /u'ranu/ m Uranus

**urbanis|mo** /urba'nizmu/ m town

planning; **~ta** m/f town planner

**urbani|zado** /urbani'zadu/ a built-up; **~zar** vt urbanize

**urbano** /ur'banu/ a (da cidade) urban; (refinado) urbane

**urdir** /ur'dʒir/ vt weave; (maquinar) hatch

**urdu** /ur'du/ m Urdu

**ur|gência** /ur'ʒẽsia/ f urgency; **~gente** a urgent; **~gir** vi be urgent; <tempo> press; **~ge irmos** we must go urgently

**uri|na** /u'rina/ f urine; **~nar** vt pass □ vi urinate; **~nol** (pl **~nóis**) m (penico) chamber pot; (em banheiro) urinal

**urna** /'urna/ f (para cinzas) urn; (para votos) ballot box; pl (fig) polls

**ur|rar** /u'xar/ vt/i roar; **~ro** m roar

**urso** /'ursu/ m bear; **~-branco** (pl **~s-brancos**) m polar bear

**urti|cária** /urtʃi'karia/ f nettle rash; **~ga** f nettle

**urubu** /uru'bu/ m black vulture

**Uruguai** /uru'gwaj/ m Uruguay

**uruguaio** /uru'gwaju/ a & m Uruguayan

**urze** /'urzi/ f heather

**usado** /u'zadu/ a used; <roupa> worn; <palavra> common

**usar** /u'zar/ vt wear <roupa, óculos, barba etc>; **~ (de)** (utilizar) use

**usina** /u'zina/ f plant; **~ termonuclear** nuclear power station

**uso** /'uzu/ m use; (de palavras, linguagem) usage; (praxe) practice

**usu|al** /uzu'aw/ (pl **~ais**) a common; **~ário** m user; **~fruir** vt enjoy <coisas boas>; have the use of <prédio, jardim etc>; **~fruto** m use

**usurário** /uzu'rariu/ a money-grubbing □ m money-lender

**usurpar** /uzur'par/ vt usurp

**uten|sílio** /utẽ'siliu/ m utensil; **~te** m/f (Port) user

**útero** /'uteru/ m uterus, womb

**UTI** /ute'i/ f intensive care unit

**útil** /'utʃiw/ (pl **úteis**) a useful; **dia ~** workday

**utili|dade** /utʃili'dadʒi/ f usefulness; (uma) utility; **~tário** a utilitarian; **~zar** vt (empregar) use; (tornar útil) utilize; **~zável** (pl **~záveis**) a usable

**utopia** /uto'pia/ f Utopia

**utópico** /u'tɔpiku/ a Utopian

**uva** /'uva/ f grape

**úvula** /'uvula/ f uvula

# V

**vaca** /'vaka/ f cow

**vaci|lante** /vasi'lãtʃi/ a wavering; <luz> flickering; **~lar** vi waver;

vacina 174 variz

<*luz*> flicker; (*fam: bobear*) slip up

**vaci|na** /va'sina/ *f* vaccine; **~nação** *f* vaccination; **~nar** *vt* vaccinate

**vácuo** /'vakuu/ *m* vacuum

**va|diar** /vadʒi'ar/ *vi* (*viver ocioso*) laze around; (*fazer cera*) mess about; **~dio** *a* idle □ *m* idler

**vaga** /'vaga/ *f* (*posto*) vacancy; (*para estacionar*) parking place

**vagabun|dear** /vagabũdʒi'ar/ *vi* (*perambular*) roam; (*vadiar*) laze around; **~do** *a* <*pessoa, vida*> shoddy □ *m* tramp; (*pessoa vadia*) bum

**vaga-lume** /vaga'lumi/ *m* glow-worm

**va|gão** /va'gãw/ *m* (*de passageiros*) carriage, (*Amer*) car; (*de carga*) wagon; **~gão-leito** (*pl* **~gões-leitos**) *m* sleeping car; **~gão-restaurante** (*pl* **~gões-restaurantes**) *m* dining car

**vagar**[1] /va'gar/ *vi* <*pessoa*> wander about; <*barco*> drift

**vagar**[2] /va'gar/ *vi* <*cargo, apartamento*> become vacant

**vagaroso** /vaga'rozu/ *a* slow

**vagem** /'vaʒẽ/ *f* green bean

**vagi|na** /va'ʒina/ *f* vagina; **~nal** (*pl* **~nais**) *a* vaginal

**vago**[1] /'vagu/ *a* (*indefinido*) vague

**vago**[2] /'vagu/ *a* (*desocupado*) vacant; <*tempo*> spare

**vaguear** /vagi'ar/ *vi* roam

**vai|a** /'vaja/ *f* boo; **~ar** *vi* boo

**vai|dade** /vaj'dadʒi/ *f* vanity; **~doso** *a* vain

**vaivém** /vaj'vẽj/ *m* comings and goings, toing and froing

**vala** /'vala/ *f* ditch; **~ comum** mass grave

**vale**[1] /'vali/ *m* (*de rio etc*) valley

**vale**[2] /'vali/ *m* (*ficha*) voucher; **~ postal** postal order

**valen|tão** /valẽ'tãw/ *a* (*f* **~tona**) tough □ *m* tough guy; **~te** *a* brave; **~tia** *f* bravery; (*uma*) feat

**valer** /va'ler/ *vt* be worth □ *vi* be valid; **~ aco a alg** earn s.o. sth; **~se de** avail o.s. of; **~ a pena** be worth it; **vale a pena tentar** it's worth trying; **mais vale desistir** it's better to give up; **vale tudo** anything goes; **fazer ~** enforce <*lei*>; **stand up for** <*direitos*>; **para ~** (*a sério*) for real; (*muito*) really

**vale|-refeição** /valirefej'sãw/ (*pl* **~s-refeição**) *m* luncheon voucher

**valeta** /va'leta/ *f* gutter

**valete** /va'letʃi/ *m* jack

**valia** /va'lia/ *f* value

**validar** /vali'dar/ *vt* validate

**válido** /'validu/ *a* valid

**valioso** /vali'ozu/ *a* valuable

**valise** /va'lizi/ *f* travelling bag

**valor** /va'lor/ *m* value; (*valentia*) valour; *pl* (*títulos*) securities; **no ~ de** to the value of; **sem ~** worthless; **objetos de ~** valuables; **~ nominal** face value

**valori|zação** /valoriza'sãw/ *f* (*apreciação*) valuing; (*aumento no valor*) increase in value; **~zado** *a* highly valued; **~zar** *vt* (*apreciar*) value; (*aumentar o valor de*) increase the value of; **~zar-se** *vt* <*coisa*> increase in value; <*pessoa*> value o.s.

**val|sa** /'vawsa/ *f* waltz; **~sar** *vi* waltz

**válvula** /'vawvula/ *f* valve

**vampiro** /vã'piru/ *m* vampire

**vandalismo** /vãda'lizmu/ *m* vandalism

**vândalo** /'vãdalu/ *m* vandal

**vangloriar-se** /vãglori'arsi/ *vpr* brag (*de about*)

**vanguarda** /vã'gwarda/ *f* vanguard; (*de arte*) avant-garde

**vanta|gem** /vã'taʒẽ/ *f* advantage; **contar ~gem** boast; **levar ~gem** have the advantage (**a** over); **tirar ~gem de** take advantage of; **~joso** /o/ *a* advantageous

**vão** /vãw/ (*pl* **~s**) *a* (*f* **vã**) vain □ *m* gap; **em ~** in vain

**vapor** /va'por/ *m* (*fumaça*) steam; (*gás*) vapour; (*barco*) steamer; **máquina a ~** steam engine; **a todo ~** at full blast

**vaporizar** /vapori'zar/ *vt* vaporize; (*com spray*) spray

**vaqueiro** /va'keru/ *m* cowboy

**vaquinha** /va'kiɲa/ *f* collection, whip-round

**vara** /'vara/ *f* rod; **~ cívil** civil district; **~ mágica** *ou* **de condão** magic wand

**va|ral** /va'raw/ (*pl* **~rais**) *m* washing line

**varanda** /va'rãda/ *f* veranda

**varão** /va'rãw/ *m* male

**varar** /va'rar/ *vt* (*furar*) pierce; (*passar por*) sweep through

**varejão** /vare'ʒão/ *m* wholesale store

**varejeira** /vare'ʒera/ *f* bluebottle

**vare|jista** /vare'ʒista/ *a* retail □ *m/f* retailer; **~jo** /e/ *m* retail trade; **vender a ~jo** sell retail

**vari|ação** /varia'sãw/ *f* variation; **~ado** *a* varied; **~ante** *a & f* variant; **~ar** *vt/i* vary; **para ~ar** for a change; **~ável** (*pl* **~áveis**) *a* variable; <*tempo*> changeable

**varicela** /vari'sɛla/ *f* chickenpox

**variedade** /varie'dadʒi/ *f* variety

**vários** /'varius/ *a pl* several

**varíola** /va'riola/ *f* smallpox

**variz** /va'ris/ *f* varicose vein

**varo|nil** /varo'niw/ (*pl* ~**nis**) *a* manly

**var|rer** /va'xer/ *vt* sweep; (*fig*) sweep away; ~**rido a um doido** ~**rido** a raving lunatic

**Varsóvia** /var'sɔvia/ *f* Warsaw

**vasculhar** /vasku'ʎar/ *vt* search through

**vasectomia** /vazekto'mia/ *f* vasectomy

**vaselina** /vaze'lina/ *f* vaseline

**vasilha** /va'ziʎa/ *f* jug

**vaso** /'vazu/ *m* pot; (*para flores*) vase; ~ **sanguíneo** blood vessel

**vassoura** /va'sora/ *f* broom

**vas|tidão** /vastʃi'dãw/ *f* vastness; ~**to** *a* vast

**vatapá** /vata'pa/ *m* spicy North-Eastern dish

**Vaticano** /vatʃi'kanu/ *m* Vatican

**vati|cinar** /vatʃisi'nar/ *vt* prophesy; ~**cínio** *m* prophecy

**va|zamento** /vaza'mẽtu/ *m* leak; ~**zante** *f* ebb tide; ~**zão** *m* outflow; **dar** ~**zão a** (*fig*) give vent to; ~**zar** *vt/i* leak

**vazio** /va'ziu/ *a* empty □ *m* emptiness; (*um*) void

**veado** /vi'adu/ *m* deer

**ve|dação** /veda'sãw/ *f* (*de casa, janela*) insulation; (*em motor etc*) gasket; ~**dar** *vt* seal <*recipiente, abertura*>; stanch <*sangue*>; seal off <*saída, área*>; ~**dar aco (a alg)** prohibit sth (for s.o.)

**vedete** /ve'dɛte/ *f* star

**vee|mência** /vee'mẽsia/ *f* vehemence; ~**mente** *a* vehement

**vege|tação** /veʒeta'sãw/ *f* vegetation; ~**tal** (*pl* ~**tais**) *a* & *m* vegetable; ~**tar** *vi* vegetate; ~**tariano** *a* & *m* vegetarian

**veia** /'veja/ *f* vein

**veicular** /veiku'lar/ *vt* convey; place <*anúncios*>

**veículo** /ve'ikulu/ *m* vehicle; (*de comunicação etc*) medium

**vela**[1] /'vɛla/ *f* (*de barco*) sail; (*esporte*) sailing

**vela**[2] /'vɛla/ *f* candle; (*em motor*) spark plug; **segurar a** ~ (*fam*) play gooseberry

**velar**[1] /ve'lar/ *vt* (*cobrir*) veil

**velar**[2] /ve'lar/ *vt* watch over □ *vi* keep vigil

**veleidade** /velej'dadʒi/ *f* whim

**ve|leiro** /ve'leru/ *m* sailing boat; ~**lejar** *vi* sail

**velhaco** /ve'ʎaku/ *a* crooked □ *m* crook

**ve|lharia** /veʎa'ria/ *f* old thing; ~**lhice** *f* old age; ~**lho** /ɛ/ *a* old □ *m* old man; ~**lhote** /ɔ/ *m* old man

**velocidade** /velosi'dadʒi/ *f* speed;

(*Port: marcha*) gear; **a toda** ~ at full speed; ~ **máxima** speed limit

**velocímetro** /velo'simetru/ *m* speedometer

**velocista** /velo'sista/ *m/f* sprinter

**velório** /ve'lɔriu/ *m* wake

**veloz** /ve'los/ *a* fast

**veludo** /ve'ludu/ *m* velvet; ~ **cotelê** corduroy

**ven|cedor**[1] /vẽse'dor/ *a* winning □ *m* winner; ~**cer** *vt* win over <*adversário etc*>; win <*partida, corrida, batalha*> □ *vi* (*triunfar*) win; <*prestação, aluguel, dívida*> fall due; <*contrato, passaporte, prazo*> expire; <*apólice*> mature; ~**cido** *a* **dar-se por** ~**cido** give in; ~**cimento** *m* (*de dívida, aluguel*) due date; (*de contrato, prazo*) expiry date; (*de alimento, remédio etc*) best before date; (*salário*) payment; *pl* earnings

**venda**[1] /'vẽda/ *f* sale; (*loja*) general store; **à** ~ on sale; **pôr à** ~ put up for sale

**ven|da**[2] /'vẽda/ *f* blindfold; ~**dar** *vt* blindfold

**venda|val** /vẽda'vaw/ (*pl* ~**vais**) *m* gale, storm

**ven|dável** /vẽ'davew/ (*pl* ~**dáveis**) *a* saleable; ~**dedor** *m* (*de loja*) shop assistant; (*em geral*) seller; ~**der** *vt/i* sell; **estar** ~**dendo saúde** be bursting with health

**vendeta** /vẽ'deta/ *f* vendetta

**veneno** /ve'nenu/ *m* poison; (*de cobra etc, malignidade*) venom; ~**so** /o/ *a* poisonous; (*maldoso*) venomous

**vene|ração** /venera'sãw/ *f* reverence; (*de Deus etc*) worship; ~**rar** *vt* revere; worship <*Deus etc*>

**vené|reo** /ve'nɛriu/ *a* **doença** ~**rea** venereal disease

**Veneza** /ve'neza/ *f* Venice

**veneziana** /venezi'ana/ *f* shutter

**Venezuela** /venezu'ɛla/ *f* Venezuela

**venezuelano** /venezue'lanu/ *a* & *m* Venezuelan

**venta** /'vẽta/ *f* nostril

**ven|tania** /vẽta'nia/ *f* gale; ~**tar** *vi* be windy; ~**tarola** /ɔ/ *f* fan

**venti|lação** /vẽtʃila'sãw/ *f* ventilation; ~**lador** *m* fan; ~**lar** *vt* ventilate; air <*sala, roupa*>

**ven|to** /'vẽtu/ *m* wind; **de** ~**to em popa** smoothly; ~**toinha** *f* (*cata-vento*) weather vane; (*Port: ventilador*) fan; ~**tosa** /ɔ/ *f* sucker; ~**toso** /o/ *a* windy

**ven|tre** /'vẽtri/ *m* belly; ~**tríloquo** *m* ventriloquist

**Vênus** /'venus/ *f* Venus

**ver** /ver/ *vt* see; watch <*televisão*>; (*resolver*) see to □ *vi* see □ *m* **a meu** ~ in my view; ~**-se** *vpr* (*no espelho*) *etc*) see o.s.; (*em estado, condição*) find o.s.; (*um ao outro*) see each other; **ter a ~ com** have to do with; **vai ~ que ela não sabe** (*fam*) I bet she doesn't know; **vê se você não volta tarde** see you don't get back late; **viu?** (*fam*) right?

**veracidade** /verasi'dadʒi/ *f* truthfulness

**vera|near** /verani'ar/ *vi* spend the summer; **~neio** *m* summer holiday, (*Amer*) summer vacation; **~nista** *m/f* holidaymaker, (*Amer*) vacationer

**verão** /ve'rãw/ *m* summer

**veraz** /ve'ras/ *a* truthful

**verbas** /'vɛrbas/ *f pl* funds

**ver|bal** /ver'baw/ (*pl* ~**bais**) *a* verbal; **~bete** /e/ *m* entry; **~bo** *m* verb; **~borragia** *f* waffle; **~boso** /o/ *a* verbose

**verda|de** /ver'dadʒi/ *f* truth; **de ~de** <*coisa*> real; <*fazer*> really; **na ~de** actually; **para falar a ~de** to tell the truth; **~deiro** *a* <*declaração, pessoa*> truthful; (*real*) true

**verde** /'verdʒi/ *a & m* green; **jogar ~ para colher maduro** fish for information; **~-abacate** *a invar* avocado; **~-amarelo** *a* yellow and green; (*brasileiro*) Brazilian; (*nacionalista*) nationalistic; **~-esmeralda** *a invar* emerald green; **~jar** *vi* turn green

**verdu|ra** /ver'dura/ *f* (*para comer*) greens; (*da natureza*) greenery; **~reiro** *m* greengrocer, (*Amer*) produce dealer

**vereador** /veria'dor/ *m* councillor

**vereda** /ve'reda/ *f* path

**veredito** /vere'dʒitu/ *m* verdict

**vergar** /ver'gar/ *vt/i* bend

**vergo|nha** /ver'goɲa/ *f* (*pudor*) shame; (*constrangimento*) embarrassment; (*timidez*) shyness; (*uma*) disgrace; **ter ~nha** be ashamed; be embarrassed; be shy; **cria** *ou* **tome ~nha na cara!** you should be ashamed of yourself!; **~nhoso** *a* shameful

**verídico** /ve'ridʒiku/ *a* true

**verificar** /verifi'kar/ *vt* check, verify <*fatos, dados etc*>; **~ que** ascertain that; **~ se** check that; **~-se** *vpr* <*previsão etc*> come true; <*acidente etc*> happen

**verme** /'vɛrmi/ *m* worm

**verme|lhidão** /vermeʎi'dãw/ *f* redness; **~lho** /e/ *a & m* red; **no ~lho** (*endividado*) in the red

**vernáculo** /ver'nakulu/ *a & m* vernacular

**verniz** /ver'nis/ *f* varnish; (*couro*) patent leather

**veros|símil** /vero'simiw/ (*pl*

**~símeis**) *a* plausible; **~similhança** *f* plausibility

**verruga** /ve'xuga/ *f* wart

**ver|sado** /ver'sadu/ *a* well-versed (**em** in); **~são** *f* version; **~sar** *vi* **~sar sobre** concern; **~sátil** (*pl* **~sáteis**) *a* versatile; **~satilidade** *f* versatility; **~sículo** *m* (*da Bíblia*) verse; **~so¹** /ɛ/ *m* verse

**verso²** /ɛ/ *m* (*de página*) reverse, other side; **vide ~** see over

**vértebra** /'vɛrtebra/ *f* vertebra

**verte|brado** /verte'bradu/ *a & m* vertebrate; **~bral** (*pl* **~brais**) *a* spinal

**ver|tente** /ver'tētʃi/ *f* slope; **~ter** *vt* (*derramar*) pour; shed <*lágrimas, sangue*>; (*traduzir*) render (**para** into)

**verti|cal** /vertʃi'kaw/ (*pl* ~**cais**) *a & f* vertical; **~gem** *f* dizziness; **~ginoso** /o/ *a* dizzy

**vesgo** /'vezgu/ *a* cross-eyed

**vesícula** /ve'zikula/ *f* gall bladder

**vespa** /'vespa/ *f* wasp

**véspera** /'vɛspera/ *f* **a ~** the day before; **a ~ de** the eve of; **a ~ de Natal** Christmas Eve; **nas ~s de** on the eve of

**vespertino** /vesper'tʃinu/ *a* evening

**ves|te** /'vɛstʃi/ *f* robe; **~tiário** *m* (*para se trocar*) changing room; (*para guardar roupa*) cloakroom

**vestibular** /vestʃibu'lar/ *m* university entrance exam

**vestíbulo** /ves'tʃibulu/ *m* hall(way); (*do teatro*) foyer

**vestido** /ves'tʃidu/ *m* dress □ *a* dressed (**de** in)

**vestígio** /ves'tʃiʒiu/ *m* trace

**ves|timenta** /vestʃi'mēta/ *f* (*de sacerdote*) vestments; **~tir** *vt* (*pôr*) put on; (*usar*) wear; (*pôr roupa em*) dress; (*dar roupa a*) clothe; **~tir-se** *vpr* dress; **~tir-se de branco/de padre** dress in white/as a priest; **~tuário** *m* clothing

**vetar** /ve'tar/ *vt* veto

**veterano** /vete'ranu/ *a & m* veteran

**veterinário** /veteri'nariu/ *a* veterinary □ *m* vet

**veto** /'vɛtu/ *m* veto

**véu** /vɛw/ *m* veil

**vexa|me** /ve'ʃami/ *m* disgrace; **dar um ~me** make a fool of o.s.; **~minoso** /o/ *a* disgraceful

**vexar** /ve'ʃar/ *vt* shame; **~-se** *vpr* be ashamed (**de** of)

**vez** /ves/ *f*(*ocasião*) time; (*turno*) turn; **às ~es** sometimes; **cada ~ mais** more and more; **de ~** for good; **desta ~** this time; **de ~ em quando** now and again, from time to time; **de uma ~** (*ao mesmo tempo*) at once; (*de um* golpe) in one go; **de uma ~ por todas** once and for all; **duas ~es** twice; **em ~ de** instead of; **fazer as ~es de** take the place of; **mais uma ~, outra ~** again; **muitas ~es** (*com muita frequência*) often; (*repetidamente*) many times; **raras ~es** seldom; **repetidas ~es** repeatedly; **uma ~** once; **uma ~ que** since

**via** /'via/ *f* (*estrada*) road; (*rumo, meio*) way; (*exemplar*) copy; *pl* (*trâmites*) channels □ *prep* via; **em ~s de** on the point of; **por ~** (*Amer*) overland **aérea/marítima** by air/sea; **por ~ das dúvidas** just in case; **por ~ de regra** as a rule; **Via Láctea** Milky Way

**viabili|dade** /viabili'dadʒi/ *f* feasibility; **~zar** *vt* make feasible

**viação** /via'sãw/ *f* (*transporte*) road transport; (*estradas*) road network; (*companhia*) bus company

**viaduto** /via'dutu/ *m* viaduct; (*rodoviário*) flyover, (*Amer*) overpass

**via|gem** /vi'aʒẽ/ *f* (*uma*) trip, journey; (*em geral*) travelling; *pl* (*de uma pessoa*) travels; (*em geral*) travel; **boa ~gem!** have a good trip!; **~gem de negócios** business trip; **~jado** *a* well-travelled; **~jante** *a* travelling □ *m/f* traveller; **~jar** *vi* travel; **estar ~jando** (*fam*) (*com o pensamento longe*) be miles away

**viário** /vi'ariu/ *a* road; **anel ~** ring road

**viatura** /via'tura/ *f* vehicle

**viá|vel** /vi'avew/ (*pl* **~veis**) *a* feasible

**víbora** /'vibora/ *f* viper

**vi|bração** /vibra'sãw/ *f* vibration; (*fig*) thrill; **~brante** *a* vibrant; **~brar** *vt* shake □ *vi* vibrate; (*fig*) be thrilled (**com** by)

**vice** /'visi/ *m/f* deputy

**vice-cam|peão** /visikãpi'ãw/ *m* (*f* **~peã**) runner-up

**vicejar** /vise'ʒar/ *vi* flourish

**vice-presiden|te** /visiprezi'dẽtʃi/ *m* (*f* **~ta**) vice-president

**vice-rei** /visi'xej/ *m* viceroy

**vice-versa** /visi'versa/ *adv* vice-versa

**vici|ado** /visi'adu/ *a* addicted (**em** to) □ *m* addict; **um ~ado em drogas** a drug addict; **~ar** *vt* (*falsificar*) tamper with; (*estragar*) ruin □ *vi* <*droga*> be addictive; **~ar-se** *vpr* get addicted (**em** to)

**vício** /'visiu/ *m* vice

**vicioso** /visi'ozu/ *a* **círculo ~** vicious circle

**vicissitudes** /visisi'tudʒis/ *f pl* ups and downs

**viço** /'visu/ *m* (*de plantas*) exuberance; (*de pessoa, pele*) freshness; **~so** /o/ *a* <*planta*> lush; <*pele, pessoa*> fresh

**vida** /'vida/ *f* life; **sem ~** lifeless; **dar ~ a** liven up

**videira** /vi'dera/ *f* vine

**vidente** /vi'dẽtʃi/ *m/f* clairvoyant

**vídeo** /'vidʒiu/ *m* video; (*tela*) screen

**video|cassete** /vidʒiuka'setʃi/ *m* (*fita*) video tape; (*aparelho*) video, (*Amer*) VCR; **~clipe** *m* video; **~clube** *m* video club; **~game** *m* videogame; **~teipe** *m* video tape

**vidra|ça** /vi'drasa/ *f* window pane; **~çaria** *f* (*fábrica*) glassworks; (*vidraças*) glazing; **~ceiro** *m* glazier

**vi|drado** /vi'dradu/ *a* glazed; **estar ~drado em** *ou* **por** (*fam*) love; **~drar** *vt* glaze □ *vi* (*fam*) fall in love (**em** *ou* **por** with); **~dro** *m* (*material*) glass; (*pote*) jar; (*janela*) window; **~dro fumê** tinted glass

**viela** /vi'ɛla/ *f* alley

**Viena** /vi'ena/ *f* Vienna

**Vietnã** /vietʃ'nã/ *m*, (*Port*) **Vietname** /viet'nam/ *m* Vietnam

**vietnamita** /vietna'mita/ *a* & *m/f* Vietnamese

**viga** /'viga/ *f* joist

**vigarice** /viga'risi/ *f* swindle

**vigário** /vi'gariu/ *m* vicar

**vigarista** /viga'rista/ *m/f* swindler, con artist

**vi|gência** /vi'ʒẽsia/ *f* (*qualidade*) force; (*tempo*) period in force; **~gente** *a* in force

**vigésimo** /vi'ʒɛzimu/ *a* twentieth

**vigi|a** /vi'ʒia/ *f* (*guarda*) watch; (*em navio*) porthole □ *m* night watchman; **~ar** *vt* (*observar*) watch; (*cuidar de*) watch over; (*como sentinela*) guard □ *vi* keep watch

**vigi|lância** /viʒi'lãsia/ *f* vigilance; **~lante** *a* vigilant

**vigília** /vi'ʒilia/ *f* vigil

**vigor** /vi'gor/ *m* vigour; **em ~** in force

**vigo|rar** /vigo'rar/ *vi* be in force; **~roso** *a* vigorous

**vil** /viw/ (*pl* **vis**) *a* base, despicable

**vila** /'vila/ *f* (*cidadezinha*) small town; (*casa elegante*) villa; (*conjunto de casas*) housing estate; **~ olímpica** Olympic village

**vi|lania** /vila'nia/ *f* villainy; **~lão** *m* (*f* **~lã**) villain

**vilarejo** /vila'reʒu/ *m* village

**vilipendiar** /vilipẽdʒi'ar/ *vt* disparage

**vime** /'vimi/ *m* wicker

**vina|gre** /vi'nagri/ *m* vinegar; **~grete** /ɛ/ *m* vinaigrette

**vin|car** /vĩ'kar/ *vt* crease; line <*rosto*>; **~co** *m* crease; (*no rosto*) line

**vincular** /vĩku'lar/ *vt* bond, tie

**vínculo** /'vĩkulu/ *m* link, bond; **~ empregatício** contract of employment

**vinda** /'vĩda/ f coming; **dar as boas ~s** a welcome

**vindicar** /vĩdʒi'kar/ vt vindicate

**vindima** /vĩ'dʒima/ f vintage

**vin|do** /'vĩdu/ pp e pres de **vir**; **~douro** a coming

**vin|gança** /vĩ'gãsa/ f vengeance, revenge; **~gar** vt revenge □ vi <flores> thrive; <criança> survive; <plano, empreendimento> be successful; **~gar-se** vpr take one's revenge (**de** for; **em** on); **~gativo** a vindictive

**vinha** /'viɲa/ f vineyard

**vinhedo** /vi'ɲedu/ m vineyard

**vinheta** /vi'ɲeta/ f (na TV etc) sequence

**vinho** /'viɲu/ m wine □ a invar maroon; **~ do Porto** port

**vinícola** /vi'nikola/ a wine-growing

**vinicul|tor** /vinikuw'tor/ m wine grower; **~tura** f wine growing

**vinil** /vi'niw/ m vinyl

**vinte** /'vĩtʃi/ a & m twenty; **~na** /e/ f score

**viola** /vi'ɔla/ f viola

**violação** /viola'sãw/ f violation

**violão** /vio'lãw/ m guitar

**violar** /vio'lar/ vt violate

**vio|lência** /vio'lẽsia/ f violence; (uma) act of violence; **~lentar** vt rape <mulher>; **~lento** a violent

**violeta** /vio'leta/ f violet □ a invar violet

**violi|nista** /violi'nista/ m/f violinist; **~no** m violin

**violonce|lista** /violõse'lista/ m/f cellist; **~lo** /ɛ/ m cello

**vir** /vir/ vi come; **o ano que vem** next year; **venho lendo os jornais** I have been reading the papers; **vem cá** come here; (fam) listen; **isso não vem ao caso** that's irrelevant; **~ a ser** turn out to be; **~ com** give <argumento etc>

**virabrequim** /virabre'kĩ/ m crankshaft

**viração** /vira'sãw/ f breeze

**vira-casaca** /viraka'zaka/ m/f turncoat

**vira|da** /vi'rada/ f turn; **~do** a <roupa> inside out; (de cabeça para baixo) upside down; **~do para** facing

**vira-lata** /vira'lata/ m mongrel

**virar** /vi'rar/ vt turn; turn over <disco, barco etc>; turn inside out <roupa>; turn out <bolsos>; tip <balde, água etc> □ vi turn; <barco> turn over; (tornar-se) become; **~-se** vpr turn round; (na vida) get by, cope; **~-se para** turn to; **vira e mexe** every so often

**viravolta** /vira'vɔwta/ f about-turn

**virgem** /'virʒẽ/ a <fita> blank; <floresta, noiva etc> virgin □ f virgin; **Virgem** (signo) Virgo

**virgindade** /virʒĩ'dadʒi/ f virginity

**vírgula** /'virgula/ f comma; (decimal) point

**vi|ril** /vi'riw/ (pl **~ris**) a virile

**virilha** /vi'riʎa/ f groin

**virilidade** /virili'dadʒi/ f virility

**virtu|al** /virtu'aw/ (pl **~ais**) a virtual

**virtude** /vir'tudʒi/ f virtue

**virtuo|sismo** /virtuo'zizmu/ m virtuosity; **~so** /o/ a virtuous □ m virtuoso

**virulento** /viru'lẽtu/ a virulent

**vírus** /'virus/ m invar virus

**visão** /vi'zãw/ f vision; (aspecto, ponto de vista) view

**visar** /vi'zar/ vt aim at <caça, alvo>; **~ (a)** aim for <objetivo>; <medida, ação> be aimed at

**vísceras** /'viseras/ f pl innards

**viscon|de** /vis'kõdʒi/ m viscount; **~dessa** /e/ f viscountess

**viscoso** /vis'kozu/ a viscous

**viseira** /vi'zera/ f visor

**visibilidade** /vizibili'dadʒi/ f visibility

**visionário** /vizio'nariu/ a & m visionary

**visi|ta** /vi'zita/ f visit; (visitante) visitor; **fazer uma ~ta a alg** pay s.o. a visit; **~tante** a visiting □ m/f visitor; **~tar** vt visit

**visí|vel** /vi'zivew/ (pl **~veis**) a visible

**vislum|brar** /vizlũ'brar/ vt (entrever) glimpse; (imaginar) envisage; **~bre** m glimpse

**visom** /vi'zõ/ m mink

**visor** /vi'zor/ m viewfinder

**vis|ta** /'vista/ f sight; (dos olhos) eyesight; (panorama) view; **à ~ta** (visível) in view; (em dinheiro) in cash; **à primeira ~ta** at first sight; **pôr à ~ta** put on show; **de ~ta** <conhecer> by sight; **em ~ta de** in view of; **ter em ~ta** have in view; **dar na ~ta** attract attention; **fazer ~ta** look nice; **fazer ~ta grossa** turn a blind eye (a to); **perder de ~ta** lose sight of; **a perder de ~ta** as far as the eye can see; **uma ~ta de olhos** a quick look; **~to** a seen □ m visa; **pelo ~to** by the looks of things; **~to que** seeing that

**visto|ria** /visto'ria/ f inspection; **~riar** vt inspect

**vistoso** /vis'tozu/ a eye-catching

**visu|al** /vizu'aw/ (pl **~ais**) a visual □ m look; **~alizar** vt visualize

**vi|tal** /vi'taw/ (pl **~tais**) a vital; **~talício** a for life; **~talidade** f vitality

**vita|mina** /vita'mina/ f vitamin; (*bebida*) liquidized fruit drink; **~minado** a with added vitamins; **~mínico** a vitamin

**vitela** /vi'tɛla/ f (*carne*) veal

**viticultura** /vitʃikuw'tura/ f viticulture

**vítima** /'vitʃima/ f victim

**viti|mar** /vitʃi'mar/ vt (*matar*) claim the life of; **ser ~mado por** fall victim to

**vitória** /vi'tɔria/ f victory

**vitorioso** /vitori'ozu/ a victorious

**vi|tral** /vi'traw/ (*pl* **~trais**) m stained glass window

**vitrine** /vi'trini/ f shop window

**vitrola** /vi'trɔla/ f jukebox

**viú|va** /vi'uva/ f widow; **~vo** a widowed □ m widower

**viva** /'viva/ f cheer □ *int* hurray; **~ a rainha** long live the queen

**vivacidade** /vivasi'dadʒi/ f vivacity

**vivalma** /vi'vawma/ f **não há ~ lá fora** there's not a soul outside

**vivar** /vi'var/ vt/i cheer

**vivaz** /vi'vas/ a lively, vivacious; <*planta*> hardy

**viveiro** /vi'veru/ m (*de plantas*) nursery; (*de peixes*) fishpond; (*de aves*) aviary; (*fig*) breeding ground

**vivência** /vi'vēsia/ f experience

**vívido** /'vividu/ a vivid

**viver** /vi'ver/ vt/i live (**de on**) □ m life; **ele vive reclamando** he's always complaining

**víveres** /'viveris/ m pl provisions

**vivissecção** /vivisek'sãw/ f vivisection

**vivo** /'vivu/ a (*que vive*) living; (*animado*) lively; <*cor*> bright □ m os **~s** the living; **ao ~** live; **estar ~** be alive; **dinheiro ~** cash

**vizi|nhança** /vizi'ɲãsa/ f neighbourhood; **~nho** a neighbouring □ m neighbour

**vo|ador** /voa'dor/ a flying; **~ar** vi fly; (*explodir*) blow up; **sair ~ando** rush off

**vocabulário** /vokabu'lariu/ m vocabulary

**vocábulo** /vo'kabulu/ m word

**voca|ção** /voka'sãw/ f vocation; **~cional** (*pl* **~cionais**) a vocational; **orientação ~cional** careers guidance

**vo|cal** /vo'kaw/ (*pl* **~cais**) a vocal

**você** /vo'se/ *pron* you; **~s** *pron* you

**vociferar** /vosife'rar/ vi shout abuse

**vodca** /'vɔdʒka/ f vodka

**voga** /'vɔga/ f (*moda*) vogue

**vo|gal** /vo'gaw/ (*pl* **~gais**) f vowel

**volante** /vo'lãtʃi/ m (*de carro*) steering wheel

**volá|til** /vo'latʃiw/ (*pl* **~teis**) a volatile

**vôlei** /'volej/ m, **voleibol** /volej'bɔw/ m volleyball

**volt** /'vɔwtʃi/ (*pl* **~s**) m volt

**volta** /'vɔwta/ f (*retorno*) return; (*da pista*) lap; (*resposta*) response; **às ~s com** tied up with; **de ~** back; **em ~ de** around; **na ~** on the way back; **na ~ do correio** by return of post; **por ~ de** around; **dar a ~ ao mundo** go round the world; **dar a ~ por cima** make a comeback; **dar meia ~** turn round; **dar uma ~** (*a pé*) go for a walk; (*de carro*) go for a drive; **dar uma ~ em** turn round; **dar ~s** spin round; **ter ~** get a response; **~ e meia** every so often; **~do a ~do para** geared towards

**voltagem** /vow'taʒē/ f voltage

**voltar** /vow'tar/ vi go/come back, return □ vt rewind <*fita*>; **~-se** vpr turn round; **~-se para/contra** turn to/against; **~ a si** come to; **~ a fazer** do again; **~ atrás** backtrack

**volu|me** /vo'lumi/ m volume; **~moso** a sizeable; <*som*> loud

**voluntário** /volū'tariu/ a & m volunteer

**volúpia** /vo'lupia/ f sensuality, lust

**voluptuoso** /voluptu'ozu/ a sensual; <*mulher*> voluptuous

**volú|vel** /vo'luvew/ (*pl* **~veis**) a fickle

**vomitar** /vomi'tar/ vt/i vomit

**vômito** /'vomitu/ m vomit; *pl* vomiting

**vontade** /võ'tadʒi/ f will; **à ~** (*bem*) at ease; (*quanto quiser*) as much as one likes; **fique à ~** make yourself at home; **tem comida à ~** there's plenty of food; **estar com ~ de** feel like; **isso me dá ~ de chorar** it makes me feel like crying; **fazer a ~ de alg** do what s.o. wants

**vôo** /'vou/ m flight; **levantar ~** take off; **~ livre** hang-gliding

**voraz** /vo'ras/ a voracious

**vos** /vus/ *pron* you; (*a vocês*) to you

**vós** /vɔs/ *pron* you

**vosso** /'vɔsu/ a your □ *pron* yours

**vo|tação** /vota'sãw/ f vote; **~tante** m/f voter; **~tar** vt vote on <*lei etc*>; (*dedicar*) devote; (*prometer*) vow □ vi vote (**em for**)

**voto** /'vɔtu/ m (*em votação*) vote; (*promessa*) vow; *pl* (*desejos*) wishes

**vo|vó** /vo'vɔ/ f grandma; **~vô** m grandpa

**voz** /vɔs/ f voice; **dar ~ de prisão a alg** place s.o. under arrest

**vozeirão** /voze'rãw/ m loud voice

**vozerio** /voze'riu/ m shouting

**vul|cânico** /vuw'kaniku/ a volcanic; **~cão** m volcano

**vul|gar** /vuw'gar/ a ordinary; (*baixo*) vulgar; **~garizar** vt popularize; (*tornar baixo*) vulgarize; **~go** adv commonly known as

**vulne|rabilidade** /vuwnerabili-'dadʒi/ f vulnerability; **~rável** (*pl* **~ráveis**) a vulnerable

**vul|to** /'vuwtu/ m (*figura*) figure; (*tamanho*) bulk; (*importância*) importance; **de ~to** important; **~toso** /o/ a bulky; (*importante*) important

# W

**walkie-talkie** /uɔki'tɔki/ (*pl* **~s**) m walkie-talkie

**walkman** /uɔk'mɛn/ m invar walkman

**watt** /u'ɔtʃi/ (*pl* **~s**) m watt

**windsur|fe** /uʃ'surfi/ m windsurfing; **~fista** m/f windsurfer

# X

**xadrez** /ʃa'dres/ m (*jogo*) chess; (*desenho*) check; (*fam: prisão*) prison □ a invar check

**xale** /'ʃali/ m shawl

**xampu** /ʃã'pu/ m shampoo

**xará** /ʃa'ra/ m/f namesake

**xarope** /ʃa'rɔpi/ m syrup

**xaxim** /ʃa'ʃĩ/ m plant fibre

**xenofobia** /ʃenofo'bia/ f xenophobia

**xenófobo** /ʃe'nɔfobu/ a xenophobic □ m xenophobe

**xepa** /'ʃepa/ f scraps

**xeque¹** /'ʃɛki/ m (*árabe*) sheikh

**xeque²** /'ʃɛki/ m (*no xadrez*) check; **~-mate** m checkmate

**xere|ta** /ʃe'reta/ (*fam*) a nosy □ m/f nosy parker; **~tar** (*fam*) vi nose around

**xerez** /ʃe'res/ m sherry

**xerife** /ʃe'rifi/ m sheriff

**xerocar** /ʃero'kar/ vt photocopy

**xerox** /ʃe'rɔks/ m invar photocopy

**xexelento** /ʃeʃe'lẽtu/ (*fam*) a scruffy □ m scruff

**xícara** /'ʃikara/ f cup

**xiita** /ʃi'ita/ a & m/f Shiite

**xilofone** /ʃilo'foni/ m xylophone

**xingar** /ʃĩ'gar/ vt swear at □ vi swear

**xis** /ʃis/ m invar letter X; **o ~ do problema** the crux of the problem

**xixi** /ʃi'ʃi/ (*fam*) m wee; **fazer ~** do a wee

**xô** /ʃo/ int shoo

**xucro** /'ʃukru/ a ignorant

# Z

**zagueiro** /za'geru/ m fullback

**Zaire** /'zajri/ m Zaire

**Zâmbia** /'zãbia/ f Zambia

**zan|gado** /zã'gadu/ a cross, annoyed; **~gar** vt annoy; **~garse** vpr get cross, get annoyed (**com** with)

**zanzar** /zã'zar/ vi wander

**zarpar** /zar'par/ vi set off; (*de navio*) set sail

**zebra** /'zebra/ f zebra; (*pessoa*) fool; (*resultado*) upset

**ze|lador** /zela'dor/ m caretaker, (*Amer*) janitor; **~lar** vt **~lar (por)** take care of; **~lo** /e/ m zeal; **~lo por** devotion to; **~loso** /o/ a zealous

**zero** /'zeru/ m zero; (*em escores*) nil; **~-quilômetro** a invar brand new

**ziguezague** /zigi'zagi/ m zigzag; **~ar** vi zigzag

**Zimbábue** /zĩ'babui/ m Zimbabwe

**zinco** /'zĩku/ m zinc

**zíper** /'ziper/ m zip, zipper

**zodíaco** /zo'dʒiaku/ m zodiac

**zoeira** /zo'era/ f din

**zom|bador** /zõba'dor/ a mocking; **~bar** vi **~bar (de)** mock; **~baria** f mockery

**zona** /'zona/ f (*área*) zone; (*de cidade*) district; (*desordem*) mess; (*tumulto*) commotion; (*bairro do meretrício*) red-light district

**zonzo** /'zõzo/ a dizzy

**zôo** /'zou/ m zoo

**zoo|logia** /zoolo'ʒia/ f zoology; **~lógico** a zoological

**zoólogo** /zo'ɔlogu/ m zoologist

**zulu** /zu'lu/ a & m/f Zulu

**zum** /zũ/ m zoom lens

**zumbi** /zũ'bi/ m zombie

**zum|bido** /zũ'bidu/ m buzz; (*no ouvido*) ringing; **~bir** vi buzz

**zu|nido** /zu'nidu/ m (*de vento, bala*) whistle; (*de inseto*) buzz; **~nir** vi <*vento, bala*> whistle; <*inseto*> buzz

**zunzum** /zũ'zũ/ m rumour

**Zurique** /zu'riki/ f Zurich

**zurrar** /zu'xar/ vi bray

# ENGLISH-PORTUGUESE

# INGLÊS-PORTUGUÊS

## A

**a** /ə/; *emphatic* /eɪ/ (*before vowel* **an** /ən/; *emphatic* /æn/) *a* um. **two pounds a metre** duas libras o metro. **sixty miles an hour** sessenta milhas por hora, (P) à hora. **once a year** uma vez por ano

**aback** /ə'bæk/ *adv* **taken ∼** descocertado, (P) surpreendido

**abandon** /ə'bændən/ *vt* abandonar □ *n* abandono *m*. **∼ed** *a* abandonado; (*behaviour*) livre, dissoluto. **∼ment** *n* abandono *m*

**abashed** /ə'bæʃt/ *a* confuso, (P) atrapalhado

**abate** /ə'beɪt/ *vt/i* abater, abrandar, diminuir. **∼ment** *n* abrandamento *m*, diminuição *f*

**abattoir** /'æbətwa:(r)/ *n* matadouro *m*

**abbey** /'æbɪ/ *n* abadia *f*, mosteiro *m*

**abbreviat|e** /ə'bri:vɪeɪt/ *vt* abreviar. **∼ion** /-'eɪʃn/ *n* abreviação *f*; (*short form*) abreviatura *f*

**abdicat|e** /'æbdɪkeɪt/ *vt/i* abdicar. **∼ion** /-'keɪʃn/ *n* abdicação *f*

**abdom|en** /'æbdəmən/ *n* abdômen *m*, (P) abdómen *m*. **∼inal** /-'dɒmɪnl/ *a* abdominal

**abduct** /æb'dʌkt/ *vt* raptar. **∼ion** /-ʃn/ *n* rapto *m*. **∼or** *n* raptor, -a *mf*

**aberration** /æbə'reɪʃn/ *n* aberração *f*

**abet** /ə'bet/ *vt* (*pt* **abetted**) (*jur*) instigar; (*aid*) auxiliar

**abeyance** /ə'beɪəns/ *n* **in ∼** (*matter*) em suspenso; (*custom*) em desuso

**abhor** /əb'hɔ:(r)/ *vt* (*pt* **abhorred**) abominar, ter horror a. **∼rence** /-'hɒrəns/ *n* horror *m*. **∼rent** /-'hɒrənt/ *a* abominável, execrável

**abide** /ə'baɪd/ *vt* (*pt* **abided**) suportar, tolerar. **∼ by** (*promise*) manter; (*rules*) acatar

**abiding** /ə'baɪdɪŋ/ *a* eterno, perpétuo

**ability** /ə'bɪlətɪ/ *n* capacidade *f* (**to do** para *or* de fazer); (*cleverness*) habilidade *f*, esperteza *f*

**abject** /'æbdʒekt/ *a* abjeto, (P) abjecto

**ablaze** /ə'bleɪz/ *a* em chamas; (*fig*) aceso, (P) excitado

**abl|e** /'eɪbl/ *a* (**∼er**, **∼est**) capaz (**to** de). **be ∼e to** (*have power, opportunity*) ser capaz de, poder; (*know how*

*to*) ser capaz de, saber. **∼y** *adv* habilmente

**ablutions** /ə'blu:ʃnz/ *npl* ablução *f*, abluções *fpl*

**abnormal** /æb'nɔ:ml/ *a* anormal. **∼ity** /-'mælətɪ/ *n* anormalidade *f*. **∼ly** *adv* (*unusually*) excepcionalmente

**aboard** /ə'bɔ:d/ *adv* a bordo □ *prep* a bordo de

**abode** /ə'bəʊd/ *n* (*old use*) habitação *f*. **place of ∼** domicílio *m*

**aboli|sh** /ə'bɒlɪʃ/ *vt* abolir, extinguir. **∼tion** /æbə'lɪʃn/ *n* abolição *f*, extinção *f*

**abominable** /ə'bɒmməbl/ *a* abominável, detestável

**abominat|e** /ə'bɒmmeɪt/ *vt* abominar, detestar. **∼ion** /-'neɪʃn/ *n* abominação *f*

**abort** /ə'bɔ:t/ *vt/i* (fazer) abortar. **∼ive** *a* (*attempt etc*) abortado, malogrado

**abortion** /ə'bɔ:ʃn/ *n* aborto *m*. **have an ∼** fazer um aborto, ter um aborto. **∼ist** *n* abortad/or, -eira *mf*

**abound** /ə'baʊnd/ *vi* abundar (**in** em)

**about** /ə'baʊt/ *adv* (*approximately*) aproximadamente, cerca de; (*here and there*) aqui e ali; (*all round*) por todos os lados, em roda, em volta; (*in existence*) por aí □ *prep* acerca de, sobre; (*round*) em torno de; (*somewhere in*) em, por. **∼-face**, **∼-turn** *ns* reviravolta *f*. **∼ here** por aqui. **be ∼ to** estar prestes a. **he was ∼ to eat** ia comer. **how** *or* **what ∼ leaving?** e se nós fôssemos embora? **know/talk ∼** saber/falar sobre

**above** /ə'bʌv/ *adv* acima, por cima □ *prep* sobre. **he's not ∼ lying** ele não éde mentir. **∼ all** sobretudo. **∼-board** *a* franco, honesto □ *adv* com lisura. **∼-mentioned** *a* acima, supracitado

**abrasion** /ə'breɪʒn/ *n* atrito *m*; (*injury*) escoriação *f*, esfoladura *f*

**abrasive** /ə'breɪsɪv/ *a* abrasivo; (*fig*) agressivo □ *n* abrasivo *m*

**abreast** /ə'brest/ *adv* lado a lado. **keep ∼ of** manter-se a par de

**abridge** /ə'brɪdʒ/ *vt* abreviar. **∼ment**

*n* abreviação *f*, abreviatura *f*, redução *f*; (*abridged text*) resumo *m*

**abroad** /ə'brɔːd/ *adv* no estrangeiro; (*far and wide*) por todo o lado. **go ~** ir para o estrangeiro

**abrupt** /ə'brʌpt/ *a* (*sudden, curt*) brusco; (*steep*) abrupto. **~ly** *adv* (*suddenly*) bruscamente; (*curtly*) com brusquidão. **~ness** *n* brusquidão *f*; (*steepness*) declive *m*

**abscess** /'æbsɪs/ *n* abscesso *m*, (*P*) abcesso *m*

**abscond** /əb'skɒnd/ *vi* evadir-se, andar fugido

**absen|t**[1] /'æbsənt/ *a* ausente; (*look etc*) distraído. **~ce** *n* ausência *f*; (*lack*) falta *f*. **~t-minded** *a* distraído. **~t-mindedness** *n* distração *f*, (*P*) distracção *f*

**absent**[2] /əb'sent/ *v refl* **~ o.s.** ausentar-se

**absentee** /æbsen'tiː/ *n* ausente *mf*, (*P*) absentista *mf*. **~ism** *n* absenteísmo *m*, (*P*) absentismo *m*

**absolute** /'æbsəluːt/ *a* absoluto; (*colloq: coward etc*) autêntico, (*P*) verdadeiro. **~ly** *adv* absolutamente

**absolution** /æbsə'luːʃn/ *n* absolvição *f*

**absolve** /əb'zɒlv/ *vt* (*from sin*) absolver (**from** de); (*from vow*) desligar (**from** de)

**absor|b** /əb'sɔːb/ *vt* absorver. **~ption** *n* absorção *f*

**absorbent** /əb'sɔːbənt/ *a* absorvente. **~ cotton** (*Amer*) algodão hidrófilo *m*

**abst|ain** /əb'steɪn/ *vi* abster-se (**from** de). **~ention** /-'stenʃn/ *n* abstenção *f*

**abstemious** /əb'stiːmɪəs/ *a* abstêmio, (*P*) abstémio, sóbrio

**abstinen|ce** /'æbstɪnəns/ *n* abstinência *f*. **~t** *a* abstinente

**abstract**[1] /'æbstrækt/ *a* abstrato, (*P*) abstracto

**abstract**[2] /əb'strækt/ *vt* (*take out*) extrair; (*separate*) abstrair. **~ed** *a* distraído. **~ion** /-ʃn/ *n* (*of mind*) distração *f*, (*P*) distracção *f*; (*idea*) abstração *f*, (*P*) abstracção *f*

**absurd** /əb'sɜːd/ *a* absurdo. **~ity** *n* absurdo *m*

**abundan|t** /ə'bʌndənt/ *a* abundante. **~ce** *n* abundância *f*

**abuse**[1] /ə'bjuːz/ *vt* (*misuse*) abusar de; (*ill-treat*) maltratar; (*insult*) injuriar, insultar

**abus|e**[2] /ə'bjuːs/ *n* (*wrong use*) abuso *m* (**of** de); (*insults*) insultos *m pl*. **~ive** *a* injurioso, ofensivo

**abysmal** /ə'bɪzməl/ *a* abismal; (*colloq: bad*) abissal

**abyss** /ə'bɪs/ *n* abismo *m*

**academic** /ækə'demɪk/ *a* acadêmico, (*P*) académico, universitário; (*schol-*)

*arly*) intelectual; (*pej*) acadêmico, (*P*) teórico □ *n* universitário

**academy** /ə'kædəmɪ/ *n* academia *f*

**accede** /ək'siːd/ *vi* **~ to** (*request*) aceder a; (*post*) assumir; (*throne*) ascender a, subir a

**accelerat|e** /ək'seləreɪt/ *vt* acelerar □ *vi* acelerar-se; (*auto*) acelerar. **~ion** /-'reɪʃn/ *n* aceleração *f*

**accelerator** /ək'seləreɪtə(r)/ *n* (*auto*) acelerador *m*

**accent**[1] /'æksənt/ *n* acento *m*; (*local pronunciation*) sotaque *m*

**accent**[2] /æk'sent/ *vt* acentuar

**accentuate** /æk'sentʃʊeɪt/ *vt* acentuar

**accept** /ək'sept/ *vt* aceitar. **~able** *a* aceitável. **~ance** *n* aceitação *f*; (*approval*) aprovação *f*

**access** /'ækses/ *n* acesso *m* (**to** a). **~ible** /ək'sesəbl/ *a* acessível

**accessory** /ək'sesərɪ/ *a* acessório □ *n* acessório *m*; (*jur: person*) cúmplice *m*

**accident** /'æksɪdənt/ *n* acidente *m*, desastre *m*; (*chance*) acaso *m*. **~al** /-'dentl/ *a* acidental, fortuito. **~ally** /-'dentəlɪ/ *adv* acidentalmente, por acaso

**acclaim** /ə'kleɪm/ *vt* aclamar □ *n* aplauso *m*, aclamações *fpl*

**acclimatiz|e** /ə'klaɪmətaɪz/ *vt/i* aclimatar(-se). **~ation** /-'zeɪʃn/ *n* aclimatação *f*

**accommodat|e** /ə'kɒmədeɪt/ *vt* acomodar; (*lodge*) alojar; (*adapt*) adaptar; (*supply*) fornecer; (*oblige*) fazer a vontade de. **~ing** *a* obsequioso, amigo de fazer vontades. **~ion** /-'deɪʃn/ *n* acomodação *f*; (*rooms*) alojamento *m*, quarto *m*

**accompan|y** /ə'kʌmpənɪ/ *vt* acompanhar. **~iment** *n* acompanhamento *m*. **~ist** *n* (*mus*) acompanhador/or, (*B*) -eira *mf*

**accomplice** /ə'kʌmplɪs/ *n* cúmplice *mf*

**accomplish** /ə'kʌmplɪʃ/ *vt* (*perform*) executar, realizar; (*achieve*) realizar, conseguir fazer. **~ed** *a* acabado. **~ment** *n* realização *f*; (*ability*) talento *m*, dote *m*

**accord** /ə'kɔːd/ *vi* concordar □ *vt* conceder □ *n* acordo *m*. **of one's own ~** por vontade própria, espontaneamente. **~ance** *n* **in ~ance with** em conformidade com, de acordo com

**according** /ə'kɔːdɪŋ/ *adv* **~ to** conforme. **~ly** *adv* (*therefore*) por conseguinte, por consequência; (*appropriately*) conformemente

**accordion** /ə'kɔːdɪən/ *n* acordeão *m*

**accost** /ə'kɒst/ *vt* abordar, abeirar-se de

**account** /ə'kaʊnt/ *n* (*comm*) conta *f*; (*description*) relato *m*; (*importance*) importância *f* □ *vt* considerar. **~ for** dar contas de, explicar. **on ~ of** por causa de. **on no ~** em caso algum. **take into ~** ter *or* levar em conta.

**~able** /-əbl/ *a* responsável (**for** por). **~ability** /-ə'bɪlətɪ/ *n* responsabilidade *f*

**accountant** /ə'kauntənt/ *n* contador(a) *m/f*, (*P*) contabilista *m*

**accrue** /ə'kru:/ *vi* acumular-se. **~ to** reverter em favor de

**accumulat|e** /ə'kju:mjʊleɪt/ *vt/i* acumular(-se). **~ion** /-'leɪʃn/ *n* acumulação *f*, acréscimo *m*

**accumulator** /ə'kju:mjʊleɪtə(r)/ *n* (*electr*) acumulador *m*

**accura|te** /'ækjərət/ *a* exato, (*P*) exacto, preciso. **~cy** *n* exatidão *f*, (*P*) exactidão *f*, precisão *f*. **~tely** *adv* com exatidão, (*P*) exactidão

**accus|e** /ə'kju:z/ *vt* acusar. **the ~ed** o acusado. **~ation** /ækju:'zeɪʃn/ *n* acusação *f*

**accustom** /ə'kʌstəm/ *vt* acostumar, habituar. **~ed** *a* acostumado, habituado. **get ~ed to** acostumar-se a, habituar-se a

**ace** /eɪs/ *n* ás *m*

**ache** /eɪk/ *n* dor *f* □ *vi* doer. **my leg ~s** dói-me a perna, tenho dores na perna

**achieve** /ə'tʃi:v/ *vt* realizar, efetuar; (*success*) alcançar. **~ment** *n* realização *f*; (*feat*) feito *m*, façanha *f*, sucesso *m*

**acid** /'æsɪd/ *a* ácido; (*wine*) azedo; (*words*) áspero □ *n* ácido *m*. **~ity** /ə'sɪdətɪ/ *n* acidez *f*

**acknowledge** /ək'nɒlɪdʒ/ *vt* reconhecer. **~ (receipt of)** acusar a recepção de. **~ment** *n* reconhecimento *m*; (*letter etc*) acusação *f* de recebimento, (*P*) aviso *m* de recepção

**acne** /'æknɪ/ *n* acne *mf*

**acorn** /'eɪkɔ:n/ *n* bolota *f*, glande *f*

**acoustic** /ə'ku:stɪk/ *a* acústico. **~s** *npl* acústica *f*

**acquaint** /ə'kweɪnt/ *vt* **~ s.o. with sth** pôr alg a par de alg coisa. **be ~ed with** (*person, fact*) conhecer. **~ance** *n* (*knowledge, person*) conhecimento *m*; (*person*) conhecido *m*

**acquiesce** /ækwɪ'es/ *vi* consentir. **~nce** /ækwɪ'esns/ *n* aquiescência *f*, consentimento *m*

**acqui|re** /ə'kwaɪə(r)/ *vt* adquirir. **~sition** /ækwɪ'zɪʃn/ *n* aquisição *f*

**acquit** /ə'kwɪt/ *vt* (*pt* **acquitted**) absolver. **~ o.s. well** sair-se bem. **~tal** *n* absolvição *f*

**acrid** /'ækrɪd/ *a* acre

**acrimon|ious** /ækrɪ'məʊnɪəs/ *a* acrimonioso. **~y** /'ækrɪmənɪ/ *n* acrimónia *f*, (*P*) acrimónia *f*

**acrobat** /'ækrəbæt/ *n* acrobata *mf*.

**~ic** /-'bætɪk/ *a* acrobático. **~ics** /-'bætɪks/ *npl* acrobacia *f*

**acronym** /'ækrənɪm/ *n* sigla *f*

**across** /ə'krɒs/ *adv & prep* (*side to side*) de lado a lado (de), de um lado para o outro (de); (*on the other side*) do outro lado (de); (*crosswise*) através (de), de través. **go** *or* **walk ~** atravessar. **swim ~** atravessar a nado

**act** /ækt/ *n* (*deed, theatr*) ato *m*, (*P*) acto *m*; (*in variety show*) número *m*; (*decree*) lei *f* □ *vi* agir, atuar, (*P*) actuar; (*theatr*) representar; (*function*) funcionar; (*pretend*) fingir □ *vt* (*part, role*) desempenhar. **~ as** servir de. **~ing** *a* interino □ *n* (*theatr*) desempenho *m*

**action** /'ækʃn/ *n* ação *f*, (*P*) acção *f*; (*mil*) combate *m*. **out of ~** fora de combate; (*techn*) avariado. **take ~** agir, atuar, (*P*) actuar

**activ|e** /'æktɪv/ *a* ativo, (*P*) activo; (*interest*) vivo; (*volcano*) em atividade, (*P*) actividade. **~ity** /-'tɪvətɪ/ *n* atividade *f*, (*P*) actividade *f*

**ac|tor** /'æktə(r)/ *n* ator *m*, (*P*) actor *m*. **~tress** *n* atriz *f*, (*P*) actriz *f*

**actual** /'æktʃʊəl/ *a* real, verdadeiro; (*example*) concreto. **the ~ pen which** a própria caneta que. **~ity** /-'æləti/ *n* realidade *f*. **~ly** *adv* (*in fact*) na realidade

**acumen** /ə'kju:men/ *n* agudeza *f*, perspicácia *f*

**acupunctur|e** /'ækjʊpʌŋktʃə(r)/ *n* acupuntura *f*, (*P*) acupunctura *f*. **~ist** *n* acupunturador *m*, (*P*) acupuncturista *mf*

**acute** /ə'kju:t/ *a* agudo; (*mind*) perspicaz; (*emotion*) intenso, vivo; (*shortage*) grande. **~ly** *adv* vivamente.

**ad** /æd/ *n* (*colloq*) anúncio *m*

**AD** *abbr* dC

**adamant** /'ædəmənt/ *a* inflexível

**adapt** /ə'dæpt/ *vt/i* adaptar(-se). **~ation** /ædæp'teɪʃn/ *n* adaptação *f*. **~or** (*electr*) *n* adaptador *m*

**adaptab|le** /ə'dæptəbl/ *a* adaptável. **~ility** /-'bɪlətɪ/ *n* adaptabilidade *f*

**add** /æd/ *vt/i* acrescentar. **~ (up)** somar. **~ up to** (*total*) elevar-se a

**adder** /'ædə(r)/ *n* víbora *f*

**addict** /'ædɪkt/ *n* viciado *m*. **drug ~** (*B*) viciado em droga, viciado da droga, (*P*) toxicodependente *mf*

**addict|ed** /ə'dɪktɪd/ *a* **be ~ed to** (*drink, drugs; fig*) ter o vício de. **~ion** /-ʃn/ *n* (*med*) dependência *f*; (*fig*) vício *m*. **~ive** *a* que produz dependência

**addition** /ə'dɪʃn/ *n* adição *f*. **in ~** além disso. **in ~ to** além de. **~al** /-ʃənl/ *a* adicional, suplementar

**address** /əˈdres/ *n* endereço *m*; (*speech*) discurso *m* □ *vt* endereçar; (*speak to*) dirigir-se a

**adenoids** /ˈædmɔɪdz/ *npl* adenóides *mpl*

**adept** /ˈædept/ *a* & *n* especialista (*mf*), perito (*m*) (at em)

**adequa|te** /ˈædɪkwət/ *a* adequado; (*satisfactory*) satisfatório. ~**cy** *n* adequação *f*; (*of person*) competência *f*. ~**tely** *adv* adequadamente

**adhere** /ədˈhɪə(r)/ *vi* aderir (to a)

**adhesive** /ədˈhiːsɪv/ *a* & *n* adesivo (*m*). ~ **plaster** esparadrapo *m*, (P) adesivo *m*

**adjacent** /əˈdʒeɪsnt/ *a* adjacente, contíguo (to a)

**adjective** /ˈædʒektɪv/ *n* adjetivo *m*, (P) adjectivo *m*

**adjoin** /əˈdʒɔɪn/ *vt* confinar com, ficar contíguo a

**adjourn** /əˈdʒɜːn/ *vt* adiar □ *vi* suspender a sessão. ~ **to** (*go*) passar a, ir para

**adjudicate** /əˈdʒuːdɪkeɪt/ *vt/i* julgar; (*award*) adjudicar

**adjust** /əˈdʒʌst/ *vt/i* (*alter*) ajustar, regular; (*arrange*) arranjar. ~ (**o.s.**) **to** adaptar-se a. ~**able** *a* regulável. ~**ment** *n* (*techn*) regulação *f*, afinação *f*; (*of person*) adaptação *f*

**ad lib** /ædˈlɪb/ *vi* (*pt* ad libbed) (*colloq*) improvisar □ *adv* à vontade

**administer** /ədˈmɪnɪstə(r)/ *vt* administrar

**administrat|e** /ədˈmɪnɪstreɪt/ *vt* administrar, gerir. ~**ion** /-ˈstreɪʃn/ *n* administração *f*. ~**or** *n* administrador *m*

**administrative** /ədˈmɪnɪstrətɪv/ *a* administrativo

**admirable** /ˈædmərəbl/ *a* admirável

**admiral** /ˈædmərəl/ *n* almirante *m*

**admir|e** /ədˈmaɪə(r)/ *vt* admirar. ~**ation** /-ˈmɪˈreɪʃn/ *n* admiração *f*. ~**er** /-ˈmaɪərə(r)/ *n* admirador *m*

**admission** /ədˈmɪʃn/ *n* admissão *f*; (*to museum, theatre, etc*) ingresso *m*, (P) entrada *f*; (*confession*) confissão *f*

**admit** /ədˈmɪt/ *vt* (*pt* admitted) (*let in*) admitir, permitir a entrada a; (*acknowledge*) reconhecer, admitir. ~ **to** confessar. ~**tance** *n* admissão *f*

**admoni|sh** /ədˈmɒnɪʃ/ *vt* admoestar. ~**tion** /-əˈnɪʃn/ *n* admoestação *f*

**adolescen|t** /ædəˈlesnt/ *a* & *n* adolescente (*mf*). ~**ce** *n* adolescência *f*

**adopt** /əˈdɒpt/ *vt* adotar, (P) adoptar. ~**ed child** filho adotado, (P) adoptivo. ~**ion** /-ʃn/ *n* adoção *f*, (P) adopção *f*

**ador|e** /əˈdɔː(r)/ *vt* adorar. ~**able** *a* adorável. ~**ation** /ædəˈreɪʃn/ *n* adoração *f*

**adorn** /əˈdɔːn/ *vt* adornar, enfeitar

**adrenalin** /əˈdrenəlɪn/ *n* adrenalina *f*

**adrift** /əˈdrɪft/ *a* & *adv* à deriva

**adult** /ˈædʌlt/ *a* & *n* adulto (*m*). ~**hood** *n* idade *f* adulta, (P) maioridade *f*

**adulterat|e** /əˈdʌltəreɪt/ *vt* adulterar. ~**ion** /-reɪʃn/ *n* adulteração *f*

**adulter|y** /əˈdʌltərɪ/ *n* adultério *m*. ~**er**, ~**ess** *ns* adúlter/o, -a *mf*. ~**ous** *a* adúltero

**advance** /ədˈvɑːns/ *vt/i* avançar □ *n* avanço *m*; (*payment*) adiantamento *m* □ *a* (*payment, booking*) adiantado. **in** ~ com antecedência. ~**d** *a* avançado. ~**ment** *n* promoção *f*, ascensão *f*

**advantage** /ədˈvɑːntɪdʒ/ *n* vantagem *f*. **take** ~ **of** aproveitar-se de, tirar partido de; (*person*) explorar. ~**ous** /ædvənˈteɪdʒəs/ *a* vantajoso

**adventur|e** /ədˈventʃə(r)/ *n* aventura *f*. ~**er** *n* aventureiro *m*, explorador *m*. ~**ous** *a* aventuroso

**adverb** /ˈædvɜːb/ *n* advérbio *m*

**adversary** /ˈædvəsərɪ/ *n* adversário *m*, antagonista *mf*

**advers|e** /ˈædvɜːs/ *a* (*contrary*) adverso; (*unfavourable*) desfavorável. ~**ity** /ədˈvɜːsətɪ/ *n* adversidade *f*

**advert** /ˈædvɜːt/ *n* (*colloq*) anúncio *m*

**advertise** /ˈædvətaɪz/ *vt/i* anunciar, fazer publicidade (de); (*sell*) pôr um anúncio (para). ~ **for** procurar; ~**r** /-ə(r)/ *n* anunciante *mf*

**advertisement** /ədˈvɜːtɪsmənt/ *n* anúncio *m*; (*advertising*) publicidade *f*

**advice** /ədˈvaɪs/ *n* conselho(s) *mpl*; (*comm*) aviso *m*

**advis|e** /ədˈvaɪz/ *vt* aconselhar; (*inform*) avisar, informar. ~**e against** desaconselhar. ~**able** *a* aconselhável. ~**er** *n* conselheiro *m*; (*in business*) consultor *m*. ~**ory** *a* consultivo

**advocate**[1] /ˈædvəkət/ *n* (*jur*) advogado *m*; (*supporter*) defensor(a) *m/f*

**advocate**[2] /ˈædvəkeɪt/ *vt* advogar, defender

**aerial** /ˈeərɪəl/ *a* aéreo □ *n* antena *f*

**aerobatics** /eərəˈbætɪks/ *npl* acrobacia *f* aérea

**aerobics** /eəˈrəʊbɪks/ *n* ginástica *f* aeróbica

**aerodynamic** /eərəʊdaɪˈnæmɪk/ *a* aerodinâmico

**aeroplane** /ˈeərəpleɪn/ *n* avião *m*

**aerosol** /ˈeərəsɒl/ *n* aerossol *m*

**aesthetic** /iːsˈθetɪk/ *a* estético.

**affair** /əˈfeə(r)/ *n* (*business*) negócio *m*; (*romance*) ligação *f*, aventura *f*; (*matter*) assunto *m*. **love** ~ paixão *f*

**affect** /əˈfekt/ *vt* afetar, (P) afectar. ~**ation** /æfekˈteɪʃn/ *n* afetação *f*, (P) afecetação f. ~ed a afetado, (P) afectado, pretencioso

**affection** /ə'fekʃn/ n afeição f, afeto m, (P) afecto m

**affectionate** /ə'fekʃənət/ a afetuoso, (P) afectuoso, carinhoso

**affiliat|e** /ə'fɪlɪeɪt/ vt afiliar. ~ed company filial f. ~ion /-'eɪʃn/ n afiliação f

**affirm** /ə'fɜ:m/ vt afirmar. ~ation /æfə'meɪʃn/ n afirmação f

**affirmative** /ə'fɜ:mətɪv/ a afirmativo □ n afirmativa f

**afflict** /ə'flɪkt/ vt afligir. ~ion /-ʃn/ n aflição f

**affluen|t** /'æfluənt/ a rico, afluente. ~ce n riqueza f, afluência f

**afford** /ə'fɔ:d/ vt (have money for) permitir-se, ter meios (para). can you afford the time? você teria tempo? I can't afford a car eu não posso comprar um carro. we can't afford to lose não podemos perder

**affront** /ə'frʌnt/ n afronta f □ vt insultar

**afield** /ə'fi:ld/ adv far ~ longe

**afloat** /ə'fləʊt/ adv & a à tona, a flutuar; (at sea) no mar; (business) lançado, (P) sem dívidas

**afraid** /ə'freɪd/ a be ~ ter medo (of, to do; that que); (be sorry) lamentar, ter muita pena. I'm ~ (that) (regret to say) lamento or tenho muita pena de dizer que

**afresh** /ə'freʃ/ adv de novo

**Africa** /'æfrɪkə/ n áfrica f. ~n a & n africano (m)

**after** /'a:ftə(r)/ adv depois □ prep depois de □ conj depois que. ~ all afinal de contas. ~ doing, depois de fazer. be ~ (seek) querer, pretender. ~-effect n sequela f, (P) sequela f, efeito m retardado; (of drug) efeito m secundário

**aftermath** /'a:ftəmæθ/ n consequências fpl

**afternoon** /a:ftə'nu:n/ n tarde f

**aftershave** /'a:ftəʃeɪv/ n loção f após-barba, (P) loção f para a barba

**afterthought** /'a:ftəθɔ:t/ n reflexão f posterior. as an ~ pensando melhor

**afterwards** /'a:ftəwədz/ adv depois, mais tarde

**again** /ə'gen/ adv de novo, outra vez; (on the other hand) por outro lado. then ~ além disso

**against** /ə'genst/ prep contra

**age** /eɪdʒ/ n idade f; (period) época f, idade f □ vt/i (pres p ageing) envelhecer. ~s (colloq: very long time) há séculos mpl. of ~ (jur) maior. ten years of ~ com/de dez anos. under ~ menor. ~-group n faixa etária f. ~less a sempre jovem

**aged**[1] /eɪdʒd/ a ~ six de seis anos de idade

**aged**[2] /'eɪdʒɪd/ a idoso, velho

**agen|cy** /'eɪdʒənsɪ/ n agência f; (means) intermédio m. ~t n agente mf

**agenda** /ə'dʒendə/ n ordem f do dia

**aggravat|e** /'ægrəveɪt/ vt agravar; (colloq: annoy) irritar. ~ion /-'veɪʃn/ n (worsening) agravamento m; (exasperation) irritação f; (colloq: trouble) aborrecimentos mpl

**aggregate** /'ægrɪgeɪt/ vt/i agregar (-se) □ a /'ægrɪgət/ total, global □ n (total, mass, materials) agregado m. in the ~ no todo

**aggress|ive** /ə'gresɪv/ a agressivo; (weapons) ofensivo. ~ion /-ʃn/ n agressão f. ~iveness n agressividade f. ~or n agressor m

**aggrieved** /ə'gri:vd/ a (having a grievance) lesado

**agil|e** /'ædʒaɪl/ a ágil. ~ity /ə'dʒɪlətɪ/ n agilidade f

**agitat|e** /'ædʒɪteɪt/ vt agitar. ~ion /-'teɪʃn/ n agitação f. ~or n agitador m

**agnostic** /æg'nɒstɪk/ a & n agnóstico (m)

**ago** /ə'gəʊ/ adv há. a month ~ há um mês. long ~ há muito tempo

**agon|y** /'ægənɪ/ n agonia f; (mental) angústia f. ~ize vi atormentar-se, torturar-se. ~izing a angustiante, (P) doloroso

**agree** /ə'gri:/ vt/i concordar; (of figures) acertar. ~ that reconhecer que. ~ to do concordar em or aceitar fazer. ~ to sth concordar com alguma coisa. seafood doesn't ~ with me não me dou bem com mariscos. ~d a (time, place) combinado. be ~d estar de acordo

**agreeable** /ə'gri:əbl/ a agradável. be ~ to estar de acordo com

**agreement** /ə'gri:mənt/ n acordo m; (gramm) concordância f; (contract) contrato m. in ~ de acordo

**agricultur|e** /'ægrɪkʌltʃə(r)/ n agricultura f. ~al /-'kʌltʃərəl/ a agrícola

**aground** /ə'graʊnd/ adv run ~ (of ship) encalhar

**ahead** /ə'hed/ adv à frente, adiante; (in advance) adiantado. ~ of sb diante de alguém, à frente de alguém. ~ of time antes da hora, adiantado. straight ~ sempre em frente

**aid** /eɪd/ vt ajudar □ n ajuda f. ~ and abet ser cúmplice de. in ~ of em auxílio de, a favor de

**AIDS** /eɪdz/ n (med) AIDS f, (P) sida m

**ail** /eɪl/ vt what ~s you? o que é que você tem? ~ing a doente. ~ment n doença f, achaque m

**aim** /eɪm/ vt (*gun*) apontar; (*efforts*) dirigir; (*send*) atirar (**at** para) □ vi visar □ n alvo m. ~ **at** visar. ~ **to** aspirar a, tencionar. **take** ~ fazer pontaria. ~**less** a, ~**lessly** adv sem objetivo, (P) objectivo

**air** /eə(r)/ n ar m □ vt arejar; (*views*) expor □ a (*base etc*) aéreo. **in the** ~ (*rumour*) espalhado; (*plans*) no ar. **on the** ~ (*radio*) no ar. ~**conditioned** a com ar condicionado. ~**conditioning** n condicionamento m do ar, (P) ar m condicionado. ~ **force** Força f Aérea. ~ **hostess** aeromoça f, (P) hospedeira f de bordo. ~ **raid** ataque m aéreo

**airborne** /ˈeəbɔːn/ a (*aviat: in flight*) no ar; (*diseases*) levado pelo ar; (*freight*) por transporte aéreo

**aircraft** /ˈeəkrɑːft/ n (pl invar) avião m. ~**carrier** n porta-aviões m

**airfield** /ˈeəfiːld/ n campo m de aviação

**airgun** /ˈeəɡʌn/ n espingarda f de pressão

**airlift** /ˈeəlɪft/ n ponte f aérea □ vt transportar em ponte aérea

**airline** /ˈeəlaɪn/ n linha f aérea

**airlock** /ˈeəlɒk/ n câmara f de vácuo; (*in pipe*) bolha f de ar

**airmail** /ˈeəmeɪl/ n correio m aéreo. **by** ~ por avião

**airport** /ˈeəpɔːt/ n aeroporto m

**airsick** /ˈeəsɪk/ a enjoado. ~**ness** /-nɪs/ n enjôo m, (P) enjoo m

**airstrip** /ˈeəstrɪp/ n pista f de aterrissagem, (P) pista f de aterragem

**airtight** /ˈeətaɪt/ a hermético

**airy** /ˈeərɪ/ a (-**ier, -iest**) arejado; (*manner*) desenvolto

**aisle** /aɪl/ n (*of church*) nave f lateral; (*gangway*) coxia f

**ajar** /əˈdʒɑː(r)/ adv & a entreaberto

**alabaster** /ˈæləbɑːstə(r)/ n alabastro m

**à la carte** /ɑːlɑːˈkɑːt/ adv & a à la carte, (P) à lista

**alarm** /əˈlɑːm/ n alarme m; (*clock*) campainha f □ vt alarmar. ~**clock** n despertador m. ~**bell** n campainha f de alarme. ~**ing** a alarmante. ~**ist** n alarmista mf

**alas** /əˈlæs/ int ai! ai de mim!

**albatross** /ˈælbətrɒs/ n albatroz m

**album** /ˈælbəm/ n álbum m

**alcohol** /ˈælkəhɒl/ n álcool m. ~**ic** /-ˈhɒlɪk/ a (*person, drink*) alcoólico □ n alcoólico m. ~**ism** n alcoolismo m

**alcove** /ˈælkəʊv/ n recesso m, alcova f

**ale** /eɪl/ n cerveja f inglesa

**alert** /əˈlɜːt/ a (*lively*) vivo; (*watchful*) vigilante □ n alerta m □ vt alertar. **be on the** ~ estar alerta

**algebra** /ˈældʒɪbrə/ n álgebra f. ~**ic** /-ˈbreɪk/ a algébrico

**Algeria** /ælˈdʒɪərɪə/ n Argélia f. ~**n** a & n argelino (m)

**alias** /ˈeɪlɪæs/ n (pl **-ases**) outro nome m, nome falso m, (P) pseudónimo m □ adv aliás

**alibi** /ˈælɪbaɪ/ n (pl **-is**) álibi m, (P) alibi m

**alien** /ˈeɪlɪən/ n & a estrangeiro (m). ~ **to** (*contrary*) contrário a; (*differing*) alheio a, estranho a

**alienat|e** /ˈeɪlɪəneɪt/ vt alienar. ~**ion** /-ˈneɪʃn/ n alienação f

**alight**[1] /əˈlaɪt/ vi descer; (*bird*) pousar

**alight**[2] /əˈlaɪt/ a (*on fire*) em chamas; (*lit up*) aceso

**align** /əˈlaɪn/ vt alinhar. ~**ment** n alinhamento m

**alike** /əˈlaɪk/ a semelhante, parecido □ adv da mesma maneira. **look** or **be** ~ parecer-se

**alimony** /ˈælɪmənɪ/ n pensão f alimentar, (P) de alimentos

**alive** /əˈlaɪv/ a vivo. ~ **to** sensível a. ~ **with** fervilhando de, (P) a fervilhar de

**alkali** /ˈælkəlaɪ/ n (pl **-is**) álcalis m, (P) alcali m

**all** /ɔːl/ a & pron todo (f & pl **-a, -os, -as**) □ pron (*everything*) tudo □ adv completamente, de todo □ n tudo m. ~ **the better/less/more/worse** etc tanto melhor/menos/mais/pior etc. ~ (**the**) **men** todos os homens. ~ **of us** todos nós. ~ **but** quase, todos menos. ~ **in** (*colloq: exhausted*) estafado. ~**in** a tudo incluído. ~**out** a fundo, (P) completamente. ~**out** a (*effort*) máximo. ~ **over** (*in one's body*) todo; (*finished*) acabado; (*in all parts of*) por todo. ~ **right** bem; (*as a response*) está bem. ~ **round** em tudo; (*for all*) para todos. ~**round** a geral. ~ **the same** apesar de tudo. **it's** ~ **the same to me** (para mim) tanto faz

**allay** /əˈleɪ/ vt acalmar

**allegation** /ælɪˈɡeɪʃn/ n alegação f

**allege** /əˈledʒ/ vt alegar. ~**dly** /-ɪdlɪ/ adv segundo dizem, alegadamente

**allegiance** /əˈliːdʒəns/ n fidelidade f, lealdade f

**allegor|y** /ˈælɪɡərɪ/ n alegoria f. ~**ical** /-ˈɡɒrɪkl/ a alegórico

**allerg|y** /ˈælədʒɪ/ n alergia f. ~**ic** /əˈlɜːdʒɪk/ a alérgico

**alleviate** /əˈliːvɪeɪt/ vt aliviar

**alley** /ˈælɪ/ n (pl **-eys**) (*street*) viela f; (*for bowling*) pista f

**alliance** /əˈlaɪəns/ n aliança f

**allied** /ˈælaɪd/ a aliado

**alligator** /ˈælɪɡeɪtə(r)/ n jacaré m

**allocat|e** /ˈæləkeɪt/ vt (*share out*) distribuir; (*assign*) destinar. ~**ion** /-ˈkeɪʃn/ n atribuição f

**allot** /ə'lɒt/ vt (pt **allotted**) atribuir. **~ment** n atribuição f; (share) distribuição f; (land) horta f alugada

**allow** /ə'laʊ/ vt permitir; (grant) conceder, dar; (reckon on) contar com; (agree) admitir, reconhecer. **~ sb to** (+ inf) permitir a alg (+ inf or que + subj). **~ for** levar em conta

**allowance** /ə'laʊəns/ n (for employees) ajudas fpl de custo; (monthly, for wife, child) benefício m; (tax) desconto m. **make ~s for** (person) levar em consideração, ser indulgente para com; (take into account) atender a, levar em consideração

**alloy** /ə'lɔɪ/ n liga f

**allude** /ə'luːd/ vi **~ to** aludir a

**allure** /ə'lʊə(r)/ vt seduzir, atrair

**allusion** /ə'luːʒn/ n alusão f

**ally¹** /'ælaɪ/ n (pl **-lies**) aliado m

**ally²** /ə'laɪ/ vt aliar. **~ oneself with/to** aliar-se com/a

**almanac** /'ɔːlmənæk/ n almanaque m

**almighty** /ɔːl'maɪtɪ/ a todo-poderoso; (collog) grande, formidável

**almond** /'aːmənd/ n amêndoa f. **~ paste** maçapão m

**almost** /'ɔːlməʊst/ adv quase

**alone** /ə'ləʊn/ a & adv só. **leave ~** (abstain from interfering with) deixar em paz. **let ~** (without considering) sem or para não falar de

**along** /ə'lɒŋ/ prep ao longo de □ adv (onward) para diante. **all ~** durante todo o tempo. **~ with** com. **move ~, please** ande, por favor

**alongside** /əlɒŋ'saɪd/ adv (naut) atracado. **come ~** acostar □ prep ao lado de

**aloof** /ə'luːf/ adv à parte □ a distante. **~ness** n reserva f

**aloud** /ə'laʊd/ adv em voz alta

**alphabet** /'ælfəbet/ n alfabeto m. **~ical** /-'betɪkl/ a alfabético

**alpine** /'ælpaɪn/ a alpino, alpestre

**Alps** /ælps/ npl the **~** os Alpes mpl

**already** /ɔːl'redɪ/ adv já

**also** /'ɔːlsəʊ/ adv também

**altar** /'ɔːltə(r)/ n altar m

**alter** /'ɔːltə(r)/ vt/i alterar(-se), modificar(-se). **~ation** /-'reɪʃn/ n alteração f; (to garment) modificação f

**alternate¹** /ɔːl'tɜːnət/ a alternado. **~ly** adv alternadamente

**alternat|e²** /'ɔːltəneɪt/ vt/i alternar (-se). **~ing current** (elect) corrente f alterna. **~or** n (elect) alternador m

**alternative** /ɔːl'tɜːnətɪv/ a alternativo □ n alternativa f. **~ly** adv em alternativa. **or ~ly** ou então

**although** /ɔːl'ðəʊ/ conj embora, conquanto

**altitude** /'æltɪtjuːd/ n altitude f

**altogether** /ɔːltə'geðə(r)/ adv (completely) completamente; (in total) ao todo; (on the whole) de modo geral

**aluminium** /æljʊ'mɪnɪəm/ (Amer **aluminum** /ə'luːmɪnəm/) n alumínio m

**always** /'ɔːlweɪz/ adv sempre

**am** /æm/ see **be**

**a.m.** /eɪ'em/ adv da manhã

**amalgamate** /ə'mælgəmeɪt/ vt/i amalgamar(-se); (comm) fundir

**amass** /ə'mæs/ vt amontoar, juntar

**amateur** /'æmətə(r)/ n & a amador (m). **~ish** a (pej) de amador, (P) amadorístico

**amaz|e** /ə'meɪz/ vt assombrar, espantar. **~ed** a assombrado. **~ement** n assombro m. **~ingly** adv espantosamente

**Amazon** /'æməzən/ n the **~** o Amazonas

**ambassador** /æm'bæsədə(r)/ n embaixador m

**amber** /'æmbə(r)/ n âmbar m; (traffic light) luz f amarela

**ambigu|ous** /æm'bɪgjʊəs/ a ambíguo. **~ity** /-'gjuːətɪ/ n ambigüidade f, (P) ambiguidade f

**ambiti|on** /æm'bɪʃn/ n ambição f. **~ous** a ambicioso

**ambivalen|t** /æm'bɪvələnt/ a ambivalente. **~ce** n ambivalência f

**amble** /'æmbl/ vi caminhar sem pressa

**ambulance** /'æmbjʊləns/ n ambulância f

**ambush** /'æmbʊʃ/ n emboscada f □ vt fazer uma emboscada para, (P) fazer uma emboscada a

**amenable** /ə'miːnəbl/ a **~ to** (responsive) sensível a

**amend** /ə'mend/ vt emendar, corrigir. **~ment** n (to rule) emenda f. **~s** n **make ~s for** reparar, compensar

**amenities** /ə'miːnətɪz/ npl (pleasant features) atrativos mpl, (P) atractivos mpl; (facilities) confortos mpl, comodidades fpl

**America** /ə'merɪkə/ n América f. **~n** a & n americano (m). **~nism** /-nɪzəm/ n americanismo m. **~nize** vt americanizar

**amiable** /'eɪmɪəbl/ a amável

**amicable** /'æmɪkəbl/ a amigável, amigo

**amid(st)** /ə'mɪd(st)/ prep entre, no meio de

**amiss** /ə'mɪs/ a & adv mal. **sth ~** qq coisa que não está bem. **take sth ~** levar qq coisa a mal

**ammonia** /ə'məʊnɪə/ n amoníaco m

**ammunition** /æmjʊ'nɪʃn/ n munições fpl

**amnesia** /æm'niːzɪə/ n amnésia f

**amnesty** /'æmnəstɪ/ n anistia f, (P) amnistia f

**amok** /ə'mɒk/ adv run ~ enlouquecer; (crowd) correr desordenadamente

**among(st)** /ə'mʌŋ(st)/ prep entre, no meio de. ~ **ourselves** (aqui) entre nós

**amoral** /eɪ'mɒrəl/ a amoral

**amorous** /'æmərəs/ a amoroso

**amount** /ə'maʊnt/ n quantidade f; (total) montante m; (sum of money) quantia f □ vi ~ **to** elevar-se a; (fig) equivaler a

**amp** /æmp/ n (colloq) ampère m

**amphibi|an** /æm'fɪbɪən/ n anfíbio m. ~ous a anfíbio

**ampl|e** /'æmpl/ a (-er, -est) (large, roomy) amplo; (enough) suficiente, bastante. ~y adv amplamente

**amplif|y** /'æmplɪfaɪ/ vt ampliar, amplificar. ~ier n amplificador m

**amputat|e** /'æmpjʊteɪt/ vt amputar. ~ion /-'teɪʃn/ n amputação f

**amus|e** /ə'mjuːz/ vt divertir. ~ement n divertimento m. ~ing a divertido

**an** /ən, æn/ see **a**

**anachronism** /ə'nækrənɪzəm/ n anacronismo m

**anaem|ia** /ə'niːmɪə/ n anemia f. ~ic a anêmico, (P) anémico

**anaesthetic** /ænɪs'θetɪk/ n anestético m, (P) anestésico m. **give an** ~ **to** anestesiar

**anaesthetist** /ə'niːsθətɪst/ n anestesista mf

**anagram** /'ænəgræm/ n anagrama m

**analog(ue)** /'ænəlɒg/ a análogo

**analogy** /ə'nælədʒɪ/ n analogia f

**analys|e** /'ænəlaɪz/ vt analisar. ~t /-ɪst/ n analista mf

**analysis** /ə'næləsɪs/ n (pl -yses) /-əsiːz/ análise f

**analytic(al)** /ænə'lɪtɪk(l)/ a analítico

**anarch|y** /'ænəkɪ/ n anarquia f. ~ist n anarquista mf

**anatom|y** /ə'nætəmɪ/ n anatomia f. ~ical /ænə'tɒmɪkl/ a anatômico, (P) anatómico

**ancest|or** /'ænsestə(r)/ n antepassado m. ~ral /-'sestrəl/ a ancestral (pl -ais)

**ancestry** /'ænsestrɪ/ n ascendência f, estirpe f

**anchor** /'æŋkə(r)/ n âncora f □ vt/i ancorar. ~age /-rɪdʒ/ n ancoradouro m

**anchovy** /'æntʃəvɪ/ n enchova f, (P) anchova f

**ancient** /'eɪnʃənt/ a antigo

**ancillary** /æn'sɪlərɪ/ a ancilar, (P) subordinado

**and** /ənd/; emphatic /ænd/ conj e. **go** ~ **see** vá ver. **better** ~ **better**/ **less** ~ **less** etc cada vez melhor/menos etc

**anecdote** /'ænɪkdəʊt/ n anedota f

**angel** /'eɪndʒl/ n anjo m. ~ic /æn'dʒelɪk/ a angélico, angelical

**anger** /'æŋgə(r)/ n cólera f, zanga f □ vt irritar

**angle**[1] /'æŋgl/ n ângulo m

**angle**[2] /'æŋgl/ vi (fish) pescar (à linha). ~ **for** (fig: compliments, information) andar à procura de. ~r /-ə(r)/ n pescador m

**anglicism** /'æŋglɪsɪzəm/ n anglicismo m

**Anglo-** /'æŋgləʊ/ pref anglo-

**Anglo-Saxon** /'æŋgləʊ'sæksn/ a & n anglo-saxão (m)

**angr|y** /'æŋgrɪ/ a (-ier, -iest) zangado. **get** ~y zangar-se (with com). ~ily adv furiosamente

**anguish** /'æŋgwɪʃ/ n angústia f

**angular** /'æŋgjʊlə(r)/ a angular; (features) anguloso

**animal** /'ænɪml/ a & n animal (m)

**animate**[1] /'ænɪmət/ a animado

**animat|e**[2] /'ænɪmeɪt/ vt animar. ~ion /-'meɪʃn/ n animação f. ~ed cartoon filme m de bonecos animados, (P) de desenhos animados

**animosity** /ænɪ'mɒsətɪ/ n animosidade f

**aniseed** /'ænɪsiːd/ n semente f de anis

**ankle** /'æŋkl/ n tornozelo m. ~ sock meia f soquete

**annex** /ə'neks/ vt anexar. ~ation /ænek'seɪʃn/ n anexação f

**annexe** /'æneks/ n anexo m

**annihilate** /ə'naɪəleɪt/ vt aniquilar

**anniversary** /ænɪ'vɜːsərɪ/ n aniversário m

**announce** /ə'naʊns/ vt anunciar. ~ment n anúncio m. ~r /-ə(r)/ n (radio, TV) locutor m

**annoy** /ə'nɔɪ/ vt irritar, aborrecer. ~ance n aborrecimento m. ~ed a aborrecido (with com). **get** ~ed aborrecer-se. ~ing a irritante

**annual** /'ænjʊəl/ a anual □ n (bot) planta f anual; (book) anuário m. ~ly adv anualmente

**annuity** /ə'njuːətɪ/ n anuidade f

**annul** /ə'nʌl/ vt (pt annulled) anular. ~ment n anulação f

**anomal|y** /ə'nɒməlɪ/ n anomalia f. ~ous a anômalo, (P) anómalo

**anonym|ous** /ə'nɒnɪməs/ a anônimo, (P) anónimo. ~ity /ænə'nɪmətɪ/ n anonimato m

**anorak** /'ænəræk/ n anoraque m, anorak m

**another** /ə'nʌðə(r)/ a & pron (um) outro. ~ **ten minutes** mais dez minutos. **to one** ~ um ao outro, uns aos outros

**answer** /'ɑːnsə(r)/ n resposta f; (solution) solução f □ vt responder a;

(*prayer*) atender a □ *vi* responder. ~ **the door** atender à porta. ~ **back** retrucar, (*P*) responder torto. ~ **for** responder por. ~**able** *a* responsável (for por; to perante). ~**ing machine** *n* secretária *f* eletrónica

**ant** /ænt/ *n* formiga *f*

**antagonis|m** /æn'tægənɪzəm/ *n* antagonismo *m*. ~**t** *n* antagonista *mf*. ~**tic** /-'nɪstɪk/ *a* antagônico, (*P*) antagónico, hostil

**antagonize** /æn'tægənaɪz/ *vt* antagonizar, hostilizar

**Antarctic** /æn'taːktɪk/ *n* Antártico, (*P*) Antárctico *m* □ *a* antártico, (*P*) antárctico

**ante-** /ænti/ *pref* ante-

**antecedent** /æntɪ'siːdnt/ *a* & *n* antecedente (*m*)

**antelope** /'æntɪləʊp/ *n* antílope *m*

**antenatal** /æntɪ'neɪtl/ *a* pré-natal

**antenna** /æn'tenə/ *n* (*pl* -ae /-iː/) antena *f*

**anthem** /'ænθəm/ *n* cântico *m*. **national** ~ hino *m* nacional

**anthology** /æn'θɒlədʒɪ/ *n* antologia *f*

**anthropolog|y** /ænθrə'pɒlədʒɪ/ *n* antropologia *f*. ~**ist** *n* antropólogo *m*

**anti-** /ænti/ *pref* anti-. ~**aircraft** /-eəkraːft/ *a* antiaéreo

**antibiotic** /æntɪbaɪ'ɒtɪk/ *n* antibiótico *m*

**antibody** /'æntɪbɒdɪ/ *n* anticorpo *m*

**anticipat|e** /æn'tɪsɪpeɪt/ *vt* (*foresee, expect*) prever; (*forestall*) anteciparse a. ~**ion** /-'peɪʃn/ *n* antecipação *f*; (*expectation*) expectativa *f*. **in** ~**ion of** na previsão *or* expectativa de

**anticlimax** /æntɪ'klaɪmæks/ *n* anticlímax *m*; (*let-down*) decepção *f*. **it was an** ~ não correspondeu à expectativa

**anticlockwise** /æntɪ'klɒkwaɪz/ *adv* & *a* no sentido contrário ao dos ponteiros dum relógio

**antics** /'æntɪks/ *npl* (*of clown*) palhaçadas *fpl*; (*behaviour*) comportamento *m* bizarro

**anticyclone** /ˌæntɪ'saɪkləʊn/ *n* anticiclone *m*

**antidote** /'æntɪdəʊt/ *n* antídoto *m*

**antifreeze** /'æntɪfriːz/ *n* anticongelante *m*

**antihistamine** /æntɪ'hɪstəmiːn/ *a* & *n* anti-histamínico (*m*)

**antipathy** /æn'tɪpəθɪ/ *n* antipatia *f*

**antiquated** /'æntɪkweɪtɪd/ *a* antiquado

**antique** /æn'tiːk/ *a* antigo □ *n* antiguidade *f*. ~ **dealer** antiquário *m*. ~ **shop** loja *f* de antiguidades, (*P*) antiquário *m*

**antiquity** /æn'tɪkwətɪ/ *n* antiguidade *f*

**antiseptic** /æntɪ'septɪk/ *a* & *n* anti-séptico (*m*)

**antisocial** /æntɪ'səʊʃl/ *a* anti-social; (*unsociable*) insociável

**antithesis** /æn'tɪθəsɪs/ *n* (*pl* -eses) /-siːz/ antítese *f*.

**antlers** /'æntləz/ *npl* chifres *mpl*, esgalhos *mpl*

**antonym** /'æntənɪm/ *n* antônimo *m*, (*P*) antónimo *m*

**anus** /'eɪnəs/ *n* ânus *m*

**anvil** /'ænvɪl/ *n* bigorna *f*

**anxiety** /æŋ'zaɪətɪ/ *n* ansiedade *f*; (*eagerness*) ânsia *f*

**anxious** /'æŋkʃəs/ *a* (*worried, eager*) ansioso (to de, por). ~**ly** *adv* ansiosamente; (*eagerly*) impacientemente

**any** /'enɪ/ *a* & *pron* qualquer, quaisquer; (*in neg and interr sentences*) algum, alguns; (*in neg sentences*) nenhum, nenhuns; (*every*) todo. **at** ~ **moment** a qualquer momento. **at** ~ **rate** de qualquer modo, em todo o caso. **in** ~ **case** em todo o caso. **have you** ~ **money/friends?** você tem (algum) dinheiro/(alguns) amigos? **I don't have** ~ **time** não tenho nenhum tempo *or* tempo nenhum *or* po algum. **has she** ~? ela tem algum? **she doesn't have** ~ ela não tem nenhum □ *adv* (*at all*) de modo algum *or* nenhum; (*a little*) um pouco. ~ **the less/the worse** *etc* menos/pior *etc*

**anybody** /'enɪbɒdɪ/ *pron* qualquer pessoa; (*somebody*) alguém; (*after negative*) ninguém. **he didn't see** ~ ele não viu ninguém

**anyhow** /'enɪhaʊ/ *adv* (*no matter how*) de qualquer modo; (*badly*) de qualquer maneira, ao acaso; (*in any case*) em todo o caso. **you can try,** ~ em todo o caso, você pode tentar

**anyone** /'enɪwʌn/ *pron* = **anybody**

**anything** /'enɪθɪŋ/ *pron* (*something*) alguma coisa; (*no matter what*) qualquer coisa; (*after negative*) nada. **he didn't say** ~ não disse nada. **it is** ~ **but cheap** é tudo menos barato. ~ **you do** tudo o que você fizer

**anyway** /'enɪweɪ/ *adv* de qualquer modo; (*in any case*) em todo o caso

**anywhere** /'enɪweə(r)/ *adv* (*somewhere*) em qualquer parte; (*after negative*) em parte alguma/nenhuma. ~ **else** em qualquer outro lado. ~ **you go** onde quer que você vá. **he doesn't go** ~ ele não vai a lado nenhum

**apart** /ə'paːt/ *adv* à parte; (*separated*) separado; (*into pieces*) aos bocados. ~ **from** a parte, além de. **ten metres** ~ a dez metros de distância entre si. **come** ~ desfazer-se. **keep** ~ manter separado. **take** ~ desmontar

**apartment** /ə'pɑːtmənt/ n (Amer) apartamento m. **~s** aposentos mpl

**apath|y** /'æpəθɪ/ n apatia f. **~etic** /-'θetɪk/ a apático

**ape** /eɪp/ n macaco m □ vt macaquear

**aperitif** /ə'perətɪf/ n aperitivo m

**aperture** /'æpətʃə(r)/ n abertura f

**apex** /'eɪpeks/ n ápice m, cume m

**apiece** /ə'piːs/ adv cada, por cabeça

**apologetic** /əpɒlə'dʒetɪk/ a (tone etc) apologético, de desculpas. **be ~** desculpar-se. **~ally** /-əlɪ/ adv desculpando-se

**apologize** /ə'pɒlədʒaɪz/ vi desculpar-se (for de, por; to junto de, perante), pedir desculpa (for, por; to, a)

**apology** /ə'pɒlədʒɪ/ n desculpa f; (defence of belief) apologia f

**apostle** /ə'pɒsl/ n apóstolo m

**apostrophe** /ə'pɒstrəfɪ/ n apóstrofe f

**appal** /ə'pɔːl/ vt (pt appalled) estarrecer. **~ling** a estarrecedor

**apparatus** /æpə'reɪtəs/ n aparelho m

**apparent** /ə'pærənt/ a aparente. **~ly** adv aparentemente

**apparition** /æpə'rɪʃn/ n aparição f

**appeal** /ə'piːl/ vi (jur) apelar (to para); (attract) atrair (to a); (for funds) angariar □ n apelo m; (attractiveness) atrativo m, (P) atractivo m; (for funds) angariação f. **~ to sb for sth** pedir uma coisa a alg. **~ing** a (attractive) atraente

**appear** /ə'pɪə(r)/ vi aparecer; (seem) parecer; (in court, theatre) apresentar-se. **~ance** n aparição f; (aspect) aparência f; (in court) comparecimento m, (P) comparência f

**appease** /ə'piːz/ vt apaziguar

**appendage** /ə'pendɪdʒ/ n apêndice m

**appendicitis** /əpendɪ'saɪtɪs/ n apendicite f

**appendix** /ə'pendɪks/ n (pl -ices /-siːz/) (of book) apêndice m; (pl -ixes /-ksɪz/) (anat) apêndice m

**appetite** /'æpɪtaɪt/ n apetite m

**appetizer** /'æpɪtaɪzə(r)/ n (snack) tira-gosto m; (drink) aperitivo m

**appetizing** /'æpɪtaɪzɪŋ/ a apetitoso

**applau|d** /ə'plɔːd/ vt/i aplaudir. **~se** n aplauso(s) m(pl)

**apple** /'æpl/ n maçã f. **~ tree** macieira f

**appliance** /ə'plaɪəns/ n aparelho m, instrumento m, utensílio m. **household ~s** utensílios mpl domésticos

**applicable** /'æplɪkəbl/ a aplicável

**applicant** /'æplɪkənt/ n candidato m (for a)

**application** /æplɪ'keɪʃn/ n aplicação f; (request) pedido m; (form) formulário m; (for job) candidatura f

**appl|y** /ə'plaɪ/ vt aplicar □ vi **~y to** (refer) aplicar-se a; (ask) dirigir-se a.

**~y for** (job, grant) candidatar-se a. **~y o.s. to** aplicar-se a. **~ied** a aplicado

**appoint** /ə'pɔɪnt/ vt (to post) nomear; (time, date) marcar. **well-~ed** a bem equipado, bem provido. **~ment** n nomeação f; (meeting) entrevista f; (with friends) encontro m; (with doctor etc) consulta f, (P) marcação f; (job) posto m

**apprais|e** /ə'preɪz/ vt avaliar. **~al** n avaliação f

**appreciable** /ə'priːʃəbl/ a apreciável

**appreciat|e** /ə'priːʃɪeɪt/ vt (value) apreciar; (understand) compreender; (be grateful for) estar/ficar grato por □ vi encarecer. **~ion** /-'eɪʃn/ n apreciação f; (rise in value) encarecimento m; (gratitude) reconhecimento m. **~ive** /ə'priːʃɪətɪv/ a apreciador; (grateful) reconhecido

**apprehen|d** /æprɪ'hend/ vt (seize, understand) apreender; (dread) recear. **~sion** n apreensão f

**apprehensive** /æprɪ'hensɪv/ a apreensivo

**apprentice** /ə'prentɪs/ n aprendiz, -a mf □ vt pôr como aprendiz (to de). **~ship** n aprendizagem f

**approach** /ə'prəʊtʃ/ vt aproximar; (with request or offer) abordar □ vi aproximar-se □ n aproximação f. **~ to** (problem) abordagem f de; (place) acesso m a; (person) diligência junto de. **~able** a acessível

**appropriate¹** /ə'prəʊprɪət/ a apropriado, próprio. **~ly** adv apropriadamente, a propósito

**appropriate²** /ə'prəʊprɪeɪt/ vt apropriar-se de

**approval** /ə'pruːvl/ n aprovação f. **on ~** (comm) sob condição, à aprovação

**approv|e** /ə'pruːv/ vt/i aprovar. **~e of** aprovar. **~ingly** adv com ar de aprovação

**approximate¹** /ə'prɒksɪmət/ a aproximado. **~ly** adv aproximadamente

**approximat|e²** /ə'prɒksɪmeɪt/ vt/i aproximar(-se) de. **~ion** /-'meɪʃn/ n aproximação f

**apricot** /'eɪprɪkɒt/ n damasco m

**April** /'eɪprəl/ n Abril m. **~ Fool's Day** o primeiro de Abril, o dia das mentiras. **make an ~ fool of** pregar uma mentira em, (P) pregar uma mentira a

**apron** /'eɪprən/ n avental m

**apt** /æpt/ a apto; (pupil) dotado. **be ~ to** ser propenso a. **~ly** adv apropriadamente

**aptitude** /'æptɪtjuːd/ n aptidão f, (P) aptitude f

**aqualung** /'ækwəlʌŋ/ n escafandro autônomo, (P) autónomo m

**aquarium** /ə'kwɛərɪəm/ n (pl -ums) aquário m

**Aquarius** /ə'kwɛərɪəs/ n (astr) Aquário m

**aquatic** /ə'kwætɪk/ a aquático; (sport) náutico, aquático

**aqueduct** /'ækwɪdʌkt/ n aqueduto m

**Arab** /'ærəb/ a & n árabe (mf). **~ic** a & n (lang) árabe (m), arábico (m). **a~ic numerals** algarismos mpl árabes or arábicos

**Arabian** /ə'reɪbɪən/ a árabe

**arable** /'ærəbl/ a arável

**arbitrary** /'ɑːbɪtrərɪ/ a arbitrário

**arbitrat|e** /'ɑːbɪtreɪt/ vi arbitrar. **~ion** /-'treɪʃn/ n arbitragem f. **~or** n árbitro m

**arc** /ɑːk/ n arco m. **~ lamp** lâmpada f de arco. **~ welding** soldadura f a arco

**arcade** /ɑː'keɪd/ n (shop) arcada f. **amusement ~** fliperama m

**arch** /ɑːtʃ/ n arco m; (vault) abóbada f □ vt/i arquear(-se)

**arch-** /ɑːtʃ/ pref arqui-.

**archaeolog|y** /ɑːkɪ'ɒlədʒɪ/ n arqueologia f. **~ical** /-ə'lɒdʒɪkl/ a arqueológico. **~ist** n arqueólogo m

**archaic** /ɑː'keɪɪk/ a arcaico

**archbishop** /ɑːtʃ'bɪʃəp/ n arcebispo m

**arch-enemy** /ɑːtʃ'enəmɪ/ n inimigo m número um

**archer** /'ɑːtʃə(r)/ n arqueiro m. **~y** n tiro m ao arco

**archetype** /'ɑːkɪtaɪp/ n arquétipo m

**architect** /'ɑːkɪtekt/ n arquiteto m, (P) arquitecto m

**architectur|e** /'ɑːkɪtektʃə(r)/ n arquitetura f, (P) arquitectura f. **~al** /-'tektʃərəl/ a arquitetônico, (P) arquitectónico

**archiv|es** /'ɑːkaɪvz/ npl arquivo m. **~ist** /-ɪvɪst/ n arquivista mf

**archway** /'ɑːtʃweɪ/ n arcada f

**Arctic** /'ɑːktɪk/ n ártico m, (P) árctico m □ a ártico, (P) árctico. **~ weather** tempo m glacial

**ardent** /'ɑːdnt/ a ardente. **~ly** adv ardentemente

**ardour** /'ɑːdə(r)/ n ardor m

**arduous** /'ɑːdjʊəs/ a árduo

**are** /ə(r)/; emphatic /ɑː(r)/ see **be**

**area** /'eərɪə/ n área f

**arena** /ə'riːnə/ n arena f

**aren't** /ɑːnt/ = are not

**Argentin|a** /ɑːdʒən'tiːnə/ n Argentina f. **~ian** /-'tɪnɪən/ a & n argentino (m)

**argu|e** /'ɑːgjuː/ vi discutir; (reason) argumentar, arguir □ vt (debate) discutir. **~e that** alegar que. **~able** a alegável. **it's ~able that** pode-se sustentar que

**argument** /'ɑːgjʊmənt/ n (dispute) disputa f; (reasoning) argumento m. **~ative** /-'mentətɪv/ a que gosta de discutir, argumentativo

**arid** /'ærɪd/ a árido

**Aries** /'eəriːz/ n (astr) Áries m, Carneiro m

**arise** /ə'raɪz/ vi (pt arose, pp arisen) surgir. **~ from** resultar de

**aristocracy** /ærɪ'stɒkrəsɪ/ n aristocracia f

**aristocrat** /'ærɪstəkræt/ n aristocrata mf. **~ic** /-'krætɪk/ a aristocrático

**arithmetic** /ə'rɪθmətɪk/ n aritmética f

**ark** /ɑːk/ n **Noah's ~** arca f de Noé

**arm¹** /ɑːm/ n braço m. **~ in ~** de braço dado

**arm²** /ɑːm/ vt armar □ n (mil) arma f. **~ed robbery** assalto m à mão armada

**armament** /'ɑːməmənt/ n armamento m

**armchair** /'ɑːmtʃeə(r)/ n cadeira f de braços, poltrona f

**armistice** /'ɑːmɪstɪs/ n armistício m

**armour** /'ɑːmə(r)/ n armadura f; (on tanks etc) blindagem f. **~ed** a blindado

**armoury** /'ɑːmərɪ/ n arsenal m

**armpit** /'ɑːmpɪt/ n axila f, sovaco m

**arms** /ɑːmz/ npl armas fpl. **coat of ~** brasão m

**army** /'ɑːmɪ/ n exército m

**aroma** /ə'rəʊmə/ n aroma m. **~tic** /ærə'mætɪk/ a aromático

**arose** /ə'rəʊz/ see **arise**

**around** /ə'raʊnd/ adv em redor, em volta; (here and there) por aí □ prep em redor de, em torno de, em volta de; (approximately) aproximadamente. **~ here** por aqui

**arouse** /ə'raʊz/ vt despertar; (excite) excitar

**arrange** /ə'reɪndʒ/ vt arranjar; (time, date) combinar. **~ to do sth** combinar fazer alg coisa. **~ment** n arranjo m; (agreement) acordo m. **make ~ments (for)** (plans) tomar disposições (para); (preparations) fazer preparativos (para)

**array** /ə'reɪ/ vt revestir □ n **an ~ of** (display) um leque de, uma série de

**arrears** /ə'rɪəz/ npl dívidas fpl em atraso, atrasos mpl. **in ~** em atraso

**arrest** /ə'rest/ vt (by law) deter, prender; (process, movement) deter □ n captura f. **under ~** sob prisão

**arrival** /ə'raɪvl/ n chegada f. **new ~** recém-chegado m

**arrive** /ə'raɪv/ vi chegar

**arrogan|t** /'ærəgənt/ a arrogante. **~ce** n arrogância f. **~tly** adv com arrogância

**arrow** /'ærəʊ/ n flecha f, seta f

**arsenal** /'a:sənl/ n arsenal m

**arsenic** /'a:snɪk/ n arsênico m, (P) arsénico m

**arson** /'a:sn/ n fogo m posto. **~ist** n incendiário m

**art**[1] /a:t/ n arte f. **the ~s** (univ) letras fpl. **fine ~s** belas-artes fpl. **~ gallery** museu m (de arte); (private) galeria f de arte

**artery** /'a:tərɪ/ n artéria f

**artful** /'a:tfl/ a manhoso. **~ness** n manha f

**arthritis** /a:'θraɪtɪs/ n artrite f

**artichoke** /'a:tɪtʃəʊk/ n alcachofra f. **Jerusalem ~** topinambo m

**article** /'a:tɪkl/ n artigo m. **~d** a (jur) em estágio, (P) a estagiar

**articulate**[1] /a:'tɪkjʊlət/ a que se exprime com clareza; (speech) bem articulado

**articulat|e**[2] /a:'tɪkjʊleɪt/ vt/i articular. **~ed lorry** camião m articulado. **~ion** /-'leɪʃn/ n articulação f

**artifice** /'a:tɪfɪs/ n artifício m

**artificial** /a:tɪ'fɪʃl/ a artificial

**artillery** /a:'tɪlərɪ/ n artilharia f

**artisan** /a:tɪ'zæn/ n artífice mf, artesão m, artesã f

**artist** /'a:tɪst/ n artista mf. **~ic** /-'tɪstɪk/ a artístico. **~ry** n arte f

**artiste** /a:'ti:st/ n artista mf

**artless** /'a:tlɪs/ a ingênuo, (P) ingénuo, simples

**as** /əz/; emphatic /æz/ adv & conj como; (while) enquanto; (when) quando. **~ a gift** de presente. **~ tall as** tão alto quanto, (P) tão alto como □ pron que. **I ate the same ~ he** comi o mesmo que ele. **~ for, ~ to** quanto a. **~ from** a partir de. **~ if** como se. **~ much** tanto, tantos. **~ many** quanto, quantos. **~ soon as** logo que. **~ well** (also) também. **~ well as** (in addition to) assim como

**asbestos** /æz'bestəs/ n asbesto m, amianto m

**ascend** /ə'send/ vt/i subir. **~ the throne** ascender ou subir ao trono

**ascent** /ə'sent/ n ascensão f; (slope) subida f, rampa f

**ascertain** /æsə'teɪn/ vt certificar-se de. **~ that** certificar-se de que

**ascribe** /ə'skraɪb/ vt atribuir

**ash**[1] /æʃ/ n **~(-tree)** freixo m

**ash**[2] /æʃ/ n cinza f. **A~ Wednesday** Quarta-feira f de Cinzas. **~en** a pálido

**ashamed** /ə'ʃeɪmd/ a **be ~** ter vergonha, ficar envergonhado (of de, por)

**ashore** /ə'ʃɔ:(r)/ adv em terra. **go ~** desembarcar

**ashtray** /'æʃtreɪ/ n cinzeiro m

**Asia** /'eɪʃə/ n ásia f. **~n** a & n asiático (m)

**aside** /ə'saɪd/ adv de lado, de parte □ n (theat) aparte m. **~ from** (Amer) à parte

**ask** /a:sk/ vt/i pedir; (a question) perguntar; (invite) convidar. **~ sb sth** pedir uma coisa a alguém. **~ about** informar-se de. **~ after sb** pedir notícias de alg, perguntar por alg. **~ for** pedir. **~ sb in** mandar entrar alg. **~ sb to do sth** pedir alguém para fazer alguma coisa

**askew** /ə'skju:/ adv & a de través, de esguelha

**asleep** /ə'sli:p/ adv & a adormecido; (numb) dormente. **fall ~** adormecer

**asparagus** /ə'spærəgəs/ n (plant) aspargo m, (P) espargo m; (culin) aspargos mpl, (P) espargo m

**aspect** /'æspekt/ n aspecto m; (direction) exposição f

**aspersions** /ə'spɜ:ʃnz/ npl **cast ~ on** caluniar

**asphalt** /'æsfælt/ n asfalto m □ vt asfaltar

**asphyxiat|e** /əs'fɪksɪeɪt/ vt/i asfixiar. **~ion** /-'eɪʃn/ n asfixia f

**aspir|e** /əs'paɪə(r)/ vi **~e to** aspirar a. **~ation** /æspə'reɪʃn/ n aspiração f

**aspirin** /'æsprɪn/ n aspirina f

**ass** /æs/ n burro m. **make an ~ of o.s.** fazer papel de palhaço, (P) fazer figura de parvo

**assail** /ə'seɪl/ vt assaltar, agredir. **~ant** n assaltante mf, agressor m

**assassin** /ə'sæsɪn/ n assassino m

**assassinat|e** /ə'sæsmeɪt/ vt assassinar. **~ion** /-'eɪʃn/ n assassinato m

**assault** /ə'sɔ:lt/ n assalto m □ vt assaltar, atacar

**assemble** /ə'sembl/ vt (people) reunir; (fit together) montar □ vi reunir-se

**assembly** /ə'semblɪ/ n assembléia f, (P) assembleia f. **~ line** linha f de montagem

**assent** /ə'sent/ n assentimento m □ vi **~ to** consentir em

**assert** /ə'sɜ:t/ vt afirmar; (one's rights) reivindicar. **~ o.s.** impor-se. **~ion** /-ʃn/ n asserção f. **~ive** a dogmático, peremptório. **~iveness** n assertividade f, (P) firmeza f

**assess** /ə'ses/ vt avaliar; (payment) estabelecer o montante de. **~ment** n avaliação f. **~or** n (valuer) avaliador m

**asset** /'æset/ n (advantage) vantagem f. **~s** (comm) ativo m, (P) activo m; (possessions) bens mpl

**assiduous** /ə'sɪdjʊəs/ a assíduo

**assign** /ə'saɪn/ vt atribuir, destinar;

(*jur*) transmitir. ~ **sb to** designar alg para

**assignation** /æsıg'neıʃn/ *n* combinação *f* (de hora e local) de encontro

**assignment** /ə'saınmənt/ *n* tarefa *f*, missão *f*; (*jur*) transmissão *f*

**assimilat|e** /ə'sımıleıt/ *vt/i* assimilar(-se). ~**ion** /-'eıʃn/ *n* assimilação *f*

**assist** /ə'sıst/ *vt/i* ajudar. ~**ance** *n* ajuda *f*, assistência *f*

**assistant** /ə'sıstənt/ *n* (*helper*) assistente *mf*, auxiliar *mf*; (*in shop*) ajudante *mf*, empregado *m* □ *a* adjunto

**associat|e¹** /ə'səʊʃıeıt/ *vt* associar □ *vi* ~**e with** conviver com. ~**ion** /-'eıʃn/ *n* associação *f*

**associate²** /ə'səʊʃıət/ *a* & *n* associado (*m*)

**assort|ed** /ə'sɔːtıd/ *a* variados; (*foods*) sortidos. ~**ment** *n* sortimento *m*, (*P*) sortido *m*

**assume** /ə'sjuːm/ *vt* assumir; (*presume*) supor, presumir

**assumption** /ə'sʌmpʃn/ *n* suposição *f*

**assurance** /ə'ʃʊərəns/ *n* certeza *f*, garantia *f*; (*insurance*) seguro *m*; (*self-confidence*) segurança *f*, confiança *f*

**assure** /ə'ʃʊə(r)/ *vt* assegurar. ~**d** *a* certo, garantido. **rest** ~**d that** ficar certo que

**asterisk** /'æstərısk/ *n* asterisco *m*

**asthma** /'æsmə/ *n* asma *f*. ~**tic** /-'mætık/ *a* & *n* asmático (*m*)

**astonish** /ə'stɒnıʃ/ *vt* espantar. ~**ingly** *adv* espantosamente. ~**ment** *n* espanto *m*

**astound** /ə'staʊnd/ *vt* assombrar

**astray** /ə'streı/ *adv* & *a* **go** ~ perder-se, extraviar-se. **lead** ~ desencaminhar

**astride** /ə'straıd/ *adv* & *prep* escarranchado (em)

**astringent** /ə'strındʒənt/ *a* & *n* adstringente (*m*)

**astrolog|y** /ə'strɒlədʒı/ *n* astrologia *f*. ~**er** *n* astrólogo *m*

**astronaut** /'æstrənɔːt/ *n* astronauta *mf*

**astronom|y** /ə'strɒnəmı/ *n* astronomia *f*. ~**er** *n* astrônomo *m*, (*P*) astrónomo *m*. ~**ical** /æstrə'nɒmıkl/ *a* astronômico *m*, (*P*) astronómico

**astute** /ə'stjuːt/ *a* astuto, astucioso. ~**ness** *n* astúcia *f*

**asylum** /ə'saıləm/ *n* asilo *m*

**at** /ət/; *emphatic* /æt/ *prep* a, em. ~ **home** em casa. ~ **night** à noite. ~ **once** imediatamente; (*simultaneously*) ao mesmo tempo. ~ **school** na escola. ~ **sea** no mar. ~ **the door** na porta. ~ **times** às vezes. **angry/ surprised** ~ zangado/surpreendido

com. **not** ~ **all** de nada. **no wind** ~ **all** nenhum vento

**ate** /et/ *see* **eat**

**atheis|t** /'eıθııst/ *n* ateu *m*. ~**m** /-zəm/ *n* ateísmo *m*

**athlet|e** /'æθliːt/ *n* atleta *mf*. ~**ic** /-'letık/ *a* atlético. ~**ics** /-'letıks/ *n*(*pl*) atletismo *m*

**Atlantic** /ət'læntık/ *a* atlântico □ *n* ~ (**Ocean**) Atlântico *m*

**atlas** /'ætləs/ *n* atlas *m*

**atmospher|e** /'ætməsfıə(r)/ *n* atmosfera *f*. ~**ic** /-'ferık/ *a* atmosférico

**atom** /'ætəm/ *n* átomo *m*. ~**ic** /ə'tɒmık/ *a* atômico, (*P*) atómico. ~(**ic**) **bomb** bomba *f* atômica, (*P*) atómica

**atomize** /'ætəmaız/ *vt* atomizar, vaparizar, pulverizar. ~**r** /-ə(r)/ *n* pulverizador *m*, vaporizador *m*

**atone** /ə'təʊn/ *vi* ~ **for** expiar. ~**ment** *n* expiação *f*

**atrocious** /ə'trəʊʃəs/ *a* atroz

**atrocity** /ə'trɒsətı/ *n* atrocidade *f*

**atrophy** /'ætrəfı/ *n* atrofia *f* □ *vt/i* atrofiar(-se)

**attach** /ə'tætʃ/ *vt/i* (*affix*) ligar(-se), prender(-se); (*join*) juntar(-se). ~**ed** *a* (*document*) junto, anexo. **be** ~**ed to** (*like*) estar apegado a. ~**ment** *n* ligação *f*; (*affection*) apego *m*; (*accessory*) acessório *m*

**attaché** /ə'tæʃeı/ *n* (*pol*) adido *m*. ~ **case** pasta *f*

**attack** /ə'tæk/ *n* ataque *m* □ *vt/i* atacar. ~**er** *n* atacante *mf*

**attain** /ə'teın/ *vt* atingir. ~**able** *a* atingível. ~**ment** *n* consecução *f*. ~**ments** *npl* conhecimentos *mpl*, talentos *mpl* adquiridos

**attempt** /ə'tempt/ *vt* tentar □ *n* tentativa *f*

**attend** /ə'tend/ *vt/i* atender (**to** a); (*escort*) acompanhar; (*look after*) tratar; (*meeting*) comparecer a; (*school*) freqüentar, (*P*) frequentar. ~**ance** *n* comparecimento *m*; (*times present*) freqüência *f*, (*P*) frequência *f*; (*people*) assistência *f*

**attendant** /ə'tendənt/ *a* concomitante, que acompanha □ *n* empregado *m*; (*servant*) servidor *m*

**attention** /ə'tenʃn/ *n* atenção *f*. ~! (*mil*) sentido! **pay** ~ prestar atenção (**to** a)

**attentive** /ə'tentıv/ *a* atento; (*considerate*) atencioso

**attest** /ə'test/ *vt/i* ~ (**to**) atestar. ~ **a signature** reconhecer uma assinatura. ~**ation** /ætə'steıʃn/ *n* atestação *f*, prova *f*

**attic** /'ætık/ *n* sótão *m*, águafurtada *f*

**attitude** /'ætıtjuːd/ *n* atitude *f*

**attorney** /əˈtɜːnɪ/ n (pl -eys) procurador m; (Amer) advogado m

**attract** /əˈtrækt/ vt atrair. ~ion /-ʃn/ n atração f, (P) atracção f; (charm) atrativo m, (P) atractivo m

**attractive** /əˈtræktɪv/ a atraente. ~ly adv atraentemente, agradavelmente

**attribute**[1] /əˈtrɪbjuːt/ vt ~ to atribuir a

**attribute**[2] /ˈætrɪbjuːt/ n atributo m

**attrition** /əˈtrɪʃn/ n war of ~ guerra f de desgaste

**aubergine** /ˈəʊbəʒiːn/ n berinjela f

**auburn** /ˈɔːbən/ a cor de acaju, castanho-avermelhado

**auction** /ˈɔːkʃn/ n leilão m □ vt leiloar. ~eer /-ˈnɪə(r)/ n leiloeiro m, (P) pregoeiro m

**audaci|ous** /ɔːˈdeɪʃəs/ a audacioso, audaz. ~ty /-ˈæsətɪ/ n audácia f

**audible** /ˈɔːdəbl/ a audível

**audience** /ˈɔːdɪəns/ n auditório m; (theat, radio; interview) audiência f

**audiovisual** /ɔːdɪəʊˈvɪʒʊəl/ a audiovisual

**audit** /ˈɔːdɪt/ n auditoria f □ vt fazer uma auditoria

**audition** /ɔːˈdɪʃn/ n audição f □ vt dar/fazer uma audição

**auditor** /ˈɔːdɪtə(r)/ n perito-contador m, (P) perito-contabilista m

**auditorium** /ɔːdɪˈtɔːrɪəm/ n auditório m

**augment** /ɔːgˈment/ vt/i aumentar (-se)

**augur** /ˈɔːgə(r)/ vi ~ well/ill ser de bom ou mau agouro

**August** /ˈɔːgəst/ n Agosto m

**aunt** /ɑːnt/ n tia f

**au pair** /əʊˈpeə(r)/ n au pair f

**aura** /ˈɔːrə/ n aura f, emanação f

**auspices** /ˈɔːspɪsɪz/ npl under the ~ of sob os auspícios or o patrocínio de

**auspicious** /ɔːˈspɪʃəs/ a auspicioso

**auster|e** /ɔːˈstɪə(r)/ a austero. ~ity /-erətɪ/ n austeridade f

**Australia** /ɒˈstreɪlɪə/ n Austrália f. ~n a & n australiano (m)

**Austria** /ˈɒstrɪə/ n áustria f. ~n a & n austríaco (m)

**authentic** /ɔːˈθentɪk/ a autêntico. ~ity /-ənˈtɪsətɪ/ n autenticidade f

**authenticate** /ɔːˈθentɪkeɪt/ vt autenticar

**author** /ˈɔːθə(r)/ n autor m, autora f. ~ship n (origin) autoria f

**authoritarian** /ɔːθɒrɪˈteərɪən/ a autoritário

**authorit|y** /ɔːˈθɒrətɪ/ n autoridade f; (permission) autorização f. ~ative /-ɪtətɪv/ a (trusted) autorizado; (manner) autoritário

**authoriz|e** /ˈɔːθəraɪz/ vt autorizar. ~ation /-ˈzeɪʃn/ n autorização f

**autistic** /ɔːˈtɪstɪk/ a autista, autístico

**autobiography** /ɔːtəˈbaɪɒgrəfɪ/ n autobiografia f

**autocrat** /ˈɔːtəkræt/ n autocrata mf. ~ic /-ˈkrætɪk/ a autocrático

**autograph** /ˈɔːtəgrɑːf/ n autógrafo m □ vt autografar

**automat|e** /ˈɔːtəmeɪt/ vt automatizar. ~ion /ɔːtəˈmeɪʃn/ n automação f

**automatic** /ɔːtəˈmætɪk/ a automático □ n (car) automático m. ~ally /-klɪ/ adv automaticamente

**automobile** /ˈɔːtəməbiːl/ n (Amer) automóvel m

**autonom|y** /ɔːˈtɒnəmɪ/ n autonomia f. ~ous a autónomo, (P) autônomo

**autopsy** /ˈɔːtɒpsɪ/ n autópsia f

**autumn** /ˈɔːtəm/ n outono m. ~al /-ˈtʌmnəl/ a outonal

**auxiliary** /ɔːgˈzɪlɪərɪ/ a & n auxiliar (mf). ~ verb verbo m auxiliar

**avail** /əˈveɪl/ vt ~ o.s. of servir-se de □ vi (be of use) valer □ n of no ~ inútil. to no ~ sem resultado, em vão

**availab|le** /əˈveɪləbl/ a disponível. ~ility /-ˈbɪlətɪ/ n disponibilidade f

**avalanche** /ˈævəlɑːnʃ/ n avalanche f

**avaric|e** /ˈævərɪs/ n avareza f. ~ious /-ˈrɪʃəs/ a avarento

**avenge** /əˈvendʒ/ vt vingar

**avenue** /ˈævənjuː/ n avenida f; (fig: line of approach) via f

**average** /ˈævərɪdʒ/ n média f □ a médio □ vt tirar a média de; (produce, do) fazer em média □ vi ~ out at dar de média, dar uma média de. on ~ em média

**avers|e** /əˈvɜːs/ a be ~e to ser avesso a. ~ion /-ʃn/ n aversão f, repugnância f

**avert** /əˈvɜːt/ vt (turn away) desviar; (ward off) evitar

**aviary** /ˈeɪvɪərɪ/ n aviário m

**aviation** /eɪvɪˈeɪʃn/ n aviação f

**avid** /ˈævɪd/ a ávido

**avocado** /ævəˈkɑːdəʊ/ n (pl -s) abacate m

**avoid** /əˈvɔɪd/ vt evitar. ~able a que se pode evitar, evitável. ~ance n evitação f

**await** /əˈweɪt/ vt aguardar

**awake** /əˈweɪk/ vt/i (pt awoke, pp awoken) acordar □ a be ~ estar acordado

**awaken** /əˈweɪkən/ vt/i despertar. ~ing n despertar m

**award** /əˈwɔːd/ vt atribuir, conferir; (jur) adjudicar □ n recompensa f, prêmio m, (P) prémio m; (scholarship) bolsa f

**aware** /əˈweə(r)/ a ciente, cônscio. be ~ of estar consciente de or ter con-

ciência de. **become** ~ **of** tomar consciência de. **make sb** ~ **of** sensibili-
zar alg para. **~ness** n consciência f
**away** /ə'weɪ/ adv (at a distance) longe;
(to a distance) para longe; (absent)
fora; (persistently) sem parar; (entirely) completamente. **eight miles**
~ a oito milhas (de distância). **four
days** ~ daí a quatro dias □ a & n ~
**(match)** jogo m fora de casa
**awe** /ɔː/ n assombro m, admiração f
reverente, terror m respeitoso.
**~some** a assombroso. **~struck** a as-
sombrado, aterrado
**awful** /'ɔːfl/ a terrível. **~ly** adv muito, terrivelmente
**awhile** /ə'waɪl/ adv por algum tempo
**awkward** /'ɔːkwəd/ a difícil; (clumsy,
difficult to use) desajeitado, maljei-
toso; (inconvenient) inconveniente;
(embarrassing) embaraçoso; (embarrassed ) embaraçado. **an ~ customer**
(colloq) um preguês perigoso or intratável
**awning** /'ɔːnɪŋ/ n toldo m
**awoke, awoken** /ə'wəʊk, ə'wəʊkən/
see awake
**awry** /ə'raɪ/ adv torto. **go** ~ dar
errado. **be** ~ estar torto
**axe** /æks/ n machado m □ vt (pres p
**axing**) (reduce) cortar; (dismiss) despedir
**axiom** /'æksɪəm/ n axioma m
**axis** /'æksɪs/ n (pl **axes** /-iːz/) eixo m
**axle** /'æksl/ n eixo (de roda) m
**Azores** /ə'zɔːz/ n Açores mpl

# B

**BA** abbr see **Bachelor of Arts**
**babble** /'bæbl/ vi balbuciar; (baby)
palrar; (stream) murmurar □ n balbú-
cio m; (of baby) palrice f; (of stream)
murmúrio m
**baboon** /bə'buːn/ n babuíno m
**baby** /'beɪbɪ/ n bebé m, (P) bebé m. **~
carriage** (Amer) carrinho m de bebê,
(P) bebé. **~-sit** vi tomar conta de
crianças. **~-sitter** n baby-sitter mf,
babá f
**babyish** /'beɪbɪʃ/ a infantil
**bachelor** /'bætʃələ(r)/ n solteiro m.
**B~ of Arts/Science** Bacharel m em
Letras/Ciências
**back** /bæk/ n (of person, hand, chair)
costas fpl; (of animal) dorso m; (of car,
train) parte f traseira; (of house,
room) fundo m; (of coin) reverso m;
(of page) verso m; (football ) beque
m; zagueiro m, (P) defesa m □ a traseiro, posterior; (taxes) em atraso □
adv atrás, para trás; (returned ) de volta □ vt (support) apoiar; (horse) apos-

tar em; (car) (fazer) recuar □ vi
recuar. **at the** ~ **of beyond** em casa
do diabo, no fim do mundo. **~-
bencher** n (pol) deputado m sem
pasta. ~ **down** desistir (from de). ~
**number** número m atrasado. ~ **out**
(of an undertaking etc) fugir (ao combinado etc). ~ **up** (auto) fazer marcha
à ré, (P) atrás; (comput) tirar um
back-up de. **~-up** n apoio m; (comput)
back-up m; (Amer: traffic-jam) engarrafamento m □ a de reserva; (comput)
back-up
**backache** /'bækeɪk/ n dor f nas costas
**backbiting** /'bækbaɪtɪŋ/ n maledicência f
**backbone** /'bækbəʊn/ n espinha f
dorsal
**backdate** /bæk'deɪt/ vt antedatar
**backer** /'bækə(r)/ n (of horse) aposta-
dor m; (of cause) partidário m,
apoiante mf; (comm) patrocinador m,
financiador m
**backfire** /bæk'faɪə(r)/ vi (auto) dar ex-
plosões no tubo de escape; ( fig) sair o
tiro pela culatra
**background** /'bækɡraʊnd/ n (of picture) fundo m, segundo-plano m; (context) contexto m; (environment) meio
m; (experience) formação f
**backhand** /'bækhænd/ n (tennis) esquerda f. **~ed** a com as costas da
mão. **~ed compliment** cumprimento
m ambíguo. **~er** n /-'hændə(r)/ n (sl:
bribe) suborno m, (P) luvas fpl
(colloq)
**backing** /'bækɪŋ/ n apoio m; (comm)
patrocínio m
**backlash** /'bæklæʃ/ n ( fig) reação f
violenta, repercussões fpl
**backlog** /'bæklɒɡ/ n acúmulo m (de
trabalho etc)
**backside** /'bæksaɪd/ n (colloq: buttocks) traseiro m
**backstage** /bæk'steɪdʒ/ a & adv por
detrás dos bastidores
**backstroke** /'bækstrəʊk/ n nado m de
costas
**backtrack** /'bæktræk/ vi ( fig) voltar
atrás
**backward** /'bækwəd/ a retrógrado;
(retarded ) atrasado; (step, look, etc)
para trás
**backwards** /'bækwədz/ adv para
trás; (walk) para trás; ( fall ) de
costas, para trás; (in reverse order)
de trás para diante, às avessas. **go** ~
**and forwards** ir e vir, andar para
trás e para a frente. **know sth** ~ saber alg coisa de trás para a frente
**backwater** /'bækwɔːtə(r)/ n (pej:
place) lugar m atrasado
**bacon** /'beɪkən/ n toucinho m defumado; (in rashers) bacon m

**bacteria** /bæk'tɪərɪə/ *npl* bactérias *fpl*. ~l *a* bacteriano

**bad** /bæd/ *a* (**worse, worst**) mau; (*accident*) grave; (*food*) estragado; (*ill*) doente. **feel ~** sentir-se mal. **~ language** palavrões *mpl*. **~-mannered** *a* mal educado. **~-tempered** *a* mal humorado. **~ly** *adv* mal; (*seriously*) gravemente. **want ~ly** (*desire*) desejar imensamente, ter grande vontade de; (*need*) precisar muito de

**badge** /bædʒ/ *n* emblema *m*; (*policeman's*) crachá *m*, (*P*) distintivo *m*

**badger** /'bædʒə(r)/ *n* texugo *m* □ *vt* atormentar; (*pester*) importunar

**badminton** /'bædmɪntən/ *n* badminton *m*

**baffle** /'bæfl/ *vt* atrapalhar, desconcertar

**bag** /bæg/ *n* saco *m*; (*handbag*) bolsa *f*, carteira *f*. ~s (*luggage*) malas *fpl* □ *vt* (*pt* **bagged**) ensacar; (*colloq: take*) embolsar

**baggage** /'bægɪdʒ/ *n* bagagem *f*

**baggy** /'bægɪ/ *a* (*clothes*) muito largo, bufante

**bagpipes** /'bægpaɪps/ *npl* gaita *f* de foles

**Bahamas** /bə'hɑːməz/ *npl* **the ~** as Bahamas *fpl*

**bail**[1] /beɪl/ *n* fiança *f* □ *vt* pôr em liberdade sob fiança. **be out on ~** estar solto sob fiança

**bail**[2] /beɪl/ *vt* **~ (out)** (*naut*) esgotar, tirar água de

**bailiff** /'beɪlɪf/ *n* (*officer*) oficial *m* de diligências; (*of estate*) feitor *m*

**bait** /beɪt/ *n* isca *f* □ *vt* pôr isca; (*fig*) atormentar (com insultos), atazanar

**bak|e** /beɪk/ *vt/i* cozer (no forno); (*bread, cakes, etc*) assar; (*in the sun*) torrar. **~er** *n* padeiro *m*; (*of cakes*) doceiro *m*. **~ing** *n* cozedura *f*; (*batch*) fornada *f*. **~ing-powder** *n* fermento *m* em pó. **~ing tin** forma *f*

**bakery** /'beɪkərɪ/ *n* padaria *f*; (*cakes*) confeitaria *f*

**balance** /'bæləns/ *n* equilíbrio *m*; (*scales*) balança *f*; (*sum*) saldo *m*; (*comm*) balanço *m*. **~ of power** equilíbrio *m* político. **~ of trade** balança *f* comercial. **~-sheet** *n* balanço *m* □ *vt* equilibrar; (*weigh up*) pesar; (*budget*) equilibrar □ *vi* equilibrar-se. **~d** *a* equilibrado

**balcony** /'bælkənɪ/ *n* balcão *m*; (*in a house*) varanda *f*

**bald** /bɔːld/ *a* (**-er, -est**) calvo, careca; (*tyre*) careca. **~ing** *a* **be ~ing** ficar calvo. **~ly** *adv* a nu e cru, (*P*) secamente. **~ness** *n* calvície *f*

**bale**[1] /beɪl/ *n* (*of straw*) fardo *m*; (*of cotton*) balote *m* □ *vt* enfardar

**bale**[2] /beɪl/ *vi* **~ out** saltar em pára-quedas

**balk** /bɔːk/ *vt* frustrar, contrariar □ *vi* **~ at** assustar-se com, recuar perante

**ball**[1] /bɔːl/ *n* bola *f*. **~-bearing** *n* rolamento *m* de esferas. **~-cock** *n* válvula *f* de depósito de água. **~-point** *n* esferográfica *f*

**ball**[2] /bɔːl/ *n* (*dance*) baile *m*

**ballad** /'bæləd/ *n* balada *f*

**ballast** /'bæləst/ *n* lastro *m*

**ballerina** /bælə'riːnə/ *n* bailarina *f*

**ballet** /'bæleɪ/ *n* balé *m*, (*P*) ballet *m*, bailado *m*

**balloon** /bə'luːn/ *n* balão *m*

**ballot** /'bælət/ *n* escrutínio *m*. **~(-paper)** *n* cédula *f* eleitoral, (*P*) boletim *m* de voto. **~-box** *n* urna *f* □ *vi* (*pt* **balloted**) (*pol*) votar □ *vt* (*members*) consultar por voto secreto

**ballroom** /'bɔːlruːm/ *n* salão *m* de baile

**balm** /bɑːm/ *n* bálsamo *m*. **~y** *a* balsâmico; (*mild*) suave

**balustrade** /bælə'streɪd/ *n* balaustrada *f*

**bamboo** /bæm'buː/ *n* bambu *m*

**ban** /bæn/ *vt* (*pt* **banned**) banir. **~ from** proibir de □ *n* proibição *f*

**banal** /bə'nɑːl/ *a* banal. **~ity** /-ælətɪ/ *n* banalidade *f*

**banana** /bə'nɑːnə/ *n* banana *f*

**band** /bænd/ *n* (*for fastening*) cinta *f*, faixa *f*; (*strip*) tira *f*, banda *f*; (*mus: mil*) banda *f*; (*mus: dance, jazz*) conjunto *m*; (*group*) bando *m* □ *vi* **~ together** juntar-se

**bandage** /'bændɪdʒ/ *n* atadura *f*, (*P*) ligadura *f* □ *vt* ligar

**bandit** /'bændɪt/ *n* bandido *m*

**bandstand** /'bændstænd/ *n* coreto *m*

**bandwagon** /'bændwægən/ *n* **climb on the ~** (*fig*) apanhar o trem

**bandy** /'bændɪ/ *vt* trocar. **~ a story about** espalhar uma história

**bandy-legged** /'bændɪlegd/ *a* cambaio, de pernas tortas

**bang** /bæŋ/ *n* (*blow*) pancada *f*; (*loud noise*) estouro *m*, estrondo *m*; (*of gun*) detonação *f* □ *vt/i* (*hit, shut*) bater □ *vi* explodir □ *int* pum. **~ in the middle** jogar no meio. **shut the door with a ~** bater (com) a porta

**banger** /'bæŋə(r)/ *n* (*firework*) bomba *f*; (*sl: sausage*) salsicha *f*, (*old*) **~** (*sl: car*) calhambeque *m* (*colloq*)

**bangle** /'bæŋgl/ *n* pulseira *f*, bracelete *m*

**banish** /'bænɪʃ/ *vt* banir, desterrar

**banisters** /'bænɪstəz/ *npl* corrimão *m*

**banjo** /'bændʒəʊ/ *pl* (**-os**) banjo *m*

**bank**[1] /bæŋk/ *n* (*of river*) margem *f*; (*of earth*) talude *m*; (*of sand*) banco *m*

□ *vt* amontoar □ *vi* (*aviat*) inclinar-se numa curva

**bank**[2] /bæŋk/ *n* (*comm*) banco *m* □ *vt* depositar no banco. ~ **account** conta *f* bancária. ~ **holiday** feriado *m* nacional. ~ **on** contar com. ~ **rate** taxa *f* bancária. ~ **with** ter conta em

**bank|er** /'bæŋkə(r)/ *n* banqueiro *m*. ~**ing** /-ɪŋ/ *n* operações *fpl* bancárias; (*career*) carreira *f* bancária, banca *f*

**banknote** /'bæŋknəʊt/ *n* nota *f* de banco

**bankrupt** /'bæŋkrʌpt/ *a* & *n* falido (*m*). go ~ falir □ *vt* levar à falência. ~**cy** *n* falência *f*, bancarrota *f*

**banner** /'bænə(r)/ *n* bandeira *f*, estandarte *m*

**banns** /bænz/ *npl* proclamas *mpl*, (P) banhos *mpl*

**banquet** /'bæŋkwɪt/ *n* banquete *m*

**banter** /'bæntə(r)/ *n* gracejo *m*, brincadeira *f* □ *vi* gracejar, brincar

**baptism** /'bæptɪzəm/ *n* batismo *m*, (P) baptismo *m*

**Baptist** /'bæptɪst/ *n* batista *mf*, (P) baptista *mf*

**baptize** /bæp'taɪz/ *vt* batizar, (P) baptizar

**bar** /ba:(r)/ *n* (*of chocolate*) tablette *f*, barra *f*; (*of metal, soap, sand etc*) barra *f*; (*of door, window*) tranca *f*; (*in pub*) bar *m*; (*counter*) balcão *m*, bar *m*; (*mus*) barra *f* de compasso; (*fig: obstacle*) barreira *f*; (*in lawcourt*) teia *f*. **the B~** a advocacia *f* □ *vt* (*pt* **barred**) (*obstruct*) barrar; (*prohibit*) proibir (**from** de); (*exclude*) excluir; (*door, window*) trancar □ *prep* salvo, exceto, (P) excepto. ~ **none** sem exceção, (P) excepção. ~ **code** código *m* de barra. **behind** ~**s** na cadeia

**Barbados** /ba:'beɪdɒs/ *n* Barbados *mpl*

**barbarian** /ba:'beərɪən/ *n* bárbaro *m*

**barbari|c** /ba:'bærɪk/ *a* bárbaro. ~**ty** /-ətɪ/ *n* barbaridade *f*

**barbarous** /'ba:bərəs/ *a* bárbaro

**barbecue** /'ba:bɪkju:/ *n* (*grill*) churrasqueira *f*; (*occasion, food*) churrasco *m* □ *vt* assar

**barbed** /ba:bd/ *a* ~ **wire** arame *m* farpado

**barber** /'ba:bə(r)/ *n* barbeiro *m*

**barbiturate** /ba:'bɪtjʊərət/ *n* barbitúrico *m*

**bare** /beə(r)/ *a* (**-er, -est**) nu; (*room*) vazio; (*mere*) mero □ *vt* pôr à mostra, pôr a nu, descobrir

**bareback** /'beəbæk/ *adv* em pêlo

**barefaced** /'beəfeɪst/ *a* descarado

**barefoot** /'beə(r)fʊt/ *adv* descalço

**barely** /'beəlɪ/ *adv* apenas, mal

**bargain** /'ba:gɪn/ *n* (*deal*) negócio *m*; (*good buy*) pechincha *f* □ *vi* negociar; (*haggle*) regatear. ~ **esperar for**

**barge** /ba:dʒ/ *n* barcaça *f* □ *vi* ~ **in** interromper (despropositadamente); (*into room*) irromper

**bark**[1] /ba:k/ *n* (*of tree*) casca *f*

**bark**[2] /ba:k/ *n* (*of dog*) latido *m* □ *vi* latir. **his ~ is worse than his bite** cão que ladra não morde

**barley** /'ba:lɪ/ *n* cevada *f*. ~ **sugar** *n* açúcar *m* de cevada. ~ **water** *n* água *f* de cevada

**barmaid** /'ba:meɪd/ *n* empregada *f* de bar

**barman** /'ba:mən/ *n* (*pl* **-men**) barman *m*, empregado *m* de bar

**barmy** /'ba:mɪ/ *a* (*sl*) maluco

**barn** /ba:n/ *n* celeiro *m*

**barometer** /bə'rɒmɪtə(r)/ *n* barômetro *m*, (P) barómetro *m*

**baron** /'bærən/ *n* barão *m*. ~**ess** *n* baronesa *f*

**baroque** /bə'rɒk/ *a* & *n* barroco (*m*)

**barracks** /'bærəks/ *n* quartel *m*, caserna *f*

**barrage** /'bæra:ʒ/ *n* barragem *f*; (*fig*) enxurrada *f*; (*mil*) fogo *m* de barragem

**barrel** /'bærəl/ *n* (*of oil, wine*) barril *m*; (*of gun*) cano *m*. ~**-organ** *n* realejo *m*

**barren** /'bærən/ *a* estéril; (*soil*) árido, estéril

**barricade** /bærɪ'keɪd/ *n* barricada *f* □ *vt* barricar

**barrier** /'bærɪə(r)/ *n* barreira *f*; (*hindrance*) entrave *m*, barreira *f*

**barring** /'ba:rɪŋ/ *prep* salvo, exceto, (P) excepto

**barrister** /'bærɪstə(r)/ *n* advogado *m*

**barrow** /'bærəʊ/ *n* carrinho *m* de mão

**barter** /'ba:tə(r)/ *n* troca *f* □ *vt* trocar

**base** /beɪs/ *n* base *f* □ *vt* basear (**on** em) □ *a* baixo, ignóbil. ~**less** *a* infundado

**baseball** /'beɪsbɔ:l/ *n* beisebol *m*

**basement** /'beɪsmənt/ *n* porão *m*, (P) cave *f*

**bash** /bæʃ/ *vt* bater com violência □ *n* pancada *f* forte. **have a ~ at** (*sl*) experimentar

**bashful** /'bæʃfl/ *a* tímido

**basic** /'beɪsɪk/ *a* básico, elementar, fundamental. ~**ally** *adv* basicamente, no fundo

**basil** /'bæzl/ *n* mangericão *m*

**basin** /'beɪsn/ *n* bacia *f*; (*for food*) tigela *f*; (*naut*) ante-doca *f*; (*for washing*) pia *f*

**basis** /'beɪsɪs/ *n* (*pl* **bases** /-si:z/) base *f*

**bask** /ba:sk/ *vi* ~ **in the sun** apanhar sol

**basket** /'ba:skɪt/ *n* cesto *m*

**basketball** /'ba:skɪtbɔːl/ n basquete(-bol) m

**Basque** /ba:sk/ a & n basco (m)

**bass**¹ /bæs/ n (pl **bass**) (fish) perca f

**bass**² /beɪs/ a (mus) grave □ n (pl **basses**) (mus) baixo m

**bassoon** /bə'suːn/ n fagote m

**bastard** /'ba:stəd/ n (illegitimate child) bastardo m; (sl: pej) safado (sl) m; (colloq: not pej) cara (colloq) m

**baste** /beɪst/ vt (culin) regar (com molho)

**bastion** /'bæstɪən/ n bastião m, baluarte m

**bat**¹ /bæt/ n (cricket) pá f, (baseball) bastão m; (table tennis) rafuete f □ vt/i (pt **batted**) bater (em). **without ~ting an eyelid** sem pestanejar

**bat**² /bæt/ n (zool) morcego m

**batch** /bætʃ/ n (loaves) fornada f; (people) monte m; (goods) remessa f; (papers, letters etc) batelada f, monte m

**bated** /'beɪtɪd/ a **with ~ breath** com a respiração em suspenso, com a respiração suspensa

**bath** /ba:θ/ n (pl ~s /ba:ðz/) banho m; (tub) banheira f. **~s** (washing) banho m público; (swimming) piscina f □ vt dar banho a □ vi tomar banho

**bathe** /beɪð/ vt dar banho em; (wound) limpar □ vi tomar banho (de mar) □ n banho m (de mar). **~r** /-ə(r)/ n banhista mf

**bathing** /'beɪðɪŋ/ n banho m de mar. **~-costume/-suit** n traje m de banho, (P) fato m de banho

**bathrobe** /'ba:θrəʊb/ n (Amer) roupão m

**bathroom** /'ba:θruːm/ n banheiro m, (P) casa f de banho

**baton** /'bætən/ n (mus) batuta f; (policeman's) cassetete m; (mil) bastão m

**battalion** /bə'tælɪən/ n batalhão m

**batter** /'bætə(r)/ vt bater, espancar, maltratar □ n (culin: for cakes) massa f de bolos; (culin: for frying) massa f de empanar. **~ed** a (car, pan) amassado; (child, wife) maltratado, espancado. **~ing** n **take a ~ing** levar pancada or uma surra

**battery** /'bætərɪ/ n (mil, auto) bateria f, (electr) pilha f

**battle** /'bætl/ n batalha f; (fig) luta f □ vi combater, batalhar, lutar

**battlefield** /'bætlfiːld/ n campo m de batalha

**battlements** /'bætlmənts/ npl ameias fpl

**battleship** /'bætlʃɪp/ n couraçado m

**baulk** /bɔːlk/ vt/i = **balk**

**bawdy** /'bɔːdɪ/ a (-ier, -iest) obsceno, indecente

**bawl** /bɔːl/ vt/i berrar

**bay**¹ /beɪ/ n (bot) loureiro m

**bay**² /beɪ/ n (geog) baía f. **~ window** janela f saliente

**bay**³ /beɪ/ n (bark) latido m □ vi latir. **at ~** (animal; fig) cercado, (P) em apuros. **keep at ~** manter à distância

**bayonet** /'beɪənɪt/ n baioneta f

**bazaar** /bə'za:(r)/ n bazar m

**BC** abbr (before Christ) a C

**be** /biː/ vi (pres **am, are, is**; pt **was, were**; pp **been**) (permanent quality/place) ser; (temporary place/state) estar; (become) ficar. **~ hot/right** etc ter calor/razão etc. **he's 30** (age) tem 30 anos. **it's fine/cold** etc (weather) faz bom tempo/frio etc. **how are you?** (health) como está? **I'm a doctor — are you?** eu sou médico — é mesmo? **it's pretty, isn't it?** é bonito, não é? **he is to come** (must) ele deve vir. **how much is it?** (cost) quanto é? **~ reading eating** etc estar lendo/comendo etc. **the money was found** o dinheiro foi encontrado. **have been to** ter ido a, ter estado em

**beach** /biːtʃ/ n praia f

**beacon** /'biːkən/ n farol m; (marker) baliza f

**bead** /biːd/ n conta f. **~ of sweat** gota f de suor

**beak** /biːk/ n bico m

**beaker** /'biːkə(r)/ n copo m de plástico com bico; (in lab) proveta f

**beam** /biːm/ n (of wood) trave f, viga f; (of light) raio m; (of torch) feixe m de luz □ vt/i (radiate) irradiar; (fig) sorrir radiante. **~ing** a radiante

**bean** /biːn/ n feijão m. **broad ~** fava f. **coffee ~s** café m em grão. **runner ~** feijão m verde

**bear**¹ /beə(r)/ n urso m

**bear**² /beə(r)/ vt (pt **bore**, pp **borne**) sustentar, suportar; (endure) agüentar, (P) aguentar; suportar; (child) dar à luz. **~ in mind** ter em mente, lembrar. **~ left** virar à esquerda. **~ on** relacionar-se com, ter a ver com. **~ out** confirmar. **~ up!** coragem! **~able** a tolerável, suportável. **~er** n portador m

**beard** /bɪəd/ n barba f. **~ed** a barbado, com barba

**bearing** /'beərɪŋ/ n (manner) porte m; (relevance) relação f; (naut) marcação f. **get one's ~s** orientar-se

**beast** /biːst/ n (animal, person) besta f, animal m; (in fables) fera f. **~ of burden** besta f de carga

**beat** /biːt/ vt/i (pt **beat**, pp **beaten**) bater □ n (med) batimento m; (mus) compasso m, ritmo m; (of drum) toque m; (of policeman) ronda f, (P) giro m. **~ about the bush** estar com rodeios. **~ a retreat** bater em retirada. **~ it**

*sl: go away*) pôr-se a andar. **it ~s me** (*colloq*) não consigo entender. **~ up** espancar. **~er** *n* (*culin*) batedeira *f*. **~ing** *n* sova *f*

**eautician** /bjuːˈtɪʃn/ *n* esteticista *mf*
**eautiful** /ˈbjuːtɪfl/ *a* belo, lindo. **~ly** *adv* lindamente
**eautify** /ˈbjuːtɪfaɪ/ *vt* embelezar
**eauty** /ˈbjuːtɪ/ *n* beleza *f*. **~ parlour** instituto *m* de beleza. **~ spot** sinal *m* no rosto, mosca *f*; (*place*) local *m* pitoresco
**eaver** /ˈbiːvə(r)/ *n* castor *m*
**ecame** /bɪˈkeɪm/ *see* become
**ecause** /bɪˈkɒz/ *conj* porque □ *adv* **~** of por causa de
**eckon** /ˈbekən/ *vt/i* **~ (to)** fazer sinal (para)
**ecome** /bɪˈkʌm/ *vt/i* (*pt* became, *pp* become) tornar-se; (*befit*) ficar bem a. **what has ~ of her?** que é feito dela?
**ecoming** /bɪˈkʌmɪŋ/ *a* que fica bem, apropriado
**ed** /bed/ *n* cama *f*; (*layer*) camada *f*; (*of sea*) fundo *m*; (*of river*) leito *m*; (*of flowers*) canteiro *m* □ *vt/i* (*pt* bedded) **~ down** ir deitar-se. **~** in plantar. **~ and breakfast (b & b)** quarto *m* com café da manhã. **~-sit(ter)** *n* (*colloq*) mixto *m* de quarto e sala. **go to ~** ir para cama. **in ~** na cama. **~ding** *n* roupa *f* de cama
**edclothes** /ˈbedkləʊðz/ *n* roupa *f* de cama
**edlam** /ˈbedləm/ *n* confusão *f*, balbúrdia *f*
**edraggled** /bɪˈdrægld/ *a* (*wet*) molhado; (*untidy*) desarrumado; (*dishevelled*) desgrenhado
**edridden** /ˈbedrɪdn/ *a* preso ao leito, doente de cama
**edroom** /ˈbedruːm/ *n* quarto *m* de dormir
**edside** /ˈbedsaɪd/ *n* cabeceira *f*. **~ manner** (*doctor's*) modos *mpl* que inspiram confiança
**edspread** /ˈbedspred/ *n* colcha *f*
**edtime** /ˈbedtaɪm/ *n* hora *f* de deitar, hora *f* de ir para a cama
**ee** /biː/ *n* abelha *f*. **make a ~-line for** ir direto a
**eech** /biːtʃ/ *n* faia *f*
**eef** /biːf/ *n* carne *f* de vaca
**eefburger** /ˈbiːfbɜːgə(r)/ *n* hambúrguer *m*
**eehive** /ˈbiːhaɪv/ *n* colméia *f*
**een** /biːn/ *see* be
**eer** /bɪə(r)/ *n* cerveja *f*
**eet** /biːt/ *n* beterraba *f*
**eetle** /ˈbiːtl/ *n* escaravelho *m*
**eetroot** /ˈbiːtruːt/ *n* (raiz de) beterraba *f*
**efore** /bɪˈfɔː(r)/ *prep* (*time*) antes de; (*place*) em frente de □ *adv* antes; (*al-*

*ready*) já □ *conj* antes que. **~ leaving** antes de partir. **~ he leaves** antes que ele parta, antes de ele partir
**beforehand** /bɪˈfɔːhænd/ *adv* de antemão, antecipadamente
**befriend** /bɪˈfrend/ *vt* tornar-se amigo de; (*be helpful to*) auxiliar
**beg** /beg/ *vt/i* (*pt* begged) mendigar; (*entreat*) suplicar. **~ sb's pardon** pedir desculpa a alg. **~ the question** fazer uma petição de princípio. **it's going ~ging** está sobrando
**began** /bɪˈgæn/ *see* begin
**beggar** /ˈbegə(r)/ *n* mendigo *m*, pedinte *mf*; (*colloq: person*) cara (*colloq*) *m*
**begin** /bɪˈgɪn/ *vt/i* (*pt* began, *pp* begun, *pres p* beginning) começar, principiar. **~ner** *n* principiante *mf*. **~ning** *n* começo *m*, princípio *m*
**begrudge** /bɪˈgrʌdʒ/ *vt* ter inveja de; (*give*) dar de má vontade. **~ doing** fazer de má vontade *or* a contragosto
**beguile** /bɪˈgaɪl/ *vt* enganar
**begun** /bɪˈgʌn/ *see* begin
**behalf** /bɪˈhaːf/ *n* **on ~ of** em nome de; (*in the interest of* ) em favor de
**behave** /bɪˈheɪv/ *vi* portar-se. **~ (o.s.)** portar-se bem
**behaviour** /bɪˈheɪvjə(r)/ *n* conduta *f*, comportamento *m*
**behead** /bɪˈhed/ *vt* decapitar
**behind** /bɪˈhaɪnd/ *prep* atrás de □ *adv* atrás; (*late*) com atraso □ *n* (*colloq: buttocks*) traseiro (*colloq*) *m*. **~ the times** antiquado, retrógrado. **leave ~** deixar para trás
**behold** /bɪˈhəʊld/ *vt* (*pt* beheld) (*old use*) ver
**beholden** /bɪˈhəʊldən/ *a* em dívida (**to** para com)
**beige** /beɪʒ/ *a* & *n* bege (*m*), (*P*) beige (*m*)
**being** /ˈbiːɪŋ/ *n* ser *m*. **bring into ~** criar. **come into ~** nascer, originar-se
**belated** /bɪˈleɪtɪd/ *a* tardio, atrasado
**belch** /beltʃ/ *vi* arrotar □ *vt* **~ out** (*smoke*) vomitar, lançar □ *n* arroto *m*
**belfry** /ˈbelfrɪ/ *n* campanário *m*
**Belgi|um** /ˈbeldʒəm/ *n* Bélgica *f*. **~an** *a* & *n* belga (*mf* )
**belief** /bɪˈliːf/ *n* crença *f*; (*trust*) confiança *f*; (*opinion*) convicção *f*
**believ|e** /bɪˈliːv/ *vt/i* acreditar. **~e in** acreditar em. **~able** *a* crível. **~er** /-ə(r)/ *n* crente *mf*
**belittle** /bɪˈlɪtl/ *vt* depreciar
**bell** /bel/ *n* sino *m*; (*small*) sineta *f*; (*on door, of phone*) campainha *f*; (*on cat, toy*) guizo *m*
**belligerent** /bɪˈlɪdʒərənt/ *a* & *n* beligerante (*mf* )

**bellow** /'beləʊ/ vt/i berrar, bramir. ~ out rugir

**bellows** /'beləʊz/ npl fole m

**belly** /'belɪ/ n barriga f, ventre m. ~-ache n dor f de barriga

**bellyful** /'belɪfʊl/ n have a ~ estar com a barriga cheia

**belong** /bɪ'lɒŋ/ vi ~ (to) pertencer (a); (club) ser sócio (de)

**belongings** /bɪ'lɒŋɪŋz/ npl pertences mpl. personal ~ objetos mpl de uso pessoal

**beloved** /bɪ'lʌvɪd/ a & n amado (m)

**below** /bɪ'ləʊ/ prep abaixo de, debaixo de □ adv abaixo, em baixo; (on page) abaixo

**belt** /belt/ n cinto m; (techn) correia f; (fig) zona f □ vt (sl: hit) zurzir □ vi (sl: rush) safar-se

**bemused** /bɪ'mju:zd/ a estonteado, confuso; (thoughtful) pensativo

**bench** /bentʃ/ n banco m; (seat, working-table) bancada f. the ~ (jur) os magistrados (no tribunal)

**bend** /bend/ vt/i (pt & pp bent) curvar(-se); (arm, leg) dobrar; (road, river) fazer uma curva, virar □ n curva f. ~ over debruçar-se or inclinar-se sobre

**beneath** /bɪ'ni:θ/ prep abaixo de, debaixo de; (fig) abaixo de □ adv debaixo, em baixo

**benediction** /benɪ'dɪkʃn/ n benção f

**benefactor** /'benɪfæktə(r)/ n benfeitor m

**beneficial** /benɪ'fɪʃl/ a benéfico, proveitoso

**benefit** /'benɪfɪt/ n (advantage, performance) benefício m; (profit) proveito m; (allowance) subsídio m □ vt/i (pt benefited, pres p benefiting) (be useful to) beneficiar (by de); (do good to) beneficiar, fazer bem a; (receive benefit) lucrar, ganhar (by, from com)

**beneficiary** /benɪ'fɪʃərɪ/ n beneficiário m

**benevolen|t** /bɪ'nevələnt/ a benevolente. ~ce n benevolência f

**benign** /bɪ'naɪn/ a (incl med) benigno

**bent** /bent/ see **bend** □ n (for para) (skill) aptidão f, jeito m; (liking) queda f □ a curvado; (twisted) torcido; (sl: dishonest) desonesto. ~ on decidido a

**bequeath** /bɪ'kwi:ð/ vt legar

**bequest** /bɪ'kwest/ n legado m

**bereave|d** /bɪ'ri:vd/ a the ~d wife/ etc a esposa/etc do falecido. the ~d family a família enlutada. ~ment n luto m

**bereft** /bɪ'reft/ a ~ of privado de

**beret** /'bereɪ/ n boina f

**Bermuda** /bə'mju:də/ n Bermudas fpl

**berry** /'berɪ/ n baga f

**berserk** /bə'sɜ:k/ a go ~ ficar louco de raiva, perder a cabeça

**berth** /bɜ:θ/ n (in ship) beliche m; (in train) couchette f; (anchorage) ancoradouro m □ vi atracar. give a wide ~ to passar ao largo, (P) de largo

**beside** /bɪ'saɪd/ prep ao lado de, junto de. ~ o.s. fora de si. be ~ the point não ter nada a ver com o assunto, não vir ao caso

**besides** /bɪ'saɪdz/ prep além de; (except) fora, salvo □ adv além disso

**besiege** /bɪ'si:dʒ/ vt sitiar, cercar. ~ with assediar

**best** /best/ a & n (the) ~ (o/a) melhor (mf) □ adv melhor. ~ man padrinho m de casamento. at (the) ~ na melhor das hipóteses. do one's ~ fazer o (melhor) que se pode. make the ~ of tirar o melhor partido de. the ~ part of a maior parte de. to the ~ of my knowledge que eu saiba

**bestow** /bɪ'stəʊ/ vt conferir. ~ praise fazer or tecer elogios

**best-seller** /best'selə(r)/ n best-seller m

**bet** /bet/ n aposta f □ vt/i (pt bet or betted) apostar (on em)

**betray** /bɪ'treɪ/ vt trair. ~al n traição f

**better** /'betə(r)/ a & adv melhor □ vt melhorar □ n our ~s os nossos superiores mpl. all the ~ tanto melhor. ~ off (richer) mais rico. he's ~ off at home é melhor para ele ficar em casa. I'd ~ go é melhor irme embora. the ~ part of it a maior parte disso. get ~ melhorar. get the ~ of sb levar a melhor em relação a alg

**betting-shop** /'betɪŋʃɒp/ n agência f de apostas

**between** /bɪ'twi:n/ prep entre □ adv in ~ no meio, no intervalo. ~ you and me aqui entre nós

**beverage** /'bevərɪdʒ/ n bebida f

**beware** /bɪ'weə(r)/ vi acautelar-se (of com), tomar cuidado (of com)

**bewilder** /bɪ'wɪldə(r)/ vt desorientar. ~ment n desorientação f, confusão f

**bewitch** /bɪ'wɪtʃ/ vt encantar, cativar

**beyond** /bɪ'jɒnd/ prep além de; (doubt, reach) fora de □ adv além. it's ~ me isso ultrapassa-me. he lives ~ his means ele vive acima dos seus meios

**bias** /'baɪəs/ n parcialidade f, (pej: prejudice) preconceito m; (sewing) viés m □ vt (pt biased) influenciar. ~ed a parcial. ~ed against de prevenção contra, (P) de pé atrás contra

**bib** /bɪb/ n babeiro m, babette m

**Bible** /'baɪbl/ n Bíblia f

**biblical** /'bɪblɪkl/ a bíblico

**bibliography** /bɪblɪ'ɒɡrəfɪ/ n bibliografia f
**bicarbonate** /baɪ'ka:bənət/ n ~ **of soda** bicarbonato m de soda
**biceps** /'baɪseps/ n bíceps m
**bicker** /'bɪkə(r)/ vi questionar, discutir
**bicycle** /'baɪsɪkl/ n bicicleta f □ vi andar de bicicleta
**bid** /bɪd/ n oferta f, lance m; (attempt) tentativa f □ vt/i (pt bid, pres p bidding) fazer uma oferta, lançar, oferecer como lance. ~**der** n licitante mf. **the highest** ~**der** quem dá or oferece mais
**bide** /baɪd/ vt ~ **one's time** esperar pelo bom momento
**bidet** /'bi:deɪ/ n bidé m, (P) bidé m
**biennial** /baɪ'enɪəl/ a bienal
**bifocals** /baɪ'fəʊklz/ npl óculos mpl bifocais
**big** /bɪɡ/ a (**bigger**, **biggest**) grande; (sl: generous) generoso □ adv (colloq) em grande. ~**-headed** a pretensioso, convencido. ~ **shot** (sl) manda-chuva m. **talk** ~ gabar-se (colloq). **think** ~ (colloq) ter grandes planos
**bigam|y** /'bɪɡəmɪ/ n bigamia f. ~**ist** n bígamo m. ~**ous** a bígamo
**bigot** /'bɪɡət/ n fanático m, intolerante mf. ~**ed** a fanático, intolerante. ~**ry** n fanatismo m, intolerância f
**bigwig** /'bɪɡwɪɡ/ n (colloq) mandachuva m
**bike** /baɪk/ n (colloq) bicicleta f
**bikini** /bɪ'ki:nɪ/ n (pl -**is**) biquíni m
**bilberry** /'bɪlbərɪ/ n arando m
**bile** /baɪl/ n bílis f
**bilingual** /baɪ'lɪŋɡwəl/ a bilíngue
**bilious** /'bɪlɪəs/ a bilioso
**bill**[1] /bɪl/ n (invoice) fatura f, (P) factura f; (in restaurant) conta f; (pol) projeto m, (P) projecto m de lei; (Amer: banknote) nota f de banco; (poster) cartaz m □ vt faturar, (P) facturar; (theatre) anunciar, pôr no programa. ~ **of exchange** letra f de câmbio. ~ **sb for** apresentar a alg a conta de
**bill**[2] /bɪl/ n (of bird) bico m
**billiards** /'bɪlɪədz/ n bilhar m
**billion** /'bɪlɪən/ n (10⁹) mil milhões; (10¹²) um milhão de milhões
**bin** /bɪn/ n (for storage) caixa f, lata f; (for rubbish) lata f do lixo, (P) caixote m
**bind** /baɪnd/ vt (pt **bound**) (tie) atar; (book) encadernar; (jur) obrigar; (cover the edge of) debruar □ n (sl: bore) chatice f (sl). **be** ~**ing on** ser obrigatório para
**binding** /'baɪndɪŋ/ n encadernação f; (braid) debrum m
**binge** /bɪndʒ/ n (sl) **go on a** ~ cair na farra; (overeat) empanturrar-se

**bingo** /'bɪŋɡəʊ/ n bingo m □ int acertei!
**binoculars** /bɪ'nɒkjʊləz/ npl binóculo m
**biochemistry** /baɪəʊ'kemɪstrɪ/ n bioquímica f
**biodegradable** /baɪəʊdɪ'ɡreɪdəbl/ a biodegradável
**biograph|y** /baɪ'ɒɡrəfɪ/ n biografia f. ~**er** n biógrafo m
**biolog|y** /baɪ'ɒlədʒɪ/ n biologia f. ~**ical** /-ə'lɒdʒɪkl/ a biológico. ~**ist** n biólogo m
**biopsy** /'baɪɒpsɪ/ n biópsia f
**birch** /bɜ:tʃ/ n (tree) bétula f; (whip) vara f de vidoeiro
**bird** /bɜ:d/ n ave f, pássaro m; (sl: girl) garota f (colloq). ~ **sanctuary** refúgio m ornitológico. ~**-watcher** n ornitófilo m
**Biro** /'baɪərəʊ/ n (pl -**os**) (caneta) esferográfica f, Bic f
**birth** /bɜ:θ/ n nascimento m. ~ **certificate** certidão f de nascimento. ~ **control/rate** controle m/índice m de natalidade. ~**-place** n lugar m de nascimento. **give** ~ **to** dar à luz
**birthday** /'bɜ:θdeɪ/ n aniversário m, (P) dia m de anos. **his** ~ **is on 9 July** ele faz anos no dia 9 de julho
**birthmark** /'bɜ:θma:k/ n sinal m
**biscuit** /'bɪskɪt/ n biscoito m, bolacha f
**bisect** /baɪ'sekt/ vt dividir ao meio
**bishop** /'bɪʃəp/ n bispo m
**bit**[1] /bɪt/ n (small piece, short time) pedaço m, bocado m; (of bridle) freio m; (of tool) broca f. **a** ~ um pouco
**bit**[2] /bɪt/ see **bite**
**bitch** /bɪtʃ/ n cadela f; (sl: woman) peste f (fig), cadela f (sl) □ vt/i (colloq: criticize) malhar, (P) cortar (em) (colloq); (colloq: grumble) resmungar. ~**y** a (colloq) maldoso
**bite** /baɪt/ vt/i (pt **bit**, pp **bitten**) morder; (insect) picar □ n mordida f; (sting) picada f. **have a** ~ (**to eat**) comer qualquer coisa
**biting** /'baɪtɪŋ/ a cortante
**bitter** /'bɪtə(r)/ a amargo; (weather) glacial. ~**ly** adv amargamente. **it's** ~**ly cold** está um frio de rachar. ~**ness** n amargura f; (resentment) ressentimento m
**bizarre** /bɪ'za:(r)/ a bizarro
**black** /blæk/ a (-**er**, -**est**) negro, preto □ n negro m, preto m. **a B**~ (person) um preto, um negro □ vt enegrecer; (goods) boicotar. ~ **and blue** coberto de nódoas negras. ~ **coffee** café m (sem leite). ~ **eye** olho m negro. ~ **ice** gelo m negro sobre o asfalto. ~ **market** mercado m negro. ~ **spot** n (place) local m perigoso, ponto m negro

**blackberry** /'blækbərɪ/ n amora f silvestre

**blackbird** /'blækbɜːd/ n melro m

**blackboard** /'blækbɔːd/ n quadro m preto

**blackcurrant** /'blækkʌrənt/ n groselha f negra

**blacken** /'blækən/ vt/i escurecer. ~ sb's name difamar, denegrir

**blackleg** /'blækleg/ n fura-greves m

**blacklist** /'blæklɪst/ n lista f negra □ vt pôr na lista negra

**blackmail** /'blækmeɪl/ n chantagem f □ vt fazer chantagem. ~er n chantagista mf

**blackout** /'blækaʊt/ n (wartime) blecaute m; (med) desmaio m; (electr) falta f de corrente; (theatr) apagar m de luzes

**blacksmith** /'blæksmɪθ/ n ferreiro m

**bladder** /'blædə(r)/ n bexiga f

**blade** /bleɪd/ n lâmina f; (of oar, propeller) pá f; (of grass) ervinha f, folhinha f de erva

**blame** /bleɪm/ vt culpar □ n culpa f. be to ~ ser o culpado. ~less a irrepreensível; (innocent) inocente

**bland** /blænd/ a (-er, -est) (of manner) suave; (mild) brando; (insipid) insípido

**blank** /blæŋk/ a (space, cheque) em branco; (look) vago; (wall) nu □ n espaço m em branco; (cartridge) cartucho m sem bala

**blanket** /'blæŋkɪt/ n cobertor m; (fig) manto m □ vt (pt blanketed) cobrir com cobertor; (cover thickly) encobrir, recobrir. wet ~ desmancha-prazeres mf

**blare** /bleə(r)/ vt/i ressoar, atroar □ n clangor m; (of horn) buzinar m

**blasé** /'blɑːzeɪ/ a blasé

**blaspheme** /blæs'fiːm/ vt/i blasfemar

**blasphem|y** /'blæsfəmɪ/ n blasfêmia f, (P) blasfémia f. ~ous a blasfemo

**blast** /blɑːst/ n (gust) rajada f; (sound) som m; (explosion) explosão f □ vt dinamitar. ~! droga! ~ed a maldito. ~-furnace n alto forno m. ~-off n (of missile) lançamento m, início m de combustão

**blatant** /'bleɪtnt/ a flagrante; (shameless) descarado

**blaze** /bleɪz/ n chamas fpl; (light) clarão m; (outburst) explosão f □ vi arder; (shine) resplandecer, brilhar. ~ a trail abrir o caminho, ser pioneiro

**blazer** /'bleɪzə(r)/ n blazer m

**bleach** /bliːtʃ/ n descolorante, descorante m; (household) água f sanitária □ vt/i branquear; (hair) oxigenar

**bleak** /bliːk/ a (-er, -est) (place) desolado; (chilly) frio; (fig) desanimador

**bleary-eyed** /'blɪərɪaɪd/ a com olhos injetados

**bleat** /bliːt/ n balido m □ vi balir

**bleed** /bliːd/ vt/i (pt bled) sangrar

**bleep** /bliːp/ n bip m. ~er n bip m

**blemish** /'blemɪʃ/ n defeito m; (on reputation) mancha f □ vt manchar

**blend** /blend/ vt/i misturar(-se); (go well together) combinar-se □ n mistura f. ~er n (culin) liquidificador m

**bless** /bles/ vt abençoar. be ~ed with ter a felicidade de ter. ~ing n bênção f; (thing one is glad of) felicidade f. it's a ~ing in disguise há males que vêm para bem

**blessed** /'blesɪd/ a bem-aventurado; (colloq: cursed) maldito

**blew** /bluː/ see blow

**blight** /blaɪt/ n doença f de plantas; (fig) influência f maligna □ vt arruinar, frustrar

**blind** /blaɪnd/ a cego □ vt cegar □ n (on window) persiana f; (deception) ardil m. ~ alley (incl fig) beco m sem saída. ~ man/woman cego m/cega f. be ~ to não ver. turn a ~ eye to fingir não ver, fechar os olhos a. ~ly adv às cegas. ~ness n cegueira f

**blindfold** /'blaɪndfəʊld/ a & adv de olhos vendados □ n venda f □ vt vendar os olhos a

**blink** /blɪŋk/ vi piscar

**blinkers** /'blɪŋkəz/ npl antolhos mpl

**bliss** /blɪs/ n felicidade f, beatitude f. ~ful a felicíssimo. ~fully adv maravilhosamente

**blister** /'blɪstə(r)/ n bolha f, empola f □ vi empolar

**blizzard** /'blɪzəd/ n tempestade f de neve, nevasca f

**bloated** /'bləʊtɪd/ a inchado

**bloater** /'bləʊtə(r)/ n arenque m salgado e defumado

**blob** /blɒb/ n pingo m grosso; (stain) mancha f

**bloc** /blɒk/ n bloco m

**block** /blɒk/ n bloco m; (buildings) quarteirão m; (in pipe) entupimento m. ~ (of flats) prédio m (de andares) □ vt bloquear, obstruir; (pipe) entupir. ~ letters maiúsculas fpl. ~age n obstrução f

**blockade** /blɒ'keɪd/ n bloqueio m □ vt bloquear

**bloke** /bləʊk/ n (colloq) sujeito m (colloq), cara m (colloq)

**blond** /blɒnd/ a & n louro (m)

**blonde** /blɒnd/ a & n loura (f)

**blood** /blʌd/ n sangue m □ a (bank, donor, transfusion, etc) de sangue; (poisoning) do sangue; (group, vessel) sangüíneo. ~-curdling a horrendo. ~ pressure tensão f arterial. ~ test exame *m* de sangue. **~less** *a* (*fig*) pacífico

**bloodhound** /'blʌdhaʊnd/ *n* sabujo *m*

**bloodshed** /'blʌdʃed/ *n* derramamento *m* de sangue, carnificina *f*

**bloodshot** /'blʌdʃɒt/ *a* injetado *or* (*P*) injectado de sangue

**bloodstream** /'blʌdstri:m/ *n* sangue *m*, fluxo *m* sangüíneo

**bloodthirsty** /'blʌdθɜ:stɪ/ *a* sanguinário

**bloody** /'blʌdɪ/ *a* (-ier, -iest) ensangüentado; (*with much bloodshed*) sangrento; (*sl*) grande, maldito □ *adv* (*sl*) pra burro. **~-minded** *a* (*colloq*) do contra (*colloq*), chato (*sl*)

**bloom** /blu:m/ *n* flor *f*; (*beauty*) frescura *f*, viço *m* □ *vi* florir; (*fig*) vicejar. **in ~** em flor

**blossom** /'blɒsəm/ *n* flor *f*. **in ~** em flor □ *vi* (*flower*) florir, desabrochar; (*develop, flourish*) florescer, desabrochar

**blot** /blɒt/ *n* mancha *f* □ *vt* (*pt* blotted) manchar; (*dry*) secar. **~ out** apagar; (*hide*) tapar, toldar. **~ter,** **~ting-paper** *n* (papel) mata-borrão *m*

**blotch** /blɒtʃ/ *n* mancha *f*. **~y** *a* manchado

**blouse** /blaʊz/ *n* blusa *f*; (*in uniform*) blusão *m*

**blow**[1] /bləʊ/ *vt/i* (*pt* blew, *pp* blown) soprar; (*fuse*) fundir-se, queimar; (*sl: squander*) esbanjar; (*trumpet etc*) tocar. **~ a whistle** apitar. **~ away** *or* **off** levar, soprar □ *vi* roar, ir pelos ares (fora). **~-dry** *vt* (*hair*) fazer um brushing □ *n* brushing *m*. **~ one's nose** assoar o nariz. **~ out** (*candle*) apagar, soprar. **~-out** *n* (*colloq: of tyre*) rebentar *m*; (*colloq: large meal*) comilança *f* (*colloq*). **~ over** passar. **~ up** *vt* (*explode*) explodir; (*tyre*) encher; (*photograph*) ampliar □ *vi* (*explode*) explodir

**blow**[2] /bləʊ/ *n* pancada *f*; (*slap*) bofetada *f*; (*punch*) murro *m*; (*fig*) golpe *m*

**blowlamp** /'bləʊlæmp/ *n* maçarico *m*

**blown** /bləʊn/ *see* blow[1]

**bludgeon** /'blʌdʒən/ *n* moca *f* □ *vt* malhar em. **~ to death** matar à pancada

**blue** /blu:/ *a* (-er, -est) azul; (*indecent*) indecente □ *n* azul *m*. **come out of the ~** ser inesperado. **~s** *n* (*mus*) blues. **have the ~s** estar deprimido (*colloq*)

**bluebell** /'blu:bel/ *n* jacinto *m* dos bosques

**bluebottle** /'blu:bɒtl/ *n* mosca *f* varejeira

**blueprint** /'blu:prɪnt/ *n* cópia *f* foto-

gráfica de planta; (*fig*) projeto *m*, (*P*) projecto *m*

**bluff** /blʌf/ *vi* blefar, (*P*) fazer bluff □ *vt* enganar (fingindo), blefar □ *n* blefe *m*, (*P*) bluff *m*

**blunder** /'blʌndə(r)/ *vi* cometer um erro crasso; (*move*) avançar às cegas *or* tateando □ *n* erro *m* crasso, (*P*) bronca *f*

**blunt** /blʌnt/ *a* (-er, -est) embotado; (*person*) direto, (*P*) directo □ *vt* embotar. **~ly** *adv* sem rodeios. **~ness-** *n* franqueza *f* rude

**blur** /blɜ:(r)/ *n* mancha *f* □ *vt* (*pt* blurred) (*smear*) manchar; (*make indistinct*) toldar

**blurb** /blɜ:b/ *n* contracapa *f*, sinopse *f* de um livro

**blurt** /blɜ:t/ *vt* **~ out** deixar escapar

**blush** /blʌʃ/ *vi* corar □ *n* rubor *m*, vermelhidão *f*

**bluster** /'blʌstə(r)/ *vi* (*wind*) soprar em rajadas; (*swagger*) andar com ar fanfarrão. **~y** *a* borrascoso

**boar** /bɔ:(r)/ *n* varrão *m*. **wild ~** javali *m*

**board** /bɔ:d/ *n* tábua *f*; (*for notices*) quadro *m*, (*P*) placard *m*; (*food*) pensão *f*; (*admin*) conselho *m* □ *vt/i* cobrir com tábuas; (*aircraft, ship, train*) embarcar (em); (*bus, train*) subir (em). **full ~** pensão *f* completa. **half ~** meia-pensão *f*. **on ~** a bordo. **~ up** entaipar. **~ with** ser pensionista em casa de. **~er** *n* pensionista *mf*; (*at school*) interno *m*. **~ing-card** *n* cartão *m* de embarque. **~ing-house** *n* pensão *f*. **~ing-school** *n* internato *m*

**boast** /bəʊst/ *vi* gabar-se □ *vt* orgulhar-se de □ *n* gabarolice *f*. **~er** *n* gabola *mf*. **~ful** *a* vaidoso. **~fully** *adv* com vaidade, gabando-se

**boat** /bəʊt/ *n* barco *m*. **in the same ~** nas mesmas circunstâncias. **~ing** *n* passear de barco

**bob** /bɒb/ *vt/i* (*pt* bobbed) (*curtsy*) inclinar-se; (*hair*) cortar pelos ombros, (*P*) cortar à Joãozinho. **~ (up and down)** andar para cima e para baixo

**bobbin** /'bɒbɪn/ *n* bobina *f*; (*sewing-machine*) canela *f*, bobina *f*

**bob-sleigh** /'bɒbsleɪ/ *n* trenó *m*

**bode** /bəʊd/ *vi* **well/ill** ser de bom/mau agouro

**bodice** /'bɒdɪs/ *n* corpete *m*

**bodily** /'bɒdɪlɪ/ *a* corporal, físico. □ *adv* (*in person*) fisicamente, em pessoa; (*lift*) em peso

**body** /'bɒdɪ/ *n* corpo *m*; (*organization*) organismo *m*. **~(work)** *n* (*of car*) carroçaria *f*. **in a ~** em massa. **the main ~ of** o grosso de. **~-building** *n* body building *m*

**bodyguard** /'bɒdɪgɑ:d/ n guarda-costas m; (escort) escolta f
**bog** /bɒg/ n pântano m □ vt get ~ged down atolar-se; ( fig) ficar emperrado
**boggle** /'bɒgl/ vi the mind ~s não da para imaginar
**bogus** /'bəʊgəs/ a falso
**boil**[1] /bɔɪl/ n (med) furúnculo m
**boil**[2] /bɔɪl/ vt/i ferver. **come to the ~** ferver. **~ down to** resumir-se a. **~ over** transbordar. **~ing hot** fervendo. **~ing point** ponto m de ebulição
**boiler** /'bɔɪlə(r)/ n caldeira f. **~ suit** macacão m, (P) fato m de macaco
**boisterous** /'bɔɪstərəs/ a turbulento; (noisy and cheerful) animado
**bold** /bəʊld/ a (-er, -est) ousado; (of colours) vivo. **~ness** n ousadia f
**Bolivia** /bə'lɪvɪə/ n Bolívia f. **~n** a & n boliviano (m)
**bollard** /'bɒləd/ n (ship) abita f; (road) poste m
**bolster** /'bəʊlstə(r)/ n travesseiro m □ vt sustentar; ajudar. **~ one's spirits** levantar o moral
**bolt** /bəʊlt/ n (on door etc) ferrolho m; ( for nut) parafuso m; (lightning) relâmpago m □ vt aferrolhar; ( food) engolir □ vi fugir, disparar. **~ up-right** reto como um fuso
**bomb** /bɒm/ n bomba f □ vt bombardear. **~er** n (aircraft) bombardeiro m; (person) bombista mf
**bombard** /bɒm'bɑ:d/ vt bombardear. **~ment** n bombardeamento m
**bombastic** /bɒm'bæstɪk/ a bombástico
**bombshell** /'bɒmʃel/ n granada f; ( fig) bomba f
**bond** /bɒnd/ n (agreement) compromisso m; (link) laço m, vínculo m; (comm) obrigação f. **in ~** em depósito na alfândega
**bondage** /'bɒndɪdʒ/ n escravidão f, servidão f
**bone** /bəʊn/ n osso m; (of fish) espinha f □ vt desossar. **~-dry** a completamente seco, ressecado. **~ idle** preguiçoso
**bonfire** /'bɒnfaɪə(r)/ n fogueira f
**bonnet** /'bɒnɪt/ n chapéu m; (auto) capô m do motor, (P) capot m
**bonus** /'bəʊnəs/ n bônus m, (P) bónus m
**bony** /'bəʊnɪ/ a (-ier, -iest) ossudo; (meat, fish) cheio de ossos/de espinhas
**boo** /bu:/ int fora □ vt/i vaiar □ n vaia f
**boob** /bu:b/ n (sl: mistake) asneira f, disparate m □ vi (sl) fazer asneira(s)
**booby** /'bu:bɪ/ n **~ prize** prêmio m de consolação. **~ trap** bomba f armadilhada

**book** /bʊk/ n livro m. **~s** (comm) contas fpl, escrita f □ vt (enter) averbar, registrar; (comm) escriturar; (reserve) marcar, reservar. **~ of matches** carteira f de fósforos. **~ of tickets** (bus, tube) caderneta f de módulos. **be fully ~ed** ter a lotação esgotada. **~ing office** bilheteria f, (P) bilheteira f
**bookcase** /'bʊkkeɪs/ n estante f
**bookkeep|er** /'bʊkki:pə(r)/ n guarda-livros m. **~ing** n contabilidade f, escrituração f
**booklet** /'bʊklɪt/ n brochura f
**bookmaker** /'bʊkmeɪkə(r)/ n book (maker) m
**bookmark** /'bʊkmɑ:k/ n marca f de livro, marcador m de página
**bookseller** /'bʊkselə(r)/ n livreiro m
**bookshop** /'bʊkʃɒp/ n livraria f
**bookstall** /'bʊkstɔ:l/ n quiosque m
**boom** /bu:m/ vi ribombar; (of trade) prosperar □ n (sound) ribombo m; (comm) boom m, prosperidade f
**boon** /bu:n/ n benção f, vantagem f
**boost** /bu:st/ vt desenvolver, promover; (morale) levantar; (price) aumentar □ n força f (colloq). **~er** n (med) dose suplementar f; (vaccine) revacinação f, (P) reforço m
**boot** /bu:t/ n bota f; (auto) portamala f □ vt ~ (up) (comput) to ~ (in addition) ainda por cima
**booth** /bu:ð/ n barraca f; (telephone, voting) cabine f
**booty** /'bu:tɪ/ n saque m, pilhagem f
**booze** /bu:z/ vi (colloq) embebedar-se (colloq), encharcar-se (colloq) □ n (colloq) pinga f (colloq)
**border** /'bɔ:də(r)/ n borda f, margem f; ( frontier) fronteira f; (garden bed) canteiro m □ vi **~ on** confinar com; (be almost the same as) atingir as raias de
**borderline** /'bɔ:dəlam/ n linha f divisória. **~ case** caso m limite
**bore**[1] /bɔ:(r)/ see **bear**[2]
**bore**[2] /bɔ:(r)/ vt/i (techn) furar, perfurar □ n (of gun barrel) calibre m
**bore**[3] /bɔ:(r)/ vt aborrecer, entediar □ n maçante m; (thing) chatice f. **be ~d** aborrecer-se, maçar-se. **~dom** n tédio m. **boring** a tedioso, maçante
**born** /bɔ:n/ a nascido. **be ~** nascer
**borne** /bɔ:n/ see **bear**[2]
**borough** /'bʌrə/ n município m
**borrow** /'bɒrəʊ/ vt pedir emprestado (from a)
**bosom** /'bʊzəm/ n peito m; (woman's; fig: midst) seio m. **~ friend** amigo m íntimo
**boss** /bɒs/ n (colloq) patrão m, patroa f, manda-chuva (colloq) m □ vt mandar. **~ sb about** (colloq) mandar em alg

**bossy** /'bɒsɪ/ *a* mandão, autoritário

**botan|y** /'bɒtənɪ/ *n* botánica *f*. ~**ical**
/bə'tænɪkl/ *a* botânico. ~**ist** /-ɪst/ *n*
botânico *m*

**botch** /bɒtʃ/ *vt* atamancar; (*spoil*) estragar, escangalhar

**both** /bəʊθ/ *a & pron* ambos, os dois □
*adv* ~ ... and não só ... mas também,
tanto ... como. ~ **of us** nós dois. ~
**the books** ambos os livros

**bother** /'bɒðə(r)/ *vt/i* incomodar(-se)
□ *n* (*inconvenience*) incômodo *m*,
(*P*) incómodo *m*, trabalho *m*; (*effort*)
custo *m*, trabalho *m*; (*worry*) preocupação *f*. **don't** ~ não se in-
comode. **I can't be** ~**ed** não posso
me dar o trabalho

**bottle** /'bɒtl/ *n* garrafa *f*; (*small*) frasco *m*; ( *for baby*) mamadeira *f*, (*P*)
biberão *m* □ *vt* engarrafar. ~**-opener**
*n* sacarolhas *m*. ~ **up** reprimir

**bottleneck** /'bɒtlnek/ *n* (*obstruction*)
entrave *m*; (*traffic-jam*) engarrafamento *m*

**bottom** /'bɒtəm/ *n* fundo *m*; (*of hill*)
sopé *m*; (*buttocks*) traseiro *m* □ *a* inferior; (*last*) último. **from top to** ~ de
alto a baixo. ~**less** *a* sem fundo

**bough** /baʊ/ *n* ramo *m*

**bought** /bɔːt/ *see* buy

**boulder** /'bəʊldə(r)/ *n* pedregulho *m*

**bounce** /baʊns/ *vi* saltar; (*of person*)
pular, dar pulos; (*sl: of cheque*) ser
devolvido □ *vt* fazer saltar □ *n* (*of
ball*) salto *m*, (*P*) ressalto *m*

**bound**[1] /baʊnd/ *vi* pular; (*move by
jumping*) ir aos pulos □ *n* pulo *m*

**bound**[2] /baʊnd/ *see* bind □ **a be** ~ **for**
ir com destino a, ir para. **be** ~ **to**
(*obliged*) ser obrigado a; (*certain*) haver de. **she's** ~ **to like it** ela há de
gostar disso

**boundary** /'baʊndrɪ/ *n* limite *m*

**bound|s** /baʊndz/ *npl* limites *mpl*.
**out of** ~**s** interdito. ~**ed by** limitado
por. ~**less** *a* sem limites

**bouquet** /bʊ'keɪ/ *n* ramo *m* de flores;
(*wine*) aroma *m*

**bout** /baʊt/ *n* período *m*; (*med*) ataque
*m*; (*boxing*) combate *m*

**boutique** /buːˈtiːk/ *n* boutique *f*

**bow**[1] /bəʊ/ *n* (*weapon, mus*) arco *m*;
(*knot*) laço *m*. ~**-legged** *a* de pernas
tortas. ~**-tie** *n* gravata borboleta *f*,
(*P*) laço *m*

**bow**[2] /baʊ/ *n* vênia *f*, (*P*) vénia *f* □ *vt/i*
inclinar(-se), curvar-se

**bow**[3] /baʊ/ *n* (*naut*) proa *f*

**bowels** /'baʊəlz/ *npl* intestinos *mpl*;
( *fig*) entranhas *fpl*

**bowl**[1] /bəʊl/ *n* (*basin*) bacia *f*; ( *for
food*) tigela *f*; (*of pipe*) fornilho *m*

**bowl**[2] /bəʊl/ *n* (*ball*) boliche *m*, (*P*)
bola *f* de madeira. ~**s** *npl* boliche *m*,

(*P*) jogo *m* com bolas de madeira □ *vt*
(*cricket*) lançar. ~ **over** siderar, varar.
~**ing** *n* boliche *m*, (*P*) bowling *m*.
~**ing-alley** *n* pista *f*

**bowler**[1] /'bəʊlə(r)/ *n* (*cricket*) lança-
dor *m*

**bowler**[2] /'bəʊlə(r)/ *n* ~ (**hat**) (chapéu
de) coco *m*

**box**[1] /bɒks/ *n* caixa *f*; (*theatr*) camarote *m* □ *vt* pôr dentro duma caixa. ~
**in** fechar. ~ **office** *n* bilheteira *f*, (*P*)
bilheteira *f*. **Boxing Day** feriado *m* no
primeiro dia útil depois do Natal

**box**[2] /bɒks/ *vt/i* (*sport*) lutar boxe. ~
**the ears of** esbofetear. ~**er** *n* pugilis-
ta *m*, boxeur *m*. ~**ing** *n* boxe *m*, pu-
gilismo *m*

**boy** /bɔɪ/ *n* rapaz *m*. ~**friend** *n* namorado *m*. ~**hood** *n* infância *f*.
~**ish** *a* de menino

**boycott** /'bɔɪkɒt/ *vt* boicotar □ *n* boi-
cote *m*

**bra** /braː/ *n* soutien *m*

**brace** /breɪs/ *n* braçadeira *f*; (*dental*)
aparelho *m*; (*tool*) berbequim *m*; (*of
birds*) par *m*. ~**s** *npl* ( *for trousers*)
suspensórios *mpl* □ *vt* apoiar, firmar.
~ **o.s.** concentrar as energias, fazer
força; ( *for blow*) preparar-se

**bracelet** /'breɪslɪt/ *n* bracelete *m*, pulseira *f*

**bracing** /'breɪsɪŋ/ *a* tonificante, esti-
mulante

**bracken** /'brækən/ *n* (*bot*) samambaia *f*, (*P*) feto *m*

**bracket** /'brækɪt/ *n* suporte *m*;
(*group*) grupo *m* □ *vt* (*pt* **bracketed**)
pôr entre parênteses; (*put together*)
pôr em pé de igualdade, agrupar.
**age/income** ~ faixa *f* etária/
salarial. **round** ~**s** parênteses *mpl*.
**square** ~**s** parênteses *mpl*, colchetes
*mpl*

**brag** /bræg/ *vi* (*pt* **bragged**) gabar-se
(**about** de)

**braid** /breɪd/ *n* galão *m*; (*of hair*)
trança *f*

**Braille** /breɪl/ *n* braile *m*

**brain** /breɪn/ *n* cérebro *m*, miolos *mpl*
(*colloq*); ( *fig*) inteligência *f*. ~**s** (*culin*) miolos *mpl*. ~**-child** *n* invenção
*f*. ~**less** *a* estúpido

**brainwash** /'breɪnwɒʃ/ *vt* fazer uma
lavagem cerebral

**brainwave** /'breɪnweɪv/ *n* idéia *f*, (*P*)
ideia *f* genial

**brainy** /'breɪnɪ/ *a* (-**ier**, -**iest**) inteligente, esperto

**braise** /breɪz/ *vt* (*culin*) estufar

**brake** /breɪk/ *n* travão *m* □ *vt/i* travar.
~ **light** farol *m* do freio

**bran** /bræn/ *n* (*husks*) farelo *m*

**branch** /braːntʃ/ *n* ramo *m*; (*of road*)
ramificação *f*; (*of railway line*) ramal

*m*; (*comm*) sucursal *f*; (*of bank*) balcão *m* □ *vi* ~ (**off**) bifurcar-se, ramificar-se

**brand** /brænd/ *n* marca *f* □ *vt* marcar. ~ **name** marca *f* de fábrica. **~-new** *a* novo em folha. ~ **sb as** tachar alg de, (*P*) rotular alg de

**brandish** /'brændɪʃ/ *vt* brandir

**brandy** /'brændɪ/ *n* aguardente *f*, conhaque *m*

**brass** /bra:s/ *n* latão *m*. **the** ~ (*mus*) os metais *mpl* □ *a* de cobre, de latão. **get down to** ~ **tacks** tratar das coisas sérias. **top** ~ (*sl*) os chefões (*colloq*)

**brassière** /'bræsɪə(r)/ *n* soutien *m*

**brat** /bræt/ *n* (*pej*) fedelho *m*

**bravado** /brə'vɑːdəʊ/ *n* bravata *f*

**brave** /breɪv/ *a* (-**er**, -**est**) bravo, valente □ *vt* arrostar. ~**ry** /-ərɪ/ *n* bravura *f*

**brawl** /brɔːl/ *n* briga *f*, rixa *f*, desordem *f* □ *vi* brigar

**brawn** /brɔːn/ *n* força *f* muscular, músculo *m*. ~**y** *a* musculoso

**bray** /breɪ/ *n* zurro *m* □ *vi* zurrar

**brazen** /'breɪzn/ *a* descarado

**brazier** /'breɪzɪə(r)/ *n* braseiro *m*

**Brazil** /brə'zɪl/ *n* Brasil *m*. ~**ian** *a* & *n* brasileiro (*m*). ~ **nut** castanha *f* do Pará

**breach** /briːtʃ/ *n* quebra *f*; (*gap*) brecha *f* □ *vt* abrir uma brecha em. ~ **of contract** quebra *f* de contrato. ~ **of the peace** perturbação *f* da ordem pública. ~ **of trust** abuso *m* de confiança

**bread** /bred/ *n* pão *m*. **~-winner** *n* ganha-pão *m*

**breadcrumbs** /'bredkrʌmz/ *npl* migalhas *fpl*; (*culin*) farinha *f* de rosca

**breadline** /'bredlaɪn/ *n* **on the** ~ na miséria

**breadth** /bredθ/ *n* largura *f*; (*of mind, view*) abertura *f*

**break** /breɪk/ *vt* (*pt* **broke**, *pp* **broken**) partir, quebrar; (*vow, silence, etc*) quebrar; (*law*) transgredir; (*journey*) interromper; (*news*) dar; (*a record*) bater □ *vi* partir-se, quebrar-se; (*voice, weather*) mudar □ *n* quebra *f*, ruptura *f*; (*interval*) intervalo *m*; (*colloq: opportunity*) oportunidade *f*, chance *f*. ~ **one's arm/leg** quebrar o braço/a perna ~ **down** *vt* analisar □ *vi* (*of person*) ir-se abaixo; (*of machine*) avariar-se. ~ **in** forçar uma entrada. ~ **off** *vt* quebrar □ *vi* desligar-se. ~ **out** rebentar. ~ **up** *vt/i* terminar *vi* (*of schools*) entrar em férias. ~**able** *a* quebrável. ~**age** *n* quebra *f*

**breakdown** /'breɪkdaʊn/ *n* (*techn*) avaria *f*, pane *f*; (*med*) esgotamento *m* nervoso; (*of figures*) análise *f* □ *a*

(*auto*) de pronto-socorro. ~ **van** pronto-socorro *m*

**breaker** /'breɪkə(r)/ *n* vaga *f* de rebentação

**breakfast** /'brekfəst/ *n* café *m* da manhã

**breakthrough** /'breɪkθruː/ *n* descoberta *f* decisiva, avanço *m*

**breakwater** /'breɪkwɔːtə(r)/ *n* quebra-mar *m*

**breast** /brest/ *n* peito *m*. **~-feed** *vt* (*pt* **-fed**) amamentar. **~-stroke** *n* estilo *m* bruços

**breath** /breθ/ *n* respiração *f*. **bad** ~ mau hálito *m*. **out of** ~ sem fôlego. **under one's** ~ num murmúrio, baixo. **~less** *a* ofegante

**breathalyser** /'breθəlaɪzə(r)/ *n* aparelho *m* para medir o nível de álcool no sangue, bafômetro *m* (*collog*)

**breath**|**e** /briːð/ *vt/i* respirar. ~ **in** inspirar. ~ **out** expirar. ~**ing** *n* respiração *f*. **~ing-space** *n* pausa *f*

**breather** /'briːðə(r)/ *n* pausa *f* de descanso, momento *m* para respirar

**breathtaking** /'breθteɪkɪŋ/ *a* assombroso, arrebatador

**bred** /bred/ *see* **breed**

**breed** /briːd/ *vt* (*pt* **bred**) criar □ *vi* reproduzir-se □ *n* raça *f*. ~**er** *n* criador *m*. ~**ing** *n* criação *f*; (*fig*) educação *f*

**breeze** /briːz/ *n* brisa *f*. ~**y** *a* fresco

**brevity** /'brevətɪ/ *n* brevidade *f*

**brew** /bruː/ *vt* (*beer*) fabricar; (*tea*) fazer; (*fig*) armar, tramar □ *vi* fermentar; (*tea*) preparar; (*fig*) armar-se, preparar-se □ *n* decocção *f*; (*tea*) infusão *f*. ~**er** *n* cervejeiro *m*. ~**ery** *n* cervejaria *f*

**bribe** /braɪb/ *n* suborno *m*, (*P*) peita *f* □ *vt* subornar. ~**ry** /-ərɪ/ *n* suborno *m*, corrupção *f*

**brick** /brɪk/ *n* tijolo *m*

**bricklayer** /'brɪkleɪə(r)/ *n* pedreiro *m*

**bridal** /'braɪdl/ *a* nupcial

**bride** /braɪd/ *n* noiva *f*

**bridegroom** /'braɪdgrʊm/ *n* noivo *m*

**bridesmaid** /'braɪdzmeɪd/ *n* dama *f* de honra, (*P*) honor

**bridge**[1] /brɪdʒ/ *n* ponte *f*; (*of nose*) cana *f* □ *vt* ~ **a gap** preencher uma lacuna

**bridge**[2] /brɪdʒ/ *n* (*cards*) bridge *m*

**bridle** /'braɪdl/ *n* cabeçada *f*, freio *m* □ *vt* refrear. **~-path** *n* atalho *m*, carreiro *m*

**brief**[1] /briːf/ *a* (-**er**, -**est**) breve. **~s** *npl* (*men's*) cueca *f*, (*P*) slip *m*; (*women's*) calcinhas *fpl*, (*P*) cuecas *fpl*. **~ly** *adv* brevemente

**brief**[2] /briːf/ *n* (*jur*) sumário *m*; (*case*) causa *f*; (*instructions*) instruções *fpl* □ *vt* dar instruções a

**briefcase** /'bri:fkeis/ *n* pasta *f*
**brigad|e** /bri'geid/ *n* brigada *f*. **~ier** /-ə'diə(r)/ *n* brigadeiro *m*
**bright** /brait/ *a* (**-er, -est**) brilhante; (*of colour*) vivo; (*of light*) forte; (*room*) claro; (*cheerful*) alegre; (*clever*) inteligente. **~ness** *n* (*sheen*) brilho *m*; (*clarity*) claridade *f*; (*intelligence*) inteligência *f*
**brighten** /'braitn/ *vt* alegrar □ *vi* (*of weather*) clarear; (*of face*) animar-se, iluminar-se
**brillian|t** /'briljənt/ *a* brilhante. **~ce** *n* brilho *m*
**brim** /brim/ *n* borda *f*; (*of hat*) aba *f* □ *vi* (*pt* **brimmed**) **~ over** transbordar, cair por fora
**brine** /brain/ *n* salmoura *f*
**bring** /briŋ/ *vt* (*pt* **brought**) trazer. **~ about** causar. **~ back** trazer (de volta); (*call to mind*) relembrar. **~ down** trazer para baixo; (*bird, plane*) abater; (*prices*) baixar. **~ forward** adiantar, apresentar. **~ it off** ser bem sucedido (em alg coisa). **~ out** (*take out*) tirar; (*show*) revelar; (*book*) publicar. **~ round** *or* **to** reanimar, fazer voltar a si. **~ to bear** (*pressure etc*) exercer. **~ up** educar; (*med*) vomitar; (*question*) levantar
**brink** /briŋk/ *n* beira *f*, borda *f*
**brisk** /brisk/ *a* (**-er, -est**) (*pace, movement*) vivo, rápido; (*business, demand*) grande
**bristl|e** /'brisl/ *n* pêlo *m*. **~y** *a* eriçado
**Britain** /'britn/ *n* Grã-Bretanha *f*
**British** /'britiʃ/ *a* britânico. **the ~** *o* povo *m* britânico, os britânicos *mpl*
**brittle** /'britl/ *a* frágil
**broach** /brəutʃ/ *vt* abordar, entabular, encetar
**broad** /brɔ:d/ *a* (**-er, -est**) largo; (*daylight*) pleno. **~ bean** fava *f*. **~-minded** *a* tolerante, liberal. **~ly** *adv* de modo geral
**broadcast** /'brɔ:dka:st/ *vt/i* (*pt* **broadcast**) transmitir, fazer uma transmissão; (*person*) cantar, falar *etc* na rádio *or* na TV □ *n* emissão *f*. **~ing** *a & n* (de) rádiodifusão (*f*)
**broaden** /'brɔ:dn/ *vt/i* alargar(-se)
**broccoli** /'brɒkəlı/ *n inv* brócolis *mpl*, (*P*) brócolos *mpl*
**brochure** /'brəuʃə(r)/ *n* brochura *f*
**broke** /brəuk/ *see* **break** □ *a* (*sl*) depenado (*sl*), liso (*sl*), (*P*) teso (*sl*)
**broken** /'brəukən/ *see* **break** □ *a* **~ English** inglês *m* estropeado. **~-hearted** *a* com o coração despedaçado
**broker** /'brəukə(r)/ *n* corretor *m*, broker *m*
**bronchitis** /brɒŋ'kaitis/ *n* bronquite *f*
**bronze** /brɒnz/ *n* bronze *m*

**brooch** /brəutʃ/ *n* broche *m*
**brood** /bru:d/ *n* ninhada *f* □ *vi* chocar; (*fig*) cismar. **~y** *a* (*hen*) choca; (*fig*) sorumbático, melancólico
**brook** /bruk/ *n* regato *m*, ribeiro *m*
**broom** /bru:m/ *n* vassoura *f*; (*bot*) giesta *f*
**broth** /brɒθ/ *n* caldo *m*
**brothel** /'brɒθl/ *n* bordel *m*
**brother** /'brʌðə(r)/ *n* irmão *m*. **~-in-law** *n* (*pl* **~s-in-law**) cunhado *m*. **~hood** *n* irmandade *f*, fraternidade *f*. **~ly** *a* fraternal
**brought** /brɔ:t/ *see* **bring**
**brow** /brau/ *n* (*forehead*) testa *f*; (*of hill*) cume *m*; (*eyebrow*) sobrancelha *f*
**browbeat** /'braubi:t/ *vt* (*pt* **-beat**, *pp* **-beaten**) intimidar
**brown** /braun/ *a* (**-er, -est**) castanho □ *n* castanho *m* □ *vt/i* acastanhar; (*in the sun*) bronzear, tostar; (*meat*) alourar
**browse** /brauz/ *vi* (*through book*) folhear; (*of animal*) pastar; (*in a shop*) olhar sem comprar
**bruise** /bru:z/ *n* hematoma *m*, contusão *f* □ *vt* causar um hematoma. **~d** *a* coberto de hematomas, contuso; (*fruit*) machucado
**brunette** /bru:'net/ *n* morena *f*
**brunt** /brʌnt/ *n* **the ~ of** o maior peso de, o pior de
**brush** /brʌʃ/ *n* escova *f*; (*painter's*) pincel *m*; (*skirmish*) escaramuça *f*. **~ against** roçar. **~ aside** não fazer caso de. **~ off** (*colloq: reject*) mandar passear (*colloq*). **~ up (on)** aperfeiçoar
**brusque** /bru:sk/ *a* brusco
**Brussels** /'brʌslz/ *n* Bruxelas *f*. **~ sprouts** couve-de-Bruxelas *f*
**brutal** /'bru:tl/ *a* brutal. **~ity** /'tælətı/ *n* brutalidade *f*
**brute** /bru:t/ *n & a* (*animal, person*) bruto (*m*). **by ~ force** por força bruta
**B Sc** *abbr see* **Bachelor of Science**
**bubb|le** /'bʌbl/ *n* bolha *f*; (*of soap*) bola *f* de sabão □ *vi* borbulhar. **~le gum** *n* chiclete *m*, (*P*) pastilha *f* elástica. **~le over** transbordar. **~ly** *a* efervescente
**buck**[1] /bʌk/ *n* macho *m* □ *vi* dar galões, (*P*) corcovear. **~ up** *vt/i* (*sl*) animar(-se); (*sl: rush*) apressar-se, despachar-se
**buck**[2] /bʌk/ *n* (*Amer sl*) dólar *m*
**buck**[3] /bʌk/ *n* **pass the ~** (*sl*) fazer o jogo do empurra
**bucket** /'bʌkit/ *n* balde *m*
**buckle** /'bʌkl/ *n* fivela *f* □ *vt/i* afivelar(-se); (*bend*) torcer(-se), vergar. **~ down to** empenhar-se
**bud** /bʌd/ *n* botão *m*, rebento *m* □ *vi* (*pt* **budded**) rebentar. **in ~** em botão

**Buddhis|t** /'bʊdɪst/ a & n budista (mf ). **~m** /-zəm/ n budismo m

**budding** /'bʌdɪŋ/ a nascente, em botão, incipiente

**budge** /bʌdʒ/ vt/i mexer(-se)

**budgerigar** /'bʌdʒərɪga:(r)/ n periquito m

**budget** /'bʌdʒɪt/ n orçamento m □ vi (pt **budgeted**) ~ **for** prever no orçamento m

**buff** /bʌf/ n (colour) côr f de camurça; (colloq) fanático m, entusiasta mf □ vt polir

**buffalo** /'bʌfələʊ/ n (pl -oes) búfalo m; (Amer) bisão m

**buffer** /'bʌfə(r)/ n pára-choque m

**buffet**[1] /'bʊfeɪ/ n (meal, counter) bufê m, (P) bufete m

**buffet**[2] /'bʌfɪt/ vt (pt **buffeted**) esbofetear; (by wind, rain; fig) fustigar

**buffoon** /bə'fu:n/ n palhaço m

**bug** /bʌg/ n (insect) bicho m; (bed-bug) percevejo m; (sl: germ) virus m; (sl: device) microfone m de escuta; (sl: defect) defeito m □ vt (pt **bugged**) grampear; (Amer sl: annoy) chatear (sl)

**bugbear** /'bʌgbeə(r)/ n papão m

**buggy** /'bʌgɪ/ n ( for baby) carrinho m

**bugle** /'bju:gl/ n clarim m, corneta f

**build** /bɪld/ vt/i (pt **built**) construir, edificar □ n físico m, compleição f. ~ **up** vt/i criar; (increase) aumentar; (accumulate) acumular(-se). **~-up** n acumulação f, ( fig) publicidade f. **~er** n construtor m, empreiteiro m; (workman) operário m

**building** /'bɪldɪŋ/ n edifício m, prédio m. ~ **site** canteiro m de obras. ~ **society** sociedade f de investimentos imobiliários

**built** /bɪlt/ see **build**. **~-in** a incorporado. **~-in wardrobe** armário m embutido na parede. **~-up** a urbanizado

**bulb** /bʌlb/ n bolbo m; (electr) lâmpada f. **~ous** a bolboso

**Bulgaria** /bʌl'geərɪə/ n Bulgária f. **~n** a & n búlgaro (m)

**bulg|e** /bʌldʒ/ n bojo m, saliência f □ vi inchar; ( jut out) fazer uma saliência. **~ing** a inchado; (pocket etc) cheio

**bulk** /bʌlk/ n quantidade f, volume m. **in** ~ por grosso; (loose) a granel. **the** ~ **of** a maior parte de. **~y** a volumoso

**bull** /bʊl/ n touro m. **~'s-eye** n (of target) centro m do alvo, mosca f

**bulldog** /'bʊldɒg/ n buldogue m

**bulldoze** /'bʊldəʊz/ vt terraplanar. **~r** /-ə(r)/ n bulldozer m

**bullet** /'bʊlɪt/ n bala f. **~-proof** a à prova de balas; (vehicle) blindado

**bulletin** /'bʊlətɪn/ n boletim m

**bullfight** /'bʊlfaɪt/ n tourada f, corri-

da f de touros. **~er** n toureiro m. **~ing** n tauromaquia f

**bullring** /'bʊlrɪŋ/ n arena f, (P) praça f de touros

**bully** /'bʊlɪ/ n mandão m, pessoa f prepotente; (schol) terror m, o mau □ vt intimidar; (treat badly) atormentar; (coerce) forçar (**into** a)

**bum**[1] /bʌm/ n (sl: buttocks) traseiro m, bunda f (sl)

**bum**[2] /bʌm/ n (Amer sl) vagabundo m

**bump** /bʌmp/ n choque m, embate m; (swelling) inchaço m; (on head) galo m □ vt/i bater, chocar. ~ **into** bater em, chocar com; (meet) esbarrar com, encontrar. **~y** a (surface) irregular; (ride) aos solavancos

**bumper** /'bʌmpə(r)/ n pára-choques m inv □ a excepcional

**bun** /bʌn/ n pãozinho m doce com passas; (hair) coque m

**bunch** /bʌntʃ/ n (of flowers) ramo m; (of keys) molho m; (of people) grupo m; (of grapes) cacho m

**bundle** /'bʌndl/ n molho m □ vt atar num molho; (push) despachar

**bung** /bʌŋ/ n batoque m, rolha f □ vt rolhar; (sl: throw) atirar, deitar. ~ **up** entupir

**bungalow** /'bʌŋgələʊ/ n chalé m; (outside Europe) bungalô m, (P) bungalow m

**bungle** /'bʌŋgl/ vt fazer mal feito, estragar

**bunion** /'bʌnjən/ n (med) joanete m

**bunk** /bʌŋk/ n (in train) couchette f; (in ship) beliche m. **~-beds** npl beliches mpl

**bunker** /'bʌŋkə(r)/ n (mil) abrigo m, casamata f, bunker m; (golf ) obstáculo m em cova de areia

**buoy** /bɔɪ/ n bóia f □ vt ~ **up** animar

**buoyan|t** /'bɔɪənt/ a flutuante; ( fig) alegre. **~cy** n ( fig) alegria f, exuberância f

**burden** /'bɜ:dn/ n fardo m □ vt collegar, sobrecarregar. **~some** a pesado

**bureau** /'bjʊərəʊ/ n (pl -eaux) /-əʊz/ (desk) secretária f; (office) secção f, (P) secção f

**bureaucracy** /bjʊə'rɒkrəsɪ/ n burocracia f

**bureaucrat** /'bjʊərəkræt/ n burocrata mf. **~ic** /-'krætɪk/ a burocrático

**burger** /'bɜ:gə(r)/ n hambúrguer m

**burglar** /'bɜ:glə(r)/ n ladrão m, assaltante mf. **~ alarm** n alarme m contra ladrões. **~ize** vt (Amer) assaltar. **~y** n assalto m

**burgle** /'bɜ:gl/ vt assaltar

**burial** /'berɪəl/ n enterro m

**burlesque** /bɜ:'lesk/ n paródia f

**burly** /'bɜ:lɪ/ a (-ier, -iest) robusto e corpulento, forte

**Burm|a** /'bɜːmə/ n Birmânia f. **~ese**
/-'miːz/ a & n birmanês (m)
**burn** /bɜːn/ vt (pt burned or burnt)
queimar □ vi queimar(-se), arder □ n
queimadura f. **~ down** reduzir a
cinzas. **~er** n (of stove) bico m de
gás. **~ing** a (thirst, desire) ardente;
(topic) candente
**burnish** /'bɜːnɪʃ/ vt polir, brunir
**burnt** /bɜːnt/ see **burn**
**burp** /bɜːp/ n (colloq) arroto m □ vi
(colloq) arrotar
**burrow** /'bʌrəʊ/ n toca f □ vi cavar,
fazer uma toca
**burst** /bɜːst/ vt/i (pt burst) arreben-
tar □ n estouro m, rebentar m; (of
anger, laughter) explosão f; (of firing)
rajada f; (of energy) acesso m. **~ into**
(flames, room, etc) irromper em. **~
into tears** desatar num choro, desfazer-se em lágrimas. **~ out laughing**
desatar a rir
**bury** /'beri/ vt sepultar, enterrar;
(hide) esconder; (engross, thrust) mergulhar
**bus** /bʌs/ n (pl buses) ônibus m, (P)
autocarro m. **~-stop** n paragem f
**bush** /bʊʃ/ n arbusto m; (land) mato
m. **~y** a espesso
**business** /'bɪznɪs/ n (trade, shop,
affair) negócio m; (task) função f;
(occupation) ocupação f. **have no
~ to** não ter o direito de. **it's no ~
of yours** não é da sua conta. **mind
your own ~** cuide da sua vida.
**that's my ~** isso é meu problema.
**~like** a eficiente, sistemático.
**~man** n homem m de negócios, comerciante m
**busker** /'bʌskə(r)/ n músico m ambulante
**bust**[1] /bʌst/ n busto m
**bust**[2] /bʌst/ vt/i (pt busted or bust)
(sl) = **burst, break** □ a falido. **~-up** n
(sl) discussão f, (P) bulha f. **go ~** (sl)
falir
**bustl|e** /'bʌsl/ vi andar numa azáfa-
ma; (hurry) apressar-se □ n azáfama
f. **~ing** a animado, movimentado
**bus|y** /'bɪzɪ/ a (-ier, -iest) ocupado;
(street) movimentado; (day) atarefado
□ vt **~y o.s. with** ocupar-se com.
**~ily** adv ativamente, atarefadamente
**busybody** /'bɪzɪbɒdɪ/ n intrometido
m, pessoa f abelhuda
**but** /bʌt/ conj mas □ prep exceto, (p)
excepto, senão □ adv apenas, só. **all
~** todos menos; (nearly) quaze, por
pouco não. **~ for** sem, se não fosse.
**last ~ one/two** penúltimo/antepe-
núltimo. **nobody ~** ninguém a não
ser
**butcher** /'bʊtʃə(r)/ n açougueiro m,
(P) homem m do talho; (fig) carrasco

m □ vt chacinar. **the ~'s** açougue m,
(P) talho m. **~y** n chacina f
**butler** /'bʌtlə(r)/ n mordomo m
**butt** /bʌt/ n (of gun) coronha f; (of
cigarette) ponta f; (target) alvo m de
troça, de ridículo etc; (cask) barril m
□ vt/i dar cabeçada em. **~ in** interromper
**butter** /'bʌtə(r)/ n manteiga f □ vt pôr
manteiga em. **~-bean** n feijão m
branco
**buttercup** /'bʌtəkʌp/ n botão-de-ouro m
**butterfly** /'bʌtəflaɪ/ n borboleta f
**buttock** /'bʌtək/ n nádega f
**button** /'bʌtn/ n botão m □ vt/i abo-
toar(-se)
**buttonhole** /'bʌtnhəʊl/ n casa f de
botão; (in lapel) botoeira f □ vt (fig)
obrigar a ouvir
**buttress** /'bʌtrɪs/ n contraforte m;
(fig) esteio m □ vt sustentar
**buxom** /'bʌksəm/ a roliço, rechonchudo
**buy** /baɪ/ vt (pt bought) comprar
(from a); (sl: believe) engolir (colloq)
□ n compra f. **~er** n comprador m
**buzz** /bʌz/ n zumbido m □ vi zumbir.
**~ off** (sl) pôr-se a andar. **~er** n campainha f
**by** /baɪ/ prep (near) junto de, perto de;
(along, past, means) por; (according
to) conforme; (before) antes de. **~
land/sea/air** por terra/mar/ar. **~
bike/car** etc de bicicleta/carro etc.
**~ day/night** de dia/noite. **~ the
kilo** por quilo. **~ now** a esta hora. **~
accident/mistake** sem querer. **~
oneself** sozinho □ adv (near) perto. **~
and ~** muito em breve. **~ and large**
no conjunto. **~-election** n eleição f
suplementar. **~-law** n regulamento
m. **~-product** n derivado m
**bye(-bye)** /'baɪ(baɪ)/ int (colloq) adeus,
adeusinho
**bygone** /'baɪɡɒn/ a passado. **let ~s be
~s** o que passou, passou
**bypass** /'baɪpaːs/ n (estrada) secundária f, desvio m; (med) by-pass m,
ponte f de safema □ vt fazer um desvio; (fig) contornar
**bystander** /'baɪstændə(r)/ n circums-
tante mf, espectador m
**byte** /baɪt/ n

# C

**cab** /kæb/ n táxi m; (of lorry, train)
cabina f, cabine f
**cabaret** /'kæbəreɪ/ n variedades fpl,
cabaré n
**cabbage** /'kæbɪdʒ/ n couve f, repolho m
**cabin** /'kæbɪn/ n cabana f; (in plane)
cabina f; (in ship) camarote m

**cabinet** /'kæbmɪt/ n armário m. **C~** (pol) gabinete m

**cable** /'keɪbl/ n cabo m. **~-car** n funicular m, teleférico m. **~ railway** funicular m. **~ television** televisão f a cabo

**cache** /kæʃ/ n (esconderijo m de) tesouro m, armas fpl, provisões f pl

**cackle** /'kækl/ n cacarejo m □ vi cacarejar

**cactus** /'kæktəs/ n (pl ~es or cacti /-taɪ/) cacto m

**caddie** /'kædɪ/ n (golf) caddie m

**caddy** /'kædɪ/ n lata f para o chá

**cadet** /kə'det/ n cadete m

**cadge** /kædʒ/ vt/i filar, (P) cravar

**Caesarean** /sɪ'zeərɪən/ a ~ (section) cesariana f

**café** /'kæfeɪ/ n café m

**cafeteria** /kæfɪ'tɪərɪə/ n cafeteria f, restaurante m self-service

**caffeine** /'kæfi:n/ n cafeína f

**cage** /keɪdʒ/ n gaiola f

**cagey** /'keɪdʒɪ/ a (colloq: secretive) misterioso, reservado

**cajole** /kə'dʒəʊl/ vt ~ sb into doing sth convencer alguém (com lábia ou lisonjas) a fazer alg coisa

**cake** /keɪk/ n bolo m. **~d** a empastado. his shoes were ~d with mud tinha os sapatos cobertos de lama. **a piece of ~** (sl) canja f (sl)

**calamity** /kə'læmətɪ/ n calamidade f

**calcium** /'kælsɪəm/ n cálcio m

**calculat|e** /'kælkjʊleɪt/ vt/i calcular; (Amer: suppose) supor. **~ed** a (action) deliberado, calculado. **~ing** a calculista. **~ion** /-'leɪʃn/ n cálculo m. **~or** n calculador m, (P) maquina f de calcular

**calendar** /'kælmdə(r)/ n calendário m

**calf¹** /ka:f/ n (pl calves) (young cow or bull) vitelo m, bezerro m; (of other animals) cria f

**calf²** /ka:f/ n (pl calves) (of leg) barriga f da perna

**calibrat|e** /'kælɪbreɪt/ vt calibrar. **~ion** /-breɪʃn/ n calibragem f

**calibre** /'kælɪbə(r)/ n calibre m

**calico** /'kælɪkəʊ/ n pano m de algodão; (printed) chita f, algodão m

**call** /kɔ:l/ vt/i chamar; (summon) convocar; (phone) telefonar. ~ (in or round) (visit) passar por casa de □ n chamada f; (bird's cry) canto m; (shout) brado m, grito m. be ~ed (named) chamar-se. be on ~ estar de serviço. ~ back (phone) tornar a telefonar; (visit) voltar. ~ for (demand) pedir, requerer; (fetch) ir buscar. ~ off cancelar. ~ on (visit) visitar, fazer uma visita a. ~ out (to) chamar. ~ up (mil) mobilizar, recrutar; (phone) telefonar. **~-box** n

cabina f telefônica, (P) telefónica. **~er** n visitante f, visita f; (phone) chamador m, (P) pessoa f que faz a chamada. **~ing** n vocação f

**callous** /'kæləs/ a insensível. **~ly** adv sem piedade

**callow** /'kæləʊ/ a (-er, -est) inexperiente, verde

**calm** /ka:m/ a (-er, -est) calmo □ n calma f □ vt/i ~ (down) acalmar (-se). **~ness** n calma f

**calorie** /'kælərɪ/ n caloria f

**camber** /'kæmbə(r)/ n (of road) abaulamento m

**camcorder** /'kæmkɔ:də(r)/ n câmera f de filmar

**came** /keɪm/ see come

**camel** /'kæml/ n camelo m

**camera** /'kæmərə/ n máquina f fotográfica; (cine, TV) câmera f. **~man** n (pl -men) operador m

**camouflage** /'kæməfla:ʒ/ n camuflagem f □ vt camuflar

**camp¹** /kæmp/ n acampamento m □ vi acampar. **~-bed** n cama f de campanha. **~er** n campista mf; (car) auto-caravana f. **~ing** n campismo m

**camp²** /kæmp/ a afetado, efeminado

**campaign** /kæm'peɪn/ n campanha f □ vi fazer campanha

**campsite** /'kæmpsaɪt/ n área f de camping, (P) parque m de campismo

**campus** /'kæmpəs/ n (pl -puses /-pəsɪz/) campus m, (P) cidade f universitária

**can¹** /kæn/ n vasilha f de lata; (for food) lata f (de conserva) □ vt (pt canned) enlatar. **~ned music** música f em fita para locais públicos. **~-opener** n abridor m de latas, (P) abrelatas m

**can²** /kæn/ v aux (be able to) poder, ser capaz de; (know how to) saber. I **~not/~'t** go não posso ir

**Canad|a** /'kænədə/ n Canadá m. **~ian** /kə'neɪdɪən/ a & n canadense (mf), (P) canadiano (m)

**canal** /kə'næl/ n canal m

**canary** /kə'neərɪ/ n canário m. **C~ Islands** npl as (Ilhas) Canárias

**cancel** /'kænsl/ vt (pt cancelled) cancelar; (cross out) riscar; (stamps) inutilizar. ~ out vi (fig) neutralizar-se mutuamente. **~lation** /-'leɪʃn/ n cancelamento m

**cancer** /'kænsə(r)/ n câncer m, cancro m. **C~** (astrol) Caranguejo m, Câncer m. **~ous** a canceroso

**candid** /'kændɪd/ a franco. **~ly** adv francamente

**candida|te** /'kændɪdeɪt/ n candidato m. **~cy** /-əsɪ/ n candidatura f

**candle** /'kændl/ n vela f; (in church) vela f, círio m. **~-light** n luz f de velas

**candlestick** /'kændlstɪk/ *n* castiçal *m*

**candour** /'kændə(r)/ *n* franqueza *f*, candura *f*

**candy** /'kændɪ/ *n* bala *f*, (P) açúcar cândti; (*Amer: sweet, sweets*) doce(s) *m* (*pl*). **~-floss** *n* algodão-doce *m*

**cane** /keɪn/ *n* cana *f*; (*walking-stick*) bengala *f*; (*for baskets*) verga *f*; (*school: for punishment*) vergasta *f* □ *vt* vergastar

**canine** /'keɪnaɪn/ *a* & *n* canino (*m*)

**canister** /'kænɪstə(r)/ *n* lata *f*

**cannabis** /'kænəbɪs/ *n* cânhamo *m*, maconha *f*

**cannibal** /'kænɪbl/ *n* canibal *mf*. **~ism** /-zəm/ *n* canibalismo *m*

**cannon** /'kænən/ *n inv* canhão *m*. **~-ball** *n* bala *f* de canhão

**cannot** /'kænət/ = can not

**canny** /'kænɪ/ *a* (-ier, -iest) astuto, manhoso

**canoe** /kə'nu:/ *n* canoa *f* □ *vi* andar de canoa. **~ing** *n* (*sport*) canoagem *f*. **~ist** *n* canoeiro *m*, (P) canoísta *mf*

**canon** /'kænən/ *n* cônego *m*, (P) cónego *m*; (*rule*) cânone *m*

**canonize** /'kænənaɪz/ *vt* canonizar

**canopy** /'kænəpɪ/ *n* dossel *m*; (*over doorway*) toldo *m*, marquise *f*; (*fig*) abóbada *f*

**can't** /ka:nt/ = can not

**cantankerous** /kæn'tæŋkərəs/ *a* irascível, intratável

**canteen** /kæn'ti:n/ *n* cantina *f*; (*flask*) cantil *m*; (*for cutlery*) estojo *m*

**canter** /'kæntə(r)/ *n* meio galope *m*, cânter *m* □ *vi* andar a meio galope

**canton** /'kænton/ *n* cantão *m*

**canvas** /'kænvəs/ *n* lona *f*; (*for painting or tapestry*) tela *f*

**canvass** /'kænvəs/ *vt/i* angariar votos *or* fregueses

**canyon** /'kænjən/ *n* canhão *m*, (P) desfiladeiro *m*

**cap** /kæp/ *n* (*with peak*) boné *m*; (*without peak*) barrete *m*; (*of nurse*) touca *f*; (*of bottle, pen, tube, etc*) tampa *f*; (*mech*) tampa *f*, tampão *m* □ *vt* (*pt capped*) (*bottle, pen, tube, etc*) tapar, tampar; (*rates*) impôr um limite a; (*outdo*) suplantar; (*sport*) selecionar, (P) seleccionar. **~ped with** encimado de, coroado de

**capab|le** /'keɪpəbl/ *a* (*person*) capaz (of de); (*things, situations*) suscetível, (P) susceptível (of de). **~ility** /-'bɪlətɪ/ *n* capacidade *f*. **~ly** *adv* capazmente

**capacity** /kə'pæsətɪ/ *n* capacidade *f*. **in one's ~ as** na (sua) qualidade de

**cape¹** /keɪp/ *n* (*cloak*) capa *f*

**cape²** /keɪp/ *n* (*geog*) cabo *m*

**caper¹** /'keɪpə(r)/ *vi* andar aos pinotes

**caper²** /'keɪpə(r)/ *n* (*culin*) alcaparra *f*

**capillary** /kə'pɪlərɪ/ *n* (*pl* -ies) vaso *m* capilar

**capital** /'kæpɪtl/ *a* capital □ *n* (*town*) capital *f*; (*money*) capital *m*. **~ (letter)** maiúscula *f*. **~ punishment** pena *f* de morte

**capitalis|t** /'kæpɪtəlɪst/ *a* & *n* capitalista (*mf*). **~m** /-zəm/ *n* capitalismo *m*

**capitalize** /'kæpɪtəlaɪz/ *vi* capitalizar; (*finance*) financiar; (*writing*) escrever com maiúscula. **~ on** tirar partido de

**capitulat|e** /kə'pɪtʃʊleɪt/ *vi* capitular. **~ion** /-'leɪʃn/ *n* capitulação *f*

**capricious** /kə'prɪʃəs/ *a* caprichoso

**Capricorn** /'kæprɪkɔ:n/ *n* (*astrol*) Capricórnio *m*

**capsicum** /'kæpsɪkəm/ *n* pimento *m*

**capsize** /kæp'saɪz/ *vt/i* virar(-se)

**capsule** /'kæpsju:l/ *n* cápsula *f*

**captain** /'kæptɪn/ *n* capitão *m*; (*navy*) capitão-de-mar-e-guerra *m* □ *vt* capitanear, comandar

**caption** /'kæpʃn/ *n* legenda *f*; (*heading*) título *m*

**captivate** /'kæptɪveɪt/ *vt* cativar

**captiv|e** /'kæptɪv/ *a* & *n* cativo (*m*), prisioneiro (*m*). **~ity** /-'tɪvətɪ/ *n* cativeiro *m*

**captor** /'kæptə(r)/ *n* captor *m*

**capture** /'kæptʃə(r)/ *vt* capturar; (*attention*) prender □ *n* captura *f*

**car** /ka:(r)/ *n* carro *m*. **~ ferry** barca *f* para carros. **~-park** *n* (parque *m* de) estacionamento (*m*). **~ phone** telefone *m* de carro. **~-wash** *n* estação *f* de lavagem

**carafe** /kə'ræf/ *n* garrafa *f* para água ou vinho

**caramel** /'kærəmel/ *n* caramelo *m*

**carat** /'kærət/ *n* quilate *m*

**caravan** /'kærəvæn/ *n* caravana *f*, reboque *m*

**caraway** /'kærəweɪ/ *n* ~ **seed** cariz *f*

**carbohydrate** /ka:bəʊ'haɪdreɪt/ *n* hidrato *m* de carbono

**carbon** /'ka:bən/ *n* carbono *m*. **~ copy** cópia *f* em papel carbono, (P) químico. **~ monoxide** óxido *m* de carbono. **~ paper** papel *m* carbono, (P) químico

**carburettor** /ka:bjʊ'retə(r)/ *n* carburador *m*

**carcass** /'ka:kəs/ *n* carcaça *f*

**card** /ka:d/ *n* cartão *m*; (*postcard*) postal *m*; (*playing-card*) carta *f*. **~-game(s)** *n*(*pl*) jogo(s) *m*(*pl*) de cartas. **~ index** *n* fichário *m*, (P) ficheiro *m*

**cardboard** /'ka:dbɔ:d/ *n* cartão *m*, papelão *m*

**cardiac** /'ka:dɪæk/ *a* cardíaco

**cardigan** /'ka:dɪgən/ *n* casaco *m* de lã

**cardinal** /'ka:dml/ *a* cardeal, principal. ~ **number** numeral *m* cardinal □ *n* (*relig*) cardeal *m*

**care** /keə(r)/ *n* cuidado *m*; (*concern*) interesse *m* □ *vi* ~ **about** (*be interested*) estar interessado por; (*be worried*) estar preocupado com. ~ **for** (*like*) gostar de; (*look after*) tomar conta de. **take** ~ tomar cuidado. **take** ~ **of** cuidar de; (*deal with*) tratar de. **he couldn't** ~ **less** ele está pouco ligando, ele não dá a menor (*colloq*)

**career** /kə'rɪə(r)/ *n* carreira *f* □ *vi* ir a toda a velocidade, ir numa carreira

**carefree** /'keəfri:/ *a* despreocupado

**careful** /'keəfl/ *a* cuidadoso; (*cautious*) cauteloso. ~! cuidado! ~**ly** *adv* cuidadosamente, (*cautiously*) cautelosamente

**careless** /'keəlɪs/ *a* descuidado (**about** com). ~**ly** *adv* descuidadamente. ~**ness** *n* descuido *m*, negligência *f*

**caress** /kə'res/ *n* carícia *f* □ *vt* acariciar

**caretaker** /'keəteɪkə(r)/ *n* zelador *m* duma casa vizia; (*janitor*) zelador *m*, (*P*) porteiro *m*

**cargo** /'ka:gəʊ/ *n* (*pl* -**oes**) carregamento *m*, carga *f*

**Caribbean** /kærɪ'bi:ən/ *a* caraíba. **the** ~ as Caraíbas *fpl*

**caricature** /'kærɪkətʃʊə(r)/ *n* caricatura *f* □ *vt* caricaturar

**caring** /'keərɪŋ/ *a* carinhoso, afetuoso, (*P*) afectuoso

**carnage** /'ka:nɪdʒ/ *n* carnificina *f*

**carnation** /ka:'neɪʃn/ *n* cravo *m*

**carnival** /'ka:nɪvl/ *n* carnaval *m*

**carol** /'kærəl/ *n* cântico *m* or canto *m* de Natal

**carp**¹ /ka:p/ *n inv* carpa *f*

**carp**² /ka:p/ *vi* ~ (**at**) criticar

**carpent|er** /'ka:pɪntə(r)/ *n* carpinteiro *m*. ~**ry** *n* carpintaria *f*

**carpet** /'ka:pɪt/ *n* tapete *m* □ *vt* (*pt* **carpeted**) atapetar. **with fitted** ~**s** (estar) atapetado. **be on the** ~ (*colloq*) ser chamado à ordem. ~-**sweeper** *n* limpador *m* de tapetes

**carport** /'ka:pɔ:t/ *n* abrigo *m*, (*P*) telheiro *m* para automóveis

**carriage** /'kærɪdʒ/ *n* carruagem *f*; (*of goods*) frete *m*, transporte *m*; (*cost, bearing*) porte *m*

**carriageway** /'kærɪdʒweɪ/ *n* faixa *f* de rodagem, pista *f*

**carrier** /'kærɪə(r)/ *n* transportador *m*; (*company*) transportadora *f*; (*med*) portador *m*. ~ (**bag**) saco *m* de plástico

**carrot** /'kærət/ *n* cenoura *f*

**carry** /'kærɪ/ *vt/i* levar; (*goods*) transportar; (*involve*) acarretar; (*have for*

*sale*) ter à venda. **be carried away** entusiasmar-se, deixar-se levar. ~-**cot** *n* moisés *m*. ~ **off** levar à força; (*prize*) incluir. ~ **it off** sair-se bem (de). ~ **on** continuar; (*colloq: flirt*) flertar; (*colloq: behave*) portar-se (mal). ~ **out** executar; (*duty*) cumprir. ~ **through** levar a cabo

**cart** /ka:t/ *n* carroça *f*, carro *m* □ *vt* acarretar; (*colloq*) carregar com

**cartilage** /'ka:tɪlɪdʒ/ *n* cartilagem *f*

**carton** /'ka:tn/ *n* embalagem *f* de cartão or de plástico; (*of yogurt*) embalagem *f*, pote *m*; (*of milk*) pacote *m*

**cartoon** /ka:'tu:n/ *n* desenho *m* humorístico, caricatura *f*; (*strip*) estória *f* em quadrinhos, (*P*) banda *f* desenhada; (*film*) desenhos *mpl* animados. ~**ist** *n* caricaturista *mf*; (*of strip, film*) desenhador *m*

**cartridge** /'ka:trɪdʒ/ *n* cartucho *m*

**carv|e** /ka:v/ *vt* esculpir, talhar; (*meat*) trinchar. ~**ing** *n* obra *f* de talha; (*on tree-trunk*) incisão *f*. ~**ing knife** faca *f* de trinchar, trinchante *m*

**cascade** /kæs'keɪd/ *n* cascata *f* □ *vi* cair em cascata

**case**¹ /keɪs/ *n* caso *m*; (*jur*) causa *f*, processo *m*; (*phil*) argumentos *mpl*. **in any** ~ em todo caso. **in** ~ (**of**) no caso de. **in that** ~ nesse caso

**case**² /keɪs/ *n* caixa *f*; (*crate*) caixa *f*, caixote *m*; (*for camera, jewels, spectacles, etc*) estojo *m*; (*suitcase*) mala *f*; (*for cigarettes*) cigarreira *f*

**cash** /kæʃ/ *n* dinheiro *m*, numerário *m*, cash *m* □ *vt* (*obtain money for*) cobrar, receber; (*give money for*) pagar. **be short of** ~ ter pouco dinheiro. ~ **a cheque** (*receive/give*) cobrar/descontar um cheque. ~ **in** receber. ~ **in** (**on**) aproveitar-se de. **in** ~ em dinheiro. **pay** ~ pagar em dinheiro. ~ **desk** caixa *f*. ~ **dispenser** caixa *f* electrónica. ~-**flow** *n* cash-flow *m*. ~ **register** caixa *f* registadora, (*P*) registadora *f*

**cashew** /kæ'ʃu:/ *n* caju *m*

**cashier** /kæ'ʃɪə(r)/ *n* caixa *mf*

**cashmere** /kæʃ'mɪə(r)/ *n* caxemira *f*

**casino** /kə'si:nəʊ/ *n* (*pl* -**os**) casino *m*

**cask** /ka:sk/ *n* casco *m*, barril *m*

**casket** /'ka:skɪt/ *n* pequeno cofre *m*; (*Amer: coffin*) caixão *m*

**casserole** /'kæsərəʊl/ *n* caçarola *f*; (*stew*) estufado *m*

**cassette** /kə'set/ *n* cassette *f*. ~ **player** gravador *m*. ~ **recorder** *n*

**cast** /ka:st/ *vt* (*pt* **cast**) lançar, arremessar; (*shed*) despojar-se de; (*vote*) dar; (*metal*) fundir; (*shadow*) projetar, (*P*) projectar □ *n* (*theatr*) elenco *m*; (*mould*) molde *m*; (*med*) aparelho *m* de gesso. **~ iron** *n* ferro *m* fundido. **~-iron** *a* de ferro fundido; (*fig*) muito forte. **~-offs** *npl* roupa *f* velha

**castanets** /ˌkæstə'nets/ *npl* castanholas *fpl*

**castaway** /'ka:stəweɪ/ *n* náufrago *m*

**caste** /ka:st/ *n* casta *f*

**castigate** /'kæstɪgeɪt/ *vt* castigar

**castle** /'ka:sl/ *n* castelo *m*; (*chess*) torre *f*

**castor** /'ka:stə(r)/ *n* roda *f* de pé de móvel. **~ sugar** açúcar *m* em pó

**castrat|e** /kæ'streɪt/ *vt* castrar. **~ion** /-ʃn/ *n* castração *f*

**casual** /'kæʒuəl/ *a* (*chance: meeting*) casual; (*careless, unmethodical*) descuidado; (*informal*) informal. **~ clothes** roupa *f* prática *or* de lazer. **~ work** trabalho *m* ocasional. **~ly** *adv* casualmente; (*carelessly*) sem cuidado

**casualty** /'kæʒuəltɪ/ *n* (*dead*) morto *m*; (*death*) morte *f*; (*injured*) ferido *m*; (*victim*) vítima *f*; (*mil*) baixa *f*

**cat** /kæt/ *n* gato *m*. **~'s-eyes** *npl* (*P*) reflectores *mpl*

**Catalonia** /kætə'ləʊnɪə/ *n* Catalunha *f*

**catalogue** /'kætəlɒg/ *n* catálogo *m* □ *vt* catalogar

**catalyst** /'kætəlɪst/ *n* catalisador *m*

**catapult** /'kætəpʌlt/ *n* (*child's*) atiradeira *f*, (*P*) fisga *f* □ *vt* catapultar

**cataract** /'kætərækt/ *f* (*waterfall & med*) catarata *f*

**catarrh** /kə'ta:(r)/ *n* catarro *m*

**catastroph|e** /kə'tæstrəfi/ *n* catástrofe *f*. **~ic** /kætəs'trɒfɪk/ *a* catastrófico

**catch** /kætʃ/ *vt* (*pt* caught) apanhar; (*grasp*) agarrar; (*hear*) perceber □ *vi* prender-se (**in** em); (*get stuck*) ficar preso □ *n* apanha *f*, (*of fish*) pesca *f*; (*trick*) ratoeira *f*; (*snag*) problema *m*; (*on door*) trinco *m*; (*fastener*) fecho *m*. **~ fire** pegar fogo, (*P*) incendiar-se. **~ on** (*colloq*) pegar, tornar-se popular. **~ sb's eye** atrair a atenção de alg. **~ sight of** avistar. **~ up** (**with**) pôr-se a par (**com**); (*work*) pôr em dia. **~-phrase** *n* cliché *m*

**catching** /'kætʃɪŋ/ *a* contagioso, infeccioso

**catchment** /'kætʃmənt/ *n* **~ area** (*geog*) bacia *f* de captação; (*fig: of school, hospital*) área *f*

**catchy** /'kætʃɪ/ *a* (*tune*) que pega fácil

**categorical** /kætɪ'gɒrɪkl/ *a* categórico

**category** /'kætɪgərɪ/ *n* categoria *f*

**cater** /'keɪtə(r)/ *vi* fornecer comida (para clubes, casamentos, etc). **~ for** (*pander to*) satisfazer; (*consumers*) dirigir-se a. **~er** *n* fornecedor *m*. **~ing** *n* catering *m*

**caterpillar** /'kætəpɪlə(r)/ *n* lagarta *f*

**cathedral** /kə'θi:drəl/ *n* catedral *f*

**catholic** /'kæθəlɪk/ *a* universal; (*eclectic*) eclético, (*P*) ecléctico. **C~** *a & n* católico (*m*). **C~ism** /kə'θɒlɪsɪzəm/ *n* catolicismo *m*

**cattle** /'kætl/ *npl* gado *m*

**catty** /'kætɪ/ *a* (dissimuladamente) maldoso, com perfídia

**caught** /kɔ:t/ *see* **catch**

**cauldron** /'kɔ:ldrən/ *n* caldeirão *m*

**cauliflower** /'kɒlɪflaʊə(r)/ *n* couveflor *f*

**cause** /kɔ:z/ *n* causa *f* □ *vt* causar. **~ sth to grow/move** *etc* fazer crescer/mexer *etc* alg coisa

**causeway** /'kɔ:zweɪ/ *n* estrada *f* elevada, caminho *m* elevado

**caustic** /'kɔ:stɪk/ *a* cáustico

**cauti|on** /'kɔ:ʃn/ *n* cautela *f*; (*warning*) aviso *m* □ *vt* avisar. **~ous** /'kɔ:ʃəs/ *a* cauteloso. **~ously** *adv* cautelosamente

**cavalry** /'kævəlrɪ/ *n* cavalaria *f*

**cave** /keɪv/ *n* caverna *f*, gruta *f* □ *vi* **~ in** desabar, dar de si

**caveman** /'keɪvmæn/ *n* (*pl* -men) troglodita *m*, homem *m* das cavernas; (*fig*) (tipo) primário *m*

**cavern** /'kævən/ *n* caverna *f*. **~ous** *a* cavernoso

**caviare** /'kævɪɑː(r)/ *n* caviar *m*

**caving** /'keɪvɪŋ/ *n* espeleologia *f*

**cavity** /'kævətɪ/ *n* cavidade *f*

**cavort** /kə'vɔ:t/ *vi* curvetear; (*person*) andar aos pinotes

**CD** /si:'di:/ *see* **compact disc**

**cease** /si:s/ *vt/i* cessar. **~-fire** *n* cessar-fogo *m*. **~less** *a* incessante

**cedar** /'si:də(r)/ *n* cedro *m*

**cedilla** /sɪ'dɪlə/ *n* cedilha *f*

**ceiling** /'si:lɪŋ/ *n* (*lit & fig*) teto *m*, (*P*) tecto *m*

**celebrat|e** /'selɪbreɪt/ *vt/i* celebrar, festejar. **~ion** /'breɪʃn/ *n* celebração *f*, festejo *m*

**celebrated** /'selɪbreɪtɪd/ *a* célebre

**celebrity** /sɪ'lebrətɪ/ *n* celebridade *f*

**celery** /'selərɪ/ *n* aipo *m*

**celiba|te** /'selɪbət/ *a* celibatário. **~cy** *n* celibato *m*

**cell** /sel/ *n* (*of prison, convent*) cela *f*; (*biol, pol, electr*) célula *f*

**cellar** /'selə(r)/ *n* porão *m*, cave *f*; (*for wine*) adega *f*, cave *f*

**cell|o** /'tʃeləʊ/ *n* (*pl* -os) violoncelo *m*. **~ist** *n* violoncelista *m/f*

**Cellophane** /'seləfeɪn/ *n* (*p*) celofane *m*

**cellular** /'seljʊlə(r)/ *a* celular

**Celt** /kelt/ *n* celta *m/f*. **~ic** *a* celta, céltico

**cement** /sɪ'ment/ *n* cimento *m* □ *vt* cimentar. **~-mixer** *n* betoneira *f*

**cemetery** /'semətrı/ *n* cemitério *m*

**censor** /'sensə(r)/ *n* censor *m* □ *vt* censurar. **~ship** *n* censura *f*

**censure** /'senʃə(r)/ *n* censura *f*, crítica *f* □ *vt* censurar, criticar

**census** /'sensəs/ *n* recenseamento *m*, censo *m*

**cent** /sent/ *n* cêntimo *m*

**centenary** /sen'ti:nərı/ *n* centenário *m*

**centigrade** /'sentıɡreıd/ *a* centígrado

**centilitre** /'sentıli:tə(r)/ *n* centilitro *m*

**centimetre** /'sentımi:tə(r)/ *n* centímetro *m*

**centipede** /'sentıpi:d/ *n* centopéia *f*, (P) centopeia *f*

**central** /'sentrəl/ *a* central. **~ heating** aquecimento *m* central. **~ize** *vt* centralizar. **~ly** *adv* no centro

**centre** /'sentə(r)/ *n* centro *m* □ *vt* (*pt* centred) centrar □ *vi* **~ on** concentrar-se em, fixar-se em

**centrifugal** /sen'trıfjʊɡl/ *a* centrífugo

**century** /'sentʃərı/ *n* século *m*

**ceramic** /sı'ræmık/ *a* (*object*) em cerâmica. **~s** *n* cerâmica *f*

**cereal** /'sıərıəl/ *n* cereal *m*

**cerebral** /'serıbrəl/ *a* cerebral

**ceremonial** /serı'məʊnıəl/ *a* de cerimônia □ *n* cerimonial *m*

**ceremon|y** /'serımənı/ *n* cerimônia *f*, (P) cerimónia *f*. **~ious** /-'məʊnıəs/ *a* cerimonioso

**certain** /'sɜ:tn/ *a* certo. **be ~** ter a certeza. **for ~** com certeza, ao certo. **make ~** confirmar, verificar. **~ly** *adv* com certeza, certamente. **~ty** *n* certeza *f*

**certificate** /sə'tıfıkət/ *n* certificado *m*; (*birth, marriage*) certidão *f*; (*health*) atestado *m*

**certif|y** /'sɜ:tıfaı/ *vt/i* certificar. **~ied** *a* (*as insane*) declarado

**cervical** /sɜ:'vaıkl/ *a* cervical; (*of cervix*) do útero

**cesspit, cesspool** /'sespıt, 'sespu:l/ *ns* fossa *f* sanitária

**chafe** /tʃeıf/ *vt/i* esfregar; (*make/become sore*) esfolar/ficar esfolado; (*fig*) irritar(-se)

**chaff** /tʃɑ:f/ *vt* brincar com □ *n* brincadeira *f*; (*husk*) casca *f*

**chaffinch** /'tʃæfıntʃ/ *n* tentilhão *m*

**chagrin** /'ʃæɡrın/ *n* decepção *f*, desgosto *m*, aborrecimento *m*

**chain** /tʃeın/ *n* corrente *f*, cadeia *f*; (*series*) cadeia *f* □ *vt* acorrentar. **~ reaction** reação *f*, (P) reacção *f* em cadeia. **~-smoke** *vi* fumar cigarros um atrás do outro. **~ store** loja *f* pertencente a uma cadeia

**chair** /tʃeə(r)/ *n* cadeira *f*; (*position of chairman*) presidência *f*; (*univ*) cátedra *f* □ *vt* presidir

**chairman** /'tʃeəmən/ *n* (*pl* -men) presidente *mf*

**chalet** /'ʃæleı/ *n* chalé *m*

**chalk** /tʃɔ:k/ *n* greda *f*, cal *f*; (*for writing*) giz *m* □ *vt* traçar com giz

**challeng|e** /'tʃælmdʒ/ *n* desafio *m*; (*by sentry*) interpelação *f* □ *vt* desafiar; (*question truth of*) contestar. **~er** *n* (*sport*) pretendente *mf* (ao título). **~ing** *a* estimulante, que constitui um desafio

**chamber** /'tʃeımbə(r)/ *n* (*old use*) aposento *m*. **~-maid** *n* arrumadeira *f*. **~ music** música *f* de câmara. **C~ of Commerce** Câmara *f* de Comércio

**chamois** /'ʃæmı/ *n* **~(-leather)** camurça *f*

**champagne** /ʃæm'peın/ *n* champanhe *m*

**champion** /'tʃæmpıən/ *n* campeão *m*, campeã *f* □ *vt* defender. **~ship** *n* campeonato *m*

**chance** /tʃɑ:ns/ *n* acaso *m*; (*luck*) sorte *f*; (*opportunity*) oportunidade *f*, chance *f*; (*likelihood*) hipótese *f*, probabilidade *f*; (*risk*) risco *m* □ *a* casual, fortuito □ *vi* calhar □ *vt* arriscar. **by ~** por acaso

**chancellor** /'tʃɑ:nsələ(r)/ *n* chanceler *m*. **C~ of the Exchequer** Ministro *m* das Finanças

**chancy** /'tʃɑ:nsı/ *a* arriscado

**chandelier** /ʃændə'lıə(r)/ *n* lustre *m*

**change** /tʃemdʒ/ *vt* mudar; (*exchange*) trocar (**for** por); (*clothes, house, trains, etc*) mudar de □ *vi* mudar; (*clothes*) mudar-se, mudar de roupa □ *n* mudança *f*; (*money*) troco *m*. **a ~ of clothes** uma muda de roupa. **~ hands** (*ownership*) mudar de dono. **~ into** (*a butterfly etc*) transformar-se em; (*evening dress etc*) pôr. **~ one's mind** mudar de idéia. **~ over** passar, mudar (**to** para). **~-over** *n* mudança *f*. **~able** *a* variável

**channel** /'tʃænl/ *n* canal *m* □ *vt* (*pt* channelled) canalizar. **the C~ Islands** as Ilhas do Canal da Mancha. **the (English) C~** o Canal da Mancha

**chant** /tʃɑ:nt/ *n* cântico *m*; (*of crowd etc*) *vt/i* cantar, entoar

**chao|s** /'keıɒs/ *n* caos *m*. **~tic** /-'ɒtık/ *a* caótico

**chap** /tʃæp/ *n* (*colloq*) sujeito *m*, (B) cara *m*, (P) tipo *m*

**chapel** /'tʃæpl/ *n* capela *f*

**chaperon** /'ʃæpərəʊn/ *n* pau-de-cabeleira *m*, chaperon *m* □ *vt* servir de pau-de-cabeleira *or* de chaperon

**chaplain** /'tʃæplın/ *n* capelão *m*. **~cy** *n* capelania *f*

**chapter** /'tʃæptə(r)/ *n* capítulo *m*

**char** /tʃɑ:(r)/ *vt* (*pt* charred) carbonizar

**character** /'kærəktə(r)/ *n* caráter *m*,
(P) carácter *m*; (*in novel, play*) perso-
nagem *m*; (*reputation*) fama *f*; (*eccentric person*) excêntrico *m*; (*letter*)
caractere *m*, (P) carácter *m*. **~ize** *vt*
caracterizar

**characteristic** /kærəktə'rɪstɪk/ *a*
característico □ *n* característica *f*.
**~ally** *adv* tipicamente

**charade** /ʃə'rɑːd/ *n* charada *f*

**charcoal** /'tʃɑːkəʊl/ *n* carvão *m* de
lenha

**charge** /tʃɑːdʒ/ *n* preço *m*; (*electr, mil*)
carga *f*; (*jur*) acusação *f*; (*task, custody*) cargo *m* □ *vt/i* (*price*) cobrar;
(*enemy*) atacar; (*jur*) incriminar. **be
in ~ of** ter a cargo. **take ~ of** encarregar-se de

**chariot** /'tʃærɪət/ *n* carro *m* de guerra *or* triunfal

**charisma** /kə'rɪzmə/ *n* carisma *m*.
**~tic** /kærɪz'mætɪk/ *a* carismático

**charit|y** /'tʃærətɪ/ *n* caridade *f*; (*so-
ciety*) instituição *f* de caridade.
**~able** *a* caridoso

**charlatan** /'ʃɑːlətən/ *n* charlatão *m*

**charm** /tʃɑːm/ *n* encanto *m*, charme
*m*; (*spell*) feitiço *m*; (*talisman*) amuleto *m* □ *vt* encantar. **~ing** *a* encantador

**chart** /tʃɑːt/ *n* (*naut*) carta *f*; (*table*)
mapa *m*, gráfico *m*, tabela *f* □ *vt* fazer
o mapa de

**charter** /'tʃɑːtə(r)/ *n* carta *f*. **~
(flight)** (voo) charter *m* □ *vt* fretar.
**~ed accountant** *n* perito *m* contador, (P) perito *m* de contabilidade

**charwoman** /'tʃɑːwʊmən/ *n* (*pl
-women*) faxineira *f*, (P) mulher *f* a
dias

**chase** /tʃeɪs/ *vt* perseguir □ *vi* (*colloq*)
correr (*after* atrás de) □ *n* caça *f*,
perseguição *f*. **~ away** *or* **off** afugentar, expulsar

**chasm** /'kæzm/ *n* abismo *m*

**chassis** /'ʃæsɪ/ *n* chassi *m*

**chaste** /tʃeɪst/ *a* casto

**chastise** /tʃæs'taɪz/ *vt* castigar

**chastity** /'tʃæstətɪ/ *n* castidade *f*

**chat** /tʃæt/ *n* conversa *f* □ *vi* (*pt
chatted*) conversar, cavaquear. **have
a ~** bater um papo, (P) dar dois dedos
de conversa. **~ty** *a* conversador

**chatter** /'tʃætə(r)/ *vi* tagarelar. **his
teeth are ~ing** seus dentes estão ti-
ritando □ *n* tagarelice *f*

**chauffeur** /'ʃəʊfə(r)/ *n* motorista *m*,
chofer (particular) *m*, chauffeur *m*

**chauvinis|t** /'ʃəʊvɪnɪst/ *n* chauvinis-
ta *mf*. **male ~t** (*pej*) machista *m*.
**~m** /-zəm/ *n* chauvinismo *m*

**cheap** /tʃiːp/ *a* (*-er, -est*) barato; (*fare,
rate*) reduzido. **~(ly)** *adv* barato.
**~ness** *n* barateza *f*

**cheapen** /'tʃiːpən/ *vt* depreciar

**cheat** /tʃiːt/ *vt* enganar, trapacear □ *vi*
(*at games*) roubar, (P) fazer batota; (*in
exams*) copiar □ *n* intrujão *m*; (*at
games*) trapaceiro *m*, (P) batoteiro *m*

**check**[1] /tʃek/ *vt/i* (*examine*) verificar;
(*tickets*) revisar; (*restrain*) controlar,
refrear □ *n* verificação *f*; (*tickets*) controle *m*; (*curb*) freio *m*; (*chess*) xeque
*m*; (*Amer: bill*) conta *f*; (*Amer:
cheque*) cheque *m*. **~ in** assinar o registro; (*at airport*) fazer o check-in.
**~-in** *n* check-in *m*. **~ out** pagar a
conta. **~-out** *n* caixa *f*. **~-up** *n* exame
*m* médico, check-up *m*

**check**[2] /tʃek/ *n* (*pattern*) xadrez *m*.
**~ed** *a* de xadrez

**checkmate** /'tʃekmeɪt/ *n* xeque-mate
*m*

**cheek** /tʃiːk/ *n* face *f*; (*fig*) descaramento *m*. **~y** *a* descarado

**cheer** /tʃɪə(r)/ *n* alegria *f*; (*shout*) viva
*m* □ *vt/i* aclamar, aplaudir. **~s!** à sua,
(P) vossa (saúde)!; (*thank you*)
obrigadinho. **~ (up)** animar(-se).
**~ful** *a* bem disposto; alegre

**cheerio** /tʃɪərɪ'əʊ/ *int* (*colloq*) até logo,
(P) adeusinho

**cheese** /tʃiːz/ *n* queijo *m*

**cheetah** /'tʃiːtə/ *n* chita *f*, lobo-tigre *m*

**chef** /ʃef/ *n* cozinheiro-chefe *m*

**chemical** /'kemɪkl/ *a* químico □ *n*
produto *m* químico

**chemist** /'kemɪst/ *n* farmacêutico *m*;
(*scientist*) químico *m*. **~'s (shop)** *n*
farmácia *f*. **~ry** *n* química *f*

**cheque** /tʃek/ *n* cheque *m*. **~-book** *n*
talão *m* de cheques. **~-card** *n* cartão
*m* de banco

**cherish** /'tʃerɪʃ/ *vt* estimar, querer;
(*hope*) acalentar

**cherry** /'tʃerɪ/ *n* cereja *f*. **~-tree** *n*
cerejeira *f*

**chess** /tʃes/ *n* jogo *m* de xadrez. **~-
board** *n* tabuleiro *m* de xadrez

**chest** /tʃest/ *n* peito *m*; (*for money,
jewels*) cofre *m*. **~ of drawers**
cômoda *f*, (P) cómoda *f*

**chestnut** /'tʃesnʌt/ *n* castanha *f*. **~-
tree** *n* castanheiro *m*

**chew** /tʃuː/ *vt* mastigar. **~ing-gum** *n*
chiclete *m*, (P) pastilha *f* elástica

**chic** /ʃiːk/ *a* chique

**chick** /tʃɪk/ *n* pinto *m*

**chicken** /'tʃɪkɪn/ *n* galinha *f* □ *vi* **~
out** (*sl*) acovardar-se. **~-pox** *n* catapora *f*, (P) varicela *f*

**chicory** /'tʃɪkərɪ/ *n* (*for coffee*) chi-
cória *f*; (*for salad*) endívia *f*

**chief** /tʃiːf/ *n* chefe *m* □ *a* principal.
**~ly** *adv* principalmente

**chilblain** /'tʃɪlbleɪn/ *n* frieira *f*

**child** /tʃaɪld/ *n* (*pl* **children**
/'tʃɪldrən/) criança *f*; (*son*) filho *m*;

(*daughter*) filha *f*. **~hood** *n* infância *f*, meninice *f*. **~ish** *a* infantil; (*immature*) acriançado, pueril. **~less** *a* sem filhos. **~like** *a* infantil. **~-minder** *n* babá *f* que cuida de crianças em sua própria casa

**childbirth** /'tʃaɪldbɜ:θ/ *n* parto *m*

**Chile** /'tʃɪlɪ/ *n* Chile *m*. **~an** *a* & *n* chileno (*m*)

**chill** /tʃɪl/ *n* frio *m*; (*med*) resfriado *m*, (*P*) constipação *f* □ *vt/i* arrefecer; (*culin*) refrigerar. **~y** *a* frio. **be** or **feel ~y** ter frio

**chilli** /'tʃɪlɪ/ *n* (*pl* **-ies**) malagueta *f*

**chime** /tʃaɪm/ *n* carrilhão *m*; (*sound*) música *m* de carrilhão □ *vt/i* tocar

**chimney** /'tʃɪmnɪ/ *n* (*pl* **-eys**) chaminé *f*. **~-sweep** *n* limpador *m* de chaminés, (*P*) limpa-chaminés *m*

**chimpanzee** /tʃɪmpæn'zi:/ *n* chimpanzé *m*

**chin** /tʃɪn/ *n* queixo *m*

**china** /'tʃaɪnə/ *n* porcelana *f*, (*crockery*) louça *f*

**Chin|a** /'tʃaɪnə/ *n* China *f*. **~ese** /-'ni:z/ *a* & *n* chinês (*m*)

**chink**[1] /tʃɪŋk/ *n* (*crack*) fenda *f*, fresta *f*

**chink**[2] /tʃɪŋk/ *n* tinir *m* □ *vt/i* (fazer) tinir

**chip** /tʃɪp/ *n* (*broken piece*) bocado *m*; (*culin*) batata *f* frita em palitos; (*gambling*) ficha *f*; (*electronic*) chip *m*, circuito *m* integrado □ *vt/i* (*pt* **chipped**) lascar(-se)

**chipboard** /'tʃɪpbɔ:d/ *n* compensado *m* (de madeira)

**chiropodist** /kɪ'rɒpədɪst/ *n* calista *mf*

**chirp** /tʃɜ:p/ *n* pipilar *m*; (*of cricket*) cricri *m* □ *vi* pipilar; (*cricket*) cantar, fazer cricri

**chisel** /'tʃɪzl/ *n* cinzel *m*, escopro *m* □ *vt* (*pt* **chiselled**) talhar

**chivalr|y** /'ʃɪvlrɪ/ *n* cavalheirismo *m*. **~ous** *a* cavalheiresco

**chive** /tʃaɪv/ *n* cebolinho *m*

**chlorine** /'klɔ:ri:n/ *n* cloro *m*

**chocolate** /'tʃɒklɪt/ *n* chocolate *m*

**choice** /tʃɔɪs/ *n* escolha *f* □ *a* escolhido, seleto, (*P*) seleccionado

**choir** /'kwaɪə(r)/ *n* coro *m*

**choirboy** /'kwaɪəbɔɪ/ *n* menino *m* de coro, corista *m*, (*P*) coralista *m*

**choke** /tʃəʊk/ *vt/i* sufocar; (*on food*) engasgar(-se) □ *n* (*auto*) afogador *m*, (*P*) botão *m* do ar (*colloq*)

**cholesterol** /kə'lestərɒl/ *n* colesterol *m*

**choose** /tʃu:z/ *vt/i* (*pt* **chose**, *pp* **chosen**) escolher; (*prefer*) preferir. **~ to do** decidir fazer

**choosy** /'tʃu:zɪ/ *a* (*colloq*) exigente, difícil de contentar

**chop** /tʃɒp/ *vt/i* (*pt* **chopped**) cortar □

*n* (*wood*) machadada *f*; (*culin*) costeleta *f*. **~ down** abater. **~per** *n* cutelo *m*; (*sl: helicopter*) helicóptero *m*

**choppy** /'tʃɒpɪ/ *a* (*sea*) picado

**chopstick** /'tʃɒpstɪk/ *n* fachi *m*, pauzinho *m*

**choral** /'kɔ:rəl/ *a* coral

**chord** /kɔ:d/ *n* (*mus*) acorde *m*

**chore** /tʃɔ:(r)/ *n* trabalho *m*; (*unpleasant task*) tarefa *f* maçante. **household ~s** afazeres *mpl* domésticos

**choreograph|er** /kɒrɪ'ɒgrəfə(r)/ *n* coreógrafo *m*. **~y** *n* coreografia *f*

**chortle** /'tʃɔ:tl/ *n* risada *f* □ *vi* rir alto

**chorus** /'kɔ:rəs/ *n* coro *m*; (*of song*) refrão *m*, estribilho *m*

**chose, chosen** /tʃəʊz, 'tʃəʊzn/ *see* **choose**

**Christ** /kraɪst/ *n* Cristo *m*

**christen** /'krɪsn/ *vt* batizar, (*P*) baptizar. **~ing** *n* batismo *m*, (*P*) baptismo *m*

**Christian** /'krɪstʃən/ *a* & *n* cristão (*m*). **~ name** nome *m* de batismo, (*P*) baptismo. **~ity** /-stɪ'ænətɪ/ *n* cristandade *f*

**Christmas** /'krɪsməs/ *n* Natal *m* □ *a* do Natal. **~ card** cartão *m* de Boas Festas. **~ Day/Eve** dia *m*/véspera *f* de Natal. **~ tree** árvore *f* de Natal

**chrome** /krəʊm/ *n* cromo *m*

**chromosome** /'krəʊməsəʊm/ *n* cromossoma *m*

**chronic** /'krɒnɪk/ *a* crônico, (*P*) crónico

**chronicle** /'krɒnɪkl/ *n* crônica *f*

**chronological** /krɒnə'lɒdʒɪkl/ *a* cronológico

**chrysanthemum** /krɪ'sænθəməm/ *n* crisântemo *m*

**chubby** /'tʃʌbɪ/ *a* (**-ier**, **-iest**) gorducho, rechonchudo

**chuck** /tʃʌk/ *vt* (*colloq*) deitar, atirar. **~ out** (*person*) expulsar; (*thing*) jogar fora, (*P*) deitar fora

**chuckle** /'tʃʌkl/ *n* riso *m* abafado □ *vi* rir sozinho

**chum** /tʃʌm/ *n* (*colloq*) amigo *m* íntimo, camarada *mf*. **~my** *a* amigável

**chunk** /tʃʌŋk/ *n* (grande) bocado *m*, naco *m*

**church** /tʃɜ:tʃ/ *n* igreja *f*

**churchyard** /'tʃɜ:tʃjɑ:d/ *n* cemitério *m*

**churlish** /'tʃɜ:lɪʃ/ *a* grosseiro, indelicado

**churn** /tʃɜ:n/ *n* batedeira *f*; (*milk-can*) vasilha *f* de leite □ *vt* bater. **~ out** produzir em série

**chute** /ʃu:t/ *n* calha *f*; (*for rubbish*) conduta *f* de lixo

**chutney** /'tʃʌtnɪ/ *n* (*pl* **-eys**) chutney *m*

**cider** /'saɪdə(r)/ *n* sidra *f*, (*P*) cidra *f*

**cigar** /sɪ'gɑ:(r)/ *n* charuto *m*

**cigarette** /ˌsɪgəˈret/ *n* cigarro *m*. **~-case** *n* cigarreira *f*

**cinder** /ˈsɪndə(r)/ *n* brasa *f*. **burnt to a ~** estorricado

**cinema** /ˈsɪnəmə/ *n* cinema *m*

**cinnamon** /ˈsɪnəmən/ *n* canela *f*

**cipher** /ˈsaɪfə(r)/ *n* cifra *f*

**circle** /ˈsɜːkl/ *n* círculo *m*; (*theat*) balcão *m* □ *vt* dar a volta a □ *vi* descrever círculos, voltear

**circuit** /ˈsɜːkɪt/ *n* circuito *m*

**circuitous** /sɜːˈkjuːɪtəs/ *a* indireto, tortuoso

**circular** /ˈsɜːkjʊlə(r)/ *a* circular

**circulat|e** /ˈsɜːkjʊleɪt/ *vt/i* (fazer) circular. **~ion** /-ˈleɪʃn/ *n* circulação *f*; (*sales of newspaper*) tiragem *f*

**circumcis|e** /ˈsɜːkəmsaɪz/ *vt* circuncidar. **~ion** /-ˈsɪʒn/ *n* circuncisão *f*

**circumference** /səˈkʌmfərəns/ *n* circunferência *f*

**circumflex** /ˈsɜːkəmfleks/ *n* circunflexo *m*

**circumstance** /ˈsɜːkəmstəns/ *n* circunstância *f*. **~s** (*means*) situação *f* econômica, (*P*) económica

**circus** /ˈsɜːkəs/ *n* circo *m*

**cistern** /ˈsɪstən/ *n* reservatório *m*; (*of WC*) autoclismo *m*

**cit|e** /saɪt/ *vt* citar. **~ation** /-ˈteɪʃn/ *n* citação *f*

**citizen** /ˈsɪtɪzn/ *n* cidadão *m*, cidadã *f*; (*of town*) habitante *mf*. **~ship** *n* cidadania *f*

**citrus** /ˈsɪtrəs/ *n* **~ fruit** citrino *m*

**city** /ˈsɪtɪ/ *n* cidade *f*

**civic** /ˈsɪvɪk/ *a* cívico

**civil** /ˈsɪvl/ *a* civil; (*rights*) cívico; (*polite*) delicado. **~ servant** funcionário *m* público. **C~ Service** Administração *f* Pública. **~ war** guerra *f* civil. **~ity** /-ˈvɪlətɪ/ *n* civilidade *f*, cortesia *f*

**civilian** /sɪˈvɪlɪən/ *a* & *n* civil (*mf*), paisano *m*

**civiliz|e** /ˈsɪvəlaɪz/ *vt* civilizar. **~ation** /-ˈzeɪʃn/ *n* civilização *f*

**claim** /kleɪm/ *vt* reclamar; (*assert*) pretender □ *vi* (*from insurance*) reclamar □ *n* reivindicação *f*; (*assertion*) afirmação *f*; (*right*) direito *m*; (*from insurance*) reclamação *f*

**clairvoyant** /kleəˈvɔɪənt/ *n* vidente *mf* □ *a* clarividente

**clam** /klæm/ *n* molusco *m*

**clamber** /ˈklæmbə(r)/ *vi* trepar

**clammy** /ˈklæmɪ/ *a* (-**ier**, -**iest**) úmido, (*P*) húmido e pegajoso

**clamour** /ˈklæmə(r)/ *n* clamor *m*, vociferação *f* □ *vi* **~ for** exigir aos gritos

**clamp** /klæmp/ *n* grampo *m*; (*for car*) bloqueador *m* □ *vt* prender com grampo; (*a car*) bloquear. **~ down on**

apertar, suprimir; (*colloq*) cair em cima de (*colloq*)

**clan** /klæn/ *n* clã *m*

**clandestine** /klænˈdestɪn/ *a* clandestino

**clang** /klæŋ/ *n* tinir *m*

**clap** /klæp/ *vt/i* (*pt* **clapped**) aplaudir; (*put*) meter □ *n* aplauso *m*; (*of thunder*) ribombo *m*. **~ one's hands** bater palmas

**claptrap** /ˈklæptræp/ *n* parlapatice *f*

**claret** /ˈklærət/ *n* clarete *m*

**clarif|y** /ˈklærɪfaɪ/ *vt* esclarecer. **~ication** /-ɪˈkeɪʃn/ *n* esclarecimento *m*

**clarinet** /klærɪˈnet/ *n* clarinete *m*

**clarity** /ˈklærətɪ/ *n* claridade *f*

**clash** /klæʃ/ *n* choque *m*; (*sound*) estridor *m*; (*fig*) conflito *m* □ *vt/i* entrechocar(-se); (*of colours*) destoar

**clasp** /klɑːsp/ *n* (*fastener*) fecho *m*; (*hold, grip*) aperto *m* de mão □ *vt* apertar, serrar

**class** /klɑːs/ *n* classe *f* □ *vt* classificar

**classic** /ˈklæsɪk/ *a* & *n* clássico (*m*). **~s** *npl* letras *fpl* clássicas, (*P*) estudos *mpl* clássicos. **~al** *a* clássico

**classif|y** /ˈklæsɪfaɪ/ *vt* classificar. **~ication** /-ɪˈkeɪʃn/ *n* classificação *f*. **~ied advertisement** (anúncio *m*) classificado (*m*)

**classroom** /ˈklɑːsruːm/ *n* sala *f* de aulas

**clatter** /ˈklætə(r)/ *n* estardalhaço *m* □ *vi* fazer barulho

**clause** /klɔːz/ *n* cláusula *f*; (*gram*) oração *f*

**claustrophob|ia** /klɔːstrəˈfəʊbɪə/ *n* claustrofobia *f*. **~ic** *a* claustrofóbico

**claw** /klɔː/ *n* garra *f*; (*of lobster*) tenaz *f*, pinça *f* □ *vt* (*seize*) agarrar; (*scratch*) arranhar; (*tear*) rasgar

**clay** /kleɪ/ *n* argila *f*, barro *m*

**clean** /kliːn/ *a* (-**er**, -**est**) limpo □ *adv* completamente □ *vt* limpar □ *vi* **~ up** fazer a limpeza. **~-shaven** *a* de cara rapada. **~er** *n* faxineira *f*, (*P*) mulher *f* da limpeza; (*of clothes*) empregado *m* da tinturaria. **~ly** *adv* com limpeza, como deve ser

**cleans|e** /klenz/ *vt* limpar; (*fig*) purificar. **~ing cream** creme *m* de limpeza

**clear** /klɪə(r)/ *a* (-**er**, -**est**) claro; (*glass*) transparente; (*without obstacles*) livre; (*profit*) líquido; (*sky*) limpo □ *adv* claramente □ *vt* (*snow, one's name, etc*) limpar; (*the table*) tirar; (*jump*) transpor; (*debt*) saldar; (*jur*) absolver; (*through customs*) despachar □ *vi* (*fog*) dissipar-se; (*sky*) limpar. **~ of** (*away from*) afastado de. **~ off** *or* **out** (*sl*) sair andando, zarpar. **~ out** (*clean*) fazer a limpeza. ~ **up** (*tidy*) arrumar; (*mystery*) desvendar; (*of weather*) clarear, limpar. ~**ly** *adv* claramente

**clearance** /'klɪərəns/ *n* autorização *f*; (*for ship*) despacho *m*; (*space*) espaço *m* livre. ~ **sale** liquidação *f*, saldos *mpl*

**clearing** /'klɪərɪŋ/ *n* clareira *f*

**clearway** /'klɪəweɪ/ *n* rodovia *f* de estacionamento proibido

**cleavage** /'kliːvɪdʒ/ *n* divisão *f*; (*between breasts*) rego *m* (*of dress*) decote *m*

**cleaver** /'kliːvə(r)/ *n* cutelo *m*

**clef** /klef/ *n* (*mus*) clave *f*

**cleft** /kleft/ *n* fenda *f*

**clench** /klentʃ/ *vt* (*teeth, fists*) cerrar; (*grasp*) agarrar

**clergy** /'klɜːdʒɪ/ *n* clero *m*. ~**man** *n* (*pl* -men) clérigo *m*, sacerdote *m*

**cleric** /'klerɪk/ *n* clérigo *m*. ~**al** *a* (*relig*) clerical; (*of clerks*) de escritório

**clerk** /klɑːk/ *n* auxiliar *m* de escritório

**clever** /'klevə(r)/ *a* (-er, -est) esperto, inteligente; (*skilful*) hábil, habilidoso. ~**ly** *adv* inteligentemente; (*skilfully*) habilmente, habilidosamente. ~**ness** *n* esperteza *f*, inteligência *f*

**cliché** /'kliːʃeɪ/ *n* chavão *m*, lugar-comum *m*, cliché *m*

**click** /klɪk/ *n* estalido *m*, clique *m* □ *vi* dar um estalido

**client** /'klaɪənt/ *n* cliente *mf*

**clientele** /kliːənˈtel/ *n* clientela *f*

**cliff** /klɪf/ *n* penhasco *m*. ~**s** *npl* falésia *f*

**climat|e** /'klaɪmɪt/ *n* clima *m*. ~**ic** /'mætɪk/ *a* climático

**climax** /'klaɪmæks/ *n* clímax *m*, ponto *m* culminante

**climb** /klaɪm/ *vt* (*stairs*) subir; (*tree, wall*) subir em, trepar em; (*mountain*) escalar □ *vi* subir, trepar □ *n* subida *f*; (*mountain*) escalada *f*. ~ **down** descer; (*fig*) dar a mão à palmatória (*fig*). ~**er** *n* (*sport*) alpinista *mf*; (*plant*) trepadeira *f*

**clinch** /klɪntʃ/ *vt* (*deal*) fechar; (*argument*) resolver

**cling** /klɪŋ/ *vi* (*pt* clung) ~ (**to**) agarrar-se (a); (*stick*) colar-se (a)

**clinic** /'klɪnɪk/ *n* clínica *f*

**clinical** /'klɪnɪkl/ *a* clínico

**clink** /klɪŋk/ *n* tinido *m* □ *vt/i* (fazer) tilintar

**clip**[1] /klɪp/ *m* (*for paper*) clipe *m*; (*for hair*) grampo *m*, (*P*) gancho *m*; (*for tube*) braçadeira *f* □ *vt* (*pt* clipped) prender

**clip**[2] /klɪp/ *vt* (*pt* clipped) cortar; (*trim*) aparar □ *n* tosquia *f*; (*colloq: blow*) murro *m*. ~**ping** *n* recorte *m*

**clique** /kliːk/ *n* panelinha *f*, facção *f*, conventículo *m*

**cloak** /kləʊk/ *n* capa *f*, manto *m*

**cloakroom** /'kləʊkruːm/ *n* vestiário *m*; (*toilet*) toalete *m*, (*P*) lavabo *m*

**clock** /klɒk/ *n* relógio *m* □ *vt/i* ~**in/out** marcar o ponto (à entrada/à saída). ~ **up** (*colloq: miles etc*) fazer

**clockwise** /'klɒkwaɪz/ *a & adv* no sentido dos ponteiros do relógio

**clockwork** /'klɒkwɜːk/ *n* mecanismo *m*. **go like** ~ ir às mil maravilhas

**clog** /klɒg/ *n* tamanco *m*, soco *m* □ *vt/i* (*pt* clogged) entupir(-se)

**cloister** /'klɔɪstə(r)/ *n* claustro *m*

**close**[1] /kləʊs/ *a* (-er, -est) próximo (**to** de); (*link, collaboration*) estreito; (*friend*) íntimo; (*weather*) abafado □ *adv* perto. ~ **at hand**, ~ **by** muito perto. ~ **together** (*crowded*) espremido. **have a** ~ **shave** (*fig*) escapar por um triz. ~-**up** *n* grande plano *m*. ~**ly** *adv* de perto. ~**ness** *n* proximidade *f*

**close**[2] /kləʊz/ *vt/i* fechar(-se); (*end*) terminar; (*of shop etc*) fechar □ *n* fim *m*. ~**d shop** organização *f* que só admite trabalhadores sindicalizados

**closet** /'klɒzɪt/ *n* (*Amer*) armário *m*

**closure** /'kləʊʒə(r)/ *n* encerramento *m*

**clot** /klɒt/ *n* coágulo *m* □ *vi* (*pt* clotted) coagular

**cloth** /klɒθ/ *n* pano *m*; (*tablecloth*) toalha *f* de mesa

**cloth|e** /kləʊð/ *vt* vestir. ~**ing** *n* vestuário *m*, roupa *f*

**clothes** /kləʊðz/ *npl* roupa *f*, vestuário *m*. ~-**line** *n* varal *m* para roupa

**cloud** /klaʊd/ *n* núvem *f* □ *vt/i* toldar(-se). ~**y** *a* nublado, toldado; (*liquid*) turvo

**clout** /klaʊt/ *n* cascudo *m*, (*P*) carolo *m*; (*colloq: power*) poder *m* efectivo □ *vt* (*colloq*) bater

**clove** /kləʊv/ *n* cravo *m*. ~ **of garlic** dente *m* de alho

**clover** /'kləʊvə(r)/ *n* trevo *m*

**clown** /klaʊn/ *n* palhaço *m* □ *vi* fazer palhaçadas

**club** /klʌb/ *n* clube *m*; (*weapon*) cacete *m*. ~**s** (*cards*) paus *mpl* □ *vt/i* (*pt* clubbed) dar bordoadas *or* cacetadas (em). ~ **together** (*share costs*) cotizar-se

**cluck** /klʌk/ *vi* cacarejar

**clue** /kluː/ *n* indício *m*, pista *f*; (*in crossword*) definição *f*. **not have a** ~ (*colloq*) não fazer a menor idéia

**clump** /klʌmp/ *n* maciço *m*, tufo *m*

**clumsy** /'klʌmzɪ/ *a* (-ier, -iest) desajeitado

**clung** /klʌŋ/ *see* cling

**cluster** /'klʌstə(r)/ *n* (pequeno) grupo *m*; (*bot*) cacho *m* □ *vt/i* agrupar(-se)

**clutch** /klʌtʃ/ *vt* agarrar (em), apertar □ *vi* agarrar-se (**at** a) □ *n* (*auto*) embreagem *f*, (*P*) embraiagem *f*. **~es** *npl* garras *fpl*

**clutter** /'klʌtə(r)/ *n* barafunda *f*, desordem *f* □ *vt* atravancar

**coach** /kəʊtʃ/ *n* ônibus *m*, (*P*) camioneta *f*; (*of train*) carruagem *f*; (*sport*) treinador *m* □ *vt* (*tutor*) dar aulas a; (*sport*) treinar

**coagulate** /kəʊ'ægjʊleɪt/ *vt/i* coagular(-se)

**coal** /kəʊl/ *n* carvão *m*

**coalfield** /'kəʊlfiːld/ *n* região *f* carbonífera

**coalition** /kəʊə'lɪʃn/ *n* coligação *f*

**coarse** /kɔːs/ *a* (**-er**, **-est**) grosseiro

**coast** /kəʊst/ *n* costa *f* □ *vi* costear; (*cycle*) descer em roda-livre; (*car*) ir em ponto morto. **~al** *a* costeiro

**coastguard** /'kəʊstgaːd/ *n* polícia *f* marítima

**coastline** /'kəʊstlam/ *n* litoral *m*

**coat** /kəʊt/ *n* casaco *m*; (*of animal*) pêlo *m*; (*of paint*) camada *f*, demão *f* □ *vt* cobrir. **~ of arms** brasão *m*. **~ing** *n* camada *f*

**coax** /kəʊks/ *vt* levar com afagos ou lisonjas, convencer

**cobble** /'kɒbl/ *n* **~(-stone)** *n* pedra *f* de calçada

**cobweb** /'kɒbweb/ *n* teia *f* de aranha

**cocaine** /kəʊ'kem/ *n* cocaína *f*

**cock** /kɒk/ *n* (*male bird*) macho *m*; (*rooster*) galo *m* □ *vt* (*gun*) engatilhar; (*ears*) fitar. **~-eyed** *a* (*sl: askew*) de esguelha

**cockerel** /'kɒkərəl/ *n* frango *m*, galo *m* novo

**cockle** /'kɒkl/ *n* berbigão *m*

**cockney** /'kɒknɪ/ *n* (*pl* **-eys**) (*person*) londrino *m*; (*dialect*) dialeto *m* do leste de Londres

**cockpit** /'kɒkpɪt/ *n* cabine *f*

**cockroach** /'kɒkrəʊtʃ/ *n* barata *f*

**cocktail** /'kɒkteɪl/ *n* cocktail *m*, coquetel *m*. **fruit ~** salada *f* de fruta

**cocky** /'kɒkɪ/ *a* (**-ier**, **-iest**) convencido (*colloq*)

**cocoa** /'kəʊkəʊ/ *n* cacau *m*

**coconut** /'kəʊkənʌt/ *n* coco *m*

**cocoon** /kə'kuːn/ *n* casulo *m*

**cod** /kɒd/ *n* (*pl invar*) bacalhau *m*. **~-liver oil** óleo *m* de fígado de bacalhau

**code** /kəʊd/ *n* código *m* □ *vt* codificar

**coeducational** /kəʊedʒʊ'keɪʃənl/ *a* misto

**coerc|e** /kəʊ'ɜːs/ *vt* coagir. **~ion** /-ʃn/ *n* coação *f*, (*P*) coacção *f*

**coexist** /kəʊɪg'zɪst/ *vi* coexistir. **~ence** *n* coexistência *f*

**coffee** /'kɒfɪ/ *n* café *m*. **~ bar** café *m*.

**~-pot** *n* cafeteira *f*. **~-table** *n* mesa *f* baixa

**coffin** /'kɒfɪn/ *n* caixão *m*

**cog** /kɒg/ *n* dente *m* de roda. **a ~ in the machine** (*fig*) uma rodinha numa engrenagem

**cogent** /'kəʊdʒənt/ *a* convincente; (*relevant*) pertinente

**cognac** /'kɒnjæk/ *n* conhaque *m*

**cohabit** /kəʊ'hæbɪt/ *vi* coabitar

**coherent** /kə'hɪərənt/ *a* coerente

**coil** /kɔɪl/ *vt/i* enrolar(-se) □ *n* rolo *m*; (*electr*) bobina *f*, (*one ring*) espiral *f*; (*contraceptive*) dispositivo *m* intrauterino, DIU

**coin** /kɔm/ *n* moeda *f* □ *vt* cunhar

**coincide** /kəʊɪn'saɪd/ *vi* coincidir

**coinciden|ce** /kəʊ'ɪnsɪdəns/ *n* coincidência *f*. **~tal** /'dentl/ *a* que acontece por coincidência

**colander** /'kʌləndə(r)/ *n* peneira *f*, (*P*) coador *m*

**cold** /kəʊld/ *a* (**-er**, **-est**) frio □ *n* frio *m*; (*med*) resfriado *m*, constipação *f*. **be** *or* **feel ~** estar com frio. **it's ~** está frio. **~-blooded** *a* (*person*) insensível; (*deed*) a sangue frio. **~cream** creme *m* para a pele. **~ness** *n* frio *m*; (*of feeling*) frieza *f*

**coleslaw** /'kəʊlslɔː/ *n* salada *f* de repolho cru

**colic** /'kɒlɪk/ *n* cólica(s) *f* (*pl*)

**collaborat|e** /kə'læbəreɪt/ *vi* colaborar. **~ion** /-'reɪʃn/ *n* colaboração *f*. **~or** *n* colaborador *m*

**collapse** /kə'læps/ *vi* desabar; (*med*) ter um colapso □ *n* colapso *m*

**collapsible** /kə'læpsəbl/ *a* desmontável, dobrável

**collar** /'kɒlə(r)/ *n* gola *f*; (*of shirt*) colarinho *m*; (*of dog*) coleira *f* □ *vt* (*collog*) pôr a mão a. **~-bone** *n* clavícula *f*

**colleague** /'kɒliːg/ *n* colega *mf*

**collect** /kə'lekt/ *vt* (*gather*) juntar; (*fetch*) ir/vir buscar; (*money, rent*) cobrar; (*as hobby*) colecionar, (*P*) coleccionar □ *vi* juntar-se. **call ~** (*Amer*) chamar a cobrar. **~ion** /-ʃn/ *n* coleção *f*, (*P*) colecção *f*; (*in church*) coleta *f*, (*P*) colecta *f*; (*of mail*) tiragem *f*, coleta *f*, (*P*) abertura *f*. **~or** *n* (*as hobby*) colecionador *m*, (*P*) coleccionador *m*

**collective** /kə'lektɪv/ *a* coletivo, (*P*) colectivo

**college** /'kɒlɪdʒ/ *n* colégio *m*

**collide** /kə'laɪd/ *vi* colidir

**colliery** /'kɒlɪərɪ/ *n* mina *f* de carvão

**collision** /kə'lɪʒn/ *n* colisão *f*, choque *m*; (*fig*) conflito *m*

**colloquial** /kə'ləʊkwɪəl/ *a* coloquial. **~ism** *n* expressão *f* coloquial

**collusion** /kə'luːʒn/ *n* conluio *m*

**colon** /'kəʊlən/ *n* (*gram*) dois pontos *mpl*; (*anat*) cólon *m*

**colonel** /'kɜːnl/ n coronel m
**colonize** /'kɒlənaɪz/ vt colonizar
**colon|y** /'kɒlənɪ/ n colónia f, (P) colónia f. ~**ial** /kə'ləʊnɪəl/ a & n colonial (mf)
**colossal** /kə'lɒsl/ a colossal
**colour** /'kʌlə(r)/ n cor f □ a (photo, TV, etc) a cores; (film) colorido □ vt colorir, dar cor a □ vi (blush) corar. ~-**blind** a daltónico, (P) daltónico. ~**ful** a colorido. ~**ing** n (of skin) cor f; (in food) corante m. ~**less** a descolorido
**coloured** /'kʌləd/ a (pencil, person) de cor □ n pessoa f de cor
**column** /'kɒləm/ n coluna f
**columnist** /'kɒləmnɪst/ n colunista mf
**coma** /'kəʊmə/ n coma m
**comb** /kəʊm/ n pente m □ vt pentear; (search) vasculhar. ~ **one's hair** pentear-se
**combat** /'kɒmbæt/ n combate m □ vt (pt **combated**) combater
**combination** /kɒmbɪ'neɪʃn/ n combinação f
**combine** /kəm'baɪn/ vt/i combinar (-se), juntar(-se), reunir(-se)
**combustion** /kəm'bʌstʃən/ n combustão f
**come** /kʌm/ vi (pt **came**, pp **come**) vir; (arrive) chegar; (occur) suceder. ~ **about** acontecer. ~ **across** encontrar, dar com. ~ **away** or **off** soltar-se. ~ **back** voltar. ~-**back** n regresso m; (retort) réplica f. ~ **by** obter. ~-**down** descer; (price) baixar. ~-**down** n humilhação f. ~ **from** vir de. ~ **in** entrar. ~ **into** (money) herdar. ~ **off** (succeed) ter êxito; (fare) sair-se. ~ **on!** vamos! ~ **out** sair. ~ **round** (after fainting) voltar a si; (be converted) deixar-se convencer. ~ **to** (amount to) montar a. ~ **up** subir; (seeds) despontar; (fig) surgir. ~ **up with** (idea) vir com, propor. ~-**uppance** n castigo m merecido
**comedian** /kə'miːdɪən/ n comediante mf
**comedy** /'kɒmədɪ/ n comédia f
**comet** /'kɒmɪt/ n cometa m
**comfort** /'kʌmfət/ n conforto m □ vt confortar, consolar. ~**able** a confortável
**comic** /'kɒmɪk/ a cómico, (P) cómico □ n cómico m, (P) cómico m; (periodical) estórias fpl em quadrinhos, (P) revista f de banda desenhada. ~ **strip** estória f em quadrinhos, (p) banda f desenhada. ~**al** a cómico, (P) cómico
**coming** /'kʌmɪŋ/ n vinda f □ a próximo. ~**s and goings** idas e vindas fpl
**comma** /'kɒmə/ n vírgula f
**command** /kə'maːnd/ n (mil) comando m; (order) ordem f; (mastery) domínio m □ vt comandar; (respect) inspirar, impor. ~**er** n comandante m. ~**ing** a imponente
**commandeer** /kɒmən'dɪə(r)/ vt requisitar
**commandment** /kə'maːndmənt/ n mandamento m
**commemorat|e** /kə'meməreɪt/ vt comemorar. ~**ion** /-'reɪʃn/ n comemoração f. ~**ive** a comemorativo
**commence** /kə'mens/ vt/i começar. ~**ment** n começo m
**commend** /kə'mend/ vt louvar; (entrust) confiar. ~**able** a louvável. ~**ation** /kɒmen'deɪʃn/ n louvor m
**comment** /'kɒment/ n comentário m □ vi comentar. ~ **on** comentar, fazer comentários
**commentary** /'kɒməntrɪ/ n comentário m; (radio, TV) relato m
**commentat|e** /'kɒmənteɪt/ vi fazer um relato. ~**or** n (radio, TV) comentarista mf, (P) comentador m
**commerce** /'kɒmɜːs/ n comércio m
**commercial** /kə'mɜːʃl/ a comercial □ n publicidade (comercial) f. ~**ize** vt comercializar
**commiserat|e** /kə'mɪzəreɪt/ vi ~ **with** compadecer-se de. ~**ion** /-'reɪʃn/ n comiseração f, pesar m
**commission** /kə'mɪʃn/ n comissão f; (order for work) encomenda f □ vt encomendar; (mil) nomear. ~ **to do** encarregar de fazer. **out of** ~ fora de serviço activo, (P) activo. ~**er** n comissário m; (police) chefe m
**commit** /kə'mɪt/ vt (pt **committed**) cometer; (entrust) confiar. ~ **o.s.** comprometer-se, empenhar-se. ~ **suicide** suicidar-se. ~ **to memory** decorar. ~**ment** n compromisso m
**committee** /kə'mɪtɪ/ n comissão f, comitê m, (P) comité m
**commodity** /kə'mɒdətɪ/ n artigo m, mercadoria f
**common** /'kɒmən/ a (-er, -est) comum; (usual) usual, corrente; (pej: ill-bred) ordinário □ n prado m público, (P) baldio m. ~ **law** direito m consuetudinário. **C~ Market** Mercado m Comum. ~-**room** n sala f dos professores. ~ **sense** bom senso m, senso m comum. **House of C~s** Câmara f dos Comuns. **in** ~ em comum. ~**ly** adv mais comum
**commoner** /'kɒmənə(r)/ n plebeu m
**commonplace** /'kɒmənpleɪs/ a banal □ n lugar-comum m
**commotion** /kə'məʊʃn/ n agitação f, confusão f, barulheira f
**communal** /'kɒmjʊnl/ a (of a commune) comunal; (shared) comum

**commune** /'kɒmju:n/ *n* comuna *f*

**communicat|e** /kə'mju:nɪkeɪt/ *vt/i* comunicar. **~ion** /-'keɪʃn/ *n* comunicação *f*. **~ion cord** sinal *m* de alarme. **~ive** /-ətɪv/ *a* comunicativo

**communion** /kə'mju:nɪən/ *n* comunhão *f*

**communis|t** /'kɒmjʊnɪst/ *n* comunista *mf* □ *a* comunista. **~m** /-zəm/ *n* comunismo *m*

**community** /kə'mju:nəti/ *n* comunidade *f*. **~ centre** centro *m* comunitário

**commute** /kə'mju:t/ *vi* viajar diariamente para o trabalho. **~r** /-ə(r)/ *n* pessoa *f* que viaja diariamente para o trabalho

**compact**¹ /kəm'pækt/ *a* compacto. **~ disc** /'kɒmpækt/ cd *m*

**compact**² /'kɒmpækt/ *n* estojo *m* de pó-de-arróz, (*P*) caixa *f*

**companion** /kəm'pænɪən/ *n* companheiro *m*. **~ship** *n* companhia *f*, convívio *m*

**company** /'kʌmpəni/ *n* companhia *f*; (*guests*) visitas *fpl*. **keep sb ~** fazer companhia a alg

**comparable** /'kɒmpərəbl/ *a* comparável

**compar|e** /kəm'peə(r)/ *vt/i* comparar(-se) (**to, with** com). **~ative** /'pærətɪv/ *a* comparativo; (*comfort etc*) relativo

**comparison** /kəm'pærɪsn/ *n* comparação *f*

**compartment** /kəm'pa:tmənt/ *n* compartimento *m*

**compass** /'kʌmpəs/ *n* bússola *f*. **~es** compasso *m*

**compassion** /kəm'pæʃn/ *n* compaixão *f*. **~ate** *a* compassivo

**compatib|le** /kəm'pætəbl/ *a* compatível. **~ility** /-'bɪləti/ *n* compatibilidade *f*

**compel** /kəm'pel/ *vt* (*pt* **compelled**) compelir, forçar. **~ling** *a* irresistível, convincente

**compensat|e** /'kɒmpənseɪt/ *vt/i* compensar. **~ion** /'seɪʃn/ *n* compensação *f*; (*financial*) indenização *f*, (*P*) indemnização *f*

**compete** /kəm'pi:t/ *vi* competir. **~ with** rivalizar com

**competen|t** /'kɒmpɪtənt/ *a* competente. **~ce** *n* competência *f*

**competition** /kɒmpə'tɪʃn/ *n* competição *f*; (*comm*) concorrência *f*

**competitive** /kəm'petɪtɪv/ *a* (*sport, prices*) competitivo. **~ examination** concurso *m*

**competitor** /kəm'petɪtə(r)/ *n* competidor *m*, concorrente *mf*

**compile** /kəm'paɪl/ *vt* compilar, coligir. **~r** /-ə(r)/ *n* compilador *m*

**complacen|t** /kəm'pleɪsnt/ *a* satisfeito consigo mesmo, (*P*) complacente. **~cy** *n* (auto-)satisfação *f*, (*P*) complacência *f*

**complain** /kəm'pleɪn/ *vi* queixar-se (**about, of** de)

**complaint** /kəm'pleɪnt/ *n* queixa *f*; (*in shop*) reclamação *f*; (*med*) doença *f*, achaque *m*

**complement** /'kɒmplɪmənt/ *n* complemento *m* □ *vt* completar, complementar. **~ary** /-'mentrɪ/ *a* complementar

**complet|e** /kəm'pli:t/ *a* completo; (*finished*) acabado; (*downright*) perfeito □ *vt* completar; (*a form*) preencher. **~ely** *adv* completamente. **~ion** /-ʃn/ *n* conclusão *f*, feitura *f*, realização *f*

**complex** /'kɒmpleks/ *a* complexo □ *n* complexo *m*. **~ity** /kəm'pleksəti/ *n* complexidade *f*

**complexion** /kəm'plekʃn/ *n* cor *f* da tez; (*fig*) caráter *m*, (*P*) carácter *m*, aspecto *m*

**compliance** /kəm'plaɪəns/ *n* docilidade *f*; (*agreement*) conformidade *f*. **in ~ with** em conformidade com

**complicat|e** /'kɒmplɪkeɪt/ *vt* complicar. **~ed** *a* complicado. **~ion** /-'keɪʃn/ *n* complicação *f*

**compliment** /'kɒmplɪmənt/ *n* cumprimento *m* □ *vt* /'kɒmplɪment/ cumprimentar

**complimentary** /kɒmplɪ'mentrɪ/ *a* amável, elogioso. **~ copy** oferta *f*. **~ ticket** bilhete *m* grátis

**comply** /kəm'plaɪ/ *vi* **~ with** agir em conformidade com

**component** /kəm'pəʊnənt/ *n* componente *m*; (*of machine*) peça *f* □ *a* componente, constituinte

**compose** /kəm'pəʊz/ *vt* compor. **~ o.s.** acalmar-se, dominar-se. **~d** *a* calmo, senhor de si. **~r** /-ə(r)/ *n* compositor *m*

**composition** /kɒmpə'zɪʃn/ *n* composição *f*

**compost** /'kɒmpɒst/ *n* húmus *m*, adubo *m*

**composure** /kəm'pəʊʒə(r)/ *n* calma *f*, domínio *m* de si mesmo

**compound** /'kɒmpaʊnd/ *n* composto *m*; (*enclosure*) cercado *m*, recinto *m* □ *a* composto. **~ fracture** fratura *f*, (*P*) fractura *f* exposta

**comprehen|d** /kɒmprɪ'hend/ *vt* compreender. **~sion** /-ʃn/ *n* compreensão *f*

**comprehensive** /kɒmprɪ'hensɪv/ *a* compreensivo, vasto; (*insurance*) contra todos os riscos. **~ school** escola *f* de ensino secundário técnico e académico, (*P*) académico

compress /kəm'pres/ vt comprimir.
~ion /-ʃn/ n compressão f
comprise /kəm'praɪz/ vt compreender, abranger
compromise /'kɒmprəmaɪz/ n compromisso m □ vi comprometer □ vi chegar a um meio-termo
compulsion /kəm'pʌlʃn/ n (constraint) coação f; (psych) desejo m irresistível
compulsive /kəm'pʌlsɪv/ a (psych) compulsivo; (liar, smoker etc) inveterado
compulsory /kəm'pʌlsərɪ/ a obrigatório, compulsório
computer /kəm'pjuːtə(r)/ n computador m. ~ science informática f. ~ize vt computerizar
comrade /'kɒmreɪd/ n camarada mf. ~ship n camaradagem f
con¹ /kɒn/ vt (pt conned) (sl) enganar □ n (sl) intrujice f, vigarice f, burla f. ~ man (sl) intrujão m, vigarista m, burlão m
con² /kɒn/ see pro
concave /'kɒnkeɪv/ a côncavo
conceal /kən'siːl/ vt ocultar, esconder. ~ment n encobrimento m
concede /kən'siːd/ vt conceder, admitir; (in a game etc) ceder
conceit /kən'siːt/ n presunção f. ~ed a presunçoso, presumido, cheio de si
conceivabl|e /kən'siːvəbl/ a concebível. ~y adv possivelmente
conceive /kən'siːv/ vt/i conceber
concentrat|e /'kɒnsntreɪt/ vt/i concentrar(-se). ~ion /-'treɪʃn/ n concentração f
concept /'kɒnsept/ n conceito m
conception /kən'sepʃn/ n concepção f
concern /kən'sɜːn/ n (worry) preocupação f; (business) negócio m □ vt dizer respeito a, respeitar. ~ o.s. with, be ~ed with interessar-se por, ocupar-se de; (regard) dizer respeito a. it's no ~ of mine não me diz respeito. ~ing prep sobre, respeitante a
concerned /kən'sɜːnd/ a inquieto, preocupado (about com)
concert /'kɒnsət/ n concerto m
concerted /kən'sɜːtɪd/ a concertado
concession /kən'seʃn/ n concessão f
concise /kən'saɪs/ a conciso. ~ly adv concisamente
conclu|de /kən'kluːd/ vt concluir □ vi terminar. ~ding a final. ~sion n conclusão f
conclusive /kən'kluːsɪv/ a conclusivo. ~ly adv de forma conclusiva
concoct /kən'kɒkt/ vt preparar por mistura; (fig: invent) fabricar. ~ion /-ʃn/ n mistura f; (fig) invenção f, mentira f

concrete /'kɒnkriːt/ n concreto m, (P) cimento m □ a concreto □ vt concretar, (P) cimentar
concur /kən'kɜː(r)/ vi (pt concurred) concordar; (of circumstances) concorrer
concussion /kən'kʌʃn/ n comoção f cerebral
condemn /kən'dem/ vt condenar. ~ation /kɒndem'neɪʃn/ n condenação f
condens|e /kən'dens/ vt/i condensar(-se). ~ation /kɒnden'seɪʃn/ n condensação f
condescend /kɒndɪ'send/ vi condescender; (lower o.s.) rebaixar-se
condition /kən'dɪʃn/ n condição f □ vt condicionar. on ~ that com a condição de que. ~al a condicional. ~er n (for hair) condicionador m, creme m rinse
condolences /kən'dəʊlənsɪz/ npl condolências fpl, pêsames mpl, sentimentos mpl
condom /'kɒndəm/ n preservativo m
condone /kən'dəʊn/ vt desculpar, fechar os olhos a
conducive /kən'djuːsɪv/ a be ~ to contribuir para, ser propício a
conduct¹ /kən'dʌkt/ vt conduzir, dirigir; (orchestra) reger
conduct² /'kɒndʌkt/ n conduta f
conductor /kən'dʌktə(r)/ n maestro m; (electr; of bus) condutor m
cone /kəʊn/ n cone m; (bot) pinha f; (for ice-cream) casquinha f, (P) cone m
confectioner /kən'fekʃnə(r)/ n confeiteiro m, (P) pasteleiro m. ~y n confeitaria f, (P) pastelaria f
confederation /kənfedə'reɪʃn/ n confederação f
confer /kən'fɜː(r)/ (pt conferred) vt conferir, outorgar □ vi conferenciar
conference /'kɒnfərəns/ n conferência f. in ~ em reunião f
confess /kən'fes/ vt/i confessar; (relig) confessar(-se). ~ion /-ʃn/ n confissão f. ~ional n confessionário m. ~or n confessor m
confetti /kən'fetɪ/ n confetes mpl, (P) confetti mpl
confide /kən'faɪd/ vt confiar □ vi ~ in confiar em
confiden|t /'kɒnfɪdənt/ a confiante, confiado. ~ce n confiança f; (boldness) confiança f em si; (secret) confidência f. ~ce trick vigarice f. in ~ce em confidência
confidential /kɒnfr'denʃl/ a confidencial
confine /kən'faɪn/ vt fechar; (limit) limitar (to a). ~ment n detenção f; (med) parto m

**confirm** /kən'fɜːm/ vt confirmar. ~ation /kɒnfə'meɪʃn/ n confirmação f. ~ed a (bachelor) inveterado

**confiscat|e** /'kɒnfɪskeɪt/ vt confiscar. ~ion /-'keɪʃn/ n confiscação f

**conflict¹** /'kɒnflɪkt/ n conflito m

**conflict²** /kən'flɪkt/ vi estar em contradição. ~ing a contraditório

**conform** /kən'fɔːm/ vt/i conformar (-se)

**confound** /kən'faʊnd/ vt confundir. ~ed a (collog) maldito

**confront** /kən'frʌnt/ vt confrontar, defrontar, enfrentar. ~ with confrontar-se com. ~ation /kɒnfrʌn'teɪʃn/ n confrontação f

**confus|e** /kən'fjuːz/ vt confundir. ~ed a confuso. ~ing a que faz confusão. ~ion /-ʒn/ n confusão f

**congeal** /kən'dʒiːl/ vt/i congelar, solidificar

**congenial** /kən'dʒiːnɪəl/ a (agreeable) simpático

**congenital** /kən'dʒenɪtl/ a congênito, (P) congénito

**congest|ed** /kən'dʒestɪd/ a congestionado. ~ion /-tʃn/ n (traffic) congestionamento m; (med) congestão f

**congratulat|e** /kən'grætjʊleɪt/ vt felicitar, dar os parabéns (on por). ~ions /-'leɪʃnz/ npl felicitações fpl, parabéns mpl

**congregat|e** /'kɒŋgrɪgeɪt/ vi reunir-se. ~ion /-'geɪʃn/ n (in church) congregação f, fiéis mpl

**congress** /'kɒŋgres/ n congresso m. C~ (Amer) Congresso m

**conjecture** /kən'dʒektʃə(r)/ n conjetura f, (P) conjectura f □ vt/i conjeturar, (P) conjecturar

**conjugal** /'kɒndʒʊgl/ a conjugal

**conjugat|e** /'kɒndʒʊgeɪt/ vt conjugar. ~ion /-'geɪʃn/ n conjugação f

**conjunction** /kən'dʒʌŋkʃn/ n conjunção f

**conjur|e** /'kʌndʒə(r)/ vi fazer truques mágicos □ vt ~ up fazer aparecer. ~or n mágico m, prestidigitador m

**connect** /kə'nekt/ vt/i ligar(-se); (of train) fazer ligação. ~ed a ligado. be ~ed with estar relacionado com

**connection** /kə'nekʃn/ n relação f; (rail; phone call) ligação f; (electr) contacto m

**connoisseur** /kɒnə'sɜː(r)/ n conhecedor m, apreciador m

**connotation** /kɒnə'teɪʃn/ n conotação f

**conquer** /'kɒŋkə(r)/ vt vencer; (country) conquistar. ~or n conquistador m

**conquest** /'kɒŋkwest/ n conquista f

**conscience** /'kɒnʃəns/ n consciência f

**conscientious** /kɒnʃɪ'enʃəs/ a consciencioso

**conscious** /'kɒnʃəs/ a consciente. ~ly adv conscientemente. ~ness n consciência f

**conscript¹** /kən'skrɪpt/ vt recrutar. ~ion /-ʃn/ n serviço m militar obrigatório

**conscript²** /'kɒnskrɪpt/ n recruta m

**consecrate** /'kɒnsɪkreɪt/ vt consagrar

**consecutive** /kən'sekjʊtɪv/ a consecutivo, seguido

**consensus** /kən'sensəs/ n consenso m

**consent** /kən'sent/ vi consentir (to em) □ n consentimento m

**consequence** /'kɒnsɪkwəns/ n conseqüência f, (P) consequência f

**consequent** /'kɒnsɪkwənt/ a resultante (on, upon de). ~ly adv por consequência, (P) consequência, por conseguinte

**conservation** /kɒnsə'veɪʃn/ n conservação f

**conservative** /kən'sɜːvətɪv/ a conservador; (estimate) moderado. C~ a & n conservador (m)

**conservatory** /kən'sɜːvətrɪ/ n (greenhouse) estufa f; (house extension) jardim m de inverno

**conserve** /kən'sɜːv/ vt conservar

**consider** /kən'sɪdə(r)/ vt considerar; (allow for) levar em consideração. ~ation /-'reɪʃn/ n consideração f. ~ing prep em vista de, tendo em conta

**considerabl|e** /kən'sɪdərəbl/ a considerável; (much) muito. ~y adv consideravelmente

**considerate** /kən'sɪdərət/ a atencioso, delicado

**consign** /kən'saɪn/ vt consignar. ~ment n consignação f

**consist** /kən'sɪst/ vi consistir (of, in, em)

**consisten|t** /kən'sɪstənt/ a (unchanging) constante; (not contradictory) coerente. ~t with conforme com. ~cy n consistência f; (fig) coerência f. ~tly adv regularmente

**consol|e** /kən'səʊl/ vt consolar. ~ation /kɒnsə'leɪʃn/ n consolação f. ~ation prize prêmio m de consolação

**consolidat|e** /kən'sɒlɪdeɪt/ vt/i consolidar(-se). ~ion /-'deɪʃn/ n consolidação f

**consonant** /'kɒnsənənt/ n consoante f

**consortium** /kən'sɔːtɪəm/ n (pl -tia) consórcio m

**conspicuous** /kən'spɪkjʊəs/ a conspícuo, visível; (striking) notável. **make o.s.** ~ fazer-se notar, chamar a atenção

**conspira|cy** /kən'spɪrəsɪ/ n conspiração f. **~tor** n conspirador m

**conspire** /kən'spaɪə(r)/ vi conspirar

**constable** /'kʌnstəbl/ n polícia m

**constant** /'kɒnstənt/ a constante. **~ly** adv constantemente

**constellation** /kɒnstə'leɪʃn/ n constelação f

**consternation** /kɒnstə'neɪʃn/ n consternação f

**constipation** /kɒnstɪ'peɪʃn/ n prisão f de ventre

**constituency** /kən'stɪtjʊənsɪ/ n (pl -cies) círculo m eleitoral

**constituent** /kən'stɪtjʊənt/ a & n constituinte (m)

**constitut|e** /'kɒnstɪtjuːt/ vt constituir. **~ion** /-'tjuːʃn/ n constituição f. **~ional** /-'tjuːʃənl/ a constitucional

**constrain** /kən'strem/ vt constranger

**constraint** /kən'streɪnt/ n constrangimento m

**constrict** /kən'strɪkt/ vt constringir, apertar. **~ion** /-ʃn/ n constrição f

**construct** /kən'strʌkt/ vt construir. **~ion** /-ʃn/ n construção f. **under ~ion** em construção

**constructive** /kən'strʌktɪv/ a construtivo

**consul** /'kɒnsl/ n cônsul m

**consulate** /'kɒnsjʊlət/ n consulado m

**consult** /kən'sʌlt/ vt consultar. **~ation** /kɒnsl'teɪʃn/ n consulta f

**consultant** /kən'sʌltənt/ n consultor m; (med) especialista mf

**consume** /kən'sjuːm/ vt consumir. **~r** /-ə(r)/ n consumidor m

**consumption** /kən'sʌmpʃn/ n consumo m

**contact** /'kɒntækt/ n contacto m; (person) relação f. **~ lenses** lentes fpl de contacto □ vt contactar

**contagious** /kən'teɪdʒəs/ a contagioso

**contain** /kən'tem/ vt conter. **~ o.s.** conter-se. **~er** n recipiente m; (for transport) contentor m

**contaminat|e** /kən'tæmmeɪt/ vt contaminar. **~ion** /-'neɪʃn/ n contaminação f

**contemplat|e** /'kɒntempleɪt/ vt contemplar; (intend) ter em vista; (consider) esperar, pensar em. **~ion** /-'pleɪʃn/ n contemplação f

**contemporary** /kən'temprərɪ/ a & n contemporâneo (m)

**contempt** /kən'tempt/ n desprezo m. **~ible** a desprezível. **~uous** /-tʃʊəs/ a desdenhoso

**contend** /kən'tend/ vt afirmar, sustentar □ vi **~ with** lutar contra. **~er** n adversário m, contendor m

**content**[1] /kən'tent/ a satisfeito, contente □ vt contentar. **~ed** a satisfeito,

contente. **~ment** n contentamento m, satisfação f

**content**[2] /'kɒntent/ n conteúdo m. **(table of) ~s** indice m

**contention** /kən'tenʃn/ n disputa f, contenda f; (assertion) argumento m

**contest**[1] /'kɒntest/ n competição f; (struggle) luta f

**contest**[2] /kən'test/ vt contestar; (compete for) disputar. **~ant** n concorrente mf

**context** /'kɒntekst/ n contexto m

**continent** /'kɒntmənt/ n continente m. **the C~** a Europa (continental) f. **~al** /-'nentl/ a continental; (of mainland Europe) europeu. **~al breakfast** café m da manhã europeu, (P) pequeno almoço m europeu. **~al quilt** edredom m, (P) edredão m

**contingen|t** /kən'tmdʒənt/ a & n contingente (m). **~cy** n contingência f. **~cy plan** plano m de emergência

**continual** /kən'tmjʊəl/ a contínuo. **~ly** adv continuamente

**continu|e** /kən'tmjuː/ vt/i continuar. **~ation** /-tmjʊ'eɪʃn/ n continuação f.

**continuity** /kɒntr'njuːətɪ/ n continuidade f

**continuous** /kən'tmjʊəs/ a contínuo. **~ly** adv continuamente

**contort** /kən'tɔːt/ vt contorcer; (fig) distorcer. **~ion** /-ʃn/ n contorção f

**contour** /'kɒntʊə(r)/ n contorno m

**contraband** /'kɒntrəbænd/ n contrabando m

**contraception** /kɒntrə'sepʃn/ n contracepção f

**contraceptive** /kɒntrə'septɪv/ a & n contraceptivo (m)

**contract**[1] /'kɒntrækt/ n contrato m

**contract**[2] /kən'trækt/ vt/i contrair (-se); (make a contract) contratar. **~ion** /-ʃn/ n contração f, (P) contracção f

**contractor** /kən'træktə(r)/ n empreiteiro m; (firm) firma f empreiteira de serviços, (P) recrutadora f de mão de obra temporária

**contradict** /kɒntrə'dɪkt/ vt contradizer. **~ion** /-ʃn/ n contradição f. **~ory** a contraditório

**contraflow** /'kɒntrəfləʊ/ n fluxo m em sentido contrário

**contrary**[1] /'kɒntrərɪ/ a & n (opposite) contrário (m) □ adv **~ to** contrariamente a. **on the ~** ao ou pelo contrário

**contrary**[2] /kən'treərɪ/ a (perverse) do contra, embirrento

**contrast**[1] /'kɒntraːst/ n contraste m

**contrast**[2] /kən'traːst/ vt/i contrastar. **~ing** a contrastante

**contraven|e** /kɒntrə'viːn/ vt infringir. **~tion** /-'venʃn/ n contravenção f

**contribut|e** /kən'trɪbjuːt/ *vt/i* contribuir (**to** para); (*to newspaper etc*) colaborar (**to** em). **~ion** /kɒntrɪ-'bjuːʃn/ *n* contribuição *f*. **~or** /-'trɪbjutə(r)/ *n* contribuinte *mf*; (*to newspaper*) colaborador *m*

**contrivance** /kən'traɪvəns/ *n* (*invention*) engenho *m*; (*device*) engenhoca *f*; (*trick*) maquinação *f*

**contrive** /kən'traɪv/ *vt* imaginar, inventar. **~ to do** conseguir fazer

**control** /kən'trəʊl/ *vt* (*pt* controlled) (*check, restrain*) controlar; (*firm etc*) dirigir □ *n* controle *m*; (*management*) direcção *f*, (*P*) direcção *f*. **~s** (*of car, plane*) comandos *mpl*; (*knobs*) botões *mpl*. **be in ~ of** dirigir. **under ~** sob controle

**controversial** /kɒntrə'vɜːʃl/ *a* controverso, discutível

**controversy** /'kɒntrəvɜːsɪ/ *n* controvérsia *f*

**convalesce** /kɒnvə'les/ *vi* convalescer. **~nce** *n* convalescença *f*. **~nt** /-nt/ *a & n* convalescente (*mf*). **~nt home** casa *f* de repouso

**convene** /kən'viːn/ *vt* convocar □ *vi* reunir-se

**convenience** /kən'viːnɪəns/ *n* conveniência *f*. **~s** (*appliances*) comodidades *fpl*; (*lavatory*) privada *f*, (*P*) casa *f* de banho. **at your ~** quando (e como) lhe convier. **~ foods** alimentos *mpl* semiprontos

**convenient** /kən'viːnɪənt/ *a* conveniente. **be ~ for** convir a. **~ly** *adv* sem inconveniente; (*situated*) bem; (*arrive*) a propósito

**convent** /'kɒnvənt/ *n* convento *m*. **~ school** colégio *m* de freiras

**convention** /kən'venʃn/ *n* convenção *f*; (*custom*) uso *m*, costume *m*. **~al** *a* convencional

**converge** /kən'vɜːdʒ/ *vi* convergir

**conversant** /kən'vɜːsnt/ *a* **be ~ with** conhecer; (*fact*) saber; (*machinery*) estar familiarizado com

**conversation** /kɒnvə'seɪʃn/ *n* conversa *f*. **~al** *a* de conversa, coloquial

**converse**[1] /kən'vɜːs/ *vi* conversar

**converse**[2] /'kɒnvɜːs/ *a & n* inverso (*m*). **~ly** /kən'vɜːslɪ/ *adv* ao invés, inversamente

**conver|t**[1] /kən'vɜːt/ *vt* converter; (*house*) transformar. **~sion** /-ʃn/ *n* conversão *f*; (*house*) transformação *f*. **~tible** *a* convertível, conversível □ *n* (*auto*) conversível *m*

**convert**[2] /'kɒnvɜːt/ *n* convertido *m*, converso *m*

**convex** /'kɒnveks/ *a* convexo

**convey** /kən'veɪ/ *vt* transmitir; (*goods*) transportar; (*idea, feeling*) comunicar. **~ance** *n* transporte *m*.

**~or belt** tapete *m* rolante, correia *f* transportadora

**convict**[1] /kən'vɪkt/ *vt* declarar culpado. **~ion** /-ʃn/ *n* condenação *f*; (*opinion*) convicção *f*

**convict**[2] /'kɒnvɪkt/ *n* condenado *m*

**convinc|e** /kən'vɪns/ *vt* convencer. **~ing** *a* convincente

**convoluted** /kɒnvə'luːtɪd/ *a* retorcido; (*fig*) complicado; (*bot*) convoluto

**convoy** /'kɒnvɔɪ/ *n* escolta *f*

**convuls|e** /kən'vʌls/ *vt* convulsionar; (*fig*) abalar. **be ~ed with laughter** torcer-se de riso. **~ion** /-ʃn/ *n* convulsão *f*

**coo** /kuː/ *vi* (*pt* cooed) arrulhar □ *n* arrulho *m*

**cook** /kʊk/ *vt/i* cozinhar □ *n* cozinheira *f*, cozinheiro *m*. **~ up** (*colloq*) cozinhar (*fig*), fabricar

**cooker** /'kʊkə(r)/ *n* fogão *m*

**cookery** /'kʊkərɪ/ *n* cozinha *f*. **~ book** livro *m* de culinária

**cookie** /'kʊkɪ/ *n* (*Amer*) biscoito *m*

**cool** /kuːl/ *a* (-er, -est) fresco; (*calm*) calmo; (*unfriendly*) frio □ *n* frescura *f*; (*sl: composure*) sangue-frio *m* □ *vt/i* arrefecer. **~-box** *n* geladeira *f* portátil. **in the ~** no fresco. **~ly** /'kuːllɪ/ *adv* calmamente; (*fig*) friamente. **~ness** *n* frescura *f*; (*fig*) frieza *f*

**coop** /kuːp/ *n* galinheiro *m* □ *vt* **~ up** engaislar, fechar

**co-operat|e** /kəʊ'ɒpəreɪt/ *vi* cooperar. **~ion** /-'reɪʃn/ *n* cooperação *f*

**cooperative** /kəʊ'ɒpərətɪv/ *a* cooperativo □ *n* cooperativa *f*

**coordinat|e** /kəʊ'ɔːdɪmeɪt/ *vt* coordenar. **~ion** /-'neɪʃn/ *n* coordenação *f*

**cop** /kɒp/ *n* (*sl*) porco *m* (*sl*), (*P*) xui *m* (*sl*)

**cope** /kəʊp/ *vi* aguentar-se, arranjar-se. **~ with** poder com, dar conta de

**copious** /'kəʊpɪəs/ *a* copioso

**copper**[1] /'kɒpə(r)/ *n* cobre *m* □ *a* de cobre

**copper**[2] /'kɒpə(r)/ *n* (*sl*) porco *m* (*sl*), (*P*) xui *m* (*sl*)

**coppice** /'kɒpɪs/, **copse** /kɒps/ *ns* mata *f* de corte

**copulat|e** /'kɒpjʊleɪt/ *vi* copular. **~ion** /-'leɪʃn/ *n* cópula *f*

**copy** /'kɒpɪ/ *n* cópia *f*; (*of book*) exemplar *m*; (*of newspaper*) número *m* □ *vt/i* copiar

**copyright** /'kɒpɪraɪt/ *n* direitos *mpl* autorais

**coral** /'kɒrəl/ *n* coral *m*

**cord** /kɔːd/ *n* cordão *m*; (*electr*) fio *m*

**cordial** /'kɔːdɪəl/ *a & n* cordial (*m*)

**cordon** /'kɔːdn/ *n* cordão *m* □ *vt* **~ off** fechar (com um cordão de isolamento)

**corduroy** /'kɔːdərɔɪ/ *n* veludo *m* cotelé

core /kɔː(r)/ n âmago m; (of apple, pear) coração m

cork /kɔːk/ n cortiça f; (for bottle) rolha f □ vt rolhar

corkscrew /ˈkɔːkskruː/ n sacarolhas m

corn[1] /kɔːn/ n trigo m; (Amer: maize) milho m; (seed) grão m. ~ on the cob espiga f de milho

corn[2] /kɔːn/ n (hard skin) calo m

corned /kɔːnd/ a ~ beef carne f de vaca enlatada

corner /ˈkɔːnə(r)/ n canto m; (of street) esquina f; (bend in road) curva f □ vt encurralar; (market) monopolizar □ vi dar uma curva, virar

cornet /ˈkɔːnɪt/ n (mus) cornetim m; (for ice-cream) casquinha f, (P) cone m

cornflakes /ˈkɔːnfleɪks/ npl cornflakes mpl, cereais mpl

cornflour /ˈkɔːnflaʊə(r)/ n fécula f de milho, maisena f

Corn|wall /ˈkɔːnwəl/ n Cornualha f. ~ish a da Cornualha

corny /ˈkɔːnɪ/ a (colloq) batido, (P) estafado

coronary /ˈkɒrənrɪ/ n ~ (thrombosis) infarto m, enfarte m

coronation /kɒrəˈneɪʃn/ n coroação f

coroner /ˈkɒrənə(r)/ n magistrado m que investiga os casos de morte suspeita

corporal[1] /ˈkɔːpərəl/ n (mil) cabo m

corporal[2] /ˈkɔːpərəl/ a ~ punishment castigo m corporal

corporate /ˈkɔːpərət/ a coletivo, (P) colectivo; (body) corporativo

corporation /kɔːpəˈreɪʃn/ n corporação f; (of town) municipalidade f

corps /kɔː(r)/ n (pl corps /kɔːz/) corpo m

corpse /kɔːps/ n cadáver m

corpuscle /ˈkɔːpʌsl/ n corpúsculo m

correct /kəˈrekt/ a correto, (P) correcto. the ~ time a hora certa. you are ~ você tem razão □ vt corrigir. ~ion /-ʃn/ n correção f, (P) correcção f, emenda f

correlat|e /ˈkɒrəleɪt/ vt/i correlacionar(-se). ~ion /-ˈleɪʃn/ n correlação f

correspond /kɒrɪˈspɒnd/ vi corresponder (to, with, a); (write letters) corresponder-se (with, com). ~ence n correspondência f. ~ent n correspondente mf. ~ing a correspondente

corridor /ˈkɒrɪdɔː(r)/ n corredor m

corroborate /kəˈrɒbəreɪt/ vt corroborar

corro|de /kəˈrəʊd/ vt/i corroer(-se). ~sion n corrosão f

corrugated /ˈkɒrəgeɪtɪd/ a corru-

gado. ~ cardboard cartão m canelado. ~ iron chapa f ondulada

corrupt /kəˈrʌpt/ a corrupto □ vt corromper. ~ion /-ʃn/ n corrupção f

corset /ˈkɔːsɪt/ n espartilho m; (elasticated) cinta f elástica

Corsica /ˈkɔːsɪkə/ n Córsega f

cosmetic /kɒzˈmetɪk/ n cosmético m □ a cosmético; (fig) superficial

cosmonaut /ˈkɒzmənɔːt/ n cosmonauta mf

cosmopolitan /kɒzməˈpɒlɪtən/ a & n cosmopolita (mf)

cosset /ˈkɒsɪt/ vt (pt cosseted) proteger

cost /kɒst/ vt (pt cost) custar; (pt costed) fixar o preço de □ n custo m. ~s (jur) custos mpl. at all ~s custe o que custar. to one's ~ à sua custa. ~ of living custo m de vida

costly /ˈkɒstlɪ/ a (-ier, -iest) a caro; (valuable) precioso

costume /ˈkɒstjuːm/ n traje m

cos|y /ˈkəʊzɪ/ a (-ier, -iest) confortável, íntimo □ n abafador m (do bule do chá). ~iness n conforto m

cot /kɒt/ n cama f de bêbê, berço m

cottage /ˈkɒtɪdʒ/ n pequena casa f de campo. ~ cheese requeijão m, ricota f. ~ industry artesanato m. ~ pie empada f de carne picada

cotton /ˈkɒtn/ n algodão m; (thread) fio m, linha f. ~ wool algodão m hidrófilo

couch /kaʊtʃ/ n divã m

couchette /kuːˈʃet/ n couchette f

cough /kɒf/ vi tossir □ n tosse f

could /kʊd, kəd/ pt of can[2]

couldn't /ˈkʊdnt/ = could not

council /ˈkaʊnsl/ n conselho m. ~ house casa f de bairro popular

councillor /ˈkaʊnsələ(r)/ n vereador m

counsel /ˈkaʊnsl/ n conselho m; (pl invar) (jur) advogado m. ~lor n conselheiro m

count[1] /kaʊnt/ vt/i contar □ n conta f. ~-down n (rocket) contagem f regressiva. ~ on contar com

count[2] /kaʊnt/ n (nobleman) conde m

counter[1] /ˈkaʊntə(r)/ n (in shop) balcão m; (in game) ficha f, (P) tento m

counter[2] /ˈkaʊntə(r)/ adv ~ to contrário a; (in the opposite direction) em sentido contrário a □ a oposto □ vt opor; (blow) aparar □ vi ripostar

counter- /ˈkaʊntə(r)/ pref contra-

counteract /kaʊntərˈækt/ vt neutralizar, frustrar

counter-attack /ˈkaʊntərətæk/ n contra-ataque m □ vt/i contra-atacar

counterbalance /ˈkaʊntəbæləns/ n contrapeso m □ vt contrabalançar

**counterfeit** /'kaʊntəfɪt/ *a* falsificado, falso □ *n* falsificação *f* □ *vt* falsificar

**counterfoil** /'kaʊntəfɔɪl/ *n* talão *m*, canhoto *m*

**counterpart** /'kaʊntəpa:t/ *n* equivalente *m*; (*person*) homólogo *m*

**counter-productive** /'kaʊntəprədʌktɪv/ *a* contraproducente

**countersign** /'kaʊntəsam/ *vt* subscrever documento já assinado; (*cheque*) contrassinar

**countess** /'kaʊntɪs/ *n* condessa *f*

**countless** /'kaʊntlɪs/ *a* sem conta, incontável, inúmero

**country** /'kʌntrɪ/ *n* país *m*; (*homeland*) pátria *f*; (*countryside*) campo *m*

**countryside** /'kʌntrɪsaɪd/ *n* campo *m*

**county** /'kaʊntɪ/ *n* condado *m*

**coup** /ku:/ *n* ~ (**d'état**) golpe *m* (de estado)

**couple** /'kʌpl/ *n* par *m*, casal *m* □ *vt/i* unir(-se), ligar(-se); (*techn*) acoplar. **a** ~ **of** um par de

**coupon** /'ku:pɒn/ *n* cupão *m*

**courage** /'kʌrɪdʒ/ *n* coragem *f*. ~**ous** /kə'reɪdʒəs/ *a* corajoso

**courgette** /kʊə'ʒet/ *n* abobrinha *f*

**courier** /'kʊrɪə(r)/ *n* correio *m*; (*for tourists*) guia *mf*; (*for parcels, mail*) estafeta *m*

**course** /kɔ:s/ *n* curso *m*; (*series*) série *f*; (*culin*) prato *m*; (*for golf*) campo *m*; (*fig*) caminho *m*. **in due** ~ na altura devida, oportunamente. **in the** ~ **of** durante. **of** ~ está claro, com certeza

**court** /kɔ:t/ *n* (*of monarch*) corte *f*; (*courtyard*) pátio *m*; (*tennis*) court *m*, quadra *f*, (*P*) campo *m*; (*jur*) tribunal *m* □ *vt* cortejar; (*danger*) provocar. ~ **martial** (*pl* **courts martial**) conselho *m* de guerra

**courteous** /'kɜːtɪəs/ *a* cortês, delicado

**courtesy** /'kɜːtəsɪ/ *n* cortesia *f*

**courtship** /'kɔ:tʃɪp/ *n* namoro *m*, corte *f*

**courtyard** /'kɔ:tja:d/ *n* pátio *m*

**cousin** /'kʌzn/ *n* primo *m*. **first/second** ~ primo *m* em primeiro/segundo grau

**cove** /kəʊv/ *n* angra *f*, enseada *f*

**covenant** /'kʌvənənt/ *n* convenção *f*, convénio *m*; (*jur*) contrato *m*; (*relig*) aliança *f*

**cover** /'kʌvə(r)/ *vt* cobrir □ *n* cobertura *f*; (*for bed*) colcha *f*; (*for book, furniture*) capa *f*; (*lid*) tampa *f*; (*shelter*) abrigo *m*. ~ **charge** serviço *m*. ~ **up** tapar; (*fig*) encobrir. ~**-up** *n* (*fig*) encobrimento *m*. **take** ~ abrigar-se. **under separate** ~ em separado. ~**ing** *n* cobertura *f*. ~**ing letter** carta *f* (que acompanha um documento)

**coverage** /'kʌvərɪdʒ/ *n* (*of events*) reportagem *f*, cobertura *f*

**covet** /'kʌvɪt/ *vt* cobiçar

**cow** /kaʊ/ *n* vaca *f*

**coward** /'kaʊəd/ *n* covarde *mf*. ~**ly** *a* covarde

**cowardice** /'kaʊədɪs/ *n* covardia *f*

**cowboy** /'kaʊbɔɪ/ *n* cowboy *m*, vaqueiro *m*

**cower** /'kaʊə(r)/ *vi* encolher-se (de medo)

**cowshed** /'kaʊʃed/ *n* estábulo *m*

**coy** /kɔɪ/ *a* (**-er, -est**) (falsamente) tímido

**crab** /kræb/ *n* caranguejo *m*

**crack** /kræk/ *n* fenda *f*; (*in glass*) rachadura *f*; (*noise*) estalo *m*; (*sl: joke*) piada *f*; (*drug*) crack *m* □ *a* (*colloq*) de élite □ *vt/i* estalar; (*nut*) quebrar; (*joke*) contar; (*problem*) resolver; (*voice*) mudar. ~ **down on** (*colloq*) cair em cima de, arrochar. **get** ~**ing** (*colloq*) pôr mãos à obra

**cracker** /'krækə(r)/ *n* busca-pé *m*, bomba *f* de estalo; (*culin*) bolacha *f* de água e sal

**crackers** /'krækəz/ *a* (*sl*) desmiolado, maluco

**crackle** /'krækl/ *vi* crepitar □ *n* crepitação *f*

**crackpot** /'krækpɒt/ *n* (*sl*) desmiolado, maluco

**cradle** /'kreɪdl/ *n* berço *m* □ *vt* embalar

**craft**[1] /kra:ft/ *n* ofício *m*; (*technique*) arte *f*; (*cunning*) manha *f*, astúcia *f*

**craft**[2] /kra:ft/ *n* (*invar*) (*boat*) embarcação *f*

**craftsman** /'kra:ftsmən/ *n* (*pl* **-men**) artífice *mf*. ~**ship** *n* arte *f*

**crafty** /'kra:ftɪ/ *a* (**-ier, -iest**) manhoso, astucioso

**crag** /kræg/ *n* penhasco *m*. ~**gy** *a* escarpado, íngreme

**cram** /kræm/ *vt* (*pt* **crammed**) ~ (**for an exam**) decorar, (*P*) empinar. ~ **into/with** entulhar com

**cramp** /kræmp/ *n* cãimbra *f* □ *vt* restringir, tolher. ~**ed** *a* apertado

**crane** /kreɪn/ *n* grua *f*; (*bird*) grou *m* □ *vt* (*neck*) esticar

**crank**[1] /kræŋk/ *n* (*techn*) manivela *f*. ~**shaft** *n* (*techn*) cambota *f*

**crank**[2] /kræŋk/ *n* excêntrico *m*. ~**y** *a* excêntrico

**crash** /kræʃ/ *n* acidente *m*; (*noise*) estrondo *m*; (*comm*) falência *f*; (*financial*) colapso *m*, crash *m* □ *vt/i* (*fall/strike*) cair/bater com estrondo; (*two cars*) chocar, bater; (*comm*) abrir falência; (*plane*) cair □ *a* (*course, programme*) intensivo. ~**-helmet** *n* capacete *m*. ~**-land** *vi* fazer uma aterrissagem forçada

**crate** /kreɪt/ n engradado m
**crater** /'kreɪtə(r)/ n cratera f
**crav|e** /kreɪv/ vt/i ~e (for) ansiar
por. ~ing n desejo m irresistível,
ânsia f
**crawl** /krɔːl/ vi rastejar; (of baby) engatinhar, (P) andar de gatas; (of car)
mover-se lentamente □ n rastejo m;
(swimming) crawl m. be ~ing with
fervilhar de, estar cheio de
**crayfish** /'kreɪfɪʃ/ n (pl invar) lagos-
tim m
**crayon** /'kreɪən/ n crayon m, lápis m
de pastel
**craze** /kreɪz/ n moda f, febre f
**craz|y** /'kreɪzɪ/ a (-ier, -iest) doido,
louco (about por). ~iness n loucura
f
**creak** /kriːk/ n rangido m □ vi ranger
**cream** /kriːm/ n (milk fat; fig) nata f;
(cosmetic; culin) creme m □ a creme
invar □ vt desnatar. ~ cheese queijo-
creme m. ~y a cremoso
**crease** /kriːs/ n vinco m □ vt/i amar-
rotar(-se)
**creat|e** /kriː'eɪt/ vt criar. ~ion /-ʃn/ n
criação f. ~ive a criador. ~or n criador m
**creature** /'kriːtʃə(r)/ n criatura f
**crèche** /kreɪʃ/ n creche f
**credentials** /krɪ'denʃlz/ npl creden-
ciais fpl; (of competence etc) referências fpl
**credib|le** /'kredəbl/ a crível, verosí-
mil, (P) verossímil. ~ility /-'bɪlətɪ/ n
credibilidade f
**credit** /'kredɪt/ n crédito m; (honour)
honra f. ~s (cinema) créditos mpl □ vt
(pt credited) acreditar em; (comm)
creditar. ~ card cartão m de crédito.
~ sb with atribuir a alg. ~or n cre-
dor m
**creditable** /'kredɪtəbl/ a louvável,
honroso
**credulous** /'kredjʊləs/ a crédulo
**creed** /kriːd/ n credo m
**creek** /kriːk/ n enseada f estreita. be
up the ~ (sl) estar frito (sl)
**creep** /kriːp/ vi (pt crept) rastejar;
(move stealthily) mover-se furtivamente □ n (sl) cara m nojento. give
sb the ~s dar arrepios a alg. ~er n
(planta f) trepadeira (f). ~y a arrepiante
**cremat|e** /krɪ'meɪt/ vt cremar. ~ion
/-ʃn/ n cremação f
**crematorium** /kremə'tɔːrɪəm/ n (pl
-ia) crematório m
**crêpe** /kreɪp/ n crepe m. ~ paper papel m crepom, (P) plissado
**crept** /krept/ see creep
**crescent** /'kresnt/ n crescente m;
(street) rua f em semicírculo
**cress** /kres/ n agrião m

**crest** /krest/ n (of bird, hill) crista f;
(on coat of arms) timbre m
**Crete** /kriːt/ n Creta f
**crevasse** /krɪ'væs/ n fenda f (em geleira)
**crevice** /'krevɪs/ n racha f, fenda f
**crew**[1] /kruː/ see crow
**crew**[2] /kruː/ n tripulação f; (gang)
bando m. ~-cut n corte m à esco-
vinha. ~-neck n gola f redonda e un
pouco subida
**crib**[1] /krɪb/ n berço m; (Christmas)
presépio m
**crib**[2] /krɪb/ vt/i (pt cribbed) (colloq)
colar (sl), (P) cabular (sl) □ n cópia f,
plágio m; (translation) burro m (sl)
**cricket**[1] /'krɪkɪt/ n críquete m. ~er n
jogador m de críquete
**cricket**[2] /'krɪkɪt/ n (insect) grilo m
**crime** /kraɪm/ n crime m; (minor) delito m; (collectively) criminalidade f
**criminal** /'krɪmɪnl/ a & n criminoso
(m)
**crimp** /krɪmp/ vt preguear; (hair) frisar
**crimson** /'krɪmzn/ a & n carmesim (m)
**cring|e** /krɪndʒ/ vi encolher-se. ~ing
a servil
**crinkle** /'krɪŋkl/ vt/i enrugar(-se) □ n
vinco m, ruga f
**cripple** /'krɪpl/ n aleijado m, coxo m □
vt estropiar; (fig) paralisar
**crisis** /'kraɪsɪs/ n (pl crises /-siːz/)
crise f
**crisp** /krɪsp/ a (-er, est) (culin) crocante; (air) fresco; (manners, reply)
decidido. ~s npl batatas fpl fritas re-
dondas
**criterion** /kraɪ'tɪərɪən/ n (pl -ia)
critério m
**critic** /'krɪtɪk/ n crítico m. ~al a
crítico. ~ally adv de forma crítica;
(ill) gravemente
**criticism** /'krɪtɪsɪzəm/ n crítica f
**criticize** /'krɪtɪsaɪz/ vt/i criticar
**croak** /krəʊk/ n ( frog) coaxar
m; (raven) crocitar m, crocito m □ vi
( frog) coaxar; (raven) crocitar
**crochet** /'krəʊʃeɪ/ n crochê m □ vt
fazer em crochê
**crockery** /'krɒkərɪ/ n louça f
**crocodile** /'krɒkədaɪl/ n crocodilo m
**crocus** /'krəʊkəs/ n (pl -uses /-sɪz/)
croco m
**crony** /'krəʊnɪ/ n camarada mf,
amigão m, parceiro m
**crook** /krʊk/ n (colloq: criminal) vigarista mf; (stick) cajado m
**crooked** /'krʊkɪd/ a torcido; (winding) tortuoso; (askew) torto; (colloq:
dishonest) desonesto. ~ly adv de
través
**crop** /krɒp/ n colheita f; ( fig) quantidade f; (haircut) corte m rente □ vt (pt

**cropped)** cortar □ *vi* ~ **up** aparecer, surgir

**croquet** /'krəʊkeɪ/ *n* croquet *m*, croqué *m*

**cross** /krɒs/ *n* cruz *f* □ *vt/i* cruzar; (*cheque*) cruzar, (*P*) barrar; (*oppose*) contrariar; (*of paths*) cruzar-se □ *a* zangado. ~ **off** *or* **out** riscar. ~ **o.s.** benzer-se. ~ **sb's mind** passar pela cabeça *or* pelo espírito de alg, ocorrer a alg. **talk at ~ purposes** falar sem se entender. ~**-country** *a & adv* a corta-mato. ~**-examine** *vt* fazer o contra-interrogatório (de testemunhas). ~**-eyed** *a* vesgo, estrábico. ~**-fire** *n* fogo *m* cruzado. ~**-reference** *n* nota *f* remissiva. ~**-section** *n* corte *m* transversal; (*fig*) grupo *m or* sector *m* representativo. ~**ly** *adv* irritadamente

**crossbar** /'krɒsbɑ:(r)/ *n* barra *f* transversal *f*; (*of bicycle*) travessão *m*

**crossing** /'krɒsɪŋ/ *n* cruzamento *m*; (*by boat*) travessia *f*; (*on road*) passagem *f*

**crossroads** /'krɒsrəʊdz/ *n* encruzilhada *f*, cruzamento *m*

**crossword** /'krɒswɜ:d/ *n* palavras *fpl* cruzadas

**crotch** /krɒtʃ/ *n* entrepernas *fpl*

**crotchet** /'krɒtʃɪt/ *n* (*mus*) semínima *f*

**crouch** /kraʊtʃ/ *vi* agachar-se

**crow** /krəʊ/ *n* corvo *m* □ *vi* (*cock*) (*pt* crew) cantar; (*fig*) rejubilar-se (over com). **as the ~ flies** em linha reta, (*P*) recta

**crowbar** /'krəʊbɑ:(r)/ *n* alavanca *f*, pé-de-cabra *m*

**crowd** /kraʊd/ *n* multidão *f* □ *vi* afluir □ *vt* encher. ~ **into** apinhar-se em. ~**ed** *a* cheio, apinhado

**crown** /kraʊn/ *n* coroa *f*; (*of hill*) topo *m*, cume *m* □ *vt* coroar; (*tooth*) pôr uma coroa em

**crucial** /'kru:ʃl/ *a* crucial

**crucifix** /'kru:sɪfɪks/ *n* crucifixo *m*

**crucif|y** /'kru:sɪfaɪ/ *vt* crucificar. ~**ixion** /-'fɪkʃn/ *n* crucificação *f*

**crude** /kru:d/ *a* (**-er, -est**) (*raw*) bruto; (*rough, vulgar*) grosseiro. ~ **oil** petróleo *m* bruto

**cruel** /krʊəl/ *a* (**crueller, cruellest**) cruel. ~**ty** *n* crueldade *f*

**cruis|e** /kru:z/ *n* cruzeiro *m* □ *vi* cruzar; (*of tourists*) fazer um cruzeiro; (*of car*) ir a velocidade de cruzeiro. ~**er** *n* cruzador *m*. ~**ing speed** velocidade *f* de cruzeiro

**crumb** /krʌm/ *n* migalha *f*, farelo *m*

**crumble** /'krʌmbl/ *vt/i* desfazer(-se); (*bread*) esmigalhar(-se); (*collapse*) desmoronar-se

**crumple** /'krʌmpl/ *vt/i* amarrotar (-se)

**crunch** /krʌntʃ/ *vt* trincar; (*under one's feet*) fazer ranger

**crusade** /kru:'seɪd/ *n* cruzada *f*. ~**r** /-ə(r)/ *n* cruzado *m*; (*fig*) militante *mf*

**crush** /krʌʃ/ *vt* esmagar; (*clothes, papers*) amassar, amarrotar □ *n* aperto *m*. **a ~ on** (*sl*) uma paixonite, (*P*) paixoneta por.

**crust** /krʌst/ *n* côdea *f*, crosta *f*. ~**y** *a* crocante

**crutch** /krʌtʃ/ *n* muleta *f*; (*crotch*) entrepernas *fpl*

**crux** /krʌks/ *n* (*pl* **cruxes**) o ponto crucial

**cry** /kraɪ/ *n* grito *m* □ *vi* (*weep*) chorar; (*call out*) gritar. **a far ~ from** muito diferente de.

**crying** /'kraɪŋ/ *a* **a ~ shame** uma grande vergonha

**crypt** /krɪpt/ *n* cripta *f*

**cryptic** /'krɪptɪk/ *a* críptico, enigmático

**crystal** /'krɪstl/ *n* cristal *m*. ~**lize** *vt/i* cristalizar(-se)

**cub** /kʌb/ *n* cria *f*, filhote *m*. **C~** (Scout) lobito *m*

**Cuba** /'kju:bə/ *n* Cuba *f*. ~**n** *a & n* cubano (*m*)

**cubby-hole** /'kʌbɪhəʊl/ *n* cochicho *m*; (*snug place*) cantinho *m*

**cub|e** /kju:b/ *n* cubo *m*. ~**ic** *a* cúbico

**cubicle** /'kju:bɪkl/ *n* cubículo *m*, compartimento *m*; (*at swimming-pool*) cabine *f*

**cuckoo** /'kʊku:/ *n* cuco *m*

**cucumber** /'kju:kʌmbə(r)/ *n* pepino *m*

**cuddl|e** /'kʌdl/ *vt/i* abraçar com carinho; (*nestle*) aninhar(-se) □ *n* abracinho *m*, festinha *f*. ~**y** *a* fofo, aconchegante

**cudgel** /'kʌdʒl/ *n* cacete *m*, moca *f* □ *vt* (*pt* cudgelled) dar cacetadas em

**cue**[1] /kju:/ *n* (*theat*) deixa *f*; (*hint*) sugestão *f*, sinal *m*

**cue**[2] /kju:/ *n* (*billiards*) taco *m*

**cuff** /kʌf/ *n* punho *m*; (*blow*) sopapo *m* □ *vt* dar um sopapo. ~**-link** *n* botão *m* de punho. **off the ~** de improviso

**cul-de-sac** /'kʌldəsæk/ *n* (*pl* **culs-de-sac**) beco *m* sem saída

**culinary** /'kʌlɪnərɪ/ *a* culinário

**cull** /kʌl/ *vt* (*select*) escolher; (*kill*) abater seletivamente, (*P*) selectivamente □ *n* abate *m*

**culminat|e** /'kʌlmɪneɪt/ *vi* ~**e in** acabar em. ~**ion** /-'neɪʃn/ *n* auge *m*, ponto *m* culminante

**culprit** /'kʌlprɪt/ *n* culpado *m*

**cult** /kʌlt/ *n* culto *m*

**cultivat|e** /'kʌltɪveɪt/ *vt* cultivar. ~**ion** /-'veɪʃn/ *n* cultivo *m*, cultivação *f*

cultural /'kʌltʃərəl/ a cultural

culture /'kʌltʃə(r)/ n cultura f. ~d a culto

cumbersome /'kʌmbəsəm/ a (unwieldy) pesado, incômodo, (P) incómodo

cumulative /'kju:mjʊlətɪv/ a cumulativo

cunning /'kʌnɪŋ/ a astuto, manhoso □ n astúcia f, manha f

cup /kʌp/ n xícara f, (P) chávena f; (prize) taça f. C~ Final Final de Campeonato f

cupboard /'kʌbəd/ n armário m

cupful /'kʌpfʊl/ n xícara f cheia, (P) chávena f (cheia)

curable /'kjʊərəbl/ a curável

curator /kjʊə'reɪtə(r)/ n (museum) conservador m; (jur) curador m

curb /kɜ:b/ n freio m □ vt refrear; (price increase etc) sustar

curdle /'kɜ:dl/ vt/i coalhar

cure /kjʊə(r)/ vt curar □ n cura f

curfew /'kɜ:fju:/ n toque m de recolher

curio /'kjʊərɪəʊ/ n (pl -os) curiosidade f

curi|ous /'kjʊərɪəs/ a curioso. ~osity /-'ɒsətɪ/ n curiosidade f

curl /kɜ:l/ vt/i encaracolar(-se) □ n caracol m. ~ up enroscar(-se)

curler /'kɜ:lə(r)/ n rolo m

curly /'kɜ:lɪ/ a (-ier, -iest) encaracolado, crespo

currant /'kʌrənt/ n passa f de Corinto

currency /'kʌrənsɪ/ n moeda f corrente; (general use) circulação f. foreign ~ moeda f estrangeira

current /'kʌrənt/ a (common) corrente; (event, price, etc) atual, (P) actual □ n corrente f. ~ account conta f corrente. ~ affairs atualidades fpl, (P) actualidades fpl. ~ly adv atualmente, (P) actualmente

curriculum /kə'rɪkjʊləm/ n (pl -la) currículo m, programa m de estudos. ~ vitae n curriculum vitae m

curry¹ /'kʌrɪ/ n caril m

curry² /'kʌrɪ/ vt ~ favour with procurar agradar a

curse /kɜ:s/ n maldição f, praga f; (bad language) palavrão m □ vt amaldiçoar, praguejar contra □ vi praguejar; (swear) dizer palavrões

cursor /'kɜ:sə(r)/ n cursor m

cursory /'kɜ:sərɪ/ a apressado, superficial. a ~ look uma olhada superficial

curt /kɜ:t/ a brusco

curtail /kɜ:'teɪl/ vt abreviar; (expenses etc) reduzir

curtain /'kɜ:tn/ n cortina f; (theat) pano m

curtsy /'kɜ:tsɪ/ n reverência f □ vi fazer uma reverência

curve /kɜ:v/ n curva f □ vt/i curvar (-se); (of road) fazer uma curva

cushion /'kʊʃn/ n almofada f □ vt (a blow) amortecer; (fig) proteger

cushy /'kʊʃɪ/ a (-ier, -iest) (colloq) fácil, agradável. ~ job sinecura f, boca f (fig)

custard /'kʌstəd/ n creme m

custodian /kʌ'stəʊdɪən/ n guarda m

custody /'kʌstədɪ/ n (safe keeping) custódia f; (jur) detenção f; (of child) tutela f

custom /'kʌstəm/ n costume m; (comm) freguesia f, clientela f. ~ary a habitual

customer /'kʌstəmə(r)/ n freguês m, cliente mf

customs /'kʌstəmz/ npl alfândega f □ a alfandegário. ~ clearance desembaraço m alfandegário. ~ officer funcionário m da alfândega

cut /kʌt/ vt/i (pt cut, pres p cutting) cortar; (prices etc) reduzir □ n corte m, golpe m; (of clothes, hair) corte m; (piece) pedaço m; (prices etc) redução f, corte m; (sl: share) comissão f, (P) talhada f (sl). ~ back or down (on) reduzir. ~-back n corte m. ~ in intrometer-se; (auto) cortar. ~ off cortar; (fig) isolar. ~ out recortar; (leave out) suprimir. ~-out n figura f para recortar. ~-price a a preço(s) reduzido(s). ~ short encurtar, (P) atalhar

cute /kju:t/ a (-er, -est) (colloq: clever) esperto; (attractive) bonito, (P) giro (colloq)

cuticle /'kju:tɪkl/ n cutícula f

cutlery /'kʌtlərɪ/ n talheres mpl

cutlet /'kʌtlɪt/ n costeleta f

cutting /'kʌtɪŋ/ a cortante □ n (from newspaper) recorte m; (plant) estaca f. ~ edge gume m

CV abbr see curriculum vitae

cyanide /'saɪənaɪd/ n cianeto m

cycl|e /'saɪkl/ n ciclo m; (bicycle) bicicleta f □ vi andar de bicicleta. ~ing n ciclismo m. ~ist n ciclista mf

cyclone /'saɪkləʊn/ n ciclone m

cylind|er /'sɪlɪndə(r)/ n cilindro m. ~rical /-'lɪndrɪkl/ a cilíndrico

cymbals /'sɪmblz/ npl (mus) pratos mpl

cynic /'sɪnɪk/ n cínico m. ~al a cínico. ~ism /-sɪzəm/ n cinismo m

Cypr|us /'saɪprəs/ n Chipre m. ~iot /'sɪprɪət/ a & n cipriota (mf)

cyst /sɪst/ n quisto m

Czech /tʃek/ a & n tcheco (m), (P) checo (m)

# D

**dab** /dæb/ *vt* (*pt* **dabbed**) aplicar levemente □ *n* **a ~ of** uma aplicaçãozinha de. **~ sth on** aplicar qq coisa em gestos leves

**dabble** /'dæbl/ *vi* **~ in** interessar-se por, fazer um pouco de (como amador). **~r** /-ə(r)/ *n* amador *m*

**dad** /dæd/ *n* (*colloq*) paizinho *m*. **~dy** *n* (*children's use*) papai *m*, (*P*) papá *m*. **~dy-long-legs** *n* pernilongo *m*

**daffodil** /'dæfədɪl/ *n* narciso *m*

**daft** /da:ft/ *a* (*-er, -est*) doido, maluco

**dagger** /'dægə(r)/ *n* punhal *m*. **at ~s drawn** prestes a lutar (**with** com)

**daily** /'deɪlɪ/ *a* diário, quotidiano □ *adv* diariamente, todos os dias □ *n* (*newspaper*) diário *m*; (*colloq: charwoman*) faxineira *f*, (*P*) mulher *f* a dias

**dainty** /'deɪntɪ/ *a* (*-ier, -iest*) delicado; (*pretty, neat*) gracioso

**dairy** /'deərɪ/ *n* leiteria *f*. **~ products** laticínios *mpl*

**daisy** /'deɪzɪ/ *n* margarida *f*

**dam** /dæm/ *n* barragem *f*, represa *f* □ *vt* (*pt* **dammed**) represar

**damage** /'dæmɪdʒ/ *n* estrago(s) *mpl*. **~es** (*jur*) perdas *fpl* e danos *mpl* □ *vt* estragar, danificar; (*fig*) prejudicar. **~ing** *a* prejudicial

**dame** /deɪm/ *n* (*old use*) dama *f*; (*Amer sl*) mulher *f*

**damn** /dæm/ *vt* (*relig*) condenar aõ inferno; (*swear at*) amaldiçoar, maldizer; (*fig: condemn*) condenar □ *int* raios!, bolas! □ *n* **not care a ~** (*colloq*) estar pouco ligando (*colloq*), (*P*) estar-se marimbando (*colloq*) □ *a* (*colloq*) do diabo, danado □ *adv* (*colloq*) muitíssimo. **I'll be ~ed if** que um raio me atinja se. **~ation** /-'neɪʃn/ *n* danação *f*, condenação *f*. **~ing** *a* comprometedor, condenatório

**damp** /dæmp/ *n* umidade *f*, (*P*) humidade *f* □ *a* (*-er, -est*) úmido, (*P*) húmido □ *vt* umedecer, (*P*) humedecer. **~en** *vt* = **damp**. **~ness** *n* umidade *f*, (*P*) humidade *f*

**dance** /da:ns/ *vt/i* dançar □ *n* dança *f*. **~ hall** sala *f* de baile. **~r** /-ə(r)/ *n* dançarino *m*; (*professional*) bailarino *m*

**dandelion** /'dændɪlaɪən/ *n* dente-de-leão *m*

**dandruff** /'dændrʌf/ *n* caspa *f*

**Dane** /deɪn/ *n* dinamarquês *m*

**danger** /'deɪndʒə(r)/ *n* perigo *m*. **be in ~ of** correr o risco de. **~ous** *a* perigoso

**dangle** /'dæŋgl/ *vi* oscilar, pender □ *vt*

ter *or* trazer dependurado; (*hold*) balançar; (*fig: hopes, etc*) acenar com

**Danish** /'deɪnɪʃ/ *a* dinamarquês □ *n* (*lang*) dinamarquês *m*

**dank** /dæŋk/ *a* (*-er, -est*) frio e úmido, (*P*) húmido

**dare** /deə(r)/ *vt* **~ to do** ousar fazer. **~ sb to do** desafiar alg a fazer □ *n* desafio *m*. **I ~ say** creio

**daredevil** /'deədevl/ *n* louco *m*, temerário *m*

**daring** /'deərɪŋ/ *a* audacioso □ *n* audácia *f*

**dark** /da:k/ *a* (*-er, -est*) escuro, sombrio; (*gloomy*) sombrio; (*of colour*) escuro; (*of skin*) moreno □ *n* escuridão *f*, escuro *m*; (*nightfall*) anoitecer *m*, cair *m* da noite. **~ horse** concorrente *mf* que é uma incógnita. **~-room** *n* câmara *f* escura. **be in the ~ about** (*fig*) ignorar. **~ness** *n* escuridão *f*

**darken** /'da:kən/ *vt/i* escurecer

**darling** /'da:lɪŋ/ *a & n* querido (*m*)

**darn** /da:n/ *vt* serzir, remendar

**dart** /da:t/ *n* dardo *m*, flecha *f*. **~s** (*game*) jogo *m* de dardos □ *vi* lançar-se

**dartboard** /'da:tbɔ:d/ *n* alvo *m*

**dash** /dæʃ/ *vi* precipitar-se □ *vt* arremessar; (*hopes*) destruir □ *n* corrida *f*; (*stroke*) travessão *m*; (*Morse*) traço *m*. **a ~ of** um pouco de. **~ off** partir a toda a velocidade; (*letter*) escrever às pressas

**dashboard** /'dæʃbɔ:d/ *n* painel *m* de instrumentos, quadro *m* de bordo

**data** /'deɪtə/ *npl* dados *mpl*. **~ capture** aquisição *f* de informações, recolha *f* de dados. **~base** *n* base *f* de dados. **~ processing** processamento *m* or tratamento *m* de dados

**date**[1] /deɪt/ *n* data *f*; (*colloq*) encontro *m* marcado □ *vt/i* datar; (*colloq*) andar com. **out of ~** desatualizado, (*P*) desactualizado. **to ~** até a data. **up to ~** (*style*) moderno; (*information etc*) em dia. **~d** *a* antiquado

**date**[2] /deɪt/ *n* (*fruit*) tâmara *f*

**daub** /dɔ:b/ *vt* borrar, pintar toscamente

**daughter** /'dɔ:tə(r)/ *n* filha *f*. **~-in-law** *n* (*pl* **~s-in-law**) nora *f*

**daunt** /dɔ:nt/ *vt* assustar, intimidar, desencorajar

**dawdle** /'dɔ:dl/ *vi* perder tempo

**dawn** /dɔ:n/ *n* madrugada *f* □ *vi* madrugar, amanhecer. **~ on** (*fig*) fazer-se luz no espírito de, começar a perceber

**day** /deɪ/ *n* dia *m*; (*period*) época *f*, tempo *m*. **~-dream** *n* devaneio *m* □ *vi* devanear. **the ~ before** a véspera

**daybreak** /'deɪbreɪk/ *n* romper *m* do dia, aurora *f*, amanhecer *m*

**daylight** /'deɪlaɪt/ n luz f do dia. ~ **robbery** roubar descaradamente

**daytime** /'deɪtaɪm/ n dia m, dia m claro

**daze** /deɪz/ vt aturdir □ n in a ~ aturdido

**dazzle** /'dæzl/ vt deslumbrar; (with headlights) ofuscar

**dead** /ded/ a morto; (numb) dormente □ adv completamente, de todo □ n in the ~ of the night a horas mortas, na calada da noite. the ~ os mortos. in the ~ centre bem no meio. stop ~ estacar. ~ beat a (colloq) morto de cansaço. ~ end beco m sem saída. ~-pan a inexpressivo

**deaden** /'dedn/ vt (sound, blow) amortecer; (pain) aliviar

**deadline** /'dedlaɪn/ n prazo m final

**deadlock** /'dedlɒk/ n impasse m

**deadly** /'dedlɪ/ a (-ier, -iest) mortal; (weapon) mortífero

**deaf** /def/ a (-er, -est) surdo. turn a ~ ear fingir que não ouve. ~ mute surdo-mudo m. ~ness n surdez f

**deafen** /'defn/ vt ensurdecer. ~ing a ensurdecedor

**deal** /di:l/ vt (pt dealt) distribuir; (a blow, cards) dar □ vi negociar □ n negócio m; (cards) vez de dar f. a great ~ muito (of de). ~ in negociar em. ~ with (person) tratar (com); (affair) tratar de. ~er n comerciante m; (agent) concessionário m; representante m

**dealings** /'di:lɪŋz/ npl relações fpl; (comm) negócios mpl

**dealt** /delt/ see deal

**dean** /di:n/ n decano m

**dear** /dɪə(r)/ a (-er, -est) (cherished) caro, querido; (expensive) caro □ n amor m □ adv caro □ int oh ~! meu Deus! ~ly adv (very much) muito; (pay) caro

**dearth** /dɜ:θ/ n escassez f

**death** /deθ/ n morte f. ~ certificate certidão f de óbito. ~ penalty pena f de morte. ~ rate taxa f de mortalidade. ~-trap n lugar m perigoso, ratoeira f. ~ly a da morte, mortal

**debase** /dɪ'beɪs/ vt degradar

**debat|e** /dɪ'beɪt/ n debate m □ vt debater. ~able a discutível

**debauchery** /dɪ'bɔ:tʃərɪ/ n deboche m, devassidão f

**debility** /dɪ'bɪlətɪ/ n debilidade f

**debit** /'debɪt/ n débito m □ vt (pt debited) debitar

**debris** /'deɪbri:/ n destroços mpl

**debt** /det/ n dívida f. in ~ endividado. ~or n devedor m

**debunk** /di:'bʌŋk/ vt (colloq) desmitificar

**début** /'deɪbju:/ n (of actor, play etc) estréia f

**decade** /dekeɪd/ n década f

**decaden|t** /'dekədənt/ a decadente. ~ce n decadência f

**decaffeinated** /di:'kæfɪmeɪtɪd/ a sem cafeína

**decanter** /dɪ'kæntə(r)/ n garrafa f para vinho, de vidro ou cristal

**decapitate** /dɪ'kæpɪteɪt/ vt decapitar

**decay** /dɪ'keɪ/ vi apodrecer, estragar-se; (food; fig) deteriorar-se; (building) degradar-se □ n apodrecimento m; (of tooth) cárie f, (fig) declínio m, decadência f

**deceased** /dɪ'si:st/ a & n falecido (m), defunto (m)

**deceit** /dɪ'si:t/ n engano m. ~ful a enganador

**deceive** /dɪ'si:v/ vt enganar, iludir

**December** /dɪ'sembə(r)/ n dezembro m

**decen|t** /'di:snt/ a decente; (colloq: good) (bastante) bom; (colloq: likeable) simpático. ~cy n decência f

**decentralize** /di:'sentrəlaɪz/ vt descentralizar

**decept|ive** /dɪ'septɪv/ a enganador, ilusório. ~ion /-ʃn/ n engano m

**decibel** /'desɪbel/ n decibel m

**decide** /dɪ'saɪd/ vt/i decidir. ~ on decidir-se por. ~ to do decidir fazer. ~d /-ɪd/ a decidido; (clear) definido, nítido. ~dly /-ɪdlɪ/ adv decididamente

**decimal** /'desɪml/ a decimal □ n (fração f, (P) fracção f) decimal m. ~ point vírgula f decimal

**decipher** /dɪ'saɪfə(r)/ vt decifrar

**decision** /dɪ'sɪʒn/ n decisão f

**decisive** /dɪ'saɪsɪv/ a decisivo; (manner) decidido. ~ly adv decisivamente

**deck** /dek/ n convés m; (of cards) baralho m. ~-chair n espreguiçadeira f

**declar|e** /dɪ'kleə(r)/ vt declarar. ~ation /deklə'reɪʃn/ n declaração f

**decline** /dɪ'klaɪn/ vt (refuse) declinar, recusar delicadamente; (gram) declinar □ vi (deteriorate) declinar; (fall) baixar □ n declínio m; (fall) abaixamento m

**decode** /di:'kəʊd/ vt descodificar

**decompos|e** /di:kəm'pəʊz/ vt/i decompor(-se). ~ition /-ɒmpə'zɪʃn/ n decomposição f

**décor** /'deɪkɔ:(r)/ n decoração f

**decorat|e** /'dekəreɪt/ vt decorar, enfeitar; (paint) pintar; (paper) pôr papel em. ~ion /-'reɪʃn/ n decoração f; (medal etc) condecoração f. ~ive /-ətɪv/ a decorativo

**decorum** /dɪ'kɔ:rəm/ n decoro m

**decoy**[1] /'di:kɔɪ/ n chamariz m, engodo m; (trap) armadilha f

**decoy**[2] /dɪˈkɔɪ/ *vt* atrair, apanhar
**decrease**[1] /diːˈkriːs/ *vt/i* diminuir
**decrease**[2] /ˈdiːkriːs/ *n* diminuição *f*
**decree** /dɪˈkriː/ *n* decreto *m*; (*jur*) decisão *f* judicial □ *vt* decretar
**decrepit** /dɪˈkrepɪt/ *a* decrépito
**dedicat|e** /ˈdedɪkeɪt/ *vt* dedicar. ~ed *a* dedicado. ~ion /-ˈkeɪʃn/ *n* dedicação *f*; (*in book*) dedicatória *f*
**deduce** /dɪˈdjuːs/ *vt* deduzir
**deduct** /dɪˈdʌkt/ *vt* deduzir; (*from pay*) descontar
**deduction** /dɪˈdʌkʃn/ *n* dedução *f*; (*from pay*) desconto *m*
**deed** /diːd/ *n* ato *m*; (*jur*) contrato *m*
**deem** /diːm/ *vt* julgar, considerar
**deep** /diːp/ *a* (-er, -est) profundo □ *adv* profundamente. ~-freeze *n* congelador *m* □ *vt* congelar. **take a ~ breath** respirar fundo. ~ly *adv* profundamente
**deepen** /ˈdiːpən/ *vt/i* aprofundar(-se); (*mystery, night*) adensar-se
**deer** /dɪə(r)/ *n* (*pl invar*) veado *m*
**deface** /dɪˈfeɪs/ *vt* danificar, degradar
**defamation** /defəˈmeɪʃn/ *n* difamação *f*
**default** /dɪˈfɔːlt/ *vi* faltar □ *n* **by ~** à revelia. **win by ~** (*sport*) ganhar por não comparecimento, (*P*) comparência □ *a* (*comput*) default *m*
**defeat** /dɪˈfiːt/ *vt* derrotar; (*thwart*) malograr □ *n* derrota *f*; (*of plan, etc*) malogro *m*
**defect**[1] /ˈdiːfekt/ *n* defeito *m*. ~ive /dɪˈfektɪv/ *a* defeituoso
**defect**[2] /dɪˈfekt/ *vi* desertar. ~ion *n* defecção *m*. ~or *n* trânsfuga *mf*, dissidente *mf*; (*political*) asilado *m* político
**defence** /dɪˈfens/ *n* defesa *f*. ~less *a* indefeso
**defend** /dɪˈfend/ *vt* defender. ~ant *n* (*jur*) réu *m*, acusado *m*. ~er *n* advogado *m* de defesa, defensor *m*
**defensive** /dɪˈfensɪv/ *a* defensivo □ *n* **on the ~** na defensiva *f*; (*person, sport*) na retranca *f* (*colloq*)
**defer** /dɪˈfɜː(r)/ *vt* (*pt* deferred) adiar, diferir □ *vi* ~ **to** ceder, deferir
**deferen|ce** /ˈdefərəns/ *n* deferência *f*. ~tial /-ˈrenʃl/ *a* deferente
**defian|ce** /dɪˈfaɪəns/ *n* desafio *m*. **in ~ of** sem respeito por. ~t *a* de desafio. ~tly *adv* com ar de desafio
**deficien|t** /dɪˈfɪʃnt/ *a* deficiente. **be ~t in** ter falta de. ~cy *n* deficiência *f*
**deficit** /ˈdefɪsɪt/ *n* déficit *m*
**define** /dɪˈfaɪn/ *vt* definir
**definite** /ˈdefɪnət/ *a* definido; (*clear*) categórico, claro; (*certain*) certo. ~ly *adv* decididamente; (*clearly*) claramente
**definition** /defɪˈnɪʃn/ *n* definição *f*

**definitive** /dɪˈfɪnətɪv/ *a* definitivo
**deflat|e** /dɪˈfleɪt/ *vt* esvaziar; (*person*) desemproar, desinchar. ~ion /-ʃn/ *n* esvaziamento *m*; (*econ*) deflação *f*
**deflect** /dɪˈflekt/ *vt/i* desviar(-se)
**deform** /dɪˈfɔːm/ *vt* deformar. ~ed *a* deformado, disforme. ~ity *n* deformidade *f*
**defraud** /dɪˈfrɔːd/ *vt* defraudar
**defrost** /diːˈfrɒst/ *vt* descongelar
**deft** /deft/ *a* (-er, -est) hábil
**defunct** /dɪˈfʌŋkt/ *a* (*law etc*) caduco, extinto
**defuse** /diːˈfjuːz/ *vt* (*a bomb*) desativar, (*P*) desactivar; (*a situation*) acalmar
**defy** /dɪˈfaɪ/ *vt* desafiar; (*attempts*) resistir a; (*the law*) desobedecer a; (*public opinion*) opor-se a
**degenerate** /dɪˈdʒenəreɪt/ *vi* degenerar (**into** em)
**degrad|e** /dɪˈɡreɪd/ *vt* degradar. ~ation /deɡrəˈdeɪʃn/ *n* degradação *f*
**degree** /dɪˈɡriː/ *n* grau *m*; (*univ*) diploma *m*. **to a ~** ao mais alto grau, muito
**dehydrate** /diːˈhaɪdreɪt/ *vt/i* desidratar(-se)
**de-ice** /diːˈaɪs/ *vt* descongelar, degelar; (*windscreen*) tirar o gelo de
**deign** /deɪn/ *vt* ~ **to do** dignar-se (a) fazer
**deity** /ˈdiːɪtɪ/ *n* divindade *f*
**dejected** /dɪˈdʒektɪd/ *a* abatido
**delay** /dɪˈleɪ/ *vt* atrasar; (*postpone*) retardar □ *vi* atrasar-se □ *n* atraso *m*, demora *f*
**delegate**[1] /ˈdelɪɡət/ *n* delegado *m*
**delegat|e**[2] /ˈdelɪɡeɪt/ *vt* delegar. ~ion /-ˈɡeɪʃn/ *n* delegação *f*
**delet|e** /dɪˈliːt/ *vt* riscar. ~ion /-ʃn/ *n* rasura *f*
**deliberate**[1] /dɪˈlɪbərət/ *a* deliberado; (*steps etc*) compassado. ~ly *adv* deliberadamente, de propósito
**deliberat|e**[2] /dɪˈlɪbəreɪt/ *vt/i* deliberar. ~ion /-ˈreɪʃn/ *n* deliberação *f*
**delica|te** /ˈdelɪkət/ *a* delicado. ~cy *n* delicadeza *f*; (*food*) guloseima *f*, iguaria *f*, (*P*) acepipe *m*
**delicatessen** /delɪkəˈtesn/ *n* (*shop*) mercearias *fpl* finas
**delicious** /dɪˈlɪʃəs/ *a* delicioso
**delight** /dɪˈlaɪt/ *n* grande prazer *m*, delícia *f*; (*thing*) delícia *f*, encanto *m* □ *vt* deliciar □ *vi* ~ **in** deliciar-se com. ~ed *a* deliciado, encantado. ~ful *a* delicioso, encantador
**delinquen|t** /dɪˈlɪŋkwənt/ *a* & *n* delinquente *mf*, (*P*) delinquente *mf*. ~cy *n* delinquência *f*, (*P*) delinquência *f*
**deliri|ous** /dɪˈlɪrɪəs/ *a* delirante. **be ~ous** delirar. ~um /-əm/ *n* delírio *m*
**deliver** /dɪˈlɪvə(r)/ *vt* entregar;

**delude**        234        **depth**

(*letters*) distribuir; (*free*) libertar; (*med*) fazer o parto. **~ance** *n* libertação *f*. **~y** *n* entrega *f*; (*letters*) distribuição *f*; (*med*) parto *m*

**delu|de** /dɪˈluːd/ *vt* enganar. **~de o.s.** ter ilusões. **~sion** /-ʒn/ *n* ilusão *f*

**deluge** /ˈdeljuːdʒ/ *n* dilúvio *m* □ *vt* inundar

**de luxe** /dɪˈlʌks/ *a* de luxo

**delve** /delv/ *vi* **~ into** pesquisar, re-buscar

**demand** /dɪˈmɑːnd/ *vt* exigir; (*ask to be told*) perguntar □ *n* exigência *f*; (*comm*) procura *f*; (*claim*) reivindi-cação *f*. **in ~** procurado. **~ing** *a* exi-gente; (*work*) puxado, custoso

**demean** /dɪˈmiːn/ *vt* **~ o.s.** rebaixar-se

**demeanour** /dɪˈmiːnə(r)/ *n* comporta-mento *m*, conduta *f*

**demented** /dɪˈmentɪd/ *a* louco, de-mente. **become ~** enlouquecer

**demo** /ˈdeməʊ/ *n* (*pl* **-os**) (*colloq*) manifestação *f*, (*P*) manif *f*

**democracy** /dɪˈmɒkrəsɪ/ *n* democra-cia *f*

**democrat** /ˈdeməkræt/ *n* democrata *mf*. **~ic** /ˈkrætɪk/ *a* democrático

**demoli|sh** /dɪˈmɒlɪʃ/ *vt* demolir. **~tion** /deməˈlɪʃn/ *n* demolição *f*

**demon** /ˈdiːmən/ *n* demônio *m*

**demonstrat|e** /ˈdemənstreɪt/ *vt* demonstrar □ *vi* (*pol*) fazer uma manifestação, manifestar-se. **~ion** /-ˈstreɪʃn/ *n* demonstração *f*; (*pol*) manifestação *f*. **~or** *n* (*pol*) manifes-tante *mf*

**demonstrative** /dɪˈmɒnstrətɪv/ *a* de-monstrativo

**demoralize** /dɪˈmɒrəlaɪz/ *vt* desmora-lizar

**demote** /dɪˈməʊt/ *vt* fazer baixar de posto, rebaixar

**demure** /dɪˈmjʊə(r)/ *a* recatado, mo-desto

**den** /den/ *n* antro *m*, covil *m*; (*room*) cantinho *m*, recanto *m*

**denial** /dɪˈnaɪəl/ *n* negação *f*; (*refusal*) recusa *f*; (*statement*) desmentido *m*

**denigrate** /ˈdenɪgreɪt/ *vt* denegrir

**denim** /ˈdenɪm/ *n* brim *m*. **~s** (*jeans*) blue-jeans *mpl*

**Denmark** /ˈdenmɑːk/ *n* Dinamarca *f*

**denomination** /dɪnɒmɪˈneɪʃn/ *n* de-nominação *f*; (*relig*) confissão *f*, seita *f*; (*money*) valor *m*

**denote** /dɪˈnəʊt/ *vt* denotar

**denounce** /dɪˈnaʊns/ *vt* denunciar

**dens|e** /dens/ *a* (**-er**, **-est**) denso; (*col-loq: person*) obtuso. **~ely** *adv* (*packed etc*) muito. **~ity** *n* densidade *f*

**dent** /dent/ *n* mossa *f*, depressão *f* □ *vt* dentear

**dental** /ˈdentl/ *a* dentário, dental

**dentist** /ˈdentɪst/ *n* dentista *mf*. **~ry** *n* odontologia *f*

**denture** /ˈdentʃə(r)/ *n* dentadura *f* (postiça)

**denunciation** /dɪnʌnsɪˈeɪʃn/ *n* de-núncia *f*

**deny** /dɪˈnaɪ/ *vt* negar; (*rumour*) des-mentir; (*disown*) renegar; (*refuse*) re-cusar

**deodorant** /diːˈəʊdərənt/ *n & a* desodorante (*m*), (*P*) desodorizante (*m*)

**depart** /dɪˈpɑːt/ *vi* partir. **~ from** (*de-viate*) afastar-se de, desviar-se de

**department** /dɪˈpɑːtmənt/ *n* departa-mento *m*; (*in shop, office*) seção *f*, (*P*) secção *f*; (*government*) repartição *f*. **~ store** loja *f* de departamentos, (*P*) grande armazém *m*

**departure** /dɪˈpɑːtʃə(r)/ *n* partida *f*. **a ~ from** (*custom, diet etc*) uma mu-dança de. **a new ~** uma nova orien-tação

**depend** /dɪˈpend/ *vi* **~ on** depender de; (*trust*) contar com. **~able** *a* de confiança. **~ence** *n* dependência *f*. **~ent (on)** *a* dependente (de)

**dependant** /dɪˈpendənt/ *n* dependente *mf*

**depict** /dɪˈpɪkt/ *vt* descrever; (*in pic-tures*) representar

**deplete** /dɪˈpliːt/ *vt* reduzir; (*use up*) esgotar

**deplor|e** /dɪˈplɔː(r)/ *vt* deplorar. **~able** *a* deplorável

**deport** /dɪˈpɔːt/ *vt* deportar. **~ation** /diːpɔːˈteɪʃn/ *n* deportação *f*

**depose** /dɪˈpəʊz/ *vt* depor

**deposit** /dɪˈpɒzɪt/ *vt* (*pt* **deposited**) depositar □ *n* depósito *m*. **~ account** conta *f* de depósito a prazo. **~or** *n* depositante *mf*

**depot** /ˈdepəʊ/ *n* (*mil*) depósito *m*; (*buses*) garagem *f*; (*Amer: station*) rodoviária *f*, estação *f* de trem, (*P*) de comboio

**deprav|e** /dɪˈpreɪv/ *vt* depravar. **~ity** /-ˈprævətɪ/ *n* depravação *f*

**depreciat|e** /dɪˈpriːʃɪeɪt/ *vt/i* depre-ciar(-se). **~ion** /-ˈeɪʃn/ *n* depreciação *f*

**depress** /dɪˈpres/ *vt* deprimir; (*press down*) carregar em. **~ion** /-ʃn/ *n* depressão *f*

**deprivation** /deprɪˈveɪʃn/ *n* privação *f*

**deprive** /dɪˈpraɪv/ *vt* **~ of** privar de. **~d** *a* privado; (*underprivileged*) de-serdado (da sorte), destituído; (*child*) carente

**depth** /depθ/ *n* profundidade *f*. **be out of one's ~** perder pé, (*P*) não ter pé; (*fig*) ficar desnorteado, estar perdido. **in the ~(s) of** no mais fundo de, nas profundezas de

deputation /depjʊ'teɪʃn/ n delegação
f
deputy /'depjʊtɪ/ n (pl -ies) delegado
m □ a adjunto. ~ chairman vice-presidente m
derail /dɪ'reɪl/ vt descarrilhar. be
~ed descarrilhar. ~ment n descar-
rilhamento m
deranged /dɪ'reɪndʒd/ a (mind) transtornado, louco
derelict /'derəlɪkt/ a abandonado
deri|de /dɪ'raɪd/ vt escarnecer de.
~sion /-'rɪʒn/ n escárnio m. ~sive a
escarninho. ~sory a escarninho; (offer etc) irrisório
derivative /dɪ'rɪvətɪv/ a derivado;
(work) pouco original □ n derivado
m
deriv|e /dɪ'raɪv/ vt ~e from tirar de □
vi ~e from derivar de. ~ation
/derɪ'veɪʃn/ n derivação f
derogatory /dɪ'rɒɡətrɪ/ a pejorativo;
(remark) depreciativo
derv /dɜːv/ n gasóleo m
descend /dɪ'send/ vt/i descer, descender. be ~ed from descender de.
~ant n descendente mf
descent /dɪ'sent/ n descida f; (lineage)
descendência f, origem f
descri|be /dɪ'skraɪb/ vt descrever.
~ption /-'krɪpʃn/ n descrição f;
~ptive /-'krɪptɪv/ a descritivo
desecrat|e /'desɪkreɪt/ vt profanar.
~ion /-'kreɪʃn/ n profanação f
desert[1] /'dezət/ a & n deserto (m). ~
island ilha f deserta
desert[2] /dɪ'zɜːt/ vt/i desertar. ~ed a
abandonado. ~er n desertor m.
~ion /-ʃn/ n deserção f
deserv|e /dɪ'zɜːv/ vt merecer. ~edly
/dɪ'zɜːvɪdlɪ/ adv merecidamente, a justo título. ~ing a (person) merecedor;
(action) meritório
design /dɪ'zaɪn/ n desenho m; (artis-
tic) design m; (style of dress) modelo
m; (pattern) padrão m, motivo m □ vt
desenhar; (devise) conceber. ~er n
desenhador m; (of dresses) costureiro
m; (of machine) inventor m
designat|e /'dezɪɡneɪt/ vt designar.
~ion /-'neɪʃn/ n designação f
desir|e /dɪ'zaɪə(r)/ n desejo m □ vt
desejar. ~able a desejável, atraente
desk /desk/ n secretária f; (of pupil)
carteira f; (in hotel) recepção f; (in
bank) caixa f
desolat|e /'desələt/ a desolado. ~ion
/-'leɪʃn/ n desolação f
despair /dɪ'speə(r)/ n desespero m □
vi desesperar (of de)
desperate /'despərət/ a desesperado;
(criminal) capaz de tudo. be ~ for
ter uma vontade doida de. ~ly adv
desesperadamente

desperation /despə'reɪʃn/ n desespero m
despicable /dɪ'spɪkəbl/ a desprezível
despise /dɪ'spaɪz/ vt desprezar
despite /dɪ'spaɪt/ prep apesar de, a
despeito de, mau grado
desponden|t /dɪ'spɒndənt/ a desani-
mado. ~cy n desânimo m
despot /'despɒt/ n déspota mf
dessert /dɪ'zɜːt/ n sobremesa f. ~-
spoon n colher f de sobremesa
destination /destɪ'neɪʃn/ n destino
m, destinação f
destine /'destɪn/ vt destinar
destiny /'destɪnɪ/ n destino m
destitute /'destɪtjuːt/ a destituído, in-
digente
destr|oy /dɪ'strɔɪ/ vt destruir.
~uction /-'strʌkʃn/ n destruição f.
~uctive a destrutivo, destruidor
detach /dɪ'tætʃ/ vt separar, arrancar.
~able a separável; (lining etc) solto.
~ed a separado; (impartial) imparcial; (unemotional) desprendido.
~ed house casa f sem parede-meia
com outra
detachment /dɪ'tætʃmənt/ n separação f; (indifference) desprendimento
m; (mil) destacamento m; (impartial-
ity) imparcialidade f
detail /'diːteɪl/ n pormenor m, detalhe
m □ vt detalhar; (troops) destacar.
~ed a detalhado
detain /dɪ'teɪn/ vt reter; (in prison)
deter. ~ee /diːteɪ'niː/ n detido m
detect /dɪ'tekt/ vt detectar. ~ion /-ʃn/
n detecção f. ~or n detector m
detective /dɪ'tektɪv/ n detective m. ~
story romance m policial
detention /dɪ'tenʃn/ n detenção f. be
given a ~ (school) ficar de castigo na
escola
deter /dɪ'tɜː(r)/ vt (pt deterred) dissuadir; (hinder) impedir
detergent /dɪ'tɜːdʒənt/ a & n detergente (m)
deteriorat|e /dɪ'tɪərɪəreɪt/ vi deterio-
rar(-se). ~ion /-'reɪʃn/ n deterioração
f
determin|e /dɪ'tɜːmɪn/ vt determinar.
~e to do decidir fazer. ~ation /-'neɪ-
ʃn/ n determinação f. ~ed a determinado. ~ed to do decidido a fazer
deterrent /dɪ'terənt/ n dissuasivo m
detest /dɪ'test/ vt detestar. ~able a
detestável
detonat|e /'detəneɪt/ vt/i detonar.
~ion /-'neɪʃn/ n detonação f. ~or n
espoleta f, detonador m
detour /'diːtʊə(r)/ n desvio m
detract /dɪ'trækt/ vi ~ from depreciar, menosprezar
detriment /'detrɪmənt/ n detrimento
m. ~al /-'mentl/ a prejudicial

**devalu|e** /di:'vælju:/ vt desvalorizar. **~ation** /-'eɪʃn/ n desvalorização f

**devastat|e** /'devəsteɪt/ vi devastar; ( fig: overwhelm) arrasar. **~ing** a devastador; (criticism) de arrasar

**develop** /dɪ'veləp/ vt/i ( pt developed) desenvolver(-se); (get) contrair; (build on) urbanizar; ( film) revelar. **~ into** tornar-se. **~ing country** país m subdesenvolvido. **~ment** n desenvolvimento m; ( film) revelação f; (of land ) urbanização f

**deviat|e** /'di:vɪeɪt/ vi desviar-se. **~ion** /-'eɪʃn/ n desvio m

**device** /dɪ'vaɪs/ n dispositivo m; (scheme) processo m. **left to one's own ~s** entregue a si mesmo

**devil** /devl/ n diabo m

**devious** /'di:vɪəs/ a tortuoso; ( fig: means) escuso; ( fig: person) pouco franco

**devise** /dɪ'vaɪz/ vt imaginar, inventar

**devoid** /dɪ'vɔɪd/ a **~ of** desprovido de, destituído de

**devot|e** /dɪ'vəʊt/ vt dedicar, devotar. **~ed** a dedicado, devotado. **~ion** /-ʃn/ n devoção f

**devotee** /devə'ti:/ n **~ of** adepto m de, entusiasta mf de

**devour** /dɪ'vaʊə(r)/ vt devorar

**devout** /dɪ'vaʊt/ a devota; ( prayer) fervoroso

**dew** /dju:/ n orvalho m

**dext|erity** /dek'sterətɪ/ n destreza f, jeito m. **~rous** /'dekstrəs/ a destro, hábil

**diabet|es** /daɪə'bi:ti:z/ n diabetes f. **~ic** /-'betɪk/ a & n diabético (m)

**diabolical** /daɪə'bɒlɪkl/ a diabólico

**diagnose** /'daɪəgnəʊz/ vt diagnosticar

**diagnosis** /daɪəg'nəʊsɪs/ n ( pl -oses /-si:z/) diagnóstico m

**diagonal** /daɪ'ægənl/ a & n diagonal ( f )

**diagram** /'daɪəgræm/ n diagrama m, esquema m

**dial** /'daɪəl/ n mostrador m □ vt ( pt dialled) (number) marcar, discar. **~ling code** código m de discagem. **~ling tone** sinal m de discar

**dialect** /'daɪəlekt/ n dialeto m, (P) dialecto m

**dialogue** /'daɪəlɒg/ n diálogo m

**diameter** /daɪ'æmɪtə(r)/ n diâmetro m

**diamond** /'daɪəmənd/ n diamante m, brilhante m; (shape) losango m. **~s** (cards) ouros mpl

**diaper** /'daɪəpə(r)/ n (Amer) fralda f

**diaphragm** /'daɪəfræm/ n diafragma m

**diarrhoea** /daɪə'rɪə/ n diarréia f, (P) diarreia f

**diary** /'daɪərɪ/ n agenda f; (record ) diário m

**dice** /daɪs/ n ( pl invar) dado m

**dictat|e** /dɪk'teɪt/ vt/i ditar. **~ion** /-ʃn/ n ditado m

**dictator** /dɪk'teɪtə(r)/ n ditador m. **~ship** n ditadura f

**diction** /'dɪkʃn/ n dicção f

**dictionary** /'dɪkʃənrɪ/ n dicionário m

**did** /dɪd/ see **do**

**diddle** /'dɪdl/ vt (colloq) trapacear, enganar

**didn't** /'dɪdnt/ = **did not**

**die** /daɪ/ vi ( pres p dying) morrer. **be dying to** estar doido para. **~ down** diminuir, baixar. **~ out** desaparecer, extinguir-se

**diesel** /'di:zl/ n diesel m. **~ engine** motor m diesel

**diet** /'daɪət/ n dieta f □ vi fazer dieta, estar de dieta

**differ** /'dɪfə(r)/ vi diferir; (disagree) discordar

**differen|t** /'dɪfrənt/ a diferente. **~ce** n diferença f; (disagreement) desacordo m. **~ly** adv diferentemente

**differentiate** /dɪfə'renʃɪeɪt/ vt/i diferençar(-se), diferenciar(-se)

**difficult** /'dɪfɪkəlt/ a difícil. **~y** n dificuldade f

**diffiden|t** /'dɪfɪdənt/ a acanhado, inseguro. **~ce** n acanhamento m, insegurança f

**diffuse**[1] /dɪ'fju:s/ a difuso

**diffus|e**[2] /dɪ'fju:z/ vt difundir. **~ion** /-ʒn/ n difusão f

**dig** /dɪg/ vt/i ( pt dug, pres p digging) cavar; (thrust) espetar □ n (with elbow) cotovelada f; (with finger) cutucada f, (P) espetadela f; (remark) ferroada f; (archaeol) escavação f. **~s** (colloq) quarto m alugado. **~ up** desenterrar

**digest** /dɪ'dʒest/ vt/i digerir. **~ible** a digerível, digestível. **~ion** /-ʃn/ n digestão f

**digestive** /dɪ'dʒestɪv/ a digestivo

**digit** /'dɪdʒɪt/ n dígito m

**digital** /'dɪdʒɪtl/ a digital. **~ clock** relógio m digital

**dignif|y** /'dɪgnɪfaɪ/ vt dignificar. **~ied** a digno

**dignitary** /'dɪgnɪtərɪ/ n dignitário m

**dignity** /'dɪgnətɪ/ n dignidade f

**digress** /daɪ'gres/ vi digressar, divagar. **~ from** desviar-se de. **~ion** /-ʃn/ n digressão f

**dike** /daɪk/ n dique m

**dilapidated** /dɪ'læpɪdeɪtɪd/ a (house) arruinado, degradado; (car) estragado

**dilat|e** /daɪ'leɪt/ vt/i dilatar(-se). **~ion** /-ʃn/ n dilatação f

**dilemma** /dɪ'lemə/ n dilema m

**diligen|t** /'dɪlɪdʒənt/ a diligente, aplicado. **~ce** n diligência f, aplicação f

**dilute** /dar'lju:t/ *vt* diluir □ *a* diluído
**dim** /dɪm/ *a* (**dimmer, dimmest**)
(*weak*) fraco; (*dark*) sombrio; (*indistinct*) vago; (*colloq: stupid*) burro
(*colloq*) □ *vt/i* (*pt* **dimmed**) (*light*)
baixar. **~ly** *adv* (*shine*) fracamente;
(*remember*) vagamente
**dime** /daɪm/ *n* (*Amer*) moeda *f* de dez
centavos
**dimension** /dar'menʃn/ *n* dimensão *f*
**diminish** /dɪ'mɪnɪʃ/ *vt/i* diminuir
**diminutive** /dɪ'mɪnjʊtɪv/ *a* diminuto
□ *n* diminutivo *m*
**dimple** /'dɪmpl/ *n* covinha *f*
**din** /dɪn/ *n* barulheira *f*, (*P*) chinfrim *m*
**dine** /daɪn/ *vi* jantar. **~r** /-ə(r)/ *n*
(*person*) comensal *m*; (*rail*) vagão-
restaurante *m*; (*Amer: restaurant*)
lanchonete *f*
**dinghy** /'dɪŋgɪ/ *n* (*pl* -**ghies**) bote *m*;
(*inflatable*) bote *m* de borracha, (*P*)
barco *m* de borracha
**dingy** /'dɪndʒɪ/ *a* (-**ier, -iest**) com ar
sujo, esquálido
**dining-room** /'daɪnɪŋruːm/ *n* sala *f*
de jantar
**dinner** /'dɪnə(r)/ *n* jantar *m*; (*lunch*)
almoço *m*. **~-jacket** *n* smoking *m*
**dinosaur** /'daɪnəsɔ:(r)/ *n* dinossauro
*m*
**dip** /dɪp/ *vt/i* (*pt* **dipped**) mergulhar;
(*lower*) baixar □ *n* mergulho *m*;
(*bathe*) banho *m* rápido, mergulho *m*;
(*slope*) descida *f*; (*culin*) molho *m*. **~
into** (*book*) folhear. **~ one's headlights** baixar para médios
**diphtheria** /dɪf'θɪərɪə/ *n* difteria *f*
**diphthong** /'dɪfθɒŋ/ *n* ditongo *m*
**diploma** /dɪ'pləʊmə/ *n* diploma *m*
**diplomacy** /dɪ'pləʊməsɪ/ *n* diplomacia *f*
**diplomat** /'dɪpləmæt/ *n* diplomata *mf*.
**~ic** /-'mætɪk/ *a* diplomático
**dire** /daɪə(r)/ *a* (-**er, -est**) terrível;
(*need, poverty*) extremo
**direct** /dɪ'rekt/ *a* direto, (*P*) directo □
*adv* diretamente, (*P*) directamente □
*vt* dirigir. **~ sb to** indicar a alg o
caminho para
**direction** /dɪ'rekʃn/ *n* direção *f*, (*P*)
direcção *f*, sentido *m*. **~s** instruções
*fpl*. **~s for use** modo *m* de emprego
**directly** /dɪ'rektlɪ/ *adv* diretamente,
(*P*) directamente; (*at once*) imediatamente, logo
**director** /dɪ'rektə(r)/ *n* diretor *m*, (*P*)
director *m*
**directory** /dɪ'rektərɪ/ *n* (**telephone**)
**~** lista *f* telefónica, (*P*) telefónica
**dirt** /dɜ:t/ *n* sujeira *f*. **~ cheap** (*colloq*) baratíssimo
**dirty** /'dɜ:tɪ/ *a* (-**ier, -iest**) sujo; (*word*)
obsceno □ *vt/i* sujar(-se). **~ trick**
golpe *m* baixo, (*P*) boa partida *f*

**disability** /dɪsə'bɪlətɪ/ *n* deficiência *f*
**disable** /dɪs'eɪbl/ *vt* incapacitar. **~d** *a*
inválido, deficiente
**disadvantage** /dɪsəd'va:ntɪdʒ/ *n* desvantagem *f*
**disagree** /dɪsə'gri:/ *vi* discordar
(**with** de). **~ with** (*food, climate*)
não fazer bem. **~ment** *n* desacordo
*m*; (*quarrel*) desentendimento *m*
**disagreeable** /dɪsə'gri:əbl/ *a* desagradável
**disappear** /dɪsə'pɪə(r)/ *vi* desaparecer. **~ance** *n* desaparecimento *m*
**disappoint** /dɪsə'pɔɪnt/ *vt* desapontar,
decepcionar. **~ment** *n* desapontamento *m*, decepção *f*
**disapprov|e** /dɪsə'pru:v/ *vi* **~e (of)**
desaprovar. **~al** *n* desaprovação *f*
**disarm** /dɪs'a:m/ *vt/i* desarmar.
**~ament** *n* desarmamento *m*
**disast|er** /dɪ'za:stə(r)/ *n* desastre *m*.
**~rous** *a* desastroso
**disband** /dɪs'bænd/ *vt/i* debandar;
(*troops*) dispersar
**disbelief** /dɪsbɪ'li:f/ *n* incredulidade *f*
**disc** /dɪsk/ *n* disco *m*. **~ jockey**
disc(o) jockey *m*
**discard** /dɪs'ka:d/ *vt* pôr de lado, des-
cartar(-se) de; (*old clothes etc*) desfazer-se de
**discern** /dɪ'sɜ:n/ *vt* discernir. **~ible** *a*
perceptível. **~ing** *a* perspicaz.
**~ment** *n* discernimento *m*, perspicácia *f*
**discharge**[1] /dɪs'tʃa:dʒ/ *vt* descarregar; (*dismiss*) despedir, mandar embora; (*duty*) cumprir; (*liquid*) vazar,
(*P*) deitar; (*patient*) dar alta a;
(*prisoner*) absolver, pôr em liberdade; (*pus*) purgar, (*P*) deitar
**discharge**[2] /'dɪstʃa:dʒ/ *n* descarga *f*;
(*dismissal*) despedimento *m*; (*of patient*) alta *f*; (*of prisoner*) absolvição *f*;
(*med*) secreção *f*
**disciple** /dɪ'saɪpl/ *n* discípulo *m*
**disciplin|e** /'dɪsɪplɪn/ *n* disciplina *f*
□ *vt* disciplinar; (*punish*) castigar.
**~ary** *a* disciplinar
**disclaim** /dɪs'kleɪm/ *vt/i* (*jur*) repudiar; (*deny*) negar. **~er** *n* desmentido
*m*
**disclos|e** /dɪs'kləʊz/ *vt* revelar. **~ure**
/-ʒə(r)/ *n* revelação *f*
**disco** /'dɪskəʊ/ *n* (*pl* -**os**) (*colloq*) discoteca *f*
**discolour** /dɪs'kʌlə(r)/ *vt/i* descolo-
rir(-se); (*in sunlight*) desbotar(-se)
**discomfort** /dɪs'kʌmfət/ *n* malestar
*m*; (*lack of comfort*) desconforto *m*
**disconcert** /dɪskən'sɜ:t/ *vt* desconcertar. **~ing** *a* desconcertante
**disconnect** /dɪskə'nekt/ *vt* desligar
**discontent** /dɪskən'tent/ *n* desconten-
tamento *m*. **~ed** *a* descontente

**discontinue** /dɪskən'tɪnju:/ vt descontinuar, suspender

**discord** /'dɪskɔːd/ n discórdia f. ~ant /-'skɔːdənt/ a discordante

**discothèque** /'dɪskətek/ n discoteca f

**discount**[1] /'dɪskaʊnt/ n desconto m

**discount**[2] /dɪs'kaʊnt/ vt descontar; (disregard) dar o desconto a

**discourage** /dɪs'kʌrɪdʒ/ vt desencorajar

**discourte|ous** /dɪs'kɜːtɪəs/ a indelicado. ~sy /-sɪ/ n indelicadeza f

**discover** /dɪs'kʌvə(r)/ vt descobrir. ~y n descoberta f; (of island etc) descobrimento m

**discredit** /dɪs'kredɪt/ vt (pt discredited) desacreditar □ n descrédito m

**discreet** /dɪ'skriːt/ a discreto

**discrepancy** /dɪs'krepənsɪ/ n discrepância f

**discretion** /dɪ'skreʃn/ n discrição f; (prudence) prudência f

**discriminat|e** /dɪs'krɪmɪneɪt/ vt/i discriminar. ~e against tomar partido contra, fazer discriminação contra. ~ing a discriminador; (having good taste) com discernimento. ~ion /-'neɪʃn/ n discernimento m; (bias) discriminação f

**discus** /'dɪskəs/ n disco m

**discuss** /dɪ'skʌs/ vt discutir. ~ion /-ʃn/ n discussão f

**disdain** /dɪs'deɪn/ n desdém m □ vt desdenhar. ~ful a desdenhoso

**disease** /dɪ'ziːz/ n doença f. ~d a (plant) atacado por doença; (person, animal) doente

**disembark** /dɪsɪm'baːk/ vt/i desembarcar

**disembodied** /dɪsɪm'bɒdɪd/ a desencarnado

**disenchant** /dɪsɪn'tʃaːnt/ vt desencantar. ~ment n desencantamento m

**disengage** /dɪsɪn'geɪdʒ/ vt desprender, soltar; (mech) desengatar

**disentangle** /dɪsɪn'tæŋgl/ vt desembaraçar, desenredar

**disfavour** /dɪs'feɪvə(r)/ n desfavor m, desgraça f

**disfigure** /dɪs'fɪgə(r)/ vt desfigurar

**disgrace** /dɪs'greɪs/ n vergonha f; (disfavour) desgraça f □ vt desonrar. ~ful a vergonhoso

**disgruntled** /dɪs'grʌntld/ a descontente

**disguise** /dɪs'gaɪz/ vt disfarçar □ n disfarce m. in ~ disfarçado

**disgust** /dɪs'gʌst/ n repugnância f □ vt repugnar. ~ing a repugnante

**dish** /dɪʃ/ n prato m □ vt ~ out (colloq) distribuir. ~ up servir. the ~es (crockery) a louça f

**dishcloth** /'dɪʃklɒθ/ n pano m de prato

**dishearten** /dɪs'haːtn/ vt desencorajar, desalentar

**dishevelled** /dɪ'ʃevld/ a desgrenhado

**dishonest** /dɪs'ɒnɪst/ a desonesto. ~y n desonestidade f

**dishonour** /dɪs'ɒnə(r)/ n desonra f □ vt desonrar. ~able a desonroso

**dishwasher** /'dɪʃwɒʃə(r)/ n lavadora f de pratos, (P) máquina f de lavar a louça

**disillusion** /dɪsɪ'luːʒn/ vt desiludir. ~ment n desilusão f

**disinfect** /dɪsɪn'fekt/ vt desinfetar, (P) desinfectar. ~ant n desinfetante m, (P) desinfectante m

**disinherit** /dɪsɪn'herɪt/ vt deserdar

**disintegrate** /dɪs'ɪntɪgreɪt/ vt/i desintegrar(-se)

**disinterested** /dɪs'ɪntrəstɪd/ a desinteressado

**disjointed** /dɪs'dʒɔɪntɪd/ a (talk) descosido, desconexo

**disk** /dɪsk/ n (comput) disco m; (Amer) = **disc**. ~ **drive** unidade f de disco

**dislike** /dɪs'laɪk/ n aversão f, antipatia f □ vt não gostar de, antipatizar com

**dislocat|e** /'dɪsləkeɪt/ vt (limb) deslocar. ~ion /-'keɪʃn/ n deslocação f

**dislodge** /dɪs'lɒdʒ/ vt desalojar

**disloyal** /dɪs'lɔɪəl/ a desleal. ~ty n deslealdade f

**dismal** /'dɪzməl/ a tristonho

**dismantle** /dɪs'mæntl/ vt desmantelar

**dismay** /dɪs'meɪ/ n consternação f □ vt consternar

**dismiss** /dɪs'mɪs/ vt despedir; (from mind) afastar, pôr de lado. ~al n despedimento m

**dismount** /dɪs'maʊnt/ vi desmontar

**disobedien|t** /dɪsə'biːdɪənt/ a desobediente. ~ce n desobediência f

**disobey** /dɪsə'beɪ/ vt/i desobedecer (a)

**disorder** /dɪs'ɔːdə(r)/ n desordem f; (med) perturbações fpl, disfunção f. ~ly a desordenado; (riotous) desordeiro

**disorganize** /dɪs'ɔːgənaɪz/ vt desorganizar

**disorientate** /dɪs'ɔːrɪənteɪt/ vt desorientar

**disown** /dɪs'əʊn/ vt repudiar

**disparaging** /dɪ'spærɪdʒɪŋ/ a depreciativo

**disparity** /dɪ'spærətɪ/ n disparidade f

**dispatch** /dɪ'spætʃ/ vt despachar □ n despacho m

**dispel** /dɪ'spel/ vt (pt dispelled) dissipar

**dispensary** /dɪ'spensərɪ/ n dispensário m, farmácia f

**dispense** /dɪ'spens/ vt dispensar □ vi

**~ with** dispensar, passar sem. **~r** /-ə(r)/ n (container) distribuidor m

**dispers|e** /dɪˈspɜːs/ vt/i dispersar (-se). **~al** n dispersão f

**dispirited** /dɪˈspɪrɪtɪd/ a desanimado

**displace** /dɪsˈpleɪs/ vt deslocar; (take the place of) substituir. **~d person** deslocado m de guerra

**display** /dɪsˈpleɪ/ vt exibir, mostrar; (feeling) manifestar, dar mostras de □ n exposição f; (of computer) apresentação f visual; (comm) objetos mpl expostos

**displeas|e** /dɪsˈpliːz/ vt desagradar a. **~ed with** descontente com. **~ure** /ˈpleʒə(r)/ n desagrado m

**disposable** /dɪsˈpəʊzəbl/ a descartável

**dispos|e** /dɪsˈpəʊz/ vt dispor □ vi **~e of** desfazer-se de. **well ~ed towards** bem disposto para com. **~al** n (of waste) eliminação f. **at sb's ~al** à disposição de alg

**disposition** /dɪspəˈzɪʃn/ n disposição f; (character) índole f

**disproportionate** /dɪsprəˈpɔːʃənət/ a desproporcionado

**disprove** /dɪsˈpruːv/ vt refutar

**dispute** /dɪsˈpjuːt/ vt contestar; (fight for, quarrel) disputar □ n disputa f; (industrial, pol) conflito m. **in ~** em questão

**disqualif|y** /dɪsˈkwɒlɪfaɪ/ vt tornar inapto; (sport) desqualificar. **~y from driving** aprender a carteira de motorista. **~ication** /-ɪˈkeɪʃn/ n desqualificação f

**disregard** /dɪsrɪˈɡɑːd/ vt não fazer caso de □ n indiferença f (for por)

**disrepair** /dɪsrɪˈpeə(r)/ n mau estado m, abandono m, degradação f

**disreputable** /dɪsˈrepjʊtəbl/ a pouco recomendável; (in appearance) com mau aspecto; (in reputation) vergonhoso, de má fama

**disrepute** /dɪsrɪˈpjuːt/ n descrédito m

**disrespect** /dɪsrɪˈspekt/ n falta f de respeito. **~ful** a desrespeitoso, irreverente

**disrupt** /dɪsˈrʌpt/ vt perturbar; (plans) transtornar; (break up) dividir. **~ion** /-ʃn/ n perturbação f. **~ive** a perturbador

**dissatisf|ied** /dɪˈsætɪsfaɪd/ a descontente. **~action** /dɪsætɪsˈfækʃn/ n descontentamento m

**dissect** /dɪˈsekt/ vt dissecar. **~ion** /-ʃn/ n dissecação f

**dissent** /dɪˈsent/ vi dissentir, discordar □ n dissensão f, desacordo m

**dissertation** /dɪsəˈteɪʃn/ n dissertação f

**disservice** /dɪsˈsɜːvɪs/ n **do sb a ~** prejudicar alg

**dissident** /ˈdɪsɪdənt/ a & n dissidente (mf)

**dissimilar** /dɪˈsɪmɪlə(r)/ a diferente

**dissipate** /ˈdɪsɪpeɪt/ vt dissipar; (efforts, time) desperdiçar. **~d** a dissoluto

**dissociate** /dɪˈsəʊʃɪeɪt/ vt dissociar, desassociar

**dissolution** /dɪsəˈluːʃn/ n dissolução f

**dissolve** /dɪˈzɒlv/ vt/i dissolver(-se)

**dissuade** /dɪˈsweɪd/ vt dissuadir

**distance** /ˈdɪstəns/ n distância f. **from a ~** de longe. **in the ~** ao longe, à distância

**distant** /ˈdɪstənt/ a distante; (relative) afastado

**distaste** /dɪsˈteɪst/ n aversão f. **~ful** a desagradável

**distemper** /dɪsˈtempə(r)/ n pintura f a têmpera; (animal disease) cinomose f □ vt pintar a têmpera

**distend** /dɪsˈtend/ vt/i distender(-se)

**distil** /dɪsˈtɪl/ vt (pt distilled) destilar. **~lation** /ˈleɪʃn/ n destilação f

**distillery** /dɪsˈtɪlərɪ/ n destilaria f

**distinct** /dɪsˈtɪŋkt/ a distinto; (marked) claro, nítido. **~ion** /-ʃn/ n distinção f. **~ive** a distintivo, característico. **~ly** adv distintamente; (markedly) claramente

**distinguish** /dɪsˈtɪŋɡwɪʃ/ vt/i distinguir. **~ed** a distinto

**distort** /dɪsˈtɔːt/ vt distorcer; (misrepresent) deturpar. **~ion** /-ʃn/ n distorção f; (misrepresentation) deturpação f

**distract** /dɪsˈtrækt/ vt distrair. **~ed** a (distraught) desesperado, fora de si. **~ing** a enlouquecedor. **~ion** /-ʃn/ n distração f, (P) distracção f

**distraught** /dɪsˈtrɔːt/ a desesperado, fora de si

**distress** /dɪsˈtres/ n (physical) dor f; (anguish) aflição f; (poverty) miséria f; (danger) perigo m □ vt afligir. **~ing** a aflitivo, doloroso

**distribut|e** /dɪsˈtrɪbjuːt/ vt distribuir. **~ion** /-ˈbjuːʃn/ n distribuição f. **~or** n distribuidor m

**district** /ˈdɪstrɪkt/ n região f; (of town) zona f

**distrust** /dɪsˈtrʌst/ n desconfiança f □ vt desconfiar de

**disturb** /dɪsˈtɜːb/ vt perturbar; (move) desarrumar; (bother) incomodar. **~ance** n (noise, disorder) distúrbio m. **~ed** a perturbado. **~ing** a perturbador

**disused** /dɪsˈjuːzd/ a fora de uso, desusado, em desuso

**ditch** /dɪtʃ/ n fosso m □ vt (sl: abandon) abandonar, largar

**dither** /ˈdɪðə(r)/ vi hesitar

**ditto** /'dɪtəʊ/ *adv* idem

**div|e** /daɪv/ *vi* mergulhar; (*rush*) precipitar-se □ *n* mergulho *m*; (*of plane*) picada *f*; (*sl: place*) espelunca *f*. ~**er** *n* mergulhador *m*. ~**ing-board** *n* prancha *f* de saltos. ~**ing-suit** *n* escafandro *m*

**diverge** /daɪ'vɜ:dʒ/ *vi* divergir

**divergent** /daɪ'vɜ:dʒənt/ *a* divergente

**diverse** /daɪ'vɜ:s/ *a* diverso

**diversify** /daɪ'vɜ:sɪfaɪ/ *vt* diversificar

**diversity** /daɪ'vɜ:sətɪ/ *n* diversidade *f*

**diver|t** /daɪ'vɜ:t/ *vt* desviar; (*entertain*) divertir. ~**sion** /-ʃn/ *n* diversão *f*; (*traffic*) desvio *m*

**divide** /dɪ'vaɪd/ *vt/i* dividir(-se). ~ **in two** (*branch, river, road*) bifurcar-se

**dividend** /'dɪvɪdend/ *n* dividendo *m*

**divine** /dɪ'vaɪn/ *a* divino

**divinity** /dɪ'vɪnətɪ/ *n* divindade *f*; (*theology*) teologia *f*

**division** /dɪ'vɪʒn/ *n* divisão *f*

**divorce** /dɪ'vɔ:s/ *n* divórcio *m* □ *vt/i* divorciar(-se) de. ~**d** *a* divorciado

**divorcee** /dɪvɔ:'si:/ *n* divorciado *m*

**divulge** /daɪ'vʌldʒ/ *vt* divulgar

**DIY** *abbr see* **do-it-yourself**

**dizz|y** /'dɪzɪ/ *a* (-**ier**, -**iest**) tonto. **be or feel** ~**y** ter tonturas, sentir-se tonto. ~**iness** *n* tontura *f*, vertigem *f*

**do** /du:/ *vt/i* (*3 sing pres* **does**, *pt* **did**, *pp* **done**) fazer; (*be suitable*) servir; (*be enough*) bastar (a); (*sl: swindle*) enganar, levar (*colloq*). **how** ~ **you** ~? como vai? **well done** muito bem!, (*P*) bravo!; (*culin*) bem passado. **done for** (*colloq*) liquidado (*colloq*), (*P*) anumado (*colloq*) □ *v aux* ~ **you see?** vê?; **I** ~ **not smoke** não fumo. **don't you?, doesn't he?** *etc* não é? □ *n* (*pl* **dos** *or* **do's**) festa *f*. ~**-it-yourself** *a* faça-você-mesmo. ~ **away with** eliminar, suprimir. ~ **in** (*sl*) matar, liquidar (*colloq*). ~ **out** limpar. ~ **up** (*fasten*) fechar; (*house*) renovar. **I could** ~ **with a cup of tea** apetecia-me uma xícara de chá. **it could** ~ **with a wash** precisa de uma lavagem

**docile** /'dəʊsaɪl/ *a* dócil

**dock¹** /dɒk/ *n* doca *f* □ *vt* levar à doca □ *vi* entrar na doca. ~**er** *n* estivador *m*

**dock²** /dɒk/ *n* (*jur*) banco *m* dos réus

**dockyard** /'dɒkjɑ:d/ *n* estaleiro *m*

**doctor** /'dɒktə(r)/ *n* médico *m*, doutor *m*; (*univ*) doutor *m* □ *vt* (*cat*) capar; (*fig*) adulterar, falsificar

**doctorate** /'dɒktərət/ *n* doutorado *m*, (*P*) doutoramento *m*

**doctrine** /'dɒktrɪn/ *n* doutrina *f*

**document** /'dɒkjʊmənt/ *n* documento *m* □ *vt* documentar. ~**ary** /-'mentrɪ/ *a* documental □ *n* documentário *m*

**dodge** /dɒdʒ/ *vt/i* esquivar(-se), furtar(-se) a □ *n* (*colloq*) truque *m*

**dodgy** /'dɒdʒɪ/ *a* (-**ier**, -**iest**) (*colloq*) delicado, difícil, embaraçoso

**does** /dʌz/ *see* **do**

**doesn't** /'dʌznt/ = **does not**

**dog** /dɒg/ *n* cão *m* □ *vt* (*pt* **dogged**) ir no encalço de, perseguir. ~**-eared** *a* com os cantos dobrados

**dogged** /'dɒgɪd/ *a* obstinado, persistente

**dogma** /'dɒgmə/ *n* dogma *m*. ~**tic** /-'mætɪk/ *a* dogmático

**dogsbody** /'dɒgzbɒdɪ/ *n* (*colloq*) paupara-toda-obra *m* (*colloq*), factótum *m*

**doldrums** /'dɒldrəmz/ *npl* **be in the** ~ estar com a neura; (*business*) estar parado

**dole** /dəʊl/ *vt* ~ **out** distribuir □ *n* (*colloq*) auxílio *m* desemprego. **on the** ~ (*colloq*) desempregado (titular de auxílio)

**doleful** /'dəʊlfl/ *a* tristonho, melancólico

**doll** /dɒl/ *n* boneca *f* □ *vt/i* ~ **up** (*colloq*) embonecar(-se)

**dollar** /'dɒlə(r)/ *n* dólar *m*

**dolphin** /'dɒlfɪn/ *n* golfinho *m*

**domain** /də'ʊmeɪn/ *n* domínio *m*

**dome** /dəʊm/ *n* cúpula *f*; (*vault*) abóbada *f*

**domestic** /də'mestɪk/ *a* (*of home, animal, flights*) doméstico; (*trade*) interno; (*news*) nacional. ~**ated** /-keɪtɪd/ *a* (*animal*) domesticado; (*person*) que gosta de trabalhos caseiros

**dominant** /'dɒmɪnənt/ *a* dominante

**dominat|e** /'dɒmɪneɪt/ *vt/i* dominar. ~**ion** /-'neɪʃn/ *n* dominação *f*, domínio *m*

**domineer** /dɒmɪ'nɪə(r)/ *vi* ~ **over** mandar (em), ser autocrático (para com). ~**ing** *a* mandão, autocrático

**dominion** /də'mɪnjən/ *n* domínio *m*

**domino** /'dɒmɪnəʊ/ *n* (*pl* -**oes**) dominó *m*

**donat|e** /də'ʊneɪt/ *vt* fazer doação de, doar, dar. ~**ion** /-ʃn/ *n* donativo *m*

**done** /dʌn/ *see* **do**

**donkey** /'dɒŋkɪ/ *n* burro *m*

**donor** /'dəʊnə(r)/ *n* (*of blood*) doador *m*, (*P*) dador *m*

**don't** /dəʊnt/ = **do not**

**doodle** /'du:dl/ *vi* rabiscar

**doom** /du:m/ *n* ruína *f*; (*fate*) destino *m*. **be** ~**ed to** ser/estar condenado a. ~**ed (to failure)** condenado ao fracasso

**door** /dɔ:(r)/ *n* porta *f*

**doorman** /'dɔ:mən/ *n* (*pl* -**men**) porteiro *m*

**doormat** /'dɔ:mæt/ *n* capacho *m*

**doorstep** /'dɔ:step/ *n* degrau *m* da porta

**doorway** /'dɔːweɪ/ n vão m da porta, (P) entrada f

**dope** /dəʊp/ n (colloq) droga f; (sl: idiot) imbecil mf □ vt dopar, drogar

**dormant** /'dɔːmənt/ a dormente; (inactive) inativo, (P) inactivo; (latent) latente

**dormitory** /'dɔːmɪtrɪ/ n dormitório m; (Amer univ) residência f

**dormouse** /'dɔːmaʊs/ n (pl -mice) arganaz m

**dos|e** /dəʊs/ n dose f □ vt medicar. ~age n dosagem f; (on label) posologia f

**doss** /dɒs/ vi ~ (down) dormir sem conforto. ~-house n pensão f miserável, asilo m noturno, (P) nocturno. ~er n vagabundo m

**dot** /dɒt/ n ponto m. on the ~ no momento preciso □ vt be ~ted with estar semeado de. ~ted line linha f pontilhada

**dote** /dəʊt/ vi ~ on ser louco por, adorar

**double** /'dʌbl/ a duplo; (room, bed) de casal □ adv duas vezes mais □ n dobro m. ~s (tennis) dupla f, (P) pares mpl □ vt/i dobrar, duplicar; (fold) dobrar em dois. at the ~ a passo acelerado. ~-bass n contrabaixo m. ~ chin papada f. ~-cross vt enganar. ~-dealing n jogo m duplo. ~-decker n ónibus m, (P) autocarro m de dois andares. ~ Dutch algaraviada f, fala f incompreensível. ~ glazing (janela f de) vidro (m) duplo. doubly adv duplamente

**doubt** /daʊt/ n dúvida f □ vt duvidar de. ~ if or that duvidar que. ~ful a duvidoso; (hesitant) que tem dúvidas. ~less adv sem dúvida, indubitavelmente

**dough** /dəʊ/ n massa f

**doughnut** /'dəʊnʌt/ n sonho n, (P) bola f de Berlim

**dove** /dʌv/ n pomba f

**dowdy** /'daʊdɪ/ a (-ier, -iest) sem graça, sem gosto

**down**[1] /daʊn/ n (feathers, hair) penugem f

**down**[2] /daʊn/ adv (to lower place) abaixo, para baixo; (in lower place) em baixo. be ~ (level, price) descer; (sun) estar posto □ prep por (+n) (n+) abaixo. ~ the hill/street etc pelo monte/pela rua etc abaixo □ vt (colloq: knock down) jogar abaixo; (colloq: drink) esvaziar. come or go ~ descer. ~-and-out n marginal m. ~-hearted a desencorajado, desanimado. ~-to-earth a terra-a-terra invar. ~ under na Austrália. ~ with abaixo

**downcast** /'daʊnkɑːst/ a abatido, deprimido, desmoralizado

**downfall** /'daʊnfɔːl/ n queda f, ruína f

**downhill** /daʊn'hɪl/ adv go ~ descer; (fig) ir abaixo □ a /'daʊnhɪl/ a descer, descendente

**downpour** /'daʊnpɔː(r)/ n aguaceiro m forte, (P) chuvada f

**downright** /'daʊnraɪt/ a franco; (utter) autêntico, verdadeiro □ adv positivamente

**downstairs** /daʊn'steəz/ adv (at/to) em/para baixo, no/para o andar de baixo □ a /'daʊnsteəz/ (flat etc) de baixo, do andar de baixo

**downstream** /'daʊnstriːm/ adv rio abaixo

**downtown** /'daʊntaʊn/ a & adv (de, em, para) o centro da cidade. ~ Boston o centro de Boston

**downtrodden** /'daʊntrɒdn/ a espezinhado, oprimido

**downward** /'daʊnwəd/ a descendente. ~(s) adv para baixo

**dowry** /'daʊərɪ/ n dote m

**doze** /dəʊz/ vi dormitar. ~ off cochilar □ n soneca f, cochilo m

**dozen** /'dʌzn/ n dúzia f. ~s of (colloq) dezenas de, dúzias de

**Dr** abbr (Doctor) Dr

**drab** /dræb/ a insípido; (of colour) morto, apagado

**draft**[1] /drɑːft/ n rascunho m; (comm) ordem f de pagamento □ vt fazer o rascunho de; (draw up) redigir. the ~ (Amer: mil) recrutamento m

**draft**[2] /drɑːft/ n (Amer) = **draught**

**drag** /dræg/ vt/i (pt dragged) arrastar(-se); (river) dragar; (pull away) arrancar □ n (colloq: task) chatice f (sl); (colloq: person) estorvo m; (sl: clothes) travesti m

**dragon** /'drægən/ n dragão m

**dragonfly** /'drægənflaɪ/ n libélula f

**drain** /dreɪn/ vt drenar; (vegetables) escorrer; (glass, tank) esvaziar; (use up) esgotar □ vi ~ (off) escoar-se □ n cano m. ~s npl (sewers) esgotos mpl. ~age n drenagem f. ~(-pipe) cano m de esgoto. ~ing-board n escorredouro m

**drama** /'drɑːmə/ n arte f dramática; (play, event) drama m. ~tic /drə'mætɪk/ a dramático. ~tist /'dræmətɪst/ n dramaturgo m. ~tize /'dræmətaɪz/ vt dramatizar

**drank** /dræŋk/ see **drink**

**drape** /dreɪp/ vt ~ round/over dispor (tecido) em pregas à volta de or sobre. ~s npl (Amer) cortinas fpl

**drastic** /'dræstɪk/ a drástico, violento

**draught** /drɑːft/ n corrente f de ar; (naut) calado m. ~s (game) (jogo m das) damas fpl. ~ beer chope m, (P)

cerveja *f* à caneca, imperial *f* (*colloq*).
~y *a* com correntes de ar, ventoso

**draughtsman** /'drɑːftsmən/ *n* (*pl*
-men) desenhista *m*, (*P*) desenhador *m*

**draw** /drɔː/ *vt* (*pt* drew, *pp* drawn)
puxar; (*attract*) atrair; (*picture*) desenhar; (*in lottery*) tirar à sorte; (*line*)
traçar; (*open curtains*) abrir; (*close
curtains*) fechar □ *vi* desenhar; (*sport*)
empatar; (*come*) vir □ *n* (*sport*) empate
*m*; (*lottery*) sorteio *m*. ~ **back** recuar.
~ **in** (*of days*) diminuir. ~ **near**
aproximar-se. ~ **out** (*money*) levantar. ~ **up** deter-se, parar; (*document*)
redigir; (*chair*) aproximar, chegar

**drawback** /'drɔːbæk/ *n* inconveniente *m*, desvantagem *f*

**drawer** /drɔː(r)/ *n* gaveta *f*

**drawing** /'drɔːɪŋ/ *n* desenho *m*. ~-
**board** *n* prancheta *f*. ~-**pin** *n* percevejo *m*

**drawl** /drɔːl/ *n* fala *f* arrastada

**drawn** /drɔːn/ *see* draw

**dread** /dred/ *n* terror *m* □ *vt* temer

**dreadful** /'dredfl/ *a* medonho, terrível. ~**ly** *adv* terrivelmente

**dream** /driːm/ *n* sonho *m* □ *vt/i* (*pt*
dreamed *or* dreamt) sonhar (**of** com)
□ *a* (*ideal*) dos seus sonhos. ~ **up**
imaginar. ~**er** *n* sonhador *m*. ~**y** *a*
sonhador; (*music*) romântico

**dreary** /'drɪərɪ/ *a* (-ier, -iest) tristonho; (*boring*) aborrecido

**dredge** /dredʒ/ *n* draga *f* □ *vt/i* dragar.
~**r** /-ə(r)/ *n* draga *f*; (*for sugar*) pol-
vilhador *m*

**dregs** /dregz/ *npl* depósito *m*, sedimento *m*; (*fig*) escória *f*

**drench** /drentʃ/ *vt* encharcar

**dress** /dres/ *n* vestido *m*; (*clothing*)
roupa *f* □ *vt/i* vestir(-se); (*food*) temperar; (*wound*) fazer curativo, (*P*)
pensar, (*P*) tratar. ~ **rehearsal** ensaio *m* geral. ~ **up as** fantasiar-se
de. **get** ~**ed** vestir-se

**dresser** /'dresə(r)/ *n* (*furniture*) guar-
da-louça *m*

**dressing** /'dresɪŋ/ *n* (*sauce*) tempero
*m*; (*bandage*) curativo *m*, (*P*) penso
*m*. ~-**gown** *n* roupão *m*. ~-**room** *n*
(*sport*) vestiário *m*; (*theat*) camarim
*m*. ~-**table** *n* toucador *m*

**dressmak|er** /'dresmeɪkə(r)/ *n* cos-
tureira *f*, modista *f*. ~**ing** *n* costura
*f*

**dressy** /'dresɪ/ *a* (-ier, -iest) elegante,
chique *invar*

**drew** /druː/ *see* draw

**dribble** /'drɪbl/ *vi* pingar; (*person*)
babar-se; (*football*) driblar

**dried** /draɪd/ *a* (*fruit etc*) seco

**drier** /'draɪə(r)/ *n* secador *m*

**drift** /drɪft/ *vi* ir à deriva; (*pile up*)
amontoar-se □ *n* força *f* da corrente;

(*pile*) monte *m*; (*of events*) rumo *m*;
(*meaning*) sentido *m*. ~**er** *n* pessoa *f*
sem rumo

**drill** /drɪl/ *n* (*tool*) broca *f*; (*training*)
exercício *m*, treino *m*; (*routine procedure*) exercícios *mpl* □ *vt* furar, perfurar; (*train*) treinar; (*tooth*) abrir □
*vi* treinar-se

**drink** /drɪŋk/ *vt/i* (*pt* drank, *pp*
drunk) beber □ *n* bebida *f*. **a** ~ **of
water** um copo de água. ~**able** *a* potável; (*palatable*) bebível. ~**er** *n* be-
bedor *m*. ~**ing water** água *f* potável

**drip** /drɪp/ *vi* (*pt* dripped) pingar □ *n*
pingar *m*; (*sl: person*) banana *mf*
(*colloq*). ~-**dry** *vt* deixar escorrer □
*a* que não precisa passar

**dripping** /'drɪpɪŋ/ *n* gordura *f* do assado

**drive** /draɪv/ *vt* (*pt* drove, *pp* driven
/'drɪvn/) empurrar, impelir, levar;
(*car, animal*) dirigir, conduzir, (*P*)
guiar; (*machine*) acionar, (*P*) accionar
□ *vi* dirigir, conduzir, (*P*) guiar □ *n*
passeio *m* de carro; (*private road*)
entrada *f* para veículos; (*fig*) energia
*f*; (*psych*) drive *m*, compulsão *f*, impulso *m*; (*campaign*) campanha *f*. ~
**at** chegar a. ~ **away** (*car*) partir. ~
**in** (*force in*) enterrar. ~-**in** *n* (*bank,
cinema etc*) banco *m*, cinema *m* etc em
que se é atendido no carro, drive-in
*m*. ~ **mad** (*fazer*) enlouquecer, pôr
fora de si

**drivel** /'drɪvl/ *n* baboseira *f*, bobagem
*f*

**driver** /'draɪvə(r)/ *n* condutor *m*; (*of
taxi, bus*) chofer *m*, motorista *mf*

**driving** /'draɪvɪŋ/ *n* condução *f*. ~-
**licence** *n* carteira *f* de motorista, (*P*)
carta *f* de condução. ~-**school** auto-
escola *f*, (*P*) escola *f* de condução. ~-
**test** exame *m* de motorista, (*P*) de
condução

**drizzle** /'drɪzl/ *n* chuvisco *m* □ *vi* chuviscar

**drone** /drəʊn/ *n* zumbido *m*; (*male
bee*) zangão *m* □ *vi* zumbir; (*fig*) falar
monotonamente

**drool** /druːl/ *vi* babar(-se)

**droop** /druːp/ *vi* pender, curvar-se

**drop** /drɒp/ *n* gota *f*; (*fall*) queda *f*;
(*distance*) altura *f* de queda □ *vt/i* (*pt*
dropped) (*deixar*) cair; (*fall, lower*)
baixar. ~ (**off**) (*person from car*)
deixar, largar. ~ **a line** escrever (*on*
duas linhas (**to a**). ~ **in** passar por (**on
em** casa de). ~ **off** (*doze*) adormecer. ~
**out** (*withdraw*) retirar-se; (*of student*)
abandonar. ~-**out** *n* marginal *mf*,
marginalizado *m*

**droppings** /'drɒpɪŋz/ *npl* excremen-
tos *mpl* de animal; (*of birds*) cocô *m*
(*colloq*), porcaria *f* (*colloq*)

**dross** /drɒs/ n escória f; (refuse) lixo m

**drought** /draʊt/ n seca f

**drove** /drəʊv/ see **drive**

**drown** /draʊn/ vt/i afogar(-se)

**drowsy** /'draʊzɪ/ a sonolento. **be or feel ~** ter vontade de dormir

**drudge** /drʌdʒ/ n mouro m de trabalho. **~ry** /-ərɪ/ n trabalho m penoso e monótono, estafa f

**drug** /drʌg/ n droga f; (med) medicamento m, remédio m □ vt (pt **drugged**) drogar. **~ addict** drogado m, tóxico-dependente m

**drugstore** /'drʌgstɔː(r)/ n (Amer) farmácia f que vende também sorvetes etc

**drum** /drʌm/ n (mus) tambor m; (for oil) barril m, tambor m. **~s** (mus) bateria f □ vi (pt **drummed**) tocar tambor; (with one's fingers) tamborilar □ vt **~ into sb** fazer entrar na cabeça de alg. **~ up** (support) conseguir obter; (business) criar. **~mer** n tambor m; (in pop group etc) baterista m, (P) bateria f

**drunk** /drʌŋk/ see **drink** □ a embriagado, bêbedo. **get ~** embebedar-se, embriagar-se □ n bêbedo m. **~ard** n alcoólico m, bêbedo m. **~en** a embriagado, bêbedo; (habitually) bêbedo

**dry** /draɪ/ a (**drier, driest**) seco; (day) sem chuva □ vt/i secar. **be or feel ~** ter sede. **~-clean** vt limpar a seco. **~-cleaner's** n (loja de) lavagem f a seco, lavandaria f. **~ up** (dishes) secar a louça f; (of supplies) esgotar-se. **~ness** n secura f

**dual** /'djuːəl/ a duplo. **~ carriageway** estrada f dividida por faixa central. **~-purpose** a com fim duplo

**dub** /dʌb/ vt (pt **dubbed**) (film) dobrar; (nickname) apelidar de

**dubious** /'djuːbɪəs/ a duvidoso; (character, compliment) dúbio. **feel ~ about** ter dúvidas quanto a

**duchess** /'dʌtʃɪs/ n duquesa f

**duck** /dʌk/ n pato m □ vi abaixar-se rapidamente □ vt (head) baixar; (person) batizar, pregar uma amona em. **~ling** n patinho m

**duct** /dʌkt/ n canal m, tubo m

**dud** /dʌd/ a (sl: thing) que não presta ou não funciona; (sl: coin) falso; (sl: cheque) sem fundos, (P) careca (sl)

**due** /djuː/ a devido; (expected) esperado □ adv **~ east/etc** exatamente, (P) exactamente a leste/etc □ n devido m. **~s** direitos mpl; (of club) cota f. **~ to** devido a, por causa de. **in ~ course** no tempo devido

**duel** /'djuːəl/ n duelo m

**duet** /djuˈet/ n dueto m

**duffel** /'dʌfl/ a **~ bag** saco m de lona. **~-coat** n casaco m de tecido de lã

**dug** /dʌg/ see **dig**

**duke** /djuːk/ n duque m

**dull** /dʌl/ a (**-er, -est**) (boring) enfadonho; (colour) morto; (mirror) embaçado; (weather) encoberto; (sound) surdo; (stupid) burro

**duly** /'djuːlɪ/ adv devidamente; (in due time) no tempo devido

**dumb** /dʌm/ a (**-er, -est**) mudo; (colloq: stupid) bronco, burro

**dumbfound** /dʌmˈfaʊnd/ vt pasmar

**dummy** /'dʌmɪ/ n imitação f, coisa f simulada; (of tailor) manequim m; (of baby) chupeta f

**dump** /dʌmp/ vt (rubbish) jogar fora; (put down) deixar cair; (colloq: abandon) largar □ n monte m de lixo; (tip) lixeira f; (mil) depósito m; (colloq) buraco m

**dunce** /dʌns/ n burro m. **~'s cap** orelhas fpl de burro

**dune** /djuːn/ n duna f

**dung** /dʌŋ/ n esterco m; (manure) estrume m

**dungarees** /dʌŋgəˈriːz/ npl macacão m, (P) fato m de macaco

**dungeon** /'dʌndʒən/ n calabouço m, masmorra f

**dupe** /djuːp/ vt enganar □ n trouxa m

**duplicate**[1] /'djuːplɪkət/ n duplicado m □ a idêntico

**duplicate**[2] /'djuːplɪkeɪt/ vt duplicar, fazer em duplicado; (on machine) fotocopiar

**duplicity** /djuːˈplɪsətɪ/ n duplicidade f

**durable** /'djʊərəbl/ a resistente; (enduring) duradouro, durável

**duration** /djʊˈreɪʃn/ n duração f

**duress** /djʊˈres/ n **under ~** sob coação f, (P) coacção f

**during** /'djʊərɪŋ/ prep durante

**dusk** /dʌsk/ n crepúsculo m, anoitecer m

**dusky** /'dʌskɪ/ a (**-ier, -iest**) escuro, sombrio

**dust** /dʌst/ n pó m, poeira f □ vt limpar o pó de; (sprinkle) polvilhar. **~-jacket** n sobrecapa f de livro

**dustbin** /'dʌstbɪn/ n lata f do lixo, (P) caixote m

**duster** /'dʌstə(r)/ n pano m do pó

**dustman** /'dʌstmən/ n (pl **-men**) lixeiro m, (P) homem m do lixo

**dusty** /'dʌstɪ/ a (**-ier, -iest**) poeirento, empoeirado

**Dutch** /dʌtʃ/ a holandês □ n (lang) holandês m. **~man** n holandês m. **~woman** n holandesa f. **go ~** pagar cada um a sua despesa

**dutiful** /'djuːtɪfl/ a cumpridor; (showing respect) respeitador

**dut|y** /'dju:tɪ/ n dever m; (tax) impostos mpl. **~ies** (of official etc) funções fpl. **off ~y** de folga. **on ~y** de serviço. **~y-free** a isento de impostos. **~y-free shop** free shop m

**duvet** /'dju:veɪ/ n edredom m, (P) edredão m de penas

**dwarf** /dwɔːf/ n (pl **-fs**) anão m

**dwell** /dwel/ vi (pt **dwelt**) morar. **~ on** alongar-se sobre. **~er** n habitante. **~ing** n habitação f

**dwindle** /'dwɪndl/ vi diminuir, reduzir-se

**dye** /daɪ/ vt (pres p **dyeing**) tingir □ n tinta f

**dying** /'daɪɪŋ/ see **die**

**dynamic** /dar'næmɪk/ a dinâmico

**dynamite** /'daməmaɪt/ n dinamite f □ vt dinamitar

**dynamo** /'daməməʊ/ n (pl **-os**) dínamo m

**dynasty** /'dɪnəstɪ/ n dinastia f

**dysentery** /'dɪsəntrɪ/ n disenteria f

**dyslex|ia** /dɪs'leksɪə/ n dislexia f. **~ic** a disléxico

# E

**each** /iːtʃ/ a & pron cada. **~ one** cada um. **~ other** um ao outro, uns aos outros. **they like ~ other** gostam um do outro/uns dos outros. **know/love/etc ~ other** conhecer-se/amar-se/etc

**eager** /'iːgə(r)/ a ansioso (to por), desejoso (for de); (supporter) entusiástico. **be ~ to** ter vontade de. **~ly** adv com impaciência, ansiosamente; (keenly) com entusiasmo. **~ness** n ansiedade f, desejo m; (keenness) entusiasmo m

**eagle** /'iːgl/ n águia f

**ear** /ɪə(r)/ n ouvido m; (external part) orelha f. **~-drum** n tímpano m. **~-ring** n brinco m

**earache** /'ɪəreɪk/ n dor f de ouvidos

**earl** /ɜːl/ n conde m

**early** /'ɜːlɪ/ (-ier, -iest) adv cedo □ a primeiro; (hour) matinal; (fruit) temporão; (retirement) antecipado. **have an ~ dinner** jantar cedo. **in ~ summer** no princípio do verão

**earmark** /'ɪəmɑːk/ vt destinar, reservar (for para)

**earn** /ɜːn/ vt ganhar; (deserve) merecer

**earnest** /'ɜːnɪst/ a sério. **in ~** a sério

**earnings** /'ɜːnɪŋz/ npl salário m; (profits) ganhos mpl, lucros mpl

**earshot** /'ɪəʃɒt/ n **within ~** ao alcance da voz

**earth** /ɜːθ/ n terra f □ vt (electr) ligar à terra. **why on ~?** por que diabo?, por que cargas d'água? **~ly** a terrestre, terreno

**earthenware** /'ɜːθənweə(r)/ n louça f de barro, faiança f

**earthquake** /'ɜːθkweɪk/ n tremor m de terra, terremoto m

**earthy** /'ɜːθɪ/ a terroso, térreo; (coarse) grosseiro

**earwig** /'ɪəwɪg/ n lacrainha f, (P) bicha-cadela f

**ease** /iːz/ n facilidade f; (comfort) bem-estar m □ vt/i (from pain, anxiety) acalmar(-se); (slow down) afrouxar; (slide) deslizar. **at ~** à vontade; (mil) descansar. **ill at ~** pouco à vontade. **with ~** facilmente. **~ in/out** fazer entrar/sair com cuidado

**easel** /'iːzl/ n cavalete m

**east** /iːst/ n este m, leste m, pas-cente m, oriente m. **the E~** o Oriente □ a este, (de) leste, oriental □ adv a/para leste. **~ of** para o leste de **~erly** a oriental, leste, a/de leste **~ward** a, **~ward(s)** adv para leste

**Easter** /'iːstə(r)/ n Páscoa f. **~ egg** ovo m de Páscoa

**eastern** /'iːstən/ a oriental, leste

**easy** /'iːzɪ/ a (-ier, -iest) fácil; (relaxed) natural, descontraído. **take it ~** levar as coisas com calma. **~ chair** poltrona f. **~-going** a bonacheirão. **easily** adv facilmente

**eat** /iːt/ vt/i (pt **ate**, pp **eaten**) comer. **~ into** corroer. **~able** a comestível

**eaves** /iːvz/ npl beiral m

**eavesdrop** /'iːvzdrɒp/ vi (pt **-dropped**) escutar por detrás da porta

**ebb** /eb/ n vazante f, baixa-mar m □ vi vazar; (fig) declinar

**EC** /iː'siː/ n (abbr of European Community) CE f

**eccentric** /ɪk'sentrɪk/ a & n excêntrico (m). **~ity** /eksen'trɪsətɪ/ n excentricidade f

**ecclesiastical** /ɪkliːzɪ'æstɪkl/ a eclesiástico

**echo** /'ekəʊ/ n (pl **-oes**) eco m □ vt/i (pt **echoed**, pres p **echoing**) ecoar; (fig) repetir

**eclipse** /ɪ'klɪps/ n eclipse m □ vt eclipsar

**ecolog|y** /iː'kɒlədʒɪ/ n ecologia f. **~ical** /iːkə'lɒdʒɪkl/ a ecológico

**economic** /iːkə'nɒmɪk/ a económico, (P) económico; (profitable) rentável. **~al** a económico, (P) económico. **~s** n economia f política

**economist** /ɪ'kɒnəmɪst/ n economista mf

**econom|y** /ɪ'kɒnəmɪ/ n economia f. **~ize** vt/i economizar

**ecstasy** /'ekstəsɪ/ n êxtase m

**ecstatic** /ɪk'stætɪk/ a extático, extasiado

**ecu** /'eɪkju:/ n unidade f monetária européia

**eczema** /'ɛksɪmə/ n eczema m

**edge** /edʒ/ n borda f, beira f; (of town) periferia f, limite m; (of knife) fio m □ vt debruar □ vi (move) avançar pouco a pouco

**edging** /'edʒɪŋ/ n borda f, (P) bordadura f

**edgy** /'edʒɪ/ a irritadiço, nervoso

**edible** /'edɪbl/ a comestível

**edict** /'i:dɪkt/ n édito m

**edifice** /'edɪfɪs/ n edifício m

**edit** /'edɪt/ vt (pt edited) (newspaper) dirigir; (text) editar

**edition** /ɪ'dɪʃn/ n edição f

**editor** /'edɪtə(r)/ n (of newspaper) diretor m, (P) director m, editor m responsável; (of text) organizador m de texto. **the ~ (in chief)** redatorchefe m, (P) redactor-chefe m. **~ial** /edɪ'tɔ:rɪəl/ a & n editorial (m)

**educat|e** /'edʒʊkeɪt/ vt instruir; (mind, public) educar. **~ed** a instruído; educado. **~ion** /-'keɪʃn/ n educação f; (schooling) ensino m. **~ional** /'keɪʃənl/ a educativo, pedagógico

**EEC** /i:i:'si:/ n (abbr of European Economic Community) CEE f

**eel** /i:l/ n enguia f

**eerie** /'ɪərɪ/ a (-ier, -iest) arrepiante, misterioso

**effect** /ɪ'fekt/ n efeito m □ vt efetuar, (P) efectuar. **come into ~** entrar em vigor. **in ~** na realidade. **take ~** ter efeito

**effective** /ɪ'fektɪv/ a eficaz, eficiente; (striking) sensacional; (actual) efetivo, (P) efectivo. **~ly** adv (efficiently) eficazmente; (strikingly) de forma sensacional; (actually) efetivamente, (P) efectivamente. **~ness** n eficácia f

**effeminate** /ɪ'femɪnət/ a efeminado, afeminado

**effervescent** /efə'vesnt/ a efervescente

**efficien|t** /ɪ'fɪʃnt/ a eficiente, eficaz. **~cy** n eficiência f. **~tly** adv eficientemente

**effigy** /'efɪdʒɪ/ n efígie f

**effort** /'efət/ n esforço m. **~less** a fácil, sem esforço

**effrontery** /ɪ'frʌntərɪ/ n desfaçatez f

**effusive** /ɪ'fju:sɪv/ a efusivo, expansivo

**e.g.** /i:'dʒi:/ abbr por ex

**egg¹** /eg/ n ovo m. **~-cup** n copinho m para ovo quente, oveiro m. **~-plant** n beringela f

**egg²** /eg/ vt **~ on** (colloq) incitar

**eggshell** /'egʃel/ n casca f de ovo

**ego** /'egəʊ/ n (pl -os) ego m, eu m. **~ism** n egoísmo m. **~ist** n egoísta mf. **~tism** n egotismo m. **~tist** n egotista mf

**Egypt** /'i:dʒɪpt/ n Egito m. **~ian** /ɪ'dʒɪpʃn/ a & n egípcio (m)

**eh** /eɪ/ int (colloq) hã?

**eiderdown** /'aɪdədaʊn/ n edredão m, edredom m

**eight** /eɪt/ a & n oito (m). **eighth** /eɪtθ/ a & n oitavo (m)

**eighteen** /eɪ'ti:n/ a & n dezoito (m). **~th** a & n décimo-oitavo (m)

**eight|y** /'eɪtɪ/ a & n oitenta (m). **~ieth** a & n octogésimo (m)

**either** /'aɪðə(r)/ a & pron um e outro; (with negative) nem um nem outro; (each) cada □ adv também não □ conj **~ ... or** ou ... ou; (with negative) nem ... nem

**ejaculate** /ɪ'dʒækjʊleɪt/ vt/i ejacular; (exclaim) exclamar

**eject** /ɪ'dʒekt/ vt expelir; (expel) expulsar, despejar

**elaborate¹** /ɪ'læbərət/ a elaborado, rebuscado, minucioso

**elaborate²** /ɪ'læbəreɪt/ vt elaborar □ vi entrar em pormenores. **~ on** estender-se sobre

**elapse** /ɪ'læps/ vi decorrer

**elastic** /ɪ'læstɪk/ a & n elástico (m). **~ band** elástico m

**elat|ed** /ɪ'leɪtɪd/ a radiante, exultante. **~ion** n exultação f

**elbow** /'elbəʊ/ n cotovelo m

**elder¹** /'eldə(r)/ a mais velho. **~s** npl pessoas fpl mais velhas

**elder²** /'eldə(r)/ n (tree) sabugueiro m

**elderly** /'eldəlɪ/ a idoso. **the ~** as pessoas de idade

**eldest** /'eldɪst/ a & n o mais velho (m)

**elect** /ɪ'lekt/ vt eleger □ a eleito. **~ion** /-kʃn/ n eleição f

**electric** /ɪ'lektrɪk/ a elétrico, (P) eléctrico. **~al** a elétrico, (P) eléctrico

**electrician** /ɪlek'trɪʃn/ n eletricista m, (P) electricista m

**electricity** /ɪlek'trɪsətɪ/ n eletricidade f, (P) electricidade f

**electrify** /ɪ'lektrɪfaɪ/ vt eletrificar, (P) electrificar; (fig: excite) eletrizar, (P) electrizar

**electrocute** /ɪ'lektrəkju:t/ vt eletrocutar, (P) electrocutar

**electronic** /ɪlek'trɒnɪk/ a eletrônico, (P) electrónico. **~s** n eletrônica f, (P) electrónica f

**elegan|t** /'elɪgənt/ a elegante. **~ce** n elegância f. **~tly** adv elegantemente, com elegância

**element** /'elɪmənt/ n elemento m; (of heater etc) resistência f. **~ary** /-'mentrɪ/ a elementar; (school) primário

**elephant** /'elɪfənt/ n elefante m

**elevat|e** /'elɪveɪt/ vt elevar. **~ion** /'veɪʃn/ n elevação f

**elevator** /'elɪveɪtə(r)/ n (Amer: lift) elevador m, ascensor m

**eleven** /ɪˈlevn/ *a & n* onze (*m*). ~th *a & n* décimo primeiro (*m*). **at the ~th hour** à última hora

**elf** /elf/ *n* (*pl* **elves**) elfo *m*, duende *m*

**elicit** /ɪˈlɪsɪt/ *vt* extrair, obter

**eligible** /ˈelɪdʒəbl/ *a* (*for office*) idôneo, (*P*) idóneo (*for para*); (*desirable*) aceitável. **be ~ for** (*entitled to*) ter direito a

**eliminat|e** /ɪˈlɪmɪneɪt/ *vt* eliminar. ~**ion** /-ˈneɪʃn/ *n* eliminação *f*

**élite** /eɪˈliːt/ *n* elite *f*

**ellip|se** /ɪˈlɪps/ *n* elipse *f.* ~**tical** *a* elíptico

**elm** /elm/ *n* olmo *m*, ulmeiro *m*

**elocution** /eləˈkjuːʃn/ *n* elocução *f*

**elongate** /ˈiːlɒŋgeɪt/ *vt* alongar

**elope** /ɪˈləʊp/ *vi* fugir. ~**ment** *n* fuga *f* (de amantes), (*P*) (de amorosos)

**eloquen|t** /ˈeləkwənt/ *a* eloqüente, (*P*) eloquente. ~**ce** *n* eloqüência *f*, (*P*) eloquência *f*

**else** /els/ *adv* mais. **everybody ~** todos os outros. **nobody ~** mais ninguém. **nothing ~** nada mais. **or ~** ou então, senão. **somewhere ~** noutro lado qualquer. ~**where** *adv* noutro lado

**elude** /ɪˈluːd/ *vt* escapar a; (*a question*) evadir

**elusive** /ɪˈluːsɪv/ *a* (*person*) esquivo, difícil de apanhar; (*answer*) evasivo

**emaciated** /ɪˈmeɪʃɪeɪtɪd/ *a* emaciado, macilento

**emancipat|e** /ɪˈmænsɪpeɪt/ *vt* emancipar. ~**ion** /-ˈpeɪʃn/ *n* emancipação *f*

**embalm** /ɪmˈbɑːm/ *vt* embalsamar

**embankment** /ɪmˈbæŋkmənt/ *n* (*of river*) dique *m*; (*of railway*) terrapleno *m*, talude *m*, (*P*) aterro *m*

**embargo** /ɪmˈbɑːgəʊ/ *n* (*pl* **-oes**) embargo *m*

**embark** /ɪmˈbɑːk/ *vt/i* embarcar. ~ **on** (*business etc*) embarcar em, meter-se em (*colloq*); (*journey*) começar

**embarrass** /ɪmˈbærəs/ *vt* embaraçar, confundir. ~**ment** *n* embaraço *m*, atrapalhação *f*

**embassy** /ˈembəsɪ/ *n* embaixada *f*

**embellish** /ɪmˈbelɪʃ/ *vt* embelezar, enfeitar. ~**ment** *n* embelezamento *m*, enfeite *m*

**embezzle** /ɪmˈbezl/ *vt* desviar (fundos). ~**ment** *n* desfalque *m*

**embitter** /ɪmˈbɪtə(r)/ *vt* (*person*) amargurar; (*situation*) azedar

**emblem** /ˈembləm/ *n* emblema *m*

**embod|y** /ɪmˈbɒdɪ/ *vt* encarnar; (*include*) incorporar, incluir. ~**iment** *n* personificação *f*

**emboss** /ɪmˈbɒs/ *vt* (*metal*) gravar em relevo; (*paper*) gofrar

**embrace** /ɪmˈbreɪs/ *vt/i* abraçar(-se); (*offer, opportunity*) acolher □ *n* abraço *m*

**embroider** /ɪmˈbrɔɪdə(r)/ *vt* bordar. ~**y** *n* bordado *m*

**embryo** /ˈembrɪəʊ/ *n* (*pl* **-os**) embrião *m*. ~**nic** /-ˈɒnɪk/ *a* embrionário

**emerald** /ˈemərəld/ *n* esmeralda *f*

**emerge** /ɪˈmɜːdʒ/ *vi* emergir, surgir

**emergency** /ɪˈmɜːdʒənsɪ/ *n* emergência *f*; (*urgent case*) urgência *f*. ~ **exit** saída *f* de emergência. **in an ~** em caso de urgência

**emigrant** /ˈemɪgrənt/ *n* emigrante *mf*

**emigrat|e** /ˈemɪgreɪt/ *vi* emigrar. ~**ion** /ˈgreɪʃn/ *n* emigração *f*

**eminen|t** /ˈemɪnənt/ *a* eminente. ~**tly** *adv* eminentemente

**emi|t** /ɪˈmɪt/ *vt* (*pt* **emitted**) emitir. ~**ssion** /-ʃn/ *n* emissão *f*

**emotion** /ɪˈməʊʃn/ *n* emoção *f.* ~**al** *a* (*person, shock*) emotivo; (*speech, scene*) emocionante

**emperor** /ˈempərə(r)/ *n* imperador *m*

**emphasis** /ˈemfəsɪs/ *n* ênfase *f.* **lay ~ on** pôr em relevo

**emphasize** /ˈemfəsaɪz/ *vt* enfatizar, sublinhar; (*syllable, word*) acentuar

**emphatic** /ɪmˈfætɪk/ *a* enfático; (*manner*) enérgico. ~**ally** *adv* enfaticamente

**empire** /ˈempaɪə(r)/ *n* império *m*

**employ** /ɪmˈplɔɪ/ *vt* empregar. ~**ee** /emplɔɪˈiː/ *n* empregado *m*. ~**er** *n* patrão *m*. ~**ment** *n* emprego *m*. ~**ment agency** agência *f* de empregos

**empower** /ɪmˈpaʊə(r)/ *vt* autorizar (**to do** a fazer)

**empress** /ˈemprɪs/ *n* imperatriz *f*

**empt|y** /ˈemptɪ/ *a* vazio; (*promise*) falso □ *vt/i* esvaziar(-se). **on an ~y stomach** com o estômago vazio, em jejum. ~**ies** *npl* garrafas *fpl* vazias. ~**iness** *n* vazio *m*

**emulate** /ˈemjʊleɪt/ *vt* imitar, rivalizar com, emular com

**emulsion** /ɪˈmʌlʃn/ *n* emulsão *f*

**enable** /ɪˈneɪbl/ *vt* ~ **sb to do** permitir a alg fazer

**enact** /ɪˈnækt/ *vt* (*jur*) decretar; (*theat*) representar

**enamel** /ɪˈnæml/ *n* esmalte *m* □ *vt* (*pt* **enamelled**) esmaltar

**enamoured** /ɪˈnæməd/ *a* ~ **of** enamorado de, apaixonado por

**encase** /ɪnˈkeɪs/ *vt* encerrar (**in** em); (*cover*) revestir (**in** de)

**enchant** /ɪnˈtʃɑːnt/ *vt* encantar. ~**ing** *a* encantador. ~**ment** *n* encantamento *m*

**encircle** /ɪnˈsɜːkl/ *vt* cercar, rodear

**enclose** /ɪnˈkləʊz/ *vt* (*land*) cercar; (*with letter*) enviar incluso/junto. ~**d** *a* (*space*) fechado; (*with letter*) anexo, incluso, junto

**enclosure** /ɪnˈkləʊʒə(r)/ n cercado m, recinto m; (with letter) documento m anexo

**encompass** /ɪnˈkʌmpəs/ vt abranger

**encore** /ɒŋˈkɔː(r)/ int & n bis (m)

**encounter** /ɪnˈkaʊntə(r)/ vt encontrar, deparar com □ n encontro m

**encourage** /ɪnˈkʌrɪdʒ/ vt encorajar. ~ment n encorajamento m

**encroach** /ɪnˈkrəʊtʃ/ vi ~ on (land) invadir; (time) abusar de

**encumb|er** /ɪnˈkʌmbə(r)/ vt estorvar; (burden) sobrecarregar. ~rance n estorvo m, empecilho m; (burden) ônus m, (P) ónus m, encargo m

**encycloped|ia** /ɪnsaɪkləˈpiːdɪə/ n enciclopédia f. ~ic a enciclopédico

**end** /end/ n fim m; (farthest part) extremo m, ponta f □ vt/i acabar, terminar. ~ up (arrive finally) ir parar (in a/em). ~ up doing acabar por fazer. **in the** ~ por fim. **no** ~ **of** (colloq) muito, enorme, imenso. **on** ~ (upright) em pé; (consecutive) a fio, de seguida

**endanger** /ɪnˈdeɪndʒə(r)/ vt pôr em perigo

**endear|ing** /ɪnˈdɪərɪŋ/ a cativante. ~ment n palavra f meiga; (act) carinho m

**endeavour** /ɪnˈdevə(r)/ n esforço m □ vi esforçar-se (to por)

**ending** /ˈendɪŋ/ n fim m; (of word) terminação f

**endless** /ˈendlɪs/ a interminável; (times) sem conta; (patience) infinito

**endorse** /ɪnˈdɔːs/ vt (document) endossar; (action) aprovar. ~ment n (auto) averbamento m

**endow** /ɪnˈdaʊ/ vt doar. ~ment n doação f

**endur|e** /ɪnˈdjʊə(r)/ vt suportar □ vi durar. ~able a suportável. ~ance n resistência f

**enemy** /ˈenəmɪ/ n & a inimigo (m)

**energetic** /enəˈdʒetɪk/ a enérgico

**energy** /ˈenədʒɪ/ n energia f

**enforce** /ɪnˈfɔːs/ vt aplicar

**engage** /ɪnˈgeɪdʒ/ vt (staff) contratar; (mech) engrenar □ vi ~ **in** envolver-se em, lançar-se em. ~**d** a (to) noivo; (busy) ocupado. ~ment n noivado m; (undertaking, appointment) compromisso m; (mil) combate m

**engender** /ɪnˈdʒendə(r)/ vt engendrar, produzir, causar

**engine** /ˈendʒɪn/ n motor m; (of train) locomotiva f

**engineer** /endʒɪˈnɪə(r)/ n engenheiro m □ vt engenhar. ~ing n engenharia f

**England** /ˈɪŋglənd/ n Inglaterra f

**English** /ˈɪŋglɪʃ/ a inglês □ n (lang) inglês m. **the** ~ os ingleses mpl.

~**man** n inglês m. ~-**speaking** a de lingua inglesa f. ~**woman** n inglesa f

**engrav|e** /ɪnˈgreɪv/ vt gravar. ~-**ing** n gravura f

**engrossed** /ɪnˈgrəʊst/ a absorto (**in** em)

**engulf** /ɪnˈgʌlf/ vt engolfar, tragar

**enhance** /ɪnˈhɑːns/ vt aumentar; (heighten) realçar

**enigma** /ɪˈnɪgmə/ n enigma m. ~**tic** /enɪgˈmætɪk/ a enigmático

**enjoy** /ɪnˈdʒɔɪ/ vt gostar de; (benefit from) gozar de. ~ **o.s.** divertir-se. ~**able** a agradável. ~**ment** n prazer m

**enlarge** /ɪnˈlɑːdʒ/ vt/i aumentar. ~ **upon** alargar-se sobre. ~**ment** n ampliação f

**enlighten** /ɪnˈlaɪtn/ vt esclarecer. ~**ment** n esclarecimento m, elucidação f

**enlist** /ɪnˈlɪst/ vt recrutar; (fig) aliciar, granjear □ vi alistar-se

**enliven** /ɪnˈlaɪvn/ vt animar

**enmity** /ˈenmətɪ/ n inimizade f

**enormous** /ɪˈnɔːməs/ a enorme

**enough** /ɪˈnʌf/ a, adv & n bastante (m), suficiente (m) □ int basta!, chega! **have** ~ **of** estar farto de

**enquir|e** /ɪnˈkwaɪə(r)/ vt/i perguntar, indagar. ~**e about** informar-se de, pedir informações sobre. ~**y** n pedido m de informações

**enrage** /ɪnˈreɪdʒ/ vt enfurecer, enraivecer

**enrich** /ɪnˈrɪtʃ/ vt enriquecer

**enrol** /ɪnˈrəʊl/ vt/i (pt **enrolled**) inscrever(-se); (schol) matricular(-se). ~**ment** n inscrição f; (schol) matrícula f

**ensemble** /ɒnˈsɒmbl/ n conjunto m

**ensign** /ˈensən/ n pavilhão m; (officer) guarda-marinha m

**ensu|e** /ɪnˈsjuː/ vi seguir-se. ~**ing** a decorrente

**ensure** /ɪnˈʃʊə(r)/ vt assegurar. ~ **that** assegurar-se de que

**entail** /ɪnˈteɪl/ vt acarretar

**entangle** /ɪnˈtæŋgl/ vt emaranhar, enredar

**enter** /ˈentə(r)/ vt (room, club etc) entrar em; (register) registar; (data) entrar com □ vi entrar (**into** em). ~ **for** inscrever-se em

**enterprise** /ˈentəpraɪz/ n empresa f, empreendimento m; (fig) iniciativa f

**enterprising** /ˈentəpraɪzɪŋ/ a empreendedor

**entertain** /entəˈteɪn/ vt entreter; (guests) receber; (ideas) alimentar, nutrir. ~**er** n artista mf. ~**ment** n entretenimento m; (performance) espetáculo m, (P) espectáculo m

**enthral** /mˈθrɔːl/ vt (pt **enthralled**) fascinar

**enthuse** /mˈθjuːz/ vi ~ **over** entusiasmar-se por

**enthusias|m** /mˈθjuːzɪæzm/ n entusiasmo m. ~**t** n entusiasta mf. ~**tic** /-ˈæstɪk/ a entusiástico. ~**tically** /-ˈæstɪkəlɪ/ adv entusiasticamente

**entice** /mˈtaɪs/ vt atrair. ~ **to do** induzir a fazer. ~**ment** n tentação f, engodo m

**entire** /mˈtaɪə(r)/ a inteiro. ~**ly** adv inteiramente

**entirety** /mˈtaɪərətɪ/ n **in its** ~ por inteiro, na (sua) totalidade

**entitle** /mˈtaɪtl/ vt dar direito. ~**d** a (book) intitulado. **be** ~**d to sth** ter direito a alg coisa. ~**ment** n direito m

**entity** /ˈentətɪ/ n entidade f

**entrance** /ˈentrəns/ n entrada f (**to** para); (right to enter) admissão f

**entrant** /ˈentrənt/ n (sport) concorrente mf; (in exam) candidato m

**entreat** /mˈtriːt/ vt rogar, suplicar. ~**y** n rogo m, súplica f

**entrench** /mˈtrentʃ/ vt (mil) entrincheirar; (fig) fincar

**entrust** /mˈtrʌst/ vt confiar

**entry** /ˈentrɪ/ n entrada f; (on list) item m; (in dictionary) verbete m. ~**form** ficha f de inscrição, (P) boletim m de inscrição. **no** ~ entrada proibida

**enumerate** /ˈnjuːməreɪt/ vt enumerar

**envelop** /mˈveləp/ vt (pt **enveloped**) envolver

**envelope** /ˈenvələʊp/ n envelope m, sobrescrito m

**enviable** /ˈenvɪəbl/ a invejável

**envious** /ˈenvɪəs/ a invejoso. **be** ~ **of** ter inveja de. ~**ly** adv invejosamente, com inveja

**environment** /mˈvaɪərənmənt/ n meio m; (ecological) meio-ambiente m. ~**al** /-ˈmentl/ a do meio; (ecological) do ambiente

**envisage** /mˈvɪzɪdʒ/ vt encarar; (foresee) prever

**envoy** /ˈenvɔɪ/ n enviado m

**envy** /ˈenvɪ/ n inveja f □ vt invejar, ter inveja de

**enzyme** /ˈenzaɪm/ n enzima f

**epic** /ˈepɪk/ n epopéia f □ a épico

**epidemic** /epɪˈdemɪk/ n epidemia f

**epilep|sy** /ˈepɪlepsɪ/ n epilepsia f. ~**tic** /ˈleptɪk/ a & n epiléptico (m)

**episode** /ˈepɪsəʊd/ n episódio m

**epitaph** /ˈepɪtɑːf/ n epitáfio m

**epithet** /ˈepɪθet/ n epíteto m

**epitom|e** /ˈpɪtəmɪ/ n (summary) epítome m; (embodiment) modelo m. ~**ize** vt (fig) representar, encarnar; (summarize) resumir

**epoch** /ˈiːpɒk/ n época f. ~**-making** a que marca uma época

**equal** /ˈiːkwəl/ a & n igual (m) □ vt (pt **equalled**) igualar, ser igual a. ~ **to** (task) à altura de. ~**ity** /iːˈkwɒlətɪ/ n igualdade f. ~**ly** adv igualmente; (similarly) de igual modo

**equalize** /ˈiːkwəlaɪz/ vt/i igualar; (sport) empatar

**equanimity** /ekwəˈnɪmətɪ/ n equanimidade f, serenidade f

**equate** /ɪˈkweɪt/ vt equacionar (**with** com); (treat as equal) equiparar (**with** a)

**equation** /ɪˈkweɪʒn/ n equação f

**equator** /ɪˈkweɪtə(r)/ n equador m. ~**ial** /ekwəˈtɔːrɪəl/ a equatorial

**equilibrium** /iːkwɪˈlɪbrɪəm/ n equilíbrio m

**equip** /ɪˈkwɪp/ vt (pt **equipped**) equipar (**with** com), munir (**with** de). ~**ment** n equipamento m

**equitable** /ˈekwɪtəbl/ a eqüitativo, (P) equitativo

**equity** /ˈekwətɪ/ n eqüidade f, (P) equidade f

**equivalent** /ɪˈkwɪvələnt/ a & n eqüivalente (m), (P) equivalente (m)

**equivocal** /ɪˈkwɪvəkl/ a equívoco

**era** /ˈɪərə/ n era f, época f

**eradicate** /ɪˈrædɪkeɪt/ vt erradicar, suprimir

**erase** /ɪˈreɪz/ vt apagar. ~**r** /-ə(r)/ n borracha f (de apagar)

**erect** /ɪˈrekt/ a erecto, (P) erecto □ vt erigir. ~**ion** /-ʃn/ n ereção f, (P) erecção f; (building) construção f, edifício m

**ero|de** /ɪˈrəʊd/ vt corroer. ~**sion** /ɪˈrəʊʒn/ n erosão f

**erotic** /ɪˈrɒtɪk/ a erótico

**err** /ɜː(r)/ vi (pt **erred**) errar

**errand** /ˈerənd/ n recado m

**erratic** /ɪˈrætɪk/ a errático, irregular; (person) variável, imprevisível

**erroneous** /ɪˈrəʊnɪəs/ a errôneo, (P) erróneo, errado

**error** /ˈerə(r)/ n erro m

**erudit|e** /ˈeruːdaɪt/ a erudito. ~**ion** /-ˈdɪʃn/ n erudição f

**erupt** /ɪˈrʌpt/ vi (war, fire) irromper; (volcano) entrar em erupção. ~**ion** /-ʃn/ n erupção f

**escalat|e** /ˈeskəleɪt/ vt/i intensificar (-se); (of prices) subir em espiral. ~**ion** /ˈleɪʃn/ n escalada f

**escalator** /ˈeskəleɪtə(r)/ n escada f rolante

**escapade** /eskəˈpeɪd/ n peripécia f

**escape** /ɪˈskeɪp/ vi escapar-se □ vt escapar a □ n fuga f; (of prisoner) evasão f, fuga f. ~ **from sb** escapar de alguém. ~ **to** fugir para. **have a lucky** or **narrow** ~ escapar por um tris escapism /ɪ'skeɪpɪzəm/ n escapismo m

escort¹ /'eskɔ:t/ n escolta f; (of woman) cavalheiro m, acompanhante m

escort² /ɪ'skɔ:t/ vt escoltar; (accompany) acompanhar

escudo /es'kjudəʊ/ n (pl -os) escudo m

Eskimo /'eskɪməʊ/ n (pl -os) esquimó mf

especial /ɪ'speʃl/ a especial. ~ly adv especialmente

espionage /'espɪənɑ:ʒ/ n espionagem f

espouse /ɪ'spaʊz/ vt (a cause etc) abraçar

espresso /e'spressəʊ/ n (pl -os) (coffee) expresso m

essay /'eseɪ/ n ensaio m; (schol) redação f, (P) redacção f

essence /'esns/ n essência f

essential /ɪ'senʃl/ a essencial □ n the ~s o essencial m. ~ly adv essencialmente

establish /ɪ'stæblɪʃ/ vt estabelecer; (business, state) fundar; (prove) provar, apurar. ~ment n estabelecimento m; (institution) instituição f. the E~ment o Establishment m, a classe f dirigente

estate /ɪ'steɪt/ n propriedade f; (possessions) bens mpl; (inheritance) herança f. ~ agent agente m imobiliário. (housing) ~ conjunto m habitacional. ~ car perua f

esteem /ɪ'sti:m/ vt estimar □ n estima f

estimate¹ /'estɪmət/ n cálculo m, avaliação f; (comm) orçamento m, estimativa f

estimat|e² /'estɪmeɪt/ vt calcular, estimar. ~ion /-'meɪʃn/ n opinião f

estuary /'estʃʊərɪ/ n estuário m

etc abbr = et cetera /ɪt'setərə/ etc

etching /'etʃɪŋ/ n água-forte f

eternal /ɪ'tɜ:nl/ a eterno

eternity /ɪ'tɜ:nətɪ/ n eternidade f

ethic /'eθɪk/ n ética f. ~s ética f. ~al a ético

ethnic /'eθnɪk/ a étnico

etiquette /'etɪket/ n etiqueta f

etymology /etɪ'mɒlədʒɪ/ n etimologia f

eulogy /'ju:lədʒɪ/ n elogio m

euphemism /'ju:fəmɪzəm/ n eufemismo m

euphoria /ju:'fɔ:rɪə/ n euforia f

Europe /'jʊərəp/ n Europa f. ~an /-'pɪən/ a & n europeu (m)

euthanasia /ju:θə'neɪzɪə/ n eutanásia f

evacuat|e /ɪ'vækjʊeɪt/ vt evacuar. ~ion /-'eɪʃn/ n evacuação f

evade /ɪ'veɪd/ vt evadir, esquivar-se a

evaluate /ɪ'væljʊeɪt/ vt avaliar

evangelical /i:væn'dʒelɪkl/ a evangélico

evaporat|e /ɪ'væpəreɪt/ vt/i evaporar(-se). ~ed milk leite m evaporado. ~ion /-'reɪʃn/ n evaporação f

evasion /ɪ'veɪʒn/ n evasão f

evasive /ɪ'veɪsɪv/ a evasivo

eve /i:v/ n véspera f

even /'i:vn/ a regular; (surface) liso, plano; (amounts) igual; (number) par □ vt/i ~ up igualar(-se), acertar □ adv mesmo. ~ better ainda melhor. get ~ with ajustar contas com. ~ly adv uniformemente; (amounts) em partes iguais

evening /'i:vnɪŋ/ n entardecer m, anoitecer m; (whole evening) serão m. ~ class aula f à noite (para adultos). ~ dress traje m de cerimónia, (P) trajo m de cerimónia or de rigor; (woman's) vestido m de noite

event /ɪ'vent/ n acontecimento m. in the ~ of no caso de. ~ful a movimentado, memorável

eventual /ɪ'ventʃʊəl/ a final. ~ity /-'ælətɪ/ n eventualidade f. ~ly adv por fim; (in future) eventualmente

ever /'evə(r)/ adv jamais; (at all times) sempre. do you ~ go? você já foi alguma vez?, vais alguma vez? the best I ~ saw o melhor que já vi. ~ since adv desde então □ prep desde □ conj desde que. ~ so (colloq) muitíssimo, tão. hardly ~ quase nunca

evergreen /'evəgri:n/ n sempre-verde f, planta f de folhas persistentes □ a persistente

everlasting /'evəlɑ:stɪŋ/ a eterno

every /'evrɪ/ a cada. ~ now and then de vez em quando, volta e meia. ~ one cada um. ~ other day dia sim dia não, de dois em dois dias. ~ three days de três em três dias

everybody /'evrɪbɒdɪ/ pron todo mundo, todos

everyday /'evrɪdeɪ/ a cotidiano, (P) quotidiano, diário; (common) do dia a dia, vulgar

everyone /'evrɪwʌn/ pron todo mundo, todos

everything /'evrɪθɪŋ/ pron tudo

everywhere /'evrɪweə(r)/ adv (position) em todo lugar, em toda parte; (direction) a todo lugar, a toda parte

evict /ɪ'vɪkt/ vt expulsar, despejar. ~ion /-ʃn/ n despejo m

evidence /'evɪdəns/ n evidência f; (proof) prova f; (testimony) testemunho m, depoimento m. ~ of sinal de. give ~ testemunhar. in ~ em evidência

evident /'evɪdənt/ a evidente. ~ly adv evidentemente

**evil** /'iːvl/ *a* mau □ *n* mal *m*
**evo|ke** /ɪ'vəʊk/ *vt* evocar. **~cative** /ɪ'vɒkətɪv/ *a* evocativo
**evolution** /iːvə'luːʃn/ *n* evolução *f*
**evolve** /ɪ'vɒlv/ *vi* evolucionar, evoluir □ *vt* desenvolver, produzir
**ex-** /eks/ *pref* ex-
**exacerbate** /ɪg'zæsəbeɪt/ *vt* exacerbar
**exact** /ɪg'zækt/ *a* exato, (P) exacto □ *vt* exigir (**from** de). **~ing** *a* exigente; (*task*) difícil. **~ly** *adv* exatamente, (P) exactamente
**exaggerat|e** /ɪg'zædʒəreɪt/ *vt/i* exagerar. **~ion** /-'reɪʃn/ *n* exagero *m*
**exam** /ɪg'zæm/ *n* (*colloq*) exame *m*
**examination** /ɪgzæmɪ'neɪʃn/ *n* exame *m*; (*jur*) interrogatório *m*
**examine** /ɪg'zæmɪn/ *vt* examinar; (*witness etc*) interrogar. **~r** /-ə(r)/ *n* examinador *m*
**example** /ɪg'zaːmpl/ *n* exemplo *m*. **for ~** por exemplo. **make an ~ of** castigar para servir de exemplo
**exasperat|e** /ɪg'zæspəreɪt/ *vt* exasperar. **~ion** /-'reɪʃn/ *n* exaspero *m*
**excavat|e** /'ekskəveɪt/ *vt* escavar; (*uncover*) desenterrar. **~ion** /-'veɪʃn/ *n* escavação *f*
**exceed** /ɪk'siːd/ *vt* exceder; (*speed limit*) ultrapassar, exceder
**excel** /ɪk'sel/ *vi* (*pt* **excelled**) distinguir-se □ *vt* superar, ultrapassar
**excellen|t** /'eksələnt/ *a* excelente. **~ce** *n* excelência *f*. **~tly** *adv* excelentemente
**except** /ɪk'sept/ *prep* exceto, (P) excepto, fora □ *vt* excetuar, (P) exceptuar. **~ for** a não ser, menos, salvo. **~ing** *prep* à exceção de, (P) à excepção de. **~ion** /-ʃn/ *n* exceção *f*, (P) excepção *f*. **take ~ion to** (*object to*) achar inaceitável; (*be offended by*) achar ofensivo
**exceptional** /ɪk'sepʃənl/ *a* excepcional. **~ly** *adv* excepcionalmente
**excerpt** /'eksɜːpt/ *n* trecho *m*, excerto *m*
**excess¹** /ɪk'ses/ *n* excesso *m*
**excess²** /'ekses/ *a* excedente, em excesso. **~ fare** excesso *m*, suplemento *m*. **~ luggage** excesso *m* de peso
**excessive** /ɪk'sesɪv/ *a* excessivo. **~ly** *adv* excessivamente
**exchange** /ɪks'tʃeɪndʒ/ *vt* trocar □ *n* troca *f*; (*of currency*) câmbio *m*. (**telephone**) **~** central *f* telefónica, (P) telefónica. **~ rate** taxa *f* de câmbio
**excise** /'eksaɪz/ *n* imposto *m* (indireto, (P) indirecto)
**excit|e** /ɪk'saɪt/ *vt* excitar; (*rouse*) despertar; (*enthuse*) entusiasmar. **~able** *a* excitável. **~ed** *a* excitado. **get ~ed** excitar-se, entusiasmar-se. **~ement** *n* excitação *f*. **~ing** *a* excitante, emocionante

**exclaim** /ɪk'skleɪm/ *vi* exclamar
**exclamation** /eksklə'meɪʃn/ *n* exclamação *f*. **~ mark** ponto *m* de exclamação
**exclu|de** /ɪk'skluːd/ *vt* excluir. **~ding** *prep* excluído. **~sion** /ɪk'skluːʒn/ *n* exclusão *f*
**exclusive** /ɪk'skluːsɪv/ *a* (*rights etc*) exclusivo; (*club etc*) seleto, (P) selecto; (*news item*) (em) exclusivo. **~ of** sem incluir. **~ly** *adv* exclusivamente
**excruciating** /ɪk'skruːʃɪeɪtɪŋ/ *a* excruciante, atroz
**excursion** /ɪk'skɜːʃn/ *n* excursão *f*
**excus|e¹** /ɪk'skjuːz/ *vt* desculpar. **~e me!** desculpe!, com licença! **~e from** (*exempt*) dispensar de. **~able** *a* desculpável
**excuse²** /ɪk'skjuːs/ *n* desculpa *f*
**ex-directory** /eksdɪ'rektərɪ/ *a* que não vem no anuário, (P) na lista
**execute** /'eksɪkjuːt/ *vt* executar
**execution** /eksɪ'kjuːʃn/ *n* execução *f*
**executive** /ɪg'zekjʊtɪv/ *a & n* executivo (*m*)
**exemplary** /ɪg'zemplərɪ/ *a* exemplar
**exemplify** /ɪg'zemplɪfaɪ/ *vt* exemplificar, ilustrar
**exempt** /ɪg'zempt/ *a* isento (**from** de) □ *vt* dispensar, eximir. **~ion** /-ʃn/ *n* isenção *f*
**exercise** /'eksəsaɪz/ *n* exercício *m* □ *vt* (*powers, restraint etc*) exercer; (*dog*) levar para passear □ *vi* fazer exercício. **~ book** caderno *m*
**exert** /ɪg'zɜːt/ *vt* empregar, exercer. **~ o.s.** esforçar-se, fazer um esforço. **~ion** /-ʃn/ *n* esforço *m*
**exhaust** /ɪg'zɔːst/ *vt* esgotar □ *n* (*auto*) (tubo de) escape *m*. **~ed** *a* esgotado, exausto. **~ion** /-stʃən/ *n* esgotamento *m*, exaustão *f*
**exhaustive** /ɪg'zɔːstɪv/ *a* exaustivo, completo
**exhibit** /ɪg'zɪbɪt/ *vt* exibir, mostrar; (*thing, collection*) expor □ *n* objeto *m*, (P) objecto *m* exposto
**exhibition** /eksɪ'bɪʃn/ *n* exposição *f*; (*act of showing*) demonstração *f*
**exhilarat|e** /ɪg'zɪləreɪt/ *vt* regozijar; (*invigorate*) animar, estimular. **~ion** /-'reɪʃn/ *n* animação *f*, alegria *f*
**exhort** /ɪg'zɔːt/ *vt* exortar
**exile** /'eksaɪl/ *n* exílio *m*; (*person*) exilado *m* □ *vt* exilar, desterrar
**exist** /ɪg'zɪst/ *vi* existir. **~ence** *n* existência *f*. **be in ~ence** existir
**exit** /'eksɪt/ *n* saída *f*
**exonerate** /ɪg'zɒnəreɪt/ *vt* exonerar
**exorbitant** /ɪg'zɔːbɪtənt/ *a* exorbitante
**exorcize** /'eksɔːsaɪz/ *vt* esconjurar, exorcisar
**exotic** /ɪg'zɒtɪk/ *a* exótico

**expan|d** /ɪk'spænd/ vt/i expandir(-se); (extend) estender(-se), alargar(-se); (gas, liquid, metal) dilatar(-se). **~sion** /ɪk'spænʃn/ n expansão f; (extension) alargamento m; (of gas etc) dilatação f

**expanse** /ɪk'spæns/ n extensão f

**expatriate** /eks'pætrɪət/ a & n expatriado (m)

**expect** /ɪk'spekt/ vt esperar; (suppose) crer, supor; (require) contar com, esperar; (baby) esperar. **~ to do** contar fazer. **~ation** /ekspek'teɪʃn/ n expectativa f

**expectan|t** /ɪk'spektənt/ a **~t mother** gestante f. **~cy** n expectativa f

**expedient** /ɪk'spiːdɪənt/ a oportuno □ n expediente m

**expedition** /ekspɪ'dɪʃn/ n expedição f

**expel** /ɪk'spel/ vt (pt expelled) expulsar; (gas, poison etc) expelir

**expend** /ɪk'spend/ vt despender. **~able** a descartável

**expenditure** /ɪk'spendɪtʃə(r)/ n despesa f, gasto m

**expense** /ɪk'spens/ n despesa f; (cost) custo m. **at sb's ~** à custa de alg. **at the ~ of** (fig) à custa de

**expensive** /ɪk'spensɪv/ a caro, dispendioso; (tastes, habits) de luxo

**experience** /ɪk'spɪərɪəns/ n experiência f □ vt experimentar; (feel) sentir. **~d** a experiente

**experiment** /ɪk'sperɪmənt/ n experiência f □ vi /ɪk'sperɪment/ fazer uma experiência. **~al** /-'mentl/ a experimental

**expert** /'eksp3ːt/ a & n perito (m). **~ly** adv com perícia, habilmente

**expertise** /eksp3ː'tiːz/ n perícia f, competência f

**expir|e** /ɪk'spaɪə(r)/ vi expirar. **~y** n fim m de prazo, expiração f

**expl|ain** /ɪk'spleɪn/ vt explicar. **~anation** /eksplə'neɪʃn/ n explicação f. **~anatory** /ɪk'splænətrɪ/ a explicativo

**expletive** /ɪk'spliːtɪv/ n imprecação f, praga f

**explicit** /ɪk'splɪsɪt/ a explícito

**explo|de** /ɪk'spləʊd/ vt/i (fazer) explodir. **~sion** /ɪk'spləʊʒn/ n explosão f. **~sive** a & n explosivo (m)

**exploit**[1] /'eksplɔɪt/ n façanha f

**exploit**[2] /ɪk'splɔɪt/ vt explorar. **~ation** /eksplɔɪ'teɪʃn/ n exploração f

**exploratory** /ɪk'splɒrətrɪ/ a exploratório; (talks) preliminar

**explor|e** /ɪk'splɔː(r)/ vt explorar; (fig) examinar. **~ation** /eksplə'reɪʃn/ n exploração f. **~er** n explorador m

**exponent** /ɪk'spəʊnənt/ n (person) expoente mf; (math) expoente m

**export**[1] /ɪk'spɔːt/ vt exportar. **~er** n exportador m

**export**[2] /'ekspɔːt/ n exportação f. **~s** npl exportações fpl

**expos|e** /ɪk'spəʊz/ vt expor; (disclose) revelar; (unmask) desmascarar. **~ure** /-ʒə(r)/ n exposição f; (cold) frio m

**expound** /ɪk'spaʊnd/ vt explanar, expor

**express**[1] /ɪk'spres/ a expresso, categórico □ adv (por) expresso □ n (train) rápido m, expresso m. **~ly** adv expressamente

**express**[2] /ɪk'spres/ vt exprimir. **~ion** /-ʃn/ n expressão f. **~ive** a expressivo

**expulsion** /ɪk'spʌlʃn/ n expulsão f

**exquisite** /'ekskwɪzɪt/ a requintado

**extempore** /ek'stempərɪ/ a improvisado □ adv de improviso, sem preparação prévia

**exten|d** /ɪk'stend/ vt (stretch) estender; (enlarge) aumentar, ampliar; (prolong) prolongar; (grant) oferecer □ vi (stretch) estender-se; (in time) prolongar-se. **~sion** /ɪk'stenʃn/ n (incl phone) extensão f; (of deadline) prorrogação f; (building) anexo m

**extensive** /ɪk'stensɪv/ a extenso; (damage, study) vasto. **~ly** adv muito

**extent** /ɪk'stent/ n extensão f; (degree) medida f. **to some ~** até certo ponto, em certa medida. **to such an ~ that** a tal ponto que

**exterior** /ɪk'stɪərɪə(r)/ a & n exterior (m)

**exterminat|e** /ɪk'st3ːmɪneɪt/ vt exterminar. **~ion** /'neɪʃn/ n exterminação f, extermínio m

**external** /ɪk'st3ːnl/ a externo. **~ly** adv exteriormente

**extinct** /ɪk'stɪŋkt/ a extinto. **~ion** /-ʃn/ n extinção f

**extinguish** /ɪk'stɪŋgwɪʃ/ vt extinguir, apagar. **~er** n extintor m

**extol** /ɪk'stəʊl/ vt (pt extolled) exaltar, elogiar, louvar

**extort** /ɪk'stɔːt/ vt extorquir (from a). **~ion** /-ʃn/ n extorsão f

**extortionate** /ɪk'stɔːʃənət/ a exorbitante

**extra** /'ekstrə/ a extra, adicional □ adv extra, excepcionalmente. **~ strong** extra-forte □ n extra m; (cine, theat) extra mf, figurante mf. **~ time** (football) prorrogação f

**extra-** /'ekstrə/ pref extra-

**extract**[1] /ɪk'strækt/ vt extrair; (promise, tooth) arrancar; (fig) obter. **~ion** /-ʃn/ n extracção f, (P) extracção f; (descent) origem f

**extract**[2] /'ekstrækt/ n extrato m, (P) extracto m

**extradit|e** /'ekstrədaɪt/ vt extraditar. **~ion** /-'dɪʃn/ n extradição f

**extramarital** /ekstrə'mærɪtl/ a extraconjugal, extramatrimonial

**extraordinary** /ɪk'strɔːdnrɪ/ a extraordinário

**extravagan|t** /ɪk'strævəgənt/ a extravagante; (*wasteful*) esbanjador. ~ce n extravagância f; (*wastefulness*) esbanjamento m

**extrem|e** /ɪk'striːm/ a & n extremo (m). ~ely adv extremamente. ~ist n extremista mf

**extremity** /ɪk'stremətɪ/ n extremidade f

**extricate** /'ekstrɪkeɪt/ vt desembaraçar, livrar

**extrovert** /'ekstrəvɜːt/ n extrovertido m

**exuberan|t** /ɪg'zjuːbərənt/ a exuberante. ~ce n exuberância f

**exude** /ɪg'zjuːd/ vt (*charm etc*) destilar, ressumar, (P) transpirar

**exult** /ɪg'zʌlt/ vi exultar

**eye** /aɪ/ n olho m □ vt (pt eyed, pres p eyeing) olhar. keep an ~ on vigiar. see ~ to ~ concordar inteiramente. ~-opener n revelação f. ~-shadow n sombra f

**eyeball** /'aɪbɔːl/ n globo m ocular

**eyebrow** /'aɪbraʊ/ n sobrancelha f

**eyelash** /'aɪlæʃ/ n pestana f

**eyelid** /'aɪlɪd/ n pálpebra f

**eyesight** /'aɪsaɪt/ n vista f

**eyesore** /'aɪsɔː(r)/ n monstruosidade f, horror m

**eyewitness** /'aɪwɪtnɪs/ n testemunha f ocular

# F

**fable** /'feɪbl/ n fábula f

**fabric** /'fæbrɪk/ n tecido m; (*structure*) edifício m

**fabricat|e** /'fæbrɪkeɪt/ vt fabricar; (*invent*) urdir, inventar. ~ion /-'keɪʃn/ n fabrico m; (*invention*) invenção f

**fabulous** /'fæbjʊləs/ a fabuloso

**façade** /fə'saːd/ n fachada f

**face** /feɪs/ n face f, cara f, rosto m; (*expression*) face f; (*grimace*) careta f; (*of clock*) mostrador m □ vt (*look towards*) encarar; (*confront*) enfrentar □ vi (*be opposite*) estar de frente para. ~ up to enfrentar. ~ to face cara a cara, frente a frente. in the ~ of em vista de. on the ~ of it a julgar pelas aparências. pull ~s fazer caretas. ~-cloth n toalha f de rosto, (P) toalhete m de rosto. ~-lift n cirurgia f plástica do rosto. ~-pack n máscara de beleza f

**faceless** /'feɪslɪs/ a (*fig*) anônimo, (P) anónimo

**facet** /'fæsɪt/ n faceta f

**facetious** /fə'siːʃəs/ a faceto; (*pej*) engraçadinho (*colloq pej*)

**facial** /'feɪʃl/ a facial

**facile** /'fæsaɪl/ a fácil; (*superficial*) superficial

**facilitate** /fə'sɪlɪteɪt/ vt facilitar

**facilit|y** /fə'sɪlətɪ/ n facilidade f. ~ies (*means*) facilidades fpl; (*installations*) instalações fpl

**facing** /'feɪsɪŋ/ n revestimento m

**facsimile** /fæk'sɪməlɪ/ n fac-símile m

**fact** /fækt/ n fato m, (P) facto m. in ~, as a matter of ~ na realidade

**faction** /'fækʃn/ n facção f

**factor** /'fæktə(r)/ n fator m, (P) factor m

**factory** /'fæktərɪ/ n fábrica f

**factual** /'fæktʃʊəl/ a concreto, real

**faculty** /'fækltɪ/ n faculdade f

**fad** /fæd/ n capricho m, mania f, (*craze*) moda f

**fade** /feɪd/ vt/i (*colour*) desbotar; (*sound*) diminuir; (*disappear*) apagar(-se)

**fag** /fæg/ n (*colloq: chore*) estafa f; (*sl: cigarette*) cigarro m. ~ged a estafado

**fail** /feɪl/ vt/i falhar; (*in an examination*) reprovar; (*omit, neglect*) deixar de; (*comm*) falir □ n without ~ sem falta

**failing** /'feɪlɪŋ/ n deficiência f □ prep na falta de, à falta de

**failure** /'feɪljə(r)/ n fracasso m, (P) falhanço m; (*of engine*) falha f; (*of electricity*) falta f; (*person*) fracassado m.

**faint** /feɪnt/ a (-er, -est) (*indistinct*) apagado; (*weak*) fraco; (*giddy*) tonto □ vi desmaiar □ n desmaio m. ~-hearted a tímido. ~ly adv vagamente. ~ness n debilidade f; (*indistinctness*) apagado m

**fair¹** /feə(r)/ n feira f. ~-ground n parque m de diversões, (P) largo m de feira

**fair²** /feə(r)/ a (-er, -est) (*of hair*) louro; (*weather*) bom; (*moderate quality*) razoável; (*just*) justo. ~ play jogo m limpo, fair-play m. ~ly adv razoavelmente. ~ness n justiça f

**fairy** /'feərɪ/ n fada f. ~ story, ~ tale conto m de fadas

**faith** /feɪθ/ n fé f; (*religion*) religião f; (*loyalty*) lealdade f. in good ~ de boa fé, (P) à boa fé. ~-healer n curandeiro m

**faithful** /'feɪθfl/ a fiel. ~ly adv fielmente. yours ~ly atenciosamente. ~ness n fidelidade f

**fake** /feɪk/ n (*thing*) imitação f; (*person*) impostor m □ a falsificado □ vt falsificar; (*pretend*) simular, fingir

**falcon** /'fɔːlkən/ n falcão m

**fall** /fɔːl/ vi (pt fell, pp fallen) cair □ n quedas f; (*Amer: autumn*) outono m.

~s *npl* (*waterfall*) queda-d'água *f*. ~ **back** bater em retirada. ~ **back on** recorrer a. ~ **behind** atrasar-se (with em). ~ **down** *or* **off** cair. ~ **flat** falhar, não resultar. ~ **flat on one's face** estatelar-se. ~ **for** (*a trick*) cair em, deixar-se levar por; (*colloq: a person*) apaixonar-se por, ficar caído por (*colloq*). ~ **in** (*roof*) ruir; (*mil*) alinhar-se, pôr-se em forma. ~ **out** brigar, (*P*) zangar-se (with com). ~**out** *n* poeira *f* radioactiva, (*P*) radioactiva. ~ **through** (*of plans*) falhar

**fallac|y** /'fæləsɪ/ *n* falácia *f*, engano *m*. ~**ious** /fə'leɪʃəs/ *a* errôneo

**fallen** /'fɔːlən/ *see* **fall**

**fallible** /'fæləbl/ *a* falível

**fallow** /'fæləʊ/ *a* (*of ground*) de pousio; (*uncultivated*) inculto

**false** /fɔːls/ *a* falso. ~ **teeth**. ~**ly** *adv* falsamente. ~**ness** *n* falsidade *f*

**falsehood** /'fɔːlshʊd/ *n* falsidade *f*, mentira *f*

**falsify** /'fɔːlsɪfaɪ/ *vt* (*pt* **-fied**) falsificar; (*a story*) deturpar

**falter** /'fɔːltə(r)/ *vi* vacilar; (*of the voice*) hesitar

**fame** /feɪm/ *n* fama *f*. ~**d** *a* afamado

**familiar** /fə'mɪlɪə(r)/ *a* familiar; (*intimate*) íntimo. **be** ~ **with** estar familiarizado com

**familiarity** /fəmɪlɪ'ærɪtɪ/ *n* familiaridade *f*

**familiarize** /fə'mɪlɪəraɪz/ *vt* familiarizar (**with/to** com); (*make well known*) tornar conhecido

**family** /'fæməlɪ/ *n* família *f*. ~ **doctor** médico *m* da família. ~ **tree** árvore *f* genealógica

**famine** /'fæmɪn/ *n* fome *f*

**famished** /'fæmɪʃt/ *a* esfomeado, faminto. **be** ~ (*colloq*) estar morrendo de fome, (*P*) estar a morrer de fome

**famous** /'feɪməs/ *a* famoso

**fan**[1] /fæn/ *n* (*in the hand*) leque *m*; (*mechanical*) ventilador *m*, (*P*) ventoínha *f* □ *vt* (*pt* **fanned**) abanar; (*a fire; fig*) atiçar □ *vi* ~ **out** abrir-se em leque. ~ **belt** correia *f* da ventoínhas

**fan**[2] /fæn/ *n* (*colloq*) fã *mf*. ~ **mail** correio *m* de fãs

**fanatic** /fə'nætɪk/ *n* fanático *m*. ~**al** *a* fanático. ~**ism** /-sɪzəm/ *n* fanatismo *m*

**fanciful** /'fænsɪfl/ *a* fantasioso, fantasista

**fancy** /'fænsɪ/ *n* fantasia *f*; (*liking*) gosto *m* □ *a* extravagante, fantástico; (*of buttons etc*) de fantasia; (*of prices*) exorbitante □ *vt* imaginar; (*colloq: like*) gostar de; (*colloq: want*) apetecer. **it took my** ~ gostei disso,

(*P*) deu-me no gosto. **a passing** ~ um entusiasmo passageiro. ~ **dress** traje *m* fantasia, (*P*) trajo *m* de fantasia

**fanfare** /'fænfeə(r)/ *n* fanfarra *f*

**fang** /fæŋ/ *n* presa *f*, dente *m* canino

**fantastic** /fæn'tæstɪk/ *a* fantástico

**fantas|y** /'fæntəsɪ/ *n* fantasia *f*. ~**ize** *vt* fantasiar, imaginar

**far** /fɑː(r)/ *adv* longe; (*much, very*) muito □ *a* distante, longínquo; (*end, side*) outro. ~ **away**, ~ **off** ao longe. **as** ~ **as** (*up to*) até. **as** ~ **as I know** tanto quanto saiba. **the F**~ **East** o Extremo-Oriente *m*. ~**-away** *a* distante, longínquo. ~**-fetched** *a* forçado; (*unconvincing*) pouco plausível. ~**-reaching** *a* de grande alcance

**farc|e** /fɑːs/ *n* farsa *f*. ~**ical** *a* de farsa; ridículo

**fare** /feə(r)/ *n* preço *m* da passagem; (*in taxi*) tarifa *f*, preço *m* da corrida; (*passenger*) passageiro *m*; (*food*) comida *f* □ *vi* (*get on*) dar-se

**farewell** /feə'wel/ *int* & *n* adeus (*m*)

**farm** /fɑːm/ *n* quinta *f*, fazenda *f* □ *vt* cultivar □ *vi* ser fazendeiro, (*P*) lavrador. ~ **out** (*of work*) delegar a tarefeiros. ~**-hand** *n* trabalhador *m* rural. ~**er** *n* fazendeiro *m*, (*P*) lavrador *m*. ~**ing** *n* agricultura *f*, lavoura *f*

**farmhouse** /'fɑːmhaʊs/ *n* casa *f* da fazenda, (*P*) quinta

**farmyard** /'fɑːmjɑːd/ *n* quintal de fazenda *m*, (*P*) pátio *m* de quinta

**farth|er** /'fɑːðə(r)/ *adv* mais longe □ *a* mais distante. ~**est** *adv* mais longe □ *a* o mais distante

**fascinat|e** /'fæsɪneɪt/ *vt* fascinar. ~**ion** /-'neɪʃn/ *n* fascínio *m*, fascinação *f*

**fascis|t** /'fæʃɪst/ *n* fascista *mf*. ~**m** /-zəm/ *n* fascismo *m*

**fashion** /'fæʃn/ *n* moda *f*; (*manner*) maneira *f* □ *vt* amoldar, (*P*) moldar. ~**able** *a* na moda, (*P*) à moda. ~**ably** *adv* na moda, (*P*) à moda

**fast**[1] /fɑːst/ *a* (**-er, -est**) rápido; (*colour*) fixo, que não desbota □ *adv* depressa; (*firmly*) firmemente. **be** ~ (*of clock*) adiantar-se, estar adiantado. ~ **asleep** profundamente adormecido, ferrado no sono. ~ **food** *n* fast-food *f*

**fast**[2] /fɑːst/ *vi* jejuar □ *n* jejum *m*

**fasten** /'fɑːsn/ *vt/i* prender; (*door, window*) fechar(-se); (*seat-belt*) apertar. ~**er**, ~**ing** *ns* fecho *m*

**fastidious** /fə'stɪdɪəs/ *a* exigente

**fat** /fæt/ *n* gordura *f* □ *a* (**fatter, fattest**) gordo. ~**ness** *n* gordura *f*

**fatal** /'feɪtl/ *a* fatal. ~ **injuries** ferimentos *mpl* mortais. ~**ity** /fə'tælətɪ/ *n* fatalidade *f*. ~**ly** *adv* fatalmente, mortalmente

**fate** /feɪt/ *n* (*destiny*) destino *m*; (*one's lot*) destino *m*, sorte *f*. ~**ful** *a* fatídico

**fated** /'feɪtɪd/ *a* predestinado; (*doomed*) condenado (**to, a**)

**father** /'fɑːðə(r)/ *n* pai *m* □ *vt* gerar. ~**-in-law** *n* (*pl* ~**s-in-law**) sogro *m*. ~**ly** *a* paternal

**fathom** /'fæðəm/ *n* braça *f* □ *vt* ~ (**out**) (*comprehend*) compreender

**fatigue** /fə'tiːɡ/ *n* fadiga *f* □ *vt* fatigar

**fatten** /'fætn/ *vt/i* engordar. ~**ing** *a* que engorda

**fatty** /'fætɪ/ *a* (**-ier, -iest**) gorduroso; (*tissue*) adiposo

**fault** /fɔːlt/ *n* defeito *m*, falha *f*; (*blame*) falta *f*, culpa *f*; (*geol*) falha *f*. **at** ~ culpado. **it's your** ~ é culpa sua. ~**less** *a* impecável. ~**y** *a* defeituoso

**favour** /'feɪvə(r)/ *n* favor *m* □ *vt* favorecer; (*prefer*) preferir. **do sb a** ~ fazer um favor a alg. ~**able** *a* favorável. ~**ably** *adv* favoravelmente

**favourit|e** /'feɪvərɪt/ *a* & *n* favorito (*m*). ~**ism** /-ɪzəm/ *n* favoritismo *m*

**fawn**[1] /fɔːn/ *n* cervo *m* novo □ *a* (*colour*) castanho claro

**fawn**[2] /fɔːn/ *vi* ~ **on** adular, bajular

**fax** /fæks/ *n* fax *m*, fac-símile *m* □ *vt* mandar um fax. ~ **machine** fax *m*

**fear** /fɪə(r)/ *n* medo *m*, receio *m*, temor *m*; (*likelihood*) perigo *m* □ *vt* recear, ter medo de. **for** ~ **of/that** com medo de/que. ~**ful** *a* (*terrible*) medonho; (*timid*) medroso, receoso. ~**less** *a* destemido, intrépido

**feasib|le** /'fiːzəbl/ *a* factível, praticável; (*likely*) plausível. ~**ility** /-'bɪlətɪ/ *n* possibilidade *f*; (*plausibility*) plausibilidade *f*

**feast** /fiːst/ *n* festim *m*; (*relig; fig*) festa *f* □ *vt/i* festejar; (*eat and drink*) banquetear-se. ~ **on** regalar-se com

**feat** /fiːt/ *n* feito *m*, façanha *f*

**feather** /'feðə(r)/ *n* pena *f*, pluma *f*

**feature** /'fiːtʃə(r)/ *n* feição *f*, traço *m*; (*quality*) característica *f*; (*film*) longa metragem *f*, (*article*) artigo *m* em destaque □ *vt* representar; (*film*) ter como protagonista □ *vi* figurar

**February** /'februərɪ/ *n* Fevereiro *m*

**fed** /fed/ *see* **feed** □ *a* **be** ~ **up** estar farto (*colloq*) (**with** de)

**federa|l** /'fedərəl/ *a* federal. ~**tion** /-'reɪʃn/ *n* federação *f*

**fee** /fiː/ *n* preço *m*. ~**(s)** (*of doctor, lawyer etc*) honorários *mpl*; (*member's subscription*) quota *f*; (*univ*) (*P*) propinas *fpl*. (errolment/registration) matrícula *f* **school** ~**s** mensalidades *fpl* escolares, (*P*) mensalidades *fpl*

**feeble** /'fiːbl/ *a* (**-er, -est**) débil, fraco. ~**-minded** *a* débil mental, (*P*) deficiente

**feed** /fiːd/ *vt* (*pt* **fed**) alimentar, dar de comer a; (*suckle*) alimentar; (*supply*) alimentar, abostecer □ *vi* alimentar-se □ *n* comida *f*; (*breast-feeding*) mamada *f*; (*mech*) alimentação *f*

**feedback** /'fiːdbæk/ *n* reação *f*, (*P*) reacção *f*; (*electr*) regeneração *f*

**feel** /fiːl/ *vt* (*pt* **felt**) sentir; (*touch*) apalpar, tatear □ *vi* (*tired, lonely etc*) sentir-se. ~ **hot/thirsty** ter calor/sede. ~ **as if** ter a impressão (de) que. ~ **like** ter vontade de

**feeler** /'fiːlə(r)/ *n* antena *f*

**feeling** /'fiːlɪŋ/ *n* sentimento *m*; (*physical*) sensação *f*

**feet** /fiːt/ *see* **foot**

**feign** /feɪn/ *vt* fingir

**feline** /'fiːlaɪn/ *a* felino

**fell**[1] /fel/ *vt* abater, derrubar

**fell**[2] /fel/ *see* **fall**

**fellow** /'feləʊ/ *n* companheiro *m*, camarada *m*; (*of society, college*) membro *m*; (*colloq*) cara *m*, (*P*) tipo *m* (*colloq*). ~**-traveller** *n* companheiro *m* de viagem. ~**-ship** *n* companheirismo *m*, camaradagem *f*; (*group*) associação *f*

**felt**[1] /felt/ *n* feltro *m*

**felt**[2] /felt/ *see* **feel**

**female** /'fiːmeɪl/ *a* (*animal etc*) fêmea *f*; (*voice, sex etc*) feminino □ *n* mulher *f*; (*animal*) fêmea *f*

**feminin|e** /'femənɪn/ *a* & *n* feminino (*m*). ~**ity** /-'nɪnətɪ/ *n* feminilidade *f*

**feminist** /'femɪnɪst/ *n* feminista *mf*

**fenc|e** /fens/ *n* tapume *m*, cerca *f* □ *vt* cercar □ *vi* esgrimir. ~**er** *n* esgrimista *mf*. ~**ing** *n* esgrima *f*; (*fences*) tapume *m*

**fend** /fend/ *vi* ~ **for o.s.** defender-se, virar-se (*colloq*), governar-se □ *vt* ~ **off** defender-se de

**fender** /'fendə(r)/ *n* guarda-fogo *m*; (*Amer: mudguard*) pára-lama *m*, guarda-lama *m*, (*P*) pára-choques *m*

**fennel** /'fenl/ *n* (*herb*) funcho *m*, erva-doce *f*

**ferment**[1] /fə'ment/ *vt/i* fermentar; (*excite*) excitar. ~**ation** /fɜːmen-'teɪʃn/ *n* fermentação *f*

**ferment**[2] /'fɜːment/ *n* fermento *m*; (*fig*) efervescência *f*

**fern** /fɜːn/ *n* feto *m*

**feroc|ious** /fə'rəʊʃəs/ *a* feroz. ~**ity** /-'rɒsətɪ/ *n* ferocidade *f*

**ferret** /'ferɪt/ *n* furão *m* □ *vi* (*pt* **ferreted**) caçar com furões □ *vt* ~ **out** desenterrar

**ferry** /'ferɪ/ *n* barco *m* de travessia, ferry(-boat) *m* □ *vt* transportar

**fertil|e** /'fɜːtaɪl/ *a* fértil, fecundo. ~**ity** /fə'tɪlətɪ/ *n* fertilidade *f*, fecundidade *f*. ~**ize** /-əlaɪz/ *vt* fertilizar, fecundar

**fertilizer** /'fɜːtəlaɪzə(r)/ *n* adubo *m*, fertilizante *m*

**fervent** /'fɜ:vənt/ a fervoroso

**fervour** /'fɜ:və(r)/ n fervor m, ardor m

**fester** /'festə(r)/ vt/i infectar; ( fig) envenenar

**festival** /'festɪvl/ n festival m; (relig) festa f

**festiv|e** /'festɪv/ a festivo. ~e season período m das festas. ~ity /fes'tɪvətɪ/ n festividade f, regozijo m. ~ities festas fpl, festividades fpl

**festoon** /fe'stu:n/ vt engrinaldar

**fetch** /fetʃ/ vt (go for) ir buscar; (bring) trazer; (be sold for) vender-se por, render

**fetching** /'fetʃɪŋ/ a atraente

**fête** /feɪt/ n festa f or feira f de caridade ao ar livre □ vt festejar

**fetish** /'fetɪʃ/ n fetiche m, ídolo m; (obsession) mania f

**fetter** /'fetə(r)/ vt agrilhoar. ~s npl ferros mpl, grilhões mpl, grilhetas fpl

**feud** /fju:d/ n discórdia f, inimizade f. ~al a feudal

**fever** /'fi:və(r)/ n febre f. ~ish a febril

**few** /fju:/ a & n poucos (mpl). ~ books poucos livros. they are ~ são poucos. a ~ a & n alguns (mpl). a good ~, quite a ~ bastantes. ~er a & n menos (de). they were ~er eram menos numerosos. ~est a & n o menor número (de)

**fiancé** /fɪ'ɑnseɪ/ n noivo m. ~e n noiva f

**fiasco** /fɪ'æskəʊ/ n (pl -os) fiasco m

**fib** /fɪb/ n lorota f, cascata f, peta f, (P) mentira f □ vi (pt fibbed)

**fibre** /'faɪbə(r)/ n fibra f

**fibreglass** /'faɪbəglɑ:s/ n fibra f de vidro

**fickle** /'fɪkl/ a leviano, inconstante

**fiction** /'fɪkʃn/ n ficção f. (works of) ~ romances mpl, obras fpl de ficção. ~al a de ficção, fictício

**fictitious** /fɪk'tɪʃəs/ a fictício

**fiddle** /'fɪdl/ n (colloq) violino m; (sl: swindle) trapaça f □ vi (sl) trapacear (sl) □ vt (sl: falsify) falsificar, cozinhar (sl). ~ with (colloq) brincar com, remexer em, (P) estar a brincar com, estar a (re)mexer em. ~r /-ə(r)/ n (colloq) violinista m/f

**fidelity** /fɪ'delətɪ/ n fidelidade f

**fidget** /'fɪdʒɪt/ vi (pt fidgeted) estar irrequieto, remexer-se. ~ with remexer em. ~y a irrequieto; (impatient) impaciente

**field** /fi:ld/ n campo m □ vt/i (cricket) (estar pronto para) apanhar ou interceptar a bola. ~-day n grande dia m. ~-glasses npl binóculo m. F~ Marshal marechal-de-campo m

**fieldwork** /'fi:ldwɜːk/ n trabalho m de campo; (mil) fortificação f de campanha

**fiend** /fi:nd/ n diabo m, demônio m, (P) demónio m. ~ish a diabólico

**fierce** /fɪəs/ a (-er, -est) feroz; (storm, attack) violento; (heat) intenso, abrasador. ~ness n ferocidade f; (of storm, attack) violência f; (of heat) intensidade f

**fiery** /'faɪərɪ/ a (-ier, -iest) ardente; (temper, speech) inflamado

**fifteen** /fɪf'ti:n/ a & n quinze (m). ~th a & n décimo quinto (m)

**fifth** /fɪfθ/ a & n quinto (m)

**fift|y** /'fɪftɪ/ a & n cinqüenta (m), (P) cinquenta (m). ~y-~y a meias. ~ieth a & n qüinquagésimo (m), (P) quinquagésimo (m)

**fig** /fɪg/ n figo m. ~-tree n figueira f

**fight** /faɪt/ vi (pt fought) lutar, combater □ vt lutar contra, combater □ n luta f; (quarrel, brawl) briga f. ~ over sth lutar por alg coisa. ~ shy of esquivar-se de, fugir de. ~er n lutador m; (mil) combatente m/f; (plane) caça m. ~ing n combate m

**figment** /'fɪgmənt/ n ~ of the imagination fruto m or produto m da imaginação

**figurative** /'fɪgjərətɪv/ a figurado. ~ly adv em sentido figurado

**figure** /'fɪgə(r)/ n (number) algarismo m; (diagram, body) figura f. ~s npl (arithmetic) contas fpl, aritmética f □ vt imaginar, supor □ vi (appear) figurar (in em). ~ of speech figura f de retórica. ~ out compreender. ~-head n figura f de proa; (pej: person) testa-de-ferro m, chefe m nominal

**filament** /'fɪləmənt/ n filamento m

**fil|e¹** /faɪl/ n (tool) lixa f, lima f □ vt lixar, limar. ~ings npl limalha f

**fil|e²** /faɪl/ n fichário m, (P) dossier m; (box, drawer) fichário m, (P) ficheiro m; (comput) arquivo m (line) fila f □ vt arquivar □ vi ~e (past) desfilar, marchar em fila. ~e in/out entrar/sair em fila. (in) single ~e (em) fila indiana. ~ing cabinet fichário m, (P) ficheiro m

**fill** /fɪl/ vt/i encher(-se); (vacancy) preencher □ n eat one's ~ comer o que quiser. have one's ~ estar farto. ~ in (form) preencher. ~ out (get fat) engordar. ~ up encher até cima; (auto) encher o tanque

**fillet** /'fɪlɪt/ n (meat, fish) filé m, (P) filete m □ vt (pt filleted) (meat, fish) cortar em filés, (P) filetes

**filling** /'fɪlɪŋ/ n recheio m; (of tooth) obturação f, (P) chumbo m. ~ station posto m de gasolina

**film** /fɪlm/ n filme m □ vt/i filmar. ~ star estrela f or vedete f or (P) vedeta f de cinema, astro m

**filter** /'fɪltə(r)/ n filtro m □ vt/i filtrar

(-se). ~ **coffee** café *m* filtro. ~-**tip** *n* cigarro *m* com filtro

**filth** /fɪlθ/ *n* imundície *f*; (*fig*) obscenidade *f*. ~**y** *a* imundo; (*fig*) obsceno

**fin** /fɪn/ *n* barbatana *f*

**final** /'faɪnl/ *a* final; (*conclusive*) decisivo □ *n* (*sport*) final *f*. ~**s** *npl* (*exams*) finais *fpl*. ~**ist** *n* finalista *mf*. ~**ly** *adv* finalmente, por fim; (*once and for all*) definitivamente

**finale** /fɪ'nɑːlɪ/ *n* final *m*

**finalize** /'faɪnəlaɪz/ *vt* finalizar

**financ|e** /'faɪnæns/ *n* finança(s) *f* (*pl*) □ *a* financeiro □ *vt* financiar. ~**ier** /-'nænsɪə(r)/ *n* financeiro *m*

**financial** /faɪ'nænʃl/ *a* financeiro. ~**ly** *adv* financeiramente

**find** /faɪnd/ *vt* (*pt* **found**) (*sth lost*) achar, encontrar; (*think*) achar; (*discover*) descobrir; (*jur*) declarar □ *n* achado *m*. ~ **out** *vt* apurar, descobrir □ *vi* informar-se (**about** sobre)

**fine**[1] /faɪn/ *n* multa *f* □ *vt* multar

**fine**[2] /faɪn/ *a* (**-er, -est**) fino; (*splendid*) belo, lindo □ *adv* (muito) bem; (*small*) fino, fininho. ~ **arts** belas artes *fpl*. ~ **weather** bom tempo. ~**ly** *adv* lindamente; (*cut*) fininho, aos bocadinhos

**finesse** /fɪ'nes/ *n* finura *f*, sutileza *f*

**finger** /'fɪŋɡə(r)/ *n* dedo *m* □ *vt* apalpar. ~-**mark** *n* dedada *f*. ~-**nail** *n* unha *f*

**fingerprint** /'fɪŋɡəprɪnt/ *n* impressão *f* digital

**fingertip** /'fɪŋɡətɪp/ *n* ponta *f* do dedo

**finicky** /'fɪnɪkɪ/ *a* meticuloso, miudinho

**finish** /'fɪnɪʃ/ *vt/i* acabar, terminar □ *n* fim *m*; (*of race*) chegada *f*; (*on wood, clothes*) acabamento *m*. ~ **doing** acabar de fazer. ~ **up doing** acabar por fazer. ~ **up in** ir parar a, acabar em

**finite** /'faɪnaɪt/ *a* finito

**Fin|land** /'fɪnlənd/ *n* Finlândia *f*. ~**n** *n* finlandês *m*. ~**nish** *a* & *n* (*lang*) finlandês (*m*)

**fir** /fɜː(r)/ *n* abeto *m*

**fire** /'faɪə(r)/ *n* fogo *m*; (*conflagration*) incêndio *m*; (*heater*) aquecedor *m* □ *vt* (*bullet, gun, etc*) disparar; (*dismiss*) despedir; (*fig: stimulate*) inflamar □ *vi* atirar, fazer fogo (**at** sobre). **on ~** em chamas. **set ~ to** pôr fogo em. ~-**alarm** *n* alarme *m* de incêndio. ~-**brigade** bombeiros *mpl*. ~-**engine** *n* carro *m* de bombeiro, (*P*) da bomba. ~-**escape** *n* saída *f* de incêndio. ~ **extinguisher** *n* extintor *m* de incêndio. ~ **station** quartel *m* dos bombeiros

**firearm** /'faɪərɑːm/ *n* arma *f* de fogo

**fireman** /'faɪəmən/ *n* (*pl* -**men**) bombeiro *m*

**fireplace** /'faɪəpleɪs/ *n* chaminé *f*, lareira *f*

**firewood** /'faɪəwʊd/ *n* lenha *f*

**firework** /'faɪəwɜːk/ *n* fogo *m* de artifício

**firing-squad** /'faɪərɪŋskwɒd/ *n* pelotão *m* de execução

**firm**[1] /fɜːm/ *n* firma *f* comercial

**firm**[2] /fɜːm/ *a* (**-er, -est**) firme; (*belief*) firme, inabalável. ~**ly** *adv* firmemente. ~**ness** *n* firmeza *f*

**first** /fɜːst/ *a* & *n* primeiro (*m*); (*auto*) primeira (*f*) □ *adv* primeiro, em primeiro lugar. **at ~** a princípio, no início. ~ **of all** antes de mais nada. **for the ~ time** pela primeira vez. ~ **aid** primeiros socorros *mpl*. ~-**class** *a* de primeira classe. ~ **name** nome de batismo *m*, (*P*) baptismo *m*. ~-**rate** *a* excelente. ~**ly** *adv* primeiramente, em primeiro lugar

**fiscal** /'fɪskl/ *a* fiscal

**fish** /fɪʃ/ *n* (*pl usually invar*) peixe *m* □ *vt/i* pescar. ~ **out** (*colloq*) tirar. ~**ing** *n* pesca *f*. **go** ~**ing** ir pescar, (*P*) ir à pesca. ~**ing-rod** *n* vara *f* de pescar. ~**y** *a* de peixe; (*fig: dubious*) suspeito

**fisherman** /'fɪʃəmən/ *n* (*pl* -**men**) pescador *m*

**fishmonger** /'fɪʃmʌŋɡə(r)/ *n* dono *m*/empregado *m* de peixaria. ~**'s (shop)** peixaria *f*

**fission** /'fɪʃn/ *n* fissão *f*, cisão *f*

**fist** /fɪst/ *n* punho *m*, mão *f* fechada, (*P*) punho *m*

**fit**[1] /fɪt/ *n* acesso *m*, ataque *m*; (*of generosity*) rasgo *m*

**fit**[2] /fɪt/ *a* (**fitter, fittest**) de boa saúde, em forma; (*proper*) próprio; (*good enough*) em condições; (*able*) capaz □ *vt/i* (*pt* **fitted**) (*clothes*) assentar, ficar bem (a); (*into space*) (*match*) ajustar (-se) (a); (*install*) instalar □ *n* **be a good ~** assentar bem. **be a tight ~** estar justo. ~ **out** equipar. ~-**ted carpet** carpete *m*, (*P*) alcatifa *f*. ~-**ness** *n* saúde *f*, (*P*) condição *f* física

**fitful** /'fɪtfl/ *a* intermitente

**fitment** /'fɪtmənt/ *n* móvel *m* de parede

**fitting** /'fɪtɪŋ/ *a* apropriado □ *n* (*clothes*) prova *f*. ~**s** (*fixtures*) instalações *fpl*; (*fitments*) mobiliário *m*. ~ **room** cabine *f*

**five** /faɪv/ *a* & *n* cinco *m*

**fix** /fɪks/ *vt* fixar; (*mend, prepare*) arranjar □ *n* **in a** ~ em apuros, (*P*) numa alhada. ~ **sb up with sth** conseguir alg coisa para alguém. ~**ed** *a* fixo

**fixation** /fɪk'seɪʃn/ *n* fixação *f*; (*obsession*) obsessão *f*

**fixture** /'fɪkstʃə(r)/ *n* equipamento *m*,

instalação f; (sport) (data f marcada para) competição f

**fizz** /fɪz/ vi efervescer, borbulhar □ n efervescência f. ~y a gasoso

**fizzle** /'fɪzl/ vi ~ out (plan etc) acabar em nada or (P) em águas de bacalhau (colloq)

**flab** /flæb/ n (colloq) gordura f, banha f (colloq). ~by a flácido

**flabbergasted** /'flæbəgɑːstɪd/ a (colloq) espantado, pasmado (colloq)

**flag¹** /flæg/ n bandeira f □ vt (pt flagged) fazer sinal. ~ down fazer sinal para parar. ~-pole n mastro m (de bandeira)

**flag²** /flæg/ vi (pt flagged) (droop) cair, pender, tombar; (of person) emorecer

**flagrant** /'fleɪgrənt/ a flagrante

**flagstone** /'flægstəʊn/ n laje f

**flair** /fleə(r)/ n jeito m, habilidade f

**flak|e** /fleɪk/ n floco m; (paint) lasca f □ vi descamar-se, lascar-se. ~y a (paint) descamado, lascado

**flamboyant** /flæm'bɔɪənt/ a flamejante; (showy) flamante, vistoso; (of manner) extravagante

**flame** /fleɪm/ n chama f, labareda f □ vi flamejar. **burst into** ~s incendiar-se

**flamingo** /flə'mɪŋgəʊ/ n (pl -os) flamingo m

**flammable** /'flæməbl/ a inflamável

**flan** /flæn/ n torta f, (P) tarte f

**flank** /flæŋk/ n flanco m □ vt flanquear

**flannel** /'flænl/ n flanela f; (for face) toalha f, (P) toalhete m de rosto

**flap** /flæp/ vi (pt flapped) bater □ vt ~ its wings bater as asas □ n (of table, pocket) aba f; (sl: panic) pânico m

**flare** /fleə(r)/ vi ~ up irromper em chamas; (of war) rebentar; (fig: of person) enfurecer-se □ n chamejar m; (dazzling light) clarão m; (signal) foguete m de sinalização. ~d a (skirt) evasé

**flash** /flæʃ/ vi brilhar subitamente; (on and off) piscar; (auto) fazer sinal com o pisca-pisca □ vt fazer brilhar; (send) lançar, dardejar; (flaunt) fazer alarde de, ostentar □ n clarão m, lampejo m; (photo) flash m. ~ past passar como uma bala, (P) passar como um bólide

**flashback** /'flæʃbæk/ n cena f retrospectiva, flashback m

**flashlight** /'flæʃlaɪt/ n lanterna f elétrica, (P) eléctrica

**flashy** /'flæʃɪ/ a espalhafatoso, que dá na vista

**flask** /flɑːsk/ n frasco m; (vacuum flask) garrafa f térmica, (P) garrafa f termos

**flat** /flæt/ a (flatter, flattest) plano, chato; (tyre) arriado, vazio; (battery) fraco; (refusal) categórico; (fare, rate) fixo; (monotonous) monótono; (mus) bemol; (out of tune) desafinado □ n apartamento m; (colloq: tyre) furo m no preu; (mus) bemol m. ~ out (drive); (work) a dar tudo por tudo. ~ly adv categoricamente

**flatter** /'flætə(r)/ vt lisonjear, adular. ~er n lisonjeiro m, adulador m. ~ing a lisonjeiro, adulador. ~y n lisonja f

**flatulence** /'flætjʊləns/ n flatulência f

**flaunt** /flɔːnt/ vt/i pavonear(-se), ostentar

**flavour** /'fleɪvə(r)/ n sabor m (of a) □ vt dar sabor a, temperar. ~ing n aroma m sintético; (seasoning) tempero m

**flaw** /flɔː/ n falha f, imperfeição f. ~ed a imperfeito. ~less a perfeito

**flea** /fliː/ n pulga f

**fled** /fled/ see flee

**fledged** /fledʒd/ a fully-~ (fig) treinado, experiente

**flee** /fliː/ vi (pt fled) fugir □ vt fugir de

**fleece** /fliːs/ n lã f de carneiro, velo m □ vt (fig) esfolar, roubar

**fleet** /fliːt/ n (of warships) esquadra f; (of merchant ships, vehicles) frota f

**fleeting** /'fliːtɪŋ/ a curto, fugaz

**Flemish** /'flemɪʃ/ a & n (lang) flamengo (m)

**flesh** /fleʃ/ n carne f; (of fruit) polpa f. ~y a carnudo

**flew** /fluː/ see fly²

**flex¹** /fleks/ vt flexionar

**flex²** /fleks/ n (electr) fio f flexível

**flexib|le** /'fleksəbl/ a flexível. ~ility /-'bɪlətɪ/ n flexibilidade f

**flexitime** /'fleksɪtaɪm/ n horário m flexível

**flick** /flɪk/ n (light blow) safanão m; (with fingertip) piparote m □ vt dar um safanão em; (with fingertip) dar um piparote a. ~-knife n navalha f de ponta e mola. ~ through folhear

**flicker** /'flɪkə(r)/ vi vacilar, oscilar, tremular □ n oscilação f, tremular m; (light) luz f oscilante

**flier** /'flaɪə(r)/ n = flyer

**flies** /flaɪz/ npl (of trousers) braguilha f

**flight¹** /flaɪt/ n (flying) voo m. ~ of stairs lance m, (P) lanço m de escada. ~-deck n cabine f, (P) cabina f

**flight²** /flaɪt/ n (fleeing) fuga f. put to ~ pôr em fuga. take ~ pôr-se em fuga

**flimsy** /'flɪmzɪ/ a (-ier, -iest) (material) fino; (object) frágil; (excuse etc) fraco, esfarrapado

**flinch** /flɪntʃ/ vi (wince) retrair-se; (draw back) recuar; (hesitate) hesitar

**fling** /flɪŋ/ vt/i (pt **flung**) atirar(-se), arremessar(-se); (rush) precipitar-se

**flint** /flɪnt/ n sílex m; ( for lighter) pedra f

**flip** /flɪp/ vt (pt **flipped**) fazer girar com o dedo e o polegar □ n pancadinha f. ~ **through** folhear

**flippant** /'flɪpənt/ a irreverente, petulante

**flipper** /'flɪpə(r)/ n (of seal) nadadeira f; (of swimmer) pé-de-pato m

**flirt** /flɜːt/ vt namoriscar, flertar, (P) flartar □ n namorador m, namoradeira f. ~**ation** /-'teɪʃn/ n namorico m, flerte m, (P) flirt m. ~**atious** a namorador m, namoradeira f

**flit** /flɪt/ vi (pt **flitted**) esvoaçar

**float** /fləʊt/ vt/i (fazer) flutuar; (company) lançar □ n bóia f; (low cart) carro m de alegórico

**flock** /flɒk/ n (of sheep; congregation) rebanho m; (of birds) bando m; (crowd) multidão f □ vi afluir, juntar-se

**flog** /flɒg/ vt (pt **flogged**) açoitar; (sl: sell) vender

**flood** /flʌd/ n inundação f, cheia f; (of tears) dilúvio m □ vt inundar, alagar □ vi estar inundado; (river) transbordar; ( fig: people) afluir

**floodlight** /'flʌdlaɪt/ n projetor m, (P) projector m, holofote m □ vt (pt **floodlit**) iluminar

**floor** /flɔː(r)/ n chão m, soalho m; ( for dancing) pista f; (storey) andar m □ vt assoalhar; (baffle) desconcertar, embatucar

**flop** /flɒp/ vi (pt **flopped**) (drop) (deixar-se) cair; (move helplessly) debater-se; (sl: fail) ser um fiasco □ n (sl) fiasco m. ~**py** a mole, tombado. ~**py (disk)** disquete m

**floral** /'flɔːrəl/ a floral

**florid** /'flɒrɪd/ a florido

**florist** /'flɒrɪst/ n florista mf

**flounce** /flaʊns/ n babado m, debrum m

**flounder** /'flaʊndə(r)/ vi esbracejar, debater-se; ( fig) meter os pés pelas mãos

**flour** /'flaʊə(r)/ n farinha f. ~**y** a farinhento

**flourish** /'flʌrɪʃ/ vi florescer, prosperar □ vt brandir □ n floreado m; (movement) gesto m elegante. ~**ing** a próspero

**flout** /flaʊt/ vt escarnecer (de)

**flow** /fləʊ/ vi correr, fluir; (traffic) mover-se; (hang loosely) flutuar; (gush) jorrar □ n corrente f; (of tide; fig) enchente f. ~ **into** (of river) desaguar em. ~ **chart** organograma m, (P) organigrama m

**flower** /'flaʊə(r)/ n flor f □ vi florir, florescer. ~**-bed** n canteiro m. ~**ed** a de flores, (P) florido, às flores. ~**y** a florido

**flown** /fləʊn/ see **fly²**

**flu** /fluː/ n (colloq) gripe f

**fluctuat|e** /'flʌktʃʊeɪt/ vi flutuar, oscilar. ~**ion** /-'eɪʃn/ n flutuação f, oscilação f

**flue** /fluː/ n cano m de chaminé

**fluen|t** /'fluːənt/ a fluente. **be** ~**t (in a language)** falar correntemente (uma língua). ~**cy** n fluência f. ~**tly** adv fluentemente

**fluff** /flʌf/ n cotão m; (down) penugem f □ vt (colloq: bungle) estender-se em (sl), executar mal. ~**y** a penugento, fofo

**fluid** /'fluːɪd/ a & n fluido (m)

**fluke** /fluːk/ n bambúrrio (colloq) m, golpe m de sorte

**flung** /flʌŋ/ see **fling**

**flunk** /flʌŋk/ vt/i (Amer colloq) levar pau (colloq), (P) chumbar (colloq)

**fluorescent** /flʊə'resnt/ a fluorescente

**fluoride** /'flʊəraɪd/ n flúor m, fluor m

**flurry** /'flʌrɪ/ n rajada f, rabanada f, lufada f; ( fig) atrapalhação f, agitação f

**flush¹** /flʌʃ/ vi corar, ruborizar-se □ vt lavar com água, (P) lavar a jorros de água □ n rubor m, vermelhidão f; ( fig) excitação f; (of water) jorro m □ a a ~ **with** ao nível de, rente a. ~ **the toilet** dar descarga

**flush²** /flʌʃ/ vt ~ **out** desalojar

**fluster** /'flʌstə(r)/ vt atarantar, perturbar, enervar

**flute** /fluːt/ n flauta f

**flutter** /'flʌtə(r)/ vi esvoaçar; (wings) bater; (heart) palpitar □ vt bater. ~ **one's eyelashes** pestanejar □ n (of wings) batimento m; ( fig) agitação f

**flux** /flʌks/ n **in a state of** ~ em mudança f contínua

**fly¹** /flaɪ/ n mosca f

**fly²** /flaɪ/ vi (pt **flew**, pp **flown**) voar; (passengers) ir de/viajar de avião; (rush) correr □ vt pilotar; (passengers, goods) transportar por avião; ( flag) hastear, (P) arvorar □ n (of trousers) braguilha f

**flyer** /'flaɪə(r)/ n aviador m; (Amer: circular) prospecto m

**flying** /'flaɪŋ/ a voador. **with** ~ **colours** com grande êxito, esplendidamente. ~ **saucer** disco m voador. ~ **start** bom arranque m. ~ **visit** visita f de médico

**flyleaf** /'flaɪliːf/ n (pl -**leaves**) guarda f, folha f em branco

**flyover** /'flaɪəʊvə(r)/ n viaduto m

**foal** /fəʊl/ n potro m

**foam** /fəʊm/ n espuma f □ vi espumar.
~ **(rubber)** n espuma f de borracha

**fob** /fɒb/ vt (pt **fobbed**) ~ **off** iludir,
entreter com artifícios. ~ **off on** impingir a

**focus** /'fəʊkəs/ n (pl **-cuses** or **-ci**
/-saɪ/) foco m □ vt/i (pt **focused**) focar; (,fig) concentrar(-se). **in** ~ focado, em foco. **out of** ~ desfocado

**fodder** /'fɒdə(r)/ n forragem f

**foetus** /'fiːtəs/ n (pl **-tuses**) feto m

**fog** /fɒg/ n nevoeiro m □ vt/i (pt
**fogged**) enevoar(-se). ~**-horn** n sereia f de nevoeiro. ~**gy** a enevoado,
brumoso. **it is** ~**gy** está nevoento

**foible** /'fɔɪbl/ n fraqueza f, ponto m
fraco

**foil**[1] /fɔɪl/ n papel m de alumínio; (fig)
contraste m

**foil**[2] /fɔɪl/ vt frustrar

**foist** /fɔɪst/ vt impingir (**on** a)

**fold** /fəʊld/ vt/i dobrar(-se); (arms)
cruzar; (colloq: fail) falir □ n dobra f.
~**er** n pasta f; (leaflet) prospecto m
(desdobrável). ~**ing** a dobrável, dobradiço

**foliage** /'fəʊlɪdʒ/ n folhagem f

**folk** /fəʊk/ n povo m. ~**s** (family, people) gente f (colloq) □ a folclórico,
popular. ~**lore** n folclore m

**follow** /'fɒləʊ/ vt/i seguir. **it** ~**s that**
quer dizer que. ~ **suit** (cards) servir
o naipe jogado; (fig) seguir o exemplo, fazer o mesmo. ~ **up** (letter etc)
dar seguimento a. ~**er** n partidário
m, seguidor m. ~**ing** n partidários
mpl □ a seguinte □ prep em seguimento a

**folly** /'fɒlɪ/ n loucura f

**fond** /fɒnd/ a (**-er -est**) carinhoso;
(hope) caro. **be** ~ **of** gostar de, ser
amigo de. ~**ness** n (for people)
afeição f; (for thing) gosto m

**fondle** /'fɒndl/ vt acariciar

**font** /fɒnt/ n pia f batismal, (P) baptismal

**food** /fuːd/ n alimentação f, comida f;
(nutrient) alimento m □ a alimentar.
~ **poisoning** envenenamento m alimentar

**fool** /fuːl/ n idiota mf, parvo m □ vt
enganar □ vi ~ **around** andar sem
fazer nada

**foolhardy** /'fuːlhaːdɪ/ a imprudente,
atrevido

**foolish** /'fuːlɪʃ/ a idiota, parvo. ~**ly**
adv parvamente. ~**ness** n idiotice f,
parvoíce f

**foolproof** /'fuːlpruːf/ a infalível

**foot** /fʊt/ n (pl **feet**) (of person, bed,
stairs) pé m; (of animal) pata f;
(measure) pé m (= 30,48 cm) □ vt ~
**the bill** pagar a conta. **on** ~ a pé. **on**
or **to one's feet** de pé. **put one's** ~

**in it** fazer uma gafe. **to be under sb's
feet** atrapalhar alg. ~**-bridge** n passarela f

**football** /'fʊtbɔːl/ n bola f de futebol;
(game) futebol m. ~ **pools** loteria f
esportiva, (P) totobola m. ~**er** n futebolista mf, jogador m de futebol

**foothills** /'fʊthɪlz/ npl contrafortes
mpl

**foothold** /'fʊthəʊld/ n ponto m de
apoio

**footing** /'fʊtɪŋ/ n: **firm** ~ stor. **on an
equal** ~ em pé de igualdade

**footlights** /'fʊtlaɪts/ npl ribalta f

**footnote** /'fʊtnəʊt/ n nota f de rodapé

**footpath** /'fʊtpaːθ/ n (pavement) calçada f, (P) passeio m; (in open country) atalho m, caminho m

**footprint** /'fʊtprɪnt/ n pegada f

**footstep** /'fʊtstep/ n passo m

**footwear** /'fʊtweə(r)/ n calçado m

**for** /fə(r)/; emphatic /fɔː(r)/ prep para;
(in favour of; in place of ) por; (during) durante □ conj porque, visto
que. **a liking** ~ gosto por. **he has
been away** ~ **two years** há dois anos
que ele está fora. ~ **ever** para sempre

**forage** /'fɒrɪdʒ/ vi forragear; (rummage) remexer à procura (de) □ n forragem f

**forbade** /fə'bæd/ see **forbid**

**forbear** /fɔː'beə(r)/ vt/i (pt **forbore**,
pp **forborne**) abster-se (**from** de).
~**ance** n paciência f, tolerância f

**forbid** /fə'bɪd/ vt (pt **forbade**, pp **forbidden**) proibir. **you are** ~**den to
smoke** você está proibido de fumar,
(P) estás proibido de fumar. ~**ding** a
severo, intimidante

**force** /fɔːs/ n força f □ vt forçar. ~
**into** fazer entrar à força. ~ **on** impor
a. **come into** ~ entrar em vigor. **the**
~**s** as Forças Armadas. ~**d** a
forçado. ~**ful** a enérgico

**force-feed** /'fɔːsfiːd/ vt (pt **-fed**) alimentar à força

**forceps** /'fɔːseps/ n (pl invar) fórceps
m

**forcibl|e** /'fɔːsəbl/ a convincente;
(done by force) à força. ~**y** adv à força

**ford** /fɔːd/ n vau m □ vt passar a vau,
vadear

**fore** /fɔː(r)/ a dianteiro □ n **to the** ~
em evidência

**forearm** /'fɔːraːm/ n antebraço m

**foreboding** /fɔː'bəʊdɪŋ/ n pressentimento m

**forecast** /'fɔːkaːst/ vt (pt **forecast**)
prever □ n previsão f. **weather** ~
boletim m meteorológico, previsão f
do tempo

**forecourt** /'fɔːkɔːt/ n pátio m de entrada; (of garage) área f das bombas
de gasolina

**forefinger** /'fɔ:fɪŋəg(r)/ n (dedo) indicador m

**forefront** /'fɔ:frʌnt/ n vanguarda f

**foregone** /'fɔ:gɒn/ a ~ **conclusion** resultado m previsto

**foreground** /'fɔ:graʊnd/ n primeiro plano m

**forehead** /'fɒrɪd/ n testa f

**foreign** /'fɒrən/ a estrangeiro; (trade) externo; (travel) ao/no estrangeiro. F~ **Office** Ministério m dos Negócios Estrangeiros. ~**er** n estrangeiro m.

**foreman** /'fɔ:mən/ n (pl **foremen**) contramestre m; (of jury) primeiro jurado m

**foremost** /'fɔ:məʊst/ a principal, primeiro □ adv **first and** ~ antes de mais nada, em primeiro lugar

**forename** /'fɔ:neɪm/ n

**forensic** /fə'rensɪk/ a forense. ~ **medicine** medicina f legal

**forerunner** /'fɔ:rʌnə(r)/ n precursor m

**foresee** /fɔ:'si:/ vt (pt -**saw**, pp -**seen**) prever. ~**able** a previsível

**foreshadow** /fɔ:'ʃædəʊ/ vt prefigurar, pressagiar

**foresight** /'fɔ:saɪt/ n previsão f, previdência f

**forest** /'fɒrɪst/ n floresta f

**forestall** /fɔ:'stɔ:l/ vt (do first) antecipar-se a; (prevent) prevenir; (anticipate) antecipar

**forestry** /'fɒrɪstrɪ/ n silvicultura f

**foretell** /fɔ:'tel/ vt (pt **foretold**) predizer, profetizar

**forever** /fə'revə(r)/ adv (endlessly) constantemente

**foreword** /'fɔ:wɜ:d/ n prefácio m

**forfeit** /'fɔ:fɪt/ n penalidade f, preço m; (in game) prenda f □ vt perder

**forgave** /fə'geɪv/ see **forgive**

**forge**[1] /fɔ:dʒ/ vi ~ **ahead** tomar a dianteira, avançar

**forge**[2] /fɔ:dʒ/ n forja f □ vt (metal, friendship) forjar; (counterfeit) falsificar, forjar. ~**r** /-ə(r)/ n falsificador m, forjador m. ~**ry** /-ərɪ/ n falsificação f

**forget** /fə'get/ vt/i (pt **forgot**, pp **forgotten**) esquecer. ~ **o.s.** portar-se com menos dignidade, esquecer-se de quem é. ~**-me-not** n miosótis m. ~**ful** a esquecido. ~**fulness** n esquecimento m

**forgive** /fə'gɪv/ vt (pt **forgave**, pp **forgiven**) perdoar (sb for sth alg coisa a alg). ~**ness** n perdão m

**forgo** /fɔ:'gəʊ/ vt (pt **forwent**, pp **forgone**) renunciar a

**fork** /fɔ:k/ n garfo m; (for digging etc) forquilha f; (in road) bifurcação f □ vi bifurcar. ~ **out** (sl) desembolsar. ~**-lift truck** empilhadeira f. ~**ed** a bifurcado; (lightning) em zigzag

**forlorn** /fə'lɔ:n/ a abandonado, desolado

**form** /fɔ:m/ n forma f; (document) impresso m, formulário m; (schol) classe f □ vt/i formar(-se)

**formal** /'fɔ:ml/ a formal; (dress) de cerimónia, (P) cerimónia. ~**ity** /-'mælətɪ/ n formalidade f. ~**ly** adv formalmente

**format** /'fɔ:mæt/ n formato m □ vt (pl **formatted**) (disk) formatar

**formation** /fɔ:'meɪʃn/ n formação f

**former** /'fɔ:mə(r)/ a antigo; (first of two) primeiro. **the** ~ aquele. ~**ly** adv antigamente

**formidable** /'fɔ:mɪdəbl/ a formidável, tremendo

**formula** /'fɔ:mjʊlə/ n (pl -**ae** /-i:/ or -**as**) fórmula f

**formulate** /'fɔ:mjʊleɪt/ vt formular

**forsake** /fə'seɪk/ vt (pt **forsook**, pp **forsaken**) abandonar

**fort** /fɔ:t/ n (mil) forte m

**forth** /fɔ:θ/ adv adiante, para a frente. **and so** ~ e assim por diante, etcetera. **go back and** ~ andar de trás para diante.

**forthcoming** /fɔ:θ'kʌmɪŋ/ a que está para vir, próximo; (communicative) comunicativo, receptivo; (book) no prelo

**forthright** /'fɔ:θraɪt/ a franco, direto, (P) directo

**fortify** /'fɔ:tɪfaɪ/ vt fortificar. ~**ication** /-ɪ'keɪʃn/ n fortificação f

**fortitude** /'fɔ:tɪtju:d/ n fortitude f, fortaleza f

**fortnight** /'fɔ:tnaɪt/ n quinze dias mpl, (P) quinzena f. ~**ly** a quinzenal □ adv de quinze em quinze dias

**fortress** /'fɔ:trɪs/ n fortaleza f

**fortuitous** /fɔ:'tju:ɪtəs/ a fortuito, acidental

**fortunate** /'fɔ:tʃənət/ a feliz, afortunado. **be** ~ ter sorte. ~**ly** adv felizmente

**fortune** /'fɔ:tʃən/ n sorte f; (wealth) fortuna f. **have the good** ~ **to** ter a sorte de. ~**-teller** n cartomante mf

**fort|y** /'fɔ:tɪ/ a & n quarenta (m). ~**ieth** a &n quadragésimo (m)

**forum** /'fɔ:rəm/ n fórum m, foro m

**forward** /'fɔ:wəd/ a (in front) dianteiro; (towards the front) para a frente; (advanced) adiantado; (pert) atrevido □ n (sport) atacante m, (P) avançado m □ adv ~(**s**) para a frente, para diante □ vt (letter) remeter; (goods) expedir; (fig: help) favorecer. **come** ~ apresentar-se. **go** ~ avançar. ~**ness** n adiantamento m; (pertness) atrevimento m

**fossil** /'fɒsl/ a & n fóssil (m)

**foster** /'fɒstə(r)/ vt fomentar; (child)

criar. **~-child** n filho m adotivo, (P) adoptivo. **~-mother** n mãe f adotiva, (P) adoptiva

**fought** /fɔ:t/ see **fight**

**foul** /faul/ a (-er, -est) infecto; (language) obsceno; (weather) mau □ n (football) falta f □ vt sujar, emporcalhar. **~-mouthed** a de linguagem obscena. **~ play** jogo m desleal; (crime) crime m

**found¹** /faund/ see **find**

**found²** /faund/ vt fundar. **~ation** /-'deɪʃn/ n fundação f; (basis) fundamento m. **~ations** npl (of building) alicerces mpl

**founder¹** /'faundə(r)/ n fundador m

**founder²** /'faundə(r)/ vi afundar-se

**foundry** /'faundrɪ/ n fundição f

**fountain** /'fauntɪn/ n fonte f. **~-pen** n caneta-tinteiro f, (P) caneta f de tinta permanente

**four** /fɔ:(r)/ a & n quatro (m). **~fold** a quádruplo □ adv quadruplamente. **~th** a & n quarto (m)

**foursome** /'fɔ:səm/ n grupo m de quatro pessoas

**fourteen** /fɔ:'ti:n/ a & n catorze (m). **~th** a & n décimo quarto (m)

**fowl** /faul/ n ave f de capoeira

**fox** /fɒks/ n raposa f □ vt (colloq) mistificar, enganar. **be ~ed** ficar perplexo

**foyer** /'fɔɪeɪ/ n foyer m

**fraction** /'frækʃn/ n fração f, (P) fracção f; (small bit) bocadinho m, partícula f

**fracture** /'fræktʃə(r)/ n fratura f, (P) fractura f □ vt/i fraturar(-se), (P) fracturar(-se)

**fragile** /'frædʒaɪl/ a frágil

**fragment** /'frægmənt/ n fragmento m. **~ary** /'frægməntrɪ/ a fragmentário

**fragran|t** /'freɪɡrənt/ a fragrante, perfumado. **~ce** n fragrância f, perfume m

**frail** /freɪl/ a (-er, -est) frágil

**frame** /freɪm/ n (techn; of spectacles) armação f; (of picture) moldura f, (of window) caixilho m; (body) corpo m, (P) estrutura f □ vt colocar a armação em; (picture) emoldurar; (fig) formular; (sl) incriminar falsamente, tramar. **~ of mind** estado m de espírito

**framework** /'freɪmwɜ:k/ n estrutura f; (context) quadro m, esquema m

**France** /frɑ:ns/ n França f

**franchise** /'fræntʃaɪz/ n (pol) direito m de voto; (comm) concessão f, franchise f

**frank¹** /fræŋk/ a franco. **~ly** adv francamente. **~ness** n franqueza f

**frank²** /fræŋk/ vt franquear

**frantic** /'fræntɪk/ a frenético

**fraternal** /frə'tɜ:nl/ a fraternal

**fraternize** /'frætənaɪz/ vi confraternizar

**fraud** /frɔ:d/ n fraude f; (person) impostor m. **~ulent** /'frɔ:djulənt/ a fraudulento

**fraught** /frɔ:t/ a **~ with** cheio de

**fray¹** /freɪ/ n rixa f

**fray²** /freɪ/ vt/i desfiar(-se), puir, esgarçar(-se)

**freak** /fri:k/ n aberração f, anomalia f □ a anormal. **~ of nature** aborto m da natureza. **~ish** a anormal

**freckle** /'frekl/ n sarda f. **~d** a sardento

**free** /fri:/ a (freer, freest) livre; (gratis) grátis; (lavish) liberal □ vt (pt freed) libertar (from de); (rid) livrar (of de). **~ of charge** grátis, de graça. **a ~ hand** carta f branca. **~-lance** a independente, free-lance. **~-range** a (egg) de galinha criada em galinheiro. **~ly** adv livremente

**freedom** /'fri:dəm/ n liberdade f

**freez|e** /fri:z/ vt/i (pt froze, pp frozen) gelar; (culin; finance) congelar (-se) □ n gelo m; (culin; finance) congelamento m. **~er** n congelador m. **~ing** a gélido, glacial. **below ~ing** abaixo de zero

**freight** /freɪt/ n frete m

**French** /frentʃ/ a francês □ n (lang) francês m. **the ~** os franceses. **~man** n francês m. **~-speaking** a francófono. **~ window** porta f envidraçada. **~woman** n francesa f

**frenz|y** /'frenzɪ/ n frenesi m. **~ied** a frenético

**frequen|t¹** /'fri:kwənt/ a freqüente, (P) frequente. **~cy** n freqüência f, (P) frequência f. **~tly** adv freqüentemente, (P) frequentemente

**frequent²** /frɪ'kwent/ vt freqüentar, (P) frequentar

**fresh** /freʃ/ a (-er, -est) fresco; (different, additional) novo; (colloq: cheeky) descarado, atrevido. **~ly** adv recentemente. **~ness** n frescura f

**freshen** /'freʃn/ vt/i refrescar. **~ up** refrescar-se

**fret** /fret/ vt/i (pt fretted) ralar(-se). **~ful** a rabugento

**friar** /'fraɪə(r)/ n frade m; (before name) frei m

**friction** /'frɪkʃn/ n fricção f

**Friday** /'fraɪdɪ/ n sexta-feira f. **Good ~** sexta-feira f santa

**fridge** /frɪdʒ/ n (colloq) geladeira f, (P) frigorífico m

**fried** /fraɪd/ see **fry** □ a frito

**friend** /frend/ n amigo m. **~ship** n amizade f

**friendl|y** /'frendlɪ/ a (-ier, -iest)

amigável, amigo, simpático. ~iness *n*
simpatia *f*, gentileza *f*
**frieze** /fri:z/ *n* friso *m*
**frigate** /'frɪgət/ *n* fragata *f*
**fright** /fraɪt/ *n* medo *m*, susto *m*. **give
sb a** ~ pregar um susto em alguém.
~ful *a* medonho, assustador
**frighten** /'fraɪtn/ *vt* assustar. ~ **off**
afugentar. ~ed *a* assustado. **be** ~ed
(**of**) ter medo (de)
**frigid** /'frɪdʒɪd/ *a* frígido. ~ity
/-'dʒɪdətɪ/ *n* frigidez *f*, frieza *f*; (*psych*)
frigidez *f*
**frill** /frɪl/ *n* babado *m*, (*P*) folho *m*
**fringe** /frɪndʒ/ *n* franja *f*; (*of area*)
borda *f*; (*of society*) margem *f*. ~ **be-
nefits** (*work*) regalias *fpl* extras. ~
**theatre** teatro *m* alternativo, teatro
*m* de vanguarda
**frisk** /frɪsk/ *vi* pular, brincar □ *vt* revistar
**fritter**¹ /'frɪtə(r)/ *n* bolinho *m* frito,
(*P*) frito *m*
**fritter**² /'frɪtə(r)/ *vt* ~ **away** desperdiçar
**frivol|ous** /'frɪvələs/ *a* frívolo. ~ity
/-'vɒlətɪ/ *n* frivolidade *f*
**fro** /frəʊ/ *see* **to and fro**
**frock** /frɒk/ *n* vestido *m*
**frog** /frɒg/ *n* rã *f*
**frogman** /'frɒgmən/ *n* (*pl* -**men**)
homem-rã *m*
**frolic** /'frɒlɪk/ *vi* (*pt* **frolicked**) brincar, fazer travessuras □ *n* brincadeira
*f*, travessura *f*
**from** /frəm/; *emphatic* /frɒm/ *prep* de;
(*with time, prices etc*) de, a partir de;
(*according to*) por, a julgar por
**front** /frʌnt/ *n* (*meteo, mil, pol; of car,
train*) frente *f*; (*of shirt*) peitilho *m*; (*of
building; fig*) fachada *f*; (*promenade*)
calçada *f* à beiramar □ *a* da frente;
(*first*) primeiro. **in** ~ (**of**) em frente
(de). ~ **door** porta *f* da rua. ~-**wheel
drive** tração *f*, (*P*) tracção *f* dianteira.
~**age** *n* frontaria *f*. ~**al** *a* frontal
**frontier** /'frʌntɪə(r)/ *n* fronteira *f*
**frost** /frɒst/ *n* gelo *m*, temperatura *f*
abaixo de zero; (*on ground, plants etc*)
geada *f* □ *vt/i* cobrir(-se) de geada. ~-
**bite** *n* queimadura *f* de frio. ~-**bitten**
*a* queimado pelo frio. ~**ed** *a* (*glass*)
fosco. ~**y** *a* glacial
**froth** /frɒθ/ *n* espuma *f* □ *vi* espumar,
fazer espuma. ~**y** *a* espumoso
**frown** /fraʊn/ *vi* franzir as sobrancelhas □ *n* franzir *m* de sobrancelhas. ~
**on** desaprovar
**froze, frozen** /frəʊz, 'frəʊzn/ *see*
**freeze**
**frugal** /'fru:gl/ *a* poupado; (*meal*)
frugal. ~**ly** *adv* frugalmente
**fruit** /fru:t/ *n* fruto *m*; (*collectively*)
fruta *f*. ~ **machine** caça-níqueis *ms/*

*pl.* ~ **salad** salada *f* de frutas. ~**y** *a*
que tem gosto *or* cheiro de fruta
**fruit|ful** /'fru:tfl/ *a* frutífero, pro-
dutivo. ~**less** *a* infrutífero
**fruition** /fru:'ɪʃn/ *n* **come to** ~ realizar-se
**frustrat|e** /frʌ'streɪt/ *vt* frustrar.
~**ion** /-ʃn/ *n* frustração *f*
**fry** /fraɪ/ *vt/i* (*pt* **fried**) fritar. ~**ing-
pan** *n* frigideira *f*
**fudge** /fʌdʒ/ *n* (*culin*) doce *m* de leite,
(*P*) doce *m* acaramelado □ *vt/i* ~ (**the
issue**) lançar a confusão
**fuel** /'fju:əl/ *n* combustível *m*; (*for
car*) carburante *m* □ *vt* (*pt* **fuelled**)
abastecer de combustível; (*fig*) atear
**fugitive** /'fju:dʒətɪv/ *a & n* fugitivo
(*m*)
**fulfil** /fʊl'fɪl/ *vt* (*pt* **fulfilled**) cumprir,
realizar; (*condition*) satisfazer. ~ **o.s.**
realizar-se. ~**ling** *a* satisfatório.
~**ment** *n* realização *f*; (*of condition*)
satisfação *f*
**full** /fʊl/ *a* (-**er**, -**est**) cheio; (*meal*)
completo; (*price*) total, por inteiro;
(*skirt*) rodado □ *adv* **in** ~
integralmente. **at** ~ **speed** a toda
velocidade. **to the** ~ ao máximo. **be**
~ **up** (*colloq: after eating*) estar cheio
(*colloq*). ~ **moon** lua *f* cheia. ~-**scale**
*a* em grande. ~-**size** *a* em tamanho
natural. ~ **stop** ponto *m* final. ~-
**time** *a & adv* a tempo integral, full-
time. ~**y** *adv* completamente
**fulsome** /'fʊlsəm/ *a* excessivo
**fumble** /'fʌmbl/ *vi* tatear, (*P*) tactear;
(*in the dark*) andar tateando. ~ **with**
estar atrapalhado com, andar às voltas com
**fume** /fju:m/ *vi* defumar, (*P*) deitar
fumo, fumegar; (*with anger*) ferver.
~**s** *npl* gases *mpl*
**fumigate** /'fju:mɪgeɪt/ *vt* fumigar
**fun** /fʌn/ *n* divertimento *m*. **for** ~ de
brincadeira. **make** ~ **of** zombar de,
fazer troça de. ~-**fair** *n* parque *m* de
diversões, (*P*) feira *f* de diversões, (*P*)
feira *f* popular
**function** /'fʌŋkʃn/ *n* função *f* □ *vi*
funcionar. ~**al** *a* funcional
**fund** /fʌnd/ *n* fundos *mpl* □ *vt* financiar
**fundamental** /fʌndə'mentl/ *a* fundamental
**funeral** /'fju:nərəl/ *n* enterro *m*, funeral *m* □ *a* fúnebre
**fungus** /'fʌŋgəs/ *n* (*pl* -**gi** /-gaɪ/) fungo
*m*
**funnel** /'fʌnl/ *n* funil *m*; (*of ship*)
chaminé *f*
**funn|y** /'fʌnɪ/ *a* (-**ier**, -**iest**) engraçado,
divertido; (*odd*) esquisito. ~**ily** *adv*
comicamente; (*oddly*) estranhamente.
~**ily enough** por incrível que pareça

**fur** /fɜː(r)/ n pêlo m; ( for clothing) pele f; (in kettle) depósito m, crosta f. ~ **coat** casaco m de pele

**furious** /'fjʊəriəs/ a furioso. ~**ly** adv furiosamente

**furnace** /'fɜːnɪs/ n fornalha f

**furnish** /'fɜːnɪʃ/ vt mobiliar, (P) mobilar; (supply) prover (**with** de). ~**ings** npl mobiliário m e equipamento m

**furniture** /'fɜːnɪtʃə(r)/ n mobília f

**furrow** /'fʌrəʊ/ n sulco m; (wrinkle) ruga f □ vt sulcar; (wrinkle) enrugar

**furry** /'fɜːrɪ/ a (-ier, -iest) peludo; (toy) de pelúcia

**furth|er** /'fɜːðə(r)/ a mais distante; (additional) adicional, suplementar □ adv mais longe; (more) mais □ vt promover. ~**er education** ensino m supletivo, cursos mpl livres, (P) educação f superior. ~**est** a o mais distante □ adv mais longe

**furthermore** /fɜːðə'mɔː(r)/ adv além disso

**furtive** /'fɜːtɪv/ a furtivo

**fury** /'fjʊəri/ n fúria f, furor m

**fuse¹** /fjuːz/ vt/i fundir(-se); (fig) amalgamar □ n fusível m. **the lights** ~**d** os fusíveis queimaram

**fuse²** /fjuːz/ n (of bomb) espoleta f

**fuselage** /'fjuːzəlɑːʒ/ n fuselagem f

**fusion** /'fjuːʒn/ n fusão f

**fuss** /fʌs/ n história(s) f(pl), escarcéu m □ vi preocupar-se com ninharias. **make a ~ of** ligar demasiado para, criar caso com, fazer um espalhafato com. ~**y** a exigente, complicado

**futile** /'fjuːtaɪl/ a fútil

**future** /'fjuːtʃə(r)/ a & n futuro (m). **in ~** no futuro, de agora em diante

**futuristic** /fjuːtʃə'rɪstɪk/ a futurista, futurístico

**fuzz** /fʌz/ n penugem f; (hair) cabelo m frisado

**fuzzy** /'fʌzɪ/ a (hair) frisado; (photo) pouco nítido, desfocado

# G

**gab** /gæb/ n (colloq) **have the gift of the ~** ter o dom da palavra

**gabble** /'gæbl/ vt/i tagarelar, falar, ler muito depressa □ n tagarelice f, algaravia f

**gable** /'geɪbl/ n empena f, oitão m

**gad** /gæd/ vi (pt gadded) ~ **about** (colloq) badalar

**gadget** /'gædʒɪt/ n pequeno utensílio m; (fitting) dispositivo m; (device) engenhoca f (colloq)

**Gaelic** /'geɪlɪk/ n galês m

**gaffe** /gæf/ n gafe f

**gag** /gæg/ n mordaça f; (joke) gag m, piada f □ vt (pt gagged) amordaçar

**gaiety** /'geɪətɪ/ n alegria f

**gaily** /'geɪlɪ/ adv alegremente

**gain** /geɪn/ vt ganhar □ vi (of clock) adiantar-se. ~ **weight** aumentar de peso. ~ **on** (get closer to) aproximar-se de □ n ganho m; (increase) aumento m. ~**ful** a lucrativo, proveitoso

**gait** /geɪt/ n (modo de) andar m

**gala** /'gɑːlə/ n gala m; (sport) festival m

**galaxy** /'gæləksɪ/ n galáxia f

**gale** /geɪl/ n vento m forte

**gall** /gɔːl/ n bílis f; ( fig) fel m; (sl: impudence) descaramento m, desplante m, (P) lata f (sl). ~**bladder** n vesícula f biliar. ~**stone** n cálculo m biliar

**gallant** /'gælənt/ a galhardo, valente; (chivalrous) galante, cortês. ~**ry** n galhardia f, valentia f; (chivalry) galanteria f, cortesia f

**gallery** /'gælərɪ/ n galeria f

**galley** /'gælɪ/ n (pl -eys) galera f; (ship's kitchen) cozinha f

**gallivant** /gælɪ'vænt/ vi (colloq) vadiar, (P) andar na paródia

**gallon** /'gælən/ n galão m (= 4,546 litros; Amer = 3.785 litros)

**gallop** /'gæləp/ n galope m □ vi (pt galloped) galopar

**gallows** /'gæləʊz/ npl forca f

**galore** /gə'lɔː(r)/ adv à beça, em abundância

**galvanize** /'gælvənaɪz/ vt galvanizar

**gambit** /'gæmbɪt/ n gambito m

**gamb|le** /'gæmbl/ vt/i jogar □ n jogo (de azar) m; ( fig) risco m. ~**e on** apostar em. ~**er** n jogador m. ~**ing** n jogo m (de azar)

**game** /geɪm/ n jogo m; ( football) desafio m; (animals) caça f □ a bravo. ~ **for** pronto para

**gamekeeper** /'geɪmkiːpə(r)/ n guarda-florestal m

**gammon** /'gæmən/ n presunto m defumado

**gamut** /'gæmət/ n gama f

**gang** /gæŋ/ n bando m, gang m; (of workmen) turma f, (P) grupo m □ vi ~ **up** ligar-se (on contra)

**gangling** /'gæŋglɪŋ/ a desengonçado

**gangrene** /'gæŋgriːn/ n gangrena f

**gangster** /'gæŋstə(r)/ n gângster m, bandido m

**gangway** /'gæŋweɪ/ n passagem f; (aisle) coxia f; (on ship) portaló m; ( from ship to shore) passadiço m

**gaol** /dʒeɪl/ n & vt = **jail**

**gap** /gæp/ n abertura f, brecha f; (in time) intervalo m; (deficiency) lacuna f

**gap|e** /geɪp/ vi ficar boquiaberto or embasbacado. ~**ing** a escancarado

**garage** /'gærɑːʒ/ n garagem f; (service station) posto m de gasolina, (P) estação f de serviço □ vt pôr na garagem

**garbage** /'ga:bɪdʒ/ n lixo m. ~ **can** (*Amer*) lata f do lixo, (P) caixote m do lixo

**garble** /'ga:bl/ vt deturpar

**garden** /'ga:dn/ n jardim m □ vi jardinar. ~**er** n jardineiro m. ~**ing** n jardinagem f

**gargle** /'ga:gl/ vi gargarejar □ n gargarejo m

**gargoyle** /'ga:gɔɪl/ n gárgula f

**garish** /'geərɪʃ/ a berrante, espalhafatoso

**garland** /'ga:lənd/ n grinalda f

**garlic** /'ga:lɪk/ n alho m

**garment** /'ga:mənt/ n peça f de vestuário, roupa f

**garnish** /'ga:nɪʃ/ vt enfeitar, guarnecer □ n guarnição f

**garrison** /'gærɪsn/ n guarnição f □ vt guarnecer

**garrulous** /'gærələs/ a tagarela

**garter** /'ga:tə(r)/ n liga f. ~-**belt** n (*Amer*) cinta f de ligas

**gas** /gæs/ n (*pl* gases) gás m; (*med*) anestésico m; (*Amer colloq: petrol*) gasolina f □ vt (*pt* gassed) asfixiar; (*mil*) gasear □ vi (*colloq*) fazer conversa fiada. ~ **fire** aquecedor m a gás. ~ **mask** máscara f anti-gás. ~ **meter** medidor m do gás

**gash** /gæʃ/ n corte m, lanho m □ vt cortar

**gasket** /'gæskɪt/ n junta f

**gasoline** /'gæsəli:n/ n (*Amer*) gasolina f

**gasp** /ga:sp/ vi arfar, arquejar; (*fig: with rage, surprise*) ficar sem ar □ n arquejo m

**gassy** /'gæsɪ/ a gasoso; (*full of gas*) cheio de gás

**gastric** /'gæstrɪk/ a gástrico

**gastronomy** /gæ'strɒnəmɪ/ n gastronomia f

**gate** /geɪt/ n portão m; (*of wood*) cancela f; (*barrier*) barreira f; (*airport*) porta f

**gateau** /'gætəʊ/ n (*pl* ~x /-təʊz/) bolo m grande com creme

**gatecrash** /'geɪtkræʃ/ vt/i entrar (numa festa) sem convite

**gateway** /'geɪtweɪ/ n (porta de) entrada f

**gather** /'gæðə(r)/ vt reunir, juntar; (*pick up, collect*) apanhar; (*amass, pile up*) acumular, juntar; (*conclude*) deduzir; (*cloth*) franzir □ vi reunir-se; (*pile up*) acumular-se. ~ **speed** ganhar velocidade. ~**ing** n reunião f

**gaudy** /'gɔ:dɪ/ a (-ier, -iest) (*bright*) berrante; (*showy*) espalhafatoso

**gauge** /geɪdʒ/ n medida f padrão; (*device*) indicador m; (*railway*) bitola f □ vt medir, avaliar

**gaunt** /gɔ:nt/ a emagrecido, macilento; (*grim*) lúgubre, desolado

**gauntlet** /'gɔ:ntlɪt/ n run the ~ of (*fig*) expor-se a. throw down the ~ lançar um desafio, (P) atirar a luva

**gauze** /gɔ:z/ n gaze f

**gave** /geɪv/ *see* give

**gawky** /'gɔ:kɪ/ a (-ier, -iest) desajeitado

**gay** /geɪ/ a (-er, -est) alegre; (*colloq: homosexual*) homosexual, gay

**gaze** /geɪz/ vi ~ (at) olhar fixamente (para) □ n contemplação f

**gazelle** /gə'zel/ n gazela f

**GB** *abbr of* Great Britain

**gear** /gɪə(r)/ n equipamento m; (*techn*) engrenagem f; (*auto*) velocidade f □ vt equipar; (*adapt*) adaptar. in ~ engrenado. out of ~ em ponto morto. ~-**lever** n alavanca f de mudanças

**gearbox** /'gɪəbɒks/ n caixa f de mudança, caixa f de transmissão, (P) caixa f de velocidades

**geese** /gi:s/ *see* goose

**gel** /dʒel/ n geléia f, (P) geleia f

**gelatine** /'dʒelæti:n/ n gelatina f

**gelignite** /'dʒelɪgnaɪt/ n gelignite f

**gem** /dʒem/ n gema f, pedra f preciosa

**Gemini** /'dʒemɪnaɪ/ n (*astr*) Gêmeos *mpl*, (P) Gémeos *mpl*

**gender** /'dʒendə(r)/ n gênero m, (P) género m

**gene** /dʒi:n/ n gene m

**genealogy** /dʒi:nɪ'ælədʒɪ/ n genealogia f

**general** /'dʒenrəl/ a geral □ n general m. ~ **election** eleições *fpl* legislativas. ~ **practitioner** n clínicogeral m, (P) médico m de família. in ~ em geral. ~**ly** adv geralmente

**generaliz|e** /'dʒenrəlaɪz/ vt/i generalizar. ~**ation** /-'zeɪʃn/ n generalização f

**generate** /'dʒenəreɪt/ vt gerar, produzir

**generation** /dʒenə'reɪʃn/ n geração f

**generator** /'dʒenəreɪtə(r)/ n gerador m

**gener|ous** /'dʒenərəs/ a generoso; (*plentiful*) abundante. ~**osity** /-'rɒsətɪ/ n generosidade f

**genetic** /dʒɪ'netɪk/ a genético. ~**s** n genética f

**genial** /'dʒi:nɪəl/ a agradável

**genital** /'dʒenɪtl/ a genital. ~**s** *npl* órgãos *mpl* genitais

**genius** /'dʒi:nɪəs/ n (*pl* -uses) gênio m, (P) génio m

**genocide** /'dʒenəsaɪd/ n genocídio m

**gent** /dʒent/ n the G~s (*colloq*) banheiros *mpl* de homens, (P) lavabos *mpl* para homens

**genteel** /dʒen'ti:l/ a elegante, fino, refinado

**gentl|e** /'dʒentl/ a (~er, ~est) brando, suave. ~eness n brandura f, suavidade f. ~y adv brandamente, suavemente

**gentleman** /'dʒentlmən/ n (pl -men) senhor m; (well-bred) cavalheiro m

**genuine** /'dʒenjʊɪn/ a genuíno, verdadeiro; (belief) sincero

**geograph|y** /dʒɪ'ɒɡrəfɪ/ n geografia f. ~er n geógrafo m. ~ical /dʒɪə-'ɡræfɪkl/ a geográfico

**geolog|y** /dʒɪ'ɒlədʒɪ/ n geologia f. ~ical /dʒɪə'lɒdʒɪkl/ a geológico. ~ist n geólogo m

**geometr|y** /dʒɪ'ɒmətrɪ/ n geometria f. ~ic(al) /dʒɪə'metrɪk(l)/ a geométrico

**geranium** /dʒə'reɪnɪəm/ n gerânio m

**geriatric** /dʒerɪ'ætrɪk/ a geriátrico

**germ** /dʒɜ:m/ n germe m, micróbio m

**German** /'dʒɜ:mən/ a & n alemão (m), alemã (f); (lang) alemão (m). ~ measles rubéola f. ~ic /dʒə'mænɪk/ a germânico. ~y n Alemanha f

**germinate** /'dʒɜ:mɪneɪt/ vi germinar

**gestation** /dʒe'steɪʃn/ n gestação f

**gesticulate** /dʒe'stɪkjʊleɪt/ vi gesticular

**gesture** /'dʒestʃə(r)/ n gesto m

**get** /ɡet/ vt (pt got, pres p getting) (have) ter; (receive) receber; (catch) apanhar; (earn, win) ganhar; (fetch) ir buscar; (find) achar; (colloq: understand) entender. ~ sb to do sth fazer com que alguém faça alg coisa □ vi ir, chegar; (become) ficar. ~ married/ready casar-se/aprontar-se. ~ about andar dum lado para o outro. ~ across atravessar. ~ along or by (manage) ir indo. ~ along or on with entender-se com. ~ at (reach) chegar a; (attack) atacar; (imply) insinuar. ~ away ir-se embora; (escape) fugir. ~ back vi voltar □ vt recuperar. ~ by (pass) passar, escapar; (manage) aguentar-se. ~ down descer. ~ in entrar. ~ off vi descer; (leave) partir; (jur) ser absolvido □ vt (remove) tirar. ~ on (succeed) fazer progressos, ir; (be on good terms) dar-se bem. ~ out sair. ~ out of (fig) fugir de. ~ over (illness) restabelecer-se de. ~ round (person) convencer; (rule) contornar. ~ up vi levantar-se □ vt (mount) montar. ~-up n (colloq) apresentação f

**getaway** /'ɡetəweɪ/ n fuga f

**geyser** /'ɡi:zə(r)/ n aquecedor m; (geol) gêiser m, (P) géiser m

**Ghana** /'ɡɑ:nə/ n Gana m

**ghastly** /'ɡɑ:stlɪ/ a (-ier, -iest) horrível; (pale) lívido

**gherkin** /'ɡɜ:kɪn/ n pepino m pequeno para conservas, cornichão m

**ghetto** /'ɡetəʊ/ n (pl -os) gueto m, ghetto m

**ghost** /ɡəʊst/ n fantasma m, espectro m. ~ly a fantasmagórico, espectral

**giant** /'dʒaɪənt/ a & n gigante (m)

**gibberish** /'dʒɪbərɪʃ/ n algaravia f, linguagem f incompreensível

**gibe** /dʒaɪb/ n zombaria f □ vi ~ (at) zombar (de)

**giblets** /'dʒɪblɪts/ npl miúdos mpl, miudezas fpl

**giddy** /'ɡɪdɪ/ a (-ier, -iest) estonteante, vertiginoso. be or feel ~ ter tonturas or vertigens

**gift** /ɡɪft/ n presente m, dádiva f; (ability) dom m, dote m. ~-wrap vt (pt -wrapped) fazer um embrulho de presente

**gifted** /'ɡɪftɪd/ a dotado

**gig** /ɡɪɡ/ n (colloq) show m, sessão f de jazz etc

**gigantic** /dʒaɪ'ɡæntɪk/ a gigantesco

**giggle** /'ɡɪɡl/ vi dar risadinhas nervosas □ n risinho m nervoso

**gild** /ɡɪld/ vt dourar

**gills** /ɡɪlz/ npl guelras fpl

**gilt** /ɡɪlt/ a & n dourado (m). ~-edged a de toda a confiança

**gimmick** /'ɡɪmɪk/ n truque m, artifício m

**gin** /dʒɪn/ n gin m, genebra f

**ginger** /'dʒɪndʒə(r)/ n gengibre m □ a louro-avermelhado, ruivo. ~ ale, ~ beer cerveja f de gengibre, (P) ginger ale m

**gingerbread** /'dʒɪndʒəbred/ n pão m de gengibre

**gingerly** /'dʒɪndʒəlɪ/ adv cautelosamente

**gipsy** /'dʒɪpsɪ/ n = gypsy

**giraffe** /dʒɪ'rɑ:f/ n girafa f

**girder** /'ɡɜ:də(r)/ n trave f, viga f

**girdle** /'ɡɜ:dl/ n cinto m; (corset) cinta f □ vt rodear

**girl** /ɡɜ:l/ n (child) menina f; (young woman) moça f, (P) rapariga f. ~-friend n amiga f; (of boy) namorada f. ~hood n (of child) meninice f; (youth) juventude f

**giro** /'dʒaɪrəʊ/ n sistema m de transferência de crédito entre bancos; (cheque) cheque m pago pelo governo a desempregados ou doentes

**girth** /ɡɜ:θ/ n circumferência f, perímetro m

**gist** /dʒɪst/ n essencial m

**give** /ɡɪv/ vt/i (pt gave, pp given) dar; (bend, yield) ceder. ~ away dar; (secret) revelar, trair. ~ back devolver. ~ in dar-se por vencido, render-se. ~ off emitir. ~ out vt anunciar □ vi esgotar-se. ~ up vt/i desistir (de), renunciar (a). ~ **o.s. up** entregar-se. ~ **way** ceder; (*traffic*) dar prioridade; (*collapse*) dar de si

**given** /'gɪvn/ *see* give □ *a* dado. ~ **name** nome *m* de batismo, (*P*) baptismo

**glacier** /'glæsɪə(r)/ *n* glaciar *m*, geleira *f*

**glad** /glæd/ *a* contente. ~**ly** *adv* com (todo o) prazer

**gladden** /'glædn/ *vt* alegrar

**glam|our** /'glæmə(r)/ *n* fascinação *f*, encanto *m*. ~**orize** *vt* tornar fascinante. ~**orous** *a* fascinante, sedutor

**glance** /glɑːns/ *n* relance *m*, olhar *m* □ *vi* ~ **at** dar uma olhada a. **at first** ~ à primeira vista

**gland** /glænd/ *n* glândula *f*

**glar|e** /gleə(r)/ *vi* brilhar intensamente, faiscar □ *n* luz *f* crua; (*fig*) olhar *m* feroz. ~**e at** olhar ferozmente para. ~**ing** *a* brilhante; (*obvious*) flagrante

**glass** /glɑːs/ *n* vidro *m*; (*vessel, its contents*) copo *m*; (*mirror*) espelho *m*. ~**es** óculos *mpl*. ~**y** *a* vítreo

**glaze** /gleɪz/ *vt* (*door etc*) envidraçar; (*pottery*) vidrar □ *n* vidrado *m*

**gleam** /gliːm/ *n* raio *m* de luz frouxa; (*fig*) vislumbre *m* □ *vi* luzir, brilhar

**glean** /gliːn/ *vt* catar

**glee** /gliː/ *n* alegria *f*. ~**ful** *a* cheio de alegria

**glib** /glɪb/ *a* que tem a palavra fácil, verboso. ~**ly** *adv* fluentemente, sem hesitação. ~**ness** *n* verbosidade *f*

**glide** /glaɪd/ *vi* deslizar; (*bird, plane*) planar. ~**r** /-ə(r)/ *n* planador *m*

**glimmer** /'glɪmə(r)/ *n* luz *f* trêmula □ *vi* tremular

**glimpse** /glɪmps/ *n* vislumbre *m*. **catch a** ~ **of** entrever, ver de relance

**glint** /glɪnt/ *n* brilho *m*, reflexo *m* □ *vi* brilhar, cintilar

**glisten** /'glɪsn/ *vi* reluzir

**glitter** /'glɪtə(r)/ *vi* luzir, resplandecer □ *n* esplendor *m*, cintilação *f*

**gloat** /gləʊt/ *vi* ~ **over** ter um prazer maligno em, exultar com

**global** /'gləʊbl/ *a* global

**globe** /gləʊb/ *n* globo *m*

**gloom** /gluːm/ *n* obscuridade *f*; (*fig*) tristeza *f*. ~**y** *a* sombrio; (*sad*) triste; (*pessimistic*) pessimista

**glorif|y** /'glɔːrɪfaɪ/ *vt* glorificar. **a** ~**ied waitress**/*etc* pouco mais que uma garçonete/*etc*

**glorious** /'glɔːrɪəs/ *a* glorioso

**glory** /'glɔːrɪ/ *n* glória *f*; (*beauty*) esplendor *m* □ *vi* ~ **in** orgulhar-se de

**gloss** /glɒs/ *n* brilho *m* □ *a* brilhante □ *vt* ~ **over** minimizar, encobrir. ~**y** *a* brilhante

**glossary** /'glɒsərɪ/ *n* (*pl* -**ries**) glossário *m*

**glove** /glʌv/ *n* luva *f*. ~ **compartment** porta-luvas *m*. ~**d** *a* enluvado

**glow** /gləʊ/ *vi* arder; (*person*) resplandecer; (*eyes*) brilhar □ *n* brasa *f*. ~**ing** *a* (*fig*) entusiástico

**glucose** /'gluːkəʊs/ *n* glucose *f*

**glue** /gluː/ *n* cola *f* □ *vt* (*pres p* gluing) colar

**glum** /glʌm/ *a* (**glummer, glummest**) sorumbático; (*dejected*) abatido

**glut** /glʌt/ *n* superabundância *f*

**glutton** /'glʌtn/ *n* glutão *m*. ~**ous** *a* glutão. ~**y** *n* gula *f*

**gnarled** /nɑːld/ *a* nodoso

**gnash** /næʃ/ *vt* ~ **one's teeth** ranger os dentes

**gnat** /næt/ *n* mosquito *m*

**gnaw** /nɔː/ *vt/i* roer

**gnome** /nəʊm/ *n* gnomo *m*

**go** /gəʊ/ *vi* (*pt* went, *pp* gone) ir; (*leave*) ir, ir-se; (*mech*) andar, funcionar; (*become*) ficar; (*be sold*) vender-se; (*vanish*) ir-se, desaparecer □ *n* (*pl* goes) (*energy*) dinamismo *m*; (*try*) tentativa *f*; (*success*) sucesso *m*; (*turn*) vez *f*. ~ **riding** ir andar *or* montar a cavalo. ~ **shopping** ir às compras. **be** ~**ing to do** ir fazer. ~ **ahead** ir para diante. ~ **away** ir-se embora. ~ **back** voltar atrás (**on** com). ~ **bad** estragar-se. ~ **by** (*pass*) passar. ~ **down** descer; (*sun*) pôr-se; (*ship*) afundar-se. ~ **for** ir buscar; (*like*) gostar de; (*sl: attack*) atirar-se a, ir-se a (*colloq*). ~ **in** entrar. ~ **in for** (*exam*) apresentar-se a. ~ **off** ir-se; (*explode*) rebentar; (*sound*) soar; (*decay*) estragar-se. ~ **on** continuar; (*happen*) acontecer. ~ **out** sair; (*light*) apagar-se. ~ **over** *or* **through** verificar, examinar. ~ **round** (**be** *enough*) chegar. ~ **under** ir abaixo. ~ **up** subir. ~ **without** passar sem. **on the** ~ em grande atividade, (*P*) actividade. ~-**ahead** *n* luz *f* verde □ *a* dinâmico, empreendedor. ~-**between** *n* intermediário *m*. ~-**kart** *n* kart *m*. ~-**slow** *n* operação *f* tartaruga, (*P*) greve *f* de zelo

**goad** /gəʊd/ *vt* aguilhoar, espicaçar

**goal** /gəʊl/ *n* meta *f*; (*area*) baliza *f*; (*score*) gol *m*, (*P*) golo *m*. ~-**post** *n* trave *f*

**goalkeeper** /'gəʊlkiːpə(r)/ *n* goleiro *m*, (*P*) guarda-redes *m*

**goat** /gəʊt/ *n* cabra *f*

**gobble** /'gɒbl/ *vt* comer com sofreguidão, devorar

**goblet** /'gɒblɪt/ *n* taça *f*, cálice *m*

**goblin** /'gɒblɪn/ *n* duende *m*

**God** /gɒd/ *n* Deus *m*. ~-**forsaken** *a* miserável, abandonado

**god** /gɒd/ *n* deus *m*. **~-daughter** *n* afilhada *f*. **~dess** *n* deusa *f*. **~father** *n* padrinho *m*. **~ly** *a* devoto. **~mother** *n* madrinha *f*. **~son** *n* afilhado *m*

**godsend** /'gɒdsend/ *n* achado *m*, dádiva *f* do céu

**goggles** /'gɒglz/ *npl* óculos *mpl* de proteção, (*P*) protecção

**going** /'gəʊɪŋ/ *n* **it is slow/hard ~** é demorado/difícil □ *a* (*price, rate*) corrente, atual, (*P*) actual. **~s-on** *npl* acontecimentos *mpl* estranhos

**gold** /gəʊld/ *n* ouro *m* □ *a* de/em ouro. **~-mine** *n* mina *f* de ouro

**golden** /'gəʊldən/ *a* de ouro; (*like gold*) dourado; (*opportunity*) único. **~ wedding** bodas *fpl* de ouro

**goldfish** /'gəʊldfɪʃ/ *n* peixe *m* dourado/vermelho

**goldsmith** /'gəʊldsmɪθ/ *n* ourives *m inv*

**golf** /gɒlf/ *n* golfe *m*. **~ club** clube *m* de golfe, associação *f* de golfe; (*stick*) taco *m*. **~-course** *n* campo *m* de golfe. **~er** *n* jogador *m* de golfe

**gone** /gɒn/ *see* go □ *a* ido, passado. **~ six o'clock** depois das seis

**gong** /gɒŋ/ *n* gongo *m*

**good** /gʊd/ *a* (**better, best**) bom □ *n* bem *m*. **as ~ as** praticamente. **for ~** para sempre. **it is no ~** não adianta. **it is no ~ shouting/**etc não adianta gritar/etc. **~ afternoon** *int* boa(s) tarde(s). **~ evening/night** *int* boa(s) noite(s). **G~ Friday** Sexta-feira *f* Santa. **~-looking** *a* bonito. **~ morning** *int* bom dia. **~ name** bom nome *m*

**goodbye** /gʊd'baɪ/ *int & n* adeus (*m*)

**goodness** /'gʊdnɪs/ *n* bondade *f*. **my ~ness!** meu Deus!

**goods** /gʊdz/ *npl* (*comm*) mercadorias *fpl*. **~ train** trem *m* de carga, (*P*) comboio *m* de mercadorias

**goodwill** /gʊd'wɪl/ *n* boa vontade *f*

**goose** /gu:s/ *n* (*pl* geese) ganso *m*. **~-flesh, ~-pimples** *ns* pele *f* de galinha

**gooseberry** /'gʊzbərɪ/ *n* (*fruit*) groselha *f*; (*bush*) groselheira *f*

**gore**[1] /gɔ:(r)/ *n* sangue *m* coagulado

**gore**[2] /gɔ:(r)/ *vt* perfurar

**gorge** /gɔ:dʒ/ *n* desfiladeiro *m*, garganta *f* □ *vt* **~ o.s.** empanturrar-se

**gorgeous** /'gɔ:dʒəs/ *a* magnífico, maravilhoso

**gorilla** /gə'rɪlə/ *n* gorila *m*

**gormless** /'gɔ:mlɪs/ *a* (*sl*) estúpido

**gorse** /gɔ:s/ *n* giesta *f*, tojo *m*, urze *f*

**gory** /'gɔ:rɪ/ *a* (**-ier, -iest**) sangrento

**gosh** /gɒʃ/ *int* puxa!, (*P*) caramba!

**gospel** /'gɒspl/ *n* evangelho *m*

**gossip** /'gɒsɪp/ *n* bisbilhotice *f*, fofoca *f*; (*person*) bisbilhoteiro *m*, fofoqueiro *m* □ *vi* (*pt* gossiped) bisbilhotar. **~y** *a* bisbilhoteiro, fofoqueiro

**got** /gɒt/ *see* **get**. **have ~** ter. **have to do** ter de *or* que fazer

**Gothic** /'gɒθɪk/ *a* gótico

**gouge** /gaʊdʒ/ *vt* **~ out** arrancar

**gourmet** /'gʊəmeɪ/ *n* gastrônomo *m*, (*P*) gastrónomo *m*, gourmet *m*

**gout** /gaʊt/ *n* gota *f*

**govern** /'gʌvn/ *vt/i* governar. **~ess** *n* preceptora *f*. **~or** *n* governador *m*; (*of school, hospital etc*) diretor *m*, (*P*) director *m*

**government** /'gʌvənmənt/ *n* governo *m*. **~al** /-'mentl/ *a* governamental

**gown** /gaʊn/ *n* vestido *m*; (*of judge, teacher*) toga *f*

**GP** *abbr see* **general practitioner**

**grab** /græb/ *vt* (*pt* grabbed) agarrar, apanhar

**grace** /greɪs/ *n* graça *f* □ *vt* honrar; (*adorn*) ornar. **say ~** dar graças. **~ful** *a* gracioso

**gracious** /'greɪʃəs/ *a* gracioso; (*kind*) amável, afável

**grade** /greɪd/ *n* categoria *f*; (*of goods*) classe *f*, qualidade *f*; (*on scale*) grau *m*; (*school mark*) nota *f* □ *vt* classificar

**gradient** /'greɪdɪənt/ *n* gradiente *m*, declive *m*

**gradual** /'grædʒʊəl/ *a* gradual, progressivo. **~ly** *adv* gradualmente

**graduate**[1] /'grædʒʊət/ *n* diplomado *m*, graduado *m*, licenciado *m*

**graduate**[2] /'grædʒʊeɪt/ *vt/i* formar (-se). **~ion** /-'eɪʃn/ *n* colação *f* de grau, (*P*) formatura *f*

**graffiti** /grə'fi:ti:/ *npl* graffiti *mpl*

**graft** /grɑ:ft/ *n* (*med, bot*) enxerto *m*; (*work*) batalha *f* □ *vt* enxertar; (*work*) batalhar

**grain** /greɪn/ *n* grão *m*; (*collectively*) cereais *mpl*; (*in wood*) veio *m*. **against the ~** (*fig*) contra a maneira de ser

**gram** /græm/ *n* grama *m*

**gramm|ar** /'græmə(r)/ *n* gramática *f*. **~atical** /grə'mætɪkl/ *a* gramatical

**grand** /grænd/ *a* (**-er, -est**) grandioso, magnífico; (*duke, master*) grão. **~ piano** piano *m* de cauda.

**grand|child** /'græntʃaɪld/ *n* (*pl* -children) neto *m*. **~daughter** *n* neta *f*. **~father** *n* avô *m*. **~mother** *n* avó *f*. **~parents** *npl* avós *mpl*. **~son** *n* neto *m*

**grandeur** /'grændʒə(r)/ *n* grandeza *f*

**grandiose** /'grændɪəʊs/ *a* grandioso

**grandstand** /'grændstænd/ *n* tribuna *f* principal

**granite** /'grænɪt/ *n* granito *m*

**grant** /grɑ:nt/ *vt* conceder; (*a request*) ceder a; (*admit*) admitir (**that** que) □ *n* subsídio *m*; (*univ*) bolsa *f*. **take for**

**~ed** ter como coisa garantida, contar com

**grape** /greɪp/ *n* uva *f*

**grapefruit** /'greɪpfru:t/ *n inv* grapefruit *m*, toronja *f*

**graph** /gra:f/ *n* gráfico *m*

**graphic** /'græfɪk/ *a* gráfico; ( *fig*) vívido. **~s** *npl* (*comput*) gráficos *mpl*

**grapple** /'græpl/ *vi* **~ with** estar engalfinhado com; ( *fig*) estar às voltas com

**grasp** /gra:sp/ *vt* agarrar; (*understand*) compreender □ *n* domínio *m*; (*reach*) alcance *m*; ( *fig: understanding*) compreensão *f*

**grasping** /'gra:spɪŋ/ *a* ganancioso

**grass** /gra:s/ *n* erva *f*; (*lawn*) grama *f*, (*P*) relva *f*; (*pasture*) pastagem *f*; (*sl: informer*) delator *m* □ *vt* cobrir com grama; (*sl: betray*) delatar. **~ roots** (*pol*) bases *fpl*. **~y** *a* coberto de erva

**grasshopper** /'gra:shɒpə(r)/ *n* gafanhoto *m*

**grate**[1] /greɪt/ *n* ( *fireplace*) lareira *f*; ( *frame*) grelha *f*

**grate**[2] /greɪt/ *vt* ralar □ *vi* ranger. **~ one's teeth** ranger os dentes. **~r** /-ə(r)/ *n* ralador *m*

**grateful** /'greɪtfl/ *a* grato, agradecido. **~ly** *adv* com reconhecimento, com gratidão

**gratify** /'grætɪfaɪ/ *vt* ( *pt* **-fied**) contentar, satisfazer. **~ing** *a* gratificante

**grating** /'greɪtɪŋ/ *n* grade *f*

**gratis** /'greɪtɪs/ *a* & *adv* grátis (*invar*), de graça

**gratitude** /'grætɪtju:d/ *n* gratidão *f*, reconhecimento *m*

**gratuitous** /grə'tju:ɪtəs/ *a* gratuito; (*uncalled-for*) sem motivo

**gratuity** /grə'tju:əti/ *n* gratificação *f*, gorjeta *f*

**grave**[1] /greɪv/ *n* cova *f*, sepultura *f*, túmulo *m*

**grave**[2] /greɪv/ *a* (**-er, -est**) grave, sério. **~ly** *adv* gravemente

**grave**[3] /gra:v/ *a* **~ accent** acento *m* grave

**gravel** /'grævl/ *n* cascalho *m* miúdo, saibro *m*

**gravestone** /'greɪvstəʊn/ *n* lápide *f*, campa *f*

**graveyard** /'greɪvja:d/ *n* cemitério *m*

**gravity** /'grævəti/ *n* gravidade *f*

**gravy** /'greɪvɪ/ *n* molho *m* (de carne)

**graze**[1] /greɪz/ *vt/i* pastar

**graze**[2] /greɪz/ *vt* roçar; (*scrape*) esfolar □ *n* esfoladura *f*, (*P*) esfoladela *f*

**greas|e** /gri:s/ *n* gordura *f* □ *vt* engordurar; (*culin*) untar; (*mech*) lubrificar. **~e-proof paper** papel *m* vegetal. **~y** *a* gorduroso

**great** /greɪt/ *a* (**-er, -est**) grande; (*colloq: splendid*) esplêndido. **G~** Brit-

**ain** Grã-Bretanha *f*. **~-grandfather** *n* bisavô *m*. **~-grandmother** *f* bisavó *f*. **~-ly** *adv* grandemente, muito. **~ness** *n* grandeza *f*

**Great Britain** /greɪt'brɪtən/ *n* Grã-Bretanha *f*

**Greece** /gri:s/ *n* Grécia *f*

**greed** /gri:d/ *n* cobiça *f*, ganância *f*; ( *for food*) gula *f*. **~y** *a* cobiçoso, ganancioso; ( *for food*) guloso

**Greek** /gri:k/ *a* & *n* grego (*m*)

**green** /gri:n/ *a* (**-er, -est**) verde □ *n* verde *m*; (*grass*) gramado *m*, (*P*) relvado *m*. **~s** hortaliças *fpl*. **~ belt** zona *f* verde, paisagem *f* protegida. **~ light** luz *f* verde. **~ery** *n* verdura *f*

**greengrocer** /'gri:ŋgrəʊsə(r)/ *n* quitandeiro *m*, (*P*) vendedor *m* de hortaliças

**greenhouse** /'gri:nhaʊs/ *n* estufa *f*. **~ effect** efeito estufa

**Greenland** /'gri:nlənd/ *n* Groenlândia *f*

**greet** /gri:t/ *vt* acolher. **~ing** *n* saudação *f*; (*welcome*) acolhimento *m*. **~ings** *npl* cumprimentos *mpl*; (*Christmas etc*) votos *mpl*, desejos *mpl*

**gregarious** /grɪ'geərɪəs/ *a* gregário; (*person*) sociável

**grenade** /grɪ'neɪd/ *n* granada *f*

**grew** /gru:/ *see* **grow**

**grey** /greɪ/ *a* (**-er, -est**) cinzento; (*of hair*) grisalho □ *n* cinzento *m*

**greyhound** /'greɪhaʊnd/ *n* galgo *m*

**grid** /grɪd/ *n* (*grating*) gradeamento *m*, grade *f*; (*electr*) rede *f*

**grief** /gri:f/ *n* dor *f*. **come to ~** acabar mal

**grievance** /'gri:vns/ *n* razão *f* de queixa

**grieve** /gri:v/ *vt* sofrer, afligir □ *vi* sofrer. **~ for** chorar por

**grill** /grɪl/ *n* grelha *f*; ( *food*) grelhado *m*; (*place*) grill *m* □ *vt* grelhar; (*question*) submeter a interrogatório cerrado, apertar com perguntas □ *vi* grelhar

**grille** /grɪl/ *n* grade *f*; (*of car*) grelha *f*

**grim** /grɪm/ *a* (**grimmer, grimmest**) sinistro; (*without mercy*) implacável

**grimace** /grɪ'meɪs/ *n* careta *f* □ *vi* fazer careta(s)

**grim|e** /graɪm/ *n* sujeira *f*. **~y** *a* encardido, sujo

**grin** /grɪn/ *vi* ( *pt* **grinned**) sorrir abertamente, dar um sorriso largo □ *n* sorriso *m* aberto

**grind** /graɪnd/ *vt* ( *pt* **ground**) triturar; (*coffee*) moer; (*sharpen*) amolar, afiar. **~ one's teeth** ranger os dentes. **~ to a halt** parar freando lentamente

**grip** /grɪp/ *vt* ( *pt* **gripped**) agarrar;

(*interest*) prender □ *n* (*of hands*) aperto *m*; (*control*) controle *m*, domínio *m*. **come to ~s with** arcar com. **~ping** *a* apaixonante

**grisly** /'grɪzlɪ/ *a* (-ier, -iest) macabro, horrível

**gristle** /'grɪsl/ *n* cartilagem *f*

**grit** /grɪt/ *n* areia *f*, grão *m* de areia; (*fig: pluck*) coragem *f*, fortaleza *f* □ *vt* (*pt* gritted) (*road*) jogar areia em; (*teeth*) cerrar

**groan** /grəʊn/ *vi* gemer □ *n* gemido *m*

**grocer** /'grəʊsə(r)/ *n* dono/a *m/f* de mercearia. **~ies** *npl* artigos *mpl* de mercearia. **~y** *n* (*shop*) mercearia *f*

**groggy** /'grɒgɪ/ *a* (-ier, -iest) grogue, fraco das pernas

**groin** /grɔɪn/ *n* virilha *f*

**groom** /gru:m/ *n* noivo *m*; (*for horses*) moço *m* de estrebaria □ *vt* (*horse*) tratar de; (*fig*) preparar

**groove** /gru:v/ *n* ranhura *f*; (*for door, window*) calha *f*; (*in record*) estria *f*; (*fig*) rotina *f*

**grope** /grəʊp/ *vi* tatear. **~ for** procurar às cegas

**gross** /grəʊs/ *a* (-er, -est) (*vulgar*) grosseiro; (*flagrant*) flagrante; (*of error*) crasso; (*of weight, figure etc*) bruto □ *n* (*pl invar*) grosa *f*. **~ly** *adv* grosseiramente; (*very*) extremamente

**grotesque** /grəʊ'tesk/ *a* grotesco

**grotty** /'grɒtɪ/ *a* (*sl*) sórdido

**grouch** /graʊtʃ/ *vi* (*colloq*) ralhar. **~y** *a* (*colloq*) rabugento

**ground**[1] /graʊnd/ *n* chão *m*, solo *m*; (*area*) terreno *m*; (*reason*) razão *f*, motivo *m*. **~s** jardins *mpl*; (*of coffee*) borra(s) *f* (*pl*) □ *vt/i* (*naut*) encalhar; (*plane*) reter em terra. **~ floor** térreo *m*, (*P*) rés-do-chão *m*. **~less** *a* infundado, sem fundamento

**ground**[2] /graʊnd/ *see* grind

**grounding** /'graʊndɪŋ/ *n* bases *fpl*, conhecimentos *mpl* básicos

**groundsheet** /'graʊndʃi:t/ *n* impermeável *m* para o chão

**groundwork** /'graʊndwɜ:k/ *n* trabalhos *mpl* de base *or* preliminares

**group** /gru:p/ *n* grupo *m* □ *vt/i* agrupar(-se)

**grouse**[1] /graʊs/ *n* (*pl invar*) galo *m* silvestre

**grouse**[2] /graʊs/ *vi* (*colloq: grumble*) resmungar; (*colloq: complain*) queixar-se

**grovel** /'grɒvl/ *vi* (*pt* grovelled) humilhar-se; (*fig*) rebaixar-se

**grow** /grəʊ/ *vi* (*pt* grew, *pp* grown) crescer; (*become*) tornar-se □ *vt* cultivar. **~ old** envelhecer. **~ up** crescer, tornar-se adulto. **~er** *n* cultivador *m*, produtor *m*. **~ing** *a* crescente

**growl** /graʊl/ *vi* rosnar □ *n* rosnadela *f*

**grown** /grəʊn/ *see* grow □ *a* **~ man** homem feito. **~-up** *a* adulto □ (*increase*) aumento *m*; (*med*) tumor *m*

**grub** /grʌb/ *n* larva *f*; (*sl: food*) papança *f* (*colloq*) (*B*) bóia (*sl*) *f*, (*P*) alimento *m*

**grubby** /'grʌbɪ/ *a* (-ier, -iest) sujo, porco

**grudge** /grʌdʒ/ *vt* dar/reconhecer de má vontade □ *n* má vontade *f*. **~ doing** fazer de má vontade. **~ sb sth** dar alg a alguém má vontade. **have a ~ against** ter ressentimento contra.

**grudgingly** *adv* relutantemente

**gruelling** /'gru:əlɪŋ/ *a* estafante, extenuante

**gruesome** /'gru:səm/ *a* macabro

**gruff** /grʌf/ *a* (-er, -est) carrancudo, rude

**grumble** /'grʌmbl/ *vi* resmungar (**at** contra, **por**)

**grumpy** /'grʌmpɪ/ *a* (-ier, -iest) malhumorado, rabugento

**grunt** /grʌnt/ *vi* grunhir □ *n* grunhido *m*

**guarantee** /gærən'ti:/ *n* garantia *f* □ *vt* garantir

**guard** /ga:d/ *vt* guardar, proteger □ *vi* **~ against** precaver-se contra □ *n* guarda *f*; (*person*) guarda *m*; (*on train*) condutor *m*. **~ian** *n* guardião *m*, defensor *m*; (*of orphan*) tutor *m*

**guarded** /'ga:dɪd/ *a* cauteloso, circunspeto, (*P*) circunspecto

**guerrilla** /gə'rɪlə/ *n* guerrilheiro *m*, (*P*) guerrilha *m*. **~ warfare** guerrilha *f*, guerra *f* de guerrilhas

**guess** /ges/ *vt/i* adivinhar; (*suppose*) supor □ *n* suposição *f*, conjetura *f*, (*P*) conjectura *f*

**guesswork** /'geswɜ:k/ *n* suposição *f*, conjetura(s) *f* (*pl*), (*P*) conjectura(s) *f* (*pl*)

**guest** /gest/ *n* convidado *m*; (*in hotel*) hóspede *mf*. **~-house** *n* pensão *f*

**guffaw** /gə'fɔ:/ *n* gargalhada *f* □ *vi* rir à(s) gargalhada(s)

**guidance** /'gaɪdns/ *n* orientação *f*, direção *f*, (*P*) direcção *f*

**guide** /gaɪd/ *n* guia *mf* □ *vt* guiar. **~d missile** míssil *m* guiado; (*remote-control*) míssil *m* teleguiado. **~-dog** *n* cão *m* de cego, cão-guia *m*. **~-lines** *npl* diretrizes *fpl*, (*P*) directrizes *fpl*

**Guide** /gaɪd/ *n* Guia *f*

**guidebook** /'gaɪdbʊk/ *n* guia *m* (turístico)

**guild** /gɪld/ *n* corporação *f*

**guile** /gaɪl/ *n* astúcia *f*, manha *f*

**guilt** /gɪlt/ *n* culpa *f*. **~y** *a* culpado

**guinea-pig** /'gɪnɪpɪg/ n cobaia f, porquinho-da-India m
**guitar** /gɪ'ta:(r)/ n guitarra f, violão m, (P) viola f. **~ist** n guitarrista mf, tocador m de violão, (P) de viola
**gulf** /gʌlf/ n golfo m; (hollow) abismo m
**gull** /gʌl/ n gaivota f
**gullible** /'gʌləbl/ a crédulo
**gully** /'gʌlɪ/ n barranco m; (drain) sarjeta f
**gulp** /gʌlp/ vt engolir, devorar □ vi engolir em seco □ n trago m
**gum**[1] /gʌm/ n (anat) gengiva f
**gum**[2] /gʌm/ n goma f; (chewing-gum) chiclete m, goma f elástica, (P) pastilha f □ vt (pt gummed) colar
**gumboot** /'gʌmbu:t/ n bota f de borracha
**gumption** /'gʌmpʃn/ n (colloq) iniciativa f e bom senso m, cabeça f, juizo m
**gun** /gʌn/ n (pistol) pistola f; (rifle) espingarda f; (cannon) canhão m □ vt (pt gunned) **~ down** abater a tiro
**gunfire** /'gʌnfaɪə(r)/ n tiroteio m
**gunman** /'gʌnmən/ n (pl -men) bandido m armado
**gunpowder** /'gʌnpaʊdə(r)/ n pólvora f
**gunshot** /'gʌnʃɒt/ n tiro m
**gurgle** /'gɜ:gl/ n gorgolejo m □ vi gorgolejar
**gush** /gʌʃ/ vi jorrar □ n jorro m. **~ing** a efusivo, derretido
**gust** /gʌst/ n (of wind) rajada f; (of smoke) nuvem f. **~y** a ventoso
**gusto** /'gʌstəʊ/ n gosto m, entusiasmo m
**gut** /gʌt/ n tripa f. **~s** (belly) barriga f; (colloq: courage) coragem f □ vt (pt gutted) estripar; (fish) limpar; (fire) destruir o interior de
**gutter** /'gʌtə(r)/ n calha f, canaleta f; (in street) sarjeta f, valeta f
**guy** /gaɪ/ n (sl: man) cara m, (P) tipo m (colloq)
**guzzle** /'gʌzl/ vt/i comer/beber com sofreguidão, encher-se (de)
**gym** /dʒɪm/ n (colloq: gymnasium) ginásio m; (colloq: gymnastics) ginástica f. **~slip** n uniforme m escolar
**gym|nasium** /dʒɪm'neɪzɪəm/ n ginásio m. **~nast** /'dʒɪmnæst/ n ginasta mf. **~nastics** /-'næstɪks/ npl ginástica f
**gynaecolog|y** /gaɪnɪ'kɒlədʒɪ/ n ginecologia f. **~ist** n ginecologista mf
**gypsy** /'dʒɪpsɪ/ n cigano m
**gyrate** /dʒaɪ'reɪt/ vi girar

# H

**haberdashery** /'hæbədæʃərɪ/ n armarinho m, (P) retrosaria f
**habit** /'hæbɪt/ n hábito m, costume m; (costume) hábito m. **be in/get into the ~ of** ter/apanhar o hábito de
**habit|able** /'hæbɪtəbl/ a habitável. **~ation** /-'teɪʃn/ n habitação f
**habitat** /'hæbɪtæt/ n habitat m
**habitual** /hə'bɪtʃʊəl/ a habitual, costumeiro; (smoker, liar) inveterado. **~ly** adv habitualmente
**hack**[1] /hæk/ n (horse) cavalo m de aluguel; (writer) escrevinhador (pej) m
**hack**[2] /hæk/ vt cortar, despedaçar. **~ to pieces** cortar em pedaços
**hackneyed** /'hæknɪd/ a banal, batido
**had** /hæd/ see have
**haddock** /'hædək/ n invar hadoque m, eglefim m. **smoked ~** hadoque m fumado
**haemorrhage** /'hemərɪdʒ/ n hemorragia f
**haemorrhoids** /'hemərɔɪdz/ npl hemorróidas fpl
**haggard** /'hægəd/ a desfigurado, com o rosto desfeito, magro e macilento
**haggle** /'hægl/ vi **~ (over)** regatear
**hail**[1] /heɪl/ vt saudar; (taxi) fazer sinal para, chamar □ vi **~ from** vir de
**hail**[2] /heɪl/ n granizo m, (P) saraiva f, (P) chuva de pedra f □ vi chover granizo, (P) saraivar
**hailstone** /'heɪlstəʊn/ n pedra f de granizo
**hair** /heə(r)/ n (on head) cabelo(s) m(pl); (on body) pêlos mpl; (single strand) cabelo m; (of animal) pêlo m. **~-do** n (colloq) penteado m. **~-dryer** n secador m de cabelo. **~-raising** a horripilante, de pôr os cabelos em pé. **~-style** n estilo m de penteado
**hairbrush** /'heəbrʌʃ/ n escova f para o cabelo
**haircut** /'heəkʌt/ n corte m de cabelo
**hairdresser** /'heədresə(r)/ n cabeleireiro m, cabeleireira f
**hairpin** /'heəpɪn/ n grampo m, (P) gancho m para o cabelo. **~ bend** curva f fechada, quase em W
**hairy** /'heərɪ/ a (-ier, -iest) peludo, cabeludo; (sl: terrifying) de pôr os cabelos em pé, horripilante
**hake** /heɪk/ n (pl invar) abrótea f
**half** /ha:f/ n (pl halves /ha:vz/) metade f, meio m □ a meio □ adv ao meio. **~ a dozen** meia dúzia. **~ an hour** meia hora. **~-caste** n mestiço m. **~-hearted** a sem grande

entusiasmo. ~-term *n* férias *fpl* no meio do trimestre. ~-time *n* meio-tempo *m*. ~-way *a* & *adv* a meio caminho. ~-wit *n* idiota *mf*. go halves dividir as despesas

**halibut** /'hælɪbət/ *n* (*pl invar*) halibute *m*

**hall** /hɔːl/ *n* sala *f*; (*entrance*) vestíbulo *m*, entrada *f*; (*mansion*) solar *m*. ~ of residence residência *f* de estudantes

**hallmark** /'hɔːlmɑːk/ *n* (*on gold etc*) marca *f* do contraste; (*fig*) cunho *m*, selo *m*

**hallo** /hə'ləʊ/ *int* & *n* (*greeting, surprise*) olá; (*on phone*) está

**hallow** /'hæləʊ/ *vt* consagrar, santificar

**Halloween** /hæləʊ'iːn/ *n* véspera *f* do Dia de Todos os Santos

**hallucination** /həluːsɪˈneɪʃn/ *n* alucinação *f*

**halo** /'heɪləʊ/ *n* (*pl* -oes) halo *m*, auréola *f*

**halt** /hɔːlt/ *n* parada *f*, (*P*) paragem *f* □ *vt* deter, fazer parar □ *vi* fazer· alto, parar

**halve** /hɑːv/ *vt* dividir ao meio; (*time etc*) reduzir à metade

**ham** /hæm/ *n* presunto *m*

**hamburger** /'hæmbɜːɡə(r)/ *n* hambúrguer *m*, (*P*) hamburgo *m*

**hamlet** /'hæmlɪt/ *n* aldeola *f*, lugarejo *m*

**hammer** /'hæmə(r)/ *n* martelo *m* □ *vt/i* martelar; (*fig*) bater com força

**hammock** /'hæmək/ *n* rede *f* (de dormir)

**hamper**[1] /'hæmpə(r)/ *n* cesto *m*, (*P*) cabaz *m*

**hamper**[2] /'hæmpə(r)/ *vt* dificultar, atrapalhar

**hamster** /'hæmstə(r)/ *n* hamster *m*

**hand** /hænd/ *n* mão *f*; (*of clock*) ponteiro *m*; (*writing*) letra *f*; (*worker*) trabalhador *m*; (*cards*) mão *f*; (*measure*) palmo *m*. (*helping*) ~ ajuda *f*, mão *f* □ *vt* dar, entregar. at ~ à mão. ~-baggage *n* bagagem *f* de mão. ~ in *or* over entregar. ~ out distribuir. ~-out *n* impresso *m*, folheto *m*; (*money*) esmola *f*, donativo *m*. on the one ~... on the other ~ por um lado ... por outro. out of ~ incontrolável. to ~ à mão

**handbag** /'hændbæg/ *n* carteira *f*, bolsa de mão *f*, mala de mão *f*

**handbook** /'hændbʊk/ *n* manual *m*

**handbrake** /'hændbreɪk/ *n* freio *m* de mão, (*P*) travão *m* de mão

**handcuffs** /'hændkʌfs/ *npl* algemas *fpl*

**handful** /'hændfʊl/ *n* mão-cheia *f*, punhado *m*; (*a few*) punhado *m*; (*diffi-*

*cult task*) mão-de-obra *f*. she's a ~ (*colloq*) ela é danada

**handicap** /'hændɪkæp/ *n* (*in competition*) handicap *m*; (*disadvantage*) desvantagem *f* □ *vt* (*pt* handicapped) prejudicar. ~ped *a* deficiente. mentally ~ped deficiente mental

**handicraft** /'hændɪkrɑːft/ *n* artesanato *m*, trabalho *m* manual

**handiwork** /'hændɪwɜːk/ *n* obra *f*, trabalho *m*

**handkerchief** /'hæŋkətʃɪf/ *n* lenço *m*

**handle** /'hændl/ *n* (*of door etc*) maçaneta *f*, puxador *m*; (*of cup etc*) asa *f*; (*of implement*) cabo *m*; (*of pan etc*) alça *f*, (*P*) pega *f* □ *vt* (*touch*) manusear, tocar; (*operate with hands*) manejar; (*deal in*) negociar em; (*deal with*) tratar de; (*person*) lidar com. fly off the ~ (*colloq*) perder as estribeiras

**handlebar** /'hændlbɑː(r)/ *n* guidão *m*, (*P*) guiador *m*

**handmade** /'hændmeɪd/ *a* feito à mão

**handshake** /'hændʃeɪk/ *n* aperto *m* de mão

**handsome** /'hænsəm/ *a* bonito; (*fig*) generoso

**handwriting** /'hændraɪtɪŋ/ *n* letra *f*, caligrafia *f*

**handy** /'hændɪ/ *a* (-ier, -iest) *a* (*convenient, useful*) útil, prático; (*person*) jeitoso; (*near*) à mão

**handyman** /'hændɪmæn/ *n* (*pl* -men) faz-tudo *m*

**hang** /hæŋ/ *vt* (*pt* hung) pendurar, suspender; (*head*) baixar; (*pt* hanged) (*criminal*) enfo.car □ *vi* estar dependurado, pender; (*criminal*) ser enforcado. get the ~ of (*colloq*) pegar o jeito de, (*P*) apanhar. ~ about andar por aí. ~ back hesitar. ~-gliding *n* asa *f* delta. ~ on (*wait*) aguardar. ~ on to (*hold tightly*) agarrar-se a. ~ out (*sl: live*) morar. ~ up (*phone*) desligar. ~-up *n* (*sl*) complexo *m*

**hangar** /'hæŋə(r)/ *n* hangar *m*

**hanger** /'hæŋə(r)/ *n* (*for clothes*) cabide *m*. ~-on *n* parasita *mf*

**hangover** /'hæŋəʊvə(r)/ *n* (*from drinking*) ressaca *f*

**hanker** /'hæŋkə(r)/ *vi* ~ after ansiar por, suspirar por

**haphazard** /hæp'hæzəd/ *a* ~ ly *adv* ao acaso, à sorte

**happen** /'hæpən/ *vi* acontecer, suceder. he ~s to be out por acaso ele não está. ~ing *n* acontecimento *m*

**happ|y** /'hæpɪ/ *a* (-ier, -iest) feliz. be ~y with estar contente com. ~y-go-lucky *a* despreocupado. ~ily *adv* com satisfação; (*fortunately*) felizmente. **she smiled** ~**ily** ela sorriu feliz. ~**iness** n felicidade f

**harass** /'hærəs/ vt amofinar, atormentar, perseguir. ~**ment** n amofinação f, perseguição f. **sexual** ~**ment** assédio m sexual

**harbour** /'ha:bə(r)/ n porto m; (*shelter*) abrigo m □ vt abrigar, dar asilo a; (*fig: in the mind*) ocultar, obrigar

**hard** /ha:d/ a (-er, -est) duro; (*difficult*) difícil □ adv muito, intensamente; (*look*) fixamente; (*pull*) com força; (*think*) a fundo, a sério. ~**back** n livro m encadernado ~**boiled egg** ovo m cozido. **by** muito perto. ~ **disk** disco m rígido. ~**headed** a realista, prático. ~ **of hearing** meio surdo. ~ **shoulder** acostamento m, (P) berma f alcatroada. ~ **up** (*colloq*) sem dinheiro, teso (*sl*), liso (*sl*). ~ **water** água f dura

**hardboard** /'ha:dbo:d/ n madeira f compensada, madeira f prensada, (P) tabopan m

**harden** /'ha:dn/ vt/i endurecer. ~**ed** a (*callous*) calejado; (*robust*) enrijado

**hardly** /'ha:dlɪ/ adv mal, dificilmente, a custo. ~ **ever** quase nunca

**hardship** /'ha:dʃɪp/ n provação f, adversidade f; (*suffering*) sofrimento m; (*financial*) privação f

**hardware** /'ha:dweə(r)/ n ferragens fpl; (*comput*) hardware m

**hardy** /'ha:dɪ/ a (-ier, -iest) resistente

**hare** /heə(r)/ n lebre f

**hark** /ha:k/ vi ~ **back to** voltar a, recordar

**harm** /ha:m/ n mal m □ vt prejudicar, fazer mal a. ~**ful** a prejudicial, nocivo. ~**less** a inofensivo. **out of** ~**'s way** a salvo. **there's no** ~ **in** não há mal em

**harmonica** /ha:'mɒnɪkə/ n gaita f de boca, (P) beiços

**harmon|y** /'ha:mənɪ/ n harmonia f. ~**ious** /-'məʊnɪəs/ a harmonioso. ~**ize** vt/i harmonizar(-se)

**harness** /'ha:nɪs/ n arreios mpl □ vt arrear; (*fig: use*) aproveitar, utilizar

**harp** /ha:p/ n harpa f □ vi ~ **on** (*about*) repisar. ~**ist** n harpista mf

**harpoon** /ha:'pu:n/ n arpão m

**harpsichord** /'ha:psɪkɔ:d/ n cravo m

**harrowing** /'hærəʊɪŋ/ a dilacerante, lancinante

**harsh** /ha:ʃ/ a (-er, -est) duro, severo; (*texture, voice*) áspero; (*light*) cru; (*colour*) gritante; (*climate*) rigoroso. ~**ly** adv duramente. ~**ness** n dureza f

**harvest** /'ha:vɪst/ n colheita f, ceifa f □ vt colher, ceifar

**has** /hæz/ see **have**

**hash** /hæʃ/ n picadinho m, carne f cozida; (*fig: jumble*) bagunça f. **make a** ~ **of** fazer uma bagunça

**hashish** /'hæʃɪʃ/ n haxixe m

**hassle** /'hæsl/ n (*colloq: quarrel*) discussão f, (*colloq: struggle*) dificuldade f □ vt (*colloq*) aborrecer

**haste** /heɪst/ n pressa f. **make** ~ apressar-se

**hasten** /'heɪsn/ vt/i apressar(-se)

**hast|y** /'heɪstɪ/ a (-ier, -iest) apressado; (*too quick*) precipitado. ~**ily** adv às pressas, precipitadamente

**hat** /hæt/ n chapéu m

**hatch**[1] /hætʃ/ n (*for food*) postigo m; (*naut*) escotilha f

**hatch**[2] /hætʃ/ vt/i chocar; (*a plot etc*) tramar, urdir

**hatchback** /'hætʃbæk/ n carro m de três ou cinco portas

**hatchet** /'hætʃɪt/ n machadinha f

**hate** /heɪt/ n ódio m □ vt odiar, detestar. ~**ful** a odioso, detestável

**hatred** /'heɪtrɪd/ n ódio m

**haughty** /'hɔ:tɪ/ a (-ier, -iest) altivo, soberbo, arrogante

**haul** /hɔ:l/ vt arrastar, puxar; (*goods*) transportar em camião □ n (*booty*) presa f; (*fish caught*) apanha f; (*distance*) percurso m. ~**age** n transporte m de cargas. ~**ier** n (*firm*) transportadora f rodoviária; (*person*) fretador m

**haunt** /hɔ:nt/ vt rondar, freqüentar; (P) frequentar; (*ghost*) assombrar; (*thought*) obcecar □ n lugar m favorito. ~**ed house** casa f malassombrada

**have** /hæv/ vt (3 sing pres **has**, pt **had**) ter; (*bath etc*) tomar; (*meal*) fazer; (*walk*) dar □ v aux ter. ~ **done** ter feito. ~ **it out (with)** pôr a coisa em pratos limpos, pedir uma explicação (para). ~ **sth done** mandar fazer alg coisa

**haven** /'heɪvn/ n porto m; (*refuge*) refúgio m

**haversack** /'hævəsæk/ n mochila f

**havoc** /'hævək/ n estragos mpl. **play** ~ **with** causar estragos em

**hawk**[1] /hɔ:k/ n falcão m

**hawk**[2] /hɔ:k/ vt vender de porta em porta. ~**er** n vendedor m ambulante

**hawthorn** /'hɔ:θɔ:n/ n pirilteiro m, estrepeiro m

**hay** /heɪ/ n feno m. ~ **fever** febre f do feno

**haystack** /'heɪstæk/ n palheiro m, (P) meda f de feno

**haywire** /'heɪwaɪə(r)/ a **go** ~ (*colloq*) ficar transtornado

**hazard** /'hæzəd/ n risco m □ vt arriscar. ~ **warning lights** pisca-alerta m. ~**ous** a arriscado

**haze** /heɪz/ *n* bruma *f*, neblina *f*, cerração *f*

**hazel** /'heɪzl/ *n* aveleira *f*. **~-nut** *n* avelã *f*

**hazy** /'heɪzɪ/ *a* (-ier, -iest) brumoso, encoberto; (*fig: vague*) vago

**he** /hi:/ *pron* ele □ *n* macho *m*

**head** /hed/ *n* cabeça *f*; (*chief*) chefe *m*; (*of beer*) espuma *f* □ *a* principal □ *vt* encabeçar, estar à frente de □ *vi* **~ for** dirigir-se para. **~-dress** *n* toucador *m*. **~ first** de cabeça. **~-on** *a* frontal □ *adv* de frente. **~s or tails?** cara ou coroa? **~ waiter** chefe de garçons *m*, (*P*) dos criados. **~er** *n* (*football*) cabeçada *f*

**headache** /'hedeɪk/ *n* dor *f* de cabeça

**heading** /'hedɪŋ/ *n* cabeçalho *m*, título *m*; (*subject category*) rubrica *f*

**headlamp** /'hedlæmp/ *n* farol *m*

**headland** /'hedlənd/ *n* promontório *m*

**headlight** /'hedlaɪt/ *n* farol *m*

**headline** /'hedlaɪn/ *n* título *m*, cabeçalho *m*

**headlong** /'hedlɒŋ/ *a* de cabeça; (*rash*) precipitado □ *adv* de cabeça; (*rashly*) precipitadamente

**head|master** /hed'ma:stə(r)/ *n* diretor *m*, (*P*) director *m*. **~mistress** *n* diretora *f*, (*P*) directora *f*

**headphone** /'hedfəʊn/ *n* fone *m* de cabeça, (*P*) auscultador *m*

**headquarters** /hed'kwɔ:təz/ *npl* sede *f*, (*mil*) quartel *m* general

**headrest** /'hedrest/ *n* apoio *m* para a cabeça

**headroom** /'hedru:m/ *n* (*auto*) espaço *m* para a cabeça; (*bridge*) limite *m* de altura, altura *f* máxima

**headstrong** /'hedstrɒŋ/ *a* teimoso

**headway** /'hedweɪ/ *n* progresso *m*. **make ~** fazer progressos

**heady** /'hedɪ/ *a* (-ier, -iest) empolgante

**heal** /hi:l/ *vt/i* curar(-se), sarar; (*wound*) cicatrizar

**health** /helθ/ *n* saúde *f*. **~ centre** posto *m* de saúde. **~ foods** alimentos *mpl* naturais. **~y** *a* saudável, sadio

**heap** /hi:p/ *n* monte *m*, pilha *f* □ *vt* amontoar, empilhar. **~s of money** (*colloq*) dinheiro aos montes (*colloq*)

**hear** /hɪə(r)/ *vt/i* (*pt* heard /hɜ:d/) ouvir. **~, hear!** apoiado! **~ from** ter notícias de. **~ of or about** ouvir falar de. **I won't ~ of it** nem quero ouvir falar nisso. **~ing** *n* ouvido *m*, audição *f*; (*jur*) audiência *f*. **~ing-aid** *n* aparelho *m* de audição

**hearsay** /'hɪəseɪ/ *n* boato *m*. **it's only ~** é só por ouvir dizer

**hearse** /hɜ:s/ *n* carro *m* funerário

**heart** /hɑ:t/ *n* coração *m*. **~s** (*cards*) copas *fpl*. **at ~** no fundo. **by ~** de cor. **~ attack** ataque *m* de coração. **~-beat** *n* pulsação *f*, batida *f*. **~-breaking** *a* de cortar o coração. **~-broken** *a* com o coração partido, desfeito. **~-to-heart** *a* com o coração nas mãos. **lose ~** perder a coragem, desanimar

**heartburn** /'hɑ:tbɜ:n/ *n* azia *f*

**hearten** /'hɑ:tn/ *vt* animar, encorajar

**heartfelt** /'hɑ:tfelt/ *a* sincero, sentido

**hearth** /hɑ:θ/ *n* lareira *f*

**heartless** /'hɑ:tlɪs/ *a* insensível, desalmado, cruel

**heart|y** /'hɑ:tɪ/ *a* (-ier, -iest) caloroso; (*meal*) abundante. **~ily** *adv* calorosamente; (*eat, laugh*) com vontade

**heat** /hi:t/ *n* calor *m*; (*fig*) ardor *m*; (*contest*) eliminatória *f* □ *vt/i* aquecer. **~stroke** *n* insolação *f*. **~wave** *n* onda *f* de calor. **~er** *n* aquecedor *m*. **~ing** *n* aquecimento *m*

**heated** /'hi:tɪd/ *a* (*fig*) acalorado, aceso

**heathen** /'hi:ðn/ *n* pagão *m*, pagã *f*

**heather** /'heðə(r)/ *n* urze *f*

**heave** /hi:v/ *vt/i* (*lift*) içar; (*a sigh*) soltar; (*retch*) ter náuseas; (*colloq: throw*) atirar

**heaven** /'hevn/ *n* céu *m*. **~ly** *a* celestial; (*colloq*) divino

**heav|y** /'hevɪ/ *a* (-ier, -iest) pesado; (*blow, rain*) forte; (*cold, drinker*) grande; (*traffic*) intenso. **~ily** *adv* pesadamente; (*drink, smoke etc*) inveterado

**heavyweight** /'hevɪweɪt/ *n* (*boxing*) peso-pesado *m*

**Hebrew** /'hi:bru:/ *a* hebreu, hebraico □ *n* (*lang*) hebreu *m*

**heckle** /'hekl/ *vt* interromper, interpelar

**hectic** /'hektɪk/ *a* muito agitado, febril

**hedge** /hedʒ/ *n* sebe *f* □ *vt* cercar □ *vi* (*in answering*) usar de evasivas. **~ one's bets** (*fig*) resguardar-se

**hedgehog** /'hedʒhɒg/ *n* ouriço-cacheiro *m*

**heed** /hi:d/ *vt* prestar atenção a, escutar □ *n* **pay ~ to** prestar atenção a, dar ouvidos a. **~less** *a* **~less of** indiferente a, sem prestar atenção a

**heel** /hi:l/ *n* calcanhar *m*; (*of shoe*) salto *m*; (*sl*) canalha *m*

**hefty** /'heftɪ/ *a* (-ier, -iest) robusto e corpulento

**height** /haɪt/ *n* altura *f*; (*of mountain, plane*) altitude *f*; (*fig*) auge *m*, cúmulo *m*

**heighten** /'haɪtn/ *vt/i* aumentar, elevar(-se)

**heir** /eə(r)/ *n* herdeiro *m*. **~ess** *n* herdeira *f*

**heirloom** /'eəlu:m/ n peça f de família, (P) relíquia f de família
**held** /held/ see **hold**[1]
**helicopter** /'helikɒptə(r)/ n helicóptero m
**hell** /hel/ n inferno m. **for the ~ of it** só por gozo. ~**bent** a decidido a todo o custo (**on** a). ~**ish** a infernal
**hello** /hə'ləʊ/ int & n = **hallo**
**helm** /helm/ n leme m
**helmet** /'helmɪt/ n capacete m
**help** /help/ vt/i ajudar □ n ajuda f. **home ~** empregada f, faxineira f, (P) mulher f a dias. ~ **o.s. to** servir-se de. **he cannot ~ laughing** ele não pode conter o riso. **it can't be ~ed** não há remédio. ~**er** n ajudante mf. ~**ful** a útil; (*serviceable*) de grande ajuda. ~**less** a impotente
**helping** /'helpɪŋ/ n porção f, dose f
**hem** /hem/ n bainha f □ vt (pt **hemmed**) fazer a bainha. ~ **in** cercar, encurralar
**hemisphere** /'hemɪsfɪə(r)/ n hemisfério m
**hemp** /hemp/ n cânhamo m
**hen** /hen/ n galinha f
**hence** /hens/ adv ( *from now*) a partir desta altura; ( *for this reason*) daí, por isso. **a week ~** daqui a uma semana. ~**forth** adv de agora em diante, doravante
**henpecked** /'henpekt/ a mandado, (P) dominado pela mulher
**her** /hз:(r)/ pron a (a ela); (*after prep*) ela. (**to**) ~ lhe. **I know ~** conheço-a □ a seu(s), sua(s); dela
**herald** /'herəld/ vt anunciar
**heraldry** /'herəldrɪ/ n heráldica f
**herb** /hз:b/ n erva f culinária or medicinal
**herd** /hз:d/ n manada f; (*of pigs*) vara f □ vi ~ **together** juntar-se em rebanho
**here** /hɪə/ adv aqui □ int tome; aqui está. **to/from ~** para aqui/daqui
**hereafter** /hɪər'ɑ:ftə(r)/ adv de/para o futuro, daqui em diante □ n **the ~** a vida de além-túmulo, (P) a vida futura
**hereby** /hɪə'baɪ/ adv ( *jur*) pelo presente ato ou decreto, etc, (P) pelo presente acto ou decreto, etc
**hereditary** /hɪ'redɪtrɪ/ a hereditário
**heredity** /hɪ'redɪtɪ/ n hereditariedade f
**here|sy** /'herəsɪ/ n heresia f. ~**tic** n herege mf. ~**tical** /hɪ'retɪkl/ a herético
**heritage** /'herɪtɪdʒ/ n herança f, patrimônio m, (P) património m
**hermit** /'hз:mɪt/ n eremita m
**hernia** /'hз:nɪə/ n hérnia f
**hero** /'hɪərəʊ/ n (pl -oes) herói m
**heroic** /hɪ'rəʊɪk/ a heróico

**heroin** /'herəʊɪn/ n heroína f
**heroine** /'herəʊɪn/ n heroína f
**heroism** /'herəʊɪzəm/ n heroísmo m
**heron** /'herən/ n garça f
**herring** /'herɪŋ/ n arenque m
**hers** /hз:z/ poss pron o(s) seu(s), a(s) sua(s), o(s) dela, a(s) dela. **it is ~** é (o) dela or o seu
**herself** /hз:'self/ pron ela mesma; (*reflexive*) se. **by ~** sozinha. **for ~** para si mesma. **to ~** a/para si mesma. **Mary ~ said so** foi a própria Maria que o disse
**hesitant** /'hezɪtənt/ a hesitante
**hesitat|e** /'hezɪteɪt/ vt hesitar. ~**ion** /-'teɪʃn/ n hesitação f
**heterosexual** /hetərəʊ'seksjʊəl/ a & n heterossexual (mf)
**hexagon** /'heksəgən/ n hexágono m. ~**al** /-'æɡənl/ a hexagonal
**hey** /heɪ/ int eh, olá
**heyday** /'heɪdeɪ/ n auge m, apogeu m
**hi** /haɪ/ int olá, viva
**hibernat|e** /'haɪbəneɪt/ vi hibernar. ~**ion** /-'neɪʃn/ n hibernação f
**hiccup** /'hɪkʌp/ n soluço m □ vi soluçar, estar com soluços
**hide**[1] /haɪd/ vt/i (pt **hid**, pp **hidden**) esconder(-se) (**from** de). ~**-and-seek** n (*game*) esconde-esconde m. ~**out** n (*colloq*) esconderijo m
**hide**[2] /haɪd/ n pele f, couro m
**hideous** /'hɪdɪəs/ a horrendo, medonho
**hiding** /'haɪdɪŋ/ n (*colloq: thrashing*) sova f, surra f. **go into ~** esconder-se. ~**-place** n esconderijo m
**hierarchy** /'haɪərɑ:kɪ/ n hierarquia f
**hi-fi** /'haɪfaɪ/ a & n (de) alta fidelidade ( f )
**high** /haɪ/ a (-er, -est) alto; ( *price, number*) elevado; (*voice, pitch*) agudo □ n alta f □ adv alto. **two metres ~** com dois metros de altura. ~ **chair** cadeira f alta para crianças. ~**handed** a autoritário, prepotente. ~ **jump** salto m em altura. ~**-rise building** edifício m alto, (P) torre f. ~ **school** escola f secundária. **in the ~ season** em plena estação. ~**-speed** a ultra-rápido. ~**-spirited** a animado, vivo. ~ **spot** (*sl*) ponto m culminante. ~ **street** rua f principal. ~ **tide** maré f alta. ~**er education** ensino m superior
**highbrow** /'haɪbraʊ/ a & n (*colloq*) intelectual (m)
**highlight** /'haɪlaɪt/ n ( *fig*) ponto m alto □ vt salientar, pôr em relevo, realçar
**highly** /'haɪlɪ/ adv altamente, extremamente. ~**-strung** a muito sensível, nervoso, tenso. **speak ~ of** falar bem de

**Highness** /'haɪnɪs/ n Alteza f

**highway** /'haɪweɪ/ n estrada f, rodovia f. **H~ Code** Código m Nacional de Trânsito

**hijack** /'haɪdʒæk/ vt seqüestrar, (P) sequestrar □ n seqüestro m, (P) sequestro m. **~er** n (of plane) pirata m (do ar)

**hike** /haɪk/ n caminhada no campo f □ vi fazer uma caminhada. **~r** /-ə(r)/ n excursionista mf, caminhante mf

**hilarious** /hɪ'leərɪəs/ a divertido, desopilante

**hill** /hɪl/ n colina f, monte m; (slope) ladeira f, subida f. **~y** a acidentado

**hillside** /'hɪlsaɪd/ n encosta f, vertente f

**hilt** /hɪlt/ n punho m. **to the ~** completamente, inteiramente

**him** /hɪm/ pron o (a ele); (after prep) ele. **(to) ~** lhe. **I know ~** conheço-o

**himself** /hɪm'self/ pron ele mesmo; (reflexive) se. **by ~** sozinho. **for ~** para si mesmo. **to ~** a/para si mesmo. **Peter ~ saw it** foi o próprio Pedro que o viu

**hind** /haɪnd/ a traseiro, posterior

**hind|er** /'hɪndə(r)/ vt empatar, estorvar; (prevent) impedir. **~rance** n estorvo m

**hindsight** /'haɪndsaɪt/ n **with ~** em retrospecto

**Hindu** /hɪn'duː/ n & a hindu (mf). **~ism** /-zəm/ n hinduísmo m

**hinge** /hɪndʒ/ n dobradiça f □ vi **~ on** depender de

**hint** /hɪnt/ n insinuação f, indireta f, (P) indirecta f; (advice) sugestão f, dica f (colloq) □ vt dar a entender, insinuar □ vi **~ at** fazer alusão a

**hip** /hɪp/ n quadril m

**hippie** /'hɪpɪ/ n hippie mf

**hippopotamus** /hɪpə'pɒtəməs/ n (pl -muses) hipopótamo m

**hire** /'haɪə(r)/ vt alugar; (person) contratar □ n aluguel m, (P) aluguer m. **~-purchase** n compra f a prestações, (P) crediário m

**hirsute** /'hɜːsjuːt/ a hirsuto

**his** /hɪz/ a seu(s), sua(s), dele □ poss pron o(s) seu(s), a(s) sua(s), o(s) dele, a(s) dele. **it is ~** é (o) dele or o seu

**Hispanic** /hɪs'pænɪk/ a hispânico

**hiss** /hɪs/ n silvo m; (for disapproval) assobio m, vaia f □ vt/i sibilar; (for disapproval) assobiar, vaiar

**historian** /hɪ'stɔːrɪən/ n historiador m

**histor|y** /'hɪstərɪ/ n história f. **~ic(al)** /hɪ'stɒrɪk(l)/ a histórico

**hit** /hɪt/ vt (pt hit, pres p hitting) atingir, bater em; (knock against, collide with) chocar com, ir de encontro a; (strike a target) acertar em; (find)

descobrir; (affect) atingir □ vi **~ on** dar com □ n pancada f; (fig: success) sucesso m. **~ it off** dar-se bem (with com). **~-and-run** a (driver) que foge depois do desastre. **~-or-miss** a ao acaso

**hitch** /hɪtʃ/ vt atar, prender; (to a hook) enganchar □ n sacão m; (snag) problema m. **~ a lift**, **~-hike** viajar de carona, (P) boleia. **~-hiker** n o que viaja de carona, boleia. **~ up** puxar para cima

**hive** /haɪv/ n colméia f □ vt **~ off** separar e tornar independente

**hoard** /hɔːd/ vt juntar, açambarcar □ n provisão f; (of valuables) tesouro m

**hoarding** /'hɔːdɪŋ/ n tapume m, outdoor m

**hoarse** /hɔːs/ a (-er, -est) rouco. **~ness** n rouquidão f

**hoax** /həʊks/ n (malicious) logro m, embuste m; (humorous) trote m □ vt (malicious) engancer, lograr; passar um trote, pregar uma peça

**hob** /hɒb/ n placa f de aquecimento (do fogão)

**hobble** /'hɒbl/ vi coxear □ vt pear

**hobby** /'hɒbɪ/ n passatempo m favorito. **~-horse** n (fig) tópico m favorito

**hock** /hɒk/ n vinho m branco do Reno

**hockey** /'hɒkɪ/ n hóquei m

**hoe** /həʊ/ n enxada f □ vt trabalhar com enxada

**hog** /hɒg/ n porco m; (greedy person) glutão m □ vt (pt hogged) (colloq) açambarcar

**hoist** /hɔɪst/ vt içar □ n guindaste m, (P) monta-cargas m

**hold**[1] /həʊld/ vt (pt held) segurar; (contain) levar; (possess) ter, possuir; (occupy) ocupar; (keep, maintain) conservar, manter; (affirm) manter □ vi (of rope etc) agüentar(-se), (P) aguentar(-se) □ n (influence) domínio m. **get ~ of** pôr as mãos em; (fig) apanhar. **~ back** reter. **~ on** (colloq) esperar. **~ on to** guardar; (cling to) agarrar-se a. **~ one's breath** suster a respiração. **~ one's tongue** calar-se. **~ the line** não desligar. **~ out** resistir. **~ up** (support) sustentar; (delay) demorar; (rob) assaltar. **~-up** n atraso m; (auto) engarrafamento m; (robbery) assalto m. **~ with** agüentar, (P) aguentar. **~er** n detentor m; (of post, title etc) titular mf; (for object) suporte m

**hold**[2] /həʊld/ n (of ship, plane) porão m

**holdall** /'həʊldɔːl/ n saco m de viagem

**holding** /'həʊldɪŋ/ n (land) propriedade f; (comm) ações fpl, (P) acções fpl, valores mpl, holding m

**hole** /həʊl/ n buraco m □ vt abrir buraco(s) em, esburacar

**holiday** /'hɒlədeɪ/ n férias fpl; (day off; public) feriado m □ vi passar férias. ~-**maker** n pessoa f em férias; (in summer) veranista mf, (P) veraneante mf

**holiness** /'həʊlmɪs/ n santidade f

**Holland** /'hɒlənd/ n Holanda f

**hollow** /'hɒləʊ/ a oco, vazio; (fig) falso; (cheeks) fundo; (sound) surdo □ n (in the ground) cavidade f; (in the hand) cova f

**holly** /'hɒlɪ/ n azevinho m

**holster** /'həʊlstə(r)/ n coldre m

**holy** /'həʊlɪ/ a (-ier, -iest) santo, sagrado; (water) benta. **H~ Ghost, H~ Spirit** Espírito m Santo

**homage** /'hɒmɪdʒ/ n homenagem f. **pay ~ to** prestar homenagem a

**home** /həʊm/ n casa f, lar m; (institution) lar m, asilo m; (country) país m natal □ a caseiro, doméstico; (of family) de família; (pol) nacional, interno; (football match) em casa □ adv (at) ~ em casa. **come/go ~** vir/ir para casa. **make oneself at ~** não fazer cerimónia, (P) cerimónia. ~-**made** a caseiro. **H~ Office** Ministério m do Interior. ~ **town** cidade f or terra f natal. ~ **truth** dura verdade f, verdade(s) f (pl) amarga(s). ~**less** a sem casa, desabrigado

**homeland** /'həʊmlænd/ n pátria f

**homely** /'həʊmlɪ/ a (-ier, -iest) (simple) simples; (Amer: ugly) sem graça

**homesick** /'həʊmsɪk/ a **be ~** ter saudades

**homeward** /'həʊmwəd/ a (journey) de regresso

**homework** /'həʊmwɜːk/ n trabalho m de casa, dever m de casa

**homicide** /'hɒmɪsaɪd/ n homicídio m; (person) homicida mf

**homoeopath|y** /həʊmɪ'ɒpəθɪ/ n homeopatia f.~**ic** a homeopático

**homosexual** /hɒmə'sekʃʊəl/ a & n homossexual (mf)

**honest** /'ɒnɪst/ a honesto; (frank) franco. ~**ly** adv honestamente; (frankly) francamente. ~**y** n honestidade f

**honey** /'hʌnɪ/ n mel m; (colloq: darling) querido m, querida f, meu bem m

**honeycomb** /'hʌnɪkəʊm/ n favo m de mel

**honeymoon** /'hʌnɪmuːn/ n lua de mel f

**honorary** /'ɒnərərɪ/ a honorário

**honour** /'ɒnə(r)/ n honra f □ vt honrar. ~**able** a honrado, honroso

**hood** /hʊd/ n capuz m; (car roof) capota f, (P) tejadilho m; (Amer: bonnet) capô m, (P) capot m

**hoodwink** /'hʊdwɪŋk/ vt enganar

**hoof** /huːf/ n (pl -fs) casco m

**hook** /hʊk/ n gancho m; (on garment) colchete m; (for fishing) anzol m □ vt enganchar; (fish) apanhar, pescar. **off the ~** livre de dificuldades; (phone) desligado

**hooked** /hʊkt/ a **be ~ on** (sl) ter o vício de, estar viciado em

**hookey** /'hʊkɪ/ n **play ~** (Amer sl) fazer gazeta

**hooligan** /'huːlɪgən/ n desordeiro m

**hoop** /huːp/ n arco m; (of cask) cinta f

**hooray** /hu:'reɪ/ int & n = **hurrah**

**hoot** /hu:t/ n (of owl) pio m de mocho; (of horn) buzinada f; (jeer) apupo m □ vi (of owl) piar; (of horn) buzinar; (jeer) apupar. ~**er** n buzina f; (of factory) sereia f

**Hoover** /'hu:və(r)/ n aspirador de pó m, (P) aspirador m □ vt passar o aspirador

**hop**[1] /hɒp/ vi (pt hopped) saltar num pé só, (P) ao pé coxinho □ n salto m. ~ **in** (colloq) subir, saltar (colloq). ~ **it** (sl) pôr-se a andar (colloq). ~ **out** (colloq) descer, saltar (colloq)

**hop**[2] /hɒp/ n (plant) lúpulo m. ~**s** espigas fpl de lúpulo

**hope** /həʊp/ n esperança f □ vt/i esperar. ~ **for** esperar (ter). ~**ful** a esperançoso; (promising) promissor. **be ~ful (that)** ter esperança (que), confiar (em que). ~**fully** adv esperançosamente; (it is hoped that) é de esperar que. ~**less** a desesperado, sem esperança; (incompetent) incapaz

**horde** /hɔːd/ n horda f

**horizon** /hə'raɪzn/ n horizonte m

**horizontal** /hɒrɪ'zɒntl/ a horizontal

**hormone** /'hɔːməʊn/ n hormônio m, (P) hormona f

**horn** /hɔːn/ n chifre m, corno m; (of car) buzina f, (mus) trompa f. ~**y** a caloso, calejado

**hornet** /'hɔːnɪt/ n vespão m

**horoscope** /'hɒrəskəʊp/ n horóscopo m, (P) horoscópio m

**horrible** /'hɒrəbl/ a horrível, horroroso

**horrid** /'hɒrɪd/ a horrível, horripilante

**horrific** /hə'rɪfɪk/ a horrífico

**horr|or** /'hɒrə(r)/ n horror m □ a (film etc) de terror. ~**ify** vt horrorizar, horripilar

**horse** /hɔːs/ n cavalo m. ~-**chestnut** n castanha f da Índia. ~-**racing** n corrida f de cavalos, hipismo m. ~-**radish** n rábano m

**horseback** /'hɔːsbæk/ n **on ~** a cavalo

**horseplay** /'hɔ:spleɪ/ n brincadeira f grosseira, abrutalhada f
**horsepower** /'hɔ:spaʊə(r)/ n cavalo-vapor m
**horseshoe** /'hɔ:sʃu:/ n ferradura f
**horticultur|e** /'hɔ:tɪkʌltʃə(r)/ n horticultura f. ~**al** /-'kʌltʃərəl/ a hortícola
**hose** /həʊz/ n ~(-pipe) mangueira f □ vt regar com a mangueira
**hospice** /'hɒspɪs/ n hospício m; (for travellers) hospedaria f
**hospit|able** /hə'spɪtəbl/ a hospitaleiro. ~**ality** /-'tælətɪ/ n hospitalidade f
**hospital** /'hɒspɪtl/ n hospital m
**host**[1] /həʊst/ n anfitrião m, dono m da casa. ~**ess** n anfitriã f, dona f da casa
**host**[2] /həʊst/ n a ~ of uma multidão de, um grande número de
**host**[3] /həʊst/ n (relig) hóstia f
**hostage** /'hɒstɪdʒ/ n refém m
**hostel** /'hɒstl/ n residência f de estudantes etc
**hostil|e** /'hɒstaɪl/ a hostil. ~**ity** /hɒ'stɪlətɪ/ n hostilidade f
**hot** /hɒt/ a (hotter, hottest) quente; (culin) picante. **be** or **feel** ~ estar com or ter calor. **it is** ~ está or faz calor □ vt/i (pt hotted) ~ **up** (colloq) aquecer. ~ **dog** cachorro-quente m. ~ **line** linha directa f, (P) directa esp entre chefes de estado. ~**-water bottle** saco m de água quente
**hotbed** /'hɒtbed/ n (fig) foco m
**hotchpotch** /'hɒtʃpɒtʃ/ n misturada f, (P) salgalhada f
**hotel** /həʊ'tel/ n hotel m. ~**ier** /-ɪə(r)/ n hoteleiro m
**hound** /haʊnd/ n cão m de caça e de corrida, sabujo m □ vt acossar, perseguir
**hour** /'aʊə(r)/ n hora f. ~**ly** adv de hora em hora □ a de hora em hora. ~**ly pay** retribuição f horária. **paid** ~**ly** pago por hora
**house**[1] /haʊs/ n (pl ~s /'haʊzɪz/) n casa f; (pol) câmara f. **on the** ~ por conta da casa. ~**-warming** n inauguração f da casa
**house**[2] /haʊz/ vt alojar; (store) arrecadar, guardar
**houseboat** /'haʊsbəʊt/ n casa f flutuante
**household** /'haʊshəʊld/ n família f, agregado m familiar. ~**er** n ocupante mf; (owner) proprietário m
**housekeep|er** /'haʊskɪːpə(r)/ n governanta f. ~**ing** n (work) tarefas fpl domésticas
**housewife** /'haʊswaɪf/ n (pl -wives) dona f de casa
**housework** /'haʊswɜːk/ n tarefas fpl domésticas

**housing** /'haʊzɪŋ/ n alojamento m. ~ **estate** zona f residencial
**hovel** /'hɒvl/ n casebre m, tugúrio m
**hover** /'hɒvə(r)/ vi pairar; (linger) deixar-se ficar, demorar-se
**hovercraft** /'hɒvəkra:ft/ n invar aerobarco m, hovercraft m
**how** /haʊ/ adv como. ~ **long/old is...?** que comprimento/idade tem...? ~ **far?** a que distância? ~ **many?** quantos? ~ **much?** quanto? ~ **often?** com que frequência, (P) frequência? ~ **pretty it is** como é lindo. ~ **about a walk?** e se fôssemos dar uma volta? ~ **are you?** como vai? ~ **do you do?** muito prazer! **and** ~! oh se é!
**however** /haʊ'evə(r)/ adv de qualquer maneira; (though) contudo, no entanto, todavia. ~ **small it may be** por menor que seja
**howl** /haʊl/ n uivo m □ vi uivar
**HP** abbr see **hire-purchase**
**hp** abbr see **horsepower**
**hub** /hʌb/ n cubo m da roda; (fig) centro m. ~**-cap** n calota f, (P) tampão m da roda
**hubbub** /'hʌbʌb/ n chinfrim m
**huddle** /'hʌdl/ vt/i apinhar(-se). ~ **together** aconchegar-se
**hue**[1] /hju:/ n matiz f, tom m
**hue**[2] /hju:/ n ~ **and cry** clamor m, alarido m
**huff** /hʌf/ n **in a** ~ com raiva, zangado
**hug** /hʌg/ vt (pt hugged) abraçar, apertar nos braços; (keep close to) chegar-se a □ n abraço m
**huge** /hju:dʒ/ a enorme
**hulk** /hʌlk/ n casco (esp de navio desmantelado) m. ~**ing** a (colloq) desajeitadão m
**hull** /hʌl/ n (of ship) casco m
**hullo** /hə'ləʊ/ int & n = **hallo**
**hum** /hʌm/ vt/i (pt hummed) cantar com a boca fechada; (of insect, engine) zumbir □ n zumbido m
**human** /'hju:mən/ a humano □ n ~ **(being)** ser m humano
**humane** /hju:'meɪn/ a humano, compassivo
**humanitarian** /hju:mænɪ'teərɪən/ a humanitário
**humanity** /hju:'mænətɪ/ n humanidade f
**humbl|e** /'hʌmbl/ a (-er, -est) humilde □ vt humilhar. ~**y** adv humildemente
**humdrum** /'hʌmdrʌm/ a monótono, rotineiro
**humid** /'hju:mɪd/ a úmido, (P) húmido. ~**ity** /-'mɪdətɪ/ n umidade f, (P) humidade f
**humiliat|e** /hju:'mɪlɪeɪt/ vt humilhar. ~**ion** /-'eɪʃn/ n humilhação f

**humility** /hju:'mɪlətɪ/ n humildade f

**humorist** /'hju:mərɪst/ n humorista mf

**hum|our** /'hju:mə(r)/ n humor m □ vt fazer a vontade de. **~orous** a humorístico; (person) divertido, espirituoso

**hump** /hʌmp/ n corcova f; (of the back) corcunda f □ vt corcovar, arquear. **the ~** (sl) a neura (colloq)

**hunch**[1] /hʌntʃ/ vt curvar. **~ed up** curvado

**hunch**[2] /hʌntʃ/ n (colloq) palpite m

**hunchback** /'hʌntʃbæk/ n corcunda mf

**hundred** /'hʌndrəd/ a cem □ n centena f, cento m. **~s of** centenas de. **~fold** a cêntuplo □ adv cem vezes mais. **~th** a & n centésimo (m)

**hundredweight** /'hʌndrədweɪt/ n quintal m (= 50,8 kg; Amer 45,36 kg)

**hung** /hʌŋ/ see **hang**

**Hungar|y** /'hʌŋgərɪ/ n Hungria f. **~ian** /-'geərɪən/ a & n húngaro (m)

**hunger** /'hʌŋgə(r)/ n fome f □ vi **~ for** ter fome de; (fig) desejar vivamente, ansiar por

**hungr|y** /'hʌŋgrɪ/ a (ier, -iest) esfomeado, faminto. **be ~y** ter fome, estar com fome. **~ily** adv avidamente

**hunk** /hʌŋk/ n grande naco m

**hunt** /hʌnt/ vt/i caçar. □ n caça f. **~ for** andar à caça de, andar à procura de. **~er** n caçador m. **~ing** n caça f, caçada f

**hurdle** /'hɜ:dl/ n obstáculo m

**hurl** /hɜ:l/ vt arremessar, lançar com força

**hurrah, hurray** /hʊ'ra:, hʊ'reɪ/ int & n hurra (m), viva (m)

**hurricane** /'hʌrɪkən/ n furacão m

**hurried** /'hʌrɪd/ a apressado. **~ly** adv apressadamente, às pressas

**hurry** /'hʌrɪ/ vt/i apressar(-se), despachar(-se) □ n pressa f. **be in a ~** estar com or ter pressa. **do sth in a ~** fazer alg coisa às pressas. **~ up!** ande logo

**hurt** /hɜ:t/ vt (pt hurt) fazer mal a; (injure, offend) magoar, ferir □ vi doer □ a magoado, ferido □ n mal m; (feelings) mágoa f. **~ful** a prejudicial; (remark etc) que magoa

**hurtle** /'hɜ:tl/ vi despenhar-se; (move rapidly) precipitar-se □ vt arremessar

**husband** /'hʌzbənd/ n marido m, esposo m

**hush** /hʌʃ/ vt (fazer) calar. **~!** silencio! □ vi calar-se □ n silêncio m. **~-hush** a (colloq) muito em segredo. **~ up** abafar, encobrir

**husk** /hʌsk/ n casca f

**husky** /'hʌskɪ/ a (-ier, -iest) (hoarse) rouco, enrouquecido; (burly) corpulento □ n cão m esquimó

**hustle** /'hʌsl/ vt empurrar, dar encon-

trões a □ n empurrão m. **~ and bustle** grande movimento m

**hut** /hʌt/ n cabana f, barraca f de madeira

**hutch** /hʌtʃ/ n coelheira f

**hyacinth** /'haɪəsɪnθ/ n jacinto m

**hybrid** /'haɪbrɪd/ a & n híbrido (m)

**hydrant** /'haɪdrənt/ n hidrante m

**hydraulic** /har'drɔ:lɪk/ a hidráulico

**hydroelectric** /haɪdrəʊ'lektrɪk/ a hidrelétrico, (P) hidroeléctrico

**hydrofoil** /'haɪdrəʊfɔɪl/ n

**hydrogen** /'haɪdrədʒən/ n hidrogênio m, (P) hidrogénio m

**hyena** /har'i:nə/ n hiena f

**hygiene** /'haɪdʒi:n/ n higiene f

**hygienic** /har'dʒi:nɪk/ a higiênico, (P) higiénico

**hymn** /hɪm/ n hino m, cântico m

**hyper-** /'haɪpə(r)/ pref hiper-

**hypermarket** /'haɪpəma:kɪt/ n hipermercado m

**hyphen** /'haɪfn/ n hífen m, traço-de-união m. **~ate** vt unir com hífen

**hypno|sis** /hɪp'nəʊsɪs/ n hipnose f. **~tic** /-'nɒtɪk/ a hipnótico

**hypnot|ize** /'hɪpnətaɪz/ vt hipnotizar. **~ism** /-ɪzəm/ n hipnotismo m

**hypochondriac** /haɪpə'kɒndrɪæk/ n hipocondríaco m

**hypocrisy** /hɪ'pɒkrəsɪ/ n hipocrisia f

**hypocrit|e** /'hɪpəkrɪt/ n hipócrita mf. **~ical** /-'krɪtɪkl/ a hipócrita

**hypodermic** /haɪpə'dɜ:mɪk/ a hipodérmico □ n seringa f

**hypothe|sis** /har'pɒθəsɪs/ n (pl -theses /-si:z/) hipótese f. **~tical** /-ə'θetɪkl/ a hipotético

**hyster|ia** /hɪ'stɪərɪə/ n histeria f. **~ical** /hɪ'sterɪkl/ a histérico

# I

**I** /aɪ/ pron eu

**Iberian** /aɪ'bɪərɪən/ a ibérico □ n íbero m

**ice** /aɪs/ n gelo m □ vt/i gelar; (cake) cobrir com glacê □ vi **~ up** gelar. **~-box** n (Amer) geladeira f, (P) frigorífico m. **~-(cream)** n sorvete m, (P) gelado m. **~-cube** n cubo m or pedra f de gelo. **~ hockey** hóquei m sobre o gelo. **~ lolly** picolé m. **~-pack** n saco m de gelo. **~-rink** n rimque m de patinação, (P) patinagem f no gelo. **~ skating** n patinação f, (P) patinagem f no gelo

**iceberg** /'aɪsbɜ:g/ n iceberg m; (fig) pedaço m de gelo

**Iceland** /'aɪslənd/ n Islândia f. **~er** n islandês m. **~ic** /-'lændɪk/ a & n islandês (m)

**icicle** /'aɪsɪkl/ n pingente m de gelo

**icing** /'aɪsɪŋ/ n (culin) cobertura f de açúcar, glacê m

**icy** /'aɪsɪ/ a (-ier, -iest) gelado, gélido, glacial; (road) com gelo

**idea** /ar'dɪə/ n idéia f, (P) ideia f

**ideal** /ar'dɪəl/ a & n ideal (m). ~ize vt idealizar. ~ly adv idealmente

**idealis|t** /ar'dɪəlɪst/ n idealista mf. ~m /-zəm/ n idealismo m. ~tic /-'lɪstɪk/ a idealista

**identical** /ar'dentɪkl/ a idêntico

**identif|y** /ar'dentɪfaɪ/ vt identificar □ vi ~y with identificar-se com. ~ication /-ɪ'keɪʃn/ n identificação f; (papers) documentos mpl de identificação

**identity** /ar'dentətɪ/ n identidade f. ~ card carteira f de identidade

**ideolog|y** /aɪdɪ'ɒlədʒɪ/ n ideologia f. ~ical a /-ɪə'lɒdʒɪkl/ a ideológico

**idiom** /'ɪdɪəm/ n idioma m; (phrase) expressão f idiomática. ~atic /-'mætɪk/ a idiomático

**idiosyncrasy** /ɪdɪə'sɪŋkrəsɪ/ n idiossincrasia f, peculiaridade f

**idiot** /'ɪdɪət/ n idiota mf. ~ic /-'ɒtɪk/ a idiota

**idl|e** /'aɪdl/ a (-er, -est) (not active; lazy) ocioso; (unemployed) sem trabalho; (of machines) parado; (fig: useless) inútil □ vt/i (of engine) estar em ponto morto, P estar no ralenti. ~eness n ociosidade f. ~y adv ociosamente

**idol** /'aɪdl/ n ídolo m. ~ize vt idolatrar

**idyllic** /ɪ'dɪlɪk/ a idílico

**i.e.** abbr isto é, quer dizer

**if** /ɪf/ conj se

**igloo** /'ɪɡlu:/ n iglu m

**ignite** /ɪɡ'naɪt/ vt/i inflamar(-se), acender; (catch fire) pegar fogo; (set fire to) atear fogo a, (P) deitar fogo a

**ignition** /ɪɡ'nɪʃn/ n (auto) ignição f. ~ (key) chave f de ignição

**ignoran|t** /'ɪɡnərənt/ a ignorante. ~ce n ignorância f. be ~t of ignorar

**ignore** /ɪɡ'nɔ:(r)/ vt não fazer caso de, passar por cima de; (person in the street etc) fingir não ver

**ill** /ɪl/ a (sick) doente; (bad) mau □ adv mal □ n mal m. ~-advised a pouco aconselhável. ~ at ease pouco à vontade. ~-bred a mal educado. ~-fated a malfadado. ~-treat vt maltratar. ~ will má vontade f, animosidade f

**illegal** /ɪ'li:ɡl/ a ilegal

**illegible** /ɪ'ledʒəbl/ a ilegível

**illegitima|te** /ɪlɪ'dʒɪtɪmət/ a ilegítimo. ~cy n ilegitimidade f

**illitera|te** /ɪ'lɪtərət/ a analfabeto; (uneducated) iletrado. ~cy n analfabetismo m

**illness** /'ɪlnɪs/ n doença f

**illogical** /ɪ'lɒdʒɪkl/ a ilógico

**illuminat|e** /ɪ'lu:mɪneɪt/ vt iluminar; (explain) esclarecer. ~ion /-'neɪʃn/ n iluminação f. ~ions npl luminárias fpl

**illusion** /ɪ'lu:ʒn/ n ilusão f

**illusory** /ɪ'lu:sərɪ/ a ilusório

**illustrat|e** /'ɪləstreɪt/ vt ilustrar. ~ion /-'streɪʃn/ n ilustração f. ~ive /-ətɪv/ a ilustrativo

**illustrious** /ɪ'lʌstrɪəs/ a ilustre

**image** /'ɪmɪdʒ/ n imagem f. (public) ~ imagem f pública

**imaginary** /ɪ'mædʒɪnərɪ/ a imaginário

**imaginat|ion** /ɪmædʒɪ'neɪʃn/ n imaginação f. ~ive /ɪ'mædʒɪnətɪv/ a imaginativo

**imagin|e** /ɪ'mædʒɪn/ vt imaginar. ~able a imaginável

**imbalance** /ɪm'bæləns/ n desequilíbrio m

**imbecile** /'ɪmbəsi:l/ a & n imbecil (mf)

**imbue** /ɪm'bju:/ vt imbuir, impregnar

**imitat|e** /'ɪmɪteɪt/ vt imitar. ~ion /-'teɪʃn/ n imitação f

**immaculate** /ɪ'mækjulət/ a imaculado; (impeccable) impecável

**immaterial** /ɪmə'tɪərɪəl/ a (of no importance) irrelevante. that's ~ to me para mim tanto faz

**immature** /ɪmə'tjʊə(r)/ a imaturo

**immediate** /ɪ'mi:dɪət/ a imediato. ~ly adv imediatamente □ conj logo que, assim que

**immens|e** /ɪ'mens/ a imenso. ~ely /-slɪ/ adv imensamente. ~ity n imensidade f

**immers|e** /ɪ'mɜ:s/ vt mergulhar, imergir. be ~ed in (fig) estar imerso em. ~ion /-ʃn/ n imersão f. ~ion heater aquecedor m de água elétrico, (P) eléctrico

**immigr|ate** /'ɪmɪɡreɪt/ vi imigrar. ~ant n & a imigrante (mf), imigrado (m). ~ation /-'ɡreɪʃn/ n imigração f

**imminen|t** /'ɪmɪnənt/ a iminente. ~ce n iminência f

**immobil|e** /ɪ'məʊbaɪl/ a imóvel. ~ize /-əlaɪz/ vt imobilizar

**immoderate** /ɪ'mɒdərət/ a imoderado, descomedido

**immoral** /ɪ'mɒrəl/ a imoral. ~ity /ɪmə'rælətɪ/ n imoralidade f

**immortal** /ɪ'mɔ:tl/ a imortal. ~ity /-'tælətɪ/ n imortalidade f. ~ize vt imortalizar

**immun|e** /ɪ'mju:n/ a imune, imunizado (from, to contra). ~ity n imunidade f

**imp** /ɪmp/ n diabrete m

**impact** /'ɪmpækt/ n impacto m

**impair** /ɪm'peə(r)/ *vt* deteriorar; (*damage*) prejudicar

**impale** /ɪm'peɪl/ *vt* empalar

**impart** /ɪm'paːt/ *vt* comunicar, transmitir (**to a**)

**impartial** /ɪm'paːʃl/ *a* imparcial. ~**ity** /-ʃɪ'ælətɪ/ *n* imparcialidade *f*

**impassable** /ɪm'paːsəbl/ *a* (*road, river*) impraticável, intransitável; (*barrier etc*) intransponível

**impasse** /'æmpaːs/ *n* impasse *m*

**impatien|t** /ɪm'peɪʃnt/ *a* impaciente. ~**ce** *n* impaciência *f*. ~**tly** *adv* impacientemente

**impeach** /ɪm'piːtʃ/ *vt* incriminar, acusar

**impeccable** /ɪm'pekəbl/ *a* impecável

**impede** /ɪm'piːd/ *vt* impedir, estorvar

**impediment** /ɪm'pedɪmənt/ *n* impedimento *m*, obstáculo *m*. (**speech**) ~ defeito *m* (na fala)

**impel** /ɪm'pel/ *vt* (*pt* **impelled**) impelir, forçar (**to do a fazer**)

**impending** /ɪm'pendɪŋ/ *a* iminente

**impenetrable** /ɪm'penɪtrəbl/ *a* impenetrável

**imperative** /ɪm'perətɪv/ *a* imperativo; (*need etc*) imperioso □ *n* imperativo *m*

**imperceptible** /ɪmpə'septəbl/ *a* imperceptível

**imperfect** /ɪm'pɜːfɪkt/ *a* imperfeito. ~**ion** /-ə'fekʃn/ *n* imperfeição *f*

**imperial** /ɪm'pɪərɪəl/ *a* imperial; (*of measures*) legal (na *GB*). ~**ism** /-lɪzəm/ *n* imperialismo *m*

**imperious** /ɪm'pɪərɪəs/ *a* imperioso

**impersonal** /ɪm'pɜːsənl/ *a* impessoal

**impersonat|e** /ɪm'pɜːsəneɪt/ *vt* fazerse passar por; (*theat*) fazer *or* representar (o papel) de. ~**ion** /'neɪʃn/ *n* imitação *f*

**impertinen|t** /ɪm'pɜːtɪmənt/ *a* impertinente. ~**ce** *n* impertinência *f*. ~**tly** *adv* com impertinência

**impervious** /ɪm'pɜːvɪəs/ *a* ~ **to** (*water*) impermeável a; (*fig*) insensível a

**impetuous** /ɪm'petʃʊəs/ *a* impetuoso

**impetus** /'ɪmpɪtəs/ *n* ímpeto *m*

**impinge** /ɪm'pɪndʒ/ *vi* ~ **on** afetar, *P* afectar; (*encroach*) infringir

**impish** /'ɪmpɪʃ/ *a* travesso, malicioso

**implacable** /ɪm'plækəbl/ *a* implacável

**implant** /ɪm'plaːnt/ *vt* implantar

**implement**[1] /'ɪmplɪmənt/ *n* instrumento *m*, utensílio *m*

**implement**[2] /'ɪmplɪment/ *vt* implementar, executar

**implicat|e** /'ɪmplɪkeɪt/ *vt* implicar. ~**ion** /-'keɪʃn/ *n* implicação *f*

**implicit** /ɪm'plɪsɪt/ *a* implícito; (*unquestioning*) absoluto, incondicional

**implore** /ɪm'plɔː(r)/ *vt* implorar, suplicar, rogar

**imply** /ɪm'plaɪ/ *vt* implicar; (*hint*) sugerir, dar a entender, insinuar

**impolite** /ɪmpə'laɪt/ *a* indelicado, incorreto, (*P*) incorrecto

**import**[1] /ɪm'pɔːt/ *vt* importar. ~**ation** /-'teɪʃn/ *n* importação *f*. ~**er** *n* importador *m*

**import**[2] /'ɪmpɔːt/ *n* importação *f*; (*meaning*) significado *m*; (*importance*) importância *f*

**importan|t** /ɪm'pɔːtnt/ *a* importante. ~**ce** *n* importância *f*

**impos|e** /ɪm'pəʊz/ *vt* impôr, (*inflict*) infligir □ *vi* ~**e on** abusar de. ~**ition** /-ə'zɪʃn/ *n* imposição *f*; (*unfair burden*) abuso *m*

**imposing** /ɪm'pəʊzɪŋ/ *a* imponente

**impossib|le** /ɪm'pɒsəbl/ *a* impossível. ~**ility** /-'bɪlətɪ/ *n* impossibilidade *f*

**impostor** /ɪm'pɒstə(r)/ *n* impostor *m*

**impoten|t** /'ɪmpətənt/ *a* impotente. ~**ce** *n* impotência *f*

**impound** /ɪm'paʊnd/ *vt* apreender, confiscar

**impoverish** /ɪm'pɒvərɪʃ/ *vt* empobrecer

**impracticable** /ɪm'præktɪkəbl/ *a* impraticável

**impractical** /ɪm'præktɪkl/ *a* pouco prático

**imprecise** /ɪmprɪ'saɪs/ *a* impreciso

**impregnable** /ɪm'pregnəbl/ *a* inexpugnável; (*fig*) inabalável, irrefutável

**impregnate** /'ɪmpregneɪt/ *vt* impregnar (**with** de)

**impresario** /ɪmprɪ'saːrɪəʊ/ *n* (*pl* **-os**) empresário *m*

**impress** /ɪm'pres/ *vt* impressionar, causar impressão a; (*imprint*) imprimir. ~ **on s.o.** inculcar algo em alguém

**impression** /ɪm'preʃn/ *n* impressão *f*. ~**able** *a* impressionável. ~**ist** *n* impressionista *mf*

**impressive** /ɪm'presɪv/ *a* impressionante, imponente

**imprint**[1] /'ɪmprɪnt/ *n* impressão *f*, marca *f*

**imprint**[2] /ɪm'prɪnt/ *vt* imprimir

**imprison** /ɪm'prɪzn/ *vt* prender, aprisionar. ~**ment** *n* aprisionamento *m*, prisão *f*

**improbab|le** /ɪm'prɒbəbl/ *a* improvável. ~**ility** /-'bɪlətɪ/ *n* improbabilidade *f*

**impromptu** /ɪm'prɒmptjuː/ *a* & *adv* de improviso □ *n* impromptu *m*

**improper** /ɪm'prɒpə(r)/ *a* impróprio; (*indecent*) indecente, pouco decente; (*wrong*) incorreto, (*P*) incorrecto

**improve** /ɪm'pruːv/ *vt/i* melhorar. ~ **on** aperfeiçoar. ~**ment** *n* melhoria *f*;

(*in house etc*) melhoramento *m*; (*in health*) melhoras *fpl*

**improvis|e** /'ɪmprəvaɪz/ *vt/i* improvisar. **~ation** /-'zeɪʃn/ *n* improvisação *f*

**imprudent** /ɪm'pruːdnt/ *a* imprudente

**impuden|t** /'ɪmpjʊdənt/ *a* descarado, insolente. **~ce** *n* descaramento *m*, insolência *f*

**impulse** /'ɪmpʌls/ *n* impulso *m*

**impulsive** /ɪm'pʌlsɪv/ *a* impulsivo

**impur|e** /ɪm'pjʊə(r)/ *a* impuro. **~ity** *n* impureza *f*

**in** /ɪn/ *prep* em, dentro de □ *adv* dentro; (*at home*) em casa; (*in fashion*) na moda. **~ Lisbon/English** em Lisboa/inglês. **~ winter** no inverno. **~ an hour** (*at end of, within*) numa hora. **~ the rain** na chuva. **~ doing** ao fazer. **~ the evening** à tardinha. **the best ~** o melhor em. **we are ~ for** vamos ter. **~-laws** *npl* (*colloq*) sogros *mpl*. **~-patient** *n* doente em internado. **the ~s and outs** meandros *mpl*

**inability** /ɪnə'bɪlətɪ/ *n* incapacidade *f* (**to do** para fazer)

**inaccessible** /ɪnæk'sesəbl/ *a* inacessível

**inaccura|te** /ɪn'ækjərət/ *a* inexato, (*P*) inexacto. **~cy** *n* inexatidão *f*, (*P*) inexactidão *f*, falta *f* de rigor

**inaction** /ɪn'ækʃn/ *n* inação *f*, (*P*) inacção *f*

**inactiv|e** /ɪn'æktɪv/ *a* inativo, (*P*) inactivo. **~ity** /-'tɪvətɪ/ *n* inação *f*, (*P*) inacção *f*

**inadequa|te** /ɪn'ædɪkwət/ *a* inadequado, impróprio; (*insufficient*) insuficiente. **~cy** *n* inadequação *f*; (*insufficiency*) insuficiência *f*

**inadmissible** /ɪnəd'mɪsəbl/ *a* inadmissível

**inadvertently** /ɪnəd'vɜːtəntlɪ/ *adv* inadvertidamente; (*unintentionally*) sem querer, sem ser por mal

**inadvisable** /ɪnəd'vaɪzəbl/ *a* desaconselhável, não aconselhável

**inane** /ɪ'neɪn/ *a* tolo, oco

**inanimate** /ɪn'ænɪmət/ *a* inanimado

**inappropriate** /ɪnə'prəʊprɪət/ *a* impróprio, inadequado

**inarticulate** /ɪnɑː'tɪkjʊlət/ *a* inarticulado; (*of person*) incapaz de se exprimir claramente

**inattentive** /ɪnə'tentɪv/ *a* desatento

**inaugural** /ɪ'nɔːgjʊrəl/ *a* inaugural

**inaugurat|e** /ɪ'nɔːgjʊreɪt/ *vt* inaugurar. **~ion** /-'reɪʃn/ *n* inauguração *f*

**inauspicious** /ɪnɔː'spɪʃəs/ *a* pouco auspicioso

**inborn** /ɪn'bɔːn/ *a* inato

**inbred** /ɪn'bred/ *a* inato, congênito, (*P*) congénito

**incalculable** /ɪn'kælkjʊləbl/ *a* incalculável

**incapable** /ɪn'keɪpəbl/ *a* incapaz

**incapacit|y** /ɪnkə'pæsətɪ/ *n* incapacidade *f*. **~ate** *vt* incapacitar

**incarnat|e** /ɪn'kɑːneɪt/ *a* encarnado. **the devil ~e** o diabo em pessoa. **~ion** /-'neɪʃn/ *n* encarnação *f*

**incendiary** /ɪn'sendɪərɪ/ *a* incendiário □ *n* bomba *f* incendiária

**incense**[1] /'ɪnsens/ *n* incenso *m*

**incense**[2] /ɪn'sens/ *vt* exasperar, enfurecer

**incentive** /ɪn'sentɪv/ *n* incentivo, estímulo

**incessant** /ɪn'sesənt/ *a* incessante. **~ly** *adv* incessantemente, sem cessar

**incest** /'ɪnsest/ *n* incesto *m*. **~uous** /ɪn'sestjʊəs/ *a* incestuoso

**inch** /ɪntʃ/ *n* polegada *f* (= 2.54 cm) □ *vt/i* avançar palmo a palmo *or* pouco a pouco. **within an ~** of a um passo de

**incidence** /'ɪnsɪdəns/ *n* incidência *f*; (*rate*) percentagem *f*

**incident** /'ɪnsɪdənt/ *n* incidente *m*

**incidental** /ɪnsɪ'dentl/ *a* incidental, acessório; (*casual*) eventuais; (*expenses*) eventuais; (*music*) de cena, incidental. **~ly** *adv* incidentalmente; (*by the way*) a propósito

**incinerat|e** /ɪn'sɪnəreɪt/ *vt* incinerar. **~or** *n* incinerador *m*

**incision** /ɪn'sɪʒn/ *n* incisão *f*

**incisive** /ɪn'saɪsɪv/ *a* incisivo

**incite** /ɪn'saɪt/ *vt* incitar, instigar. **~ment** *n* incitamento *m*

**inclination** /ɪnklɪ'neɪʃn/ *n* inclinação *f*, tendência *f*

**incline**[1] /ɪn'klaɪn/ *vt/i* inclinar(-se). **be ~d to** inclinar-se para; (*have tendency*) ter tendência para

**incline**[2] /'ɪnklaɪn/ *n* inclinação *f*, declive *m*

**inclu|de** /ɪn'kluːd/ *vt* incluir; (*in letter*) enviar junto *or* em anexo. **~ding** *prep* inclusive. **~sion** *n* inclusão *f*

**inclusive** /ɪn'kluːsɪv/ *a* & *adv* inclusive. **be ~ of** incluir

**incognito** /ɪnkɒg'niːtəʊ/ *a* & *adv* incógnito

**incoherent** /ɪnkə'hɪərənt/ *a* incoerente

**income** /'ɪŋkʌm/ *n* rendimento *m*. **~ tax** imposto sobre a renda, (*P*) sobre o rendimento

**incoming** /'ɪnkʌmɪŋ/ *a* (*tide*) enchente; (*tenant etc*) novo

**incomparable** /ɪn'kɒmpərəbl/ *a* incomparável

**incompatible** /ɪnkəm'pætəbl/ *a* incompatível

**incompeten|t** /ɪn'kɒmpɪtənt/ *a* incompetente. **~ce** *n* incompetência *f*

**incomplete** /ɪnkəm'pliːt/ *a* incompleto

**incomprehensible** /ɪnkɒmprɪ'hensəbl/ *a* incompreensível

**inconceivable** /ɪnkən'siːvəbl/ *a* inconcebível

**inconclusive** /ɪnkən'kluːsɪv/ *a* inconcludente

**incongruous** /ɪn'kɒŋgrʊəs/ *a* incongruente; (*absurd*) absurdo

**inconsequential** /ɪnkɒnsɪ'kwenʃl/ *a* sem importância

**inconsiderate** /ɪnkən'sɪdərət/ *a* impensado, inconsiderado; (*lacking in regard*) pouco atencioso, sem consideração (pelos sentimentos *etc* de outrem)

**inconsisten|t** /ɪnkən'sɪstənt/ *a* incoerente; (*at variance*) contraditório. ~t with incompatível com. ~cy *n* incoerência *f*. ~cies *npl* contradições *fpl*

**inconspicuous** /ɪnkən'spɪkjʊəs/ *a* que não dá nas vistas, que não chama a atenção

**incontinen|t** /ɪn'kɒntmənt/ *a* incontinente. ~ce *n* incontinência *f*

**inconvenien|t** /ɪnkən'viːnɪənt/ *a* inconveniente, incómodo. ~ce *n* inconveniência *f*; (*drawback*) inconveniente *m* □ *vt* incomodar

**incorporate** /ɪn'kɔːpəreɪt/ *vt* incorporar; (*include*) incluir

**incorrect** /ɪnkə'rekt/ *a* incorreto, (*P*) incorrecto

**incorrigible** /ɪn'kɒrɪdʒəbl/ *a* incorrigível

**increas|e¹** /ɪn'kriːs/ *vt/i* aumentar. ~ing *a* crescente. ~ingly *adv* cada vez mais

**increase²** /'ɪnkriːs/ *n* aumento *m*. on the ~ aumentando, crescendo

**incredible** /ɪn'kredəbl/ *a* incrível

**incredulous** /ɪn'kredjʊləs/ *a* incrédulo

**increment** /'ɪŋkrəmənt/ *n* incremento *m*, aumento *m*

**incriminat|e** /ɪn'krɪmɪneɪt/ *vt* incriminar. ~ing *a* comprometedor

**incubat|e** /'ɪŋkjʊbeɪt/ *vt* incubar. ~ion /-'beɪʃn/ *n* incubação *f*. ~or *n* incubadora *f*

**inculcate** /'ɪnkʌlkeɪt/ *vt* inculcar

**incumbent** /ɪn'kʌmbənt/ *n* (*pol, relig*) titular *mf* □ *a* be ~ on incumbir a, caber a

**incur** /ɪn'kɜːr/ *vt* (*pt* incurred) (*displeasure, expense etc*) incorrer em; (*debts*) contrair

**incurable** /ɪn'kjʊərəbl/ *a* incurável, que não tem cura

**indebted** /ɪn'detɪd/ *a* ~ to s.o. em dívida (para) com alg (for por)

**indecen|t** /ɪn'diːsnt/ *a* indecente. ~t

**assault** atentado *m* contra o pudor. ~cy *n* indecência *f*

**indecision** /ɪndɪ'sɪʒn/ *n* indecisão *f*

**indecisive** /ɪndɪ'saɪsɪv/ *a* inconcludente, não decisivo; (*hesitating*) indeciso

**indeed** /ɪn'diːd/ *adv* realmente, deveras, mesmo; (*in fact*) de fato, (*P*) facto. **very much** ~ muitíssimo

**indefinite** /ɪn'defnət/ *a* indefinido; (*time*) indeterminado. ~ly *adv* indefinidamente

**indelible** /ɪn'deləbl/ *a* indelével

**indemnify** /ɪn'demnɪfaɪ/ *vt* indenizar, (*P*) indemnizar (for de); (*safeguard*) garantir (against contra)

**indemnity** /ɪn'demnətɪ/ *n* (*legal exemption*) isenção *f*; (*compensation*) indenização *f*, (*P*) indemnização *f*; (*safeguard*) garantia *f*

**indent** /ɪn'dent/ *vt* (*notch*) recortar; (*typ*) entrar. ~ation /-'teɪʃn/ *n* recorte *m*; (*typ*) entrada *f*

**independen|t** /ɪndɪ'pendənt/ *a* independente. ~ce *n* independência *f*. ~tly *adv* independentemente

**indescribable** /ɪndɪ'skraɪbəbl/ *a* indescritível

**indestructible** /ɪndɪ'strʌktəbl/ *a* indestrutível

**indeterminate** /ɪndɪ'tɜːmmət/ *a* indeterminado

**index** /'ɪndeks/ *n* (*pl* indexes) *n* (*in book*) índice *m*; (*in library*) catálogo *m* □ *vt* indexar. ~ card ficha *f* (de fichário). ~ finger index *m*, (dedo) indicador *m*. ~-linked *a* ligado ao índice de inflação

**India** /'ɪndɪə/ *n* índia *f*. ~n *a & n* (*of India*) indiano (*m*); (*American*) índio (*m*)

**indicat|e** /'ɪndɪkeɪt/ *vt* indicar. ~ion /-'keɪʃn/ *n* indicação *f*. ~or *n* indicador *m*; (*auto*) pisca-pisca *m*; (*board*) quadro *m*

**indicative** /ɪn'dɪkətɪv/ *a & n* indicativo (*m*)

**indict** /ɪn'daɪt/ *vt* acusar. ~ment *n* acusação *f*

**indifferen|t** /ɪn'dɪfrənt/ *a* indiferente; (*not good*) medíocre. ~ce *n* indiferença *f*

**indigenous** /ɪn'dɪdʒɪnəs/ *a* indígena, natural, nativo (to de)

**indigest|ion** /ɪndɪ'dʒestʃən/ *n* indigestão *f*. ~ible /-'təbl/ *a* indigesto

**indign|ant** /ɪn'dɪgnənt/ *a* indignado. ~ation /-'neɪʃn/ *n* indignação *f*

**indirect** /ɪndɪ'rekt/ *a* indireto, (*P*) indirecto. ~ly *adv* indiretamente, (*P*) indirectamente

**indiscr|eet** /ɪndɪ'skriːt/ *a* indiscreto; (*not wary*) imprudente. ~etion

/-'eʃn/ n indiscrição f; (action, remark etc) deslize m

**indiscriminate** /mdr'skrmmət/ a que tem falta de discernimento; (random) indiscriminado. ~ly adv sem discernimento; (at random) indiscriminadamente, ao acaso

**indispensable** /mdr'spensəbl/ a indispensável

**indispos|ed** /mdr'spəʊzd/ a indisposto. ~ition /-ə'zɪʃn/ n indisposição f

**indisputable** /mdr'spjuːtəbl/ a indisputável, incontestável

**indistinct** /mdr'stɪŋkt/ a indistinto

**indistinguishable** /mdr'stɪŋgwɪʃəbl/ a indistinguível, imperceptível; (identical) indiferenciável

**individual** /mdr'vɪdʒʊəl/ a individual □ n indivíduo m. ~ity /-'ælətɪ/ n individualidade f. ~ly adv individualmente

**indivisible** /mdr'vɪzəbl/ a indivisível

**indoctrinat|e** /m'dɒktrɪneɪt/ vt (en)doutrinar. ~ion /-'neɪʃn/ n (en)doutrinação f

**indolen|t** /'mdələnt/ a indolente. ~ce n indolência f

**indoor** /'mdɔː(r)/ a (de) interior, interno; (under cover) coberto; (games) de salão. ~s /m'dɔːz/ adv dentro de casa, no interior

**induce** /m'djuːs/ vt induzir, levar; (cause) causar, provocar. ~ment n incentivo m, encorajamento m

**indulge** /m'dʌldʒ/ vt satisfazer; (spoil) fazer a(s) vontade(s) de □ vi ~ in entregar-se a

**indulgen|t** /m'dʌldʒənt/ a indulgente. ~ce n (leniency) indulgência f; (desire) satisfação f

**industrial** /m'dʌstrɪəl/ a industrial; (unrest etc) trabalhista; (action) reivindicativo. ~ estate zona f industrial. ~ist n industrial m. ~ized a industrializado

**industrious** /m'dʌstrɪəs/ a trabalhador, aplicado

**industry** /'mdəstrɪ/ n indústria f; (zeal) aplicação f, diligência f, zelo m

**inebriated** /ɪ'niːbrɪeɪtɪd/ a embriagado, ébrio

**inedible** /ɪ'nedɪbl/ a não comestível

**ineffective** /mr'fektɪv/ a ineficaz; (person) ineficiente, incapaz

**ineffectual** /mr'fektʃʊəl/ a ineficaz, improfícuo

**inefficien|t** /mr'fɪʃnt/ a ineficiente. ~cy n ineficiência f

**ineligible** /m'elɪdʒəbl/ a inelegível; (undesirable) indesejável. be ~ for não ter direito a

**inept** /r'nept/ a inepto

**inequality** /mr'kwɒlətɪ/ n desigualdade f

**inert** /r'nɜːt/ a inerte. ~ia /-ʃə/ n inércia f

**inevitable** /m'evɪtəbl/ a inevitável, fatal

**inexcusable** /mɪk'skjuːzəbl/ a indesculpável, imperdoável

**inexhaustible** /mɪg'zɔːstəbl/ a inesgotável, inexaurível

**inexorable** /m'eksərəbl/ a inexorável

**inexpensive** /mɪk'spensɪv/ a barato, em conta

**inexperience** /mɪk'spɪərɪəns/ n inexperiência f, falta de experiência f. ~d a inexperiente

**inexplicable** /m'eksplɪkəbl/ a inexplicável

**inextricable** /m'ekstrɪkəbl/ a inextricável

**infallib|le** /m'fæləbl/ a infalível. ~ility /'bɪlətɪ/ n infalibilidade f

**infam|ous** /'mfəməs/ a infame. ~y n infâmia f

**infan|t** /'mfənt/ n bebê m, (P) bebé m; (child) criança f. ~cy n infância f; (babyhood) primeira infância f

**infantile** /'mfəntaɪl/ a infantil

**infantry** /'mfəntrɪ/ n infantaria f

**infatuat|ed** /m'fætʃʊeɪtɪd/ a ~ed with cego or perdido por. ~ion /-'eɪʃn/ n cegueira f, paixão f

**infect** /m'fekt/ vt infectar. ~ s.o. with contagiar or contaminar alg com. ~ion /-ʃn/ n infecção f, contágio m. ~ious /-ʃəs/ a infeccioso, contagioso

**infer** /m'fɜː(r)/ vt (pt inferred) inferir, deduzir. ~ence /'mfərəns/ n inferência f

**inferior** /m'fɪərɪə(r)/ a inferior; (work etc) de qualidade inferior □ n inferior mf; (in rank) subalterno m. ~ity /-'ɒrətɪ/ n inferioridade f

**infernal** /m'fɜːnl/ a infernal

**infertil|e** /m'fɜːtaɪl/ a infértil, estéril. ~ity /-ə'tɪlətɪ/ n infertilidade f, esterilidade f

**infest** /m'fest/ vt infestar (with de). ~ation n infestação f

**infidelity** /mfr'delətɪ/ n infidelidade f

**infiltrat|e** /'mfɪltreɪt/ vt/i infiltrar(-se). ~ion /-'treɪʃn/ n infiltração f

**infinite** /'mfmət/ a & n infinito (m). ~ly adv infinitamente

**infinitesimal** /mfmr'tesɪml/ a infinitesimal, infinitésimo

**infinitive** /m'fmətɪv/ n infinitivo m

**infinity** /m'fmətɪ/ n infinidade f, infinito m

**infirm** /m'fɜːm/ a débil, fraco. ~ity n (illness) enfermidade f; (weakness) fraqueza f

**inflam|e** /m'fleɪm/ vt inflamar. ~mable /-æməbl/ a inflamável. ~mation /-ə'meɪʃn/ n inflamação f

**inflate** /ɪn'fleɪt/ vt (balloon etc) encher de ar; (prices) causar inflação de
**inflation** /ɪn'fleɪʃn/ n inflação f. ~**ary** a inflacionário
**inflection** /ɪn'flekʃn/ n inflexão f; (gram) flexão f, desinência f
**inflexible** /ɪn'fleksəbl/ a inflexível
**inflict** /ɪn'flɪkt/ vt infligir, impor (**on** a)
**influence** /'ɪnflʊəns/ n influência f □ vt influenciar, influir sobre
**influential** /ɪnflʊ'enʃl/ a influente
**influenza** /ɪnflʊ'enzə/ n gripe f
**influx** /'ɪnflʌks/ n afluência f, influxo m
**inform** /ɪn'fɔːm/ vt informar. ~ **against** or **on** denunciar. **keep** ~**ed** manter ao corrente or a par. ~**ant** n informante mf. ~**er** n delator m, denunciante mf
**informal** /ɪn'fɔːml/ a informal; (simple) simples, sem cerimônia, (P) cerimónia; (unofficial) oficioso; (colloquial) familiar; (dress) de passeio, à vontade; (dinner, gathering) íntimo. ~**ity** /-'mælətɪ/ n informalidade f; (simplicity) simplicidade f, (intimacy) intimidade f. ~**ly** adv informalmente, sem cerimônia, (P) cerimónia, à vontade
**information** /ɪnfə'meɪʃn/ n informação f; (facts, data) informações fpl. ~ **technology** tecnologia f da informação
**informative** /ɪn'fɔːmətɪv/ a informativo
**infra-red** /ɪnfrə'red/ a infravermelho
**infrequent** /ɪn'friːkwənt/ a pouco frequente, (P) frequente. ~**ly** adv raramente
**infringe** /ɪn'frɪndʒ/ vt infringir. ~ **on** transgredir; (rights) violar. ~**ment** n infração f, (P) infracção f; (rights) violação f
**infuriate** /ɪn'fjʊərɪeɪt/ vt enfurecer, enraivecer. ~**ing** a enfurecedor, de enfurecer, de dar raiva
**infuse** /ɪn'fjuːz/ vt infundir, incutir; (herbs, tea) pôr de infusão. ~**ion** /-ʒn/ n infusão f
**ingenious** /ɪn'dʒiːnɪəs/ a engenhoso, bem pensado. ~**uity** /-ɪ'njuːətɪ/ n engenho m, habilidade f, imaginação f
**ingenuous** /ɪn'dʒenjʊəs/ a cândido, ingênuo, (P) ingénuo
**ingot** /'ɪŋgət/ n barra f, lingote m
**ingrained** /ɪn'greɪnd/ a arraigado, enraizado; (dirt) entranhado
**ingratiate** /ɪn'greɪʃɪeɪt/ vt ~ **o.s. with** insinuar-se junto de, cair nas or ganhar as boas graças de
**ingratitude** /ɪn'grætɪtjuːd/ n ingratidão f

**ingredient** /ɪn'griːdɪənt/ n ingrediente m
**inhabit** /ɪn'hæbɪt/ vt habitar. ~**able** a habitável. ~**ant** n habitante mf
**inhale** /ɪn'heɪl/ vt inalar, aspirar. ~**r** /-ə(r)/ n inalador m
**inherent** /ɪn'hɪərənt/ a inerente. ~**ly** adv inerentemente, em si
**inherit** /ɪn'herɪt/ vt herdar (**from** de). ~**ance** n herança f
**inhibit** /ɪn'hɪbɪt/ vt inibir; (prevent) impedir. **be** ~**ed** ser (um) inibido. ~**ion** /-'bɪʃn/ n inibição f
**inhospitable** /ɪn'hɒspɪtəbl/ a inóspito; (of person) inospitaleiro, pouco/nada hospitaleiro
**inhuman** /ɪn'hjuːmən/ a desumano. ~**ity** /-'mænətɪ/ n desumanidade f
**inhumane** /ɪnhjuː'meɪn/ a inumano, cruel
**inimitable** /ɪ'nɪmɪtəbl/ a inimitável
**iniquitous** /ɪ'nɪkwɪtəs/ a iníquo
**initial** /ɪ'nɪʃl/ a & n inicial (f) □ vt (pt **initialled**) assinar com as iniciais, rubricar. ~**ly** adv inicialmente
**initiat|e** /ɪ'nɪʃɪeɪt/ vt iniciar (**into** em); (scheme) lançar. ~**ion** /-'eɪʃn/ n iniciação f; (start) início m
**initiative** /ɪ'nɪʃɪətɪv/ n iniciativa f
**inject** /ɪn'dʒekt/ vt injetar, (P) injectar; (fig) insuflar. ~**ion** /-ʃn/ n injeção f, (P) injecção f
**injure** /'ɪndʒə(r)/ vt (harm) fazer mal a, prejudicar, lesar; (hurt) ferir
**injury** /'ɪndʒərɪ/ n ferimento m, lesão f; (wrong) mal m
**injustice** /ɪn'dʒʌstɪs/ n injustiça f
**ink** /ɪŋk/ n tinta f. ~-**well** n tinteiro m. ~**y** a sujo de tinta
**inkling** /'ɪŋklɪŋ/ n idéia f, (P) ideia f, suspeita f
**inlaid** /ɪn'leɪd/ see **inlay**[1]
**inland** /'ɪnlənd/ a interior □ adv /ɪn'lænd/ no interior, para o interior. **the I**~ **Revenue** o Fisco, a Receita Federal
**inlay**[1] /ɪn'leɪ/ vt (pt **inlaid**) embutir, incrustar
**inlay**[2] /'ɪnleɪ/ n incrustação f, obturação f
**inlet** /'ɪnlet/ n braço m de mar, enseada f; (techn) admissão f
**inmate** /'ɪnmeɪt/ n residente mf; (in hospital) internado m; (in prison) presidiário m
**inn** /ɪn/ n estalagem f
**innards** /'ɪnədz/ npl (colloq) tripas (colloq) fpl
**innate** /ɪ'neɪt/ a inato
**inner** /'ɪnə(r)/ a interior, interno; (fig) íntimo. ~ **city** centro m da cidade. ~**most** a mais profundo, mais íntimo. ~ **tube** n câmara f de ar

**innings** /'mɪŋz/ *n* (*cricket*) vez *f* de bater; (*pol*) período *m* no poder

**innocen|t** /'ɪnəsnt/ *a & n* inocente (*mf*). **~ce** *n* inocência *f*

**innocuous** /ɪ'nɒkjʊəs/ *a* inócuo, inofensivo

**innovat|e** /'ɪnəveɪt/ *vi* inovar. **~ion** /-'veɪʃn/ *n* inovação *f*. **~or** *n* inovador *m*

**innuendo** /ɪnjuː'endəʊ/ *n* (*pl* -oes) insinuação *f*, indireta *f*, (*P*) indirecta *f*

**innumerable** /ɪ'njuːmərəbl/ *a* inumerável

**inoculat|e** /ɪ'nɒkjʊleɪt/ *vt* inocular. **~ion** /-'leɪʃn/ *n* inoculação *f*, vacina *f*

**inoffensive** /ɪnə'fensɪv/ *a* inofensivo

**inoperative** /ɪn'ɒpərətɪv/ *a* inoperante, ineficaz

**inopportune** /ɪn'ɒpətjuːn/ *a* inoportuno

**inordinate** /ɪ'nɔːdɪnət/ *a* excessivo, desmedido. **~ly** *adv* excessivamente, desmedidamente

**input** /'ɪnpʊt/ *n* (*data*) dados mpl; (*electr: power*) energia *f*; (*computer process*) entrada *f*, dados mpl

**inquest** /'ɪnkwest/ *n* inquérito *m*

**inquir|e** /ɪn'kwaɪə(r)/ *vi* informar-se □ *vt* perguntar, indagar, inquirir. **~e about** procurar informações sobre, indagar. **~e into** inquirir, indagar. **~ing** *a* (*look*) interrogativo; (*mind*) inquisitivo. **~y** *n* (*question*) pergunta *f*; (*jur*) inquérito *m*; (*investigation*) investigação *f*

**inquisition** /ɪnkwɪ'zɪʃn/ *n* inquisição *f*

**inquisitive** /ɪn'kwɪzətɪv/ *a* curioso, inquisitivo; (*prying*) intrometido, bisbilhoteiro

**insan|e** /ɪn'seɪn/ *a* louco, doido. **~ity** /ɪn'sænətɪ/ *n* loucura *f*, demência *f*

**insanitary** /ɪn'sænɪtrɪ/ *a* insalubre, anti-higiénico, (*P*) anti-higiénico

**insatiable** /ɪn'seɪʃəbl/ *a* insaciável

**inscri|be** /ɪn'skraɪb/ *vt* inscrever; (*book*) dedicar. **~ption** /-ɪpʃn/ *n* inscrição *f*; (*in book*) dedicatória *f*

**inscrutable** /ɪn'skruːtəbl/ *a* impenetrável, misterioso

**insect** /'ɪnsekt/ *n* inseto *m*, (*P*) insecto *m*

**insecur|e** /ɪnsɪ'kjʊə(r)/ *a* (*not firm*) inseguro, mal seguro; (*unsafe; psych*) inseguro. **~ity** *n* insegurança *f*, falta *f* de segurança

**insensible** /ɪn'sensəbl/ *a* insensível; (*unconscious*) inconsciente

**insensitive** /ɪn'sensətɪv/ *a* insensível

**inseparable** /ɪn'seprəbl/ *a* inseparável

**insert**[1] /ɪn'sɜːt/ *vt* inserir; (*key*) meter, colocar; (*add*) pôr, inserir. **~ion** /-ʃn/ *n* inserção *f*

**insert**[2] /'ɪnsɜːt/ *n* coisa *f* inserida

**inside** /ɪn'saɪd/ *n* interior *m*. **~s** (*colloq*) tripas fpl (*colloq*) □ *a* interior, interno □ *adv* no interior, dentro, por dentro □ *prep* dentro de; (*of time*) em menos de. **~ out** de dentro para fora, do avesso; (*thoroughly*) por dentro e por fora, a fundo

**insidious** /ɪn'sɪdɪəs/ *a* insidioso

**insight** /'ɪnsaɪt/ *n* penetração *f*, perspicácia *f*; (*glimpse*) vislumbre *m*

**insignificant** /ɪnsɪg'nɪfɪkənt/ *a* insignificante

**insincer|e** /ɪnsɪn'sɪə(r)/ *a* insincero. **~ity** /-'serətɪ/ *n* insinceridade *f*, falta *f* de sinceridade

**insinuat|e** /ɪn'sɪnjʊeɪt/ *vt* insinuar. **~ion** /-'eɪʃn/ *n* (*act*) insinuação *f*; (*hint*) indireta *f*, (*P*) indirecta *f*, insinuação *f*

**insipid** /ɪn'sɪpɪd/ *a* insípido, sem sabor

**insist** /ɪn'sɪst/ *vt/i* **~ (on/that)** insistir (em/em que)

**insisten|t** /ɪn'sɪstənt/ *a* insistente. **~ce** *n* insistência *f*. **~tly** *adv* insistentemente

**insolen|t** /'ɪnsələnt/ *a* insolente. **~ce** *n* insolência *f*

**insoluble** /ɪn'sɒljʊbl/ *a* insolúvel

**insolvent** /ɪn'sɒlvənt/ *a* insolvente

**insomnia** /ɪn'sɒmnɪə/ *n* insônia *f*, (*P*) insónia *f*

**inspect** /ɪn'spekt/ *vt* inspecionar, (*P*) inspeccionar, examinar; (*tickets*) fiscalizar; (*passport*) controlar; (*troops*) passar revista a. **~ion** /-ʃn/ *n* inspeção *f*, (*P*) inspecção *f*, exame *m*; (*ticket*) fiscalização *f*; (*troops*) revista *f*. **~or** *n* inspetor *m*, (*P*) inspector *m*; (*on train*) fiscal *m*

**inspir|e** /ɪn'spaɪə(r)/ *vt* inspirar. **~ation** /-ə'reɪʃn/ *n* inspiração *f*

**instability** /ɪnstə'bɪlətɪ/ *n* instabilidade *f*

**install** /ɪn'stɔːl/ *vt* instalar; (*heater etc*) montar, instalar. **~ation** /-ə'leɪʃn/ *n* instalação *f*

**instalment** /ɪn'stɔːlmənt/ *n* prestação *f*; (*of serial*) episódio *m*

**instance** /'ɪnstəns/ *n* exemplo *m*, caso *m*. **for ~** por exemplo. **in the first ~** em primeiro lugar

**instant** /'ɪnstənt/ *a* imediato; (*food*) instantâneo □ *n* instante *m*. **~ly** *adv* imediatamente, logo

**instantaneous** /ɪnstən'teɪnɪəs/ *a* instantâneo

**instead** /ɪn'sted/ *adv* em vez disso, em lugar disso. **~ of** em vez de, em lugar de

**instigat|e** /'ɪnstɪgeɪt/ *vt* instigar, incitar. **~ion** /-'geɪʃn/ *n* instigação *f*. **~or** *n* instigador *m*

**instil** /ɪnˈstɪl/ *vt* (*pt* **instilled**) instilar, insuflar

**instinct** /ˈɪnstɪŋkt/ *n* instinto *m*. **~ive** /ɪnˈstɪŋktɪv/ *a* instintivo

**institut|e** /ˈɪnstɪtjuːt/ *n* instituto *m* □ *vt* instituir; (*legal proceedings*) intentar; (*inquiry*) ordenar. **~ion** /-ˈtjuːʃn/ *n* instituição *f*; (*school*) estabelecimento *m* de ensino; (*hospital*) estabelecimento *m* hospitalar

**instruct** /ɪnˈstrʌkt/ *vt* instruir; (*order*) mandar, ordenar; (*a solicitor etc*) dar instruções a. **~ s.o. in sth** ensinar alg coisa a alguém. **~ion** /-ʃn/ *n* instrução *f*. **~ions** /-ʃnz/ *npl* instruções *fpl*, modo *m* de emprego; (*orders*) ordens *fpl*. **~ive** *a* instrutivo. **~or** *n* instrutor *m*

**instrument** /ˈɪnstrʊmənt/ *n* instrumento *m*. **~ panel** painel *m* de instrumentos

**instrumental** /ɪnstrʊˈmentl/ *a* instrumental. **be ~ in** ter um papel decisivo em. **~ist** *n* instrumentalista *mf*

**insubordinat|e** /ɪnsəˈbɔːdɪnət/ *a* insubordinado. **~ion** /-ˈneɪʃn/ *n* insubordinação *f*

**insufferable** /ɪnˈsʌfrəbl/ *a* intolerável, insuportável

**insufficient** /ɪnsəˈfɪʃnt/ *a* insuficiente

**insular** /ˈɪnsjʊlə(r)/ *a* insular; (*fig: narrow-minded*) bitolado, limitado, (*P*) tacanho

**insulat|e** /ˈɪnsjʊleɪt/ *vt* isolar. **~ing tape** fita *f* isolante. **~ion** /-ˈleɪʃn/ *n* isolamento *m*

**insulin** /ˈɪnsjʊlɪn/ *n* insulina *f*

**insult**[1] /ˈɪnsʌlt/ *vt* insultar, injuriar. **~ing** *a* insultante, injurioso

**insult**[2] /ˈɪnsʌlt/ *n* insulto *m*, injúria *f*

**insur|e** /ɪnˈʃʊə(r)/ *vt* segurar, pôr no seguro; (*Amer*) = **ensure**. **~ance** *n* seguro *m*. **~ance policy** apólice *f* de seguro

**insurmountable** /ɪnsəˈmaʊntəbl/ *a* insuperável

**intact** /ɪnˈtækt/ *a* intato, (*P*) intacto

**intake** /ˈɪnteɪk/ *n* admissão *f*; (*techn*) admissão *f*, entrada *f*; (*of food*) ingestão *f*

**intangible** /ɪnˈtændʒəbl/ *a* intangível

**integral** /ˈɪntɪɡrəl/ *a* integral. **be an ~ part of** ser parte integrante de

**integrat|e** /ˈɪntɪɡreɪt/ *vt/i* integrar (-se). **~ed circuit** circuito *m* integrado. **~ion** /-ˈɡreɪʃn/ *n* integração *f*

**integrity** /ɪnˈteɡrətɪ/ *n* integridade *f*

**intellect** /ˈɪntəlekt/ *n* intelecto *m*, inteligência *f*. **~ual** /-ˈlektʃʊəl/ *a & n* intelectual (*mf*)

**intelligen|t** /ɪnˈtelɪdʒənt/ *a* inteligente. **~ce** *n* inteligência *f*; (*mil*) informações *fpl*. **~tly** *adv* inteligentemente

**intelligible** /ɪnˈtelɪdʒəbl/ *a* inteligível

**intend** /ɪnˈtend/ *vt* tencionar; (*destine*) reservar, destinar. **~ed** *a* intencional, propositado

**intens|e** /ɪnˈtens/ *a* intenso; (*person*) emotivo. **~ely** *adv* intensamente; (*very*) extremamente. **~ity** *n* intensidade *f*

**intensif|y** /ɪnˈtensɪfaɪ/ *vt* intensificar. **~ication** /-ɪˈkeɪʃn/ *n* intensificação *f*

**intensive** /ɪnˈtensɪv/ *a* intensivo. **~ care** tratamento *m* intensivo

**intent** /ɪnˈtent/ *n* intento *m*, desígnio *m*, propósito *m* □ *a* atento, concentrado. **~ on** absorto em; (*intending to*) decidido a. **~ly** *adv* atentamente

**intention** /ɪnˈtenʃn/ *n* intenção *f*. **~al** *a* intencional. **~ally** *adv* de propósito

**inter** /ɪnˈtɜː(r)/ *vt* (*pt* **interred**) enterrar

**inter-** /ˈɪntə(r)/ *pref* inter-

**interact** /ɪntərˈækt/ *vi* agir uns sobre os outros. **~ion** /-ʃn/ *n* interação *f*, (*P*) interacção *f*

**intercede** /ɪntəˈsiːd/ *vi* interceder

**intercept** /ɪntəˈsept/ *vt* interceptar

**interchange**[1] /ɪntəˈtʃeɪndʒ/ *vt* permutar, trocar. **~able** *a* permutável

**interchange**[2] /ˈɪntətʃeɪndʒ/ *n* permuta *f*, intercâmbio *m*; (*road junction*) trevo *m* de trânsito, (*P*) nó *m*

**intercom** /ˈɪntəkɒm/ *n* interfone *m*, (*P*) intercomunicador *m*

**interconnected** /ɪntəkəˈnektɪd/ *a* (*facts, events etc*) ligado, relacionado

**intercourse** /ˈɪntəkɔːs/ *n* (*sexual*) relações *fpl* sexuais

**interest** /ˈɪntrəst/ *n* interesse *m*; (*legal share*) título *m*; (*in finance*) juro(s) *m(pl)*. **rate of ~** taxa *f* de juros □ *vt* interessar. **~ed** *a* interessado. **be ~ed in** interessar-se por. **~ing** *a* interessante

**interface** /ˈɪntəfeɪs/ *n* interface *f*

**interfer|e** /ɪntəˈfɪə(r)/ *vi* interferir, intrometer-se (**in** em); (*meddle, hinder*) interferir (**with** com); (*tamper*) mexer indevidamente (**with** em). **~ence** *n* interferência *f*

**interim** /ˈɪntərɪm/ *n* **in the ~** nesse/neste ínterim *m*, (*P*) interim *m* □ *a* interino, provisório

**interior** /ɪnˈtɪərɪə(r)/ *a & n* interior (*m*)

**interjection** /ɪntəˈdʒekʃn/ *n* interjeição *f*

**interlock** /ɪntəˈlɒk/ *vt/i* entrelaçar; (*pieces of puzzle etc*) encaixar(-se); (*mech: wheels*) engrenar, engatar

**interloper** /ˈɪntələʊpə(r)/ *n* intruso *m*

**intermarr|iage** /mtə'mærɪdʒ/ *n* casamento *m* entre membros de diferentes famílias, raças etc; (*between near relations*) casamento *m* consangüíneo, (*P*) consanguíneo. **~y** *vi* ligar-se por casamento

**intermediary** /mtə'mi:dɪərɪ/ *a & n* intermediário (*m*)

**intermediate** /mtə'mi:dɪət/ *a* intermédio, intermediário

**interminable** /m'tɜ:mməbl/ *a* interminável, infindável

**intermission** /mtə'mɪʃn/ *n* intervalo *m*

**intermittent** /mtə'mɪtnt/ *a* intermitente. **~ly** *adv* intermitentemente

**intern** /m'tɜ:n/ *vt* internar. **~ee** /-'ni:/ *n* internado *m*. **~ment** *n* internamento *m*

**internal** /m'tɜ:nl/ *a* interno, interior. **~ly** *adv* internamente, interiormente

**international** /mtə'næʃnəl/ *a & n* internacional (*mf*)

**interpolate** /m'tɜ:pəleɪt/ *vt* interpolar

**interpret** /m'tɜ:prɪt/ *vt/i* interpretar. **~ation** /-'teɪʃn/ *n* interpretação *f*. **~er** *n* intérprete *mf*

**interrelated** /mtərɪ'leɪtɪd/ *a* interrelacionado, correlacionado

**interrogat|e** /m'terəgeɪt/ *vt* interrogar. **~ion** /'geɪʃn/ *n* interrogação *f*; (*of police etc*) interrogatório *m*

**interrogative** /mtə'rɒgətɪv/ *a* interrogativo □ *n* (*pronoun*) pronome *m* interrogativo

**interrupt** /mtə'rʌpt/ *vt* interromper. **~ion** /-ʃn/ *n* interrupção *f*

**intersect** /mtə'sekt/ *vt/i* intersectar (-se); (*roads*) cruzar-se. **~ion** /-ʃn/ *n* intersecção *f*; (*crossroads*) cruzamento *m*

**intersperse** /mtə'spɜ:s/ *vt* entremear, intercalar; (*scatter*) espalhar

**interval** /'mtəvl/ *n* intervalo *m*. **at ~s** a intervalos

**interven|e** /mtə'vi:n/ *vi* (*interfere*) intervir; (*of time*) passar-se, decorrer; (*occur*) sobrevir, intervir. **~tion** /-'venʃn/ *n* intervenção *f*

**interview** /'mtəvju:/ *n* entrevista *f* □ *vt* entrevistar. **~ee** *n* entrevistado *m*. **~er** *n* entrevistador *m*

**intestin|e** /m'testɪn/ *n* intestino *m*. **~al** *a* intestinal

**intima|te¹** /'mtɪmət/ *a* íntimo; (*detailed*) profundo. **~cy** *n* intimidade *f*. **~tely** *adv* intimamente

**intimate²** /'mtɪmeɪt/ *vt* (*announce*) dar a conhecer, fazer saber; (*imply*) dar a entender

**intimidat|e** /m'tɪmɪdeɪt/ *vt* intimidar. **~ion** /-'deɪʃn/ *n* intimidação *f*

**into** /'mtə/; *emphatic* /'mtu/ *prep* para dentro de. **divide ~ three** dividir em três. **~ pieces** aos bocados. **translate ~** traduzir para

**intolerable** /m'tɒlərəbl/ *a* intolerável, insuportável

**intoleran|t** /m'tɒlərənt/ *a* intolerante. **~ce** *n* intolerância *f*

**intonation** /mtə'neɪʃn/ *n* entonação *f*, entoação *f*, inflexão *f*

**intoxicat|ed** /m'tɒksɪkeɪtɪd/ *a* embriagado, etilizado. **~ion** /'keɪʃn/ *n* embriaguez *f*

**intra-** /mtrə/ *pref* intra-

**intractable** /m'træktəbl/ *a* intratável, difícil

**intransigent** /m'trænsɪdʒənt/ *a* intransigente

**intransitive** /m'trænsətɪv/ *a* (*verb*) intransitivo

**intravenous** /mtrə'vi:nəs/ *a* intravenoso

**intrepid** /m'trepɪd/ *a* intrépido, arrojado

**intrica|te** /'mtrɪkət/ *a* intrincado, complexo. **~cy** *n* complexidade *f*

**intrigu|e** /m'tri:g/ *vt/i* intrigar □ *n* intriga *f*. **~ing** *a* intrigante, curioso

**intrinsic** /m'trmsɪk/ *a* intrínseco. **~ally** /-klɪ/ *adv* intrinsecamente

**introduce** /mtrə'dju:s/ *vt* (*programme, question*) apresentar; (*bring in, insert*) introduzir; (*initiate*) iniciar. **~ sb to sb** (*person*) apresentar alg a alguém

**introduct|ion** /mtrə'dʌkʃn/ *n* introdução *f*; (*of/to person*) apresentação *f*. **~ory** /-tərɪ/ *a* introdutório, de introdução; (*letter, words*) de apresentação

**introspective** /mtrə'spektɪv/ *a* introspectivo

**introvert** /'mtrəvɜ:t/ *n & a* introvertido (*m*)

**intru|de** /m'tru:d/ *vi* intrometer-se, ser a mais. **~der** *n* intruso *m*. **~sion** *n* intrusão *f*. **~sive** *a* intruso

**intuit|ion** /mtju:'ɪʃn/ *n* intuição *f*. **~ive** /m'tju:ɪtɪv/ *a* intuitivo

**inundate** /'mʌndeɪt/ *vt* inundar (**with** de)

**invade** /m'veɪd/ *vt* invadir. **~r** /-ə(r)/ *n* invasor *m*

**invalid¹** /'mvəlɪd/ *n* inválido *m*

**invalid²** /m'vælɪd/ *a* inválido. **~ate** *vt* invalidar

**invaluable** /m'væljuəbl/ *a* inestimável

**invariabl|e** /m'veərɪəbl/ *a* invariável. **~y** *adv* invariavelmente

**invasion** /m'veɪʒn/ *n* invasão *f*

**invective** /m'vektɪv/ *n* invectiva *f*

**invent** /ɪn'vent/ *vt* inventar. **~ion** *n* invenção *f*. **~ive** *a* inventivo. **~or** *n* inventor *m*

**inventory** /'ɪnvəntrɪ/ *n* inventário *m*

**inverse** /ɪn'vɜːs/ *a* & *n* inverso (*m*). **~ly** *adv* inversamente

**inver|t** /ɪn'vɜːt/ *vt* inverter. **~ted commas** aspas *fpl*. **~sion** *n* inversão *f*

**invest** /ɪn'vest/ *vt* investir; (*time, effort*) dedicar □ *vi* fazer um investimento. **~ in** (*colloq: buy*) gastar dinheiro em. **~ment** *n* investimento *m*. **~or** *n* investidor *m*, financiador *m*

**investigat|e** /ɪn'vestɪgeɪt/ *vt* investigar. **~ion** /-'geɪʃn/ *n* investigação *f*. **under ~ion** em estudo. **~or** *n* investigador *m*

**inveterate** /ɪn'vetərət/ *a* inveterado

**invidious** /ɪn'vɪdɪəs/ *a* antipático, odioso

**invigorate** /ɪn'vɪgəreɪt/ *vt* revigorar; (*encourage*) estimular

**invincible** /ɪn'vɪnsəbl/ *a* invencível

**invisible** /ɪn'vɪzəbl/ *a* invisível

**invit|e** /ɪn'vaɪt/ *vt* convidar; (*bring on*) pedir, provocar. **~ation** /ɪnvɪ'teɪʃn/ *n* convite *m*. **~ing** *a* (*tempting*) tentador; (*pleasant*) acolhedor, convidativo

**invoice** /'ɪnvɔɪs/ *n* fatura *f*, (*P*) factura *f* □ *vt* faturar, (*P*) facturar

**invoke** /ɪn'vəʊk/ *vt* invocar

**involuntary** /ɪn'vɒləntrɪ/ *a* involuntário

**involve** /ɪn'vɒlv/ *vt* implicar, envolver. **~d** *a* (*complex*) complicado; (*at stake*) em jogo; (*emotionally*) envolvido. **~d in** implicado em. **~ment** *n* envolvimento *m*, participação *f*

**invulnerable** /ɪn'vʌlnərəbl/ *a* invulnerável

**inward** /'ɪnwəd/ *a* interior; (*thought etc*) íntimo. **~(s)** *adv* para dentro, para o interior. **~ly** *adv* interiormente, intimamente

**iodine** /'aɪədiːn/ *n* iodo *m*; (*antiseptic*) tintura *f* de iodo

**IOU** /aɪəʊ'juː/ *n abbr* vale *m*

**IQ** /aɪ'kjuː/ *abbr* (*intelligence quotient*) Q I *m*

**Iran** /ɪ'rɑːn/ *n* Irã *m*. **~ian** /ɪ'reɪnɪən/ *a* & *n* iraniano (*m*)

**Iraq** /ɪ'rɑːk/ *n* Iraque *m*. **~i** *a* & *n* iraquiano (*m*)

**irascible** /ɪ'ræsəbl/ *a* irascível

**irate** /aɪ'reɪt/ *a* irado, enraivecido

**Ireland** /'aɪələnd/ *n* Irlanda *f*

**iris** /'aɪərɪs/ *n* (*anat, bot*) íris *f*

**Irish** /'aɪərɪʃ/ *a* & *n* (*language*) irlandês (*m*). **~man** *n* irlandês *m*. **~woman** *n* irlandesa *f*

**irk** /ɜːk/ *vt* aborrecer, ncomodar. **~some** *a* aborrecido

**iron** /'aɪən/ *n* ferro *m*; (*appliance*) ferro *m* de engomar □ *a* de ferro □ *vt* passar a ferro. **~ out** fazer desaparecer; (*fig*) aplanar, resolver. **~ing** *n* do the **~ing** passar a roupa. **~ing-board** *n* tábua *f* de passar roupa, (*P*) tábua *f* de engomar

**ironic(al)** /aɪ'rɒnɪk(l)/ *a* irônico, (*P*) irónico

**ironmonger** /'aɪənmʌŋgə(r)/ *n* ferreiro *m*, (*P*) ferrageiro *m*. **~'s** *n* (*shop*) loja *f* de ferragens

**irony** /'aɪərənɪ/ *n* ironia *f*

**irrational** /ɪ'ræʃənl/ *a* irracional; (*person*) ilógico, que não raciocina

**irreconcilable** /ɪrekən'saɪləbl/ *a* irreconciliável

**irrefutable** /ɪrɪ'fjuːtəbl/ *a* irrefutável

**irregular** /ɪ'regjʊlə(r)/ *a* irregular. **~ity** /-'lærətɪ/ *n* irregularidade *f*

**irrelevant** /ɪ'reləvənt/ *a* irrelevante, que não é pertinente

**irreparable** /ɪ'repərəbl/ *a* irreparável, irremediável

**irreplaceable** /ɪrɪ'pleɪsəbl/ *a* insubstituível

**irresistible** /ɪrɪ'zɪstəbl/ *a* irresistível

**irresolute** /ɪ'rezəluːt/ *a* irresoluto

**irrespective** /ɪrɪ'spektɪv/ *a* **~ of** sem levar em conta, independente de

**irresponsible** /ɪrɪ'spɒnsəbl/ *a* irresponsável

**irretrievable** /ɪrɪ'triːvəbl/ *a* irreparável

**irreverent** /ɪ'revərənt/ *a* irreverente

**irreversible** /ɪrɪ'vɜːsəbl/ *a* irreversível; (*decision*) irrevogável

**irrigat|e** /'ɪrɪgeɪt/ *vt* irrigar. **~ion** /-'geɪʃn/ *n* irrigação *f*

**irritable** /'ɪrɪtəbl/ *a* irritável, irascível

**irritat|e** /'ɪrɪteɪt/ *vt* irritar. **~ion** /-'teɪʃn/ *n* irritação *f*

**is** /ɪz/ *see* **be**

**Islam** /'ɪzlaːm/ *n* Islã *m*. **~ic** /ɪz'læmɪk/ *a* islâmico

**island** /'aɪlənd/ *n* ilha *f*. **traffic ~** abrigo *m* de pedestres, (*P*) placa *f* de refugio

**isolat|e** /'aɪsəleɪt/ *vt* isolar. **~ion** /-'leɪʃn/ *n* isolamento *m*

**Israel** /'ɪzreɪl/ *n* Israel *m*. **~i** /ɪz'reɪlɪ/ *a* & *n* israelense (*mf*), (*P*) israelita (*mf*)

**issue** /'ɪʃuː/ *n* questão *f*; (*outcome*) resultado *m*; (*of magazine etc*) número *m*; (*of stamps, money etc*) emissão *f* □ *vt* distribuir, dar; (*stamps, money etc*) emitir; (*orders*) dar □ *vi* **~ from** sair de. **at ~** em questão. **take ~ with** entrar em discussão com, discutir com

**it** /ɪt/ *pron* (*subject*) ele, ela; (*object*) o, a; (*non-specific*) isto, isso, aquilo. ~ **is cold** está *or* faz frio. ~ **is the 6th of May** hoje é seis de maio. **that's** ~ é isso. **take** ~ leva isso. **who is** ~? quem é?

**italic** /ɪ'tælɪk/ *a* itálico. ~**s** *npl* itálico *m*

**Ital|y** /'ɪtəlɪ/ *n* Itália *f.* ~**ian** /ɪ'tælɪən/ *a* & *n* (*person, lang*) italiano (*m*)

**itch** /ɪtʃ/ coceira *f*, (P) comichão *f*; (*fig: desire*) desejo *m* ardente □ *vi* coçar, sentir comichão, comichar. **my arm** ~**es** estou com coceira no braço. **I am** ~**ing to** estou morto por (*colloq*). ~**y** *a* que dá coceira

**item** /'aɪtəm/ *n* item *m*, artigo *m*; (*on programme*) número *m*; (*on agenda*) ponto *m.* **news** ~ notícia *f.* ~**ize** /-aɪz/ *vt* discriminar, especificar

**itinerant** /aɪ'tɪnərənt/ *a* itinerante; (*musician, actor*) ambulante

**itinerary** /aɪ'tɪnərərɪ/ *n* itinerário *m*

**its** /ɪts/ *a* seu, sua, seus, suas

**it's** /ɪts/ = **it is, it has**

**itself** /ɪt'self/ *pron* ele mesmo, ele próprio, ela mesma, ela própria; (*reflexive*) se; (*after prep*) si mesmo, si próprio, si mesma, si própria. **by** ~ sozinho, por si

**ivory** /'aɪvərɪ/ *n* marfim *m*

**ivy** /'aɪvɪ/ *n* hera *f*

# J

**jab** /dʒæb/ *vt* (*pt* **jabbed**) espetar □ *n* espetadela *f*; (*colloq: injection*) picada *f*

**jabber** /'dʒæbə(r)/ *vi* tagarelar; (*indistinctly*) falar confusamente □ *n* tagarelice *f*; (*indistinct speech*) algaravia *f*; (*indistinct voices*) algaraviada *f*

**jack** /dʒæk/ *n* (*techn*) macaco *m*; (*cards*) valete *m* □ *vt* ~ **up** levantar com macaco. **the Union J**~ a bandeira *f* inglesa

**jackal** /'dʒækl/ *n* chacal *m*

**jackdaw** /'dʒækdɔ:/ *n* gralha *f*

**jacket** /'dʒækɪt/ *n* casaco (curto) *m*; (*of book*) sobrecapa *f*; (*of potato*) casca *f*

**jack-knife** /'dʒæknaɪf/ *vi* (*lorry*) perder o controle

**jackpot** /'dʒækpɒt/ *n* sorte *f* grande. **hit the** ~ ganhar a sorte grande

**Jacuzzi** /dʒə'ku:zi:/ *n* (P) jacuzzi *m*, banheira *f* de hidromassagem

**jade** /dʒeɪd/ *n* (*stone*) jade *m*

**jaded** /'dʒeɪdɪd/ *a* (*tired*) estafado; (*bored*) enfastiado

**jagged** /'dʒægɪd/ *a* recortado, denteado; (*sharp*) pontiagudo

**jail** /dʒeɪl/ *n* prisão *f* □ *vt* prender,

colocar na cadeia. ~**er** *n* carcereiro *m*

**jam**¹ /dʒæm/ *n* geléia *f*, compota *f*

**jam**² /dʒæm/ *vt/i* (*pt* **jammed**) (*wedge*) entalar; (*become wedged*) entalar-se; (*crowd*) apinhar(-se); (*mech*) bloquear; (*radio*) provocar interferências em □ *n* (*crush*) aperto *m*; (*traffic*) engarrafamento *m*; (*colloq: difficulty*) apuro *m*, aperto *m.* ~ **one's brakes on** (*colloq*) pôr o pé no freio, (P) no travão subitamente, apertar o freio subitamente. ~-**packed** *a* (*colloq*) abarrotado (**with** de)

**Jamaica** /dʒə'meɪkə/ *n* Jamaica *f*

**jangle** /'dʒæŋgl/ *n* som *m* estridente □ *vi* retinir

**janitor** /'dʒænɪtə(r)/ *n* porteiro *m*; (*caretaker*) zelador *m*

**January** /'dʒænjʊərɪ/ *n* Janeiro *m*

**Japan** /dʒə'pæn/ *n* Japão *m.* ~**ese** /dʒæpə'ni:z/ *a* & *n* japonês (*m*)

**jar**¹ /dʒɑ:(r)/ *n* pote *m.* **jam-**~ *n* frasco *m* de geléia

**jar**² /dʒɑ:(r)/ *vt/i* (*pt* **jarred**) ressoar, bater ruidosamente (**against** contra); (*of colours*) destoar; (*disagree*) discorder (**with** de) □ *n* (*shock*) choque *m.* ~**ring** *a* dissonante

**jargon** /'dʒɑ:gən/ *n* jargão *m*, gíria *f* profissional

**jaundice** /'dʒɔ:ndɪs/ *n* icterícia *f.* ~**d** *a* (*fig*) invejoso, despeitado

**jaunt** /dʒɔ:nt/ *n* (*trip*) passeata *f*

**jaunty** /'dʒɔ:ntɪ/ *a* (-ier, -iest) (*cheerful*) alegre, jovial; (*sprightly*) desenvolto

**javelin** /'dʒævlɪn/ *n* dardo *m*

**jaw** /dʒɔ:/ *n* maxilar *m*, mandíbula *f*

**jay** /dʒeɪ/ *n* gaio *m.* ~-**walker** *n* pedestre *m* imprudente, (P) peão *m* indisciplinado

**jazz** /dʒæz/ *n* jazz *m* □ *vt* ~ **up** animar. ~**y** *a* (*colloq*) espalhafatoso

**jealous** /'dʒeləs/ *a* ciumento; (*envious*) invejoso. ~**y** *n* ciúme *m*; (*envy*) inveja *f*

**jeans** /dʒi:nz/ *npl* (blue-)jeans *mpl*, calça *f* de zuarte, (P) calças *fpl* de ganga

**jeep** /dʒi:p/ *n* jipe *m*

**jeer** /dʒɪə(r)/ *vt/i* ~ **at** (*laugh*) fazer troça de; (*scorn*) escarnecer de; (*boo*) vaiar □ *n* (*mockery*) troça *f*; (*booing*) vaia *f*

**jell** /dʒel/ *vi* tomar consistência, gelatinizar-se

**jelly** /'dʒelɪ/ *n* gelatina *f.*

**jellyfish** /'dʒelɪfɪʃ/ *n* água-viva *f*

**jeopard|y** /'dʒepədɪ/ *n* perigo *m.* ~**ize** *vt* comprometer, pôr em perigo

**jerk** /dʒɜ:k/ *n* solavanco *m*, (P) sacão *m*; (*sl: fool*) idiota *mf* □ *vt/i* sacudir; (*move*) mover-se aos solavancos, (P) mover(-se) aos sacões. ~y *a* sacudido

**jersey** /'dʒɜːzɪ/ *n* (*pl* **-eys**) camisola *f*, pulôver *m*, suéter *m*; (*fabric*) jérsei *m*

**jest** /dʒest/ *n* gracejo *m*, graça *f* □ *vi* gracejar, brincar

**Jesus** /'dʒiːzəs/ *n* Jesus *m*

**jet**¹ /dʒet/ *n* azeviche *m*. ~**-black** *a* negro de azeviche

**jet**² /dʒet/ *n* jato *m*, (*P*) jacto *m*; (*plane*) (avião a) jato *m*, (*P*) jacto *m*. ~ **lag** cansaço *m* provocado pela diferença de fuso horário. ~**-propelled** *a* de propulsão a jato, (*P*) jacto

**jettison** /'dʒetɪsn/ *vt* alijar; (*discard*) desfazer-se de; (*fig*) abandonar

**jetty** /'dʒetɪ/ *n* (*breakwater*) quebramar *m*; (*landing-stage*) desembarcadouro *m*, cais *m*

**Jew** /dʒuː/ *n* judeu *m*

**jewel** /'dʒuːəl/ *n* jóia *f*. ~**ler** *n* joalheiro *m*. ~**ler's** (**shop**) joalheria *f*. ~**lery** *n* jóias *fpl*

**Jewish** /'dʒuːɪʃ/ *a* judeu

**jib** /dʒɪb/ *vi* (*pt* **jibbed**) recusar-se a avançar; (*of a horse*) empacar. ~ **at** (*fig*) opor-se a, ter relutância em □ *n* (*sail*) bujarrona *f*

**jig** /dʒɪg/ *n* jiga *f*

**jiggle** /'dʒɪgl/ *vt* (*rock*) balançar; (*jerk*) sacolejar

**jigsaw** /'dʒɪgsɔː/ *n* ~(**-puzzle**) puzzle *m*, quebra-cabeça *m*, (*P*) quebracabeças *m*

**jilt** /dʒɪlt/ *vt* deixar, abandonar, dar um fora em (*colloq*), (*P*) mandar passear (*colloq*)

**jingle** /'dʒɪŋgl/ *vt/i* tilintar, tinir □ *n* tilintar *m*, tinido *m*; (*advertising etc*) música *f* de anúncio

**jinx** /dʒɪŋks/ *n* (*colloq*) pessoa *f* or coisa *f* azarenta; (*fig: spell*) azar *m*

**jitter**|**s** /'dʒɪtəz/ *npl* **the** ~**s** (*colloq*) nervos *mpl*. ~**y** /-ərɪ/ *a* **be** ~**y** (*colloq*) estar nervoso, ter os nervos a flor da pele (*colloq*)

**job** /dʒɒb/ *n* trabalho *m*; (*post*) emprego *m*. **have a** ~ **doing** ter dificuldade em fazer. **it is a good** ~ **that** felizmente que. ~**less** *a* desempregado

**jobcentre** /'dʒɒbsentə(r)/ *n* posto *m* de desemprego

**jockey** /'dʒɒkɪ/ *n* (*pl* **-eys**) jóquei *m*

**jocular** /'dʒɒkjʊlə(r)/ *a* jocoso, galhofeiro, brincalhão

**jog** /dʒɒg/ *vt* (*pt* **jogged**) dar um leve empurrão em, tocar em; (*memory*) refrescar □ *vi* (*sport*) fazer jogging. ~**ging** *n* jogging *m*

**join** /dʒɔɪn/ *vt* juntar, unir; (*become member*) fazer-se sócio de, entrar para. ~ **sb** juntar-se a alg □ *vi* (*of roads*) juntar-se, entroncar-se; (*of rivers*) confluir □ *n* junção *f*, junta *f*.

~ **in** *vt/i* participar (em). ~ **up** alistar-se

**joiner** /'dʒɔɪnə(r)/ *n* marceneiro *m*

**joint** /dʒɔɪnt/ *a* comum, conjunto; (*effort*) conjunto □ *n* junta *f*, junção *f*; (*anat*) articulação *f*; (*culin*) quarto *m*; (*roast meat*) carne *f* assada; (*sl: place*) espelunca *f*. ~ **author** co-autor *m*. ~**ly** *adv* conjuntamente

**joist** /dʒɔɪst/ *n* trave *f*, barrote *m*

**jok**|**e** /dʒəʊk/ *n* piada *f*, gracejo *m* □ *vi* gracejar. ~**er** *n* brincalhão *m*; (*cards*) curinga *f* de baralho, (*P*) diabo *m*. ~**ingly** *adv* brincadeira

**joll**|**y** /'dʒɒlɪ/ *a* (**-ier**, **-iest**) alegre, bem disposto □ *adv* (*colloq*) muito. ~**ity** *n* festança *f*, pândega *f*

**jolt** /dʒəʊlt/ *vt* sacudir, sacolejar □ *vi* ir aos solavancos □ *n* solavanco *m*; (*shock*) choque *m*, sobressalto *m*

**jostle** /'dʒɒsl/ *vt* dar um encontrão or encontrões em, empurrar □ *vi* empurrar, acotovelar-se

**jot** /dʒɒt/ *n* (**not a**) ~ nada □ *vt* (*pt* **jotted**) ~ (**down**) apontar, tomar nota de. ~**ter** *n* (*pad*) bloco *m* de notas

**journal** /'dʒɜːnl/ *n* diário *m*; (*newspaper*) jornal *m*; (*periodical*) periódico *m*, revista *f*. ~**ism** *n* jornalismo *m*. ~**ist** *n* jornalista *mf*

**journey** /'dʒɜːnɪ/ *n* (*pl* **-eys**) viagem *f*; (*distance*) trajeto *m*, (*P*) trajecto *m* □ *vi* viajar

**jovial** /'dʒəʊvɪəl/ *a* jovial

**joy** /dʒɔɪ/ *n* alegria *f*. ~**-ride** *n* passeio *m* em carro roubado. ~**ful**, ~**ous** *adjs* alegre

**jubil**|**ant** /'dʒuːbɪlənt/ *a* cheio de alegria, jubiloso. ~**ation** /'leɪʃn/ *n* júbilo *m*, regozijo *m*

**jubilee** /'dʒuːbɪliː/ *n* jubileu *m*

**Judaism** /'dʒuːdeɪzəm/ *n* judaísmo *m*

**judder** /'dʒʌdə(r)/ *vi* trepidar, vibrar □ *n* trepidação *f*, vibração *f*

**judge** /dʒʌdʒ/ *n* juiz *m* □ *vt* julgar. ~**ment** *n* (*judging*) julgamento *m*, juízo *m*; (*opinion*) juízo *m*; (*decision*) julgamento *m*

**judic**|**iary** /dʒuː'dɪʃərɪ/ *n* magistratura *f*; (*system*) judiciário *m*. ~**ial** *a* judiciário

**judicious** /dʒuː'dɪʃəs/ *a* judicioso

**judo** /'dʒuːdəʊ/ *n* judô *m*, (*P*) judo *m*

**jug** /dʒʌg/ *n* (*tall*) jarro *m*; (*round*) botija *f*; **milk-**~ *n* leiteira *f*

**juggernaut** /'dʒʌgənɔːt/ *n* (*lorry*) jainanta *f*, (*P*) camião *m* TIR

**juggle** /'dʒʌgl/ *vt/i* fazer malabarismos (**with** com). ~**r** /-ə(r)/ *n* malabarista *mf*

**juic**|**e** /dʒuːs/ *n* suco *m*, (*P*) sumo *m*. ~**y** *a* suculento; (*colloq: story etc*) picante

**juke-box** /'dʒu:kbɒks/ n juke-box m, (P) máquina f de música
**July** /dʒu:'laɪ/ n julho m
**jumble** /'dʒʌmbl/ vt misturar □ n mistura f. ~ **sale** venda f de caridade de objetos usados
**jumbo** /'dʒʌmbəʊ/ a ~ **jet** (avião) jumbo m
**jump** /dʒʌmp/ vt/i saltar; (start) sobressaltar(-se); (of prices etc) subir repentinamente □ n salto m; (start) sobressalto m; (of prices) alta f. ~ **at** aceitar imediatamente. ~ **the gun** agir prematuramente. ~ **the queue** furar a fila. ~ **to conclusions** tirar conclusões apressadas
**jumper** /'dʒʌmpə(r)/ n pulôver m, suéter m, (P) camisada f de lã
**jumpy** /'dʒʌmpɪ/ a nervoso
**junction** /'dʒʌŋkʃn/ n junção f; (of roads etc) entroncamento m
**June** /dʒu:n/ n junho m
**jungle** /'dʒʌŋgl/ n selva f, floresta f
**junior** /'dʒu:nɪə(r)/ a júnior; (in age) mais novo (to que); (in rank) subalterno; (school) primária □ n o mais novo m; (sport) júnior mf. ~ **to** (in rank) abaixo de
**junk** /dʒʌŋk/ n ferro-velho m, velharias fpl; (rubbish) lixo m. ~ **food** comida f sem valor nutritivo. ~ **mail** material m impresso, enviado por correio, sem ter sido solicitado. ~ **shop** loja f de ferro-velho, bricabraque m
**junkie** /'dʒʌŋkɪ/ n (sl) drogado m
**jurisdiction** /dʒʊərɪs'dɪkʃn/ n jurisdição f
**juror** /'dʒʊərə(r)/ n jurado m
**jury** /'dʒʊərɪ/ n júri m
**just** /dʒʌst/ a justo □ adv justamente, exatamente, (P) exactamente; (only) só. **he has ~ left** ele acabou de sair. ~ **listen!** escuta só! ~ **as** assim como; (with time) assim que. ~ **as tall as** exatamente, (P) exactamente tão alto quanto. ~ **as well that** ainda bem que. ~ **before** um momento antes (de). ~**ly** adv com justiça, justamente
**justice** /'dʒʌstɪs/ n justiça f. **J~ of the Peace** juiz m de paz
**justifiabl|e** /'dʒʌstɪfaɪəbl/ a justificável. ~**y** adv com razão, justificadamente
**justif|y** /'dʒʌstɪfaɪ/ vt justificar. ~**ication** /-ɪ'keɪʃn/ n justificação f
**jut** /dʒʌt/ vi (pt jutted) ~ **out** fazer saliência, sobressair
**juvenile** /'dʒu:vənaɪl/ a (youthful) juvenil; (childish) pueril; (delinquent) jovem; (court) de menores □ n jovem mf
**juxtapose** /dʒʌkstə'pəʊz/ vt justapor

# K

**kaleidoscope** /kə'laɪdəskəʊp/ n caleidoscópio m
**kangaroo** /kæŋgə'ru:/ n canguru m
**karate** /kə'ra:tɪ/ n klaratê m
**kebab** /kə'bæb/ n churrasquinho m, espetinho m
**keel** /ki:l/ n quilha f □ vi ~ **over** virar-se
**keen** /ki:n/ a (-er, -est) (sharp) agudo; (eager) entusiástico; (of appetite) devorador; (of intelligence) vivo; (of wind) cortante. ~**ly** adv vivamente; (eagerly) com entusiasmo. ~**ness** n vivacidade f; (enthusiasm) entusiasmo m
**keep** /ki:p/ (pt kept) vt guardar; (family) sustentar; (animals) ter, criar; (celebrate) festejar; (conceal) esconder; (delay) demorar; (prevent) impedir (from de); (promise) cumprir; (shop) ter □ vi manter-se, conservar-se; (remain) ficar. ~ **(on)** continuar (doing fazendo) □ n sustento m; (of castle) torre f de menagem. ~ **back** vt (withhold) reter □ vi manter-se afastado. ~ **in/out** impedir de entrar/de sair. ~ **up** conservar. ~ **up (with)** acompanhar. ~**er** n guarda mf
**keeping** /'ki:pɪŋ/ n guarda f, cuidado m. **in ~ with** em harmonia com, (P) de harmonia com
**keepsake** /'ki:pseɪk/ n (thing) lembrança f, recordação f
**keg** /keg/ n barril m pequeno
**kennel** /'kenl/ n casota f (de cão). ~**s** npl canil m
**kept** /kept/ see keep
**kerb** /kɜ:b/ n meio fio m, (P) borda f do passeio
**kernel** /'kɜ:nl/ n (of nut) miolo m
**kerosene** /'kerəsi:n/ n (paraffin) querosene m, (P) petróleo m; (aviation fuel) gasolina f
**ketchup** /'ketʃəp/ n molho m de tomate, ketchup m
**kettle** /'ketl/ n chaleira f
**key** /ki:/ n chave f; (of piano etc) tecla f; (mus) clave f □ a chave. ~**-ring** n chaveiro m, porta-chaves m invar □ vt ~ **in** digitar, bater. ~**ed up** tenso
**keyboard** /'ki:bɔ:d/ n teclado m
**keyhole** /'ki:həʊl/ n buraco m da fechadura
**khaki** /'ka:kɪ/ a & n cáqui (invar m), (P) caqui (invar m)
**kick** /kɪk/ vt/i dar um pontapé or pontapés (a, em); (ball) chutar (em); (of horse) dar um coice or coices, escoicear □ n pontapé m; (of gun, horse) coice m; (colloq: thrill) excitação f,

prazer *m*. **~-off** *n* chute *m* inicial, kick-off *m*. **~ out** (*colloq*) pôr na rua. **~ up** (*colloq: fuss, racket*) fazer

**kid** /kɪd/ *n* (*goat*) cabrito *m*; (*sl: child*) garoto *m*; (*leather*) pelica *f* □ *vt/i* (*pt* **kidded**) (*colloq*) brincar (com)

**kidnap** /ˈkɪdnæp/ *vt* (*pt* **kidnapped**) raptar. **~ping** *n* rapto *m*

**kidney** /ˈkɪdnɪ/ *n* rim *m*

**kill** /kɪl/ *vt* matar; (*fig: put an end to*) acabar com □ *n* matança *f*. **~er** *n* assassino *m*. **~ing** *n* matança *f*, massacre *m*; (*of game*) caçada *f* □ *a* (*colloq: funny*) de morrer de rir; (*colloq: exhausting*) de morte

**killjoy** /ˈkɪldʒɔɪ/ *n* desmancha-prazeres *mf*

**kiln** /kɪln/ *n* forno *m*

**kilo** /ˈkiːləʊ/ *n* (*pl* **-os**) quilo *m*

**kilogram** /ˈkɪləgræm/ *n* quilograma *m*

**kilometre** /ˈkɪləmiːtə(r)/ *n* quilômetro *m*, (*P*) quilómetro *m*

**kilowatt** /ˈkɪləwɒt/ *n* quilowatt *m*, (*P*) quilovate *m*

**kilt** /kɪlt/ *n* kilt *m*, saiote *m* escocês

**kin** /kɪn/ *n* família *f*, parentes *mpl*. **next of ~** os parentes mais próximos

**kind**[1] /kaɪnd/ *n* espécie *f*, gênero *m*, (*P*) género *m*, natureza *f*. **in ~** em gêneros, (*P*) géneros; (*fig: in the same form*) na mesma moeda. **~ of** (*colloq: somewhat*) de certo modo, um pouco

**kind**[2] /kaɪnd/ *a* (**-er**, **-est**) (*good*) bom; (*friendly*) gentil, amável. **~-hearted** *a* bom, bondoso. **~ness** *n* bondade *f*

**kindergarten** /ˈkɪndəgɑːtn/ *n* jardim de infância *m*, (*P*) infantil

**kindle** /ˈkɪndl/ *vt/i* acender(-se), atear(-se)

**kindly** /ˈkaɪndlɪ/ *a* (**-ier**, **-iest**) benévolo, bondoso □ *adv* bondosamente, gentilmente, com simpatia. **~ wait** tenha a bondade de esperar

**kindred** /ˈkɪndrɪd/ *a* aparentado; (*fig: connected*) afim. **~ spirit** espírito *m* congênere, alma *f* gêmea

**kinetic** /krˈnetɪk/ *a* cinético

**king** /kɪŋ/ *n* rei *m*. **~-size(d)** *a* de tamanho grande

**kingdom** /ˈkɪŋdəm/ *n* reino *m*

**kingfisher** /ˈkɪŋfɪʃə(r)/ *n* pica-peixe *m*, martim-pescador *m*

**kink** /kɪŋk/ *n* (*in rope*) volta *f*, nó *m*; (*fig*) perversão *f*. **~y** *a* (*colloq*) excêntrico, pervertido; (*of hair*) encarapinhado

**kiosk** /ˈkiːɒsk/ *n* quiosque *m*. **telephone ~** cabine telefônica, (*P*) telefónica

**kip** /kɪp/ *n* (*sl*) sono *m* □ *vi* (*pt* **kipped**) (*sl*) dormir

**kipper** /ˈkɪpə(r)/ *n* arenque *m* defumado

**kiss** /kɪs/ *n* beijo *m* □ *vt/i* beijar(-se)

**kit** /kɪt/ *n* equipamento *m*; (*set of tools*) ferramenta *f*; (*for assembly*) kit *m* □ *vt* (*pt* **kitted**) **~ out** equipar

**kitbag** /ˈkɪtbæg/ *n* mochila *f* (de soldado etc); saco *m* de viagem

**kitchen** /ˈkɪtʃɪn/ *n* cozinha *f*. **~ garden** horta *f*. **~ sink** pia *f*, (*P*) lava-louças *m*

**kite** /kaɪt/ *n* (*toy*) pipa *f*, (*P*) papagaio *m* de papel

**kith** /kɪθ/ *n* **~ and kin** parentes e amigos *mpl*

**kitten** /ˈkɪtn/ *n* gatinho *m*

**kitty** /ˈkɪtɪ/ *n* (*fund*) fundo *m* comum, vaquinha *f*; (*cards*) bolo *m*

**knack** /næk/ *n* jeito *m*

**knapsack** /ˈnæpsæk/ *n* mochila *f*

**knead** /niːd/ *vt* amassar

**knee** /niː/ *n* joelho *m*

**kneecap** /ˈniːkæp/ *n* rótula *f*

**kneel** /niːl/ *vi* (*pt* **knelt**) **~ (down)** ajoelhar(-se)

**knelt** /nelt/ *see* **kneel**

**knew** /njuː/ *see* **know**

**knickers** /ˈnɪkəz/ *npl* calcinhas (de senhora) *fpl*

**knife** /naɪf/ *n* (*pl* **knives**) faca *f* □ *vt* esfaquear, apunhalar

**knight** /naɪt/ *n* cavaleiro *m*; (*chess*) cavalo *m*. **~hood** *n* grau *m* de cavaleiro

**knit** /nɪt/ *vt* (*pt* **knitted** *or* **knit**) tricotar □ *vi* tricotar, fazer tricô; (*fig: unite*) unir-se; (*of bones*) soldar-se. **~ one's brow** franzir as sobrancelhas. **~ting** *n* malha *f*, tricô *m*

**knitwear** /ˈnɪtweə(r)/ *n* roupa *f* de malha, malhas *fpl*

**knob** /nɒb/ *n* (*of door*) maçaneta *f*; (*of drawer*) puxador *m*; (*of radio, TV etc*) botão *m*; (*of butter*) noz *f*. **~bly** *a* nodoso

**knock** /nɒk/ *vt/i* bater (em); (*sl: criticize*) desancar (em). **~ about** *vt* tratar mal □ *vi* (*wander*) andar a esmo. **~ down** (*chair, pedestrian*) deitar no chão, derrubar; (*demolish*) jogar abaixo; (*colloq: reduce*) baixar, reduzir; (*at auction*) adjudicar (the a). **~-down** *a* (*price*) muito baixo. **~-kneed** *a* de pernas de tesoura. **~ off** *vt* (*colloq: complete quickly*) despachar; (*sl: steal*) roubar □ *vi* (*colloq*) parar de trabalhar, fechar a loja (*colloq*). **~ out** pôr fora de combate, eliminar; (*stun*) assombrar. **~-out** *n* (*boxing*) nocaute *m*, KO *m*. **~ over** entornar. **~ up** (*meal etc*) arranjar às pressas. **~er** *n* aldrava *f*

**knot** /nɒt/ *n* nó *m* □ *vt* (*pt* **knotted**) atar com nó, dar nó *or* nós em

**knotty** /ˈnɒtɪ/ *a* (**-ier**, **-iest**) nodoso, cheio de nós; (*difficult*) complicado, espinhoso

**know** /nəʊ/ vt/i (pt **knew**, pp **known**) saber (**that** que); (*person, place*) conhecer □ n **in the ~** (*colloq*) por dentro. **~ about** (*cars etc*) saber sobre, saber de. **~-all** n sabe-tudo m (*colloq*). **~-how** n know-how m, conhecimentos mpl técnicos, culturais etc. **~ of** ter conhecimento de, ter ouvido falar de. **~ingly** adv com ar conhecedor; (*consciously*) conscientemente

**knowledge** /'nɒlɪdʒ/ n conhecimento m; (*learning*) saber m. **~able** a conhecedor, entendido, versado

**known** /nəʊn/ see **know** □ a conhecido

**knuckle** /'nʌkl/ n nó m dos dedos □ vi **~ under** ceder, submeter-se

**Koran** /kə'ra:n/ n Alcorão m, Corão m

**Korea** /kə'rɪə/ n Coréia f

**kosher** /'kəʊʃə(r)/ a aprovado pela lei judaica; (*colloq*) como deve ser

**kowtow** /kaʊ'taʊ/ vi prosternar-se (**to** diante de); (*act obsequiously*) bajular

# L

**lab** /læb/ n (*colloq*) laboratório m

**label** /'leɪbl/ n (*on bottle etc*) rótulo m; (*on clothes, luggage*) etiqueta f □ vt (pt **labelled**) rotular; etiquetar, pôr etiqueta em

**laboratory** /lə'bɒrətrɪ/ n laboratório m

**laborious** /lə'bɔ:rɪəs/ a laborioso, trabalhoso

**labour** /'leɪbə(r)/ n trabalho m, labuta f; (*workers*) mão-de-obra f □ vi trabalhar; (*try hard*) esforçar-se □ vt alongar-se sobre, insistir em. **in ~** em trabalho de parto. **~ed** a (*writing*) laborioso, sem espontaneidade; (*breathing, movement*) difícil. **~-saving** a que poupa trabalho

**Labour** /'leɪbə(r)/ n (*party*) Partido m Trabalhista, os trabalhistas □ a trabalhista

**labourer** /'leɪbərə(r)/ n trabalhador m; (*on farm*) trabalhador m rural

**labyrinth** /'læbərɪnθ/ n labirinto m

**lace** /leɪs/ n renda f; (*of shoe*) cordão m de sapato, (P) atacador m □ vt atar; (*drink*) juntar um pouco (de aguardente, rum etc)

**lacerate** /'læsəreɪt/ vt lacerar, rasgar

**lack** /læk/ n falta f □ vt faltar (a), não ter. **be ~ing** faltar. **be ~ing in** carecer de

**lackadaisical** /lækə'deɪzɪkl/ a lânguido, apático, desinteressado

**laconic** /lə'kɒnɪk/ a lacônico, (P) lacónico

**lacquer** /'lækə(r)/ n laca f

**lad** /læd/ n rapaz m, moço m

**ladder** /'lædə(r)/ n escada de mão f, (P) escadote m; (*in stocking*) fio m corrido, (P) malha f caída □ vi deixar correr um fio, (P) cair uma malha □ vt fazer malhas em

**laden** /'leɪdn/ a carregado (**with** de)

**ladle** /'leɪdl/ n concha (de sopa) f

**lady** /'leɪdɪ/ n senhora f, (*title*) Lady f. **~-in-waiting** n dama f de companhia, (P) dama f de honor. **young ~** jovem f. **~like** a senhoril, elegante. **Ladies** n (*toilets*) toalete m das Senhoras

**ladybird** /'leɪdɪbɜ:d/ n joaninha f

**lag**[1] /læg/ vi (pt **lagged**) atrasar-se, ficar para trás □ n atraso m

**lag**[2] /læg/ vt (pt **lagged**) (*pipes etc*) revestir com isolante térmico

**lager** /'la:gə(r)/ n cerveja f leve e clara, "loura" f (*sl*)

**lagoon** /lə'gu:n/ n lagoa f

**laid** /leɪd/ see **lay**[2]

**lain** /leɪn/ see **lie**[2]

**lair** /leə(r)/ n toca f, covil m

**laity** /'leɪətɪ/ n leigos mpl

**lake** /leɪk/ n lago m

**lamb** /læm/ n cordeiro m, carneiro m; (*meat*) carneiro m

**lambswool** /'læmzwʊl/ n lã f

**lame** /leɪm/ a (**-er, -est**) coxo; (*fig: unconvincing*) fraco. **~ness** n claudicação f, coxeadura f

**lament** /lə'ment/ n lamento m, lamentação f □ vt/i lamentar(-se) (de). **~able** a lamentável

**laminated** /'læmɪneɪtɪd/ a laminado

**lamp** /læmp/ n lâmpada f

**lamppost** /'læmppəʊst/ n poste m (do candeeiro) (de iluminação pública)

**lampshade** /'læmpʃeɪd/ n abajur m, quebra-luz m

**lance** /la:ns/ n lança f □ vt lancetar

**lancet** /'la:nsɪt/ n bisturi m, (P) lanceta f

**land** /lænd/ n terra f; (*country*) país m; (*plot*) terreno m; (*property*) terras fpl □ a de terra, terrestre; (*policy etc*) agrário □ vt/i desembarcar; (*aviat*) aterrissar, (P) aterrar; (*fall*) ir parar (**on** em); (*colloq: obtain*) arranjar; (*a blow*) aplicar, mandar. **~-locked** a rodeado de terra

**landing** /'lændɪŋ/ n desembarque m; (*aviat*) aterrissagem m, (P) aterragem f; (*top of stairs*) patamar m. **~-stage** n cais m flutuante

**land|lady** /'lændleɪdɪ/ n (*of rented house*) senhoria f, proprietária f; (*who lets rooms*) dona f da casa; (*of boarding-house*) dona f da pensão; (*of inn etc*) proprietária f, estalajadeira f. **~lord** n (*of rented house*) senhorio *m*, proprietário *m*; (*of inn etc*) proprietário *m*, estalajadeiro *m*

**landmark** /'lændma:k/ *n* (*conspicuous feature*) ponto *m* de referência; (*fig*) marco *m*

**landscape** /'lændskeɪp/ *n* paisagem *f* □ *vt* projetar, (*P*) projectar paisagisticamente

**landslide** /'lændsleɪd/ *n* desabamento *m* or desmoronamento *m* de terras; (*fig: pol*) vitoria *f* esmagadora

**lane** /leɪn/ *n* senda *f*, caminho *m*; (*in country*) estrada *f* pequena; (*in town*) viela *f*, ruela *f*; (*of road*) faixa *f*, pista *f*; (*of traffic*) fila *f*, (*aviat*) corredor *m*; (*naut*) rota *f*

**language** /'læŋgwɪdʒ/ *n* língua *f*, (*speech, style*) linguagem *f*. **bad** ~ linguagem *f* grosseira. ~ **lab** laboratório *m* de línguas

**languid** /'læŋgwɪd/ *a* lânguido

**languish** /'læŋgwɪʃ/ *vi* elanguescer

**lank** /læŋk/ *a* (*of hair*) escorrido, liso

**lanky** /'læŋkɪ/ *a* (-ier, -iest) desengonçado, escaninhado

**lantern** /'læntən/ *n* lanterna *f*

**lap**[1] /læp/ *n* colo *m*; (*sport*) volta *f* completa. ~-**dog** *n* cãozinho *m* de estimação

**lap**[2] /læp/ *vt* ~ **up** beber lambendo □ *vi* marulhar

**lapel** /lə'pel/ *n* lapela *f*

**lapse** /læps/ *vi* decair, degenerar-se; (*expire*) caducar □ *n* lapso *m*; (*jur*) prescrição *f*. ~ **into** (*thought*) mergulhar em; (*bad habit*) adquirir

**larceny** /'la:sənɪ/ *n* furto *m*

**lard** /la:d/ *n* banha de porco *f*

**larder** /'la:də(r)/ *n* despensa *f*

**large** /la:dʒ/ *a* (-er, -est) grande. **at** ~ à solta, em liberdade. **by and** ~ em geral. ~**ly** *adv* largamente, em grande parte. ~**ness** *n* grandeza *f*

**lark**[1] /la:k/ *n* (*bird*) cotovia *f*

**lark**[2] /la:k/ *n* (*colloq*) pândega *f*, brincadeira *f* □ *vi* ~ **about** (*colloq*) fazer travessuras, brincar

**larva** /'la:və/ *n* (*pl* -**vae** /-vi:/) larva *f*

**laryngitis** /lærɪn'dʒaɪtɪs/ *n* laringite *f*

**larynx** /'lærɪŋks/ *n* laringe *f*

**lascivious** /lə'sɪvɪəs/ *a* lascivo, sensual

**laser** /'leɪzə(r)/ *n* laser *m*. ~ **printer** impressora *f* a laser

**lash** /læʃ/ *vt* chicotear, açoitar; (*rain*) fustigar □ *n* chicote *m*; (*stroke*) chicotada *f*; (*eyelash*) pestana *f*, cílio *m*. ~ **out** atacar, atirar-se a; (*colloq: spend*) esbanjar dinheiro em algo

**lashings** /'læʃɪŋz/ *npl* ~ **of** (*sl*) montes de (*colloq*)

**lasso** /læ'su:/ *n* (*pl* -os) laço *m* □ *vt* laçar

**last**[1] /la:st/ *a* último □ *adv* no fim, em

último lugar; (*most recently*) a última vez □ *n* último *m*. **at (long)** ~ por fim, finalmente. ~-**minute** *a* de última hora. ~ **night** ontem à noite, a noite passada. **the** ~ **straw** a gota d'água. **to the** ~ até o fim. ~**ly** *adv* finalmente, em último lugar

**last**[2] /la:st/ *vt/i* durar, continuar. ~**ing** *a* duradouro, durável

**latch** /lætʃ/ *n* trinco *m*

**late** /leɪt/ *a* (-er, -est) atrasado; (*recent*) recente; (*former*) antigo, ex-, anterior; (*hour, fruit etc*) tardio; (*deceased*) falecido □ *adv* tarde. **in** ~ **July** no fim de julho. **of** ~ ultimamente. **at the** ~**st** o mais tardar. ~**ness** *n* atraso *m*

**lately** /'leɪtlɪ/ *adv* nos últimos tempos, ultimamente

**latent** /'leɪtnt/ *a* latente

**lateral** /'lætərəl/ *a* lateral

**lathe** /leɪð/ *n* torno *m*

**lather** /'la:ðə(r)/ *n* espuma *f* de sabão □ *vt* ensaboar □ *vi* fazer espuma

**Latin** /'lætɪn/ *n* (*lang*) latim *m* □ *a* latino. ~ **America** *n* América *f* Latina. ~ **American** *a* & *n* latino-americano (*m*)

**latitude** /'lætɪtjuːd/ *n* latitude *f*

**latter** /'lætə(r)/ *a* último, mais recente □ **the** ~ este, esta. ~**ly** *adv* recentemente

**lattice** /'lætɪs/ *n* treliça *f*, (*P*) gradeamento *m* de ripas

**laudable** /'lɔːdəbl/ *a* louvável

**laugh** /la:f/ *vi* rir (**at** de). ~ **off** disfarçar com uma piada □ *n* riso *m*. ~**able** *a* irrisório, ridículo. ~**ing-stock** *n* objeto *m*, (*P*) objecto *m* de troça

**laughter** /'la:ftə(r)/ *n* riso *m*, risada *f*

**launch**[1] /lɔːntʃ/ *vt* lançar □ *n* lançamento *m*. ~ **into** lançar-se or meter-se em. ~**ing pad** plataforma *f* de lançamento

**launch**[2] /lɔːntʃ/ *n* (*boat*) lancha *f*

**launder** /'lɔːndə(r)/ *vt* lavar e passar

**launderette** /lɔːn'dret/ *n* lavanderia *f* automática

**laundry** /'lɔːndrɪ/ *n* lavanderia *f*, (*clothes*) roupa *f*. **do the** ~ lavar a roupa

**laurel** /'lɒrəl/ *n* loureiro *m*, louro *m*

**lava** /'la:və/ *n* lava *f*

**lavatory** /'lɒvətrɪ/ *n* privada *f*, (*P*) retrete *f*; (*room*) toalete *m*, (*P*) lavabo *m*

**lavender** /'lævəndə(r)/ *n* alfazema *f*, lavanda *f*

**lavish** /'lævɪʃ/ *a* pródigo; (*plentiful*) copioso, generoso; (*lush*) suntuoso □ *vt* ser pródigoem, encher de. ~**ly** *adv* prodigamente; copiosamente; suntuosamente

**law** /lɔː/ *n* lei *f*; (*profession, study*) direito *m*. ~-**abiding** *a* cumpridor da lei, respeitador da lei. ~ **and order** ordem *f* pública. ~-**breaker** *n* transgressor *m* da lei. ~**ful** *a* legal, legítimo. ~**fully** *adv* legalmente. ~**less** *a* sem lei; (*act*) ilegal; (*person*) rebelde

**lawcourt** /ˈlɔːkɔːt/ *n* tribunal *m*

**lawn** /lɔːn/ *n* gramado *m*, (P) relvado *m*. ~-**mower** *n* cortador *m* de grama, (P) máquina *f* de cortar a relva

**lawsuit** /ˈlɔːsuːt/ *n* processo *m*, ação *f*, (P) acção *f* judicial

**lawyer** /ˈlɔːjə(r)/ *n* advogado *m*

**lax** /læks/ *a* negligente; (*discipline*) frouxo; (*morals*) relaxado. ~**ity** *n* negligência *f*, (*of discipline*) frouxidão *f*; (*of morals*) relaxamento *m*

**laxative** /ˈlæksətɪv/ *n* laxante *m*, laxativo *m*

**lay**[1] /leɪ/ *a* leigo. ~ **opinion** opinião *f* de um leigo

**lay**[2] /leɪ/ *vt* (*pt* **laid**) pôr, colocar; (*trap*) preparar, pôr; (*eggs, table, siege*) pôr; (*plan*) fazer □ *vi* pôr (*ovos*). ~ **aside** pôr de lado. ~ **down** pousar; (*condition, law, rule*) impôr; (*arms*) depor; (*one's life*) oferecer; (*policy*) ditar. ~ **hold of** agarrar(-se a). ~ **off** *vt* (*worker*) suspender do trabalho □ *vi* (*colloq*) parar, desistir. ~-**off** *n* suspensão *f* temporária. ~ **on** (*gas, water etc*) instalar, ligar; (*entertainment etc*) organizar, providenciar; (*food*) servir. ~ **out** (*design*) traçar, planejar; (*spread out*) estender, espalhar; (*money*) gastar. ~ **up** *vt* (*store*) juntar; (*ship, car*) pôr fora de serviço

**lay**[3] /leɪ/ *see* **lie**

**layabout** /ˈleɪəbaʊt/ *n* (*sl*) vadio *m*

**lay-by** /ˈleɪbaɪ/ *n* acostamento *m*, (P) berma *f*

**layer** /ˈleɪə(r)/ *n* camada *f*

**layman** /ˈleɪmən/ *n* (*pl* -**men**) leigo *m*

**layout** /ˈleɪaʊt/ *n* disposição *f*; (*typ*) composição *f*

**laze** /leɪz/ *vi* descansar, vadiar

**laz|y** /ˈleɪzɪ/ *a* (-**ier**, -**iest**) preguiçoso. ~**iness** *n* preguiça *f*. ~**y-bones** *n* (*colloq*) vadio *m*, vagabundo *m*

**lead**[1] /liːd/ *vt/i* (*pt* **led**) conduzir, guiar, levar; (*team etc*) chefiar, liderar; (*life*) levar; (*choir, band etc*) dirigir □ *n* (*distance*) avanço *m*; (*first place*) dianteira *f*; (*clue*) indício *m*, pista *f*; (*leash*) coleira *f*; (*electr*) cabo *m*; (*theatr*) papel *m* principal; (*example*) exemplo *m*. **in the** ~ na frente. ~ **away** levar. ~ **on** (*fig*) encorajar. ~ **the way** ir na frente. ~ **up to** conduzir a

**lead**[2] /led/ *n* chumbo *m*; (*of pencil*) grafite *f*. ~**en** *a* de chumbo; (*of colour*) plúmbeo

**leader** /ˈliːdə(r)/ *n* chefe *m*, líder *m*; (*of country, club, union etc*) dirigente *mf*; (*pol*) líder; (*of orchestra*) regente *mf*, maestro *m*; (*in newspaper*) editorial *m*. ~**ship** *n* direção *f*, (P) direcção *f*, liderança *f*

**leading** /ˈliːdɪŋ/ *a* principal. ~ **article** artigo *m* de fundo, editorial *m*

**leaf** /liːf/ *n* (*pl* **leaves**) folha *f*; (*flap of table*) aba *f* □ *vi* ~ **through** folhear. ~**y** *a* frondoso

**leaflet** /ˈliːflɪt/ *n* prospecto *m*, folheto *m* informativo

**league** /liːg/ *n* liga *f*; (*sport*) campeonato *m* da Liga. **in** ~ **with** de coligação com, em conluio com

**leak** /liːk/ *n* (*escape*) fuga *f*; (*hole*) buraco *m* □ *vt/i* (*roof, container*) pingar; (*eletr gas*) ter um escapamento, (P) ter uma fuga; (*naut*) fazer água. ~ (**out**) (*fig: divulge*) divulgar; (*fig: become known*) transpirar, divulgar-se. ~**age** *n* vazamento *m*. ~**y** *a* que tem um vazamento

**lean**[1] /liːn/ *a* (-**er**, -**est**) magro. ~**ness** *n* magreza *f*

**lean**[2] /liːn/ *vt/i* (*pt* **leaned** *or* **leant** /lent/) encostar(-se), apoiar-se (**on** em); (*be slanting*) inclinar(-se). ~ **back/forward** *or* **over** inclinar-se para trás/para a frente. ~ **on** (*colloq*) pressionar. ~ **to** *n* alpendre *m*

**leaning** /ˈliːnɪŋ/ *a* inclinado □ *n* inclinação *f*

**leap** /liːp/ *vt* (*pt* **leaped** *or* **leapt**/ lept/) galgar, saltar por cima de □ *vi* saltar □ *n* salto *m*, pulo *m*. ~-**frog** *n* eixo-badeixo *m*, (P) jogo *m* do eixo. ~ **year** ano *m* bissexto

**learn** /lɜːn/ *vt/i* (*pt* **learned** *or* **learnt**) aprender; (*be told*) vir a saber, ouvir dizer. ~**er** *n* principiante *mf*, aprendiz *m*

**learn|ed** /ˈlɜːnɪd/ *a* erudito. ~**ing** *n* saber *m*, erudição *f*

**lease** /liːs/ *n* arrendamento *m*, aluguel *m*, (P) aluguer *m* □ *vt* arrendar, (P) alugar

**leash** /liːʃ/ *n* coleira *f*

**least** /liːst/ *a* o menor □ *n* o mínimo *m*, o menos *m* □ *adv* o menos. **at** ~ pelo menos. **not in the** ~ de maneira alguma

**leather** /ˈleðə(r)/ *n* couro *m*, cabedal *m*

**leave** /liːv/ *vt/i* (*pt* **left**) deixar; (*depart from*) sair/partir (de), ir-se (de) □ *n* licença *f*, permissão *f*. **be left** (**over**) restar, sobrar. ~ **alone** deixar em paz, não tocar. ~ **out** omitir. ~ **of absence** licença *f*. **on** ~ (*mil*) de licença. **take one's** ~ despedir-se (**of de**)

**leavings** /ˈliːvɪŋz/ *npl* restos *mpl*

**Leban|on** /'lebənən/ *n* Líbano *m*. **~ese** /'ni:z/ *a & n* libanês (*m*)

**lecherous** /'letʃərəs/ *a* lascivo

**lectern** /'lektən/ *n* estante *f* (de coro de igreja)

**lecture** /'lektʃə(r)/ *n* conferência *f*; (*univ*) aula *f* teórica; (*fig*) sermão *m* □ *vi* dar uma conferência; (*univ*) dar aula(s) □ *vt* pregar um sermão a alg (*colloq*). **~r** /-ə(r)/ *n* conferente *mf*, conferencista *mf*; (*univ*) professor *m*

**led** /led/ *see* **lead¹**

**ledge** /ledʒ/ *n* rebordo *m*, saliência *f*; (*of window*) peitoril *m*

**ledger** /'ledʒə(r)/ *n* livro-mestre *m*, razão *m*

**leech** /li:tʃ/ *n* sanguessuga *f*

**leek** /li:k/ *n* alho-poró *m*, (*P*) alho-porro *m*

**leer** /lɪə(r)/ *vi* **~ (at)** olhar de modo malicioso *or* manhoso (para) □ *n* olhar *m* malicioso *or* manhoso

**leeway** /'li:weɪ/ *n* (*naut*) deriva *f*; (*fig*) liberdade *f* de ação, (*P*) acção, margem *f* (*colloq*)

**left¹** /left/ *see* **leave**. **~ luggage (office)** depósito *m* de bagagens. **~overs** *npl* restos *mpl*, sobras *fpl*

**left²** /left/ *a* esquerdo; (*pol*) de esquerda □ *n* esquerda *f* □ *adv* à/para à esquerda. **~-hand** *a* da esquerda; (*position*) à esquerda. **~-handed** *a* canhoto. **~-wing** *a* (*pol*) de esquerda

**leg** /leg/ *n* perna *f*; (*of table*) pé *m*, perna *f*; (*of journey*) etapa *f*. **pull sb's ~** brincar *or* mexer com alg. **stretch one's ~s** esticar as pernas. **~-room** *n* espaço *m* para as pernas

**legacy** /'legəsɪ/ *n* legado *m*

**legal** /'li:gl/ *a* legal; (*affairs etc*) jurídico. **~ adviser** advogado *m*. **~ity** /li:'gælətɪ/ *n* legalidade *f*. **~ly** *adv* legalmente

**legalize** /'li:gəlaɪz/ *vt* legalizar

**legend** /'ledʒənd/ *n* lenda *f*. **~ary** /'ledʒəndrɪ/ *a* lendário

**leggings** /'legɪŋz/ *npl* perneiras *fpl*; (*women's*) legging *m*

**legib|le** /'ledʒəbl/ *a* legível. **~ility** /-'bɪlətɪ/ *n* legibilidade *f*

**legion** /'li:dʒən/ *n* legião *f*

**legislat|e** /'ledʒɪsleɪt/ *vi* legislar. **~ion** /-'leɪʃn/ *n* legislação *f*

**legislat|ive** /'ledʒɪslətɪv/ *a* legislativo. **~ure** /-eɪtʃə(r)/ *n* corpo *m* legislativo

**legitima|te** /lɪ'dʒɪtɪmət/ *a* legítimo. **~cy** *n* legitimidade *f*

**leisure** /'leʒə(r)/ *n* lazer *m*, tempo livre *m*. **at one's ~** ao bel prazer, (*P*) a seu belo prazer. **~ centre** centro *m* de lazer. **~ly** *a* pausado, compassado □ *adv* sem pressa, devagar

**lemon** /'lemən/ *n* limão *m*

**lemonade** /lemə'neɪd/ *n* limonada *f*

**lend** /lend/ *vt* (*pt* **lent**) emprestar; (*contribute*) dar. **~ a hand to** (*help*) ajudar. **~ itself to** prestar-se a. **~er** *n* pessoa *f* que empresta. **~ing** *n* empréstimo *m*

**length** /leŋθ/ *n* comprimento *m*; (*in time*) período *m*; (*of cloth*) corte *m*. **at ~ extensamente**; (*at last*) por fim, finalmente. **~ of** *a* longo, demorado

**lengthen** /'leŋθən/ *vt/i* alongar(-se)

**lengthways** /'leŋθweɪz/ *adv* ao comprido, em comprimento, longitudinalmente

**lenien|t** /'li:nɪənt/ *a* indulgente, clemente. **~cy** *n* indulgência *f*, clemência *f*

**lens** /lenz/ *n* (*of spectacles*) lente *f*; (*photo*) objetiva *f*, (*P*) objectiva *f*

**lent** /lent/ *see* **lend**

**Lent** /lent/ *n* Quaresma *f*

**lentil** /'lentl/ *n* lentilha *f*

**Leo** /'li:əʊ/ *n* (*astr*) Leão *m*

**leopard** /'lepəd/ *n* leopardo *m*

**leotard** /'li:əʊta:d/ *n* collant(s) *m* (*pl*), (*P*) maillot *m* de ginástica ou dança

**leper** /'lepə(r)/ *n* leproso *m*

**leprosy** /'leprəsɪ/ *n* lepra *f*

**lesbian** /'lezbɪən/ *a* lésbico □ *n* lésbica *f*

**less** /les/ *a* (*in number*) menor (**than** que); (*in quantity*) menos (**than** que) □ *n, adv & prep* menos. **~ and ~** cada vez menos

**lessen** /'lesn/ *vt/i* diminuir

**lesser** /'lesə(r)/ *a* menor. **to a ~ degree** em menor grau

**lesson** /'lesn/ *n* lição *f*

**let** /let/ *vt* (*pt* **let**, *pres p* **letting**) deixar, permitir; (*lease*) alugar, arrendar □ *v aux* **~'s go** vamos. **~ him do it** que o faça ele. **~ me know** diga-me, avise-me □ *n* aluguel *m*, (*P*) aluguer *m*. **~ alone** deixar em paz; (*not to mention*) sem falar em, para não falar em. **~ down** baixar; (*deflate*) esvaziar; (*disappoint*) desapontar; (*fail to help*) deixar na mão. **~-down** *n* desapontamento *m*. **~ go** *vt/i* soltar. **~ in** deixar entrar. **~ o.s. in for** (*task, trouble*) meter-se em. **~ off** (*gun*) disparar; (*firework*) soltar, (*P*) deitar; (*excuse*) desculpar. **~ on** (*colloq*) *vt* revelar (**that** que) □ *vi* descoser-se (*colloq*), (*P*) descair-se (*colloq*). **~ out** deixar sair. **~ through** deixar passar. **~ up** (*colloq*) abrandar, diminuir. **~-up** *n* (*colloq*) pausa *f*, trégua *f*

**lethal** /'li:θl/ *a* fatal, mortal

**letharg|y** /'leθədʒɪ/ *n* letargia *f*, apatia *f*. **~ic** /li'θa:dʒɪk/ *a* letárgico, apático

**letter** /'letə(r)/ *n* (*symbol*) letra *f*; (*message*) carta *f*. **~-bomb** *n* carta-bomba *f*. **~-box** *n* caixa *f* do correio. **~ing** *n* letras *fpl*

**lettuce** /'letɪs/ n alface f
**leukaemia** /luː'kiːmɪə/ n leucemia f
**level** /'levl/ a plano; (on surface) horizontal; (in height) no mesmo nível (with que); (spoonful etc) raso □ n nível m □ vt (pt **levelled**) nivelar; (gun, missile) apontar; (accusation) dirigir. **on the ~** (colloq) franco, sincero. **~ crossing** passagem f de nível. **~-headed** a equilibrado, sensato
**lever** /'liːvə(r)/ n alavanca f □ vt **~ up** levantar com alavanca
**leverage** /'liːvərɪdʒ/ n influência f
**levity** /'levətɪ/ n frivolidade f, leviandade f
**levy** /'levɪ/ vt (tax) cobrar □ n imposto m
**lewd** /luːd/ a (-er, -est) libidinoso, obsceno
**liabilit|y** /laɪə'bɪlətɪ/ n responsabilidade f; (colloq: handicap) desvantagem f. **~ies** dívidas fpl
**liable** /'laɪəbl/ a **~ to do** suscetível, (P) susceptível de fazer; **~ to** (illness etc) suscetível, (P) susceptível a; (fine) sujeito a. **~ for** responsável por
**liaise** /lɪ'eɪz/ vi (colloq) servir de intermediário (**between** entre), fazer a ligação (**with** com)
**liaison** /lɪ'eɪzn/ n ligação f
**liar** /'laɪə(r)/ n mentiroso m
**libel** /'laɪbl/ n difamação f □ vt (pt **libelled**) difamar
**liberal** /'lɪbərəl/ a liberal. **~ly** adv liberalmente
**Liberal** /'lɪbərəl/ a & n liberal (mf)
**liberat|e** /'lɪbəreɪt/ vt libertar. **~ion** /-'reɪʃn/ n libertação f; (of women) emancipação f
**libert|y** /'lɪbətɪ/ n liberdade f. **at ~y to** livre de. **take ~ies** tomar liberdades
**libido** /lɪ'biːdəʊ/ n (pl -os) libido m
**Libra** /'liːbrə/ n (astr) Balança f, Libra f
**librar|y** /'laɪbrərɪ/ n biblioteca f. **~ian** /-'breərɪən/ n bibliotecário m
**Libya** /'lɪbɪə/ n Líbia f. **~n** a & n líbio (m)
**lice** /laɪs/ n see **louse**
**licence** /'laɪsns/ n licença f; d (for TV) taxa f; (for driving) carteira f, (P) carta f; (behaviour) libertinagem f
**license** /'laɪsns/ vt dar licença para, autorizar □ n (Amer) = **licence**. **~plate** placa f do carro, (P) placa f de matrícula
**licentious** /laɪ'senʃəs/ a licencioso
**lichen** /'laɪkən/ n líquen m
**lick** /lɪk/ vt lamber; (sl: defeat) bater (colloq), dar uma surra em (colloq) □ n lambidela f. **a ~ of paint** uma mão de pintura

**lid** /lɪd/ n tampa f
**lido** /'liːdəʊ/ n (pl ~os) piscina f pública ao ar livre
**lie¹** /laɪ/ n mentira f □ vi (pt **lied**, pres p **lying**) mentir. **give the ~ to** desmentir
**lie²** /laɪ/ vi (pt **lay**, pp **lain**, pres p **lying**) estar deitado; (remain) ficar; (be situated) estar, encontrar-se; (in grave, on ground) jazer. **~ down** descansar. **~ in, have a ~-in** dormir até tarde. **~ low** (colloq: hide) andar escondido
**lieu** /luː/ n **in ~ of** em vez de
**lieutenant** /lef'tenənt/ n (army) tenente m; (navy) 1º tenente m
**life** /laɪf/ n (pl **lives**) vida f. **~ cycle** ciclo m vital. **~ expectancy** probabilidade f de vida. **~-guard** n salvavidas m. **~ insurance** seguro m de vida. **~-jacket** n colete m salva-vidas. **~-size(d)** a (de) tamanho natural invar
**lifebelt** /'laɪfbelt/ n cinto m salvavidas, (P) cinto m de salvação
**lifeboat** /'laɪfbəʊt/ n barco m salvavidas
**lifebuoy** /'laɪfbɔɪ/ n bóia f salva-vidas, (P) bóia f de salvação
**lifeless** /'laɪflɪs/ a sem vida
**lifelike** /'laɪflaɪk/ a natural, real; (of portrait) muito parecido
**lifelong** /'laɪflɒŋ/ a de toda a vida, perpétuo
**lifestyle** /'laɪfstaɪl/ n estilo m de vida
**lifetime** /'laɪftaɪm/ n vida f. **the chance of a ~** uma oportunidade única
**lift** /lɪft/ vt/i levantar(-se), erguer(-se); (colloq: steal) roubar, surripiar (colloq); (of fog) levantar, dispersar-se □ n ascensor m, elevador m. **give a ~ to** dar carona, (P) boleia a (colloq). **~off** n decolagem f, (P) descolagem f
**ligament** /'lɪgəmənt/ n ligamento m
**light¹** /laɪt/ n luz f; (lamp) lâmpada f; (on vehicle) farol m; (spark) lume m □ a claro □ vt (pt **lit** or **lighted**) (ignite) acender; (illuminate) iluminar. **bring to ~** trazer à luz, revelar. **come to ~** vir à luz. **~ up** iluminar(-se), acender(-se). **~-year** n ano-luz m
**light²** /laɪt/ a & adv (-er, -est) leve. **~headed** a (dizzy) estonteado, tonto; (frivolous) leviano. **~-hearted** a alegre, despreocupado. **~ly** adv de leve, levemente, ligeiramente. **~ness** n leveza f
**lighten¹** /'laɪtn/ vt/i iluminar(-se); (make brighter) clarear
**lighten²** /'laɪtn/ vt/i (load etc) aligeirar(-se), tornar mais leve
**lighter** /'laɪtə(r)/ n isqueiro m
**lighthouse** /'laɪthaʊs/ n farol m

**lighting** /'laɪtɪŋ/ n iluminação f
**lightning** /'laɪtnɪŋ/ n relâmpago m; (*thunderbolt*) raio m □ a muito rápido. **like ~** como um relâmpago
**lightweight** /'laɪtweɪt/ a leve
**like**[1] /laɪk/ a semelhante (a), parecido (com) □ *prep* como □ *conj* (*colloq*) como □ n igual m, coisa f parecida. **~-minded** a da mesma opinião. **the ~s of you** gente como você(s).
**like**[2] /laɪk/ vt gostar (de). **~s** npl gostos mpl. **I would ~** gostaria (de), queria. **if you ~** se quiser. **would you ~?** gostaria?, queria? **~able** a simpático
**like|ly** /'laɪklɪ/ a (-ier, -iest) provável □ adv provavelmente. **he is ~ly to come** é provável que ele venha. **not ~ly!** (*colloq*) nem morto, nem por sonhos. **~lihood** n probabilidade f
**liken** /'laɪkn/ vt comparar (**to** com)
**likeness** /'laɪknɪs/ n semelhança f
**likewise** /'laɪkwaɪz/ adv também; (*in the same way*) da mesma maneira
**liking** /'laɪkɪŋ/ n gosto m, inclinação f; (*for person*) afeição f. **take a ~ to** (*thing*) tomar gosto por; (*person*) simpatizar com
**lilac** /'laɪlək/ n lilás m □ a lilás invar
**lily** /'lɪlɪ/ n lírio m, lis m. **~ of the valley** lírio m do vale
**limb** /lɪm/ n membro m
**limber** /'lɪmbə(r)/ vi **~ up** fazer exercícios para desenferrujar (*colloq*)
**lime**[1] /laɪm/ n cal f
**lime**[2] /laɪm/ n (*fruit*) limão m
**lime**[3] /laɪm/ n **~(-tree)** tília f
**limelight** /'laɪmlaɪt/ n **be in the ~** estar em evidência
**limerick** /'lɪmərɪk/ n poema m humorístico (*de cinco versos*)
**limit** /'lɪmɪt/ n limite m □ vt limitar. **~ation** /-'teɪʃn/ n limitação f. **~ed company** sociedade f anônima, (P) anónima de responsabilidade limitada
**limousine** /'lɪməziːn/ n limusine f
**limp**[1] /lɪmp/ vi mancar, coxear □ n **have a ~** coxear
**limp**[2] /lɪmp/ a (-er, -est) mole, frouxo
**line**[1] /laɪn/ n linha f; (*string*) fio m; (*rope*) corda f; (*row*) fila f; (*of poem*) verso m; (*wrinkle*) ruga f; (*of business*) ramo m; (*of goods*) linha f. (*Amer: queue*) fila f, (P) bicha f □ vt marcar com linhas; (*streets etc*) ladear, enfileirar-se ao longo de. **~d paper** papel m pautado. **in ~ with** de acordo com. **~ up** alinhar(-se), enfileirar(-se); (*in queue*) pôr(-se) em fila, (P) bicha. **~-up** n (*players*) formação f
**line**[2] /laɪn/ vt (*garment*) forrar (**with** de)
**lineage** /'lɪnɪdʒ/ n linhagem f
**linear** /'lɪnɪə(r)/ a linear

**linen** /'lɪnɪn/ n (*sheets etc*) roupa f (branca) de cama; (*material*) linho m
**liner** /'laɪnə(r)/ n navio m de linha regular, (P) paquete m
**linesman** /'laɪnzmən/ n (*football, tennis*) juiz m de linha
**linger** /'lɪŋɡə(r)/ vi demorar-se, deixar-se ficar; (*of smells etc*) persistir
**lingerie** /'lænʒərɪ/ n roupa f de baixo (de senhora), lingerie f
**linguist** /'lɪŋɡwɪst/ n lingüista mf, (P) linguista mf
**linguistic** /lɪŋ'ɡwɪstɪk/ a lingüístico, (P) linguístico. **~s** n lingüística f, (P) linguística f
**lining** /'laɪnɪŋ/ n forro m
**link** /lɪŋk/ n laço m; (*of chain; fig*) elo m □ vt unir, ligar; (*relate*) ligar; (*arm*) enfiar. **~ up** (*of roads*) juntar-se (**with** a). **~age** n ligação f
**lino, linoleum** /'laɪnəʊ, lɪ'nəʊlɪəm/ n linóleo m
**lint** /lɪnt/ n (*med*) curativo m de fibra de algodão; (*fluff*) cotão m
**lion** /'laɪən/ n leão m. **~ess** n leoa f
**lip** /lɪp/ n lábio m, beiço m; (*edge*) borda f; (*of jug etc*) bico m. **~-read** vt/i entender pelos movimentos dos lábios. **pay ~-service to** fingir pena, admiração etc
**lipstick** /'lɪpstɪk/ n batom m, (P) bâton m
**liquefy** /'lɪkwɪfaɪ/ vt/i liquefazer(-se)
**liqueur** /lɪ'kjʊə(r)/ n licor m
**liquid** /'lɪkwɪd/ n & a líquido (m). **~ize** vt liqüidificar, (P) liquidificar. **~izer** n liqüidificador m, (P) liquidificador m
**liquidat|e** /'lɪkwɪdeɪt/ vt liquidar. **~ion** /-'deɪʃn/ n liquidação f
**liquor** /'lɪkə(r)/ n bebida f alcoólica
**liquorice** /'lɪkərɪs/ n alcaçuz m
**Lisbon** /'lɪzbən/ n Lisboa f
**lisp** /lɪsp/ n ceceio m □ vi cecear
**list**[1] /lɪst/ n lista f □ vt fazer uma lista de; (*enter*) pôr na lista
**list**[2] /lɪst/ vi (*of ship*) adernar □ n adernamento m
**listen** /'lɪsn/ vi escutar, prestar atenção. **~ to, ~ in (to)** escutar, pôr-se à escuta. **~er** n ouvinte mf
**listless** /'lɪstlɪs/ a sem energia, apático
**lit** /lɪt/ see **light**[1]
**literal** /'lɪtərəl/ a literal. **~ly** adv literalmente
**litera|te** /'lɪtərət/ a alfabetizado. **~cy** n alfabetização f, instrução f
**literature** /'lɪtrətʃə(r)/ n literatura f; (*colloq: leaflets etc*) folhetos mpl
**lithe** /laɪð/ a ágil, flexível
**litigation** /lɪtɪ'ɡeɪʃn/ n litígio m
**litre** /'liːtə(r)/ n litro m
**litter** /'lɪtə(r)/ n lixo m; (*animals*) ninhada f □ vt cobrir de lixo. **~ed**

**with** coberto de. **~-bin** n lata f, (P) caixote m do lixo

**little** /'lɪtl/ a pequeno; (not much) pouco □ n pouco m □ adv pouco, mal, nem. **a ~** um pouco (de). **he ~ knows** ele mal/nem sabe. **~ by ~** pouco a pouco

**liturgy** /'lɪtədʒɪ/ n liturgia f

**live**[1] /laɪv/ a vivo; (wire) eletrizado; (broadcast) em direto, (P) directo, ao vivo

**live**[2] /lɪv/ vt/i viver; (reside) habitar, morar, viver. **~ down** fazer esquecer. **~ it up** cair na farra. **~ on** viver de; (continue) continuar a viver. **~ up to** mostrar-se à altura de; (fulfil) cumprir

**livelihood** /'laɪvlɪhʊd/ n modo m de vida

**livel**|**y** /'laɪvlɪ/ a (-ier, -iest) vivo, animado. **~iness** n vivacidade f, animação f

**liven** /'laɪvn/ vt/i **~ up** animar(-se)

**liver** /'lɪvə(r)/ n fígado m

**livery** /'lɪvərɪ/ n libré f

**livestock** /'laɪvstɒk/ n gado m

**livid** /'lɪvɪd/ a lívido; (colloq: furious) furioso

**living** /'lɪvɪŋ/ a vivo □ n vida f; (livelihood) modo de vida m, sustento m. **earn** or **make a ~** ganhar a vida. **standard of ~** nível m de vida. **~-room** n sala f de estar

**lizard** /'lɪzəd/ n lagarto m

**llama** /'la:mə/ n lama m

**load** /ləʊd/ n carga f; (of lorry, ship) carga f, carregamento m; (weight, strain) peso m. **~s of** (colloq) montes de (colloq) □ vt carregar. **~ed** a (dice) viciado; (sl: rich) cheio da nota

**loaf**[1] /ləʊf/ n (pl loaves) pão m

**loaf**[2] /ləʊf/ vi vadiar. **~er** n preguiçoso m, vagabundo m

**loan** /ləʊn/ n empréstimo m □ vt emprestar. **on ~** emprestado

**loath** /ləʊθ/ a sem vontade de, pouco disposto a, relutante em

**loath**|**e** /ləʊð/ vt detestar. **~ing** n repugnância f, aversão f. **~some** a repugnante

**lobby** /'lɒbɪ/ n entrada f, vestíbulo m; (pol) lobby m, grupo m de pressão □ vt fazer pressão sobre

**lobe** /ləʊb/ n lóbulo m

**lobster** /'lɒbstə(r)/ n lagosta f

**local** /'ləʊkl/ a local; (shops etc) do bairro □ n pessoa f do lugar; (colloq: pub) taberna f/pub m do bairro. **~ government** administração f municipal. **~ly** adv localmente; (nearby) na vizinhança

**locale** /ləʊ'ka:l/ n local m

**locality** /ləʊ'kælətɪ/ n localidade f; (position) lugar m

**localized** /'ləʊkəlaɪzd/ a localizado

**locat**|**e** /ləʊ'keɪt/ vt localizar; (situate) situar. **~ion** /-ʃn/ n localização f. **on ~ion** (cinema) em external, (P) no exterior

**lock**[1] /lɒk/ n (hair) mecha f de cabelo

**lock**[2] /lɒk/ n (on door etc) fecho m, fechadura f; (on canal) comporta f □ vt/i fechar à chave; (auto: wheels) imobilizar(-se). **~ in** fechar à chave, encerrar. **~ out** fechar a porta para, deixar na rua. **~-out** n lockout m. **~ up** fechar a casa. **under ~ and key** a sete chaves

**locker** /'lɒkə(r)/ n compartimento m com chave

**locket** /'lɒkɪt/ n medalhão m

**locksmith** /'lɒksmɪθ/ n serralheiro m, chaveiro m

**locomotion** /ləʊkə'məʊʃn/ n locomoção f

**locomotive** /'ləʊkəməʊtɪv/ n locomotiva f

**locum** /'ləʊkəm/ n (med) substituto m

**locust** /'ləʊkəst/ n gafanhoto m

**lodge** /lɒdʒ/ n casa f do guarda numa propriedade; (of porter) portaria f □ vt alojar; (money) depositar. **~ a complaint** apresentar uma queixa □ vi estar alojado (with em casa de); (become fixed) alojar-se. **~r** /-ə(r)/ n hóspede mf

**lodgings** /'lɒdʒɪŋz/ n quarto m mobiliado; (flat) apartamento m

**loft** /lɒft/ n sótão m

**lofty** /'lɒftɪ/ a (-ier, -iest) elevado; (haughty) altivo

**log** /lɒg/ n tronco m, toro m. **~ (-book)** n (naut) diário m de bordo; (aviat) diario m de vôo. **sleep like a ~** dormir como uma pedra □ vt (pt logged) (naut/aviat) lançar no diário de bordo. **~ off** acabar de usar. **~ on** começar a usar

**loggerheads** /'lɒgəhedz/ npl **at ~** às turras (with com)

**logic** /'lɒdʒɪk/ a lógico. **~al** a lógico. **~ally** adv logicamente

**logistics** /lə'dʒɪstɪks/ n logística f

**logo** /'ləʊgəʊ/ n (pl -os) (colloq) emblema m, logotipo m, (P) logótipo m

**loin** /lɔɪn/ n (culin) lombo m, alcatra f

**loiter** /'lɔɪtə(r)/ vi andar vagarosamente; (stand about) rondar

**loll** /lɒl/ vi refestelar-se

**loll**|**ipop** /'lɒlɪpɒp/ n pirulito m, (P) chupa-chupa m. **~y** n (colloq) pirulito m, (P) chupa-chupa m; (sl: money) grana f

**London** /'lʌndən/ n Londres

**lone** /ləʊn/ a solitário. **~r** /-ə(r)/ n solitário m. **~some** a solitário

**lonely** /'ləʊnlɪ/ a (-ier, -iest) solitário; (person) só, solitário

**long**[1] /lɒŋ/ a (-er, -est) longo, comprido □ adv muito tempo, longamente. **how ~ is...?** (in size) qual é o comprimento de...? **how ~?** (in time) quanto tempo? **he will not be ~** ele não vai demorar. **a ~ time** muito tempo. **a ~ way** longe. **as** or **so ~ as** contanto que, desde que. **~ ago** há muito tempo. **before ~** (future) daqui a pouco, dentro em pouco; (past) pouco (tempo) depois. **in the ~ run** no fim de contas. **~ before** muito (tempo) antes. **~-distance** a (flight) de longa distância; (phone call) interurbano. **~ face** cara f triste. **~ jump** salto m em distância. **~-playing record** LP m. **~-range** a de longo alcance; (forecast) a longo prazo. **~-sighted** a que enxerga mal à distância. **~-standing** a de longa data. **~-suffering** a com paciência exemplar/de santo. **~-term** a a longo prazo. **~ wave** ondas fpl longas. **~-winded** a prolixo. **so ~!** (colloq) até logo!

**long**[2] /lɒŋ/ vi **~ for** ansiar por, ter grande desejo de. **~ to** desejar. **~ing** n desejo m ardente

**longevity** /lɒnˈdʒevətɪ/ n longevidade f, vida f longa

**longhand** /ˈlɒŋhænd/ n escrita f à mão

**longitude** /ˈlɒndʒɪtjuːd/ n longitude f

**loo** /luː/ n (colloq) banheiro m, (P) casa f de banho

**look** /lʊk/ vt/i olhar; (seem) parecer □ n olhar m; (appearance) ar m, aspecto m. **(good) ~s** beleza f. **~ after** tomar conta de, olhar por. **~ at** olhar para. **~ down on** desprezar. **~ for** procurar. **~ forward to** aguardar com impaciência. **~ in on** visitar. **~ into** examinar, investigar. **~ like** parecer-se com, ter ar de. **~ on** (as spectator) ver, assistir; (regard as) considerar. **~ out** ter cautela. **~ out for** procurar; (watch) estar à espreita de. **~-out** n (mil) posto m de observação; (watcher) vigia m. **~ round** olhar em redor. **~ up** (word) procurar; (visit) ir ver. **~ up to** respeitar

**loom**[1] /luːm/ n tear m

**loom**[2] /luːm/ vi surgir indistintamente; (fig) ameaçar

**loony** /ˈluːnɪ/ n & a (sl) maluco (m), doido (m)

**loop** /luːp/ n laçada f; (curve) volta f, arco m; (aviat) loop m □ vt dar uma laçada

**loophole** /ˈluːphəʊl/ n (in rule) saída f, furo m

**loose** /luːs/ a (-er, -est) (knot etc) frouxo; (page etc) solto; (clothes) folgado; (not packed) a granel; (inexact) vago; (morals) dissoluto, imoral. **at a ~ end** sem saber o que fazer, sem

ocupação definida. **break ~** soltar-se. **~ly** adv sem apertar; (roughly) vagamente

**loosen** /ˈluːsn/ vt (slacken) soltar, desapertar; (untie) desfazer, desatar

**loot** /luːt/ n saque m □ vt pilhar, saquear. **~er** n assaltante mf. **~ing** n pilhagem f, saque m

**lop** /lɒp/ vt (pt lopped) **~ off** cortar, podar

**lop-sided** /lɒpˈsaɪdɪd/ a torto, inclinado para um lado

**lord** /lɔːd/ n senhor m; (title) lord m. **the L~** o Senhor. **the L~'s Prayer** o Pai-Nosso. **(good) L~!** meu Deus! **~ly** a magnífico, nobre; (haughty) altivo, arrogante

**lorry** /ˈlɒrɪ/ n camião m, caminhão m

**lose** /luːz/ vt/i (pt lost) perder. **get lost** perder-se. **get lost** (sl) vai passear! (colloq). **~r** /-ə(r)/ n perdedor m

**loss** /lɒs/ n perda f. **be at a ~** estar perplexo. **at a ~ for words** sem saber o que dizer

**lost** /lɒst/ see **lose** □ a perdido. **~ property** objetos mpl, (P) objectos mpl perdidos (e achados)

**lot**[1] /lɒt/ n sorte f; (at auction, land) lote m. **draw ~s** tirar à sorte

**lot**[2] /lɒt/ n **the ~** tudo; (people) todos mpl. **a ~ (of), ~s (of)** (colloq) uma porção (de) (colloq). **quite a ~ (of)** (colloq) uma boa porção (de) (colloq)

**lotion** /ˈləʊʃn/ n loção f

**lottery** /ˈlɒtərɪ/ n loteria f, (P) lotaria f

**loud** /laʊd/ a (-er, -est) alto, barulhento, ruidoso; (of colours) berrante □ adv alto. **~hailer** n megafone m. **out ~** em voz alta. **~ly** adv alto

**loudspeaker** /laʊdˈspiːkə(r)/ n alto-falante m

**lounge** /laʊndʒ/ vi recostar-se preguiçosamente □ n sala f, salão m

**louse** /laʊs/ n (pl lice) piolho m

**lousy** /ˈlaʊzɪ/ a (-ier, -iest) piolhento; (sl: very bad) péssimo

**lout** /laʊt/ n pessoa f grosseira, arruaceiro m

**lovable** /ˈlʌvəbl/ a amoroso, adorável

**love** /lʌv/ n amor m; (tennis) zero m, nada m □ vt amar, estar apaixonado por; (like greatly) gostar muito de. **in ~** apaixonado (with por). **~ affair** aventura f amorosa. **she sends you her ~** ela lhe manda lembranças

**lovely** /ˈlʌvlɪ/ a (-ier, -iest) lindo; (colloq: delightful) encantador, delicioso

**lover** /ˈlʌvə(r)/ n namorado m, apaixonado m; (illicit) amante m; (devotee) admirador m, apreciador m

**lovesick** /ˈlʌvsɪk/ a perdido de amor

**loving** /ˈlʌvɪŋ/ a amoroso, terno, extremoso

**low** /ləʊ/ *a* (**-er**, **-est**) baixo □ *adv* baixo □ *n* baixa *f*; (*low pressure*) área de baixa pressão *f*. **~-cut** *a* decotado. **~-down** *a* baixo, reles □ *n* (*colloq*) a verdade autêntica, (*P*) a verdade nua e crua. **~-fat** *a* de baixo teor de gordura. **~-key** *a* (*fig*) moderado, discreto

**lower** /ˈləʊə(r)/ *a & adv see* **low** □ *vt* baixar. **~ o.s.** (re)baixar-se (**to** a)

**lowlands** /ˈləʊləndz/ *npl* planície(s) *f* (*pl*)

**lowly** /ˈləʊlɪ/ *a* (**-ier**, **-iest**) humilde, modesto

**loyal** /ˈlɔɪəl/ *a* leal. **~ly** *adv* lealmente. **~ty** *n* lealdade *f*

**lozenge** /ˈlɒzɪndʒ/ *n* (*shape*) losango *m*; (*tablet*) pastilha *f*

**LP** *abbr see* **long-playing record**

**lubric|ate** /ˈluːbrɪkeɪt/ *vt* lubrificar. **~ant** *n* lubrificante *m*. **~ation** /-ˈkeɪ/ *n* lubrificação *f*

**lucid** /ˈluːsɪd/ *a* lúcido. **~ity** /luːˈsɪdətɪ/ *n* lucidez *f*

**luck** /lʌk/ *n* sorte *f*. **bad ~** pouca sorte *f*. **for ~** para dar sorte. **good ~!**

**luck|y** /ˈlʌkɪ/ *a* (**-ier**, **-iest**) sortudo, com sorte; (*event etc*) feliz; (*number etc*) que dá sorte. **~ily** *adv* felizmente

**lucrative** /ˈluːkrətɪv/ *a* lucrativo, rentável

**ludicrous** /ˈluːdɪkrəs/ *a* ridículo, absurdo

**lug** /lʌg/ *vt* (*pt* **lugged**) arrastar

**luggage** /ˈlʌgɪdʒ/ *n* bagagem *f*. **~-rack** *n* porta-bagagem *m*. **~-van** *n* furgão *m*

**lukewarm** /ˈluːkwɔːm/ *a* morno; (*fig*) sem entusiasmo, indiferente

**lull** /lʌl/ *vt* (*send to sleep*) embalar; (*suspicions*) acalmar □ *n* calmaria *f*, (*P*) acalmia *f*

**lullaby** /ˈlʌləbaɪ/ *n* canção *f* de embalar

**lumbago** /lʌmˈbeɪgəʊ/ *n* lumbago *m*

**lumber** /ˈlʌmbə(r)/ *n* trastes *mpl* velhos; (*wood*) madeira *f* cortada □ *vt* **~ sb with**

**luminous** /ˈluːmɪnəs/ *a* luminoso

**lump** /lʌmp/ *n* bocado *m*; (*swelling*) caroço *m*; (*in the throat*) nó *m*; (*in liquid*) grumo *m*; (*of sugar*) torrão *m* □ *vt* **~ together** amontoar, juntar indiscriminadamente. **~ sum** quantia *f* total; (*payment*) pagamento *m* de uma vez. **~y** *a* grumoso, encaroçado

**lunacy** /ˈluːnəsɪ/ *n* loucura *f*

**lunar** /ˈluːnə(r)/ *a* lunar

**lunatic** /ˈluːnətɪk/ *n* lunático *m*. **~ asylum** manicômio *m*, (*P*) manicómio *m*

**lunch** /lʌntʃ/ *n* almoço *m* □ *vi* almoçar. **~-time** *n* hora *f* do almoço

**luncheon** /ˈlʌntʃən/ *n* (*formal*) almoço *m*. **~ meat** carne *f* enlatada, (*P*) 'merenda' *f*. **~ voucher** senha *f* de almoço

**lung** /lʌŋ/ *n* pulmão *m*

**lunge** /lʌndʒ/ *n* mergulho *m*, movimento *m* súbito para a frente; (*thrust*) arremetida *f* □ *vi* mergulhar, arremessar-se (**at** para cima de, contra)

**lurch**[1] /lɜːtʃ/ *n* **leave sb in the ~** deixar alg em apuros

**lurch**[2] /lɜːtʃ/ *vi* ir aos ziguezagues, dar guinadas; (*stagger*) cambalear

**lure** /lʊə(r)/ *vt* atrair, tentar □ *n* chamariz *m*, engodo *m*. **the ~ of the sea** a atração do mar

**lurid** /ˈlʊərɪd/ *a* berrante; (*fig: sensational*) sensacional; (*fig: shocking*) horrífico

**lurk** /lɜːk/ *vi* esconder-se à espreita; (*prowl*) rondar; (*be latent*) estar latente

**luscious** /ˈlʌʃəs/ *a* apetitoso; (*voluptuous*) desejável

**lush** /lʌʃ/ *a* viçoso, luxuriante

**Lusitanian** /luːsɪˈteɪnɪən/ *a & n* lusitano (*m*)

**lust** /lʌst/ *n* luxúria *f*, sensualidade *f*; (*fig*) cobiça *f*, desejo *m* ardente □ *vi* **~ after** cobiçar, desejar ardentemente. **~ful** *a* sensual

**lustre** /ˈlʌstə(r)/ *n* lustre *m*; (*fig*) prestígio *m*

**lusty** /ˈlʌstɪ/ *a* (**-ier**, **-iest**) robusto, vigoroso

**lute** /luːt/ *n* alaúde *m*

**Luxembourg** /ˈlʌksəmbɜːg/ *n* Luxemburgo *m*

**luxuriant** /lʌgˈʒʊərɪənt/ *a* luxuriante

**luxurious** /lʌgˈʒʊərɪəs/ *a* luxuoso

**luxury** /ˈlʌkʃərɪ/ *n* luxo *m* □ *a* de luxo

**lying** /ˈlaɪŋ/ *see* **lie**[1], **lie**[2]

**lynch** /lɪntʃ/ *vt* linchar

**lynx** /lɪŋks/ *n* lince *m*

**lyre** /ˈlaɪə(r)/ *n* lira *f*

**lyric** /ˈlɪrɪk/ *a* lírico. **~s** *npl* (*mus*) letra *f*. **~al** *a* lírico

# M

**MA** *abbr see* **Master of Arts**

**mac** /mæk/ *n* (*colloq*) impermeável *m*, gabardine *f*

**macabre** /məˈkɑːbrə/ *a* macabro

**macaroni** /mækəˈrəʊnɪ/ *n* macarrão *m*

**macaroon** /mækəˈruːn/ *n* bolinho *m* seco de amêndoa ralada

**mace**[1] /meɪs/ *n* (*staff*) maça *f*

**mace**[2] /meɪs/ *n* (*spice*) macis *m*

**machination** /mækɪ'neɪʃn/ *n* maquinação *f*

**machine** /mə'ʃiːn/ *n* máquina *f* □ *vt* fazer à máquina; (*sewing*) coser à máquina. ~**-gun** *n* metralhadora *f*. ~**-readable** *a* em linguagem de máquina. ~ **tool** máquina-ferramenta *f*

**machinery** /mə'ʃiːnərɪ/ *n* maquinaria *f*; (*working parts; fig*) mecanismo *m*

**machinist** /mə'ʃiːnɪst/ *n* maquinista *m*

**macho** /'mætʃəʊ/ *a* machista

**mackerel** /'mækrəl/ *n* (*pl invar*) cavala *f*

**mackintosh** /'mækɪntɒʃ/ *n* impermeável *m*, gabardine *f*

**mad** /mæd/ *a* (**madder, maddest**) doido, louco; (*dog*) raivoso; (*colloq: angry*) furioso (*colloq*). **be ~ about** ser doido por. **like ~** como (um) doido. ~**ly** *adv* loucamente; (*frantically*) enlouquecidamente. ~**ness** *n* loucura *f*

**Madagascar** /mædə'gæskə(r)/ *n* Madagáscar *m*

**madam** /'mædəm/ *n* senhora *f*. **no, ~** não senhora

**madden** /'mædn/ *vt* endoidecer, enlouquecer. **it's ~ing** é de enlouquecer

**made** /meɪd/ *see* **make**. ~ **to measure** feito sob medida

**Madeira** /mə'dɪərə/ *n* Madeira *f*; (*wine*) Madeira *m*

**madman** /'mædmən/ *n* (*pl* -**men**) doido *m*

**madrigal** /'mædrɪgl/ *n* madrigal *m*

**Mafia** /'mæfɪə/ *n* Máfia *f*

**magazine** /mægə'ziːn/ *n* revista *f*, magazine *m*; (*of gun*) carregador *m*

**magenta** /mə'dʒentə/ *a & n* magenta (*m*), carmin (*m*)

**maggot** /'mægət/ *n* larva *f*. ~**y** *a* bichento

**Magi** /'meɪdʒaɪ/ *npl* **the ~** os Reis *mpl* Magos

**magic** /'mædʒɪk/ *n* magia *f* □ *a* mágico. ~**al** *a* mágico

**magician** /mə'dʒɪʃn/ *n* (*conjuror*) prestidigitador *m*; (*wizard*) feiticeiro *m*

**magistrate** /'mædʒɪstreɪt/ *n* magistrado *m*

**magnanim|ous** /mæg'nænɪməs/ *a* magnânimo. ~**ity** /-ə'nɪmətɪ/ *n* magnanimidade *f*

**magnate** /'mægneɪt/ *n* magnata *m*

**magnet** /'mægnɪt/ *n* ímã *m*, (*P*) íman *m*. ~**ic** /-'netɪk/ *a* magnético. ~**ism** /-ɪzəm/ *n* magnetismo *m*. ~**ize** *vt* magnetizar

**magnificen|t** /mæg'nɪfɪsnt/ *a* magnífico. ~**ce** *n* magnificência *f*

**magnif|y** /'mægnɪfaɪ/ *vt* aumentar; (*sound*) ampliar, amplificar. ~**ication** /-ɪ'keɪʃn/ *n* aumento *m*, ampliação *f*. ~**ying glass** lupa *f*

**magnitude** /'mægnɪtjuːd/ *n* magnitude *f*

**magpie** /'mægpaɪ/ *n* pega *f*

**mahogany** /mə'hɒgənɪ/ *n* mogno *m*

**maid** /meɪd/ *n* criada *f*, empregada *f*. **old ~** solteirona *f*

**maiden** /'meɪdn/ *n* (*old use*) donzela *f* □ *a* (*aunt*) solteira; (*speech, voyage*) inaugural. ~ **name** nome *m* de solteira

**mail**[1] /meɪl/ *n* correio *m*; (*letters*) correio *m*, correspondência *f* □ *a* postal □ *vt* postar, pôr no correio; (*send by mail*) mandar pelo correio. ~**-bag** *n* mala *f* postal. ~**-box** *n* (*Amer*) caixa *f* do correio. ~**ing-list** *n* lista *f* de endereços. ~ **order** *n* encomenda *f* por correspondência, (*P*) por correio

**mail**[2] /meɪl/ *n* (*armour*) cota *f* de malha

**mailman** /'meɪlmæn/ *n* (*pl* -**men**) (*Amer*) carteiro *m*

**maim** /meɪm/ *vt* mutilar, aleijar

**main**[1] /meɪn/ *a* principal □ *n* **in the ~** em geral, essencialmente. ~ **road** estrada *f* principal. ~**ly** *adv* principalmente, sobretudo

**main**[2] /meɪn/ *n* (**water/gas**) ~ cano *m* de água/gás. **the ~s** (*electr*) a rede *f* elétrica

**mainland** /'meɪnlənd/ *n* continente *m*

**mainstay** /'meɪnsteɪ/ *n* (*fig*) esteio *m*

**mainstream** /'meɪnstriːm/ *n* tendência *f* dominante, linha *f* principal

**maintain** /meɪn'teɪn/ *vt* manter, sustentar; (*rights*) defender, manter

**maintenance** /'meɪntənəns/ *n* (*care, continuation*) manutenção *f*; (*allowance*) pensão *f*

**maisonette** /meɪzə'net/ *n* dúplex *m*

**maize** /meɪz/ *n* milho *m*

**majestic** /mə'dʒestɪk/ *a* majestoso. ~**ally** *adv* majestosamente

**majesty** /'mædʒəstɪ/ *n* majestade *f*

**major** /'meɪdʒə(r)/ *a* maior; (*very important*) de vulto □ *n* maior *m* □ *vi* ~ **in** (*Amer: univ*) especializar-se em. ~ **road** estrada *f* principal

**Majorca** /mə'dʒɔːkə/ *n* Maiorca *f*

**majority** /mə'dʒɒrətɪ/ *n* maioria *f*; (*age*) maioridade *f* □ *a* majoritário, (*P*) maioritário. **the ~ of people** a maioria *or* a maior parte das pessoas

**make** /meɪk/ *vt/i* (*pt* **made**) fazer; (*decision*) tomar; (*destination*) chegar a; (*cause to*) fazer (+ *inf*) *or* (*com*) que (+ *subj*). **you ~ me angry** você me aborrece □ *n* (*brand*) marca *f*. **on the ~** (*sl*) oportunista. **be made of** ser feito de. ~ **o.s. at home** estar à vontade/

como em sua casa. ~ **it** chegar; (*succeed*) triunfar. **I** ~ **it two o'clock** são duas pelo meu relógio. ~ **as if to** fazer *ou* fingir que. ~ **believe** fingir. ~**-believe** *a* fingido □ *n* fantasia *f*. ~ **do with** arranjar-se com, contentar-se com. ~ **for** dirigir-se para; (*contribute to*) ajudar a. ~ **good** *vi* triunfar □ *vt* compensar; (*repair*) reparar. ~ **off** fugir (**with com**). ~ **out** avistar, distinguir; (*understand*) entender; (*claim*) pretender; (*a cheque*) passar, emitir. ~ **over** ceder, transferir. ~ **up** *vt* fazer, compor; (*story*) inventar; (*deficit*) suprir □ *vi* fazer as pazes. ~ **up** (**one's face**) maquilar-se, (*P*) maquilhar-se. ~**-up** *n* maquilagem *f*, (*P*) maquilhagem *f*; (*of object*) composição *f*; (*psych*) maneira *f* de ser, natureza *f*. ~ **up for** compensar. ~ **up one's mind** decidir-se

**maker** /'meɪkə(r)/ *n* fabricante *mf*

**makeshift** /'meɪkʃɪft/ *n* solução *f* temporária □ *a* provisório

**making** /'meɪkɪŋ/ *n* **be the ~ of** fazer, ser a causa do sucesso de. **in the ~** em formação. **he has the ~s of** ele tem as qualidades essenciais de

**maladjusted** /mælə'dʒʌstɪd/ *a* desajustado, inadaptado

**maladministration** /mælədmɪnɪ-'streɪʃn/ *n* mau governo *m*, má gestão *f*

**malaise** /mæ'leɪz/ *n* mal-estar *m*

**malaria** /mə'leərɪə/ *n* malária *f*

**Malay** /mə'leɪ/ *a* & *n* malaio (*m*). **~sia** /-ʒə/ *n* Malásia *f*

**male** /meɪl/ *a* (*voice, sex*) masculino; (*biol, techn*) macho □ *n* (*human*) homem *m*, indivíduo *m* do sexo masculino; (*arrival*) macho *m*

**malevolen|t** /mə'levələnt/ *a* malévolo. ~**ce** *n* malevolência *f*, má vontade *f*

**malform|ation** /mælfɔː'meɪʃn/ *n* malformação *f*, deformidade *f*. ~**ed** *a* deformado

**malfunction** /mæl'fʌŋkʃn/ *n* mau funcionamento *m* □ *vi* funcionar mal

**malice** /'mælɪs/ *n* maldade *f*, malícia *f*. **bear sb** ~ guardar rancor a alg

**malicious** /mə'lɪʃəs/ *a* maldoso, malicioso. ~**ly** *adv* maldosamente, maliciosamente

**malign** /mə'laɪn/ *vt* caluniar, difamar

**malignan|t** /mə'lɪgnənt/ *a* (*tumour*) maligno; (*malevolent*) malévolo. ~**cy** *n* malignidade *f*; malevolência *f*

**malinger** /mə'lɪŋɡə(r)/ *vi* fingir-se doente. ~**er** *n* pessoa *f* que se finge doente

**mallet** /'mælɪt/ *n* maço *m*

**malnutrition** /mælnjuː'trɪʃn/ *n* desnutrição *f*, subalimentação *f*

**malpractice** /mæl'præktɪs/ *n* abuso *m*; (*incompetence*) incompetência *f* profissional, negligência *f*

**malt** /mɔːlt/ *n* malte *m*

**Malt|a** /'mɔːltə/ *n* Malta *f*. ~**ese** /-'tiːz/ *a* & *n* maltês (*m*)

**maltreat** /mæl'triːt/ *vt* maltratar. ~**ment** *n* mau(s) trato(s) *m* (*pl*)

**mammal** /'mæml/ *n* mamífero *m*

**mammoth** /'mæməθ/ *n* mamute *m* □ *a* gigantesco, colossal

**man** /mæn/ *n* (*pl* **men**) homem *m*; (*in sports team*) jogador *m*; (*chess*) peça *f* □ *vt* (*pt* **manned**) prover de pessoal; (*mil*) guarnecer; (*naut*) guarnecer, equipar, tripular; (*be on duty at*) estar de serviço em. ~ **in the street** o homem da rua. ~**-hour** *n* hora *f* de trabalho por capita, homem-hora *f*. ~**-hunt** *n* caça *f* ao homem. ~**-made** *a* artificial. ~ **to man** de homem para homem

**manage** /'mænɪdʒ/ *vt* (*household*) governar; (*tool*) manejar; (*boat, affair, crowd*) manobrar; (*shop*) dirigir, gerir. **I could** ~ **another drink** (*colloq*) até que tomaria mais um drinque (*colloq*) □ *vi* arranjar-se. ~ **to do** conseguir fazer. ~**able** *a* manejável; (*easily controlled*) controlável. ~**ment** *n* gerência *f*, direção *f*, (*P*) direcção *f*. **managing director** diretor *m*, (*P*) director *m* geral

**manager** /'mænɪdʒə(r)/ *n* diretor *m*, (*P*) director *m*; (*of bank, shop*) gerente *m*; (*of actor*) empresário *m*; (*sport*) treinador *m*. ~**ess** /-'res/ *n* diretora *f*, (*P*) directora *f*; gerente *f*. ~**ial** /-'dʒɪərɪəl/ *a* diretivo, (*P*) directivo, administrativo. ~**ial staff** gestores *mpl*

**mandarin** /'mændərɪn/ *n* mandarim *m*. ~ (**orange**) mandarina *f*, tangerina *f*

**mandate** /'mændeɪt/ *n* mandato *m*

**mandatory** /'mændətrɪ/ *a* obrigatório

**mane** /meɪn/ *n* crina *f*, (*of lion*) juba *f*

**mangle**¹ /'mæŋɡl/ *n* calandra *f* □ *vt* espremer (com a calandra)

**mangle**² /'mæŋɡl/ *vt* (*mutilate*) mutilar, estropiar

**mango** /'mæŋɡəʊ/ *n* (*pl* **-oes**) manga *f*

**manhandle** /'mænhændl/ *vt* mover à força de braço; (*treat roughly*) tratar com brutalidade

**manhole** /'mænhəʊl/ *n* poço *m* de inspeção, (*P*) inspecção *f*

**manhood** /'mænhʊd/ *n* idade adulta *f*; (*quality*) virilidade *f*

**mania** /'meɪnɪə/ *n* mania *f*. ~**c** /-ɪæk/ *n* maníaco *m*

**manicur|e** /'mænɪkjʊə(r)/ *n* manicure *f* □ *vt* fazer. ~**ist** *n* manicure *m*

**manifest** /'mænɪfest/ *a* manifes to □ *vt* manifestar. **~ation** /-'steɪʃn/ *n* manifestação *f*

**manifesto** /mænɪ'festəʊ/ *n* (*pl* **-os**) manifesto *m*

**manipulat|e** /mə'nɪpjʊleɪt/ *vt* manipular. **~ion** /-'leɪʃn/ *n* manipulação *f*

**mankind** /mæn'kaɪnd/ *n* humanidade *f*, gênero *m*, (*P*) género *m* humano

**manly** /'mænlɪ/ *a* viril, másculo

**manner** /'mænə(r)/ *n* maneira *f*, modo *m*; (*attitude*) modo(s) *m* (*pl*); (*kind*) espécie *f*. **~s** maneiras *fpl*. **bad ~s** má-criação *f*, falta *f* de educação. **good ~s** (boa) educação *f*. **~ed** *a* afetado.

**mannerism** /'mænərɪzəm/ *n* maneirismo *m*

**manoeuvre** /mə'nu:və(r)/ *n* manobra *f* □ *vt/i* manobrar

**manor** /'mænə(r)/ *n* solar *m*

**manpower** /'mænpaʊə(r)/ *n* mão-de-obra *f*

**mansion** /'mænʃn/ *n* mansão *f*

**manslaughter** /'mænslɔ:tə(r)/ *n* homicídio *m* involuntário

**mantelpiece** /'mæntlpi:s/ *n* (*shelf*) consolo *m* da lareira, (*P*) prateleira *f* da chaminé

**manual** /'mænjʊəl/ *a* manual □ *n* manual *m*

**manufacture** /mænjʊ'fæktʃə(r)/ *vt* fabricar □ *n* fabrico *m*, fabricação *f*. **~r** /-ə(r)/ *n* fabricante *mf*

**manure** /mə'njʊə(r)/ *n* estrume *m*

**manuscript** /'mænjʊskrɪpt/ *n* manuscrito *m*

**many** /'menɪ/ *a* (**more, most**) muitos □ *n* muitos; (*many people*) muita gente *f*. **a great ~** muitíssimos. **~ a man/tear/etc** muitos homens/muitas lágrimas/*etc*. **you may take as ~ as you want** você pode levar quantos quiser. **~ of us/them/you** muitos de nós/deles/de vocês. **how ~?** quantos? **one too ~** um a mais

**map** /mæp/ *n* mapa *m* □ *vt* (*pt* **mapped**) fazer mapa de. **~ out** planear em pormenor; (*route*) traçar

**maple** /'meɪpl/ *n* bordo *m*

**mar** /ma:(r)/ *vt* (*pt* **marred**) estragar; (*beauty*) desfigurar

**marathon** /'mærəθən/ *n* maratona *f*

**marble** /'ma:bl/ *n* mármore *m*; (*for game*) bola *f* de gude, (*P*) berlinde *f*

**March** /ma:tʃ/ *n* março *m*

**march** /ma:tʃ/ *vi* marchar □ *vt* **~ off** fazer marchar, conduzir à força. **he was ~ed off to prison** fizeram-no marchar para a prisão □ *n* marcha *f*. **~-past** *n* desfile *m* em revista militar

**mare** /meə(r)/ *n* égua *f*

**margarine** /ma:dʒə'ri:n/ *n* margarina *f*

**margin** /'ma:dʒɪn/ *n* margem *f*. **~al** *a* marginal. **~al seat** (*pol*) lugar *m* ganho com pequena maioria. **~ally** *adv* por uma pequena margem, muito pouco

**marigold** /'mærɪɡəʊld/ *n* cravo-de-defunto *m*, (*P*) malmequer *m*

**marijuana** /mærɪ'wa:nə/ *n* maconha *f*

**marina** /mə'ri:nə/ *n* marina *f*

**marinade** /mærɪ'neɪd/ *n* vinha d'alho, escalabeche *m* □ *vt* pôr na vinha d'alho

**marine** /mə'ri:n/ *a* marinho; (*of ship, trade etc*) marítimo □ *n* (*shipping*) marinha *f*; (*sailor*) fuzileiro *m* naval

**marionette** /mærɪə'net/ *n* fantoche *m*, marionete *f*

**marital** /'mærɪtl/ *a* marital, conjugal, matrimonial. **~ status** estado *m* civil

**maritime** /'mærɪtaɪm/ *a* marítimo

**mark**[1] /ma:k/ *n* (*currency*) marco *m*

**mark**[2] /ma:k/ *n* marca *f*; (*trace*) marca *f*, sinal *m*; (*stain*) mancha *f*; (*schol*) nota *f*; (*target*) alvo *m* □ *vt* marcar; (*exam etc*) marcar, classificar. **~ out** marcar. **~ out for** escolher para, designar para. **~ time** marcar passo. **make one's ~** ganhar nome. **~er** *n* marcador *m*. **~ing** *n* marcas *fpl*, marcação *f*

**marked** /ma:kt/ *a* marcado. **~ly** /-ɪdlɪ/ *adv* manifestamente, visivelmente

**market** /'ma:kɪt/ *n* mercado *m* □ *vt* vender; (*launch*) comercializar, lançar. **~ garden** horta *f* de legumes para venda. **~-place** *n* mercado *m*. **~ research** pesquisa *f* de mercado. **on the ~** à venda. **~ing** *n* marketing *m*

**marksman** /'ma:ksmən/ *n* (*pl* **-men**) atirador *m* especial

**marmalade** /'ma:məleɪd/ *n* compota *f* de laranja

**maroon** /mə'ru:n/ *a* & *n* bordô (*m*), (*P*) bordeaux (*m*)

**marooned** /mə'ru:nd/ *a* abandonado em ilha, costa deserta etc; (*fig: stranded*) encalhado (*fig*)

**marquee** /ma:'ki:/ *n* barraca *f ou* tenda *f* grande; (*Amer: awning*) toldo *m*

**marriage** /'mærɪdʒ/ *n* casamento *m*, matrimônio *m*, (*P*) matrimónio *m*. **~ certificate** certidão *f*. de casamento. **~able** *a* casadouro

**marrow** /'mærəʊ/ *n* (*of bone*) tutano *m*, medula *f*; (*vegetable*) abóbora *f*. **chilled to the ~** gelado até os ossos

**marr|y** /'mærɪ/ *vt* casar(-se) com; (*give or unite in marriage*) casar □ *vi* casar-se. **~ied** *a* casado; (*life*) de casado, conjugal. **get ~ied** casar-se

**Mars** /ma:z/ *n* Marte *m*

**marsh** /ma:ʃ/ n pântano m. ~y a pantanoso

**marshal** /'ma:ʃl/ n (mil) marechal m; (steward) mestre m de cerimónias, (P) cerimónias □ vt (pt **marshalled**) dispor em ordem, ordenar; (usher) conduzir, escoltar

**marshmallow** /ma:ʃ'mæləu/ n marshmallow m

**martial** /'ma:ʃl/ a marcial. ~ **law** lei f marcial

**martyr** /'ma:tə(r)/ n mártir mf □ vt martirizar. ~**dom** n martírio m

**marvel** /'ma:vl/ n maravilha f, prodígio m □ vi (pt **marvelled**) (feel wonder) maravilhar-se (**at** com); (be astonished) pasmar (**at** com)

**marvellous** /'ma:vələs/ a maravilhoso

**Marxis|t** /'ma:ksɪst/ a & n marxista (mf). ~**m** /-zəm/ n marxismo m

**marzipan** /'ma:zɪpæn/ n maçapão m

**mascara** /mæ'ska:rə/ n rímel m

**mascot** /'mæskət/ n mascote f

**masculin|e** /'mæskjʊlɪn/ a masculino □ n masculino m. ~**ity** /'lmætɪ/ n masculinidade f

**mash** /mæʃ/ n (pulp) papa f □ vt esmagar. ~**ed potatoes** purê m de batata(s)

**mask** /ma:sk/ n máscara f □ vt mascarar

**masochis|t** /'mæsəkɪst/ n masoquista mf. ~**m** /-zəm/ n masoquismo m

**mason** /'meɪsn/ n maçom m; (building) pedreiro m. ~**ry** n maçonaria f; (building) alvenaria f

**Mason** /'meɪsn/ n Maçónico m, (P) Maçónico m. ~**ic** /mə'sɒnɪk/ a Maçónico, (P) Maçónico

**masquerade** /mæ:skə'reɪd/ n mascarada f □ vi ~ **as** mascarar-se de, disfarçar-se de

**mass**[1] /mæs/ n (relig) missa f

**mass**[2] /mæs/ n massa f; (heap) montão m □ vt/i aglomerar(-se), reunir(-se) em massa. ~-**produce** vt produzir em série. **the** ~**es** as massas, a grande massa

**massacre** /'mæsəkə(r)/ n massacre m □ vt massacrar

**massage** /'mæsa:ʒ/ n massagem f □ vt massagear, fazer massagens em, (P) dar massagens a

**masseu|r** /mæ'sɜ:(r)/ n massagista m. ~**se** /mæ'sɜ:z/ n massagista f

**massive** /'mæsɪv/ a (heavy) maciço; (huge) enorme

**mast** /ma:st/ n mastro m; (for radio etc) antena f

**master** /'ma:stə(r)/ n (in school) professor m, (P) (expert) mestre m; (boss) patrão m; (owner) dono m. **M**~ (boy) menino m □ vt dominar. ~-**key** n chave-mestra f. ~-**mind** n (of scheme etc) cérebro m □ vt planejar, dirigir. **M**~ **of Arts**/etc Licenciado m em Letras/etc. ~-**stroke** n golpe m de mestre. ~**y** n domínio m (**over** sobre); (knowledge) conhecimento m; (skill) perícia f

**masterly** /'ma:stəlɪ/ a magistral

**masterpiece** /'ma:stəpi:s/ n obra-prima f

**masturbat|e** /'mæstəbeɪt/ vi masturbar-se. ~**ion** /'beɪʃn/ n masturbação f

**mat** /mæt/ n tapete m pequeno; (at door) capacho m. (**table-**)~ n (of cloth) paninho m de mesa; (for hot dishes) descanso m para pratos

**match**[1] /mætʃ/ n fósforo m

**match**[2] /mætʃ/ n (contest) competição f, torneio m; (game) partida f; (equal) par m, parceiro m, igual mf; (fig: marriage) casamento m; (marriage partner) partido m □ vt/i (set against) contrapôr (**against** a); (equal) igualar; (go with) condizer; (be alike) ir com, emparceirar com. **her shoes** ~**ed her bag** os sapatos dela combinavam com a bolsa. ~**ing** a condizente, a condizer

**matchbox** /'mætʃbɒks/ n caixa f de fósforos

**mat|e**[1] /meɪt/ n companheiro m, camarada mf; (of birds, animals) macho m, fêmea f; (assistant) ajudante mf □ vt/i acasalar(-se) (**with** com). ~**ing season** n época f de cio

**mate**[2] /meɪt/ n (chess) mate m, xeque-mate m

**material** /mə'tɪərɪəl/ n material m; (fabric) tecido m; (equipment) apetrechos mpl □ a material; (significant) importante

**materialis|m** /mə'tɪərɪəlɪzəm/ n materialismo m. ~**tic** /'lɪstɪk/ a materialista

**materialize** /mə'tɪərɪəlaɪz/ vi realizar-se, concretizar-se; (appear) aparecer

**maternal** /mə'tɜ:nəl/ a maternal

**maternity** /mə'tɜ:nətɪ/ n maternidade f □ a (clothes) de grávida. ~ **hospital** maternidade f. ~ **leave** licença f de maternidade

**mathematic|s** /mæθə'mætɪks/ n matemática f. ~**al** a matemático. ~**ian** /-ə'tɪʃn/ n matemático m.

**maths** /mæθs/ n (colloq) matemática f

**matinée** /'mætɪneɪ/ n matinê f, (P) matinée f

**matrimon|y** /'mætrɪmənɪ/ n matrimónio m, (P) matrimónio m. ~**ial** /'məʊnɪəl/ a matrimonial, conjugal

**matrix** /'meɪtrɪks/ n (pl **matrices** /-si:z/) matriz f

**matron** /'meɪtrən/ n matrona f; (in school) inspetora f; (former use: senior nursing officer) enfermeira-chefe f. ~ly a respeitável, muito digno

**matt** /mæt/ a fosco, sem brilho

**matted** /'mætɪd/ a emaranhado

**matter** /'mætə(r)/ n (substance) matéria f; (affair) assunto m, caso m, questão f; (pus) pus m □ vi importar. **as a ~ of fact** na verdade. **it does not ~** não importa. **~-of-fact** a prosaico, terra-a-terra. **no ~ what happens** não importa o que acontecer. **what is the ~?** o que é que há? **what is the ~ with you?** o que é que você tem?

**mattress** /'mætrɪs/ n colchão m

**matur|e** /mə'tjʊə(r)/ a maduro, amadurecido □ vt/i amadurecer; (comm) vencer-se. **~ity** n madureza f, maturidade f; (comm) vencimento m

**maul** /mɔːl/ vt maltratar, atacar

**Mauritius** /mə'rɪʃəs/ n Ilha f Maurícia

**mausoleum** /mɔːsə'lɪəm/ n mausoléu m

**mauve** /məʊv/ a & n lilás (m)

**maxim** /'mæksɪm/ n máxima f

**maxim|um** /'mæksɪməm/ a & n (pl -ima) máximo (m). **~ize** vt aumentar ao máximo, maximizar

**may** /meɪ/ v aux (pt **might**) poder. he ~/**might come** talvez venha/viesse. **you might have** podia ter. **you ~ leave** pode ir. **~ I smoke?** posso fumar?, dá licença que eu fume? **~ he be happy** que ele seja feliz. **I ~ or might as well go** talvez seja or fosse melhor eu ir

**May** /meɪ/ n maio n. **~ Day** o primeiro de maio

**maybe** /'meɪbiː/ adv talvez

**mayhem** /'meɪhem/ n (disorder) distúrbios mpl violentos; (havoc) estragos mpl

**mayonnaise** /meɪə'neɪz/ n maionese f

**mayor** /meə(r)/ n prefeito m. **~ess** n prefeita f; (mayor's wife) mulher f do prefeito

**maze** /meɪz/ n labirinto m

**me** /miː/ pron me; (after prep) mim. **with ~** comigo. **he knows ~** ele me conhece. **it's ~** sou eu

**meadow** /'medəʊ/ n prado m, campina f

**meagre** /'miːgə(r)/ a (thin) magro; (scanty) escasso

**meal¹** /miːl/ n refeição f

**meal²** /miːl/ n (grain) farinha f grossa

**mean¹** /miːn/ a (-er, -est) mesquinho; (unkind) mau. **~ness** n mesquinhez f

**mean²** /miːn/ a médio □ n média f. **Greenwich ~ time** tempo m médio de Greenwich

**mean³** /miːn/ vt (pt **meant**) (intend) tencionar or ter (a) intenção (**to de**); (signify) querer dizer, significar; (entail) dar em resultado, resultar provavelmente em; (refer to) referir-se a. **be meant for** destinar-se a. **I didn't ~ it** desculpe, foi sem querer. **he ~s what he says** ele está falando sério

**meander** /mɪ'ændə(r)/ vi serpentear; (wander) perambular

**meaning** /'miːnɪŋ/ n sentido m, significado m. **~ful** a significativo. **~less** a sem sentido

**means** /miːnz/ n meio(s) m(pl) □ npl meios mpl pecuniários, recursos mpl. **by all ~** com certeza. **by ~ of** por meio de, através de. **by no ~** de modo nenhum

**meant** /ment/ see **mean³**

**mean|time** /'miːntaɪm/ adv (**in the**) **~time** entretanto. **~while** /-waɪl/ adv entretanto

**measles** /'miːzlz/ n sarampo m. **German ~** rubéola f

**measly** /'miːzlɪ/ a (sl) miserável, ínfimo

**measurable** /'meʒərəbl/ a mensurável

**measure** /'meʒə(r)/ n medida f □ vt/i medir. **made to ~** feito sob medida. **~ up to** mostrar-se à altura de. **~d** a medido, calculado. **~ment** n medida f

**meat** /miːt/ n carne f. **~y** a carnudo; (fig: substantial) substancial

**mechanic** /mɪ'kænɪk/ n mecânico m

**mechanic|al** /mɪ'kænɪkl/ a mecânico. **~s** n mecânica f; npl mecanismo m

**mechan|ism** /'mekənɪzəm/ n mecanismo m. **~ize** vt mecanizar

**medal** /'medl/ n medalha f. **~list** n condecorado m. **be a gold ~list** ser medalha de ouro

**medallion** /mɪ'dælɪən/ n medalhão m

**meddle** /'medl/ vi (interfere) imiscuir-se, intrometer-se (**in em**); (tinker) mexer (**with em**). **~some** a intrometido, abelhudo

**media** /'miːdɪə/ see **medium** □ npl **the ~** a mídia, os meios de comunicação social or de massa

**mediat|e** /'miːdɪeɪt/ vi servir de intermediário, mediar. **~ion** /-'eɪʃn/ n mediação f. **~or** n mediador m, intermediário m

**medical** /'medɪkl/ a médico □ n (colloq: examination) exame m médico

**medicat|ed** /'medɪkeɪtɪd/ a medicinal. **~ion** /-'keɪʃn/ n medicamentação f

**medicinal** /mɪ'dɪsɪnl/ a medicinal

**medicine** /'medsn/ n medicina f; (substance) remédio m, medicamento m

**medieval** /medɪ'iːvl/ a medieval

**mediocr|e** /miːdɪ'əʊkə(r)/ a medíocre. **~ity** /-'ɒkrətɪ/ n mediocridade f

**meditat|e** /'medɪteɪt/ *vt/i* meditar. **~ion** /-'teɪʃn/ *n* meditação *f*

**Mediterranean** /medɪtə'reɪnɪən/ *a* mediterrâneo □ *n* the **~** o Mediterrâneo

**medium** /'miːdɪəm/ *n* (*pl* **media**) meio *m*; (*pl* **mediums**) (*person*) médium *mf* □ *a* médio. **~ wave** (*radio*) onda *f* média. **the happy ~** o meio-termo

**medley** /'medlɪ/ *n* (*pl* **-eys**) miscelânea *f*

**meek** /miːk/ *a* (**-er, -est**) manso, submisso, sofrido

**meet** /miːt/ *vt* (*pt* **met**) encontrar; (*intentionally*) encontrar-se com, ir ter com; (*at station etc*) ir esperar, ir buscar; (*make the acquaintance of*) conhecer; (*conform with*) ir ao encontro de, satisfazer; (*opponent, obligation etc*) fazer face a; (*bill, expenses*) pagar □ *vi* encontrar-se; (*get acquainted*) familiarizar-se; (*in session*) reunir-se. **~ with** encontrar; (*accident, misfortune*) sofrer, ter

**meeting** /'miːtɪŋ/ *n* reunião *f*, encontro *m*; (*between two people*) encontro *m*. **~-place** *n* ponto *m* de encontro

**megalomania** /megələʊ'meɪnɪə/ *n* megalomania *f*, mania *f* de grandezas

**megaphone** /'megəfəʊn/ *n* megafone *m*, porta-voz *m*

**melancholy** /'melənkɒlɪ/ *n* melancolia *f* □ *a* melancólico

**mellow** /'meləʊ/ *a* (**-er, -est**) (*fruit, person*) amadurecido, maduro; (*sound, colour*) quente, suave □ *vt/i* amadurecer; (*soften*) suavizar

**melodious** /mɪ'ləʊdɪəs/ *a* melodioso

**melodrama** /'melədrɑːmə/ *n* melodrama *m*. **~tic** /-ə'mætɪk/ *a* melodramático

**melod|y** /'melədɪ/ *n* melodia *f*. **~ic** /mɪ'lɒdɪk/ *a* melódico

**melon** /'melən/ *n* melão *m*

**melt** /melt/ *vt/i* (*metals*) fundir(-se); (*butter, snow etc*) derreter (-se); (*fade away*) desvanecer (-se). **~ing-pot** *n* cadinho *m*

**member** /'membə(r)/ *n* membro *m*; (*of club etc*) sócio *m*. **M~ of Parliament** deputado *m*. **~ship** *n* qualidade *f* de sócio; (*members*) número *m* de sócios; (*fee*) cota *f*. **~ship card** carteira *f*, (*P*) cartão *m* de sócio

**membrane** /'membreɪn/ *n* membrana *f*

**memento** /mɪ'mentəʊ/ *n* (*pl* **-oes**) lembrança *f*, recordação *f*

**memo** /'meməʊ/ *n* (*pl* **-os**) (*colloq*) nota *f*, apontamento *m*, lembrete *m*

**memoir** /'memwɑː(r)/ *n* (*record, essay*) memória *f*, memorial *m*; **~s** *npl* (*autobiography*) memórias *fpl*

**memorable** /'memərəbl/ *a* memorável

**memorandum** /memə'rændəm/ *n* (*pl* **-da** *or* **-dums**) nota *f*, lembrete *m*; (*diplomatic*) memorando *m*

**memorial** /mɪ'mɔːrɪəl/ *n* monumento *m* comemorativo □ *a* comemorativo

**memorize** /'meməraɪz/ *vt* decorar, memorizar, aprender de cor

**memory** /'memərɪ/ *n* memória *f*. **from ~** de memória, de cor. **in ~ of** em memória de

**men** /men/ *see* **man**

**menac|e** /'menəs/ *n* ameaça *f*; (*nuisance*) praga *f*, chaga *f* □ *vt* ameaçar. **~ingly** *adv* ameaçadoramente, de modo ameaçador

**menagerie** /mɪ'nædʒərɪ/ *n* coleção *f*, (*P*) colecção *f* de animais ferozes em jaulas

**mend** /mend/ *vt* consertar, reparar; (*darn*) remendar □ *n* conserto *m*; (*darn*) remendo *m*. **~ one's ways** corrigir-se, emendar-se. **on the ~** melhorando

**menial** /'miːnɪəl/ *a* humilde

**meningitis** /menɪn'dʒaɪtɪs/ *n* meningite *f*

**menopause** /'menəpɔːz/ *n* menopausa *f*

**menstruation** /menstrʊ'eɪʃn/ *n* menstruação *f*

**mental** /'mentl/ *a* mental; (*hospital*) de doentes mentais, psiquiátrico

**mentality** /men'tælətɪ/ *n* mentalidade *f*

**mention** /'menʃn/ *vt* mencionar □ *n* menção *f*. **don't ~ it!** não tem de quê, de nada

**menu** /'menjuː/ *n* (*pl* **-us**) menu *m*, (*P*) ementa *f*

**mercenary** /'mɜːsnərɪ/ *a & n* mercenário (*m*)

**merchandise** /'mɜːtʃəndaɪz/ *n* mercadorias *fpl* □ *vt/i* negociar

**merchant** /'mɜːtʃənt/ *n* mercador *m* □ *a* (*ship, navy*) mercante. **~ bank** banco *m* comercial

**merciful** /'mɜːsɪfl/ *a* misericordioso

**merciless** /'mɜːsɪlɪs/ *a* impiedoso, sem dó

**mercury** /'mɜːkjʊrɪ/ *n* mercúrio *m*

**mercy** /'mɜːsɪ/ *n* piedade *f*, misericórdia *f*. **at the ~ of** à mercê de

**mere** /mɪə(r)/ *a* mero, simples. **~ly** *adv* meramente, simplesmente, apenas

**merge** /mɜːdʒ/ *vt/i* fundir(-se), amalgamar(-se); (*comm: companies*) fundir(-se). **~r** /-ə(r)/ *n* fusão *f*

**meringue** /mə'ræŋ/ *n* merengue *m*, suspiro *m*

**merit** /'merɪt/ *n* mérito *m* □ *vt* (*pt* **merited**) merecer

**mermaid** /'mɜːmeɪd/ n sereia f

**merriment** /'merɪmənt/ n divertimento m, alegria f, folguedo m

**merry** /'merɪ/ a (-ier, -iest) alegre, divertido. ~ **Christmas** Feliz Natal. ~**-go-round** n carrossel m. ~**-making** n festa f, divertimento m. **merrily** adv alegremente

**mesh** /meʃ/ n malha f. ~**es** npl (network; fig) malhas fpl.

**mesmerize** /'mezməraɪz/ vt hipnotizar

**mess** /mes/ n (disorder) desordem f, trapalhada f; (trouble) embrulhada f, trapalhada f; (dirt) porcaria f; (mil: place) cantina f; (mil: food) rancho m □ vt ~ **up** (make untidy) desarrumar; (make dirty) sujar; (confuse) atrapalhar, estragar □ vi ~ **about** (behave foolishly) fazer asneiras. ~ **about with** (tinker with) entreter-se com, andar às voltas com. **make a** ~ **of** estragar

**message** /'mesɪdʒ/ n mensagem f; (informal) recado m

**messenger** /'mesɪndʒə(r)/ n mensageiro m

**Messiah** /mɪ'saɪə/ n Messias m

**messy** /'mesɪ/ a (-ier, -iest) desarrumado, bagunçado; (dirty) sujo, porco

**met** /met/ see **meet**

**metabolism** /mɪ'tæbəlɪzm/ n metabolismo m

**metal** /'metl/ n metal m □ a de metal. ~**lic** /mɪ'tælɪk/ a metálico; (paint, colour) metalizado

**metamorphosis** /metə'mɔːfəsɪs/ n (pl -phoses /-siːz/) metamorfose f

**metaphor** /'metəfə(r)/ n metáfora f. ~**ical** /'fɒrɪkl/ a metafórico

**meteor** /'miːtɪə(r)/ n meteoro m

**meteorolog|y** /miːtɪə'rɒlədʒɪ/ n meteorologia f. ~**ical** /-ə'lɒdʒɪkl/ a meteorológico

**meter**[1] /'miːtə(r)/ n contador m

**meter**[2] /'miːtə(r)/ n (Amer) = **metre**

**method** /'meθəd/ n método m

**methodical** /mɪ'θɒdɪkl/ a metódico

**Methodist** /'meθədɪst/ n metodista mf

**methylated** /'meθɪleɪtɪd/ a ~ **spirit** álcool m metílico

**meticulous** /mɪ'tɪkjʊləs/ a meticuloso

**metre** /'miːtə(r)/ n metro m

**metric** /'metrɪk/ a métrico. ~**ation** /-'keɪʃn/ n conversão f para o sistema métrico

**metropol|is** /mə'trɒpəlɪs/ n metrópole f. ~**itan** /metrə'pɒlɪtən/ a metropolitano

**mettle** /'metl/ n têmpera f, caráter m; (P) carácter m; (spirit) brio m

**mew** /mjuː/ n miado m □ vi miar

**Mexic|o** /'meksɪkəʊ/ n México m. ~**an** a & n mexicano (m)

**miaow** /miː'aʊ/ n & vi = **mew**

**mice** /maɪs/ see **mouse**

**mickey** /'mɪkɪ/ n **take the** ~ **out of** (sl) fazer troça de, gozar (colloq)

**micro-** /'maɪkrəʊ/ pref micro-

**microbe** /'maɪkrəʊb/ n micróbio m

**microchip** /'maɪkrəʊtʃɪp/ n microchip m

**microcomputer** /'maɪkrəʊkəmpjuːtə(r)/ n microcomputador m

**microfilm** /'maɪkrəʊfɪlm/ n microfilme m

**microlight** /'maɪkrəʊlaɪt/ n (aviat) ultraleve m

**microphone** /'maɪkrəfəʊn/ n microfone m

**microprocessor** /maɪkrəʊ'prəʊsesə(r)/ n microprocessador m

**microscop|e** /'maɪkrəskəʊp/ n microscópio m. ~**ic** /'skɒpɪk/ a microscópico

**microwave** /'maɪkrəʊweɪv/ n microonda f. ~ **oven** forno m de microondas

**mid** /mɪd/ a meio. **in** ~**-air** no ar, em pleno vôo. **in** ~**-March** em meados de março

**midday** /mɪd'deɪ/ n meio-dia m

**middle** /'mɪdl/ a médio, meio; (quality) médio, mediano □ n meio m. **in the** ~ **of** no meio de. ~**-aged** a de meia idade. **M**~ **Ages** Idade f Média. ~ **class** classe f média. ~**-class** a burguês. **M**~ **East** Médio Oriente m. ~ **name** segundo nome m

**middleman** /'mɪdlmæn/ n (pl -men) intermediário m

**midge** /mɪdʒ/ n mosquito m

**midget** /'mɪdʒɪt/ n anão m □ a minúsculo

**Midlands** /'mɪdləndz/ npl região f do centro da Inglaterra

**midnight** /'mɪdnaɪt/ n meia-noite f

**midriff** /'mɪdrɪf/ n diafragma m; (abdomen) ventre m

**midst** /mɪdst/ n **in the** ~ **of** no meio de

**midsummer** /mɪd'sʌmə(r)/ n pleno verão m; (solstice) solstício m do verão

**midway** /mɪd'weɪ/ adv a meio caminho

**midwife** /'mɪdwaɪf/ n (pl -wives) parteira f

**might**[1] /maɪt/ n potência f; (strength) força f. ~**y** a poderoso; (fig: great) imenso □ adv (colloq) muito

**might**[2] /maɪt/ see **may**

**migraine** /'miːgreɪn/ n enxaqueca f

**migrant** /'maɪgrənt/ a migratório □ n (person) migrante mf, emigrante mf

**migrat|e** /maɪ'greɪt/ vi migrar. ~**ion** /-ʃn/ n migração f

**mike** /maɪk/ n (colloq) microfone m

**mild** /maɪld/ a (-er, -est) brando, manso; (*illness, taste*) leve; (*climate*) temperado; (*weather*) ameno. ~ly adv brandamente, mansamente. **to put it ~ly** para não dizer coisa pior. ~ness n brandura f

**mildew** /ˈmɪldju:/ n bolor m, mofo m; (*in plants*) míldio m

**mile** /maɪl/ n milha f (= 1.6 km). ~s **too big/etc** (*colloq*) grande demais. ~age n (*loosely*) quilometragem f

**milestone** /ˈmaɪlstəʊn/ n marco m miliário; (*fig*) data f or acontecimento m importante

**militant** /ˈmɪlɪtənt/ a & n militante (mf)

**military** /ˈmɪlɪtrɪ/ a militar

**militate** /ˈmɪlɪteɪt/ vi militar. ~ **against** militar contra

**milk** /mɪlk/ n leite m □ a (*product*) lácteo □ vt ordenhar; (*fig: exploit*) explorar. ~-**shake** n milk-shake m, leite m batido. ~y a (*like milk*) leitoso; (*tea etc*) com muito leite. **M~ Way** Via f Láctea

**milkman** /ˈmɪlkmən/ n (pl -men) leiteiro m

**mill** /mɪl/ n moinho m; (*factory*) fábrica f □ vt moer □ vi ~ **around** aglomerar-se; (*crowd*) apinhar-se, (P) agitar-se. ~er n moleiro m. **pepper-~** n moedor m de pimenta

**millennium** /mɪˈlenɪəm/ n (pl -iums or -ia) milênio m, (P) milénio m

**millet** /ˈmɪlɪt/ n painço m, milhete m

**milli-** /ˈmɪlɪ/ pref mili-

**milligram** /ˈmɪlɪgræm/ n miligrama m

**millilitre** /ˈmɪlɪliːtə(r)/ n mililitro m

**millimetre** /ˈmɪlɪmiːtə(r)/ n milímetro m

**million** /ˈmɪljən/ n milhão m. **a ~ pounds** um milhão de libras. ~**aire** /-ˈneə(r)/ n milionário m

**millstone** /ˈmɪlstəʊn/ n mó f. **a ~ round one's neck** um peso nos ombros

**mime** /maɪm/ n mímica f; (*actor*) mímico m □ vt/i exprimir por mímica, mimar

**mimic** /ˈmɪmɪk/ vt (pt **mimicked**) imitar □ n imitador m, parodiante mf. ~**ry** n imitação f.

**mince** /mɪns/ vt picar □ n carne f moída, (P) carne f picada. ~-**pie** n pastel m recheado com massa de passas, amêndoas, especiarias etc. ~r n máquina f de moer

**mincemeat** /ˈmɪnsmiːt/ n massa f de passas, amêndoas, especiarias etc usada para recheio. **make ~ of** (*colloq*) arrasar, aniquilar

**mind** /maɪnd/ n espírito m, mente f; (*intellect*) intelecto m; (*sanity*) razão f □ vt (*look after*) tomar conta de, tratar de; (*heed*) prestar atenção a; (*object to*) importar-se com, incomodar-se com. **do you ~ if I smoke?** você se incomoda que eu fume? **do you ~ helping me?** quer fazer o favor de me ajudar? **never ~** não se importe, não tem importância. **to be out of one's ~** estar fora de si. **have a good ~ to** estar disposto a. **make up one's ~** decidir-se. **presence of ~** presença f de espírito. **to my ~** a meu ver. ~**ful** of atento a, consciente de. ~**less** a insensato

**minder** /ˈmaɪndə(r)/ n pessoa f que toma conta mf; (*bodyguard*) guarda-costa mf, (P) guarda-costas mf

**mine**[1] /maɪn/ poss pron o(s) meu(s), a(s) minha(s). **it is ~** é (o) meu or (a) minha

**min|e**[2] /maɪn/ n mina f □ vt escavar, explorar; (*extract*) extrair; (*mil*) minar. ~**er** n mineiro m. ~**ing** n exploração f mineira □ a mineiro

**minefield** /ˈmaɪnfiːld/ n campo m minado

**mineral** /ˈmɪnərəl/ n mineral m; (*soft drink*) bebida f gasosa. ~ **water** água f mineral

**minesweeper** /ˈmaɪnswiːpə(r)/ n caça-minas m

**mingle** /ˈmɪŋgl/ vt/i misturar(-se) (with com)

**mingy** /ˈmɪndʒɪ/ a (-ier, -iest) (*colloq*) sovina, unha(s)-de-fome (*colloq*)

**mini-** /ˈmɪnɪ/ pref mini-

**miniature** /ˈmɪnɪtʃə(r)/ n miniatura f □ a miniatural

**minibus** /ˈmɪnɪbʌs/ n (*public*) microônibus m, (P) autocarro m pequeno

**minim** /ˈmɪnɪm/ n (*mus*) mínima f

**minim|um** /ˈmɪnɪməm/ a & n (pl -ma) mínimo (m). ~**al** a mínimo. ~**ize** vt minimizar, dar pouca importância a

**miniskirt** /ˈmɪnɪskɜːt/ n minissaia f

**minist|er** /ˈmɪnɪstə(r)/ n ministro m; (*relig*) pastor m. ~**erial** /-ˈstɪərɪəl/ a ministerial. ~**ry** n ministério m

**mink** /mɪŋk/ n (*fur*) marta f, visão m

**minor** /ˈmaɪnə(r)/ a & n menor (mf)

**minority** /maɪˈnɒrətɪ/ n minoria f □ a minoritário

**mint**[1] /mɪnt/ n the **M~** a Casa da Moeda. **a ~** uma fortuna □ vt cunhar. **in ~ condition** em perfeito estado, como novo, impecável

**mint**[2] /mɪnt/ n (*plant*) hortelã f; (*sweet*) pastilha f de hortelã

**minus** /ˈmaɪnəs/ prep menos; (*colloq: without*) sem □ n menos m

**minute**[1] /ˈmɪnɪt/ n minuto m. ~**s** (*of meeting*) ata f, (P) acta f

**minute²** /maɪˈnjuːt/ *a* diminuto, minúsculo; (*detailed*) minucioso

**mirac|le** /ˈmɪrəkl/ *n* milagre *m*. ~ulous /mɪˈrækjʊləs/ *a* milagroso, miraculoso

**mirage** /ˈmɪrɑːʒ/ *n* miragem *f*

**mire** /maɪə(r)/ *n* lodo *m*, lama *f*

**mirror** /ˈmɪrə(r)/ *n* espelho *m*; (*in car*) retrovisor *m* □ *vt* refletir, (*P*) reflectir, espelhar

**mirth** /mɜːθ/ *n* alegria *f*, hilaridade *f*

**misadventure** /mɪsədˈventʃə(r)/ *n* desgraça *f*. **death by** ~ morte *f* acidental

**misanthropist** /mɪsˈænθrəpɪst/ *n* misantropo *m*

**misapprehension** /mɪsæprɪˈhenʃn/ *n* mal-entendido *m*

**misbehav|e** /mɪsbɪˈheɪv/ *vi* portar-se mal, proceder mal. ~**iour** /-ˈheɪvɪə(r)/ *n* mau comportamento *m*, má conduta *f*

**miscalculat|e** /mɪsˈkælkjʊleɪt/ *vi* calcular mal, enganar-se. ~**ion** /-ˈleɪʃn/ *n* erro *m* de cálculo

**miscarr|y** /mɪsˈkærɪ/ *vi* abortar, ter um aborto; (*fail*) falhar, malograr-se. ~**iage** /-ɪdʒ/ *n* aborto *m*. ~**iage of justice** erro *m* judiciário

**miscellaneous** /mɪsəˈleɪnɪəs/ *a* variado, diverso

**mischief** /ˈmɪstʃɪf/ *n* (*of children*) diabrura *f*, travessura *f*; (*harm*) mal *m*, dano *m*. **get into** ~ fazer disparates. **make** ~ criar *or* semear discórdias

**mischievous** /ˈmɪstʃɪvəs/ *a* endiabrado, travesso

**misconception** /mɪskənˈsepʃn/ *n* idéia *f* errada, falso conceito *m*

**misconduct** /mɪsˈkɒndʌkt/ *n* conduta *f* imprópria

**misconstrue** /mɪskənˈstruː/ *vt* interpretar mal

**misdeed** /mɪsˈdiːd/ *n* má ação *f*, (*P*) acção *f*; (*crime*) crime *m*

**misdemeanour** /mɪsdɪˈmiːnə(r)/ *n* delito *m*

**miser** /ˈmaɪzə(r)/ *n* avarento *m*, sovina *mf*. ~**ly** *a* avarento, sovina

**miserable** /ˈmɪzrəbl/ *a* infeliz; (*wretched, mean*) desgraçado, miserável

**misery** /ˈmɪzərɪ/ *n* infelicidade *f*

**misfire** /mɪsˈfaɪə(r)/ *vi* (*plan, gun, engine*) falhar

**misfit** /ˈmɪsfɪt/ *n* inadaptado *m*

**misfortune** /mɪsˈfɔːtʃən/ *n* desgraça *f*, infelicidade *f*, pouca sorte *f*

**misgiving(s)** /mɪsˈgɪvɪŋ(z)/ *n*(*pl*) dúvida(s) *f*(*pl*), receio(s) *m*(*pl*)

**misguided** /mɪsˈgaɪdɪd/ *a* (*mistaken*) desencaminhado; (*misled*) mal aconselhado, enganado

**mishap** /ˈmɪshæp/ *n* contratempo *m*, desastre *m*

**misinform** /mɪsɪnˈfɔːm/ *vt* informar mal

**misinterpret** /mɪsɪnˈtɜːprɪt/ *vt* interpretar mal

**misjudge** /mɪsˈdʒʌdʒ/ *vt* julgar mal

**mislay** /mɪsˈleɪ/ *vt* (*pt* **mislaid**) perder, extraviar

**mislead** /mɪsˈliːd/ *vt* (*pt* **misled**) induzir em erro, enganar. ~**ing** *a* enganador

**mismanage** /mɪsˈmænɪdʒ/ *vt* dirigir mal. ~**ment** *n* má gestão *f*, desgoverno *m*

**misnomer** /mɪsˈnəʊmə(r)/ *n* termo *m* impróprio

**misogynist** /mɪˈsɒdʒɪnɪst/ *n* misógino *m*

**misprint** /ˈmɪsprɪnt/ *n* erro *m* tipográfico

**mispronounce** /mɪsprəˈnaʊns/ *vt* pronunciar mal

**misquote** /mɪsˈkwəʊt/ *vt* citar incorretamente

**misread** /mɪsˈriːd/ *vt* (*pt* **misread** /-ˈred/) ler *or* interpretar mal

**misrepresent** /mɪsreprɪˈzent/ *vt* deturpar, desvirtuar

**miss** /mɪs/ *vt/i* (*chance, bus etc*) perder; (*target*) errar, falhar; (*notice the loss of*) dar pela falta de; (*regret the absence of*) sentir a falta de, ter saudades de. **he** ~**es her/Portugal**/*etc* ele sente a falta *or* tem saudades dela/de Portugal/*etc* □ *n* falha *f*. **it was a near** ~ foi *or* escapou por um triz. ~ **out** omitir. ~ **the point** não compreender

**Miss** /mɪs/ *n* (*pl* **Misses**) Senhorita *f*, (*P*) Senhora *f*

**misshapen** /mɪsˈʃeɪpn/ *a* disforme

**missile** /ˈmɪsaɪl/ *n* míssil *m*; (*object thrown*) projétil *m*, (*P*) projéctil *m*

**missing** /ˈmɪsɪŋ/ *a* que falta; (*lost*) perdido; (*person*) desaparecido. **a book with a page** ~ um livro com uma página a menos

**mission** /ˈmɪʃn/ *n* missão *f*

**missionary** /ˈmɪʃənrɪ/ *n* missionário *m*

**misspell** /mɪsˈspel/ *vt* (*pt* **misspelt** *or* **misspelled**) escrever mal

**mist** /mɪst/ *n* neblina *f*, névoa *f*, bruma *f*; (*fig*) névoa *f* □ *vt/i* enevoar(-se); (*window*) embaçar(-se)

**mistake** /mɪsˈteɪk/ *n* engano *m*, erro *m* □ *vt* (*pt* **mistook**, *pp* **mistaken**) compreender mal; (*choose wrongly*) enganar-se em. ~ **for** confundir com, tomar por. ~**n** /-ən/ *a* errado. **be** ~**n** enganar-se. ~**nly** /-ənlɪ/ *adv* por engano

**mistletoe** /ˈmɪsltəʊ/ *n* visco *m*

**mistreat** /mɪsˈtriːt/ *vt* maltratar. ~**ment** *n* mau trato *m*

**mistress** /'mɪstrɪs/ *n* senhora *f*, dona *f*; (*teacher*) professora *f*; (*lover*) amante *f*

**mistrust** /mɪs'trʌst/ *vt* desconfiar de, duvidar de □ *n* desconfiança *f*

**misty** /'mɪstɪ/ *a* (**-ier, -iest**) enevoado, brumoso; (*window*) embaçado; (*indistinct*) indistinto

**misunderstand** /mɪsʌndə'stænd/ *vt* (*pt* **-stood**) compreender mal. **~ing** *n* mal-entendido *m*

**misuse**[1] /mɪs'juːz/ *vt* empregar mal; (*power etc*) abusar de

**misuse**[2] /mɪs'juːs/ *n* mau uso *m*; (*abuse*) abuso *m*; (*of funds*) desvio *m*

**mitigat|e** /'mɪtɪgeɪt/ *vt* atenuar, mitigar. **~ing circumstances** circunstâncias *fpl* atenuantes

**mitten** /'mɪtn/ *n* luva *f* com uma única divisão entre o polegar e os dedos

**mix** /mɪks/ *vt/i* misturar(-se) □ *n* mistura *f*. **~ up** misturar bem; (*fig: confuse*) confundir. **~-up** *n* trapalhada *f*, confusão *f*. **~ with** associar-se com. **~er** *n* (*culin*) batedeira *f*

**mixed** /mɪkst/ *a* (*school etc*) misto; (*assorted*) sortido. **be ~ up** (*colloq*) estar confuso

**mixture** /'mɪkstʃə(r)/ *n* mistura *f*. **cough ~** xarope *m* para a tosse

**moan** /məʊn/ *n* gemido *m* □ *vi* gemer; (*complain*) queixar-se, lastimar-se (*about* de). **~er** *n* pessoa *f* lamurienta

**moat** /məʊt/ *n* fosso *m*

**mob** /mɒb/ *n* multidão *f*; (*tumultuous*) turba *f*; (*sl: gang*) bando *m* □ *vt* (*pt* **mobbed**) cercar, assediar

**mobil|e** /'məʊbaɪl/ *a* móvel. **~e home** caravana *f*, trailer *m*. **~ity** /-'bɪlətɪ/ *n* mobilidade *f*

**mobiliz|e** /'məʊbɪlaɪz/ *vt/i* mobilizar. **~ation** /-'zeɪʃn/ *n* mobilização *f*

**moccasin** /'mɒkəsɪn/ *n* mocassim *m*

**mock** /mɒk/ *vt/i* zombar de, gozar □ *a* falso. **~-up** *n* modelo *m*, maqueta *f*

**mockery** /'mɒkərɪ/ *n* troça *f*, gozação *f*. **a ~ of** uma gozação de

**mode** /məʊd/ *n* modo *m*; (*fashion*) moda *f*

**model** /'mɒdl/ *n* modelo *m* □ *a* modelo; (*exemplary*) exemplar; (*toy*) em miniatura □ *vt* (*pt* **modelled**) modelar; (*clothes*) apresentar □ *vi* ser or trabalhar como modelo

**modem** /'məʊdem/ *n* modem *m*

**moderate**[1] /'mɒdərət/ *a & n* moderado (*m*). **~ly** *adv* moderadamente. **~ly good** sofrível

**moderat|e**[2] /'mɒdəreɪt/ *vt/i* moderar (-se). **~ion** /-'reɪʃn/ *n* moderação *f*. **in ~ion** com moderação

**modern** /'mɒdn/ *a* moderno. **~ languages** línguas *fpl* vivas. **~ize** *vt* modernizar

**modest** /'mɒdɪst/ *a* modesto. **~y** *n* modéstia *f*. **~ly** *adv* modestamente

**modicum** /'mɒdɪkəm/ *n* **a ~ of** um pouco de

**modif|y** /'mɒdɪfaɪ/ *vt* modificar. **~ication** /-ɪ'keɪʃn/ *n* modificação *f*

**modulat|e** /'mɒdjʊleɪt/ *vt/i* modular. **~ion** /-'leɪʃn/ *n* modulação *f*

**module** /'mɒdjuːl/ *n* módulo *m*

**mohair** /'məʊheə(r)/ *n* mohair *m*

**moist** /mɔɪst/ *a* (**-er, -est**) úmido, (*P*) húmido. **~ure** /'mɔɪstʃə(r)/ *n* umidade *f*, (*P*) humidade *f*. **~urizer** /-tʃəraɪzə(r)/ *n* creme *m* hidratante

**moisten** /'mɔɪsn/ *vt/i* umedecer, (*P*) humedecer

**molasses** /mə'læsɪz/ *n* melaço *m*

**mole**[1] /məʊl/ *n* (*on skin*) sinal na pele *m*

**mole**[2] /məʊl/ *n* (*animal*) toupeira *f*

**molecule** /'mɒlɪkjuːl/ *n* molécula *f*

**molest** /mə'lest/ *vt* meter-se com, molestar

**mollusc** /'mɒləsk/ *n* molusco *m*

**mollycoddle** /'mɒlɪkɒdl/ *vt* mimar

**molten** /'məʊltən/ *a* fundido

**moment** /'məʊmənt/ *n* momento *m*

**momentar|y** /'məʊməntrɪ/ *a* momentâneo. **~ily** /'məʊməntrəlɪ/ *adv* momentâneamente

**momentous** /mə'mentəs/ *a* grave, importante

**momentum** /mə'mentəm/ *n* ímpeto *m*, velocidade *f* adquirida

**Monaco** /'mɒnəkəʊ/ *n* Mônaco *m*

**monarch** /'mɒnək/ *n* monarca *mf*. **~y** *n* monarquia *f*

**monast|ery** /'mɒnəstrɪ/ *n* mosteiro *m*, convento *m*. **~ic** /mə'næstɪk/ *a* monástico

**Monday** /'mʌndɪ/ *n* segunda-feira *f*

**monetary** /'mʌnɪtrɪ/ *a* monetário

**money** /'mʌnɪ/ *n* dinheiro *m*. **~-box** *n* cofre *m*. **~-lender** *n* agiota *mf*. **~ order** der vale *m* postal

**mongrel** /'mʌŋgrəl/ *n* (*cão*) vira-lata *m*, (*P*) rafeiro *m*

**monitor** /'mɒnɪtə(r)/ *n* chefe *m* de turma; (*techn*) monitor *m* □ *vt* controlar; (*a broadcast*) monitorar (a transmissão)

**monk** /mʌŋk/ *n* monge *m*, frade *m*

**monkey** /'mʌŋkɪ/ *n* (*pl* **-eys**) macaco *m*. **~-nut** *n* amendoim *m*. **~-wrench** *n* chave *f* inglesa

**mono** /'mɒnəʊ/ *n* (*pl* **-os**) gravação *f* mono □ *a* mono *invar*

**monocle** /'mɒnəkl/ *n* monóculo *m*

**monogram** /'mɒnəgræm/ *n* monograma *m*

**monologue** /'mɒnəlɒg/ *n* monólogo *m*

**monopol|y** /mə'nɒpəlɪ/ *n* monopólio *m*. **~ize** *vt* monopolizar

**monosyllab|le** /'mɒnəsɪləbl/ *n*

**monossílabo** *m.* **~ic** /-'læbɪk/ *a* monossilábico

**monotone** /'mɒnətəʊn/ *n* tom *m* uniforme

**monoton|ous** /mə'nɒtənəs/ *a* monótono. **~y** *n* monotonia *f*

**monsoon** /mɒn'su:n/ *n* monção *f*

**monst|er** /'mɒnstə(r)/ *n* monstro *m*. **~rous** *a* monstruoso

**monstrosity** /mɒn'strɒsətɪ/ *n* monstruosidade *f*

**month** /mʌnθ/ *n* mês *m*

**monthly** /'mʌnθlɪ/ *a* mensal □ *adv* mensalmente □ *n* (*periodical*) revista *f* mensal

**monument** /'mɒnjʊmənt/ *n* monumento *m*. **~al** /-'mentl/ *a* monumental

**moo** /mu:/ *n* mugido *m* □ *vi* mugir

**mood** /mu:d/ *n* humor *m*, disposição *f*. **in a good/bad ~** de bom/mau humor. **~y** *a* de humor instável; (*sullen*) carrancudo

**moon** /mu:n/ *n* lua *f*

**moon|light** /'mu:nlaɪt/ *n* luar *m*. **~lit** *a* iluminado pela lua, enluarado

**moonlighting** /'mu:nlaɪtɪŋ/ *n* (*colloq*) segundo emprego *m*, esp à noite

**moor**[1] /mʊə(r)/ *n* charneca *f*

**moor**[2] /mʊə(r)/ *vt* amarrar, atracar. **~ings** *npl* amarras *fpl*; (*place*) amarradouro *m*, fundeadouro *m*

**moose** /mu:s/ *n* (*pl invar*) alce *m*

**moot** /mu:t/ *a* discutível □ *vt* levantar

**mop** /mɒp/ *n* esfregão *m* □ *vt* (*pt* **mopped**) **~ (up)** limpar. **~ of hair** trunfa *f*

**mope** /məʊp/ *vi* estar *or* andar abatido e triste

**moped** /'məʊped/ *n* (bicicleta) motorizada *f*

**moral** /'mɒrəl/ *a* moral □ *n* moral *f*. **~s** moral *f*, bons costumes *mpl*. **~ize** *vi* moralizar. **~ly** *adv* moralmente

**morale** /mə'ra:l/ *n* moral *m*

**morality** /mə'rælətɪ/ *n* moralidade *f*

**morass** /mə'ræs/ *n* pântano *m*

**morbid** /'mɔ:bɪd/ *a* mórbido

**more** /mɔ:(r)/ *a* & *adv* mais (**than** (do) que) □ *n* mais *m.* (**some**) **~ tea/pens/***etc* mais chá/canetas/*etc.* **there is no ~ bread** não há mais pão. **~ or less** mais ou menos

**moreover** /mɔ:'rəʊvə(r)/ *adv* além disso, de mais a mais

**morgue** /mɔ:g/ *n* morgue *f*, necrotério *m*

**moribund** /'mɒrɪbʌnd/ *a* moribundo, agonizante

**morning** /'mɔ:nɪŋ/ *n* manhã *f*. **in the ~** de manhã

**Morocc|o** /mə'rɒkəʊ/ *n* Marrocos *m*. **~an** *a* & *n* marroquino (*m*)

**moron** /'mɔ:rɒn/ *n* idiota *mf*

**morose** /mə'rəʊs/ *a* taciturno e insociável, carrancudo

**morphine** /'mɔ:fi:n/ *n* morfina *f*

**Morse** /mɔ:s/ *n* **~ (code)** (alfabeto) Morse *m*

**morsel** /'mɔ:sl/ *n* bocado *m* (esp *de* comida)

**mortal** /'mɔ:tl/ *a* & *n* mortal (*mf*). **~ity** /mɔ:'tælətɪ/ *n* mortalidade *f*

**mortar** /'mɔ:tə(r)/ *n* argamassa *f*; (*bowl*) almofariz *m*; (*mil*) morteiro *m*

**mortgage** /'mɔ:gɪdʒ/ *n* hipoteca *f* □ *vt* hipotecar

**mortify** /'mɔ:tɪfaɪ/ *vt* mortificar

**mortuary** /'mɔ:tʃərɪ/ *n* casa *f* mortuária

**mosaic** /məʊ'zeɪk/ *n* mosaico *m*

**Moscow** /'mɒskəʊ/ *n* Moscou *m*, (*P*) Moscovo *m*

**mosque** /mɒsk/ *n* mesquita *f*

**mosquito** /mə'ski:təʊ/ *n* (*pl* **-oes**) mosquito *m*

**moss** /mɒs/ *n* musgo *m*. **~y** *a* musgoso

**most** /məʊst/ *a* o mais, o maior; (*majority*) a maioria de, a maior parte de □ *n* mais *m*; (*majority*) a maioria, a maior parte, o máximo □ *adv* o mais; (*very*) muito. **at ~** no máximo. **for the ~ part** na maior parte, na grande maioria. **make the ~ of** aproveitar ao máximo, tirar o melhor partido de. **~ly** *adv* sobretudo

**motel** /məʊ'tel/ *n* motel *m*

**moth** /mɒθ/ *n* mariposa *f*, (*P*) borboleta *f* nocturna. (**clothes-**)**~** *n* traça *f*. **~-ball** *n* bola *f* de naftalina. **~-eaten** *a* roído por traças

**mother** /'mʌðə(r)/ *n* mãe *f* □ *vt* tratar como a um filho. **~hood** *n* maternidade *f*. **~-in-law** *n* (*pl* **~s-in-law**) sogra *f*. **~-of-pearl** *n* madrepérola *f*. **M~'s Day** o Dia das Mães. **~-to-be** *n* futura mãe *f*. **~ly** *a* maternal

**motif** /məʊ'ti:f/ *n* tema *m*

**motion** /'məʊʃn/ *n* movimento *m*; (*proposal*) moção *f* □ *vt/i* **~ (to) sb to** fazer sinal a alg para. **~less** *a* imóvel

**motivat|e** /'məʊtɪveɪt/ *vt* motivar. **~ion** /-'veɪʃn/ *n* motivação *f*

**motive** /'məʊtɪv/ *n* motivo *m*

**motor** /'məʊtə(r)/ *n* motor *m*; (*car*) automóvel *m* □ *a* (*anat*) motor; (*boat*) a motor □ *vi* ir de automóvel. **~ bike** (*colloq*) moto *f* (*colloq*). **~ car** carro *m*. **~ cycle** motocicleta *f*. **~ cyclist** motociclista *mf*. **~ vehicle** veículo *m* automóvel. **~ing** *n* automobilismo *m*. **~ized** *a* motorizado

**motorist** /'məʊtərɪst/ *n* motorista *mf*, automobilista *mf*

**motorway** /'məʊtəweɪ/ *n* autoestrada *f*

**mottled** /'mɒtld/ a sarapintado, pintalgado

**motto** /'mɒtəʊ/ n (pl -oes) divisa f, lema m

**mould**[1] /məʊld/ n (container) forma f, molde m; (culin) forma f □ vt moldar. ~ing n (archit) moldura f

**mould**[2] /məʊld/ n (fungi) bolor m, mofo m. ~y a bolorento

**moult** /məʊlt/ vi estar na muda

**mound** /maʊnd/ n monte m de terra or de pedras; (small hill) montículo m

**mount** /maʊnt/ vt/i montar □ n (support) suporte m; (for gem etc) engaste m. ~ up aumentar, subir

**mountain** /'maʊntɪn/ n montanha f. ~ bike mountain bike f. ~ous a montanhoso

**mountaineer** /maʊntɪ'nɪə(r)/ n alpinista mf. ~ing n alpinismo m

**mourn** /mɔːn/ vt/i ~ (for) chorar (a morte de). ~ (over) sofrer (por). ~er n pessoa f que acompanha o enterro. ~ing n luto m. in ~ing de luto

**mournful** /'mɔːnfl/ a triste; (sorrowful) pesaroso

**mouse** /maʊs/ n (pl mice) camundongo m

**mousetrap** /'maʊstræp/ n ratoeira f

**mousse** /muːs/ n mousse f

**moustache** /mə'staːʃ/ n bigode m

**mouth**[1] /maʊθ/ n boca f. ~-organ n gaita f de boca, (P) beiços

**mouth**[2] /maʊð/ vt/i declamar; (silently) articular sem som

**mouthful** /'maʊθful/ n bocado m

**mouthpiece** /'maʊθpiːs/ n (mus) bocal m, boquilha f; (fig: person) porta-voz mf

**mouthwash** /'maʊθwɒʃ/ n líquido m para bochecho

**movable** /'muːvəbl/ a móvel

**move** /muːv/ vt/i mover(-se), mexer(-se), deslocar(-se); (emotionally) comover; (incite) convencer, levar a; (act) agir; (propose) propor; (depart) ir, partir; (go forward) avançar. ~ (out) mudar-se, sair □ n movimento m; (in game) jogada f; (player's turn) vez f; (house change) mudança f. ~ back recuar. ~ forward avançar. ~ in mudar-se para. ~ on! circulem! ~ over, please chegue-se para lá, por favor. on the ~ em marcha

**movement** /'muːvmənt/ n movimento m

**movie** /'muːvɪ/ n (Amer) filme m. the ~s o cinema

**moving** /'muːvɪŋ/ a (touching) comovente; (movable) móvil; (in motion) em movimento

**mow** /məʊ/ vt (pp mowed or mown) ceifar; (lawn) cortar a grama, (P) relva. ~ down ceifar. ~er n (for lawn) máquina f de cortar a grama, (P) relva

**MP** abbr see **Member of Parliament**

**Mr** /'mɪstə(r)/ n (pl **Messrs**) Senhor m. ~ **Smith** o Sr Smith

**Mrs** /'mɪsɪz/ n Senhora f. ~ **Smith** a Sra Smith. **Mr and** ~ **Smith** o Sr Smith e a mulher

**Ms** /mɪz/ n Senhora D f

**much** /mʌtʃ/ (**more**, **most**) a, adv & n muito (m). **very** ~ muito, muitíssimo. **you may have as** ~ **as you need** você pode levar o que precisar. ~ **of it** muito or grande parte dele. **so** ~ **the better/worse** tanto melhor/pior. **how** ~? quanto? **not** ~ não muito. **too** ~ demasiado, demais. **he's not** ~ **of a gardener** não é lá grande jardineiro

**muck** /mʌk/ n estrume m; (colloq: dirt) porcaria f □ vi ~ **about** (sl) entreter-se, perder tempo. ~ **in** (sl) ajudar, dar uma mão □ vt ~ **up** (sl) estragar. ~y a sujo

**mucus** /'mjuːkəs/ n muco m

**mud** /mʌd/ n lama f. ~dy a lamacento, enlameado

**muddle** /'mʌdl/ vt baralhar, atrapalhar, confundir □ vi ~ **through** sair-se bem, desenrascar-se (sl) □ n desordem f; (mix-up) confusão f, trapalhada f

**mudguard** /'mʌdgaːd/ n para-lama m

**muff** /mʌf/ n (for hands) regalo m

**muffle** /'mʌfl/ vt abafar. ~ (up) agasalhar(-se). ~d **sounds** sons mpl abafados. ~r /-ə(r)/ n cachecol m

**mug** /mʌg/ n caneca f; (sl: face) cara f; (sl: fool) trouxa mf (colloq) □ vt (pt mugged) assaltar, agredir. ~ger n assaltante mf. ~ging n assalto m

**muggy** /'mʌgɪ/ a abafado

**mule** /mjuːl/ n mulo m; (female) mula f

**mull** /mʌl/ vt ~ **over** ruminar; (fig) matutar em

**multi-** /'mʌltɪ/ pref mult(i)-

**multicoloured** /'mʌltɪkʌləd/ a multicolor

**multinational** /mʌltɪ'næʃnəl/ a & n multinacional (f)

**multiple** /'mʌltɪpl/ a & n múltiplo (m)

**multipl|y** /'mʌltɪplaɪ/ vt/i multiplicar(-se). ~ication /-ɪ'keɪʃn/ n multiplicação f

**multi-storey** /mʌltɪ'stɔːrɪ/ a (car park) em vários níveis

**multitude** /'mʌltɪtjuːd/ n multidão f

**mum**[1] /mʌm/ a **keep** ~ (colloq) ficar calado

**mum**[2] /mʌm/ (B) mamãe f (colloq) n (colloq) (P) mamã

**mumble** /'mʌmbl/ vt/i resmungar, resmonear

**mummy**[1] /'mʌmɪ/ n (*body*) múmia *f*
**mummy**[2] /'mʌmɪ/ n (*esp child's lang*) mamã (*B*) mamãe *f* (*colloq*) mãezinha *f* (*colloq*), (*P*)
**mumps** /mʌmps/ n parotidite *f*, papeira *f*
**munch** /mʌntʃ/ *vt* mastigar
**mundane** /mʌn'deɪn/ *a* banal; (*worldly*) mundano
**municipal** /mju:'nɪsɪpl/ *a* municipal. **~ity** /-'pælətɪ/ n municipalidade *f*
**munitions** /mju:'nɪʃnz/ *npl* munições *fpl*
**mural** /'mjʊərəl/ *a & n* mural (*m*)
**murder** /'mɜ:də(r)/ n assassínio *m*, assassinato *m* □ *vt* assassinar. **~er** n assassino *m*, assassina *f*. **~ous** *a* assassino, sanguinário; (*of weapon*) mortífero
**murky** /'mɜ:kɪ/ *a* (-ier, -iest) escuro, sombrio
**murmur** /'mɜ:mə(r)/ n murmúrio *m* □ *vt/i* murmurar
**muscle** /'mʌsl/ n músculo *m* □ *vi* ~ in (*colloq*) impor-se, intrometer-se
**muscular** /'mʌskjʊlə(r)/ *a* muscular; (*brawny*) musculoso
**muse** /mju:z/ *vi* meditar, cismar
**museum** /mju:'zɪəm/ n museu *m*
**mush** /mʌʃ/ n papa *f* de farinha de milho. **~y** *a* mole; (*sentimental*) piegas *inv*
**mushroom** /'mʌʃrʊm/ n cogumelo *m* □ *vi* pulular, multiplicar-se com rapidez
**music** /'mju:zɪk/ n música *f*. **~al** *a* musical □ n (*show*) comédia *f* musical, musical *m*. **~al box** n caixa *f* de música. **~-stand** n estante *f* de música
**musician** /mju:'zɪʃn/ n músico *m*
**musk** /mʌsk/ n almíscar *m*
**Muslim** /'mʊzlɪm/ *a & n* muçulmano (*m*)
**muslin** /'mʌzlɪn/ n musselina *f*
**mussel** /'mʌsl/ n mexilhão *m*
**must** /mʌst/ *v aux* dever. **you ~ go** é necessário que você parta. **he ~ be old** ele deve ser velho. **I ~ have done it** eu devo tê-lo feito □ n **be a ~** (*colloq*) ser imprescindível
**mustard** /'mʌstəd/ n mostarda *f*
**muster** /'mʌstə(r)/ *vt/i* juntar(-se), reunir(-se). **pass ~** ser aceitável
**musty** /'mʌstɪ/ *a* (-ier, -iest) mofado, bolorento
**mutation** /mju:'teɪʃn/ n mutação *f*
**mute** /mju:t/ *a & n* mudo (*m*)
**muted** /'mju:tɪd/ *a* (*sound*) em surdina; (*colour*) suave
**mutilat|e** /'mju:tɪleɪt/ *vt* mutilar. **~ion** /-'leɪʃn/ n mutilação *f*
**mutin|y** /'mju:tɪnɪ/ n motim *f* □ *vi* amotinar-se. **~ous** *a* amotinado

**mutter** /'mʌtə(r)/ *vt/i* resmungar
**mutton** /'mʌtn/ n (carne de) carneiro *m*
**mutual** /'mju:tʃʊəl/ *a* mútuo; (*colloq: common*) comum. **~ly** *adv* mutuamente
**muzzle** /'mʌzl/ n focinho *m*; (*device*) focinheira *f*; (*of gun*) boca *f* □ *vt* amordaçar; (*dog*) pôr focinheira em
**my** /maɪ/ *a* meu(s), minha(s)
**myself** /maɪ'self/ *pron* eu mesmo, eu próprio; (*reflexive*) me; (*after prep*) mim (próprio, mesmo). **by ~** sozinho
**mysterious** /mɪ'stɪərɪəs/ *a* misterioso
**mystery** /'mɪstərɪ/ n mistério *m*
**mystic** /'mɪstɪk/ *a & n* místico (*m*). **~al** *a* místico. **~ism** /-sɪzəm/ n misticismo *m*
**mystify** /'mɪstɪfaɪ/ *vt* deixar perplexo
**mystique** /mɪ'sti:k/ n mística *f*
**myth** /mɪθ/ n mito *m*. **~ical** *a* mítico
**mytholog|y** /mɪ'θɒlədʒɪ/ n mitologia *f*. **~ical** /mɪθə'lɒdʒɪkl/ *a* mitológico

# N

**nab** /næb/ *vt* (*pt* **nabbed**) (*sl*) apanhar em flagrante, apanhar com a boca na botija (*colloq*), pilhar
**nag** /næg/ *vt/i* (*pt* **nagged**) implicar (com), criticar constantemente; (*pester*) apoquentar
**nagging** /'nægɪŋ/ *a* implicante; (*pain*) constante, contínuo
**nail** /neɪl/ n prego *m*; (*of finger, toe*) unha *f* □ *vt* pregar. **~-brush** n escova *f* de unhas. **~-file** n lixa *f* de unhas. **~-polish** esmalte *m*, (*P*) verniz *m* para as unhas. **hit the ~ on the head** acertar em cheio. **on the ~** sem demora
**naïve** /naɪ'i:v/ *a* ingênuo, (*P*) ingénuo
**naked** /'neɪkɪd/ *a* nu. **to the ~ eye** a olho nu, à vista desarmada **~ness** *f* nudez *f*
**name** /neɪm/ n nome *m*; (*fig*) reputação *f*, fama *f* □ *vt* (*mention; appoint*) nomear; (*give a name to*) chamar, dar o nome de; (*a date*) marcar. **be ~d after** ter o nome de. **~less** *a* sem nome, anônimo, (*P*) anónimo
**namely** /'neɪmlɪ/ *adv* a saber
**namesake** /'neɪmseɪk/ n homônimo *m* (*P*) homónimo
**nanny** /'nænɪ/ n ama *f*, babá *f*
**nap**[1] /næp/ n soneca *f* □ *vi* (*pt* **napped**) dormitar, tirar um cochilo. **catch ~ping** apanhar desprevenido
**nap**[2] /næp/ n (*of material*) felpa *f*
**nape** /neɪp/ n nuca *f*
**napkin** /'næpkɪn/ n guardanapo *m*; (*for baby*) fralda *f*

**nappy** /'næpɪ/ *n* fralda *f*. **~-rash** *n* assadura *f*

**narcotic** /na:'kɒtɪk/ *a* & *n* narcótico(*m*)

**narrat|e** /nə'reɪt/ *vt* narrar. **~ion** /-ʃn/ *n* narrativa *f*. **~or** *n* narrador *m*

**narrative** /'nærətɪv/ *n* narrativa *f* □ *a* narrativo

**narrow** /'nærəʊ/ *a* (-er, -est) estreito; (*fig*) restrito □ *vt/i* estreitar(-se); (*limit*) limitar(-se). **~ly** *adv* (*only just*) por pouco; (*closely, carefully*) de perto, com cuidado. **~-minded** *a* bitolado, de visão limitada. **~ness** *n* estreiteza *f*

**nasal** /'neɪzl/ *a* nasal

**nast|y** /'na:stɪ/ *a* (-ier, -iest) (*malicious, of weather*) mau; (*unpleasant*) desagradável, intragável; (*rude*) grosseiro. **~ily** *adv* maldosamente; (*unpleasantly*) desagradavelmente. **~iness** *n* (*malice*) maldade *f*; (*rudeness*) grosseria *f*

**nation** /'neɪʃn/ *n* nação *f*. **~-wide** *a* em todo o país, em escala *or* a nível nacional

**national** /'næʃnəl/ *a* nacional □ *n* natural *mf*. **~ anthem** hino *m* nacional. **~ism** *n* nacionalismo *m*. **~ize** *vt* nacionalizar. **~ly** *adv* em escala nacional

**nationality** /næʃə'næləti/ *n* nacionalidade *f*

**native** /'neɪtɪv/ *n* natural *mf*, nativo *m* □ *a* nativo; (*country*) natal; (*inborn*) inato. **be a ~ of** ser natural de. **~ language** língua *f* materna. **~ speaker of Portuguese** pessoa *f* de língua portuguesa, falante *m* nativo de Português

**Nativity** /nə'tɪvətɪ/ *n* **the ~** a Natividade *f*

**natter** /'nætə(r)/ *vi* fazer conversa fiada, falar à toa, tagarelar

**natural** /'nætʃrəl/ *a* natural. **~ history** história *f* natural. **~ist** *n* naturalista *mf*. **~ly** *adv* naturalmente; (*by nature*) por natureza

**naturaliz|e** /'nætʃrəlaɪz/ *vt/i* naturalizar(-se); (*animal, plant*) aclimatar(-se). **~ation** /-'zeɪʃn/ *n* naturalização *f*

**nature** /'neɪtʃə(r)/ *n* natureza *f*; (*kind*) género *m*, (*P*) género *m*; (*of person*) índole *f*

**naughty** /'nɔ:tɪ/ *a* (-ier, -iest) (*child*) levado; (*indecent*) picante

**nause|a** /'nɔ:sɪə/ *n* náusea *f*. **~ate** /'nɔ:sɪeɪt/ *vt* nausear. **~ating**, **~ous** *a* nauseabundo, repugnante

**nautical** /'nɔ:tɪkl/ *a* náutico. **~ mile** milha *f* marítima

**naval** /'neɪvl/ *a* naval; (*officer*) de marinha

**nave** /neɪv/ *n* nave *f*

**navel** /'neɪvl/ *n* umbigo *m*

**navigable** /'nævɪgəbl/ *a* navegável

**navigat|e** /'nævɪgeɪt/ *vt* (*sea etc*) navegar; (*ship*) pilotar □ *vi* navegar. **~ion** /-'geɪʃn/ *n* navegação *f*. **~or** *n* navegador *m*

**navy** /'neɪvɪ/ *n* marinha *f* de guerra. **~ (blue)** azul-marinho *m invar*

**near** /nɪə(r)/ *adv* perto, quaze □ *prep* perto de □ *a* próximo □ *vt* aproximar-se de, chegar-se a. **draw ~** aproximar(-se) **(to** de). **~ by** *adv* perto, próximo. **N~ East** Oriente *m* Próximo. **~ to** perto de. **~ness** *n* proximidade *f*

**nearby** /'nɪəbaɪ/ *a* & *adv* próximo, perto

**nearly** /'nɪəlɪ/ *adv* quase, por pouco. **not ~ as pretty**/*etc* **as** longe de ser tão bonita/*etc* como

**neat** /ni:t/ *a* (-er, -est) (bem) cuidado; (*room*) bem arrumado; (*spirits*) puro, sem gelo. **~ly** *adv* (*with care*) com cuidado; (*cleverly*) habilmente. **~ness** *n* aspecto *m* cuidado

**nebulous** /'nebjʊləs/ *a* nebuloso; (*vague*) vago, confuso

**necessar|y** /'nesəsərɪ/ *a* necessário. **~ily** *adv* necessariamente

**necessitate** /nɪ'sesɪteɪt/ *vt* exigir, obrigar a, tornar necessário

**necessity** /nɪ'sesətɪ/ *n* necessidade *f*; (*thing*) coisa *f* indispensável, artigo *m* de primeira necessidade

**neck** /nek/ *n* pescoço *m*; (*of dress*) gola *f*. **~ and neck** emparelhados

**necklace** /'neklɪs/ *n* colar *m*

**neckline** /'neklaɪn/ *n* decote *m*

**nectarine** /'nektərɪn/ *n* pêssego *m*

**née** /neɪ/ *a* em solteira. **Ann Jones ~ Drewe** Ann Jones cujo nome de solteira era Drewe

**need** /ni:d/ *n* necessidade *f* □ *vt* precisar de, necessitar de. **you ~ not come** não temde *or* não precisa vir. **~less** *a* inútil, desnecessário. **~lessly** *adv* inutilmente, sem necessidade

**needle** /'ni:dl/ *a* agulha *f* □ *vt* (*colloq*: *provoke*) provocar

**needlework** /'ni:dlwɜ:k/ *n* costura *f*; (*embroidery*) bordado *m*

**needy** /'ni:dɪ/ *a* (-ier, -iest) necessitado, carenciado

**negation** /nɪ'geɪʃn/ *n* negação *f*

**negative** /'negətɪv/ *a* negativo □ *n* negativa *f*, negação *f*; (*photo*) negativo *m*. **in the ~** (*answer*) na negativa; (*gram*) na forma negativa. **~ly** *adv* negativamente

**neglect** /nɪ'glekt/ *vt* descuidar; (*opportunity*) desprezar; (*family*) não cuidar de, abandonar; (*duty*) não cumprir □ *n* falta *f* de cuidado(s), descuido *m*. **(state of) ~** abandono *m.* ~ **to** (*omit to*) esquecer-se de. ~**ful** *a* negligente

**negligen|t** /ˈneɡlɪdʒənt/ *a* negligente. ~**ce** *n* negligência *f*, desleixo *m*

**negligible** /ˈneɡlɪdʒəbl/ *a* insignificante, ínfimo

**negotiable** /nɪˈɡəʊʃəbl/ *a* negociável

**negotiat|e** /nɪˈɡəʊʃɪeɪt/ *vt/i* negociar; (*obstacle*) transpor; (*difficulty*) vencer. ~**ion** /-sɪˈeɪʃn/ *n* negociação *f*. ~**or** *n* negociador *m*

**Negro** /ˈniːɡrəʊ/ *a* & *n* (*pl* -**oes**) negro (*m*), preto (*m*)

**neigh** /neɪ/ *n* relincho *m* □ *vi* relinchar

**neighbour** /ˈneɪbə(r)/ *n* vizinho *m*. ~**hood** *n* vizinhança *f*. ~**ing** *a* vizinho. ~**ly** *a* de boa vizinhança

**neither** /ˈnaɪðə(r)/ *a* & *pron* nenhum(a) (de dois *ou* duas), nem um nem outro, nem uma nem outra □ *adv* tampouco, também não □ *conj* nem. ~ **big nor small** nem grande nem pequeno. ~ **am** I nem eu

**neon** /ˈniːɒn/ *n* néon *m* □ *a* (*lamp etc*) de néon

**nephew** /ˈnevjuː/ *n* sobrinho *m*

**nerve** /nɜːv/ *n* nervo *m*; ( *fig: courage*) coragem *f*; (*colloq: impudence*) descaramento *m*, (*P*) lata *f* (*colloq*). **get on sb's nerves** irritar, dar nos nervos de alg. ~**-racking** *a* de arrasar os nervos, enervante

**nervous** /ˈnɜːvəs/ *a* nervoso. **be or feel** ~ (*afraid*) ter receio/um certo medo. ~ **breakdown** esgotamento *m* nervoso. ~**ly** *adv* nervosamente. ~**ness** *n* nervosismo *m*; ( *fear*) receio *m*

**nest** /nest/ *n* ninho *m* □ *vi* aninhar-se, fazer *or* ter ninho. ~**-egg** *n* pé-de-meia *m*

**nestle** /ˈnesl/ *vi* aninhar-se

**net**[1] /net/ *n* rede *f* □ *vt* (*pt* netted) apanhar na rede. ~**ting** *n* rede *f*. **wire** ~**ting** rede *f* de arame

**net**[2] /net/ *a* (*weight etc*) líquido

**Netherlands** /ˈneðələndz/ *npl* **the** ~ os Países Baixos

**nettle** /ˈnetl/ *n* urtiga *f*

**network** /ˈnetwɜːk/ *n* rede *f*, cadeia *f*

**neuro|sis** /njʊəˈrəʊsɪs/ *n* (*pl* -**oses** /-siːz/) neurose *f*. ~**tic** /-ˈrɒtɪk/ *a* & *n* neurótico (*m*)

**neuter** /ˈnjuːtə(r)/ *a* & *n* neutro (*m*) □ *vt* castrar, capar

**neutral** /ˈnjuːtrəl/ *a* neutro. ~ (**gear**) ponto *m* morto. ~**ity** /-ˈtrælətɪ/ *n* neutralidade *f*

**never** /ˈnevə(r)/ *adv* nunca; (*colloq: not*) não. **he** ~ **refuses** ele nunca recusa. **I** ~ **saw him** (*colloq*) nunca o vi. ~ **mind** não faz mal, deixe para lá. ~**-ending** *a* interminável

**nevertheless** /nevəðəˈles/ *adv* & *conj* contudo, no entanto

**new** /njuː/ *a* (-**er**, -**est**) novo. ~**-born** *a* recém-nascido. ~ **moon** lua *f* nova. ~ **year** ano *m* novo. **N~ Year's Day** dia *m* de Ano Novo. **N~ Year's Eve** véspera *f* de Ano Novo. **N~ Zealand** Nova Zelândia *f*. **N~ Zealander** neozelandês *m*. ~**ness** *n* novidade *f*

**newcomer** /ˈnjuːkʌmə(r)/ *n* recém-chegado *m*, (*P*) recém-vindo *m*

**newfangled** /njuːˈfæŋɡld/ *a* (*pej*) moderno

**newly** /ˈnjuːlɪ/ *adv* há pouco, recentemente. ~**-weds** *npl* recém-casados *mpl*

**news** /njuːz/ *n* notícia *f*(*pl*); (*radio*) noticiário *m*, notícias *fpl*; (*TV*) telejornal *m*. ~**-caster**, ~**-reader** *n* locutor *m*. ~**-flash** *n* notícia *f* de última hora

**newsagent** /ˈnjuːzeɪdʒənt/ *n* jornaleiro *m*

**newsletter** /ˈnjuːzletə(r)/ *n* boletim *m* informativo

**newspaper** /ˈnjuːzpeɪpə(r)/ *n* jornal *m*

**newsreel** /ˈnjuːzriːl/ *n* atualidades *fpl*, (*P*) actualidades *fpl*

**newt** /njuːt/ *n* tritão *m*

**next** /nekst/ *a* próximo; (*adjoining*) pegado, ao lado, contíguo; ( *following*) seguinte □ *adv* a seguir □ *n* seguinte *mf*. ~**-door** *a* do lado. ~ **of kin** parente *m* mais próximo. ~ **to** ao lado de. ~ **to nothing** quase nada

**nib** /nɪb/ *n* bico *m*, (*P*) aparo *m*

**nibble** /ˈnɪbl/ *vt* mordiscar, dar dentadinhas em

**nice** /naɪs/ *a* (-**er**, -**est**) agradável, bom; (*kind*) simpático, gentil; (*pretty*) bonito; (*respectable*) bem educado, correto, (*P*) correcto; (*subtle*) fino, subtil. ~**ly** *adv* agradavelmente; (*well*) bem

**nicety** /ˈnaɪsətɪ/ *n* sutileza *f*, (*P*) subtileza *f*

**niche** /nɪtʃ/ *n* nicho *m*; ( *fig*) bom lugar *m*

**nick** /nɪk/ *n* corte *m*, chanfradura *f*; (*sl: prison*) cadeia *f* □ *vt* dar um corte em; (*sl: steal*) roubar, limpar (*colloq*); (*sl: arrest*) apanhar, pôr a mão em (*colloq*). **in good** ~ (*colloq*) em boa forma, em bom estado. **in the** ~ **of time** mesmo a tempo

**nickel** /ˈnɪkl/ *n* níquel *m*; (*Amer*) moeda *f* de cinco cêntimos

**nickname** /ˈnɪknem/ *n* apelido *m*, (*P*) alcunha *f*; (*short form*) diminutivo *m* □ *vt* apelidar de

**nicotine** /ˈnɪkətiːn/ *n* nicotina *f*

**niece** /niːs/ *n* sobrinha *f*

**Nigeria** /naɪˈdʒɪərɪə/ *n* Nigéria *f*. ~**n** *a* & *n* nigeriano (*m*)

**niggardly** /'nɪgədlɪ/ a miserável
**night** /naɪt/ n noite f □ a de noite,
noturno, (P) nocturno. **at ~** à/de
noite. **by ~** de noite. **~-cap** n (drink)
bebida f na hora de deitar. **~-club** n
boate f, (P) boîte f. **~-dress, ~-gown**
ns camisola f de dormir, (P) camisa f
de noite. **~-life** n vida f noturna, (P)
nocturna. **~-school** n escola f noturna, (P) nocturna. **~-time** n noite f. **~-
watchman** n guarda-noturno m, (P)
guarda-nocturno m
**nightfall** /'naɪtfɔːl/ n anoitecer m
**nightingale** /'naɪtɪŋgeɪl/ n rouxinol
m
**nightly** /'naɪtlɪ/ a noturno, (P) nocturno □ adv de noite, à noite, todas as
noites
**nightmare** /'naɪtmeə(r)/ n pesadelo
m
**nil** /nɪl/ n nada m; (sport) zero m □ a
nulo
**nimble** /'nɪmbl/ a (-er, -est) ágil, ligeiro
**nin|e** /naɪn/ a & n nove (m). **~th** a & n
nono (m)
**nineteen** /naɪn'tiːn/ a & n dezenove
(m), (P) dezanove (m). **~th** a & n décimo nono (m)
**ninet|y** /'naɪntɪ/ a & n noventa (m).
**~ieth** a & n nonagésimo (m)
**nip** /nɪp/ vt/i (pt nipped) apertar, beliscar; (colloq: rush) ir correndo, ir
num pulo (colloq) □ n aperto m,
beliscão m; (drink) gole m, trago m.
**a ~ in the air** um frio cortante. **~ in
the bud** cortar pela raiz
**nipple** /'nɪpl/ n mamilo m
**nippy** /'nɪpɪ/ a (-ier, -iest) (colloq:
quick) rápido; (colloq: chilly) cortante
**nitrogen** /'naɪtrədʒən/ n azoto m,
nitrogénio m, (P) nitrogénio m
**nitwit** /'nɪtwɪt/ n (colloq) imbecil m
**no** /nəʊ/ a nenhum □ adv não □ n (pl
noes) não m. **~ entry** entrada f
proibida. **~ money/time/** etc nenhum dinheiro/tempo/etc. **~ man's
land** terra f de ninguém. **~ one =
nobody. ~ smoking** é proibido
fumar. **~ way!** (colloq) de modo nenhum!
**nob|le** /'nəʊbl/ a (-er, -est) nobre.
**~ility** /-'bɪlətɪ/ n nobreza f
**nobleman** /'nəʊblmən/ n (pl -men)
nobre m, fidalgo m
**nobody** /'nəʊbɒdɪ/ pron ninguém □ n
nulidade f. **he knows ~** ele não conhece ninguém. **~ is there** não tem
ninguém lá
**nocturnal** /nɒk'tɜːnl/ a noturno, (P)
nocturno
**nod** /nɒd/ vt/i (pt nodded) **~ (one's
head)** acenar (com) a cabeça; **~ (off)**
cabecear □ n aceno m com a cabeça

(para dizer que sim or para cumprimentar)
**noise** /nɔɪz/ n ruído m, barulho m.
**~less** a silencioso
**nois|y** /'nɔɪzɪ/ a (-ier, -iest) ruidoso,
barulhento. **~ily** adv ruidosamente
**nomad** /'nəʊmæd/ n nômade mf, (P)
nómade mf. **~ic** /'mædɪk/ a nômade,
(P) nómade
**nominal** /'nɒmɪnl/ a nominal; (fee,
sum) simbólico
**nominat|e** /'nɒmɪneɪt/ vt (appoint)
nomear; (put forward) propor. **~ion**
/-'neɪʃn/ n nomeação f
**non-** /nɒn/ pref não, sem, in-, a-, anti-,
des-. **~-skid** a antiderrapante. **~-
stick** a não-aderente
**nonchalant** /'nɒnʃələnt/ a indiferente, desinteressado
**non-commissioned** /nɒnkə'mɪʃnd/ a
**~ officer** sargento m, cabo m
**non-committal** /nɒnkə'mɪtl/ a evasivo
**nondescript** /'nɒndɪskrɪpt/ a insignificante, medíocre, indefinível
**none** /nʌn/ pron (person) nenhum,
ninguém; (thing) nenhum, nada. **~
of us** nenhum de nós. **I have ~** não
tenho nenhum. **~ of that!** nada disso!
□ adv **~ too** não muito. **he is ~ the
happier** nem por isso ele é mais feliz.
**~ the less** contudo, no entanto, apesar disso
**nonentity** /nɒ'nentətɪ/ n nulidade f,
zero m à esquerda, João Ninguém m
**non-existent** /nɒnɪg'zɪstənt/ a inexistente
**nonplussed** /nɒn'plʌst/ a perplexo,
pasmado
**nonsens|e** /'nɒnsns/ n absurdo m,
disparate m. **~ical** /-'sensɪkl/ a absurdo, disparatado
**non-smoker** /nɒn'sməʊkə(r)/ n não-
fumante m, (P) não-fumador m
**non-stop** /nɒn'stɒp/ a ininterrupto,
contínuo; (train) direto, (P) directo;
(flight) sem escala □ adv sem parar
**noodles** /'nuːdlz/ npl talharim m, (P)
macarronete m
**nook** /nʊk/ n (re)canto m
**noon** /nuːn/ n meio-dia m
**noose** /nuːs/ n laço m corrediço
**nor** /nɔː(r)/ conj & adv nem, também
não. **~ do I** nem eu
**norm** /nɔːm/ n norma f
**normal** /'nɔːml/ a & n normal (m).
**above/below ~** acima/abaixo do
normal. **~ity** /nɔː'mælɪtɪ/ n normalidade f. **~ly** adv normalmente
**north** /nɔːθ/ n norte m □ a norte, do
norte; (of country, people etc) setentrional □ adv a, ao/para o norte. **N~
America** América f do Norte. **N~
American** a & n norte-americano

(*m*). ~**-east** *n* nordeste *m*. ~**erly** /'nɔ:ðəlɪ/ *a* do norte. ~**ward** *a* ao norte. ~**ward(s)** *adv* para o norte. ~**-west** *n* noroeste *m*
**northern** /'nɔ:ðən/ *a* do norte
**Norw|ay** /'nɔ:weɪ/ *n* Noruega *f*. ~**egian** /nɔ:'wi:dʒən/ *a* & *n* norueguês (*m*)
**nose** /nəʊz/ *n* nariz *m*; (*of animal*) focinho *m* □ *vi* ~ **about** farejar. **pay through the** ~ pagar um preço exorbitante
**nosebleed** /'nəʊzbli:d/ *n* hemorragia *f* nasal *or* pelo nariz
**nosedive** /'nəʊzdaɪv/ *n* vôo *m* picado
**nostalg|ia** /nɒ'stældʒə/ *n* nostalgia *f*. ~**ic** *a* nostálgico
**nostril** /'nɒstrəl/ *n* narina *f*; (*of horse*) venta *f* (*usually pl*)
**nosy** /'nəʊzɪ/ *a* (**-ier, -iest**) (*colloq*) bisbilhoteiro
**not** /nɒt/ *adv* não. ~ **at all** nada, de modo nenhum; (*reply to thanks*) de nada. **he is** ~ **at all bored** ele não está nem um pouco entediado. ~ **yet** ainda não. **I suppose** ~ creio que não
**notable** /'nəʊtəbl/ *a* notável □ *n* notabilidade *f*
**notably** /'nəʊtəblɪ/ *adv* notavelmente; (*particularly*) especialmente
**notch** /nɒtʃ/ *n* corte *m* em V □ *vt* marcar com cortes. ~ **up** (*score etc*) marcar
**note** /nəʊt/ *n* nota *f*; (*banknote*) nota (de banco) *f*; (*short letter*) bilhete *m* □ *vt* notar
**notebook** /'nəʊtbʊk/ *n* livrinho *m* de notas, (*P*) bloco-notas *m*
**noted** /'nəʊtɪd/ *a* conhecido, famoso
**notepaper** /'nəʊtpeɪpə(r)/ *n* papel *m* de carta
**noteworthy** /'nəʊtwɜ:ðɪ/ *a* notável
**nothing** /'nʌθɪŋ/ *n* nada *m*; (*person*) nulidade *f*, zero *m* □ *adv* nada, de modo algum *or* nenhum, de maneira alguma *or* nenhuma. **he eats** ~ ele não come nada. **big/**etc **nada (de)** grande/*etc*. ~ **else** nada mais. ~ **much** pouca coisa. **for** ~ ( *free*) de graça; (*in vain*) em vão
**notice** /'nəʊtɪs/ *n* anúncio *m*, notícia *f*; (*in street, on wall*) letreiro *m*; (*warning*) aviso *m*; (*attention*) atenção *f*. (**advance**) ~ pré-aviso *m* □ *vt* notar, reparar. **at short** ~ num prazo curto. **a week's** ~ o prazo de uma semana. ~**-board** *n* quadro *m* para afixar anúncios etc. **hand in one's** ~ pedir demissão. **take** ~ reparar (**of** em). **take no** ~ não fazer caso (**of** de)
**noticeabl|e** /'nəʊtɪsəbl/ *a* visível. ~**y** *adv* visivelmente
**notif|y** /'nəʊtɪfaɪ/ *vt* participar, noti-

ficar. ~**ication** /-ɪ'keɪʃn/ *n* participação *f*, notificação *f*
**notion** /'nəʊʃn/ *n* noção *f*
**notor|ious** /nəʊ'tɔ:rɪəs/ *a* notório. ~**iety** /-ə'raɪətɪ/ *n* fama *f*
**notwithstanding** /nɒtwɪθ'stændɪŋ/ *prep* apesar de, não obstante □ *adv* mesmo assim, ainda assim □ *conj* embora, conquanto, apesar de que
**nougat** /'nu:ga:/ *n* nugá *m*, torrone *m*
**nought** /nɔ:t/ *n* zero *m*
**noun** /naʊn/ *n* substantivo *m*, nome *m*
**nourish** /'nʌrɪʃ/ *vt* alimentar, nutrir. ~**ing** *a* alimentício, nutritivo. ~**ment** *n* alimento *m*, sustento *m*
**novel** /'nɒvl/ *n* romance *m* □ *a* novo, original. ~**ist** *n* romancista *mf*. ~**ty** *n* novidade *f*
**November** /nəʊ'vembə(r)/ *n* novembro *m*
**novice** /'nɒvɪs/ *n* (*beginner*) noviço *m*, novato *m*; (*relig*) noviço *m*
**now** /naʊ/ *adv* agora □ *conj* ~ (**that**) agora que. **by** ~ a estas horas, por esta altura. **from** ~ **on** de agora em diante. ~ **and again**, ~ **and then** de vez em quando. **right** ~ já
**nowadays** /'naʊədeɪz/ *adv* hoje em dia, presentemente, atualmente, (*P*) actualmente
**nowhere** /'nəʊweə(r)/ *adv* (*position*) em lugar nenhum, em lado nenhum; (*direction*) a lado nenhum, a parte alguma *or* nenhuma
**nozzle** /'nɒzl/ *n* bico *m*, bocal *m*; (*of hose*) agulheta *f*
**nuance** /'nju:a:ns/ *n* nuance *f*, matiz *m*
**nuclear** /'nju:klɪə(r)/ *a* nuclear
**nucleus** /'nju:klɪəs/ *n* (*pl* **-lei** /-lɪaɪ/) núcleo *m*
**nud|e** /nju:d/ *a* & *n* nu (*m*). **in the** ~**e** nu. ~**ity** *n* nudez *f*
**nudge** /nʌdʒ/ *vt* tocar com o cotovelo, cutucar □ *n* ligeira cotovelada *f*, cutucada *f*
**nudis|t** /'nju:dɪst/ *n* nudista *mf*. ~**m** /-zəm/ *n* nudismo *m*
**nuisance** /'nju:sns/ *n* aborrecimento *m*, chatice *f* (*sl*); (*person*) chato *m* (*sl*)
**null** /nʌl/ *a* nulo. ~ **and void** (*jur*) írrito e nulo. ~**ify** *vt* anular, invalidar
**numb** /nʌm/ *a* entorpecido, dormente □ *vt* entorpecer, adormecer
**number** /'nʌmbə(r)/ *n* número *m*; (*numeral*) algarismo *m* □ *vt* numerar; (*amount to*) ser em número de; (*count*) contar, incluir. ~**-plate** *n* chapa (do carro) *f*
**numeral** /'nju:mərəl/ *n* número *m*, algarismo *m*
**numerate** /'nju:mərət/ *a* que tem conhecimentos básicos de matemática

**numerical** /njuː'merɪkl/ a numérico

**numerous** /'njuːmərəs/ a numeroso

**nun** /nʌn/ n freira f, religiosa f

**nurs|e** /nɜːs/ n enfermeira f, enfermeiro m; (*nanny*) ama(-seca) f, babá f □ vt cuidar de, tratar de; (*hopes etc*) alimentar, acalentar. **~ing** n enfermagem f. **~ing home** clínica f de repouso

**nursery** /'nɜːsərɪ/ n quarto m de crianças; (*for plants*) viveiro m. **(day)** ~ creche f. ~ **rhyme** poema m or canção f infantil. ~ **school** jardim m de infância

**nurture** /'nɜːtʃə(r)/ vt educar

**nut** /nʌt/ n (*bot*) noz f; (*techn*) porca f de parafuso

**nutcrackers** /'nʌtkrækəz/ npl quebra-nozes m invar

**nutmeg** /'nʌtmeg/ n noz-moscada f

**nutrient** /'njuːtrɪənt/ n substância f nutritiva, nutriente m

**nutrit|ion** /njuː'trɪʃn/ n nutrição f. **~ious** a nutritivo

**nutshell** /'nʌtʃel/ n casca f de noz. in a ~ em poucas palavras

**nuzzle** /'nʌzl/ vt esfregar com o focinho

**nylon** /'naɪlɒn/ n nylon m. ~**s** meias fpl de nylon

# O

**oaf** /əʊf/ n (pl **oafs**) imbecil m, idiota m

**oak** /əʊk/ n carvalho m

**OAP** abbr see **old-age pensioner**

**oar** /ɔː(r)/ n remo m

**oasis** /əʊ'eɪsɪs/ n (pl **oases** /-siːz/) oásis m

**oath** /əʊθ/ n juramento m; (*swearword*) praga f

**oatmeal** /'əʊtmiːl/ n farinha f de aveia; (*porridge*) papa f de aveia

**oats** /əʊts/ npl aveia f

**obedien|t** /ə'biːdɪənt/ a obediente. **~ce** n obediência f. **~tly** adv obedientemente

**obes|e** /əʊ'biːs/ a obeso. **~ity** n obesidade f

**obey** /ə'beɪ/ vt/i obedecer (a)

**obituary** /ə'bɪtʃʊərɪ/ n necrológio m, (*P*) necrologia f

**object**[1] /'ɒbdʒɪkt/ n objeto m, (*P*) objecto m; (*aim*) objetivo m, (*P*) objectivo m; (*gram*) complemento m

**object**[2] /əb'dʒekt/ vt/i objetar, (*P*) objectar (que). ~ **to** opor-se a, discordar de. **~ion** /-ʃn/ n objeção f, (*P*) objecção f

**objectionable** /əb'dʒekʃnəbl/ a censurável; (*unpleasant*) desagradável

**objectiv|e** /əb'dʒektɪv/ a objetivo, (*P*) objectivo. **~ity** /-'tɪvətɪ/ n objetividade f, (*P*) objectividade f

**obligation** /ɒblɪ'geɪʃn/ n obrigação f. **be under an** ~ **to sb** dever favores a alg

**obligatory** /ə'blɪgətrɪ/ a obrigatório

**oblig|e** /ə'blaɪdʒ/ vt obrigar; (*do a favour*) fazer um favor a, obsequiar. **~ed** a obrigado (**to** a). **~ed to sb** em dívida (para) com alg. **~ing** a prestável, amável. **~ingly** adv amavelmente

**oblique** /ə'bliːk/ a oblíquo

**obliterat|e** /ə'blɪtəreɪt/ vt obliterar. **~ion** /-'reɪʃn/ n obliteração f

**oblivion** /ə'blɪvɪən/ n esquecimento m

**oblivious** /ə'blɪvɪəs/ a esquecido, sem consciência (**of/to** de)

**oblong** /'ɒblɒŋ/ a oblongo □ n retângulo m, (*P*) rectângulo m

**obnoxious** /əb'nɒkʃəs/ a ofensivo, detestável

**oboe** /'əʊbəʊ/ n oboé m

**obscen|e** /əb'siːn/ a obsceno. **~ity** /-'enətɪ/ n obscenidade f

**obscur|e** /əb'skjʊə(r)/ a obscuro □ vt obscurecer; (*conceal*) encobrir. **~ity** n obscuridade f

**obsequious** /əb'siːkwɪəs/ a demasiado obsequioso, subserviente

**observan|t** /əb'zɜːvənt/ a observador. **~ce** n observância f, cumprimento m

**observatory** /əb'zɜːvətrɪ/ n observatório m

**observ|e** /əb'zɜːv/ vt observar. **~ation** /ɒbzə'veɪʃn/ n observação f. **keep under ~ation** vigiar. **~er** n observador m

**obsess** /əb'ses/ vt obcecar. **~ion** /-ʃn/ n obsessão f. **~ive** a obsessivo

**obsolete** /'ɒbsəliːt/ a obsoleto, antiguado

**obstacle** /'ɒbstəkl/ n obstáculo m

**obstetric|s** /əb'stetrɪks/ n obstetrícia f. **~ian** /ɒbstɪ'trɪʃn/ n obstetra mf

**obstina|te** /'ɒbstɪnət/ a obstinado. **~cy** n obstinação f

**obstruct** /əb'strʌkt/ vt obstruir, bloquear; (*hinder*) estorvar, obstruir. **~ion** /-ʃn/ n obstrução f; (*thing*) obstáculo m

**obtain** /əb'teɪn/ vt obter □ vi prevalecer, estar em vigor. **~able** a que se pode obter

**obtrusive** /əb'truːsɪv/ a importuno; (*thing*) demasiado em evidência, que dá muito na vista (*colloq*)

**obvious** /'ɒbvɪəs/ a óbvio, evidente. **~ly** adv obviamente

**occasion** /ə'keɪʒn/ n ocasião f; (*event*) acontecimento m □ vt ocasionar. **on** ~ de vez em quando, ocasionalmente

**occasional** /ə'keɪʒənl/ a ocasional.

**~ly** *adv* de vez em quando, ocasionalmente

**occult** /ɒˈkʌlt/ *a* oculto

**occupation** /ɒkjʊˈpeɪʃn/ *n* ocupação *f*. **~al** *a* profissional; (*therapy*) ocupacional

**occupy** /ˈɒkjʊpaɪ/ *vt* ocupar. **~ant**, **~ier** *ns* ocupante *mf*

**occur** /əˈkɜː(r)/ *vi* (*pt* **occurred**) ocorrer, acontecer, dar-se; (*arise*) apresentar-se, aparecer. **~ to sb** ocorrer a alg

**occurrence** /əˈkʌrəns/ *n* acontecimento *m*, ocorrência *f*

**ocean** /ˈəʊʃn/ *n* oceano *m*

**o'clock** /əˈklɒk/ *adv* **it is one ~** é uma hora. **it is six ~** são seis horas

**octagon** /ˈɒktəɡən/ *n* octógono *m*. **~al** /-ˈtæɡənl/ *a* octogonal

**octave** /ˈɒktɪv/ *n* oitava *f*

**October** /ɒkˈtəʊbə(r)/ *n* outubro *m*

**octopus** /ˈɒktəpəs/ *n* (*pl* **-puses**) polvo *m*

**odd** /ɒd/ *a* (**-er, -est**) estranho, singular; (*number*) ímpar; (*left over*) de sobra; (*not of set*) desemparelhado; (*occasional*) ocasional. **~ jobs** (*paid*) biscates *mpl*; (*in garden etc*) trabalhos *mpl* diversos. **twenty ~** vinte e tantos. **~ity** *n* singularidade *f*; (*thing*) curiosidade *f*. **~ly** *adv* de modo estranho

**oddment** /ˈɒdmənt/ *n* resto *m*, artigo *m* avulso

**odds** /ɒdz/ *npl* probabilidades *fpl*; (*in betting*) ganhos *mpl* líquidos. **at ~** em desacordo; (*quarrelling*) de mal, brigado. **it makes no ~** não faz diferença. **~ and ends** artigos *mpl* avulsos, coisas *fpl* pequenas

**odious** /ˈəʊdɪəs/ *a* odioso

**odour** /ˈəʊdə(r)/ *n* odor *m*. **~less** *a* inodoro

**of** /əv/; *emphatic* /ɒv/ *prep* de. **a friend ~ mine** um amigo meu. **the fifth ~ June** (no dia) cinco de junho. **take six ~ them** leve seis deles

**off** /ɒf/ *adv* embora, fora; (*switched off*) apagado, desligado; (*taken off*) tirado, desligado; (*cancelled*) cancelado; (*food*) estragado □ *prep* (fora) de; (*distant from*) a alguma distância de. **be ~** (*depart*) ir-se embora, partir. **be well ~** ser abastado. **be better/worse ~** estar em melhor/pior situação. **a day ~** um dia de folga. **20% ~** redução de 20%. **on the ~ chance that** no caso de. **~ colour** indisposto, adoentado. **~-licence** *n* loja *f* de bebidas alcoólicas. **~-load** *vt* descarregar. **~-putting** *a* desconcertante, (*P*) frequentemente. **~-stage** *adv* fora de cena. **~-white** *a* branco-sujo

**offal** /ˈɒfl/ *n* miudezas *fpl*, fressura *f*

**offence** /əˈfens/ *n* (*feeling*) ofensa *f*; (*crime*) delito *m*, transgressão *f*. **give ~ to** ofender. **take ~** ofender-se (**at com**)

**offend** /əˈfend/ *vt* ofender. **be ~ed** ofender-se (**at com**). **~er** *n* delinquente *mf*, (*P*) delinquente *mf*

**offensive** /əˈfensɪv/ *a* ofensivo; (*disgusting*) repugnante □ *n* ofensiva *f*

**offer** /ˈɒfə(r)/ *vt* (*pt* **offered**) oferecer □ *n* oferta *f*. **on ~** em promoção. **~ing** *n* oferenda *f*

**offhand** /ɒfˈhænd/ *a* espontâneo; (*curt*) seco □ *adv* de improviso, sem pensar

**office** /ˈɒfɪs/ *n* escritório *m*; (*post*) cargo *m*; (*branch*) filial *f*. **~ hours** horas *fpl* de expediente. **in ~** no poder. **take ~** assumir o cargo

**officer** /ˈɒfɪsə(r)/ *n* oficial *m*; (*policeman*) agente *m*

**official** /əˈfɪʃl/ *a* oficial □ *n* funcionário *m*. **~ly** *adv* oficialmente

**officiate** /əˈfɪʃɪeɪt/ *vi* (*relig*) oficiar. **~ as** presidir, exercer as funções de

**officious** /əˈfɪʃəs/ *a* intrometido

**offing** /ˈɒfɪŋ/ *n* **in the ~** (*fig*) em perspectiva

**offset** /ˈɒfset/ *vt* (*pt* **-set**, *pres p* **-setting**) compensar, contrabalançar

**offshoot** /ˈɒfʃuːt/ *n* rebento *m*; (*fig*) efeito *m* secundário

**offshore** /ˈɒfʃɔː(r)/ *a* ao largo da costa

**offside** /ɒfˈsaɪd/ *a* & *adv* offside, em impedimento, (*P*) fora de jogo

**offspring** /ˈɒfsprɪŋ/ *n* (*pl invar*) descendência *f*, prole *f*

**often** /ˈɒfn/ *adv* muitas vezes, frequentemente, (*P*) frequentemente. **every so ~** de vez em quando. **how ~?** quantas vezes?

**oh** /əʊ/ *int* oh, ah

**oil** /ɔɪl/ *n* óleo *m*; (*petroleum*) petróleo *m* □ *vt* lubrificar. **~-painting** *n* pintura *f* a óleo. **~ rig** plataforma *f* de poço de petróleo. **~ well** poço *m* de petróleo. **~y** *a* oleoso; (*food*) gorduroso

**oilfield** /ˈɔɪlfiːld/ *n* campo *m* petrolífero

**oilskins** /ˈɔɪlskɪnz/ *npl* roupa *f* de oleado

**ointment** /ˈɔɪntmənt/ *n* pomada *f*

**OK** /əʊˈkeɪ/ *a* & *adv* (*colloq*) (está) bem, (está) certo, (está) legal

**old** /əʊld/ *a* (**-er, -est**) velho; (*person*) velho, idoso; (*former*) antigo. **how ~ is he?** que idade tem ele? **he is eight years ~** ele tem oito anos (de idade). **of ~** (d)antes, antigamente. **~ age** velhice *f*. **~-age pensioner** reformado *m*, aposentado *m*, pessoa *f* de terceira idade. **~ boy** antigo aluno *m*. **~-fashioned** *a* fora de moda. **~ girl** antiga aluna *f*. **~ maid** solteirona *f*.

~ **man** homem *m* idoso, velho *m*. ~
-**time** *a* antigo. ~ **woman** mulher *f*
idosa, velha *f*
**olive** /'ɒlɪv/ *n* azeitona *f* □ *a* de
azeitona. ~ **oil** azeite *m*
**Olympic** /ə'lɪmpɪk/ *a* olímpico. ~**s**
*npl* Olimpíadas *fpl*. ~ **Games** Jogos
*mpl* Olímpicos
**omelette** /'ɒmlɪt/ *n* omelete *f*
**omen** /'əʊmən/ *n* agouro *m*, presságio
*m*
**ominous** /'ɒmɪnəs/ *a* agourento; ( *fig:
threatening*) ameaçador
**omi|t** /ə'mɪt/ *vt* ( *pt* **omitted**) omitir.
~**ssion** /-ʃn/ *n* omissão *f*
**on** /ɒn/ *prep* sobre, em cima de, de, em
□ *adv* para diante, para a frente;
( *switched on*) aceso, ligado; ( *tap*) aberto; ( *machine*) em funcionamento; ( *put
on*) posto; ( *happening*) em curso. ~
**arrival** na chegada, ao chegar. ~
**foot** *etc* a pé *etc.* ~ **doing** ao fazer. ~
**time** na hora, dentro do horário. ~
**Tuesday** na terça-feira. ~ **Tuesdays**
às terças-feiras. **walk**/*etc* ~ continuar a andar/*etc.* **be** ~ **at** ( *film, TV*)
estar levando *or* passando. ~ **and off**
de vez em quando. ~ **and** ~ sem
parar
**once** /wʌns/ *adv* uma vez; ( *formerly*)
noutro(s) tempo(s) □ *conj* uma vez
que, desde que. **all at** ~ de repente;
( *simultaneously*) todos ao mesmo
tempo. **just this** ~ só esta vez. ~
**(and) for all** duma vez para sempre.
~ **upon a time** era uma vez. ~-**over**
*n* ( *collog*) vista *f* de olhos.
**oncoming** /'ɒnkʌmɪŋ/ *a* que se apro-
xima, próximo. **the** ~ **traffic** o trânsito que vem do sentido oposto, (P) no
sentido contrário
**one** /wʌn/ *a* um(a); ( *sole*) único □ *n*
um(a) *mf* □ *pron* um(a) *mf*; ( *impersonal*) se. ~ **by** ~ um a um. **a big/
red**/*etc* ~ um grande/vermelho/*etc.*
**this/that** ~ este/esse. ~ **another**
um ao outro, uns aos outros. ~-
**sided** *a* parcial. ~-**way** *a* ( *street*)
mão única; ( *ticket*) simples
**oneself** /wʌn'self/ *pron* si, si mesmo/
próprio; ( *reflexive*) se. **by** ~ sozinho
**onion** /'ʌnɪən/ *n* cebola *f*
**onlooker** /'ɒnlʊkə(r)/ *n* espectador *m*,
circunstante *mf*
**only** /'əʊnlɪ/ *a* único □ *adv* apenas,
só, somente □ *conj* só que. **an** ~
**child** um filho único. **he** ~ **has six**
ele só tem seis. **not** ~ ... **but also** não
só ... mas também. ~ **too** muito, mais
que
**onset** /'ɒnset/ *n* começo *m*; ( *attack*)
ataque *m*
**onslaught** /'ɒnslɔːt/ *n* ataque *m* violento, assalto *m*

**onward(s)** /'ɒnwəd(z)/ *adv* para a
frente/diante
**ooze** /uːz/ *vt/i* escorrer, verter
**opal** /'əʊpl/ *n* opala *f*
**opaque** /əʊ'peɪk/ *a* opaco, tosco
**open** /'əʊpən/ *a* aberto; ( *view*) aberto,
amplo; ( *free to all*) aberto ao público;
( *attempt*) franco □ *vt/i* abrir(-se); ( *of
shop, play*) abrir. **in the** ~ **air** ao ar
livre. **keep** ~ **house** receber muito,
abrir a porta para todos. ~ **on to** dar
para. ~ **out** *or* **up** abrir(-se). ~-**heart**
*a* ( *of surgery*) de coração aberto. ~-
**minded** *a* imparcial. ~-**plan** *a* sem
divisórias. ~ **secret** segredo *m* de
polichinelo. ~ **sea** mar *m* alto.
~**ness** *n* abertura *f*; ( *frankness*) franqueza *f*
**opener** /'əʊpənə(r)/ *n* ( *tins*) abridor *m*
de latas; ( *bottles*) saca-rolhas *m invar*
**opening** /'əʊpənɪŋ/ *n* abertura *f*; ( *beginning*) começo *m*; ( *opportunity*)
oportunidade *f*; ( *job*) vaga *f*
**openly** /'əʊpənlɪ/ *adv* abertamente
**opera** /'ɒprə/ *n* ópera *f*. ~-**glasses** *npl*
binóculo (de teatro) *m*, (P) binóculos
*mpl*. ~-**tic** /ɒp'rætɪk/ *a* de ópera
**operat|e** /'ɒpəreɪt/ *vt/i* operar; ( *techn*)
(pôr a) funcionar. ~**e on** ( *med*)
operar. ~**ing-theatre** *n* ( *med*) anfiteatro *m*, sala *f* de operações. ~**ion**
/-'reɪʃn/ *n* operação *f*. **in** ~**ion** em
vigor; ( *techn*) em funcionamento.
~**ional** /'reɪʃənl/ *a* operacional. ~**or**
*n* operador *m*; ( *telephonist*) telefonista
*mf*
**operative** /'ɒpərətɪv/ *a* ( *surgical*)
operatório; ( *law etc*) em vigor
**opinion** /ə'pɪnɪən/ *n* opinião *f*, parecer *m*. **in my** ~ a meu ver. ~ **poll** *n*
sondagem (de opinião) *f*. ~**ated**
/-ertɪd/ *a* dogmático
**opium** /'əʊpɪəm/ *n* ópio *m*
**Oporto** /ə'pɔːtəʊ/ *n* Porto *m*
**opponent** /ə'pəʊnənt/ *n* adversário *m*,
antagonista *mf*, oponente *mf*
**opportune** /'ɒpətjuːn/ *a* oportuno
**opportunity** /ɒpə'tjuːnətɪ/ *n* oportunidade *f*
**oppos|e** /ə'pəʊz/ *vt* opor-se a. ~**ed to**
oposto a. ~**ing** *a* oposto
**opposite** /'ɒpəzɪt/ *a* & *n* oposto (*m*),
contrário (*m*) □ *adv* em frente □ *prep*
~ **(to)** em frente de
**opposition** /ɒpə'zɪʃn/ *n* oposição *f*
**oppress** /ə'pres/ *vt* oprimir. ~**ion**
/-ʃn/ *n* opressão *f*. ~**ive** *a* opressivo.
~**or** *n* opressor *m*
**opt** /ɒpt/ *vi* ~ **for** optar por. ~ **out**
recusar-se a participar (of de). ~ **to**
**do** escolher fazer
**optical** /'ɒptɪkl/ *a* óptico. ~ **illusion**
ilusão *f* óptica
**optician** /ɒp'tɪʃn/ *n* oculista *mf*

**optimis|t** /'ɒptɪmɪst/ n otimista mf,
(P) optimista mf. **~m** /-zəm/ n otimis-
mo m, (P) optimismo m. **~tic**
/-'mɪstɪk/ a otimista, (P) optimista.
**~tically** /-'mɪstɪklɪ/ adv com otimis-
mo, (P) optimismo

**optimum** /'ɒptɪməm/ a & n (pl -ima)
ótimo (m), (P) óptimo (m)

**option** /'ɒpʃn/ n escolha f, opção f.
**have no ~ (but)** não ter outro remédio (senão)

**optional** /'ɒpʃənl/ a opcional, faculta-
tivo

**opulen|t** /'ɒpjʊlənt/ a opulento. **~ce**
n opulência f

**or** /ɔ:(r)/ conj ou; (with negative) nem.
**~ else** senão

**oracle** /'ɒrəkl/ n oráculo m

**oral** /'ɔ:rəl/ a oral

**orange** /'ɒrɪndʒ/ n laranja f; (colour)
laranja m, cor f de laranja □ a de
laranja; (colour) alaranjado, cor de
laranja

**orator** /'ɒrətə(r)/ n orador m. **~y** n
oratória f

**orbit** /'ɔ:bɪt/ n órbita f □ vt (pt or-
bited) gravitar em torno de

**orchard** /'ɔ:tʃəd/ n pomar m

**orchestra** /'ɔ:kɪstrə/ n orquestra f. **~l**
/'kestrəl/ a orquestral

**orchestrate** /'ɔ:kɪstreɪt/ vt orquestrar

**orchid** /'ɔ:kɪd/ n orquídea f

**ordain** /ɔ:'deɪn/ vt decretar; (relig) ordenar

**ordeal** /ɔ:'di:l/ n prova f, provação f

**order** /'ɔ:də(r)/ n ordem f, (comm) encomenda f, pedido m □ vt ordenar;
(goods etc) encomendar. **in ~ that**
para que. **in ~ to** para

**orderly** /'ɔ:dəlɪ/ a ordenado, em ordem; (not unruly) ordeiro □ n (mil)
ordenança f; (med) servente m de hospital

**ordinary** /'ɔ:dɪnrɪ/ a normal, ordinário, vulgar. **out of the ~** fora do comum

**ordination** /ɔ:dɪ'neɪʃn/ n (relig)
ordenação f

**ore** /ɔ:(r)/ n minério m

**organ** /'ɔ:gən/ n órgão m. **~ist** n or-
ganista mf

**organic** /ɔ:'gænɪk/ a orgânico

**organism** /'ɔ:gənɪzəm/ n organismo
m

**organiz|e** /'ɔ:gənaɪz/ vt organizar.
**~ation** /-'zeɪʃn/ n organização f.
**~er** n organizador m

**orgasm** /'ɔ:gæzəm/ n orgasmo m

**orgy** /'ɔ:dʒɪ/ n orgia f

**Orient** /'ɔ:rɪənt/ n the **~** o Oriente m.
**~al** /-'entl/ a & n oriental (mf)

**orientat|e** /'ɔ:rɪənteɪt/ vt orientar.
**~ion** /-'teɪʃn/ n orientação f

**orifice** /'ɒrɪfɪs/ n orifício m

**origin** /'ɒrɪdʒɪn/ n origem f

**original** /ə'rɪdʒənl/ a original; (not
copied) original. **~ity** /-'nælətɪ/ n ori-
ginalidade f. **~ly** adv originalmente;
(in the beginning) originariamente

**originat|e** /ə'rɪdʒəneɪt/ vt/i originar
(-se). **~e from** provir de. **~or** n ini-
ciador m, criador m, autor m

**ornament** /'ɔ:nəmənt/ n ornamento
m; (object) peça f decorativa. **~al**
/-'mentl/ a ornamental. **~ation**
/-en'teɪʃn/ n ornamentação f

**ornate** /ɔ:'neɪt/ a florido, floreado

**ornitholog|y** /ɔ:nɪ'θɒlədʒɪ/ n ornito-
logia f. **~ist** n ornitólogo m

**orphan** /'ɔ:fn/ n órfã(o) f(m) □ vt deixar órfão. **~age** n orfanato m

**orthodox** /'ɔ:θədɒks/ a ortodoxo

**orthopaedic** /ɔ:θə'pi:dɪk/ a ortopédi-
co

**oscillate** /'ɒsɪleɪt/ vi oscilar, vacilar

**ostensibl|e** /ɒs'tensəbl/ a aparente,
pretenso. **~y** adv aparentemente,
pretensamente

**ostentati|on** /ɒsten'teɪʃn/ n osten-
tação f. **~ous** /-'teɪʃəs/ a ostentoso,
ostensivo

**osteopath** /'ɒstɪəpæθ/ n osteopata mf

**ostracize** /'ɒstrəsaɪz/ vt pôr de lado,
marginalizar

**ostrich** /'ɒstrɪtʃ/ n avestruz mf

**other** /'ʌðə(r)/ a, n & pron outro (m) □
adv. **~ than** diferente de, senão.
(some) **~s** outros. the **~ day** no
outro dia. the **~ one** o outro

**otherwise** /'ʌðəwaɪz/ adv de outro
modo □ conj senão, caso contrário

**otter** /'ɒtə(r)/ n lontra f

**ouch** /aʊtʃ/ int ai!, ui!

**ought** /ɔ:t/ v aux (pt ought) dever.
**you ~ to stay** você devia ficar. **he
~ to succeed** ele deve vencer. **I ~
to have done it** eu devia tê-lo feito

**ounce** /aʊns/ n onça f (= 28,35g)

**our** /'aʊə(r)/ a nosso(s), nossa(s)

**ours** /'aʊəz/ poss pron o(s) nosso(s),
a(s) nossa(s)

**ourselves** /aʊə'selvz/ pron nós mes-
mos/próprios; (reflexive) nos. **by ~**
sozinhos

**oust** /aʊst/ vt expulsar, obrigar a sair

**out** /aʊt/ adv fora; (of light, fire) apagado; (in blossom) aberto, desabrocha-
do; (of tide) baixo. **be ~** não estar em
casa, estar fora (de casa); (wrong) enganar-se. **be ~ to** estar resolvido a.
**run/etc ~** sair correndo/etc. **~-and-
~** a completo, rematado. **~ of** fora
de; (without) sem. **~ of pity/etc** por
pena/etc. **made ~ of** feito de or em.
**take ~ of** tirar de. **5 ~ of 6** 5 (de)
entre 6. **~ of date** fora de moda; (not
valid) fora do prazo. **~ of doors** ao ar
livre. **~ of one's mind** doido. **~ of**

order quebrado. ~ of place deslocado. ~ of the way afastado. ~-patient n doente mf de consulta externa

outboard /'aʊtbɔ:d/ a ~ motor motor m de popa

outbreak /'aʊtbreɪk/ n (of flu etc) surto m, epidemia f; (of war) deflagração f

outburst /'aʊtbɜ:st/ n explosão f

outcast /'aʊtkɑ:st/ n pária m

outcome /'aʊtkʌm/ n resultado m

outcry /'aʊtkraɪ/ n clamor m; (protest) protesto m

outdated /aʊt'deɪtɪd/ a fora da moda, ultrapassado

outdo /aʊt'du:/ vt (pt -did, pp -done) ultrapassar, superar

outdoor /'aʊtdɔ:(r)/ a ao ar livre. ~s /-'dɔ:z/ adv fora de casa, ao ar livre

outer /'aʊtə(r)/ a exterior. ~ space espaço (cósmico) m

outfit /'aʊtfɪt/ n equipamento m; (clothes) roupa f

outgoing /'aʊtgəʊɪŋ/ a que vai sair; (of minister etc) demissionário; (fig) sociável. ~s npl despesas fpl

outgrow /aʊt'grəʊ/ vt (pt -grew, pp -grown) crescer mais do que; (clothes) já não caber em

outhouse /'aʊthaʊs/ n anexo m, dependência f

outing /'aʊtɪŋ/ n saída f, passeio m

outlandish /aʊt'lændɪʃ/ a exótico, estranho

outlaw /'aʊtlɔ:/ n fora-da-lei mf, bandido m □ vt banir, proscrever

outlay /'aʊtleɪ/ n despesa(s) f(pl)

outlet /'aʊtlet/ n saída f, escoadouro m; (for goods) mercado m, saída f; (for feelings) escape m, vazão m; (electr) tomada f

outline /'aʊtlaɪn/ n contorno m; (summary) plano m geral, esquema m, esboço m □ vt contornar; (summarize) descrever em linhas gerais

outlive /aʊt'lɪv/ vt sobreviver a

outlook /'aʊtlʊk/ n (view) vista f; (mental attitude) visão f; (future prospects) perspectiva(s) f(pl)

outlying /'aʊtlaɪɪŋ/ a afastado, remoto

outnumber /aʊt'nʌmbə(r)/ vt ultrapassar em número

outpost /'aʊtpəʊst/ n posto m avançado

output /'aʊtpʊt/ n rendimento m; (of computer) saída f, output m

outrage /'aʊtreɪdʒ/ n atrocidade f, crime m; (scandal) escândalo m □ vt ultrajar

outrageous /aʊt'reɪdʒəs/ a (shocking) escandaloso; (very cruel) atroz

outright /'aʊtraɪt/ adv completamente; (at once) imediatamente;

(frankly) abertamente □ a completo; (refusal) claro

outset /'aʊtset/ n início m, começo m, princípio m

outside¹ /aʊt'saɪd/ n exterior m □ adv (lá) (por) fora □ prep (para) fora de, além de; (in front of) diante de. at the ~ no máximo

outside² /'aʊtsaɪd/ a exterior

outsider /aʊt'saɪdə(r)/ n estranho m; (in race) cavalo m com poucas probabilidades, azarão m

outsize /'aʊtsaɪz/ a tamanho extra invar

outskirts /'aʊtskɜ:ts/ npl arredores mpl, subúrbios mpl

outspoken /aʊt'spəʊkn/ a franco

outstanding /aʊt'stændɪŋ/ a saliente, proeminente; (debt) por saldar; (very good) notável, destacado

outstretched /aʊt'stretʃt/ a (arm) estendido, esticado

outstrip /aʊt'strɪp/ vt (pt -stripped) ultrapassar, passar à frente de

outward /'aʊtwəd/ a para o exterior; (sign etc) exterior; (journey) de ida. ~ly adv exteriormente. ~s adv para o exterior

outwit /aʊt'wɪt/ vt (pt -witted) ser mais esperto que, enganar

oval /'əʊvl/ n & a oval (m)

ovary /'əʊvərɪ/ n ovário m

ovation /əʊ'veɪʃn/ n ovação f

oven /'ʌvn/ n forno m

over /'əʊvə(r)/ prep sobre, acima de, por cima de; (across) de para o/do outro lado de; (during) durante, em; (more than) mais de □ adv por cima; (too) demais, demasiadamente; (ended) acabado. the film is ~ o filme já acabou. jump/etc ~ saltar/ etc por cima. he has some ~ ele tem uns de sobra. all ~ the country em/ por todo o país. all ~ the table por toda a mesa. ~ and above (besides, in addition to) (para) além de. ~ and ~ repetidas vezes. ~ there ali, lá acolá

over- /'əʊvə(r)/ pref sobre-, super-; (excessively) demais, demasiado

overall¹ /'əʊvərɔ:l/ n bata f. ~s macacão m, (P) fato-macaco m

overall² /'əʊvərɔ:l/ a global; (length etc) total □ adv globalmente

overawe /əʊvər'ɔ:/ vt intimidar

overbalance /əʊvə'bæləns/ vt/i (fazer) perder o equilíbrio

overbearing /əʊvə'beərɪŋ/ a autoritário, despótico; (arrogant) arrogante

overboard /'əʊvəbɔ:d/ adv (pela) borda fora

overcast /əʊvə'kɑ:st/ a encoberto, nublado

overcharge /əʊvə'tʃɑ:dʒ/ vt ~ sb (for) cobrar demais a alg (por)

**overcoat** /'əʊvəkəʊt/ n casacão m; ( for men) sobretudo m

**overcome** /əʊvə'kʌm/ vt ( pt **-came**, pp **-come**) superar, vencer. ~ **by** sucumbindo a, dominado or vencido por

**overcrowded** /əʊvə'kraʊdɪd/ a apinhado, superlotado; (country) superpovoado

**overdo** /əʊvə'du:/ vt ( pt **-did**, pp **-done**) exagerar, levar longe demais. ~ne (culin) cozinhado demais

**overdose** /'əʊvədəʊs/ n dose f excessiva

**overdraft** /'əʊvədra:ft/ n saldo m negativo

**overdraw** /əʊvə'drɔ:/ vt ( pt **-drew**, pp **-drawn**) sacar a descoberto

**overdue** /əʊvə'dju:/ a em atraso, atrasado; (belated) tardio

**overestimate** /əʊvər'estɪmeɪt/ vt sobreestimar, atribuir valor excessivo a

**overexpose** /əʊvərɪk'spəʊz/ vt expor demais

**overflow**[1] /əʊvə'fləʊ/ vt/i extravasar, transbordar (**with** de)

**overflow**[2] /'əʊvəfləʊ/ n (outlet) descarga f; (excess) excesso m

**overgrown** /əʊvə'grəʊn/ a que cresceu demais; (garden etc) invadido pela vegetação

**overhang** /əʊvə'hæŋ/ vt ( pt **-hung**) estar sobranceiro a, pairar sobre □ vi projetar-se para fora □ n saliência f

**overhaul**[1] /əʊvə'hɔ:l/ vt fazer uma revisão em

**overhaul**[2] /'əʊvəhɔ:l/ n revisão f

**overhead**[1] /əʊvə'hed/ adv em or por cima, ao or no alto

**overhead**[2] /'əʊvəhed/ a aéreo. ~s npl despesas fpl gerais

**overhear** /əʊvə'hɪə(r)/ vt ( pt **-heard**) (eavesdrop) ouvir sem conhecimento do falante; (hear by chance) ouvir por acaso

**overjoyed** /əʊvə'dʒɔɪd/ a radiante, felicíssimo

**overlap** /əʊvə'læp/ vt/i ( pt **-lapped**) sobrepor(-se) parcialmente; ( fig) coincidir

**overleaf** /əʊvə'li:f/ adv no verso

**overload** /əʊvə'ləʊd/ vt sobrecarregar

**overlook** /əʊvə'lʊk/ vt deixar passar; (of window) dar para; (of building) dominar

**overnight** /əʊvə'naɪt/ adv durante a noite; ( fig) dum dia para o outro □ a (train) da noite; (stay, journey, etc) noite, noturno; ( fig) súbito

**overpass** /əʊvə'pa:s/ n passagem f superior

**overpay** /əʊvə'peɪ/ vt ( pt **-paid**) pagar em excesso

**overpower** /əʊvə'paʊə(r)/ vt dominar, subjugar; ( fig) esmagar. ~ing a esmagador; (heat) sufocante, insuportável

**overpriced** /əʊvə'praɪst/ a muito caro

**overrate** /əʊvə'reɪt/ vt sobreestimar, exagerar o valor de

**override** /əʊvə'raɪd/ vt ( pt **-rode**, pp **-ridden**) prevalecer sobre, passar por cima de. ~ing a primordial, preponderante; (importance) maior

**overripe** /'əʊvəraɪp/ a demasiado maduro

**overrule** /əʊvə'ru:l/ vt anular, rejeitar; (claim) indeferir

**overrun** /əʊvə'rʌn/ vt ( pt **-ran**, pp **-run**, pres p **-running**) invadir; (a limit) exceder, ultrapassar

**overseas** /əʊvə'si:z/ a ultramarino; (abroad) estrangeiro □ adv no ultramar, no estrangeiro

**oversee** /əʊvə'si:/ vt ( pt **-saw**, pp **-seen**) supervisionar. ~r /'əʊvəsɪə(r)/ n capataz m

**overshadow** /əʊvə'ʃædəʊ/ vt ( fig) eclipsar, ofuscar

**oversight** /'əʊvəsaɪt/ n lapso m

**oversleep** /əʊvə'sli:p/ vi ( pt **-slept**) acordar tarde, dormir demais

**overt** /'əʊvɜ:t/ a manifesto, claro, patente

**overtake** /əʊvə'teɪk/ vt/i ( pt **-took**, pp **-taken**) ultrapassar

**overthrow** /əʊvə'θrəʊ/ vt ( pt **-threw**, pp **-thrown**) derrubar □ n /'əʊvəθrəʊ/ (pol) derrubada f

**overtime** /'əʊvətaɪm/ n horas fpl extras

**overtones** /'əʊvətəʊnz/ npl ( fig) tom m, implicação f

**overture** /'əʊvətjʊə(r)/ n (mus) abertura f; ( fig) proposta f, abordagem f

**overturn** /əʊvə'tɜ:n/ vt/i virar(-se); (car, plane) capotar, virar-se

**overweight** /əʊvə'weɪt/ a be ~ ter excesso de peso

**overwhelm** /əʊvə'welm/ vt oprimir; (defeat) esmagar; (amaze) assoberbar. ~ing a esmagador; (urge) irresistível

**overwork** /əʊvə'wɜ:k/ vt/i sobrecarregar(-se) com trabalho □ n excesso m de trabalho

**overwrought** /əʊvə'rɔ:t/ a muito agitado, superexcitado

**owe** /əʊ/ vt dever. ~ing a devido. ~ing to devido a

**owl** /aʊl/ n coruja f

**own**[1] /əʊn/ a próprio. a house/etc of one's ~ uma casa/etc própria. get one's ~ back (colloq) ir à forra, (P) desforrar-se. hold one's ~ aguentarse, (P) aguentar-se. on one's ~ sozinho

**own**[2] /əʊn/ vt possuir. ~ up (to) (colloq) confessar. ~er n proprietário m, dono m. ~ership n posse f, propriedade f

**ox** /ɒks/ n (pl oxen) boi m

**oxygen** /ˈɒksɪdʒən/ n oxigénio m, (P) oxigénio m

**oyster** /ˈɔɪstə(r)/ n ostra f

**ozone** /ˈəʊzəʊn/ n ozónio m, (P) ozono m. ~ layer camada f de ozónio, (P) ozono m

# P

**pace** /peɪs/ n passo m; (fig) ritmo m □ vt percorrer passo a passo □ vi ~ up and down andar de um lado para o outro. keep ~ with acompanhar, manter-se a par de

**pacemaker** /ˈpeɪsmeɪkə(r)/ n (med) marcapasso m, (P) pacemaker m

**Pacific** /pəˈsɪfɪk/ a pacífico □ n ~ (Ocean) (Oceano) Pacífico m

**pacifist** /ˈpæsɪfɪst/ n pacifista mf

**pacify** /ˈpæsɪfaɪ/ vt pacificar, apaziguar

**pack** /pæk/ n pacote m, (mil) mochila f; (of hounds) matilha f; (of lies) porção f; (of cards) baralho m □ vt empacotar; (suitcase) fazer; (box, room) encher; (press down) atulhar, encher até não caber mais □ vi fazer as malas. ~ into (cram) apinhar em, comprimir em. send ~ing pôr a andar, mandar passear. ~ed a apinhado. ~ed lunch merenda f

**package** /ˈpækɪdʒ/ n pacote m, embrulho m □ vt embalar. ~ deal pacote m de propostas. ~ holiday pacote m turístico, (P) viagem f organizada

**packet** /ˈpækɪt/ n pacote m; (of cigarettes) maço m

**pact** /pækt/ n pacto m

**pad** /pæd/ n (in clothing) chumaço m; (for writing) bloco m de papel/de notas; (for ink) almofada (de carimbo) f. (launching) ~ rampa f de lançamento □ vt (pt padded) enchumaçar, acolchoar; (fig: essay etc) encher linguiça. ~ding n chumaço m; (fig) linguiça f

**paddle**[1] /ˈpædl/ n remo m de canoa. ~-steamer n vapor m movido a rodas

**paddle**[2] /ˈpædl/ vi chapinhar, molhar os pés. ~ing pool piscina f de plástico para crianças

**paddock** /ˈpædək/ n cercado m; (at racecourse) paddock m

**padlock** /ˈpædlɒk/ n cadeado m □ vt fechar com cadeado

**paediatrician** /piːdɪəˈtrɪʃn/ n pediatra mf

**pagan** /ˈpeɪɡən/ a & n pagão (m), pagã (f)

**page**[1] /peɪdʒ/ n (of book etc) página f

**page**[2] /peɪdʒ/ vt mandar chamar

**pageant** /ˈpædʒənt/ n espetáculo m, (P) espectáculo m (histórico); (procession) cortejo m. ~ry n pompa f

**pagoda** /pəˈɡəʊdə/ n pagode m

**paid** /peɪd/ see pay □ a put ~ to (colloq: end) pôr fim a

**pail** /peɪl/ n balde m

**pain** /peɪn/ n dor f. ~s esforços mpl □ vt magoar. be in ~ sofrer, ter dores. ~-killer n analgésico m. take ~s to esforçar-se por. ~ful a doloroso; (grievous, laborious) penoso. ~less a sem dor, indolor

**painstaking** /ˈpeɪnzteɪkɪŋ/ a cuidadoso, esmerado, meticuloso

**paint** /peɪnt/ n tinta f. ~s (in box) tintas fpl □ vt/i pintar. ~er n pintor m. ~ing n pintura f

**paintbrush** /ˈpeɪntbrʌʃ/ n pincel m

**pair** /peə(r)/ n par m. a ~ of scissors uma tesoura. a ~ of trousers um par de calças. in ~s aos pares □ vi ~ off formar pares

**Pakistan** /pɑːkɪˈstɑːn/ n Paquistão m. ~i a & n paquistanês (m)

**pal** /pæl/ n (colloq) colega mf, amigo m

**palace** /ˈpælɪs/ n palácio m

**palat|e** /ˈpælət/ n palato m. ~able a saboroso, gostoso; (fig) agradável

**palatial** /pəˈleɪʃl/ a suntuoso, (P) sumptuoso

**pale** /peɪl/ a (-er, -est) pálido; (colour) claro □ vi empalidecer. ~ness n palidez f

**Palestin|e** /ˈpælɪstaɪn/ n Palestina f. ~ian /-ˈstɪnɪən/ a & n palestino (m)

**palette** /ˈpælɪt/ n paleta f. ~-knife n espátula f

**pall** /pɔːl/ vi tornar-se enfadonho, perder o interesse (on para)

**pallid** /ˈpælɪd/ a pálido

**palm** /pɑːm/ n (of hand) palma f; (tree) palmeira f □ vt ~ off impingir (on a). P~ Sunday Domingo m de Ramos

**palpable** /ˈpælpəbl/ a palpável

**palpitat|e** /ˈpælpɪteɪt/ vi palpitar. ~ion /-ˈteɪʃn/ n palpitação f

**paltry** /ˈpɔːltrɪ/ a (-ier, -iest) irrisório

**pamper** /ˈpæmpə(r)/ vt mimar, paparicar

**pamphlet** /ˈpæmflɪt/ n panfleto m, folheto m

**pan** /pæn/ n panela f; (for frying) frigideira f □ vt (pt panned) (colloq) criticar severamente

**panacea** /pænəˈsɪə/ n panacéia f

**panache** /pæˈnæʃ/ n brio m, estilo m, panache m

**pancake** /ˈpænkeɪk/ n crepe m, panqueca f

**pancreas** /'pæŋkrɪəs/ n pâncreas m

**panda** /'pændə/ n panda m

**pandemonium** /ˌpændɪ'məʊnɪəm/ n pandemônio m, (P) pandemónio m, caos m

**pander** /'pændə(r)/ vi ~ to prestar-se a servir, ir ao encontro de, fazer concessões a

**pane** /peɪn/ n vidraça f

**panel** /'pænl/ n painel m; (jury) júri m; (speakers) convidados mpl. (instrument) ~ painel m de instrumentos, (P) de bordo. ~led a apainelado. ~ling n apainelamento m. ~list n convidado m

**pang** /pæŋ/ n pontada f, dor f aguda e súbita. ~s (of hunger) ataques mpl de fome. ~s of conscience remorsos mpl

**panic** /'pænɪk/ n pânico m □ vt/i (pt panicked) desorientar(-se), (fazer) entrar em pânico. ~-stricken a tomado de pânico

**panoram|a** /ˌpænə'rɑːmə/ n panorama m. ~ic /-'ræmɪk/ a panorâmico

**pansy** /'pænzɪ/ n amor-perfeito m

**pant** /pænt/ vi ofegar, arquejar

**panther** /'pænθə(r)/ n pantera f

**panties** /'pæntɪz/ npl (colloq) calcinhas fpl

**pantomime** /'pæntəmaɪm/ n pantomima f

**pantry** /'pæntrɪ/ n despensa f

**pants** /pænts/ npl (colloq: underwear) cuecas fpl; (colloq: trousers) calças fpl

**papal** /'peɪpl/ a papal

**paper** /'peɪpə(r)/ n papel m; (newspaper) jornal m; (exam) prova f escrita; (essay) comunicação f. ~s npl (for identification) documentos mpl □ vt forrar com papel. on ~ por escrito. ~-clip n clipe m

**paperback** /'peɪpəbæk/ a & n ~ (book) livro m de capa mole

**paperweight** /'peɪpəweɪt/ n pesa-papéis m invar, (P) pisa-papéis m invar

**paperwork** /'peɪpəwɜːk/ n trabalho m de secretária; (pej) papelada f

**paprika** /'pæprɪkə/ n páprica f, pimentão m doce

**par** /pɑː(r)/ n be below ~ estar abaixo do padrão desejado. on a ~ with em igualdade com

**parable** /'pærəbl/ n parábola f

**parachut|e** /'pærəʃuːt/ n pára-quedas m invar □ vi descer de pára-quedas. ~ist n pára-quedista mf

**parade** /pə'reɪd/ n (mil) parada f militar; (procession) procissão f □ vi desfilar □ vt alardear, exibir

**paradise** /'pærədaɪs/ n paraíso m

**paradox** /'pærədɒks/ n paradoxo m. ~ical /-'dɒksɪkl/ a paradoxal

**paraffin** /'pærəfɪn/ n querosene m, (P) petróleo m

**paragon** /'pærəgən/ n modelo m de perfeição

**paragraph** /'pærəgrɑːf/ n parágrafo m

**parallel** /'pærəlel/ a & n paralelo (m) □ vt (pt paralleled) comparar(-se) a

**paralyse** /'pærəlaɪz/ vt paralisar

**paraly|sis** /pə'ræləsɪs/ n paralisia f. ~tic /-'lɪtɪk/ a & n paralítico (m)

**parameter** /pə'ræmɪtə(r)/ n parâmetro m

**paramount** /'pærəmaʊnt/ a supremo, primordial

**parapet** /'pærəpɪt/ n parapeito m

**paraphernalia** /ˌpærəfə'neɪlɪə/ n equipamento m, tralha f (colloq)

**paraphrase** /'pærəfreɪz/ n paráfrase f □ vt parafrasear

**paraplegic** /ˌpærə'pliːdʒɪk/ n paraplégico m

**parasite** /'pærəsaɪt/ n parasita mf

**parasol** /'pærəsɒl/ n sombrinha f; (on table) pára-sol m, guarda-sol m

**parcel** /'pɑːsl/ n embrulho m; (for post) encomenda f

**parch** /pɑːtʃ/ vt ressecar. be ~ed estar com muita sede

**parchment** /'pɑːtʃmənt/ n pergaminho m

**pardon** /'pɑːdn/ n perdão m; (jur) perdão m, indulto m □ vt (pt pardoned) perdoar. I beg your ~ perdão, desculpe. (I beg your) ~? como?

**pare** /peə(r)/ vt aparar, cortar; (peel) descascar

**parent** /'peərənt/ n pai m, mãe f. ~s npl pais mpl. ~al /pə'rentl/ a dos pais, paterno, materno

**parenthesis** /pə'renθəsɪs/ n (pl -theses) /-siːz/ parêntese m, parêntesis m

**Paris** /'pærɪs/ n Paris m

**parish** /'pærɪʃ/ n paróquia f; (municipal) freguesia f. ~ioner /pə'rɪʃənə(r)/ n paroquiano m

**parity** /'pærətɪ/ n paridade f

**park** /pɑːk/ n parque m □ vt estacionar. ~ing n estacionamento m. no ~ing estacionamento proibido. ~ing-meter n parquímetro m

**parliament** /'pɑːləmənt/ n parlamento m, assembléia f. ~ary /-'mentrɪ/ a parlamentar

**parochial** /pə'rəʊkɪəl/ a paroquial; (fig) provinciano, tacanho

**parody** /'pærədɪ/ n paródia f □ vt parodiar

**parole** /pə'rəʊl/ n on ~ em liberdade condicional □ vt pôr em liberdade condicional

**parquet** /'pɑːkeɪ/ n parquê m, parquete m

**parrot** /'pærət/ *n* papagaio *m*
**parry** /'pærɪ/ *vt* (a)parar □ *n* parada *f*
**parsimonious** /ˌpaːsɪˈməʊnɪəs/ *a* parco; *(mean)* avarento
**parsley** /'paːslɪ/ *n* salsa *f*
**parsnip** /'paːsnɪp/ *n* cherovia *f*, pastinaga *f*
**parson** /'paːsn/ *n* pároco *m*, pastor *m*
**part** /paːt/ *n* parte *f*; *(of serial)* episódio *m*; *(of machine)* peça *f*; *(theatre)* papel *m*; *(side in dispute)* partido *m* □ *a* parcial □ *adv* em parte □ *vt/i* separar (-se) *(from* de). **in ~** em parte. **on the ~ of** da parte de. **~-exchange** *n* troca *f* parcial. **~ of speech** categoria *f* gramatical. **~-time** *a* & *adv* a tempo parcial, part-time. **take ~ in** tomar parte em. **these ~s** estas partes
**partial** /'paːʃl/ *a* (incomplete, biased) parcial. **be ~ to** gostar de. **~ity** /-ɪˈrælətɪ/ *n* parcialidade *f*; *(liking)* predileção *f*, (P) predilecção *f* *(for* por). **~ly** *adv* parcialmente
**participate** /paːˈtɪsɪpeɪt/ *vi* participar *(in* em). **~ant** *n* /-ənt/ participante *mf*. **~ation** /-ˈpeɪʃn/ *n* participação *f*
**participle** /'paːtɪsɪpl/ *n* particípio *m*
**particle** /'paːtɪkl/ *n* partícula *f*; *(of dust)* grão *m*; *(fig)* mínimo *m*
**particular** /pəˈtɪkjʊlə(r)/ *a* especial, particular; *(fussy)* exigente; *(careful)* escrupuloso. **~s** *npl* pormenores *mpl*. **in ~** *adv* em especial, particularmente. **~ly** *adv* particularmente
**parting** /'paːtɪŋ/ *n* separação *f*; *(in hair)* risca *f* □ *a* de despedida
**partisan** /paːtɪˈzæn/ *n* partidário *m*; *(mil)* guerrilheiro *m*
**partition** /paːˈtɪʃn/ *n* (of room) tabique *m*, divisória *f*; *(pol: division)* partilha *f*, divisão *f* □ *vt* dividir, repartir. **~ off** dividir por meio de tabique
**partly** /'paːtlɪ/ *adv* em parte
**partner** /'paːtnə(r)/ *n* sócio *m*; *(cards, sport)* parceiro *m*; *(dancing)* par *m*. **~ship** *n* associação *f*; *(comm)* sociedade *f*
**partridge** /'paːtrɪdʒ/ *n* perdiz *f*
**party** /'paːtɪ/ *n* festa *f*, reunião *f*; *(group)* grupo *m*; *(pol)* partido *m*; *(jur)* parte *f*. **~ line** *(telephone)* linha *f* coletiva, (P) colectiva
**pass** /paːs/ *vt/i* (pt **passed**) passar; *(overtake)* ultrapassar; *(exam)* passar; *(approve)* passar; *(law)* aprovar. **~ (by)** passar por □ *n* (permit, sport) passe *m*; *(geog)* desfiladeiro *m*, garganta *f*; *(in exam)* aprovação *f*. **make a ~ at** *(colloq)* atirar-se para *(colloq)*. **~ away** falecer. **~ out** *or* **round** distribuir. **~ out** *(colloq: faint)* perder os sentidos, desmaiar. **~ over** *(disre-*

gard, overlook) passar por cima de. **~ up** *(colloq: forgo)* deixar perder
**passable** /'paːsəbl/ *a* passável; *(road)* transitável
**passage** /'pæsɪdʒ/ *n* passagem *f*; *(voyage)* travessia *f*; *(corridor)* corredor *m*, passagem *f*
**passenger** /'pæsɪndʒə(r)/ *n* passageiro *m*
**passer-by** /paːsəˈbaɪ/ *n* (pl **passers-by**) transeunte *mf*
**passion** /'pæʃn/ *n* paixão *f*. **~ate** *a* apaixonado, exaltado
**passive** /'pæsɪv/ *a* passivo. **~ness** *n* passividade *f*
**Passover** /'paːsəʊvə(r)/ *n* Páscoa *f* dos judeus
**passport** /'paːspɔːt/ *n* passaporte *m*
**password** /'paːswɜːd/ *n* senha *f*
**past** /paːst/ *a* passado; *(former)* antigo □ *n* passado □ *prep* para além de; *(in time)* mais de; *(in front of)* diante de □ *adv* em frente. **be ~ it** já não ser capaz. **it's five ~ eleven** são onze e cinco. **these ~ months** estes últimos meses
**pasta** /'pæstə/ *n* prato *m* de massa(s)
**paste** /peɪst/ *n* cola *f*; *(culin)* massa(s) *f(pl)*; *(dough)* massa *f*, *(jewellery)* strass *m* □ *vt* colar
**pastel** /'pæstl/ *n* pastel *m* □ *a* pastel *invar*
**pasteurize** /'pæstʃəraɪz/ *vt* pasteurizar
**pastille** /'pæstɪl/ *n* pastilha *f*
**pastime** /'paːstaɪm/ *n* passatempo *m*
**pastoral** /'paːstərəl/ *a* & *n* pastoral (*f*)
**pastry** /'peɪstrɪ/ *n* massa *f* (de pastelaria); *(tart)* pastel *m*
**pasture** /'paːstʃə(r)/ *n* pastagem *f*
**pasty**[1] /'pæstɪ/ *n* empadinha *f*
**pasty**[2] /'peɪstɪ/ *a* pastoso
**pat** /pæt/ *vt* (pt **patted**) *(hit gently)* dar pancadinhas em; *(caress)* fazer festinhas a □ *n* pancadinha *f*; *(caress)* festinha *f* □ *adv* a propósito; *(readily)* prontamente □ *a* preparado, pronto
**patch** /pætʃ/ *n* remendo *m*; *(over eye)* tapa-ôlho *m*; *(spot)* mancha *f*; *(small area)* pedaço *m*; *(of vegetables)* canteiro *m*, (P) leira *f* □ *vt* **~ up** remendar. **~ up a quarrel** fazer as pazes. **bad ~** mau bocado *m*. **not be a ~ on** não chegar aos pés de. **~-work** *n* obra *f* de retalhos. **~y** *a* desigual
**pâté** /'pæteɪ/ *n* patê *m*
**patent** /'peɪtnt/ *a* & *n* patente (*f*) □ *vt* patentear. **~ leather** verniz *m*, polimento *m*. **~ly** *adv* claramente
**paternal** /pəˈtɜːnl/ *a* paternal; *(relative)* paterno
**paternity** /pəˈtɜːnətɪ/ *n* paternidade *f*

**path** /pa:θ/ n (pl -s /pa:ðz/) caminho m, trilha f; (in park) aléia f; (of rocket) trajetória f, (P) trajectória f

**pathetic** /pə'θetɪk/ a patético; (colloq: contemptible) desgraçado (colloq)

**patholog|y** /pə'θɒlədʒɪ/ n patologia f. ~**ist** n patologista mf

**pathos** /'peɪθɒs/ n patos m, patético m

**patience** /'peɪʃns/ n paciência f

**patient** /'peɪʃnt/ a paciente □ n doente mf, paciente mf. ~**ly** adv pacientemente

**patio** /'pætɪəʊ/ n (pl -os) pátio m

**patriot** /'pætrɪət/ n patriota mf. ~**ic** /-'ɒtɪk/ a patriótico. ~**ism** /-ɪzəm/ n patriotismo m

**patrol** /pə'trəʊl/ n patrulha f □ vt/i patrulhar. ~ **car** carro m de patrulha

**patron** /'peɪtrən/ n (of the arts etc) patrocinador m, protetor m, (P) protector m; (of charity) benfeitor m; (customer) freguês m, cliente mf. ~ **saint** padroeiro m, patrono m

**patron|age** /'pætrənɪdʒ/ n freguesia f, clientela f; (support) patrocínio m. ~**ize** vt ser cliente de; (support) patrocinar; (condescend) tratar com ares de superioridade

**patter**[1] /'pætə(r)/ n (of rain) tamborilar m, rufo m. ~ **of steps** som m leve de passos miúdos, corridinha f leve

**patter**[2] /'pætə(r)/ n (of class, profession) gíria f, jargão m; (chatter) conversa f fiada

**pattern** /'pætn/ n padrão m; (for sewing) molde m; (example) modelo m

**paunch** /pɔ:ntʃ/ n pança f

**pause** /pɔ:z/ n pausa f □ vi pausar, fazer (uma) pausa

**pav|e** /peɪv/ vt pavimentar. ~**e the way** preparar o caminho (**for** para). ~**ing-stone** n paralelepípedo m, laje f

**pavement** /'peɪvmənt/ n passeio m

**pavilion** /pə'vɪlɪən/ n pavilhão m

**paw** /pɔ:/ n pata f □ vt dar patadas em; (horse) escarvar; (colloq: person) pôr as patas em cima de

**pawn**[1] /pɔ:n/ n (chess) peão m; (fig) joguete m

**pawn**[2] /pɔ:n/ vt empenhar. ~-**shop** casa f de penhores, prego m (colloq)

**pawnbroker** /'pɔ:nbrəʊkə(r)/ n penhorista mf, dono m de casa de penhores, agiota mf

**pay** /peɪ/ vt/i (pt paid) pagar; (interest) render; (visit, compliment) fazer □ n pagamento m; (wages) vencimento m, ordenado m, salário m. **in the** ~ **of** em pagamento de. ~ **attention** prestar atenção. ~ **back** restituir. ~ **for** pagar. ~ **homage** prestar homenagem. ~ **in** depositar. ~-**slip** n contracheque m, (P) folha f de pagamento

**payable** /'peɪəbl/ a pagável

**payment** /'peɪmənt/ n pagamento m; (fig: reward) recompensa f

**payroll** /'peɪrəʊl/ n folha f de pagamentos. **be on the** ~ fazer parte da folha de pagamento de uma firma

**pea** /pi:/ n ervilha f

**peace** /pi:s/ n paz f. **disturb the** ~ perturbar a ordem pública. ~**able** a pacífico

**peaceful** /'pi:sfl/ a pacífico; (calm) calmo, sereno

**peacemaker** /'pi:smeɪkə(r)/ n mediador m, pacificador m

**peach** /pi:tʃ/ n pêssego m

**peacock** /'pi:kɒk/ n pavão m

**peak** /pi:k/ n pico m, cume m, cimo m; (of cap) pala f; (maximum) máximo m. ~ **hours** horas fpl de ponta; (electr) horas fpl de carga máxima. ~**ed cap** boné m de pala

**peaky** /'pi:kɪ/ a com ar doentio

**peal** /pi:l/ n (of bells) repique m; (of laughter) gargalhada f, risada f

**peanut** /'pi:nʌt/ n amendoim m. ~**s** (sl: small sum) uma bagatela f

**pear** /peə(r)/ n pera f

**pearl** /pɜ:l/ n pérola f. ~**y** a nacarado

**peasant** /'peznt/ n camponês m, aldeão m

**peat** /pi:t/ n turfa f

**pebble** /'pebl/ n seixo m, calhau m

**peck** /pek/ vt/i bicar; (attack) dar bicadas (em) □ n bicada f; (colloq: kiss) beijo m seco. ~**ing order** hierarquia f, ordem f de importância

**peckish** /'pekɪʃ/ a **be** ~ (colloq) ter vontade de comer

**peculiar** /pɪ'kju:lɪə(r)/ a bizarro, singular; (special) peculiar (**to** a), característico (**to** de). ~**ity** /-'ærətɪ/ n singularidade f; (feature) peculiaridade f

**pedal** /'pedl/ n pedal m □ vi (pt pedalled) pedalar

**pedantic** /pɪ'dæntɪk/ a pedante

**peddle** /'pedl/ vt vender de porta em porta; (drugs) fazer tráfico de

**pedestal** /'pedɪstl/ n pedestal m

**pedestrian** /pɪ'destrɪən/ n pedestre mf, (P) peão m □ a pedestre; (fig) prosaico. ~ **crossing** faixa f para pedestres, (P) passadeira f

**pedigree** /'pedɪgri:/ n estirpe f, linhagem f; (of animal) raça f □ a de raça

**pedlar** /'pedlə(r)/ n vendedor m ambulante

**peek** /pi:k/ vi espreitar □ n espreitadela f

**peel** /pi:l/ n casca f □ vt descascar □ vi (skin) pelar; (paint) escamar-se, descascar; (wallpaper) descolar-se. ~**ings** npl cascas fpl

**peep** /pi:p/ vi espreitar □ n espreitadela *f*. **~-hole** *n* vigia *f*; (*in door*) olho *m* mágico

**peer**[1] /pɪə(r)/ *vi* ~ **at/into** (*searchingly*) perscrutar; (*with difficulty*) esforçar-se por ver

**peer**[2] /pɪə(r)/ *n* (*equal, noble*) par *m*. **~age** *n* pariato *m*

**peeved** /piːvd/ *a* (*sl*) irritado, chateado (*sl*)

**peevish** /ˈpiːvɪʃ/ *a* irritável

**peg** /peg/ *n* cavilha *f*; (*for washing*) pregador *m* de roupa, (*P*) mola *f*; (*for coats etc*) cabide *m*; (*for tent*) □ *vt* (*pt* **pegged**) prender com estacas. **off the ~** — prêt-à-porter

**pejorative** /prɪˈdʒɒrətɪv/ *a* pejorativo

**pelican** /ˈpelɪkən/ *n* pelicano *m*. **~ crossing** passagem *f* com sinais manobrados pelos pedestres

**pellet** /ˈpelɪt/ *n* bolinha *f*; (*for gun*) grão *m* de chumbo

**pelt**[1] /pelt/ *n* pele *f*

**pelt**[2] /pelt/ *vt* bombardear (**with** com) □ *vi* chover a cântaros; (*run fast*) correr em disparada

**pelvis** /ˈpelvɪs/ *n* (*anat*) pélvis *m*, bacia *f*

**pen**[1] /pen/ *n* (*enclosure*) cercado *m*. **play-~** *n* cercado *m*, (*P*) pargue *m* □ *vt* (*pt* **penned**) encurralar

**pen**[2] /pen/ *n* caneta *f* □ *vt* (*pt* **penned**) escrever. **~-friend** *n* correspondente *mf*. **~-name** *n* pseudônimo *m*, (*P*) pseudónimo *m*

**penal** /ˈpiːnl/ *a* penal. **~ize** *vt* impôr uma penalidadea; (*sport*) penalizar

**penalty** /ˈpenltɪ/ *n* pena *f*; (*fine*) multa *f*; (*sport*) penalidade *f*. **~ kick** pênalti *m*, (*P*) grande penalidade *f*

**penance** /ˈpenəns/ *n* penitência *f*

**pence** /pens/ *see* **penny**

**pencil** /ˈpensl/ *n* lápis *m* □ *vt* (*pt* **pencilled**) escrever *or* desenhar a lápis. **~-sharpener** *n* apontador *m*, (*P*) apara-lápis *m invar*

**pendant** /ˈpendənt/ *n* berloque *m*

**pending** /ˈpendɪŋ/ *a* pendente □ *prep* (*during*) durante; (*until*) até

**pendulum** /ˈpendjʊləm/ *n* pêndulo *m*

**penetrat|e** /ˈpenɪtreɪt/ *vt/i* penetrar (em). **~ing** *a* penetrante. **~ion** /-ˈtreɪʃn/ *n* penetração *f*

**penguin** /ˈpeŋgwɪn/ *n* pingüim *m*, (*P*) pinguim *m*

**penicillin** /penɪˈsɪlɪn/ *n* penicilina *f*

**peninsula** /pəˈnɪnsjʊlə/ *n* península *f*

**penis** /ˈpiːnɪs/ *n* pênis *m*, (*P*) pénis *m*

**peniten|t** /ˈpenɪtənt/ *a* & *n* penitente (*mf*). **~ce** *n* /-əns/ contrição *f*, penitência *f*

**penitentiary** /penɪˈtenʃərɪ/ *n* (*Amer*) penitenciária *f*, cadeia *f*

**penknife** /ˈpennaɪf/ *n* (*pl* **-knives**) canivete *m*

**penniless** /ˈpenɪlɪs/ *a* sem vintém, sem um tostão

**penny** /ˈpenɪ/ *n* (*pl* **pennies** *or* **pence**) pêni *m*, (*P*) péni *m*; (*fig*) centavo *m*, vintém *m*

**pension** /ˈpenʃn/ *n* pensão *f*; (*in retirement*) aposentadoria *f*, (*P*) reforma *f* □ *vt* **~ off** reformar, aposentar. **~er** *n* (**old-age**) **~er** reformado *m*

**pensive** /ˈpensɪv/ *a* pensativo

**Pentecost** /ˈpentɪkɒst/ *n* Pentecostes *m*

**penthouse** /ˈpenthaʊs/ *n* cobertura *f*, (*P*) apartamento de luxo (no último andar)

**pent-up** /ˈpentʌp/ *a* reprimido

**penultimate** /penˈʌltɪmət/ *a* penúltimo

**people** /ˈpiːpl/ *npl* pessoas *fpl* □ *n* gente *f*, povo *m* □ *vt* povoar. **the Portuguese ~** os portugueses *mpl*. **~ say** dizem, diz-se

**pep** /pep/ *n* vigor *m* □ *vt* **~ up** animar. **~ talk** discurso *m* de encorajamento

**pepper** /ˈpepə(r)/ *n* pimenta *f*; (*vegetable*) pimentão *m*, (*P*) pimento *m* □ *vt* apimentar. **~y** *a* apimentado, picante

**peppermint** /ˈpepəmɪnt/ *n* hortelã-pimenta *f*; (*sweet*) bala *f*, (*P*) pastilha *f* de hortelã-pimenta

**per** /pɜː(r)/ *prep* por. **~ annum** por ano. **~ cent** por cento. **~ kilo/etc** o quilo/*etc*

**perceive** /pəˈsiːv/ *vt* perceber; (*notice*) aperceber-se de

**percentage** /pəˈsentɪdʒ/ *n* percentagem *f*

**perceptible** /pəˈseptəbl/ *a* perceptível

**percept|ion** /pəˈsepʃn/ *n* percepção *f*. **~ive** /-tɪv/ *a* perceptivo, penetrante, perspicaz

**perch**[1] /pɜːtʃ/ *n* poleiro *m* □ *vi* empoleirar-se, pousar

**perch**[2] /pɜːtʃ/ *n* (*fish*) perca *f*

**percolat|e** /ˈpɜːkəleɪt/ *vt/i* filtrar(-se), passar. **~or** *n* máquina *f* de café com filtro, cafeteira *f*

**percussion** /pəˈkʌʃn/ *n* percussão *f*

**peremptory** /pəˈremptərɪ/ *a* peremptório, decisivo

**perennial** /pəˈrenɪəl/ *a* perene; (*plant*) perene

**perfect**[1] /ˈpɜːfɪkt/ *a* perfeito. **~ly** *adv* perfeitamente

**perfect**[2] /pəˈfekt/ *vt* aperfeiçoar. **~ion** /-ʃn/ *n* perfeição *f*. **~ionist** *n* perfeccionista *mf*

**perforat|e** /ˈpɜːfəreɪt/ *vt* perfurar. **~ion** /ˈreɪʃn/ *n* perfuração *f*; (*line of holes*) pontilhado *m*, picotado *m*

**perform** /pəˈfɔːm/ *vt* (*a task; mus*) executar; (*a function; theat*) desempenhar □ *vi* representar; (*function*) funcionar. **~ance** *n* (*of task; mus*) execução f; (of function; theat) desempenho m; (of car) performance f, comportamento m, rendimento m; (colloq: fuss) drama m, cena f. **~er** n artista mf

**perfume** /'pɜːfjuːm/ n perfume m

**perfunctory** /pə'fʌŋktərɪ/ a superficial, negligente

**perhaps** /pə'hæps/ adv talvez

**peril** /'perəl/ n perigo m. **~ous** a perigoso

**perimeter** /pə'rɪmɪtə(r)/ n perímetro m

**period** /'pɪərɪəd/ n período m, época f; (era) época f; (lesson) hora f de aula, período m letivo, (P) lectivo; (med) período m; (full stop) ponto (final) m □ a (of novel) de costumes; (of furniture) de estilo. **~ic** /-'ɒdɪk/ a periódico. **~ical** /-'ɒdɪkl/ n periódico m. **~ically** /-'ɒdɪklɪ/ adv periodicamente

**peripher|y** /pə'rɪfərɪ/ n periferia f. **~al** a periférico; (fig) marginal, à margem

**perish** /'perɪʃ/ vi morrer, perecer; (rot) estragar-se, deteriorar-se. **~able** a deteriorável

**perjur|e** /'pɜːdʒə(r)/ vpr **~e o.s.** jurar falso, perjurar. **~y** n perjúrio m

**perk**[1] /pɜːk/ vt/i **~ up** (colloq) arrebitar(-se). **~y** a (colloq) vivo, animado

**perk**[2] /pɜːk/ n (colloq) regalia f, extra m

**perm** /pɜːm/ n permanente f □ vt **have one's hair ~ed** fazer uma permanente

**permanen|t** /'pɜːmənənt/ a permanente. **~ce** n permanência f. **~tly** adv permanentemente, a título permanente

**permeable** /'pɜːmɪəbl/ a permeável

**permeate** /'pɜːmɪeɪt/ vt/i permear, penetrar

**permissible** /pə'mɪsəbl/ a permissível, admissível

**permission** /pə'mɪʃn/ n permissão f, licença f

**permissive** /pə'mɪsɪv/ a permissivo. **~ society** sociedade f permissiva. **~ness** n permissividade f

**permit**[1] /pə'mɪt/ vt (pt permitted) permitir, consentir (**sb to** a alguém que)

**permit**[2] /'pɜːmɪt/ n licença f; (pass) passe m

**permutation** /pɜːmjuː'teɪʃn/ n permutação f

**pernicious** /pə'nɪʃəs/ a pernicioso, prejudicial

**perpendicular** /pɜːpən'dɪkjʊlə(r)/ a & n perpendicular (f)

**perpetrat|e** /'pɜːpɪtreɪt/ vt perpetrar. **~or** n autor m

**perpetual** /pə'petʃʊəl/ a perpétuo

**perpetuate** /pə'petʃʊeɪt/ vt perpetuar

**perplex** /pə'pleks/ vt deixar perplexo. **~ed** a perplexo. **~ing** a confuso. **~ity** n perplexidade f

**persecut|e** /'pɜːsɪkjuːt/ vt perseguir. **~ion** n /-'kjuːʃn/ n perseguição f

**persever|e** /pɜːsɪ'vɪə(r)/ vi perseverar. **~ance** n perseverança f

**Persian** /'pɜːʃn/ a & n (lang) persa (m)

**persist** /pə'sɪst/ vi persistir (**in doing** em fazer). **~ence** n persistência f. **~ent** a persistente; (obstinate) teimoso; (continual) contínuo, constante. **~ently** adv persistentemente

**person** /'pɜːsn/ n pessoa f. **in ~** em pessoa

**personal** /'pɜːsənl/ a pessoal; (secretary) particular. **~ stereo** estereo m pessoal. **~ly** adv pessoalmente

**personality** /pɜːsə'nælətɪ/ n personalidade f; (on TV) vedete f

**personify** /pə'sɒnɪfaɪ/ vt personificar

**personnel** /pɜːsə'nel/ n pessoal m

**perspective** /pə'spektɪv/ n perspectiva f

**perspir|e** /pə'spaɪə(r)/ vi transpirar. **~ation** /-ə'reɪʃn/ n transpiração f

**persua|de** /pə'sweɪd/ vt persuadir (**to a**). **~sion** /-'sweɪʒn/ n persuasão f; (belief) crença f, convicção f. **~sive** /-'sweɪsɪv/ a persuasivo

**pert** /pɜːt/ a (saucy) atrevido, descarado; (lively) vivo

**pertain** /pə'teɪn/ vi **~ to** pertencer a; (be relevant) ser pertinente a, (P) ser próprio de

**pertinent** /'pɜːtɪnənt/ a pertinente

**perturb** /pə'tɜːb/ vt perturbar, transtornar

**Peru** /pə'ruː/ n Peru m. **~vian** a & n peruano (m), (P) peruviano (m)

**peruse** /pə'ruːz/ vt ler com atenção

**perva|de** /pə'veɪd/ vt espalhar-se por, invadir. **~sive** a penetrante

**pervers|e** /pə'vɜːs/ a que insiste no erro; (wicked) perverso; (wayward) caprichoso. **~ity** n obstinação f; (wickedness) perversidade f; (waywardness) capricho m, birra f

**perver|t**[1] /pə'vɜːt/ vt perverter. **~sion** n perversão f

**pervert**[2] /'pɜːvɜːt/ n pervertido m

**peseta** /pə'seɪtə/ n peseta f

**pessimis|t** /'pesɪmɪst/ n pessimista mf. **~m** /-zəm/ n pessimismo m. **~tic** /-'mɪstɪk/ a pessimista

**pest** /pest/ n inseto m, (P) insecto m nocivo; (animal) animal m daninho; (person) peste f

**pester** /'pestə(r)/ vt incomodar (colloq)

**pesticide** /'pestɪsaɪd/ n pesticida m

**pet** /pet/ *n* animal *m* de estimação; (*favourite*) preferido *m*, querido *m* □ *a* (*rabbit etc*) de estimação □ *vt* (*pt* **petted**) acariciar. ~ **name** nome *m* usado em família

**petal** /'petl/ *n* pétala *f*

**peter** /'pi:tə(r)/ *vi* ~ **out** extinguir-se, acabar pouco a pouco, morrer (*fig*)

**petition** /pɪ'tɪʃn/ *n* petição *f* □ *vt* requerer

**petrify** /'petrɪfaɪ/ *vt* petrificar

**petrol** /'petrəl/ *n* gasolina *f*. ~ **pump** bomba *f* de gasolina. ~ **station** posto *m* de gasolina. ~ **tank** tanque *m* de gasolina

**petroleum** /pɪ'trəʊliəm/ *n* petróleo *m*

**petticoat** /'petɪkəʊt/ *n* combinação *f*, anágua *f*

**petty** /'petɪ/ *a* (-ier, -iest) pequeno, insignificante; (*mean*) mesquinho. ~ **cash** fundo *m* para pequenas despesas, caixa *f* pequena

**petulan|t** /'petjʊlənt/ *a* irritável. ~**ce** *n* irritabilidade *f*

**pew** /pju:/ *n* banco (de igreja) *m*

**pewter** /'pju:tə(r)/ *n* estanho *m*

**phallic** /'fælɪk/ *a* fálico

**phantom** /'fæntəm/ *n* fantasma *m*

**pharmaceutical** /fa:mə'sju:tɪkl/ *a* farmacêutico

**pharmac|y** /'fa:məsɪ/ *n* farmácia *f*. ~**ist** *n* farmacêutico *m*

**phase** /feɪz/ *n* fase *f* □ *vt* ~ **in/out** introduzir/retirar progressivamente

**PhD** *abbr of* Doctor of Philosophy *n* doutorado *m*

**pheasant** /'feznt/ *n* faisão *m*

**phenomen|on** /fɪ'nɒmɪnən/ *n* (*pl* -ena) fenômeno *m*, (*P*) fenómeno *m*. ~**al** *a* fenomenal

**philanthrop|ist** /fɪ'lænθrəpɪst/ *n* filantropo *m*. ~**ic** /-ən'θrɒpɪk/ *a* filantrópico

**Philippines** /'fɪlɪpi:nz/ *npl* **the** ~ as Filipinas *fpl*

**philistine** /'fɪlɪstaɪn/ *n* filisteu *m*

**philosoph|y** /fɪ'lɒsəfɪ/ *n* filosofia *f*. ~**er** *n* filósofo *m*. ~**ical** /-ə'sɒfɪkl/ *a* filosófico

**phlegm** /flem/ *n* (*med*) catarro *m*, fleuma *f*

**phobia** /'fəʊbɪə/ *n* fobia *f*

**phone** /fəʊn/ *n* (*colloq*) telefone *m* □ *vt/i* (*colloq*) telefonar (para). **on the** ~ no telefone. ~ **back** voltar a telefonar, ligar de volta. ~ **book** lista *f* telefônica, (*P*) telefónica. ~ **box** cabine *f* telefônica, (*P*) telefónica. ~ **call** chamada *f*, telefonema *m*. ~**in** *n* programa *m* de rádio ou tv com participação dos ouvintes

**phonecard** /'fəʊnka:d/ *n* cartão *m* para uso em telefone público

**phonetic** /fə'netɪk/ *a* fonetico. ~**s** *n* fonética *f*

**phoney** /'fəʊnɪ/ *a* (-ier, -iest) (*sl*) falso, fingido □ *n* (*sl: person*) fingido *m*; (*sl: thing*) falso *m*, (*P*) falsificação *f*

**phosphate** /'fɒsfeɪt/ *n* fosfato *m*

**phosphorus** /'fɒsfərəs/ *n* fósforo *m*

**photo** /'fəʊtəʊ/ *n* (*pl* -os) (*colloq*) retrato *m*, foto *f*

**photocop|y** /'fəʊtəʊkɒpɪ/ *n* fotocópia *f* □ *vt* fotocopiar. ~**ier** *n* fotocopiadora *f*

**photogenic** /fəʊtəʊ'dʒenɪk/ *a* fotogênico, (*P*) fotogénico

**photograph** /'fəʊtəgra:f/ *n* fotografia *f* □ *vt* fotografar. ~**er** /fə'tɒgrəfə(r)/ *n* fotógrafo *m*. ~**ic** /-'græfɪk/ *a* fotográfico. ~**y** /fə'tɒgrəfɪ/ *n* fotografia *f*

**phrase** /freɪz/ *n* expressão *f*, frase *f*; (*gram*) locução *f*, frase *f* elíptica □ *vt* exprimir. ~**-book** *n* livro *m* de expressões idiomáticas

**physical** /'fɪzɪkl/ *a* físico

**physician** /fɪ'zɪʃn/ *n* médico *m*

**physicist** /'fɪzɪsɪst/ *n* físico *m*

**physics** /'fɪzɪks/ *n* física *f*

**physiology** /fɪzɪ'ɒlədʒɪ/ *n* fisiologia *f*

**physiotherap|y** /fɪzɪəʊ'θerəpɪ/ *n* fisioterapia *f*. ~**ist** *n* fisioterapeuta *mf*

**physique** /fɪ'zi:k/ *n* físico *m*

**pian|o** /'prænəʊ/ *n* (*pl* -os) piano *m*. ~**ist** /'pɪənɪst/ *n* pianista *mf*

**pick**[1] /pɪk/ *n* (*tool*) picareta *f*

**pick**[2] /pɪk/ *vt* escolher; (*flowers, fruit etc*) colher; (*lock*) forçar; (*teeth*) palitar □ *n* escolha *f*; (*best*) o/a melhor. ~ **a quarrel with** puxar uma briga com. ~ **holes in an argument** descobrir os pontos fracos dum argumento. ~ **sb's pocket** bater a carteira de alg. ~ **off** tirar, arrancar. ~ **on** implicar com. ~ **out** escolher; (*identify*) identificar, reconhecer. ~ **up** apanhar; (*speed*) ganhar. **take one's** ~ escolher livremente

**pickaxe** /'pɪkæks/ *n* picareta *f*

**picket** /'pɪkɪt/ *n* piquete *m*; (*single striker*) grevista *mf* de piquete □ *vt* (*pt* **picketed**) colocar um piquete em □ *vi* fazer piquete

**pickings** /'pɪkɪŋz/ *npl* restos *mpl*

**pickle** /'pɪkl/ *n* vinagre *m*. ~**s** picles *mpl*, (*P*) pickles *mpl* □ *vt* conservar em vinagre. **in a** ~ (*colloq*) numa encrenca (*colloq*)

**pickpocket** /'pɪkpɒkɪt/ *n* batedor *m* de carteiras, (*P*) carteirista *m*

**picnic** /'pɪknɪk/ *n* piquenique *m* □ *vi* (*pt* **picnicked**) piquenicar, (*P*) fazer um piquenique

**pictorial** /pɪk'tɔ:rɪəl/ *a* ilustrado

**picture** /'pɪktʃə(r)/ *n* imagem *f*; (*illustration*) estampa *f*, ilustração *f*; (*painting*) quadro *m*, pintura *f*;

(*photo*) fotografia *f*, retrato *m*; (*drawing*) desenho *m*; (*fig*) descrição *f*, quadro *m* □ *vt* imaginar; (*describe*) pintar, descrever. **the ~s** o cinema

**picturesque** /pɪktʃə'resk/ *a* pitoresco

**pidgin** /'pɪdʒɪn/ *a* ~ **English** inglês *m* estropiado

**pie** /paɪ/ *n* torta *f*, (*P*) tarte *f*; (*of meat*) empada *f*

**piece** /piːs/ *n* pedaço *m*, bocado *m*; (*of machine, in game*) peça *f*; (*of currency*) moeda *f* □ *vt* ~ **together** juntar, montar. **a ~ of advice/furniture/** *etc* um conselho/um móvel/*etc*. ~-**work** *n* trabalho *m* por, (*P*) a peça or por, (*P*) a tarefa. **take to ~s** desmontar

**piecemeal** /'piːsmiːl/ *a* aos poucos, pouco a pouco

**pier** /pɪə(r)/ *n* molhe *m*

**pierc**|**e** /pɪəs/ *vt* furar, penetrar. ~**ing** *a* penetrante; (*of scream, pain*) lancinante

**piety** /'paɪətɪ/ *n* piedade *f*, devoção *f*

**pig** /pɪg/ *n* porco *m*. ~-**headed** *a* cabeçudo, teimoso

**pigeon** /'pɪdʒɪn/ *n* pombo *m*. ~-**hole** *n* escaninho *m*

**piggy** /'pɪgɪ/ *a* como um porco. ~-**back** *adv* nas costas. ~ **bank** cofre *m* de criança

**pigment** /'pɪgmənt/ *n* pigmento *m*. ~**ation** /-'teɪʃn/ *n* pigmentação *f*

**pigsty** /'pɪgstaɪ/ *n* pocilga *f*, chiqueiro *m*

**pigtail** /'pɪgteɪl/ *n* trança *f*

**pike** /paɪk/ *n* (*pl invar*) (*fish*) lúcio *m*

**pilchard** /'pɪltʃəd/ *n* peixe *m* pequeno da família do arenque, sardinha *f* européia

**pile** /paɪl/ *n* pilha *f*; (*of carpet*) pêlo *m* □ *vt/i* amontoar(-se), empilhar(-se) (**into** em). **a ~ of** (*colloq*) um monte de (*colloq*). ~ **up** acumular(-se). ~-**up** *n* choque *m* em cadeia

**piles** /paɪlz/ *npl* hemorróidas *fpl*

**pilfer** /'pɪlfə(r)/ *vt* furtar. ~**age** *n* furto *m* (de coisas pequenas or em pequenas quantidades)

**pilgrim** /'pɪlgrɪm/ *n* peregrino *m*, romeiro *m*. ~**age** *n* peregrinação *f*, romaria *f*

**pill** /pɪl/ *n* pílula *f*, comprimido *m*

**pillage** /'pɪlɪdʒ/ *n* pilhagem *f*, saque *m* □ *vt* pilhar, saquear

**pillar** /'pɪlə(r)/ *n* pilar *m*. ~-**box** *n* marco *m* do correio

**pillion** /'pɪlɪən/ *n* assento *m* traseiro de motorizada. **ride ~** ir no assento de trás

**pillow** /'pɪləʊ/ *n* travesseiro *m*

**pillowcase** /'pɪləʊkeɪs/ *n* fronha *f*

**pilot** /'paɪlət/ *n* piloto *m* □ *vt* (*pt* **piloted**) pilotar. ~-**light** *n* piloto *m*;

(*electr*) lâmpada *f* testemunho; (*gas*) piloto *m*

**pimento** /pɪ'mentəʊ/ *n* (*pl* -**os**) pimentão *m* vermelho

**pimple** /'pɪmpl/ *n* borbulha *f*, espinha *f*

**pin** /pɪn/ *n* alfinete *m*; (*techn*) cavilha *f* □ *vt* (*pt* **pinned**) pregar or prender com alfinete(s); (*hold down*) prender, segurar. **have ~s and needles** estar com cãibra. ~ **sb down** (*fig*) obrigar alg a definir-se, apertar alg (*fig*). ~-**point** *vt* localizar com precisão. ~-**stripe** *a* de listras finas. ~ **up** pregar. ~-**up** *n* (*colloq*) pin-up *f*

**pinafore** /'pɪnəfɔː(r)/ *n* avental *m*. ~ **dress** veste *f*

**pincers** /'pɪnsəz/ *npl* (*tool*) torquês *f*, (*P*) alicate *m*; (*med*) pinça *f*; (*zool*) pinça(s) *f*(*pl*), tenaz(es) *f* (*pl*)

**pinch** /pɪntʃ/ *vt* apertar; (*sl: steal*) surripiar (*colloq*) □ *n* aperto *m*; (*tweak*) beliscão *m*; (*small amount*) pitada *f*. **at a ~** em caso de necessidade

**pine**[1] /paɪn/ *n* (*tree*) pinheiro *m*; (*wood*) pinho *m*

**pine**[2] /paɪn/ *vi* ~ **away** definhar, consumir-se. ~ **for** suspirar por

**pineapple** /'paɪnæpl/ *n* abacaxi *m*, (*P*) ananás *m*

**ping-pong** /'pɪŋpɒŋ/ *n* pingue-pongue *m*

**pink** /pɪŋk/ *a* & *n* rosa (*m*)

**pinnacle** /'pɪnəkl/ *n* pináculo *m*

**pint** /paɪnt/ *n* quartilho *m* (= 0,57*l*; *Amer = 0,47l*)

**pioneer** /paɪə'nɪə(r)/ *n* pioneiro *m* □ *vt* ser o pioneiro em, preparar o caminho para

**pious** /'paɪəs/ *a* piedoso, devoto

**pip** /pɪp/ *n* (*seed*) pevide *f*

**pipe** /paɪp/ *n* cano *m*, tubo *m*; (*of smoker*) cachimbo *m* □ *vt* encanar, canalizer ~ **down** calar a boca

**pipeline** /'paɪplaɪn/ *n* (*for oil*) oleoduto *m*; (*for gas*) gaseoduto *m*, (*P*) gasoduto *m*. **in the ~** (*fig*) encaminhado

**piping** /'paɪpɪŋ/ *n* tubagem *f*. ~ **hot** muito quente

**piquant** /'piːkənt/ *a* picante

**pira**|**te** /'paɪərət/ *n* pirata *m*. ~**cy** *n* pirataria *f*

**Pisces** /'paɪsiːz/ *n* (*astr*) Peixe *m*, (*P*) Pisces *m*

**pistol** /'pɪstl/ *n* pistola *f*

**piston** /'pɪstən/ *n* êmbolo *m*, pistão *m*

**pit** /pɪt/ *n* (*hole*) cova *f*, fosso *m*; (*mine*) poço *m*; (*quarry*) pedreira *f* □ *vt* (*pt* **pitted**) picar, esburacar; (*fig*) opor. ~ **o.s. against** (*struggle*) medir-se com

**pitch**[1] /pɪtʃ/ *n* breu *m*. ~-**black** *a* escuro como breu

**pitch²** /pɪtʃ/ *vt* (*throw*) lançar; (*tent*) armar □ *vi* cair □ *n* (*slope*) declive *m*; (*of sound*) som *m*; (*of voice*) altura *f*; (*sport*) campo *m*

**pitchfork** /'pɪtʃfɔ:k/ *n* forcado *m*

**pitfall** /'pɪtfɔ:l/ *n* (*fig*) cilada *f*, perigo *m* inesperado

**pith** /pɪθ/ *n* (*of orange*) parte *f* branca da casca, mesocarpo *m*; (*fig: essential part*) cerne *m*, âmago *m*

**pithy** /'pɪθɪ/ *a* (**-ier, -iest**) preciso, conciso

**piti|ful** /'pɪtɪfl / *a* lastimoso; (*contemptible*) miserável. **~less** *a* impiedoso

**pittance** /'pɪtns/ *n* salário *m* miserável, miséria *f*

**pity** /'pɪtɪ/ *n* dó *m*, pena *f*, piedade *f* □ *vt* compadecer-se de. **it's a ~** é uma pena. **take ~ on** ter pena de. **what a ~!** que pena!

**pivot** /'pɪvət/ *n* eixo *m* □ *vt* (*pt* **pivoted**) girar em torno de

**placard** /'plæka:d/ *n* (*poster*) cartaz *m*

**placate** /plə'keɪt/ *vt* apaziguar, aplacar

**place** /pleɪs/ *n* lugar *m*, sítio *m*; (*house*) casa *f*; (*seat, rank etc*) lugar *m* □ *vt* colocar, pôr. **~ an order** fazer uma encomenda. **at/to my ~** em a *or* na minha casa. **~-mat** *n* pano *m* de mesa individual, (*P*) napperon *m* à americana

**placid** /'plæsɪd/ *a* plácido

**plagiar|ize** /'pleɪdʒəraɪz/ *vt* plagiar. **~ism** *n* plágio *m*

**plague** /pleɪg/ *n* peste *f*; (*of insects*) praga *f* □ *vt* atormentar, atazanar

**plaice** /pleɪs/ *n* (*pl invar*) solha *f*

**plain** /pleɪn/ *a* (**-er, -est**) claro; (*candid*) franco; (*simple*) simples; (*not pretty*) sem beleza; (*not patterned*) liso □ *adv* com franqueza □ *n* planície *f*. **in ~ clothes** à paisana. **~ly** *adv* claramente; (*candidly*) francamente

**plaintiff** /'pleɪntɪf/ *n* queixoso *m*

**plaintive** /'pleɪntɪv/ *a* queixoso

**plait** /plæt/ *vt* entrançar □ *n* trança *f*

**plan** /plæn/ *n* plano *m*, projeto *m*, (*P*) projecto *m*; (*of a house, city etc*) plano *m*, planta *f* □ *vt* (*pt* **planned**) planear, planejar □ *vi* fazer planos. **~ to do** ter a intenção de fazer

**plane¹** /pleɪn/ *n* (*level*) plano *m*; (*aeroplane*) avião *m* □ *a* plano

**plane²** /pleɪn/ *n* (*tool*) plaina *f* □ *vt* aplainar

**planet** /'plænɪt/ *n* planeta *m*

**plank** /plæŋk/ *n* prancha *f*

**planning** /'plænɪŋ/ *n* planeamento *m*, planejamento *m*. **~ permission** permissão *f* para construir

**plant** /pla:nt/ *n* planta *f*; (*techn*) aparelhagem *f*; (*factory*) fábrica *f* □ *vt*

plantar. **~ a bomb** colocar uma bomba. **~ation** /-'teɪʃn/ *n* plantação *f*

**plaque** /pla:k/ *n* placa *f*; (*on teeth*) tártaro *m*, pedra *f*

**plaster** /'pla:stə(r)/ *n* reboco *m*; (*adhesive*) esparadrapo *m*, band-aid *m* □ *vt* rebocar; (*cover*) cobrir (**with** com, de). **in ~** engessado. **~ of Paris** gesso *m*. **~er** *n* rebocador *m*, caiador *m*

**plastic** /'plæstɪk/ *a* plástico □ *n* plástica *f*. **~ surgery** cirurgia *f* plástica

**plate** /pleɪt/ *n* prato *m*; (*in book*) gravura *f* □ *vt* revestir de metal

**plateau** /'plætəʊ/ *n* (*pl* **-eaux** /-əʊz/) planalto *m*, platô *m*

**platform** /'plætfɔ:m/ *n* estrado *m*; (*for speaking*) tribuna *f*; (*rail*) plataforma *f*, cais *m*; (*fig*) programa *m* de partido político. **~ ticket** bilhete *m* de gare

**platinum** /'plætɪnəm/ *n* platina *f*

**platitude** /'plætɪtju:d/ *n* banalidade *f*, lugar-comum *m*

**platonic** /plə'tɒnɪk/ *a* platônico, (*P*) platónico

**plausible** /'plɔ:zəbl/ *a* plausível; (*person*) convincente

**play** /pleɪ/ *vt/i* (*for amusement*) brincar; (*instrument*) tocar; (*cards, game*) jogar; (*opponent*) jogar contra; (*match*) disputar □ *n* jogo *m*; (*theatre*) peça *f*; (*movement*) folga *f*, margem *f*. **~ down** minimizar. **~ on** (*take advantage of*) aproveitar-se de. **~ safe** jogar pelo seguro. **~ up** (*colloq*) dar problemas (a). **~-group** *n* jardim *m* de infância, (*P*) jardim *m* infantil. **~-pen** *n* cercado *m* para crianças

**playboy** /'pleɪbɔɪ/ *n* play-boy *m*

**player** /'pleɪə(r)/ *n* jogador *m*; (*theat*) artista *mf*; (*mus*) artista *mf*, executante *mf*, instrumentista *mf*

**playful** /'pleɪfl/ *a* brincalhão *m*

**playground** /'pleɪgraʊnd/ *n* pátio *m* de recreio

**playing** /'pleɪŋ/ *n* atuação *f*, (*P*) actuação *f*. **~-card** *n* carta *f* de jogar. **~-field** *n* campo *m* de jogos

**playwright** /'pleɪraɪt/ *n* dramaturgo *m*

**plc** *abbr* (*of public limited company*) SARL

**plea** /pli:/ *n* súplica *f*; (*reason*) pretexto *m*, desculpa *f*; (*jur*) alegação *f* da defesa

**plead** /pli:d/ *vt/i* pleitear; (*as excuse*) alegar. **~ guilty** confessar-se culpado. **~ with** implorar a

**pleasant** /'pleznt/ *a* agradável

**pleas|e** /pli:z/ *vt/i* agradar (a), dar prazer (a) □ *adv* por favor, (*P*) se faz favor. **they ~e themselves, they do as they ~e** eles fazem como bem entendem. **~ed** *a* contente, satisfeito (with com). **~ing** *a* agradável

**pleasur|e** /'pleʒə(r)/ *n* prazer *m*. **~able** *a* agradável

**pleat** /pli:t/ *n* prega *f* □ *vt* preguear

**pledge** /pledʒ/ *n* penhor *m*, garantia *f*; (*fig*) promessa *f* □ *vt* prometer; (*pawn*) empenhar

**plentiful** /'plentɪfl/ *a* abundante

**plenty** /'plentɪ/ *n* abundância *f*, fartura *f*. **~ (of)** muito (de); (*enough*) bastante (de)

**pliable** /'plaɪəbl/ *a* flexível

**pliers** /'plaɪəz/ *npl* alicate *m*

**plight** /plaɪt/ *n* triste situação *f*

**plimsoll** /'plɪmsəl/ *n* alpargata *f*, ténis *m*, (P) ténis *m*

**plinth** /plɪnθ/ *n* plinto *m*

**plod** /plɒd/ *vi* (*pt* **plodded**) caminhar lentamente; (*work*) trabalhar, marrar (*sl*). **~der** *n* trabalhador *m* lento mas perseverante. **~ding** *a* lento

**plonk** /plɒŋk/ *n* (*sl*) vinho *m* ordinário, (P) carrascão *m*

**plot** /plɒt/ *n* complô *m*, conspiração *f*; (*of novel etc*) trama *f*; (*of land*) lote *m* □ *vt/i* (*pt* **plotted**) conspirar; (*mark out*) traçar

**plough** /plaʊ/ *n* arado *m* □ *vt/i* arar. **~ back** reinvestir. **~ into** colidir. **~ through** abrir caminho por

**ploy** /plɔɪ/ *n* (*colloq*) estratagema *m*

**pluck** /plʌk/ *vt* apanhar; (*bird*) depenar; (*eyebrows*) depilar; (*mus*) tanger □ *n* coragem *f*. **~ up courage** ganhar coragem. **~y** *a* corajoso

**plug** /plʌg/ *n* tampão *m*; (*electr*) tomada *f*, (P) ficha *f* □ *vt* (*pt* **plugged**) tapar com tampão; (*colloq: publicize*) fazer grande propaganda de □ *vi* **~ away** (*colloq*) trabalhar com afinco. **~ in** (*electr*) ligar. **~-hole** *n* buraco *m* do cano

**plum** /plʌm/ *n* ameixa *f*

**plumb** /plʌm/ *adv* exatamente, (P) exactamente, mesmo □ *vt* sondar. **~-line** *n* fio *m* de prumo

**plumb|er** /'plʌmə(r)/ *n* bombeiro *m*, encanador *m*, (P) canalizador *m*. **~ing** *n* encanamento *m*, (P) canalização *f*

**plummet** /'plʌmɪt/ *vi* (*pt* **plummeted**) despencar

**plump** /plʌmp/ *a* (**-er, -est**) rechonchudo, roliço □ *vi* **~ for** optar por. **~ness** *n* gordura *f*

**plunder** /'plʌndə(r)/ *vt* pilhar, saquear □ *n* pilhagem *f*, saque *m*; (*goods*) despojo *m*

**plunge** /plʌndʒ/ *vt/i* mergulhar, atirar(-se), afundar(-se) □ *n* mergulho *m*. **take the ~** (*fig*) decidir-se, dar o salto (*fig*)

**plunger** /'plʌndʒə(r)/ *n* (*of pump*) êmbolo *m*, pistão *m*; (*for sink etc*) desentupidor *m*

**pluperfect** /plu:'pɜ:fɪkt/ *n* mais-que-perfeito *m*

**plural** /'plʊərəl/ *a* plural; (*noun*) no plural □ *n* plural *m*

**plus** /plʌs/ *prep* mais □ *a* positivo □ *n* sinal +; (*fig*) qualidade *f* positiva

**plush** /plʌʃ/ *n* pelúcia *f* □ *a* de pelúcia; (*colloq*) de luxo

**ply** /plaɪ/ *vt* (*tool*) manejar; (*trade*) exercer □ *vi* (*ship, bus*) fazer carreira entre dois lugares. **~ sb with drink** encher alguém de bebidas

**plywood** /'plaɪwʊd/ *n* madeira *f* compensada

**p.m.** /pi:'em/ *adv* da tarde, da noite

**pneumatic** /nju:'mætɪk/ *a* pneumático. **~ drill** broca *f* pneumática

**pneumonia** /nju:'məʊnɪə/ *n* pneumonia *f*

**PO** *abbr see* **Post Office**

**poach** /pəʊtʃ/ *vt/i* (*steal*) caçar/pescar em propriedade alheia; (*culin*) fazer pochê, (P) escalfar. **~ed eggs** ovos *mpl* pochês, (P) ovos *mpl* escalfados

**pocket** /'pɒkɪt/ *n* bolso *m*, algibeira *f* □ *a* de algibeira □ *vt* meter no bolso. **~-book** *n* (*notebook*) livro *m* de apontamentos; (*Amer: handbag*) carteira *f*. **~-money** *n* (*monthly*) mesada *f*; (*weekly*) semanada *f*, dinheiro *m* para pequenas despesas

**pod** /pɒd/ *n* vagem *f*

**poem** /'pəʊɪm/ *n* poema *m*

**poet** /'pəʊɪt/ *n* poeta *m*, poetisa *f*. **~ic** /-'etɪk/ *a* poético

**poetry** /'pəʊɪtrɪ/ *n* poesia *f*

**poignant** /'pɔɪnjənt/ *a* pungente, doloroso

**point** /pɔɪnt/ *n* ponto *m*; (*tip*) ponta *f*; (*decimal point*) vírgula *f*; (*meaning*) sentido *m*, razão *m*; (*electr*) tomada *f*. **~s** (*rail*) agulhas *fpl* □ *vt/i* (*aim*) apontar (**at** para); (*show*) apontar, indicar (**at/to** para). **on the ~ of** prestes a, quase a. **~-blank** *a & adv* à queima-roupa; (*fig*) categórico. **~ of view** ponto *m* de vista. **~ out** apontar, fazer ver. **that is a good ~** (*remark*) é uma boa observação. **to the ~** a propósito. **what is the ~?** de que adianta?

**pointed** /'pɔɪntɪd/ *a* ponteagudo; (*of remark*) intencional, contundente

**pointer** /'pɔɪntə(r)/ *n* ponteiro *m*; (*colloq: hint*) sugestão *f*

**pointless** /'pɔɪntlɪs/ *a* inútil, sem sentido

**poise** /pɔɪz/ *n* equilíbrio *m*; (*carriage*) porte *m*; (*fig: self-possession*) presença *f*, segurança *f*. **~d** *a* equilibrado; (*person*) seguro de si

**poison** /'pɔɪzn/ n veneno m, peçonha f □ vt envenenar. **blood-~ing** n envenenamento m do sangue. **food-~ing** n intoxicação f alimentar. **~ous** a venenoso

**poke** /pəʊk/ vt/i espetar; (with elbow) acotovelar; ( fire) atiçar □ n espetadela f; (with elbow) cotovelada f. **~ about** esgaravatar, remexer, procurar. **~ fun at** fazer troça/pouco de. **~ out** (head) enfiar

**poker**[1] /'pəʊkə(r)/ n atiçador m

**poker**[2] /'pəʊkə(r)/ n (cards) pôquer m, (P) póquer m

**poky** /'pəʊkɪ/ a (-ier, -iest) acanhado, apertado

**Poland** /'pəʊlənd/ n Polônia f, (P) Polónia f

**polar** /'pəʊlə(r)/ a polar. **~ bear** urso m branco

**polarize** /'pəʊləraɪz/ vt polarizar

**pole**[1] /pəʊl/ n vara f; ( for flag) mastro m; (post) poste m

**pole**[2] /pəʊl/ n (geog) pólo m

**Pole** /pəʊl/ n polaco m

**polemic** /pə'lemɪk/ n polêmica f, (P) polémica f

**police** /pə'liːs/ n polícia f □ vt policiar. **~ state** estado m policial. **~ station** distrito m, delegacia f, (P) esquadra f de polícia

**police|man** /pə'liːsmən/ n (pl -men) policial m, (P) polícia m, guarda m, agente m de polícia. **~-woman** (pl -women) n polícia f feminina, (P) mulher-polícia f

**policy**[1] /'pɒlɪsɪ/ n (plan of action) política f

**policy**[2] /'pɒlɪsɪ/ n (insurance) apólice f de seguro

**polio** /'pəʊlɪəʊ/ n polio f

**polish** /'pɒlɪʃ/ vt polir, dar lustro em; (shoes) engraxar; ( floor) encerar □ n ( for shoes) graxa f; ( for floor) cera f; ( for nails) esmalte m, (P) verniz m; (shine) polimento m; ( fig) requinte m. **~ off** acabar (rapidamente). **~ up** (language) aperfeiçoar. **~ed** a requintado, elegante

**Polish** /'pəʊlɪʃ/ a & n polonês (m), (P) polaco (m)

**polite** /pə'laɪt/ a polido, educado, delicado. **~ly** adv delicadamente. **~ness** n delicadeza f, cortesia f

**political** /pə'lɪtɪkl/ a político

**politician** /pɒlɪ'tɪʃn/ n político m

**politics** /'pɒlɪtɪks/ n política f

**polka** /'pɒlkə/ n polca f. **~ dots** bolas fpl

**poll** /pəʊl/ n votação f; (survey) sondagem f, pesquisa f □ vt (votes) obter. **go to the ~s** votar, ir às urnas. **~ing-booth** n cabine f de voto

**pollen** /'pɒlən/ n pólen m

**pollut|e** /pə'luːt/ vt poluir. **~ion** /-ʃn/ n poluição f

**polo** /'pəʊləʊ/ n pólo m. **~ neck** gola f rolê

**polyester** /pɒlɪ'estə/ n poliéster m

**polytechnic** /pɒlɪ'teknɪk/ n politécnica f

**polythene** /'pɒlɪθiːn/ n politeno m. **~ bag** n saco m de plástico

**pomegranate** /'pɒmɪgrænɪt/ n romã f

**pomp** /pɒmp/ n pompa f

**pompon** /'pɒmpɒn/ n pompom m

**pomp|ous** /'pɒmpəs/ a pomposo. **~osity** /-'pɒsətɪ/ n imponência f

**pond** /pɒnd/ n lagoa f, lago m; (artificial) tanque m, lago m

**ponder** /'pɒndə(r)/ vt/i ponderar, meditar (over sobre)

**pong** /pɒŋ/ n (sl) pivete m □ vi (sl) cheirar mal, tresandar

**pony** /'pəʊnɪ/ n pônei m, (P) pónei m. **~-tail** n rabo m de cavalo. **~-trekking** n passeio m de pônei, (P) pónei

**poodle** /'puːdl/ n cão m de água, caniche m

**pool**[1] /puːl/ n (puddle) charco m, poça f; ( for swimming) piscina f

**pool**[2] /puːl/ n ( fund) fundo m comum; (econ, comm) pool m; (game) forma f de bilhar. **~s** loteca f, (P) totobola m □ vt pôr num fundo comum

**poor** /pʊə(r)/ a (-er, -est) pobre; (not good) medíocre. **~ly** adv mal □ a doente

**pop**[1] /pɒp/ n estalido m, ruído m seco □ vt/i (pt popped) dar um estalido, estalar; (of cork) saltar. **~ in/out/off** entrar/sair/ir-se embora. **~ up** aparecer de repente, saltar

**pop**[2] /pɒp/ n música f pop □ a pop invar

**popcorn** /'pɒpkɔːn/ n pipoca f

**pope** /pəʊp/ n papa m

**poplar** /'pɒplə(r)/ n choupo m, álamo m

**poppy** /'pɒpɪ/ n papoula f

**popular** /'pɒpjʊlə(r)/ a popular; (in fashion) em voga, na moda. **be ~ with** ser popular entre. **~ity** /-'lærətɪ/ n popularidade f. **~ize** vt popularizar, vulgarizar

**populat|e** /'pɒpjʊlert/ vt povoar. **~ion** /-'leɪʃn/ n população f

**populous** /'pɒpjʊləs/ a populoso

**porcelain** /'pɔːslɪn/ n porcelana f

**porch** /pɔːtʃ/ n alpendre m; (Amer) varanda f

**porcupine** /'pɔːkjʊpam/ n porco-espinho m

**pore**[1] /pɔː(r)/ n poro m

**pore**[2] /pɔː(r)/ vi **~ over** examinar, estudar

**pork** /pɔːk/ n carne f de porco

**pornograph|y** /pɔ:'nɒgrəfɪ/ *n* pornografia *f*. **~ic** /-ə'græfɪk/ *a* pornográfico

**porous** /'pɔ:rəs/ *a* poroso

**porpoise** /'pɔ:pəs/ *n* toninha *f*, (*P*) golfinho *m*

**porridge** /'pɒrɪdʒ/ *n* (papa *f* de) flocos *mpl* de aveia

**port**[1] /pɔ:t/ *n* (*harbour*) porto *m*

**port**[2] /pɔ:t/ *n* (*wine*) (vinho do) Porto *m*

**portable** /'pɔ:təbl/ *a* portátil

**porter**[1] /'pɔ:tə(r)/ *n* (*carrier*) carregador *m*

**porter**[2] /'pɔ:tə(r)/ *n* (*doorkeeper*) porteiro *m*

**portfolio** /pɔ:t'fəʊlɪəʊ/ *n* (*pl* **-os**) (*case*, *post*) pasta *f*; (*securities*) carteira *f* de investimentos

**porthole** /'pɔ:θəʊl/ *n* vigia *f*

**portion** /'pɔ:ʃn/ *n* (*share*, *helping*) porção *f*; (*part*) parte *f*

**portly** /'pɔ:tlɪ/ *a* (**-ier, -iest**) corpulento e digno

**portrait** /'pɔ:trɪt/ *n* retrato *m*

**portray** /pɔ:'treɪ/ *vt* retratar, pintar; (*fig*) descrever. **~al** *n* retrato *m*

**Portug|al** /'pɔ:tjʊgl/ *n* Portugal *m*. **~uese** /-'gi:z/ *a* & *n invar* português (*m*)

**pose** /pəʊz/ *vt/i* (fazer) posar; (*question*) fazer □ *n* pose *f*, postura *f*. **~ as** fazer-se passar por

**poser** /'pəʊzə(r)/ *n* quebra-cabeças *m*

**posh** /pɒʃ/ *a* (*sl*) chique *invar*

**position** /pə'zɪʃn/ *n* posição *f*; (*job*) lugar *m*, colocação *f*; (*state*) situação *f* □ *vt* colocar

**positive** /'pɒzətɪv/ *a* positivo; (*definite*) categórico, definitivo; (*colloq: downright*) autêntico. **she's ~ that** ela tem certeza que. **~ly** *adv* positivamente; (*absolutely*) completamente

**possess** /pə'zes/ *vt* possuir. **~ion** /-ʃn/ *n* posse *f*; (*thing possessed*) possessão *f*. **~or** *n* possuidor *m*

**possessive** /pə'zesɪv/ *a* possessivo

**possib|le** /'pɒsəbl/ *a* possível. **~ility** /-'bɪlətɪ/ *n* possibilidade *f*

**possibly** /'pɒsəblɪ/ *adv* possivelmente, talvez. **if I ~ can** se me fôr possível. **I cannot ~ leave** estou impossibilitado de partir

**post**[1] /pəʊst/ *n* (*pole*) poste *m* □ *vt* (*notice*) afixar, pregar

**post**[2] /pəʊst/ *n* (*station, job*) posto *m* □ *vt* colocar; (*appoint*) colocar

**post**[3] /pəʊst/ *n* (*mail*) correio *m* □ *a* postal □ *vt* mandar pelo correio. **keep ~ed** manter informado. **~-code** *n* código *m* postal. **P~ Office** agência *f* dos correios, (*P*) estação *f* dos correios; (*corporation*) Departamento *m* dos Correios e Telégrafos, (*P*) Correios, Telégrafos e Telefones *mpl* (CTT)

**post-** /pəʊst/ *pref* pós-

**postage** /'pəʊstɪdʒ/ *n* porte *m*

**postal** /'pəʊstl/ *a* postal. **~ order** vale *m* postal

**postcard** /'pəʊstka:d/ *n* cartão-postal *m*, (*P*) (bilhete) postal *m*

**poster** /'pəʊstə(r)/ *n* cartaz *m*

**posterity** /pɒ'sterətɪ/ *n* posteridade *f*

**postgraduate** /pəʊst'grædʒʊet/ *n* pós-graduado *m*

**posthumous** /'pɒstjʊməs/ *a* póstumo. **~ly** *adv* a título póstumo

**postman** /'pəʊstmən/ *n* (*pl* **-men**) carteiro *m*

**postmark** /'pəʊstma:k/ *n* carimbo *m* do correio

**post-mortem** /pəʊst'mɔ:təm/ *n* autópsia *f*

**postpone** /pə'spəʊn/ *vt* adiar. **~ment** *n* adiamento *m*

**postscript** /'pəʊsskrɪpt/ *n* post scriptum *m*

**postulate** /'pɒstjʊleɪt/ *vt* postular

**posture** /'pɒstʃə(r)/ *n* postura *f*, posição *f* □ *vi* posar

**post-war** /'pəʊstwɔ:(r)/ *a* de após-guerra

**posy** /'pəʊzɪ/ *n* raminho *m* de flores

**pot** /pɒt/ *n* pote *m*; (*for cooking*) panela *f*; (*for plants*) vaso *m*; (*sl: marijuana*) maconha *f* □ *vt* (*pt* **potted**) (**~ up**) plantar em vaso. **go to ~** (*sl: business*) arruinar, degringolar (*colloq*); (*sl: person*) estar arruinado or liquidado. **~-belly** *n* pança *f*, barriga *f*. **take ~ luck** aceitar o que houver. **take a ~-shot** dar um tiro de perto (**at em**); (*at random*) dar um tiro a esmo (**at em**)

**potato** /pə'teɪtəʊ/ *n* (*pl* **-oes**) batata *f*

**poten|t** /'pəʊtnt/ *a* potente, poderoso; (*drink*) forte. **~cy** *n* potência *f*

**potential** /pə'tenʃl/ *a* & *n* potencial (*m*). **~ly** *adv* potencialmente

**pothol|e** /'pɒθəʊl/ *n* caverna *f*, caldeirão *m*; (*in road*) buraco *m*. **~ing** *n* espeleologia *f*

**potion** /'pəʊʃn/ *n* poção *f*

**potted** /'pɒtɪd/ *a* (*of plant*) de vaso; (*preserved*) de conserva

**potter**[1] /'pɒtə(r)/ *n* oleiro *m*, ceramista *mf*. **~y** *n* olaria *f*, cerâmica *f*

**potter**[2] /'pɒtə(r)/ *vi* entreter-se com isto ou aquilo

**potty**[1] /'pɒtɪ/ *a* (**-ier, -iest**) (*sl*) doido, pirado (*sl*), (*P*) chanfrado (*colloq*)

**potty**[2] /'pɒtɪ/ *n* (**-ties**) (*colloq*) penico *m* de criança

**pouch** /paʊtʃ/ *n* bolsa *f*; (*for tobacco*) tabaqueira *f*

**poultice** /'pəʊltɪs/ *n* cataplasma *f*

**poultry** /'pəʊltrɪ/ *n* aves *fpl* domésticas

**pounce** /paʊns/ *vi* atirar-se (**on** sobre, para cima de) □ *n* salto *m*

**pound**[1] /paʊnd/ *n* (*weight*) libra *f* (= 453 *g*); (*money*) libra *f*

**pound**[2] /paʊnd/ *n* (*for dogs*) canil municipal *m*; (*for cars*) parque de viaturas rebocadas *m*

**pound**[3] /paʊnd/ *vt/i* (*crush*) esmagar, pisar; (*of heart*) bater com força; (*bombard*) bombardear; (*on piano etc*) martelar

**pour** /pɔː(r)/ *vt* deitar □ *vi* correr; (*rain*) chover torrencialmente. ~ **in/ out** (*of people*) afluir/sair em massa. ~ **off** *or* **out** esvaziar, vazar. ~**ing rain** chuva *f* torrencial

**pout** /paʊt/ *vt/i* ~ (**one's lips**) (*sulk*) fazer beicinho; (*in annoyance*) ficar de trombas □ *n* beicinho *m*

**poverty** /'pɒvətɪ/ *n* pobreza *f*, miséria *f*. ~**-stricken** *a* pobre

**powder** /'paʊdə(r)/ *n* pó *m*; (*for face*) pó-de-arroz *m* □ *vt* polvilhar; (*face*) empoar. ~**ed** *a* em pó. ~**-room** *n* toalete *m*, toucador *m*. ~**y** *a* como pó

**power** /'paʊə(r)/ *n* poder *m*; (*maths, mech*) potência *f*; (*energy*) energia *f*; (*electr*) corrente *f*. ~ **cut** corte *m* de energia, blecaute *m*. ~ **station** central *f* elétrica, (*P*) eléctrica. ~**ed by** movido a; (*jet etc*) de propulsão. ~**ful** *a* poderoso; (*mech*) potente. ~**less** *a* impotente

**practicable** /'præktɪkəbl/ *a* viável

**practical** /'præktɪkl/ *a* prático. ~ **joke** brincadeira *f* de mau gosto

**practically** /'præktɪklɪ/ *adv* praticamente

**practice** /'præktɪs/ *n* prática *f*; (*of law etc*) exercício *m*; (*sport*) treino *m*; (*clients*) clientela *f*. **in** ~ (*in fact*) na prática; (*well-trained*) em forma. **out of** ~ destreinado, sem prática. **put into** ~ pôr em prática

**practis|e** /'præktɪs/ *vt/i* (*skill, sport*) praticar, exercitar-se em; (*profession*) exercer; (*put into practice*) pôr em prática. ~**ed** *a* experimentado, experiente. ~**ing** *a* (*Catholic etc*) praticante

**practitioner** /præk'tɪʃənə(r)/ *n* praticante *mf*. **general** ~ médico *m* de clínica geral *or* de família

**pragmatic** /præg'mætɪk/ *a* pragmático

**prairie** /'preərɪ/ *n* pradaria *f*

**praise** /preɪz/ *vt* louvar, elogiar □ *n* elogio(s) *m*(*pl*), louvor(es) *m*(*pl*)

**praiseworthy** /'preɪzwɜːðɪ/ *a* louvável, digno de louvor

**pram** /præm/ *n* carrinho *m* de bebê, (*P*) bebé

**prance** /praːns/ *vi* (*of horse*) curvetear, empinar-se; (*of person*) pavonear-se

**prank** /præŋk/ *n* brincadeira *f* de mau gosto

**prattle** /'prætl/ *vi* tagarelar

**prawn** /prɔːn/ *n* camarão *m* grande, (*P*) gamba *f*

**pray** /preɪ/ *vi* rezar, orar

**prayer** /preə(r)/ *n* oração *f*. **the Lord's P~** o Padre-Nosso. ~**-book** *n* missal *m*

**pre-** /priː/ *pref* pré-

**preach** /priːtʃ/ *vt/i* pregar (**at, to** a). ~**er** *n* pregador *m*

**preamble** /priː'æmbl/ *n* preâmbulo *m*

**prearrange** /priːə'reɪndʒ/ *vt* combinar *or* arranjar de antemão

**precarious** /prɪ'keərɪəs/ *a* precário; (*of position*) instável, inseguro

**precaution** /prɪ'kɔːʃn/ *n* precaução *f*. ~**ary** *a* de precaução

**preced|e** /prɪ'siːd/ *vt* preceder. ~**ing** *a* precedente

**precedent** /'presɪdənt/ *n* precedente *m*

**precinct** /'priːsɪŋkt/ *n* precinto *m*; (*Amer: district*) circunscrição *f*. (**pedestrian**) ~ área *f* de pedestres, (*P*) zona *f* para peões

**precious** /'preʃəs/ *a* precioso

**precipice** /'presɪpɪs/ *n* precipício *m*

**precipitat|e** /prɪ'sɪpɪteɪt/ *vt* precipitar □ *a* /-ɪtət/ precipitado. ~**ion** /-'teɪʃn/ *n* precipitação *f*

**precis|e** /prɪ'saɪs/ *a* preciso; (*careful*) meticuloso. ~**ely** *adv* precisamente. ~**ion** /-'sɪʒn/ *n* precisão *f*

**preclude** /prɪ'kluːd/ *vt* evitar, excluir, impedir

**precocious** /prɪ'kəʊʃəs/ *a* precoce

**preconc|eived** /priːkən'siːvd/ *a* preconcebido. ~**eption** /priːkən'sepʃn/ *n* idéia *f* preconcebida

**precursor** /priː'kɜːsə(r)/ *n* precursor *m*

**predator** /'predətə(r)/ *n* animal *m* de rapina, predador *m*. ~**y** *a* predatório

**predecessor** /'priːdɪsesə(r)/ *n* predecessor *m*

**predicament** /prɪ'dɪkəmənt/ *n* situação *f* difícil

**predict** /prɪ'dɪkt/ *vt* predizer, prognosticar. ~**able** *a* previsível. ~**ion** /-ʃn/ *n* predição *f*, prognóstico *m*

**predominant** /prɪ'dɒmɪnənt/ *a* predominante, preponderante. ~**ly** *adv* predominantemente, preponderantemente

**predominate** /prɪ'dɒmɪneɪt/ *vi* predominar

**pre-eminent** /priː'emɪnənt/ *a* preeminente, superior

**pre-empt** /priː'empt/ *vt* adquirir por

preempção. ~ive *a* antecipado; (*mil*) preventivo

**preen** /pri:n/ *vt* alisar. ~ **o.s.** enfeitar-se

**prefab** /'pri:fæb/ *n* (*colloq*) casa *f* pré-fabricada. ~**ricated** /-'fæbrɪkeɪtɪd/ *a* pré-fabricado

**preface** /'prefɪs/ *n* prefácio *m*

**prefect** /'pri:fekt/ *n* aluno *m* autorizado a disciplinar outros; (*official*) prefeito *m*

**prefer** /prɪ'fɜ:(r)/ *vt* (*pt* preferred) preferir. ~**able** /'prefrəbl/ *a* preferível

**preferen|ce** /'prefrəns/ *n* preferência *f*. ~**tial** /-ə'renʃl/ *a* preferencial, privilegiado

**prefix** /'pri:fɪks/ *n* (*pl* -ixes) prefixo *m*

**pregnan|t** /'pregnənt/ *a* (*woman*) grávida; (*animal*) prenhe. ~**cy** *n* gravidez *f*

**prehistoric** /pri:hɪ'stɒrɪk/ *a* pré-histórico

**prejudice** /'predʒʊdɪs/ *n* preconceito *m*, idéia *f* preconcebida, prejuízo *m*; (*harm*) prejuízo *m* □ *vt* influenciar. ~**d** *a* com preconceitos

**preliminar|y** /prɪ'lɪmɪnəri/ *a* preliminar. ~**ies** *npl* preliminares *mpl*, preâmbulos *mpl*

**prelude** /'prelju:d/ *n* prelúdio *m*

**premarital** /pri:'mærɪtl/ *a* antes do casamento, pré-marital

**premature** /'premətjʊə(r)/ *a* prematuro

**premeditated** /pri:'medɪteɪtɪd/ *a* premeditado

**premier** /'premɪə(r)/ *a* primeiro □ *n* (*pol*) primeiro-ministro *m*

**premises** /'premɪsɪz/ *npl* local *m*, edifício *m*. **on the ~** neste estabelecimento, no local

**premium** /'pri:mɪəm/ *n* prêmio *m*, (*P*) prémio *m*. **at a ~** a peso de ouro

**premonition** /pri:mə'nɪʃn/ *n* pressentimento *m*

**preoccup|ation** /priːɒkjʊ'peɪʃn/ *n* preocupação *f*. ~**ied** /-'ɒkjʊpaɪd/ *a* preocupado

**preparation** /prepə'reɪʃn/ *n* preparação *f*. ~**s** preparativos *mpl*

**preparatory** /prɪ'pærətrɪ/ *a* preparatório. ~ **school** escola *f* primária particular

**prepare** /prɪ'peə(r)/ *vt/i* preparar(-se) (**for** para). ~**d to** pronto a, preparado para

**preposition** /prepə'zɪʃn/ *n* preposição *f*

**preposterous** /prɪ'pɒstərəs/ *a* absurdo, disparatado, ridículo

**prerequisite** /pri:'rekwɪzɪt/ *n* condição *f* prévia

**prerogative** /prɪ'rɒgətɪv/ *n* prerrogativa *f*

**Presbyterian** /prezbɪ'tɪərɪən/ *a & n* presbiteriano (*m*)

**prescri|be** /prɪ'skraɪb/ *vt* prescrever; (*med*) receitar, prescrever. ~**ption** /-ɪpʃn/ *n* prescrição *f*; (*med*) receita *f*

**presence** /'prezns/ *n* presença *f*. ~ **of mind** presença *f* de espírito

**present**[1] /'preznt/ *a & n* presente (*mf*). **at** ~ no momento, presentemente

**present**[2] /'preznt/ *n* (*gift*) presente *m*

**present**[3] /prɪ'zent/ *vt* apresentar; (*film etc*) dar. ~ **sb with** oferecer a alg. ~**able** *a* apresentável. ~**ation** /prezn'teɪʃn/ *n* apresentação *f*. ~**er** *n* apresentador *m*

**presently** /'prezntlɪ/ *adv* dentro em pouco, daqui a pouco; (*Amer: now*) neste momento

**preservative** /prɪ'zɜ:vətɪv/ *n* preservativo *m*

**preserv|e** /prɪ'zɜ:v/ *vt* preservar; (*maintain; culin*) conservar □ *n* reserva *f*; (*fig*) área *f*, terreno *m*; (*jam*) compota *f*. ~**ation** /prezə'veɪʃn/ *n* conservação *f*

**preside** /prɪ'zaɪd/ *vi* presidir (**over** a)

**presiden|t** /'prezɪdənt/ *n* presidente *mf*. ~**cy** *n* presidência *f*. ~**tial** /-'denʃl/ *a* presidencial

**press** /pres/ *vt/i* carregar (**on** em); (*squeeze*) espremer; (*urge*) pressionar; (*iron*) passar a ferro □ *n* imprensa *f*; (*mech*) prensa *f*; (*for wine*) lagar *m*. **be ~ed for** estar apertado com falta de. ~ **on** (**with**) continuar (com), prosseguir (com). ~ **conference** entrevista *f* coletiva. ~-**stud** *n* mola *f*, botão *m* de pressão

**pressing** /'presɪŋ/ *a* premente, urgente

**pressure** /'preʃə(r)/ *n* pressão *f* □ *vt* fazer pressão sobre. ~-**cooker** *n* panela *f* de pressão. ~ **group** grupo *m* de pressão

**pressurize** /'preʃəraɪz/ *vt* pressionar, fazer pressão sobre

**prestige** /pre'sti:ʒ/ *n* prestígio *m*

**prestigious** /pre'stɪdʒəs/ *a* prestigioso

**presumably** /prɪ'zju:məblɪ/ *adv* provavelmente

**presum|e** /prɪ'zju:m/ *vt* presumir. ~**e to** tomar a liberdade de, atrever-se a. ~**ption** /-'zʌmpʃn/ *n* presunção *f*

**presumptuous** /prɪ'zʌmptʃʊəs/ *a* presunçoso

**pretence** /prɪ'tens/ *n* fingimento *m*; (*claim*) pretensão *f*; (*pretext*) desculpa *f*, pretexto *m*

**pretend** /prɪ'tend/ *vt/i* fingir (**to do** fazer). ~ **to** (*lay claim to*) ter pretensões a, ser pretendente a; (*profess to have*) pretender ter

**pretentious** /prɪˈtenʃəs/ a pretencioso

**pretext** /ˈpriːtekst/ n pretexto m

**pretty** /ˈprɪtɪ/ a (-ier, -iest) bonito, lindo □ adv bastante

**prevail** /prɪˈveɪl/ vi prevalecer. ~ on sb to convencer alguéma. ~ing a dominante

**prevalen|t** /ˈprevələnt/ a geral, dominante. ~ce n frequência f

**prevent** /prɪˈvent/ vt impedir (from doing de fazer). ~able a que se pode evitar, evitável. ~ion /-ʃn/ n prevenção f. ~ive a preventivo

**preview** /ˈpriːvjuː/ n pré-estréia f, (P) ante-estréia f

**previous** /ˈpriːvɪəs/ a precedente, anterior. ~ to antes de. ~ly adv antes, anteriormente

**pre-war** /priːˈwɔː(r)/ a do pré-guerra, (P) de antes da guerra

**prey** /preɪ/ n presa f □ vi ~ on dar caça a; (worry) preocupar, atormentar. bird of ~ ave f de rapina, predador m

**price** /praɪs/ n preço m □ vt marcar o preço de. ~less a inestimável; (colloq: amusing) impagável

**prick** /prɪk/ vt picar, furar □ n picada f. ~ up one's ears arrebitar a(s) orelha(s)

**prickl|e** /ˈprɪkl/ n pico m, espinho m; (sensation) picada f. ~y a espinhoso, que pica; (person) irritável

**pride** /praɪd/ n orgulho m □ vpr ~ o.s. on orgulhar-se de

**priest** /priːst/ n padre m, sacerdote m. ~hood n sacerdócio m; (clergy) clero m

**prim** /prɪm/ a (primmer, primmest) formal, cheio de nove-horas; (prudish) pudico

**primary** /ˈpraɪmərɪ/ a primário; (chief, first) primeiro. ~ school escola f primária

**prime**[1] /praɪm/ a primeiro, principal; (first-rate) de primeira qualidade. P~ Minister Primeiro-Ministro m. ~ number número m primo

**prime**[2] /praɪm/ vt aprontar, aprestar; (with facts) preparar; (surface) preparar, aparelhar. ~r /-ə(r)/ n (paint) aparelho m

**primeval** /praɪˈmiːvl/ a primitivo

**primitive** /ˈprɪmɪtɪv/ a primitivo

**primrose** /ˈprɪmrəʊz/ n primavera f, prímula f

**prince** /prɪms/ n príncipe m

**princess** /prɪnˈses/ n princesa f

**principal** /ˈprɪnsəpl/ a principal □ n (schol) diretor m, (P) director m. ~ly adv principalmente

**principle** /ˈprɪnsəpl/ n princípio m. in/on ~ em/por princípio

**print** /prɪnt/ vt imprimir; (write) escrever em letra de imprensa □ n marca f, impressão f; (letters) letra f de imprensa; (photo) prova (fotográfica) f; (engraving) gravura f. out of ~ esgotado. ~-out n cópia f impressa. ~ed matter impressos mpl

**print|er** /ˈprɪntə(r)/ n tipógrafo m; (comput) impressora f. ~ing n impressão f, tipografia f

**prior** /ˈpraɪə(r)/ a anterior, precedente. ~ to antes de

**priority** /praɪˈɒrətɪ/ n prioridade f

**prise** /praɪz/ vt forçar (com alavanca). ~ open arrombar

**prison** /ˈprɪzn/ n prisão f. ~er n prisioneiro m

**pristine** /ˈprɪstiːn/ a primitivo; (condition) perfeito, como novo

**privacy** /ˈprɪvəsɪ/ n privacidade f, intimidade f; (solitude) isolamento m

**private** /ˈpraɪvət/ a privado; (confidential) confidencial; (lesson, life, house etc) particular; (ceremony) íntimo □ n soldado m raso. in ~ em particular; (of ceremony) na intimidade. ~ly adv particularmente; (inwardly) no fundo, interiormente

**privet** /ˈprɪvɪt/ n (bot) alfena f, ligustro m

**privilege** /ˈprɪvəlɪdʒ/ n privilégio m. ~d a privilegiado. be ~d to ter o privilégio de

**prize** /praɪz/ n prêmio m, (P) prémio m □ a premiado; (fool etc) perfeito □ vt ter em grande apreço, apreciar muito. ~-giving n distribuição f de prêmios, (P) prémios. ~-winner n premiado m, vencedor m

**pro**[1] /prəʊ/ n the ~s and cons os prós e os contras

**pro-** /prəʊ/ pref (acting for) pro-; (favouring) pró-

**probab|le** /ˈprɒbəbl/ a provável. ~ility /-ˈbɪlətɪ/ n probabilidade f. ~ly adv provavelmente

**probation** /prəˈbeɪʃn/ n (testing) estágio m, tirocínio m; (jur) liberdade f condicional. ~ary a probatório

**probe** /prəʊb/ n (med) sonda f; (fig: investigation) inquérito m □ vt/i ~ (into) sondar, investigar

**problem** /ˈprɒbləm/ n problema m □ a difícil. ~atic /-ˈmætɪk/ a problemático

**procedure** /prəˈsiːdʒə(r)/ n procedimento m, processo m, norma f

**proceed** /prəˈsiːd/ vi prosseguir, ir para diante, avançar. ~ to do passar a fazer. ~ with sth continuar or avançar com alguma coisa. ~ing n procedimento m

**proceedings** /prəˈsiːdɪŋz/ npl (jur) processo m; (report) ata f, (P) acta f

**proceeds** /ˈprəʊsiːdz/ *npl* produto *m*, luco *m*, proventos *mpl*

**process** /ˈprəʊses/ *n* processo *m* □ *vt* tratar; (*photo*) revelar. **in ~** em curso. **in the ~ of doing** sendo feito

**procession** /prəˈseʃn/ *n* procissão *f*, cortejo *m*

**procl|aim** /prəˈkleɪm/ *vt* proclamar. **~amation** /prɒkləˈmeɪʃn/ *n* proclamação *f*

**procure** /prəˈkjʊə(r)/ *vt* obter

**prod** /prɒd/ *vt/i* (*pt* **prodded**) (*push*) empurrar; (*poke*) espetar; (*fig: urge*) incitar □ *n* espetadela *f*; (*fig*) incitamento *m*

**prodigal** /ˈprɒdɪgl/ *a* pródigo

**prodigious** /prəˈdɪdʒəs/ *a* prodigioso

**prodigy** /ˈprɒdɪdʒɪ/ *n* prodígio *m*

**produc|e[1]** /prəˈdjuːs/ *vt/i* produzir; (*bring out*) tirar, extrair; (*show*) apresentar, mostrar; (*cause*) causar, provocar; (*theat*) pôr em cena. **~er** *n* produtor *m*, (P) -'dʌkʃn/ *n* produção *f*; (*theat*) encenação *f*

**produce[2]** /ˈprɒdjuːs/ *n* produtos (agrícolas) *mpl*

**product** /ˈprɒdʌkt/ *n* produto *m*

**productive** /prəˈdʌktɪv/ *a* produtivo. **~ity** /prɒdʌkˈtɪvətɪ/ *n* produtividade *f*

**profan|e** /prəˈfeɪn/ *a* profano; (*blasphemous*) blasfemo. **~ity** /-ˈfænətɪ/ *n* profanidade *f*

**profess** /prəˈfes/ *vt* professar. **~ to do** alegar fazer

**profession** /prəˈfeʃn/ *n* profissão *f*. **~al** *a* profissional; (*well done*) de profissional; (*person*) que exerce uma profissão liberal □ *n* profissional *mf*

**professor** /prəˈfesə(r)/ *n* professor (universitário) *m*

**proficien|t** /prəˈfɪʃnt/ *a* proficiente, competente. **~cy** *n* proficiência *f*, competência *f*

**profile** /ˈprəʊfaɪl/ *n* perfil *m*

**profit** /ˈprɒfɪt/ *n* proveito *m*; (*money*) lucro *m* □ *vi* (*pt* **profited**) **~ by** aproveitar-se de; **~ from** tirar proveito de. **~able** *a* proveitoso; (*of business*) lucrativo, rentável

**profound** /prəˈfaʊnd/ *a* profundo. **~ly** *adv* profundamente

**profus|e** /prəˈfjuːs/ *a* profuso. **~ely** *adv* profusamente, em abundância. **~ion** /-ʒn/ *n* profusão *f*

**program** /ˈprəʊgræm/ *n* (*computer*) **~** programa *m* □ *vt* (*pt* **programmed**) programar. **~mer** *n* programador *m*

**programme** /ˈprəʊgræm/ *n* programa *m*

**progress[1]** /ˈprəʊgres/ *n* progresso *m*. **in ~** em curso, em andamento

**progress[2]** /prəˈgres/ *vi* progredir. **~ion** /-ʃn/ *n* progressão *f*

**progressive** /prəˈgresɪv/ *a* progressivo; (*reforming*) progressista. **~ly** *adv* progressivamente

**prohibit** /prəˈhɪbɪt/ *vt* proibir (**sb from doing** alg de fazer)

**project[1]** /prəˈdʒekt/ *vt* projetar, (P) projectar □ *vi* ressaltar, sobressair. **~ion** /-ʃn/ *n* projeção *f*, (P) projecção *f*; (*protruding*) saliência *f*, ressalto *m*

**project[2]** /ˈprɒdʒekt/ *n* projeto *m*, (P) projecto *m*

**projectile** /prəˈdʒektaɪl/ *n* projétil *m*, (P) projéctil *m*

**projector** /prəˈdʒektə(r)/ *n* projetor *m*, (P) projector *m*

**proletari|at** /prəʊlɪˈteərɪət/ *n* proletariado *m*. **~an** *a* & *n* proletário (*m*)

**proliferat|e** /prəˈlɪfəreɪt/ *vi* proliferar. **~ion** /-ˈreɪʃn/ *n* proliferação *f*

**prolific** /prəˈlɪfɪk/ *a* prolífico

**prologue** /ˈprəʊlɒg/ *n* prólogo *m*

**prolong** /prəˈlɒŋ/ *vt* prolongar

**promenade** /prɒməˈnɑːd/ *n* passeio *m* □ *vt/i* passear

**prominen|t** /ˈprɒmɪnənt/ *a* (*projecting; important*) proeminente; (*conspicuous*) bem à vista, conspícuo. **~ce** *n* proeminência *f*. **~tly** *adv* bem à vista

**promiscu|ous** /prəˈmɪskjʊəs/ *a* promíscuo, de costumes livres. **~ity** /prɒmɪsˈkjuːətɪ/ *n* promiscuidade *f*, liberdade *f* de costumes

**promis|e** /ˈprɒmɪs/ *n* promessa *f* □ *vt/i* prometer. **~ing** *a* prometedor, promissor

**promot|e** /prəˈməʊt/ *vt* promover. **~ion** /-ˈməʊʃn/ *n* promoção *f*

**prompt** /prɒmpt/ *a* pronto, rápido, imediato; (*punctual*) pontual □ *adv* em ponto □ *vt* levar; (*theat*) soprar, servir de ponto para. **~er** *n* ponto *m*. **~ly** *adv* prontamente; pontualmente. **~ness** *n* prontidão *f*

**prone** /prəʊn/ *a* deitado (de bruços). **~ to** propenso a

**prong** /prɒŋ/ *n* (*of fork*) dente *m*

**pronoun** /ˈprəʊnaʊn/ *n* pronome *m*

**pron|ounce** /prəˈnaʊns/ *vt* pronunciar; (*declare*) declarar. **~ounced** *a* pronunciado. **~ouncement** *n* declaração *f*. **~unciation** /-ʌnsɪˈeɪʃn/ *n* pronúncia *f*

**proof** /pruːf/ *n* prova *f*; (*of liquor*) teor *m* alcoólico, graduação *f* □ *a* **~ against** à prova de

**prop[1]** /prɒp/ *n* suporte *m*; (*lit & fig*) apoio *m*, esteio *m* □ *vt* (*pt* **propped**) sustentar, suportar, apoiar. **~ against** apoiar contra

**prop**[2] /prɒp/ *n* (*colloq: theat*) acessório *m*, (*P*) adereço *m*

**propaganda** /prɒpə'gændə/ *n* propaganda *f*

**propagat|e** /'prɒpəgeɪt/ *vt/i* propagar(-se). **~ion** /-'geɪʃn/ *n* propagação *f*

**propel** /prə'pel/ *vt* (*pt* **propelled**) propulsionar, impelir

**propeller** /prə'pelə(r)/ *n* hélice *f*

**proper** /'prɒpə(r)/ *a* correto, (*P*) correcto; (*seemly*) conveniente; (*real*) propriamente dito; (*colloq: thorough*) belo. **~ly** *adv* corretamente, (*P*) correctamente; (*rightly*) com razão, acertadamente; (*accurately*) apropriadamente

**property** /'prɒpətɪ/ *n* (*house*) imóvel *m*; (*land, quality*) propriedade *f*; (*possessions*) bens *mpl*

**prophecy** /'prɒfəsɪ/ *n* profecia *f*

**prophesy** /'prɒfɪsaɪ/ *vt/i* profetizar. **~ that** predizer que

**prophet** /'prɒfɪt/ *n* profeta *m*. **~ic** /prə'fetɪk/ *a* profético

**proportion** /prə'pɔːʃn/ *n* proporção *f*. **~al, ~ate** *adjs* proporcional

**proposal** /prə'pəʊzl/ *n* proposta *f*; (*of marriage*) pedido *m* de casamento

**propos|e** /prə'pəʊz/ *vt* propor □ *vi* pedir em casamento. **~e to do** propor-se fazer. **~ition** /prɒpə'zɪʃn/ *n* proposição *f*; (*colloq: matter*) caso *m*, questão *f*

**propound** /prə'paʊnd/ *vt* propor

**proprietor** /prə'praɪətə(r)/ *n* proprietário *m*

**propriety** /prə'praɪətɪ/ *n* propriedade *f*, correção *f*, (*P*) correcção *f*

**propulsion** /prə'pʌlʃn/ *n* propulsão *f*

**prosaic** /prə'zeɪk/ *a* prosaico

**prose** /prəʊz/ *n* prosa *f*

**prosecut|e** /'prɒsɪkjuːt/ *vt* (*jur*) processar. **~ion** /-'kjuːʃn/ *n* (*jur*) acusação *f*

**prospect**[1] /'prɒspekt/ *n* perspectiva *f*

**prospect**[2] /prə'spekt/ *vt/i* pesquisar, prospectar

**prospective** /prə'spektɪv/ *a* futuro; (*possible*) provável

**prosper** /'prɒspə(r)/ *vi* prosperar

**prosper|ous** /'prɒspərəs/ *a* próspero. **~ity** /-'sperətɪ/ *n* prosperidade *f*

**prostitut|e** /'prɒstɪtjuːt/ *n* prostituta *f*. **~ion** /-'tjuːʃn/ *n* prostituição *f*

**prostrate** /'prɒstreɪt/ *a* prostrado

**protect** /prə'tekt/ *vt* proteger. **~ion** /-ʃn/ *n* proteção *f*, (*P*) protecção *f*. **~ive** *a* protetor, (*P*) protector. **~or** *n* protetor *m*, (*P*) protector *m*

**protégé** /'prɒtɪʒeɪ/ *n* protegido *m*. **~e** *n* protegida *f*

**protein** /'prəʊtiːn/ *n* proteína *f*

**protest**[1] /'prəʊtest/ *n* protesto *m*

**protest**[2] /prə'test/ *vt/i* protestar. **~er** *n* (*pol*) manifestante *mf*

**Protestant** /'prɒtɪstənt/ *a & n* protestante (*mf*). **~ism** /-ɪzəm/ *n* protestantismo *m*

**protocol** /'prəʊtəkɒl/ *n* protocolo *m*

**prototype** /'prəʊtətaɪp/ *n* protótipo *m*

**protract** /prə'trækt/ *vt* prolongar, arrastar

**protrud|e** /prə'truːd/ *vi* sobressair, sair do alinhamento. **~ing** *a* saliente

**proud** /praʊd/ *a* (**er, -est**) orgulhoso. **~ly** *adv* orgulhosamente

**prove** /pruːv/ *vt* provar, demonstrar □ *vi* **~ (to be) easy**/*etc* verificar-se ser fácil/*etc*. **~ o.s.** dar provas de si. **~n** /-n/ *a* provado

**proverb** /'prɒvɜːb/ *n* provérbio *m*. **~ial** /prə'vɜːbɪəl/ *a* proverbial

**provid|e** /prə'vaɪd/ *vt* prover, munir (**sb with sth** alg de alguma coisa) □ *vi* **~ for** providenciar para; (*person*) prover de, cuidar de; (*allow for*) levar em conta. **~ed, ~ing (that)** *conj* desde que, contanto que

**providence** /'prɒvɪdəns/ *n* providência *f*

**province** /'prɒvɪns/ *n* província *f*; (*fig*) competência *f*

**provincial** /prə'vɪnʃl/ *a* provincial; (*rustic*) provinciano

**provision** /prə'vɪʒn/ *n* provisão *f*; (*stipulation*) disposição *f*. **~s** (*pl food*) provisões *fpl*

**provisional** /prə'vɪʒənl/ *a* provisório. **~ly** *adv* provisoriamente

**proviso** /prə'vaɪzəʊ/ *n* (*pl* **-os**) condição *f*

**provo|ke** /prə'vəʊk/ *vt* provocar. **~cation** /prɒvə'keɪʃn/ *n* provocação *f*. **~cative** /-'vɒkətɪv/ *a* provocante

**prowess** /'praʊɪs/ *n* proeza *f*, façanha *f*

**prowl** /praʊl/ *vi* rondar □ *n* **be on the ~** andar à espreita. **~er** *n* pessoa *f* que anda à espreita

**proximity** /prɒk'sɪmətɪ/ *n* proximidade *f*

**proxy** /'prɒksɪ/ *n* **by ~** por procuração

**prude** /pruːd/ *n* puritano *m*, pudico *m*

**pruden|t** /'pruːdnt/ *a* prudente. **~ce** *n* prudência *f*

**prune**[1] /pruːn/ *n* ameixa *f* seca

**prune**[2] /pruːn/ *vt* podar

**pry** /praɪ/ *vi* bisbilhotar. **~ into** meter o nariz em, intrometer-se em

**psalm** /sɑːm/ *n* salmo *m*

**pseudo-** /'sjuːdəʊ/ *pref* pseudo-

**pseudonym** /'sjuːdənɪm/ *n* pseudônimo *m*, (*P*) pseudónimo *m*

**psychiatr|y** /saɪ'kaɪətrɪ/ *n* psiquiatria *f*. **~ic** /-ɪ'rætrɪk/ *a* psiquiátrico. **~ist** *n* psiquiatra *mf*

**psychic** /'saɪkɪk/ a psíquico; (*person*) com capacidade de telepatia

**psychoanalys|e** /saɪkəʊ'ænəlaɪz/ vt psicanalisar. ~**t** /-ɪst/ n psicanalista mf

**psychoanalysis** /saɪkəʊə'næləsɪs/ n psicanálise f

**psycholog|y** /saɪ'kɒlədʒɪ/ n psicologia f. ~**ical** /-ə'lɒdʒɪkl/ a psicológico. ~**ist** n psicólogo m

**psychopath** /'saɪkəʊpæθ/ n psicopata mf

**pub** /pʌb/ n pub m

**puberty** /'pjuːbətɪ/ n puberdade f

**public** /'pʌblɪk/ a público; (*holiday*) feriado. **in ~** em público. **~ house** pub m. **~ relations** relações fpl públicas. **~ school** escola f particular; (*Amer*) escola f oficial. **~-spirited** a de espírito cívico, patriótico. **~ly** adv publicamente

**publication** /pʌblɪ'keɪʃn/ n publicação f

**publicity** /pʌ'blɪsətɪ/ n publicidade f

**publicize** /'pʌblɪsaɪz/ vt fazer publicidade de

**publish** /'pʌblɪʃ/ vt publicar. ~**er** n editor m. ~**ing** n publicação f. ~**ing house** editora f

**pucker** /'pʌkə(r)/ vt/i franzir

**pudding** /'pʊdɪŋ/ n pudim m; (*dessert*) doce m

**puddle** /'pʌdl/ n poça f de água, charco m

**puerile** /'pjʊəraɪl/ a pueril

**puff** /pʌf/ n baforada f □ vt/i lançar baforadas; (*breathe hard*) arquejar, ofegar. **~ at** (*cigar etc*) dar baforadas em. **~ out** (*swell*) inchar(-se). **~-pastry** n massa f folhada

**puffy** /'pʌfɪ/ a inchado

**pugnacious** /pʌg'neɪʃəs/ a belicoso, combativo

**pull** /pʊl/ vt/i puxar; (*muscle*) distender □ n puxão m; (*fig: influence*) influência f, empenho m. **give a ~** dar um puxão. **~ a face** fazer uma careta. **~ one's weight** (*fig*) fazer a sua quota-parte. **~ sb's leg** brincar com alguém, meter-se com alguém. **~ away or out** (*auto*) arrancar. **~ down** puxar para baixo; (*building*) demolir. **~ in** (*auto*) encostar-se. **~ off** tirar; (*fig*) sair-se bem em, conseguir alcançar. **~ out** partir; (*extract*) arrancar, tirar. **~ through** sair-se bem. **~ o.s. together** recompor-se, refazer-se. **~ up** puxar para cima; (*uproot*) arrancar; (*auto*) parar

**pulley** /'pʊlɪ/ n roldana f

**pullover** /'pʊləʊvə(r)/ n pulôver m

**pulp** /pʌlp/ n polpa f; (*for paper*) pasta f de papel

**pulpit** /'pʊlpɪt/ n púlpito m

**pulsat|e** /pʌl'seɪt/ vi pulsar, bater, palpitar. ~**ion** /-'seɪʃn/ n pulsação f

**pulse** /pʌls/ n pulso m. **feel sb's ~** tirar o pulso de alguém

**pulverize** /'pʌlvəraɪz/ vt (*grind, defeat*) pulverizar

**pummel** /'pʌml/ vt (*pt* **pummelled**) esmurrar

**pump**[1] /pʌmp/ n bomba f □ vt/i bombear; (*person*) arrancar or extrair informações de. **~ up** encher com bomba

**pump**[2] /pʌmp/ n (*shoe*) sapato m

**pumpkin** /'pʌmpkɪn/ n abóbora f

**pun** /pʌn/ n trocadilho m, jogo m de palavras

**punch**[1] /pʌntʃ/ vt esmurrar, dar um murro or soco; (*perforate*) furar, perfurar; (*a hole*) fazer □ n murro m, soco m; (*device*) furador m. **~-line** n remate m. **~-up** n (*colloq*) pancadaria f

**punch**[2] /pʌntʃ/ n (*drink*) ponche m

**punctual** /'pʌŋktʃʊəl/ a pontual. ~**ity** /-'ælətɪ/ n pontualidade f

**punctuat|e** /'pʌŋktʃʊeɪt/ vt pontuar. ~**ion** /-'eɪʃn/ n pontuação f

**puncture** /'pʌŋktʃə(r)/ n (*in tyre*) furo m □ vt/i furar

**pundit** /'pʌndɪt/ n autoridade f, sumidade f

**pungent** /'pʌndʒənt/ a acre, pungente

**punish** /'pʌnɪʃ/ vt punir, castigar. ~**able** a punível. ~**ment** n punição f, castigo m

**punitive** /'pjuːnɪtɪv/ a (*expedition, measure etc*) punitivo; (*taxation etc*) penalizador

**punt** /pʌnt/ n (*boat*) chalana f

**punter** /'pʌntə(r)/ n (*gambler*) jogador m; (*colloq: customer*) freguês m

**puny** /'pjuːnɪ/ a (-ier, -iest) fraco, débil

**pup(py)** /'pʌp(ɪ)/ n cachorro m, cachorrinho m

**pupil** /'pjuːpl/ n aluno m; (*of eye*) pupila f

**puppet** /'pʌpɪt/ n (*lit & fig*) fantoche m, marionete f

**purchase** /'pɜːtʃəs/ vt comprar (**from sb** de alg) □ n compra f. ~**r** /-ə(r)/ n comprador m

**pur|e** /'pjʊə(r)/ a (-er, -est) puro. ~**ely** adv puramente. ~**ity** n pureza f

**purgatory** /'pɜːgətrɪ/ n purgatório m

**purge** /pɜːdʒ/ vt purgar; (*pol*) sanear □ n (*med*) purgante m; (*pol*) saneamento m

**purif|y** /'pjʊərɪfaɪ/ vt purificar. ~**ication** /-ɪ'keɪʃn/ n purificação f

**puritan** /'pjʊərɪtən/ n puritano m. ~**ical** /-'tænɪkl/ a puritano

**purple** /'pɜːpl/ a roxo, purpúreo □ n roxo m, púrpura f

**purport** /pə'pɔːt/ *vt* dizer-se, (P) dar a entender. ~ **to be** pretender ser

**purpose** /'pɜːpəs/ *n* propósito *m*; (*determination*) firmeza *f*. **on** ~ de propósito. **to no** ~ em vão. ~**-built** *a* construído especialmente.

**purposely** /'pɜːpəslɪ/ *adv* de propósito, propositadamente

**purr** /pɜːr/ *n* ronrom *m* □ *vi* ronronar

**purse** /pɜːs/ *n* carteira *f*; (*Amer*) bolsa *f* □ *vt* franzir

**pursue** /pə'sjuː/ *vt* perseguir; (*go on with*) prosseguir; (*engage in*) entregar-se a, dedicar-se a. ~**r** /-ə(r)/ *n* perseguidor *m*

**pursuit** /pə'sjuːt/ *n* perseguição *f*, (*fig*) atividade *f*, (P) actividade *f*

**pus** /pʌs/ *n* pus *m*

**push** /pʊʃ/ *vt/i* empurrar; (*button*) apertar; (*thrust*) enfiar; (*colloq: recommend*) insistir □ *n* empurrão *m*; (*effort*) esforço *m*; (*drive*) energia *f*. **be** ~**ing thirty/etc** (*colloq*) estar beirando os trinta/*etc*. **give the** ~ **to** (*sl*) dar o fora em alguém. ~ **s.o. around** fazer alguém de bobo. ~ **back** repelir. ~**-chair** *n* carrinho *m* (de criança). ~**er** *n* fornecedor *m* (de droga). ~ **off** (*sl*) dar o fora. ~ **on** continuar. ~**-over** *n* canja *f*, coisa *f* fácil. ~ **up** (*lift*) levantar; (*prices*) forçar o aumento de. ~**-up** *n* (*Amer*) flexão *f*. ~**y** *a* (*colloq*) agressivo, furão

**put** /pʊt/ *vt/i* (*pt* put, *pres p* putting) colocar, pôr; (*question*) fazer. ~ **the damage at a million** estimar os danos em um milhão. **I'd** ~ **it at a thousand** eu diria mil. ~ **sth tactfully** dizer alg coisa com tato. ~ **across** comunicar. ~ **away** guardar. ~ **back** repor; (*delay*) retardar, atrasar. ~ **by** pôr de lado. ~ **down** pôr em lugar baixo; (*write*) anotar; (*pay*) pagar; (*suppress*) sufocar, reprimir. ~ **forward** (*plan*) submeter. ~ **in** (*insert*) introduzir; (*fix*) instalar; (*submit*) submeter. ~ **in for** fazer um pedido, candidatar-se. ~ **off** (*postpone*) adiar; (*disconcert*) desanimar; (*displease*) desagradar. ~ **s.o. off sth** tirar o gosto de alguém por alg coisa. ~ **on** (*clothes*) pôr; (*radio*) ligar; (*light*) acender; (*speed*, *weight*) ganhar; (*accent*) adotar. ~ **out** pôr para fora; (*stretch*) esticar; (*extinguish*) extinguir, apagar; (*disconcert*) desconcertar; (*inconvenience*) incomodar. ~ **up** levantar; (*building*) erguer, construir; (*notice*) colocar; (*price*) aumentar; (*guest*) hospedar; (*offer*) oferecer. ~**-up job** embuste *m*. ~ **up with** suportar

**putrefy** /'pjuːtrɪfaɪ/ *vi* putrefazer-se, apodrecer

**putty** /'pʌtɪ/ *n* massa de vidraceiro *f*, betume *m*

**puzzl|e** /'pʌzl/ *n* puzzle *m*, quebra-cabeça *m* □ *vt* deixar perplexo, intrigar □ *vi* quebrar a cabeça. ~**ing** *a* intrigante

**pygmy** /'pɪgmɪ/ *n* pigmeu *m*

**pyjamas** /pə'dʒɑːməz/ *npl* pijama *m*

**pylon** /'paɪlɒn/ *n* poste *m*

**pyramid** /'pɪrəmɪd/ *n* pirâmide *f*

**python** /'paɪθn/ *n* píton *m*

# Q

**quack**[1] /kwæk/ *n* (*of duck*) grasnido *m* □ *vi* grasnar

**quack**[2] /kwæk/ *n* charlatão *m*

**quadrangle** /'kwɒdræŋgl/ *n* quadrângulo *m*; (*of college*) pátio *m* quadrangular

**quadruped** /'kwɒdrʊped/ *n* quadrúpede *m*

**quadruple** /'kwɒdrʊpl/ *a* & *n* quádruplo (*m*) □ *vt/i* /kwɒ'drʊpl/ quadruplicar. ~**ts** /-plɪts/ *npl* quadrigêmeos *mpl*, (P) quadrigémeos *mpl*

**quagmire** /'kwægmaɪə(r)/ *n* pântano *m*, lamaçal *m*

**quail** /kweɪl/ *n* codorniz *f*

**quaint** /kweɪnt/ *a* (-er, -est) pitoresco; (*whimsical*) estranho, bizarro

**quake** /kweɪk/ *vi* tremer □ *n* (*colloq*) tremor *m* de terra

**Quaker** /'kweɪkə(r)/ *n* quaker *mf*, quacre *m*

**qualification** /kwɒlɪfɪ'keɪʃn/ *n* qualificação *f*; (*accomplishment*) habilitação *f*, (*diploma*) diploma *m*, título *m*; (*condition*) requisito *m*, condição *f*; (*fig*) restrição *f*, reserva *f*

**qualif|y** /'kwɒlɪfaɪ/ *vt* qualificar; (*fig: moderate*) atenuar, moderar; (*fig: limit*) pôr ressalvas or restrições a □ *vi* (*fig: be entitled to*) ter os requisitos (**for** para); (*sport*) classificar-se. **he** ~**ied as a vet** ele formou-se em veterinária. ~**ied** *a* formado; (*able*) qualificado, habilitado; (*moderated*) atenuado; (*limited*) limitado

**quality** /'kwɒlətɪ/ *n* qualidade *f*

**qualm** /kwɑːm/ *n* escrúpulo *m*

**quandary** /'kwɒndərɪ/ *n* dilema *m*

**quantity** /'kwɒntətɪ/ *n* quantidade *f*

**quarantine** /'kwɒrəntiːn/ *n* quarentena *f*

**quarrel** /'kwɒrəl/ *n* zanga *f*, questão *f*, discussão *f* □ *vi* (*pt* quarrelled) zangar-se, questionar, discutir. ~**some** *a* conflituoso, brigão

**quarry**[1] /'kwɒrɪ/ *n* (*prey*) presa *f*, caça *f*

**quarry**[2] /'kwɒrɪ/ *n* (*excavation*) pedreira *f*

**quarter** /'kwɔːtə(r)/ *n* quarto *m*; (*of year*) trimestre *m*; (*Amer: coin*) quarto *m* de dólar, 25 cêntimos *mpl*; (*district*) bairro *m*, quarteirão *m*. ~s (*lodgings*) alojamento *m*, residência *f*; (*mil*) quartel *m* □ *vt* dividir em quarto; (*mil*) aquartelar. **from all** ~s de todos os lados. ~ **of an hour** quarto *m* de hora. (**a**) ~ **past six** seis e quinze. (**a**) ~ **to seven** quinze para as sete. ~-**final** *n* (*sport*) quarta *f* de final. ~**ly** *a* trimestral □ *adv* trimestralmente

**quartet** /kwɔː'tet/ *n* quarteto *m*

**quartz** /kwɔːts/ *n* quartzo *m* □ *a* (*watch etc*) de quartzo

**quash** /kwɒʃ/ *vt* reprimir; (*jur*) revogar

**quaver** /'kweɪvə(r)/ *vi* tremer, tremular □ *n* (*mus*) colcheia *f*

**quay** /kiː/ *n* cais *m*

**queasy** /'kwiːzɪ/ *a* delicado. **feel** ~ estar enjoado

**queen** /kwiːn/ *n* rainha *f*; (*cards*) dama *f*

**queer** /kwɪə(r)/ *a* (-**er**, -**est**) estranho; (*slightly ill*) indisposto; (*sl: homosexual*) bicha, maricas (*sl*); (*dubious*) suspeito □ *n* (*sl*) bicha *m*, maricas *m* (*sl*)

**quell** /kwel/ *vt* reprimir, abafar, sufocar

**quench** /kwentʃ/ *vt* (*fire, flame*) apagar; (*thirst*) matar, saciar

**query** /'kwɪərɪ/ *n* questão *f* □ *vt* pôr em dúvida

**quest** /kwest/ *n* busca *f*, procura *f*. **in** ~ **of** em demanda de

**question** /'kwestʃən/ *n* pergunta *f*, interrogação *f*; (*problem, affair*) questão *f* □ *vt* perguntar, interrogar; (*doubt*) pôr em dúvida *or* em causa. **in** ~ em questão *or* em causa. **out of the** ~ fora de toda a questão. **there's no** ~ **of** nem pensar em. **without** ~ sem dúvida. ~ **mark** ponto *m* de interrogação. ~**able** *a* discutível

**questionnaire** /kwestʃə'neə(r)/ *n* questionário *m*

**queue** /kjuː/ *n* fila *f*, (P) bicha *f* □ *vi* (*pres p* **queuing**) fazer fila, (P) fazer bicha

**quibble** /'kwɪbl/ *vi* tergiversar, usar de evasivas; (*raise petty objections*) discutir por coisas insignificantes

**quick** /kwɪk/ *a* (-**er**, -**est**) rápido □ *adv* depressa. **be** ~ despachar-se. **have a** ~ **temper** exaltar-se facilmente. ~**ly** *adv* rapidamente, depressa. ~**ness** *n* rapidez *f*

**quicken** /'kwɪkən/ *vt/i* apressar(-se)

**quicksand** /'kwɪksænd/ *n* areia *f* movediça

**quid** /kwɪd/ *n invar* (*sl*) libra *f*

**quiet** /'kwaɪət/ *a* (-**er**, -**est**) quieto, sossegado, tranquilo □ *n* quietude *f*, sossego *m*, tranqüilidade *f*. **keep** ~ calar-se. **on the** ~ às escondidas, na calada. ~**ly** *adv* sossegadamente, silenciosamente. ~**ness** *n* sossego *m*, tranquilidade *f*, calma *f*

**quieten** /'kwaɪətn/ *vt/i* sossegar, acalmar(-se)

**quilt** /kwɪlt/ *n* coberta *f* acolchoada. (**continental**) ~ edredão *m* de penas □ *vt* acolchoar

**quince** /kwɪns/ *n* marmelo *m*

**quintet** /kwɪn'tet/ *n* quinteto *m*

**quintuplets** /kwɪn'tjuːplɪts/ *npl* quíntuplos *mpl*

**quip** /kwɪp/ *n* piada *f* □ *vt* contar piadas

**quirk** /kwɜːk/ *n* mania *f*, singularidade *f*

**quit** /kwɪt/ *vt* (*pt* **quitted**) deixar □ *vi* ir-se embora; (*resign*) demitir-se. ~ **doing** (*Amer*) parar de fazer

**quite** /kwaɪt/ *adv* completamente, absolutamente; (*rather*) bastante. ~ (**so**)! isso mesmo!, exatamente! ~ **a few** bastante, alguns/algumas. ~ **a lot** bastante

**quiver** /'kwɪvə(r)/ *vi* tremer, estremecer □ *n* tremor *m*, estremecimento *m*

**quiz** /kwɪz/ *n* (*pl* **quizzes**) teste *m*; (*game*) concurso *m* □ *vt* (*pt* **quizzed**) interrogar

**quizzical** /'kwɪzɪkl/ *a* zombeteiro

**quorum** /'kwɔːrəm/ *n* quorum *m*

**quota** /'kwəʊtə/ *n* cota *f*, quota *f*

**quotation** /kwəʊ'teɪʃn/ *n* citação *f*; (*estimate*) orçamento *m*. ~ **marks** aspas *fpl*

**quote** /kwəʊt/ *vt* citar; (*estimate*) fazer um orçamento □ *n* (*colloq: passage*) citação *f*; (*colloq: estimate*) orçamento *m*

# R

**rabbi** /'ræbaɪ/ *n* rabino *m*

**rabbit** /'ræbɪt/ *n* coelho *m*

**rabble** /'ræbl/ *n* turba *f*. **the** ~ a ralé, a gentalha, o povinho

**rabid** /'ræbɪd/ *a* (*fig*) fanático, ferrenho; (*dog*) raivoso

**rabies** /'reɪbiːz/ *n* raiva *f*

**race**[1] /reɪs/ *n* corrida *f* □ *vt* (*horse*) fazer correr □ *vi* correr, dar uma corrida; (*rush*) ir em grande *or* a toda (a) velocidade. ~-**track** *n* pista *f*

**race**[2] /reɪs/ *n* (*group*) raça *f* □ *a* racial

**racecourse** /'reɪskɔːs/ *n* hipódromo *m*

**racehorse** /'reɪshɔ:s/ n cavalo m de corrida

**racial** /'reɪʃl/ a racial

**racing** /'reɪsɪŋ/ n corridas fpl. ~ **car** carro m de corridas

**racis|t** /'reɪsɪst/ a & n racista (mf). ~**m** /-zəm/ n racismo m

**rack¹** /ræk/ n (for luggage) porta-bagagem m, bagageiro m; (for plates) escorredor m de prato □ vt ~ **one's brains** dar tratos à imaginação

**rack²** /ræk/ n **go to** ~ **and ruin** arruinar-se; (of buildings etc) cair em ruínas

**racket¹** /'rækɪt/ n (sport) raquete f, (P) raqueta f

**racket²** /'rækɪt/ n (din) barulheira f; (swindle) roubalheira f; (sl: business) negociata f (colloq)

**racy** /'reɪsɪ/ a (-ier, -iest) vivo, vigoroso

**radar** /'reɪda:(r)/ n radar m □ a de radar

**radian|t** /'reɪdɪənt/ a radiante. ~**ce** n brilho m

**radiator** /'reɪdɪeɪtə(r)/ n radiador m

**radical** /'rædɪkl/ a & n radical (m)

**radio** /'reɪdɪəʊ/ n (pl -os) rádio f, (set) (aparelho de) rádio m □ vt transmitir pelo rádio. ~ **station** estação f de rádio, emissora f

**radioactiv|e** /reɪdɪəʊ'æktɪv/ a radioativo, (P) radioactivo. ~**ity** /'tɪvətɪ/ n radioatividade f, (P) radioactividade f

**radiograph|er** /reɪdɪ'ɒɡrəfə(r)/ n radiologista mf. ~**y** n radiografia f

**radish** /'rædɪʃ/ n rabanete m

**radius** /'reɪdɪəs/ n (pl -dii /-dɪaɪ/) raio m

**raffle** /'ræfl/ n rifa f □ vt rifar

**raft** /ra:ft/ n jangada f

**rafter** /'ra:ftə(r)/ n trave f, viga f

**rag¹** /ræɡ/ n farrapo m; (for wiping) trapo m; (pej: newspaper) jornaleco m. ~**s** npl farrapos mpl, andrajos mpl. **in** ~**s** maltrapilho. ~ **doll** boneca f de trapos

**rag²** /ræɡ/ vt (pt **ragged**) zombar de

**rage** /reɪdʒ/ n raiva f, fúria f □ vi estar furioso; (of storm) rugir; (of battle) estar acesa. **be all the** ~ (colloq) fazer furor, estar na moda (colloq)

**ragged** /'ræɡɪd/ a (clothes, person) esfarrapado, roto; (edge) esfiapado, esgarçado

**raid** /reɪd/ n (mil) ataque m; (by police) batida f; (by criminals) assalto m □ vt fazer um ataque or uma batida or um assalto. ~**er** n atacante m, assaltante m

**rail** /reɪl/ n (of stairs) corrimão m; (of ship) amurada f; (on balcony) parapeito m; (for train) trilho m; (for cur-tain) varão m. **by** ~ por estrada, (P) caminho de ferro

**railings** /'reɪlɪŋz/ npl grade f

**railroad** /'reɪlrəʊd/ n (Amer) = **railway**

**railway** /'reɪlweɪ/ n estrada f, (P) caminho m de ferro. ~ **line** linha f do trem. ~ **station** estação f ferroviária, (P) estação f de caminho de ferro

**rain** /reɪn/ n chuva f □ vi chover. ~ **forest** floresta f tropical. ~**-storm** n tempestade f com chuva. ~**-water** n água f da chuva

**rainbow** /'reɪnbəʊ/ n arco-íris m

**raincoat** /'reɪnkəʊt/ n impermeável m

**raindrop** /'reɪndrɒp/ n pingo m de chuva

**rainfall** /'reɪnfɔ:l/ n precipitação f, pluviosidade f

**rainy** /'reɪnɪ/ a (-ier, -iest) chuvoso

**raise** /reɪz/ vt levantar, erguer; (breed) criar; (voice) levantar; (question) fazer; (price etc) aumentar, subir; (funds) angariar; (loan) obter □ n (Amer) aumento m

**raisin** /'reɪzn/ n passa f

**rake** /reɪk/ n ancinho m □ vt juntar, alisar com ancinho; (search) revolver, remexer. ~ **in** (money) ganhar a rodos. ~**-off** n (colloq) percentagem f (colloq). ~ **up** desenterrar, ressuscitar

**rally** /'rælɪ/ vt/i reunir(-se); (reassemble) reagrupar(-se), reorganizar(-se); (health) restabelecer(-se); (strength) recuperar as forças □ n (recovery) recuperação f; (meeting) comício m, assembléia f; (auto) rally m, rali m

**ram** /ræm/ n (sheep) carneiro m □ vt (pt **rammed**) (beat down) calcar; (push) meter à força; (crash into) bater contra

**rambl|e** /'ræmbl/ n caminhada f, perambulação f □ vi perambular, vaguear. ~**e on** divagar. ~**er** n caminhante mf; (plant) trepadeira f. ~**ing** a (speech) desconexo

**ramp** /ræmp/ n rampa f

**rampage** /ræm'peɪdʒ/ vi causar distúrbios violentos

**rampant** /'ræmpənt/ a **be** ~ vicejar, florescer; (diseases etc) grassar

**rampart** /'ræmpa:t/ n baluarte m; (fig) defesa f

**ramshackle** /'ræmʃækl/ a (car) desconjuntado; (house) caindo aos pedaços

**ran** /ræn/ see **run**

**ranch** /ra:ntʃ/ n rancho m, estância f. ~**er** n rancheiro m

**rancid** /'rænsɪd/ a rançoso

**rancour** /'ræŋkə(r)/ n rancor m

**random** /'rændəm/ a feito, tirado etc ao acaso □ n at ~ ao acaso, a esmo, aleatoriamente

**randy** /'rændɪ/ a (-ier, -iest) lascivo, sensual

**rang** /ræŋ/ see ring

**range** /reɪndʒ/ n (distance) alcance m; (scope) âmbito m; (variety) gama f, variedade f; (stove) fogão m; (of voice) registo m, (P) registo m; (of temperature) variação f □ vt dispor, ordenar □ vi estender-se; (vary) variar. ~ of mountains cordilheira f, serra f. ~r n guarda m florestal

**rank**[1] /ræŋk/ n fila f, fileira f; (mil) posto m; (social position) classe f, categoria f □ vt/i ~ among contar(-se) entre. **the ~ and file** a massa

**rank**[2] /ræŋk/ a (-er, -est) (plants) luxuriante; (smell) fétido; (out-and-out) total

**ransack** /'rænsæk/ vt (search) espionar, revistar, remexer; (pillage) pilhar, saquear

**ransom** /'rænsəm/ n resgate m □ vt resgatar. **hold to ~** prender como refém

**rant** /rænt/ vi usar linguagem bombástica

**rap** /ræp/ n pancadinha f seca □ vt/i (pt rapped) bater, dar uma pancada seca em

**rape** /reɪp/ vt violar, estuprar □ n violação f, estupro m

**rapid** /'ræpɪd/ a rápido. ~ity /rə-'pɪdətɪ/ n rapidez f

**rapids** /'ræpɪdz/ npl rápidos mpl

**rapist** /'reɪpɪst/ n violador m, estuprador m

**rapport** /ræ'pɔː(r)/ n bom relacionamento m

**rapt** /ræpt/ a absorto. ~ **in** mergulhado em

**raptur|e** /'ræptʃə(r)/ n êxtase m. ~ous a extático; (welcome etc) entusiástico

**rar|e**[1] /reə(r)/ a (-er, -est) raro. ~ely adv raramente, raras vezes. ~ity n raridade f

**rare**[2] /reə(r)/ a (-er, -est) (culin) mal passado

**rarefied** /'reərɪfaɪd/ a rarefeito; (refined) requintado

**raring** /'reərɪŋ/ a ~ **to** (colloq) impaciente por, louco por (colloq)

**rascal** /'rɑːskl/ n (dishonest) patife m; (mischievous) maroto m

**rash**[1] /ræʃ/ n erupção f cutânea, irritação f na pele (colloq)

**rash**[2] /ræʃ/ a (-er, -est) imprudente, precipitado. ~ly adv imprudentemente, precipitadamente

**rasher** /'ræʃə(r)/ n fatia f (de presunto or de bacon)

**rasp** /rɑːsp/ n lixa f grossa, (P) lima f grossa

**raspberry** /'rɑːzbrɪ/ n framboesa f

**rasping** /'rɑːspɪŋ/ a áspero

**rat** /ræt/ n rato m, (P) ratazana f. ~ **race** (fig) luta renhida para vencer na vida, arrivismo m

**rate** /reɪt/ n (ratio) razão f; (speed) velocidade f; (price) tarifa f; (of exchange) (taxa m de) câmbio m; (of interest) taxa f. ~s (taxes) impostos mpl municipais, taxas fpl □ vt avaliar; (fig: consider) considerar. **at any ~** de qualquer modo, pelo menos. **at the ~ of** à razão de. **at this ~** desse jeito, desse modo

**ratepayer** /'reɪtpeɪə(r)/ n contribuinte mf

**rather** /'rɑːðə(r)/ adv (by preference) antes; (fairly) muito, bastante; (a little) um pouco. **I would ~ go** preferia ir

**ratif|y** /'rætɪfaɪ/ vt ratificar. ~ication /-ɪ'keɪʃn/ n ratificação f

**rating** /'reɪtɪŋ/ n (comm) rating m, (P) valor m; (sailor) praça f, marinheiro m; (radio, TV) índice m de audiência

**ratio** /'reɪʃɪəʊ/ n (pl -os) proporção f

**ration** /'ræʃn/ n ração f □ vt racionar

**rational** /'ræʃnəl/ a racional; (person) sensato, razoável. ~**ize** vt racionalizar

**rattle** /'rætl/ vt/i matraquear; (of door, window) bater; (of bottles) chocalhar; (colloq) agitar, mexer com os nervos de □ n (baby's toy) guizo m, chocalho m; (of football fan) matraca f; (sound) matraquear m, chocalhar m. ~ **off** despejar (colloq)

**rattlesnake** /'rætlsneɪk/ n cobra f cascavel

**raucous** /'rɔːkəs/ a áspero, rouco

**ravage** /'rævɪdʒ/ vt devastar, causar estragos a. ~**s** npl devastação f, estragos mpl

**rave** /reɪv/ vi delirar; (in anger) urrar. ~ **about** delirar (de entusiasmo) com

**raven** /'reɪvn/ n corvo m

**ravenous** /'rævənəs/ a esfomeado; (greedy) voraz

**ravine** /rə'viːn/ n ravina f, barranco m

**raving** /'reɪvɪŋ/ a ~ **lunatic** doido m varrido □ adv ~ **mad** loucamente

**ravish** /'rævɪʃ/ vt (rape) violar; (enrapture) arrebatar, encantar. ~**ing** a arrebatador, encantador

**raw** /rɔː/ a (-er, -est) cru; (not processed) bruto; (wound) em carne viva; (weather) frio e úmido, (P) húmido; (immature) inexperiente, verde. ~ **deal** tratamento m injusto. ~ **material** matéria-prima f

**ray** /reɪ/ n raio m

**raze** /reɪz/ vt arrasar

**razor** /'reɪzə(r)/ n navalha f de barba. **~-blade** n lâmina f de barbear

**re** /riː/ prep a respeito de, em referência a, relativo a

**re-** /riː/ pref re-

**reach** /riːtʃ/ vt chegar a atingir; (contact) contatar; (pass) passar □ vi estender-se, chegar □ n alcance m. **out of ~** fora de alcance. **~ for** estender a mão para agarrar. **within ~ of** ao alcance de; (close to) próximo de

**react** /rɪ'ækt/ vi reagir

**reaction** /rɪ'ækʃn/ n reação f, (P) reacção f. **~ary** a & n reacionário (m), (P) reaccionário (m)

**reactor** /rɪ'æktə(r)/ n reator m, (P) reactor m

**read** /riːd/ vt/i (pt read /red/) ler; (fig: interpret) interpretar; (study) estudar; (of instrument) marcar, indicar □ n (colloq) leitura f. **~ about** ler um artigo sobre. **~ out** ler em voz alta. **~able** a agradável or fácil de ler; (legible) legível. **~er** n leitor m; (book) livro m de leitura. **~ing** n leitura f; (of instrument) registro m, (P) registo m

**readily** /'redɪlɪ/ adv de boa vontade, prontamente; (easily) facilmente

**readiness** /'redmɪs/ n prontidão f. **in ~** pronto (for para)

**readjust** /riːə'dʒʌst/ vt reajustar □ vi readaptar-se

**ready** /'redɪ/ a (-ier, -iest) pronto □ n **at the ~** pronto para disparar. **~-made** a pronto. **~ money** dinheiro m vivo, (P) dinheiro m de contado, pagamento m à vista. **~-to-wear** a prêt-à-porter

**real** /rɪəl/ a real, verdadeiro; (genuine) autêntico □ adv (Amer: colloq) realmente. **~ estate** bens mpl imobiliários

**realis|t** /'rɪəlɪst/ n realista mf. **~m** /-zəm/ n realismo m. **~tic** /'lɪstɪk/ a realista. **~tically** /'lɪstɪkəlɪ/ adv realisticamente

**reality** /rɪ'ælətɪ/ n realidade f

**realiz|e** /'rɪəlaɪz/ vt dar-se conta de, aperceber-se de, perceber; (fulfil; turn into cash) realizar. **~ation** /-'zeɪʃn/ n consciência f, noção f; (fulfilment) realização f

**really** /'rɪəlɪ/ adv realmente, na verdade

**realm** /relm/ n reino m; (fig) domínio m, esfera f

**reap** /riːp/ vt (cut) ceifar; (gather; fig) colher

**reappear** /riːə'pɪə(r)/ vi reaparecer. **~ance** n reaparição f

**rear**[1] /rɪə(r)/ n traseira f, retaguarda f □ a traseiro, de trás, posterior. **bring up the ~** ir na retaguarda, fechar a marcha. **~-view mirror** espelho m retrovisor

**rear**[2] /rɪə(r)/ vt levantar, erguer; (children, cattle) criar □ vi (of horse etc) empinar-se. **~ one's head** levantar a cabeça

**rearrange** /riːə'reɪndʒ/ vt arranjar doutro modo, reorganizar

**reason** /'riːzn/ n razão f □ vt/i raciocinar, argumentar. **~ with sb** procurar convencer alguém. **within ~** razoável. **~ing** n raciocínio m

**reasonable** /'riːznəbl/ a razoável

**reassur|e** /riːə'ʃʊə(r)/ vt tranqüilizar, sossegar. **~ance** n garantia f. **~ing** a animador, reconfortante

**rebate** /'riːbeɪt/ n (refund) reimbolso m; (discount) desconto m, abatimento m

**rebel**[1] /'rebl/ n rebelde mf

**rebel**[2] /rɪ'bel/ vi (pt rebelled) rebelar-se, revoltar-se, sublevar-se. **~lion** n rebelião f, revolta f. **~lious** a rebelde

**rebound**[1] /rɪ'baʊnd/ vi repercutir, ressoar; (fig: backfire) recair (on sobre)

**rebound**[2] /'riːbaʊnd/ n ricochete m

**rebuff** /rɪ'bʌf/ vt receber mal, repelir (colloq) □ n rejeição f

**rebuild** /riː'bɪld/ vt (pt rebuilt) reconstruir

**rebuke** /rɪ'bjuːk/ vt repreender □ n reprimenda f

**recall** /rɪ'kɔːl/ vt chamar, mandar regressar; (remember) lembrar-se de □ n (summons) ordem f de regresso

**recant** /rɪ'kænt/ vi retratar-se, (P) retractar-se

**recap** /'riːkæp/ vt/i (pt recapped) (colloq) recapitular □ n recapitulação f

**recapitulat|e** /riːkə'pɪtʃʊleɪt/ vt/i recapitular. **~ion** /-'leɪʃn/ n recapitulação f

**reced|e** /rɪ'siːd/ vi recuar, retroceder. **his hair is ~ing** ele está ficando com entradas. **~ing** a (forehead, chin) recuado, voltado para dentro

**receipt** /rɪ'siːt/ n recibo m; (receiving) recepção f. **~s** (comm) receitas fpl

**receive** /rɪ'siːv/ vt receber. **~r** n (of stolen goods) receptador m; (phone) fone m, (P) auscultador m; (radio/TV) receptor m. **(official) ~r** síndico m de massa falida

**recent** /'riːsnt/ a recente. **~ly** adv recentemente

**receptacle** /rɪ'septəkl/ n recipiente m, receptáculo m

**reception** /rɪ'sepʃn/ n recepção f; (welcome) acolhimento m. **~ist** n recepcionista mf

**receptive** /rɪ'septɪv/ a receptivo

**recess** /rɪ'ses/ n recesso m; (of legisla-

*ture*) recesso *m*; (*Amer: schol*) recreio *m*

**recession** /rɪˈseʃn/ *n* recessão *f*, depressão *f*

**recharge** /riːˈtʃɑːdʒ/ *vt* tornar a carregar, recarregar

**recipe** /ˈresəpɪ/ *n* (*culin*) receita *f*

**recipient** /rɪˈsɪpɪənt/ *n* recipiente *mf*; (*of letter*) destinatário *m*

**reciprocal** /rɪˈsɪprəkl/ *a* recíproco

**reciprocate** /rɪˈsɪprəkeɪt/ *vt/i* reciprocar(-se), retribuir, fazer o mesmo

**recital** /rɪˈsaɪtl/ *n* (*music etc*) recital *m*

**recite** /rɪˈsaɪt/ *vt* recitar; (*list*) enumerar

**reckless** /ˈreklɪs/ *a* inconsciente, imprudente, estouvado

**reckon** /ˈrekən/ *vt/i* calcular; (*judge*) considerar; (*think*) supor, pensar. ~ **on** contar com, depender de. ~ **with** contar com, levar em conta. ~**ing** *n* conta(s) *f* (*pl*)

**reclaim** /rɪˈkleɪm/ *vt* (*demand*) reclamar; (*land*) recuperar

**reclin|e** /rɪˈklaɪn/ *vt/i* reclinar(-se). ~**ing** *a* (*person*) reclinado; (*chair*) reclinável

**recluse** /rɪˈkluːs/ *n* solitário *m*, recluso *m*

**recognition** /rekəgˈnɪʃn/ *n* reconhecimento *m*. **beyond** ~ irreconhecível. **gain** ~ ganhar nome, ser reconhecido

**recogniz|e** /ˈrekəgnaɪz/ *vt* reconhecer. ~**able** /ˈrekəgnaɪzəbl/ *a* reconhecível

**recoil** /rɪˈkɔɪl/ *vi* recuar; (*gun*) dar coice □ *n* recuo *m*; (*gun*) coice *m*. ~ **from doing** recusar-se a fazer

**recollect** /rekəˈlekt/ *vt* recordar-se de. ~**ion** /-ʃn/ *n* recordação *f*

**recommend** /rekəˈmend/ *vt* recomendar. ~**ation** /-ˈdeɪʃn/ *n* recomendação *f*

**recompense** /ˈrekəmpens/ *vt* recompensar □ *n* recompensa *f*

**reconcil|e** /ˈrekənsaɪl/ *vt* (*people*) reconciliar; (*facts*) conciliar. ~**e o.s. to** resignar-se a, conformar-se com. ~**iation** /-sɪlɪˈeɪʃn/ *n* reconciliação *f*

**reconnaissance** /rɪˈkɒnɪsns/ *n* reconhecimento *m*

**reconnoitre** /rekəˈnɔɪtə(r)/ *vt/i* (*pres p* -**tring**) (*mil*) reconhecer, fazer um reconhecimento (de)

**reconsider** /riːkənˈsɪdə(r)/ *vt* reconsiderar

**reconstruct** /riːkənˈstrʌkt/ *vt* reconstruir. ~**ion** /-ʃn/ *n* reconstrução *f*

**record**[1] /rɪˈkɔːd/ *vt* registar; (*disc, tape etc*) gravar. ~ **that** referir/relatar que. ~**ing** *n* (*disc, tape etc*) gravação *f*

**record**[2] /ˈrekɔːd/ *n* (*register*) registro *m*, (*P*) registo *m*; (*mention*) menção *f*, nota *f*; (*file*) arquivo *m*; (*mus*) disco

*m*; (*sport*) record(e) *m* □ *a* record(e) *invar*. **have a (criminal)** ~ ter cadastro. **off the** ~ (*unofficial*) oficioso; (*secret*) confidencial. ~**-player** *n* toca-discos *m invar*, (*P*) gira-discos *m invar*

**recorder** /rɪˈkɔːdə(r)/ *n* (*mus*) flauta *f* de ponta; (*techn*) instrumento *m* registrador

**recount** /rɪˈkaʊnt/ *vt* narrar em pormenor, relatar

**re-count** /ˈriːkaʊnt/ *n* (*pol*) nova contagem *f*

**recoup** /rɪˈkuːp/ *vt* compensar; (*recover*) recuperar

**recourse** /rɪˈkɔːs/ *n* recurso *m*. **have** ~ **to** recorrer a

**recover** /rɪˈkʌvə(r)/ *vt* recuperar □ *vi* restabelecer-se. ~**y** *n* recuperação *f*; (*health*) recuperação *f*, restabelecimento *m*

**recreation** /rekrɪˈeɪʃn/ *n* recreação *f*, recreio *m*; (*pastime*) passatempo *m*. ~**al** *a* recreativo

**recrimination** /rɪkrɪmɪˈneɪʃn/ *n* recriminação *f*

**recruit** /rɪˈkruːt/ *n* recruta *m* □ *vt* recrutar. ~**ment** *n* recrutamento *m*

**rectang|le** /ˈrektæŋgl/ *n* retângulo *m*, (*P*) rectângulo *m*. ~**ular** /-ˈtæŋgjʊlə(r)/ *a* retangular, (*P*) rectangular

**rectify** /ˈrektɪfaɪ/ *vt* retificar, (*P*) rectificar

**recuperate** /rɪˈkjuːpəreɪt/ *vt/i* recuperar(-se)

**recur** /rɪˈkɜː(r)/ *vi* (*pt* **recurred**) repetir-se; (*come back*) voltar (**to** a)

**recurren|t** /rɪˈkʌrənt/ *a* freqüente, (*P*) frequente, repetido, periódico. ~**ce** *n* repetição *f*

**recycle** /riːˈsaɪkl/ *vt* reciclar

**red** /red/ *a* (**redder**, **reddest**) encarnado, vermelho; (*hair*) ruivo □ *n* encarnado *m*, vermelho *m*. **in the** ~ em déficit. ~ **carpet** (*fig*) recepção *f* solene, tratamento *m* especial. **R~ Cross** Cruz *f* Vermelha. ~**-handed** *a* em flagrante (delito), com a boca na botija (*colloq*). ~ **herring** (*fig*) pista *f* falsa. ~**-hot** *a* escaldante, incandescente. ~ **light** luz *f* vermelha. ~ **tape** (*fig*) papelada *f*, burocracia *f*. ~ **wine** vinho *m* tinto

**redden** /ˈredn/ *vt/i* avermelhar(-se); (*blush*) corar, ruborizar-se

**redecorate** /riːˈdekəreɪt/ *vt* decorar/pintar de novo

**red|eem** /rɪˈdiːm/ *vt* (*sins etc*) redimir; (*sth pawned*) tirar do prego (*colloq*); (*voucher etc*) resgatar. ~**emption** /rɪˈdempʃn/ *n* resgate *m*; (*of honour*) salvação *f*

**redirect** /riːdaɪˈrekt/ *vt* (*letter*) reendereçar

**redness** /'rednɪs/ n vermelhidão f, cor f vermelha

**redo** /riː'duː/ vt (pt -did, pp -done) refazer

**redress** /rɪ'dres/ vt reparar; (set right) remediar, emendar. ~ **the balance** restabelecer o equilíbrio □ n reparação f

**reduc|e** /rɪ'djuːs/ vt reduzir; (temperature etc) baixar. ~**tion** /rɪ'dʌkʃən/ n redução f

**redundan|t** /rɪ'dʌndənt/ a redundante, supérfluo; (worker) desempregado. **be made** ~**t** ficar desempregado. ~**cy** n demissão f por excesso de pessoal

**reed** /riːd/ n cana f, junco m; (mus) palheta f

**reef** /riːf/ n recife m

**reek** /riːk/ n mau cheiro m □ vi cheirar mal, tresandar. **he** ~**s of wine** ele está com cheiro de vinho

**reel** /riːl/ n carretel m; (spool) bobina f □ vi cambalear, vacilar □ vt ~ **off** recitar (colloq)

**refectory** /rɪ'fektərɪ/ n refeitório m

**refer** /rɪ'fɜː(r)/ vt/i (pt referred) ~ **to** referir-se a; (concern) aplicar-se a, dizer respeito a; (consult) consultar; (direct) remeter a

**referee** /refə'riː/ n árbitro m; (for job) pessoa f que dá referências □ vt (pt refereed) arbitrar

**reference** /'refrəns/ n referência f; (testimonial) referências fpl. **in** ~ or **with** ~ **to** com referência a. ~ **book** livro m de consulta

**referendum** /refə'rendəm/ n (pl -dums or -da) referendo m, plebiscito m

**refill[1]** /riː'fɪl/ vt encher de novo; (pen etc) pôr carga nova em

**refill[2]** /'riːfɪl/ n (pen etc) carga f nova, (P) recarga f

**refine** /rɪ'faɪn/ vt refinar. ~**d** a refinado; (taste, manners etc) requintado. ~**ment** n (taste, manners etc) refinamento m, requinte m; (tech) refinação f. ~**ry** /-ərɪ/ n refinaria f

**reflect** /rɪ'flekt/ vt/i refletir, (P) reflectir (**on/upon** em). ~**ion** /-ʃn/ n reflexão f; (image) reflexo m. ~**or** n refletor m, (P) reflector m

**reflective** /rɪ'flektɪv/ a refletor, (P) reflector; (thoughtful) refletido, (P) reflectido, ponderado

**reflex** /'riːfleks/ a & n reflexo (m)

**reflexive** /rɪ'fleksɪv/ a (gram) reflexivo, (P) reflexo

**reform** /rɪ'fɔːm/ vt/i reformar(-se) □ n reforma f. ~**er** n reformador m

**refract** /rɪ'frækt/ vt refratar, (P) refractar

**refrain[1]** /rɪ'freɪn/ n refrão m, estribilho m

**refrain[2]** /rɪ'freɪn/ vi abster-se (**from** de)

**refresh** /rɪ'freʃ/ vt refrescar; (of rest etc) restaurar. ~ **one's memory** avivar or refrescar a memória. ~**ing** a refrescante; (of rest etc) reparador. ~**ments** npl refeição f leve; (drinks) refrescos mpl

**refresher** /rɪ'freʃə(r)/ n ~ **course** curso m de reciclagem

**refrigerat|e** /rɪ'frɪdʒəreɪt/ vt refrigerar. ~**or** n frigorífico m, refrigerador m, geladeira f

**refuel** /riː'fjuːəl/ vt/i (pt refuelled) reabastecer(-se) (de combustível)

**refuge** /'refjuːdʒ/ n refúgio m, asilo m. **take** ~ refugiar-se

**refugee** /refjuː'dʒiː/ n refugiado m

**refund[1]** /rɪ'fʌnd/ vt reembolsar

**refund[2]** /'riːfʌnd/ n reembolso m

**refus|e[1]** /rɪ'fjuːz/ vt/i recusar(-se). ~**al** n recusa f. **first** ~**al** preferência f, primeira opção f

**refuse[2]** /'refjuːs/ n refugo m, lixo m. ~**-collector** n lixeiro m, (P) homem m do lixo

**refute** /rɪ'fjuːt/ vt refutar

**regain** /rɪ'geɪn/ vt recobrar, recuperar

**regal** /'riːgl/ a real, régio

**regalia** /rɪ'geɪlɪə/ npl insígnias fpl

**regard** /rɪ'gɑːd/ vt considerar; (gaze) olhar □ n consideração f, estima f; (gaze) olhar m. ~**s** cumprimentos mpl; (less formally) lembranças fpl, saudades fpl. **as** ~**s**, ~**ing** prep no que diz respeito a, quanto a. ~**less** adv apesar de tudo. ~**less of** apesar de

**regatta** /rɪ'gætə/ n regata f

**regenerate** /rɪ'dʒenəreɪt/ vt regenerar

**regen|t** /'riːdʒənt/ n regente mf. ~**cy** n regência f

**regime** /reɪ'ʒiːm/ n regime m

**regiment** /'redʒɪmənt/ n regimento m. ~**al** /-'mentl/ a de regimento, regimental. ~**ation** /-en'teɪʃn/ n arregimentação f, disciplina f excessiva

**region** /'riːdʒən/ n região f. **in the** ~ **of** por volta de. ~**al** a regional

**regist|er** /'redʒɪstə(r)/ n registro m, (P) registo m □ vt (record) anotar; (notice) fixar, registar, prestar atenção a; (birth, letter) registrar, (P) registar; (vehicle) matricular; (emotions etc) exprimir □ vi inscrever-se. ~**er office** registro m, (P) registo m. ~**ration** /-'streɪʃn/ n registro m, (P) registo m; (for course) inscrição f, matrícula f. ~**ration (number)** número m de placa

**registrar** /redʒɪ'strɑː(r)/ n oficial m do registro, (P) registo civil; (univ) secretário m

**regret** /rɪˈgret/ n pena f, pesar m; (*repentance*) remorso m. **I have no ~s** não estou arrependido □ vt (*pt regretted*) lamentar, sentir (**to do fazer**); (*feel repentance*) arrepender-se de, lamentar. **~fully** adv com pena, pesarosamente. **~table** a lamentável. **~tably** adv infelizmente

**regular** /ˈregjʊlə(r)/ a regular; (*usual*) normal; (*colloq: thorough*) perfeito, verdadeiro, autêntico □ n (*colloq: client*) cliente mf habitual. **~ity** /-ˈlærəti/ n regularidade f. **~ly** adv regularmente

**regulat|e** /ˈregjʊleɪt/ vt regular. **~ion** /-ˈleɪʃn/ n regulação f; (*rule*) regulamento m, regra f

**rehabilitat|e** /riːəˈbɪlɪteɪt/ vt reabilitar. **~ion** /-ˈteɪʃn/ n reabilitação f

**rehash¹** /riːˈhæʃ/ vt apresentar sob nova forma, (P) cozinhar (*colloq*)

**rehash²** /ˈriːhæʃ/ n (*fig*) apanhado m, (P) cozinhado m (*colloq*)

**rehears|e** /rɪˈhɜːs/ vt ensaiar. **~al** n ensaio m. **dress ~al** ensaio m geral

**reign** /reɪn/ n reinado m □ vi reinar (**over** em)

**reimburse** /riːɪmˈbɜːs/ vt reembolsar. **~ment** n reembolso m

**rein** /reɪn/ n rédea f

**reincarnation** /riːmkaːˈneɪʃn/ n reencarnação f

**reindeer** /ˈreɪndɪə(r)/ n invar rena f

**reinforce** /riːɪnˈfɔːs/ vt reforçar. **~ment** n reforço m. **~ments** reforços mpl. **~d concrete** concreto m armado, (P) cimento m or betão m armado

**reinstate** /riːɪnˈsteɪt/ vt reintegrar

**reiterate** /riːˈɪtəreɪt/ vt reiterar

**reject¹** /rɪˈdʒekt/ vt rejeitar. **~ion** /-ʃn/ n rejeição f

**reject²** /ˈriːdʒekt/ n (artigo de) refugo m

**rejoic|e** /rɪˈdʒɔɪs/ vi regozijar-se (**at/over** com). **~ing** n regozijo m

**rejuvenate** /riːˈdʒuːvəneɪt/ vt rejuvenescer

**relapse** /rɪˈlæps/ n recaída f □ vi recair

**relate** /rɪˈleɪt/ vt relatar; (*associate*) relacionar □ vi **~ to** ter relação com, dizer respeito a; (*get on with*) entender-se com. **~d** a aparentado; (*ideas etc*) afim, relacionado

**relation** /rɪˈleɪʃn/ n relação f; (*person*) parente mf. **~ship** n parentesco m; (*link*) relação f; (*affair*) ligação f

**relative** /ˈrelətɪv/ n parente mf □ a relativo. **~ly** adv relativamente

**relax** /rɪˈlæks/ vt/i relaxar(-se); (*fig*) descontrair(-se). **~ation** /riːlækˈseɪʃn/ n relaxamento m; (*fig*) descontração f, (P) descontracção f;

(*recreation*) distração f, (P) distracção f **~ing** a relaxante

**relay¹** /ˈriːleɪ/ n turma f, (P) turno m. **~ race** corrida f de revezamento, (P) estafetas

**relay²** /rɪˈleɪ/ vt (*message*) retransmitir

**release** /rɪˈliːs/ vt libertar, soltar; (*mech*) desengatar, soltar; (*bomb, film, record*) lançar; (*news*) dar, publicar; (*gas, smoke*) soltar □ n libertação f; (*mech*) desengate m; (*bomb, film, record*) lançamento m; (*news*) publicação f; (*gas, smoke*) emissão f. **new ~** estréia f

**relegate** /ˈrelɪgeɪt/ vt relegar

**relent** /rɪˈlent/ vi ceder. **~less** a implacável, inexorável, inflexível

**relevan|t** /ˈreləvənt/ a relevante, pertinente, a propósito. **be ~ to** ter a ver com. **~ce** n pertinência f, relevância f

**reliab|le** /rɪˈlaɪəbl/ a de confiança, com que se pode contar; (*source etc*) fidedigno; (*machine etc*) seguro, confiável. **~ility** /-ˈbɪləti/ n confiabilidade f

**reliance** /rɪˈlaɪəns/ n (*dependence*) segurança f; (*trust*) confiança f, fé f (**on** em)

**relic** /ˈrelɪk/ n relíquia f. **~s** vestígios mpl, ruínas fpl

**relief** /rɪˈliːf/ n alívio m; (*assistance*) auxílio m, assistência f; (*outline, design*) relevo m. **~ road** estrada f alternativa

**relieve** /rɪˈliːv/ vt aliviar; (*help*) socorrer; (*take over from*) revezar, substituir; (*mil*) render

**religion** /rɪˈlɪdʒən/ n religião f

**religious** /rɪˈlɪdʒəs/ a religioso

**relinquish** /rɪˈlɪŋkwɪʃ/ vt abandonar, renunciar a

**relish** /ˈrelɪʃ/ n prazer m, gosto m; (*culin*) molho m condimentado □ vt saborear, apreciar, gostar de

**relocate** /riːləʊˈkeɪt/ vt/i transferir (-se), mudar(-se)

**reluctan|t** /rɪˈlʌktənt/ a relutante (**to** em), pouco inclinado (**to** a). **~ce** n relutância f. **~tly** adv a contragosto, relutantemente

**rely** /rɪˈlaɪ/ vi **~ on** contar com; (*depend*) depender de

**remain** /rɪˈmeɪn/ vi ficar, permanecer. **~s** npl restos mpl; (*ruins*) ruínas fpl. **~ing** a restante

**remainder** /rɪˈmeɪndə(r)/ n restante m, remanescente m

**remand** /rɪˈmaːnd/ vt reconduzir à prisão para detenção provisória □ n **on ~** sob prisão preventiva

**remark** /rɪˈmaːk/ n observação f, comentário m □ vt observar, comentar □ *vi* ~ **on** fazer observações *or* comentários sobre. ~**able** *a* notável

**remarr|y** /ri:ˈmærɪ/ *vt/i* tornar a casar(-se) (com). ~**iage** *n* novo casamento *m*

**remed|y** /ˈremədɪ/ *n* remédio *m* □ *vt* remediar. ~**ial** /rɪˈmiːdɪəl/ *a* (*med*) corretivo, (*P*) correctivo

**rememb|er** /rɪˈmembə(r)/ *vt* lembrar-se de, recordar-se de. ~**rance** *n* lembrança *f*, recordação *f*

**remind** /rɪˈmaɪnd/ *vt* (fazer) lembrar (**sb of sth** alg coisa a alguém). ~ **sb to do** lembrar a alguém que faça. ~**er** *n* o que serve para fazer lembrar; (*note*) lembrete *m*

**reminisce** /remɪˈnɪs/ *vi* (re)lembrar (coisas passadas). ~**nces** *npl* reminiscências *fpl*

**reminiscent** /remɪˈnɪsnt/ *a* ~ **of** que faz lembrar, evocativo de

**remiss** /rɪˈmɪs/ *a* negligente, descuidado

**remission** /rɪˈmɪʃn/ *n* remissão *f*; (*jur*) comutação *f* (de pena)

**remit** /rɪˈmɪt/ *vt* (*pt* **remitted**) (*money*) remeter. ~**tance** *n* remessa *f* (de dinheiro)

**remnant** /ˈremnənt/ *n* resto *m*; (*trace*) vestígio *m*; (*of cloth*) retalho *m*

**remorse** /rɪˈmɔːs/ *n* remorso *m*. ~**ful** *a* arrependido, com remorsos. ~**less** *a* implacável

**remote** /rɪˈməʊt/ *a* remoto, distante; (*person*) distante; (*slight*) vago, leve. ~ **control** comando *m* à distância, telecomando *m*. ~**ly** *adv* de longe; vagamente

**remov|e** /rɪˈmuːv/ *vt* tirar, remover; (*lead away*) levar; (*dismiss*) demitir; (*get rid of*) eliminar; ~**al** *n* remoção *f*; (*dismissal*) demissão *f*; (*from house*) mudança *f*

**remunerat|e** /rɪˈmjuːnəreɪt/ *vt* remunerar. ~**ion** /-ˈreɪʃn/ *n* remuneração *f*

**rename** /riːˈneɪm/ *vt* rebatizar, (*P*) rebaptizar

**render** /ˈrendə(r)/ *vt* retribuir; (*services*) prestar; (*mus*) interpretar; (*translate*) traduzir. ~**ing** *n* (*mus*) interpretação *f*; (*plaster*) reboco *m*

**renegade** /ˈrenɪɡeɪd/ *n* renegado *m*

**renew** /rɪˈnjuː/ *vt* renovar; (*resume*) retomar. ~**able** *a* renovável. ~**al** *n* renovação *f*; (*resumption*) reatamento *m*

**renounce** /rɪˈnaʊns/ *vt* renunciar a; (*disown*) renegar, repudiar

**renovat|e** /ˈrenəveɪt/ *vt* renovar. ~**ion** /-ˈveɪʃn/ *n* renovação *f*

**renown** /rɪˈnaʊn/ *n* renome *m*. ~**ed** *a* conceituado, célebre, de renome

**rent** /rent/ *n* aluguel *m*, (*P*) aluguer *m*, renda *f* □ *vt* alugar, arrendar. ~**al** *n* (*charge*) aluguel *m*, (*P*) aluguer *m*, renda *f*; (*act of renting*) aluguel *m*, (*P*) aluguer *m*

**renunciation** /rɪnʌnsɪˈeɪʃn/ *n* renúncia *f*

**reopen** /riːˈəʊpən/ *vt/i* reabrir(-se). ~**ing** *n* reabertura *f*

**reorganize** /riːˈɔːɡənaɪz/ *vt/i* reorganizar(-se)

**rep** /rep/ *n* (*colloq*) vendedor *m*, caixeiro-viajante *m*

**repair** /rɪˈpeə(r)/ *vt* reparar, consertar □ *n* reparo *m*, conserto *m*. **in good** ~ em bom estado (de conservação)

**repartee** /repaːˈtiː/ *n* resposta *f* pronta e espirituosa

**repatriat|e** /riːˈpætrɪeɪt/ *vt* repatriar. ~**ion** /ˈeɪʃn/ *n* repatriamento *m*

**repay** /riːˈpeɪ/ *vt* (*pt* **repaid**) pagar, devolver, reembolsar; (*reward*) recompensar. ~**ment** *n* pagamento *m*, reembolso *m*

**repeal** /rɪˈpiːl/ *vt* revogar □ *n* revogação *f*

**repeat** /rɪˈpiːt/ *vt/i* repetir(-se) □ *n* repetição *f*; (*broadcast*) retransmissão *f*. ~**edly** *adv* repetidas vezes, repetidamente

**repel** /rɪˈpel/ *vt* (*pt* **repelled**) repelir. ~**lent** *a* & *n* repelente (*m*)

**repent** /rɪˈpent/ *vi* arrepender-se (**of** de). ~**ance** *n* arrependimento *m*. ~**ant** *a* arrependido

**repercussion** /riːpəˈkʌʃn/ *n* repercussão *f*

**repertoire** /ˈrepətwaː(r)/ *n* repertório *m*

**repertory** /ˈrepətrɪ/ *n* repertório *m*

**repetit|ion** /repɪˈtɪʃn/ *n* repetição *f*. ~**ious** /-ˈtɪʃəs/, ~**ive** /rɪˈpetətɪv/ *a* repetitivo

**replace** /rɪˈpleɪs/ *vt* colocar no mesmo lugar, repor; (*take the place of*) substituir. ~**ment** *n* reposição *f*; (*substitution*) substituição *f*; (*person*) substituto *m*

**replenish** /rɪˈplenɪʃ/ *vt* voltar a encher, reabastecer; (*renew*) renovar

**replica** /ˈreplɪkə/ *n* réplica *f*, cópia *f*, reprodução *f*

**reply** /rɪˈplaɪ/ *vt/i* responder, replicar □ *n* resposta *f*, réplica *f*

**report** /rɪˈpɔːt/ *vt* relatar; (*notify*) informar; (*denounce*) denunciar, apresentar queixa de □ *vi* fazer um relatório. ~ **(on)** (*news item*) fazer uma reportagem (sobre). ~ **to** (*go*) apresentar-se a □ *n* (*in newspapers*) reportagem *f*; (*of company, doctor*) relatório *m*; (*schol*) boletim *m* escolar; (*sound*) detonação *f*; (*rumour*) rumores *mpl*. ~**edly** *adv* segundo consta. ~**er** *n* repórter *m*

**repose** /rɪ'pəʊz/ n repouso m

**repossess** /ri:pə'zes/ vt reapossar-se de, retomar de

**represent** /reprɪ'zent/ vt representar. **~ation** /-'teɪʃn/ n representação f

**representative** /reprɪ'zentətɪv/ a representativo □ n representante mf

**repress** /rɪ'pres/ vt reprimir. **~ion** /-ʃn/ n repressão f. **~ive** a repressor, repressivo

**reprieve** /rɪ'pri:v/ n suspensão f temporária; (temporary relief) tréguas fpl □ vt suspender temporariamente; (fig) dar tréguas a

**reprimand** /'reprɪmɑ:nd/ vt repreender □ n repreensão f, reprimenda f

**reprint** /'ri:prɪnt/ n reimpressão f, reedição f □ vt /ri:'prɪnt/

**reprisals** /rɪ'praɪzlz/ npl represálias fpl

**reproach** /rɪ'prəʊtʃ/ vt censurar, repreender (sb for sth alguém por alg coisa, alg coisa a alguém) □ n censura f. **above ~** irrepreensível. **~ful** a repreensivo, reprovador. **~fully** adv reprovadoramente

**reproduc|e** /ri:prə'dju:s/ vt/i reproduzir(-se). **~tion** /-'dʌkʃn/ n reprodução f. **~tive** /-'dʌktɪv/ a reprodutivo, reprodutor

**reptile** /'reptaɪl/ n réptil m

**republic** /rɪ'pʌblɪk/ n república f. **~an** a & n republicano (m)

**repudiate** /rɪ'pju:dɪeɪt/ vt repudiar, rejeitar

**repugnan|t** /rɪ'pʌgnənt/ a repugnante. **~ce** n repugnância f

**repuls|e** /rɪ'pʌls/ vt repelir, repulsar. **~ion** /-ʃn/ n repulsa f. **~ive** a repulsivo, repelente, repugnante

**reputable** /'repjʊtəbl/ a respeitado, honrado; (firm, make etc) de renome, conceituado

**reputation** /repjʊ'teɪʃn/ n reputação f

**repute** /rɪ'pju:t/ n reputação f. **~d** /-ɪd/ a suposto, putativo. **~dly** /-ɪdlɪ/ adv segundo consta, com fama de

**request** /rɪ'kwest/ n pedido m □ vt pedir, solicitar (of, from a)

**requiem** /'rekwɪəm/ n réquiem m; (mass) missa f de réquiem

**require** /rɪ'kwaɪə(r)/ vt requerer. **~d** a requerido; (needed) necessário, preciso. **~ment** n (fig) requisito m; (need) necessidade f; (demand) exigência f

**requisite** /'rekwɪzɪt/ a necessário □ n coisa necessária f, requisito m. **~s** (for travel etc) artigos mpl

**requisition** /rekwɪ'zɪʃn/ n requisição f □ vt requisitar

**resale** /'ri:seɪl/ n revenda f

**rescue** /'reskju:/ vt salvar, socorrer (from de) □ n salvamento m; (help) socorro m, ajuda f. **~r** /-ə(r)/ n salvador m

**research** /rɪ'sɜ:tʃ/ n pesquisa f, investigação f □ vt/i pesquisar, fazer investigação (into sobre). **~er** n investigador m

**resembl|e** /rɪ'zembl/ vt assemelhar-se a, parecer-se com. **~ance** n semelhança f, similaridade f (to com)

**resent** /rɪ'zent/ vt ressentir(-se de), ficar ressentido com. **~ful** a ressentido. **~ment** n ressentimento m

**reservation** /rezə'veɪʃn/ n (booking) reserva f; (Amer) reserva f (de índios)

**reserve** /rɪ'zɜ:v/ vt reservar □ n reserva f; (sport) suplente mf. **in ~** de reserva. **~d** a reservado

**reservoir** /'rezəvwɑ:(r)/ n (lake, supply etc) reservatório m; (container) depósito m

**reshape** /ri:'ʃeɪp/ vt remodelar

**reshuffle** /ri:'ʃʌfl/ vt (pol) remodelar □ n (pol) reforma f (do Ministério)

**reside** /rɪ'zaɪd/ vi residir

**residen|t** /'rezɪdənt/ a residente □ n morador m, habitante mf; (foreigner) residente mf; (in hotel) hóspede mf. **~ce** n residência f; (of students) residência f, lar m. **~ce permit** visto m de residência

**residential** /rezɪ'denʃl/ a residencial

**residue** /'rezɪdju:/ n resíduo m

**resign** /rɪ'zaɪn/ vt (post) demitir-se. **~ o.s.** to resignar-se a □ vi demitir-se de. **~ation** /rezɪg'neɪʃn/ n resignação f; (from job) demissão f. **~ed** a resignado

**resilien|t** /rɪ'zɪlɪənt/ a (springy) elástico; (person) resistente. **~ce** n elasticidade f; (of person) resistência f

**resin** /'rezɪn/ n resina f

**resist** /rɪ'zɪst/ vt/i resistir (a). **~ance** n resistência f. **~ant** a resistente

**resolut|e** /'rezəlu:t/ a resoluto. **~ion** /-'lu:ʃn/ n resolução f

**resolve** /rɪ'zɒlv/ vt resolver. **~ to do** resolver fazer □ n resolução f. **~d** a (resolute) resoluto; (decided) resolvido (to a)

**resonan|t** /'rezənənt/ a ressonante. **~ce** n ressonância f

**resort** /rɪ'zɔ:t/ vi **~ to** recorrer a, valer-se de □ n recurso m; (place) estância f, local m turístico. **as a last ~** em último recurso. **seaside ~** praia f, balneário m, (P) estância f balnear

**resound** /rɪ'zaʊnd/ vi reboar, ressoar (with com). **~ing** a ressoante; (fig) retumbante

**resource** /rɪ'sɔ:s/ n recurso m. **~s** recursos mpl, riquezas fpl. **~ful** a

expedito, engenhoso, desembaraçado.
**~fulness** *n* expediente *m*, engenho *m*
**respect** /rɪ'spekt/ *n* respeito *m* □ *vt*
respeitar. **with ~ to** a respeito de,
com respeito a, relativamente a.
**~ful** *a* respeitoso
**respectab|le** /rɪ'spektəbl/ *a* respeitá-
vel; (*passable*) passável, aceitável.
**~ility** /-'bɪlətɪ/ *n* res-peitabilidade *f*
**respective** /rɪ'spektɪv/ *a* respectivo.
**~ly** *adv* respectivamente
**respiration** /respə'reɪʃn/ *n* respiração *f*
**respite** /'respaɪt/ *n* pausa *f*, trégua *f*,
folga *f*
**respond** /rɪ'spɒnd/ *vi* responder (**to**
a); (*react*) reagir (**to** a)
**response** /rɪ'spɒns/ *n* resposta *f*; (*reaction*) reação *f*, (*P*) reacção *f*
**responsib|le** /rɪ'spɒnsəbl/ *a* respon-
sável; (*job*) de responsabilidade.
**~ility** /-'bɪlətɪ/ *n* responsabilidade
*f*
**responsive** /rɪ'spɒnsɪv/ *a* receptivo,
que reage bem. **~ to** sensível a
**rest**[1] /rest/ *vt/i* descansar, repousar;
(*lean*) apoiar(-se) □ *n* descanso *m*, repouso *m*; (*support*) suporte *m*. **~-
room** *n* (*Amer*) banheiro *m*, (*P*) toa-
letes *mpl*
**rest**[2] /rest/ *vi* (*remain*) ficar □ *n* (*remainder*) resto *m* (**of** de). **the ~** (**of
the**) (*others*) os outros. **it ~s with
him** cabe a ele
**restaurant** /'restrɒnt/ *n* restaurante
*m*
**restful** /'restfl/ *a* sossegado, repou-
sante, tranqüilo, (*P*) tranquilo
**restitution** /restɪ'tjuːʃn/ *n* restituição
*f*; (*for injury*) indenização *f*, (*P*)
indemnização *f*
**restless** /'restlɪs/ *a* agitado, desassos-
segado
**restor|e** /rɪ'stɔː(r)/ *vt* restaurar; (*give
back*) restituir, devolver. **~ation**
/restə'reɪʃn/ *n* restauração *f*
**restrain** /rɪ'streɪn/ *vt* conter, reprimir. **~ o.s.** controlar-se. **~ sb
from** impedir alguém de. **~ed** *a* comedido, reservado. **~t** *n* controle *m*;
(*moderation*) moderação *f*, comedi-
mento *m*
**restrict** /rɪ'strɪkt/ *vt* restringir,
limitar. **~ion** /-ʃn/ *n* restrição *f*.
**~ive** *a* restritivo
**result** /rɪ'zʌlt/ *n* resultado *m* □ *vi* resultar (**from** de). **~ in** resultar em
**resum|e** /rɪ'zjuːm/ *vt/i* reatar, reto-
mar; (*work, travel*) recomeçar.
**~ption** /rɪ'zʌmpʃn/ *n* reatamento *m*,
retomada *f*, (*of work*) recomeço *m*
**résumé** /'rezjuːmeɪ/ *n* resumo *m*
**resurgence** /rɪ'sɜːdʒəns/ *n* reapareci-
mento *m*, ressurgimento *m*

**resurrect** /rezə'rekt/ *vt* ressuscitar.
**~ion** /-ʃn/ *n* ressureição *f*
**resuscitat|e** /rɪ'sʌsɪteɪt/ *vt* ressusci-
tar, reanimar. **~ion** /-'teɪʃn/ *n*
reanimação *f*
**retail** /'riːteɪl/ *n* retalho *m* □ *a* & *adv* a
retalho □ *vt/i* vender(-se) a retalho.
**~er** *n* retalhista *mf*
**retain** /rɪ'teɪn/ *vt* reter; (*keep*) conservar, guardar
**retaliat|e** /rɪ'tælɪeɪt/ *vi* retaliar, exer-
cer represálias, desforrar-se. **~ion**
/-'eɪʃn/ *n* retaliação *f*, represália *f*,
desforra *f*
**retarded** /rɪ'tɑːdɪd/ *a* retardado, atrasado
**retch** /retʃ/ *vi* fazer esforço para vomitar, estar com ânsias de vômito
**retention** /rɪ'tenʃn/ *n* retenção *f*
**retentive** /rɪ'tentɪv/ *a* retentivo. **~
memory** boa memória *f*
**reticen|t** /'retɪsnt/ *a* reticente. **~ce** *n*
reticência *f*
**retina** /'retɪnə/ *n* retina *f*
**retinue** /'retɪnjuː/ *n* séquito *m*, comitiva *f*
**retire** /rɪ'taɪə(r)/ *vi* reformar-se,
aposentar-se; (*withdraw*) retirar-se;
(*go to bed*) ir deitar-se □ *vt*
reformar, aposentar. **~d** *a* reformado,
aposentado. **~ment** *n* reforma *f*,
aposentadoria *f*, (*P*) aposentação *f*
**retiring** /rɪ'taɪərɪŋ/ *a* reservado, retraído
**retort** /rɪ'tɔːt/ *vt/i* retrucar, retorquir
□ *n* réplica *f*
**retrace** /riː'treɪs/ *vt* **~ one's steps**
refazer o mesmo caminho; (*fig*) recordar, recapitular
**retract** /rɪ'trækt/ *vt/i* retratar(-se);
(*wheels*) recolher; (*claws*) encolher, recolher
**retreat** /rɪ'triːt/ *vi* retirar-se; (*mil*) retirar, bater em retirada □ *n* retirada *f*;
(*seclusion*) retiro *m*
**retrial** /riː'traɪəl/ *n* novo julgamento
*m*
**retribution** /retrɪ'bjuːʃn/ *n* castigo
(merecido) *m*; (*vengeance*) vingança *f*
**retriev|e** /rɪ'triːv/ *vt* ir buscar; (*res-
cue*) salvar; (*recover*) recuperar; (*put
right*) reparar. **~al** *n* recuperação *f*.
**information ~al** (*comput*) acesso *m*
à informação. **~er** *n* (*dog*) perdi-
gueiro *m*, (*P*) cobrador *m*
**retrograde** /'retrəgreɪd/ *a* retrógrado
□ *vt* retroceder, recuar
**retrospect** /'retrəspekt/ *n* **in ~** em
retrospecto, (*P*) retrospectivamente.
**~ive** /-'spektɪv/ *a* retrospectivo; (*of
law, payment*) retroativo, (*P*) retroac-
tivo
**return** /rɪ'tɜːn/ *vi* voltar, regressar, re-
tornar (**to**, a) □ *vt* devolver; (*compli-*

*ment, visit*) retribuir; (*put back*) pôr de volta □ *n* volta *f*, regresso *m*, retorno *m*; (*profit*) lucro *m*, rendimento *m*; (*restitution*) devolução *f*. **in ~ for** em troca de. **~ journey** viagem *f* de volta. **~ match** (*sport*) desafio *m* de desforra. **~ ticket** bilhete *m* de ida e volta. **many happy ~s (of the day)** muitos parabéns

**reunion** /riːˈjuːnɪən/ *n* reunião *f*

**reunite** /riːjuːˈnaɪt/ *vt* reunir

**rev** /rev/ *n* (*colloq: auto*) rotação *f* □ *vt/i* (*pt* **revved**) **~ (up)** (*colloq: auto*) acelerar (o motor)

**reveal** /rɪˈviːl/ *vt* revelar; (*display*) expor. **~ing** *a* revelador

**revel** /ˈrevl/ *vi* (*pt* **revelled**) divertir-se. **~ in** deleitar-se com. **~ry** *n* festas *fpl*, festejos *mpl*

**revelation** /revəˈleɪʃn/ *n* revelação *f*

**revenge** /rɪˈvendʒ/ *n* vingança *f*; (*sport*) desforra *f* □ *vt* vingar

**revenue** /ˈrevənjuː/ *n* receita *f*, rendimento *m*. **Inland R~** Fisco *m*

**reverberate** /rɪˈvɜːbəreɪt/ *vi* ecoar, repercutir

**revere** /rɪˈvɪə(r)/ *vt* reverenciar, venerar

**reverend** /ˈrevərənd/ *a* reverendo. **R~** Reverendo

**reveren|t** /ˈrevərənt/ *a* reverente. **~ce** *n* reverência *f*, veneração *f*

**revers|e** /rɪˈvɜːs/ *a* contrário, inverso □ *n* contrário *m*; (*back*) reverso *m*; (*gear*) marcha *f* à ré, (*P*) atrás □ *vt* virar ao contrário; (*order*) inverter; (*turn inside out*) virar do avesso; (*decision*) anular □ *vi* (*auto*) fazer marcha à ré, (*P*) atrás. **~al** *n* inversão *f*, mudança *f* em sentido contrário; (*of view etc*) mudança *f*

**revert** /rɪˈvɜːt/ *vi* **~ to** reverter a

**review** /rɪˈvjuː/ *n* (*inspection; magazine*) revista *f*; (*of a situation*) revisão *f*; (*critique*) crítica *f* □ *vt* revistar, passar revista em; (*situation*) rever; (*book, film etc*) fazer a crítica de. **~er** *n* crítico *m*

**revis|e** /rɪˈvaɪz/ *vt* rever; (*amend*) corrigir. **~ion** /-ɪʒn/ *n* revisão *f*; (*amendment*) correção *f*

**reviv|e** /rɪˈvaɪv/ *vt/i* ressuscitar, reavivar; (*play*) reapresentar; (*person*) reanimar(-se). **~al** *n* reflorescimento *m*, renascimento *m*

**revoke** /rɪˈvəʊk/ *vt* revogar, anular, invalidar

**revolt** /rɪˈvəʊlt/ *vt/i* revoltar(-se) □ *n* revolta *f*

**revolting** /rɪˈvəʊltɪŋ/ *a* (*disgusting*) repugnante

**revolution** /revəˈluːʃn/ *n* revolução *f*. **~ary** *a & n* revolucionário (*m*). **~ize** *vt* revolucionar

**revolv|e** /rɪˈvɒlv/ *vi* girar. **~ing door** porta *f* giratória

**revolver** /rɪˈvɒlvə(r)/ *n* revólver *m*

**revulsion** /rɪˈvʌlʃn/ *n* repugnância *f*, repulsa *f*

**reward** /rɪˈwɔːd/ *n* prêmio *m*, (*P*) prémio *m*; (*for criminal, for lost/stolen property*) recompensa *f* □ *vt* recompensar. **~ing** *a* compensador; (*task etc*) gratificante

**rewind** /riːˈwaɪnd/ *vt* (*pt* **rewound**) rebobinar

**rewrite** /riːˈraɪt/ *vt* (*pt* **rewrote**, *pp* **rewritten**) reescrever

**rhetoric** /ˈretərɪk/ *n* retórica *f*. **~al** /rɪˈtɒrɪkl/ *a* retórico; (*question*) pro forma

**rheumati|c** /ruːˈmætɪk/ *a* reumático. **~sm** /ˈruːmətɪzm/ *n* reumatismo *m*

**rhinoceros** /raɪˈnɒsərəs/ *n* (*pl* **-oses**) rinoceronte *m*

**rhubarb** /ˈruːbɑːb/ *n* ruibarbo *m*

**rhyme** /raɪm/ *n* rima *f*; (*poem*) versos *mpl* □ *vt/i* (fazer) rimar

**rhythm** /ˈrɪðəm/ *n* ritmo *m*. **~ic(al)** /ˈrɪðmɪk(l)/ *a* rítmico, compassado

**rib** /rɪb/ *n* costela *f*

**ribbon** /ˈrɪbən/ *n* fita *f*. **in ~s** em tiras

**rice** /raɪs/ *n* arroz *m*

**rich** /rɪtʃ/ *a* (**-er, -est**) rico; (*food*) rico em açúcar e gordura. **~es** *npl* riquezas *fpl*. **~ly** *adv* ricamente. **~ness** *n* riqueza *f*

**rickety** /ˈrɪkətɪ/ *a* (*shaky*) desconjuntado

**ricochet** /ˈrɪkəʃeɪ/ *n* ricochete *m* □ *vi* (*pt* **ricocheted** /-ʃeɪd/) fazer ricochete, ricochetear

**rid** /rɪd/ *vt* (*pt* **rid**, *pres p* **ridding**) desembaraçar (**of** de). **get ~ of** desembaraçar-se de, livrar-se de

**riddance** /ˈrɪdns/ *n* **good ~**! que alívio!, vai com Deus!

**ridden** /ˈrɪdn/ *see* **ride**

**riddle**[1] /ˈrɪdl/ *n* enigma *m*; (*puzzle*) charada *f*

**riddle**[2] /ˈrɪdl/ *vt* **~ with** crivar de

**ride** /raɪd/ *vt/i* (*pt* **rode**, *pp* **ridden**) andar (de bicicleta, a cavalo, de carro) □ *vt* (*horse*) montar; (*bicycle*) andar de; (*distance*) percorrer □ *n* passeio *m or* volta *f* (de carro, a cavalo etc); (*distance*) percurso *m*. **~r** /-ə(r)/ *n* cavaleiro *m*, amazona *f*; (*cyclist*) ciclista *mf*; (*in document*) aditamento *m*

**ridge** /rɪdʒ/ *n* aresta *f*; (*of hill*) cume *m*

**ridicule** /ˈrɪdɪkjuːl/ *n* ridículo *m* □ *vt* ridicularizar

**ridiculous** /rɪˈdɪkjuləs/ *a* ridículo

**riding** /ˈraɪdɪŋ/ *n* equitação *f*

**rife** /raɪf/ *a* **be ~** estar espalhado; (*of illness*) grassar. **~ with** cheio de

**riff-raff** /'rɪfræf/ n gentinha f, povinho m, ralé f

**rifle** /'raɪfl/ n espingarda f □ vt revistar e roubar, saquear

**rift** /rɪft/ n fenda f, brecha f; ( fig: dissension) desacordo m, desavença f, desentendimento m

**rig**[1] /rɪg/ vt (pt rigged) equipar □ n ( for oil) plataforma f de poço de petróleo. ~ **out** enfarpelar (colloq). ~**-out** n (colloq) roupa f, farpela f (colloq). ~ **up** arranjar

**rig**[2] /rɪg/ vt (pt rigged) (pej) manipular. ~**ged** a (election) fraudulento

**right** /raɪt/ a (correct, moral) certo, correto, (P) correcto; ( fair) justo; (not left) direito; (suitable) certo, próprio □ n (entitlement) direito m; (not left) direita f; (not evil) o bem □ vt (a wrong) reparar; (sth fallen) endireitar □ adv (not left) à direita; (directly) direito; (exactly) mesmo, bem; (completely) completamente. **be** ~ (person) ter razão (to em). **be in the** ~ ter razão. **on the** ~ à direita. **put** ~ acertar, corrigir. ~ **of way** (auto) prioridade f. ~ **angle** n ângulo reto m, (P) recto. ~ **away** logo, imediatamente. ~**-hand** a à or de direita. ~**-handed** a (person) destro. ~**-wing** a (pol) de direita

**righteous** /'raɪtʃəs/ a justo, virtuoso

**rightful** /'raɪtfl/ a legítimo. ~**ly** adv legitimamente, legalmente

**rightly** /'raɪtlɪ/ adv devidamente, corretamente, (P) correctamente; (with reason) justificadamente

**rigid** /'rɪdʒɪd/ a rígido. ~**ity** /rɪ-'dʒɪdətɪ/ n rigidez f

**rigmarole** /'rɪgmərəʊl/ n (speech: procedure) embrulhada f

**rig|our** /'rɪgə(r)/ n rigor m. ~**orous** a rigoroso

**rile** /raɪl/ vt (colloq) irritar, exasperar

**rim** /rɪm/ n borda f; (of wheel) aro m

**rind** /raɪnd/ n (on cheese, fruit) casca f; (on bacon) pele f

**ring**[1] /rɪŋ/ n (on finger) anel m; ( for napkin, key etc) argola f; (circle) roda f, círculo m; (boxing) ringue m; (arena) arena f; (of people) quadrilha f □ vt rodear, cercar. ~ **road** n estrada f periférica or perimetral

**ring**[2] /rɪŋ/ vt/i (pt rang, pp rung) tocar; (of words etc) soar □ n toque m; (colloq: phone call) telefonadela f (colloq). ~ **the bell** tocar a campainha. ~ **back** telefonar de volta. ~ **off** desligar. ~ **up** telefonar (a)

**ringleader** /'rɪŋliːdə(r)/ n cabeça m, cérebro m

**rink** /rɪŋk/ n rinque m de patinação

**rinse** /rɪns/ vt passar uma água, enxaguar □ n enxaguadura f, (P) enxuagadela f; (hair tint) rinsagem f

**riot** /'raɪət/ n distúrbio m, motim m, (of colours) festival m □ vi fazer distúrbios or motins. **run** ~ desenfrear-se, descontrolar-se; (of plants) crescer em matagal. ~**er** n desordeiro m

**riotous** /'raɪətəs/ a desenfreado, turbulento, desordeiro

**rip** /rɪp/ vt/i (pt ripped) rasgar(-se) □ n rasgão m. ~ **off** (sl: defraud) defraudar, enrolar (sl). ~**-off** n (sl) roubalheira f (colloq)

**ripe** /raɪp/ a (-er, -est) maduro. ~**ness** n madureza f, (P) amadurecimento m

**ripen** /'raɪpən/ vt/i amadurecer

**ripple** /'rɪpl/ n ondulação f leve; (sound) murmúrio m □ vt/i encrespar(-se), agitar(-se), ondular

**rise** /raɪz/ vi (pt rose, pp risen) subir, elevar-se; (stand up) erguer-se, levantar-se; (rebel) sublevar-se; (sun) nascer; (curtain, prices) subir □ n (increase) aumento m; (slope) subida f, ladeira f; (origin) origem f. **give** ~ **to** originar, causar, dar origem a. ~**r** /-ə(r)/ n **early** ~**r** madrugador m

**rising** /'raɪzɪŋ/ n (revolt) insurreição f □ a (sun) nascente

**risk** /rɪsk/ n risco m □ vt arriscar. **at** ~ em risco, em perigo. **at one's own** ~ por sua conta e risco. ~ **doing** (venture) arriscar-se a fazer. ~**y** a arriscado

**risqué** /'riːskeɪ/ a picante

**rite** /raɪt/ n rito m. **last** ~**s** últimos sacramentos mpl

**ritual** /'rɪtʃʊəl/ a & n ritual (m)

**rival** /'raɪvl/ n & a rival (mf); ( fig) concorrente (mf), competidor (m) □ vt (pt rivalled) rivalizar com. ~**ry** n rivalidade f

**river** /'rɪvə(r)/ n rio m □ a fluvial

**rivet** /'rɪvɪt/ n rebite m □ vt (pt riveted) rebitar; ( fig) prender, cravar. ~**ing** a fascinante

**road** /rəʊd/ n estrada f; (in town) rua f; (small; fig) caminho m. ~**-block** n barricada f. ~**-map** n mapa m das estradas. ~ **sign** n sinal m, placa f de sinalização. ~ **tax** imposto m de circulação. ~**-works** npl obras fpl

**roadside** /'rəʊdsaɪd/ n beira f da estrada

**roadway** /'rəʊdweɪ/ n pista f de rolamento, (P) rodagem

**roadworthy** /'rəʊdwɜːðɪ/ a em condições de ser utilizado na rua/estrada

**roam** /rəʊm/ vi errar, andar sem destino □ vt percorrer

**roar** /rɔː(r)/ n berro m, rugido m; (of thunder) ribombo m, troar m; (of sea, *wind*) bramido *m* □ *vt/i* berrar, rugir; (*of lion*) rugir; (*of thunder*) ribombar, troar; (*of sea, wind*) bramir. **~ with laughter** rir às gargalhadas

**roaring** /'rɔːrɪŋ/ *a* (*trade*) florescente; (*success*) enorme; (*fire*) com grandes chamas

**roast** /rəʊst/ *vt/i* assar □ *a & n* assado (*m*)

**rob** /rɒb/ *vt* (*pt* **robbed**) roubar (**sb of sth** alg coisa de alguém); (*bank*) assaltar; (*deprive*) privar (of de). **~ber** *n* ladrão *m*. **~bery** *n* roubo *m*; (*of bank*) assalto *m*

**robe** /rəʊb/ *n* veste *f* comprida e solta; (*dressing-gown*) robe *m*. **~s** *npl* (*of judge etc*) toga *f*

**robin** /'rɒbɪn/ *n* papo-roxo *m*, (*P*) pintarroxo *m*

**robot** /'rəʊbɒt/ *n* robô *m*, (*P*) robot *m*, autômato *m*, (*P*) autómato *m*

**robust** /rəʊ'bʌst/ *a* robusto

**rock**[1] /rɒk/ *n* rocha *f*; (*boulder*) penhasco *m*, rochedo *m*; (*sweet*) pirulito *m*, (*P*) chupa-chupa *m* comprido. **on the ~s** (*colloq: of marriage*) em crise; (*colloq: of drinks*) com gelo. **~-bottom** *n* ponto *m* mais baixo □ *a* (*of prices*) baixíssimo (*colloq*)

**rock**[2] /rɒk/ *vt/i* balouçar(-se); (*shake*) abanar, sacudir; (*child*) embalar □ *n* (*mus*) rock *m*. **~ing-chair** *n* cadeira *f* de balanço, (*P*) cadeira *f* de baloiço. **~ing-horse** *n* cavalo *m* de balanço, (*P*) cavalo *m* de baloiço

**rocket** /'rɒkɪt/ *n* foguete *m*

**rocky** /'rɒkɪ/ *a* (**-ier, -iest**) (*ground*) pedregoso; (*hill*) rochoso; (*colloq: unsteady*) instável; (*colloq: shaky*) tremido (*colloq*)

**rod** /rɒd/ *n* vara *f*, vareta *f*; (*mech*) haste *f*; (*for curtains*) bastão *m*, (*P*) varão *m*; (*for fishing*) vara (de pescar) *f*

**rode** /rəʊd/ *see* **ride**

**rodent** /'rəʊdnt/ *n* roedor *m*

**rodeo** /rəʊ'deɪəʊ/ *n* (*pl* **-os**) rode(i)o *m*

**roe** /rəʊ/ *n* ova(s) *f* (*pl*) de peixe

**rogue** /rəʊg/ *n* (*dishonest*) patife *m*, velhaco *m*; (*mischievous*) brincalhão *m*

**role** /rəʊl/ *n* papel *m*

**roll** /rəʊl/ *vt/i* (fazer) rolar; (*into ball or cylinder*) enrolar(-se) □ *n* rolo *m*; (*list*) rol *m*, lista *f*; (*bread*) pãozinho *m*; (*of ship*) balanço *m*; (*of drum*) rufar *m*; (*of thunder*) ribombo *m*. **be ~ing in money** (*colloq*) nadar em dinheiro (*colloq*). **~ over** (*turn over*) virar-se ao contrário. **~ up** *vi* (*colloq*) aparecer □ *vt* (*sleeves*) arregaçar; (*umbrella*) fechar. **~-call** *n* chamada *f*. **~ing-pin** *n* rolo *m* de pastel

**roller** /'rəʊlə(r)/ *n* cilindro *m*; (*wave*)

vagalhão *m*; (*for hair*) rolo *m*. **~-blind** *n* estore *m*. **~-coaster** *n* montanha *f* russa. **~-skate** *n* patim *m* de rodas

**rolling** /'rəʊlɪŋ/ *a* ondulante

**Roman** /'rəʊmən/ *a & n* romano (*m*). **R~ Catholic** *a & n* católico (*m*). **~ numerals** algarismos *mpl* romanos

**romance** /rəʊ'mæns/ *n* (*love affair*) romance *m*; (*fig*) poesia *f*

**Romania** /rʊ'meɪnɪə/ *n* Romênia *f*, (*P*) Roménia *f*. **~n** *a & n* romeno (*m*)

**romantic** /rəʊ'mæntɪk/ *a* romântico. **~ally** *adv* românticamente. **~ism** *n* romantismo *m*. **~ize** *vi* fazer romance □ *vt* romantizar

**romp** /rɒmp/ *vi* brincar animadamente □ *n* brincadeira *f* animada. **~ers** *npl* macacão *m* de bebê, (*P*) fato *m* de bebé

**roof** /ruːf/ *n* (*pl* **roofs**) telhado *m*; (*of car*) teto *m*, (*P*) capota *f*; (*of mouth*) palato *m*, céu *m* da boca □ *vt* cobrir com telhado. **hit the ~** (*colloq*) ficar furioso. **~ing** *n* material *m* para telhados. **~-rack** *n* porta-bagagem *m*. **~-top** *n* cimo *m* do telhado

**rook**[1] /rʊk/ *n* (*bird*) gralha *f*

**rook**[2] /rʊk/ *n* (*chess*) torre *f*

**room** /ruːm/ *n* quarto *m*, divisão *f*; (*bedroom*) quarto *m* de dormir; (*large hall*) sala *f*; (*space*) espaço *m*, lugar *m*. **~s** (*lodgings*) apartamento *m*, cômodos *mpl*. **~-mate** *n* companheiro *m* de quarto. **~y** *a* espaçoso; (*clothes*) amplo, largo

**roost** /ruːst/ *n* poleiro *m* □ *vi* empoleirar-se. **~er** *n* (*Amer*) galo *m*

**root**[1] /ruːt/ *n* raiz *f*; (*fig*) origem *f* □ *vt/i* enraizar(-se), radicar(-se). **~ out** extirpar, erradicar. **take ~** criar raízes. **~less** *a* sem raízes, desenraizado

**root**[2] /ruːt/ *vi* **~ about** revolver, remexer. **~ for** (*Amer sl*) torcer por

**rope** /rəʊp/ *n* corda *f* □ *vt* atar. **know the ~s** estar por dentro (do assunto). **~ in** convencer a participar de

**rosary** /'rəʊzərɪ/ *n* rosário *m*

**rose**[1] /rəʊz/ *n* rosa *f*; (*nozzle*) ralo *m* (de regador). **~-bush** *n* roseira *f*

**rose**[2] /rəʊz/ *see* **rise**

**rosé** /'rəʊzeɪ/ *n* rosé *m*

**rosette** /rəʊ'zet/ *n* roseta *f*

**rosewood** /'rəʊzwʊd/ *n* pau-rosa *m*

**roster** /'rɒstə(r)/ *n* lista (de serviço) *f*, escala *f* (de serviço)

**rostrum** /'rɒstrəm/ *n* tribuna *f*; (*for conductor*) estrado *m*; (*sport*) podium *m*

**rosy** /'rəʊzɪ/ *a* (**-ier, -iest**) rosado; (*fig*) risonho

**rot** /rɒt/ *vt/i* (*pt* **rotted**) apodrecer □ *n*

putrefação f, podridão f; (sl: nonsense)
disparate m, asneiras fpl

**rota** /'rəʊtə/ n escala f de serviço

**rotary** /'rəʊtərɪ/ a rotativo, giratório

**rotat|e** /rəʊ'teɪt/ vt/i (fazer) girar,
(fazer) revolver; (change round)
alternar. **~ing** a rotativo. **~ion** /-ʃn/
n rotação f

**rote** /rəʊt/ n **by ~** de cor, maquinal-
mente

**rotten** /'rɒtn/ a podre; (corrupt) corrupto; (colloq: bad) mau, ruim. **~
eggs** ovos mpl podres. **feel ~** (ill)
não se sentir nada bem

**rotund** /rəʊ'tʌnd/ a rotundo, redondo

**rough** /rʌf/ a (-er, -est) rude; (to
touch) áspero, rugoso; (of ground)
acidentado, irregular; (violent) violento; (of sea) agitado, encapelado; (of
weather) tempestuoso; (not perfect)
tosco, rudimentar; (of estimate etc)
aproximado □ n (ruffian) rufia m, desordeiro m □ adv (live) ao relento;
(play) bruto □ vt **~ it** viver de modo
primitivo, não ter onde morar
(colloq). **~ out** fazer um esboço
preliminar de. **~-and-ready** a grosseiro mas eficiente. **~ paper** rascunho m, borrão m. **~ly** adv
asperamente, rudemente; (approximately) aproximadamente. **~ness** n
rudeza f, aspereza f; (violence) brutalidade f

**roughage** /'rʌfɪdʒ/ n alimentos mpl
fibrosos

**roulette** /ruː'let/ n roleta f

**round** /raʊnd/ a (-er, -est) redondo □
n (circle) círculo m; (slice) fatia f;
(postman's) entrega f; (patrol) ronda
f; (of drinks) rodada f; (competition)
partida f, rodada f; (boxing) round
m; (of talks) ciclo m, série f □ prep a
adv em volta (de), em torno (de) □ vt
arredondar; (cape, corner) dobrar,
virar. **come ~** (into consciousness)
voltar a si. **go or come ~ to** (a friend
etc) dar um pulo na casa de. **~ about**
(nearby) por aí; (fig) mais ou menos.
**~ of applause** salva f de palmas. **~
off** terminar. **~-shouldered** a
curvado. **~ the clock** noite e dia
sem parar. **~ trip** viagem f de ida e
volta. **~ up** (gather) juntar; (a figure)
arredondar. **~-up** n (of cattle) rodeio
m; (of suspects) captura f

**roundabout** /'raʊndəbaʊt/ n carrossel m; (for traffic) rotatória f, (P) rotunda f □ a indireto, (P) indirecto

**rous|e** /raʊz/ vt acordar, despertar. **be
~ed** (angry) exaltar-se, inflamar-se,
ser provocado. **~ing** a (speech) inflamado, exaltado; (music) vibrante;
(cheers) frenético

**rout** /raʊt/ n derrota f; (retreat) debandada f □ vt derrotar; (cause to retreat)
pôr em debandada

**route** /ruːt/ n percurso m, itinerário
m; (naut, aviat) rota f

**routine** /ruː'tiːn/ n rotina f; (theat)
número m □ a de rotina, rotineiro.
**daily ~** rotina f diária

**rov|e** /rəʊv/ vt/i errar (por), vaguear
(em/por). **~ing** a (life) errante

**row**[1] /rəʊ/ n fila f, fileira f; (in knitting) carreira f. **in a ~** (consecutive)
em fila

**row**[2] /rəʊ/ vt/i remar. **~ing** n remo m.
**~ing-boat** n barco m a remo

**row**[3] /raʊ/ n (colloq: noise) barulho m,
bagunça f, banzé m (colloq); (colloq:
quarrel) discussão f, briga f. **~
(with)** vi (colloq) brigar (com), discutir (com)

**rowdy** /'raʊdɪ/ a (-ier, -iest) desordeiro

**royal** /'rɔɪəl/ a real

**royalty** /'rɔɪəltɪ/ n família real f; (payment) direitos mpl (de autor, de patente, etc)

**rub** /rʌb/ vt/i (pt rubbed) esfregar;
(with ointment etc) esfregar, friccio-
nar □ n esfrega f; (with ointment etc)
fricção f. **~ it in** repisar/insistir em.
**~ off on** comunicar-se a, transmitir-
se a. **~ out** (with rubber) apagar

**rubber** /'rʌbə(r)/ n borracha f. **~
band** elástico m. **~ stamp** carimbo
m. **~-stamp** vt aprovar sem
questionar. **~y** a semelhante à borracha

**rubbish** /'rʌbɪʃ/ n (refuse) lixo m;
(nonsense) disparates mpl. **~ dump**
n lixeira f. **~y** a sem valor

**rubble** /'rʌbl/ n entulho m

**ruby** /'ruːbɪ/ n rubi m

**rucksack** /'rʌksæk/ n mochila f

**rudder** /'rʌdə(r)/ n leme m

**ruddy** /'rʌdɪ/ a (-ier, -iest) avermelhado; (of cheeks) corado, vermelho; (sl:
damned) maldito (colloq)

**rude** /ruːd/ a (-er, -est) mal-educado,
malcriado, grosseiro. **~ly** adv grosseiramente, malcriadamente. **~ness**
n má-educação f, má-criação f, grosseria f

**rudiment** /'ruːdɪmənt/ n rudimento
m. **~ary** /-'mentrɪ/ a rudimentar

**rueful** /'ruːfl/ a contrito, pesaroso

**ruffian** /'rʌfɪən/ n desordeiro m

**ruffle** /'rʌfl/ vt (feathers) eriçar;
(hair) despentear; (clothes) amarrotar; (fig) perturbar □ n (frill) franzi-
do m, (P) folho m

**rug** /rʌg/ n tapete m; (covering) manta
f

**rugged** /'rʌgɪd/ a rude, irregular;
(coast, landscape) acidentado; (character) forte; (features) marcado

**ruin** /'ru:m/ *n* ruína *f* □ *vt* arruinar; (*fig*) estragar. **~ous** *a* desastroso

**rule** /ru:l/ *n* regra *f*; (*regulation*) regulamento *m*; (*pol*) governo *m* □ *vt* governar; (*master*) dominar; (*jur*) decretar; (*decide*) decidir □ *vi* governar. **as a ~** regra geral, por via de regra. **~ out** excluir. **~d paper** papel *m* pautado. **~r** /-ə(r)/ *n* (*sovereign*) soberano *m*; (*leader*) governante *m*; (*measure*) régua *f*

**ruling** /'ru:lɪŋ/ *a* (*class*) dirigente; (*pol*) no poder □ *n* decisão *f*

**rum** /rʌm/ *n* rum *m*

**rumble** /'rʌmbl/ *vi* ribombar, ressoar; (*of stomach*) roncar □ *n* ribombo *m*, estrondo *m*

**rummage** /'rʌmɪdʒ/ *vt* revistar, remexer

**rumour** /'ru:mə(r)/ *n* boato *m*, rumor *m* □ *vt* **it is ~ed that** corre o boato de que, consta que

**rump** /rʌmp/ *n* (*of horse etc*) garupa *f*; (*of fowl*) mitra *f*. **~ steak** *n* bife *m* de alcatra

**run** /rʌn/ *vi* (*pt* **ran**, *pp* **run**, *pres p* **running**) correr; (*flow*) correr; (*pass*) passar; (*function*) andar, funcionar; (*melt*) derreter, pingar; (*bus etc*) circular; (*play*) estar em cartaz; (*colour*) desbotar; (*in election*) candidatar-se (**for** a) □ *vt* (*manage*) dirigir, gerir; (*a risk*) correr; (*a race*) participar em; (*water*) deixar correr; (*a car*) ter, manter □ *n* corrida *f*; (*excursion*) passeio *m*, ida *f*; (*rush*) corrida *f*, correria *f*; (*in cricket*) ponto *m*. **be on the ~** estar foragido. **have the ~ of** ter à sua disposição. **in the long ~** a longo prazo. **~ across** encontrar por acaso, dar com. **~ away** fugir. **~ down** descer correndo; (*of vehicle*) atropelar; (*belittle*) dizer mal de, denegrir. **~ down** estar exausto. **~ in** (*engine*) ligar. **~ into** (*meet*) encontrar por acaso; (*hit*) bater em, ir de encontro a. **~ off** *vt* (*copies*) tirar; (*water*) deixar correr □ *vi* fugir. **~-of-the-mill** *a* vulgar. **~ out** esgotar-se; (*lease*) expirar. **I ran out of sugar** o açúcar acabou. **~ over** (*of vehicle*) atropelar. **~ up** deixar acumular. **the ~-up to** o período que precede

**runaway** /'rʌnəweɪ/ *n* fugitivo *m* □ *a* fugitivo; (*horse*) desembestado; (*vehicle*) desarvorado; (*success*) grande

**rung**[1] /rʌŋ/ *n* (*of ladder*) degrace *m*

**rung**[2] /rʌŋ/ *see* **ring**[2]

**runner** /'rʌnə(r)/ *n* (*person*) corredor *m*; (*carpet*) passadeira *f*. **~ bean** feijão *m* verde. **~-up** *n* segundo classificado *m*

**running** /'rʌnɪŋ/ *n* corrida *f*; (*functioning*) funcionamento *m* □ *a* consecutivo, seguido; (*water*) corrente. **be in the ~** (*competitor*) ter probabilidades de êxito. **four days ~** quatro dias seguidos *or* a fio. **~ commentary** reportagem *f*, comentário *m*

**runny** /'rʌnɪ/ *a* derretido

**runway** /'rʌnweɪ/ *n* pista *f* de decolagem, (*P*) descolagem

**rupture** /'rʌptʃə(r)/ *n* ruptura *f*; (*med*) hérnia *f* □ *vt/i* romper(-se), rebentar

**rural** /'rʊərəl/ *a* rural

**ruse** /ru:z/ *n* ardil *m*, estratagema *m*, manha *f*

**rush**[1] /rʌʃ/ *n* (*plant*) junco *m*

**rush**[2] /rʌʃ/ *vi* (*move*) precipitar-se, (*be in a hurry*) apressar-se □ *vt* fazer, mandar *etc* a toda a pressa; (*person*) pressionar; (*mil*) tomar de assalto □ *n* tropel *m*; (*haste*) pressa *f*. **in a ~** as pressas. **~ hour** rush *m*, (*P*) hora *f* de ponta

**rusk** /rʌsk/ *n* bolacha *f*, biscoito *m*

**russet** /'rʌsɪt/ *a* castanho avermelhado □ *n* maçã *f* reineta

**Russia** /'rʌʃə/ *n* Rússia *f*. **~n** *a* & *n* russo (*m*)

**rust** /rʌst/ *n* (*on iron, plants*) ferrugem *f* □ *vt/i* enferrujar(-se). **~-proof** *a* inoxidável. **~y** *a* ferrugento, enferrujado; (*fig*) enferrujado

**rustic** /'rʌstɪk/ *a* rústico

**rustle** /'rʌsl/ *vt/i* restolhar, (fazer) farfalhar; (*Amer: steal*) roubar. **~ up** (*colloq: food etc*) arranjar

**rut** /rʌt/ *n* sulco *m*; (*fig*) rotina *f*. **in a ~** numa vida rotineira

**ruthless** /'ru:θlɪs/ *a* implacável

**rye** /raɪ/ *n* centeio *m*

# S

**sabbath** /'sæbəθ/ *n* (*Jewish*) sábado *m*; (*Christian*) domingo *m*

**sabbatical** /sə'bætɪkl/ *n* (*univ*) período *m* de licença

**sabot|age** /'sæbətɑ:ʒ/ *n* sabotagem *f* □ *vt* sabotar. **~eur** /-'tɜ:(r)/ *n* sabotador *m*

**sachet** /'sæʃeɪ/ *n* saché *m*

**sack** /sæk/ *n* saco *m*, saca *f* □ *vt* (*colloq*) despedir. **get the ~** (*colloq*) ser despedido

**sacrament** /'sækrəmənt/ *n* sacramento *m*

**sacred** /'seɪkrɪd/ *a* sagrado

**sacrifice** /'sækrɪfaɪs/ *n* sacrifício *m*; (*fig*) sacrifício *m* □ *vt* sacrificar

**sacrileg|e** /'sækrɪlɪdʒ/ *n* sacrilégio *m*. **~ious** /-'lɪdʒəs/ *a* sacrílego

**sad** /sæd/ *a* (**sadder**, **saddest**) (*person*) triste; (*story, news*) triste. **~ly**

*adv* tristemente; (*unfortunately*) infelizmente. **~ness** *n* tristeza *f*

**sadden** /'sædn/ *vt* entristecer

**saddle** /'sædl/ *n* sela *f* □ *vt* (*horse*) selar. **~ sb with** sobrecarregar alguém com

**sadis|m** /'seidizəm/ *n* sadismo *m*. **~t** /-ist/ *n* sádico *m*. **~tic** /sə'distik/ *a* sádico

**safe** /seif/ *a* (-er, -est) (*not dangerous*) seguro; (*out of danger*) fora de perigo; (*reliable*) confiável. **~ from** salvo de risco de □ *n* cofre *m*, caixa-forte *f*. **~ and sound** são e salvo. **~ conduct** salvo-conduto *m*. **~ keeping** custódia *f*, proteção *f*. **to be on the ~ side** por via das dúvidas. **~ly** *adv* (*arrive etc*) em segurança; (*keep*) seguro

**safeguard** /'seifga:d/ *n* salvaguarda *f* □ *vt* salvaguardar

**safety** /'seifti/ *n* segurança *f*. **~-belt** *n* cinto *m* de segurança. **~-pin** *n* alfinete *m* de fralda. **~-valve** *n* válvula *f* de segurança

**sag** /sæg/ *vi* (*pt* sagged) afrouxar

**saga** /'sa:gə/ *n* saga *f*

**sage**[1] /seidʒ/ *n* (*herb*) salva *f*

**sage**[2] /seidʒ/ *a* sensato, prudente □ *n* sábio *m*

**Sagittarius** /sædʒɪ'teərɪəs/ *n* (*astrol*) Sagitário *m*

**said** /sed/ *see* **say**

**sail** /seil/ *n* vela *f*; (*trip*) viagem *f* em barco à vela □ *vi* navegar; (*leave*) partir; (*sport*) velejar □ *vt* navegar. **~ing** *n* navegação *f* à vela. **~ing-boat** *n* barco *m* à vela

**sailor** /'seilə(r)/ *n* marinheiro *m*

**saint** /seint/ *n* santo *m*. **~ly** *a* santo, santificado

**sake** /seik/ *n* **for the ~ of** em consideração a. **for my/your/its own ~** por mim/por isso

**salad** /'sæləd/ *n* salada *f*. **~ dressing** *n* molho *m* para salada

**salary** /'sæləri/ *n* salário *m*

**sale** /seil/ *n* venda *f*; (*at reduced prices*) liquidação *f*. **for ~** "vende-se". **on ~** à venda. **~s assistant**, (*Amer*) **~s clerk** vendedor *m*. **~s department** departamento *m* de vendas

**sales|man** /'seilzmən/ *n* (*pl* -men) (*in shop*) vendedor *m*; (*traveller*) caixeiro-viajante *m*. **~woman** *n* (*pl* -women) (*in shop*) vendedora *f*; (*traveller*) caixeira-viajante *f*

**saline** /'seilain/ *a* salino □ *n* salina *f*

**saliva** /sə'laivə/ *n* saliva *f*

**sallow** /'sæləʊ/ *a* (-er, -est) amarelado

**salmon** /'sæmən/ *n* (*pl invar*) salmão *m*

**saloon** /sə'lu:n/ *n* (*on ship*) salão *m*; (*bar*) botequim *m*. **~ (car)** sedã *m*

**salt** /sɔ:lt/ *n* sal *m* □ *a* salgado □ *vt* (*season*) salgar; (*cure*) pôr em salmoura. **~-cellar** *n* saleiro *m*. **~ water** água *f* salgada, água *f* do mar. **~y** *a* salgado

**salutary** /'sæljʊtri/ *a* salutar

**salute** /sə'lu:t/ *n* saudação *f* □ *vt/i* saudar

**salvage** /'sælvidʒ/ *n* (*naut*) salvamento *m*; (*of waste*) reciclagem *f* □ *vt* salvar

**salvation** /sæl'veiʃn/ *n* salvação *f*

**same** /seim/ *a* mesmo (**as que**) □ *pron* **the ~** o mesmo □ *adv* **the ~** o mesmo. **all the ~** (*nevertheless*) mesmo assim, apesar de tudo. **at the ~ time** (*at once*) ao mesmo tempo

**sample** /'sa:mpl/ *n* amostra *f* □ *vt* experimentar, provar

**sanatorium** /sænə'tɔ:rɪəm/ *n* (*pl* -iums) sanatório *m*

**sanctify** /'sæŋktɪfai/ *vt* santificar

**sanctimonious** /sæŋktɪ'məʊnɪəs/ *a* santarrão, carola

**sanction** /'sæŋkʃn/ *n* (*approval*) aprovação *f*; (*penalty*) pena *f*, sanção *f* □ *vt* sancionar

**sanctity** /'sæŋktɪtɪ/ *n* santidade *f*

**sanctuary** /'sæŋktʃʊəri/ *n* (*relig*) santuário *m*; (*refuge*) refúgio *m*; (*for animals*) reserva *f*

**sand** /sænd/ *n* areia *f*; (*beach*) praia *f* □ *vt* (*with sandpaper*) lixar

**sandal** /'sændl/ *n* sandália *f*

**sandbag** /'sændbæg/ *n* saco *m* de areia

**sandbank** /'sændbæŋk/ *n* banco *m* de areia

**sandcastle** /'sændka:sl/ *n* castelo *m* de areia

**sandpaper** /'sændpeipə(r)/ *n* lixa *f* □ *vt* lixar

**sandpit** /'sændpit/ *n* caixa *f* de areia

**sandwich** /'sænwidʒ/ *n* sanduíche *m*, (*P*) sandes *f invar* □ *vt* **~ed between** encaixado entre. **~ course** curso *m* profissionalizante envolvendo estudo teórico e estágio em local de trabalho

**sandy** /'sændi/ *a* (-ier, iest) arenoso; (*beach*) arenoso; (*hair*) ruivo

**sane** /sein/ *a* (-er, -est) (*not mad*) são *m*; (*sensible*) sensato, ajuizado

**sang** /sæŋ/ *see* **sing**

**sanitary** /'sænitri/ *a* sanitário; (*system*) sanitário. **~ towel**, (*Amer*) **~ napkin** toalha *f* absorvente

**sanitation** /sæni'teiʃn/ *n* condições *fpl* sanitárias, saneamento *m*

**sanity** /'sæniti/ *n* sanidade *f*

**sank** /sæŋk/ *see* **sink**

**Santa Claus** /'sæntəklɔ:z/ *n* Papai Noel *m*

**sap** /sæp/ *n* seiva *f* □ *vt* (*pt* sapped) esgotar, minar

**sapphire** /'sæfaɪə(r)/ *n* safira *f*

**sarcas|m** /'sa:rkæzəm/ *n* sarcasmo *m*. **~tic** /sa:r'kæstɪk/ *a* sarcástico

**sardine** /sa:'di:n/ *n* sardinha *f*

**sardonic** /sa:'dɒnɪk/ *a* sardônico

**sash** /sæʃ/ *n* (*around waist*) cinto *m*; (*over shoulder*) faixa *f*. **~window** *n* janela *f* de guilhotina

**sat** /sæt/ *see* **sit**

**satanic** /sə'tænɪk/ *a* satânico

**satchel** /'sætʃl/ *n* sacola *f*

**satellite** /'sætəlaɪt/ *n* satélite *m*. **~dish** antena *f* de satélite. **~ television** televisão *f* via satélite

**satin** /'sætɪn/ *n* cetim *m*

**satir|e** /'sætaɪə(r)/ *n* sátira *f*. **~ical** /sə'tɪrɪkl/ *a* satirical. **~ist** /'sætərɪst/ *n* satirista *mf*. **~ize** *vt* satirizar

**satisfact|ion** /sætɪs'fækʃn/ *n* satisfação *f*. **~ory** /fæktərɪ/ *a* satisfatório

**satisfy** /'sætɪsfaɪ/ *vt* satisfazer; (*convince*) convencer; (*fulfil*) atender. **~ing** *a* satisfatório

**saturat|e** /'sætʃəreɪt/ *vt* saturar; (*fig*) **~ed** *a* (*wet*) encharcado; (*fat*) saturado. **~ion** /'reɪʃn/ *n* saturação *f*

**Saturday** /'sætədɪ/ *n* sábado *m*

**sauce** /sɔ:s/ *n* molho *m*; (*colloq: cheek*) atrevimento *m*

**saucepan** /'sɔ:spən/ *n* panela *f*, (*P*) caçarola *f*

**saucer** /'sɔ:sə(r)/ *n* pires *m invar*

**saucy** /'sɔ:sɪ/ *a* (**-ier, -iest**) picante

**Saudi Arabia** /saʊdɪə'reɪbɪə/ *n* Arábia *f* Saudita

**sauna** /'sɔ:nə/ *n* sauna *f*

**saunter** /'sɔ:ntə(r)/ *vi* perambular

**sausage** /'sɒsɪdʒ/ *n* salsicha *f*, linguiça *f*; (*precooked*) salsicha *f*

**savage** /'sævɪdʒ/ *a* (*wild*) selvagem; (*fierce*) cruel; (*brutal*) brutal □ *n* selvagem *mf* □ *vt* atacar ferozmente. **~ry** *n* selvageria *f*, ferocidade *f*

**sav|e** /seɪv/ *vt* (*rescue*) salvar; (*keep*) guardar; (*collect*) colecionar; (*money*) economizar; (*time*) ganhar; (*prevent*) evitar, impedir (**from** de) □ *n* (*sport*) salvamento *m* □ *prep* salvo, exceto. **~er** *n* poupador *m*. **~ing** *n* economia *f*, poupança *f*. **~ings** *npl* economias *fpl*

**saviour** /'seɪvɪə(r)/ *n* salvador *m*

**savour** /'seɪvə(r)/ *n* sabor *m* □ *vt* saborear. **~y** *a* (*tasty*) saboroso; (*not sweet*) salgado

**saw**[1] /sɔ:/ *see* **see**[1]

**saw**[2] /sɔ:/ *n* serra *f* □ *vt* (*pt* **sawed**, *pp* **sawn** or **sawed**) serrar

**sawdust** /'sɔ:dʌst/ *n* serragem *f*

**saxophone** /'sæksəfəʊn/ *n* saxofone *m*

**say** /seɪ/ *vt/i* (*pt* **said** /sed/) □ *n* have a **~ (in)** opinar sobre alg coisa. have

one's **~** exprimir sua opinião. **I ~!** olhe! *or* escute! **~ing** *n* ditado *m*, provérbio *m*

**scab** /skæb/ *n* casca *f*, crosta *f*; (*colloq: blackleg*) fura-greve *mf invar*

**scaffold** /'skæfəʊld/ *n* cadafalso *m*, andaime *m*. **~ing** /-əldɪŋ/ *n* andaime *m*

**scald** /skɔ:ld/ *vt* escaldar, queimar □ *n* escaldadura *f*

**scale**[1] /skeɪl/ *n* (*of fish etc*) escama *f*

**scale**[2] /skeɪl/ *n* (*ratio, size*) escala *f*; (*mus*) escala *f*, (*of salaries, charges*) tabela *f*. **on a small/large/etc ~** numa pequena/grande/*etc* escala □ *vt* (*climb*) escalar. **~ down** reduzir

**scales** /skeɪlz/ *npl* (*for weighing*) balança *f*

**scallop** /'skɒləp/ *n* (*culin*) concha *f* de vieira; (*shape*) concha *f* de vieira

**scalp** /skælp/ *n* couro *m* cabeludo □ *vt* escalpar

**scalpel** /'skælpl/ *n* bisturi *m*

**scamper** /'skæmpə(r)/ *vi* sair correndo

**scampi** /'skæmpɪ/ *npl* camarões *mpl* fritos

**scan** /skæn/ *vt* (*pt* **scanned**) (*intently*) perscrutar, esquadrinhar; (*quickly*) passar os olhos em; (*med*) examinar; (*radar*) explorar □ *n* (*med*) exame *m*

**scandal** /'skændl/ *n* (*disgrace*) escândalo *m*; (*gossip*) fofoca *f*. **~ous** *a* escandaloso

**Scandinavia** /skændɪ'neɪvɪə/ *n* Escandinávia *f*. **~n** *a & n* escandinavo (*m*)

**scanty** /'skæntɪ/ *a* (**-ier, -iest**) escasso; (*clothing*) sumário

**scapegoat** /'skeɪpgəʊt/ *n* bode *m* expiatório

**scar** /ska:(r)/ *n* cicatriz *f* □ *vt* (*pt* **scarred**) marcar; (*fig*) deixar marcas

**scarc|e** /skeəs/ *a* (**-er, -est**) escasso, raro. **make o.s. ~e** (*colloq*) sumir, dar o fora (*colloq*). **~ity** *n* escassez *f*. **~ely** *adv* mal, apenas

**scare** /skeə(r)/ *vt* assustar, apavorar. **be ~d** estar com medo (**of** de) □ *n* pavor *m*, pânico *m*. **bomb ~** pânico *m* causado por suspeita de bomba num local

**scarecrow** /'skeəkrəʊ/ *n* espantalho *m*

**scarf** /ska:f/ *n* (*pl* **scarves**) (*oblong*) cachecol *m*; (*square*) lenço *m* de cabelo

**scarlet** /'ska:lət/ *a* escarlate *m*

**scary** /'skeərɪ/ *a* (**-ier, -iest**) (*colloq*) assustador, apavorante

**scathing** /'skeɪðɪŋ/ *a* mordaz

**scatter** /'skætə(r)/ *vt* (*strew*) espalhar; (*disperse*) dispersar □ *vi* espalhar-se

**scavenge** /'skævɪndʒ/ *vi* procurar

comida *etc* no lixo. **~r** /-ə(r)/ *n* (*person*) que procura comida *etc* no lixo; (*animal*) que se alimenta de carniça
**scenario** /sɪ'nɑːrɪəʊ/ *n* (*pl* **-os**) sinopse *f*, resumo *m* detalhado
**scene** /siːn/ *n* cena *f*; (*of event*) cenário *m*; (*sight*) vista *f*, panorama *m*. **behind the ~s** nos bastidores. **make a ~** fazer um escândalo
**scenery** /'siːnərɪ/ *n* cenário *m*, paisagem *f*; (*theat*) cenário *m*
**scenic** /'siːnɪk/ *a* pitoresco, cênico
**scent** /sent/ *n* (*perfume*) perfume *m*, fragância *f*; (*trail*) rastro *m*, pista *f* □ *vt* (*discern*) sentir. **~ed** *a* perfumado
**sceptic** /'skeptɪk/ *n* cético *m*. **~al** *a* cético. **~ism** /-sɪzəm/ *n* ceticismo *m*
**schedule** /'ʃedjuːl/ *n* programa *m*; (*timetable*) horário *m* □ *vt* marcar, programar. **according to ~** conforme planejado. **behind ~** atrasado. **on ~** (*train*) na hora; (*work*) em dia. **~d flight** *n* vôo *m* regular
**scheme** /skiːm/ *n* esquema *m*; (*plan of work*) plano *m*; (*plot*) conspiração *f*, maquinação *f* □ *vi* planejar, (*P*) planear; (*pej*) intrigar, maquinar, tramar
**schism** /'sɪzəm/ *n* cisma *m*
**schizophreni|a** /skɪtsəʊ'friːnɪə/ *n* esquizofrenia *f*. **~c** /-'frenɪk/ *a* esquizofrênico, (*P*) esquizofrénico
**scholar** /'skɒlə(r)/ *n* erudito *m*, estudioso *m*, escolar *m*. **~ly** *a* erudito. **~ship** *n* erudição *f*, saber *m*; (*grant*) bolsa *f* de estudo
**school** /skuːl/ *n* escola *f*; (*of university*) escola *f*, faculdade *f* □ *a* (*age, year, holidays*) escolar □ *vt* ensinar; (*train*) treinar, adestrar. **~ing** *n* instrução *f*; (*attendance*) escolaridade *f*
**school|boy** /'skuːlbɔɪ/ *n* aluno *m*. **~girl** aluna *f*
**school|master** /'skuːlmɑːstə(r)/, **~mistress**, **~teacher** *ns* professor *m*, professora *f*
**schooner** /'skuːnə(r)/ *n* escuna *f*; (*glass*) copo *m* alto
**sciatica** /saɪ'ætɪkə/ *n* ciática *f*
**scien|ce** /'saɪəns/ *n* ciência *f*. **~ce fiction** ficção *f* científica. **~tific** /-'tɪfɪk/ *a* científico
**scientist** /'saɪəntɪst/ *n* cientista *mf*
**scintillate** /'sɪntɪleɪt/ *vi* cintilar; (*fig: person*) brilhar
**scissors** /'sɪzəz/ *npl* (**pair of**) **~** tesoura *f*
**scoff**[1] /skɒf/ *vi* **~ at** zombar de, (*P*) troçar de
**scoff**[2] /skɒf/ *vt* (*sl: eat*) devorar, tragar
**scold** /skəʊld/ *vt* ralhar com. **~ing** *n* repreensão *f*, descompostura *f*
**scone** /skɒn/ *n* (*culin*) scone *m*, bolinho *m* para o chá

**scoop** /skuːp/ *n* (*for grain, sugar etc*) pá *f*; (*ladle*) concha *f*; (*news*) furo *m* □ *vt* **~ out** (*hollow out*) escavar, tirar com concha *or* pá. **~ up** (*lift*) apanhar
**scoot** /skuːt/ *vi* (*colloq*) fugir, mandar-se (*colloq*), (*P*) pôr-se a milhas (*colloq*)
**scooter** /'skuːtə(r)/ *n* (*child's*) patinete *f*, (*P*) trotinete *m*; (*motor cycle*) motoreta *f*, lambreta *f*
**scope** /skəʊp/ *n* âmbito *m*; (*fig: opportunity*) oportunidade *f*
**scorch** /skɔːtʃ/ *vt/i* chamuscar(-se), queimar de leve. **~ing** *a* (*colloq*) escaldante, abrasador
**score** /skɔː(r)/ *n* (*sport*) contagem *f*, escore *m*; (*mus*) partitura *f* □ *vt* marcar com corte(s), riscar; (*a goal*) marcar; (*mus*) orquestrar □ *vi* marcar pontos; (*keep score*) fazer a contagem; (*football*) marcar um gol, (*P*) golo. **a ~ (of)** (*twenty*) uma vintena (de), vinte. **~s** muitos, dezenas. **on that ~** nesse respeito, quanto a isso. **~board** *n* marcador *m*. **~r** /-ə(r)/ *n* (*score-keeper*) marcador *m*; (*of goals*) autor *m*
**scorn** /skɔːn/ *n* desprezo *m* □ *vt* desprezar. **~ful** *a* desdenhoso, escarninho. **~fully** *adv* com desdém, desdenhosamente
**Scorpio** /'skɔːpɪəʊ/ *n* (*astr*) Escorpião *m*
**scorpion** /'skɔːpɪən/ *n* escorpião *m*
**Scot** /skɒt/ *n*, **~tish** *a* escocês (*m*)
**Scotch** /skɒtʃ/ *a* escocês □ *n* uísque *m*
**scotch** /skɒtʃ/ *vt* pôr fim a, frustrar
**scot-free** /skɒt'friː/ *a* impune □ *adv* impunemente
**Scotland** /'skɒtlənd/ *n* Escócia *f*
**Scots** /skɒts/ *a* escocês. **~man** *n* escocês *m*. **~woman** *n* escocesa *f*
**scoundrel** /'skaʊndrəl/ *n* patife *m*, canalha *m*
**scour**[1] /'skaʊə(r)/ *vt* (*clean*) esfregar, arear. **~er** *n* esfregão *m* de palha de aço *or* de nylon
**scour**[2] /'skaʊə(r)/ *vt* (*search*) percorrer, esquadrinhar
**scourge** /skɜːdʒ/ *n* açoite *m*; (*fig*) flagelo *m*
**scout** /skaʊt/ *n* (*mil*) explorador *m* □ *vi* **~ about (for)** andar à procura de
**Scout** /skaʊt/ *n* escoteiro *m*, (*P*) escuteiro *m*. **~ing** *n* escotismo *m*, (*P*) escutismo *m*
**scowl** /skaʊl/ *n* carranca *f*, ar *m* carrancudo □ *vi* fazer um ar carrancudo
**scraggy** /'skrægɪ/ *a* (**-ier**, **-iest**) descarnado, ossudo
**scramble** /'skræmbl/ *vi* trepar; (*crawl*) avançar de rastros, rastejar, arrastar-se □ *vt* (*eggs*) mexer □ *n* luta *f*, confusão *f*
**scrap**[1] /skræp/ *n* bocadinho *m*. **~s**

*npl* restos *mpl* □ *vt* (*pt* **scrapped**) jogar fora, (P) deitar fora; (*plan etc*) abandonar, pôr de lado. **~-book** *n* álbum *m* de recortes. **~ heap** monte *m* de ferro-velho. **~-iron** *n* ferro *m* velho, sucata *f*. **~ merchant** sucateiro *m*. **~-paper** *n* papel *m* de rascunho. **~py** *a* fragmentário

**scrap²** /skræp/ *n* (*colloq: fight*) briga *f*, pancadaria *f* (*colloq*), rixa *f*

**scrape** /skreɪp/ *vt* raspar; (*graze*) esfolar, arranhar □ *vi* (*graze, rub*) roçar □ *n* (*act of scraping*) raspagem *f*; (*mark*) raspão *m*, esfoladura *f*; (*fig*) encrenca *f*, maus lençóis *mpl*. **~ through** escapar pela tangente, (P) à tangente; (*exam*) passar pela tangente, (P) à tangente. **~ together** conseguir juntar. **~r** /-ə(r)/ *n* raspadeira *f*

**scratch** /skrætʃ/ *vt/i* arranhar(-se); (*a line*) riscar; (*to relieve itching*) coçar(-se) □ *n* arranhão *m*; (*line*) risco *m*; (*wound with claw, nail*) unhada *f*. **start from ~** começar do princípio. **up to ~** à altura, ao nível requerido

**scrawl** /skrɔːl/ *n* rabisco *m*, garrancho *m*, garatuja *f* □ *vt/i* rabiscar, fazer garranchos, garatujar

**scrawny** /'skrɔːnɪ/ *a* (-ier, -iest) descarnado, ossudo, magricela

**scream** /skriːm/ *vt/i* gritar □ *n* grito *m* (agudo)

**screech** /skriːtʃ/ *vi* guinchar, gritar; (*of brakes*) chiar, guinchar □ *n* guincho *m*, grito *m* agudo

**screen** /skriːn/ *n* écran *m*, tela *f*; (*folding*) biombo *m*; (*fig: protection*) manto *m* (*fig*), capa *f* (*fig*) □ *vt* resguardar, tapar; (*film*) passar; (*candidates etc*) fazer a triagem de. **~ing** *n* (*med*) exame *m* médico

**screw** /skruː/ *n* parafuso *m* □ *vt* aparafusar, atarraxar. **~ up** (*eyes, face*) franzir; (*sl: ruin*) estragar. **~ up one's courage** cobrar coragem

**screwdriver** /'skruːdraɪvə(r)/ *n* chave *f* de parafusos *or* de fenda

**scribble** /'skrɪbl/ *vt/i* rabiscar, garatujar □ *n* rabisco *m*, garatuja *f*

**script** /skrɪpt/ *n* escrita *f*; (*of film*) roteiro *m*, (P) guião *m*. **~-writer** *n* (*film*) roteirista *m*, (P) autor *m* do guião

**Scriptures** /'skrɪptʃəz/ *npl* the **~** a Sagrada Escritura

**scroll** /skrəʊl/ *n* rolo *m* (de papel ou pergaminho); (*archit*) voluta *f* □ *vt/i* (*comput*) passar na tela

**scrounge** /skraʊndʒ/ *vt* (*colloq: cadge*) filar (*sl*), (P) cravar (*sl*) □ *vi* (*beg*) parasitar, viver às custas de alguém. **~r** /-ə(r)/ *n* parasita *mf*, filão *m* (*sl*), (P) crava *mf* (*sl*)

**scrub¹** /skrʌb/ *n* (*land*) mato *m*

**scrub²** /skrʌb/ *vt/i* (*pt* **scrubbed**) esfregar, lavar com escova e sabão; (*colloq: cancel*) cancelar □ *n* esfrega *f*

**scruff** /skrʌf/ *n* **by the ~ of the neck** pelo cangote, (P) pelo cachaço

**scruffy** /'skrʌfɪ/ *a* (-ier, -iest) desmazelado, desleixado, mal ajambrado (*colloq*)

**scrum** /skrʌm/ *n* rixa *f*; (*Rugby*) placagem *f*

**scruple** /'skruːpl/ *n* escrúpulo *m*

**scrupulous** /'skruːpjʊləs/ *a* escrupuloso. **~ly** *adv* escrupulosamente. **~ly clean** impecavelmente limpo

**scrutin|y** /'skruːtɪnɪ/ *n* averiguação *f*, escrutínio *m*. **~ize** *vt* examinar em detalhes

**scuff** /skʌf/ *vt* (*scrape*) esfolar, safar □ *n* esfoladura *f*

**scuffle** /'skʌfl/ *n* tumulto *m*, briga *f*

**sculpt** /skʌlpt/ *vt/i* esculpir. **~or** *n* escultor *m*. **~ure** /-tʃə(r)/ *n* escultura *f* □ *vt/i* esculpir

**scum** /skʌm/ *n* (*on liquid*) espuma *f*; (*pej: people*) gentinha *f*, escumalha *f*, ralé *f*

**scurf** /skɜːf/ *n* películas *fpl*; (*dandruff*) caspa *f*

**scurrilous** /'skʌrɪləs/ *a* injurioso, insultuoso

**scurry** /'skʌrɪ/ *vi* dar corridinhas; (*hurry*) apressar-se. **~ off** escapulir-se

**scurvy** /'skɜːvɪ/ *n* escorbuto *m*

**scuttle¹** /'skʌtl/ *n* (*bucket, box*) balde *m* para carvão

**scuttle²** /'skʌtl/ *vt* (*ship*) afundar abrindo rombos *or* as torneiras de fundo

**scuttle³** /'skʌtl/ *vi* **~ away** *or* off fugir, escapulir-se

**scythe** /saɪð/ *n* gadanha *f*, foice *f* grande

**sea** /siː/ *n* mar *m* □ *a* do mar, marinho, marítimo. **at ~** no alto mar, ao largo. **all at ~** desnorteado. **by ~** por mar. **~bird** ave *f* marinha. **~-green** *a* verde-mar. **~ horse** cavalo-marinho *m*, hipocampo *m*. **~ level** nível *m* do mar. **~ lion** leão-marinho *m*. **~ shell** concha *f*. **~-shore** *n* litoral *m*; (*beach*) praia *f*. **~ water** água *f* do mar

**seaboard** /'siːbɔːd/ *n* litoral *m*, costa *f*

**seafarer** /'siːfeərə(r)/ *n* marinheiro *m*, navegante *m*

**seafood** /'siːfuːd/ *n* marisco(s) *m* (*pl*)

**seagull** /'siːɡʌl/ *n* gaivota *f*

**seal¹** /siːl/ *n* (*animal*) foca *f*

**seal²** /siːl/ *n* selo *m*, sinete *m* □ *vt* selar; (*with wax*) lacrar. **~ing-wax** *n* lacre *m*. **~ off** (*area*) vedar

**seam** /siːm/ *n* (*in cloth etc*) costura *f*; (*of mineral*) veio *m*, filão *m*. **~less** *a* sem costura

**seaman** /'si:mən/ n (pl -men) marinheiro m, marítimo m

**seamy** /'si:mɪ/ a ~ **side** lado m (do avesso); (fig) lado m sórdido

**seance** /'seɪɑːns/ n sessão f espírita

**seaplane** /'si:pleɪn/ n hidroavião m

**seaport** /'si:pɔːt/ n porto m de mar

**search** /sɜːtʃ/ vt/i revistar, dar busca (a); (one's heart, conscience etc) examinar □ n revista f, busca f; (quest) procura f, busca f; (official) inquérito m. **in ~ of** à procura de. **~ for** procurar. **~-party** n equipe f de busca. **~-warrant** n mandado m de busca. **~ing** a (of look) penetrante; (of test etc) minucioso

**searchlight** /'sɜːtʃlaɪt/ n holofote m

**seasick** /'si:sɪk/ a enjoado. **~ness** n enjôo m, P enjoo m

**seaside** /'si:saɪd/ n costa f, praia f, beira-mar f. **~ resort** n balneário m, praia f

**season** /'si:zn/ n (of year) estação f; (proper time) época f; (cricket, football etc) temporada f □ vt temperar; (wood) secar. **in ~** na época. **~able** a próprio da estação. **~al** a sazonal. **~ed** a (of people) experimentado. **~ing** n tempero m. **~-ticket** n (train etc) passe m; (theatre etc) assinatura f

**seat** /si:t/ n assento m; (place) lugar m; (of bicycle) selim m; (of chair) assento m; (of trousers) fundilho m □ vt sentar; (have seats for) ter lugares sentados para. **be ~ed, take a ~** sentar-se. **~ of learning** centro m de cultura. **~-belt** n cinto m de segurança

**seaweed** /'si:wi:d/ n alga f marinha

**seaworthy** /'si:wɜːðɪ/ a navegável, em condições de navegabilidade

**secateurs** /'sekətɜːz/ npl tesoura f de poda

**seclu|de** /sɪ'klu:d/ vt isolar. **~ded** a isolado, retirado. **~sion** /sɪ'klu:ʒn/ n isolamento m

**second¹** /'sekənd/ a segundo □ n segundo m; (in duel) testemunha f. **~ (gear)** (auto) segunda f (velocidade). **the ~ of April** dois de Abril. **~s** (goods) artigos mpl de segunda or de refugo □ adv (in race etc) em segundo lugar □ vt secundar. **~-best** a escolhido em segundo lugar. **~-class** a de segunda classe. **~-hand** a de segunda mão □ n (on clock) ponteiro m dos segundos. **~-rate** a medíocre, de segunda ordem. **~ thoughts** dúvidas fpl. **on ~ thoughts** pensando melhor. **~ly** adv segundo, em segundo lugar

**second²** /sɪ'kɒnd/ vt (transfer) destacar (**to** para)

**secondary** /'sekəndrɪ/ a secundário. **~ school** escola f secundária

**secrecy** /'si:krəsɪ/ n segredo m

**secret** /'si:krɪt/ a secreto □ n segredo m. **in ~** em segredo. **~ agent** n agente mf secreto. **~ly** adv em segredo, secretamente

**secretar|y** /'sekrətrɪ/ n secretário m, secretária f. **S~y of State** ministro m de Estado, (P) Secretário m de Estado; (Amer) ministro m dos Negócios Estrangeiros. **~ial** /-'teərɪəl/ a (work, course etc) de secretária

**secret|e** /sɪ'kri:t/ vt segregar; (hide) esconder. **~ion** /-ʃn/ n secreção f

**secretive** /'si:krətɪv/ a misterioso, reservado

**sect** /sekt/ n seita f. **~arian** /'teərɪən/ a sectário

**section** /'sekʃn/ n seção f, (P) secção f; (of country, community etc) setor m, (P) sector m; (district of town) zona f

**sector** /'sektə(r)/ n setor m, (P) sector m

**secular** /'sekjʊlə(r)/ a secular, leigo, P laico; (art, music etc) profano

**secure** /sɪ'kjʊə(r)/ a seguro, em segurança; (firm) seguro, sólido; (in mind) tranqüilo, P tranquilo □ vt prender bem or com segurança; (obtain) conseguir, arranjar; (ensure) assegurar; (windows, doors) fechar bem. **~ly** adv solidamente; (safely) em segurança

**securit|y** /sɪ'kjʊərətɪ/ n segurança f; (for loan) fiança f, caução f. **~ies** npl (finance) títulos mpl

**sedate** /sɪ'deɪt/ a sereno, comedido □ vt (med) tratar com sedativos

**sedation** /sɪ'deɪʃn/ n (med) sedação f. **under ~** sob o efeito de sedativos

**sedative** /'sedətɪv/ n (med) sedativo m

**sedentary** /'sedntrɪ/ a sedentário

**sediment** /'sedɪmənt/ n sedimento m, depósito m

**seduce** /sɪ'dju:s/ vt seduzir

**seduct|ion** /sɪ'dʌkʃn/ n sedução f. **~ive** /-tɪv/ a sedutor, aliciante

**see¹** /si:/ vt/i (pt saw, pp seen) ver; (escort) acompanhar. **~ about** or **to** tratar de, encarregar-se de. **~ off** vt (wave goodbye) ir despedir-se de; (chase) through (task) levar a cabo; (not be deceived by) não se deixar enganar por. **~ (to it) that** assegurar que, tratar de fazer com que. **~ing that** visto que, uma vez que. **~ you later!** (colloq) até logo! (colloq)

**see²** /si:/ n sé f, bispado m

**seed** /si:d/ n semente f, (fig: origin) germe(n) m; (tennis) cabeça f de série; (pip) caroço m. **go to ~** produzir sementes; (fig) desmazelar-se (colloq).

**~ling** n planta f brotada a partir da semente

**seedy** /'si:dɪ/ a (**-ier, -iest**) (com um ar) gasto, surrado; (*colloq: unwell*) abatido, deprimido, em baixo astral (*colloq*)

**seek** /si:k/ vt (pt **sought**) procurar; (*help etc*) pedir

**seem** /si:m/ vi parecer. **~ingly** adv aparentemente, ao que parece

**seemly** /'si:mlɪ/ adv decente, conveniente, próprio

**seen** /si:n/ see **see**[1]

**seep** /si:p/ vi (*ooze*) filtrar-se; (*trickle*) pingar, escorrer, passar. **~age** n infiltração f

**see-saw** /'si:sɔ:/ n gangorra f, (P) balanço m

**seethe** /si:ð/ vi ~ **with** (*anger*) ferver de; (*people*) fervilhar de

**segment** /'segmənt/ n segmento m; (*of orange*) gomo m

**segregat|e** /'segrɪgeɪt/ vt segregar, separar. **~ion** /-'geɪʃn/ n segregação f

**seize** /si:z/ vt agarrar, (P) deitar a mão a, apanhar; (*take possession by force*) apoderar-se de; (*by law*) apreender, confiscar, (P) apresar □ vi ~ **on** (*opportunity*) aproveitar. **~ up** (*engine etc*) grimpar, emperrar. **be ~d with** (*fear, illness*) ter um ataque de

**seizure** /'si:ʒə(r)/ n (*med*) ataque m, crise f; (*law*) apreensão f, captura f

**seldom** /'seldəm/ adv raras vezes, raramente, raro

**select** /sɪ'lekt/ vt escolher, selecionar, (P) seleccionar □ a seleto, (P) selecto. **~ion** /-ʃn/ n seleção f, (P) selecção f; (*comm*) sortido m

**selective** /sɪ'lektɪv/ a seletivo, (P) selectivo

**self** /self/ n (pl **selves**) the ~ o eu, o ego

**self-** /self/ pref **~-assurance** n segurança f. **~-assured** a seguro de si. **~-catering** a em que os hóspedes tem facilidades de cozinhar. **~-centred** a egocêntrico. **~-confidence** n autoconfiança f, confiança f em si mesmo. **~-confident** a que tem confiança em si mesmo. **~-conscious** a inibido, constrangido. **~-contained** a independente. **~-control** n autodomínio m. **~-controlled** a senhor de si. **~-defence** n legítima defesa f. **~-denial** n abnegação f. **~-employed** a autónomo. **~-esteem** n amor m próprio. **~-evident** a evidente. **~-indulgent** a que não resiste a tentações; (*for ease*) comodista. **~-interest** n interesse m pessoal. **~-portrait** n auto-retrato m. **~-possessed** a senhor de si. **~-reliant** a independente, seguro de si.

**~-respect** n amor m próprio. **~-righteous** a que se tem em boa conta. **~-sacrifice** n abnegação f, sacrifício m. **~-satisfied** a cheio de si, convencido (*colloq*). **~-seeking** a egoísta. **~-service** a auto-serviço, self-service. **~-styled** a pretenso. **~-sufficient** a auto-suficiente. **~-willed** a voluntarioso

**selfish** /'selfɪʃ/ a egoísta; (*motive*) interesseiro. **~ness** n egoismo m

**selfless** /'selflɪs/ a desinteressado

**sell** /sel/ vt/i (pt **sold**) vender(-se). **~-by date** ~ **off** liquidar. **be sold out** estar esgotado. **~-out** n (*show*) sucesso m; (*colloq: betrayal*) traição f. **~er** n vendedor m

**Sellotape** /'seləʊteɪp/ n fita f adesiva, (P) fitacola f

**semantic** /sɪ'mæntɪk/ a semântico. **~s** n semântica f

**semblance** /'sembləns/ n aparência f

**semen** /'si:mən/ n sêmen m, (P) sémen m, esperma m

**semester** /sɪ'mestə(r)/ n (*Amer: univ*) semestre m

**semi-** /'semɪ/ pref semi-, meio

**semibreve** /'semɪbri:v/ n (*mus*) semibreve f

**semicirc|le** /'semɪsɜ:kl/ n semicírculo m. **~ular** /-sɜ:kjʊlə(r)/ a semicircular

**semicolon** /semɪ'kəʊlən/ n ponto-e-vírgula m

**semi-detached** /semɪdɪ'tætʃt/ a ~ **house** casa f geminada

**semifinal** /semɪ'faɪnl/ n semifinal f, (P) meiafinal f

**seminar** /'semmɑ:(r)/ n seminário m

**semiquaver** /'semɪkweɪvə(r)/ n (*mus*) semicolcheia f

**Semit|e** /'si:maɪt/ a & n semita (mf). **~ic** /sɪ'mɪtɪk/ a & n (*lang*) semítico (m)

**semitone** /'semɪtəʊn/ n (*mus*) semitom m

**semolina** /semə'li:nə/ n sêmola f, (P) sémola f, semolina f

**senat|e** /'senɪt/ n senado m. **~or** /-ətə(r)/ n senador m

**send** /send/ vt/i (pt **sent**) enviar, mandar. ~ **back** devolver. ~ **for** (*person*) chamar, mandar vir; (*help*) pedir. ~ (**away** or **off**) **for** encomendar, mandar vir (por carta). **~-off** n despedida f, bota-fora m. ~ **up** (*colloq*) parodiar. **~er** n expedidor m, remetente m

**senil|e** /'si:naɪl/ a senil. **~ity** /sɪ'nɪlətɪ/ n senilidade f

**senior** /'si:nɪə(r)/ a mais velho, mais idoso (**to** que); (*in rank*) superior; (*in service*) mais antigo; (*after surname*) sênior, (P) sénior □ n pessoa f mais velha; (*schol*) finalista mf. ~ **citizen**

pessoa f de idade or da terceira idade.
**~ity** /-'prəti/ n (in age) idade f; (in service) antiguidade f

**sensation** /sen'seiʃn/ n sensação f.
**~al** a sensacional. **~alism** n sensacionalismo m

**sense** /sens/ n sentido m; (wisdom) bom senso m; (sensation) sensação f; (mental impression) sentimento m. **~s** (sanity) razão f □ vt pressentir. **make ~** fazer sentido. **make ~ of** compreender. **~less** a disparatado, sem sentido; (med) sem sentidos, inconsciente

**sensible** /'sensəbl/ a sensato, razoável; (clothes) prático

**sensitiv|e** /'sensətɪv/ a sensível (to a); (touchy) susceptível. **~ity** /-'tɪvəti/ n sensibilidade f

**sensory** /'sensərɪ/ a sensorial

**sensual** /'senʃʊəl/ a sensual. **~ity** /-'ælətɪ/ n sensualidade f

**sensuous** /'senʃʊəs/ a sensual

**sent** /sent/ see send

**sentence** /'sentəns/ n frase f; (jur: decision) sentença f; (punishment) pena f □ vt **~ to** condenar a

**sentiment** /'sentɪmənt/ n sentimento m; (opinion) modo m de ver

**sentimental** /sentɪ'mentl/ a sentimental. **~ity** /-'men'tæləti/ n sentimentalidade f, sentimentalismo m. **~ value** valor m estimativo

**sentry** /'sentrɪ/ n sentinela f

**separable** /'sepərəbl/ a separável

**separate¹** /'seprət/ a separado, diferente. **~s** npl (clothes) conjuntos mpl. **~ly** adv separadamente, em separado

**separat|e²** /'sepərett/ vt/i separar (-se). **~ion** /-'reɪʃn/ n separação f

**September** /sep'tembə(r)/ n setembro m

**septic** /'septɪk/ a séptico, infectado

**sequel** /'si:kwəl/ n resultado m, sequela f, (P) sequela f; (of novel, film) continuação f

**sequence** /'si:kwəns/ n sequência f, (P) sequência f

**sequin** /'si:kwm/ n lantejoula f

**serenade** /serə'neɪd/ n serenata f □ vt fazer uma serenata para

**seren|e** /sɪ'ri:n/ a sereno. **~ity** /-'enəti/ n serenidade f

**sergeant** /'sɑ:dʒənt/ n sargento m

**serial** /'sɪərɪəl/ n folhetim m □ a (number) de série. **~ize** /-laɪz/ vt publicar em folhetim

**series** /'sɪərɪːz/ n invar série f

**serious** /'sɪərɪəs/ a sério; (very bad, critical) grave, sério. **~ly** adv seriamente, gravemente, a sério. **take ~ly** levar a sério. **~ness** n seriedade f, gravidade f

**sermon** /'sɜ:mən/ n sermão m

**serpent** /'sɜ:pənt/ n serpente f

**serrated** /sɪ'reɪtɪd/ a (edge) serr(e)ado, com serrilha

**serum** /'sɪərəm/ n (pl -a) soro m

**servant** /'sɜ:vənt/ n criado m, criada f, empregado m, empregada f

**serv|e** /sɜ:v/ vt/i servir; (a sentence) cumprir; (jur: a writ) entregar; (mil) servir, prestar serviço; (apprenticeship) fazer □ n (tennis) saque m, (P) serviço m. **~e as/to** servir de/para. **~e its purpose** servir para o que é (colloq), servir os seus fins. **it ~es you/him etc right** é bem feito. **~ing** n (portion) dose f, porção f

**service** /'sɜ:vɪs/ n serviço m; (relig) culto m; (tennis) saque m (P) serviço m; (maintenance) revisão f. **~s** (mil) forças fpl armadas □ vt (car etc) fazer a revisão de. **of ~ to** útil a, de utilidade a. **~ area** área f de serviço. **~ charge** serviço m. **~ station** posto m de gasolina

**serviceable** /'sɜ:vɪsəbl/ a (of use, usable) útil, prático; (durable) resistente; (of person) prestável

**serviceman** /'sɜ:vɪsmən/ n (pl -men) militar m

**serviette** /sɜ:vɪ'et/ n guardanapo m

**servile** /'sɜ:vaɪl/ a servil

**session** /'seʃn/ n sessão f; (univ) ano m académico, (P) acadêmico; (Amer: univ) semestre m. **in ~** (sitting) em sessão, reunidos

**set** /set/ vt (pt set, pres p setting) pôr, colocar; (put down) pousar; (limit etc) fixar; (watch, clock) regular; (example) dar; (exam, task) marcar; (in plaster) engessar □ vi (of sun) pôr-se; (of jelly) endurecer, solidificar- □ n (of people) círculo m, roda f; (of books) colecção f, (P) colecção f; (of tools, chairs etc) jogo m; (TV, radio) aparelho m; (hair) mise f; (theat) cenário m; (tennis) partida f, set m □ a fixo; (habit) inveterado; (jelly) duro, sólido; (book) do programa, (P) adoptado; (meal) a preço fixo. **be ~ on doing** estar decidido a fazer. **~ about** or **to** começar a, pôr-se a. **~ back** (plans etc) atrasar; (sl: cost) custar. **~-back** n revés m, contratempo m, atraso m de vida (colloq). **~ fire to** atear fogo a, (P) deitar fogo a. **~ free** pôr em liberdade. **~ in** (rain etc) pegar. **~ off** or **out** partir, começar a viajar. **~ off** (mechanism) pôr para funcionar, (P) pôr a funcionar; (bomb) explodir; (by contrast) realçar. **~ out** (state) expor; (arrange) dispor. **~ sail** partir, içar as velas. **~ square** esquadro m. **~ the table** pôr a mesa. **~ theory** teoria f de conjuntos. **~-to** n briga f.

~ **up** (*establish*) fundar, estabelecer.
~**-up** *n* (*system*) sistema *m*, organização *f*; (*situation*) situação *f*
**settee** /se'tiː/ *n* sofá *m*
**setting** /'setɪŋ/ *n* (*framework*) quadro *m*; (*of jewel*) engaste *m*; (*typ*) composição *f*; (*mus*) arranjo *m* musical
**settle** /'setl/ *vt* (*arrange* ) resolver; (*date*) marcar; (*nerves*) acalmar; (*doubts*) esclarecer; (*new country*) colonizar, povoar; (*bill*) pagar □ *vi* assentar; (*in country*) estabelecer-se; (*in house, chair etc*) instalar-se; (*weather*) estabilizar-se.  ~ **down** acalmar-se; (*become orderly*) assentar; (*sit, rest*) instalar-se. ~ **for** aceitar. ~ **up (with)** fazer contas (com); (*fig*) ajustar contas (com). ~**r** /-ə(r)/ *n* colono *m*, colonizador *m*
**settlement** /'setlmənt/ *n* (*agreement*) acordo *m*; (*payment*) pagamento *m*; (*colony*) colónia *f*, (*P*) colónia *f*; (*colonization*) colonização *f*
**seven** /'sevn/ *a* & *n* sete (*m*). ~**th** *a* & *n* sétimo (*m*)
**seventeen** /sevn'tiːn/ *a* & *n* dezessete (*m*), (*P*) dezassete (*m*). ~**th** *a* & *n* décimo sétimo (*m*)
**sevent**|**y** /'sevntɪ/ *a* & *n* setenta (*m*). ~**ieth** *a* & *n* septuagésimo (*m*)
**sever** /'sevə(r)/ *vt* cortar. ~**ance** *n* corte *m*
**several** /'sevrəl/ *a* & *pron* vários, diversos
**sever**|**e** /sɪ'vɪə(r)/ *a* (-**er**, -**est**) severo; (*pain*) forte, violento; (*illness*) grave; (*winter*) rigoroso. ~**ely** *adv* severamente; (*seriously*) gravemente. ~**ity** /sɪ'verɪtɪ/ *n* severidade *f*; (*seriousness*) gravidade *f*
**sew** /səʊ/ *vt*/*i* (*pt* **sewed**, *pp* **sewn** *or* **sewed**) coser, costurar. ~**ing** *n* costura *f*. ~**ing-machine** *n* máquina *f* de costura
**sewage** /'sjuːɪdʒ/ *n* efluentes *mpl* dos esgotos, detritos *mpl*
**sewer** /'sjuːə(r)/ *n* cano *m* de esgoto
**sewn** /səʊn/ *see* **sew**
**sex** /seks/ *n* sexo *m* □ *a* sexual. **have** ~ ter relações. ~ **maniac** tarado *m* sexual. ~**y** *a* sexy *invar*, que tem sex-appeal
**sexist** /'seksɪst/ *a* & *n* sexista *mf*
**sexual** /'sekʃʊəl/ *a* sexual. ~ **harassment** assédio *m* sexual. ~ **intercourse** relações *fpl* sexuais. ~**ity** /'ælətɪ/ *n* sexualidade *f*
**shabb**|**y** /'ʃæbɪ/ *a* (-**ier**, -**iest**) (*clothes, object*) gasto, surrado; (*person*) maltrapilho, mal vestido; (*mean*) miserável. ~**ily** *adv* miseravelmente
**shack** /ʃæk/ *n* cabana *f*, barraca *f*
**shackles** /'ʃæklz/ *npl* grilhões *mpl*, algemas *fpl*

**shade** /ʃeɪd/ *n* sombra *f*; (*of colour*) tom *m*, matiz *m*; (*of opinion*) matiz *m*; ( *for lamp*) abat-jour *m*, quebra-luz *m*; (*Amer: blind*) estore *m* □ *vt* resguardar da luz; (*darken*) sombrear. **a** ~ **bigger**/*etc* ligeiramente maior/*etc*. **in the** ~ à sombra
**shadow** /'ʃædəʊ/ *n* sombra *f* □ *vt* cobrir de sombra; ( *follow*) seguir, vigiar. **S~ Cabinet** gabinete *m* formado pelo partido da oposição. ~**y** *a* ensombrado, sombreado; ( *fig*) vago, indistinto
**shady** /'ʃeɪdɪ/ *a* (-**ier**, -**iest**) sombreiro, (*P*) que dá sombra; (*in shade*) à sombra; ( *fig: dubious*) suspeito, duvidoso
**shaft** /ʃɑːft/ *n* (*of arrow, spear*) haste *f*; (*axle*) eixo *m*, veio *m*; (*of mine, lift*) poço *m*; (*of light*) raio *m*
**shaggy** /'ʃægɪ/ *a* (-**ier**, -**iest**) (*beard*) hirsuto; (*hair*) desgrenhado; (*animal*) peludo, felpudo
**shake** /ʃeɪk/ *vt* (*pt* **shook**, *pp* **shaken**) abanar, sacudir; (*bottle*) agitar; (*belief, house etc*) abalar □ *vi* estremecer, tremer □ *n* (*violent*) abanão *m*, safanão *m*; (*light*) sacudidela *f*. ~ **hands with** apertar a mão de. ~ **off** (*get rid of*) sacudir, livrar-se de. ~ **one's head** (*to say no*) fazer que não com a cabeça. ~ **up** agitar. ~**-up** *n* (*upheaval*) reviravolta *f*
**shaky** /'ʃeɪkɪ/ *a* (-**ier**, -**iest**) (*hand, voice*) trêmulo, (*P*) trémulo; (*unsteady, unsafe*) pouco firme, inseguro; (*weak*) fraco
**shall** /ʃæl/; *unstressed* /ʃəl/ *v aux* **I**/ **we** ~ **do** ( *future*) farei/faremos. **you**/**he** ~ **do** (*command*) eu hei de/ você há de/tu hás de/ele há de fazer
**shallot** /ʃə'lɒt/ *n* cebolinha *f*, (*P*) chalota *f*
**shallow** /'ʃæləʊ/ *a* (-**er**, -**est**) pouco fundo, raso; ( *fig*) superficial
**sham** /ʃæm/ *n* fingimento *m*; (*jewel etc*) imitação *f*; (*person*) impostor *m*, fingido *m* □ *a* fingido; ( *false*) falso □ *vt* (*pt* **shammed**) fingir
**shambles** /'ʃæmblz/ *npl* (*colloq: mess*) balbúrdia *f*, trapalhada *f*
**shame** /ʃeɪm/ *n* vergonha *f* □ *vt* (*fazer*) envergonhar. **it's a** ~ é uma pena. **what a** ~**!** que pena! ~**ful** *a* vergonhoso. ~**less** *a* sem vergonha, descarado; (*immodest*) despudorado, desavergonhado
**shamefaced** /'ʃeɪmfeɪst/ *a* envergonhado
**shampoo** /ʃæm'puː/ *n* xampu *m*, (*P*) champô *m*, shampoo *m* □ *vt* lavar com xampu, (*P*) champô *or* shampoo
**shan't** /ʃɑːnt/ = **shall not**
**shanty** /'ʃæntɪ/ *n* barraca *f*. ~ **town** favela *f*, (*P*) bairro(s) *m* (*pl*) da lata

**shape** /ʃeɪp/ *n* forma *f* □ *vt* moldar □ *vi* ~ (**up**) andar bem, fazer progressos. **take** ~ concretizar-se, avançar. ~**less** *a* informe, sem forma; (*of body*) deselegante, disforme

**shapely** /'ʃeɪplɪ/ *a* (-**ier**, -**iest**) (*leg, person*) bem feito, elegante

**share** /ʃeə(r)/ *n* parte *f*, porção *f*; (*comm*) ação *f*, (*P*) acção *f* □ *vt/i* partilhar (**with** com, **in** de)

**shareholder** /'ʃeəhəʊldə(r)/ *n* acionista *mf*, (*P*) accionista *f*

**shark** /ʃɑːk/ *n* tubarão *m*

**sharp** /ʃɑːp/ *a* (-**er**, -**est**) (*knife, pencil etc*) afiado; (*pin, point etc*) pontiagudo, aguçado; (*words, reply*) áspero; (*of bend*) fechado; (*acute*) agudo; (*sudden*) brusco; (*dishonest*) pouco honesto; (*well-defined*) nítido; (*brisk*) rápido, vigoroso; (*clever*) vivo □ *adv* (*stop*) de repente □ *n* (*mus*) sustenido *m*. **six o'clock** ~ seis horas em ponto. ~**ly** *adv* (*harshly*) rispidamente; (*suddenly*) de repente

**sharpen** /'ʃɑːpən/ *vt* aguçar; (*pencil*) fazer a ponta de, (*P*) afiar; (*knife etc*) afiar, amolar. ~**er** *n* afiadeira *f*; (*for pencil*) apontador *m*, (*P*) apára-lápis *m*, (*P*) afia-lápis *m*

**shatter** /'ʃætə(r)/ *vt/i* despedaçar (-se), esmigalhar(-se); (*hopes*) destruir(-se); (*nerves*) abalar(-se). ~**ed** *a* (*upset*) passado; (*exhausted*) estourado (*colloq*)

**shav|e** /ʃeɪv/ *vt/i* barbear(-se), fazer a barba (de) □ *n* **have a** ~**e** barbear-se. **have a close** ~**e** (*fig*) escapar por um triz. ~**en** *a* raspado, barbeado. ~**er** *n* aparelho *m* de barbear, (*P*) máquina *f* de barbear. ~**ing-brush** *n* pincel *m* para a barba. ~**ing-cream** *n* creme *m* de barbear

**shaving** /'ʃeɪvɪŋ/ *n* apara *f*

**shawl** /ʃɔːl/ *n* xale *m*, (*P*) xaile *m*

**she** /ʃiː/ *pron* ela □ *n* fêmea *f*

**sheaf** /ʃiːf/ *n* (*pl* **sheaves**) feixe *m*; (*of papers*) maço *m*, molho *m*

**shear** /ʃɪə(r)/ *vt* (*pp* **shorn** or **sheared**) (*sheep etc*) tosquiar

**shears** /ʃɪəz/ *npl* tesoura *f* para jardim

**sheath** /ʃiːθ/ *n* (*pl* ~**s** /ʃiːðz/) bainha *f*; (*condom*) preservativo *m*, camisa-de-Vénus *f*

**sheathe** /ʃiːð/ *vt* embainhar

**shed**[1] /ʃed/ *n* (*hut*) casinhola *f*; (*for cows*) estábulo *m*

**shed**[2] /ʃed/ (*pt* **shed**, *pres p* **shedding**) perder, deixar cair; (*spread*) espalhar; (*blood, tears*) deitar, derramar. ~ **light on** lançar luz sobre

**sheen** /ʃiːn/ *n* brilho *m*, lustre *m*

**sheep** /ʃiːp/ *n* (*pl invar*) carneiro *m*, ovelha *f*. ~-**dog** *n* cão *m* de pastor

**sheepish** /'ʃiːpɪʃ/ *a* encabulado. ~**ly** *adv* com um ar encabulado

**sheepskin** /'ʃiːpskɪn/ *n* pele *f* de carneiro; (*leather*) carneira *f*

**sheer** /ʃɪə(r)/ *a* mero, simples; (*steep*) íngreme, a pique; (*fabric*) diáfano, transparente □ *adv* a pique, verticalmente

**sheet** /ʃiːt/ *n* lençol *m*; (*of glass, metal*) chapa *f*, placa *f*; (*of paper*) folha *f*

**sheikh** /ʃeɪk/ *n* xeque *m*, sheik *m*

**shelf** /ʃelf/ *n* (*pl* **shelves**) prateleira *f*

**shell** /ʃel/ *n* (*of egg, nut etc*) casca *f*; (*of mollusc*) concha *f*; (*of ship, tortoise*) casco *m*; (*of building*) estrutura *f*, armação *f*; (*of explosive*) cartucho *m* □ *vt* descascar; (*mil*) bombardear

**shellfish** /'ʃelfɪʃ/ *n* (*pl invar*) crustáceo *m*; (*as food*) marisco *m*

**shelter** /'ʃeltə(r)/ *n* abrigo *m*, refúgio *m* □ *vt* abrigar; (*protect*) proteger; (*harbour*) dar asilo a □ *vi* abrigar-se, refugiar-se. ~**ed** *a* (*life etc*) protegido; (*spot*) abrigado

**shelve** /ʃelv/ *vt* pôr em prateleiras; (*fit with shelves*) pôr prateleiras em; (*fig*) engavetar, pôr de lado

**shelving** /'ʃelvɪŋ/ *n* (*shelves*) prateleiras *fpl*

**shepherd** /'ʃepəd/ *n* pastor *m* □ *vt* guiar. ~**'s pie** empadão *m* de batata e carne moída

**sheriff** /'ʃerɪf/ *n* xerife *m*

**sherry** /'ʃerɪ/ *n* Xerez *m*

**shield** /ʃiːld/ *n* (*armour, heraldry*) escudo *m*; (*screen*) antepara *m* □ *vt* proteger (**from** contra, de)

**shift** /ʃɪft/ *vt/i* mudar de posição, deslocar(-se); (*exchange, alter*) mudar de □ *n* mudança *f*; (*workers; work*) turno *m*. **make** ~ arranjar-se

**shiftless** /'ʃɪftlɪs/ *a* (*lazy*) molengão, preguiçoso

**shifty** /'ʃɪftɪ/ *a* (-**ier**, -**iest**) ·elhaco, duvidoso

**shimmer** /'ʃɪmə(r)/ *vi* luzir suavemente □ *n* luzir *m*

**shin** /ʃɪn/ *n* perna *f*. ~-**bone** *n* tíbia *f*, canela *f*. ~-**pad** *n* (*football*) caneleira *f*

**shin|e** /ʃaɪn/ *vt/i* (*pt* **shone**) (fazer) brilhar, (fazer) reluzir; (*shoes*) engraxar □ *n* lustro *m*. ~**e a torch** (**on**) iluminar com uma lanterna de mão. **the sun is** ~**ing** faz sol

**shingle** /'ʃɪŋgl/ *n* (*pebbles*) seixos *mpl*

**shingles** /'ʃɪŋglz/ *npl med* zona *f*, herpes-zóster *f*

**shiny** /'ʃaɪnɪ/ *a* (-**ier**, -**iest**) brilhante; (*of coat, trousers*) lustroso

**ship** /ʃɪp/ *n* barco *m*, navio *m* □ *vt* (*pt* **shipped**) transportar; (*send*) mandar por via marítima; (*load*) embarcar. ~**ment** *n* (*goods*) carregamento *m*;

(*shipping*) embarque *m*. ~**per** *n* expedidor *m*. ~**ping** *n* navegação *f*; (*ships*) navios *mpl*

**shipbuilding** /'ʃɪpbɪldɪŋ/ *n* construção *f* naval

**shipshape** /'ʃɪpʃeɪp/ *adv* & *a* em (perfeita) ordem, impecável

**shipwreck** /'ʃɪprek/ *n* naufrágio *m*. ~**ed** *a* naufragado. be ~**ed** naufragar

**shipyard** /'ʃɪpjɑːd/ *n* estaleiro *m*

**shirk** /ʃɜːk/ *vt* fugir a, furtar-se a, (*P*) baldar-se a (*sl*). ~**er** *n* parasita *mf*

**shirt** /ʃɜːt/ *n* camisa *f*; (*of woman*) blusa *f*. **in** ~-**sleeves** em mangas de camisa

**shiver** /'ʃɪvə(r)/ *vi* arrepiar-se, tiritar □ *n* arrepio *m*

**shoal** /ʃəʊl/ *n* (*of fish*) cardume *m*

**shock** /ʃɒk/ *n* choque *m*, embate *m*; (*electr*) choque *m* elétrico, (*P*) eléctrico; (*med*) choque *m* □ *a* de choque □ *vt* chocar. ~**absorber** (*mech*) amortecedor *m*. ~**ing** *a* chocante; (*colloq: very bad*) horrível

**shod** /ʃɒd/ *see* **shoe**

**shodd|y** /'ʃɒdɪ/ *a* (-**ier**, -**iest**) mal feito, ordinário, de má qualidade. ~**ily** *adv* mal

**shoe** /ʃuː/ *n* sapato *m*; (*footwear*) calçado *m*; (*horse*) ferradura *f*; (*brake*) sapata *f*, (*P*) calço *m* (de travão) □ *vt* (*pt* **shod**, *pres p* **shoeing**) (*horse*) ferrar. ~**polish** *n* pomada *f*, (*P*) graxa *f* para sapatos. ~-**shop** *n* sapataria *f*. **on a** ~-**string** (*colloq*) com/por muito pouco dinheiro, na pindaíba (*colloq*)

**shoehorn** /'ʃuːhɔːn/ *n* calçadeira *f*

**shoelace** /'ʃuːleɪs/ *n* cordão *m* de sapato, (*P*) atacador *m*

**shoemaker** /'ʃuːmeɪkə(r)/ *n* sapateiro *m*

**shone** /ʃɒn/ *see* **shine**

**shoo** /ʃuː/ *vt* enxotar □ *int* xô

**shook** /ʃʊk/ *see* **shake**

**shoot** /ʃuːt/ *vt* (*pt* **shot**) (*gun*) disparar; (*glance, missile*) lançar; (*kill*) matar a tiro; (*wound*) ferir a tiro; (*execute*) executar, fuzilar; (*hunt*) caçar; (*film*) filmar, rodar □ *vi* disparar, atirar (**at** contra, sobre); (*bot*) rebentar; (*football*) rematar □ *n* (*bot*) rebento *m*. ~**down** abater (a tiro). ~**in/out** (*rush*) entrar/sair correndo *or* disparado. ~**up** (*spurt*) jorrar; (*grow quickly*) crescer a olhos vistos, dar um pulo; (*prices*) subir em disparada. ~**ing** *n* (*shots*) tiroteio *m*. ~**ing-range** *n* carreira *f* de tiro. ~**ing star** estrela *f* cadente

**shop** /ʃɒp/ *n* loja *f*; (*workshop*) oficina *f* □ *vi* (*pt* **shopped**) fazer compras. ~**around** procurar, ver o que há. ~

**assistant** empregado *m*, caixeiro *m*; vendedor *m*. ~-**floor** *n* (*workers*) trabalhadores *mpl*. ~**per** *n* comprador *m*. ~-**soiled**, (*Amer*) ~-**worn** *adjs* enxovalhado. ~**steward** delegado *m* sindical. ~**window** vitrina *f*, (*P*) montra *f*. **talk** ~ falar de coisas profissionais

**shopkeeper** /'ʃɒpkiːpə(r)/ *n* lojista *mf*, comerciante *mf*

**shoplift|er** /'ʃɒplɪftə(r)/ *n* gatuno *m* de lojas. ~**ing** *n* furto *m* em lojas

**shopping** /'ʃɒpɪŋ/ *n* (*goods*) compras *fpl*. **go** ~ ir às compras. ~**bag** sacola *f* de compras. ~**centre** centro *m* comercial

**shore** /ʃɔː(r)/ *n* (*of sea*) praia *f*, costa *f*; (*of lake*) margem *f*

**shorn** /ʃɔːn/ *see* **shear** □ *a* tosquiado. ~**of** despojado de

**short** /ʃɔːt/ *a* (-**er**, -**est**) curto; (*person*) baixo; (*brief*) breve, curto; (*curt*) seco, brusco. **be** ~ **of** (*lack*) ter falta de □ *adv* (*abruptly*) bruscamente, de repente. **cut** ~ abreviar; (*interrupt*) interromper □ *n* (*electr*) curto-circuito *m*; (*film*) curta-metragem *f*, short *m*. ~**s** (*trousers*) calção *m*, (*P*) calções *mpl*, short *m*, (*P*) shorts *mpl*. **a** ~ **time** pouco tempo. **he is called Tom for** ~ o diminutivo dele é Tom. **in** ~ em suma. ~-**change** *vt* (*cheat*) enganar. ~**circuit** (*electr*) curto-circuito *m*. ~-**circuit** *vt/i* (*electr*) fazer *or* dar um curto-circuito (em). ~**cut** atalho *m*. ~-**handed** *a* com falta de pessoal. ~**list** pré-seleção *f*, (*P*) pré-selecção *f*. ~-**lived** *a* de pouca duração. ~-**sighted** *a* míope, (*P*) curto de vista. ~-**tempered** *a* irritadiço. ~**story** conto *m*. ~**wave** (*radio*) onda(s) *f(pl)* curta(s)

**shortage** /'ʃɔːtɪdʒ/ *n* falta *f*, escassez *f*

**shortbread** /'ʃɔːtbred/ *n* ⊃ **shortbread** *m*, biscoito *m* de massa amanteigada

**shortcoming** /'ʃɔːtkʌmɪŋ/ *n* falha *f*, imperfeição *f*

**shorten** /'ʃɔːtn/ *vt/i* encurtar(-se), abreviar(-se), diminuir

**shorthand** /'ʃɔːthænd/ *n* estenografia *f*. ~**typist** estenodactilógrafa *f*

**shortly** /'ʃɔːtlɪ/ *adv* (*soon*) em breve, dentro em pouco

**shot** /ʃɒt/ *see* **shoot** □ *n* (*firing, bullet*) tiro *m*; (*person*) atirador *m*; (*pellets*) chumbo *m*; (*photograph*) fotografia *f*; (*injection*) injeção *f*, (*P*) injecção *f*; (*golf, billiards*) tacada *f*. **go like a** ~ ir disparado. **have a** ~ (**at sth**) experimentar (fazer alg coisa). ~-**gun** *n* espingarda *f*, caçadeira *f*

**should** /ʃʊd/; *unstressed* /ʃəd/ *v aux* **you** ~ **help me** você devia me ajudar. **I** ~ **have stayed** devia ter ficado. **I ~ like to** gostaria de or gostava de. **if he ~ come** se ele vier

**shoulder** /'ʃəʊldə(r)/ n ombro m □ vt (*responsibility*) tomar, assumir; (*burden*) carregar, arcar com. **~-blade** n (*anat*) omoplata f. **~-pad** n enchimento m de ombro, ombreira f

**shout** /ʃaʊt/ n grito m, brado m; (*very loud*) berro m □ vt/i gritar (**at** com); (*very loudly*) berrar (**at** com). **~ down** fazer calar com gritos. **~ing** n gritaria f, berraria f

**shove** /ʃʌv/ n empurrão m □ vt/i empurrar; (*colloq: put*) meter, enfiar. **~ off** (*colloq: depart*) começar a andar (*colloq*), dar o fora (*colloq*), (*P*) cavar (*colloq*)

**shovel** /'ʃʌvl/ n pá f; (*machine*) escavadora f □ vt (*pt* shovelled) remover com pá

**show** /ʃəʊ/ vt (*pt* showed, *pp* shown) mostrar; (*of dial, needle*) marcar; (*put on display*) expor; (*film*) dar, passar □ vi ver-se, aparecer, estar à vista □ n mostra f, demonstração f, manifestação f; (*ostentation*) alarde m, espalhafato m; (*exhibition*) mostra f, exposição f; (*theatre, cinema*) espetáculo m, (*P*) espectáculo m, show m. **for ~** para fazer vista. **on ~** exposto, em exposição. **~-down** n confrontação f. **~-jumping** n concurso m hípico. **~ in** mandar entrar. **~ off** vt exibir, ostentar □ vi exibir-se, querer fazer figura. **~-off** n exibicionista mf. **~ out** acompanhar à porta. **~-piece** n peça f digna de se expor. **~ up** ser claramente visível, ver-se bem; (*colloq: arrive*) aparecer. **~ing** n (*performance*) atuação f, performance f; (*cinema*) exibição f

**shower** /'ʃaʊə(r)/ n (*of rain*) aguaceiro m, chuvarada f; (*of blows etc*) saraivada f; (*in bathroom*) chuveiro m, ducha f, (*P*) duche m □ vt ~ **with** cumular de, encher de □ vi tomar um banho de chuveiro or uma ducha, (*P*) um duche. **~y** a chuvoso

**showerproof** /'ʃaʊəpruːf/ a impermeável

**shown** /ʃəʊn/ see **show**

**showroom** /'ʃəʊrʊm/ n espaço m de exposição, show-room m; (*for cars*) stand m

**showy** /'ʃəʊɪ/ a (-ier, -iest) vistoso; (*too bright*) berrante; (*pej*) espalhafatoso

**shrank** /ʃræŋk/ see **shrink**

**shred** /ʃred/ n tira f, retalho m, farrapo m; (*fig*) mínimo m, sombra f □ vt (*pt* shredded) reduzir a tiras, estraçalhar; (*culin*) desfiar. **~der** n trituradora f; (*for paper*) fragmentadora f

**shrewd** /ʃruːd/ a (-er, -est) astucioso,

fino, perspicaz. **~ness** n astúcia f, perspicácia f

**shriek** /ʃriːk/ n grito m agudo, guincho m □ vt/i gritar, guinchar

**shrift** /ʃrɪft/ n **give sb short ~** tratar alguém com brusquidão, despachar alguém sem mais cerimônias, (*P*) cerimónias

**shrill** /ʃrɪl/ a estridente, agudo

**shrimp** /ʃrɪmp/ n camarão m

**shrine** /ʃraɪn/ n (*place*) santuário m; (*tomb*) túmulo m; (*casket*) relicário m

**shrink** /ʃrɪŋk/ vt/i (*pt* shrank, *pp* shrunk) encolher; (*recoil*) encolher-se. **~ from** esquivar-se a, fugir a (+ *inf*)/de (+ *noun*), retrair-se de. **~age** n encolhimento m; (*comm*) contração f

**shrivel** /'ʃrɪvl/ vt/i (*pt* shrivelled) encarquilhar(-se)

**shroud** /ʃraʊd/ n mortalha f □ vt (*veil*) encobrir, envolver

**Shrove** /ʃrəʊv/ n ~ **Tuesday** Terça-feira f gorda or de Carnaval

**shrub** /ʃrʌb/ n arbusto m. **~bery** n arbustos mpl

**shrug** /ʃrʌg/ vt (*pt* shrugged) ~ **one's shoulders** encolher os ombros □ n encolher m de ombros. **~ off** não dar importância a

**shrunk** /ʃrʌŋk/ see **shrink**. **~en** a encolhido; (*person*) mirrado, chupado

**shudder** /'ʃʌdə(r)/ vi arrepiar-se, estremecer, tremer □ n arrepio m, tremor m, estremecimento m. **I ~ to think** tremo só de pensar

**shuffle** /'ʃʌfl/ vt (*feet*) arrastar; (*cards*) embaralhar □ vi arrastar os pés □ n marcha f arrastada

**shun** /ʃʌn/ vt (*pt* shunned) evitar, fugir de

**shunt** /ʃʌnt/ vt/i (*train*) mudar de linha, manobrar

**shut** /ʃʌt/ vt (*pt* shut, *pres p* shutting) fechar □ vi fechar-se; (*shop, bank etc*) encerrar, fechar. **~ down** or **up** fechar. **~-down** n encerramento m. **~ in** or **up** trancar. **~ up** vi (*colloq: stop talking*) calar-se □ vt (*colloq: silence*) mandar calar. **~ up!** (*colloq*) cale-se!, cale a boca!

**shutter** /'ʃʌtə(r)/ n taipais mpl, (*P*) portada f de madeira; (*of laths*) persiana f; (*in shop*) taipais mpl; (*photo*) obturador m

**shuttle** /'ʃʌtl/ n (*of spaceship*) ônibus m espacial. **~ service** (*plane*) ponte f aérea; (*bus*) navete f

**shuttlecock** /'ʃʌtlkɒk/ n volante m

**shy** /ʃaɪ/ a (-er, -est) tímido, acanhado, envergonhado □ vi (*horse*) espantar-se (**at** com); (*fig*) assustar-se (**at** or **away from** com). **~ness** n timidez f, acanhamento m, vergonha f

**Siamese** /saɪə'miːz/ a & n siamês (m). ~ **cat** gato m siamês

**Sicily** /'sɪsɪlɪ/ n Sicília f

**sick** /sɪk/ a doente; (humour) negro. **be** ~ (vomit) vomitar. **be** ~ **of** estar farto de. **feel** ~ estar enjoado. ~**-bay** n enfermaria f. ~**-leave** n licença f por doença ~**-room** n quarto m de doente

**sicken** /'sɪkn/ vt (distress) desesperar; (disgust) repugnar □ vi be ~ing for flu etc começar a pegar uma gripe (colloq)

**sickle** /'sɪkl/ n foice f

**sickly** /'sɪklɪ/ a (-ier, -iest) (person) doentio, achacado; (smell) enjoativo; (pale) pálido

**sickness** /'sɪknɪs/ n doença f; (vomiting) náusea f, vômito m, (P) vómito m

**side** /saɪd/ n lado m; (of road, river) beira f; (of hill) encosta f; (sport) equipe f, (P) equipa f □ a lateral □ vi ~ **with** tomar o partido de. **on the** ~ (extra) nas horas vagas; (secretly) pela calada. ~ **by** ~ lado a lado. ~**-car** n sidecar m. ~**-effect** n efeito m secundário. ~**-show** n espetáculo m, (P) espectáculo m suplementar. ~**-step** vt (pt -stepped) evitar. ~**-track** vt (fazer) desviar dum propósito

**sideboard** /'saɪdbɔːd/ n aparador m

**sideburns** /'saɪdbɜːnz/ npl suíças fpl, costeletas fpl, (P) patilhas fpl

**sidelight** /'saɪdlaɪt/ n (auto) luz f lateral, (P) farolim m

**sideline** /'saɪdlaɪn/ n atividade f, (P) actividade f secundária; (sport) linha f lateral

**sidelong** /'saɪdlɒŋ/ adv & a de lado

**sidewalk** /'saɪdwɔːk/ n (Amer) passeio m

**sideways** /'saɪdweɪz/ adv & a de lado

**siding** /'saɪdɪŋ/ n desvio m, ramal m

**sidle** /'saɪdl/ vi ~ **up (to)** avançar furtivamente (para), chegar-se furtivamente (a)

**siege** /siːdʒ/ n cerco m

**siesta** /sɪ'estə/ n sesta f

**sieve** /sɪv/ n peneira f; (for liquids) coador m □ vt peneirar; (liquids) passar, coar

**sift** /sɪft/ vt peneirar; (sprinkle) polvilhar. ~ **through** examinar minuciosamente, esquadrinhar

**sigh** /saɪ/ n suspiro m □ vt/i suspirar

**sight** /saɪt/ n vista f; (scene) cena f; (on gun) mira f □ vt avistar, ver, divisar. **at** or **on** ~ à vista. **catch** ~ **of** avistar. **in** ~ à vista, visível. **lose** ~ **of** perder de vista. **out of** ~ longe dos olhos

**sightsee|ing** /'saɪtsiːɪŋ/ n visita f, turismo m. **go** ~**ing** visitar lugares turísticos. ~**r** /'saɪtsiːə(r)/ n turista mf

**sign** /saɪn/ n sinal m; (symbol) signo m □ vt (in writing) assinar □ vi (make a sign) fazer sinal. ~ **on** or **up** (worker) assinar contrato. ~**-board** n tabuleta f. ~ **language** n mímica f

**signal** /'sɪɡnəl/ n sinal m □ vi (pt signalled) fazer signal □ vt comunicar (por sinais); (person) fazer sinal para. ~**-box** n cabine f de sinalização

**signature** /'sɪɡnətʃə(r)/ n assinatura f. ~ **tune** indicativo m musical

**signet-ring** /'sɪɡnɪtrɪŋ/ n anel m de sinete

**significan|t** /sɪɡ'nɪfɪkənt/ a importante; (meaningful) significativo. ~**ce** n importância f; (meaning) significado m. ~**tly** adv (much) sensivelmente

**signify** /'sɪɡnɪfaɪ/ vt significar

**signpost** /'saɪnpəʊst/ n poste m de sinalização □ vt sinalizar

**silence** /'saɪləns/ n silêncio m □ vt silenciar, calar. ~**r** /-ə(r)/ n (on gun) silenciador m; (on car) silencioso m

**silent** /'saɪlənt/ a silencioso; (not speaking) calado; (film) mudo. ~**ly** adv silenciosamente

**silhouette** /sɪlu'et/ n silhueta f □ vt **be** ~**d against** estar em silhueta contra

**silicon** /'sɪlɪkən/ n silicone m. ~ **chip** circuito m integrado

**silk** /sɪlk/ n seda f. ~**en,** ~**y** adjs sedoso

**sill** /sɪl/ n (of window) parapeito m; (of door) soleira f, limiar m

**sill|y** /'sɪlɪ/ a (-ier, -iest) tolo, idiota. ~**iness** n tolice f, idiotice f

**silo** /'saɪləʊ/ n (pl -os) silo m

**silt** /sɪlt/ n aluvião m, sedimento m

**silver** /'sɪlvə(r)/ n prata f; (silverware) prataria f, pratas fpl □ a de prata. ~ **paper** papel m prateado. ~ **wedding** bodas fpl de prata. ~**y** a prateado; (sound) argentino

**silversmith** /'sɪlvəsmɪθ/ n ourives m

**silverware** /'sɪlvəweə(r)/ n prataria f, pratas fpl

**similar** /'sɪmɪlə(r)/ a ~ **(to)** semelhante (a), parecido (com). ~**ity** /-ə'lærətɪ/ n semelhança f. ~**ly** adv de igual modo, analogamente

**simile** /'sɪmɪlɪ/ n símile m, comparação f

**simmer** /'sɪmə(r)/ vt/i cozinhar em fogo brando; (fig: smoulder) ferver, fremir; ~ **down** acalmar(-se)

**simpl|e** /'sɪmpl/ a (-er, -est) simples. ~**e-minded** a simples; (feebleminded) pobre de espírito, tolo. ~**icity** /-'plɪsətɪ/ n simplicidade f.

**~y** *adv* simplesmente; (*absolutely*) absolutamente, simplesmente

**simpleton** /'sɪmpltən/ *n* simplório *m*

**simplif|y** /'sɪmplɪfaɪ/ *vt* simplificar. **~ication** /-ɪ'keɪʃn/ *n* simplificação *f*

**simulat|e** /'sɪmjʊleɪt/ *vt* simular, imitar. **~ion** /-'leɪʃn/ *n* simulação *f*, imitação *f*

**simultaneous** /sɪml'teɪnɪəs/ *a* simultâneo, concomitante. **~ly** *adv* simultaneamente

**sin** /sɪn/ *n* pecado *m* □ *vi* (*pt* sinned) pecar

**since** /sɪns/ *prep* desde □ *adv* desde então □ *conj* desde que; (*because*) uma vez que, visto que. **~ then** desde então

**sincer|e** /sɪn'sɪə(r)/ *a* sincero. **~ely** *adv* sinceramente. **~ity** /-'serətɪ/ *n* sinceridade *f*

**sinew** /'sɪnjuː/ *n* (*anat*) tendão *m*. **~s** músculos *mpl*. **~y** *a* forte, musculoso

**sinful** /'sɪnfl/ *a* (*wicked*) pecaminoso; (*shocking*) escandaloso

**sing** /sɪŋ/ *vt/i* (*pt* sang, *pp* sung) cantar. **~er** *n* cantor *m*

**singe** /sɪndʒ/ *vt* (*pres p* singeing) chamuscar

**single** /'sɪŋgl/ *a* único, só; (*unmarried*) solteiro; (*bed*) de solteiro; (*room*) individual; (*ticket*) de ida, simples □ *n* (*ticket*) bilhete *m* de ida *or* simples; (*record*) disco *m* de 45 r.p.m. **~s** (*tennis*) singulares *mpl* □ *vt* **~ out** escolher. **in ~ file** em fila indiana. **~-handed** *a* sem ajuda, sozinho. **~-minded** *a* decidido, aferrado à sua idéia, tenaz. **~ parent** pai *m* solteiro, mãe *f* solteira. **singly** *adv* um a um, um por um

**singsong** /'sɪŋsɒŋ/ *n* **have a ~** cantar em coro □ *a* (*voice*) monótono, monocórdico

**singular** /'sɪŋgjʊlə(r)/ *n* singular *m* □ *a* (*uncommon; gram*) singular; (*noun*) no singular. **~ly** *adv* singularmente

**sinister** /'sɪnɪstə(r)/ *a* sinistro

**sink** /sɪŋk/ *vt* (*pt* sank, *pp* sunk) (*ship*) afundar, ir a pique; (*well*) abrir; (*invest money*) empatar; (*lose money*) enterrar □ *vi* afundar-se; (*of ground*) ceder; (*of voice*) baixar □ *n* pia *f*, (*P*) lava-louça *m*. **~ in** (*fig*) ficar gravado, entrar (*colloq*). **~ or swim** ou vai ou racha

**sinner** /'sɪnə(r)/ *n* pecador *m*

**sinuous** /'sɪnjʊəs/ *a* sinuoso

**sinus** /'saɪnəs/ *n* (*pl* -es) (*anat*) seio (nasal) *m*. **~itis** /saɪnə'saɪtɪs/ *n* sinusite *f*

**sip** /sɪp/ *n* gole *m* □ *vt* (*pt* sipped) bebericar, beber aos golinhos

**siphon** /'saɪfn/ *n* sifão *m* □ *vt* **~ off** extrair por meio de sifão

**sir** /sɜː(r)/ *n* senhor *m*. **S~** (*title*) Sir *m*. **Dear S~** Exmo Senhor. **excuse me, ~** desculpe, senhor. **no, ~** não, senhor

**siren** /'saɪərən/ *n* sereia *f*, sirene *f*

**sirloin** /'sɜːlɔɪn/ *n* lombo *m* de vaca

**sissy** /'sɪsɪ/ *n* maricas *m*

**sister** /'sɪstə(r)/ *n* irmã *f*; (*nun*) irmã *f*, freira *f*; (*nurse*) enfermeira-chefe *f*. **~-in-law** (*pl* **~s-in-law**) cunhada *f*. **~ly** *a* fraterno, fraternal

**sit** /sɪt/ *vt/i* (*pt* sat, *pres p* sitting) sentar(-se); (*of committee etc*) reunir-se. **~ for an exam** fazer um exame, prestar uma prova. **be ~ting** estar sentado. **~ around** não fazer nada. **~ down** sentar-se. **~-in** *n* ocupação *f*. **~ting** *n* reunião *f*, sessão *f*; (*in restaurant*) serviço *m*. **~ting-room** *n* sala *f* de estar. **~ up** endireitar-se na cadeira; (*not go to bed*) passar a noite acordado

**site** /saɪt/ *n* local *m*. (**building**) **~** terreno *m* para construção, lote *m* □ *vt* localizar, situar

**situat|e** /'sɪtʃʊeɪt/ *vt* situar. **be ~ed** estar situado. **~ion** /-'eɪʃn/ *n* (*position, condition*) situação *f*; (*job*) emprego *m*, colocação *f*

**six** /sɪks/ *a & n* seis (*m*). **~th** *a & n* sexto (*m*)

**sixteen** /sɪk'stiːn/ *a & n* dezesseis *m*, (*P*) dezasseis (*m*). **~th** *a & n* décimo sexto (*m*)

**sixt|y** /'sɪkstɪ/ *a & n* sessenta (*m*). **~ieth** *a & n* sexagésimo (*m*)

**size** /saɪz/ *n* tamanho *m*; (*of person, garment etc*) tamanho *m*, medida *f*; (*of shoes*) número *m*; (*extent*) grandeza *f* □ *vt* **~ up** calcular o tamanho de; (*colloq: judge*) formar um juízo sobre, avaliar. **~able** *a* bastante grande, considerável

**sizzle** /'sɪzl/ *vi* chiar, rechinar

**skate¹** /skeɪt/ *n* (*pl invar*) (*fish*) (ar)raia *f*

**skat|e²** /skeɪt/ *n* patim *m* □ *vi* patinar. **~er** *n* patinador *m*. **~ing** *n* patinação *f*. **~ing-rink** *n* rinque *m* de patinação

**skateboard** /'skeɪtbɔːd/ *n* skate *m*

**skelet|on** /'skelɪtən/ *n* esqueleto *m*; (*framework*) armação *f*. **~on crew** *or* **staff** pessoal *m* reduzido. **~on key** chave *f* mestra. **~al** *a* esquelético

**sketch** /sketʃ/ *n* esboço *m*, croqui(s) *m*; (*theat*) sketch *m*, peça *f* curta e humorística; (*outline*) idéia *f* geral, esboço *m* □ *vt* esboçar, delinear □ *vi* fazer esboços. **~-book** *n* caderno *m* de desenho

**sketchy** /'sketʃɪ/ *a* (-ier, -iest) incompleto, esboçado

**skewer** /'skjʊə(r)/ *n* espeto *m*

**ski** /ski:/ n (pl -s) esqui m □ vi (pt
**ski'd** or **skied**, pres p **skiing**) es-
quiar; (go skiing) fazer esqui. ~**er** n
esquiador m. ~**ing** n esqui m

**skid** /skɪd/ vi (pt **skidded**) derrapar,
patinar □ n derrapagem f

**skilful** /'skɪlfl/ a hábil, habilidoso.
~**ly** adv habilmente, com perícia

**skill** /skɪl/ n habilidade f, jeito m;
(craft) arte f. ~**s** aptidões fpl. ~**ed** a
hábil, habilidoso; (worker) especializado

**skim** /skɪm/ vt (pt **skimmed**) tirar a
espuma de; (milk) desnatar, tirar a
nata de; (pass or glide over) deslizar
sobre, roçar □ vi ~ **through** ler por
alto, passar os olhos por. ~**med milk**
leite m desnatado

**skimp** /skɪmp/ vt (use too little) poupar em □ vi ser poupado

**skimpy** /'skɪmpɪ/ a (-ier, -iest)
(clothes) sumário; (meal) escasso, ra-
cionado (fig)

**skin** /skɪn/ n (of person, animal) pele
f; (of fruit) casca f □ vt (pt **skinned**)
(animal) esfolar, tirar a pele de;
(fruit) descascar. ~-**diving** n mergulho m, caça f submarina

**skinny** /'skɪnɪ/ a (-ier, -iest) magricela, escanzelado

**skint** /skɪnt/ a (sl) sem dinheiro, na
última lona (sl), (P) nas lonas

**skip**[1] /skɪp/ vi (pt **skipped**) saltar, pular; (jump about) saltitar; (with rope)
pular corda □ vt (page) saltar; (class)
faltar a □ n salto m. ~**ping rope** n
corda f de pular

**skip**[2] /skɪp/ n (container) container m
grande para entulho

**skipper** /'skɪpə(r)/ n capitão m

**skirmish** /'skɜ:mɪʃ/ n escaramuça f

**skirt** /skɜ:t/ n saia f □ vt contornar,
ladear. ~**ing-board** n rodapé m

**skit** /skɪt/ n (theat) paródia f, sketch m
satírico

**skittle** /'skɪtl/ n pino m. ~**s** npl
boliche m, (P) jogo m de laranjinha

**skive** /skaɪv/ vi (sl) eximir-se de um
dever, evitar trabalhar (sl)

**skulk** /skʌlk/ vi (move) rondar furtivamente; (hide) esconder-se

**skull** /skʌl/ n caveira f, crânio m

**skunk** /skʌŋk/ n (animal) gambá m

**sky** /skaɪ/ n céu m. ~-**blue** a & n azul-
celeste (m)

**skylight** /'skaɪlaɪt/ n clarabóia f

**skyscraper** /'skaɪskreɪpə(r)/ n arra-
nha-céus m invar

**slab** /slæb/ n (of marble) placa f; (of
paving-stone) laje f; (of metal) chapa f;
(of cake) fatia f grossa

**slack** /slæk/ a (-er, -est) (rope) bambo,
frouxo; (person) descuidado, negligente; (business) parado, fraco;

(period, season) morto □ n the ~ (in
rope) a parte bamba □ vt/i (be lazy)
estar com preguiça, fazer cera (fig)

**slacken** /'slækən/ vt/i (speed, activity
etc) afrouxar, abrandar

**slacks** /slæks/ npl calças fpl

**slag** /slæg/ n escória f

**slain** /sleɪn/ see **slay**

**slam** /slæm/ vt (pt **slammed**) bater
violentamente com; (throw) atirar;
(sl: criticize) criticar, malhar □ vi
(door etc) bater violentamente □ n
(noise) bater m, pancada f

**slander** /'slɑ:ndə(r)/ n calúnia f,
difamação f □ vt caluniar, difamar.
~**ous** a calunioso, difamatório

**slang** /slæŋ/ n calão m, gíria f. ~**y** a
de calão

**slant** /slɑ:nt/ vt/i inclinar(-se); (news)
apresentar de forma tendenciosa □ n
inclinação f; (bias) tendência f; (point
of view) ângulo m. **be** ~**ing** ser/estar
inclinado or em declive

**slap** /slæp/ vt (pt **slapped**) (strike)
bater, dar uma palmada em; (on face)
esbofetear, dar uma bofetada em; (put
forcefully) atirar com □ n palmada f,
bofetada f □ adv em cheio. ~-**up** a (sl:
excellent) excelente

**slapdash** /'slæpdæʃ/ a descuidado;
(impetuous) precipitado

**slapstick** /'slæpstɪk/ n farsa f com
palhaçadas

**slash** /slæʃ/ vt (cut) retalhar, dar
golpes em; (sever) cortar; (a garment)
golpear; (fig: reduce) reduzir drasti-
camente, fazer um corte radical em
□ n corte m, golpe m

**slat** /slæt/ n (in blind) ripa f, (P)
lâmina f

**slate** /sleɪt/ n ardósia f □ vt (colloq:
criticize) criticar severamente

**slaughter** /'slɔ:tə(r)/ vt chacinar,
massacrar; (animals) abater □ n chacina f, massacre m, mortandade f;
(animals) abate m

**slaughterhouse** /'slɔ:təhaʊs/ n matadouro m

**slave** /sleɪv/ n escravo m □ vi moure-
jar, trabalhar como um escravo. ~-
**driver** n (fig) o que obriga os outros
a trabalharem como escravos, condutor m de escravos. ~**ry** /-ərɪ/ n escra-
vatura f

**slavish** /'sleɪvɪʃ/ a servil

**slay** /sleɪ/ vt (pt **slew**, pp **slain**) matar

**sleazy** /'sli:zɪ/ a (-ier, -iest) (colloq)
esqualido, sórdido

**sledge** /sledʒ/ n trenó m. ~-**hammer**
n martelo m de forja, marreta f

**sleek** /sli:k/ a (-er, -est) liso, macio e
lustroso

**sleep** /sli:p/ n sono m □ vi (pt **slept**)
dormir □ vt ter lugar para, alojar. **go**

**to ~** ir dormir, adormecer. **put to ~** (*kill*) mandar matar. **~ around** ser promíscuo. **~er** n aquele que dorme; (*rail: beam*) dormente m; (*berth*) couchette f. **~ing-bag** n saco m de dormir. **~ing-car** n carro-dormitório m, carruagemcama f, (P) vagon-lit m. **~less** a insone; (*night*) em claro, insone. **~-walker** n sonâmbulo m

**sleep|y** /'sli:pɪ/ a (-ier, -iest) sonolento. **be ~y** ter or estar com sono. **~ily** adv meio dormindo

**sleet** /sli:t/ n geada f miúda □ vi cair geada miúda

**sleeve** /sli:v/ n manga f; (*of record*) capa f. **up one's ~** de reserva, escondido. **~less** a sem mangas

**sleigh** /sleɪ/ n trenó m

**sleight** /slaɪt/ n **~ of hand** prestidigitação f, passe m de mágica

**slender** /'slendə(r)/ a esguio, esbelto; (*fig: scanty*) escasso. **~ness** n aspecto m esguio, esbelteza f, elegância f; (*scantiness*) escassez f

**slept** /slept/ see **sleep**

**sleuth** /slu:θ/ n (*colloq*) detective m

**slew**[1] /slu:/ vi (*turn*) virar-se

**slew**[2] /slu:/ see **slay**

**slice** /slaɪs/ n fatia f □ vt cortar em fatias; (*golf, tennis*) cortar

**slick** /slɪk/ a (*slippery*) escorregadio; (*cunning*) astuto, habilidoso; (*unctuous*) melífluo □ n (*oil*) ~ mancha f de óleo

**slid|e** /slaɪd/ vt/i (*pt* slid) escorregar, deslizar □ n escorregadela f, escorregão m; (*in playground*) escorrega m; (*for hair*) prendedor m, (P) travessa f; (*photo*) diapositivo m, slide m. **~e-rule** n régua f de cálculo. **~ing** a (*door, panel*) corrediço, de correr. **~ing scale** escala f móvel

**slight** /slaɪt/ a (-er, -est) (*slender, frail*) delgado, franzino; (*inconsiderable*) leve, ligeiro □ vt desconsiderar, desfeitear □ n desconsideração f, desfeita f. **the ~est** a o/a menor. **not in the ~est** em absoluto. **~ly** adv ligeiramente, um pouco

**slim** /slɪm/ a (**slimmer, slimmest**) magro, esbelto; (*chance*) pequeno, remoto □ vi (*pt* slimmed) emagrecer. **~ness** n magreza f, esbelteza f

**slim|e** /slaɪm/ n lodo m. **~y** a lodoso; (*slippery*) escorregadio; (*fig: servile*) servil, bajulador

**sling** /slɪŋ/ n (*weapon*) funda f; (*for arm*) tipóia f □ vt (*pt* slung) atirar, lançar

**slip** /slɪp/ vt/i (*pt* slipped) escorregar; (*move quietly*) mover-se de mansinho □ n escorregadela f, escorregão m; (*mistake*) engano m, lapso m; (*petti-*

*coat*) combinação f; (*of paper*) tira f de papel. **give the ~ to** livrar-se de, escapar(-se) de. **~ away** esgueirar-se. **~ by** passar sem se dar conta, passar despercebido. **~-cover** n (*Amer*) capa f para móveis. **~ into** (*go*) entrar de mansinho, enfiar-se em; (*clothes*) enfiar. **~ of the tongue** lapso m. **~ped disc** disco m deslocado. **~-road** n acesso m a autoestrada. **~ sb's mind** passar pela cabeça de alguém. **~ up** (*colloq*) cometer uma gafe. **~-up** n (*colloq*) gafe f

**slipper** /'slɪpə(r)/ n chinelo m

**slippery** /'slɪpərɪ/ a escorregadio; (*fig: person*) que não é de confiança, sem escrúpulos

**slipshod** /'slɪpʃɒd/ a (*person*) desleixado, desmazelado; (*work*) feito sem cuidado, desleixado

**slit** /slɪt/ n fenda f; (*cut*) corte m; (*tear*) rasgão m □ vt (*pt* slit, *pres p* slitting) fender; (*cut*) fazer um corte em, cortar

**slither** /'slɪðə(r)/ vi escorregar, resvalar

**sliver** /'slɪvə(r)/ n (*of cheese etc*) fatia f; (*splinter*) lasca f

**slobber** /'slɒbə(r)/ vi babar-se

**slog** /slɒg/ vt (*pt* slogged) (*hit*) bater com força □ vi (*walk*) caminhar com passos pesados e firmes; (*work*) trabalhar duro □ n (*work*) trabalheira f; (*walk, effort*) estafa f

**slogan** /'sləʊgən/ n slogan m, lema m, palavra f de ordem

**slop** /slɒp/ vt/i (*pt* slopped) transbordar, entornar. **~s** npl (*dirty water*) água(s) f(pl) suja(s); (*liquid refuse*) despejos mpl

**slop|e** /sləʊp/ vt/i inclinar(-se), formar declive □ n (*of mountain*) encosta f; (*of street*) rampa f, ladeira f. **~ing** a inclinado, em declive

**sloppy** /'slɒpɪ/ a (-ier, -iest) (*ground*) molhado, com poças de água; (*food*) aguado; (*clothes*) desleixado; (*work*) descuidado, feito de qualquer jeito or maneira (*colloq*); (*person*) desmazelado; (*maudlin*) piegas

**slosh** /slɒʃ/ vt entornar; (*colloq: splash*) esparrinhar; (*sl: hit*) bater em, dar (uma) sova em □ vi chapinhar

**slot** /slɒt/ n ranhura f; (*in timetable*) horário m; (*TV*) espaço m; (*aviat*) slot m □ vt/i (*pt* slotted) enfiar(-se), meter(-se), encaixar (-se). **~-machine** n (*for stamps, tickets etc*) distribuidor m automático; (*for gambling*) caça-níqueis m, (P) slot machine f

**sloth** /sləʊθ/ n preguiça f, indolência f; (*zool*) preguiça f

**slouch** /slaʊtʃ/ vi (*stand, move*) andar com as costas curvadas; (*sit*) sentar em má postura

**slovenly** /'slʌvnlɪ/ a desmazelado, desleixado

**slow** /sləʊ/ a (-er, -est) lento, vagaroso □ adv devagar, lentamente □ vt/i ~ (up or down) diminuir a velocidade, afrouxar; (auto) desacelerar. be ~ (clock etc) atrasar-se, estar atrasado. in ~ motion em câmara lenta. ~ly adv devagar, lentamente, vagarosamente

**slow|coach** /'sləʊkəʊtʃ/, (Amer) ~poke ns lesma m/f, pastelão m (fig)

**sludge** /slʌdʒ/ n lama f, lodo m

**slug** /slʌg/ n lesma f

**sluggish** /'slʌgɪʃ/ a (slow) lento, moroso; (lazy) indolente, preguiçoso

**sluice** /slu:s/ n (gate) comporta f; (channel) canal m □ vt lavar com jorros de água

**slum** /slʌm/ n favela f, (P) bairro m da lata; (building) cortiço m

**slumber** /'slʌmbə(r)/ n sono m □ vi dormir

**slump** /slʌmp/ n (in prices) baixa f, descida f; (in demand) quebra f na procura; (econ) depressão f □ vi (fall limply) cair, afundar-se; (of price) baixar bruscamente

**slung** /slʌŋ/ see sling

**slur** /slɜ:(r)/ vt/i (pt slurred) (speech) pronunciar indistintamente, mastigar □ n (in speech) som m indistinto; (discredit) nódoa f, estigma m

**slush** /slʌʃ/ n (snow) neve f meio derretida. ~ fund (comm) fundo m para subornos. ~y a (road) coberto de neve derretida, lamacento

**slut** /slʌt/ n (dirty woman) porca f, desmazelada f; (immoral woman) desavergonhada f

**sly** /slaɪ/ a (slyer, slyest) (crafty) manhoso; (secretive) sonso □ n on the ~ na calada. ~ly adv (craftily) astutamente; (secretively) sonsamente

**smack**[1] /smæk/ n palmada f; (on face) bofetada f □ vt dar uma palmada or tapa em; (on the face) esbofetear, dar uma bofetada em □ adv (colloq) em cheio, direto

**smack**[2] /smæk/ vi ~ of sth cheirar a alg coisa

**small** /smɔ:l/ a (-er, -est) pequeno □ n ~ of the back zona f dos rins □ adv (cut etc) em pedaços pequenos, aos bocadinhos. ~ change trocado m, dinheiro m miúdo. ~ talk conversa f fiada, bate-papo m. ~ness n pequenez f

**smallholding** /'smɔ:lhəʊldɪŋ/ n pequena propriedade f

**smallpox** /'smɔ:lpɒks/ n varíola f

**smarmy** /'smɑ:mɪ/ a (-ier, -iest) (colloq) bajulador, puxa-saco (colloq)

**smart** /smɑ:t/ a (-er, -est) elegante; (clever) esperto, vivo; (brisk) rápido □ vi (sting) arder, picar. ~ly adv elegantemente, com elegância; (cleverly) com esperteza, vivamente; (briskly) rapidamente. ~ness n elegância f

**smarten** /'smɑ:tn/ vt/i ~ (up) arranjar, dar um ar mais cuidado a. ~ (o.s.) up embelezar-se, arrumar-se, (P) pôr-se elegante/bonito; (tidy) arranjar-se

**smash** /smæʃ/ vt/i (to pieces) despedaçar(-se), espatifar(-se) (colloq); (a record) quebrar; (opponent) esmagar; (ruin) (fazer) falir; (of vehicle) espatifar(-se) □ n (noise) estrondo m; (blow) pancada f forte, golpe m; (collision) colisão f; (tennis) smash m

**smashing** /'smæʃɪŋ/ a (colloq) formidável, estupendo (colloq)

**smattering** /'smætərɪŋ/ n leves noções fpl

**smear** /smɪə(r)/ vt (stain; discredit) manchar; (coat) untar, besuntar □ n mancha f, nódoa f; (med) esfregaço m

**smell** /smel/ n cheiro m, odor m; (sense) cheiro m, olfato m, (P) olfacto m □ vt/i (pt smelt or smelled) ~ (of) cheirar (a). ~y a malcheiroso

**smelt**[1] /smelt/ see smell

**smelt**[2] /smelt/ vt (ore) fundir

**smil|e** /smaɪl/ n sorriso m □ vi sorrir. ~ing a sorridente, risonho

**smirk** /smɜ:k/ n sorriso m falso or afetado, (P) afectado

**smithereens** /smɪðə'ri:nz/ npl to or in ~ em pedaços mpl

**smock** /smɒk/ n guarda-pó m

**smog** /smɒg/ n mistura f de nevoeiro e fumaça, smog m

**smoke** /sməʊk/ n fumo m, fumaça f □ vt fumar; (bacon etc) fumar, defumar □ vi fumar, fumegar. ~-screen n (lit & fig) cortina f de fumaça. ~less a (fuel) sem fumo. ~r /-ə(r)/ n (person) fumante mf, (P) fumador m. smoky a (air) enfumaçado, fumacento

**smooth** /smu:ð/ a (-er, -est) liso; (soft) macio; (movement) regular, suave; (manners) lisonjeiro, conciliador, suave □ vt alisar. ~ out (fig) aplanar, remover. ~ly adv suavemente, facilmente

**smother** /'smʌðə(r)/ vt (stifle) abafar, sufocar; (cover, overwhelm) cobrir (with de); (suppress) abafar, reprimir

**smoulder** /'sməʊldə(r)/ vi (lit & fig) arder, abrasar-se

**smudge** /smʌdʒ/ n mancha f, borrão m □ vt/i sujar(-se), manchar(-se), borrar(-se)

**smug** /smʌg/ a (smugger, smuggest) presunçoso, convencido (colloq). ~ly adv presunçosamente. ~ness n presunção f

**smuggl|e** /'smʌgl/ vt contrabandear, fazer contrabando de. **~er** n contrabandista mf. **~ing** n contrabando m

**smut** /smʌt/ n fuligem f. **~ty** a cheio de fuligem; (colloq: obscene) indecente, sujo (colloq)

**snack** /snæk/ n refeição f ligeira. **~-bar** n lanchonete f, (P) snack(-bar) m

**snag** /snæg/ n (obstacle) obstáculo m; (drawback) problema m, contra m; (in cloth) rasgão m; (in stocking) fio m puxado

**snail** /sneɪl/ n caracol m. **at a ~'s pace** em passo de tartaruga

**snake** /sneɪk/ n serpente f, cobra f

**snap** /snæp/ vt/i (pt snapped) (whip, fingers) (fazer) estalar; (break) estalar(-se), partir(-se) com um estalo, rebentar; (say) dizer irritadamente □ n estalo m; (photo) instantâneo m; (Amer: fastener) mola f □ a súbito, repentino. **~ at** (bite) abocanhar, tentar morder; (speak angrily) retrucar asperamente. **~ up** (buy) comprar rapidamente

**snappish** /'snæpɪʃ/ a irritadiço

**snappy** /'snæpɪ/ a (-ier, -iest) (colloq) vivo, animado. **make it ~** (colloq) vai rápido!, apresse-se! (colloq)

**snapshot** /'snæpʃɒt/ n instantâneo m

**snare** /sneə(r)/ n laço m, cilada f, armadilha f

**snarl** /snɑːl/ vi rosnar □ n rosnadela f

**snatch** /snætʃ/ vt (grab) agarrar, apanhar; (steal) roubar. **~ from sb** arrancar de alguém □ n (theft) roubo m; (bit) bocado m, pedaço m

**sneak** /sniːk/ vi (slink) esgueirar-se furtivamente; (sl: tell tales) fazer queixa, delatar □ vt (sl: steal) rapinar (colloq) □ n (sl) dedo-duro m, queixinhas mf (sl). **~ing** a secreto. **~y** a sonso

**sneer** /snɪə(r)/ n sorriso m de desdém □ vi sorrir desdenhosamente

**sneeze** /sniːz/ n espirro m □ vi espirrar

**snide** /snaɪd/ a (colloq) sarcástico

**sniff** /snɪf/ vi fungar □ vt/i **~ (at)** (smell) cheirar; (dog) farejar. **~ at** (fig: in contempt) desprezar □ n fungadela f

**snigger** /'snɪgə(r)/ n riso m abafado □ vi rir dissimuladamente

**snip** /snɪp/ vt (pt snipped) cortar com tesoura □ n pedaço m, retalho m; (sl: bargain) pechincha f

**snipe** /snaɪp/ vi dar tiros de emboscada. **~r** /-ə(r)/ n franco-atirador m

**snivel** /'snɪvl/ vi (pt snivelled) choramingar, lamuriar-se

**snob** /snɒb/ n esnobe mf, (P) snob mf. **~bery** n esnobismo m, (P) snobismo m. **~bish** a esnobe, (P) snob

**snooker** /'snuːkə(r)/ n snooker m, sinuca f

**snoop** /snuːp/ vi (colloq) bisbilhotar, meter o nariz em toda a parte. **~ on** espiar, espionar. **~er** n bisbilhoteiro m

**snooty** /'snuːtɪ/ a (-ier, -iest) (colloq) convencido, arrogante (colloq)

**snooze** /snuːz/ n (colloq) soneca f (colloq) □ vi (colloq) tirar uma soneca

**snore** /snɔː(r)/ n ronco m □ vi roncar

**snorkel** /'snɔːkl/ n tubo m de respiração, snorkel m

**snort** /snɔːt/ n resfôlego m , bufido m □ vi resfolegar, bufar

**snout** /snaʊt/ n focinho m

**snow** /snəʊ/ n neve f □ vi nevar. **be ~ed under** ( fig: be overwhelmed) estar sobrecarregado ( fig). **~-bound** a bloqueado pela neve. **~-drift** n banco m de neve. **~-plough** n limpa-neve m. **~y** a nevado, coberto de neve

**snowball** /'snəʊbɔːl/ n bola f de neve □ vi atirar bolas de neve (em); ( fig) acumular-se, ir num crescendo, aumentar rapidamente

**snowdrop** /'snəʊdrɒp/ n (bot) furaneve m

**snowfall** /'snəʊfɔːl/ n nevada f, (P) nevão m

**snowflake** /'snəʊfleɪk/ n floco m de neve

**snowman** /'snəʊmæn/ n (pl -men) boneco m de neve

**snub** /snʌb/ vt (pt snubbed) desdenhar, tratar com desdém □ n desdém m

**snuff**[1] /snʌf/ n rapé m

**snuff**[2] /snʌf/ vt **~ out** (candles, hopes etc) apagar, extinguir

**snuffle** /'snʌfl/ vi fungar

**snug** /snʌg/ a (snugger, snuggest) (cosy) aconchegado; (close-fitting) justo

**snuggle** /'snʌgl/ vt/i (nestle) aninhar-se, aconchegar-se; (cuddle) aconchegar

**so** /səʊ/ adv tão, de tal modo; (thus) assim, deste modo □ conj por isso, portanto, por consequinte. **~ am I** eu também. **~ does he** ele também. **that is ~** é isso. **I think ~** acho que sim. **five or ~** uns cinco. **~ as to** de modo a. **~ far** até agora, até aqui. **~ long!** (colloq) até já! (colloq). **~ many** tantos. **~ much** tanto. **~ that** para que, de modo que. **~-and-~** fulano m. **~-called** a pretenso, soidisant. **~-so** a & adv assim assim, mais ou menos

**soak** /səʊk/ vt/i molhar(-se), ensopar(-se), enchacar(-se). **leave to ~** pôr de molho. **~ in** or **up** vt absorver, embeber. **~ through** repassar. **~ing** a ensopado, encharcado

**soap** /səʊp/ *n* sabão *m*. (toilet) ~ sabonete *m* □ *vt* ensaboar. ~ **opera** (*radio*) novela *f* radiofônica, (*P*) radiofônica; (*TV*) telenovela *f*. ~ **flakes** flocos *mpl* de sabão. ~ **powder** sabão *m* em pó. ~**y** *a* ensaboado

**soar** /sɔː(r)/ *vi* voar alto; (*go high*) elevar-se; (*hover*) pairar

**sob** /sɒb/ *n* soluço *m* □ *vi* (*pt* **sobbed**) soluçar

**sober** /ˈsəʊbə(r)/ *a* (*not drunk, calm, of colour*) sóbrio; (*serious*) sério, grave □ *vt/i* ~ **up** (fazer) ficar sóbrio, (fazer) curar a bebedeira (*colloq*)

**soccer** /ˈsɒkə(r)/ *n* (*colloq*) futebol *m*

**sociable** /ˈsəʊʃəbl/ *a* sociável

**social** /ˈsəʊʃl/ *a* social; (*sociable*) sociável; (*gathering, life*) de sociedade □ *n* reunião *f* social. ~**ly** *adv* socialmente; (*meet*) em sociedade. ~ **security** previdência *f* social; (*for old age*) pensão *f*. ~ **worker** assistente *mf* social

**socialis|t** /ˈsəʊʃəlɪst/ *n* socialista *mf*. ~**m** /-zəm/ *n* socialismo *m*

**socialize** /ˈsəʊʃəlaɪz/ *vi* socializar-se, reunir-se em sociedade. ~ **with** freqüentar, (*P*) frequentar, conviver com

**society** /səˈsaɪətɪ/ *n* sociedade *f*

**sociolog|y** /səʊsɪˈɒlədʒɪ/ *n* sociologia *f*. ~**ical** /-əˈlɒdʒɪkl/ *a* sociológico. ~**ist** *n* sociólogo *m*

**sock**[1] /sɒk/ *n* meia *f* curta; (*men's*) meia *f* (curta), (*P*) peúga *f*; (*women's*) soquete *f*

**sock**[2] /sɒk/ *vt* (*sl: hit*) esmurrar, dar um murro em (*colloq*)

**socket** /ˈsɒkɪt/ *n* cavidade *f*; (*for lamp*) suporte *m*; (*electr*) tomada *f*; (*of tooth*) alvéolo *m*

**soda** /ˈsəʊdə/ *n* soda *f*. (**baking**) ~ (*culin*) bicarbonato *m* de soda. ~ (**-water**) água *f* gasosa, soda *f* limonada, (*P*) água *f* gaseificada

**sodden** /ˈsɒdn/ *a* ensopado, empapado

**sodium** /ˈsəʊdɪəm/ *n* sódio *m*

**sofa** /ˈsəʊfə/ *n* sofá *m*

**soft** /sɒft/ *a* (**-er, -est**) (*not hard, feeble*) mole; (*not rough, not firm*) macio; (*gentle, not loud, not bright*) suave; (*tender-hearted*) sensível; (*fruit*) sem caroço; (*wood*) de coníferas; (*drink*) não alcoólico. ~**-boiled** *a* (*egg*) quente. ~ **spot** (*fig*) fraco *m*. ~**ly** *adv* docemente. ~**ness** *n* moleza *f*; (*to touch*) maciez *f*; (*gentleness*) suavidade *f*, brandura *f*

**soften** /ˈsɒfn/ *vt/i* amaciar, amolecer; (*tone down, lessen*) abrandar

**software** /ˈsɒftweə(r)/ *n* software *m*

**soggy** /ˈsɒgɪ/ *a* (**-ier, -iest**) ensopado, empapado

**soil**[1] /sɔɪl/ *n* solo *m*, terra *f*

**soil**[2] /sɔɪl/ *vt/i* sujar(-se). ~**ed** *a* sujo

**solace** /ˈsɒlɪs/ *n* consolo *m*; (*relief*) alívio *m*

**solar** /ˈsəʊlə(r)/ *a* solar

**sold** /səʊld/ *see* **sell** □ *a* ~ **out** esgotado

**solder** /ˈsəʊldə(r)/ *n* solda *f* □ *vt* soldar

**soldier** /ˈsəʊldʒə(r)/ *n* soldado *m* □ *vi* ~ **on** (*colloq*) perseverar com afinco, batalhar (*colloq*)

**sole**[1] /səʊl/ *n* (*of foot*) planta *f*, sola *f* do pé; (*of shoe*) sola *f*

**sole**[2] /səʊl/ *n* (*fish*) solha *f*

**sole**[3] /səʊl/ *a* único. ~**ly** *adv* unicamente

**solemn** /ˈsɒləm/ *a* solene. ~**ity** /səˈlemnətɪ/ *n* solenidade *f*. ~**ly** *adv* solenemente

**solicit** /səˈlɪsɪt/ *vt* (*seek*) solicitar □ *vi* (*of prostitute*) aproximar-se de homens na rua

**solicitor** /səˈlɪsɪtə(r)/ *n* advogado *m*

**solicitous** /səˈlɪsɪtəs/ *a* solícito

**solid** /ˈsɒlɪd/ *a* sólido; (*not hollow*) maciço, cheio, compacto; (*gold etc*) maciço; (*meal*) substancial □ *n* sólido *m*. ~**s** (*food*) alimentos *mpl* sólidos. ~**ity** /səˈlɪdətɪ/ *n* solidez *f*. ~**ly** *adv* solidamente

**solidarity** /sɒlɪˈdærətɪ/ *n* solidariedade *f*

**solidify** /səˈlɪdɪfaɪ/ *vt/i* solidificar(-se)

**soliloquy** /səˈlɪləkwɪ/ *n* monólogo *m*, solilóquio *m*

**solitary** /ˈsɒlɪtrɪ/ *a* solitário, só; (*only one*) um único. ~ **confinement** prisão *f* celular, solitária *f*

**solitude** /ˈsɒlɪtjuːd/ *n* solidão *f*

**solo** /ˈsəʊləʊ/ *n* (*pl* **-os**) solo *m* □ *a* solo. ~ **flight** vôo *m* solo. ~**ist** *n* solista *mf*

**soluble** /ˈsɒljʊbl/ *a* solúvel

**solution** /səˈluːʃn/ *n* solução *f*

**solv|e** /sɒlv/ *vt* resolver, solucionar. ~**able** *a* resolúvel, solúvel

**solvent** /ˈsɒlvənt/ *a* (dis)solvente; (*comm*) solvente □ *n* (dis)solvente *m*

**sombre** /ˈsɒmbə(r)/ *a* sombrio

**some** /sʌm/ *a* (*quantity*) algum(a); (*number*) alguns, algumas, uns, umas; (*unspecified, some or other*) um(a)... qualquer, uns... quaisquer, umas... quaisquer; (*a little*) um pouco de, algum; (*a certain*) um certo; (*contrasted with others*) uns, umas, alguns, algumas, certos, certas □ *pron* uns, umas, algum(a), alguns, algumas; (*a little*) um pouco, algum □ *adv* (*approximately*) uns, umas. **will you have** ~ **coffee/***etc*? você quer café/*etc*? ~ **day** algum dia. ~ **of my friends** alguns dos meus amigos. ~ **people say**... algumas pessoas dizem... ~ **time ago** algum tempo atrás

**somebody** /'sʌmbədɪ/ *pron* alguém □ *n* **be a ~** ser alguém

**somehow** /'sʌmhaʊ/ *adv* (*in some way*) de algum modo, de alguma maneira; (*for some reason*) por alguma razão

**someone** /'sʌmwʌn/ *pron & n* = **somebody**

**somersault** /'sʌməsɔːlt/ *n* cambalhota *f*; (*in the air*) salto *m* mortal □ *vi* dar uma cambalhota/um salto mortal

**something** /'sʌmθɪŋ/ *pron & n* uma/ alguma/qualquer coisa *f*, algo. **~ good**/*etc* uma coisa boa/*etc*, qualquer coisa de bom/*etc*. **~ like** um pouco como

**sometime** /'sʌmtaɪm/ *adv* a certa altura, um dia □ *a* (*former*) antigo. **~ last summer** a certa altura no verão passado. **I'll go ~** hei de ir um dia

**sometimes** /'sʌmtaɪmz/ *adv* às vezes, de vez em quando

**somewhat** /'sʌmwɒt/ *adv* um pouco, um tanto (ou quanto)

**somewhere** /'sʌmweə(r)/ *adv* (*position*) em algum lugar; (*direction*) para algum lugar

**son** /sʌn/ *n* filho *m*. **~-in-law** *n* (*pl* **~s-in-law**) genro *m*

**sonar** /'səʊnɑː(r)/ *n* sonar *m*

**sonata** /sə'nɑːtə/ *n* (*mus*) sonata *f*

**song** /sɒŋ/ *n* canção *f*. **~-bird** *n* ave *f* canora

**sonic** /'sɒnɪk/ *a* **~ boom** estrondo *m* sônico, (*P*) sónico

**sonnet** /'sɒnɪt/ *n* soneto *m*

**soon** /suːn/ *adv* (**-er, -est**) em breve, dentro em pouco, daqui a pouco; (*early*) cedo. **as ~ as possible** o mais rápido possível. **I would ~er stay** preferia ficar. **~ after** pouco depois. **~er or later** mais cedo ou mais tarde

**soot** /sʊt/ *n* fuligem *f*. **~y** *a* coberto de fuligem

**soothe** /suːð/ *vt* acalmar, suavizar; (*pain*) aliviar. **~ing** *a* (*remedy*) calmante, suavizante; (*words*) confortante

**sophisticated** /sə'fɪstɪkeɪtɪd/ *a* sofisticado, refinado, requintado; (*machine etc*) sofisticado

**soporific** /sɒpə'rɪfɪk/ *a* soporífico

**sopping** /'sɒpɪŋ/ *a* encharcado, ensopado

**soppy** /'sɒpɪ/ *a* (**-ier, -iest**) (*colloq: sentimental*) piegas; (*colloq: silly*) bobo

**soprano** /sə'prɑːnəʊ/ *n* (*pl* **~s**) & *adj* soprano (*mf*)

**sorbet** /'sɔːbeɪ/ *n* (*water-ice*) sorvete *m* feito sem leite

**sorcerer** /'sɔːsərə(r)/ *n* feiticeiro *m*

**sordid** /'sɔːdɪd/ *a* sórdido

**sore** /sɔː(r)/ *a* (**-er, -est**) dolorido;

(*vexed*) aborrecido (**at, with** com) □ *n* ferida *f*. **have a ~ throat** ter a garganta inflamada, ter dores de garganta

**sorely** /'sɔːlɪ/ *adv* fortemente, seriamente

**sorrow** /'sɒrəʊ/ *n* dor *f*, mágoa *f*, pesar *m*. **~ful** *a* pesaroso, triste

**sorry** /'sɒrɪ/ *a* (**-ier, -iest**) (*state, sight etc*) triste. **be ~ to/that** (*regretful*) sentir muito/que, lamentar que; **be ~ about/for** (*repentant*) ter pena de, estar arrependido de. **feel ~ for** ter pena de. **~!** desculpe!, perdão!

**sort** /sɔːt/ *n* gênero *m*, (*P*) género *m*, espécie *f*, qualidade *f*. **of ~s** (*colloq*) uma espécie de (*colloq, pej*). **out of ~s** indisposto □ *vt* separar por grupos; (*tidy*) arrumar. **~ out** (*problem*) resolver; (*arrange, separate*) separar, distribuir

**soufflé** /'suːfleɪ/ *n* (*culin*) suflê *m*, (*P*) soufflé *m*

**sought** /sɔːt/ *see* **seek**

**soul** /səʊl/ *n* alma *f*. **the life and ~ of** (*fig*) a alma *f* de (*fig*)

**soulful** /'səʊlfl/ *a* emotivo, expressivo, cheio de sentimento

**sound**[1] /saʊnd/ *n* som *m*, barulho *m*, ruído *m* □ *vt/i* soar; (*seem*) dar a impressão de, parecer (**as if** que). **~ a horn** tocar uma buzina, buzinar. **~ barrier** barreira *f* de som. **~ like** parecer ser, soar como. **~-proof** *a* à prova de som □ *vt* fazer o isolamento sonoro de, isolar. **~-track** *n* (*of film*) trilha *f* sonora, (*P*) banda *f* sonora

**sound**[2] /saʊnd/ *a* (**-er, -est**) (*healthy*) saudável, sadio; (*sensible*) sensato, acertado; (*secure*) firme, sólido. **~ asleep** profundamente adormecido. **~ly** *adv* solidamente

**sound**[3] /saʊnd/ *vt* (*test*) sondar; (*med; views*) auscultar

**soup** /suːp/ *n* sopa *f*

**sour** /'saʊə(r)/ *a* (**-er, -est**) azedo □ *vt/i* azedar, envinagrar

**source** /sɔːs/ *n* fonte *f*; (*of river*) nascente *f*

**souse** /saʊs/ *vt* (*throw water on*) atirar água em cima de; (*pickle*) pôr em vinagre; (*salt*) pôr em salmoura

**south** /saʊθ/ *n* sul *m* □ *a* sul, do sul; (*of country, people etc*) meridional □ *adv* a, ao/para o sul. **S~ Africa/ America** África *f*/América *f* do Sul. **S~ African/American** *a & n* sul-africano (*m*)/sul-americano (*m*). **~-east** *n* sudeste *m*. **~erly** /'sʌðəlɪ/ *a* do sul, meridional. **~ward** *a* ao sul. **~ward(s)** *adv* para o sul. **~-west** *n* sudoeste *m*

**southern** /'sʌðən/ *a* do sul, meridional, austral

**souvenir** /suːvəˈnɪə(r)/ n recordação f, lembrança f

**sovereign** /ˈsɒvrɪn/ n & a soberano (m). ~ty n soberania f

**Soviet** /ˈsəʊvɪət/ a soviético. **the S~ Union** a União Soviética

**sow**¹ /səʊ/ vt (pt **sowed**, pp **sowed** or **sown**) semear

**sow**² /saʊ/ n (zool) porca f

**soy** /sɔɪ/ n ~ **sauce** molho m de soja

**soya** /ˈsɔɪə/ n soja f. ~**-bean** semente f de soja

**spa** /spaː/ n termas fpl

**space** /speɪs/ n espaço m; (room) lugar m; (period) espaço m, período m □ a (research etc) espacial □ vt ~ **out** espaçar

**space|craft** /ˈspeɪskraːft/ n (pl invar), ~**ship** n nave espacial f

**spacious** /ˈspeɪʃəs/ a espaçoso

**spade** /speɪd/ n (gardener's) pá f de ferro; (child's) pá f. ~**s** (cards) espadas fpl

**spadework** /ˈspeɪdwɜːk/ n (fig) trabalho m preliminar

**spaghetti** /spəˈɡetɪ/ n espaguete m, (P) esparguete m

**Spain** /speɪn/ n Espanha f

**span**¹ /spæn/ n (of arch) vão m; (of wings) envergadura f; (of time) espaço m, duração f; (measure) palmo m □ vt (pt **spanned**) (extend across) transpor; (measure) medir em palmos; (in time) abarcar, abranger, estender-se por

**span**² /spæn/ see **spick**

**Spaniard** /ˈspænɪəd/ n espanhol m

**Spanish** /ˈspænɪʃ/ a espanhol □ n (lang) espanhol m

**spaniel** /ˈspænɪəl/ n spaniel m, epagneul m

**spank** /spæŋk/ vt dar palmadas or chineladas no. ~**ing** n (with hand) palmada f; (with slipper) chinelada f

**spanner** /ˈspænə(r)/ n (tool) chave f de porcas; (adjustable) chave f inglesa

**spar** /spaː(r)/ vi (pt **sparred**) jogar boxe, esp para treino; (fig: argue) discutir

**spare** /speə(r)/ vt (not hurt; use with restraint) poupar; (afford to give) dispensar, ceder □ a (in reserve) de reserva, de sobra; (tyre) sobressalente; (bed) extra; (room) de hóspedes □ n (part) sobressalente m. ~ **time** horas fpl vagas. **have an hour to** ~ dispôr de uma hora. **have no time to** ~ não ter tempo a perder

**sparing** /ˈspeərɪŋ/ a poupado. **be** ~ **of** poupar em, ser poupado com. ~**ly** adv frugalmente

**spark** /spaːk/ n centelha f, faísca f □ vt lançar faíscas. ~ **off** (initiate)

desencadear, provocar. ~**(ing)-plug** n vela f de ignição

**sparkle** /ˈspaːkl/ vi cintilar, brilhar □ n brilho m, cintilação f

**sparkling** /ˈspaːklɪŋ/ a (wine) espumante

**sparrow** /ˈspærəʊ/ n pardal m

**sparse** /spaːs/ a esparso; (hair) ralo. ~**ly** adv (furnished etc) escassamente

**spasm** /ˈspæzəm/ n (of muscle) espasmo m; (of coughing, anger etc) ataque m, acesso m

**spasmodic** /spæzˈmɒdɪk/ a espasmódico; (at irregular intervals) intermitente

**spastic** /ˈspæstɪk/ n deficiente mf motor

**spat** /spæt/ see **spit**¹

**spate** /speɪt/ n (in river) enxurrada f, cheia f. **a** ~ **of** (letters etc) uma avalanche de

**spatter** /ˈspætə(r)/ vt salpicar (**with** de, com)

**spawn** /spɔːn/ n ovas fpl □ vi desovar □ vt gerar em quantidade

**speak** /spiːk/ vt/i (pt **spoke**, pp **spoken**) falar (**to/with sb about sth** com alguém de/sobre alg coisa); (say) dizer. ~ **out/up** falar abertamente; (louder) falar mais alto. ~ **one's mind** dizer o que se pensa. **so to** ~ por assim dizer. **English/Portuguese spoken** fala-se português/inglês

**speaker** /ˈspiːkə(r)/ n (in public) orador m; (loudspeaker) alto-falante m; (of a language) pessoa f de língua nativa

**spear** /spɪə(r)/ n lança f

**spearhead** /ˈspɪəhed/ n ponta f de lança □ vt (lead) estar à frente de, encabeçar

**special** /ˈspeʃl/ a especial. ~**ity** /-ɪˈrælətɪ/ n especialidade f. ~**ly** adv especialmente. ~**ty** n especialidade f

**specialist** /ˈspeʃəlɪst/ n especialista mf

**specialize** /ˈspeʃəlaɪz/ vi especializar-se (**in** em). ~**d** a especializado

**species** /ˈspiːʃɪz/ n (pl invar) espécie f

**specific** /spəˈsɪfɪk/ a específico. ~**ally** adv especificamente, explicitamente

**specif|y** /ˈspesɪfaɪ/ vt especificar. ~**ication** /-ɪˈkeɪʃn/ n especificação f. ~**ications** npl (of work etc) caderno m de encargos

**specimen** /ˈspesɪmɪn/ n espécime(n) m, amostra f

**speck** /spek/ n (stain) mancha f pequena; (dot) pontinho m, pinta f; (particle) grão m

**speckled** /ˈspekld/ a salpicado, manchado

**specs** /speks/ *npl* (*colloq*) óculos *mpl*

**spectacle** /'spektəkl/ *n* espetáculo *m*, (P) espectáculo *m*. (**pair of**) **~s** (par *m* de) óculos *mpl*

**spectacular** /spek'tækjʊlə(r)/ *a* espetacular, (P) espectacular

**spectator** /spek'teɪtə(r)/ *n* espectador *m*

**spectre** /'spektə(r)/ *n* espectro *m*, fantasma *m*

**spectrum** /'spektrəm/ *n* (*pl* **-tra**) espectro *m*; (*of ideas etc*) faixa *f*, gama *f*, leque *m*

**speculat|e** /'spekjʊleɪt/ *vi* especular, fazer especulações *or* conjeturas, (P) conjecturas (**about** sobre); (*comm*) especular, fazer especulação (**in** em). **~ion** /-'leɪʃn/ *n* especulação *f*, conjetura *f*, (P) conjectura *f*; (*comm*) especulação *f*. **~or** *n* especulador *m*

**speech** /spiːtʃ/ *n* (*faculty*) fala *f*; (*diction*) elocução *f*; (*dialect*) falar *m*; (*address*) discurso *m*. **~less** *a* mudo, sem fala (**with** com, de)

**speed** /spiːd/ *n* velocidade *f*, rapidez *f* □ *vt/i* (*pt* **sped** /sped/) (*move*) ir depressa *or* a grande velocidade; (*send*) despedir, mandar; (*pt* **speeded**) (*drive too fast*) ultrapassar o limite de velocidade. **~ limit** limite *m* de velocidade. **~ up** acelerar(-se). **~ing** *n* excesso *m* de velocidade

**speedometer** /spiː'dɒmɪtə(r)/ *n* velocímetro *m*, (P) conta-quilómetros *m inv*

**speed|y** /'spiːdɪ/ *a* (**-ier**, **-iest**) rápido, (*prompt*) pronto. **~ily** *adv* rapidamente; (*promptly*) prontamente

**spell**[1] /spel/ *n* (*magic*) sortilégio *m*

**spell**[2] /spel/ *vt/i* (*pt* **spelled** *or* **spelt**) escrever; (*fig: mean*) significar, ter como resultado. **~ out** soletrar; (*fig: explain*) explicar claramente. **~ing** *n* ortografia *f*

**spell**[3] /spel/ *n* (*short period*) período *m* curto, breve espaço *m* de tempo; (*turn*) turno *m*

**spend** /spend/ *vt* (*pt* **spent**) (*money, energy*) gastar (**on** em); (*time, holiday*) passar. **~er** *n* gastador *m*

**spendthrift** /'spendθrɪft/ *n* perdulário *m*, esbanjador *m*

**spent** /spent/ *see* **spend** □ *a* (*used*) gasto

**sperm** /spɜːm/ *n* (*pl* **sperms** *or* **sperm**) (*semen*) esperma *m*, sêmen *m*, (P) sémen *m*; (*cell*) espermatozóide *m*

**spew** /spjuː/ *vt/i* vomitar, lançar

**sphere** /sfɪə(r)/ *n* esfera *f*

**spherical** /'sferɪkl/ *a* esférico

**spic|e** /spaɪs/ *n* especiaria *f*, condimento *m*; (*fig*) picante *m* □ *vt* condimentar. **~y** *a* condimentado; (*fig*) picante

**spick** /spɪk/ *a* **~ and span** novo em folha, impecável

**spider** /'spaɪdə(r)/ *n* aranha *f*

**spik|e** /spaɪk/ *n* (*of metal etc*) bico *m*, espigão *m*, ponta *f*. **~y** *a* guarnecido de bicos *or* pontas

**spill** /spɪl/ *vt/i* (*pt* **spilled** *or* **spilt**) derramar(-se), entornar(-se), espalhar(-se). **~ over** transbordar, extravasar

**spin** /spɪn/ *vt/i* (*pt* **spun**, *pres p* **spinning**) (*wool, cotton*) fiar; (*web*) tecer; (*turn*) (fazer) girar, (fazer) rodopiar. **~ out** (*money, story*) fazer durar; (*time*) (fazer) parar □ *n* volta *f*; (*aviat*) parafuso *m*. **go for a ~** dar uma volta *or* um giro. **~-drier** *n* centrifugadora *f* para a roupa, secadora *f*. **~ning-wheel** *n* roda *f* de fiar. **~-off** *n* bónus *m*, (P) bónus *m* inesperado; (*by-product*) derivado *m*

**spinach** /'spɪnɪdʒ/ *n* (*plant*) espinafre *m*; (*as food*) espinafres *mpl*

**spinal** /'spaɪnl/ *a* vertebral. **~ cord** espina *f* dorsal

**spindl|e** /'spɪndl/ *n* roca *f*, fuso *m*; (*mech*) eixo *m*. **~y** *a* alto e magro; (*of plant*) espigado

**spine** /spaɪn/ *n* espinha *f*, coluna *f* vertebral; (*prickle*) espinho *m*, pico *m*; (*of book*) lombada *f*

**spineless** /'spaɪnlɪs/ *a* (*fig: cowardly*) covarde, sem fibra (*fig*)

**spinster** /'spɪnstə(r)/ *n* solteira *f*; (*pej*) solteirona *f*

**spiral** /'spaɪərəl/ *a* (em) espiral; (*staircase*) em caracol □ *n* espiral *f* □ *vi* (*pt* **spiralled**) subir em espiral

**spire** /spaɪə(r)/ *n* agulha *f*, flecha *f*

**spirit** /'spɪrɪt/ *n* espírito *m*; (*boldness*) coragem *f*, brio *m*. **~s** (*morale*) moral *m*; (*drink*) bebidas *fpl* alcoólicas, (P) bebidas *fpl* espirituosas. **in high ~s** alegre □ *vt* **~ away** dar sumiço em, arrebatar. **~-level** *n* nível *m* de bolha de ar

**spirited** /'spɪrɪtɪd/ *a* fogoso; (*attack, defence*) vigoroso, enérgico

**spiritual** /'spɪrɪtʃʊəl/ *a* espiritual

**spiritualism** /'spɪrɪtʃʊəlɪzəm/ *n* espiritismo *m*

**spit**[1] /spɪt/ *vt/i* (*pt* **spat** *or* **spit**, *pres p* **spitting**) cuspir; (*of rain*) chuviscar; (*of cat*) bufar □ *n* cuspe *m*, (P) cuspo *m*. **the ~ting image of** o retrato vivo de, a cara chapada de (*colloq*)

**spit**[2] /spɪt/ *n* (*for meat*) espeto *m*; (*of land*) restinga *f*, (P) língua *f* de terra

**spite** /spaɪt/ *n* má vontade *f*, despeito *m*, rancor *m* □ *vt* aborrecer, mortificar. **in ~ of** a despeito de, apesar de. **~ful** *a* rancoroso, maldoso. **~fully** *adv* rancorosamente, maldosamente

**spittle** /'spɪtl/ *n* cuspe *m*, (P) cuspo *m*, saliva *f*

**splash** /splæʃ/ *vt* salpicar, respingar □ *vi* esparrinhar, esparramar-se. ~ **(about)** chapinhar □ *n* (*act, mark*) salpico *m*; (*sound*) chape *m*; (*of colour*) mancha *f*. **make a** ~ (*striking display*) fazer um vistão, causar furor

**spleen** /spli:n/ *n* (*anat*) baço *m*. **vent one's** ~ **on sb** descarregar a neura em alguém (*colloq*)

**splendid** /'splendɪd/ *a* esplêndido, magnífico; (*excellent*) estupendo (*colloq*), ótimo, (P) óptimo

**splendour** /'splendə(r)/ *n* esplendor *m*

**splint** /splɪnt/ *n* (*med*) tala *f*

**splinter** /'splɪntə(r)/ *n* lasca *f*, estilhaço *m*; (*under the skin*) farpa *f*, lasca *f* □ *vi* estilhaçar-se, lascar-se. ~ **group** grupo *m* dissidente

**split** /splɪt/ *vt/i* (*pt* split, *pres p* splitting) rachar, fender(-se); (*divide, share*) dividir; (*tear*) romper(-se) □ *n* racha *f*, fenda *f*; (*share*) quinhão *m*, parte *f*; (*pol*) cisão *f*. ~ **on** (*sl: inform on*) denunciar. ~ **one's sides** rebentar de risa. ~ **up** (*of couple*) separarse. **a** ~ **second** uma fração de segundo. ~**ting headache** dor *f* de cabeça forte

**splurge** /splɜːdʒ/ *n* (*colloq*) espalhafato *m*, estardalhaço *m* □ *vi* (*colloq: spend*) gastar os tubos, (P) gastar à doida (*colloq*)

**spool** /spu:l/ *n* (*of sewing machine*) bobina *f*; (*for cotton thread*) carretel *m*, carrinho *m*; (*naut; fishing*) carretel *m*

**splutter** /'splʌtə(r)/ *vi* falar cuspindo; (*engine*) cuspir; (*fat*) crepitar

**spoil** /spɔɪl/ *vt* (*pt* spoilt *or* spoiled) estragar; (*pamper*) mimar □ *n* ~**(s)** (*plunder*) despojo(s) *m*(*pl*), espólios *mpl*. ~**-sport** *n* desmancha-prazeres *mf invar.* ~**t** *a* (*pampered*) mimado, estragado com mimos

**spoke**¹ /spəʊk/ *n* raio *m*

**spoke**², **spoken** /spəʊk, 'spəʊkən/ *see* **speak**

**spokes|man** /'spəʊksmən/ *n* (*pl* -men) ~**woman** *n* (*pl* -women) porta-voz *mf*

**sponge** /spʌndʒ/ *n* esponja *f* □ *vt* (*clean*) lavar com esponja; (*wipe*) limpar com esponja □ *vi* ~ **on** (*colloq: cadge*) viver à custa de. ~ **bag** bolsa *f* de toalete. ~ **cake** pão-de-ló *m*. ~**r** /-ə(r)/ *n* parasita *mf* (*colloq*) (*sl*). **spongy** *a* esponjoso

**sponsor** /'spɒnsə(r)/ *n* patrocinador *m*; (*for membership*) (sócio) proponente *m* □ *vt* patrocinar; (*for membership*) propor. ~**ship** *n* patrocínio *m*

**spontaneous** /spɒn'teɪnɪəs/ *a* espontâneo

**spoof** /spu:f/ *n* (*colloq*) paródia *f*

**spooky** /'spu:kɪ/ *a* (-ier, -iest) (*colloq*) fantasmagórico, que dá arrepios

**spool** /spu:l/ *n* (*of sewing machine*) bobina *f*; (*for thread, line*) carretel *m*, (P) carrinho *m*

**spoon** /spu:n/ *n* colher *f*. ~**-feed** *vt* (*pt* -fed) alimentar de colher; (*fig: help*) dar na bandeja para (*fig*). ~**ful** *n* (*pl* ~**fuls**) colherada *f*

**sporadic** /spə'rædɪk/ *a* esporádico, acidental

**sport** /spɔːt/ *n* esporte *m*, (P) desporto *m*. **(good)** ~ (*sl: person*) gente *f* fina, (P) bom tipo *m* (*colloq*), (P) tipo *m* bestial □ *vt* (*display*) exibir, ostentar. ~**s car/coat** carro *m*/casaco *m* esporte, (P) de desporto. ~**y** *a* (*colloq*) esportivo, (P) desportivo

**sporting** /'spɔːtɪŋ/ *a* esportivo, (P) desportivo. **a** ~ **chance** uma certa possibilidade de sucesso, uma boa chance

**sports|man** /'spɔːtsmən/ *n* (*pl* -men), ~**woman** (*pl* -women) desportista *mf*. ~**manship** *n* (*spirit*) espírito *m* esportivo, (P) desportivo; (*activity*) esportismo *m*, (P) desportismo *m*

**spot** /spɒt/ *n* (*mark, stain*) mancha *f*; (*in pattern*) pinta *f*, bola *f*; (*drop*) gota *f*; (*place*) lugar *m*, ponto *m*; (*pimple*) borbulha *f*, espinha *f*; (*TV*) spot *m* televisivo □ *vt* (*pt* spotted) manchar; (*colloq: detect*) descobrir, detectar (*colloq*). **a** ~ **of** (*colloq*) um pouco de. **be in a** ~ (*colloq*) estar numa encrenca (*colloq*), (P) estar metido numa alhada (*colloq*). **on the** ~ no local; (*there and then*) ali mesmo, logo ali. ~**-on** *a* (*colloq*) certo. ~ **check** inspeção *f*, (P) inspecção *f* de surpresa; (*of cars*) fiscalização *f* de surpresa. ~**ted** *a* manchado; (*with dots*) de pintas, de bolas; (*animal*) malhado. ~**ty** *a* (*with pimples*) com borbulhas

**spotless** /'spɒtlɪs/ *a* impecável, imaculado

**spotlight** /'spɒtlaɪt/ *n* foco *m*; (*cine, theat*) refletor *m*, holofote *m*

**spouse** /spaʊz/ *n* cônjuge *mf*, esposo *m*

**spout** /spaʊt/ *n* (*of vessel*) bico *m*; (*of liquid*) esguicho *m*, jorro *m*; (*pipe*) cano *m* □ *vi* jorrar, esguichar. **up the** ~ (*sl: ruined*) liquidado (*sl*)

**sprain** /spreɪn/ *n* entorse *f*, mau jeito *m* □ *vt* torcer, dar um mau jeito a

**sprang** /spræŋ/ *see* **spring**

**sprawl** /sprɔːl/ *vi* (*sit*) estirar-se, esparramar-se; (*fall*) estatelar-se; (*town*) estender-se, espraiar-se

**spray**¹ /spreɪ/ *n* (*of flowers*) raminho *m*, ramalhete *m*

**spray**[2] /spreɪ/ n (water) borrifo m, salpico m; (from sea) borrifo m de espuma; (device) bomba f, aerossol m; (for perfume) vaporizador m, atomizador m □ vt aspergir, borrifar, pulverizar; (with insecticide) pulverizar. **~-gun** n (for paint) pistola f

**spread** /spred/ vt/i (pt spread) (extend, stretch) estender(-se); (news, fear, illness etc) alastrar(-se), espalhar(-se), propagar(-se); (butter etc) passar; (wings) abrir □ n (expanse) expansão f, extensão f; (spreading) propagação f; (paste) pasta f para passar pão; (colloq: meal) banquete m. **~-eagled** a de braços e pernas abertos. **~sheet** n (comput) folha f de cálculo

**spree** /spri:/ n **go on a ~** (colloq) cair na farra

**sprig** /sprɪg/ n raminho m

**sprightly** /ˈspraɪtlɪ/ a (-ier, -iest) vivo, animado

**spring** /sprɪŋ/ vi (pt sprang, pp sprung) (arise) nascer; (jump) saltar, pular □ vt (produce suddenly) sair-se com; (a surprise) fazer (**on sb** a alguém) □ n salto m, pulo m; (device) mola f; (season) primavera f; (of water) fonte f, nascente f. **~ from** vir de, originar, provir de. **~-clean** vt fazer limpeza geral. **~ onion** cebolinha f. **~ up** surgir

**springboard** /ˈsprɪŋbɔːd/ n trampolim m

**springtime** /ˈsprɪŋtaɪm/ n primavera f

**springy** /ˈsprɪŋɪ/ a (-ier, -iest) elástico

**sprinkle** /ˈsprɪŋkl/ vt (with liquid) borrifar, salpicar; (with salt, flour) polvilhar (**with** de). **~ sand/etc** espalhar areia/etc. **~r** /-ə(r)/ n (in garden) regador m; (for fires) sprinkler m

**sprinkling** /ˈsprɪŋklɪŋ/ n (amount) pequena quantidade f; (number) pequeno número m

**sprint** /sprɪnt/ n (sport) corrida f de pequena distância, sprint m □ vi correr em sprint or a toda a velocidade; (sport) correr

**sprout** /spraʊt/ vt/i brotar, germinar; (put forth) deitar □ n (on plant etc) broto m. **(Brussels) ~s** couves f de Bruxelas

**spruce** /spruːs/ a bem arrumado □ vt **~ o.s. up** arrumar(-se)

**sprung** /sprʌŋ/ see spring □ a (mattress etc) de molas

**spry** /spraɪ/ a (spryer, spryest) vivo, ativo, (P) activo; (nimble) ágil

**spud** /spʌd/ n (sl) batata f

**spun** /spʌn/ see spin

**spur** /spɜː(r)/ n (of rider) espora f; (fig: stimulus) aguilhão m; (fig)

espora f (fig) □ vt (pt spurred) esporear, picar com esporas; (fig: incite) aguilhoar, esporear. **on the ~ of the moment** impulsivamente

**spurious** /ˈspjʊərɪəs/ a falso, espúrio

**spurn** /spɜːn/ vt desdenhar, desprezar, rejeitar

**spurt** /spɜːt/ vi jorrar, esguichar; (fig: accelerate) acelerar subitamente, dar um arranco súbito □ n jorro m, esguicho m; (of energy, speed) arranco m, surto m

**spy** /spaɪ/ n espião m □ vt (make out) avistar, descortinar □ vi **~ (on)** espiar, espionar. **~ out** descobrir. **~ing** n espionagem f

**squabble** /ˈskwɒbl/ vi discutir, brigar □ n briga f, disputa f

**squad** /skwɒd/ n (mil) pelotão m; (team) equipe f, (P) equipa f. **firing ~** pelotão m de fuzilamento. **flying ~** brigada f móvel

**squadron** /ˈskwɒdrən/ n (mil) esquadrão m; (aviat) esquadrilha f; (naut) esquadra f

**squalid** /ˈskwɒlɪd/ a esquálido, sórdido. **~or** n sordidez f

**squall** /skwɔːl/ n borrasca f

**squander** /ˈskwɒndə(r)/ vt desperdiçar

**square** /skweə(r)/ n quadrado m; (in town) largo m, praça f; (T-square) régua-tê f; (set-square) esquadro m □ a (of shape) quadrado; (metre, mile etc) quadrado; (honest) direito, honesto; (of meal) abundante, substancial. **(all) ~** (quits) quite(s) □ vt (math) elevar ao quadrado; (settle) acertar □ vi (agree) concordar. **go back to ~ one** recomeçar tudo do princípio, voltar à estaca zero. **~ brackets** parênteses mpl retos, (P) rectos. **~ up to** enfrentar. **~ly** adv diretamente, (P) directamente; (fairly) honestamente

**squash** /skwɒʃ/ vt (crush) esmagar; (squeeze) espremer; (crowd) comprimir, apertar □ n (game) squash m; (Amer: marrow) abóbora f. **lemon ~** limonada f. **orange ~** laranjada f. **~y** a mole

**squat** /skwɒt/ vi (pt squatted) acocorar-se, agachar-se; (be a squatter) ser ocupante ilegal □ a (dumpy) atarracado. **~ter** n ocupante mf ilegal de casa vazia, posseiro m

**squawk** /skwɔːk/ n grasnido m, crocito m □ vi grasnar, crocitar

**squeak** /skwiːk/ n guincho m, chio m; (of door, shoes etc) rangido m □ vi guinchar, chiar; (of door, shoes etc) ranger. **~y** a (shoe etc) que range; (voice) esganiçado

**squeal** /skwiːl/ vi dar gritos agudos,

**guinchar** □ *n* grito *m* agudo, guincho *m*. **~ (on)** (*sl: inform on*) delatar, (*P*) denunciar

**squeamish** /'skwi:mɪʃ/ *a* (*nauseated*) que enjoa à toa

**squeeze** /skwi:z/ *vt* (*lemon, sponge etc*) espremer; (*hand, arm*) apertar; (*extract*) arrancar, extorquir (**from** de) □ *vi* (*force one's way*) passar à força, meter-se por □ *n* aperto *m*, apertão *m*; (*hug*) abraço *m*; (*comm*) restrições *fpl* de crédito

**squelch** /skweltʃ/ *vi* chapinhar *or* fazer chape-chape na lama

**squid** /skwɪd/ *n* lula *f*

**squiggle** /'skwɪgl/ *n* rabisco *m*, floreado *m*

**squint** /skwɪnt/ *vi* ser estrábico *or* vesgo; (*with half-shut eyes*) franzir os olhos □ *n* (*med*) estrabismo *m*

**squirm** /skwɜːm/ *vi* (re)torcer-se, contorcer-se

**squirrel** /'skwɪrəl/ *n* esquilo *m*

**squirt** /skwɜːt/ *vt/i* esguichar □ *n* esguicho *m*

**stab** /stæb/ *vt* (*pt* **stabbed**) apunhalar; (*knife*) esfaquear □ *n* punhalada *f*; (*with knife*) facada *f*; (*of pain*) pontada *f*; (*colloq: attempt*) tentativa *f*

**stabilize** /'steɪbəlaɪz/ *vt* estabilizar

**stab|le**[1] /'steɪbl/ *a* (-er, -est) estável. **~ility** /stə'bɪlətɪ/ *n* estabilidade *f*

**stable**[2] /'steɪbl/ *n* cavalariça *f*, estrebaria *f*. **~-boy** *n* moço *m* de estrebaria

**stack** /stæk/ *n* pilha *f*, montão *m*; (*of hay etc*) meda *f* □ *vt* **~ (up)** empilhar, amontoar

**stadium** /'steɪdɪəm/ *n* estádio *m*

**staff** /stɑːf/ *n* pessoal *m*; (*in school*) professores *mpl*; (*mil*) estado-maior *m*; (*stick*) bordão *m*, cajado *m*; (*mus*) (*pl* **staves**) pauta *f* □ *vt* prover de pessoal

**stag** /stæg/ *n* veado (macho) *m*, cervo *m*. **~-party** (*colloq*) reunião *f* masculina; (*before wedding*) despedida *f* de solteiro

**stage** /steɪdʒ/ *n* (*theatre*) palco *m*; (*phase*) fase *f*, ponto *m*; (*platform in hall*) estrado *m* □ *vt* encenar, pôr em cena; (*fig: organize*) organizar. **go on the ~** seguir a carreira teatral, ir para o teatro (*colloq*). **~ door** entrada *f* dos artistas. **~-fright** *n* nervosismo *m*

**stagger** /'stægə(r)/ *vi* vacilar, cambalear □ *vt* (*shock*) atordoar, chocar; (*holidays etc*) escalonar. **~ing** *a* atordoador, chocante

**stagnant** /'stægnənt/ *a* estagnado, parado

**stagnat|e** /stæg'neɪt/ *vi* estagnar. **~ion** /-ʃn/ *n* estagnação *f*

**staid** /steɪd/ *a* sério, sensato, estável

**stain** /steɪn/ *vt* manchar, pôr nódoa em; (*colour*) tingir, dar cor a □ *n* mancha *f*, nódoa *f*; (*colouring*) corante *m*. **~ed glass window** vitral *m*. **~less steel** aço *m* inoxidável

**stair** /steə(r)/ *n* degrau *m*. **~s** escada(s) *f*(*pl*)

**stair|case** /'steəkeɪs/, **~way** /-weɪ/ *ns* escada(s) *f*(*pl*), escadaria *f*

**stake** /steɪk/ *n* (*post*) estaca *f*, poste *m*; (*wager*) parada *f*, aposta *f* □ *vt* (*area*) demarcar, delimitar; (*wager*) jogar, apostar. **at ~** em jogo. **have a ~ in** ter interesse em. **~ a claim to** reivindicar

**stale** /steɪl/ *a* (-er, -est) estragado, velho; (*bread*) duro, mofado; (*smell*) rançoso; (*air*) viciado; (*news*) velho

**stalemate** /'steɪlmeɪt/ *n* (*chess*) empate *m*; (*fig: deadlock*) impasse *m*, beco-sem-saída *m*

**stalk**[1] /stɔːk/ *n* (*of plant*) caule *m*

**stalk**[2] /stɔːk/ *vi* andar com ar empertigado □ *vt* (*prey*) perseguir furtivamente, tocaiar

**stall** /stɔːl/ *n* (*in stable*) baia *f*; (*in market*) tenda *f*, barraca *f*. **~s** (*theat*) poltronas *fpl* de orquestra; (*cinema*) platéia *f*, (*P*) plateia *f* □ *vt/i* (*auto*) enguiçar, (*P*) ir abaixo. **~ (for time)** ganhar tempo

**stalwart** /'stɔːlwət/ *a* forte, rijo; (*supporter*) fiel

**stamina** /'stæmɪnə/ *n* resistência *f*

**stammer** /'stæmə(r)/ *vt/i* gaguejar □ *n* gagueira *f*, (*P*) gaguez *f*

**stamp** /stæmp/ *vt/i* **~ (one's foot)** bater com o pé (no chão), pisar com força □ *vt* estampar; (*letter*) estampilhar, selar; (*with rubber stamp*) carimbar. **~ out** (*fire, rebellion etc*) esmagar; (*disease*) erradicar □ *n* estampa *f*; (*for postage*) selo *m*; (*fig: mark*) cunho *m*. (**rubber**) **~** carimbo *m*. **~-collecting** *n* filatelia *f*

**stampede** /stæm'piːd/ *n* (*scattering*) debandada *f*; (*of horses, cattle etc*) tresma/hada *f*; debandada *f*; (*fig: rush*) corrida *f* □ *vt/i* (*fazer*) debandar; (*horses, cattle etc*) tresmalhar

**stance** /stæns/ *n* posição *f*, postura *f*

**stand** /stænd/ *vi* (*pt* **stood**) estar em pé; (*keep upright position*) ficar em pé; (*rise*) levantar-se; (*be situated*) encontrar-se, ficar, situar-se; (*pol*) candidatar-se (**for** por) □ *vt* pôr (de pé), colocar; (*tolerate*) suportar, agüentar, (*P*) aguentar □ *n* posição *f*; (*support*) apoio *m*; (*mil*) resistência *f*; (*at fair*) stand *m*, pavilhão *m*; (*in street*) quiosque *m*; (*for spectators*) arquibancada *f*, (*P*) bancada *f*; (*Amer: witness-box*) banco *m* das testemunhas. **~ a**

chance ter uma possibilidade. ~ **back** recuar. ~ **by** or **around** estar parado sem fazer nada. ~ **by** (be ready) estar a postos; (promise, person) manter-se fiel a. ~ **down** desistir, retirar-se. ~ **for** representar, simbolizar; (colloq: tolerate) aturar. ~ **in for** substituir. ~ **out** (be conspicuous) sobressair. ~ **still** estar/ficar imóvel. ~ **still!** não se mexa!, quieto! ~ **to reason** ser lógico. ~ **up** levantar-se, pôr-se em or de pé. ~ **up for** defender, apoiar. ~ **up to** enfrentar. ~-**by** a (for emergency) de reserva; (ticket) de stand-by □ n (at airport) stand-by m. **on** ~-**by** (mil) de prontidão; (med) de plantão. ~-**in** n substituto m, suplente mf. ~-**offish** a (colloq: aloof) reservado, distante

**standard** /'stændəd/ n norma f, padrão m; (level) nível m; (flag) estandarte m, bandeira f. ~**s** (morals) princípios mpl □ a regulamentar; (average) standard, normal. ~ **lamp** abajur m de pé. ~ **of living** padrão m de vida, (P) nível m de vida

**standardize** /'stændədaɪz/ vt padronizar

**standing** /'stændɪŋ/ a em pé, de pé invar; (army, committee etc) permanente □ n posição f; (reputation) prestígio m; (duration) duração f. ~ **order** (at bank) ordem f permanente. ~-**room** n lugares mpl em pé

**standpoint** /'stændpɔɪnt/ n ponto m de vista

**standstill** /'stændstɪl/ n paralisação f. **at a** ~ parado, paralisado. **bring/ come to a** ~ (fazer) parar, paralisar(-se), imobilizar(-se)

**stank** /stæŋk/ see **stink**

**staple**[1] /'steɪpl/ n (for paper) grampo m, (P) agrafo m □ vt (paper) grampear, (P) agrafar. ~**r** /-ə(r)/ n grampeador m, (P) agrafador m

**staple**[2] /'steɪpl/ a principal, básico □ n (comm) artigo m básico

**star** /sta:(r)/ n estrela f; (cinema) estrela f, vedete f; (celebrity) celebridade f □ vt (pt starred) (of film) ter no papel principal, (P) ter como actor principal □ vi ~ **in** ser a vedete or ter o papel principal em. ~**dom** n celebridade f, estrelato m

**starch** /sta:tʃ/ n amido m, fécula f; (for clothes) goma f □ vt pôr em goma, engomar. ~**y** a (of food) farináceo, feculento; (fig: of person) rígido, formal

**stare** /steə(r)/ vi ~ **at** olhar fixamente □ n olhar m fixo

**starfish** /'sta:fɪʃ/ n (pl invar) estrela-do-mar f

**stark** /sta:k/ a (-er, -est) (desolate) ári-

do, desolado; (severe) austero, severo; (utter) completo, rematado; (fact etc) brutal □ adv completamente. ~ **naked** nu em pêlo, (P) em pelota (colloq)

**starling** /'sta:lɪŋ/ n estorninho m

**starlit** /'sta:lɪt/ a estrelado

**starry** /'sta:rɪ/ a estrelado. ~-**eyed** a (colloq) sonhador, idealista

**start** /sta:t/ vt/i começar; (machine) ligar, pôr em andamento; (fashion etc) lançar; (leave) partir; (cause) causar, provocar; (jump) sobressaltar-se, estremecer; (of car) arrancar, partir □ n começo m, início m; (of race) largada f, partida f; (lead) avanço m; (jump) sobressalto m, estremecimento m. **by fits and** ~**s** aosarrancos, intermitentemente. **for a** ~ para começar. **give sb a** sobressaltar alguém, pregar um susto a alguém. ~ **to do** começar a or pôr-se a fazer. ~**er** n (auto) arranque m; (competitor) corredor m; (culin) entrada f. ~**ing-point** n ponto m de partida

**startl|e** /'sta:tl/ vt (make jump) sobressaltar, pregar um susto a; (shock) alarmar, chocar. ~**ing** a alarmante; (surprising) surpreendente

**starv|e** /sta:v/ vi (suffer) passar fome; (die) morrer de fome. **be** ~**ing** (colloq: very hungry) ter muita fome, morrer de fome (colloq) □ vt fazer passar fome a; (deprive) privar. ~**ation** /-'veɪʃn/ n fome f

**stash** /stæʃ/ vt (sl) guardar, esconder, enfurnar (colloq)

**state** /steɪt/ n estado m, condição f; (pomp) pompa f, gala f; (pol) Estado m □ a de Estado, do Estado; (school) público; (visit etc) oficial □ vt afirmar (that que); (views) exprimir; (fix) marcar, fixar. **in a** ~ muito abalado

**stateless** /'steɪtlɪs/ a apátrida

**stately** /'steɪtlɪ/ a (-ier, -iest) majestoso. ~ **home** solar m, palácio m

**statement** /'steɪtmənt/ n declaração f; (of account) extrato m, (P) extracto m de conta

**statesman** /'steɪtsmən/ n (pl -men) homem m de estado, estadista m

**static** /'stætɪk/ a estático □ n (radio, TV) estática f, interferência f

**station** /'steɪʃn/ n (position) posto m; (rail, bus, radio) estação f; (rank) condição f, posição f social □ vt colocar. ~-**wagon** n perua f, (P) carrinha f. ~**ed at** or **in** (mil) estacionado em

**stationary** /'steɪʃnrɪ/ a estacionário, parado, imóvel; (vehicle) estacionado, parado

**stationer** /'steɪʃənə(r)/ n dono m de

papelaria. ~'s shop papelaria f. ~y n artigos mpl de papelaria; (writing-paper) papel m de carta

**statistic** /stə'tɪstɪk/ n dado m estatístico. ~s n (as a science) estatística f. ~al a estatístico

**statue** /'stætʃuː/ n estátua f

**stature** /'stætʃə(r)/ n estatura f

**status** /'steɪtəs/ n (pl -uses) situação f, posição f, categoria f; (prestige) prestígio m, importância f, status m. ~ quo status quo m. ~ symbol símbolo m de status

**statut|e** /'stætʃuːt/ n estatuto m, lei f. ~ory /-ʊtrɪ/ a estatutário, regulamentar; (holiday) legal

**staunch** /stɔːntʃ/ a (-er, -est) (friend) fiel, leal

**stave** /steɪv/ n (mus) pauta f □ vt ~ off (keep off) conjurar, evitar; (delay) adiar

**stay** /steɪ/ vi estar, ficar, permanecer; (dwell temporarily) ficar, alojar-se, hospedar-se; (spend time) demorar-se □ vt (hunger) enganar □ n estada f, visita f, permanência f. ~ behind ficar para trás. ~ in ficar em casa. ~ put (colloq) não se mexer (colloq). ~ up (late) deitar-se tarde. ~ing-power n resistência f

**stead** /sted/ n in my/your/etc ~ no meu/teu/etc lugar. stand in good ~ ser muito útil

**steadfast** /'stedfɑːst/ a firme, constante

**stead|y** /'stedɪ/ a (-ier, -iest) (stable) estável, firme, seguro; (regular) regular, constante; (hand, voice) firme □ vt firmar, fixar, estabilizar; (calm) acalmar. go ~y with (colloq) namorar. ~ily adv firmemente, (regularly) regularmente, de modo constante

**steak** /steɪk/ n bife m

**steal** /stiːl/ vt/i (pt stole, pp stolen) roubar (from sb de alguém). ~ away/in/etc sair/entrar/etc furtivamente, esgueirar-se. ~ the show pôr os outros na sombra

**stealth** /stelθ/ n by ~ furtivamente, na calada, às escondidas. ~y a furtivo

**steam** /stiːm/ n vapor m de água; (on window) condensação f □ vt (cook) cozinhar a vapor. ~ up (window) embaciar. □ vi soltar vapor, fumegar; (move) avançar. ~-engine n máquina f a vapor; (locomotive) locomotiva f a vapor. ~ iron ferro m a vapor. ~y a (heat) úmido, (P) húmido

**steamer** /'stiːmə(r)/ n (ship) (barco a) vapor m; (culin) utensílio m para cozinhar a vapor

**steamroller** /'stiːmrəʊlə(r)/ n cilindro m a vapor, rolo m compressor

**steel** /stiːl/ n aço m □ a de aço □ vpr ~ o.s. endurecer-se, fortalecer-se. ~ industry siderurgia f

**steep**[1] /stiːp/ vt (soak) mergulhar, pôr de molho; (permeate) passar, impregnar. ~ed in (fig: vice, misery etc) mergulhado em; (fig: knowledge, wisdom etc) impregnado de, repassado de

**steep**[2] /stiːp/ a (-er, -est) íngreme, escarpado; (colloq) exagerado, exorbitante. rise ~ly (slope) subir a pique; (price) disparar

**steeple** /'stiːpl/ n campanário m, torre f

**steeplechase** /'stiːpltʃeɪs/ n (race) corrida f de obstáculos

**steer** /stɪə(r)/ vt/i guiar, conduzir, dirigir; (ship) governar; (fig) guiar, orientar. ~ clear of evitar passar perto de. ~ing n (auto) direção f, (P) direcção f. ~ing-wheel n (auto) volante m

**stem**[1] /stem/ n caule m, haste f; (of glass) pé m; (of pipe) boquilha f; (of word) radical m □ vi (pt stemmed) ~ from provir de, vir de

**stem**[2] /stem/ vt (pt stemmed) (check) conter; (stop) estancar

**stench** /stentʃ/ n mau cheiro m, fedor m

**stencil** /'stensl/ n estêncil m, (P) stencil m □ vt (pt stencilled) (document) policopiar

**step** /step/ vi (pt stepped) ir andar □ vt ~ up aumentar □ n passo m, passada f; (of stair, train) degrau m; (action) medida f, passo m. ~s (ladder) escada f in ~ no mesmo passo, a passo certo; (fig) em conformidade (with com). ~ down (resign) demitir-se. ~ in (intervene) intervir. ~-ladder n escada f portátil. ~ping-stone n (fig: means to an end) ponte f, trampolim m

**stepbrother** /'stepbrʌðə(r)/ n meio-irmão m. ~daughter n nora f, (P) enteada f. ~father n padrasto m. ~mother n madrasta f. ~sister n meio-irmã f. ~son n genro m, (P) enteado m

**stereo** /'sterɪəʊ/ n (pl -os) estéreo m; (record-player etc) equipamento m or sistema m estéreo □ a estéreo invar. ~phonic /-ə'fɒnɪk/ a estereofônico, (P) estereofônico

**stereotype** /'sterɪətaɪp/ n estereótipo m. ~d a estereotipado

**steril|e** /'steraɪl/ a estéril. ~ity /stə'rɪlətɪ/ n esterilidade f

**steriliz|e** /'steraɪlaɪz/ vt esterilizar. ~ation /-'zeɪʃn/ n esterilização f

**sterling** /'stɜːlɪŋ/ n libra f esterlina □ a esterlino; (silver) de lei; (fig) excelente, de (primeira) qualidade

**stern**[1] /stɜ:n/ a (**-er, -est**) severo

**stern**[2] /stɜ:n/ n (*of ship*) popa f, ré f

**stethoscope** /'steθəskəʊp/ n estetoscópio m

**stew** /stju:/ vt/i estufar, guisar; (*fruit*) cozer □ n ensopado m. ~**ed fruit** compota f

**steward** /'stjʊəd/ n (*of club etc*) ecônomo m, (P) económo m, administrador m; (*on ship etc*) camareiro m (de bordo), (P) criado m (de bordo). ~**ess** /-'des/ n aeromoça f, (P) hospedeira f

**stick**[1] /stɪk/ n pau m; (*for walking*) bengala f; (*of celery*) talo m

**stick**[2] /stɪk/ vt (*pt* **stuck**) (*glue*) colar; (*thrust*) cravar, espetar; (*colloq: put*) enfiar, meter; (*sl: endure*) agüentar, (P) aguentar, aturar, suportar □ vi (*adhere*) colar, aderir; (*remain*) ficar enfiado or metido; (*be jammed*) emperrar, ficar engatado. ~ **in one's mind** ficar na memória. **be stuck with sb/sth** (*colloq*) não conseguir descartar-se de alguém/alg coisa (*colloq*). ~ **out** vt (*head*) esticar; (*tongue etc*) mostrar □ vi (*protrude*) sobressair. ~ **to** (*promise*) ser fiel a. ~**-up** n (*sl*) assalto m à mão armada. ~ **up for** (*colloq*) tomar o partido de, defender. ~**ing-plaster** n esparadrapo m, (P) adesivo m

**sticker** /'stɪkə(r)/ n adesivo m, etiqueta f (adesiva)

**stickler** /'stɪklə(r)/ n **be a ~ for** fazer grande questão de, insistir em

**sticky** /'stɪkɪ/ a (**-ier, -iest**) pegajoso; (*label, tape*) adesivo; (*weather*) abafado, mormacento

**stiff** /stɪf/ a (**-er, -est**) teso, hirto, rígido; (*limb, joint; hard*) duro; (*unbending*) inflexível; (*price*) elevado, puxado (*colloq*); (*penalty*) severo; (*drink*) forte; (*manner*) reservado, formal. **be bored/scared** ~ (*colloq*) estar muito aborrecido/com muito medo (*colloq*). ~ **neck** torcicolo m. ~**ness** n rigidez f

**stiffen** /'stɪfn/ vt/i (*harden*) endurecer; (*limb, joint*) emperrar

**stifl|e** /'staɪfl/ vt/i abafar, sufocar. ~**ing** a sufocante

**stigma** /'stɪgmə/ n estigma m. ~**tize** vt estigmatizar

**stile** /staɪl/ n degrau m para passar por cima de cerca

**stiletto** /stɪ'letəʊ/ n (*pl* **-os**) estilete m. ~ **heel** n salto m alto fino

**still**[1] /stɪl/ a imóvel, quieto; (*quiet*) sossegado □ n silêncio m, sossego m □ adv ainda; (*nevertheless*) apesar disso, apesar de tudo. **keep ~!** fique quieto!, não se mexa! ~ **life** natureza f morta. ~**ness** n calma f

**still**[2] /stɪl/ n (*apparatus*) alambique m

**stillborn** /'stɪlbɔ:n/ a natimorto, (P) nado-morto

**stilted** /'stɪltɪd/ a afetado, (P) afectado

**stilts** /stɪlts/ npl pernas de pau fpl, (P) andas fpl

**stimul|ate** /'stɪmjʊleɪt/ vt estimular. ~**ant** n estimulante m. ~**ating** a estimulante. ~**ation** /-'leɪʃn/ n estimulação f

**stimulus** /'stɪmjʊləs/ n (*pl* **-li** /-laɪ/) (*spur*) estímulo m

**sting** /stɪŋ/ n picada f; (*organ*) ferrão m □ vt (*pt* **stung**) picar □ vi picar, arder. ~**ing nettle** urtiga f

**stingy** /'stɪndʒɪ/ a (**-ier, -iest**) pãoduro m, sovina (**with** com)

**stink** /stɪŋk/ n fedor m, catinga f, mau cheiro m □ vi (*pt* **stank** or **stunk**, *pp* **stunk**) ~ (**of**) cheirar (a), tresandar (a) □ vt ~ **out** (*room etc*) empestar. ~**ing** a malcheiroso. ~**ing rich** (*sl*) podre de rico (*colloq*)

**stinker** /'stɪŋkə(r)/ n (*sl: person*) cara m horroroso (*colloq*); (*sl: sth difficult*) osso m duro de moer

**stint** /stɪnt/ vi ~ **on** poupar em, apertar em □ n (*work*) tarefa f, parte f, quinhão m

**stipulat|e** /'stɪpjʊleɪt/ vt estipular. ~**ion** /-'leɪʃn/ n condição f, estipulação f

**stir** /stɜ:r/ vt/i (*pt* **stirred**) (*move*) mexer(-se), mover(-se); (*excite*) excitar; (*a liquid*) mexer □ n agitação f, rebuliço m. ~ **up** (*trouble etc*) provocar, fomentar. ~**ring** a excitante

**stirrup** /'stɪrəp/ n estribo m

**stitch** /stɪtʃ/ n (*in sewing; med*) ponto m; (*in knitting*) malha f, ponto m; (*pain*) pontada f □ vt coser. **in ~es** (*colloq*) às gargalhadas (*colloq*)

**stoat** /stəʊt/ n arminho m

**stock** /stɒk/ n (*comm*) estoque m, (P) stock m, provisão f; (*finance*) valores mpl, fundos mpl; (*family*) família f, estirpe f; (*culin*) caldo m; (*flower*) goivo m □ a (*goods*) corrente, comum; (*hackneyed*) estereotipado □ vt (*shop etc*) abastecer, fornecer; (*sell*) vender □ vi ~ **up with** abastecer-se de. **in ~** em estoque. **out of ~** esgotado. **take** ~ (*fig*) fazer um balanço. ~**-car** n stock-car m. ~**-cube** n cubo m de caldo. ~ **market** Bolsa f (de Valores). ~**-still** a, adv imóvel. ~**-taking** n (*comm*) inventário m

**stockbroker** /'stɒkbrəʊkə(r)/ n corretor m da Bolsa

**stocking** /'stɒkɪŋ/ n meia f

**stockist** /'stɒkɪst/ n armazenista m

**stockpile** /'stɒkpaɪl/ n reservas fpl □ vt acumular reservas de, estocar

**stocky** /'stɒkɪ/ a (**-ier, -iest**) atarracado

**stodge** /stɒdʒ/ n (colloq) comida f pesada (colloq). ~y a (of food, book) pesado, maçudo

**stoic** /'stəʊɪk/ n estóico m. ~al a estoico. ~ism /-sɪzəm/ n estoicismo m

**stoke** /stəʊk/ vt (boiler, fire) alimentar, carregar

**stole**[1] /stəʊl/ n (garment) estola m

**stole**[2], **stolen** /stəʊl, 'stəʊlən/ see **steal**

**stomach** /'stʌmək/ n estômago m; (abdomen) barriga f, ventre m □ vt (put up with) aturar. ~-ache n dor f de estômago; (abdomen) dores fpl de barriga

**ston|e** /stəʊn/ n pedra f; (pebble) seixo m; (in fruit) caroço m; (weight) 6,348 kg; (med) cálculo m, pedra f □ vt apedrejar; (fruit) tirar o caroço de. **with-in a ~e's throw (of)** muito perto (de). **~e-cold** gelado. **~e-deaf** totalmente surdo. **~ed** a (colloq: drunk) bebão m (colloq); (colloq: drugged) drogado. ~y a pedregoso. **~y-broke** a (sl) duro, liso (sl)

**stonemason** /'stəʊnmeɪsn/ n pedreiro m

**stood** /stʊd/ see **stand**

**stooge** /stuːdʒ/ n (colloq: actor) ajudante mf; (colloq: puppet) antoche m, (P) comparsa mf, parceiro m

**stool** /stuːl/ n banco m, tamborete m

**stoop** /stuːp/ vi (bend) curvar-se, baixar-se; (condescend) condescender, dignar-se. ~ **to sth** rebaixar-se para (fazer) alg coisa □ n walk with a ~ andar curvado

**stop** /stɒp/ vt/i (pt **stopped**) parar; (prevent) impedir (**from** de); (hole, leak etc) tapar, vedar; (pain, noise etc) parar; (colloq: stay) ficar □ n (of bus) parada f, (P) paragem f; (full stop) ponto m final. **put a ~ to** pôr fim a. ~ **it!** acabe logo com isso! **~-over** n (break in journey) parada f, (P) paragem f; (port of call) escala f. **~press** n notícia f de última hora. **~-watch** n cronômetro m, (P) cronómetro m

**stopgap** /'stɒpgæp/ n substituto m provisório, tapa-buracos mpl (colloq) □ a temporário

**stoppage** /'stopɪdʒ/ n parada f, (P) paragem f; (of work) paralisação f de trabalho; (of pay) suspensão f

**stopper** /'stɒpə(r)/ n rolha f, tampa f

**storage** /'stɔːrɪdʒ/ n (of goods, food etc) armazenagem f, armazenamento m. **in cold ~** em frigorífico

**store** /stɔː(r)/ n reserva f, provisão f; (warehouse) armazém m, entreposto m; (shop) grande armazém m; (Amer) loja f; (in computer) memória f □ vt (for future) pôr de reserva, juntar, fazer provisão de; (in warehouse) armazenar. **be in ~** estar guardado. **have in ~ for** reservar para. **set ~ by** dar valor a. **~-room** n depósito m, almortarifado m, (P) armazém m

**storey** /'stɔːrɪ/ n (pl -eys) andar m

**stork** /stɔːk/ n cegonha f

**storm** /stɔːm/ n tempestade f □ vt tomar de assalto □ vi enfurecer-se. **a ~ in a teacup** uma tempestade num copo de água. ~y a tempestuoso

**story** /'stɔːrɪ/ n estória f, (P) história f; (in press) artigo m, matéria f; (Amer: storey) andar m; (colloq: lie) cascata f, (P) peta f. **~-teller** n contador m de estórias, (P) histórias

**stout** /staʊt/ a (-er, -est) (fat) gordo, corpulento; (strong, thick) resistente, sólido, grosso; (brave) resoluto □ n cerveja f preta forte

**stove** /stəʊv/ n (for cooking) fogão m (de cozinha)

**stow** /stəʊ/ vt ~ **(away)** (put away) guardar, arrumar; (hide) esconder □ vi ~ **away** viajar clandestinamente

**stowaway** /'stəʊəweɪ/ n passageiro m clandestino

**straddle** /'strædl/ vt (sit) escarranchar-se em, montar; (stand) pôr-se de pernas abertas sobre

**straggle** /'strægl/ vi (lag behind) desgarrar-se, ficar para trás; (spread) estender-se desordenadamente. **~r** /-ə(r)/ n retardatário m

**straight** /streɪt/ a (-er, -est) direito; (tidy) em ordem; (frank) franco, direto, (P) directo; (of hair) liso; (of drink) puro □ adv (in straight line) reto; (directly) direito, direto, (P) directo, diretamente, (P) directamente □ n linha f reta, (P) recta. **~ ahead** or **on** (sempre) em frente. **~ away** logo, imediatamente. **go ~** viver honestamente. **keep a ~ face** não se desmanchar, manter um ar sério

**straighten** /'streɪtn/ vt endireitar; (tidy) arrumar, pôr em ordem

**straightforward** /streɪt'fɔːwəd/ a franco, sincero; (easy) simples

**strain**[1] /streɪn/ n (breed) raça f; (streak) tendência f, veia f

**strain**[2] /streɪn/ vt (rope) esticar, puxar; (tire) cansar; (filter) filtrar, passar; (vegetables, tea etc) coar; (med) distender, torcer; (fig) forçar, pôr à prova □ vi esforçar-se □ n tensão f; (fig: effort) esforço m; (med) distensão f. ~s (music) melodias fpl. ~ **one's ears** apurar o ouvido. **~ed** a forçado; (relations) tenso. **~er** n coador m, (P) passador m

**strait** /streɪt/ n estreito m. ~s estreito m; (fig) apuros mpl, dificuldades fpl. **~-jacket** n camisa-de-força f. **~-laced** a severo, puritano

**strand** /strænd/ *n* (*thread*) fio *m*; (*lock of hair*) mecha *f*, madeixa *f*

**stranded** /'strændıd/ *a* (*person*) em dificuldades, deixado para trás, abandonado

**strange** /streındʒ/ *a* (-er, -est) estranho. ~ly *adv* estranhamente. ~ness *n* estranheza *f*

**stranger** /'streındʒə(r)/ *n* estranho *m*, desconhecido *m*

**strangle** /'stræŋgl/ *vt* estrangular, sufocar

**stranglehold** /'stræŋglhəʊld/ *n* **have a ~ on** ter domínio sobre

**strangulation** /stræŋgjʊ'leıʃn/ *n* estrangulamento *m*

**strap** /stræp/ *n* (*of leather etc*) correia *f*; (*of dress*) alça *f*; (*of watch*) pulseira *f* com correia □ *vt* (*pt* **strapped**) prender com correia

**strapping** /'stræpıŋ/ *a* robusto, grande

**strata** /'streıtə/ *see* **stratum**

**stratagem** /'strætədʒəm/ *n* estratagema *m*

**strategic** /strə'tiːdʒık/ *a* estratégico; (*of weapons*) de longo alcance

**strategy** /'strætədʒı/ *n* estratégia *f*

**stratum** /'straːtəm/ *n* (*pl* **strata**) estrato *m*, camada *f*

**straw** /strɔː/ *n* palha *f*; (*for drinking*) canudo *m*, (P) palhinha *f*. **the last ~** a última gota *f*

**strawberry** /'strɔːbrı/ *n* (*fruit*) morango *m*; (*plant*) morangueiro *m*

**stray** /streı/ *vi* (*deviate from path etc*) extraviar-se, desencaminhar-se, afastar-se (**from** de); (*lose one's way*) perder-se; (*wander*) vagar, errar □ *a* perdido, extraviado; (*isolated*) isolado, raro, esporádico □ *n* animal *m* perdido *or* vadio

**streak** /striːk/ *n* risca *f*, lista *f*; (*strain*) veia *f*; (*period*) período *m*. ~ **of lightning** relâmpago *m* □ *vt* listrar, riscar □ *vi* ir como um raio. ~**er** *n* (*colloq*) pessoa *f* que corre nua em lugares públicos. ~**y** *a* listrado, riscado. ~**y bacon** toucinho *m* entremeado com gordura

**stream** /striːm/ *n* riacho *m*, córrego *m*, regato *m*; (*current*) corrente *f*; (*fig: flow*) jorro *m*, torrente *f*; (*schol*) nível *m*, grupo *m* □ *vi* correr; (*of banner, hair*) flutuar; (*sweat*) escorrer, pingar

**streamer** /'striːmə(r)/ *n* (*of paper*) serpentina *f*; (*flag*) flâmula *f*, bandeirola *f*

**streamline** /'striːmlaın/ *vt* dar forma aerodinâmica a; (*fig*) racionalizar. ~**d** *a* (*shape*) aerodinâmico

**street** /striːt/ *n* rua *f*. **the man in the ~** (*fig*) o homem da rua. ~ **lamp** poste *m* de iluminação

**streetcar** /'striːtkaː(r)/ *n* (*Amer*) bonde *m*, (P) carro *m* eléctrico

**strength** /streŋθ/ *n* força *f*; (*of wall*) solidez *f*; (*of fabric etc*) resistência *f*. **on the ~ of** à base de, em virtude de

**strengthen** /'streŋθn/ *vt* fortificar, fortalecer, reforçar

**strenuous** /'strenjʊəs/ *a* enérgico; (*arduous*) árduo, estrênuo, (P) estrênuo; (*tiring*) fatigante, esgotante. ~**ly** *adv* esforçadamente, energicamente

**stress** /stres/ *n* acento *m*; (*pressure*) pressão *f*, tensão *f*; (*med*) stress *m* □ *vt* acentuar, sublinhar; (*sound*) acentuar. ~**ful** *a* estressante

**stretch** /stretʃ/ *vt* (*pull taut*) esticar; (*arm, leg, neck*) estender, esticar; (*clothes*) alargar; (*truth*) forçar, torcer □ *vi* estender-se; (*after sleep etc*) espreguiçar-se; (*of clothes*) alargar-se □ *n* extensão *f*, trecho *m*; (*period*) período *m*; (*of road*) troço *m* □ *a* (*of fabric*) com elasticidade. **at a ~** sem parar. ~ **one's legs** esticar as pernas

**stretcher** /'stretʃə(r)/ *n* maca *f*, padiola *f*. ~-**bearer** *n* padioleiro *m*, (P) maqueiro *m*

**strew** /struː/ *vt* (*pt* **strewed**, *pp* **strewed** *or* **strewn**) (*scatter*) espalhar; (*cover*) juncar, cobrir

**stricken** /'strıkən/ *a* ~ **with** atacado *or* acometido de

**strict** /strıkt/ *a* (-er, -est) estrito, rigoroso. ~**ly** *adv* estritamente. ~**ly speaking** a rigor. ~**ness** *n* severidade *f*, rigor *m*

**stride** /straıd/ *vi* (*pt* **strode**, *pp* **stridden**) caminhar a passos largos □ *n* passada *f*. **make great ~s** (*fig*) fazer grandes progressos. **take sth in one's ~** fazer alg coisa sem problemas

**strident** /'straıdnt/ *a* estridente

**strife** /straıf/ *n* conflito *m*, dissensão *f*, luta *f*

**strike** /straık/ *vt* (*pt* **struck**) bater (em); (*blow*) dar; (*match*) riscar, acender; (*gold etc*) descobrir; (*of clock*) soar, dar, bater (horas); (*of lightning*) atingir □ *vi* fazer greve; (*attack*) atacar □ *n* (*of workers*) greve *f*; (*mil*) ataque *m*; (*find*) descoberta *f*. **on ~** em greve. ~ **a bargain** fechar negócio. ~ **off** *or* **out** riscar. ~ **up** (*mus*) começar a tocar; (*friendship*) travar

**striker** /'straıkə(r)/ *n* grevista *mf*

**striking** /'straıkıŋ/ *a* notável, impressionante; (*attractive*) atraente

**string** /strıŋ/ *n* corda *f*, fio *m*; (*of violin, racket etc*) corda *f*; (*of pearls*) fio *m*; (*of onions, garlic*) réstia *f*; (*of lies etc*) série *f*; (*row*) fila *f* □ *vt* (*pt* **strung**) (*thread*) enfiar. **pull ~s** usar pistolão, (P) puxar os cordelinhos. ~ **out**

espaçar-se. ~ed *a* (*instrument*) de cordas. ~y *a* filamentoso, fibroso; (*meat*) com nervos

**stringent** /'strɪndʒənt/ *a* rigoroso, estrito

**strip**[1] /strɪp/ *vt/i* (*pt* **stripped**) (*undress*) despir(-se); (*machine*) desmontar; (*deprive*) despojar, privar. ~**per** *n* artista *mf* de striptease; (*solvent*) removedor *m*

**strip**[2] /strɪp/ *n* tira *f*; (*of land*) faixa *f*. ~ **comic** — história *f* em quadrinhos, (*P*) banda *f* desenhada. ~ **light** tubo *m* de luz fluorescente

**stripe** /straɪp/ *n* risca *f*, lista *f*, barra *f*. ~**d** *a* listrado, com listras

**strive** /straɪv/ *vi* (*pt* **strove**, *pp* **striven**) esforçar-se (**to** por)

**strode** /strəʊd/ *see* **stride**

**stroke**[1] /strəʊk/ *n* golpe *m*; (*of pen*) penada *f*, (*P*) traço *m*; (*in swimming*) braçada *f*; (*in rowing*) remada *f*; (*med*) ataque *m*, congestão *f*. ~ **of genius** rasgo *m* de genialidade. ~ **of luck** golpe *m* de sorte

**stroke**[2] /strəʊk/ *vt* (*with hand*) acariciar, fazer festas em

**stroll** /strəʊl/ *vi* passear, dar uma volta □ *n* volta *f*, (*P*) giro *m*. ~ **in**/*etc* entrar/*etc* tranquilamente

**strong** /strɒŋ/ *a* (**-er**, **-est**) forte; (*shoes, fabric etc*) resistente. **be a hundred**/*etc* ~ ser em número de cem/*etc*. ~**box** *n* cofre-forte *m*. ~ **language** linguagem *f* grosseira, palavrões *mpl*. ~**minded** *a* resoluto, firme. ~**room** *n* casa-forte *f*. ~**ly** *adv* (*greatly*) fortemente, grandemente; (*with energy*) com força; (*deeply*) profundamente

**stronghold** /'strɒŋhəʊld/ *n* fortaleza *f*; (*fig*) baluarte *m*, bastião *m*

**strove** /strəʊv/ *see* **strive**

**struck** /strʌk/ *see* **strike** □ *a* ~ **on** (*sl*) apaixonado por

**structur|e** /'strʌktʃə(r)/ *n* estrutura *f*; (*of building etc*) edifício *m*, construção *f*. ~**al** *a* estrutural, de estrutura, de construção

**struggle** /'strʌgl/ *vi* (*to get free*) debater-se; (*contend*) lutar; (*strive*) esforçar-se (**to, for** por) □ *n* luta *f*; (*effort*) esforço *m*. **have a** ~ **to** ter dificuldade em. ~ **to one's feet** levantar-se a custo

**strum** /strʌm/ *vt* (*pt* **strummed**) (*banjo etc*) dedilhar

**strung** /strʌŋ/ *see* **string**

**strut** /strʌt/ *n* (*support*) suporte *m*, escora *f* □ *vi* (*pt* **strutted**) (*walk*) pavonear-se

**stub** /stʌb/ *n* (*of pencil, cigarette*) ponta *f*; (*of tree*) cepo *m*, toco *m*; (*counterfoil*) talão *m*, canhoto *m* □ *vt* (*pt*

stubbed) ~ **one's toe** dar uma topada. ~ **out** esmagar

**stubble** /'stʌbl/ *n* (*on chin*) barba *f* por fazer; (*of crop*) restolho *m*

**stubborn** /'stʌbən/ *a* teimoso, obstinado. ~**ly** *adv* obstinadamente, teimosamente. ~**ness** *n* teimosia *f*, obstinação *f*

**stubby** /'stʌbɪ/ *a* (**-ier**, **-iest**) (*finger*) curto e grosso; (*person*) atarracado

**stuck** /stʌk/ *see* **stick**[2] □ *a* emperrado. ~**-up** *a* (*colloq*: *snobbish*) convencido, esnobe

**stud**[1] /stʌd/ *n* tacha *f*; (*for collar*) botão *m* de colarinho □ *vt* (*pt* **studded**) enfeitar com tachas. ~**ded with** salpicado de

**stud**[2] /stʌd/ *n* (*horses*) haras *m*. ~ (**-farm**) *n* coudelaria *f*. ~(**-horse**) *n* garanhão *m*

**student** /'stju:dnt/ *n* (*univ*) estudante *mf*, aluno *m*; (*schol*) aluno *m* □ *a* (*life, residence*) universitário

**studied** /'stʌdɪd/ *a* estudado

**studio** /'stju:dɪəʊ/ *n* (*pl* **-os**) estúdio *m*. ~ **flat** estúdio *m*

**studious** /'stju:dɪəs/ *a* (*person*) estudioso; (*deliberate*) estudado. ~**ly** *adv* (*carefully*) cuidadosamente

**study** /'stʌdɪ/ *n* estudo *m*; (*office*) escritório *m* □ *vt/i* estudar

**stuff** /stʌf/ *n* substância *f*, matéria *f*; (*sl*: *things*) coisa(s) *f* (*pl*) □ *vt* encher; (*animal*) empalhar; (*cram*) apinhar, encher ao máximo; (*culin*) rechear; (*block up*) entupir; (*put*) enfiar, meter. ~**ing** *n* enchimento *m*; (*culin*) recheio *m*

**stuffy** /'stʌfɪ/ *a* (**-ier**, **-iest**) abafado, mal arejado; (*dull*) enfadonho

**stumbl|e** /'stʌmbl/ *vi* tropeçar. ~**e across** *or* **on** dar com, encontrar por acaso, topar com. ~**ing-block** *n* obstáculo *m*

**stump** /stʌmp/ *n* (*of tree*) cepo *m*, toco *m*; (*of limb*) coto *m*; (*of pencil, cigar*) ponta *f*

**stumped** /stʌmpt/ *a* (*colloq*: *baffled*) atrapalhado, perplexo

**stun** /stʌn/ *vt* (*pt* **stunned**) aturdir, estontear

**stung** /stʌŋ/ *see* **sting**

**stunk** /stʌŋk/ *see* **stink**

**stunning** /'stʌnɪŋ/ *a* atordoador; (*colloq*: *delightful*) fantástico, sensacional

**stunt**[1] /stʌnt/ *vt* (*growth*) atrofiar. ~**ed** *a* atrofiado

**stunt**[2] /stʌnt/ *n* (*feat*) façanha *f*, proeza *f*; (*trick*) truque *m*; (*aviat*) acrobacia *f* aérea. ~ **man** *n* dublê *m*, (*P*) duplo *m*

**stupefy** /'stju:pɪfaɪ/ *vt* estupefazer, (*P*) estupeficar

**stupendous** /stju:'pendəs/ *a* estupendo, assombroso, prodigioso

**stupid** /'stju:pɪd/ *a* estúpido, obtuso. **~ity** /-'pɪdətɪ/ *n* estupidez *f*. **~ly** *adv* estupidamente

**stupor** /'stju:pə(r)/ *n* estupor *m*, torpor *m*

**sturdy** /'stɜ:dɪ/ *a* (**-ier, -iest**) robusto, vigoroso, forte

**stutter** /'stʌtə(r)/ *vi* gaguejar □ *n* gagueira *f*, (P) gaguez *f*

**sty** /staɪ/ *n* (*pigsty*) pocilga *f*, chiqueiro *m*

**stye** /staɪ/ *n* (*on eye*) terçol *m*, terçolho *m*

**styl|e** /staɪl/ *n* estilo *m*; (*fashion*) moda *f*; (*kind*) gênero *m*, (P) género *m*, tipo *m*; (*pattern*) feitio *m*, modelo *m* □ *vt* (*design*) desenhar, criar. **in ~e** (*live*) em grande estilo; (*do things*) com classe. **~e sb's hair** fazer um penteado em alguém. **~ist** *n* (*of hair*) cabeleireiro *m*

**stylish** /'staɪlɪʃ/ *a* elegante, na moda

**stylized** /'staɪlaɪzd/ *a* estilizado

**stylus** /'staɪləs/ *n* (*pl* **-uses**) (*of record-player*) agulha *f*, safira *f*

**suave** /swa:v/ *a* polido, de fala mansa, (P) melífluo

**sub-** /sʌb/ *pref* sub-

**subconscious** /sʌb'kɒnʃəs/ *a* & *n* subconsciente (*m*)

**subcontract** /sʌbkən'trækt/ *vt* dar de subempreitada

**subdivide** /sʌbdɪ'vaɪd/ *vt* subdividir

**subdue** /səb'dju:/ *vt* (*enemy, feeling*) dominar, subjugar; (*sound, voice*) abrandar. **~d** *a* (*weak*) submisso; (*quiet*) recolhido; (*light*) velado

**subject**[1] /'sʌbdʒɪkt/ *a* (*state etc*) dominado □ *n* sujeito *m*; (*schol, univ*) disciplina *f*, matéria *f*; (*citizen*) súdito *m*. **~-matter** *n* conteúdo *m*, tema *m*, assunto *m*. **~ to** sujeito a

**subject**[2] /səb'dʒekt/ *vt* submeter. **~ion** /-kʃn/ *n* submissão *f*

**subjective** /sʌb'dʒektɪv/ *a* subjetivo, (P) subjectivo

**subjunctive** /səb'dʒʌŋktɪv/ *a* & *n* subjuntivo (*m*), (P) conjuntivo (*m*)

**sublime** /sə'blaɪm/ *a* sublime

**submarine** /sʌbmə'ri:n/ *n* submarino *m*

**submerge** /səb'mɜ:dʒ/ *vt* submergir □ *vi* submergir, mergulhar

**submissive** /səb'mɪsɪv/ *a* submisso

**submi|t** /səb'mɪt/ *vt/i* (*pt* submitted) submeter(-se) (**to** a); (*jur: argue*) alegar. **~ssion** /-'mɪʃn/ *n* submissão *f*

**subnormal** /sʌb'nɔ:ml/ *a* subnormal; (*temperature*) abaixo do normal

**subordinate**[1] /sə'bɔ:dɪnət/ *a* subordinado, subalterno; (*gram*) subordinado □ *n* subordinado *m*, subalterno *m*

**subordinate**[2] /sə'bɔ:dɪneɪt/ *vt* subordinar (**to** a)

**subpoena** /səb'pi:nə/ *n* (*pl* **-as**) (*jur*) citação *f*, intimação *f*

**subscribe** /səb'skraɪb/ *vt/i* subscrever, contribuir (**to** para). **~ to** (*theory, opinion*) subscrever, aceitar; (*newspaper*) assinar. **~r** /-ə(r)/ *n* subscritor *m*, assinante *m*

**subscription** /səb'skrɪpʃn/ *n* subscrição *f*; (*to newspaper*) assinatura *f*

**subsequent** /'sʌbsɪkwənt/ *a* subseqüente, (P) subsequente, posterior. **~ly** *adv* subseqüentemente, a seguir, posteriormente

**subservient** /səb'sɜ:vɪənt/ *a* servil, subserviente

**subside** /səb'saɪd/ *vi* (*flood, noise etc*) baixar; (*land*) ceder, afundar; (*wind, storm, excitement*) abrandar. **~nce** /-əns/ *n* (*of land*) afundamento *m*

**subsidiary** /səb'sɪdɪərɪ/ *a* subsidiário □ *n* (*comm*) filial *f*, sucursal *f*

**subsid|y** /'sʌbsədɪ/ *n* subsídio *m*, subvenção *f*. **~ize** /-ɪdaɪz/ *vt* subsidiar, subvencionar

**subsist** /səb'sɪst/ *vi* subsistir. **~ on** viver de. **~ence** *n* subsistência *f*. **~ence allowance** ajudas *fpl* de custo

**substance** /'sʌbstəns/ *n* substância *f*

**substandard** /sʌb'stændəd/ *a* de qualidade inferior

**substantial** /səb'stænʃl/ *a* substancial. **~ly** *adv* substancialmente

**substantiate** /səb'stænʃɪeɪt/ *vt* comprovar, fundamentar

**substitut|e** /'sʌbstɪtju:t/ *n* (*person*) substituto *m*, suplente *mf* (**for** de); (*thing*) substituto *m* (**for** de) □ *vt* substituir (**for** por). **~ion** /'tju:ʃn/ *n* substituição *f*

**subterfuge** /'sʌbtəfju:dʒ/ *n* subterfúgio *m*

**subtitle** /'sʌbtaɪtl/ *n* subtítulo *m*

**subtle** /'sʌtl/ *a* (**-er, -est**) sutil, (P) subtil. **~ty** *n* sutileza *f*, (P) subtileza *f*

**subtotal** /'sʌbtəʊtl/ *n* soma *f* parcial

**subtract** /səb'trækt/ *vt* subtrair, diminuir. **~ion** /-kʃn/ *n* subtração *f*, diminuição *f*

**suburb** /'sʌbɜ:b/ *n* subúrbio *m*, arredores *mpl*. **~an** /sə'bɜ:bən/ *a* dos subúrbios, suburbano. **~ia** /sə'bɜ:bɪə/ *n* (*pej*) os arredores

**subver|t** /səb'vɜ:t/ *vt* subverter. **~sion** /-ʃn/ *n* subverção *f*. **~sive** /-sɪv/ *a* subversivo

**subway** /'sʌbweɪ/ *n* passagem *f* subterrânea; (*Amer: underground*) metropolitano *m*

**succeed** /sək'si:d/ *vi* ser bem sucedido, ter êxito. **~ in doing sth** conseguir fazer alg coisa □ *vt* (*follow*) suceder a. **~ing** *a* seguinte, sucessivo

**success** /sək'ses/ *n* sucesso *m*, êxito *m*

**succession** /sək'seʃn/ *n* sucessão *f*; (*series*) série *f*. **in** ~ seguidos, consecutivos

**successive** /sək'sesɪv/ *a* sucessivo, consecutivo

**successor** /sək'sesə(r)/ *n* sucessor *m*

**succinct** /sək'sɪŋkt/ *a* sucinto

**succulent** /'sakjʊlənt/ *a* suculento

**succumb** /sə'kʌm/ *vi* sucumbir

**such** /sʌtʃ/ *a & pron* tal, semelhante, assim; (*so much*) tanto □ *adv* tanto. ~ **a book/etc** um tal livro/etc ou um livro/etc assim. ~ **books/etc** tais livros/etc ou livros/etc assim. ~ **courage/etc** tanta coragem/etc. ~ **a big house** uma casa tão grande. **as** ~ como tal. ~ **as** como, tal como. **there's no** ~ **thing** uma coisa dessa não existe. ~**-and-such** *a & pron* tal e tal

**suck** /sʌk/ *vt* chupar; (*breast*) mamar. ~ **in** *or* **up** (*absorb*) absorver, aspirar; (*engulf*) tragar. ~ **up to** puxar o saco a (*colloq*). ~ **one's thumb** chupar o dedo. ~**er** *n* (*sl: greenhorn*) trouxa *mf* (*colloq*); (*bot*) broto *m*

**suckle** /'sʌkl/ *vt* amamentar, dar de mamar a

**suction** /'sʌkʃn/ *n* sucção *f*

**sudden** /'sʌdn/ *a* súbito, repentino. **all of a** ~ de repente, de súbito. ~**ly** *adv* subitamente, repentinamente. ~**ness** *n* subitaneidade *f*, brusquidão *f*

**suds** /sʌdz/ *npl* espuma *f* de sabão; (*soapy water*) água *f* de sabão

**sue** /su:/ *vt* (*pres p* **suing**) processar

**suede** /sweɪd/ *n* camurça *f*

**suet** /'su:ɪt/ *n* sebo *m*

**suffer** /'sʌfə(r)/ *vt/i* sofrer; (*tolerate*) tolerar, suportar. ~**er** *n* sofredor *m*, o que sofre; (*patient*) doente *mf*, vítima *f*. ~**ing** *n* sofrimento *m*

**suffice** /sə'faɪs/ *vi* bastar, chegar, ser suficiente

**sufficien|t** /sə'fɪʃnt/ *a* suficiente, bastante. ~**cy** *n* suficiência *f*, quantidade *f* suficiente. ~**tly** *adv* suficientemente

**suffix** /'sʌfɪx/ *n* sufixo *m*

**suffocat|e** /'sʌfəkeɪt/ *vt/i* sufocar. ~**ion** /'keɪʃn/ *n* sufocação *f*, asfixia *f*. ~**ing** *a* sufocante, asfixiante

**sugar** /'ʃʊgə(r)/ *n* açúcar *m* □ *vt* adoçar, pôr açúcar em. ~**-bowl** *n* açucareiro *m*. ~**-lump** *n* torrão *m* de açúcar, (*P*) quadradinho *m* de açúcar. **brown** ~ açúcar *m* preto, (*P*) açúcar *m* amarelo. ~**y** *a* açucarado; (*fig: too sweet*) delico-doce

**suggest** /sə'dʒest/ *vt* sugerir. ~**ion** /-tʃn/ *n* sugestão *f*. ~**ive** *a* sugestivo; (*improper*) brejeiro, picante. **be** ~**ive of** sugerir, fazer lembrar

**suicid|e** /'su:ɪsaɪd/ *n* suicídio *m*. **commit** ~**e** suicidar-se. ~**al** /-'saɪdl/ *a* suicida

**suit** /su:t/ *n* terno *m*, (*P*) fato *m*; (*woman's*) costume *m*, (*P*) saia-casaco *m*; (*cards*) naipe *m* □ *vt* convir a; (*of garment, style*) ficar bem em; (*adapt*) adaptar. **follow** ~ (*fig*) seguir o exemplo. ~**ability** *n* (*of action*) conveniência *f*, oportunidade *f*; (*of candidate*) aptidão *f*. ~**able** *a* conveniente, apropriado (**for** para). ~**ably** *adv* convenientemente. ~**ed** *a* **be** ~**ed to** ser feito para, servir para. **be well** ~**ed** (*matched*) combinar-se bem; (*of people*) ser o ideal

**suitcase** /'su:tkeɪs/ *n* mala *f* (de viagem)

**suite** /swi:t/ *n* (*of rooms; mus*) suíte *f*, (*P*) suite *f*; (*of furniture*) mobília *f*

**suitor** /'su:tə(r)/ *n* pretendente *m*

**sulk** /sʌlk/ *vi* amuar, ficar emburrado. ~**y** *a* amuado, emburrado (*colloq*)

**sullen** /'sʌlən/ *a* carrancudo

**sulphur** /'sʌlfə(r)/ *n* enxofre *m*. ~**ic** /-'fjʊərɪk/ *a* ~**ic acid** ácido *m* sulfúrico

**sultan** /'sʌltən/ *n* sultão *m*

**sultana** /sʌl'ta:nə/ *n* (*fruit*) passa *f* branca, (*P*) sultana *f*

**sultry** /'sʌltrɪ/ *a* (**-ier, -iest**) abafado, opressivo; (*fig*) sensual

**sum** /sʌm/ *n* soma *f*; (*amount of money*) soma *f*, quantia *f*, importância *f*; (*in arithmetic*) conta *f* □ *vt* (*pt* **summed**) somar. ~ **up** recapitular, resumir; (*assess*) avaliar, medir

**summar|y** /'sʌmərɪ/ *n* sumário *m*, resumo *m* □ *a* sumário. ~**ize** *vt* resumir

**summer** /'sʌmə(r)/ *n* verão *m*, estio *m* □ *a* de verão. ~**-time** *n* verão *m*, época *f* de verão. ~**y** *a* estival, próprio de verão

**summit** /'sʌmɪt/ *n* cume *m*, cimo *m*. ~ **conference** (*pol*) conferência *f* de cúpula, (*P*) reunião *f* de cimeira

**summon** /'sʌmən/ *vt* mandar chamar; (*to meeting*) convocar. ~ **up** (*strength, courage etc*) chamar a si, fazer apelo a

**summons** /'sʌmənz/ *n* (*jur*) citação *f*, intimação *f* □ *vt* citar, intimar

**sump** /sʌmp/ *n* (*auto*) cárter *m*

**sumptuous** /'sʌmptʃʊəs/ *a* suntuoso, (*P*) sumptuoso, luxuoso

**sun** /sʌn/ *n* sol *m* □ *vt* (*pt* **sunned**) ~ **o.s.** aquecer-se ao sol. ~**-glasses** *npl* óculos *mpl* de sol. ~**-roof** *n* teto *m* solar. ~**-tan** *n* bronzeado *m*. ~**-tanned** *a* bronzeado. ~**-tan oil** *n* óleo *m* de bronzear

**sunbathe** /'sʌnbeɪð/ *vi* tomar um banho de sol

**sunburn** /'sʌnbɜːn/ n queimadura f de sol. **~t** a queimado pelo sol

**Sunday** /'sʌndɪ/ n domingo m. **~ school** catecismo m

**sundial** /'sʌndaɪəl/ n relógio m de sol

**sundown** /'sʌndaʊn/ n = **sunset**

**sundr|y** /'sʌndrɪ/ a vários, diversos. **~ies** npl artigos mpl diversos. **all and ~y** todo o mundo

**sunflower** /'sʌnflaʊə(r)/ n girassol m

**sung** /sʌŋ/ see **sing**

**sunk** /sʌŋk/ see **sink**

**sunken** /'sʌŋkən/ a (ship etc) afundado; (eyes) fundo

**sunlight** /'sʌnlaɪt/ n luz f do sol, sol m

**sunny** /'sʌnɪ/ a (-ier, -iest) (room, day etc) ensolarado

**sunrise** /'sʌnraɪz/ n nascer m do sol

**sunset** /'sʌnset/ n pôr m do sol

**sunshade** /'sʌnʃeɪd/ n (awning) toldo m; (parasol) pára-sol m, (P) guarda-sol m

**sunshine** /'sʌnʃaɪn/ n sol m, luz f do sol

**sunstroke** /'sʌnstrəʊk/ n (med) insolação f

**super** /'suːpə(r)/ a (colloq: excellent) formidável

**superb** /suː'pɜːb/ a soberbo, esplêndido

**supercilious** /suːpə'sɪlɪəs/ a (haughty) altivo; (disdainful) desdenhoso

**superficial** /suːpə'fɪʃl/ a superficial. **~ity** /-ɪ'ælətɪ/ n superficialidade f. **~ly** adv superficialmente

**superfluous** /suː'pɜːflʊəs/ a supérfluo

**superhuman** /suːpə'hjuːmən/ a sobre-humano

**superimpose** /suːpərɪm'pəʊz/ vt sobrepor (on a)

**superintendent** /suːpərɪn'tendənt/ n superintendente m; (of police) comissário m, chefe m de polícia

**superior** /suː'pɪərɪə(r)/ a & n superior (m). **~ity** /-'ɒrətɪ/ n superioridade f

**superlative** /suː'pɜːlətɪv/ a supremo, superlativo □ n (gram) superlativo m

**supermarket** /'suːpəmɑːkɪt/ n supermercado m

**supernatural** /suːpə'nætʃrəl/ a sobrenatural

**superpower** /'suːpəpaʊə(r)/ n superpotência f

**supersede** /suːpə'siːd/ vt suplantar, substituir

**supersonic** /suːpə'sɒnɪk/ a supersônico, (P) supersónico

**superstiti|on** /suːpə'stɪʃn/ n superstição f. **~ous** a /-'stɪʃəs/ supersticioso

**superstore** /'suːpəstɔː(r)/ n hipermercado m

**supertanker** /'suːpətæŋkə(r)/ n superpetroleiro m

**supervis|e** /'suːpəvaɪz/ vt supervisar, fiscalizar. **~ion** /-'vɪʒn/ n supervisão f. **~or** n supervisor m; (shop) chefe mf de seção; (firm) chefe mf de serviço. **~ory** /'suːpəvaɪzərɪ/ a de supervisão

**supper** /'sʌpə(r)/ n jantar m; (late at night) ceia f

**supple** /'sʌpl/ a flexível, maleável

**supplement**[1] /'sʌplɪmənt/ n suplemento m. **~ary** /-'mentrɪ/ a suplementar

**supplement**[2] /'sʌplɪment/ vt suplementar

**supplier** /sə'plaɪə(r)/ n fornecedor m

**suppl|y** /sə'plaɪ/ vt suprir, prover; (comm) fornecer, abastecer □ n provisão f; (of goods, gas etc) fornecimento m, abastecimento m □ a (teacher) substituto. **~ies** (food) víveres mpl; (mil) suprimentos mpl. **~y and demand** oferta e procura

**support** /sə'pɔːt/ vt (hold up, endure) suportar; (provide for) sustentar, suster; (back) apoiar, patrocinar; (sport) torcer por □ n apoio m; (techn) suporte m. **~er** n partidário m; (sport) torcedor m

**suppos|e** /sə'pəʊz/ vt/i supor. **~e that** supondo que, na hipótese de que. **~ed** a suposto. **he's ~ed to do it** ele deve fazer; (believed to) consta que ele faz. **~edly** /-ɪdlɪ/ adv segundo dizem; (probably) supostamente, em princípio. **~ing** conj se. **~ition** /sʌpə'zɪʃn/ n suposição f

**suppress** /sə'pres/ vt (put an end to) suprimir; (restrain) conter, reprimir; (stifle) abafar, sufocar; (psych) recalcar. **~ion** /-ʃn/ n supressão f; (restraint) repressão f; (psych) recalque m, (P) recalcamento m

**suprem|e** /suː'priːm/ a supremo. **~acy** /-eməsɪ/ n supremacia f

**surcharge** /'sɜːtʃɑːdʒ/ n sobretaxa f; (on stamp) sobrecarga f

**sure** /ʃʊə(r)/ a (-er, -est) seguro, certo □ adv (colloq: certainly) deveras, não há dúvida que, de certeza. **be ~ about** or of ter a certeza de. **be ~ to** (not fail) não deixar de. **he is ~ to find out** ele vai descobrir com certeza. **make ~** assegurar. **~ly** adv com certeza, certamente

**surety** /'ʃʊərətɪ/ n (person) fiador m; (thing) garantia f

**surf** /sɜːf/ n (waves) ressaca f, rebentação f. **~er** n surfista mf. **~ing** n surfe m, (P) surf m, jacaré-na-praia m

**surface** /'sɜːfɪs/ n superfície f □ a superficial □ vt/i revestir; (rise, become known) emergir. **~ mail** via f marítima

**surfboard** /'sɜ:fbɔ:d/ n prancha f de surfe, (P) surf

**surfeit** /'sɜ:fɪt/ n excesso m (of de)

**surge** /sɜ:dʒ/ vi (waves) ondular, encapelar-se; (move forward) avançar ▢ n (wave) onda f, vaga f; (motion) arremetida f

**surgeon** /'sɜ:dʒən/ n cirurgião m

**surg|ery** /'sɜ:dʒərɪ/ n cirurgia f; (office) consultório m; (session) consulta f; (consulting hours) horas fpl de consulta. ~ical a cirúrgico

**surly** /'sɜ:lɪ/ a (-ier, -iest) carrancudo, trombudo

**surmise** /sə'maɪz/ vt imaginar, supor, calcular ▢ n conjetura f, (P) conjectura f; hipótese f

**surmount** /sə'maʊnt/ vt sobrepujar, vencer, (P) superar

**surname** /'sɜ:neɪm/ n sobrenome m, (P) apelido m

**surpass** /sə'pɑ:s/ vt superar, ultrapassar, exceder

**surplus** /'sɜ:pləs/ n excedente m, excesso m; (finance) saldo m positivo ▢ a excedente, em excesso

**surpris|e** /sə'praɪz/ n surpresa f ▢ vt surpreender. ~ed a surpreendido, admirado (at com).. ~ing a surpreendente. ~ingly adv surpreendentemente

**surrender** /sə'rendə(r)/ vi render-se ▢ vt (hand over; mil) entregar ▢ n (mil) rendição f; (of rights) renúncia f

**surreptitious** /sʌrep'tɪʃəs/ a subreptício, furtivo

**surrogate** /'sʌrəgeɪt/ n delegado m. ~ mother mãe f de aluguel, (P) aluguer

**surround** /sə'raʊnd/ vt rodear, cercar; (mil etc) cercar. ~ing a circundante, vizinho. ~ings npl arredores mpl; (setting) meio m, ambiente m

**surveillance** /sɜ:'veɪləns/ n vigilância f

**survey¹** /sə'veɪ/ vt (landscape etc) observar; (review) passar em revista; (inquire about) pesquisar; (land) fazer o levantamento de; (building) vistoriar, inspecionar, (P) inspeccionar. ~or n (of buildings) fiscal m; (of land) agrimensor m

**survey²** /'sɜ:veɪ/ n (inspection) vistoria f, inspeção f, (P) inspecção f; (general view) panorâmica f; (inquiry) pesquisa f

**survival** /sə'vaɪvl/ n sobrevivência f; (relic) relíquia f, vestígio m

**surviv|e** /sə'vaɪv/ vt/i sobreviver (a). ~or n sobrevivente mf

**susceptib|le** /sə'septəbl/ a (prone) susceptível (to a); (sensitive, impressionable) susceptível, sensível. ~ility /-'bɪlətɪ/ n susceptibilidade f

**suspect¹** /sə'spekt/ vt suspeitar; (doubt, distrust) desconfiar de, suspeitar de

**suspect²** /'sʌspekt/ a & n suspeito (m)

**suspen|d** /sə'spend/ vt (hang, stop) suspender; (from duty etc) suspender. ~ded sentence suspensão f de pena. ~sion n suspensão f. ~sion bridge ponte f suspensa or pênsil

**suspender** /sə'spendə(r)/ n (presilha de) liga f. ~ belt n cintaliga f, (P) cinta f de ligas. ~s (Amer: braces) suspensórios mpl

**suspense** /sə'spens/ n ansiedade f, incerteza f; (in book etc) suspense m, tensão f

**suspicion** /sə'spɪʃn/ n suspeita f; (distrust) desconfiança f; (trace) vestígio m, (P) traço m

**suspicious** /sə'spɪʃəs/ a desconfiado; (causing suspicion) suspeito. be ~ of desconfiar de. ~ly adv de modo suspeito

**sustain** /sə'steɪn/ vt (support) suster, sustentar; (suffer) sofrer; (keep up) sustentar; (jur: uphold) sancionar; (interest, effort) manter. ~ed effort esforço m contínuo

**sustenance** /'sʌstɪməns/ n (food) alimento m, sustento m

**swagger** /'swægə(r)/ vi pavonear-se, andar com arrogância

**swallow¹** /'swɒləʊ/ vt/i engolir. ~ up (absorb, engulf) devorar, tragar

**swallow²** /'swɒləʊ/ n (bird) andorinha f

**swam** /swæm/ see **swim**

**swamp** /swɒmp/ n pântano m, brejo m ▢ vt (flood, overwhelm) inundar, submergir. ~y a pantanoso

**swan** /swɒn/ n cisne m

**swank** /swæŋk/ vi (colloq: show off) gabar-se, mostrar-se (colloq)

**swap** /swɒp/ vt/i (pt swapped) (colloq) trocar (for por) ▢ n (colloq) troca f

**swarm** /swɔ:m/ n (of insects, people) enxame m ▢ vi formigar. ~ into or round invadir

**swarthy** /'swɔ:ðɪ/ a (-ier, -iest) moreno, trigueiro

**swat** /swɒt/ vt (pt swatted) (fly etc) esmagar, esborrachar

**sway** /sweɪ/ vt/i oscilar, balançar(-se); (influence) mover, influenciar ▢ n oscilação f, balanceio m; (rule) domínio m, poder m

**swear** /sweə(r)/ vt/i (pt swore, pp sworn) jurar; (curse) praguejar, rogar pragas (at contra). ~ by jurar por; (colloq: recommend) ter grande fé em. ~-word n palavrão m

**sweat** /swet/ n suor m ▢ vi suar. ~y a suado

**sweater** /'swetə(r)/ n suéter m, (P) camisola f

**sweatshirt** /'swetʃɜːt/ n suéter m de malha or algodão

**swede** /swiːd/ n couve-nabo f

**Swed|e** /swiːd/ n sueco m. **~en** n Suécia f. **~ish** a & n sueco (m)

**sweep** /swiːp/ vt/i (pt swept) varrer; (go majestically) avançar majestosamente; (carry away) arrastar; (chimney) limpar □ n (with broom) varredela f, (curve) curva f, (movement) gesto m largo. **(chimney-)~** limpa-chaminés m. **~ing** a (gesture) largo; (action) de grande alcance. **~ing statement** generalização f fácil

**sweet** /swiːt/ a (-er, -est) doce; (colloq: charming) doce, gracinha; (colloq: pleasant) agradável □ n doce m. **~ corn** milho m. **~ pea** ervilha-de-cheiro f. **~ shop** confeitaria f. **have a ~ tooth** gostar de doce. **~ly** adv docemente. **~ness** n doçura f

**sweeten** /'swiːtn/ vt adoçar; (fig: mitigate) suavizar. **~er** n (for tea, coffee) adoçante m (artificial); (colloq: bribe) agrado m

**sweetheart** /'swiːthaːt/ n namorado m, namorada f; (term of endearment) querido m, querida f, amor m

**swell** /swel/ vt/i (pt swelled, pp swollen or swelled) (expand) inchar; (increase) aumentar □ n (of sea) ondulação f □ a (colloq: excellent) excelente; (colloq : smart) chique. **~ing** n (med) inchação f, inchaço m

**swelter** /'sweltə(r)/ vi fazer um calor abrasador; (person) abafar (com calor)

**swept** /swept/ see sweep

**swerve** /swɜːv/ vi desviar-se, dar uma guinada

**swift** /swɪft/ a (-er, -est) rápido, veloz. **~ly** adv rapidamente. **~ness** n rapidez f

**swig** /swɪg/ vt (pt swigged) (colloq: drink) emborcar, beber em longos tragos □ n (colloq) trago m, gole m

**swill** /swɪl/ vt passar por água □ n (pig-food) lavagem f, (P) lavadura f

**swim** /swɪm/ vt/i (pt swam, pp swum, pres p swimming) nadar; (room, head) rodar □ vt atravessar a nado; (distance) nadar □ n banho m. **~mer** n nadador m. **~ming** n natação f. **~ming-bath**, **~ming-pool** ns piscina f. **~ming-cap** n touca f de banho. **~ming-costume**, **~-suit** ns maiô m, (P) fato m de banho. **~ming-trunks** npl calção m de banho

**swindle** /'swɪndl/ vt trapacear, fraudar, (P) vigarizar □ n vigarice f. **~r** /-ə(r)/ n vigarista mf

**swine** /swaɪn/ npl (pigs) porcos mpl □ n (pl invar) (colloq: person) animal m, canalha m (colloq)

**swing** /swɪŋ/ vt/i (pt swung) balançar(-se); (turn round) girar □ n (seat) balanço m; (of opinion) reviravolta f; (mus) swing m; (rhythm) ritmo m. **in full ~** no máximo, em plena atividade, (P) actividade. **~ round** (of person) virar-se. **~-bridge/door** ns ponte f/porta f giratória

**swipe** /swaɪp/ vt (colloq: hit) bater em, dar uma pancada em (colloq); (colloq: steal) afanar, roubar (colloq) □ n (colloq: hit) pancada f (colloq)

**swirl** /swɜːl/ vi rodopiar, redemoinhar □ n turbilhão m, redemoinho m

**swish** /swɪʃ/ vt/i sibilar, zunir, (fazer) cortar o ar; (with brushing sound) roçar □ a (colloq) chique

**Swiss** /swɪs/ a & n suiço (m)

**switch** /swɪtʃ/ n interruptor m; (change) mudança f □ vt (transfer) transferir; (exchange) trocar □ vi desviar-se. **~ off** desligar

**switchboard** /'swɪtʃbɔːd/ n (telephone) PBX m, mesa f telefónica

**Switzerland** /'swɪtsələnd/ n Suiça f

**swivel** /'swɪvl/ vt/i (pt swivelled) (fazer) girar. **~ chair** cadeira f giratória

**swollen** /'swəʊlən/ see swell □ a inchado

**swoop** /swuːp/ vi (bird) lançar-se, cair (down on sobre); (police) dar uma batida policial, (P) rusga

**sword** /sɔːd/ n espada f

**swore** /swɔː(r)/ see swear

**sworn** /swɔːn/ see swear □ a (enemy) jurado, declarado; (ally) fiel

**swot** /swɒt/ vt/i (pt swotted) (colloq: study) estudar muito, (P) marrar (sl) □ n (colloq) estudante m muito aplicado, (P) marrão m (sl)

**swum** /swʌm/ see swim

**swung** /swʌŋ/ see swing

**sycamore** /'sɪkəmɔː(r)/ n (maple) sicômoro m, (P) sicómoro m; (Amer: plane) plátano m

**syllable** /'sɪləbl/ n sílaba f

**syllabus** /'sɪləbəs/ n (pl -uses) programa m

**symbol** /'sɪmbl/ n símbolo m. **~ic(al)** /-'bɒlɪk(l)/ a simbólico. **~ism** n simbolismo m

**symbolize** /'sɪmbəlaɪz/ vt simbolizar

**symmetr|y** /'sɪmətrɪ/ n simetria f. **~ical** /sɪ'metrɪkl/ a simétrico

**sympathize** /'sɪmpəθaɪz/ vi **~ with** ter pena de, condoer-se de; (fig) compartilhar os sentimentos de. **~r** n simpatizante mf

**sympath|y** /'sɪmpəθɪ/ n (pity) pena f, compaixão f; (solidarity) solidariedade f; (condolences) pêsames mpl, condolências fpl. **be in ~y with** estar de acordo com. **~etic** /-'θetɪk/ a compensivo, simpático; (likeable) simpático; (showing pity) compassivo. **~etically** /-'θetɪklɪ/ adv compassivamente; (fig) compreensivamente

**symphon|y** /'sɪmfənɪ/ n sinfonia f □ a sinfônico, (P) sinfónico. **~ic** /-'fɒnɪk/ a sinfônico, (P) sinfónico

**symptom** /'sɪmptəm/ n sintoma m. **~atic** /-'mætɪk/ a sintomático (of de)

**synagogue** /'sɪnəgɒg/ n sinagoga f

**synchronize** /'sɪŋkrənaɪz/ vt sincronizar

**syndicate** /'sɪndɪkət/ n sindicato m

**syndrome** /'sɪndrəʊm/ n (med) síndrome m, (P) síndroma f

**synonym** /'sɪnənɪm/ n sinônimo m, (P) sinónimo m. **~ous** /sɪ'nɒnɪməs/ a sinônimo, (P) sinónimo (with de)

**synopsis** /sɪ'nɒpsɪs/ n (pl -opses /-siːz/) sinopse f, resumo m

**syntax** /'sɪntæks/ n sintaxe f

**synthesis** /'sɪnθəsɪs/ n (pl -theses /-siːz/) síntese f

**synthetic** /sɪn'θetɪk/ a sintético

**syphilis** /'sɪfɪlɪs/ n sífilis f

**Syria** /'sɪrɪə/ n Síria f. **~n** a & n sírio (m)

**syringe** /sɪ'rɪndʒ/ n seringa f □ vt seringar

**syrup** /'sɪrəp/ n (liquid) xarope m; (treacle) calda f de açúcar. **~y** a (fig) melado, enjoativo

**system** /'sɪstəm/ n sistema m; (body) organismo m; (order) método m. **~atic** /sɪstə'mætɪk/ a sistemático

# T

**tab** /tæb/ n (flap) lingueta f; (for fastening, hanging) aba f; (label) etiqueta f; (loop) argola f; (Amer colloq: bill) conta f. **keep ~s on** (colloq) vigiar

**table** /'teɪbl/ n mesa f; (list) tabela f, lista f □ vt (submit) apresentar; (postpone) adiar. **at ~** à mesa. **lay or set the ~** pôr a mesa. **~ of contents** índice m (das matérias). **turn the ~s** inverter as posições. **~-cloth** n toalha de mesa f. **~-mat** n descanso m. **~ tennis** pingue-pongue m

**tablespoon** /'teɪblspuːn/ n colher f grande de sopa. **~ful** n (pl -fuls) colher f de sopa cheia

**tablet** /'tæblɪt/ n (of stone) lápide f, placa f; (drug) comprimido m

**tabloid** /'tæblɔɪd/ n tablóide m. **~ journalism** (pej) jornalismo m sensacionalista, imprensa f marron

**taboo** /tə'buː/ n & a tabu (m)

**tacit** /'tæsɪt/ a tácito

**taciturn** /'tæsɪtɜːn/ a taciturno

**tack** /tæk/ n (nail) tacha f; (stitch)

ponto m de alinhavo; (naut) amura f; (fig: course of action) rumo m □ vt (nail) pregar com tachas; (stitch) alinhavar □ vi (naut) bordejar. **~ on** (add) acrescentar, juntar

**tackle** /'tækl/ n equipamento m, apetrechos mpl; (sport) placagem f □ vt (problem etc) atacar; (sport) placar; (a thief etc) agarrar-se a

**tacky** /'tækɪ/ a (-ier, -iest) peganhento, pegajoso

**tact** /tækt/ n tato m, (P) tacto m. **~ful** a cheio de tato, (P) tacto, diplomático. **~fully** adv com tato, (P) tacto. **~less** a sem tato, (P) tacto. **~lessly** adv sem tato, (P) tacto

**tactic** /'tæktɪk/ n (expedient) tática f, (P) táctica f. **~s** n(pl) (procedure) tática f, (P) táctica f. **~al** a tático, (P) táctico

**tadpole** /'tædpəʊl/ n girino m

**tag** /tæg/ n (label) etiqueta f; (on shoelace) agulheta f; (phrase) chavão m, clichê m □ vi (pt tagged) etiquetar; (add) juntar □ vi **~ along** (colloq) andar atrás, seguir

**Tagus** /'teɪgʌs/ n Tejo m

**tail** /teɪl/ n cauda f, rabo m; (of shirt) fralda f. **~s!** (tossing coin) coroa! □ vt (follow) seguir, vigiar □ vi **~ away or off** diminuir, baixar. **~-back** n (traffic) fila f, (P) bicha f. **~-end** n parte f traseira, cauda f. **~-light** n (auto) farolete m traseiro, (P) farolim m da rectaguarda

**tailor** /'teɪlə(r)/ n alfaiate m □ vt (garment) fazer; (fig: adapt) adaptar. **~-made** a feito sob medida, (P) por medida. **~-made for** (fig) feito para, talhado para

**tainted** /'teɪntɪd/ a (infected) contaminado; (decayed) estragado; (fig) manchado

**take** /teɪk/ vt/i (pt took, pp taken) (get hold of) agarrar em, pegar em; (capture) tomar; (a seat, a drink; train, bus etc) tomar; (carry) levar (to a, para); (contain, escort) levar; (tolerate) suportar, agüentar, (P) aguentar; (choice, exam) fazer; (photo) tirar; (require) exigir. **be ~n by or with** ficar encantado com. **be ~n ill** adoecer. **it ~s time** to leva tempo para. **~ after** parecer-se a. **~-away** n (meal) comida f para levar, takeaway m; (shop) loja f que só vende comida para ser consumida em outro lugar. **~ away** levar. **~ away from sb/sth** tirar de alguém/de alg coisa. **~ back** aceitar de volta; (return) devolver; (accompany) acompanhar; (statement) retirar, retratar. **~ down** (object) tirar para baixo; (notes) tirar, tomar. **~ in** (garment) meter para dentro; (*include*) incluir; (*cheat*) enganar, levar (*colloq*); (*grasp*) compreender; (*receive*) receber. ~ **it that** supor que. ~ **off** *vt* (*remove*) tirar; (*mimic*) imitar, macaquear □ *vi* (*aviat*) decolar, levantar vôo. ~**off** *n* imitação *f*; (*aviat*) decolagem *f*, (*P*) descolagem *f*. ~ **on** (*task*) encarregar-se de; (*staff* ) admitir, contratar. ~ **out** tirar; (*on an outing*) levar para sair. ~ **over** *vt* tomar conta de, assumir a direção, (*P*) direcção de □ *vi* tomar o poder. ~ **over from** (*relieve*) render, substituir; (*succeed*) suceder a. ~**-over** *n* (*pol*) tomada *f* de poder; (*comm*) take-over *m*. ~ **part** participar or tomar parte (in em). ~ **place** ocorrer, suceder. ~ **sides** tomar partido. ~ **sides with** tomar o partido de. ~ **to** gostar de, simpatizar com; (*activity*) tomar gosto por, entregar-se a. ~ **up** (*object*) apanhar, pegar em; (*hobby*) dedicar-se a; (*occupy*) ocupar, tomar

**takings** /'teɪkɪŋz/ *npl* receita *f*

**talcum** /'tælkəm/ *n* talco *m*. ~ **powder** pó *m* talco

**tale** /teɪl/ *n* conto *m*, história *f*

**talent** /'tælənt/ *n* talento *m*. ~**ed** *a* talentoso, bem dotado

**talk** /tɔːk/ *vt/i* falar; (*chat*) conversar □ *n* conversa *f*; (*mode of speech*) fala *f*; (*lecture*) palestra *f*. **small** ~ conversa *f* banal. ~ **into doing** convencer a fazer. ~ **nonsense** dizer disparates. ~ **over** discutir. ~ **shop** falar de assuntos profissionais. ~ **to o.s.** falar sozinho, falar com os seus botões. **there's** ~ **of** fala-se de. ~**er** *n* conversador *m*. ~**ing-to** *n* (*colloq*) descompostura *f*

**talkative** /'tɔːkətɪv/ *a* falador, conversador, tagarela

**tall** /tɔːl/ *a* (-er, -est) alto. ~ **story** (*colloq*) história *f* do arco-da-velha

**tallboy** /'tɔːlbɔɪ/ *n* cômoda *f*, (*P*) cómoda *f* alta

**tally** /'tælɪ/ *vi* corresponder (with a), conferir (with com)

**tambourine** /tæmbə'riːn/ *n* tamborim *m*, pandeiro *m*

**tame** /teɪm/ *a* (-er, -est) manso; (*domesticated*) domesticado; (*dull*) insípido □ *vt* amansar, domesticar

**tamper** /'tæmpə(r)/ *vi* ~ **with** mexer indevidamente em; (*text*) alterar

**tampon** /'tæmpən/ *n* (*med*) tampão *m*; (*sanitary towel*) toalha *f* higiênica

**tan** /tæn/ *vt/i* (*pt* **tanned**) queimar, bronzear; (*hide*) curtir □ *n* bronzeado *m* □ *a* castanho amarelado

**tandem** /'tændəm/ *n* (*bicycle*) tandem *m*. **in** ~ em tandem, um atrás do outro

**tang** /tæŋ/ *n* (*taste*) sabor *m* or gosto

*m* característico; (*smell*) cheiro *m* característico

**tangent** /'tændʒənt/ *n* tangente *f*

**tangerine** /tændʒə'riːn/ *n* tangerina *f*

**tangible** /'tændʒəbl/ *a* tangível

**tangle** /'tæŋgl/ *vt* emaranhar, enredar □ *n* emaranhado *m*. **become** ~**d** emaranhar-se, enredar-se

**tank** /tæŋk/ *n* tanque *m*, reservatório *m*; (*for petrol*) tanque *m*, (*P*) depósito *m*; (*for fish*) aquário *m*; (*mil*) tanque *m*

**tankard** /'tæŋkəd/ *n* caneca *f* grande

**tanker** /'tæŋkə(r)/ *n* carro-tanque *m*, camião-cisterna *m*; (*ship*) petroleiro *m*

**tantaliz|e** /'tæntəlaɪz/ *vt* atormentar, tantalizar. ~**ing** *a* tentador

**tantamount** /'tæntəmaʊnt/ *a* **be** ~ **to** equivaler a

**tantrum** /'tæntrəm/ *n* chilique *m*, ataque *m* de mau gênio, (*P*) génio, birra *f*

**tap**[1] /tæp/ *n* (*for water etc*) torneira *f* □ *vt* (*pt* **tapped**) (*resources*) explorar; (*telephone*) gram-pear. **on** ~ (*colloq*: *available*) disponível

**tap**[2] /tæp/ *vt/i* (*pt* **tapped**) bater levemente. ~**-dance** *n* sapateado *m*

**tape** /teɪp/ *n* (*for dressmaking*) fita *f*; (*sticky*) fita *f* adesiva. (**magnetic**) ~ fita *f* (magnética) □ *vt* (*tie*) atar, prender; (*stick*) colar; (*record*) gravar. ~**-measure** *n* fita *f* métrica. ~ **recorder** gravador *m*

**taper** /'teɪpə(r)/ *n* vela *f* comprida e fina □ *vt/i* ~ (**off**) estreitar(-se), afilar(-se). ~**ed**, ~**ing** *adjs* (*fingers etc*) afilado; (*trousers*) afunilado

**tapestry** /'tæpɪstrɪ/ *n* tapeçaria *f*

**tapioca** /tæpɪ'əʊkə/ *n* tapioca *f*

**tar** /taː(r)/ *n* alcatrão *m* □ *vt* (*pt* **tarred**) alcatroar

**target** /'taːgɪt/ *n* alvo *m* □ *vt* ter como alvo

**tariff** /'tærɪf/ *n* tarifa *f*; (*on import*) direitos *mpl* aduaneiros

**Tarmac** /'taːmæk/ *n* macadame (alcatroado) *m*; (*runway*) pista *f*

**tarnish** /'taːnɪʃ/ *vt/i* (fazer) perder o brilho; (*stain*) manchar

**tarpaulin** /taː'pɔːlɪn/ *n* lona *f* impermeável (alcatroada or encerada)

**tart**[1] /taːt/ *a* (-er, -est) ácido; ( *fig*: *cutting*) mordaz, azedo

**tart**[2] /taːt/ *n* (*culin*) torta *f* de fruta, (*P*) tarte *f*; (*sl*: *prostitute*) prostituta *f*, mulher *f* da vida (*sl*) □ *vt* ~ **up** (*colloq*) embonecar(-se)

**tartan** /'taːtn/ *n* tecido *m* escocês □ *a* escocês

**tartar** /'taːtə(r)/ *n* (*on teeth*) tártaro *m*, (*P*) pedra *f*. ~ **sauce** molho *m* tártaro

**task** /taːsk/ *n* tarefa *f*, trabalho *m*.

**take to** ~ repreender, censurar. ~ **force** (*mil*) força-tarefa *f*

**tassel** /'tæsl/ *n* borla *f*

**taste** /teɪst/ *n* gosto *m*; ( *fig: sample*) amostra *f* □ *vt* (*eat, enjoy*) saborear; (*try*) provar; (*perceive taste of* ) sentir o gosto de □ *vi* ~ **of** *or* **like** ter o sabor de. **have a** ~ **of** (*experience*) provar. **~ful** *a* de bom gosto. **~fully** *adv* com bom gosto. **~less** *a* insípido, insosso; ( *fig: not in good taste*) sem gosto; ( *fig: in bad taste*) de mau gosto

**tasty** /'teɪstɪ/ *a* (**-ier, -iest**) saboroso, gostoso

**tat** /tæt/ *see* **tit**[2]

**tatter|s** /'tætəz/ *npl* farrapos *mpl*. **~ed** /-əd/ *a* esfarrapado

**tattoo** /tə'tuː/ *vt* tatuar □ *n* tatuagem *f*

**tatty** /'tætɪ/ *a* (**-ier, -iest**) (*colloq*) enxovalhado, em mau estado

**taught** /tɔːt/ *see* **teach**

**taunt** /tɔːnt/ *vt* escarnecer de, zombar de □ *n* escárnio *m*. **~ing** *a* escarninho

**Taurus** /'tɔːrəs/ *n* (*astr*) Touro *m*, (P) Taurus *m*

**taut** /tɔːt/ *a* esticado, retesado; ( *fig: of nerves*) tenso

**tawdry** /'tɔːdrɪ/ *a* (**-ier, -iest**) espalhafatoso e ordinário

**tawny** /'tɔːnɪ/ *a* fulvo

**tax** /tæks/ *n* taxa *f*, imposto *m*; (*on income*) imposto *m* de renda, (P) sobre o rendimento □ *vt* taxar, lançar impostos sobre, tributar; ( *fig: put to test*) pôr à prova. **~-collector** *n* cobrador *m* de impostos. **~-free** *a* isento de imposto. ~ **relief** isenção *f* de imposto. ~ **return** declaração *f* do imposto de renda, (P) sobre o rendimento. ~ **year** ano *m* fiscal. **~able** *a* tributável, passível de imposto. **~ation** /-'seɪʃn/ *n* impostos *mpl*, tributação *f*. **~ing** *a* penoso, difícil

**taxi** /'tæksɪ/ *n* (*pl* **-is**) táxi *m* □ *vi* (*pt* **taxied**, *pres p* **taxiing**) (*aviat*) rolar na pista, taxiar. **~-cab** *n* táxi *m*. **~-driver** *n* motorista *mf* de táxi. **~-rank**, (*Amer*) ~ **stand** ponto *m* de táxis, (P) praça *f* de táxis

**taxpayer** /'tækspeɪə(r)/ *n* contribuinte *mf*

**tea** /tiː/ *n* chá *m*. **high** ~ refeição *f* leve à noite. **~-bag** *n* saquinho *m* de chá. **~-break** *n* intervalo *m* para o chá. **~-cosy** *n* abafador *m*. **~-leaf** *n* folha *f* de chá. **~-set** *n* serviço *m* de chá. **~-shop** *n* salão *m* or casa *f* de chá. **~-time** *n* hora *f* do chá. **~-towel** *n* pano *m* de prato

**teach** /tiːtʃ/ *vt* (*pt* **taught**) ensinar, lecionar, (P) leccionar (**sb sth** alg coisa a alguém) □ *vi* ensinar, ser professor. **~er** *n* professor *m*. **~ing** *n* ensino *m*; (*doctrines*) ensinamento(s) *m* (*pl*) □ *a* pedagógico, de ensino; (*staff*) docente

**teacup** /'tiːkʌp/ *n* xícara *f* de chá, (P) chávena *f*

**teak** /tiːk/ *n* teca *f*

**team** /tiːm/ *n* equipe *f*, (P) equipa *f*; (*of oxen*) junta *f*; (*of horses*) parelha *f* □ *vi* ~ **up** juntar-se, associar-se (**with** a). **~-work** *n* trabalho *m* de equipe, (P) equipa

**teapot** /'tiːpɒt/ *n* bule *m*

**tear**[1] /teə(r)/ *vt/i* (*pt* **tore**, *pp* **torn**) rasgar(-se); (*snatch*) arrancar, puxar; (*rush*) lançar-se, ir numa correria; ( *fig*) dividir □ *n* rasgão *m*. ~ **o.s. away** arrancar-se (**from** de)

**tear**[2] /tɪə(r)/ *n* lágrima *f*. **~-gas** *n* gases *mpl* lacrimogênios, (P) lacrimogénios

**tearful** /'tɪəfl/ *a* lacrimoso, choroso. **~ly** *adv* choroso, com (as) lágrimas nos olhos

**tease** /tiːz/ *vt* implicar; (*make fun of* ) caçoar de

**teaspoon** /'tiːspuːn/ *n* colher *f* de chá. **~ful** *n* (*pl* **-fuls**) colher *f* de chá cheia

**teat** /tiːt/ *n* (*of bottle*) bico *m*; (*of animal*) teta *f*

**technical** /'teknɪkl/ *a* técnico. **~ity** /-'kælətɪ/ *n* questão *f* de ordem técnica. **~ly** *adv* tecnicamente

**technician** /tek'nɪʃn/ *n* técnico *m*

**technique** /tek'niːk/ *n* técnica *f*

**technolog|y** /tek'nɒlədʒɪ/ *n* tecnologia *f*. **~ical** /-ə'lɒdʒɪkl/ *a* tecnológico

**teddy** /'tedɪ/ *a* ~ (**bear**) ursinho *m* de pelúcia, (P) peluche

**tedious** /'tiːdɪəs/ *a* maçante

**tedium** /'tiːdɪəm/ *n* tédio *m*

**tee** /tiː/ *n* (*golf* ) tee *m*

**teem**[1] /tiːm/ *vi* ~ (**with**) (*swarm*) pulular (de), fervilhar (de), abundar (em)

**teem**[2] /tiːm/ *vi* ~ (**with rain**) chover torrencialmente

**teenage** /'tiːneɪdʒ/ *a* juvenil, de/para adolescente. **~r** /-ə(r)/ *n* jovem *mf*, adolescente *mf*

**teens** /tiːnz/ *npl* **in one's** ~ na adolescência, entre os 13 e os 19 anos

**teeter** /'tiːtə(r)/ *vi* cambalear, vacilar

**teeth** /tiːθ/ *see* **tooth**

**teeth|e** /tiːð/ *vi* começar a ter dentes. **~ing troubles** ( *fig*) problemas *mpl* iniciais

**teetotaller** /tiː'təʊtlə(r)/ *n* abstêmio *m*, (P) abstémio *m*

**telecommunications** /telɪkəmjuːnɪ'keɪʃnz/ *npl* telecomunicações *fpl*

**telegram** /'telɪɡræm/ *n* telegrama *m*

**telegraph** /'telɪɡrɑːf/ *n* telégrafo *m*;

*a* telegráfico. **~ic** /-'græfɪk/ *a* telegráfico

**telepath|y** /tɪ'lepəθɪ/ *n* telepatia *f*. **~ic** /telɪ'pæθɪk/ *a* telepático

**telephone** /'telɪfəʊn/ *n* telefone *m* □ *vt* (*person*) telefonar a; (*message*) telefonar □ *vi* telefonar. **~ book** lista *f* telefónica, (P) telefónica, guia *m* telefónico, (P) telefónico. **~ box**, **~ booth** cabine *f* telefónica, (P) telefónica. **~ call** chamada *f*. **~ directory** lista *f* telefónica, (P) telefónica, guia *m* telefónico, (P) telefónico. **~ number** número *m* de telefone

**telephonist** /tɪ'lefənɪst/ *n* (*in exchange*) telefonista *mf*

**telephoto** /telɪ'fəʊtəʊ/ *n* **~ lens** teleobjetiva *f*, (P) teleobjectiva *f*

**telescop|e** /'telɪskəʊp/ *n* telescópio *m* □ *vt/i* encaixar(-se). **~ic** /-'skɒpɪk/ *a* telescópico

**teletext** /'telɪtekst/ *n* teletexto *m*

**televise** /'telɪvaɪz/ *vt* televisionar

**television** /'telɪvɪʒn/ *n* televisão *f*. **~ set** aparelho *m* de televisão, televisor *m*

**telex** /'teleks/ *n* telex *m* □ *vt* transmitir por telex, telexar

**tell** /tel/ *vt* (*pt* told) dizer (**sb sth** alg coisa a alguém); (*story*) contar; (*distinguish*) distinguir, diferençar □ *vi* (*know*) ver-se, saber. **I told you so** bem lhe disse. **~ of** falar de. **~ off** (*colloq: scold*) ralhar, dar uma bronca em. **~ on** (*have effect on*) afetar, (P) afectar; (*colloq: inform on*) fazer queixa de (*colloq*). **~-tale** *n* mexeriqueiro *m*, fofoqueiro *m* □ *a* (*revealing*) revelador. **tales** mexericar, fofocar

**telly** /'telɪ/ *n* (*colloq*) TV *f* (*colloq*)

**temp** /temp/ *n* (*colloq*) empregado *m* temporário

**temper** /'tempə(r)/ *n* humor *m*, disposição *f*; (*anger*) mau humor *m* □ *vt* temperar. **keep/lose one's ~** manter a calma/perder a calma *or* a cabeça, zangar-se

**temperament** /'temprəmənt/ *n* temperamento *m*. **~al** /'mentl/ *a* caprichoso

**temperance** /'tempərəns/ *n* (*in drinking*) moderação *f*, sobriedade *f*

**temperate** /'tempərət/ *a* moderado, comedido; (*climate*) temperado

**temperature** /'temprətʃə(r)/ *n* temperatura *f*. **have a ~** estar com *or* ter febre

**tempest** /'tempɪst/ *n* tempestade *f*, temporal *m*

**tempestuous** /tem'pestʃʊəs/ *a* tempestuoso

**template** /'templ(e)ɪt/ *n* molde *m*

**temple¹** /'templ/ *n* templo *m*

**temple²** /'templ/ *n* (*anat*) têmpora *f*, fonte *f*

**tempo** /'tempəʊ/ *n* (*pl* -os) (*mus*) tempo *m*; (*pace*) ritmo *m*

**temporar|y** /'temprərɪ/ *a* temporário, provisório. **~ily** *adv* temporariamente, provisoriamente

**tempt** /tempt/ *vt* tentar. **~ sb to do** dar a alguém vontade de fazer, tentar alguém a fazer. **~ation** /-'teɪʃn/ *n* tentação *f*. **~ing** *a* tentador

**ten** /ten/ *a* & *n* dez (*m*)

**tenac|ious** /tɪ'neɪʃəs/ *a* tenaz. **~ity** /-'æsətɪ/ *n* tenacidade *f*

**tenant** /'tenənt/ *n* inquilino *m*, locatário *m*

**tend¹** /tend/ *vt* tomar conta de, cuidar de

**tend²** /tend/ *vi* **~ to** (*be apt to*) tender a, ter tendência para

**tendency** /'tendənsɪ/ *n* tendência *f*

**tender¹** /'tendə(r)/ *a* (*soft, delicate*) terno; (*sore, painful*) sensível, dolorido; (*loving*) terno, meigo. **~-hearted** *a* compassivo. **~ly** *adv* (*lovingly*) ternamente, meigamente; (*delicately*) delicadamente. **~ness** *n* (*love*) ternura *f*, meiguice *f*

**tender²** /'tendə(r)/ *vt* (*money*) oferecer; (*apologies, resignation*) apresentar □ *vi* **~ (for)** apresentar orçamento (para) □ *n* (*comm*) orçamento *m*. **legal ~** (*money*) moeda *f* corrente

**tendon** /'tendən/ *n* tendão *m*

**tenement** /'tenəmənt/ *n* prédio *m* de apartamentos de renda moderada; (*Amer: slum*) prédio *m* pobre

**tenet** /'tenɪt/ *n* princípio *m*, dogma *m*

**tennis** /'tenɪs/ *n* tênis *m*, (P) ténis *m*. **~ court** quadra *f* de tênis, (P) court *m* de ténis

**tenor** /'tenə(r)/ *n* (*meaning*) teor *m*; (*mus*) tenor *m*

**tense¹** /tens/ *n* (*gram*) tempo *m*

**tense²** /tens/ *a* (-er, -est) tenso □ *vt* (*muscles*) retesar

**tension** /'tenʃn/ *n* tensão *f*

**tent** /tent/ *n* tenda *f*, barraca *f*. **~-peg** *n* estaca *f*

**tentacle** /'tentəkl/ *n* tentáculo *m*

**tentative** /'tentətɪv/ *a* provisório; (*hesitant*) hesitante. **~ly** *adv* tentativamente, a título experimental; (*hesitantly*) hesitantemente

**tenterhooks** /'tentəhʊks/ *npl* **on ~** em suspense

**tenth** /tenθ/ *a* & *n* décimo (*m*)

**tenuous** /'tenjʊəs/ *a* tênue, (P) ténue

**tepid** /'tepɪd/ *a* tépido, morno

**term** /tɜːm/ *n* (*word*) termo *m*; (*limit*) prazo *m*, termo *m*; (*schol etc*) período *m*, trimestre *m*; (*Amer*) semestre *m*; (*of imprisonment*) (duração de) pena *f*. **~s** (*conditions*) condições *fpl* □ *vt* designar, denominar, chamar. **on good/**

**bad** ~s de boas/más relações. **not on speaking** ~s de relações cortadas. **come to** ~s **with** chegar a um acordo com; (*become resigned to*) resignar-se a. ~ **of office** (*pol*) mandato *m*

**terminal** /'tɜːmɪnl/ *a* terminal, final; (*illness*) fatal, mortal □ *n* (*oil, computer*) terminal *m*; (*rail*) estação *f* terminal; (*electr*) borne *m*. **(air)** ~ terminal *m* (de avião)

**terminat|e** /'tɜːmɪneɪt/ *vt* terminar, pôr termo a □ *vi* terminar. ~**ion** /-'neɪʃn/ *n* término *m*, (*P*) terminação *f*, termo *m*

**terminology** /tɜːmɪ'nɒlədʒɪ/ *n* terminologia *f*

**terminus** /'tɜːmɪnəs/ *n* (*pl* **-ni** /-naɪ/) (*rail, coach*) estação *f* terminal

**terrace** /'terəs/ *n* terraço *m*; (*in cultivation*) socalco *m*; (*houses*) casas *fpl* em fileira contínua, lance *m* de casas. **the** ~**s** (*sport*) arquibancada *f*. ~**d house** casa *f* ladeada por outras casas

**terrain** /te'reɪn/ *n* terreno *m*

**terribl|e** /'terəbl/ *a* terrível. ~**y** *adv* terrivelmente; (*collog: very*) extremamente, espantosamente

**terrific** /tə'rɪfɪk/ *a* terrífico, tremendo; (*collog: excellent; great*) tremendo. ~**ally** *adv* (*collog: very*) tremendamente (*collog*); (*collog: very well*) lindamente, maravilhosamente

**terrif|y** /'terɪfaɪ/ *vt* aterrar, aterrorizar. **be** ~**ied of** ter pavor de

**territorial** /terɪ'tɔːrɪəl/ *a* territorial

**territory** /'terɪtərɪ/ *n* território *m*

**terror** /'terə(r)/ *n* terror *m*, pavor *m*

**terroris|t** /'terərɪst/ *n* terrorista *mf*. ~**m** /-zəm/ *n* terrorismo *m*

**terrorize** /'terəraɪz/ *vt* aterrorizar, aterrar

**terse** /tɜːs/ *a* conciso, lapidar; (*curt*) lacônico, (*P*) lacónico

**test** /test/ *n* teste *m*, exame *m*, prova *f*; (*schol*) prova *f*, teste *m*; (*of goods*) controle *m*; (*of machine etc*) ensaio *m*; (*of strength*) prova *f* □ *vt* examinar; (*check*) controlar; (*try*) ensaiar; (*pupil*) interrogar. **put to the** ~ pôr à prova. ~ **match** jogo *m* internacional. ~-**tube** *n* proveta *f*. ~-**tube baby** bebê *m* de proveta

**testament** /'testəmənt/ *n* testamento *m*. **Old/New T**~ Antigo/Novo Testamento *m*

**testicle** /'testɪkl/ *n* testículo *m*

**testify** /'testɪfaɪ/ *vt/i* testificar, testemunhar, depor

**testimonial** /testɪ'məʊnɪəl/ *n* carta *f* de recomendação

**testimony** /'testɪmənɪ/ *n* testemunho *m*

**tetanus** /'tetənəs/ *n* tétano *m*

**tether** /'teðə(r)/ *vt* prender com corda □ *n* **be at the end of one's** ~ não poder mais, estar nas últimas

**text** /tekst/ *n* texto *m*

**textbook** /'tekstbʊk/ *n* compêndio *m*, manual *m*, livro *m* de texto

**textile** /'tekstaɪl/ *n* & *a* têxtil (*m*)

**texture** /'tekstʃə(r)/ *n* (*of fabric*) textura *f*; (*of paper*) grão *m*

**Thai** /taɪ/ *a* & *n* tailandês (*m*). ~**land** *n* Tailândia *f*

**Thames** /temz/ *n* Tâmisa *m*

**than** /ðæn/; *unstressed* /ðən/ *conj* que, do que; (*with numbers*) de. **more/less** ~ **ten** mais/menos de dez

**thank** /θæŋk/ *vt* agradecer. ~ **you!** obrigado! ~**s!** (*collog*) (*P*) obrigadinho! (*collog*). ~**s** *npl* agradecimentos *mpl*. ~**s to** graças a. **T**~**sgiving (Day)** (*Amer*) Dia *m* de Ação, (*P*) Acção de Graças

**thankful** /'θæŋkfl/ *a* grato, agradecido, reconhecido (**for** por). ~**ly** *adv* com gratidão; (*happily*) felizmente

**thankless** /'θæŋklɪs/ *a* ingrato, mal agradecido

**that** /ðæt/; *unstressed* /ðət/ *a* & *pron* (*pl* **those**) esse/essa, esses/essas; (*more distant*) aquele/aquela, aqueles /aquelas; (*neuter*) isso *invar*; (*more distant*) aquilo *invar* □ *adv* tão, tanto, de tal modo □ *rel pron* que □ *conj* que. ~ **boy** esse/aquele rapaz. **what is** ~? o que é isso? **who is** ~? quem é? **is** ~ **you?** é você? **give me** ~ (**one**) dá-me esse. ~ **is (to say)** isto é, quer dizer. **after** ~ depois disso. **the day** ~ o dia em que. ~ **much** tanto assim, tanto como isto

**thatch** /θætʃ/ *n* colmo *m*. ~**ed** *a* de colmo. ~**ed cottage** casa *f* com telhado de colmo

**thaw** /θɔː/ *vt/i* derreter(-se), degelar; (*food*) descongelar □ *n* degelo *m*, derretimento *m*

**the** /*before vowel* ðɪ/, *before consonant* ðə/, *stressed* ðiː/ *a* o, a, (*pl* os, as). **of** ~, **from** ~ do, da (*pl* dos, das). **at** ~, **to** ~ ao, à (*pl* aos, às), para o/a/os/ as. **in** ~ no, na (*pl* nos, nas). **by** ~ **hour** a cada hora □ *adv* **all** ~ **better** tanto melhor. ~ **more**... ~ **more**... quanto mais... tanto mais...

**theatre** /'θɪətə(r)/ *n* teatro *m*

**theatrical** /θɪ'ætrɪkl/ *a* teatral

**theft** /θeft/ *n* roubo *m*

**their** /ðeə(r)/ *a* deles, delas, seu

**theirs** /ðeəz/ *poss pron* o(s) seu(s), a(s) sua(s), o(s) deles, a(s) delas. **it is** ~ é (o) deles/delas *or* o seu

**them** /ðem/; *unstressed* /ðəm/ *pron* os, as; (*after prep*) eles, elas. **(to)** ~ lhes

**theme** /θiːm/ *n* tema *m*

**themselves** /ðəm'selvz/ *pron* eles

mesmos/próprios, elas mesmas/ próprias; (*reflexive*) se; (*after prep*) si (mesmos, próprios). **by ~** sozinhos. **with ~** consigo

**then** /ðen/ *adv* (*at that time*) então, nessa altura; (*next*) depois, em seguida; (*in that case*) então, nesse caso; (*therefore*) então, portanto, por conseguinte □ *a* (de) então. **from ~ on** desde então

**theolog|y** /θɪˈɒlədʒɪ/ *n* teologia *f*. **~ian** /θɪəˈləʊdʒən/ *n* teólogo *m*

**theorem** /ˈθɪərəm/ *n* teorema *m*

**theor|y** /ˈθɪərɪ/ *n* teoria *f*. **~etical** /ˈretɪkl/ *a* teórico

**therapeutic** /θerəˈpjuːtɪk/ *a* terapêutico

**therap|y** /ˈθerəpɪ/ *n* terapia *f*. **~ist** *n* terapeuta *mf*

**there** /ðeə(r)/ *adv* aí, ali, lá; (*over there*) lá, acolá □ *int* (*triumphant*) pronto, aí está; (*consoling*) então, vamos lá. **he goes ~** ele vai aí *or* lá. **~ he goes** aí vai ele. **~ is**, **~ are** há. **~ you are** (*giving*) toma. **~ and then** logo ali. **~abouts** *adv* por aí. **~after** *adv* daí em diante, depois disso. **~by** *adv* desse modo

**therefore** /ˈðeəfɔː(r)/ *adv* por isso, portanto, por conseguinte

**thermal** /ˈθɜːml/ *a* térmico

**thermometer** /θəˈmɒmɪtə(r)/ *n* termômetro *m*, (*P*) termómetro *m*

**Thermos** /ˈθɜːməs/ *n* garrafa *f* térmica, (*P*) termo *m*

**thermostat** /ˈθɜːməstæt/ *n* termostato *m*

**thesaurus** /θɪˈsɔːrəs/ *n* (*pl* -ri /-raɪ/) dicionário *m* de sinônimos, (*P*) sinónimos

**these** /ðiːz/ *see* this

**thesis** /ˈθiːsɪs/ *n* (*pl* theses /-siːz/) tese *f*

**they** /ðeɪ/ *pron* eles, elas. **~ say** (that)... diz-se *or* dizem que...

**thick** /θɪk/ *a* (-er, -est) espesso, grosso; (*colloq: stupid*) estúpido □ *adv* = **thickly** □ *n* **in the ~ of** no meio de. **~-skinned** *a* insensível. **~ly** *adv* espessamente; (*spread*) em camada espessa. **~ness** *n* espessura *f*, grossura *f*

**thicken** /ˈθɪkən/ *vt/i* engrossar, espessar(-se). **the plot ~s** o enredo complica-se

**thickset** /θɪkˈset/ *a* (*person*) atarracado

**thief** /θiːf/ *n* (*pl* thieves /θiːvz/) ladrão *m*, gatuno *m*

**thigh** /θaɪ/ *n* coxa *f*

**thimble** /ˈθɪmbl/ *n* dedal *m*

**thin** /θɪn/ *a* (thinner, thinnest) (*slender*) estreito, fino, delgado; (*lean, not plump*) magro; (*sparse*) ralo, escasso;

(*flimsy*) leve, fino; (*soup*) aguado; (*hair*) ralo □ *adv* = **thinly** □ *vt/i* (*pt* **thinned**) (*of liquid*) diluir(-se); (*of fog etc*) dissipar(-se); (*of hair*) rarear. **~ out** (*in quantity*) diminuir, reduzir; (*seedlings etc*) desbastar. **~ly** *adv* (*sparsely*) esparsamente. **~ness** *n* (*of board, wire etc*) finura *f*; (*of person*) magreza *f*

**thing** /θɪŋ/ *n* coisa *f*. **~s** (*belongings*) pertences *mpl*. **the best ~ is to** o melhor é. **for one ~** em primeiro lugar. **just the ~** exatamente o que era preciso. **poor ~** coitado

**think** /θɪŋk/ *vt/i* (*pt* thought) pensar (**about, of** em); (*carefully*) refletir, (*P*) reflectir (**about, of** em). **I ~ so** eu acho que sim. **~ better of it** (*change one's mind*) pensar melhor. **~ nothing of** achar natural. **~ of** (*hold opinion of*) pensar de, achar de. **~ over** pensar bem em. **~-tank** *n* comissão *f* de peritos. **~ up** inventar. **~er** *n* pensador *m*

**third** /θɜːd/ *a* terceiro □ *n* terceiro *m*; (*fraction*) terço *m*. **~-party insurance** seguro *m* contra terceiros. **~rate** *a* inferior, medíocre. **T~ World** Terceiro Mundo *m*. **~ly** *adv* em terceiro lugar

**thirst** /θɜːst/ *n* sede *f*. **~y** *a* sequioso, sedento. **be ~y** estar com *or* ter sede. **~ily** *adv* sofregamente

**thirteen** /θɜːˈtiːn/ *a* & *n* treze (*m*). **~th** *a* & *n* décimo terceiro (*m*)

**thirt|y** /ˈθɜːtɪ/ *a* & *n* trinta (*m*). **~ieth** *a* & *n* trigésimo (*m*)

**this** /ðɪs/ *a* & *pron* (*pl* these) este, esta □ *pron* isto *invar*. **~ one** este, esta. **these ones** estes, estas. **~ boy** este rapaz. **~ is** isto é. **after ~** depois disto. **like ~** assim. **~ is the man** este é o homem. **~ far** até aqui. **~ morning** esta manhã. **~ Wednesday** esta quarta-feira

**thistle** /ˈθɪsl/ *n* cardo *m*

**thorn** /θɔːn/ *n* espinho *m*, pico *m*. **~y** *a* espinhoso; (*fig*) espinhoso

**thorough** /ˈθʌrə/ *a* consciencioso; (*deep*) completo, profundo; (*cleaning, washing*) a fundo. **~ly** *adv* (*clean, study etc*) completo, a fundo; (*very*) perfeitamente, muito bem

**thoroughbred** /ˈθʌrəbred/ *n* (*horse etc*) puro-sangue *m invar*

**thoroughfare** /ˈθʌrəfeə(r)/ *n* artéria *f*. **no ~** passagem *f* proibida

**those** /ðəʊz/ *see* that

**though** /ðəʊ/ *conj* se bem que, embora, conquanto □ *adv* (*colloq*) contudo, no entanto

**thought** /θɔːt/ *see* think □ *n* pensamento *m*; idéia *f*. **on second ~s** pensando bem

**thoughtful** /'θɔːtfl/ *a* pensativo; (*considerate*) atencioso, solícito. ~**ly** *adv* pensativamente; (*considerately*) com consideração, atenciosamente

**thoughtless** /'θɔːtlɪs/ *a* irrefletido, (P) irreflectido; (*inconsiderate*) pouco atencioso. ~**ly** *adv* sem pensar; (*inconsiderately*) sem consideração

**thousand** /'θaʊznd/ *a & n* mil(*m*). ~**s of** milhares de. ~**th** *a & n* milésimo (*m*)

**thrash** /θræʃ/ *vt* surrar, espancar; (*defeat*) dar uma surra *or* sova em. ~ **about** debater-se. ~ **out** debater a fundo, discutir bem

**thread** /θred/ *n* fio *m*; (*for sewing*) linha *f* de coser; (*of screw*) rosca *f* □ *vt* enfiar. ~ **one's way** abrir caminho, furar

**threadbare** /'θredbeə(r)/ *a* puído, surrado

**threat** /θret/ *n* ameaça *f*

**threaten** /'θretn/ *vt/i* ameaçar. ~**ingly** *adv* com ar ameaçador, ameaçadoramente

**three** /θriː/ *a & n* três (*m*)

**thresh** /θreʃ/ *vt* (*corn etc*) malhar, debulhar

**threshold** /'θreʃəʊld/ *n* limiar *m*, soleira *f*; (*fig*) limiar *m*

**threw** /θruː/ *see* **throw**

**thrift** /θrɪft/ *n* economia *f*, poupança *f*. ~**y** *a* econômico, (P) económico, poupado

**thrill** /θrɪl/ *n* arrepio *m* de emoção, frêmito *m*, (P) frémito *m* □ *vt* excitar(-se), emocionar(-se), (*fazer*) vibrar. **be** ~**ed** estar/ficar encantado. ~**ing** *a* excitante, emocionante

**thriller** /'θrɪlə(r)/ *n* livro *m or* filme *m* de suspense

**thriv**|**e** /θraɪv/ *vi* (*pt* **thrived** *or* **throve**, *pp* **thrived** *or* **thriven**) prosperar, florescer; (*grow strong*) crescer, dar-se bem (**on** com). ~**ing** *a* próspero

**throat** /θrəʊt/ *n* garganta *f*. **have a sore** ~ ter dores de garganta

**throb** /θrɒb/ *vi* (*pt* **throbbed**) (*wound, head*) latejar; (*heart*) palpitar, bater; (*engine; fig*) vibrar, trepidar □ *n* (*of pain*) latejo *m*, espasmo *m*; (*of heart*) palpitação *f*, batida *f*; (*of engine*) vibração *f*, trepidação *f*. ~**bing** *a* (*pain*) latejante

**throes** /θrəʊz/ *npl* **in the** ~ **of** (*fig*) às voltas com, no meio de

**thrombosis** /θrɒm'bəʊsɪs/ *n* trombose *f*

**throne** /θrəʊn/ *n* trono *m*

**throng** /θrɒŋ/ *n* multidão *f* □ *vt/i* apinhar(-se); (*arrive*) afluir

**throttle** /'θrɒtl/ *n* (*auto*) válvula-borboleta *f*, estrangulador *m*, acelerador *m* de mão □ *vt* estrangular

**through** /θruː/ *prep* através de, por; (*during*) durante; (*by means or way of, out of*) por; (*by reason of*) por, por causa de □ *adv* através; (*entirely*) completamente, até o fim □ *a* (*train, traffic etc*) direto, (P) directo. **be** ~ ter acabado (**with** com); (*telephone*) estar ligado. **come** *or* **go** ~ (*cross, pierce*) atravessar. **get** ~ (*exam*) passar. **be wet** ~ estar ensopado *or* encharcado

**throughout** /θruː'aʊt/ *prep* durante, por todo. ~ **the country** por todo o país afora. ~ **the day** durante todo a dia, pelo dia afora □ *adv* completamente; (*place*) por toda a parte; (*time*) durante todo o tempo

**throw** /θrəʊ/ *vt* (*pt* **threw**, *pp* **thrown**) atirar, jogar, lançar; (*colloq: baffle*) desconcertar □ *n* lançamento *m*; (*of dice*) lançe *m*. ~ **a party** (*colloq*) dar uma festa. ~ **away** jogar fora, (P) deitar fora. ~ **off** (*get rid of*) livrar-se de. ~ **out** (*person*) expulsar; (*reject*) rejeitar. ~ **over** (*desert*) abandonar, deixar. ~ **up** (*one's arms*) levantar; (*resign from*) abandonar; (*colloq: vomit*) vomitar

**thrush** /θrʌʃ/ *n* (*bird*) tordo *m*

**thrust** /θrʌst/ *vt* (*pt* **thrust**) arremeter, empurrar, impelir □ *n* empurrão *m*, arremetida *f*. ~ **into** (*put*) enfiar em, mergulhar em. ~ **upon** (*force on*) impôr a

**thud** /θʌd/ *n* som *m* surdo, baque *m*

**thug** /θʌg/ *n* bandido *m*, facínora *m*, malfeitor *m*

**thumb** /θʌm/ *n* polegar *m* □ *vt* (*book*) manusear. ~ **a lift** pedir carona, (P) boleia. **under sb's** ~ completamente dominado por alguém. ~**-index** *n* índice *m* de dedo

**thumbtack** /'θʌmtæk/ *n* (*Amer*) percevejo *m*

**thump** /θʌmp/ *vt/i* bater (em), dar pancadas (em); (*with fists*) dar murros (em); (*piano*) martelar (em); (*of heart*) bater com força □ *n* pancada *f*; (*thud*) baque *m*. ~**ing** *a* (*colloq*) enorme

**thunder** /'θʌndə(r)/ *n* trovão *m*, trovoada *f*; (*loud noise*) estrondo *m* □ *vi* (*weather, person*) trovejar. ~ **past** passar como um raio. ~**y** *a* (*weather*) tempestuoso

**thunderbolt** /'θʌndəbəʊlt/ *n* raio *m* e ribombo *m* de trovão; (*fig*) raio *m* fulminante (*fig*)

**thunderstorm** /'θʌndəstɔːm/ *n* tempestade *f* com trovoadas, temporal *m*

**Thursday** /'θɜːzdɪ/ *n* quinta-feira *f*

**thus** /ðʌs/ *adv* assim, desta maneira. ~ **far** até aqui

**thwart** /θwɔːt/ *vt* frustrar, contrariar

**thyme** /taɪm/ *n* tomilho *m*

**tiara** /tɪ'ɑːrə/ *n* tiara *f*, diadema *m*

tic                                401                           tingle

tic /tɪk/ n tique m
tick¹ /tɪk/ n (sound) tique-taque m;
(mark) sinal (V) m; (colloq: moment)
instantinho m □ vi fazer tique-taque □
vt ~ (off) marcar com sinal (V). ~
off (colloq: scold) dar uma bronca em
(colloq). ~ over (engine, factory) funcionar em marcha lenta, (P) no "ra-
lenti"
tick² /tɪk/ n (insect) carrapato m
ticket /'tɪkɪt/ n bilhete m; (label) etiqueta f; ( for traffic offence) aviso m de
multa. ~-collector n (railway) guarda m. ~-office n bilheteira f
tickle /'tɪkl/ vt fazer cócegas; ( fig:
amuse) divertir □ n cócegas fpl,
comichão m
ticklish /'tɪklɪʃ/ a coceguento, sensível
a cócegas; ( fig) delicado, melindroso
tidal /'taɪdl/ a de marés, que tem
marés. ~ wave onda f gigantesca;
( fig) onda f de sentimento popular
tiddly-winks /'tɪdlɪwɪŋks/ n (game)
jogo m da pulga
tide /taɪd/ n maré f; (of events) marcha
f, curso m. high ~ maré f cheia,
preia-mar f. low ~ maré f baixa,
baixa-mar f □ vt ~ over (help temporarily) agüentar, (P) aguentar
tid|y /'taɪdɪ/ a (-ier, -iest) (room) arru-
mado; (appearance, work) asseado,
cuidado; (methodical) bem ordenado;
(colloq: amount) belo (colloq) □ vt
arrumar, arranjar. ~ily adv com
cuidado. ~iness n arrumação f, ordem f
tie /taɪ/ vt (pres p tying) atar, amarrar, prender; (link) ligar, vincular; (a
knot) dar, fazer □ vi (sport) empatar □
n fio m, cordel m; (necktie) gravata f;
(link) laço m, vínculo m; (sport) empate m. ~ in with estar ligado com,
relacionar-se com. ~ up amarrar,
atar; (animal) prender; (money) imo-
bilizar; (occupy) ocupar
tier /tɪə(r)/ n cada fila f, camada f,
prateleira f etc colocada em cima de
outra; (in stadium) bancada f; (of
cake) andar m; (of society) camada f
tiff /tɪf/ n arrufo m
tiger /'taɪgə(r)/ n tigre m
tight /taɪt/ a (-er, -est) (clothes) apertado, justo; (rope) esticado, tenso;
(control) rigoroso; (knot, schedule,
lid) apertado; (colloq: drunk) embriagado (colloq) □ adv = tightly. be in a
~ corner ( fig) estar em apuros or
num aperto, (P) estar entalado
(colloq). ~-fisted a sovina, pão-duro,
(P) agarrado (colloq). ~ly adv bem;
(squeeze) com força
tighten /'taɪtn/ vt/i (rope) esticar;
(bolt, control) apertar. ~ up on apertar o cinto

tightrope /'taɪtrəʊp/ n corda f (de
acrobacias). ~ walker funâmbulo m
tights /taɪts/ npl collants mpl, meias-
colant fpl
tile /taɪl/ n (on wall, floor) ladrilho m,
azulejo m; (on roof ) telha f □ vt ladri-
lhar, pôr azulejos em; (roof ) telhar,
cobrir com telhas
till¹ /tɪl/ vt (land) cultivar
till² /tɪl/ prep & conj = until
till³ /tɪl/ n caixa (registadora) f
tilt /tɪlt/ vt/i inclinar(-se), pender □ n
(slope) inclinação f. (at) full ~ a toda
a velocidade
timber /'tɪmbə(r)/ n madeira f (de
construção); (trees) árvores fpl
time /taɪm/ n tempo m; (moment) momento m; (epoch) época f, tempo m;
(by clock) horas fpl; (occasion) vez f;
(rhythm) compasso m. ~s (multiply-
ing ) vezes □ vt escolher a hora para;
(measure) marcar o tempo; (sport)
cronometrar; (regulate) acertar. at
~s às vezes. for the ~ being por
agora, por enquanto. from ~ to ~
de vez em quando. have a good ~
divertir-se. have no ~ for não ter
paciência para. in no ~ num
instante. in ~ a tempo; (eventually)
com o tempo. in two days ~ daqui
a dois dias. on ~ na hora, (P) a horas.
take your ~ não se apresse. what's
the ~? que horas são? ~ bomb
bomba-relógio f. ~-limit n prazo m.
~ off tempo m livre. ~-sharing n
time-sharing m. ~ zone fuso m
horário
timeless /'taɪmlɪs/ a intemporal; (unending) eterno
timely /'taɪmlɪ/ a oportuno
timer /'taɪmə(r)/ n (techn) relógio m;
(with sand) ampulheta f
timetable /'taɪmteɪbl/ n horário m
timid /'tɪmɪd/ a tímido; (fearful) as-
sustadiço, medroso. ~ly adv timida-
mente
timing /'taɪmɪŋ/ n (measuring) crono-
metragem f; (of artist) ritmo m; (moment) cálculo m do tempo, timing m.
good/bad ~ (moment) momento m
bem/mal escolhido
tin /tɪn/ n estanho m; (container) lata f
□ vt (pt tinned) estanhar; ( food)
enlatar. ~ foil papel m de alumínio.
~-opener n abridor m de latas, (P)
abre-latas m. ~ plate lata f, folha(-de-
Flandes) f. ~ned foods conservas fpl.
~ny a (sound) metálico
tinge /tɪndʒ/ vt ~ (with) tingir (de);
( fig) dar um toque (de) □ n tom m,
matiz m; ( fig) toque m
tingle /'tɪŋgl/ vi (sting) arder;
(prickle) picar □ n ardor m; (prickle)
picadela f

**tinker** /'tɪŋkə(r)/ n latoeiro m ambulante □ vi ~ (with) mexer (em), tentar consertar

**tinkle** /'tɪŋkl/ n tinido m, tilintar m □ vt/i tilintar

**tinsel** /'tɪnsl/ n fio m prateado/dourado, enfeites mpl metálicos de Natal; ( fig) falso brilho m, ouropel m

**tint** /tɪnt/ n tom m, matiz m; ( for hair) tintura f, tinta f □ vt tingir, colorir

**tiny** /'taɪnɪ/ a (**-ier, -iest**) minúsculo, pequenino

**tip**[1] /tɪp/ n ponta f. **(have sth) on the ~ of one's tongue** ter alg coisa na ponta de língua

**tip**[2] /tɪp/ vt/i (pt **tipped**) (tilt) inclinar(-se); (overturn) virar(-se); ( pour) colocar, (P) deitar; (empty) despejar(-se) □ n (money) gorjeta f; (advice) sugestão f, dica f (colloq); ( for rubbish) lixeira f. ~ **off** avisar, prevenir. ~**-off** n (warning) aviso m; (information) informação f

**tipsy** /'tɪpsɪ/ a ligeiramente embriagado, alegre, tocado

**tiptoe** /'tɪptəʊ/ n **on ~** na ponta dos pés

**tir|e**[1] /taɪə(r)/ vt/i cansar(-se) (de). ~**eless** a incansável, infatigável. ~**ing** a fatigante, cansativo

**tire**[2] /taɪə(r)/ n (Amer) pneu m

**tired** /taɪəd/ a cansado, fatigado. ~ **out** (sick of ) farto de. ~ **out** morto de cansaço

**tiresome** /'taɪəsəm/ a maçador, aborrecido, chato (sl)

**tissue** /'tɪʃuː/ n tecido m; (handkerchief ) lenço de papel. ~**-paper** n papel m de seda

**tit**[1] /tɪt/ n (bird) chapim m, canário-da-terra m

**tit**[2] /tɪt/ n **give ~ for tat** pagar na mesma moeda

**titbit** /'tɪtbɪt/ n petisco m

**titillate** /'tɪtɪleɪt/ vt excitar, titilar, (P) dar gozo a

**title** /'taɪtl/ n título m. ~**-deed** n título m de propriedade. ~**-page** n página f de rosto, (P) frontispício m. ~**-role** n papel m principal

**titter** /'tɪtə(r)/ vi rir com riso abafado

**to** /tuː/; unstressed /tə/ prep a, para; (as far as) até; (towards) para; (of attitude) para (com) □ adv push or pull ~ (close) fechar. ~ **Portugal** ( for a short time) a Portugal; (to stay) para Portugal. ~ **the baker's** para o padeiro, (P) ao padeiro. ~ **do/sit/etc** (infinitive) fazer/sentar-se/etc; (expressing purpose) para fazer/para se sentar/etc. **it's ten ~ six** são dez para as seis, faltam dez para as seis. **go ~ and fro** andar de um lado para outro. **husband/etc-~-be** n futuro marido m/etc. ~**-do** n ( fuss) agitação f, alvoroço m

**toad** /təʊd/ n sapo m

**toadstool** /'təʊdstuːl/ n cogumelo m venenoso

**toady** /'təʊdɪ/ n lambe-botas mf, puxa-saco m □ vi puxar saco

**toast** /təʊst/ n fatia f de pão torrado, torrada f; (drink) brinde m, saúde f □ vt (bread) torrar; (drink to) brindar, beber à saúde de. ~**er** n torradeira f

**tobacco** /tə'bækəʊ/ n tabaco m

**tobacconist** /tə'bækənɪst/ n vendedor m de tabaco, homem m da tabacaria (colloq). ~**'s shop** tabacaria f

**toboggan** /tə'bɒgən/ n tobogã m, (P) toboggan m

**today** /tə'deɪ/ n & adv hoje (m)

**toddler** /'tɒdlə(r)/ n criança f que está aprendendo a andar

**toe** /təʊ/ n dedo m do pé; (of shoe, stocking) biqueira f □ vt ~ **the line** andar na linha. **on one's ~s** alerta, vigilante. ~**-hold** n apoio (precário) m. ~**-nail** n unha f do dedo do pé

**toffee** /'tɒfɪ/ n puxa-puxa m, (P) caramelo m. ~**-apple** n maçã f caramelizada

**together** /tə'geðə(r)/ adv junto, juntamente, juntos; (at the same time) ao mesmo tempo. ~ **with** juntamente com. ~**ness** n camaradagem f, companheirismo m

**toil** /tɔɪl/ vi labutar □ n labuta f, labor m

**toilet** /'tɔɪlɪt/ n banheiro m, (P) casa f de banho; (grooming) toalete f. ~**-paper** n papel m higiênico, (P) higiénico. ~**-roll** n rolo m de papel higiênico, (P) higiénico. ~ **water** água-de-colônia f

**toiletries** /'tɔɪlɪtrɪz/ npl artigos mpl de toalete

**token** /'təʊkən/ n sinal m, prova f; (voucher) cheque m; (coin) ficha f □ a simbólico

**told** /təʊld/ see **tell** □ a **all ~** (all in all) ao todo

**tolerabl|e** /'tɒlərəbl/ a tolerável; (not bad) sofrível, razoável. ~**y** adv (work, play) razoavelmente

**toleran|t** /'tɒlərənt/ a tolerante (of para com). ~**ce** n tolerância f. ~**tly** adv com tolerância

**tolerate** /'tɒləreɪt/ vt tolerar

**toll**[1] /təʊl/ n pedágio m, (P) portagem f. **death ~** número m de mortos. **take its ~** (of age) fazer sentir o seu peso

**toll**[2] /təʊl/ vt/i (of bell) dobrar

**tomato** /tə'mɑːtəʊ/ n (pl **-oes**) tomate m

**tomb** /tuːm/ n túmulo m, sepultura f

**tomboy** /'tɒmbɔɪ/ n menina f levada (E masculinizada), (P) maria-rapaz f

**tombstone** /'tu:mstəun/ *n* lápide *f*, pedra *f* tumular

**tome** /təum/ *n* tomo *m*, volume *m*

**tomfoolery** /tɒm'fu:ləri/ *n* disparates *mpl*, imbecilidades *fpl*

**tomorrow** /tə'mɒrəu/ *n & adv* amanhã (*m*). ~ **morning/night** amanhã de manhã/à noite

**ton** /tʌn/ *n* tonelada *f* (= *1016 kg*). **(metric)** ~ tonelada *f* (= *1000 kg*). ~**s of** (*colloq*) montes de (*colloq*), (*P*) carradas de (*colloq*)

**tone** /təun/ *n* tom *m*; (*of radio, telephone etc*) sinal *m*; (*colour*) tom *m*, tonalidade *f*; (*med*) tonicidade *f* □ *vt* ~ **down** atenuar □ *vi* ~ **in** combinar-se, harmonizar-se (**with** com). ~ **up** (*muscles*) tonificar. ~-**deaf** *a* sem ouvido musical

**tongs** /tɒŋz/ *n* tenaz *f*; (*for sugar*) pinça *f*; (*for hair*) pinça *f*

**tongue** /tʌŋ/ *n* língua *f*. ~-**in-cheek** *a & adv* sem ser a sério, com ironia. ~-**tied** *a* calado. ~-**twister** *n* trava-língua *m*

**tonic** /'tɒnɪk/ *n* (*med*) tônico *m*, (*P*) tónico *m*; (*mus*) tônica *f*, (*P*) tónica *f* □ *a* tônico, (*P*) tónico

**tonight** /tə'naɪt/ *adv & n* hoje à noite, logo à noite, esta noite (*f*)

**tonne** /tʌn/ *n* (*metric*) tonelada *f*

**tonsil** /'tɒnsl/ *n* amígdala *f*

**tonsillitis** /tɒnsɪ'laɪtɪs/ *n* amigdalite *f*

**too** /tu:/ *adv* demasiado, demais; (*also*) também, igualmente; (*colloq: very*) muito. ~ **many** *a* demais, demasiados. ~ **much** *a & adv* demais, demasiado

**took** /tuk/ *see* **take**

**tool** /tu:l/ *n* (*carpenter's, plumber's etc*) ferramenta *f*; (*gardener's*) utensílio *m*; (*fig: person*) joguete *m*. ~-**bag** *n* saco *m* de ferramenta

**toot** /tu:t/ *n* toque *m* de buzina □ *vt/i* ~ **(the horn)** buzinar, tocar a buzina

**tooth** /tu:θ/ *n* (*pl* **teeth**) dente *m*. ~**less** *a* desdentado

**toothache** /'tu:θeɪk/ *n* dor *f* de dentes

**toothbrush** /'tu:θbrʌʃ/ *n* escova *f* de dentes

**toothpaste** /'tu:θpeɪst/ *n* pasta *f* de dentes, dentifrício *m*

**toothpick** /'tu:θpɪk/ *n* palito *m*

**top**[1] /tɒp/ *n* (*highest point; upper part*) alto *m*, cimo *m*, topo *m*; (*of hill; fig*) cume *m*; (*upper surface*) cimo *m*, topo *m*; (*surface of table*) tampo *m*; (*lid*) tampa *f*; (*of bottle*) rolha *f*; (*of list*) cabeça *f* □ *a* (*shelf etc*) de cima, superior; (*in rank*) primeiro; (*best*) melhor; (*distinguished*) eminente; (*maximum*) máximo □ *vt* (*pt* **topped**) (*exceed*) ultrapassar, ir acima de. **from** ~ **to bottom** de alto a baixo. **on** ~ **of** em

cima de; (*fig*) além de. **on** ~ **of that** ainda por cima. ~ **gear** (*auto*) a velocidade mais alta. ~ **hat** chapéu *m* alto. ~-**heavy** *a* mais pesado na parte de cima. ~ **secret** ultra-secreto. ~ **up** encher. ~**ped with** coberto de

**top**[2] /tɒp/ *n* (*toy*) pião *m*. **sleep like a** ~ dormir como uma pedra

**topic** /'tɒpɪk/ *n* tópico *m*, assunto *m*

**topical** /'tɒpɪkl/ *a* da atualidade, (*P*) actualidade, corrente

**topless** /'tɒplɪs/ *a* com o peito nu, topless

**topple** /'tɒpl/ *vt/i* (fazer) desabar, (fazer) tombar, (fazer) cair

**torch** /tɔ:tʃ/ *n* (*electric*) lanterna *f* elétrica, (*P*) eléctrica; (*flaming*) archote *m*, facho *m*

**tore** /tɔ:(r)/ *see* **tear**[1]

**torment**[1] /'tɔ:mənt/ *n* tormento *m*

**torment**[2] /tɔ:'ment/ *vt* atormentar, torturar; (*annoy*) aborrecer, chatear

**torn** /tɔ:n/ *see* **tear**[1]

**tornado** /tɔ:'neɪdəu/ *n* (*pl* -**oes**) tornado *m*

**torpedo** /tɔ:'pi:dəu/ *n* (*pl* -**oes**) torpedo *m* □ *vt* torpedear

**torrent** /'tɒrənt/ *n* torrente *f*. ~**ial** /tə'renʃl/ *a* torrencial

**torrid** /'tɒrɪd/ *a* (*climate etc*) tórrido; (*fig*) intenso, ardente

**torso** /'tɔ:səu/ *n* (*pl* -**os**) torso *m*

**tortoise** /'tɔ:təs/ *n* tartaruga *f*

**tortoiseshell** /'tɔ:təsʃel/ *n* (*for ornaments etc*) tartaruga *f*

**tortuous** /'tɔ:tʃuəs/ *a* (*of path etc*) que dá muitas voltas, sinuoso; (*fig*) tortuoso, retorcido

**torture** /'tɔ:tʃə(r)/ *n* tortura *f*, suplício *m* □ *vt* torturar. ~**r** /-ə(r)/ *n* carrasco *m*, algoz *m*, torturador *m*

**Tory** /'tɔ:rɪ/ *a & n* (*colloq*) conservador (*m*), (*P*) tóri (*m*)

**toss** /tɒs/ *vt* atirar, jogar, (*P*) deitar; (*shake*) agitar, sacudir □ *vi* agitar-se, debater-se. ~ **a coin**, ~ **up** tirar cara ou coroa

**tot**[1] /tɒt/ *n* criancinha *f*; (*colloq: glass*) copinho *m*

**tot**[2] /tɒt/ *vt/i* (*pt* **totted**) ~ **up** (*colloq*) somar

**total** /'təutl/ *a & n* total (*m*) □ *vt* (*pt* **totalled**) (*find total of*) totalizar; (*amount to*) elevar-se a, montar a. ~**ity** /-'tæləti/ *n* totalidade *f*. ~**ly** *adv* totalmente

**totalitarian** /təutælɪ'teərɪən/ *a* totalitário

**totter** /'tɒtə(r)/ *vi* cambalear, andar aos tombos; (*of tower etc*) oscilar

**touch** /tʌtʃ/ *vt/i* tocar; (*of ends, gardens etc*) tocar-se; (*tamper with*) mexer em; (*affect*) comover □ *n* (*sense*) tato *m*, (*P*) tacto *m*; (*contact*) toque *m*; (*of* *colour*) toque *m*, retoque *m*. **a ~ of** (*small amount*) um pouco de. **get in ~ with** entrar em contato, (P) contacto com. **lose ~** perder contato, (P) contacto. **~ down** (*aviat*) aterrissar, (P) aterrar. **~ off** disparar; (*cause*) dar início a, desencadear. **~ on** (*mention*) tocar em. **~ up** retocar. **~-and-go** *a* (*risky*) arriscado; (*uncertain*) duvidoso, incerto. **~-line** *n* linha *f* lateral

**touching** /'tʌtʃɪŋ/ *a* comovente, comovedor

**touchy** /'tʌtʃɪ/ *a* melindroso, susceptível, (P) susceptível, que se ofende facilmente

**tough** /tʌf/ *a* (-er, -est) (*hard, difficult; relentless*) duro; (*strong*) forte, resistente □ *n* ~ (**guy**) valentão *m*, durão *m* (*colloq*). **~ luck!** (*colloq*) pouca sorte! **~ness** *n* dureza *f*; (*strength*) força *f*, resistência *f*

**toughen** /'tʌfn/ *vt/i* (*a person*) endurecer; (*strengthen*) reforçar

**tour** /tʊə(r)/ *n* viagem *f*, (*visit*) visita *f*, (*by team etc*) tournée *f* □ *vt* visitar. **on ~** em tournée

**tourism** /'tʊərɪzəm/ *n* turismo *m*

**tourist** /'tʊərɪst/ *n* turista *mf* □ *a* turístico. **~ office** agência *f* de turismo

**tournament** /'tʊənəmənt/ *n* torneio *m*

**tousle** /'taʊzl/ *vt* despentear, esguedelhar

**tout** /taʊt/ *vi* angariar clientes (**for** para) □ *vt* (*try to sell*) tentar revender □ *n* (*hotel etc*) angariador *m*; (*ticket*) cambista *m*, (P) revendedor *m*

**tow** /təʊ/ *vt* rebocar □ *n* reboque *m*. **on ~** a reboque. **~ away** (*vehicle*) rebocar. **~-path** *n* caminho *m* de sirga. **~-rope** *n* cabo *m* de reboque

**toward(s)** /tə'wɔːd(z)/ *prep* para, em direção, (P) direcção a, na direção, (P) direcção de; (*of attitude*) para com; (*time*) por volta de

**towel** /'taʊəl/ *n* toalha *f*, (*tea towel*) pano *m* de prato □ *vt* (*pt* towelled) esfregar com a toalha. **~-rail** *n* toalheiro *m*. **~ling** *n* atoalhado *m*, (P) pano *m* turco

**tower** /'taʊə(r)/ *n* torre *f* □ *vi* **~ above** dominar. **~ block** prédio *m* alto. **~ing** *a* muito alto; (*fig: of rage etc*) violento

**town** /taʊn/ *n* cidade *f*. **go to ~** (*colloq*) perder a cabeça (*colloq*). **~ council** município *m*. **~ hall** câmara *f* municipal. **~ planning** urbanização *f*

**toxic** /'tɒksɪk/ *a* tóxico

**toy** /tɔɪ/ *n* brinquedo *m* □ *vi* **~ with** (*object*) brincar com; (*idea*) considerar, cogitar

**trace** /treɪs/ *n* traço *m*, rastro *m*, sinal *m*; (*small quantity*) traço *m*, vestígio *m* □ *vt* seguir *or* encontrar a pista de; (*draw*) traçar; (*with tracing-paper*) decalcar

**tracing** /'treɪsɪŋ/ *n* decalque *m*, desenho *m*. **~-paper** *n* papel *m* vegetal

**track** /træk/ *n* (*of person etc*) rastro *m*, pista *f*, (*race-track, of tape*) pista *f*, (*record*) faixa *f*, (*path*) trilho *m*, carreiro *m*; (*rail*) via *f* □ *vt* seguir a pista *or* a trajetória, (P) trajectória de. **keep ~ of** manter-se em contato com; (*keep oneself informed*) seguir. **~ down** (*find*) encontrar, descobrir; (*hunt*) seguir a pista de. **~ suit** conjunto *m* de jogging, (P) fato *m* de treino

**tract** /trækt/ *n* (*land*) extensão *f*, (*anat*) aparelho *m*

**tractor** /'træktə(r)/ *n* trator *m*, (P) tractor *m*

**trade** /treɪd/ *n* comércio *m*; (*job*) ofício *m*, profissão *f*, (*swap*) troca *f* □ *vt/i* comerciar (em), negociar (em) □ *vt* (*swap*) trocar. **~ in** (*used article*) trocar. **~-in** *n* troca *f*. **~ mark** marca *f* de fábrica. **~ on** (*exploit*) tirar partido de, abusar de. **~ union** sindicato *m*. **~r** /-ə(r)/ *n* negociante *mf*, comerciante *mf*

**tradesman** /'treɪdzmən/ *n* (*pl* -men) comerciante *m*

**trading** /'treɪdɪŋ/ *n* comércio *m*. **~ estate** zona *f* industrial

**tradition** /trə'dɪʃn/ *n* tradição *f*. **~al** *a* tradicional

**traffic** /'træfɪk/ *n* (*trade*) tráfego *m*, tráfico *m*; (*on road*) trânsito *m*, tráfego *m*; (*aviat*) tráfego *m* □ *vi* (*pt* trafficked) traficar (**in** em). **~ circle** (*Amer*) giratória *f*, (P) rotunda *f*. **~ island** ilha *f* de pedestres, (P) refúgio *m* para peões. **~ jam** engarrafamento *m*. **~-lights** *npl* sinal *m* luminoso, (P) semáforo *m*. **~ warden** guarda *mf* de trânsito. **~ker** *n* traficante *mf*

**tragedy** /'trædʒədɪ/ *n* tragédia *f*

**tragic** /'trædʒɪk/ *a* trágico

**trail** /treɪl/ *vt/i* arrastar(-se), rastejar; (*of plant, on ground*) rastejar; (*of plant, over wall*) trepar; (*track*) seguir □ *n* (*of powder, smoke etc*) esteira *f*, rastro *m*, (P) rasto *m*; (*track*) pista *f*; (*beaten path*) trilho *m*

**trailer** /'treɪlə(r)/ *n* reboque *m*; (*Amer: caravan*) reboque *m*, caravana *f*, trailer *m*; (*film*) trailer *m*, apresentação *f* de filme

**train** /treɪn/ *n* (*rail*) trem *m*, (P) comboio *m*; (*procession*) fila *f*; (*of dress*) cauda *f*; (*retinue*) comitiva *f* □ *vt* (*instruct, develop*) educar, formar, treinar; (*plant*) guiar; (*sportsman, animal*) treinar; (*aim*) assestar, apon-

tar □ *vi* estudar, treinar-se. ~ed *a*
(*skilled*) qualificado; (*doctor etc*)
diplomado. ~er *n* (*sport*) treinador
*m*; (*shoe*) tênis *m*. ~ing *n* treino *m*
**trainee** /treɪ'niː/ *n* estagiário *m*
**trait** /treɪ(t)/ *n* traço *m*, característica *f*
**traitor** /'treɪtə(r)/ *n* traidor *m*
**tram** /træm/ *n* bonde *m*, (P) (carro)
eléctrico *m*
**tramp** /træmp/ *vi* marchar (com passo pesado) □ *vt* percorrer, palmilhar □
*n* som *m* de passos pesados; (*vagrant*)
vagabundo *m*, andarilho *m*; (*hike*)
longa caminhada *f*
**trample** /'træmpl/ *vt/i* ~ (**on**) pisar
com força; (*fig*) menosprezar
**trampoline** /'træmpəliːn/ *n* (lona *f*
usada como) trampolim *m*
**trance** /traːns/ *n* (*hypnotic*) transe *m*;
(*ecstasy*) êxtase *m*, arrebatamento *m*;
(*med*) estupor *m*
**tranquil** /'træŋkwɪl/ *a* tranqüilo, (P)
tranquilo, sossegado. ~lity /-'kwɪlətɪ/
*n* tranqüilidade *f*, (P) tranquilidade *f*,
sossego *m*
**tranquillizer** /'træŋkwɪlaɪzə(r)/ *n*
(*drug*) tranqüilizante *m*, (P) tranquilizante *m*, calmante *m*
**transact** /træn'zækt/ *vt* (*business*) fazer, efetuar, (P) efectuar; ~ion /-kʃn/
*n* transação *f*, (P) transacção *f*
**transcend** /træn'send/ *vt* transcender. ~ent *a* transcendente
**transcribe** /træn'skraɪb/ *vt* transcrever. ~pt, ~ption /-ɪpʃn/ *ns*
transcrição *f*
**transfer¹** /træns'fɜː(r)/ *vt* (*pt* transferred) transferir; (*power, property*)
transmitir □ *vi* mudar, ser transferido; (*change planes etc*) fazer transferência. ~ the charges (*telephone*)
ligar a cobrar
**transfer²** /'trænsfɜː(r)/ *n* transferência *f*; (*of power, property*)
transmissão *f*; (*image*) decalcomania *f*
**transfigure** /træns'fɪgə(r)/ *vt* transfigurar
**transform** /træns'fɔːm/ *vt* transformar. ~ation /-ə'meɪʃn/ *n* transformação *f*. ~er *n* (*electr*) transformador *m*
**transfusion** /træns'fjuːʒn/ *n* (*of
blood*) transfusão *f*
**transient** /'trænzɪənt/ *a* transitório,
transiente, efêmero, (P) efémero, passageiro
**transistor** /træn'zɪstə(r)/ *n* (*device,
radio*) transistor *m*
**transit** /'trænsɪt/ *n* trânsito *m*. in ~
em trânsito
**transition** /træn'zɪʃn/ *n* transição *f*.
~al *a* transitório
**transitive** /'trænsətɪv/ *a* transitivo
**transitory** /'trænsɪtərɪ/ *a* transitório

**translate** /trænz'leɪt/ *vt* traduzir.
~ion /-ʃn/ *n* tradução *f*. ~or *n* tradutor *m*
**translucent** /trænz'luːsnt/ *a* translúcido
**transmit** /trænz'mɪt/ *vt* (*pt* transmitted) transmitir. ~ssion *n*
transmissão *f*. ~tter *n* transmissor *m*
**transparent** /træns'pærənt/ *a* transparente. ~cy *n* transparência *f*;
(*photo*) diapositivo *m*
**transpire** /træn'spaɪə(r)/ *vi* (*secret
etc*) transpirar; (*happen*) suceder,
acontecer
**transplant¹** /træns'plɑːnt/ *vt* transplantar
**transplant²** /'trænsplɑːnt/ *n* (*med*)
transplantação *f*, transplante *m*
**transport¹** /træn'spɔːt/ *vt* (*carry, delight*) transportar. ~ation /'teɪʃn/ *n*
transporte *m*
**transport²** /'trænspɔːt/ *n* (*of goods,
delight etc*) transporte *m*
**transpose** /træn'spəʊz/ *vt* transpor
**transverse** /'trænzvɜːs/ *a* transversal
**transvestite** /trænz'vestaɪt/ *n* travesti *mf*
**trap** /træp/ *n* armadilha *f*, ratoeira *f*,
cilada *f* □ *vt* (*pt* trapped) apanhar na
armadilha; (*cut off*) prender,
bloquear. ~per *n* caçador *m* de armadilha (esp de peles)
**trapdoor** /træp'dɔː(r)/ *n* alçapão *m*
**trapeze** /trə'piːz/ *n* trapézio *m*
**trash** /træʃ/ *n* (*worthless stuff*) porcaria *f*; (*refuse*) lixo *m*; (*nonsense*) disparates *mpl*. ~ can *n* (*Amer*) lata *f* do
lixo, (P) caixote *m* do lixo. ~y *a* que
não vale nada, porcaria
**trauma** /'trɔːmə/ *n* trauma *m*, traumatismo *m*. ~tic /-'mætɪk/ *a* traumático
**travel** /'trævl/ *vi* (*pt* travelled) viajar; (*of vehicle, bullet, sound*) ir □ *vt*
percorrer □ *n* viagem *f*. ~ agent
agente *mf* de viagem. ~ler *n* viajante
*mf*. ~ler's cheque cheque *m* de
viagem. ~ling *n* viagem *f*, viagens
*fpl*, viajar *m*
**travesty** /'trævəstɪ/ *n* paródia *f*, caricatura *f*
**trawler** /'trɔːlə(r)/ *n* traineira *f*, (P)
arrastão *m*
**tray** /treɪ/ *n* tabuleiro *m*, bandeja *f*
**treacherous** /'tretʃərəs/ *a* traiçoeiro
**treachery** /'tretʃərɪ/ *n* traição *f*,
perfídia *f*, deslealdade *f*
**treacle** /'triːkl/ *n* melaço *m*
**tread** /tred/ *vt/i* (*pt* trod, *pp* trodden)
(*step*) pisar; (*walk*) andar, caminhar;
(*walk along*) seguir □ *n* passo *m*, maneira *f* de andar; (*of tyre*) trilho *m*. ~
sth into (*carpet*) esmigalhar alg coisa sobre/em

**treason** /'tri:zn/ n traição f

**treasure** /'treʒə(r)/ n tesouro m □ vt ter o maior apreço por; (store) guardar bem guardado. ~r n tesoureiro m

**treasury** /'treʒərɪ/ n (building) tesouraria f; (department) Ministério m das Finanças or da Fazenda; (fig) tesouro m

**treat** /tri:t/ vt/i tratar □ n (pleasure) prazer m, regalo m; (present) mimo m, gentileza f. ~ sb to sth convidar alguém para alg coisa

**treatise** /'tri:tɪz/ n tratado m

**treatment** /'tri:tmənt/ n tratamento m

**treaty** /'tri:tɪ/ n (pact) tratado m

**treble** /'trebl/ a triplo □ vt/i triplicar □ n (mus: voice) soprano m. ~y adv triplamente

**tree** /tri:/ n árvore f

**trek** /trek/ n viagem f penosa; (walk) caminhada f □ vi (pt trekked) viajar penosamente; (walk) caminhar

**trellis** /'trelɪs/ n grade f para trepadeiras, treliça f

**tremble** /'trembl/ vi tremer

**tremendous** /trɪ'mendəs/ a (fearful, huge) tremendo; (colloq: excellent) fantástico, formidável

**tremor** /'tremə(r)/ n tremor m, estremecimento m. (earth) ~ abalo (sísmico) m, tremor m de terra

**trench** /trentʃ/ n fossa f, vala f; (mil) trincheira f

**trend** /trend/ n tendência f; (fashion) moda f. ~y a (colloq) na última moda, (P) na berra (colloq)

**trepidation** /trepɪ'deɪʃn/ n (fear) receio m, apreensão f

**trespass** /'trespəs/ vi entrar ilegalmente (on em). no ~ing entrada f proibida. ~er n intruso m

**trestle** /'tresl/ n cavalete m, armação f de mesa. ~-table n mesa f de cavaletes

**trial** /'traɪəl/ n (jur) julgamento m, processo m; (test) ensaio m, experiência f, prova f; (ordeal) provação f. on ~ em julgamento. ~ and error tentativas fpl

**triangle** /'traɪæŋgl/ n triângulo m. ~ular /-'æŋgjʊlə(r)/ a triangular

**tribe** /traɪb/ n tribo f. ~al a tribal

**tribulation** /trɪbjʊ'leɪʃn/ n tribulação f

**tribunal** /traɪ'bju:nl/ n tribunal m

**tributary** /'trɪbjʊtərɪ/ n afluente m, tributário m

**tribute** /'trɪbju:t/ n tributo m. pay ~ to prestar homenagem a, render tributo a

**trick** /trɪk/ n truque m; (prank) partida f; (habit) jeito m □ vt enganar. do the ~ (colloq: work) dar resultado

**trickery** /'trɪkərɪ/ n trapaça f

**trickle** /'trɪkl/ vi pingar, gotejar, escorrer □ n fio m de água etc; (fig: small number) punhado m

**tricky** /'trɪkɪ/ a (crafty) manhoso; (problem) delicado, complicado

**tricycle** /'traɪsɪkl/ n triciclo m

**trifle** /'traɪfl/ n ninharia f, bagatela f; (sweet) sobremesa f feita de pão-de-ló e frutas e creme □ vi ~ with brincar com. a ~ um pouquinho, (P) um pouquochinho

**trifling** /'traɪflɪŋ/ a insignificante

**trigger** /'trɪgə(r)/ n (of gun) gatilho m □ vt ~ (off) (initiate) desencadear, despoletar

**trill** /trɪl/ n trinado m, gorjeio m

**trilogy** /'trɪlədʒɪ/ n trilogia f

**trim** /trɪm/ a (trimmer, trimmest) bem arranjado, bem cuidado; (figure) elegante, esbelto □ vt (pt trimmed) (cut) aparar; (sails) orientar, marear; (ornament) enfeitar, guarnecer (with com) □ n (cut) aparadela f, corte m leve; (decoration) enfeite m; (on car) acabamento(s) m(pl), estofado m. in ~ em ordem; (fit) em boa forma. ~ming(s) n(pl) (dress) enfeite m; (culin) guarnição f, acompanhamento m

**Trinity** /'trɪnətɪ/ n the (Holy) ~ a Santíssima Trindade

**trinket** /'trɪŋkɪt/ n bugiganga f; (jewel) bijuteria f, berloque m

**trio** /'tri:əʊ/ n (pl -os) trio m

**trip** /trɪp/ vi (pt tripped) (stumble) tropeçar, dar um passo em falso; (go or dance lightly) andar/dançar com passos leves □ vt ~ (up) fazer tropeçar, passar uma rasteira a □ n (journey) viagem f; (outing) passeio m, excursão f; (stumble) tropeção m, passo m em falso

**tripe** /traɪp/ n (food) dobrada f, tripas fpl; (colloq: nonsense) disparates mpl

**triple** /'trɪpl/ a triplo, tríplice □ vt/i triplicar. ~ts /-plɪts/ npl trigêmeos mpl, (P) trigêmeos mpl

**triplicate** /'trɪplɪkət/ n in ~ em triplicata

**tripod** /'traɪpɒd/ n tripé m

**trite** /traɪt/ a banal, corriqueiro

**triumph** /'traɪəmf/ n triunfo m □ vi triunfar (over sobre); (exult) exultar, rejubilar-se. ~al /-'ʌmfl/ a triunfal. ~ant /-'ʌmfənt/ a triunfante. ~antly /-'ʌmfəntlɪ/ adv em triunfo, triunfantemente

**trivial** /'trɪvɪəl/ a insignificante

**trod, trodden** /trɒd, 'trɒdn/ see tread

**trolley** /'trɒlɪ/ n carrinho m. (tea-)~ carrinho m de chá

**trombone** /trɒm'bəʊn/ n (mus) trombone m

**troop** /tru:p/ n bando m, grupo m. ~s

(*mil*) tropas *fpl* □ *vi* ~ **in/out** entrar/ sair em bando *or* grupo. ~**ing the colour** a saudação da bandeira. ~**er** *n* soldado *m* de cavalaria

**trophy** /'trəʊfɪ/ *n* troféu *m*

**tropic** /'trɒpɪk/ *n* trópico *m*. ~**s** trópicos *mpl*. ~**al** *a* tropical

**trot** /trɒt/ *n* trote *m* □ *vi* (*pt* **trotted**) trotar; (*of person*) correr em passos curtos, ir num *or* a trote (*colloq*). **on the** ~ (*colloq*) a seguir, a fio. ~ **out** (*colloq: produce*) exibir; (*colloq: state*) desfiar

**trouble** /'trʌbl/ *n* (*difficulty*) dificuldade(s) *f*(*pl*), problema(s) *m*(*pl*); (*distress*) desgosto(s) *m*(*pl*), aborrecimento(s) *m*(*pl*); (*pains, effort*) cuidado *m*, trabalho *m*, maçada *f*; (*inconvenience*) transtorno *m*, incômodo *m*, (*P*) incómodo *m*; (*med*) doença *f*. ~(**s**) (*unrest*) agitação *f*, conflito(s) *m*(*pl*) □ *vt/i* (*bother*) incomodar(-se), (*P*) maçar(-se); (*worry*) preocupar(-se); (*agitate*) perturbar. **be in** ~ estar em apuros, estar em dificuldades. **get into** ~ meter-se em encrenca/apuros. **it is not worth the** ~ não vale a pena. ~**-maker** *n* desordeiro *m*, provocador *m*. ~**-shooter** *n* mediador *m*, negociador *m*. ~**d** *a* agitado, perturbado; (*of sleep*) agitado; (*of water*) turvo

**troublesome** /'trʌblsəm/ *a* problemático, importuno, (*P*) maçador

**trough** /trɒf/ *n* (*drinking*) bebedouro *m*; (*feeding*) comedouro *m*. ~ (**of low pressure**) depressão *f*, linha *f* de baixa pressão

**trounce** /traʊns/ *vt* (*defeat*) esmagar; (*thrash*) espancar

**troupe** /truːp/ *n* (*theat*) companhia *f*, troupe *f*

**trousers** /'traʊzəz/ *npl* calça *f*, (*P*) calças *fpl*. **short** ~ calções *mpl*

**trousseau** /'truːsəʊ/ *n* (*pl* -**s** /-əʊz/) (*of bride*) enxoval *m* de noiva

**trout** /traʊt/ *n* (*pl invar*) truta *f*

**trowel** /'traʊəl/ *n* (*garden*) colher *f* de jardineiro; (*for mortar*) trolha *f*

**truan|t** /'truːənt/ *n* absenteísta *mf*, (*P*) absentista *mf*; (*schol*) gazeteiro *m*. **play** ~**t** fazer gazeta. ~**cy** *n* absenteísmo *m*, (*P*) absentismo *m*

**truce** /truːs/ *n* trégua(s) *f*(*pl*), armistício *m*

**truck** /trʌk/ *n* (*lorry*) camião *m*; (*barrow*) carro *m* de bagageiro; (*wagon*) vagão *m* aberto. ~**-driver** *n* motorista *mf* de camião, (*P*) camionista *mf*

**truculent** /'trʌkjʊlənt/ *a* agressivo, brigão

**trudge** /trʌdʒ/ *vi* caminhar com dificuldade, caminhar a custo, arrastar-se

**true** /truː/ *a* (-**er**, -**est**) verdadeiro; (*accurate*) exato, (*P*) exacto; (*faithful*) fiel. **come** ~ (*happen*) realizar-se, concretizar-se. **it is** ~ é verdade

**truffle** /'trʌfl/ *n* trufa *f*

**truism** /'truːɪzəm/ *n* truísmo *m*, verdade *f* evidente, (*P*) verdade *f* do Amigo Banana (*colloq*)

**truly** /'truːlɪ/ *adv* verdadeiramente; (*faithfully*) fielmente; (*truthfully*) sinceramente

**trump** /trʌmp/ *n* trunfo *m* □ *vt* jogar trunfo, trunfar. ~ **up** forjar, inventar. ~ **card** carta *f* de trunfo; (*colloq: valuable resource*) trunfo *m*

**trumpet** /'trʌmpɪt/ *n* trombeta *f*

**truncheon** /'trʌntʃən/ *n* cassetete *m*, (*P*) cassetête *m*

**trundle** /'trʌndl/ *vt/i* (fazer) rolar ruidosamente/pesadamente

**trunk** /trʌŋk/ *n* (*of tree, body*) tronco *m*; (*of elephant*) tromba *f*; (*box*) mala *f* grande; (*Amer; auto*) mala *f*. ~**s** (*for swimming*) calção *m* de banho. ~ **call** *n* chamada *f* interurbana. ~ **road** *n* estrada *f* nacional

**truss** /trʌs/ *n* (*med*) funda *f* □ *vt* atar, amarrar

**trust** /trʌst/ *n* confiança *f*; (*association*) truste *m*, (*P*) trust *m*, consórcio *m*; (*foundation*) fundação *f*; (*responsibility*) responsabilidade *f*; (*jur*) fideicomisso *m* □ *vt* (*rely on*) ter confiança em, confiar em; (*hope*) esperar □ *vi* ~ **in** *or* **to** confiar em. **in** ~ em fideicomisso. **on** ~ (*without proof*) sem verificação prévia; (*on credit*) a crédito. ~ **sb with** confiar em alguém. ~**ed** *a* (*friend etc*) de confiança, seguro. ~**ful**, ~**ing** *adjs* confiante. ~**y** *a* fiel

**trustee** /trʌsˈtiː/ *n* administrador *m*; (*jur*) fideicomissório *m*

**trustworthy** /'trʌstwɜːðɪ/ *a* (digno) de confiança

**truth** /truːθ/ *n* (*pl* -**s** /truːðz/) verdade *f*. ~**ful** *a* (*account etc*) verídico; (*person*) verdadeiro, que fala verdade. ~**fully** *adv* sinceramente

**try** /traɪ/ *vt/i* (*pt* **tried**) tentar, experimentar; (*be a strain on*) cansar, pôr à prova; (*jur*) julgar □ *n* (*attempt*) tentativa *f*, experiência *f*; (*Rugby*) ensaio *m*. ~ **for** (*post, scholarship*) candidatar-se a; (*record*) tentar alcançar. ~ **on** (*clothes*) provar. ~ **out** experimentar. ~ **to do** tentar fazer. ~**ing** *a* difícil

**tsar** /zɑː(r)/ *n* czar *m*

**T-shirt** /'tiːʃɜːt/ *n* T-shirt *f*, camiseta *f* de algodão de mangas curtas

**tub** /tʌb/ *n* selha *f*; (*colloq: bath*) tina *f*, banheira *f*

**tuba** /'tjuːbə/ *n* (*mus*) tuba *f*

**tubby** /'tʌbɪ/ a (-ier, -iest) baixote e gorducho

**tub|e** /tjuːb/ n tubo m; (colloq: railway) metrô m. **inner** ~e câmara f de ar. ~**ing** n tubos mpl, tubagem f

**tuber** /'tjuːbə(r)/ n tubérculo m

**tuberculosis** /tjuːbɜːkjʊ'ləʊsɪs/ n tuberculose f

**tubular** /'tjuːbjʊlə(r)/ a tubular

**tuck** /tʌk/ n (fold) prega f cosida; (for shortening or ornament) refego m □ vt/i fazer pregas; (put) guardar, meter, enfiar; (hide) esconder. ~ **in** or **into** (colloq: eat) atacar. ~ **in** (shirt) meter as fraldas para dentro; (blanket) prender em; (person) cobrir bem, aconchegar. ~-**shop** n (schol) loja f de balas, (P) pastelaria f (junto à escola)

**Tuesday** /'tjuːzdɪ/ n terça-feira f

**tuft** /tʌft/ n tufo m

**tug** /tʌg/ vt/i (pt tugged) puxar com força; (vessel) rebocar □ n (boat) rebocador m; (pull) puxão m. ~ **of war** cabo-de-guerra m, (P) jogo m da guerra

**tuition** /tjuː'ɪʃn/ n ensino m

**tulip** /'tjuːlɪp/ n tulipa f

**tumble** /'tʌmbl/ vi tombar, baquear, dar um trambolhão □ n tombo m, trambolhão m. ~-**drier** n máquina f de secar (roupa)

**tumbledown** /'tʌmbldaʊn/ a em ruínas

**tumbler** /'tʌmblə(r)/ n copo m

**tummy** /'tʌmɪ/ n (colloq: stomach) estômago m; (colloq: abdomen) barriga f. ~-**ache** n (colloq) dor f de barriga/de estômago

**tumour** /'tjuːmə(r)/ n tumor m

**tumult** /'tjuːmʌlt/ n tumulto m. ~**uous** /'mʌltʃʊəs/ a tumultuado, barulhento, agitado

**tuna** /'tjuːnə/ n (pl invar) atum m

**tune** /tjuːn/ n melodia f □ vt (engine) regular; (piano etc) afinar □ vi ~ **in** (to) (radio, TV) ligar (em), (P) sintonizar. ~ **up** afinar. **be in** ~/**out of** ~ (instrument) estar afinado/desafinado; (singer) cantar afinado/desafinado. ~**ful** a melodioso, harmonioso. ~**r** n afinador m; (radio) sintonizador m

**tunic** /'tjuːnɪk/ n túnica f

**Tunisia** /tjuː'nɪzɪə/ n Tunísia f. ~**n** a & n tunisiano (m), (P) tunisino (m)

**tunnel** /'tʌnl/ n túnel m □ vi (pt tunnelled) abrir um túnel (into em)

**turban** /'tɜːbən/ n turbante m

**turbine** /'tɜːbaɪn/ n turbina f

**turbo-** /'tɜːbəʊ/ pref turbo-

**turbot** /'tɜːbət/ n rodovalho m

**turbulen|t** /'tɜːbjʊlənt/ a turbulento. ~**ce** n turbulência f

**tureen** /tə'riːn/ n terrina f

**turf** /tɜːf/ n (pl **turfs** or **turves**) gramado m, (P) relva f, relvado m □ vt ~ **out** (colloq) jogar fora, (P) deitar fora. **the** ~ (racing) turfe m, hipismo m. ~ **accountant** corretor m de apostas

**turgid** /'tɜːdʒɪd/ a (speech, style) pomposo, empolado

**Turk** /tɜːk/ n turco m. ~**ey** n Turquia f. ~**ish** a n (lang) turco m

**turkey** /'tɜːkɪ/ n peru m

**turmoil** /'tɜːmɔɪl/ n agitação f, confusão f, desordem f. **in** ~ em ebulição

**turn** /tɜːn/ vt/i virar(-se), voltar(-se), girar; (change) transformar(-se) (**into** em); (become) ficar, tornar-se; (corner) virar, dobrar; (page) virar, voltar □ n volta f; (in road) curva f; (of mind, events) mudança f; (occasion, opportunity) vez f; (colloq) ataque m, crise f; (colloq: shock) susto m. **do a good** ~ prestar (um) serviço. **in** ~ por sua vez, sucessivamente. **speak out of** ~ dizer o que não se deve, cometer uma indiscrição. **take** ~s revezar-se. ~ **of the century** virada f do século. ~ **against** virar-se or voltar-se contra. ~ **away** vi virar-se or voltar-se para o outro lado □ vt (avert) desviar; (reject) recusar; (send back) mandar embora. ~ **back** vi (return) devolver; (vehicle) dar meia volta, voltar para trás □ vt (fold) dobrar para trás. ~ **down** recusar; (fold) dobrar para baixo; (reduce) baixar. ~ **in** (hand in) entregar; (colloq: go to bed) deitar-se. ~ **off** (light etc) apagar; (tap) fechar; (road) virar (para rua transversal). ~ **on** (light etc) acender, ligar; (tap) abrir. ~ **out** vt (light) apagar; (empty) esvaziar, despejar; (pocket) virar do avesso; (produce) produzir □ vi (transpire) vir a saber-se, descobrir-se; (colloq: come) aparecer. ~ **round** virar-se, voltar-se. ~ **up** vi aparecer, chegar; (be found) aparecer □ vt (find) desenterrar; (increase) aumentar; (collar) levantar. ~-**out** n assistência f. ~-**up** n (of trousers) dobra f

**turning** /'tɜːnɪŋ/ n rua f transversal; (corner) esquina f. ~-**point** n momento m decisivo

**turnip** /'tɜːnɪp/ n nabo m

**turnover** /'tɜːnəʊvə(r)/ n (pie, tart) pastel m, empada f; (money) faturamento m, (P) facturação f; (of staff) rotatividade f

**turnpike** /'tɜːnpaɪk/ n (Amer) autoestrada f com pedágio, (P) portagem f

**turnstile** /'tɜːnstaɪl/ n (gate) torniquete m, borboleta f

**turntable** /'tɜ:nteɪbl/ n ( for record ) prato m do toca-disco, (P) giradiscos; (record-player) toca-disco m, (P) gira-discos m

**turpentine** /'tɜ:pəntaɪn/ n terebenti-na f, aguarrás m

**turquoise** /'tɜ:kwɔɪz/ a turquesa in-var

**turret** /'tʌrɪt/ n torreão m, torrinha f

**turtle** /'tɜ:tl/ n tartaruga-do-mar f. ~-neck a de gola alta

**tusk** /tʌsk/ n (tooth) presa f; (ele-phant's) defesa f, dente m

**tussle** /'tʌsl/ n luta f, briga f

**tutor** /'tju:tə(r)/ n professor m parti-cular; (univ) professor m universitá-rio

**tutorial** /tju:'tɔ:rɪəl/ n (univ) semi-nário m

**TV** /ti:'vi:/ n tevê f

**twaddle** /'twɒdl/ n disparates mpl

**twang** /twæŋ/ n (mus) som m duma corda esticada; (in voice) nasalação f □ vt/i (mus) (fazer) vibrar, dedilhar

**tweet** /twi:t/ n pio m, pipilo m □ vi pipilar

**tweezers** /'twi:zəz/ npl pinça f

**twel|ve** /twelv/ a & n doze (m). ~ (o'clock) doze horas. ~fth a & n dé-cimo segundo (m). T~fth Night véspera f de Reis

**twent|y** /'twentɪ/ a & n vinte (m). ~ieth a & n vigésimo (m)

**twice** /twaɪs/ adv duas vezes

**twiddle** /'twɪdl/ vt/i ~ (with) ( fiddle with) torcer, brincar (com). ~ one's thumbs girar os polegares

**twig** /twɪg/ n galho m, graveto m

**twilight** /'twaɪlaɪt/ n crepúsculo m □ a crepuscular

**twin** /twɪn/ n & a gêmeo (m), (P) gê-meo (m) □ vt (pt twinned) (pair) em-parelhar, emparceirar. ~ beds par m de camas de solteiro. ~ning n empa-relhamento m

**twine** /twaɪn/ n guita f, cordel m □ vt/i (weave together) entrançar; (wind) enroscar(-se)

**twinge** /twɪndʒ/ n dor f aguda e sú-bita, pontada f; ( fig) pontada f, (P) ferroada f

**twinkle** /'twɪŋkl/ vi cintilar, brilhar □ n cintilação f, brilho m

**twirl** /twɜ:l/ vt/i (fazer) girar; (mous-tache) torcer

**twist** /twɪst/ vt torcer; (weave to-gether) entrançar; (roll) enrolar; (dis-tort) torcer, deturpar □ vi (rope etc) torcer-se, enrolar-se; (road ) dar voltas or curvas, serpentear □ n (act of twist-ing) torcedura f, (P) torcedela f; (of rope) nó m; (of events) reviravolta f. ~ sb's arm ( fig) forçar alguém

**twit** /twɪt/ n (colloq) idiota mf

**twitch** /twɪtʃ/ vt/i contrair(-se) □ n (tic) tique m; ( jerk) puxão m

**two** /tu:/ a & n dois (m). in or of ~ minds indeciso. put ~ and ~ to-gether tirar conclusões. ~-faced a de duas caras, hipócrita. ~-piece n (garment) duas-peças m invar. ~-seater n (car) carro m de dois lugares. ~-way a (of road ) mão dupla

**twosome** /'tu:səm/ n par m

**tycoon** /taɪ'ku:n/ n magnata m

**tying** /'taɪŋ/ see **tie**

**type** /taɪp/ n (example, print) tipo m; (kind ) tipo m, gênero m, (P) género m; (colloq: person) cara m, (P) tipo m (colloq) □ vt/i (write) bater à máquina, datilografar, (P) dactilografar

**typescript** /'taɪpskrɪpt/ n texto m da-tilografado, (P) dactilografado

**typewrit|er** /'taɪpraɪtə(r)/ n máquina f de escrever. ~ten /-ɪtn/ a batido à máquina, datilografado, (P) dactilo-grafado

**typhoid** /'taɪfɔɪd/ n ~ (fever) febre f tifóide

**typhoon** /taɪ'fu:n/ n tufão m

**typical** /'tɪpɪkl/ a típico. ~ly adv tipi-camente

**typify** /'tɪpɪfaɪ/ vt ser o (protó)tipo de, tipificar

**typing** /'taɪpɪŋ/ n datilografia f, (P) dactilografia f

**typist** /'taɪpɪst/ n datilógrafo f, (P) dactilógrafa f

**tyrann|y** /'tɪrənɪ/ n tirania f. ~ical /tɪ'rænɪkl/ a tirânico

**tyrant** /'taɪərənt/ n tirano m

**tyre** /'taɪə(r)/ n pneu m

# U

**ubiquitous** /ju:'bɪkwɪtəs/ a ubíquo, onipresente

**udder** /'ʌdər/ n úbere m

**UFO** /'ju:fəʊ/ n OVNI m

**ugl|y** /'ʌglɪ/ a (-ier, -iest) feio. ~iness n feiúra f, (P) fealdade f

**UK** abbr see **United Kingdom**

**ulcer** /'ʌlsə(r)/ n úlcera f

**ulterior** /ʌl'tɪərɪə(r)/ a ulterior. ~ mo-tive razão f inconfessada, segundas intenções fpl

**ultimate** /'ʌltɪmət/ a último, derra-deiro; (definitive) definitivo; (max-imum) supremo; (basic) fundamen-tal. ~ly adv finalmente

**ultimatum** /ʌltɪ'meɪtəm/ n (pl -ums) ultimato m

**ultra-** /'ʌltrə/ pref ultra-, super-

**ultraviolet** /ʌltrə'vaɪələt/ a ultravio-leta

**umbilical** /ʌm'bɪlɪkl/ a ~ cord cor-dão m umbilical

**umbrage** /'ʌmbrɪdʒ/ n take ~ (at sth) ofender-se or melindrar-se (com alg coisa)

**umbrella** /ʌm'brelə/ n guardachuva m

**umpire** /'ʌmpaɪə(r)/ n (sport) árbitro m □ vt arbitrar

**umpteen** /'ʌmptiːn/ a (sl) sem conta, montes de (colloq). **for the ~th time** (sl) pela centésima or enésima vez

**UN** abbr (United Nations) ONU f

**un-** /ʌn/ pref não, pouco

**unable** /ʌn'eɪbl/ a **be ~ to do** ser incapaz de/não poder fazer

**unabridged** /ʌnə'brɪdʒd/ a (text) integral

**unacceptable** /ʌnək'septəbl/ a inaceitável, inadmissível

**unaccompanied** /ʌnə'kʌmpənɪd/ a só, desacompanhado

**unaccountable** /ʌnə'kaʊntəbl/ a (strange) inexplicável; (not responsible) que não tem que dar contas

**unaccustomed** /ʌnə'kʌstəmd/ a desacostumado. ~ **to** não acostumado or não habituado a

**unadulterated** /ʌnə'dʌltəreɪtɪd/ a (pure, sheer) puro

**unaided** /ʌn'eɪdɪd/ a sem ajuda, sozinho, por si só

**unanim|ous** /juː'nænɪməs/ a unânime. ~**ity** /-ə'nɪmətɪ/ n unanimidade f. ~**ously** adv unânimemente, por unanimidade

**unarmed** /ʌn'ɑːmd/ a desarmado, indefeso

**unashamed** /ʌnə'ʃeɪmd/ a desavergonhado, sem vergonha. ~**ly** /-ɪdlɪ/ adv sem vergonha

**unassuming** /ʌnə'sjuːmɪŋ/ a modesto, despretencioso

**unattached** /ʌnə'tætʃt/ a (person) livre

**unattainable** /ʌnə'teməbl/ a inacessível

**unattended** /ʌnə'tendɪd/ a (person) desacompanhado; (car, luggage) abandonado

**unattractive** /ʌnə'træktɪv/ a sem atrativos, (P) atractivos; (offer) de pouco interesse

**unauthorized** /ʌn'ɔːθəraɪzd/ a não-autorizado, sem autorização

**unavoidabl|e** /ʌnə'vɔɪdəbl/ a inevitável. ~**y** adv inevitavelmente

**unaware** /ʌnə'weə(r)/ a **be ~ of** desconhecer, ignorar, não ter consciência de. ~**s** /-eəz/ adv (unexpectedly) inesperadamente. **catch sb ~s** apanhar alguém desprevenido

**unbalanced** /ʌn'bælənst/ a (mind, person) desequilibrado

**unbearable** /ʌn'beərəbl/ a insuportável

**unbeat|able** /ʌn'biːtəbl/ a imbatível. ~**en** a não vencido, invicto; (unsurpassed) insuperado

**unbeknown(st)** /ʌnbɪ'nəʊn(st)/ a ~ **to** (colloq) sem o conhecimento de

**unbelievable** /ʌnbɪ'liːvəbl/ a inacreditável, incrível

**unbend** /ʌn'bend/ vi (pt unbent) (relax) descontrair. ~**ing** a inflexível

**unbiased** /ʌn'baɪəst/ a imparcial

**unblock** /ʌn'blɒk/ vt desbloquear, desobstruir; (pipe) desentupir

**unborn** /'ʌnbɔːn/ a por nascer; (future) vindouro, futuro

**unbounded** /ʌn'baʊndɪd/ a ilimitado

**unbreakable** /ʌn'breɪkəbl/ a inquebrável

**unbridled** /ʌn'braɪdld/ a desequilibrado, (P) desenfreado

**unbroken** /ʌn'brəʊkən/ a (intact) intato, (P) intacto, inteiro; (continuous) ininterrupto

**unburden** /ʌn'bɜːdn/ vpr ~ **o.s.** (open one's heart) desabafar (**to** com)

**unbutton** /ʌn'bʌtn/ vt desabotoar

**uncalled-for** /ʌn'kɔːldfɔː(r)/ a injustificável, gratuito

**uncanny** /ʌn'kænɪ/ a (-ier, -iest) estranho, misterioso

**unceasing** /ʌn'siːsɪŋ/ a incessante

**unceremonious** /ʌnserɪ'məʊnɪəs/ a sem cerimônia, (P) cerimónia, brusco

**uncertain** /ʌn'sɜːtn/ a incerto. **be ~ whether** não saber ao certo se, estar indeciso quanto a. ~**ty** n incerteza f

**unchang|ed** /ʌn'tʃeɪndʒd/ a inalterado, sem modificação. ~**ing** a inalterável, imutável

**uncivilized** /ʌn'sɪvɪlaɪzd/ a não civilizado, bárbaro

**uncle** /'ʌŋkl/ n tio m

**uncomfortable** /ʌn'kʌmfətəbl/ a (thing) desconfortável, incômodo, (P) incómodo; (unpleasant) desagradável. **feel** or **be ~** (uneasy) sentir-se or estar pouco à vontade

**uncommon** /ʌn'kɒmən/ a pouco vulgar, invulgar, fora do comum. ~**ly** adv invulgarmente, excepcionalmente

**uncompromising** /ʌn'kɒmprəmaɪzɪŋ/ a intransigente

**unconcerned** /ʌnkən'sɜːnd/ a (indifferent) indiferente (by a)

**unconditional** /ʌnkən'dɪʃənl/ a incondicional

**unconscious** /ʌn'kɒnʃəs/ a inconsciente (**of** de). ~**ly** adv inconscientemente. ~**ness** n inconsciência f

**unconventional** /ʌnkən'venʃənl/ a não convencional, fora do comum

**uncooperative** /ʌnkəʊ'ɒpərətɪv/ a

(*person*) pouco cooperativo, do contra (*colloq*)

**uncork** /ʌn'kɔːk/ *vt* desarolhar, tirar a rolha de

**uncouth** /ʌn'kuːθ/ *a* rude, grosseiro

**uncover** /ʌn'kʌvə(r)/ *vt* descobrir, revelar

**unctuous** /'ʌŋktʃʊəs/ *a* untuoso, gorduroso; (*fig*) melifluo

**undecided** /ʌndɪ'saɪdɪd/ *a* (*irresolute*) indeciso; (*not settled*) por decidir, pendente

**undeniable** /ʌndɪ'naɪəbl/ *a* inegável, incontestável

**under** /'ʌndə(r)/ *prep* debaixo de, sob; (*less than*) com menos de; (*according to*) conforme, segundo □ *adv* por baixo, debaixo. ~ **age** menor de idade. ~ **way** em preparo

**under-** /ʌndə(r)/ *pref* sub-

**undercarriage** /'ʌndəkærɪdʒ/ *n* (*aviat*) trem *m* de aterrissagem, (P) trem *m* de aterragem

**underclothes** /'ʌndəkləʊðz/ *npl see* **underwear**

**undercoat** /'ʌndəkəʊt/ *n* (*of paint*) primeira mão *f*, (P) primeira demão *f*

**undercover** /ʌndə'kʌvə(r)/ *a* (*agent, operation*) secreto

**undercurrent** /'ʌndəkʌrənt/ *n* corrente *f* subterrânea; (*fig*) filão *m* (*fig*), tendência *f* oculta

**undercut** /ʌndə'kʌt/ *vt* (*pt* undercut, *pres p* undercutting) (*comm*) vender a preços mais baixos que

**underdeveloped** /ʌndədɪ'veləpt/ *a* atrofiado; (*country*) subdesenvolvido

**underdog** /'ʌndədɒg/ *n* desprotegido *m*, o mais fraco (*colloq*)

**underdone** /'ʌndədʌn/ *a* (*of meat*) mal passado

**underestimate** /ʌndə'restɪmeɪt/ *vt* subestimar, não dar o devido valor a

**underfed** /ʌndə'fed/ *a* subalimentado, subnutrido

**underfoot** /ʌndə'fʊt/ *adv* debaixo dos pés; (*on the ground*) no chão

**undergo** /ʌndə'gəʊ/ *vt* (*pt* -went, *pp* -gone) (*be subjected to*) sofrer; (*treatment*) ser submetido a

**undergraduate** /ʌndə'grædʒʊət/ *n* estudante *mf* universitário

**underground**[1] /ʌndə'graʊnd/ *adv* debaixo da terra; (*fig: secretly*) clandestinamente

**underground**[2] /'ʌndəgraʊnd/ *a* subterrâneo; (*fig: secret*) clandestino □ *n* (*rail*) metro(politano) *m*

**undergrowth** /'ʌndəgrəʊθ/ *n* mato *m*

**underhand** /'ʌndəhænd/ *a* (*deceitful*) sonso, dissimulado

**under|lie** /ʌndə'laɪ/ *vt* (*pt* -lay, *pp* -lain, *pres p* -lying) estar por baixo de. ~**lying** *a* subjacente

**underline** /ʌndə'laɪn/ *vt* sublinhar

**undermine** /ʌndə'maɪn/ *vt* minar, solapar

**underneath** /ʌndə'niːθ/ *prep* sob, debaixo de, por baixo de □ *adv* abaixo, em baixo, por baixo

**underpaid** /ʌndə'peɪd/ *a* mal pago

**underpants** /'ʌndəpænts/ *npl* (*man's*) cuecas *fpl*

**underpass** /'ʌndəpɑːs/ *n* (*for cars, people*) passagem *f* inferior

**underprivileged** /ʌndə'prɪvɪlɪdʒd/ *a* desfavorecido

**underrate** /ʌndə'reɪt/ *vt* subestimar, depreciar

**underside** /'ʌndəsaɪd/ *n* lado *m* inferior, base *f*

**underskirt** /'ʌndəskɜːt/ *n* anágua *f*

**understand** /ʌndə'stænd/ *vt/i* (*pt* -stood) compreender, entender. ~**able** *a* compreensível. ~**ing** *a* compreensivo □ *n* compreensão *f*; (*agreement*) acordo *m*, entendimento *m*

**understatement** /'ʌndəsteɪtmənt/ *n* versão *f* atenuada da verdade, litotes *f*

**understudy** /'ʌndəstʌdɪ/ *n* substituto *m*

**undertak|e** /ʌndə'teɪk/ *vt* (*pt* -took, *pp* -taken) empreender; (*responsibility*) assumir. ~**e to** encarregar-se de. ~**ing** *n* (*task*) empreendimento *m*; (*promise*) compromisso *m*

**undertaker** /'ʌndəteɪkə(r)/ *n* agente *m* funerário, papa-defuntos *m* (*colloq*)

**undertone** /'ʌndətəʊn/ *n* **in an** ~ a meia voz

**undervalue** /ʌndə'væljuː/ *vt* avaliar por baixo, subestimar

**underwater** /ʌndə'wɔːtə(r)/ *a* submarino □ *adv* debaixo de água

**underwear** /'ʌndəweə(r)/ *n* roupa *f* interior or de baixo

**underweight** /'ʌndəweɪt/ *a* **be** ~ estar com o peso abaixo do normal, ter peso a menos

**underwent** /ʌndə'went/ *see* **undergo**

**underworld** /'ʌndəwɜːld/ *n* (*of crime*) submundo *m*, bas-fonds *mpl*

**underwriter** /'ʌndəraɪtə(r)/ *n* segurador *m*; (*marine*) underwriter *m*

**undeserved** /ʌndɪ'zɜːvd/ *a* imerecido, injusto

**undesirable** /ʌndɪ'zaɪərəbl/ *a* indesejável, inconveniente

**undies** /'ʌndɪz/ *npl* (*colloq*) roupa *f* de baixo or interior

**undignified** /ʌn'dɪgnɪfaɪd/ *a* pouco digno, sem dignidade

**undisputed** /ʌndɪ'spjuːtɪd/ *a* incontestado

**undo** /ʌn'duː/ *vt* (*pt* -did, *pp* -done /dʌn/) desfazer; (*knot*) desfazer, desatar; (*coat, button*) abrir. **leave** ~**ne**

não fazer, deixar por fazer. ~ing n desgraça f, ruína f

**undoubted** /ʌn'dautɪd/ a indubitável. ~ly adv indubitavelmente

**undress** /ʌn'dres/ vt/i despir(-se). get ~ed despir-se

**undu|e** /ʌn'dju:/ a excessivo, indevido. ~ly adv excessivamente, indevidamente

**undulate** /'ʌndjʊleɪt/ vi ondular

**undying** /ʌn'daɪɪŋ/ a eterno, perene

**unearth** /ʌn'ɜ:θ/ vt desenterrar; (fig) descobrir

**unearthly** /ʌn'ɜ:θlɪ/ a sobrenatural, misterioso. ~ hour (colloq) hora f absurda or inconveniente

**uneasy** /ʌn'i:zɪ/ a (ill at ease) pouco à vontade; (worried) preocupado

**uneconomic** /ʌni:kə'nɒmɪk/ a antieconômico. ~al a antieconômico

**uneducated** /ʌn'edʒʊkeɪtɪd/ a (person) inculto, sem instrução

**unemploy|ed** /ʌnɪm'plɔɪd/ a desempregado. ~ment n desemprego m. ~ment benefit auxílio-desemprego m

**unending** /ʌn'endɪŋ/ a interminável, sem fim

**unequal** /ʌn'i:kwəl/ a desigual. ~led a sem igual, inigualável

**unequivocal** /ʌnɪ'kwɪvəkl/ a inequívoco, claro

**uneven** /ʌn'i:vn/ a desigual, irregular

**unexpected** /ʌnɪk'spektɪd/ a inesperado. ~ly a inesperadamente

**unfair** /ʌn'feə(r)/ a injusto (to com). ~ness n injustiça f

**unfaithful** /ʌn'feɪθfl/ a infiel

**unfamiliar** /ʌnfə'mɪlɪə(r)/ a estranho, desconhecido. be ~ with desconhecer, não conhecer, não estar familiarizado com

**unfashionable** /ʌn'fæʃənəbl/ a fora de moda

**unfasten** /ʌn'fɑ:sn/ vt (knot) desatar, soltar; (button) abrir

**unfavourable** /ʌn'feɪvərəbl/ a desfavorável

**unfeeling** /ʌn'fi:lɪŋ/ a insensível

**unfinished** /ʌn'fɪnɪʃt/ a incompleto, inacabado

**unfit** /ʌn'fɪt/ a sem preparo físico, fora de forma; (unsuitable) impróprio (for para)

**unfold** /ʌn'fəʊld/ vt desdobrar; (expose) expor, revelar □ vi desenrolar-se

**unforeseen** /ʌnfɔ:'si:n/ a imprevisto, inesperado

**unforgettable** /ʌnfə'getəbl/ a inesquecível

**unforgivable** /ʌnfə'gɪvəbl/ a imperdoável, indesculpável

**unfortunate** /ʌn'fɔ:tʃənət/ a (unlucky) infeliz; (regrettable) lamen-

tável. it was very ~ that foi uma pena que ~ly adv infelizmente

**unfounded** /ʌn'faʊndɪd/ a (rumour etc) infundado, sem fundamento

**unfriendly** /ʌn'frendlɪ/ a pouco amável, antipático, frio

**unfurnished** /ʌn'fɜ:nɪʃt/ a sem mobília

**ungainly** /ʌn'geɪnlɪ/ a desajeitado, desgracioso

**ungodly** /ʌn'gɒdlɪ/ a ímpio. ~ hour (colloq) hora f absurda, às altas horas (colloq)

**ungrateful** /ʌn'greɪtfl/ a ingrato

**unhapp|y** /ʌn'hæpɪ/ a (-ier, -iest) infeliz, triste; (not pleased) descontente, pouco contente (with com). ~ily adv infelizmente. ~iness n infelicidade f, tristeza f

**unharmed** /ʌn'hɑ:md/ a incólume, são e salvo, ileso

**unhealthy** /ʌn'helθɪ/ a (-ier, -iest) (climate etc) doentio, insalubre; (person) adoentado, com pouca saúde

**unheard-of** /ʌn'hɜ:dɒv/ a inaudito, sem precedentes

**unhinge** /ʌn'hɪndʒ/ vt (person, mind) desequilibrar

**unholy** /ʌn'həʊlɪ/ a (-ier, -iest) (person, act etc) ímpio; (colloq: great) incrível, espantoso

**unhook** /ʌn'hʊk/ vt desenganchar; (dress) desapertar

**unhoped** /ʌn'həʊpt/ a ~ for inesperado

**unhurt** /ʌn'hɜ:t/ a ileso, incólume

**unicorn** /'ju:nɪkɔ:n/ n unicórnio m

**uniform** /'ju:nɪfɔ:m/ n uniforme m □ a uniforme, sempre igual. ~ity /'fɔ:mətɪ/ n uniformidade f. ~ly adv uniformemente

**unif|y** /'ju:nɪfaɪ/ vt unificar. ~ication /-'keɪʃn/ n unificação f

**unilateral** /ju:nɪ'lætrəl/ a unilateral

**unimaginable** /ʌnɪ'mædʒɪnəbl/ a inimaginável

**unimportant** /ʌnɪm'pɔ:tnt/ a sem importância, insignificante

**uninhabited** /ʌnɪn'hæbɪtɪd/ a desabitado

**unintentional** /ʌnɪn'tenʃənl/ a involuntário, não propositado

**uninterest|ed** /ʌn'ɪntrəstɪd/ a desinteressado (in em), indiferente (in a). ~ing a desinteressante, sem interesse

**union** /'ju:nɪən/ n união f; (trade union) sindicato m. ~ist n sindicalista mf; (pol) unionista mf. U~ Jack bandeira f britânica

**unique** /ju:'ni:k/ a único, sem igual

**unisex** /'ju:nɪseks/ a unisexo

**unison** /'ju:nɪsn/ n in ~ em uníssono

**unit** /'ju:nɪt/ n unidade f; (of furniture) peça f, unidade f, (P) módulo m

**unite** /ju:'naɪt/ vt/i unir(-se). **U~d Kingdom** n Reino m Unido. **U~d Nations (Organization)** n Organização f das Nações Unidas. **U~ States (of America)** Estados mpl Unidos (da América)

**unity** /'ju:nətɪ/ n unidade f; (fig: harmony) união f

**universal** /ju:nɪ'vɜ:sl/ a universal

**universe** /'ju:nɪvɜ:s/ n universo m

**university** /ju:nɪ'vɜ:sətɪ/ n universidade f □ a universitário; (student, teacher) universitário, da universidade

**unjust** /ʌn'dʒʌst/ a injusto

**unkempt** /ʌn'kempt/ a desmazelado, desleixado; (of hair) despenteado, desgrenhado

**unkind** /ʌn'kaɪnd/ a desagradável, duro. **~ly** adv mal

**unknowingly** /ʌn'nəʊɪŋlɪ/ adv sem saber, inconscientemente

**unknown** /ʌn'nəʊn/ a desconhecido □ n the **~** o desconhecido

**unleaded** /ʌn'ledɪd/ a sem chumbo

**unless** /ʌn'les/ conj a não ser que, a menos que, salvo se, se não

**unlike** /ʌn'laɪk/ a diferente □ prep ao contrário de

**unlikely** /ʌn'laɪklɪ/ a improvável

**unlimited** /ʌn'lɪmɪtɪd/ a ilimitado

**unload** /ʌn'ləʊd/ vt descarregar

**unlock** /ʌn'lɒk/ vt abrir (com chave)

**unluck|y** /ʌn'lʌkɪ/ a (-ier, -iest) infeliz, sem sorte; (number) que dá azar. **be ~y** ter pouca sorte. **~ily** adv infelizmente

**unmarried** /ʌn'mærɪd/ a solteiro, celibatário

**unmask** /ʌn'ma:sk/ vt desmascarar

**unmistakable** /ʌnmɪs'teɪkəbl/ a (voice etc) inconfundível; (clear) claro, inequívoco

**unmitigated** /ʌn'mɪtɪgeɪtɪd/ a (absolute) completo, absoluto

**unmoved** /ʌn'mu:vd/ a impassível; (indifferent) indiferente (by a), insensível (by a)

**unnatural** /ʌn'nætʃrəl/ a que não é natural; (wicked) desnaturado

**unnecessary** /ʌn'nesəserɪ/ a desnecessário; (superfluous) supérfluo, dispensável

**unnerve** /ʌn'nɜ:v/ vt desencorajar, desmoralizar, intimidar

**unnoticed** /ʌn'nəʊtɪst/ a **go ~** passar despercebido

**unobtrusive** /ʌnəb'tru:sɪv/ a discreto

**unofficial** /ʌnə'fɪʃl/ a oficioso, que não é oficial; (strike) ilegal, inautorizado

**unorthodox** /ʌn'ɔ:θədɒks/ a pouco ortodoxo, não ortodoxo

**unpack** /ʌn'pæk/ vt (suitcase etc) desfazer; (contents) desembalar, desempacotar □ vi desfazer a mala

**unpaid** /ʌn'peɪd/ a não remunerado; (bill) a pagar

**unpalatable** /ʌn'pælətəbl/ a (food, fact etc) desagradável, intragável

**unparalleled** /ʌn'pærəleld/ a sem paralelo, incomparável

**unpleasant** /ʌn'pleznt/ a desagradável (to com); (person) antipático

**unplug** /ʌn'plʌg/ vt (pt -plugged) (electr) desligar a tomada, (P) tirar a ficha da tomada

**unpopular** /ʌn'pɒpjʊlə(r)/ a impopular

**unprecedented** /ʌn'presɪdentɪd/ a sem precedentes, inaudito, nunca visto

**unpredictable** /ʌnprə'dɪktəbl/ a imprevisível

**unprepared** /ʌnprɪ'peəd/ a sem preparação, improvisado; (person) desprevenido

**unpretentious** /ʌnprɪ'tenʃəs/ a despretencioso, sem pretensões

**unprincipled** /ʌn'prɪnsəpld/ a sem princípios, sem escrúpulos

**unprofessional** /ʌnprə'feʃənl/ a (work) de amador; (conduct) sem consciência profissional

**unprofitable** /ʌn'prɒfɪtəbl/ a não lucrativo

**unqualified** /ʌn'kwɒlɪfaɪd/ a sem habilitações; (success etc) total, absoluto. **be ~ to** não estar habilitado para

**unquestionable** /ʌn'kwestʃənəbl/ a incontestável, indiscutível

**unravel** /ʌn'rævl/ vt (pt unravelled) desenredar, desemaranhar; (knitting) desmanchar

**unreal** /ʌn'rɪəl/ a irreal

**unreasonable** /ʌn'ri:znəbl/ a pouco razoável, disparatado; (excessive) excessivo

**unrecognizable** /ʌn'rekəgnaɪzəbl/ a irreconhecível

**unrelated** /ʌnrɪ'leɪtɪd/ a (facts) desconexo, sem relação (to com); (people) não aparentado (to com)

**unreliable** /ʌnrɪ'laɪəbl/ a que não é de confiança

**unremitting** /ʌnrɪ'mɪtɪŋ/ a incessante, infatigável

**unreservedly** /ʌnrɪ'zɜ:vɪdlɪ/ adv sem reservas

**unrest** /ʌn'rest/ n agitação f, distúrbios mpl

**unrivalled** /ʌn'raɪvld/ a sem igual, incomparável

**unroll** /ʌn'rəʊl/ vt desenrolar

**unruffled** /ʌn'rʌfld/ a calmo, tranqüilo, imperturbável

**unruly** /ʌn'ru:lɪ/ a indisciplinado, turbulento

**unsafe** /ʌnˈseɪf/ a (*dangerous*) que não é seguro, perigoso; (*person*) em perigo

**unsaid** /ʌnˈsed/ a **leave ~** não mencionar, não dizer, deixar algo por dizer

**unsatisfactory** /ʌnsætɪsˈfæktərɪ/ a insatisfatório, pouco satisfatório

**unsavoury** /ʌnˈseɪvərɪ/ a desagradável, repugnante

**unscathed** /ʌnˈskeɪðd/ a ileso, incólume

**unscrew** /ʌnˈskruː/ vt desenroscar, desparafusar

**unscrupulous** /ʌnˈskruːpjʊləs/ a sem escrúpulos, pouco escrupuloso, sem consciência

**unseemly** /ʌnˈsiːmlɪ/ a inconveniente, indecoroso, impróprio

**unsettle** /ʌnˈsetl/ vt perturbar, agitar. **~d** a perturbado; (*weather*) instável, variável; (*bill*) não saldado

**unshakeable** /ʌnˈʃeɪkəbl/ a (*person, belief etc*) inabalável

**unshaven** /ʌnˈʃeɪvn/ a com a barba por fazer, por barbear

**unsightly** /ʌnˈsaɪtlɪ/ a feio

**unskilled** /ʌnˈskɪld/ a inexperiente; (*work, worker*) não especializado; (*labour*) mão-de-obra f não especializada

**unsociable** /ʌnˈsəʊʃəbl/ a insociável, misantropo

**unsophisticated** /ʌnsəˈfɪstɪkeɪtɪd/ a insofisticado, simples

**unsound** /ʌnˈsaʊnd/ a pouco sólido. **of ~ mind** (*jur*) não estar em plena posse das suas faculdades mentais (*jur*)

**unspeakable** /ʌnˈspiːkəbl/ a indescritível; (*bad*) inqualificável

**unspecified** /ʌnˈspesɪfaɪd/ a não especificado, indeterminado

**unstable** /ʌnˈsteɪbl/ a instável

**unsteady** /ʌnˈstedɪ/ a (*step*) vacilante, incerto; (*ladder*) instável; (*hand*) pouco firme

**unstuck** /ʌnˈstʌk/ a (*not stuck*) descolado. **come ~** (*colloq: fail*) falhar

**unsuccessful** /ʌnsəkˈsesfl/ a (*candidate*) mal sucedido; (*attempt*) malogrado, fracassado. **be ~** não ter êxito. **~ly** adv em vão

**unsuit|able** /ʌnˈs(j)uːtəbl/ a impróprio, pouco apropriado, inadequado (**for** para). **~ed** a inadequado (**to** para)

**unsure** /ʌnˈʃʊə(r)/ a incerto

**unsuspecting** /ʌnsəˈspektɪŋ/ a sem desconfiar de nada, insuspeitado

**untangle** /ʌnˈtæŋgl/ vt desemaranhar, desenredar

**unthinkable** /ʌnˈθɪŋkəbl/ a impensável, inconcebível

**untid|y** /ʌnˈtaɪdɪ/ a (**-ier, -iest**) (*room, desk etc*) desarrumado; (*appearance*) desleixado, desmazelado; (*hair*) despenteado. **~ily** adv sem cuidado. **~iness** n desordem f; (*of appearance*) desmazelo m

**untie** /ʌnˈtaɪ/ vt (*knot, parcel*) desatar, desfazer; (*person*) desamarrar

**until** /ənˈtɪl/ prep até. **not ~** não antes de □ conj até que

**untimely** /ʌnˈtaɪmlɪ/ a inoportuno, intempestivo; (*death*) prematuro

**untold** /ʌnˈtəʊld/ a incalculável

**untoward** /ʌntəˈwɔːd/ a inconveniente, desagradável

**untrue** /ʌnˈtruː/ a falso

**unused¹** /ʌnˈjuːzd/ a (*new*) novo, por usar; (*not in use*) não utilizado

**unused²** /ʌnˈjuːst/ a **~ to** não habituado a, não acostumado a

**unusual** /ʌnˈjuːʒʊəl/ a insólito, fora do comum. **~ly** adv excepcionalmente

**unveil** /ʌnˈveɪl/ vt descobrir; (*statue, portrait etc*) desvelar

**unwanted** /ʌnˈwɒntɪd/ a (*useless*) que já não serve; (*child*) indesejado

**unwarranted** /ʌnˈwɒrəntɪd/ a injustificado

**unwelcome** /ʌnˈwelkəm/ a desagradável; (*guest*) indesejável

**unwell** /ʌnˈwel/ a indisposto

**unwieldy** /ʌnˈwiːldɪ/ a difícil de manejar, pouco jeitoso

**unwilling** /ʌnˈwɪlɪŋ/ a relutante (**to em**), pouco disposto (**to a**)

**unwind** /ʌnˈwaɪnd/ vt/i (*pt* **unwound** /ʌnˈwaʊnd/) desenrolar(-se); (*colloq: relax*) descontrair(-se)

**unwise** /ʌnˈwaɪz/ a imprudente, insensato

**unwittingly** /ʌnˈwɪtɪŋlɪ/ adv sem querer

**unworthy** /ʌnˈwɜːðɪ/ a indigno

**unwrap** /ʌnˈræp/ vt (*pt* **unwrapped**) desembrulhar, abrir, desfazer

**unwritten** /ʌnˈrɪtn/ a (*agreement*) verbal, tácito

**up** /ʌp/ adv (*to higher place*) cima, para cima, para o alto; (*in higher place*) em cima, no alto; (*out of bed*) acordado, de pé; (*up and dressed*) pronto; (*finished*) acabado; (*sun*) alto □ prep no cimo de, em cima de, no alto de. **~ the street/river/etc** pela rua/pelo rio/etc acima □ vt (*pt* **upped**) (*increase*) aumentar. **be ~ against** defrontar, enfrentar. **be ~ in** (*colloq*) saber. **be ~ to** (*do*) estar fazendo; (*plot*) estar tramando; (*task*) estar à altura de. **feel ~ to doing** (*able*) sentir-se capaz de fazer. **it is ~ to you** depende de você. **come** or **go ~** subir. **have ~s and downs** (*fig*) ter (os seus) altos e baixos. **walk ~ and down** andar dum lado para o outro *or* para a frente e para trás. **~-and-coming** *a* prometedor. **~-market** *a* requintado, fino

**upbringing** /'ʌpbrɪŋɪŋ/ *n* educação *f*

**update** /ʌp'deɪt/ *vt* atualizar, (*P*) actualizar

**upheaval** /ʌp'hi:vl/ *n* pandemônio *m*, (*P*) pandemónio *m*, revolução *f* ( *fig*); (*social, political*) convulsão *f*

**uphill** /'ʌphɪl/ *a* ladeira acima, ascendente; ( *fig: difficult*) árduo □ *adv* /ʌp'hɪl/ **go ~** subir

**uphold** /ʌp'həʊld/ *vt* (*pt* **upheld**) sustentar, manter, apoiar

**upholster** /ʌp'həʊlstə(r)/ *vt* estofar. **~y** *n* estofados *mpl*, (*P*) estofo(s) *m* (*pl*)

**upkeep** /'ʌpki:p/ *n* manutenção *f*

**upon** /ə'pɒn/ *prep* sobre

**upper** /'ʌpə(r)/ *a* superior □ *n* (*of shoe*) gáspea *f*. **have the ~ hand** estar por cima, estar em posição de superioridade. **~ class** aristocracia *f*. **~most** *a* (*highest*) o mais alto, superior

**upright** /'ʌpraɪt/ *a* vertical; (*honourable*) honesto, honrado, (*P*) recto

**uprising** /'ʌpraɪzɪŋ/ *n* insurreição *f*, sublevação *f*, levantamento *m*

**uproar** /'ʌprɔ:(r)/ *n* tumulto *m*, alvoroço *m*

**uproot** /ʌp'ru:t/ *vt* desenraizar; ( *fig*) erradicar, desarraigar

**upset**[1] /ʌp'set/ *vt* (*pt* **upset**, *pres p* **upsetting**) (*overturn*) entornar, virar; (*plan*) contrariar, transtornar; (*stomach*) desarranjar; (*person*) contrariar, transtornar, incomodar □ *a* aborrecido

**upset**[2] /'ʌpset/ *n* transtorno *m*; (*of stomach*) indisposição *f*; (*distress*) choque *m*

**upshot** /'ʌpʃɒt/ *n* resultado *m*

**upside-down** /ʌpsaɪd'daʊn/ *adv* (*lit & fig*) ao contrário, de pernas para o ar

**upstairs** /ʌp'steəz/ *adv* (*at/to*) em/para cima, no/para o andar de cima □ *a* /'ʌpsteəz/ ( *flat etc*) de cima, do andar de cima

**upstart** /'ʌpsta:t/ *n* arrivista *mf*

**upstream** /ʌp'stri:m/ *adv* rio acima, contra a corrente

**upsurge** /'ʌpsɜ:dʒ/ *n* recrudescência *f*, recrudescimento *m*; (*of anger*) acesso *m*, ataque *m*

**uptake** /'ʌpteɪk/ *n* **be quick on the ~** pegar rapidamente as coisas; ( *fig*) ser de compreensão rápida, ser vivo

**up-to-date** /'ʌptədeɪt/ *a* moderno, atualizado, (*P*) actualizado

**upturn** /'ʌptɜ:n/ *n* melhoria *f*

**upward** /'ʌpwəd/ *a* ascendente, voltado para cima. **~s** *adv* para cima

**uranium** /jʊ'reɪnɪəm/ *n* urânio *m*

**urban** /'ɜ:bən/ *a* urbano

**urbane** /ɜ:'beɪn/ *a* delicado, cortês, urbano

**urge** /ɜ:dʒ/ *vt* aconselhar vivamente (**to** a) □ *n* (*strong desire*) grande vontade *f*. **~ on** (*impel*) incitar

**urgen|t** /'ɜ:dʒənt/ *a* urgente. **be ~t** urgir. **~cy** *n* urgência *f*

**urinal** /jʊə'raɪnl/ *n* urinol *m*

**urin|e** /'jʊərm/ *n* urina *f*. **~ate** *vi* urinar

**urn** /ɜ:n/ *n* urna *f*; ( *for tea, coffee*) espécie *f* de samovar

**us** /ʌs/; *unstressed* /əs/ *pron* nos; (*after preps*) nós. **with ~** conosco. **he knows ~** ele nos conhece

**US** *abbr* United States

**USA** *abbr* United States of America

**usable** /'ju:zəbl/ *a* utilizável

**usage** /'ju:zɪdʒ/ *n* uso *m*

**use**[1] /ju:z/ *vt* usar, utilizar, servir-se de; (*exploit*) servir-se de; (*consume*) gastar, usar, consumir. **~ up** esgotar, consumir. **~r** /-ə(r)/ *n* usuário *m*, (*P*) utente *mf*. **~r-friendly** *a* fácil de usar

**use**[2] /ju:s/ *n* uso *m*, emprego *m*. **in ~** em uso. **it is no ~ shouting**/*etc* não serve de nada *or* não adianta gritar/*etc*. **make ~ of** servir-se de. **of ~** útil

**used**[1] /ju:zd/ *a* (*second-hand*) usado

**used**[2] /ju:st/ *pt* **he ~ to** ele costumava, ele tinha por costume *or* hábito □ *a* **~ to** acostumado a, habituado a

**use|ful** /'ju:sfl/ *a* útil. **~less** *a* inútil; (*person*) incompetente

**usher** /'ʌʃə(r)/ *n* vagalume *m*, (*P*) arrumador *m* □ *vt* **~ in** mandar entrar. **~ette** *n* vagalume *m*, (*P*) arrumadora *f*

**usual** /'ju:ʒʊəl/ *a* usual, habitual, normal. **as ~** como de costume, como habitualmente. **at the ~ time** na hora de costume, (*P*) à(s) hora(s) de costume. **~ly** *adv* habitualmente, normalmente

**USSR** *abbr* URSS

**usurp** /ju:'zɜ:p/ *vt* usurpar

**utensil** /ju:'tensl/ *n* utensílio *m*

**uterus** /'ju:tərəs/ *n* útero *m*

**utilitarian** /ju:tɪlɪ'teərɪən/ *a* utilitário

**utility** /ju:'tɪlətɪ/ *n* utilidade *f*. **(public) ~** serviço *m* público. **~ room** área *f* de serviço (para as máquinas de lavar a roupa e a louça)

**utilize** /'ju:tɪlaɪz/ *vt* utilizar

**utmost** /'ʌtməʊst/ *a* ( *furthest, most intense*) extremo. **the ~ care**/*etc* (*greatest*) o maior cuidado/*etc* □ *n* **do one's ~** fazer todo o possível

**utter**[1] /'ʌtə(r)/ *a* completo, absoluto. ~**ly** *adv* completamente

**utter**[2] /'ʌtə(r)/ *vt* proferir; (*sigh, shout*) dar. ~**ance** *n* expressão *f*

**U-turn** /'juːtɜːn/ *n* retorno *m*

# V

**vacan|t** /'veɪkənt/ *a* (*post, room, look*) vago; (*mind*) vazio; (*seat, space, time*) desocupado, livre. ~**cy** *n* (*post*) vaga *f*; (*room in hotel*) vago *m*

**vacate** /və'keɪt/ *vt* vagar, deixar vago

**vacation** /və'keɪʃn/ *n* férias *fpl*

**vaccinat|e** /'væksmeɪt/ *vt* vacinar. ~**ion** /-'neɪʃn/ *n* vacinação *f*

**vaccine** /'væksiːn/ *n* vacina *f*

**vacuum** /'vækjʊəm/ *n* (*pl* -**cuums** *or* -**cua**) vácuo *m*, vazio *m*. ~ **flask** garrafa *f* térmica, (*P*) termo(s) *m*. ~ **cleaner** aspirador *m* de pó

**vagina** /və'dʒaɪnə/ *n* vagina *f*

**vagrant** /'veɪgrənt/ *n* vadio *m*, vagabundo *m*

**vague** /veɪg/ *a* (-**er**, -**est**) vago; (*outline*) impreciso. **be** ~ **about** ser vago acerca de, não precisar. ~**ly** *adv* vagamente

**vain** /veɪn/ *a* (-**er**, -**est**) (*conceited*) vaidoso; (*useless*) vão, inútil; (*fruitless*) infrutífero. **in** ~ em vão. ~**ly** *adv* em vão

**valentine** /'væləntaɪn/ *n* (*card*) cartão *m* do dia de São Valentin

**valet** /'vælɪt, 'væleɪ/ *n* (*manservant*) criado *m* de quarto; (*of hotel*) camareiro *m* □ *vt* (*car*) lavar e limpar o interior

**valiant** /'væliənt/ *a* corajoso, valente

**valid** /'vælɪd/ *a* válido. ~**ity** /və'lɪdəti/ *n* validade *f*

**validate** /'vælɪdeɪt/ *vt* validar, confirmar, ratificar

**valley** /'væli/ *n* vale *m*

**valuable** /'væljʊəbl/ *a* (*object*) valioso, de valor; (*help, time etc*) precioso. ~**s** *npl* objetos *mpl*, (*P*) objectos *mpl* de valor

**valuation** /væljʊ'eɪʃn/ *n* avaliação *f*

**value** /'væljuː/ *n* valor *m* □ *vt* avaliar; (*cherish*) dar valor a. ~ **added tax** imposto *m* de valor adicional, (*P*) acrescentado. ~**r** /-ə(r)/ *n* avaliador *m*

**valve** /vælv/ *n* (*anat, techn, of car tyre*) válvula *f*; (*of bicycle tyre*) pipo *m*; (*of radio*) lâmpada *f*, válvula *f*

**vampire** /'væmpaɪə(r)/ *n* vampiro *m*

**van** /væn/ *n* (*large*) camião *m*; (*small*) camionete *f*, comercial *m*; (*milkman's, baker's etc*) camionete *f*; (*rail*) bagageiro *m*, (*P*) furgão *m*

**vandal** /'vændl/ *n* vândalo *m*. ~**ism** /-əlɪzəm/ *n* vandalismo *m*

**vandalize** /'vændəlaɪz/ *vt* destruir, estragar

**vanguard** /'vængaːd/ *n* vanguarda *f*

**vanilla** /və'nɪlə/ *n* baunilha *f*

**vanish** /'vænɪʃ/ *vi* desaparecer, sumir-se, desvanecer-se

**vanity** /'vænəti/ *n* vaidade *f*. ~ **case** bolsa *f* de maquilagem

**vantage-point** /'vaːntɪdʒpɔɪnt/ *n* (bom) ponto *m* de observação

**vapour** /'veɪpə(r)/ *n* vapor *m*; (*mist*) bruma *f*

**vari|able** /'veərɪəbl/ *a* variável. ~**ation** /-'eɪʃn/ *n* variação *f*. ~**ed** /-ɪd/ *a* variado

**variance** /'veərɪəns/ *n* **at** ~ em desacordo (**with** com)

**variant** /'veərɪənt/ *a* diverso, diferente □ *n* variante *f*

**varicose** /'værɪkəʊs/ *a* ~ **veins** varizes *fpl*

**variety** /və'raɪəti/ *n* variedade *f*; (*entertainment*) variedades *fpl*

**various** /'veərɪəs/ *a* vários, diversos, variados

**varnish** /'vaːnɪʃ/ *n* verniz *m* □ *vt* envernizar; (*nails*) pintar

**vary** /'veərɪ/ *vt/i* variar. ~**ing** *a* variado

**vase** /vaːz/ *n* vaso *m*, jarra *f*

**vast** /vaːst/ *a* vasto, imenso. ~**ly** *adv* imensamente, infinitamente. ~**ness** *n* vastidão *f*, imensidão *f*, imensidade *f*

**vat** /væt/ *n* tonel *m*, dorna *f*, cuba *f*

**VAT** /viːeɪ'tiː, væt/ *abbr* ICM *m*, (*P*) IVA *m*

**vault**[1] /vɔːlt/ *n* (*roof*) abóbada *f*; (*in bank*) casa-forte *f*; (*tomb*) cripta *f*; (*cellar*) adega *f*

**vault**[2] /vɔːlt/ *vt/i* saltar □ *n* salto *m*

**vaunt** /vɔːnt/ *vt/i* gabar(-se), ufanar(-se) (de), vangloriar(-se)

**VD** *abbr see* **venereal disease**

**VDU** *abbr see* **visual display unit**

**veal** /viːl/ *n* (*meat*) vitela *f*

**veer** /vɪə(r)/ *vi* virar, mudar de direcção, (*P*) direcção

**vegan** /'viːgən/ *a* & *n* vegetariano (*m*) estrito

**vegetable** /'vedʒɪtəbl/ *n* hortaliça *f*, legume *m* □ *a* vegetal

**vegetarian** /vedʒɪ'teərɪən/ *a* & *n* vegetariano (*m*)

**vegetate** /'vedʒɪteɪt/ *vi* vegetar

**vegetation** /vedʒɪ'teɪʃn/ *n* vegetação *f*

**vehement** /'viːəmənt/ *a* veemente. ~**ly** *adv* veementemente

**vehicle** /'viːɪkl/ *n* veículo *m*

**veil** /veɪl/ *n* véu *m* □ *vt* velar, cobrir com véu; (*fig*) esconder, disfarçar

**vein** /veɪn/ *n* (*in body; mood*) veia *f*; (*in rock*) veio *m*, filão *m*; (*of leaf*) nervura *f*

velocity /vɪˈlɒsətɪ/ n velocidade f
velvet /ˈvelvɪt/ n veludo m. ~y a ave-
ludado
vendetta /venˈdetə/ n vendeta f
vending-machine /ˈvendɪŋməʃiːn/ n
vendedora f automática, (P) máquina
f de distribuição
vendor /ˈvendə(r)/ n vendedor m.
street ~ vendedor m ambulante
veneer /vəˈnɪə(r)/ n folheado m; (fig)
fachada f, máscara f
venerable /ˈvenərəbl/ a venerável
venereal /vəˈnɪərɪəl/ a venéreo. ~
disease doença f venérea
venetian /vəˈniːʃn/ a ~ blinds persiana f
Venezuela /venɪzˈweɪlə/ n Venezuela
f. ~n a & n venezuelano (m)
vengeance /ˈvendʒəns/ n vingança.
with a ~ furiosamente, em excesso,
com mais força do que se pretende
venison /ˈvenɪzn/ n carne f de veado
venom /ˈvenəm/ n veneno m. ~ous
/ˈvenəməs/ a venenoso
vent¹ /vent/ n (in coat) abertura f
vent² /vent/ n (hole) orifício m, abertura f; (for air) respiradouro m ◻ vt.
(anger) descarregar (on para cima
de). give ~ to (fig) desabafar, dar
vazão a
ventilat|e /ˈventɪleɪt/ vt ventilar.
~ion /-ˈleɪʃn/ n ventilação f. ~or n
ventilador m
ventriloquist /venˈtrɪləkwɪst/ n ven-
tríloquo m
venture /ˈventʃə(r)/ n emprendimen-
to m arriscado, aventura f ◻ vt/i
arriscar(-se)
venue /ˈvenjuː/ n porto m de encontro
veranda /vəˈrændə/ n varanda f
verb /vɜːb/ n verbo m
verbal /ˈvɜːbl/ a verbal; (literal) literal
verbatim /vɜːˈbeɪtɪm/ adv literalmente, palavra por palavra
verbose /vɜːˈbəʊs/ a palavroso, prolixo
verdict /ˈvɜːdɪkt/ n veredicto m;
(opinion) opinião f
verge /vɜːdʒ/ n beira f, borda f ◻ vi —
on estar à beira de. on the ~ of
doing prestes a fazer
verify /ˈverɪfaɪ/ vt verificar
veritable /ˈverɪtəbl/ a autêntico, verdadeiro
vermicelli /vɜːmɪˈselɪ/ n aletria f
vermin /ˈvɜːmɪn/ n animais mpl noci-
vos; (lice, fleas etc) parasitas mpl
vermouth /ˈvɜːməθ/ n vermute m
vernacular /vəˈnækjʊlə(r)/ n vernáculo m; (dialect) dialeto m, (P) dialecto m
versatil|e /ˈvɜːsətaɪl/ a versátil; (tool)
que serve para vários fins. ~ity
/-ˈtɪlətɪ/ n versatilidade f

verse /vɜːs/ n (poetry) verso m, poesia
f; (stanza) estrofe f; (of Bible)
versículo m
versed /vɜːst/ a ~ in versado em, conhecedor de
version /ˈvɜːʃn/ n versão f
versus /ˈvɜːsəs/ prep contra
vertebra /ˈvɜːtɪbrə/ n (pl -brae /-briː/)
vértebra f
vertical /ˈvɜːtɪkl/ a vertical. ~ly adv
verticalmente
vertigo /ˈvɜːtɪgəʊ/ n vertigem f
verve /vɜːv/ n verve f, vivacidade f
very /ˈverɪ/ adv muito ◻ a (actual)
mesmo, próprio; (exact) preciso, exato, (P) exacto. the ~ day/etc o
próprio or o mesmo dia/etc. at the
~ end mesmo or precisamente no
fim. the ~ first/best/etc (emph) o
primeiro/melhor/etc de todos. ~
much muito. ~ well muito bem
vessel /ˈvesl/ n vaso m
vest¹ /vest/ n corpete m, (P) camisola f
interior; (Amer: waistcoat) colete m
vest² /vest/ vt conferir (in a). ~ed
interests interesses mpl
vestige /ˈvestɪdʒ/ n vestígio m
vestry /ˈvestrɪ/ n sacristia f
vet /vet/ n (colloq) veterinário m ◻ vt
(pt vetted) (candidate etc) examinar
atentamente, estudar
veteran /ˈvetərən/ n veterano m.
(war) ~ veterano m de guerra
veterinary /ˈvetərɪnərɪ/ a veterinário. ~ surgeon veterinário m
veto /ˈviːtəʊ/ n (pl -oes) veto m; (right)
direito m de veto ◻ vt vetar, opor o
veto a
vex /veks/ vt aborrecer, irritar,
contrariar. ~ed question questão
f muito debatida, assunto m controverso
via /ˈvaɪə/ prep por, via
viab|le /ˈvaɪəbl/ a viável. ~ility
/-ˈbɪlətɪ/ n viabilidade f
viaduct /ˈvaɪədʌkt/ n viaduto m
vibrant /ˈvaɪbrənt/ a vibrante
vibrat|e /vaɪˈbreɪt/ vt/i (fazer) vibrar.
~ion /-ʃn/ n vibração f
vicar /ˈvɪkə(r)/ n (Anglican) pastor m;
(Catholic) vigário m, pároco m. ~age
n presbitério m
vicarious /vɪˈkeərɪəs/ a vivido indiretamente, (P) indirectamente
vice¹ /vaɪs/ n (depravity) vício m
vice² /vaɪs/ n (techn) torno m
vice- /vaɪs/ pref vice-. ~chairman
vice-presidente m. ~chancellor n
vice-chanceler m; (univ) reitor m. ~
consul n vice-cônsul m. ~president
n vice-presidente mf
vice versa /ˈvaɪsɪˈvɜːsə/ adv vice-
versa
vicinity /vɪˈsmətɪ/ n vizinhança f,

cercania(s) *fpl*, arredores *mpl*. **in the ~ of** nos arredores de

**vicious** /'vɪʃəs/ *a* (*spiteful*) mau, maldoso; (*violent*) brutal, feroz. **~ circle** círculo *m* vicioso. **~ly** *adv* maldosamente; (*violently*) brutalmente, ferozmente

**victim** /'vɪktɪm/ *n* vítima *f*

**victimiz|e** /'vɪktɪmaɪz/ *vt* perseguir. **~ation** /-'zeɪʃn/ *n* perseguição *f*

**victor** /'vɪktə(r)/ *n* vencedor *m*

**victor|y** /'vɪktərɪ/ *n* vitória *f*. **~ious** /-'tɔːrɪəs/ *a* vitorioso

**video** /'vɪdɪəʊ/ *a* vídeo □ *n* (*pl* -os) (*colloq*) vídeo □ *vt* (*record*) gravar em vídeo. **~ cassette** vídeo-cassete *f*. **~ recorder** videocassete *m*

**vie** /vaɪ/ *vi* (*pres p* **vying**) rivalizar, competir (**with** com)

**view** /vjuː/ *n* vista *f* □ *vt* ver; (*examine*) examinar; (*consider*) considerar, ver; (*a house*) visitar, ver. **in my ~** a meu ver, na minha opinião. **in ~ of** em vista de. **on ~** em exposição, à mostra; (*open to the public*) aberto ao público. **with a ~ to** com a intenção de, com o fim de. **~er** *n* (*TV*) telespectador *m*; (*for slides*) visor *m*

**viewfinder** /'vjuːfaɪndə(r)/ *n* visor *m*

**viewpoint** /'vjuːpɔɪnt/ *n* ponto *m* de vista

**vigil** /'vɪdʒɪl/ *n* vigília *f*, (*over corpse*) velório *m*; (*relig*) vigília *f*

**vigilan|t** /'vɪdʒɪlənt/ *a* vigilante. **~ce** *n* vigilância *f*. **~te** /vɪdʒɪ'læntɪ/ *n* vigilante *m*

**vig|our** /'vɪgə(r)/ *n* vigor *m*. **~orous** /'vɪgərəs/ *a* vigoroso

**vile** /vaɪl/ *a* (*base*) infame, vil; (*colloq*: *bad*) horroroso, péssimo

**vilify** /'vɪlɪfaɪ/ *vt* difamar

**villa** /'vɪlə/ *n* vivenda *f*, vila *f*, (*country residence*) casa *f* de campo

**village** /'vɪlɪdʒ/ *n* aldeia *f*, povoado *m*. **~r** *n* aldeão *m*, aldeã *f*

**villain** /'vɪlən/ *n* patife *m*, mau-caráter *m*. **~y** *n* infâmia *f*, vilania *f*

**vindicat|e** /'vɪndɪkeɪt/ *vt* vindicar, justificar. **~ion** /-'keɪʃn/ *n* justificação *f*

**vindictive** /vɪn'dɪktɪv/ *a* vingativo

**vine** /vaɪn/ *n* (*plant*) vinha *f*

**vinegar** /'vɪnɪgə(r)/ *n* vinagre *m*

**vineyard** /'vɪnjəd/ *n* vinha *f*, vinhedo *m*

**vintage** /'vɪntɪdʒ/ *n* (*year*) ano *m* de colheita de qualidade excepcional □ *a* (*wine*) de colheita excepcional e de um determinado ano; (*car*) de museu (*colloq*), fabricado entre 1917 e 1930

**vinyl** /'vaɪnɪl/ *n* vinil *m*

**viola** /vɪ'əʊlə/ *n* (*mus*) viola *f*, violeta *f*

**violat|e** /'vaɪəleɪt/ *vt* violar. **~ion** /-'leɪʃn/ *n* violação *f*

**violen|t** /'vaɪələnt/ *a* violento. **~ce** *n* violência *f*. **~tly** *adv* violentamente, com violência

**violet** /'vaɪələt/ *n* (*bot*) violeta *f*; (*colour*) violeta *m* □ *a* violeta

**violin** /vaɪə'lɪn/ *n* violino *m*. **~ist** *n* violinista *mf*

**VIP** /viːaɪ'piː/ *abbr* (*very important person*) VIP *m*, personalidade *f* importante

**viper** /'vaɪpə(r)/ *n* víbora *f*

**virgin** /'vɜːdʒɪn/ *a* & *n* virgem (*f*); **~ity** /və'dʒɪnətɪ/ *n* virgindade *f*

**Virgo** /'vɜːgəʊ/ *n* (*astr*) Virgem *f*, (P) virgo *m*

**viril|e** /'vɪraɪl/ *a* viril, varonil. **~ity** /vɪ'rɪlətɪ/ *n* virilidade *f*

**virtual** /'vɜːtʃʊəl/ *a* que é na prática embora não em teoria, verdadeiro. **a ~ failure**/*etc* praticamente um fracasso/*etc*. **~ly** *adv* praticamente

**virtue** /'vɜːtʃuː/ *n* (*goodness, chastity*) virtude *f*; (*merit*) mérito *m*. **by** *or* **in ~ of** por *or* em virtude de

**virtuos|o** /vɜːtʃʊ'əʊsəʊ/ *n* (*pl* -si /-siː/) virtuoso *m*, virtuose *mf*. **~ity** /-'ɒsətɪ/ *n* virtuosidade *f*, virtuosismo *m*

**virtuous** /'vɜːtʃʊəs/ *a* virtuoso

**virulen|t** /'vɪrʊlənt/ *a* virulento. **~ce** /-ləns/ *n* virulência *f*

**virus** /'vaɪərəs/ *n* (*pl* -es) vírus *m*; (*colloq*: *disease*) virose *f*

**visa** /'viːzə/ *n* visto *m*

**viscount** /'vaɪkaʊnt/ *n* visconde *m*. **~ess** /-ɪs/ *n* viscondessa *f*

**viscous** /'vɪskəs/ *a* viscoso

**vise** /vaɪs/ *n* (*Amer*: *vice*) torno *m*

**visib|le** /'vɪzəbl/ *a* visível. **~ility** /-'bɪlətɪ/ *n* visibilidade *f*. **~ly** *adv* visivelmente

**vision** /'vɪʒn/ *n* (*dream, insight*) visão *f*; (*seeing, sight*) vista *f*, visão *f*

**visionary** /'vɪʒənərɪ/ *a* visionário; (*plan, scheme etc*) fantasista, quimérico □ *n* visionário *m*

**visit** /'vɪzɪt/ *vt* (*pt* **visited**) (*person*) visitar, fazer uma visita a; (*place*) visitar □ *vi* estar de visita □ *n* (*tour, call*) visita *f*; (*stay*) estada *f*, visita *f*. **~or** *n* visitante *mf*; (*guest*) visita *f*

**visor** /'vaɪzə(r)/ *n* viseira *f*, (*in vehicle*) visor *m*

**vista** /'vɪstə/ *n* vista *f*, panorama *m*

**visual** /'vɪʒʊəl/ *a* visual. **~ display unit** terminal *m* de vídeo. **~ly** *adv* visualmente

**visualize** /'vɪʒʊəlaɪz/ *vt* visualizar; (*foresee*) imaginar, prever

**vital** /'vaɪtl/ *a* vital. **~ statistics** estatísticas *fpl* demográficas; (*colloq*: *woman*) medidas *fpl*

**vitality** /vaɪ'tælətɪ/ *n* vitalidade *f*

**vitamin** /'vɪtəmɪn/ *n* vitamina *f*

**vivac|ious** /vɪ'veɪʃəs/ *a* cheio de vida,

vivo, animado. ~ity /-'væsəti/ n vivacidade f, animação f

vivid /'vɪvɪd/ a vívido; (imagination) vivo. ~ly adv vividamente

vivisection /vɪvɪ'sekʃn/ n vivissecção f

vixen /'vɪksn/ n raposa f fêmea

vocabulary /və'kæbjʊləri/ n vocabulário m

vocal /'vəʊkl/ a vocal; (fig: person) eloqüente, (P) eloquente. ~ cords cordas fpl vocais. ~ist n vocalista mf

vocation /və'keɪʃn/ n vocação f; (trade) profissão f. ~al a vocacional, profissional

vociferous /və'sɪfərəs/ a vociferante

vodka /'vɒdkə/ n vodka m

vogue /vəʊg/ n voga f, moda f, popularidade f. in ~ em voga, na moda

voice /vɔɪs/ n voz f □ vt (express) exprimir

void /vɔɪd/ a vazio; (jur) nulo, sem validade □ n vácuo m, vazio m. make ~ anular, invalidar. ~ of sem, destituído de

volatile /'vɒlətaɪl/ a (substance) volátil; (fig: changeable) instável

volcan|o /vɒl'keməʊ/ n (pl -oes) vulcão m. ~ic /-ænɪk/ a vulcânico

volition /və'lɪʃn/ n of one's own ~ de sua própria vontade

volley /'vɒlɪ/ n (of blows etc) saraivada f, (of gunfire) salva f; (tennis) voleio m. ~ball n voleibol m, vôlei m

volt /vəʊlt/ n volt m. ~age n voltagem f

voluble /'vɒljʊbl/ a falante, loquaz

volume /'vɒlju:m/ n (book, sound) volume m; (capacity) capacidade f

voluntar|y /'vɒləntəri/ a voluntário; (unpaid) não-remunerado. ~ily /-trəli/ adv voluntariamente

volunteer /vɒlən'tɪə(r)/ n voluntário m □ vi oferecer-se (to do para fazer); (mil) alistar-se como voluntário □ vt oferecer espontaneamente

voluptuous /və'lʌptʃʊəs/ a voluptuoso, sensual

vomit /'vɒmɪt/ vt/i (pt vomited) vomitar □ n vômito m, (P) vómito m

voodoo /'vu:du:/ n vodu m

voraci|ous /və'reɪʃəs/ a voraz. ~ously adv vorazmente. ~ty /və-'ræsəti/ n voracidade f

vot|e /vəʊt/ n voto m; (right) direito m de voto □ vt/i votar. ~er n eleitor m. ~ing n votação f; (poll) escrutínio m

vouch /vaʊtʃ/ vi ~ for responder por, garantir

voucher /'vaʊtʃə(r)/ n (for meal, transport) vale m; (receipt) comprovante m

vow /vaʊ/ n voto m □ vt (loyalty etc) jurar (to a). ~ to do jurar fazer

vowel /'vaʊəl/ n vogal f

voyage /'vɔɪɪdʒ/ n viagem (por mar) f. ~r /-ə(r)/ n viajante m

vulgar /'vʌlgə(r)/ a ordinário, grosseiro; (in common use) vulgar. ~ity /-'gærəti/ n (behaviour) grosseria f, vulgaridade f

vulnerab|le /'vʌlnərəbl/ a vulnerável. ~ility /-'bɪləti/ n vulnerabilidade f

vulture /'vʌltʃə(r)/ n abutre m, urubu m

vying /'vaɪɪŋ/ see vie

# W

wad /wɒd/ n bucha f, tampão m; (bundle) maço m, rolo m

wadding /'wɒdɪŋ/ n enchimento m

waddle /'wɒdl/ vi bambolear-se, rebolar-se, gingar

wade /weɪd/ vi ~ through (fig) avançar a custo por; (mud, water) patinhar em

wafer /'weɪfə(r)/ n (biscuit) bolacha f de baunilha; (relig) hóstia f

waffle[1] /'wɒfl/ n (colloq: talk) lengalenga f, papo m, conversa f; (colloq: writing) □ vi (colloq) escrever muito sem dizer nada de importante

waffle[2] /'wɒfl/ n (culin) waffle m

waft /wɒft/ vi flutuar □ vt espalhar, levar suavemente

wag /wæg/ vt/i (pt wagged) abanar, agitar, sacudir

wage[1] /weɪdʒ/ vt (campaign, war) fazer

wage[2] /weɪdʒ/ n ~(s) (weekly, daily) salário m, ordenado m. ~-claim n pedido m de aumento de salário. ~-earner n trabalhador m assalariado. ~-freeze n congelamento m de salários

wager /'weɪdʒə(r)/ n (bet) aposta f □ vt apostar (that que)

waggle /'wægl/ vt/i abanar, agitar, sacudir

wagon /'wægən/ n (horse-drawn) carroça f; (rail) vagão m de mercadorias

waif /weɪf/ n criança f abandonada

wail /weɪl/ vi lamentar-se, gemer lamentosamente □ n lamentação f, gemido m lamentoso

waist /weɪst/ n cintura f. ~line n cintura f

waistcoat /'weɪskəʊt/ n colete m

wait /weɪt/ vt/i esperar □ n espera f. ~ on servir. ~ for esperar. lie in ~ (for) estar escondido à espera (de), armar uma emboscada (para). keep sb ~ing fazer alguém esperar. ~ing-list n lista *f* de espera. **~ing-room** *n* sala *f* de espera

**wait|er** /'weɪtə(r)/ *n* garçon *m*, (*P*) criado *m* (de mesa). **~ress** *n* garçonete *f*, (*P*) criada *f* (de mesa)

**waive** /weɪv/ *vt* renunciar a, desistir de

**wake**¹ /weɪk/ *vt/i* (*pt* **woke**, *pp* **woken**) **~ (up)** acordar, despertar □ *n* (*before burial*) velório *m*

**wake**² /weɪk/ *n* (*ship*) esteira (de espuma) *f*. **in the ~ of** (*following*) atrás de, em seguida a

**waken** /'weɪkən/ *vt/i* acordar, despertar

**Wales** /weɪlz/ *n* País *m* de Gales

**walk** /wɔːk/ *vi* andar, caminhar; (*not ride*) ir a pé; (*stroll*) passear □ *vt* (*streets*) andar por, percorrer; (*distance*) andar, fazer a pé, percorrer; (*dog*) levar para passear □ *n* (*stroll*) passeio *m*, volta *f*; (*excursion*) caminhada *f*; (*gait*) passo *m*, maneira *f* de andar; (*pace*) passo *m*; (*path*) caminho *m*. **it's a 5-minute ~** são 5 minutos a pé. **~ of life** meio *m*, condição *f* social. **~ out** (*go away*) sair; (*go on strike*) fazer greve. **~ out on** abandonar. **~-over** *n* vitória *f* fácil

**walker** /'wɔːkə(r)/ *n* caminhante *mf*

**walkie-talkie** /wɔːkɪ'tɔːkɪ/ *n* walkie-talkie *m*

**walking** /'wɔːkɪŋ/ *n* andar (a pé) *m*, marcha (a pé) *f* □ *a* (*colloq: dictionary*) vivo. **~-stick** *n* bengala *f*

**Walkman** /'wɔːkmæn/ *n* walkman *m*

**wall** /wɔːl/ *n* parede *f*; (*around land*) muro *m*; (*of castle, town; fig*) muralha *f*; (*of stomach etc*) paredes *f* (*pl*) □ *vt* (*city*) fortificar; (*property*) murar. **go to the ~** sucumbir, falir; (*firm*) ir à falência. **up the ~** (*colloq*) fora de si

**wallet** /'wɒlɪt/ *n* carteira *f*

**wallflower** /'wɔːlflaʊə(r)/ *n* (*bot*) goivo *m*. **be a ~** (*fig*) tomar chá de cadeira, (*P*) levar banho de cadeira

**wallop** /'wɒləp/ *vt* (*pt* **walloped**) (*sl*) espancar (*colloq*) □ *n* (*sl*) pancada *f* forte

**wallow** /'wɒləʊ/ *vi* (*in mud*) chafurdar, atolar-se; (*fig*) regozijar-se

**wallpaper** /'wɔːlpeɪpə(r)/ *n* papel *m* de parede □ *vt* forrar com papel de parede

**walnut** /'wɔːlnʌt/ *n* (*nut*) noz *f*, (*tree*) nogueira *f*

**walrus** /'wɔːlrəs/ *n* morsa *f*

**waltz** /wɔːls/ *n* valsa *f* □ *vi* valsar

**wan** /wɒn/ *a* pálido

**wand** /wɒnd/ *n* (*magic*) varinha *f* mágica *or* de condão

**wander** /'wɒndə(r)/ *vi* andar ao acaso, vagar, errar; (*river*) serpentear; (*mind, speech*) divagar; (*stray*) extra-

viar-se. **~er** *n* vagabundo *m*, andarilho *m*. **~ing** *a* errante

**wane** /weɪn/ *vi* diminuir, minguar; (*decline*) declinar □ *n* **on the ~** em declínio; (*moon*) no quarto minguante

**wangle** /'wæŋgl/ *vt* (*colloq*) conseguir algo através de pistolão

**want** /wɒnt/ *vt* querer (**to do** fazer); (*need*) precisar (de); (*ask for*) exigir, requerer □ *vi* **~ for** ter falta de □ *n* (*need*) necessidade *f*, precisão *f*; (*desire*) desejo *m*; (*lack*) falta *f*, carência *f*. **for ~ of** por falta de. **I ~ you to go** eu quero que você vá. **~ed** *a* (*criminal*) procurado pela polícia; (*in ad*) precisa(m)-se

**wanting** /'wɒntɪŋ/ *a* falho, falto (**in** de). **be found ~** não estar à altura

**wanton** /'wɒntən/ *a* (*playful*) travesso, brincalhão; (*cruelty, destruction etc*) gratuito; (*woman*) despudorado

**war** /wɔː(r)/ *n* guerra *f*. **at ~** em guerra. **on the ~-path** em pé de guerra

**warble** /'wɔːbl/ *vt/i* gorjear

**ward** /wɔːd/ *n* (*in hospital*) enfermaria *f*; (*jur: minor*) pupilo *m*; (*pol*) círculo *m* eleitoral □ *vt* **~ off** (*a blow*) aparar; (*anger*) desviar; (*danger*) prevenir, evitar

**warden** /'wɔːdn/ *n* (*of institution*) diretor *m*, (*P*) director *m*; (*of park*) guarda *m*

**warder** /'wɔːdə(r)/ *n* guarda (de prisão) *m*, carcereiro *m*

**wardrobe** /'wɔːdrəʊb/ *n* (*place*) armário *m*, guarda-roupa *m*, (*P*) guarda-fato *m*, (*P*) roupeiro *m*; (*clothes*) guarda-roupa *m*

**warehouse** /'weəhaʊs/ *n* (*pl* **-s** /-haʊzɪz/) armazém *m*, depósito *m* de mercadorias

**wares** /weəz/ *npl* (*goods*) mercadorias *fpl*, artigos *mpl*

**warfare** /'wɔːfeə(r)/ *n* guerra *f*

**warhead** /'wɔːhed/ *n* ogiva (de combate) *f*

**warlike** /'wɔːlaɪk/ *a* marcial, guerreiro; (*bellicose*) belicoso

**warm** /wɔːm/ *a* (**-er, -est**) quente; (*hearty*) caloroso, cordial. **be or feel ~** estar com *or* ter *or* sentir calor □ *vt/i* **~ (up)** aquecer(-se). **~-hearted** *a* afetuoso, (*P*) afectuoso, com calor humano. **~ly** *adv* (*heartily*) calorosamente. **wrap up ~ly** agasalhar-se bem. **~n** calor *m*

**warn** /wɔːn/ *vt* avisar, prevenir. **~ sb off sth** (*advise against*) pôr alguém de prevenção *or* de pé atrás com alg coisa; (*forbid*) proibir alg coisa a alguém. **~n** aviso *m*. **~ing light** lâmpada *f* de advertência. **without ~ing** sem aviso, sem prevenir

**warp** /wɔːp/ vt/i (wood etc) empenar; (fig: pervert) torcer, deformar, desvirtuar. ~ed a (fig) deturpado, pervertido

**warrant** /'wɒrənt/ n autorização f; (for arrest) mandato (de captura) m; (comm) título m de crédito, warrant m □ vt justificar; (guarantee) garantir

**warranty** /'wɒrəntɪ/ n garantia f

**warring** /'wɔːrɪŋ/ a em guerra; (rival) contrário, antagónico, (P) antagónico

**warrior** /'wɒrɪə(r)/ n guerreiro m

**warship** /'wɔːʃɪp/ n navio m de guerra

**wart** /wɔːt/ n verruga f

**wartime** /'wɔːtaɪm/ n in ~ em tempo de guerra

**wary** /'weərɪ/ a (-ier, -iest) cauteloso, prudente

**was** /wɒz/; unstressed /wəz/ see be

**wash** /wɒʃ/ vt/i lavar(-se); (flow over) molhar, inundar □ n lavagem f; (dirty clothes) roupa f para lavar; (of ship) esteira f; (of paint) fina camada f de tinta. **have a** ~ lavar-se. ~-**basin** n pia f, (P) lavatório m. ~-**cloth** n (Amer: face-cloth) toalha f de rosto. ~ **one's hands of** lavar as mãos de. ~ **out** (cup etc) lavar; (stain) tirar lavando. ~-**out** n (sl) fiasco m. ~-**room** n (Amer) banheiro m, (P) casa f de banho. ~ **up** lavar a louça; (Amer: wash oneself) lavar-se. ~**able** a lavável. ~**ing** n (dirty) roupa f suja; (clean) roupa f lavada. ~**ing-machine** n máquina f de lavar roupa. ~**ing-powder** n detergente m em pó. ~**ing-up** n lavagem f da louça

**washed-out** /wɒʃt'aʊt/ a (faded) desbotado; (exhausted) exausto

**washer** /'wɒʃə(r)/ n (machine) máquina f de lavar roupa, louça f, (P) loiça f; (ring) anilha f

**wasp** /wɒsp/ n vespa f

**wastage** /'weɪstɪdʒ/ n desperdício m, perda f. **natural** ~ desgaste m natural

**waste** /weɪst/ vt desperdiçar, esbanjar; (time) perder □ vi ~ **away** consumir-se □ a (useless) inútil; (material) de refugo □ n desperdício m, perda f; (of time) perda f; (rubbish) lixo m. **lay** ~ assolar, devastar. ~ (**land**) (desolate) região f desolada, ermo m; (unused) (terreno) baldio m. ~-**disposal unit** triturador m de lixo. ~ **paper** papéis mpl velhos. ~-**paper basket** cesto m de papéis

**wasteful** /'weɪstfl/ a dispendioso; (person) esbanjador, gastador, perdulário

**watch** /wɒtʃ/ vt/i ver bem, olhar com atenção, observar; (game, TV) ver; (guard, spy on) vigiar; (be careful about) tomar cuidado com □ n vigia f, vigilância f; (naut) quarto m; (for telling time) relógio m. ~-**dog** n cão m de guarda. ~ **out** (look out) estar à espreita (for de); (take care) acautelar-se. ~-**strap** n correia f, pulseira f do relógio. ~-**tower** n torre f de observação. ~**ful** a atento, vigilante

**watchmaker** /'wɒtʃmeɪkə(r)/ n relojoeiro m

**watchman** /'wɒtʃmən/ n (pl -men) (of building) guarda m. (**night-**)~ guarda-noturno m

**watchword** /'wɒtʃwɜːd/ n lema m, divisa f

**water** /'wɔːtə(r)/ n água f □ vt regar □ vi (of eyes) lacrimejar, chorar. ~ **down** juntar água a, diluir; (milk, wine) aguar, batizar, (P) baptizar (colloq); (fig: tone down) suavizar. ~-**closet** n WC m, banheiro m, (P) lavabos mpl. ~-**colour** n aquarela f. ~-**ice** n sorvete m. ~-**lily** n nenúfar m. ~-**main** n cano m principal da rede. ~-**melon** n melancia f. ~-**pistol** n pistola f de água. ~ **polo** pólo m aquático. ~-**skiing** n esqui m aquático. ~-**wheel** n roda f hidráulica

**watercress** /'wɔːtəkres/ n agrião m

**waterfall** /'wɔːtəfɔːl/ n queda f de água, cascata f

**watering-can** /'wɔːtərɪŋkæn/ n regador m

**waterlogged** /'wɔːtəlɒgd/ a saturado de água; (land) empapado, alagado; (vessel) inundado, alagado

**watermark** /'wɔːtəmaːk/ n (in paper) marca-d'água f, filigrana f

**waterproof** /'wɔːtəpruːf/ a impermeável; (watch) à prova d'água

**watershed** /'wɔːtəʃed/ n (fig) momento m decisivo; (in affairs) ponto m crítico

**watertight** /'wɔːtətaɪt/ a à prova d'água, hermético; (fig: argument etc) inequívoco, irrefutável

**waterway** /'wɔːtəweɪ/ n via f navegável

**waterworks** /'wɔːtəwɜːks/ n (place) estação f hidráulica

**watery** /'wɔːtərɪ/ a (colour) pálido; (eyes) lacrimoso; (soup) aguado; (tea) fraco

**watt** /wɒt/ n watt m

**wav|e** /weɪv/ n onda f; (in hair; radio) onda f; (sign) aceno m □ vt acenar com; (sword) brandir; (hair etc) ondular □ vi acenar (com a mão); (hair etc) ondular; (flag) tremular. ~**eband** n faixa f de onda. ~**e goodbye** dizer adeus. ~**elength** n comprimento m de onda. ~**y** a ondulado

**waver** /'weɪvə(r)/ *vi* vacilar; (*hesitate*) hesitar

**wax**¹ /wæks/ *n* cera *f* □ *vt* encerar; (*car*) polir. **~en,** **~y** *adjs* de cera

**wax**² /wæks/ *vi* (*of moon*) aumentar, crescer

**waxwork** /'wækswɜːk/ *n* (*dummy*) figura *f* de cera. **~s** *npl* (*exhibition*) museu *m* de figuras de cera

**way** /weɪ/ *n* (*road, path*) caminho *m*, estrada *f*, rua *f* (**to** para); (*distance*) percurso *m*; (*direction*) (P) direção *f*; (*manner*) modo *m*, maneira *f*; (*means*) meios *mpl*; (*respect*) respeito *m*. **~s** (*habits*) costumes *mpl* □ *adv* (*colloq*) consideravelmente, de longe. **be in the ~** atrapalhar. **be on one's or the ~** estar a caminho. **by the ~** a propósito. **by ~ of** por, via, através. **get one's own ~** conseguir o que quer. **give ~** (*yield*) ceder; (*collapse*) desabar; (*auto*) dar a preferência. **in a ~** de certo modo. **make one's ~** ir. **that ~** dessa maneira. **this ~** desta maneira. **~ in** entrada *f*. **~ out** saída *f*. **~-out** *a* (*colloq*) excêntrico

**waylay** /weɪ'leɪ/ *vt* (*pt* **-laid**) (*assail*) armar uma cilada para; (*stop*) interceptar

**wayward** /'weɪwəd/ *a* (*wilful*) teimoso; (*perverse*) caprichoso, difícil

**WC** /dʌb(ə)ljuː'siː/ *n* WC *m*, banheiro *m*, (P) casa *f* de banho

**we** /wiː/ *pron* nós

**weak** /wiːk/ *a* (**-er, -est**) fraco; (*delicate*) frágil. **~en** *vt/i* enfraquecer; (*give way*) fraquejar. **~ly** *adv* fracamente. **~ness** *n* fraqueza *f*; (*fault*) ponto *m* fraco. **a ~ness for** (*liking*) um fraco por

**weakling** /'wiːklɪŋ/ *n* fraco *m*

**wealth** /welθ/ *n* riqueza *f*; (*riches, resources*) riquezas *fpl*; (*quantity*) abundância *f*

**wealthy** /'welθɪ/ *a* (**-ier, -iest**) rico

**wean** /wiːn/ *vt* (*baby*) desmamar; (*from habit etc*) desabituar

**weapon** /'wepən/ *n* arma *f*

**wear** /weə(r)/ *vt* (*pt* **wore**, *pp* **worn**) (*have on*) usar, trazer; (*put on*) pôr; (*expression*) ter; (*damage*) gastar. **~ black/red/etc** vestir-se de preto/vermelho/*etc* □ *vi* (*last*) durar; (*become old, damaged etc*) gastar-se □ *n* (*use*) uso *m*; (*deterioration*) gasto *m*, uso *m*; (*endurance*) resistência *f*; (*clothing*) roupa *f*. **~ and tear** desgaste *m*. **~ down** gastar; (*person*) extenuar. **~ off** passar. **~ on** (*time*) passar lentamente. **~ out** gastar; (*tire*) cansar, esgotar

**wear|y** /'wɪərɪ/ *a* (**-ier, -iest**) fatigado, cansado; (*tiring*) fatigante, cansativo □ *vi* **~y of** cansar-se de. **~ily** *adv* com

lassidão, cansadamente. **~iness** *n* fadiga *f*, cansaço *m*

**weasel** /'wiːzl/ *n* doninha *f*

**weather** /'weðə(r)/ *n* tempo *m* □ *a* meteorológico □ *vt* (*survive*) agüentar, (P) aguentar, resistir a. **under the ~** (*colloq: ill*) indisposto, achacado. **~beaten** *a* curtido pelo tempo. **~ forecast** *n* boletim *m* meteorológico. **~-vane** *n* cata-vento *m*

**weathercock** /'weðəkɒk/ *n* (*lit & fig*) cata-vento *m*

**weav|e**¹ /wiːv/ *vt* (*pt* **wove**, *pp* **woven**) (*cloth etc*) tecer; (*plot*) urdir, criar □ *n* (*style*) tipo *m* de tecido. **~er** /-ə(r)/ *n* tecelão *m*, tecelã *f*. **~ing** *n* tecelagem *f*

**weave**² /wiːv/ *vi* (*move*) serpear; (*through traffic, obstacles*) ziguezaguear

**web** /web/ *n* (*of spider*) teia *f*; (*fabric*) tecido *m*; (*on foot*) membrana *f* interdigital. **~bed** *a* (*foot*) palmado. **~bing** *n* (*in chair*) tira *f* de tecido forte. **~-footed** *a* palmípede

**wed** /wed/ *vt/i* (*pt* **wedded**) casar(-se)

**wedding** /'wedɪŋ/ *n* casamento *m*. **~-cake** *n* bolo *m* de noiva. **~-ring** *n* aliança (de casamento) *f*

**wedge** /wedʒ/ *n* calço *m*, cunha *f*; (*cake*) fatia *f*; (*of lemon*) quarto *m*; (*under wheel etc*) calço *m*, cunha *f* □ *vt* calçar; (*push*) meter or enfiar à força; (*pack in*) entalar

**Wednesday** /'wenzdɪ/ *n* quartafeira *f*

**weed** /wiːd/ *n* erva *f* daninha □ *vt/i* arrancar as ervas, capinar. **~-killer** *n* herbicida *m*. **~ out** suprimir, arrancar. **~y** *a* (*fig: person*) fraco

**week** /wiːk/ *n* semana *f*. **a ~ today/ tomorrow** de hoje/de amanhã a oito dias. **~ly** *a* semanal □ *a* & *n* (*periodical*) (jornal) semanário (*m*) □ *adv* semanalmente, todas as semanas

**weekday** /'wiːkdeɪ/ *n* dia *m* de semana

**weekend** /'wiːkend/ *n* fim-de-semana *m*

**weep** /wiːp/ *vt/i* (*pt* **wept**) chorar (**for sb** por alguém). **~ing willow** (salgueiro-)chorão *m*

**weigh** /weɪ/ *vt/i* pesar. **~ anchor** levantar âncora or ferro, zarpar. **~ down** (*weight*) sobrecarregar; (*bend*) envergar; (*fig*) acabrunhar. **~ up** (*colloq: examine*) pesar

**weight** /weɪt/ *n* peso *m*. **lose ~** emagrecer. **put on ~** engordar. **~less** *a* imponderável. **~-lifter** *n* halterofilista *m*. **~-lifting** *n* halterofilia *f*. **~y** *a* pesado; (*subject etc*) de peso; (*influential*) influente

**weighting** /'weɪtɪŋ/ *n* suplemento *m* salarial

**weir** /wɪə(r)/ *n* represa *f*, açude *m*

**weird** /wɪəd/ *a* (**-er, -est**) misterioso; (*strange*) estranho, bizarro

**welcom|e** /'welkəm/ *a* agradável; (*timely*) oportuno □ *int* (seja) benvindo! □ *n* acolhimento *m* □ *vt* acolher, receber; (*as greeting*) dar as boas vindas a. **be ~e** ser bem-vindo. **you're ~e!** (*after thank you*) não tem de quê!, de nada! **~e to do** livre para fazer. **~ing** *a* acolhedor

**weld** /weld/ *vt* soldar □ *n* solda *f*. **~er** *n* soldador *m*. **~ing** *n* soldagem *f*, soldadura *f*

**welfare** /'welfeə(r)/ *n* bem-estar *m*; (*aid*) assistência *f*, previdência *f* social. **W~ State** Estado-Providência *m*

**well**[1] /wel/ *n* (*for water, oil*) poço *m*; (*of stairs*) vão *m*; (*of lift*) poço *m*

**well**[2] /wel/ *adv* (**better, best**) bem □ *a* bem (*invar*) □ *int* bem! **as ~** também. **we may as ~ go** é melhor irnos andando. **as ~ as** tão bem como; (*in addition*) assim como. **be ~** (*healthy*) ir or passar bem. **do ~** (*succeed*) sairse bem, ser bem sucedido. **very ~** muito bem. **~ done!** bravo!, muito bem! **~-behaved** *a* bem comportado, educado. **~-being** *n* bem-estar *m*. **~-bred** *a* (bem) educado. **~-done** *a* (*of meat*) bem passado. **~-dressed** *a* bem vestido. **~-heeled** *a* (*colloq: wealthy*) rico. **~-informed** *a* versado, bem informado. **~-known** *a* (bem-) conhecido. **~-meaning** *a* bem intencionado. **~-off** *a* rico, próspero. **~-read** *a* instruído. **~-spoken** *a* bem-falante. **~-timed** *a* oportuno. **~-to-do** *a* rico. **~-wisher** *n* admirador *m*, simpatizante *mf*

**wellington** /'welɪŋtən/ *n* (*boot*) bota *f* alta de borracha

**Welsh** /welʃ/ *a* galês □ *n* (*lang*) galês *m*. **~man** *n* galês *m*. **~woman** *n* galesa *f*

**wend** /wend/ *vt* **~ one's way** dirigirse, seguir o seu caminho

**went** /went/ *see* **go**

**wept** /wept/ *see* **weep**

**were** /wɜ:(r)/; *unstressed* /wə(r)/ *see* **be**

**west** /west/ *n* oeste *m*. **the W~** (*pol*) o Oeste, o Ocidente □ *a* ocidental, do oeste □ *adv* ao oeste, para o oeste. **W~ Indian** *a* & *n* antilhano (*m*). **the W~ Indies** as Antilhas. **~erly** *a* ocidental, oeste. **~ward** *a* para o oeste. **~ward(s)** *adv* para o oeste

**western** /'westən/ *a* ocidental, do oeste; (*pol*) ocidental □ *n* (*film*) filme *m* de cowboys, bangue-bangue *m*

**westernize** /'westənaɪz/ *vt* ocidentalizar

**wet** /wet/ *a* (**wetter, wettest**) molhado; (*of weather*) chuvoso, de chuva; (*colloq: person*) fraco. **get ~** molharse □ *vt* (*pt* wetted) molhar. **~ blanket** (*colloq*) desmancha-prazeres *mf invar* (*colloq*). **~ paint** pintado de fresco. **~ suit** roupa *f* de mergulho

**whack** /wæk/ *vt* (*colloq*) bater em □ *n* (*colloq*) pancada *f*. **~ed** *a* (*colloq*) morto de cansaço, rebentado (*colloq*). **~ing** *a* (*sl*) enorme, de todo o tamanho

**whale** /weɪl/ *n* baleia *f*

**wharf** /wɔ:f/ *n* (*pl* wharfs) cais *m*

**what** /wɒt/ *a* (*interr; excl*) que. **~ time is it?** que horas são? **~ an idea!** que idéia! □ *pron* (*interr*) (o) quê, como, o que, qual, quais; (*object*) o que; (*after prep*) que; (*that which*) o que, aquilo que. **~?** (o) quê?, como? **~ is it?** o que é? **~ is your address?** qual é o seu endereço? **~ is your name?** como se chama? **~ can you see?** o que é que você pode ver? **this is ~ I write with** é com isto que escrevo. **that's ~ I need** é disso que eu preciso. **do ~ you want** faça o que or aquilo que quiser. **~ about me/him/etc?** e eu/ele/etc? **~ about doing sth?** e se fizéssemos alg coisa? **~ for?** para quê?

**whatever** /wɒt'evə(r)/ *a* **~ book/etc** qualquer livro/etc que seja □ *pron* (*no matter what*) qualquer que seja; (*anything that*) o que quer que, tudo o que. **nothing ~** absolutamente nada. **~ happens** aconteça o que acontecer. **do ~ you like** faça o que quiser

**whatsoever** /wɒtsəʊ'evə(r)/ *a* & *pron* = **whatever**

**wheat** /wi:t/ *n* trigo *m*

**wheedle** /'wi:dl/ *vt* convencer, persuadir, levar a

**wheel** /wi:l/ *n* roda *f* □ *vt* empurrar □ *vi* rodar, rolar. **at the ~** (*of vehicle*) ao volante; (*helm*) ao leme

**wheelbarrow** /'wi:lbærəʊ/ *n* carrinho *m* de mão

**wheelchair** /'wi:ltʃeə(r)/ *n* cadeira *f* de rodas

**wheeze** /wi:z/ *vi* respirar ruidosamente □ *n* respiração *f* difícil

**when** /wen/ *adv, conj* & *pron* quando. **the day/moment ~** o dia/momento em que

**whenever** /wen'evə(r)/ *conj* & *adv* (*at whatever time*) quando quer que, quando; (*every time that*) (de) cada vez que, sempre que

**where** /weə(r)/ *adv, conj* & *pron* onde, aonde; (*in which place*) em que, onde; (*whereas*) enquanto que, ao passo que. **~ is he going?** aonde é que ele vai? **~abouts** *adv* onde □ *n* paradeiro *m*.

**~by** *adv* pelo que. **~upon** *adv* após o que, depois do que

**whereas** /weər'æz/ *conj* enquanto que, ao passo que

**wherever** /weər'evə(r)/ *conj & adv* onde quer que. **~ can it be?** onde pode estar?

**whet** /wet/ *vt* (*pt* **whetted**) (*appetite, desire*) aguçar, despertar

**whether** /'weðə(r)/ *conj* se. **not know ~** não saber se. **~ I go or not** caso eu vá ou não

**which** /wɪtʃ/ *interr a & pron* qual, que **~ bag is yours?** qual das malas é a sua? **~ is your coat?** qual é o seu casaco? **do you know ~ he's taken?** sabe qual/quais é que ele levou? □ *rel pron* que, o qual; (*referring to whole sentence*) o que; (*after prep*) que, o qual, cujo. **at ~** em qual/que. **from ~** do qual/que. **of ~** do qual/de que. **to ~** para o qual/o que

**whichever** /wɪtʃ'evə(r)/ *a* **~ book/** *etc* qualquer livro/*etc* que seja, seja que livro/*etc* for. **take ~ book you wish** leve o livro que quiser □ *pron* qualquer, quaisquer

**whiff** /wɪf/ *n* (*of fresh air*) sopro *m*, lufada *f*; (*smell*) baforada *f*

**while** /waɪl/ *n* (espaço de) tempo *m*, momento *m*. **once in a ~** de vez em quando □ *conj* (*when*) enquanto; (*although*) embora; (*whereas*) enquanto que □ *vt* **~ away** (*time*) passar

**whim** /wɪm/ *n* capricho *m*

**whimper** /'wɪmpə(r)/ *vi* gemer; (*baby*) choramingar □ *n* gemido *m*; (*baby*) choro *m*

**whimsical** /'wɪmzɪkl/ *a* (*person*) caprichoso; (*odd*) bizarro

**whine** /waɪn/ *vi* lamuriar-se, queixar-se; (*dog*) ganir □ *n* lamúria *f*, queixume *m*; (*dog*) ganido *m*

**whip** /wɪp/ *n* chicote *m* □ *vt* (*pt* **whipped**) chicotear; (*culin*) bater □ *vi* (*move*) ir a toda a pressa. **~-round** *n* (*colloq*) coleta *f*, vaquinha *f*. **~ up** excitar; (*cause*) provocar; (*colloq: meal*) preparar rapidamente. **~ped cream** creme *m* chantilly

**whirl** /wɜːl/ *vt/i* (fazer) rodopiar, girar □ *n* rodopio *m*

**whirlpool** /'wɜːlpuːl/ *n* redemoinho *m*

**whirlwind** /'wɜːlwɪnd/ *n* redemoinho *m* de vento, turbilhão *m*

**whirr** /wɜː(r)/ *vi* zunir, zumbir

**whisk** /wɪsk/ *vt/i* (*snatch*) levar/tirar bruscamente; (*culin*) bater; (*flies*) sacudir □ *n* (*culin*) batedeira *f*. **~ away** (*brush away*) sacudir

**whisker** /'wɪskə(r)/ *n* fio *m* de barba. **~s** *npl* (*of animal*) bigode *m*; (*beard*) barba *f*; (*sideboards*) suíças *fpl*

**whisky** /'wɪskɪ/ *n* uísque *m*

**whisper** /'wɪspə(r)/ *vt/i* sussurrar, murmurar; (*of stream, leaves*) sussurrar □ *n* sussurro *m*, murmúrio *m*. **in a ~** baixinho, em voz baixa

**whist** /wɪst/ *n* uíste *m*, (P) whist *m*

**whistle** /'wɪsl/ *n* assobio *m*; (*instrument*) apito *m* □ *vt/i* assobiar; (*with instrument*) apitar

**Whit** /wɪt/ *a* **~ Sunday** domingo *m* de Pentecostes

**white** /waɪt/ *a* (-er, -est) branco, alvo; (*pale*) pálido □ *n* (*colour; of eyes; person*) branco *m*; (*of egg*) clara (de ovo) *f*. **go ~** (*turn pale*) empalidecer; (*of hair*) branquear, embranquecer. **~ coffee** café *m* com leite. **~-collar worker** empregado *m* de escritório. **~ elephant** (*fig*) trambolho *m*, elefante *m* branco. **~ lie** mentirinha *f*. **~ness** *n* brancura *f*, alvura *f*

**whiten** /'waɪtn/ *vt/i* branquear

**whitewash** /'waɪtwɒʃ/ *n* cal *f*; (*fig*) encobrimento *m* □ *vt* caiar; (*fig*) encobrir

**Whitsun** /'wɪtsn/ *n* Pentecostes *m*

**whittle** /'wɪtl/ *vt* **~ down** aparar, cortar aparas; (*fig*) reduzir gradualmente

**whiz** /wɪz/ *vi* (*pt* **whizzed**) (*through air*) zunir, sibilar; (*rush*) passar a toda a velocidade. **~-kid** *n* (*colloq*) prodígio *m*

**who** /huː/ *interr pron* quem □ *rel pron* que, o(a) qual, os(as) quais

**whoever** /huː'evə(r)/ *pron* (*no matter who*) quem quer que, seja quem for; (*the one who*) aquele que

**whole** /həʊl/ *a* inteiro, todo; (*not broken*) intacto. **the ~ house/***etc* toda a casa/*etc* □ *n* totalidade *f*; (*unit*) todo *m*. **as a ~** no conjunto, como um todo. **on the ~** de um modo geral. **~-hearted** *a* de todo o coração; (*person*) dedicado. **~-heartedly** *adv* sem reservas, sinceramente

**wholefood** /'həʊlfuːd/ *n* comida *f* integral

**wholemeal** /'həʊlmiːl/ *a* **~ bread** pão *m* integral

**wholesale** /'həʊlseɪl/ *n* venda *f* por grosso *or* por atacado □ *a* (*firm*) por grosso, por atacado; (*fig*) sistemático, em massa □ *adv* (*in large quantities*) por atacado; (*fig*) em massa, em grande escala. **~r** /-ə(r)/ *n* grossista *mf*, atacadista *mf*

**wholesome** /'həʊlsəm/ *a* sadio, saudável

**wholewheat** /'həʊlwiːt/ *a* = **wholemeal**

**wholly** /'həʊlɪ/ *adv* inteiramente, completamente

**whom** /huːm/ *interr pron* quem □ *rel*

*pron* (*that*) que; (*after prep*) quem, que, o qual

**whooping cough** /'hu:pɪŋkɒf/ *n* coqueluche *f*

**whore** /hɔ:(r)/ *n* prostituta *f*

**whose** /hu:z/ *rel pron* & *a* cujo, de quem □ *interr pron* de quem. ~ **hat is this?**, ~ **is this hat?** de quem é este chapéu? ~ **son are you?** de quem é que o senhor é filho?

**why** /waɪ/ *adv* porque, por que motivo, por que razão, porquê. **she doesn't know** ~ **he's here** ela não sabe porque *or* por que motivo ele estáaqui. **she doesn't know** ~ ela não sabe porquê. **do you know** ~? você sabe porquê? □ *int* (*protest*) ora, ora essa; (*discovery*) oh. ~ **yes/** *etc*

**wick** /wɪk/ *n* torcida *f*, mecha *f*, pavio *m*

**wicked** /'wɪkɪd/ *a* mau, malvado; (*mischievous, spiteful*) maldoso. ~**ly** *adv* maldosamente. ~**ness** *n* maldade *f*, malvadeza *f*

**wicker** /'wɪkə(r)/ *n* verga *f*, vime *m*. ~-**work** *n* trabalho *m* de verga *or* de vime

**wicket** /'wɪkɪt/ *n* (*cricket*) arco *m*

**wide** /waɪd/ *a* (-**er**, -**est**) largo; (*extensive*) vasto, grande, extenso. **two metres** ~ com dois metros de largura □ *adv* longe; (*fully*) completamente. **open** ~ (*door, window*) abrir(-se) de par em par, escancarar(-se); (*mouth*) abrir bem. ~ **awake** desperto, acordado. **far and** ~ por toda a parte. ~**ly** *adv* largamente; (*travel, spread*) muito; (*generally*) geralmente; (*extremely*) extremamente

**widen** /'waɪdn/ *vt/i* alargar(-se)

**widespread** /'waɪdspred/ *a* muito espalhado, difundido

**widow** /'wɪdəʊ/ *n* viúva *f*. ~**ed** *a* (*man*) viúvo; (*woman*) viúva. **be** ~**ed** enviuvar, ficar viúvo *or* viúva. ~**er** *n* viúvo *m*. ~**hood** *n* viuvez *f*

**width** /wɪdθ/ *n* largura *f*

**wield** /wi:ld/ *vt* (*axe etc*) manejar; (*fig: power*) exercer

**wife** /waɪf/ *n* (*pl* **wives**) mulher *f*, esposa *f*

**wig** /wɪg/ *n* cabeleira (postiça) *f*; (*judge's etc*) peruca *f*

**wiggle** /'wɪgl/ *vt/i* remexer(-se), retorcer(-se), mexer(-se) dum lado para outro

**wild** /waɪld/ *a* (-**er**, -**est**) selvagem; (*of plant*) silvestre; (*mad*) louco; (*enraged*) furioso, violento □ *adv* a esmo; (*without control*) à solta. ~**s** *npl* regiões *fpl* selvagens. ~-**goose chase** falsa pista *f*, tentativa *f* inútil. ~**ly**

*adv* violentamente; (*madly*) loucamente

**wildcat** /'waɪldkæt/ *a* ~ **strike** greve *f* ilegal

**wilderness** /'wɪldənɪs/ *n* deserto *m*

**wildlife** /'waɪldlaɪf/ *n* animais *mpl* selvagens

**wile** /waɪl/ *n* artimanha *f*; (*cunning*) astúcia *f*, manha *f*

**wilful** /'wɪlfl/ *a* (*person*) voluntarioso; (*act*) intencional, propositado

**will**[1] /wɪl/ *v aux* **you** ~ **sing/he** ~ **do/***etc* tu cantarás/ele fará/*etc*. (*1st person: future expressing will or intention*) **I** ~ **sing/we** ~ **do/***etc* eu cantarei/nós faremos/*etc*. ~ **you have a cup of coffee?** quer tomar um cafèzinho? ~ **you shut the door?** quer fazer o favor de fechar a porta?

**will**[2] /wɪl/ *n* (*document*) testamento *m*. **at** ~ à vontade, quando *or* como se quiser □ *vt* (*wish*) querer; (*bequeath*) deixar em testamento. ~-**power** *n* força *f* de vontade

**willing** /'wɪlɪŋ/ *a* pronto, de boa vontade. ~ **to** disposto a. ~**ly** *adv* (*with pleasure*) de boa vontade, de bom grado; (*not forced*) voluntariamente. ~**ness** *n* boa vontade *f*, disposição *f* (**to do** em fazer)

**willow** /'wɪləʊ/ *n* salgueiro *m*

**willy-nilly** /'wɪlɪ'nɪlɪ/ *adv* de bom ou de mau grado, quer queira ou não

**wilt** /wɪlt/ *vi* murchar, definhar

**wily** /'waɪlɪ/ *a* (-**ier**, -**iest**) manhoso, matreiro

**win** /wɪn/ *vt/i* (*pt* **won**, *pres p* **winning**) ganhar □ *n* vitória *f*. ~ **over** *vt* convencer, conquistar

**winc|e** /wɪns/ *vi* estremecer, contrair-se. **without** ~**ing** sem pestanejar

**winch** /wɪntʃ/ *n* guincho *m* □ *vt* içar com guincho

**wind**[1] /wɪnd/ *n* vento *m*; (*breath*) fôlego *m*; (*flatulence*) gases *mpl*. **get** ~ **of** (*fig*) ouvir rumor de. **put the** ~ **up** (*sl*) assustar. **in the** ~ no ar. ~ **instrument** (*mus*) instrumento *m* de sopro. ~-**swept** *a* varrido pelo vento

**wind**[2] /waɪnd/ *vt/i* (*pt* **wound**) enrolar(-se); (*wrap*) envolver, pôr em volta; (*of path, river*) serpentear. ~ (**up**) (*clock etc*) dar corda em. ~ **up** (*end*) terminar, acabar; (*fig: speech etc*) concluir; (*firm*) liquidar. **he'll** ~ **up in jail** (*colloq*) ele vai acabar na cadeia. ~**ing** *a* (*path*) sinuoso; (*staircase*) em caracol

**windfall** /'wɪndfɔ:l/ *n* fruta *f* caída; (*fig: money*) sorte *f* grande

**windmill** /'wɪndmɪl/ *n* moinho *m* de vento

**window** /'wɪndəʊ/ *n* janela *f*; (*of shop*) vitrine *f*, (*P*) montra *f*; (*counter*) guichê *m*, (*P*) guichet *m*. **~-box** *n* jardineira *f*, (*P*) floreira *f*. **~-cleaner** *n* limpador *m* de janelas. **~-dressing** *n* decoração *f* de vitrines; (*fig*) apresentação *f* cuidadosa. **~-ledge** *n* peitoril *m*. **~-pane** *n* vidro *m*, vidraça *f*. **go ~-shopping** ir ver vitrines. **~-sill** *n* peitoril *m*

**windpipe** /ˈwɪndpaɪp/ *n* traquéia *f*, (*P*) traqueia *f*

**windscreen** /ˈwɪndskriːn/ *n* pára-brisa *m*, (*P*) pára-brisas *m invar*. **~-wiper** /-waɪpə(r)/ *n* limpador *m* de pára-brisa

**windshield** /ˈwɪndʃiːld/ *n* (*Amer*) = **windscreen**

**windsurf|er** /ˈwɪndsɜːfə(r)/ *n* surfista *mf*. **~ing** *n* surfe *m*

**windy** /ˈwɪndɪ/ *a* (**-ier, -iest**) ventoso. **it is very ~** está ventando muito

**wine** /waɪn/ *n* vinho *m*. **~ bar** bar *m* para degustação de vinhos. **~-cellar** *n* adega *f*, cave *f*. **~-grower** *n* vinicultor *m*. **~-growing** *n* vinicultura *f*. **~-list** *n* lista *f* de vinhos. **~-tasting** *n* prova *f* or degustação *f* de vinhos. **~-waiter** garçon *m*

**wineglass** /ˈwaɪnɡlɑːs/ *n* copo *m* de vinho; (*with stem*) cálice *m*

**wing** /wɪŋ/ *n* asa *f*; (*mil*) flanco *m*; (*archit*) ala *f*; (*auto*) pára-lamas *m invar*, (*P*) guarda-lamas *m invar*. **~s** (*theat*) bastidores *mpl*. **under sb's ~** debaixo das asas de alguém. **~ed** *a* alado

**wink** /wɪŋk/ *vi* piscar o olho; (*light, star*) cintilar, piscar □ *n* piscadela *f*. **not sleep a ~** não pregar olho

**winner** /ˈwɪnə(r)/ *n* vencedor *m*

**winning** /ˈwɪnɪŋ/ *see* **win** □ *a* vencedor, vitorioso; (*number*) premiado; (*smile*) encantador, atraente. **~-post** *n* meta *f*, poste de chegada *f*. **~s** *npl* ganhos *mpl*

**wint|er** /ˈwɪntə(r)/ *n* inverno *m* □ *vi* hibernar. **~ry** *a* de inverno, invernoso; (*smile*) glacial

**wipe** /waɪp/ *vt* limpar; (*dry*) enxugar, limpar □ *n* limpadela *f*. **~ off** limpar. **~ out** (*destroy*) aniquilar, limpar (*colloq*); (*cancel*) cancelar. **~ up** enxugar

**wir|e** /ˈwaɪə(r)/ *n* arame *m*; (*colloq: telegram*) telegrama *m*. (**electric**) **~** fio elétrico *m*, (*P*) eléctrico □ *vt* (*a house*) montar a instalação elétrica em; (*colloq: telegraph*) telegrafar. **~e netting** rede *f* de arame. **~ing** *n* (*electr*) instalação *f* elétrica, (*P*) eléctrica

**wireless** /ˈwaɪəlɪs/ *n* rádio *f*; (*set*) rádio *m*

**wiry** /ˈwaɪərɪ/ *a* (**-ier, -iest**) magro e rijo

**wisdom** /ˈwɪzdəm/ *n* sagacidade *f*, sabedoria *f*; (*common sense*) bom senso

*m*, sensatez *f*. **~ tooth** dente *m* (do) sizo

**wise** /waɪz/ *a* (**-er, -est**) (*person*) sábio, avisado, sensato; (*look*) entendedor. **~guy** (*colloq*) sabichão *m* (*colloq*), sabetudo *m* (*colloq*). **none the ~r** sem entender nada. **~ly** *adv* sensatamente

**wisecrack** /ˈwaɪzkræk/ *n* (*colloq*) (boa) piada *f*

**wish** /wɪʃ/ *n* (*desire, aspiration*) desejo *m*, vontade *f*; (*request*) pedido *m*; (*greeting*) desejo *m*, voto *m*. **I have no ~ to go** não tenho nenhum desejo *or* nenhuma vontade de ir □ *vt* (*desire, bid*) desejar; (*want*) apetecer, ter vontade de, desejar (**to do** fazer) □ *vi* **~ for** desejar. **~ sb well** desejar felicidades a alguém. **I don't ~ to go** não me apetece ir, não tenho vontade de ir, não desejo ir. **I ~ he'd leave** eu gostaria que ele partisse. **with best ~es** (*formal: in letter*) com os melhores cumprimentos, com saudações cordiais; (*on greeting card*) com desejos *or* votos (**for de**)

**wishful** /ˈwɪʃfl/ *a* **~ thinking** sonhar acordado

**wishy-washy** /ˈwɪʃɪwɒʃɪ/ *a* sem expressão, fraco, inexpressivo

**wisp** /wɪsp/ *n* (*of hair*) pequena mecha *f*; (*of smoke*) fio *m*

**wistful** /ˈwɪstfl/ *a* melancólico, saudoso

**wit** /wɪt/ *n* inteligência *f*; (*humour*) presença *f* de espírito, humor *m*; (*person*) senso *m* de humor. **be at one's ~'s** *or* **~s' end** não saber o que fazer. **keep one's ~s about one** estar alerta. **live by one's ~s** ganhar a vida de maneira suspeita. **scared out of one's ~s** apavorado

**witch** /wɪtʃ/ *n* feiticeira *f*, bruxa *f*. **~craft** *n* feitiçaria *f*, bruxaria *f*, magia *f*

**with** /wɪð/ *prep* com; (*having*) de; (*because of*) de; (*at the house of*) em casa de. **the man ~ the beard** o homem de barbas. **fill/etc ~** encher/*etc* de. **laughing/shaking/***etc* **~** a rir/a tremer/*etc* de. **I'm not ~ you** (*colloq*) não estou compreendendo-o

**withdraw** /wɪðˈdrɔː/ *vt/i* (*pt* **withdrew**, *pp* **withdrawn**) retirar (-se); (*money*) tirar. **~al** *n* retirada *f*; (*med*) estado *m* de privação. **~n** *a* (*person*) retraído, fechado

**wither** /ˈwɪðə(r)/ *vt/i* murchar, secar. **~ed** *a* (*person*) mirrado. **~ing** *a* (*fig: scornful*) desdenhoso

**withhold** /wɪðˈhəʊld/ *vt* (*pt* **withheld**) negar, recusar; (*retain*) reter; (*conceal, not tell*) esconder (**from** de)

**within** /wɪˈðɪn/ *prep* & *adv* dentro (de), por dentro (de); (*in distances*) a menos de. ~ **a month** (*before*) dentro de um mês. ~ **sight** à vista

**without** /wɪ'ðaʊt/ *prep* sem. ~ **fail** sem falta. **go** ~ **saying** não ser preciso dizer

**withstand** /wɪð'stænd/ *vt* (*pt* **withstood**) resistir a, opor-se a

**witness** /'wɪtnɪs/ *n* testemunha *f*; (*evidence*) testemunho *m* □ *vt* testemunhar, presenciar; (*document*) assinar como testemunha. **bear** ~ **to** testemunhar, dar testemunho de. ~-**box** *n* banco *m* das testemunhas

**witticism** /'wɪtɪsɪzəm/ *n* dito *m* espirituoso

**witty** /'wɪtɪ/ *a* (-**ier**, -**iest**) espirituoso

**wives** /waɪvz/ *see* **wife**

**wizard** /'wɪzəd/ *n* feiticeiro *m*; (*fig: genius*) gênio *m*, (*P*) génio *m*

**wizened** /'wɪznd/ *a* encarquilhado

**wobbl**|**e** /'wɒbl/ *vi* (*of jelly, voice, hand*) tremer; (*stagger*) cambalear, vacilar; (*of table, chair*) balançar. ~**y** *a* (*trembling*) trêmulo; (*staggering*) cambaleante, vacilante; (*table, chair*) pouco firme

**woe** /wəʊ/ *n* dor *f*, infortúnio *m*

**woke, woken** /wəʊk, 'wəʊkən/ *see* **wake**[1]

**wolf** /wʊlf/ *n* (*pl* **wolves** /wʊlvz/) lobo *m* □ *vt* (*food*) devorar. **cry** ~ dar alarme falso. ~-**whistle** *n* assobio *m* de admiração

**woman** /'wʊmən/ *n* (*pl* **women**) mulher *f*. ~**hood** *n* as mulheres, o sexo feminino; (*maturity*) maturidade *f*. ~**ly** *a* feminino

**womb** /wuːm/ *n* seio *m*, ventre *m*; (*med*) útero *m*; (*fig*) seio *m*

**women** /'wɪmɪn/ *see* **woman**. ~'**s movement** movimento *m* feminista

**won** /wʌn/ *see* **win**

**wonder** /'wʌndə(r)/ *n* admiração *f*; (*thing*) maravilha *f* □ *vt* perguntar-se a si mesmo (**if so**) □ *vi* admirar-se (**at** de, com), ficar admirado, espantar-se (**at** com); (*reflect*) pensar (**about** em). **it is no** ~ não admira (**that** que)

**wonderful** /'wʌndəfl/ *a* maravilhoso. ~**ly** *adv* maravilhosamente. **it works** ~**ly** funciona às mil maravilhas

**won't** /wəʊnt/ = **will not**

**wood** /wʊd/ *n* madeira *f*, pau *m*; (*for burning*) lenha *f*. ~(**s**) *n* (*pl*) (*area*) bosque *m*, mata *f*, floresta *f*. ~**ed** *a* arborizado. ~**en** *a* de or em madeira, de pau; (*fig: stiff*) rígido; (*fig: inexpressive*) inexpressivo, de pau

**woodcut** /'wʊdkʌt/ *n* gravura *f* em madeira

**woodland** /'wʊdlənd/ *n* região *f* arborizada, bosque *m*, mata *f*

**woodlouse** /'wʊdlaʊs/ *n* (*pl* -**lice** /laɪs/) baratinha *f*, tatuzinho *m*

**woodpecker** /'wʊdpekə(r)/ *n* (*bird*) pica-pau *m*

**woodwind** /'wʊdwɪnd/ *n* (*mus*) instrumentos *mpl* de sopro de madeira

**woodwork** /'wʊdwɜːk/ *n* (*of building*) madeiramento *m*; (*carpentry*) carpintaria *f*

**woodworm** /'wʊdwɜːm/ *n* caruncho *m*

**woody** /'wʊdɪ/ *a* (*wooded*) arborizado; (*like wood*) lenhoso

**wool** /wʊl/ *n* lã *f*. ~**len** *a* de lã. ~**lens** *npl* roupas *fpl* de lã. ~**ly** *a* de lã; (*vague*) confuso □ *n* (*colloq: garment*) roupa *f* de lã

**word** /wɜːd/ *n* palavra *f*; (*news*) notícia(s) *f*(*pl*); (*promise*) palavra *f* □ *vt* exprimir, formular. **by** ~ **of mouth** de viva voz. **have a** ~ **with** dizer duas palavras a. **in other** ~**s** em outras palavras. ~-**perfect** *a* que sabe de cor seu papel, a lição etc. ~ **processor** processador *m* de textos. ~**ing** *n* termos *mpl*, redação *f*, (*P*) redacção *f*. ~**y** *a* prolixo

**wore** /wɔː(r)/ *see* **wear**

**work** /wɜːk/ *n* trabalho *m*; (*product, book etc*) obra *f*; (*building etc*) obras *fpl*. **at** ~ no trabalho. **out of** ~ desempregado. ~**s** *npl* (*techn*) mecanismo *m*; (*factory*) fábrica *f* □ *vt/i* (*of person*) trabalhar; (*techn*) (fazer) funcionar, (fazer) andar; (*of drug etc*) agir, fazer efeito; (*farm, mine*) explorar; (*land*) lavrar. ~ **sb** (*make work*) fazer alguém trabalhar. ~ **in** introduzir, inserir. ~ **loose** soltar-se. ~ **off** (*get rid of*) descarregar. ~ **out** *vt* (*solve*) resolver; (*calculate*) calcular; (*devise*) planejar □ *vi* (*succeed*) resultar; (*sport*) treinar-se. ~-**station** *n* estação *f* de trabalho. ~-**to-rule** *n* greve *f* de zelo. ~ **up** *vt* criar □ *vi* (*to climax*) ir num crescendo. ~**ed up** (*person*) enervado, transtornado, agitado

**workable** /'wɜːkəbl/ *a* viável, praticável

**workaholic** /wɜːkə'hɒlɪk/ *n* **be a** ~ (*colloq*) trabalhar como um possesso (*colloq*)

**worker** /'wɜːkə(r)/ *n* trabalhador *m*, trabalhadora *f*; (*factory*) operário *m*

**working** /'wɜːkɪŋ/ *a* (*day, clothes, hypothesis, lunch etc*) de trabalho. **the** ~ **class(es)** a classe operária, a(s) class(es) trabalhadora(s), o proletariado. ~-**class** *a* operário, trabalhador. ~-**mother** mãe *f* que trabalha. ~ **party** comissão *f* consultiva, de estudo etc. ~**s** *npl* mecanismo *m*. **in** ~ **order** em condições de funcionamento

**workman** /'wɜːkmən/ *n* (*pl* -**men**)

trabalhador *m*; ( *factory*) operário *m*.
~**ship** *n* trabalho *m*, execução *f*, mão-de-obra *f*; (*skill*) arte *f*, habilidade *f*

**workshop** /'wɜːkʃɒp/ *n* oficina *f*

**world** /wɜːld/ *n* mundo *m* □ *a* mundial. **a** ~ **of** muito(s), grande quantidade de, um mundo de. ~-**wide** *a* mundial, universal

**worldly** /'wɜːldlɪ/ *a* terreno; (*devoted to the affairs of life*) mundano. ~ **goods** *mpl* materiais. ~-**wise** *a* com experiência do mundo

**worm** /wɜːm/ *n* verme *m*; (*earthworm*) minhoca *f* □ *vt* ~ **one's way into** insinuar-se, introduzir-se, enfiar-se. ~-**eaten** *a* (*wood*) carunchoso; ( *fruit*) bichado, bichoso

**worn** /wɔːn/ *see* **wear** □ *a* usado. ~-**out** *a* (*thing*) completamente gasto; ( *person*) esgotado

**worr|y** /'wʌrɪ/ *vt/i* preocupar(-se) □ *n* preocupação *f*. **don't** ~**y** fique descansado, não se preocupe. ~**ied** *a* preocupado. ~**ying** *a* preocupante, inquietante

**worse** /wɜːs/ *a & adv* pior □ *n* pior *m*. **get** ~ piorar. **from bad to** ~ de mal a pior. ~ **luck** pouca sorte, pena

**worsen** /'wɜːsn/ *vt/i* piorar

**worship** /'wɜːʃɪp/ *n* (*reverence*) reverência *f*, veneração *f*; (*religious*) culto *m* □ *vt* (*pt* **worshipped**) adorar, venerar □ *vi* fazer as suas devoções, praticar o culto. ~**per** *n* (*in church*) fiel *m*. **Your/His W~** Vossa/Sua Excelência *f*

**worst** /wɜːst/ *a & n* (**the**) ~ (o/a) pior (*mf*) □ *adv* pior. **if the** ~ **comes to the** ~ se o pior acontecer, na pior das hipóteses. **do one's** ~ fazer todo o mal que se quiser. **get the** ~ **of it** ficar a perder. **the** ~ (**thing**) **that** o pior que

**worth** /wɜːθ/ *a* **be** ~ valer; (*deserving*) merecer □ *n* valor *m*, mérito *m*. **ten pounds** ~ **of** dez libras de. **it's** ~ **it, it's** ~ **while** vale a pena. **it's not** ~ **my while** não vale a pena. **it's** ~ **waiting**/*etc* vale a pena esperar/*etc*. **for all one's** ~ (*colloq*) dando tudo por tudo. ~**less** *a* sem valor

**worthwhile** /'wɜːθwaɪl/ *a* que vale a pena; (*cause*) louvável, meritório

**worthy** /'wɜːðɪ/ *a* (**-ier, -iest**) (*deserving*) digno, merecedor (**of** de); (*laudable*) meritório, louvável □ *n* ( *person*) pessoa *f* ilustre

**would** /wʊd/; *unstressed* /wəd/ *v aux* **he** ~ **do**/**you** ~ **sing**/*etc* (*conditional tense*) ele faria/você cantaria/*etc*. **he** ~ **have done** ele teria feito. **she** ~ **come every day** (*used to*) ela vinha *or* costumava vir aqui todos os dias. ~ **you please come here?** chegue aqui

por favor. ~ **you like some tea?** você quer um chazinho? **he** ~**n't go** (*refused to*) ele não queria ir. ~-**be author/doctor/***etc* aspirante a autor/médico/*etc*

**wound**[1] /wuːnd/ *n* ferida *f* □ *vt* ferir. **the** ~**ed** os feridos *mpl*

**wound**[2] /waʊnd/ *see* **wind**[2]

**wove, woven** /wəʊv, 'wəʊvn/ *see* **weave**

**wrangle** /'ræŋgl/ *vi* disputar, discutir, brigar □ *n* disputa *f*, discussão *f*, briga *f*

**wrap** /ræp/ *vt* (*pt* **wrapped**) ~ (**up**) embrulhar (**in** em); (*in cotton wool, mystery etc*) envolver (**in** em) □ *vi* ~ **up** (*dress warmly*) abrigar-se bem, agasalhar-se bem □ *n* xale *m*. ~**ped up in** (*engrossed*) absorto em, mergulhado em. ~**per** *n* (*of sweet*) papel *m*; (*of book*) capa *f* de papel. ~**ing** *n* embalagem *f*

**wrath** /rɒθ/ *n* ira *f*. ~**ful** *a* irado

**wreak** /riːk/ *vt* ~ **havoc** (*of storm etc*) fazer estragos

**wreath** /riːθ/ *n* (*pl* **-s** /-ðz/) (*of flowers, leaves*) coroa *f*, grinalda *f*

**wreck** /rek/ *n* (*sinking*) naufrágio *m*; (*ship*) navio *m* naufragado; restos *mpl* de navio; (*remains*) destroços *mpl*; (*vehicle*) veículo *m* destroçado □ *vt* destruir; (*ship*) fazer naufragar, afundar; (*fig: hope*) acabar. **be a nervous** ~ estar com os nervos arrasados. ~**age** *n* (*pieces*) destroços *mpl*

**wren** /ren/ *n* (*bird*) carriça *f*

**wrench** /rentʃ/ *vt* (*pull*) puxar; (*twist*) torcer; (*snatch*) arrancar (**from** a) □ *n* (*pull*) puxão *m*; (*of ankle, wrist*) torcedura *f*; (*tool*) chave *f* inglesa; ( *fig*) dor *f* de separação

**wrest** /rest/ *vt* arrancar (**from** a)

**wrestl|e** /'resl/ *vi* lutar, debater-se (**with** com *or* contra). ~**er** *n* lutador *m*. ~**ing** *n* luta *f*

**wretch** /retʃ/ *n* desgraçado *m*, miserável *mf*; (*rascal*) miserável *mf*

**wretched** /'retʃɪd/ *a* (*pitiful, poor*) miserável; (*bad*) horrível, desgraçado

**wriggle** /'rɪgl/ *vt/i* remexer(-se), contorcer-se

**wring** /rɪŋ/ *vt* (*pt* **wrung**) (*twist; clothes*) torcer. ~ **out of** (*obtain from*) arrancar a. ~**ing wet** encharcado; (*of person*) encharcado até os ossos

**wrinkle** /'rɪŋkl/ *n* (*on skin*) ruga *f*; (*crease*) prega *f* □ *vt/i* enrugar(-se)

**wrist** /rɪst/ *n* pulso *m*. ~-**watch** *n* relógio *m* de pulso

**writ** /rɪt/ *n* (*jur*) mandado *m* judicial

**write** /raɪt/ *vt/i* (*pt* **wrote**, *pp* **written**) escrever. ~ **back** responder. ~ **down** escrever, tomar nota de. ~ **off** (*debt*) dar por liquidado; (*vehicle*) des-

tinar à sucata. **~-off** *n* perda *f* total. **~ out** (*in full*) escrever por extenso. **~ up** (*from notes*) redigir. **~-up** *n* relato *m*; (*review*) crítica *f*
**writer** /'raɪtə(r)/ *n* escritor *m*, autor *m*
**writhe** /raɪð/ *vi* contorcer(-se)
**writing** /'raɪtɪŋ/ *n* escrita *f*. **~(s)** (*works*) escritos *mpl*, obras *fpl*. **in ~** por escrito. **~-paper** *n* papel *m* de carta
**written** /'rɪtn/ *see* **write**
**wrong** /rɒŋ/ *a* (*incorrect, mistaken*) mal, errado; (*unfair*) injusto; (*wicked*) mau; (*amiss*) que não está bem; (*mus: note*) falso; (*clock*) que não está certo □ *adv* mal □ *n* mal *m*; (*injustice*) injustiça *f* □ *vt* (*be unfair to*) ser injusto com; (*do a wrong to*) fazer mal a. **what's ~?** qual é o problema? **what's ~ with it?** (*amiss*) o que é que não vai bem?; (*morally*) que mal há nisso?, que mal tem? **he's in the ~** (*his fault*) ele não tem razão. **go ~** (*err*) desencaminhar-se; (*fail*) ir mal; (*vehicle*) quebrar. **~ly** *adv* mal; (*blame etc*) sem razão, injustamente
**wrongful** /'rɒŋfl/ *a* injusto, ilegal
**wrote** /rəʊt/ *see* **write**
**wrought** /rɔːt/ *a* **~ iron** ferro *m* forjado. **~-up** *a* excitado
**wrung** /rʌŋ/ *see* **wring**
**wry** /raɪ/ *a* (**wryer, wryest**) torto; (*smile*) forçado. **~ face** careta *f*

# X

**Xerox** /'zɪərɒks/ *n* fotocópia *f*, xerox *m* □ *vt* fotocopiar, xerocar, tirar um xerox de
**Xmas** /'krɪsməs/ *n* Christmas
**X-ray** /'eksreɪ/ *n* raio X *m*; (*photograph*) radiografia *f* □ *vt* radiografar. **have an ~** tirar uma radiografia
**xylophone** /'zaɪləfəʊn/ *n* xilofone *m*

# Y

**yacht** /jɒt/ *n* iate *m*. **~ing** *n* iatismo *m*, andar *m* de iate; (*racing*) regata *f* de iate
**yank** /jæŋk/ *vt* (*colloq*) puxar bruscamente □ *n* (*colloq*) puxão *m*
**Yank** /jæŋk/ *n* (*colloq*) ianque *mf*
**yap** /jæp/ *vi* (*pt* **yapped**) latir
**yard**[1] /jaːd/ *n* (*measure*) jarda *f* (= 0,9144 *m*). **~age** *n* medida *f* em jardas
**yard**[2] /jaːd/ *n* (*of house*) pátio *m*; (*Amer: garden*) jardim *m*; (*for storage*) depósito *m*
**yardstick** /'jaːdstɪk/ *n* jarda *f*; (*fig*) bitola *f*, craveira *f*

**yarn** /jaːn/ *n* (*thread*) fio *m*; (*colloq: tale*) longa história *f*
**yawn** /jɔːn/ *vi* bocejar; (*be wide open*) abrir-se, escancarar-se □ *n* bocejo *m*. **~ing** *a* escancarado
**year** /jɪə(r)/ *n* ano *m*. **school/tax ~** ano *m* escolar/fiscal. **be ten/** *etc* **~s old** ter dez/*etc* anos de idade. **~-book** *n* anuário *m*. **~ly** *a* anual □ *adv* anualmente
**yearn** /jɜːn/ *vi* **~ for, to** desejar, ansiar por, suspirar por. **~ing** *n* desejo *m*, anseio *m* (**for** de)
**yeast** /jiːst/ *n* levedura *f*
**yell** /jel/ *vt/i* gritar, berrar □ *n* grito *m*, berro *m*
**yellow** /'jeləʊ/ *a* amarelo; (*colloq: cowardly*) covarde, poltrão □ *n* amarelo *m*
**yelp** /jelp/ *n* (*of dog etc*) ganido *m* □ *vi* ganir
**yen** /jen/ *n* (*colloq: yearning*) grande vontade *f* (**for** de)
**yes** /jes/ *n & adv* sim (*m*). **~-man** *n* (*colloq*) lambe-botas *m invar*, puxa-saco *m*
**yesterday** /'jestədɪ/ *n & adv* ontem (*m*). **~ morning/afternoon/evening** ontem de manhã/à tarde/à noite. **the day before ~** anteontem. **~ week** há oito dias, há uma semana
**yet** /jet/ *adv* ainda; (*already*) já □ *conj* contudo, no entanto. **as ~** até agora, por enquanto. **his best book ~** o seu melhor livro até agora
**yew** /juː/ *n* teixo *m*
**Yiddish** /'jɪdɪʃ/ *n* ídiche *m*
**yield** /jiːld/ *vt* (*produce*) produzir, dar; (*profit*) render; (*surrender*) entregar □ *vi* (*give way*) ceder □ *n* produção *f*; (*comm*) rendimento *m*
**yoga** /'jəʊgə/ *n* ioga *f*
**yoghurt** /'jɒgət/ *n* iogurte *m*
**yoke** /jəʊk/ *n* jugo *m*, canga *f*; (*of garment*) pala *f* □ *vt* jungir; (*unite*) unir, ligar
**yokel** /'jəʊkl/ *n* caipira *m*, labrego *m*
**yolk** /jəʊk/ *n* gema (de ovo) *f*
**yonder** /'jɒndə(r)/ *adv* acolá, além
**you** /juː/ *pron* (*familiar*) tu, você (*pl* vocês); (*polite*) vós, o(s) senhor(es), a(s) senhora(s); (*object: familiar*) te, lhe (*pl* vocês); (*polite*) o(s), a(s), lhes, vós, o(s) senhor(es), a(s) senhora(s) (*after prep*) ti, si, você (*pl* vocês); (*polite*) vós, o senhor, a senhora (*pl* os senhores, as senhoras); (*indefinite*) se; (*after prep*) si, você. **with ~** (*familiar*) contigo, consigo, com você (*pl* com vocês); (*polite*) com o senhor/a senhora (*pl* convosco, com os senhores/as senhoras). **I know ~** (*familiar*) eu te conheço, eu o/a conheço (*pl* eu os/as conheço); (*polite*) eu vos conheço, conheço o

senhor/a senhora (*pl* conheço os se-
nhores/as senhoras). **~ can see the
sea** você pode ver o mar

**young** /jʌŋ/ *a* (-**er**, -**est**) jovem, novo,
moço □ *n* (*people*) jovens *mpl*, a juventude *f*, a mocidade *f*; (*of animals*) crias
*fpl*, filhotes *mpl*

**youngster** /'jʌŋstə(r)/ *n* jovem *mf*,
moço *m*, rapaz *m*

**your** /jɔ:(r)/ *a* (*familiar*) teu, tua, seu,
sua (*pl* teus, tuas, seus, suas); (*polite*)
vosso, vossa, do senhor, da senhora
(*pl* vossos, vossas, dos senhores, das
senhoras)

**yours** /jɔ:z/ *poss pron* (*familiar*) o
teu, a tua, o seu, a sua (*pl* os teus, as
tuas, os seus, as suas); (*polite*) o vosso, a vossa, o/a do senhor, o/a da
senhora (*pl* os vossos, as vossas;
os/as do(s) senhor(es), os/as da(s)
senhora(s)). **a book of** ~ um livro
seu. **~ sincerely/faithfully** atenciosamente, com os cumprimentos de

**yourself** /jɔ:'self/ (*pl* -**selves** /-'selvz/)
*pron* (*familiar*) tu mesmo/a, você
mesmo/a (*pl* vocês mesmos/as);
(*polite*) vós mesmo/a, o senhor mesmo, a senhora mesma (*pl* vós mes-
mos/as, os senhores mesmos, as
senhoras mesmas); (*reflexive: familiar*) te, a ti mesmo/a, se, a si mes-
mo/a (*pl* a vocês mesmos/as);
(*polite*) ao senhor mesmo, à senhora
mesma (*pl* aos senhores mesmos,
às senhoras mesmas); (*after prep*:
*familiar*) ti mesmo/a, si mesmo/a,
você mesmo/a (*pl* vocês mesmos/as);
(*after prep*: *polite*) vós mesmo/a, o
senhor mesmo, a senhora mesma
(*pl* vós mesmos/as, os senhores
mesmos, as senhoras mesmas). **with
~** (*familiar*) contigo mesmo/a, consigo mesmo/a, com você (*pl* com
vocês); (*polite*) convosco, com o senhor, com a senhora (*pl* com os senhores, com as senhoras). **by ~**
sozinho

**youth** /ju:θ/ *n* (*pl* -**s** /-ðz/) mocidade *f*,
juventude *f*; (*young man*) jovem *m*,
moço *m*. **~ club** centro *m* de jovens.

~ **hostel** albergue *m* da juventude.
~**ful** *a* juvenil, jovem

**yo-yo** /'jəʊjəʊ/ *n* (*pl* -**os**) ioiô *m*

**Yugoslav** /'ju:gəslɑ:v/ *a* & *n* iogoslavo
(*m*), (*P*) jugoslavo (*m*). ~**ia** /-'slɑ:və/
*n* Iogoslávia *f*, (*P*) Jugoslávia *f*

# Z

**zany** /'zeɪnɪ/ *a* (-**ier**, -**iest**) tolo, bobo

**zeal** /zi:l/ *n* zelo *m*

**zealous** /'zeləs/ *a* zeloso. ~**ly** *adv* ze-
losamente

**zebra** /'zebrə, 'zi:brə/ *n* zebra *f*. ~
**crossing** faixa *f* para pedestres, (*P*)
passagem *f* para peões

**zenith** /'zenɪθ/ *n* zênite *m*, (*P*) zénite
*m*, auge *m*

**zero** /'zɪərəʊ/ *n* (*pl* -**os**) zero *m*. ~
**hour** a hora H. **below ~** abaixo de
zero

**zest** /zest/ *n* (*gusto*) entusiasmo *m*;
(*fig: spice*) sabor *m* especial; (*lemon
or orange peel*) casca *f* de limão/la-
ranja ralada

**zigzag** /'zɪgzæg/ *n* ziguezague *m* □ *a* &
*adv* em ziguezague □ *vi* (*pt* **zig-
zagged**) ziguezaguear

**zinc** /zɪŋk/ *n* zinco *m*

**zip** /zɪp/ *n* (*vigour*) energia *f*, alma *f*.
~**(-fastener)** fecho *m* ecler □ *vt* (*pt*
**zipped**) fechar o fecho eclerde □ *vi* ir
a toda a velocidade. **Z~ code** (*Amer*)
CEP de endereçamento postal *m*, (*P*)
código *m* postal

**zipper** /'zɪpə(r)/ *n* = **zip(-fastener)**

**zodiac** /'zəʊdɪæk/ *n* zodíaco *m*

**zombie** /'zɒmbɪ/ *n* zumbi *m*; (*colloq*)
zumbi *m*, (*P*) autómato *m*

**zone** /zəʊn/ *n* zona *f*

**zoo** /zu:/ *n* jardim *m* zoológico

**zoolog|y** /zəʊ'ɒlədʒɪ/ *n* zoologia *f*.
~**ical** /-ə'lɒdʒɪkl/ *a* zoológico. ~**ist** *n*
zoólogo *m*

**zoom** /zu:m/ *vi* (*rush*) sair roando ~
**lens** zum *m*, zoom *m*. ~ **off** *or* **past**
passar zunindo

**zucchini** /zu:'ki:nɪ/ *n* (*pl invar*)
(*Amer*) courgette *f*

# Portuguese Verbs · Verbos portugueses

## Introduction
Portuguese verbs can be divided into three categories: regular verbs, those with spelling peculiarities determined by their sound and irregular verbs.

## Regular verbs
in **-ar** (*e.g.* **comprar**)
*Present*: compr|o, ~as, ~a, ~amos, ~ais, ~am
*Future*: comprar|ei, ~ás, ~á, ~emos, ~eis, ~ão
*Imperfect*: compr|ava, ~avas, ~ava, ~ávamos, ~áveis, ~avam
*Preterite*: compr|ei, ~aste, ~ou, ~amos (*P*:~ámos), ~astes, ~aram
*Pluperfect*: compr|ara, ~aras, ~ara, ~áramos, ~áreis, ~aram
*Present subjunctive*: compr|e, ~es, ~e, ~emos, ~eis, ~em
*Imperfect subjunctive*: compr|asse, ~asses, ~asse, ~ássemos, ~ásseis, ~assem
*Future subjunctive*: compr|ar, ~ares, ~ar, ~armos, ~ardes, ~arem
*Conditional*: comprar|ia, ~ias, ~ia, ~íamos, ~íeis, ~iam
*Personal infinitive*: comprar, ~es, ~, ~mos, ~des, ~em
*Present participle*: comprando
*Past participle*: comprado
*Imperative*: compra, comprai

in **~er** (*e.g.* **bater**)
*Present*: bat|o, ~es, ~e, ~emos, ~eis, ~em
*Future*: bater|ei, ~ás, ~á, ~emos, ~eis, ~ão
*Imperfect*: bat|ia, ~ias, ~ia, ~íamos, ~íeis, ~iam
*Preterite*: bat|i, ~este, ~eu, ~emos, ~estes, ~eram
*Pluperfect*: bat|era, ~eras, ~era, ~êramos, ~êreis, ~eram
*Present subjunctive*: bat|a, ~as, ~a, ~amos, ~ais, ~am
*Imperfect subjunctive*: bat|esse, ~esses, ~esse, ~êssemos, ~êsseis, ~essem
*Future subjunctive*: bat|er, ~eres, ~er, ~ermos, ~erdes, ~erem
*Conditional*: bater|ia, ~ias, ~ia, ~íamos, ~íeis, ~iam
*Personal infinitive*: bater, ~es, ~, ~mos, ~des, ~em
*Present participle*: batendo
*Past participle*: batido
*Imperative*: bate, batei

in **~ir** (*e.g.* **admitir**)
*Present*: admit|o, ~es, ~e, ~imos, ~is, ~em

*Future*: admitir|ei, ~ás, ~á, ~emos, ~eis, ~ão
*Imperfect*: admit|ia, ~ias, ~ia, ~íamos, ~íeis, ~iam
*Preterite*: admit|i, ~iste, ~iu, ~imos, ~istes, ~iram
*Pluperfect*: admit|ira, ~iras, ~ira, ~íramos, ~íreis, ~iram
*Present subjunctive*: admit|a, ~as, ~a, ~amos, ~ais, ~am
*Imperfect subjunctive*: admit|isse, ~isses, ~isse, ~íssemos, ~ísseis, ~issem
*Future subjunctive*: admit|ir, ~ires, ~ir, ~irmos, ~irdes, ~irem
*Conditional*: admitir|ia, ~ias, ~ia, ~íamos, ~íeis, ~iam
*Personal infinitive*: admitir, ~es, ~, ~mos, ~des, ~em
*Present participle*: admitindo
*Past participle*: admitido
*Imperative*: admite, admiti

Regular verbs with spelling changes:

**-ar** verbs:
in **-car** (*e.g.* **ficar**)
*Preterite*: fiquei, ficaste, ficou, ficamos (*P*: ficámos), ficais, ficam
*Present subjunctive*: fique, fiques, fique, fiquemos, fiqueis, fiquem

in **-çar** (*e.g.* **abraçar**)
*Preterite*: abracei, abraçaste, abraçou, abraçamos (*P*: abraçámos), abraçastes, abraçaram
*Present subjunctive*: abrace, abraces, abrace, abracemos, abraceis, abracem

in **-ear** (*e.g.* **passear**)
*Present*: passeio, passeias, passeia, passeamos, passeais, passeiam
*Present subjunctive*: passeie, passeies, passeie, passeemos, passeeis, passeiem
*Imperative*: passeia, passeai

in **-gar** (*e.g.* **apagar**)
*Preterite*: apaguei, apagaste, apagou, apagamos (*P*: apagámos), apagastes, apagaram
*Present subjunctive*: apague, apagues, apague, apaguemos, apagueis, apaguem

in **-oar** (*e.g.* **voar**)
*Present*: vôo (*P*: voo), voas, voa, voamos, voais, voam

**averiguar**
*Preterite*: averigüei (*P*: averiguei), averiguaste, averiguou, averiguamos (*P*: averiguámos), averiguastes, averiguaram
*Present subjunctive*: averigúe, averigúes, averigúe, averigüemos (*P*: averiguemos), averigüeis (*P*: averigueis), averigüem

**enxaguar**
*Present*: enxáguo, enxáguas, enxágua, enxaguamos, enxaguais, enxáguam
*Preterite*: enxagüei (*P*: enxaguei), enxaguaste, enxaguou, enxaguamos (*P*: enxaguámos), enxaguastes, enxaguaram
*Present subjunctive*: enxágüe, enxágües, enxágüe, enxagüemos, enxagüeis, enxágüem (*P*: enxágue, enxágues, enxágue, enxaguemos, enxagueis, enxáguem)
*Similarly*: aguar, desaguar

**saudar**
*Present*: saúdo, saúdas, saúda, saudamos, saudais, saúdam
*Present subjunctive*: saúde, saúdes, saúde, saudemos, saudeis, saúdem
*Imperative*: saúda, saudai

**-er verbs:**
**in -cer** (*e.g.* **tecer**)
*Present*: teço, teces, tece, tecemos, teceis, tecem
*Present subjunctive*: teça, teças, teça, teçamos, teçais, teçam

**in -ger** (*e.g.* **proteger**)
*Present*: protejo, proteges, protege, protegemos, protegeis, protegem
*Present subjunctive*: proteja, protejas, proteja, protejamos, protejais, protejam

**in -guer** (*e.g.* **erguer**)
*Present*: ergo, ergues, ergue, erguemos, ergueis, erguem
*Present subjunctive*: erga, ergas, erga, ergamos, ergais, ergam

**in -oer** (*e.g.* **roer**)
*Present*: rôo (*P*: roo), róis, rói, roemos, roeis, roem
*Imperfect*: roía, roías, roía, roíamos, roíeis, roíam
*Preterite*: roí, roeste, roeu, roemos, roestes, roeram
*Past participle*: roído
*Imperative*: rói, roei

**-ir verbs:**
**in -ir with -e- in stem** (*e.g.* **vestir**)
*Present*: visto, vestes, veste, vestimos, vestis, vestem

*Present subjunctive*: vista, vistas, vista, vistamos, vistais, vistam
*Similarly*: mentir, preferir, refletir, repetir, seguir, sentir, servir

**in -ir with -o- in stem** (*e.g.* **dormir**)
*Present*: durmo, dormes, dorme, dormimos, dormis, dormem
*Present subjunctive*: durma, durmas, durma, durmamos, durmais, durmam
*Similarly*: cobrir, descobrir, tossir

**in -ir with -u- in the stem** (*e.g.* **subir**)
*Present*: subo, sobes, sobe, subimos, subis, sobem
*Similarly*: consumir, cuspir, fugir, sacudir, sumir

**in -air** (*e.g.* **sair**)
*Present*: saio, sais, sai, saímos, saís, saem
*Imperfect*: saía, saías, saía, saíamos, saíeis, saíam
*Preterite*: saí, saíste, saiu, saímos, saístes, saíram
*Pluperfect*: saíra, saíras, saíra, saíramos, saíreis, saíram
*Present subjunctive*: saia, saias, saia, saiamos, saiais, saiam
*Imperfect subjunctive*: saísse, saísses, saísse, saíssemos, saísseis, saíssem
*Future subjunctive*: sair, saíres, sair, sairmos, sairdes, sairem
*Personal infinitive*: sair, saíres, sair, sairmos, sairdes, sairem
*Present participle*: saindo
*Past participle*: saído
*Imperative*: sai, saí

**in -gir** (*e.g.* **dirigir**)
*Present*: dirijo, diriges, dirige, dirigimos, dirigis, dirigem
*Present subjunctive*: dirija, dirijas, dirija, dirijamos, dirijais, dirijam

**in -guir** (*e.g.* **distinguir**)
*Present*: distingo, distingues, distingue, distinguimos, distinguis, distinguem
*Present subjunctive*: distinga, distingas, distinga, distingamos, distingais, distingam

**in -uir** (*e.g.* **atribuir**)
*Present*: atribuo, atribuis, atribui, atribuímos, atribuís, atribuem
*Imperfect*: atribuía, atribuías, atribuía, atribuíamos, atribuíeis, atribuíam
*Preterite*: atribuí, atribuíste, atribuiu, atribuímos, atribuístes, atribuíram
*Pluperfect*: atribuíra, atribuíras, atribuíra, atribuíramos, atribuíreis, atribuíram

*Present subjunctive*: atribua, atribuas, atribua, atribuamos, atribuais, atribuam
*Imperfect subjunctive*: atribuísse, atribuísses, atribuísse, atribuíssemos, atribuísseis, atribuíssem
*Future subjunctive*: atribuir, atribuíres, atribuir, atribuirmos, atribuirdes, atribuírem
*Personal infinitive*: atribuir, atribuíres, atribuir, atribuirmos, atribuirdes, atribuírem
*Present participle*: atribuindo
*Past participle*: atribuído
*Imperative*: atribui, atribuí

**proibir**
*Present*: proíbo, proíbes, proíbe, proibimos, proibis, proíbem
*Present subjunctive*: proíba, proíbas, proíba, proibamos, proibais, proíbam
*Imperative*: proíbe, proibi
*Similarly*: coibir

**reunir**
*Present*: reúno, reúnes, reúne, reunimos, reunis, reúnem
*Present subjunctive*: reúna, reúnas, reúna, reunamos, reunais, reúnam
*Imperative*: reúne, reuni

**in -struir** (*e.g.* **construir**) - like atribuir except:
*Present*: construo, constróis/construis, constrói/construi, construímos, construís, constroem/construem
*Imperative*: constrói/construi, construí

**in -duzir** (*e.g.* **produzir**)
*Present*: produzo, produzes, produz, produzimos, produzis, produzem
*Imperative*: produz(e), produzi
*Similarly*: luzir, reluzir

Irregular verbs

**caber**
*Present*: caibo, cabes, cabe, cabemos, cabeis, cabem
*Preterite*: coube, coubeste, coube, coubemos, coubestes, couberam
*Pluperfect*: coubera, couberas, coubera, coubéramos, coubéreis, couberam
*Present subjunctive*: caiba, caibas, caiba, caibamos, caibais, caibam
*Imperfect subjunctive*: coubesse, coubesses, coubesse, coubéssemos, coubésseis, coubessem
*Future subjunctive*: couber, couberes, couber, coubermos, couberdes, couberem

**dar**
*Present*: dou, dás, dá, damos, dais, dão
*Preterite*: dei, deste, deu, demos, destes, deram
*Pluperfect*: dera, deras, dera, déramos, déreis, deram
*Present subjunctive*: dê, dês, dê, demos, deis, dêem
*Imperfect subjunctive*: desse, desses, desse, déssemos, désseis, dessem
*Future subjunctive*: der, deres, der, dermos, derdes, derem
*Imperative*: dá, dai

**dizer**
*Present*: digo, dizes, diz, dizemos, dizeis, dizem
*Future*: direi, dirás, dirá, diremos, direis, dirão
*Preterite*: disse, disseste, disse, dissemos, dissestes, disseram
*Pluperfect*: dissera, disseras, dissera, disséramos, disséreis, disseram
*Present subjunctive*: diga, digas, diga, digamos, digais, digam
*Imperfect subjunctive*: dissesse, dissesses, dissesse, disséssemos, dissésseis, dissessem
*Future subjunctive*: disser, disseres, disser, dissermos, disserdes, disserem
*Conditional*: diria, dirias, diria, diríamos, diríeis, diriam
*Present participle*: dizendo
*Past participle*: dito
*Imperative*: diz, dizei

**estar**
*Present*: estou, estás, está, estamos, estais, estão
*Preterite*: estive, estiveste, esteve, estivemos, estivestes, estiveram
*Pluperfect*: estivera, estiveras, estivera, estivéramos, estivéreis, estiveram
*Present subjunctive*: esteja, estejas, esteja, estejamos, estejais, estejam
*Imperfect subjunctive*: estivesse, estivesses, estivesse, estivéssemos, estivésseis, estivessem
*Future subjunctive*: estiver, estiveres, estiver, estivermos, estiverdes, estiverem
*Imperative*: está, estai

**fazer**
*Present*: faço, fazes, faz, fazemos, fazeis, fazem
*Future*: farei, farás, fará, faremos, fareis, farão
*Preterite*: fiz, fizeste, fez, fizemos, fizestes, fizeram
*Pluperfect*: fizera, fizeras, fizera, fizéramos, fizéreis, fizeram

*Present subjunctive*: faça, faças, faça, façamos, façais, façam
*Imperfect subjunctive*: fizesse, fizesses, fizesse, fizéssemos, fizésseis, fizessem
*Future subjunctive*: fizer, fizeres, fizer, fizermos, fizerdes, fizerem
*Conditional*: faria, farias, faria, faríamos, faríeis, fariam
*Present participle*: fazendo
*Past participle*: feito
*Imperative*: faz(e), fazei

**frigir**
*Present*: frijo, freges, frege, frigimos, frigis, fregem
*Present subjunctive*: frija, frijas, frija, frijamos, frijais, frijam
*Imperative*: frege, frigi

**ir**
*Present*: vou, vais, vai, vamos, ides, vão
*Imperfect*: ia, ias, ia, íamos, íeis, iam
*Preterite*: fui, foste, foi, fomos, fostes, foram
*Pluperfect*: fora, foras, fora, fôramos, fôreis, foram
*Present subjunctive*: vá, vás, vá, vamos, vades, vão
*Imperfect subjunctive*: fosse, fosses, fosse, fôssemos, fôsseis, fossem
*Future subjunctive*: for, fores, for, formos, fordes, forem
*Present participle*: indo
*Past participle*: ido
*Imperative*: vai, ide

**haver**
*Present*: hei, hás, há, hemos/havemos, haveis/heis, hão
*Preterite*: houve, houveste, houve, houvemos, houvestes, houveram
*Pluperfect*: houvera, houveras, houvera, houvéramos, houvéreis, houveram
*Present subjunctive*: haja, hajas, haja, hajamos, hajais, hajam
*Imperfect subjunctive*: houvesse, houvesses, houvesse, houvéssemos, houvésseis, houvessem
*Future subjunctive*: houver, houveres, houver, houvermos, houverdes, houverem
*Imperative*: há, havei

**ler**
*Present*: leio, lês, lê, lemos, ledes, lêem
*Imperfect*: lia, lias, lia, líamos, líeis, liam
*Preterite*: li, leste, leu, lemos, lestes, leram
*Pluperfect*: lera, leras, lera, lêramos, lêreis, leram

*Present subjunctive*: leia, leias, leia, leiamos, leiais, leiam
*Imperfect subjunctive*: lesse, lesses, lesse, lêssemos, lêsseis, lessem
*Future subjunctive*: ler, leres, ler, lermos, lerdes, lerem
*Present participle*: lendo
*Past participle*: lido
*Imperative*: lê, lede
*Similarly*: crer

**odiar**
*Present*: odeio, odeias, odeia, odiamos, odiais, odeiam
*Present subjunctive*: odeie, odeies, odeie, odiemos, odieis, odeiem
*Imperative*: odeia, odiai
*Similarly*: incendiar

**ouvir**
*Present*: ouço (*P also*: oiça), ouves, ouve, ouvimos, ouvis, ouvem
*Present subjunctive*: ouça, ouças, ouça, ouçamos, ouçais, ouçam (*P also*: oiça, oiças, oiça, oiçamos, oiçais, oiçam)

**pedir**
*Present*: peço, pedes, pede, pedimos, pedis, pedem
*Present subjunctive*: peça, peças, peça, peçamos, peçais, peçam
*Similarly*: despedir, impedir, medir

**perder**
*Present*: perco, perdes, perde, perdemos, perdeis, perdem
*Present subjunctive*: perca, percas, perca, percamos, percais, percam

**poder**
*Present*: posso, podes, pode, podemos, podeis, podem
*Preterite*: pude, pudeste, pôde, pudemos, pudestes, puderam
*Pluperfect*: pudera, puderas, pudera, pudéramos, pudéreis, puderam
*Present subjunctive*: possa, possas, possa, possamos, possais, possam
*Imperfect subjunctive*: pudesse, pudesses, pudesse, pudéssemos, pudésseis, pudessem
*Future subjunctive*: puder, puderes, puder, pudermos, puderdes, puderem

**polir**
*Present*: pulo, pules, pule, polimos, polis, pulem
*Present subjunctive*: pula, pulas, pula, pulamos, pulais, pulam
*Imperative*: pule, poli

**pôr**
*Present*: ponho, pões, põe, pomos, pondes, põem

*Future*: porei, porás, porá, poremos, poreis, porão
*Imperfect*: punha, punhas, punha, púnhamos, púnheis, punham
*Preterite*: pus, puseste, pôs, pusemos, pusestes, puseram
*Pluperfect*: pusera, puseras, pusera, puséramos, puséreis, puseram
*Present subjunctive*: ponha, ponhas, ponha, ponhamos, ponhais, ponham
*Imperfect subjunctive*: pusesse, pusesses, pusesse, puséssemos, pusésseis, pusessem
*Future subjunctive*: puser, puseres, puser, pusermos, puserdes, puserem
*Conditional*: poria, porias, poria, poríamos, poríeis, poriam
*Present participle*: pondo
*Past participle*: posto
*Imperative*: põe, ponde
*Similarly*: compor, depor, dispor, opor, supor etc

**prover**
*Present*: provejo, provês, provê, provemos, provedes, provêem
*Present subjunctive*: proveja, provejas, proveja, provejamos, provejais, provejam
*Imperative*: provê, provede

**querer**
*Present*: quero, queres, quer, queremos, quereis, querem
*Preterite*: quis, quiseste, quis, quisemos, quisestes, quiseram
*Pluperfect*: quisera, quiseras, quisera, quiséramos, quiséreis, quiseram
*Present subjunctive*: queira, queiras, queira, queiramos, queirais, queiram
*Imperfect subjunctive*: quisesse, quisesses, quisesse, quiséssemos, quisésseis, quisessem
*Future subjunctive*: quiser, quiseres, quiser, quisermos, quiserdes, quiserem
*Imperative*: quer, querei

**requerer**
*Present*: requeiro, requeres, requer, requeremos, requereis, requerem
*Present subjunctive*: requeira, requeiras, requeira, requeiramos, requeirais, requeiram
*Imperative*: requer, requerei

**rir**
*Present*: rio, ris, ri, rimos, rides, riem
*Present subjunctive*: ria, rias, ria, riamos, riais, riam
*Imperative*: ri, ride
*Similarly*: sorrir

**saber**
*Present*: sei, sabes, sabe, sabemos, sabeis, sabem
*Preterite*: soube, soubeste, soube, soubemos, soubestes, souberam
*Pluperfect*: soubera, souberas, soubera, soubéramos, soubéreis, souberam
*Present subjunctive*: saiba, saibas, saiba, saibamos, saibais, saibam
*Imperfect subjunctive*: soubesse, soubesses, soubesse, soubéssemos, soubésseis, soubessem
*Future subjunctive*: souber, souberes, souber, soubermos, souberdes, souberem
*Imperative*: sabe, sabei

**ser**
*Present*: sou, és, é, somos, sois, são
*Imperfect*: era, eras, era, éramos, éreis, eram
*Preterite*: fui, foste, foi, fomos, fostes, foram
*Pluperfect*: fora, foras, fora, fôramos, fôreis, foram
*Present subjunctive*: seja, sejas, seja, sejamos, sejais, sejam
*Imperfect subjunctive*: fosse, fosses, fosse, fôssemos, fôsseis, fossem
*Future subjunctive*: for, fores, for, formos, fordes, forem
*Present participle*: sendo
*Past participle*: sido
*Imperative*: sê, sede

**ter**
*Present*: tenho, tens, tem, temos, tendes, têm
*Imperfect*: tinha, tinhas, tinha, tínhamos, tínheis, tinham
*Preterite*: tive, tiveste, teve, tivemos, tivestes, tiveram
*Pluperfect*: tivera, tiveras, tivera, tivéramos, tivéreis, tiveram
*Present subjunctive*: tenha, tenhas, tenha, tenhamos, tenhais, tenham
*Imperfect subjunctive*: tivesse, tivesses, tivesse, tivéssemos, tivésseis, tivessem
*Future subjunctive*: tiver, tiveres, tiver, tivermos, tiverdes, tiverem
*Present participle*: tendo
*Past participle*: tido
*Imperative*: tem, tende

**trazer**
*Present*: trago, trazes, traz, trazemos, trazeis, trazem
*Future*: trarei, trarás, trará, traremos, trareis, trarão
*Preterite*: trouxe, trouxeste, trouxe, trouxemos, trouxestes, trouxeram

*Pluperfect*: trouxera, trouxeras, trouxera, trouxéramos, trouxéreis, trouxeram

*Present subjunctive*: traga, tragas, traga, tragamos, tragais, tragam

*Imperfect subjunctive*: trouxesse, trouxesses, trouxesse, trouxéssemos, trouxésseis, trouxessem

*Future subjunctive*: trouxer, trouxeres, trouxer, trouxermos, trouxerdes, trouxerem

*Conditional*: traria, trarias, traria, traríamos, traríeis, trariam

*Imperative*: traze, trazei

**valer**

*Present*: valho, vales, vale, valemos, valeis, valem

*Present subjunctive*: valha, valhas, valha, valhamos, valhais, valham

**ver**

*Present*: vejo, vês, vê, vemos, vedes, vêem

*Imperfect*: via, vias, via, víamos, víeis, viam

*Preterite*: vi, viste, viu, vimos, vistes, viram

*Pluperfect*: vira, viras, vira, víramos, víreis, viram

*Present subjunctive*: veja, vejas, veja, vejamos, vejais, vejam

*Imperfect subjunctive*: visse, visses, visse, víssemos, vísseis, vissem

*Future subjunctive*: vir, vires, vir, virmos, virdes, virem

*Present participle*: vendo

*Past participle*: visto

*Imperative*: vê, vede

**vir**

*Present*: venho, vens, vem, vimos, vindes, vêm

*Imperfect*: vinha, vinhas, vinha, vínhamos, vínheis, vinham

*Preterite*: vim, vieste, veio, viemos, viestes, vieram

*Pluperfect*: viera, vieras, viera, viéramos, viéreis, vieram

*Present subjunctive*: venha, venhas, venha, venhamos, venhais, venham

*Imperfect subjunctive*: viesse, viesses, viesse, viéssemos, viésseis, viessem

*Future subjunctive*: vier, vieres, vier, viermos, vierdes, vierem

*Present participle*: vindo

*Past participle*: vindo

*Imperative*: vem, vinde